P9-CCO-133

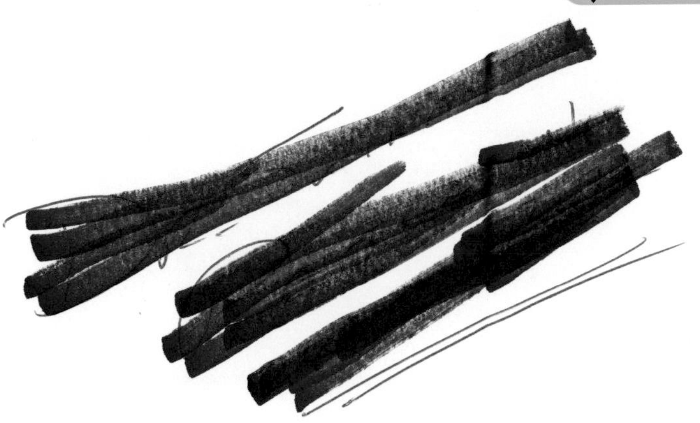

ELEVENTH EDITION

AN INTRODUCTION TO MANAGEMENT SCIENCE

QUANTITATIVE APPROACHES TO DECISION MAKING

David R. Anderson
University of Cincinnati

Dennis J. Sweeney
University of Cincinnati

Thomas A. Williams
Rochester Institute of Technology

Australia · Canada · Mexico · Singapore · Spain · United Kingdom · United States

An Introduction to Management Science:
Quantitative Approaches to Decision Making, 11e

David R. Anderson, Dennis J. Sweeney, Thomas A. Williams

Publisher:
George Werthman

Senior Acquisitions Editor:
Charles E. McCormick, Jr.

Senior Developmental Editor:
Alice C. Denny

Senior Marketing Manager:
Larry Qualls

Senior Production Editor:
Deanna R. Quinn

Media Technology Editor:
Jim Rice

Media Developmental Editor:
Chris Wittmer

Media Production Editor:
Amy Wilson

Manufacturing Coordinator:
Diane Lohman

Internal Design:
Michael H. Stratton/Chris A. Miller

Cover Design:
Chris A. Miller

Cover Image:
Digital Vision

Production House and Compositor:
BookMasters, Inc.

Printer:
Quebecor World—Versailles

Printed in the United States of America
2 3 4 5 07 06 05

For more information contact South-Western, 5191 Natorp Boulevard, Mason, Ohio 45040.
Or you can visit our Internet site at: http://www.swcollege.com

Library of Congress Control Number: 2003116699

ISBN 0-324-20231-8 (package)
ISBN 0-324-20233-4 (book)
ISBN 0-324-20234-2 (CD)

Dedicated
To Our Parents

Brief Contents

Contents

Preface

We are excited to publish the eleventh edition of a text that has been a leader in the field for over 20 years. The purpose of this eleventh edition, as with previous editions, is to provide undergraduate and graduate students with a sound conceptual understanding of the role that management science plays in the decision-making process. The text describes many of the applications where management science is used successfully. Former users of this text have told us that the applications we describe have led them to find new ways to use management science in their companies.

An Introduction to Management Science is applications oriented and continues to use the problem-scenario approach that is a hallmark of every edition of the text. Using the problem scenario-approach, we describe a problem in conjunction with the management science technique being introduced. The development of the management science technique or model includes applying it to the problem to generate a solution or recommendation. We have found that this approach helps to motivate the student by demonstrating not only how the procedure works, but also how it can contribute to the decision-making process.

From the very first edition we have been committed to the challenge of writing a textbook that would help make the mathematical and technical concepts of management science understandable and useful to students of business and economics. Judging from the responses from our teaching colleagues and thousands of students, we have successfully met the challenge. Indeed, it is the helpful comments and suggestions of many loyal users that have been a major reason why the text is so successful.

Throughout the text we have utilized generally accepted notation for the topic being covered so those students who pursue study beyond the level of this text should be comfortable reading more advanced material. To assist in further study, a references and bibliography section is included at the back of the book.

CHANGES IN THE ELEVENTH EDITION

In preparing this eleventh edition, we have been careful to maintain the overall format and approach of the previous edition. However, based on our classroom experiences and suggestions from users of previous editions, a number of changes have been made to enhance the content, managerial orientation, and readability of the text.

Decision Analysis

The student edition of TreePlan software is available on the CD accompanying the text and an appendix describing how to use it is added to Chapter 14 (Decision Analysis). TreePlan is a Microsoft® Excel add-in that allows the user to build decision trees within an Excel worksheet. Once all the probabilities and payoffs have been added to the tree, TreePlan computes the optimal decision strategy. The TreePlan software makes it easier to conduct sensitivity analysis and perform a thorough analysis of a decision analysis problem.

Management Science in Action

The Management Science in Actions are short vignettes that describe how the material covered in a chapter is used in practice. We have added 17 new Management Science in Action vignettes based on articles from *Interfaces* or *OR/MS Today.* In the previous edition we included Management Science in Practice features at the end of many chapters. These features, supplied by practitioners, described how companies had successfully used management science in practice. With this edition, we have revised these write-ups and integrated them within the chapters as additional Management Science in Actions. There are now approximately 50 Management Science in Actions integrated throughout the text.

Computer Software Integration

We have been careful to write the text so that is not dependent on any particular software package. But, we have included material that facilitates using the book with several of the more popular software packages. The Student CD accompanying the text contains Excel worksheets for most of the problem illustrations throughout the text, the TreePlan™ add-in for decision analysis, the Crystal Ball™ add-in for simulation, and the Premium Solver™ add-in for solving linear and integer programs with Excel.

All of the computer output shown in the body of the linear and integer programming chapters is from The Management Scientist version 6.0. Users of LINDO should have no difficulty interpreting this output. For instructors that prefer to use Excel Solver, we have included chapter appendixes describing how to formulate and solve linear and integer programs. In the chapters on inventory, waiting lines, and simulation, we have integrated Excel worksheets into the body of the chapter and show how these worksheets can be used to perform the analysis.

The Management Scientist 6.0

A new version of The Management Scientist software is being introduced with the text and it is free to users. The disk accompanying the book includes The Management Scientist version 6.0 (with Manual). The user interface is significantly improved with this version. For instance, users with a computer screen resolution of 1024×768 or higher can now input a linear program with up to 9 variables and 30 constraints without scrolling the input screen.

Cases and Problems

The quality of the problems and case problems is an important feature of this text. In this edition we have added approximately 30 new problems and 6 new case problems. One new case problem is added to the opening chapter, two have been added to the chapters on linear programming, one to the chapter on inventory models and two to the chapter on simulation. The new case problem in Chapter 1 does not require any specialized knowledge. It is a scheduling problem that is easy to understand, but hard to solve using a trial and error approach. It is intended to challenge the student with an interesting problem early in the course and to illustrate the value of a simple algorithm. We think it provides good motivation for learning about management science.

Other Content Changes

A variety of other changes, too numerous to mention individually, have been made throughout the text in response to suggestions of users and our students.

FEATURES AND PEDAGOGY

We have continued many of the features that appeared in previous editions. Some of the important ones are noted here.

Annotations

Annotations that highlight key points and provide additional insights for the student are a continuing feature of this edition. These annotations, which appear in the margins, are designed to provide emphasis and enhance understanding of the terms and concepts being presented in the text.

Notes and Comments

At the end of many sections, we provide Notes and Comments designed to give the student additional insights about the methodology and its application. Notes and Comments include warnings about or limitations of the methodology, recommendations for application, brief descriptions of additional technical considerations, and other matters.

Self-Test Exercises

Certain exercises are identified as self-test exercises. Completely worked-out solutions for those exercises are provided in an appendix at the end of the text. Students can attempt the self-test exercises and immediately check the solutions to evaluate their understanding of the concepts presented in the chapter.

ANCILLARY TEACHING AND LEARNING MATERIALS

As has always been the case, this new edition of *An Introduction to Management Science* has ancillaries that will increase the value of the text to both students and instructors.

- **EASYQuant Digital Tutor for Microsoft® Excel** *EasyQuant* is designed to make it easier for students to learn how to use Excel to perform quantitative analysis. In each tutorial, one of the text authors shows how Excel can be used to perform a particular management science procedure. EasyQuant is just like having a private expert tutor demonstrating the use of Excel. Information about student purchase of this online product can be found at *http://asw.swlearning.com.*
- **Study Guide** (ISBN: 0-324-22292-0) Prepared by John Loucks of St. Edward's University, the *Study Guide* will provide the student with significant supplementary

study materials. It contains an outline, review and list of formulas for each text chapter, sample exercises with step-by-step solutions, exercises with answers, and a series of self-testing questions with answers. The *Study Guide* may be purchased at a special price when bundled with the textbook.
- **LINDO** An educational version of LINDO software is available at a special price when it is packaged with the text.

The ***Instructor's Resource CD*** (ISBN: 0-324-20232-6) provides all instructor ancillaries. Adopters may request a copy online at *http://www.swlearning.com.* Included in this convenient format are:

- **Solutions Manual**—The *Solutions Manual,* prepared by the authors, includes solutions for all problems in the text. At the request of the instructor, the *Solutions Manual* can be packaged with the text for student purchase.
- **Solutions to Case Problems**—The *Solutions to Case Problems,* also prepared by the authors, contains solutions to all case problems presented in the text.
- **Microsoft® PowerPoint™ Presentation Slides**—Also prepared by John Loucks, the presentation slides contain a teaching outline that incorporates graphics to help instructors create even more stimulating lectures. The PowerPoint slides may be adapted using PowerPoint software to facilitate classroom use.
- **Test Bank**—The *Test Bank* includes objective questions and problems for each chapter. The Test Bank is provided in Microsoft® Word format on the Instructor's Resource CD.

Other teaching and learning materials will be available on our website. It may be easily reached at *http://asw.swcollege.com.*

COURSE OUTLINE FLEXIBILITY

The text is designed to enhance the instructor's flexibility in selecting topics to meet specific course needs. The single-semester and single-quarter outlines that follow are a sampling of the many options available.

One-Semester Course

Emphasis on Linear Programming, Model Development, and Applications

- Introduction (Chapter 1)
- Introduction to Linear Programming and Computer Solution (Chapters 2 and 3)
- Linear Programming Applications (Chapter 4)
- Transportation, Assignment, and Transshipment Problems (Chapter 7)
- Integer Linear Programming (Chapter 8)
- Project Scheduling: PERT/CPM (Chapter 10)
- Inventory Models (Chapter 11)
- Waiting Line Models (Chapter 12)
- Simulation (Chapter 13)
- Decision Analysis (Chapter 14)
- Multicriteria Decisions (Chapter 15)

The instructor in a one-semester course who wants to focus on model development and other applications could either spend more time on the applications in Chapter 4 or cover additional topics.

One-Quarter Course

Emphasis on Linear Programming, Model Development, and Applications

- Introduction (Chapter 1)
- Introduction to Linear Programming and Computer Solution (Chapters 2 and 3)
- Linear Programming Applications (selected portions of Chapters 4 and 7)
- Project Scheduling: PERT/CPM (Chapter 10)
- Waiting Line Models (Chapter 12)
- Simulation (Chapter 13)
- Decision Analysis (Chapter 14)

ACKNOWLEDGMENTS

We owe a debt to many of our colleagues and friends for their helpful comments and suggestions during the development of this and previous editions. Among these are:

Robert L. Armacost, University of Central Florida

Uttarayan Bagchi, University of Texas at Austin

Edward Baker, University of Miami

Norman Baker, University of Cincinnati

Oded Berman, University of Toronto

Jeffrey Camm, University of Cincinnati

Ying Chien, University of Scranton

Gerald M. Claffie, Rutgers University–Camden

Henry L. Crouch, Pittsburg State University

John Eatman, University of North Carolina–Greensboro

Ronald Ebert, University of Missouri–Columbia

Don Edwards, University of South Carolina

Ronald Ehresman, Baldwin-Wallace College

Peter Ellis, Utah State University

Lawrence Ettkin, University of Tennessee at Chattanooga

James Evans, University of Cincinnati

Michael Ford, Rochester Institute of Technology

Terri Friel, Eastern Kentucky University

Phillip Fry, Boise State University

Robert Garfinkel, University of Connecticut

Michael Gordinier, Washington University–St. Louis

Nicholas G. Hall, Ohio State University
Michael E. Hanna, University of Houston–Clear Lake
David Hott, Florida Institute of Technology
Yu-Mong Hsiao, Campbell University
Barry Kadets, Bryant College
Sriram Kannan, American Airlines
John Lawrence, Jr., California State University–Fullerton
Constantine Loucopoulos, Northeast Indiana State University
Farzin Madjidi, Pepperdine University
Ka-sing Man, Georgetown University
William G. Marchal, University of Toledo
Kamlesh Mathur, Case Western Reserve University
Joseph Mazzola, Duke University
Patrick McKeown, University of Georgia
Constance McLaren, Indiana State University
A. Erhan Mergen, Rochester Institute of Technology
Edward Minieka, University of Illinois–Chicago
Mario Miranda, The Ohio State University
Shahriar Mostashari, Campbell University
Benham Nakhai, Millersville University of Pennsylvania
Alan Neebe, University of North Carolina
Susan Norman, Northern Arizona University
David Pentico, Duquesne University
Ceyhun Qzgur, Valparaiso University
B. Madhusudan Rao, Bowling Green State University
Handanhal V. Ravinder, University of New Mexico
Donna Retzlaff-Roberts, University of Memphis
Don R. Robinson, Illinois State University
Richard Rosenthal, Naval Postgraduate School
Adriano O. Solis, University of Texas at El Paso
Antoinette Somers, Wayne State University
Minghe Sun, University of Texas at San Antonio
William Tallon, Northern Illinois University
Christopher S. Tang, University of California–Los Angeles
Giri Kumar Tayi, State University of New York–Albany
Willban Terpening, Gonzaga University
Jack A. Vaughn, University of Texas at El Paso
Edward P. Winkofsky, Mead Corporation
Sajjad Zahir, University of Lethbridge

Our associates from organizations who supplied several of the Management Science in Action vignettes make a major contribution to the text. These individuals are cited in a credit line associated with the vignette.

We are also indebted to our senior acquisitions editor, Charles McCormick, Jr.; our senior developmental editor, Alice Denny; our senior production editor, Deanna Quinn; our senior designer, Chris Miller; our senior marketing manager, Larry Qualls; and others at Thomson/South-Western for their counsel and support during the preparation of this text.

David R. Anderson
Dennis J. Sweeney
Thomas A. Williams

About the Authors

David R. Anderson. David R. Anderson is Professor of Quantitative Analysis in the College of Business Administration at the University of Cincinnati. Born in Grand Forks, North Dakota, he earned his B.S., M.S., and Ph.D. degrees from Purdue University. Professor Anderson has served as Head of the Department of Quantitative Analysis and Operations Management and as Associate Dean of the College of Business Administration. In addition, he was the coordinator of the College's first Executive Program.

At the University of Cincinnati, Professor Anderson has taught introductory statistics for business students as well as graduate-level courses in regression analysis, multivariate analysis, and management science. He has also taught statistical courses at the Department of Labor in Washington, D.C. He has been honored with nominations and awards for excellence in teaching and excellence in service to student organizations.

Professor Anderson has coauthored ten textbooks in the areas of statistics, management science, linear programming, and production and operations management. He is an active consultant in the field of sampling and statistical methods.

Dennis J. Sweeney. Dennis J. Sweeney is Professor of Quantitative Analysis and founder of the Center for Productivity Improvement at the University of Cincinnati. Born in Des Moines, Iowa, he earned a B.S.B.A. degree from Drake University and his M.B.A. and D.B.A. degrees from Indiana University where he was an NDEA Fellow. During 1978–79, Professor Sweeney worked in the management science group at Procter & Gamble; during 1981–82, he was a visiting professor at Duke University. Professor Sweeney served as Head of the Department of Quantitative Analysis and as Associate Dean of the College of Business Administration at the University of Cincinnati.

Professor Sweeney has published more than thirty articles and monographs in the area of management science and statistics. The National Science Foundation, IBM, Procter & Gamble, Federated Department Stores, Kroger, and Cincinnati Gas & Electric have funded his research, which has been published in *Management Science*, *Operations Research*, *Mathematical Programming*, *Decision Sciences*, and other journals.

Professor Sweeney has coauthored ten textbooks in the areas of statistics, management science, linear programming, and production and operations management.

Thomas A. Williams. Thomas A. Williams is Professor of Management Science in the College of Business at Rochester Institute of Technology. Born in Elmira, New York, he earned his B.S. degree at Clarkson University. He did his graduate work at Rensselaer Polytechnic Institute, where he received his M.S. and Ph.D. degrees.

Before joining the College of Business at RIT, Professor Williams served for seven years as a faculty member in the College of Business Administration at the University of Cincinnati, where he developed the undergraduate program in Information Systems and then served as its coordinator. At RIT he was the first chairman of the Decision Sciences Department. He teaches courses in management science and statistics, as well as graduate courses in regression and decision analysis.

Professor Williams is the coauthor of eleven textbooks in the areas of management science, statistics, production and operations management, and mathematics. He has been a consultant for numerous *Fortune* 500 companies and has worked on projects ranging from the use of data analysis to the development of large-scale regression models.

CHAPTER 1

Introduction

CONTENTS

Management science, an approach to decision making based on the scientific method, makes extensive use of quantitative analysis. A variety of names exists for the body of knowledge involving quantitative approaches to decision making; in addition to management science, two other widely known and accepted names are operations research and decision science. Today, many use the terms *management science, operations research,* and *decision science* interchangeably.

The scientific management revolution of the early 1900s, initiated by Frederic W. Taylor, provided the foundation for the use of quantitative methods in management. But modern management science research is generally considered to have originated during the World War II period, when teams were formed to deal with strategic and tactical problems faced by the military. These teams, which often consisted of people with diverse specialties (e.g., mathematicians, engineers, and behavioral scientists), were joined together to solve a common problem through the utilization of the scientific method. After the war, many of these team members continued their research in the field of management science.

Two developments that occurred during the post–World War II period led to the growth and use of management science in nonmilitary applications. First, continued research resulted in numerous methodological developments. Probably the most significant development was the discovery by George Dantzig, in 1947, of the simplex method for solving linear programming problems. At the same time these methodological developments were taking place, digital computers prompted a virtual explosion in computing power. Computers enabled practitioners to use the methodological advances to solve a large variety of problems. The computer technology explosion continues, and personal computers can now be used to solve problems larger than those solved on mainframe computers in the 1990s.

As stated in the Preface, the purpose of the text is to provide students with a sound conceptual understanding of the role that management science plays in the decision-making process. We also said that the text is applications oriented. To reinforce the applications nature of the text and to provide a better understanding of the variety of applications in which management science has been used successfully, Management Science in Action articles are presented throughout the text. Each Management Science in Action article summarizes an application of management science in practice. The first Management Science in Action in this chapter, Revenue Management at American Airlines, describes one of the most significant applications of management science in the airline industry.

MANAGEMENT SCIENCE IN ACTION

REVENUE MANAGEMENT AT AMERICAN AIRLINES*

One of the great success stories in management science involves the work done by the operations research (OR) group at American Airlines. In 1982, Thomas M. Cook joined a group of 12 operations research analysts at American Airlines. Under Cook's guidance, the OR group quickly grew to a staff of 75 professionals who developed models and conducted studies to support senior management decision making. Today the OR group is called Sabre and employs 10,000 professionals worldwide.

One of the most significant applications developed by the OR group came about because of the deregulation of the airline industry in the late 1970s. As a result of deregulation, a number of low-cost airlines were able to move into the market by selling seats at a fraction of the price charged by established carriers such as American Airlines. Facing the question of how to compete, the OR group suggested offering different fare classes (discount and full fare) and in the process created a new area of management science referred to as yield or revenue management.

The OR group used forecasting and optimization techniques to determine how many seats to sell at a discount and how many seats to hold for full fare. Although the initial implementation was relatively crude, the group continued to improve the forecasting and optimization models that drive the system and to obtain better data. Tom Cook counts at least four basic generations of revenue management during his tenure. Each produced in excess of $100 million in incremental profitability over its predecessor. This revenue management system at American Airlines generates nearly $1 billion annually in incremental revenue.

Today, virtually every airline uses some sort of revenue management system. The cruise, hotel, and car rental industries also now apply revenue management methods, a further tribute to the pioneering efforts of the OR group at American Airlines and its leader, Thomas M. Cook.

*Based on Peter Horner, "The Sabre Story," *OR/MS Today* (June 2000).

1.1 PROBLEM SOLVING AND DECISION MAKING

Problem solving can be defined as the process of identifying a difference between the actual and the desired state of affairs and then taking action to resolve the difference. For problems important enough to justify the time and effort of careful analysis, the problem-solving process involves the following seven steps:

1. Identify and define the problem.
2. Determine the set of alternative solutions.
3. Determine the criterion or criteria that will be used to evaluate the alternatives.
4. Evaluate the alternatives.
5. Choose an alternative.
6. Implement the selected alternative.
7. Evaluate the results to determine whether a satisfactory solution has been obtained.

Decision making is the term generally associated with the first five steps of the problem-solving process. Thus, the first step of decision making is to identify and define the problem. Decision making ends with the choosing of an alternative, which is the act of making the decision.

Let us consider the following example of the decision-making process. For the moment assume that you are currently unemployed and that you would like a position that will lead to a satisfying career. Suppose that your job search has resulted in offers from companies in Rochester, New York; Dallas, Texas; Greensboro, North Carolina; and Pittsburgh, Pennsylvania. Thus, the alternatives for your decision problem can be stated as follows:

1. Accept the position in Rochester.
2. Accept the position in Dallas.
3. Accept the position in Greensboro.
4. Accept the position in Pittsburgh.

The next step of the problem-solving process involves determining the criteria that will be used to evaluate the four alternatives. Obviously, the starting salary is a factor of some importance. If salary were the only criterion of importance to you, the alternative selected as "best" would be the one with the highest starting salary. Problems in which the objective is to find the best solution with respect to one criterion are referred to as **single-criterion decision problems.**

Suppose that you also conclude that the potential for advancement and the location of the job are two other criteria of major importance. Thus, the three criteria in your decision problem are starting salary, potential for advancement, and location. Problems that involve more than one criterion are referred to as **multicriteria decision problems.**

The next step of the decision-making process is to evaluate each of the alternatives with respect to each criterion. For example, evaluating each alternative relative to the starting

TABLE 1.1 DATA FOR THE JOB EVALUATION DECISION-MAKING PROBLEM

Alternative	Starting Salary	Potential for Advancement	Job Location
1. Rochester	$38,500	Average	Average
2. Dallas	$36,000	Excellent	Good
3. Greensboro	$36,000	Good	Excellent
4. Pittsburgh	$37,000	Average	Good

salary criterion is done simply by recording the starting salary for each job alternative. Evaluating each alternative with respect to the potential for advancement and the location of the job is more difficult to do, however, because these evaluations are based primarily on subjective factors that are often difficult to quantify. Suppose for now that you decide to measure potential for advancement and job location by rating each of these criteria as poor, fair, average, good, or excellent. The data that you compile are shown in Table 1.1.

You are now ready to make a choice from the available alternatives. What makes this choice phase so difficult is that the criteria are probably not all equally important, and no one alternative is "best" with regard to all criteria. Although we will present a method for dealing with situations like this one later in the text, for now let us suppose that after a careful evaluation of the data in Table 1.1, you decide to select alternative 3; alternative 3 is thus referred to as the **decision.**

At this point in time, the decision-making process is complete. In summary, we see that this process involves five steps:

1. Define the problem.
2. Identify the alternatives.
3. Determine the criteria.
4. Evaluate the alternatives.
5. Choose an alternative.

Note that missing from this list are the last two steps in the problem-solving process: implementing the selected alternative and evaluating the results to determine whether a satisfactory solution has been obtained. This omission is not meant to diminish the importance of each of these activities, but to emphasize the more limited scope of the term *decision making* as compared to the term *problem solving*. Figure 1.1 summarizes the relationship between these two concepts.

1.2 QUANTITATIVE ANALYSIS AND DECISION MAKING

Consider the flowchart presented in Figure 1.2. Note that it combines the first three steps of the decision-making process under the heading of "Structuring the Problem" and the latter two steps under the heading "Analyzing the Problem." Let us now consider in greater detail how to carry out the set of activities that make up the decision-making process.

Figure 1.3 shows that the analysis phase of the decision-making process may take two basic forms: qualitative and quantitative. Qualitative analysis is based primarily on the manager's judgment and experience; it includes the manager's intuitive "feel" for the problem and is more an art than a science. If the manager has had experience with similar prob-

FIGURE 1.1 THE RELATIONSHIP BETWEEN PROBLEM SOLVING AND DECISION MAKING

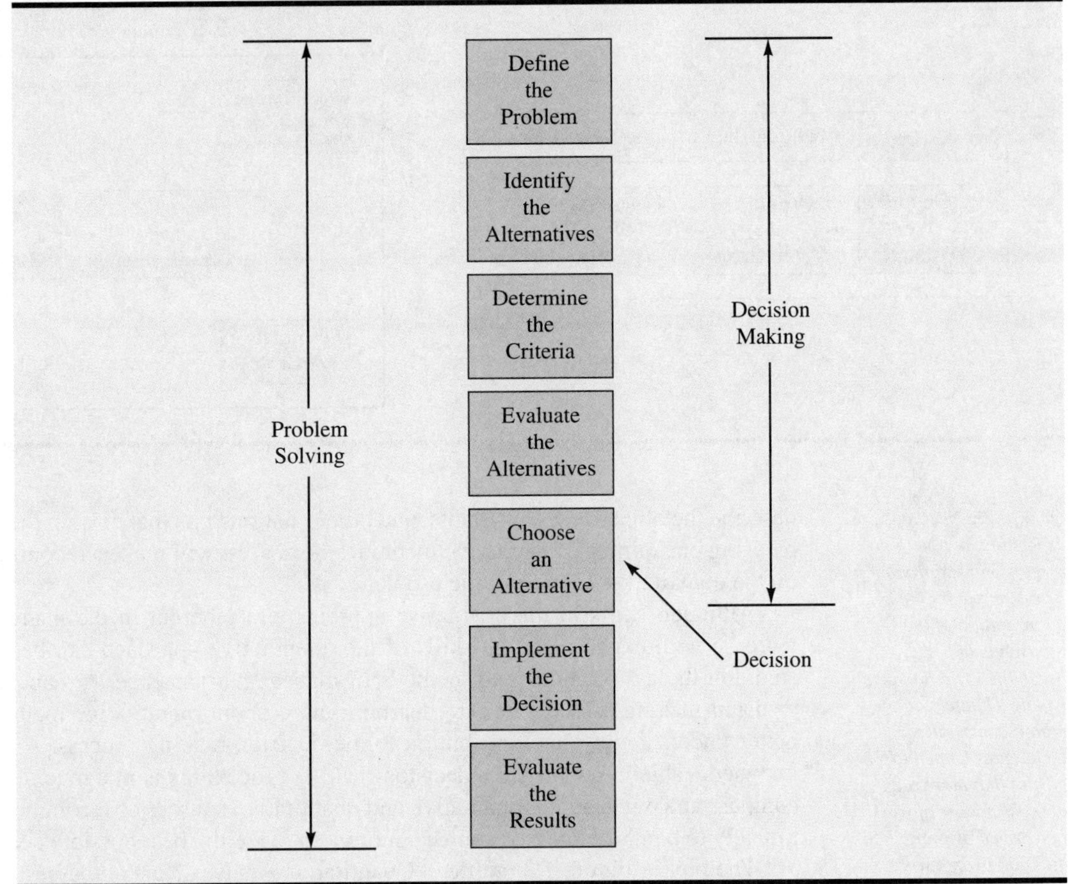

lems, or if the problem is relatively simple, heavy emphasis may be placed upon a qualitative analysis. However, if the manager has had little experience with similar problems, or if the problem is sufficiently complex, then a quantitative analysis of the problem can be an especially important consideration in the manager's final decision.

When using the quantitative approach, an analyst will concentrate on the quantitative facts or data associated with the problem and develop mathematical expressions that

FIGURE 1.2 AN ALTERNATE CLASSIFICATION OF THE DECISION-MAKING PROCESS

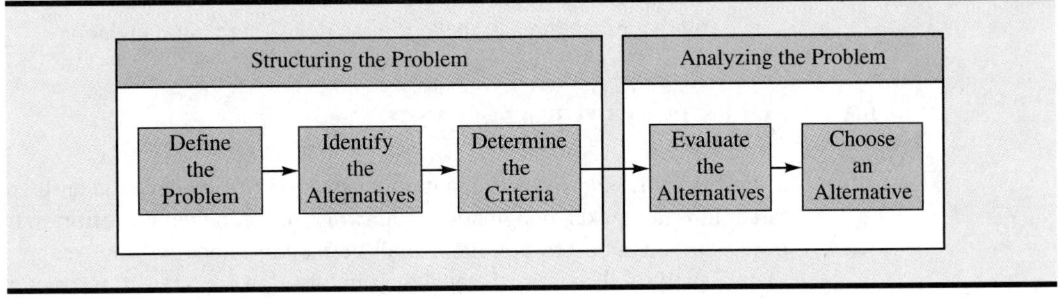

FIGURE 1.3 THE ROLE OF QUALITATIVE AND QUANTITATIVE ANALYSIS

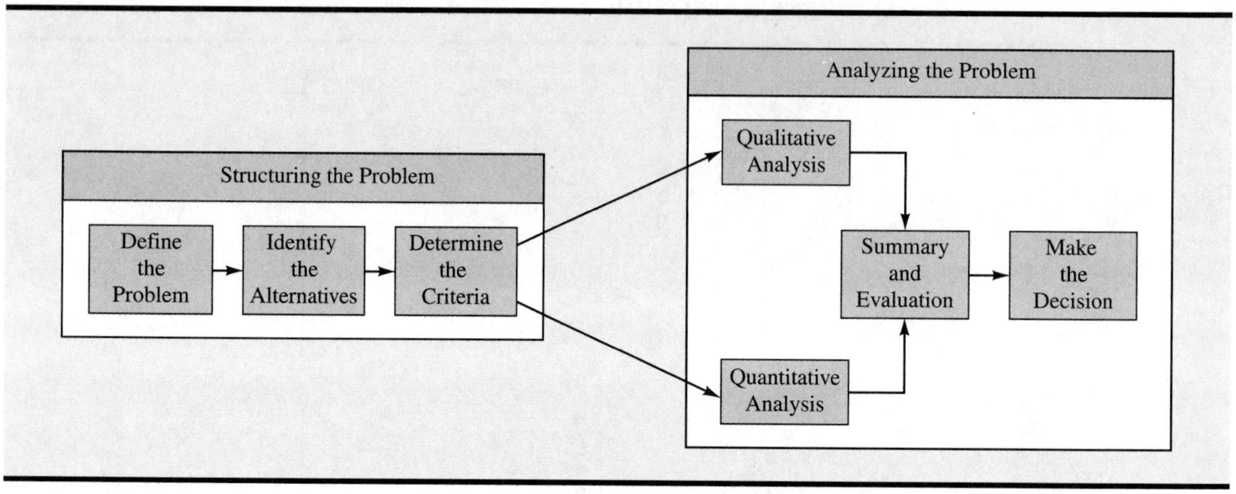

Quantitative methods are especially helpful with large, complex problems. For example, in the coordination of the thousands of tasks associated with landing Apollo 11 safely on the moon, quantitative techniques helped to ensure that more than 300,000 pieces of work performed by more than 400,000 people were integrated smoothly.

describe the objectives, constraints, and other relationships that exist in the problem. Then, by using one or more quantitative methods, the analyst will make a recommendation based on the quantitative aspects of the problem.

Although skills in the qualitative approach are inherent in the manager and usually increase with experience, the skills of the quantitative approach can be learned only by studying the assumptions and methods of management science. A manager can increase decision-making effectiveness by learning more about quantitative methodology and by better understanding its contribution to the decision-making process. A manager who is knowledgeable in quantitative decision-making procedures is in a much better position to compare and evaluate the qualitative and quantitative sources of recommendations and ultimately to combine the two sources in order to make the best possible decision.

The box in Figure 1.3 entitled "Quantitative Analysis" encompasses most of the subject matter of this text. We will consider a managerial problem, introduce the appropriate quantitative methodology, and then develop the recommended decision.

In closing this section, let us briefly state some of the reasons why a quantitative approach might be used in the decision-making process:

Try Problem 4 to test your understanding of why quantitative approaches might be needed in a particular problem.

1. The problem is complex, and the manager cannot develop a good solution without the aid of quantitative analysis.
2. The problem is especially important (e.g., a great deal of money is involved), and the manager desires a thorough analysis before attempting to make a decision.
3. The problem is new, and the manager has no previous experience from which to draw.
4. The problem is repetitive, and the manager saves time and effort by relying on quantitative procedures to make routine decision recommendations.

1.3 QUANTITATIVE ANALYSIS

From Figure 1.3 we see that quantitative analysis begins once the problem has been structured. It usually takes imagination, teamwork, and considerable effort to transform a rather general problem description into a well-defined problem that can be approached via quantitative analysis. The more the analyst is involved in the process of structuring the problem, the more likely the ensuing quantitative analysis will make an important contribution to the decision-making process.

To successfully apply quantitative analysis to decision making, the management scientist must work closely with the manager or user of the results. When both the management scientist and the manager agree that the problem has been adequately structured, work can begin on developing a model to represent the problem mathematically. Solution procedures can then be employed to find the best solution for the model. This best solution for the model then becomes a recommendation to the decision maker. The process of developing and solving models is the essence of the quantitative analysis process.

Model Development

Models are representations of real objects or situations and can be presented in various forms. For example, a scale model of an airplane is a representation of a real airplane. Similarly, a child's toy truck is a model of a real truck. The model airplane and toy truck are examples of models that are physical replicas of real objects. In modeling terminology, physical replicas are referred to as **iconic models.**

A second classification includes models that are physical in form but do not have the same physical appearance as the object being modeled. Such models are referred to as **analog models.** The speedometer of an automobile is an analog model; the position of the needle on the dial represents the speed of the automobile. A thermometer is another analog model representing temperature.

A third classification of models—the type we will primarily be studying—includes representations of a problem by a system of symbols and mathematical relationships or expressions. Such models are referred to as **mathematical models** and are a critical part of any quantitative approach to decision making. For example, the total profit from the sale of a product can be determined by multiplying the profit per unit by the quantity sold. If we let x represent the number of units sold and P the total profit, then, with a profit of \$10 per unit, the following mathematical model defines the total profit earned by selling x units:

$$P = 10x \tag{1.1}$$

The purpose, or value, of any model is that it enables us to make inferences about the real situation by studying and analyzing the model. For example, an airplane designer might test an iconic model of a new airplane in a wind tunnel to learn about the potential flying characteristics of the full-size airplane. Similarly, a mathematical model may be used to make inferences about how much profit will be earned if a specified quantity of a particular product is sold. According to the mathematical model of equation (1.1), we would expect selling three units of the product ($x = 3$) would provide a profit of $P = 10(3) = \$30$.

In general, experimenting with models requires less time and is less expensive than experimenting with the real object or situation. A model airplane is certainly quicker and less expensive to build and study than the full-size airplane. Similarly, the mathematical model in equation (1.1) allows a quick identification of profit expectations without actually requiring the manager to produce and sell x units. Models also have the advantage of reducing the risk associated with experimenting with the real situation. In particular, bad designs or bad decisions that cause the model airplane to crash or a mathematical model to project a \$10,000 loss can be avoided in the real situation.

The value of model-based conclusions and decisions is dependent on how well the model represents the real situation. The more closely the model airplane represents the real

Herbert A. Simon, a Nobel Prize winner in economics and an expert in decision making, said that a mathematical model does not have to be exact; it just has to be close enough to provide better results than can be obtained by common sense.

airplane, the more accurate the conclusions and predictions will be. Similarly, the more closely the mathematical model represents the company's true profit-volume relationship, the more accurate the profit projections will be.

Because this text deals with quantitative analysis based on mathematical models, let us look more closely at the mathematical modeling process. When initially considering a managerial problem, we usually find that the problem definition phase leads to a specific objective, such as maximization of profit or minimization of cost, and possibly a set of restrictions or **constraints,** such as production capacities. The success of the mathematical model and quantitative approach will depend heavily on how accurately the objective and constraints can be expressed in terms of mathematical equations or relationships.

A mathematical expression that describes the problem's objective is referred to as the **objective function.** For example, the profit equation $P = 10x$ would be an objective function for a firm attempting to maximize profit. A production capacity constraint would be necessary if, for instance, 5 hours are required to produce each unit and only 40 hours of production time are available per week. Let x indicate the number of units produced each week. The production time constraint is given by

$$5x \leq 40 \tag{1.2}$$

The value of $5x$ is the total time required to produce x units; the symbol $\leq$ indicates that the production time required must be less than or equal to the 40 hours available.

The decision problem or question is the following: How many units of the product should be scheduled each week to maximize profit? A complete mathematical model for this simple production problem is

$$\begin{aligned} &\text{Maximize} \quad P = 10x \quad \text{objective function} \\ &\text{subject to (s.t.)} \\ &\qquad \left.\begin{aligned} 5x &\leq 40 \\ x &\geq 0 \end{aligned}\right\} \text{constraints} \end{aligned}$$

The $x \geq 0$ constraint requires the production quantity x to be greater than or equal to zero, which simply recognizes the fact that it is not possible to manufacture a negative number of units. The optimal solution to this model can be easily calculated and is given by $x = 8$, with an associated profit of $80. This model is an example of a linear programming model. In subsequent chapters we will discuss more complicated mathematical models and learn how to solve them in situations where the answers are not nearly so obvious.

In the preceding mathematical model, the profit per unit ($10), the production time per unit (5 hours), and the production capacity (40 hours) are environmental factors that are not under the control of the manager or decision maker. Such environmental factors, which can affect both the objective function and the constraints, are referred to as **uncontrollable inputs** to the model. Inputs that are controlled or determined by the decision maker are referred to as **controllable inputs** to the model. In the example given, the production quantity x is the controllable input to the model. Controllable inputs are the decision alternatives specified by the manager and thus are also referred to as the **decision variables** of the model.

Once all controllable and uncontrollable inputs are specified, the objective function and constraints can be evaluated and the output of the model determined. In this sense, the output of the model is simply the projection of what would happen if those particular envi-

FIGURE 1.4 FLOWCHART OF THE PROCESS OF TRANSFORMING MODEL INPUTS INTO OUTPUT

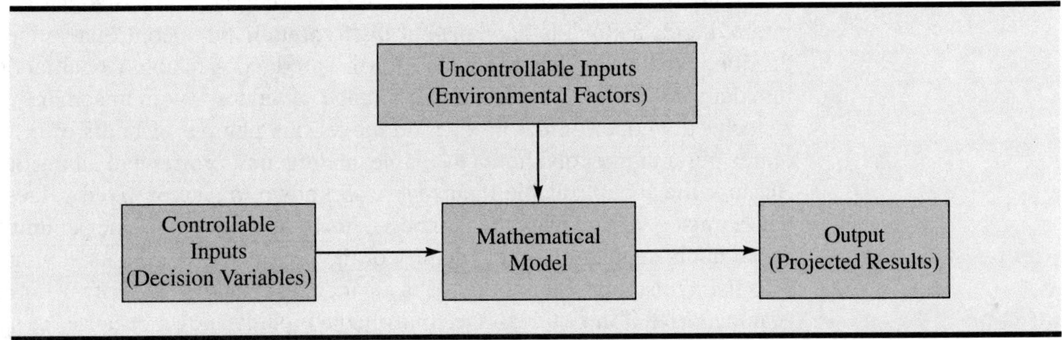

ronmental factors and decisions occurred in the real situation. A flowchart of how controllable and uncontrollable inputs are transformed by the mathematical model into output is shown in Figure 1.4. A similar flowchart showing the specific details of the production model is shown in Figure 1.5.

As stated earlier, the uncontrollable inputs are those the decision maker cannot influence. The specific controllable and uncontrollable inputs of a model depend on the particular problem or decision-making situation. In the production problem, the production time available (40) is an uncontrollable input. However, if it were possible to hire more employees or use overtime, the number of hours of production time would become a controllable input and therefore a decision variable in the model.

Uncontrollable inputs can either be known exactly or be uncertain and subject to variation. If all uncontrollable inputs to a model are known and cannot vary, the model is referred to as a **deterministic model.** Corporate income tax rates are not under the influence of the manager and thus constitute an uncontrollable input in many decision models. Because these rates are known and fixed (at least in the short run), a mathematical model with corporate income tax rates as the only uncontrollable input would be a deterministic model.

FIGURE 1.5 FLOWCHART FOR THE PRODUCTION MODEL

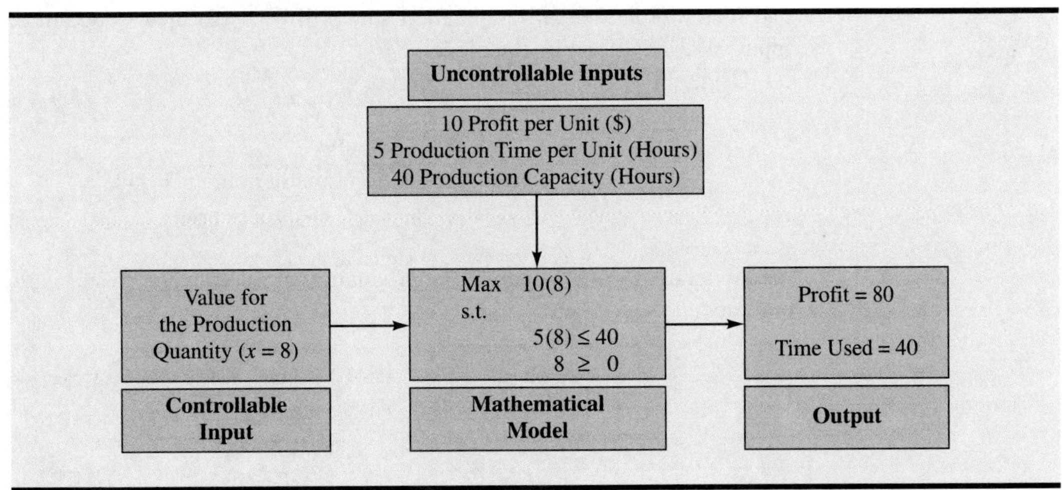

The distinguishing feature of a deterministic model is that the uncontrollable input values are known in advance.

If any of the uncontrollable inputs are uncertain and subject to variation, the model is referred to as a **stochastic** or **probabilistic model.** An uncontrollable input to many production planning models is demand for the product. A mathematical model that treats future demand—which may be any of a range of values—with uncertainty would be called a stochastic model. In the production model, the number of hours of production time required per unit, the total hours available, and the unit profit were all uncontrollable inputs. Because the uncontrollable inputs were all known to take on fixed values, the model was deterministic. If, however, the number of hours of production time per unit could vary from 3 to 6 hours depending on the quality of the raw material, the model would be stochastic. The distinguishing feature of a stochastic model is that the value of the output cannot be determined even if the value of the controllable input is known because the specific values of the uncontrollable inputs are unknown. In this respect, stochastic models are often more difficult to analyze.

Data Preparation

Another step in the quantitative analysis of a problem is the preparation of the data required by the model. Data in this sense refer to the values of the uncontrollable inputs to the model. All uncontrollable inputs or data must be specified before we can analyze the model and recommend a decision or solution for the problem.

In the production model, the values of the uncontrollable inputs or data were $10 per unit for profit, 5 hours per unit for production time, and 40 hours for production capacity. In the development of the model, these data values were known and incorporated into the model as it was being developed. If the model is relatively small and the uncontrollable input values or data required are few, the quantitative analyst will probably combine model development and data preparation into one step. In these situations the data values are inserted as the equations of the mathematical model are developed.

However, in many mathematical modeling situations, the data or uncontrollable input values are not readily available. In these situations the management scientist may know that the model will need profit per unit, production time, and production capacity data, but the values will not be known until the accounting, production, and engineering departments can be consulted. Rather than attempting to collect the required data as the model is being developed, the analyst will usually adopt a general notation for the model development step and then a separate data preparation step will be performed to obtain the uncontrollable input values required by the model.

Using the general notation

$$
\begin{aligned}
c &= \text{profit per unit} \\
a &= \text{production time in hours per unit} \\
b &= \text{production capacity in hours}
\end{aligned}
$$

the model development step of the production problem would result in the following general model:

$$
\begin{aligned}
&\text{Max} \quad cx \\
&\text{s.t.} \\
&\qquad ax \le b \\
&\qquad x \ge 0
\end{aligned}
$$

A separate data preparation step to identify the values for c, a, and b would then be necessary to complete the model.

Many inexperienced quantitative analysts assume that once the problem has been defined and a general model developed, the problem is essentially solved. These individuals tend to believe that data preparation is a trivial step in the process and can be easily handled by clerical staff. Actually, this assumption could not be further from the truth, especially with large-scale models that have numerous data input values. For example, a moderately sized linear programming model with 50 decision variables and 25 constraints could have more than 1300 data elements that must be identified in the data preparation step. The time required to prepare these data and the possibility of data collection errors will make the data preparation step a critical part of the quantitative analysis process. Often, a fairly large database is needed to support a mathematical model, and information systems specialists may become involved in the data preparation step.

Model Solution

Once the model development and data preparation steps are completed, we can proceed to the model solution step. In this step, the analyst will attempt to identify the values of the decision variables that provide the "best" output for the model. The specific decision-variable value or values providing the "best" output will be referred to as the **optimal solution** for the model. For the production problem, the model solution step involves finding the value of the production quantity decision variable x that maximizes profit while not causing a violation of the production capacity constraint.

One procedure that might be used in the model solution step involves a trial-and-error approach in which the model is used to test and evaluate various decision alternatives. In the production model, this procedure would mean testing and evaluating the model under various production quantities or values of x. Referring to Figure 1.5, note that we could input trial values for x and check the corresponding output for projected profit and satisfaction of the production capacity constraint. If a particular decision alternative does not satisfy one or more of the model constraints, the decision alternative is rejected as being **infeasible,** regardless of the objective function value. If all constraints are satisfied, the decision alternative is **feasible** and a candidate for the "best" solution or recommended decision. Through this trial-and-error process of evaluating selected decision alternatives, a decision maker can identify a good—and possibly the best—feasible solution to the problem. This solution would then be the recommended decision for the problem.

Table 1.2 shows the results of a trial-and-error approach to solving the production model of Figure 1.5. The recommended decision is a production quantity of 8 because the feasible solution with the highest projected profit occurs at $x = 8$.

Although the trial-and-error solution process is often acceptable and can provide valuable information for the manager, it has the drawbacks of not necessarily providing the best solution and of being inefficient in terms of requiring numerous calculations if many decision alternatives are tried. Thus, quantitative analysts have developed special solution procedures for many models that are much more efficient than the trial-and-error approach. Throughout this text, you will be introduced to solution procedures that are applicable to the specific mathematical models that will be formulated. Some relatively small models or problems can be solved by hand computations, but most practical applications require the use of a computer.

Model development and model solution steps are not completely separable. An analyst will want both to develop an accurate model or representation of the actual problem situation and to be able to find a solution to the model. If we approach the model development

TABLE 1.2 TRIAL-AND-ERROR SOLUTION FOR THE PRODUCTION MODEL OF FIGURE 1.5

Decision Alternative (Production Quantity) x	Projected Profit	Total Hours of Production	Feasible Solution? (Hours Used ≤ 40)
0	0	0	Yes
2	20	10	Yes
4	40	20	Yes
6	60	30	Yes
8	80	40	Yes
10	100	50	No
12	120	60	No

step by attempting to find the most accurate and realistic mathematical model, we may find the model so large and complex that it is impossible to obtain a solution. In this case, a simpler and perhaps more easily understood model with a readily available solution procedure is preferred even if the recommended solution is only a rough approximation of the best decision. As you learn more about quantitative solution procedures, you will have a better idea of the types of mathematical models that can be developed and solved.

Try Problem 8 to test your understanding of the concept of a mathematical model and what is referred to as the optimal solution to the model.

After a model solution is obtained, both the management scientist and the manager will be interested in determining how good the solution really is. Even though the analyst has undoubtedly taken many precautions to develop a realistic model, often the goodness or accuracy of the model cannot be assessed until model solutions are generated. Model testing and validation are frequently conducted with relatively small "test" problems that have known or at least expected solutions. If the model generates the expected solutions, and if other output information appears correct, the go-ahead may be given to use the model on the full-scale problem. However, if the model test and validation identify potential problems or inaccuracies inherent in the model, corrective action, such as model modification and/or collection of more accurate input data, may be taken. Whatever the corrective action, the model solution will not be used in practice until the model has satisfactorily passed testing and validation.

Report Generation

An important part of the quantitative analysis process is the preparation of managerial reports based on the model's solution. Referring to Figure 1.3, we see that the solution based on the quantitative analysis of a problem is one of the inputs the manager considers before making a final decision. Thus, the results of the model must appear in a managerial report that can be easily understood by the decision maker. The report includes the recommended decision and other pertinent information about the results that may be helpful to the decision maker.

A Note Regarding Implementation

As discussed in Section 1.2, the manager is responsible for integrating the quantitative solution with qualitative considerations in order to make the best possible decision. After completing the decision-making process, the manager must oversee the implementation and follow-up evaluation of the decision. During the implementation and follow-up, the manager should continue to monitor the contribution of the model. At times, this process may lead to requests for model expansion or refinement that will cause the management scientist to return to an earlier step of the quantitative analysis process.

Successful implementation of results is of critical importance to the management scientist as well as the manager. If the results of the quantitative analysis process are not correctly implemented, the entire effort may be of no value. It doesn't take too many unsuccessful implementations before the management scientist is out of work. Because implementation often requires people to do things differently, it often meets with resistance. People want to know, "What's wrong with the way we've been doing it?" and so on. One of the most effective ways to ensure successful implementation is to include users throughout the modeling process. A user who feels a part of identifying the problem and developing the solution is much more likely to enthusiastically implement the results. The success rate for implementing the results of a management science project is much greater for those projects characterized by extensive user involvement. The Management Science in Action, Quantitative Analysis at Merrill Lynch, discusses some of the reasons for the success Merrill Lynch has realized from using quantitative analysis.

MANAGEMENT SCIENCE IN ACTION

QUANTITATIVE ANALYSIS AT MERRILL LYNCH*

Merrill Lynch, a brokerage and financial services firm with more than 56,000 employees in 45 countries, serves its client base through two business units. The Merrill Lynch Corporate and Institutional Client Group serves more than 7,000 corporations, institutions, and governments. The Merrill Lynch Private Client Group (MLPC) serves approximately 4 million households, as well as 225,000 small to mid-sized businesses and regional financial institutions, through more than 14,000 financial consultants in 600-plus branch offices. The management science group, established in 1986, has been part of MLPC since 1991. The mission of this group is to provide high-end quantitative analysis to support strategic management decisions and to enhance the financial consultant–client relationship.

The management science group has successfully implemented models and developed systems for asset allocation, financial planning, marketing information technology, database marketing, and portfolio performance measurement. Although technical expertise and objectivity are clearly important factors in any analytical group, the management science group attributes much of its success to communications skills, teamwork, and consulting skills.

Each project begins with face-to-face meetings with the client. A proposal is then prepared to outline the background of the problem, the objectives of the project, the approach, the required resources, the time schedule, and the implementation issues. At this stage, analysts focus on developing solutions that provide significant value and are easily implemented.

As the work progresses, frequent meetings keep the clients up-to-date. Because people with different skills, perspectives, and motivations must work together for a common goal, teamwork is essential. The group's members take classes in team approaches, facilitation, and conflict resolution. They possess a broad range of multifunctional and multidisciplinary capabilities and are motivated to provide solutions that focus on the goals of the firm. This approach to problem solving and the implementation of quantitative analysis has been a hallmark of the management science group. The impact and success of the group translates into hard dollars and repeat business. The group recently received the annual Edelman award given by the Institute for Operations Research and the Management Sciences for effective use of management science for organizational success.

*Based on Russ Labe, Raj Nigam, and Steve Spence, "Management Science at Merrill Lynch Private Client Group," *Interfaces* 29, no. 2 (March/April 1999): 1–14.

NOTES AND COMMENTS

1. Developments in computer technology have increased the availability of management science techniques to decision makers. Many software packages are now available for personal computers. Versions of The Management Scientist, Microsoft Excel, and LINDO are widely used in management science courses.
2. The Management Scientist is a software package developed by the authors of this text. Version 6.0 is now available for Windows 95 through XP operating systems. This software can be used to solve problems in the text as well as small-scale problems encountered in practice. Appendix 1.1 provides an overview of the features and use of The Management Scientist.
3. Various chapter appendixes provide step-by-step instructions for using The Management Scientist, Excel, and LINDO to solve problems in the text.

1.4 MODELS OF COST, REVENUE, AND PROFIT

Some of the most basic quantitative models arising in business and economic applications are those involving the relationship between a volume variable—such as production volume or sales volume—and cost, revenue, and profit. Through the use of these models, a manager can determine the projected cost, revenue, and/or profit associated with an established production quantity or a forecasted sales volume. Financial planning, production planning, sales quotas, and other areas of decision making can benefit from such cost, revenue, and profit models.

Cost and Volume Models

The cost of manufacturing or producing a product is a function of the volume produced. This cost can usually be defined as a sum of two costs: fixed cost and variable cost. **Fixed cost** is the portion of the total cost that does not depend on the production volume; this cost remains the same no matter how much is produced. **Variable cost,** on the other hand, is the portion of the total cost that is dependent on and varies with the production volume. To illustrate how cost and volume models can be developed, we will consider a manufacturing problem faced by Nowlin Plastics.

Nowlin Plastics produces a variety of compact disc (CD) storage cases. Nowlin's best-selling product is the CD-50, a slim, plastic CD holder with a specially designed lining that protects the optical surface of the disc. Several products are produced on the same manufacturing line, and a setup cost is incurred each time a changeover is made for a new product. Suppose that the setup cost for the CD-50 is \$3000. This setup cost is a fixed cost that is incurred regardless of the number of units eventually produced. In addition, suppose that variable labor and material costs are \$2 for each unit produced. The cost-volume model for producing x units of the CD-50 can be written as

$$C(x) = 3000 + 2x \tag{1.3}$$

where

$$\begin{aligned} x &= \text{production volume in units} \\ C(x) &= \text{total cost of producing } x \text{ units} \end{aligned}$$

Once a production volume is established, the model in equation (1.3) can be used to compute the total production cost. For example, the decision to produce $x = 1200$ units would result in a total cost of $C(1200) = 3000 + 2(1200) = \$5400$.

Marginal cost is defined as the rate of change of the total cost with respect to production volume. That is, it is the cost increase associated with a one-unit increase in the production volume. In the cost model of equation (1.3), we see that the total cost $C(x)$ will increase by \$2 for each unit increase in the production volume. Thus, the marginal cost is \$2. With more complex total cost models, marginal cost may depend on the production volume. In such cases, we could have marginal cost increasing or decreasing with the production volume x.

Revenue and Volume Models

Management of Nowlin Plastics will also want information on the projected revenue associated with selling a specified number of units. Thus, a model of the relationship between revenue and volume is also needed. Suppose that each CD-50 storage unit sells for \$5. The model for total revenue can be written as

$$R(x) = 5x \tag{1.4}$$

where

$$\begin{aligned} x &= \text{sales volume in units} \\ R(x) &= \text{total revenue associated with selling } x \text{ units} \end{aligned}$$

Marginal revenue is defined as the rate of change of total revenue with respect to sales volume. That is, it is the increase in total revenue resulting from a one-unit increase in sales volume. In the model of equation (1.4), we see that the marginal revenue is \$5. In this case, marginal revenue is constant and does not vary with the sales volume. With more complex models, we may find that marginal revenue increases or decreases as the sales volume x increases.

Profit and Volume Models

One of the most important criteria for management decision making is profit. Managers need to be able to know the profit implications of their decisions. If we assume that we will only produce what can be sold, the production volume and sales volume will be equal. We can combine equations (1.3) and (1.4) to develop a profit-volume model that will determine the total profit associated with a specified production-sales volume. Total profit, denoted $P(x)$, is total revenue minus total cost; therefore, the following model provides the total profit associated with producing and selling x units:

$$\begin{aligned} P(x) &= R(x) - C(x) \\ &= 5x - (3000 + 2x) = -3000 + 3x \end{aligned} \tag{1.5}$$

Thus, the profit-volume model can be derived from the revenue-volume and cost-volume models.

Breakeven Analysis

Using equation (1.5), we can now determine the total profit associated with any production volume x. For example, suppose that a demand forecast indicates that 500 units of the product can be sold. The decision to produce and sell the 500 units results in a projected profit of

$$P(500) = -3000 + 3(500) = -1500$$

In other words, a loss of \$1500 is predicted. If sales are expected to be 500 units, the manager may decide against producing the product. However, a demand forecast of 1800 units would show a projected profit of

$$P(1800) = -3000 + 3(1800) = 2400$$

This profit may be enough to justify proceeding with the production and sale of the product.

We see that a volume of 500 units will yield a loss, whereas a volume of 1800 provides a profit. The volume that results in total revenue equaling total cost (providing \$0 profit) is called the **breakeven point.** If the breakeven point is known, a manager can quickly infer that a volume above the breakeven point will result in a profit, while a volume below the breakeven point will result in a loss. Thus, the breakeven point for a product provides valuable information for a manager who must make a yes/no decision concerning production of the product.

Let us now return to the Nowlin Plastics example and show how the total profit model in equation (1.5) can be used to compute the breakeven point. The breakeven point can be found by setting the total profit expression equal to zero and solving for the production volume. Using equation (1.5), we have

$$\begin{aligned} P(x) = -3000 + 3x &= 0 \\ 3x &= 3000 \\ x &= 1000 \end{aligned}$$

Try Problem 12 to test your ability to determine the breakeven point for a quantitative model.

With this information, we know that production and sales of the product must be greater than 1000 units before a profit can be expected. The graphs of the total cost model, the total revenue model, and the location of the breakeven point are shown in Figure 1.6. In Appendix 1.2 we also show how Excel can be used to perform a breakeven analysis for the Nowlin Plastics production example.

1.5 MANAGEMENT SCIENCE TECHNIQUES

In this section we present a brief overview of the management science techniques covered in this text. Over the years, practitioners have found numerous applications for the following techniques:

Linear Programming. Linear programming is a problem-solving approach developed for situations involving maximizing or minimizing a linear function subject to linear constraints that limit the degree to which the objective can be pursued. The production model developed in Section 1.3 (see Figure 1.5) is an example of a simple linear programming model.

Integer Linear Programming. Integer linear programming is an approach used for problems that can be set up as linear programs with the additional requirement that some or all of the decision recommendations be integer values.

FIGURE 1.6 GRAPH OF THE BREAKEVEN ANALYSIS FOR NOWLIN PLASTICS

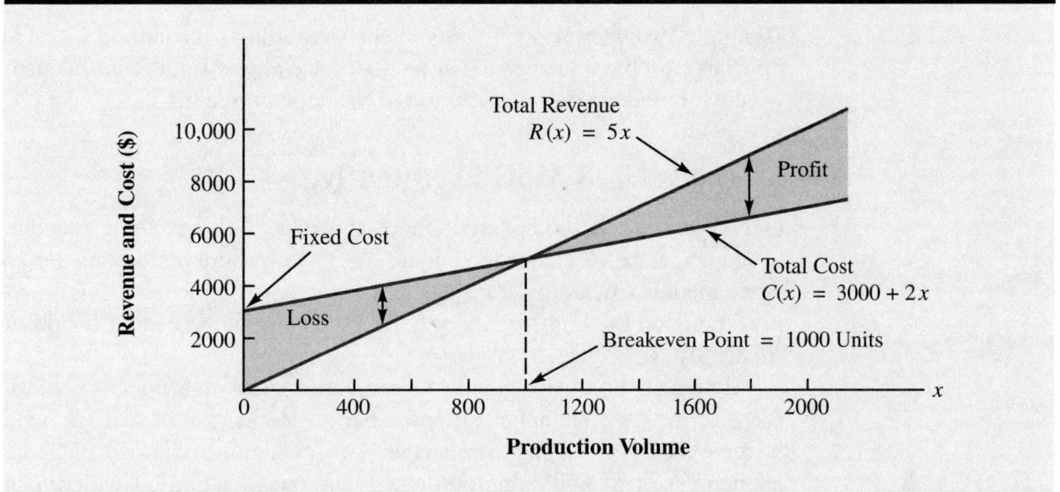

Network Models. A network is a graphical description of a problem consisting of circles called nodes that are interconnected by lines called arcs. Specialized solution procedures exist for these types of problems, enabling us to quickly solve problems in such areas as transportation system design, information system design, and project scheduling.

Project Scheduling: PERT/CPM. In many situations, managers are responsible for planning, scheduling, and controlling projects that consist of numerous separate jobs or tasks performed by a variety of departments, individuals, and so forth. The PERT (Program Evaluation and Review Technique) and CPM (Critical Path Method) techniques help managers carry out their project scheduling responsibilities.

Inventory Models. Inventory models are used by managers faced with the dual problems of maintaining sufficient inventories to meet demand for goods and, at the same time, incurring the lowest possible inventory holding costs.

Waiting Line or Queueing Models. Waiting-line or queueing models have been developed to help managers understand and make better decisions concerning the operation of systems involving waiting lines.

Simulation. Simulation is a technique used to model the operation of a system. This technique employs a computer program to model the operation and perform simulation computations.

Decision Analysis. Decision analysis can be used to determine optimal strategies in situations involving several decision alternatives and an uncertain or risk-filled pattern of events.

Goal Programming. Goal programming is a technique for solving multicriteria decision problems, usually within the framework of linear programming.

Analytic Hierarchy Process. This multicriteria decision-making technique permits the inclusion of subjective factors in arriving at a recommended decision.

Forecasting. Forecasting methods are techniques that can be used to predict future aspects of a business operation.

Markov Process Models. Markov process models are useful in studying the evolution of certain systems over repeated trials. For example, Markov processes have been used to describe the probability that a machine, functioning in one period, will function or break down in another period.

Dynamic Programming. Dynamic programming is an approach that allows us to break up a large problem in such a fashion that once all the smaller problems have been solved, we are left with an optimal solution to the large problem.

Methods Used Most Frequently

Our experience as both practitioners and educators has been that the most frequently used management science techniques are linear programming, integer programming, network models (including transportation and transshipment models), and simulation. Depending upon the industry, the other methods in the preceding list are used more or less frequently.

Helping to bridge the gap between the manager and the management scientist is a major focus of the text. We believe that the barriers to the use of management science can best be removed by increasing the manager's understanding of how management science can be applied. The text will help you develop an understanding of which management science techniques are most useful, how they are used, and, most importantly, how they can assist managers in making better decisions.

The Management Science in Action, Taco Bell's SMART Labor Management System, shows how Taco Bell was able to use management science to ensure that the maximum time customers wait in line is between three and five minutes. The SMART system consists of three models: a forecasting model, a simulation model, and an integer programming model. This system has provided Taco Bell with a major competitive advantage and is typical of the widespread role of management science in service industries. Throughout the text we will continue to illustrate the applications of management science with Management Science in Action articles.

MANAGEMENT SCIENCE IN ACTION

TACO BELL'S SMART LABOR MANAGEMENT SYSTEM*

Taco Bell turned to management science in order to develop methods for better handling customer demand while still keeping labor costs down. The company created the SMART (Scheduling Management and Restaurant Tool) Labor Management System (LMS) in order to determine a method of scheduling employees that will ensure that the maximum time customers wait in line is between three and five minutes. The SMART LMS consists of three integrated models: a forecasting model, a simulation model, and an integer programming model.

The forecasting model determines how many dollars worth of business each store will generate each day. Unlike a manufacturing plant, which makes forecasts in terms of years, months, or weeks, Taco Bell needs to develop predictions of customer arrivals based on 15-minute intervals. Then, using the predictions of how much business a store will generate the following day, a simulation model determines how many employees will be needed and how they should be positioned throughout the facility. To determine the labor table for the next day, the simulation model must take into account the differences in Taco Bell facilities, the build-to-order food preparation approach used by Taco Bell, and the randomness associated with customer demand. Using the labor table generated by the simulation model, the integer programming model determines how many people are needed on the schedule for a particular day and what their shifts should be so that payroll costs are minimized. The integer programming model also takes into account all of the customer-service responsibilities and provides Taco Bell managers with the ability to schedule other tasks such as cleaning and maintenance.

The system is used in all company-owned stores, and by 1996 had been adopted by 70 percent of franchisees. From 1993–1996, the new system resulted in labor costs savings of $40.34 million. Employee feedback is positive, and other fast-food companies have indicated that the new system has provided Taco Bell with a major competitive advantage.

*Based on Nancy Bistritz, "Taco Bell Finds Recipe for Success," *OR/MS Today* (October 1997): 20–21.

NOTES AND COMMENTS

1. Operations research analyst is listed by the Bureau of Labor Statistics as one of the fastest growing occupations for careers requiring a bachelor's degree. The predicted growth is from 57,000 jobs in 1990 to 100,000 jobs in 2005, an increase of 73%.
2. The Institute for Operations Research and the Management Sciences (INFORMS) and the Decision Sciences Institute (DSI) are two professional societies that publish journals and newsletters dealing with current research and applications of operations research and management science techniques.

SUMMARY

This text is about how management science may be used to help managers make better decisions. The focus of this text is on the decision-making process and on the role of management science in that process. We discussed the problem orientation of this process and in an overview showed how mathematical models can be used in this type of analysis.

The difference between the model and the situation or managerial problem it represents is an important point. Mathematical models are abstractions of real-world situations and, as such, cannot capture all the aspects of the real situation. However, if a model can capture the major relevant aspects of the problem and can then provide a solution recommendation, it can be a valuable aid to decision making.

One of the characteristics of management science that will become increasingly apparent as we proceed through the text is the search for a best solution to the problem. In carrying out the quantitative analysis, we shall be attempting to develop procedures for finding the "best" or optimal solution.

GLOSSARY

Problem solving The process of identifying a difference between the actual and the desired state of affairs and then taking action to resolve the difference.

Decision making The process of defining the problem, identifying the alternatives, determining the criteria, evaluating the alternatives, and choosing an alternative.

Single-criterion decision problem A problem in which the objective is to find the "best" solution with respect to just one criterion.

Multicriteria decision problem A problem that involves more than one criterion; the objective is to find the "best" solution, taking into account all the criteria.

Decision The alternative selected.

Model A representation of a real object or situation.

Iconic model A physical replica, or representation, of a real object.

Analog model Although physical in form, an analog model does not have a physical appearance similar to the real object or situation it represents.

Mathematical model Mathematical symbols and expressions used to represent a real situation.

Constraints Restrictions or limitations imposed on a problem.

Objective function A mathematical expression that describes the problem's objective.

Uncontrollable inputs The environmental factors or inputs that cannot be controlled by the decision maker.

Controllable inputs The inputs that are controlled or determined by the decision maker.

Decision variable Another term for controllable input.

Deterministic model A model in which all uncontrollable inputs are known and cannot vary.

Stochastic (probabilistic) model A model in which at least one uncontrollable input is uncertain and subject to variation; stochastic models are also referred to as probabilistic models.

Optimal solution The specific decision-variable value or values that provide the "best" output for the model.

Infeasible solution A decision alternative or solution that does not satisfy one or more constraints.

Feasible solution A decision alternative or solution that satisfies all constraints.

Fixed cost The portion of the total cost that does not depend on the volume; this cost remains the same no matter how much is produced.

Variable cost The portion of the total cost that is dependent on and varies with the volume.

Marginal cost The rate of change of the total cost with respect to volume.

Marginal revenue The rate of change of total revenue with respect to volume.

Breakeven point The volume at which total revenue equals total cost.

PROBLEMS

1. Define the terms *management science* and *operations research.*
2. List and discuss the steps of the decision-making process.
3. Discuss the different roles played by the qualitative and quantitative approaches to managerial decision making. Why is it important for a manager or decision maker to have a good understanding of both of these approaches to decision making?

4. A firm just completed a new plant that will produce more than 500 different products, using more than 50 different production lines and machines. The production scheduling decisions are critical in that sales will be lost if customer demands are not met on time. If no individual in the firm has experience with this production operation, and if new produc-

tion schedules must be generated each week, why should the firm consider a quantitative approach to the production scheduling problem?

5. What are the advantages of analyzing and experimenting with a model as opposed to a real object or situation?

6. Suppose that a manager has a choice between the following two mathematical models of a given situation: (a) a relatively simple model that is a reasonable approximation of the real situation, and (b) a thorough and complex model that is the most accurate mathematical representation of the real situation possible. Why might the model described in part (a) be preferred by the manager?

7. Suppose you are going on a weekend trip to a city that is d miles away. Develop a model that determines your round-trip gasoline costs. What assumptions or approximations are necessary to treat this model as a deterministic model? Are these assumptions or approximations acceptable to you?

8. Recall the production model from Section 1.3:

$$\begin{aligned} \text{Max} \quad & 10x \\ \text{s.t.} \quad & \\ & 5x \leq 40 \\ & x \geq 0 \end{aligned}$$

Suppose the firm in this example considers a second product that has a unit profit of \$5 and requires 2 hours of production time for each unit produced. Use y as the number of units of product 2 produced.

a. Show the mathematical model when both products are considered simultaneously.
b. Identify the controllable and uncontrollable inputs for this model.
c. Draw the flowchart of the input-output process for this model (see Figure 1.5).
d. What are the optimal solution values of x and y?
e. Is the model developed in part (a) a deterministic or a stochastic model? Explain.

9. Suppose we modify the production model in Problem 8 to obtain the following mathematical model:

$$\begin{aligned} \text{Max} \quad & 10x \\ \text{s.t.} \quad & \\ & ax \leq 40 \\ & x \geq 0 \end{aligned}$$

where a is the number of hours of production time required for each unit produced. With $a = 5$, the optimal solution is $x = 8$. If we have a stochastic model with $a = 3$, $a = 4$, $a = 5$, or $a = 6$ as the possible values for the number of hours required per unit, what is the optimal value for x? What problems does this stochastic model cause?

10. A retail store in Des Moines, Iowa, receives shipments of a particular product from Kansas City and Minneapolis. Let

x = number of units of the product received from Kansas City
y = number of units of the product received from Minneapolis

a. Write an expression for the total number of units of the product received by the retail store in Des Moines.
b. Shipments from Kansas City cost \$0.20 per unit, and shipments from Minneapolis cost \$0.25 per unit. Develop an objective function representing the total cost of shipments to Des Moines.
c. Assuming the monthly demand at the retail store is 5000 units, develop a constraint that requires 5000 units to be shipped to Des Moines.
d. No more than 4000 units can be shipped from Kansas City, and no more than 3000 units can be shipped from Minneapolis in a month. Develop constraints to model this situation.
e. Of course, negative amounts cannot be shipped. Combine the objective function and constraints developed to state a mathematical model for satisfying the demand at the Des Moines retail store at minimum cost.

11. For most products, higher prices result in a decreased demand, whereas lower prices result in an increased demand. Let

$$d = \text{annual demand for a product in units}$$
$$p = \text{price per unit}$$

Assume that a firm accepts the following price-demand relationship as being realistic:

$$d = 800 - 10p$$

where p must be between \$20 and \$70.

a. How many units can the firm sell at the \$20 per-unit price? At the \$70 per-unit price?
b. Show the mathematical model for the total revenue (TR), which is the annual demand multiplied by the unit price.
c. Based on other considerations, the firm's management will only consider price alternatives of \$30, \$40, and \$50. Use your model from part (b) to determine the price alternative that will maximize the total revenue.
d. What are the expected annual demand and the total revenue corresponding to your recommended price?

12. The O'Neill Shoe Manufacturing Company will produce a special-style shoe if the order size is large enough to provide a reasonable profit. For each special-style order, the company incurs a fixed cost of \$1000 for the production setup. The variable cost is \$30 per pair, and each pair sells for \$40.

a. Let x indicate the number of pairs of shoes produced. Develop a mathematical model for the total cost of producing x pairs of shoes.
b. Let P indicate the total profit. Develop a mathematical model for the total profit realized from an order for x pairs of shoes.
c. How large must the shoe order be before O'Neill will break even?

13. Micromedia offers computer training seminars on a variety of topics. In the seminars each student works at a personal computer, practicing the particular activity that the instructor is presenting. Micromedia is currently planning a two-day seminar on the use of Microsoft Excel in statistical analysis. The projected fee for the seminar is \$300 per student. The cost for the conference room, instructor compensation, lab assistants, and promotion is \$4,800. Micromedia rents computers for its seminars at a cost of \$30 per computer per day.

a. Develop a model for the total cost to put on the seminar. Let x represent the number of students who enroll in the seminar.
b. Develop a model for the total profit if x students enroll in the seminar.
c. Micromedia has forecasted an enrollment of 30 students for the seminar. How much profit will be earned if their forecast is accurate?
d. Compute the breakeven point.

14. Eastman Publishing Company is considering publishing a paperback textbook on spreadsheet applications for business. The fixed cost of manuscript preparation, textbook design, and production setup is estimated to be $80,000. Variable production and material costs are estimated to be $3 per book. Demand over the life of the book is estimated to be 4000 copies. The publisher plans to sell the text to college and university bookstores for $20 each.

a. What is the breakeven point?

b. What profit or loss can be anticipated with a demand of 4000 copies?

c. With a demand of 4000 copies, what is the minimum price per copy that the publisher must charge to break even?

d. If the publisher believes that the price per copy could be increased to $25.95 and not affect the anticipated demand of 4000 copies, what action would you recommend? What profit or loss can be anticipated?

15. Preliminary plans are under way for the construction of a new stadium for a major league baseball team. City officials have questioned the number and profitability of the luxury corporate boxes planned for the upper deck of the stadium. Corporations and selected individuals may buy the boxes for $100,000 each. The fixed construction cost for the upper-deck area is estimated to be $1,500,000, with a variable cost of $50,000 for each box constructed.

a. What is the breakeven point for the number of luxury boxes in the new stadium?

b. Preliminary drawings for the stadium show that space is available for the construction of up to 50 luxury boxes. Promoters indicate that buyers are available and that all 50 could be sold if constructed. What is your recommendation concerning the construction of luxury boxes? What profit is anticipated?

16. Financial Analysts, Inc., is an investment firm that manages stock portfolios for a number of clients. A new client is requesting that the firm handle an $80,000 portfolio. As an initial investment strategy, the client would like to restrict the portfolio to a mix of the following two stocks:

Stock	Price/ Share	Maximum Estimated Annual Return/Share	Possible Investment
Oil Alaska	$50	$6	$50,000
Southwest Petroleum	$30	$4	$45,000

Let

$$x = \text{number of shares of Oil Alaska}$$
$$y = \text{number of shares of Southwest Petroleum}$$

a. Develop the objective function, assuming that the client desires to maximize the total annual return.

b. Show the mathematical expression for each of the following three constraints:
(1) Total investment funds available are $80,000.
(2) Maximum Oil Alaska investment is $50,000.
(3) Maximum Southwest Petroleum investment is $45,000.

Note: Adding the $x \geq 0$ and $y \geq 0$ constraints provides a linear programming model for the investment problem. A solution procedure for this model will be discussed in Chapter 2.

17. Models of inventory systems frequently consider the relationships among a beginning inventory, a production quantity, a demand or sales, and an ending inventory. For a given production period j, let

s_{j-1} = ending inventory from the previous period (beginning inventory for period j)
x_j = production quantity in period j
d_j = demand in period j
s_j = ending inventory for period j

a. Write the mathematical relationship or model that describes how these four variables are related.
b. What constraint should be added if production capacity for period j is given by C_j?
c. What constraint should be added if inventory requirements for period j mandate an ending inventory of at least I_j?

Case Problem SCHEDULING A GOLF LEAGUE

Chris Lane, the head professional at Royal Oak Country Club, must develop a schedule of matches for the couples' golf league that begins its season at 4:00 P.M. tomorrow. Eighteen couples signed up for the league, and each couple must play every other couple over the course of the 17-week season. Chris thought it would be fairly easy to develop a schedule, but after working on it for a couple of hours, he has been unable to come up with a schedule. Because Chris must have a schedule ready by tomorrow afternoon, he asked you to help him. A possible complication is that one of the couples told Chris that they may have to cancel for the season. They told Chris they will let him know by 1:00 P.M. tomorrow whether they will be able to play this season.

Managerial Report

Prepare a report for Chris Lane. Your report should include, at a minimum, the following items:

1. A schedule that will enable each of the 18 couples to play every other couple over the 17-week season.
2. A contingency schedule that can be used if the couple that contacted Chris decides to cancel for the season.

Appendix 1.1 THE MANAGEMENT SCIENTIST SOFTWARE

Developments in computer technology play a major role in making management science techniques available to decision makers. A software package called *The Management Scientist* accompanies this text. Version 6.0 is now available for Windows 95 through Windows XP operating systems.[1] This software can be used to solve problems in the text as well as small-scale problems encountered in practice. Using The Management Scientist

[1]Version 6.0 has been designed to run optimally on computers with screen resolutions of 1024 × 768 or higher. Computers with lower screen resolutions can still run Version 6.0. Scroll bars appear when necessary for working with large problems.

will give you an understanding and appreciation of the role of the computer in applying management science to decision problems.

The Management Scientist contains 12 modules, or programs, that will enable you to solve problems in the following areas:

Chapters 2–6	Linear programming
Chapter 7	Transportation and assignment
Chapter 8	Integer linear programming
Chapter 9	Shortest route and minimal spanning tree
Chapter 10	PERT/CPM
Chapter 11	Inventory models
Chapter 12	Waiting line models
Chapter 14	Decision analysis
Chapter 16	Forecasting
Chapter 17	Markov processes

Use of The Management Scientist with the text is optional. Occasionally, we insert a figure in the text that shows the output The Management Scientist provides for a problem. However, familiarity with the use of the software is not necessary to understand the figure and the text material. The remainder of this appendix provides an overview of the features and the use of the software.

Selecting a Module

After starting The Management Scientist, you will encounter the module selection screen as shown in Figure 1.7. The choices provide access to the 12 modules. Simply click the desired module and select OK to load the requested module into the computer's memory.

FIGURE 1.7 MODULE SELECTION SCREEN FOR THE MANAGEMENT SCIENTIST VERSION 6.0

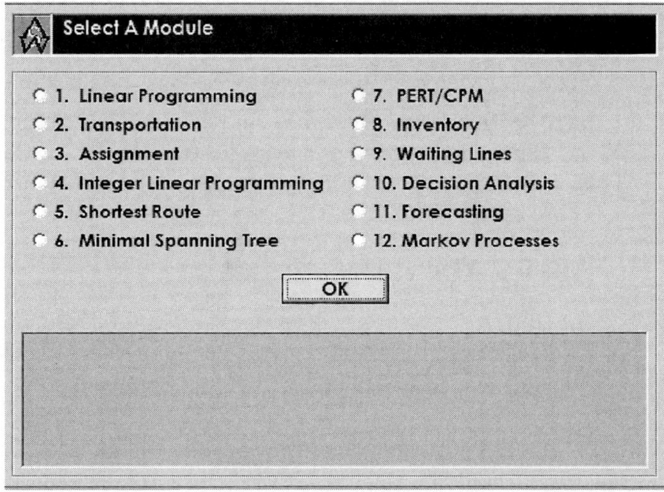

The File Menu

After a module is loaded, you will need to click the File menu to begin working with a problem. The File menu provides the following options.

New Select this option to begin a new problem. Dialog boxes and input templates will guide you through the data input process.

Open Select this option to retrieve a problem that has been previously saved. When the problem is selected it will be displayed on the screen for you to verify as the problem you want to solve.

Save Once a new problem has been entered, you may want to save it for future use or modification. The Save option will guide you through the naming and saving process. If you create a folder named Problems, the Open and Save options will take you automatically to the Problems folder.

Change Modules This option returns control to the screen in Figure 1.7 and another module may be selected.

Exit This option will exit The Management Scientist.

The Edit Menu

After a new problem has been solved, you may want to make one or more modifications to the problem before resolving. The Edit menu provides the option to display the problem and then make revisions in the problem before solving or saving. In the linear and integer programming modules, the Edit menu also includes options to change the problem size by adding or deleting variables and adding or deleting constraints. Similar options to change the problem size are provided in the Edit menu of the transportation and assignment modules.

The Solution Menu

The Solution menu provides three options.

Solve This option solves the current problem and displays the solution on the screen.

Print Once the solution is on the screen, the Print option sends the solution to a printer.

Save As Text File Once the solution is on the screen, the Save As Text File option enables the solution to be saved as a text file. The text file can be accessed later by a word processor so that the solution output may be displayed as part of a solution report.

Advice About Data Input

Any time a new problem is selected, the appropriate module will provide dialog boxes and forms for describing the features of the problem and for entering data. When using The Management Scientist, you may find the following data input suggestions helpful.

1. Do not enter commas (,) with your input data. For example, the value 104,000 should be entered with the six digits: 104000.
2. Do not enter the dollar sign ($) for profit or cost data. For example, a cost of $20.00 should be entered as 20.

3. Do not enter the percent sign (%) if percentage is requested. For example, 25% should be entered as 25, not 25% or .25.
4. Occasionally, a model may be formulated with fractional values such as ¼, ⅔, ⅚, and so on. The data input for The Management Scientist must be in decimal form. The fraction ¼ can be entered as .25. However, fractions such as ⅔ and ⅚ have repeating decimal forms. In these cases, we recommend the convention of rounding to five places such as .66667 and .83333.
5. Finally, we recommend that in general you attempt to scale extremely large input data so that smaller numbers may be input and operated on by the computer. For example, costs such as $2,500,000 may be scaled to 2.5 with the understanding that the data used in the problem reflect millions of dollars.

Appendix 1.2 USING EXCEL FOR BREAKEVEN ANALYSIS

In Section 1.4 we introduced the Nowlin Plastics production example to illustrate how quantitative models can be used to help a manager determine the projected cost, revenue, and/or profit associated with an established production quantity or a forecasted sales volume. In this appendix we introduce spreadsheet applications by showing how to use Microsoft Excel to perform a quantitative analysis of the Nowlin Plastics example.

Refer to the worksheet shown in Figure 1.8. We begin by entering the problem data into the top portion of the worksheet. The value of 3000 in cell B3 is the setup cost, the value of 2 in cell B5 is the variable labor and material costs per unit, and the value of 5 in cell B7 is

FIGURE 1.8 FORMULA WORKSHEET FOR THE NOWLIN PLASTICS PRODUCTION EXAMPLE

	A	B	C
1	**Nowlin Plastics**		
2			
3	**Fixed Cost**	3000	
4			
5	**Variable Cost Per Unit**	2	
6			
7	**Selling Price Per Unit**	5	
8			
9			
10	**Models**		
11			
12	**Production Volume**	800	
13			
14	**Total Cost**	=B3+B5*B12	
15			
16	**Total Revenue**	=B7*B12	
17			
18	**Total Profit (Loss)**	=B16-B14	
19			

the selling price per unit. In general, whenever we perform a quantitative analysis using Excel, we will enter the problem data in the top portion of the worksheet and reserve the bottom portion for model development. The label "Models" in cell A10 helps to provide a visual reminder of this convention.

Cell B12 in the models portion of the worksheet contains the proposed production volume in units. Because the values for total cost, total revenue, and total profit depend upon the value of this decision variable, we have placed a border around cell B12 and screened the cell for emphasis. Based upon the value in cell B12, the cell formulas in cells B14, B16, and B18 are used to compute values for total cost, total revenue, and total profit (loss), respectively. First, recall that the value of total cost is the sum of the fixed cost (cell B3) and the total variable cost. The total variable cost—the product of the variable cost per unit (cell B5) and the production volume (cell B12)—is given by B5*B12. Thus, to compute the value of total cost we entered the formula =B3+B5*B12 in cell B14. Next, total revenue is the product of the selling price per unit (cell B7) and the number of units produced (cell B12), which is entered in cell B16 as the formula =B7*B12. Finally, the total profit (or loss) is the difference between the total revenue (cell B16) and the total cost (cell B14). Thus, in cell B18 we have entered the formula =B16−B14. The worksheet shown in Figure 1.8 shows the formulas used to make these computations; we refer to it as a formula worksheet.

To examine the effect of selecting a particular value for the production volume, we entered a value of 800 in cell B12. The worksheet shown in Figure 1.9 shows the values obtained by the formulas; a production volume of 800 units results in a total cost of $4600, a total revenue of $4000, and a loss of $600. To examine the effect of other production vol-

FIGURE 1.9 SOLUTION USING A PRODUCTION VOLUME OF 800 UNITS FOR THE NOWLIN PLASTICS PRODUCTION EXAMPLE

	A	B	C
1	Nowlin Plastics		
2			
3	Fixed Cost	$3,000	
4			
5	Variable Cost Per Unit	$2	
6			
7	Selling Price Per Unit	$5	
8			
9			
10	Models		
11			
12	Production Volume	800	
13			
14	Total Cost	$4,600	
15			
16	Total Revenue	$4,000	
17			
18	Total Profit (Loss)	-$600	
19			

umes, we only need to enter a different value into cell B12. To examine the effect of different costs and selling prices, we simply enter the appropriate values in the data portion of the worksheet; the results will be displayed in the model section of the worksheet.

In Section 1.4 we illustrated breakeven analysis. Let us now see how Excel's Goal Seek tool can be used to compute the breakeven point for the Nowlin Plastics production example.

Determining the Breakeven Point Using Excel's Goal Seek Tool

The breakeven point is the production volume that results in total revenue equal to total cost and hence a profit of $0. One way to determine the breakeven point is to use a trial-and-error approach. For example, in Figure 1.9 we saw that a trial production volume of 800 units resulted in a loss of $600. Because this trial solution resulted in a loss, a production volume of 800 units cannot be the breakeven point. We could continue to experiment with other production volumes by simply entering different values into cell B12 and observing the resulting profit or loss in cell B18. A better approach is to use Excel's Goal Seek tool to determine the breakeven point.

Excel's Goal Seek tool allows the user to determine the value for an input cell that will cause the value of a related output cell to equal some specified value (called the *goal*). In the case of breakeven analysis, the "goal" is to set Total Profit to zero by "seeking" an appropriate value for Production Volume. Goal Seek will allow us to find the value of production volume that will set Nowlin Plastics' total profit to zero. The following steps describe how to use Goal Seek to find the breakeven point for Nowlin Plastics:

Step 1. Select the **Tools** menu
Step 2. Choose the **Goal Seek** option
Step 3. When the **Goal Seek** dialog box appears:
Enter B18 in the **Set cell** box
Enter 0 in the **To value** box
Enter B12 in the **By changing cell** box
Click **OK**

The completed Goal Seek dialog box is shown in Figure 1.10, and the worksheet obtained after selecting **OK** is shown in Figure 1.11. The Total Profit in cell B18 is zero, and the Production Volume in cell B12 has been set to the breakeven point of 1000.

FIGURE 1.10 GOAL SEEK DIALOG BOX FOR THE NOWLIN PLASTICS PRODUCTION EXAMPLE

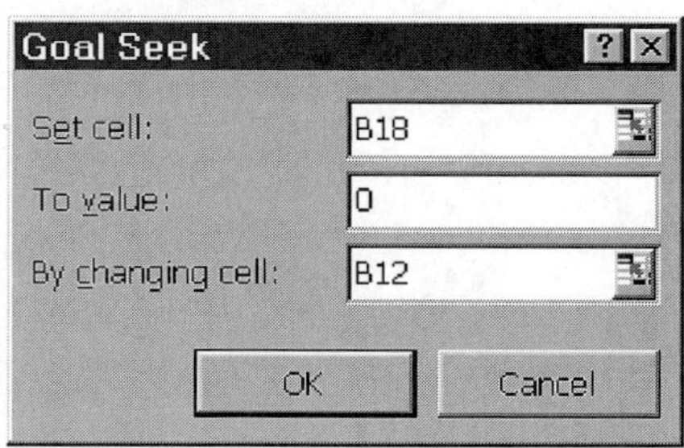

FIGURE 1.11 BREAKEVEN POINT FOUND USING EXCEL'S GOAL SEEK TOOL FOR THE NOWLIN PLASTICS PRODUCTION EXAMPLE

	A	B	C
1	Nowlin Plastics		
2			
3	Fixed Cost	$3,000	
4			
5	Variable Cost Per Unit	$2	
6			
7	Selling Price Per Unit	$5	
8			
9			
10	Models		
11			
12	Production Volume	1000	
13			
14	Total Cost	5000	
15			
16	Total Revenue	5000	
17			
18	Total Profit (Loss)	0	
19			

CHAPTER 2

An Introduction to Linear Programming

CONTENTS

Linear programming is a problem-solving approach developed to help managers make decisions. Numerous applications of linear programming can be found in today's competitive business environment. For instance, Eastman Kodak uses linear programming to determine where to manufacture products throughout their worldwide facilities, and GE Capital uses linear programming to help determine optimal lease structuring. Marathon Oil Company uses linear programming for gasoline blending and to evaluate the economics of a new terminal or pipeline. The Management Science in Action, Timber Harvesting Model at MeadWestvaco Corporation, provides another example of the use of linear programming. Later in the chapter another Management Science in Action illustrates how the Hanshin Expressway Public Corporation uses linear programming for traffic control on an urban toll expressway in Osaka, Japan.

To illustrate some of the properties that all linear programming problems have in common, consider the following typical applications:

1. A manufacturer wants to develop a production schedule and an inventory policy that will satisfy sales demand in future periods. Ideally, the schedule and policy will enable the company to satisfy demand and at the same time *minimize* the total production and inventory costs.
2. A financial analyst must select an investment portfolio from a variety of stock and bond investment alternatives. The analyst would like to establish the portfolio that *maximizes* the return on investment.
3. A marketing manager wants to determine how best to allocate a fixed advertising budget among alternative advertising media such as radio, television, newspaper, and magazine. The manager would like to determine the media mix that *maximizes* advertising effectiveness.
4. A company has warehouses in a number of locations throughout the United States. For a set of customer demands, the company would like to determine how much each warehouse should ship to each customer so that total transportation costs are *minimized.*

MANAGEMENT SCIENCE IN ACTION

TIMBER HARVESTING MODEL AT MEADWESTVACO CORPORATION*

MeadWestvaco Corporation is a major producer of premium papers for periodicals, books, commercial printing, and business forms. The company also produces pulp and lumber, designs and manufactures packaging systems for beverage and other consumables markets, and is a world leader in the production of coated board and shipping containers. Quantitative analyses at MeadWestvaco are developed and implemented by the company's Decision Analysis Department. The department assists decision makers by providing them with analytical tools of quantitative methods as well as personal analysis and recommendations.

MeadWestvaco uses quantitative models to assist with the long-range management of the company's timberland. Through the use of large-scale linear programs, timber harvesting plans are developed to cover a substantial time horizon. These models consider wood market conditions, mill pulpwood requirements, harvesting capacities, and general forest management principles. Within these constraints, the model arrives at an optimal harvesting and purchasing schedule based on discounted cash flow. Alternative schedules reflect changes in the various assumptions concerning forest growth, wood availability, and general economic conditions.

Quantitative methods are also used in the development of the inputs for the linear programming models. Timber prices and supplies as well as mill requirements must be forecast over the time horizon, and advanced sampling techniques are used to evaluate land holdings and to project forest growth. The harvest schedule is then developed using quantitative methods.

*Based on information provided by Dr. Edward P. Winkofsky of MeadWestvaco Corporation.

Linear programming was initially referred to as "programming in a linear structure." In 1948 Tjalling Koopmans suggested to George Dantzig that the name was much too long; Koopmans suggested shortening it to linear programming. George Dantzig agreed and the field we now know as linear programming was named.

These examples are only a few of the situations in which linear programming has been used successfully, but they illustrate the diversity of linear programming applications. A close scrutiny reveals one basic property they all have in common. In each example, we were concerned with *maximizing* or *minimizing* some quantity. In example 1, the manufacturer wanted to minimize costs; in example 2, the financial analyst wanted to maximize return on investment; in example 3, the marketing manager wanted to maximize advertising effectiveness; and in example 4, the company wanted to minimize total transportation costs. *In all linear programming problems, the maximization or minimization of some quantity is the objective.*

All linear programming problems also have a second property: restrictions or **constraints** that limit the degree to which the objective can be pursued. In example 1, the manufacturer is restricted by constraints requiring product demand to be satisfied and by the constraints limiting production capacity. The financial analyst's portfolio problem is constrained by the total amount of investment funds available and the maximum amounts that can be invested in each stock or bond. The marketing manager's media selection decision is constrained by a fixed advertising budget and the availability of the various media. In the transportation problem, the minimum-cost shipping schedule is constrained by the supply of product available at each warehouse. *Thus, constraints are another general feature of every linear programming problem.*

2.1 A SIMPLE MAXIMIZATION PROBLEM

Par, Inc., is a small manufacturer of golf equipment and supplies whose management has decided to move into the market for medium- and high-priced golf bags. Par's distributor is enthusiastic about the new product line and has agreed to buy all the golf bags Par produces over the next three months.

After a thorough investigation of the steps involved in manufacturing a golf bag, management determined that each golf bag produced will require the following operations:

1. Cutting and dyeing the material
2. Sewing
3. Finishing (inserting umbrella holder, club separators, etc.)
4. Inspection and packaging

The director of manufacturing analyzed each of the operations and concluded that if the company produces a medium-priced standard model, each bag will require $\frac{7}{10}$ hour in the cutting and dyeing department, $\frac{1}{2}$ hour in the sewing department, 1 hour in the finishing department, and $\frac{1}{10}$ hour in the inspection and packaging department. The more expensive deluxe model will require 1 hour for cutting and dyeing, $\frac{5}{6}$ hour for sewing, $\frac{2}{3}$ hour for finishing, and $\frac{1}{4}$ hour for inspection and packaging. This production information is summarized in Table 2.1.

Par's production is constrained by a limited number of hours available in each department. After studying departmental workload projections, the director of manufacturing estimates that 630 hours for cutting and dyeing, 600 hours for sewing, 708 hours for finishing, and 135 hours for inspection and packaging will be available for the production of golf bags during the next three months.

The accounting department analyzed the production data, assigned all relevant variable costs, and arrived at prices for both bags that will result in a profit contribution[1] of $10 for every standard bag and $9 for every deluxe bag produced. Let us now develop a mathematical model

[1]From an accounting perspective, profit contribution is more correctly described as the contribution margin per bag; for example, overhead and other shared costs have not been allocated.

TABLE 2.1 PRODUCTION REQUIREMENTS PER GOLF BAG

	Production Time (hours)	
Department	**Standard Bag**	**Deluxe Bag**
Cutting and Dyeing	$\frac{7}{10}$	1
Sewing	$\frac{1}{2}$	$\frac{5}{6}$
Finishing	1	$\frac{2}{3}$
Inspection and Packaging	$\frac{1}{10}$	$\frac{1}{4}$

It is important to understand that we are maximizing profit contribution, not profit. Overhead and other shared costs must be deducted before arriving at a profit figure.

of the Par, Inc., problem that can be used to determine the number of standard bags and the number of deluxe bags to produce in order to maximize total profit contribution.

Problem Formulation

Problem formulation or **modeling** is the process of translating the verbal statement of a problem into a mathematical statement. Formulating models is an art that can only be mastered with practice and experience. Even though every problem has some unique features, most problems also have common features. As a result, *some* general guidelines for model formulation can be helpful, especially for beginners. We will illustrate these general guidelines by developing a mathematical model for the Par, Inc., problem.

Understand the Problem Thoroughly. We selected the Par, Inc., problem to introduce linear programming because it is easy to understand. However, more complex problems will require much more thinking in order to identify the items that need to be included in the model. In such cases, read the problem description quickly to get a feel for what is involved. Taking notes will help you focus on the key issues and facts.

Describe the Objective. The objective is to maximize the total contribution to profit.

Describe Each Constraint. Four constraints relate to the number of hours of manufacturing time available; they restrict the number of standard bags and the number of deluxe bags that can be produced.

Constraint 1 Number of hours of cutting and dyeing time used must be less than or equal to the number of hours of cutting and dyeing time available.

Constraint 2 Number of hours of sewing time used must be less than or equal to the number of hours of sewing time available.

Constraint 3 Number of hours of finishing time used must be less than or equal to the number of hours of finishing time available.

Constraint 4 Number of hours of inspection and packaging time used must be less than or equal to the number of hours of inspection and packaging time available.

Define the Decision Variables. The controllable inputs for Par, Inc., are (1) the number of standard bags produced, and (2) the number of deluxe bags produced. Let

$$S = \text{number of standard bags}$$
$$D = \text{number of deluxe bags}$$

In linear programming terminology, S and D are referred to as the **decision variables.**

Write the Objective in Terms of the Decision Variables. Par's profit contribution comes from two sources: (1) the profit contribution made by producing S standard bags, and (2) the profit contribution made by producing D deluxe bags. If Par makes \$10 for every standard bag, the company will make \$10S if S standard bags are produced. Also, if Par makes \$9 for every deluxe bag, the company will make \$9D if D deluxe bags are produced. Thus, we have

$$\text{Total Profit Contribution} = 10S + 9D$$

Because the objective—maximize total profit contribution—is a function of the decision variables S and D, we refer to $10S + 9D$ as the *objective function.* Using "Max" as an abbreviation for maximize, we write Par's objective as follows:

$$\text{Max } 10S + 9D$$

Write the Constraints in Terms of the Decision Variables

Constraint 1:

$$\begin{pmatrix}\text{Hours of cutting and} \\ \text{dyeing time used}\end{pmatrix} \le \begin{pmatrix}\text{Hours of cutting and} \\ \text{dyeing time available}\end{pmatrix}$$

Every standard bag Par produces will use $\frac{7}{10}$ hour cutting and dyeing time; therefore, the total number of hours of cutting and dyeing time used in the manufacture of S standard bags is $\frac{7}{10}S$. In addition, because every deluxe bag produced uses 1 hour of cutting and dyeing time, the production of D deluxe bags will use $1D$ hours of cutting and dyeing time. Thus, the total cutting and dyeing time required for the production of S standard bags and D deluxe bags is given by

$$\text{Total hours of cutting and dyeing time used} = \tfrac{7}{10}S + 1D$$

The units of measurement on the left-hand side of the constraint must match the units of measurement on the right-hand side.

The director of manufacturing stated that Par has at most 630 hours of cutting and dyeing time available. Therefore, the production combination we select must satisfy the requirement

$$\tfrac{7}{10}S + 1D \le 630 \qquad (2.1)$$

Constraint 2:

$$\begin{pmatrix}\text{Hours of sewing} \\ \text{time used}\end{pmatrix} \le \begin{pmatrix}\text{Hours of sewing} \\ \text{time available}\end{pmatrix}$$

From Table 2.1 we see that every standard bag manufactured will require $\frac{1}{2}$ hour for sewing, and every deluxe bag will require $\frac{5}{6}$ hour for sewing. Because 600 hours of sewing time are available, it follows that

$$\tfrac{1}{2}S + \tfrac{5}{6}D \le 600 \qquad (2.2)$$

Constraint 3:

$$\begin{pmatrix}\text{Hours of finishing}\\ \text{time used}\end{pmatrix} \leq \begin{pmatrix}\text{Hours of finishing}\\ \text{time available}\end{pmatrix}$$

Every standard bag manufactured will require 1 hour for finishing, and every deluxe bag will require $\frac{2}{3}$ hour for finishing. With 708 hours of finishing time available, it follows that

$$1S + \tfrac{2}{3}D \leq 708 \qquad (2.3)$$

Constraint 4:

$$\begin{pmatrix}\text{Hours of inspection and}\\ \text{packaging time used}\end{pmatrix} \leq \begin{pmatrix}\text{Hours of inspection and}\\ \text{packaging time available}\end{pmatrix}$$

Every standard bag manufactured will require $\frac{1}{10}$ hour for inspection and packaging, and every deluxe bag will require $\frac{1}{4}$ hour for inspection and packaging. Because 135 hours of inspection and packaging time are available, it follows that

$$\tfrac{1}{10}S + \tfrac{1}{4}D \leq 135 \qquad (2.4)$$

We have now specified the mathematical relationships for the constraints associated with the four departments. Have we forgotten any other constraints? Can Par produce a negative number of standard or deluxe bags? Clearly, the answer is no. Thus, to prevent the decision variables S and D from having negative values, two constraints,

$$S \geq 0 \quad \text{and} \quad D \geq 0 \qquad (2.5)$$

must be added. These constraints ensure that the solution to the problem will contain nonnegative values for the decision variables and are thus referred to as the **nonnegativity constraints.** Nonnegativity constraints are a general feature of all linear programming problems and may be written in the abbreviated form:

$$S, D \geq 0$$

Try Problem 22(a) to test your ability to formulate a mathematical model for a maximization linear programming problem with less-than-or-equal-to constraints.

Mathematical Statement of the Par, Inc., Problem

The mathematical statement or mathematical formulation of the Par, Inc., problem is now complete. We succeeded in translating the objective and constraints of the problem into a set of mathematical relationships referred to as a **mathematical model.** The complete mathematical model for the Par problem is as follows:

$$
\begin{aligned}
\text{Max} \quad & 10S + 9D \\
\text{subject to (s.t.)} \quad & \\
& \tfrac{7}{10}S + 1D \le 630 \quad \text{Cutting and dyeing} \\
& \tfrac{1}{2}S + \tfrac{5}{6}D \le 600 \quad \text{Sewing} \\
& 1S + \tfrac{2}{3}D \le 708 \quad \text{Finishing} \\
& \tfrac{1}{10}S + \tfrac{1}{4}D \le 135 \quad \text{Inspection and packaging} \\
& S, D \ge 0
\end{aligned} \tag{2.6}
$$

Our job now is to find the product mix (i.e., the combination of S and D) that satisfies all the constraints and, at the same time, yields a value for the objective function that is greater than or equal to the value given by any other feasible solution. Once these values are calculated, we will have found the optimal solution to the problem.

This mathematical model of the Par problem is a **linear programming model,** or **linear program.** The problem has the objective and constraints that, as we said earlier, are common properties of all *linear* programs. But what is the special feature of this mathematical model that makes it a linear program? The special feature that makes it a linear program is that the objective function and all constraint functions (the left-hand sides of the constraint inequalities) are linear functions of the decision variables.

Mathematical functions in which each variable appears in a separate term and is raised to the first power are called **linear functions.** The objective function ($10S + 9D$) is linear because each decision variable appears in a separate term and has an exponent of 1. The amount of production time required in the cutting and dyeing department ($\tfrac{7}{10}S + 1D$) is also a linear function of the decision variables for the same reason. Similarly, the functions on the left-hand side of all the constraint inequalities (the constraint functions) are linear functions. Thus, the mathematical formulation of this problem is referred to as a linear program.

Try Problem 1 to test your ability to recognize the types of mathematical relationships that can be found in a linear program.

Linear *programming* has nothing to do with computer programming. The use of the word *programming* here means "choosing a course of action." Linear programming involves choosing a course of action when the mathematical model of the problem contains only linear functions.

NOTES AND COMMENTS

1. The three assumptions necessary for a linear programming model to be appropriate are proportionality, additivity, and divisibility. *Proportionality* means that the contribution to the objective function and the amount of resources used in each constraint are proportional to the value of each decision variable. *Additivity* means that the value of the objective function and the total resources used can be found by summing the objective function contribution and the resources used for all decision variables. *Divisibility* means that the decision variables are continuous. The divisibility assumption plus the nonnegativity constraints mean that decision variables can take on any value greater than or equal to zero.
2. Management scientists formulate and solve a variety of mathematical models that contain an objective function and a set of constraints. Models of this type are referred to as *mathematical programming models.* Linear programming models are a special type of mathematical programming model in that the objective function and all constraint functions are linear.

2.2 GRAPHICAL SOLUTION PROCEDURE

A linear programming problem involving only two decision variables can be solved using a graphical solution procedure. Let us begin the graphical solution procedure by developing a graph that displays the possible solutions (S and D values) for the Par problem. The graph (Figure 2.1) will have values of S on the horizontal axis and values of D on the vertical axis. Any point on the graph can be identified by the S and D values, which indicate the position of the point along the horizontal and vertical axes, respectively. Because every point (S, D) corresponds to a possible solution, every point on the graph is called a *solution point.* The solution point where $S = 0$ and $D = 0$ is referred to as the origin. Because S and D must be nonnegative, the graph in Figure 2.1 only displays solutions where $S \geq 0$ and $D \geq 0$.

Earlier, we saw that the inequality representing the cutting and dyeing constraint is

$$\tfrac{7}{10}S + 1D \leq 630$$

To show all solution points that satisfy this relationship, we start by graphing the solution points satisfying the constraint as an equality. That is, the points where $\tfrac{7}{10}S + 1D = 630$. Because the graph of this equation is a line, it can be obtained by identifying two points that satisfy the equation and then drawing a line through the points. Setting $S = 0$ and solving for D, we see that the point $(S = 0, D = 630)$ satisfies the equation. To find a second point satisfying this equation, we set $D = 0$ and solve for S. By doing so, we obtain $\tfrac{7}{10}S$ +

FIGURE 2.1 SOLUTION POINTS FOR THE TWO-VARIABLE PAR, INC., PROBLEM

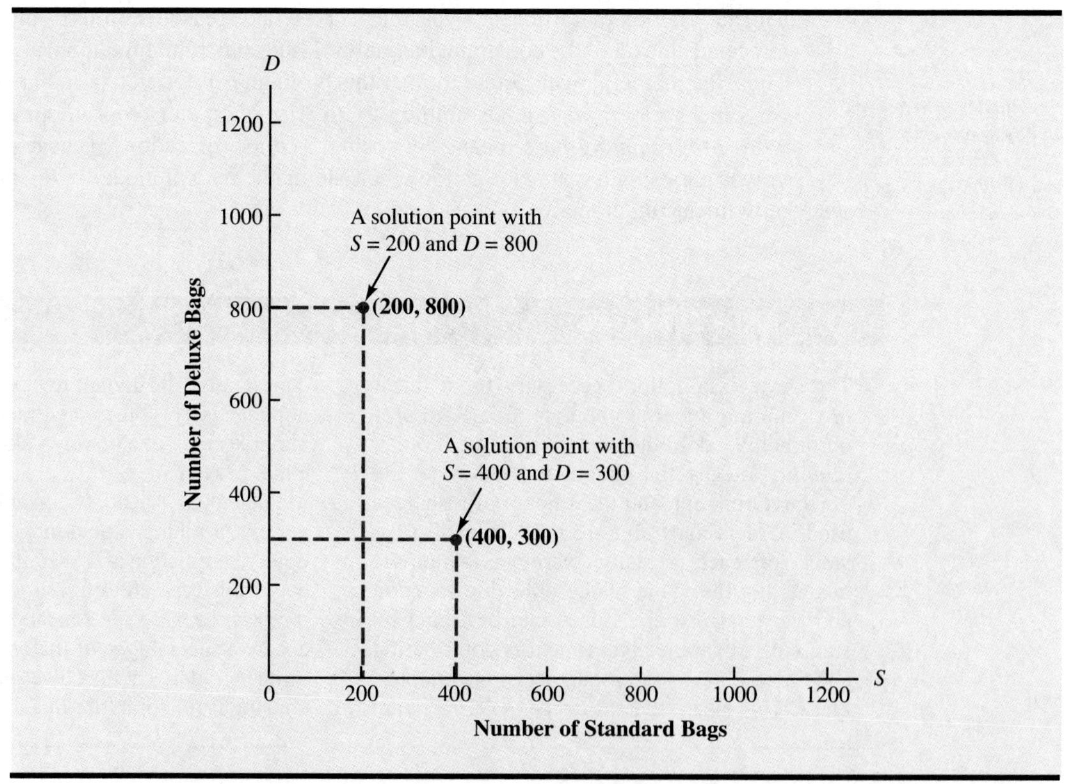

$1(0) = 630$, or $S = 900$. Thus, a second point satisfying the equation is ($S = 900$, $D = 0$). Given these two points, we can now graph the line corresponding to the equation

$$\frac{7}{10}S + 1D = 630$$

This line, which will be called the cutting and dyeing *constraint line,* is shown in Figure 2.2. We label this line "C & D" to indicate that it represents the cutting and dyeing constraint line.

Recall that the inequality representing the cutting and dyeing constraint is

$$\frac{7}{10}S + 1D \leq 630$$

Can you identify all of the solution points that satisfy this constraint? Because all points on the line satisfy $\frac{7}{10}S + 1D = 630$, we know any point on this line must satisfy the constraint. But where are the solution points satisfying $\frac{7}{10}S + 1D < 630$? Consider two solution points: ($S = 200$, $D = 200$) and ($S = 600$, $D = 500$). You can see from Figure 2.2 that the first solution point is below the constraint line and the second is above the constraint line. Which of these solutions will satisfy the cutting and dyeing constraint? For the point ($S = 200$, $D = 200$), we see that

$$\frac{7}{10}S + 1D = \frac{7}{10}(200) + 1(200) = 340$$

FIGURE 2.2 THE CUTTING AND DYEING CONSTRAINT LINE

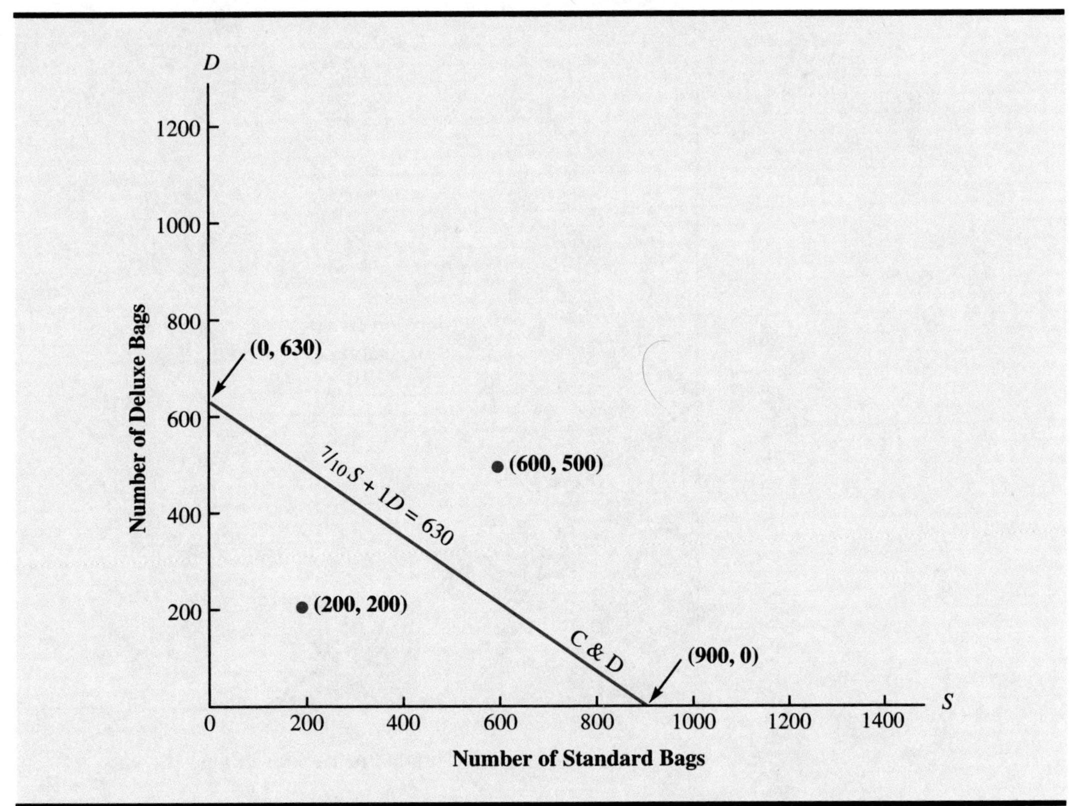

Because the 340 hours is less than the 630 hours available, the ($S = 200$, $D = 200$) production combination, or solution point, satisfies the constraint. For the point ($S = 600$, $D = 500$), we have

$$\tfrac{7}{10}S + 1D = \tfrac{7}{10}(600) + 1(500) = 920$$

The 920 hours is greater than the 630 hours available, so the ($S = 600$, $D = 500$) solution point does not satisfy the constraint and is thus not feasible.

Can you graph a constraint line and find the solution points that are feasible? Try Problem 2.

If a solution point is not feasible for a particular constraint, then all other solution points on the same side of that constraint line are not feasible. If a solution point is feasible for a particular constraint, then all other solution points on the same side of the constraint line are feasible for that constraint. Thus, one needs to evaluate the constraint function for only one solution point to determine which side of a constraint line is feasible. In Figure 2.3 we indicate all points satisfying the cutting and dyeing constraint by the shaded region.

We continue by identifying the solution points satisfying each of the other three constraints. The solutions that are feasible for each of these constraints are shown in Figure 2.4.

Four separate graphs now show the feasible solution points for each of the four constraints. In a linear programming problem, we need to identify the solution points that satisfy *all* the constraints *simultaneously.* To find these solution points, we can draw all four constraints on one graph and observe the region containing the points that do in fact satisfy all the constraints simultaneously.

FIGURE 2.3 FEASIBLE SOLUTIONS FOR THE CUTTING AND DYEING CONSTRAINT, REPRESENTED BY THE SHADED REGION

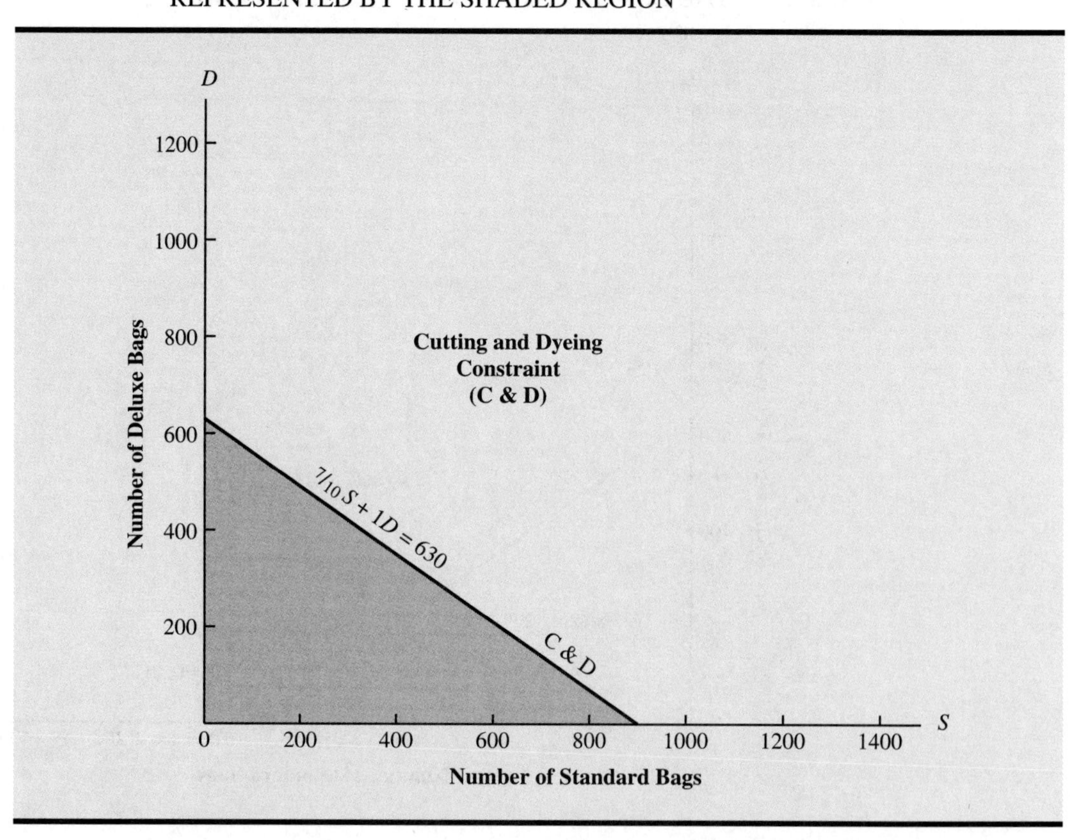

FIGURE 2.4 FEASIBLE SOLUTIONS FOR THE SEWING, FINISHING, AND INSPECTION AND PACKAGING CONSTRAINTS, REPRESENTED BY THE SHADED REGIONS

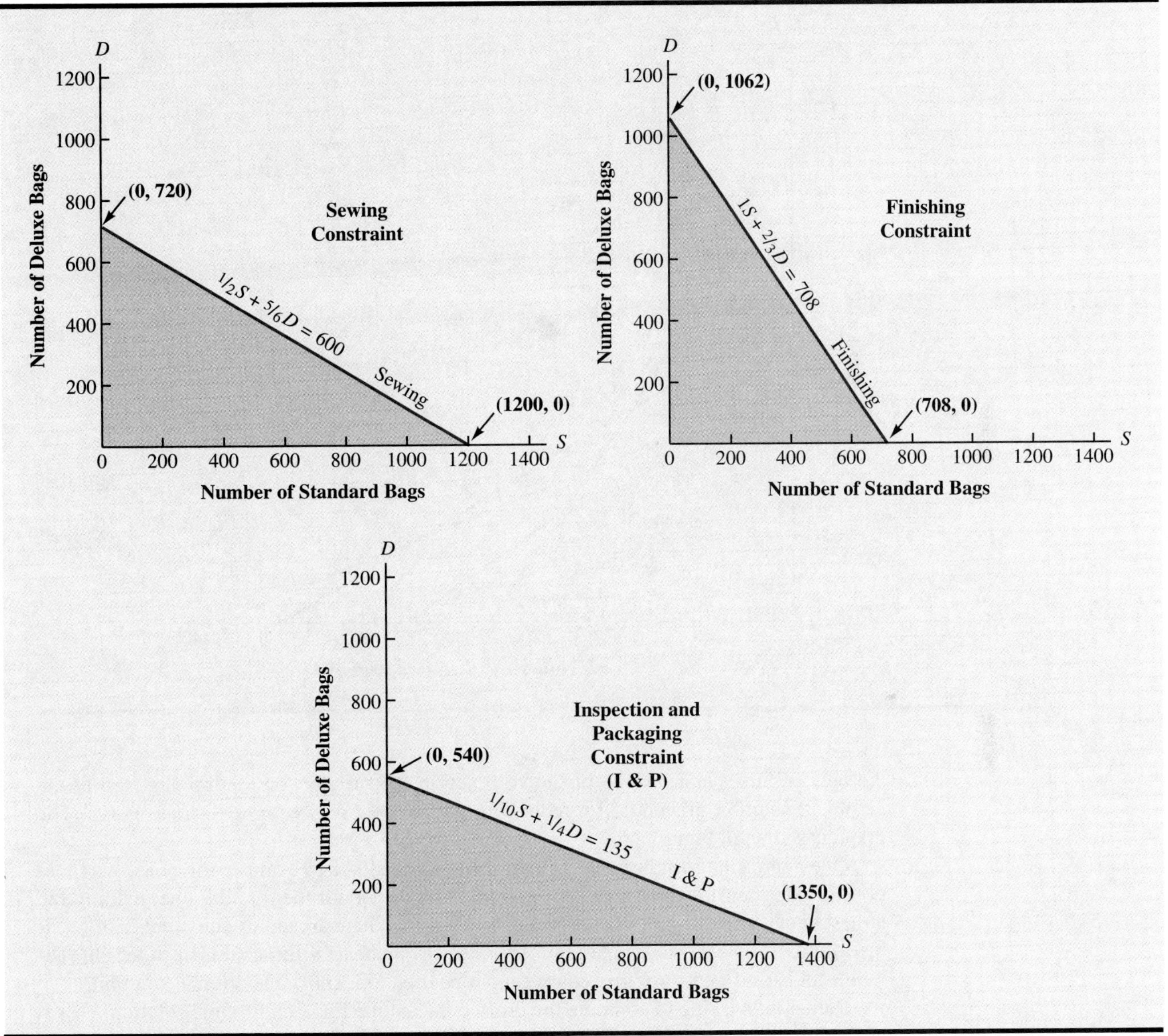

Try Problem 7 to test your ability to find the feasible region given several constraints.

The graphs in Figures 2.3 and 2.4 can be superimposed to obtain one graph with all four constraints. This combined-constraint graph is shown in Figure 2.5. The shaded region in this figure includes every solution point that satisfies all the constraints simultaneously. Solutions that satisfy all the constraints are termed **feasible solutions,** and the shaded region is called the feasible solution region, or simply the **feasible region.** Any solution point on the boundary of the feasible region or within the feasible region is a *feasible solution point.*

Now that we have identified the feasible region, we are ready to proceed with the graphical solution procedure and find the optimal solution to the Par, Inc., problem. Recall that the optimal solution for a linear programming problem is the feasible solution that provides

FIGURE 2.5 COMBINED-CONSTRAINT GRAPH SHOWING THE FEASIBLE REGION FOR THE PAR, INC., PROBLEM

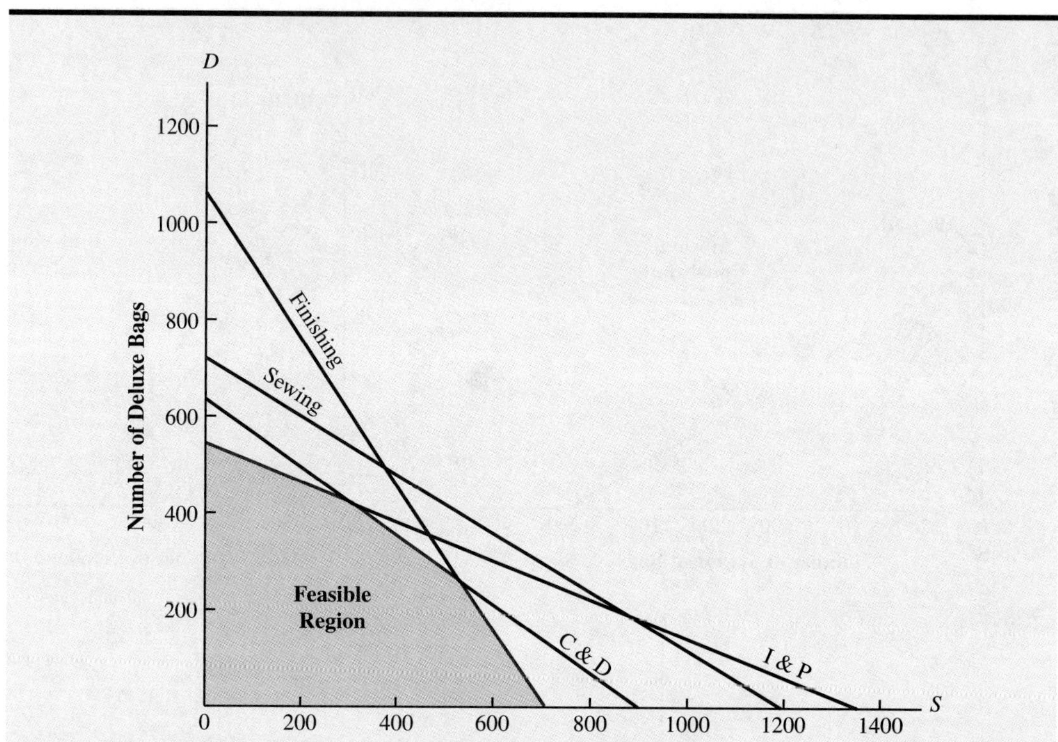

the best possible value of the objective function. Let us start the optimizing step of the graphical solution procedure by redrawing the feasible region on a separate graph. The graph is shown in Figure 2.6.

One approach to finding the optimal solution would be to evaluate the objective function for each feasible solution; the optimal solution would then be the one yielding the largest value. The difficulty with this approach is that there are an infinite number of feasible solutions; thus, because one cannot possibly evaluate an infinite number of feasible solutions, this trial-and-error procedure cannot be used to identify the optimal solution.

Rather than trying to compute the profit contribution for each feasible solution, we select an arbitrary value for profit contribution and identify all the feasible solutions (S, D) that yield the selected value. For example, what feasible solutions provide a profit contribution of \$1800? These solutions are given by the values of S and D in the feasible region that will make the objective function

$$10S + 9D = 1800$$

This expression is simply the equation of a line. Thus, all feasible solution points (S, D) yielding a profit contribution of \$1800 must be on the line. We learned earlier in this section how to graph a constraint line. The procedure for graphing the profit or objective function line is the same. Letting $S = 0$, we see that D must be 200; thus, the solution point

FIGURE 2.6 FEASIBLE REGION FOR THE PAR, INC., PROBLEM

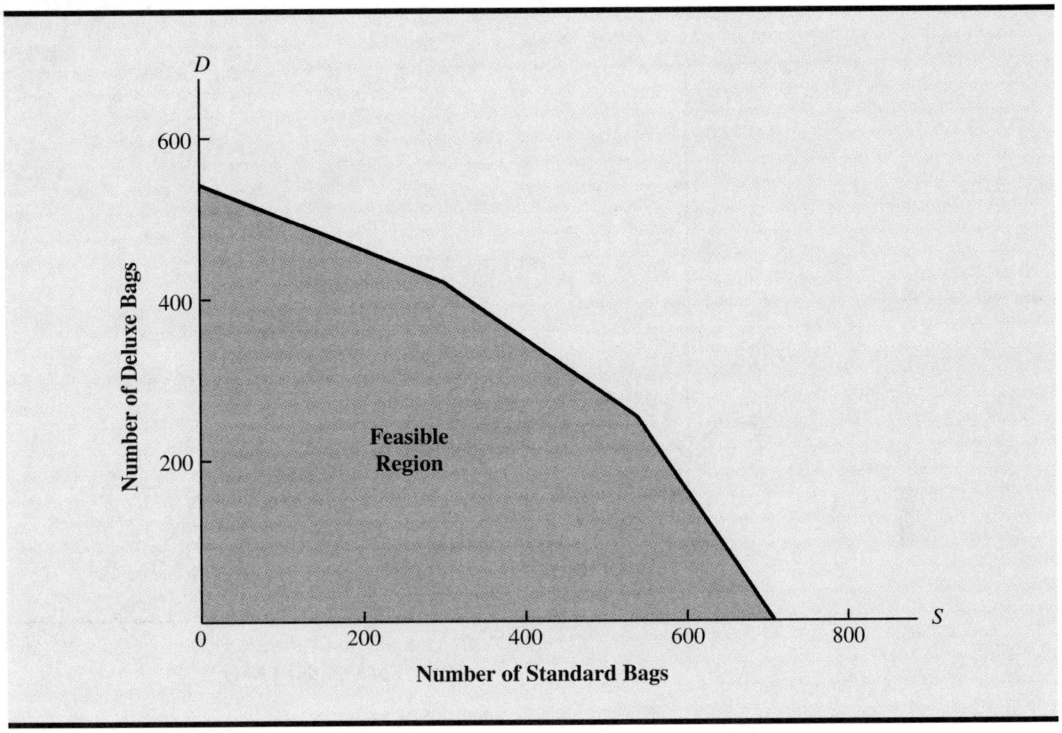

(S = 0, D = 200) is on the line. Similarly, by letting D = 0, we see that the solution point (S = 180, D = 0) is also on the line. Drawing the line through these two points identifies all the solutions that have a profit contribution of \$1800. A graph of this profit line is presented in Figure 2.7.

Because the objective is to find the feasible solution yielding the largest profit contribution, let us proceed by selecting higher profit contributions and finding the solutions yielding the selected values. For instance, let us find all solutions yielding profit contributions of \$3600 and \$5400. To do so, we must find the S and D values that are on the following lines:

$$10S + 9D = 3600$$

and

$$10S + 9D = 5400$$

Using the previous procedure for graphing profit and constraint lines, we draw the \$3600 and \$5400 profit lines as shown on the graph in Figure 2.8. Although not all solution points on the \$5400 profit line are in the feasible region, at least some points on the line are, and it is therefore possible to obtain a feasible solution that provides a \$5400 profit contribution.

Can we find a feasible solution yielding an even higher profit contribution? Look at Figure 2.8, and see what general observations you can make about the profit lines already drawn. Note the following: (1) the profit lines are *parallel* to each other, and (2) higher

FIGURE 2.7 $1800 PROFIT LINE FOR THE PAR, INC., PROBLEM

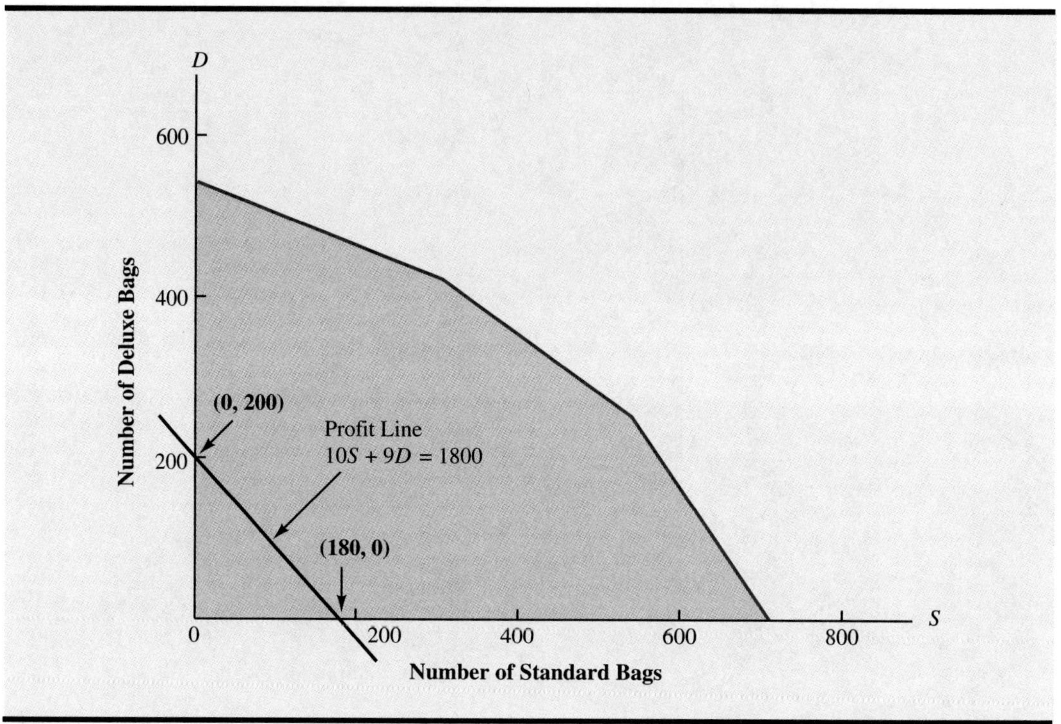

FIGURE 2.8 SELECTED PROFIT LINES FOR THE PAR, INC., PROBLEM

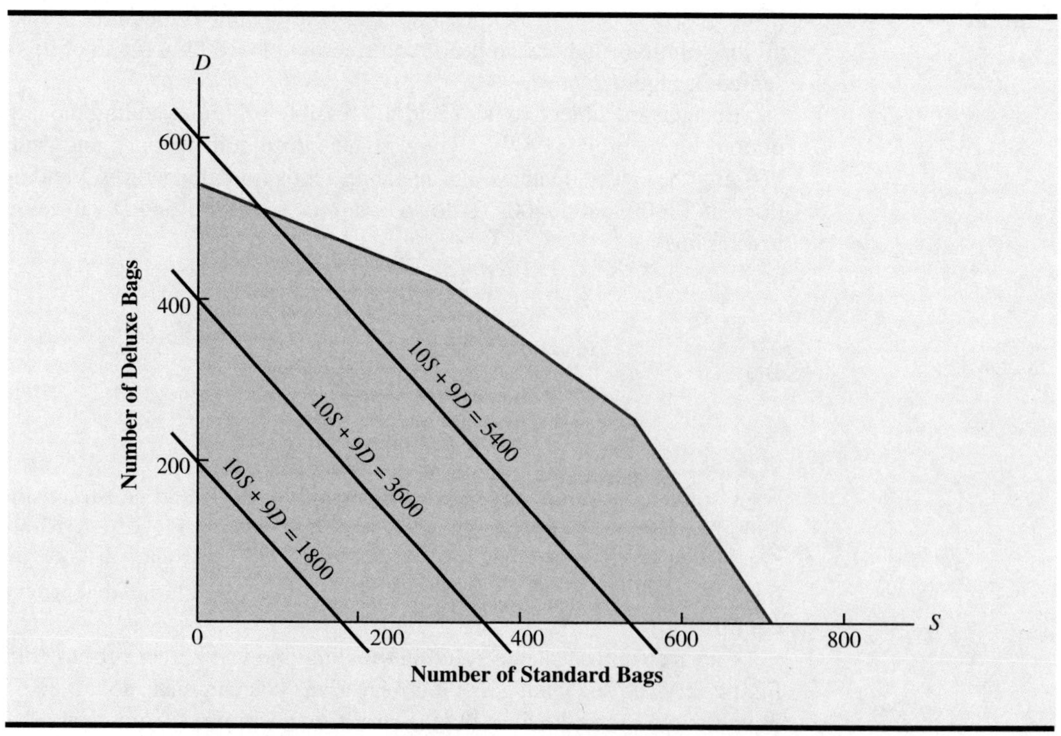

profit lines are obtained as we move farther from the origin. These observations can also be expressed algebraically. Let P represent total profit contribution. The objective function is

$$P = 10S + 9D$$

Solving for D in terms of S and P, we obtain

$$9D = -10S + P$$

$$D = -\tfrac{10}{9}S + \tfrac{1}{9}P \qquad (2.7)$$

Equation (2.7) is the *slope-intercept form* of the linear equation relating S and D. The coefficient of S, $-\tfrac{10}{9}$, is the slope of the line, and the term $\tfrac{1}{9}P$ is the D intercept (i.e., the value of D where the graph of equation [2.7] crosses the D axis). Substituting the profit contributions of $P = 1800$, $P = 3600$, and $P = 5400$ into equation (2.7) yields the following slope-intercept equations for the profit lines shown in Figure 2.8:

For $P = 1800$,

$$D = -\tfrac{10}{9}S + 200$$

For $P = 3600$,

$$D = -\tfrac{10}{9}S + 400$$

For $P = 5400$,

$$D = -\tfrac{10}{9}S + 600$$

Can you graph the profit line for a linear program? Try Problem 6.

The slope ($-\tfrac{10}{9}$) is the same for each profit line because the profit lines are parallel. Further, we see that the D intercept increases with larger profit contributions. Thus, higher profit lines are farther from the origin.

Because the profit lines are parallel and higher profit lines are farther from the origin, we can obtain solutions that yield increasingly larger values for the objective function by continuing to move the profit line farther from the origin in such a fashion that it remains parallel to the other profit lines. However, at some point we will find that any further outward movement will place the profit line completely outside the feasible region. Because solutions outside the feasible region are unacceptable, the point in the feasible region that lies on the highest profit line is the optimal solution to the linear program.

You should now be able to identify the optimal solution point for this problem. Use a ruler or the edge of a piece of paper, and move the profit line as far from the origin as you can. What is the last point in the feasible region that you reach? This point, which is the optimal solution, is shown graphically in Figure 2.9.

The optimal values of the decision variables are the S and D values at the optimal solution. Depending on the accuracy of the graph, you may or may not be able to determine the *exact* S and D values. Referring to the graph in Figure 2.9, the best we can do is conclude that the optimal production combination consists of approximately 550 standard bags (S) and approximately 250 deluxe bags (D).

FIGURE 2.9 OPTIMAL SOLUTION FOR THE PAR, INC., PROBLEM

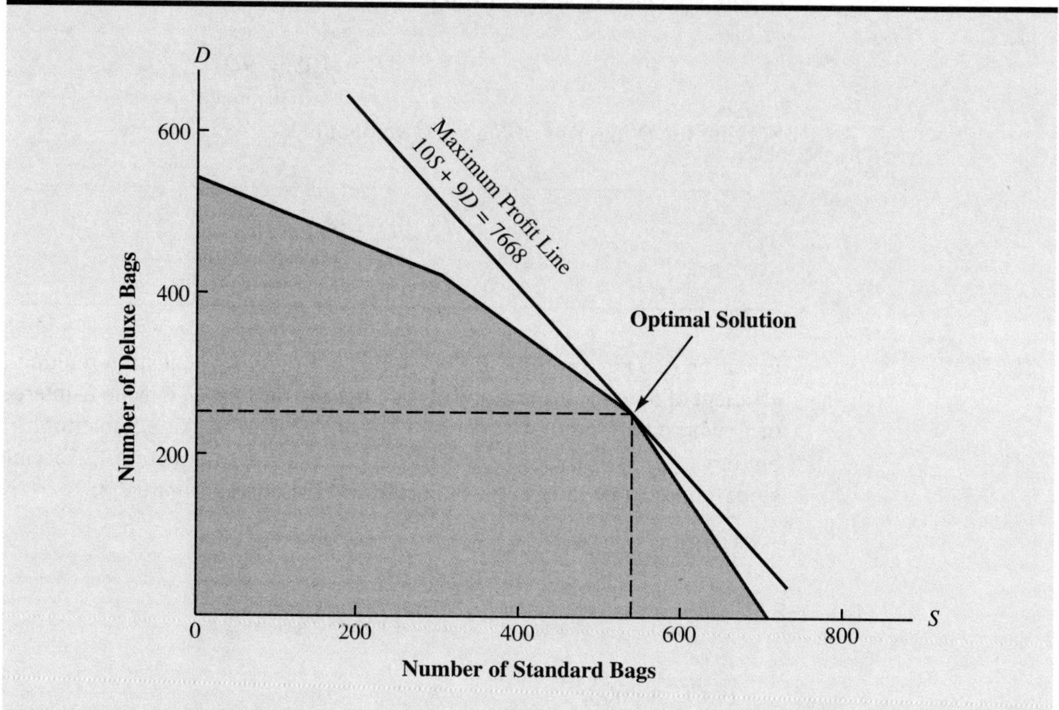

A closer inspection of Figures 2.5 and 2.9 shows that the optimal solution point is at the intersection of the cutting and dyeing and the finishing constraint lines. That is, the optimal solution point is on both the cutting and dyeing constraint line

$$\tfrac{7}{10}S + 1D = 630 \tag{2.8}$$

and the finishing constraint line

$$1S + \tfrac{2}{3}D = 708 \tag{2.9}$$

Thus, the optimal values of the decision variables S and D must satisfy both equations (2.8) and (2.9) simultaneously. Using equation (2.8) and solving for S gives

$$\tfrac{7}{10}S = 630 - 1D$$

or

$$S = 900 - \tfrac{10}{7}D \tag{2.10}$$

Substituting this expression for S into equation (2.9) and solving for D provides the following:

$$\begin{aligned} 1(900 - {}^{10}\!/\!_{7}D) + {}^{2}\!/\!_{3}D &= 708 \\ 900 - {}^{10}\!/\!_{7}D + {}^{2}\!/\!_{3}D &= 708 \\ 900 - {}^{30}\!/\!_{21}D + {}^{14}\!/\!_{21}D &= 708 \\ -{}^{16}\!/\!_{21}D &= -192 \\ D &= \frac{192}{{}^{16}\!/\!_{21}} = 252 \end{aligned}$$

Using $D = 252$ in equation (2.10) and solving for S, we obtain

$$\begin{aligned} S &= 900 - {}^{10}\!/\!_{7}(252) \\ &= 900 - 360 = 540 \end{aligned}$$

Although the optimal solution to the Par, Inc., problem consists of integer values for the decision variables, this result will not always be the case.

The exact location of the optimal solution point is $S = 540$ and $D = 252$. Hence, the optimal production quantities for Par, Inc., are 540 standard bags and 252 deluxe bags, with a resulting profit contribution of $10(540) + 9(252) = \$7668$.

For a linear programming problem with two decision variables, the exact values of the decision variables can be determined by first using the graphical solution procedure to identify the optimal solution point and then solving the two simultaneous constraint equations associated with it.

A Note on Graphing Lines

Try Problem 10 to test your ability to use the graphical solution procedure to identify the optimal solution and find the exact values of the decision variables at the optimal solution.

An important aspect of the graphical method is the ability to graph lines showing the constraints and the objective function of the linear program. The procedure we used for graphing the equation of a line is to find any two points satisfying the equation and then draw the line through the two points. For the Par, Inc., constraints, the two points were easily found by first setting $S = 0$ and solving the constraint equation for D. Then we set $D = 0$ and solved for S. For the cutting and dyeing constraint line

$${}^{7}\!/\!_{10}S + 1D = 630$$

this procedure identified the two points ($S = 0, D = 630$) and ($S = 900, D = 0$). The cutting and dyeing constraint line was then graphed by drawing a line through these two points.

All constraints and objective function lines in two-variable linear programs can be graphed if two points on the line can be identified. However, finding the two points on the line is not always as easy as shown in the Par, Inc., problem. For example, suppose a company manufactures two models of a small handheld computer: the Assistant (A) and the Professional (P). Management needs 50 units of the Professional model for its own salesforce, and expects sales of the Professional to be at most one-half of the sales of the Assistant. A constraint enforcing this requirement is

$$P - 50 \leq {}^{1}\!/\!_{2}A$$

or

$$2P - 100 \leq A$$

or

$$2P - A \leq 100$$

Using the equality form and setting $P = 0$, we find the point ($P = 0, A = -100$) is on the constraint line. Setting $A = 0$, we find a second point ($P = 50, A = 0$) on the constraint line. If we have drawn only the nonnegative ($P \geq 0, A \geq 0$) portion of the graph, the first point ($P = 0, A = -100$) cannot be plotted because $A = -100$ is not on the graph. Whenever we have two points on the line, but one or both of the points cannot be plotted in the nonnegative portion of the graph, the simplest approach is to enlarge the graph. In this example, the point ($P = 0, A = -100$) can be plotted by extending the graph to include the negative A axis. Once both points satisfying the constraint equation have been located, the line can be drawn. The constraint line and the feasible solutions for the constraint $2P - A \leq 100$ are shown in Figure 2.10.

As another example, consider a problem involving two decision variables, R and T. Suppose that the number of units of R produced had to be at least equal to the number of units of T produced. A constraint enforcing this requirement is

$$R \geq T$$

or

$$R - T \geq 0$$

FIGURE 2.10 FEASIBLE SOLUTIONS FOR THE CONSTRAINT $2P - A \leq 100$

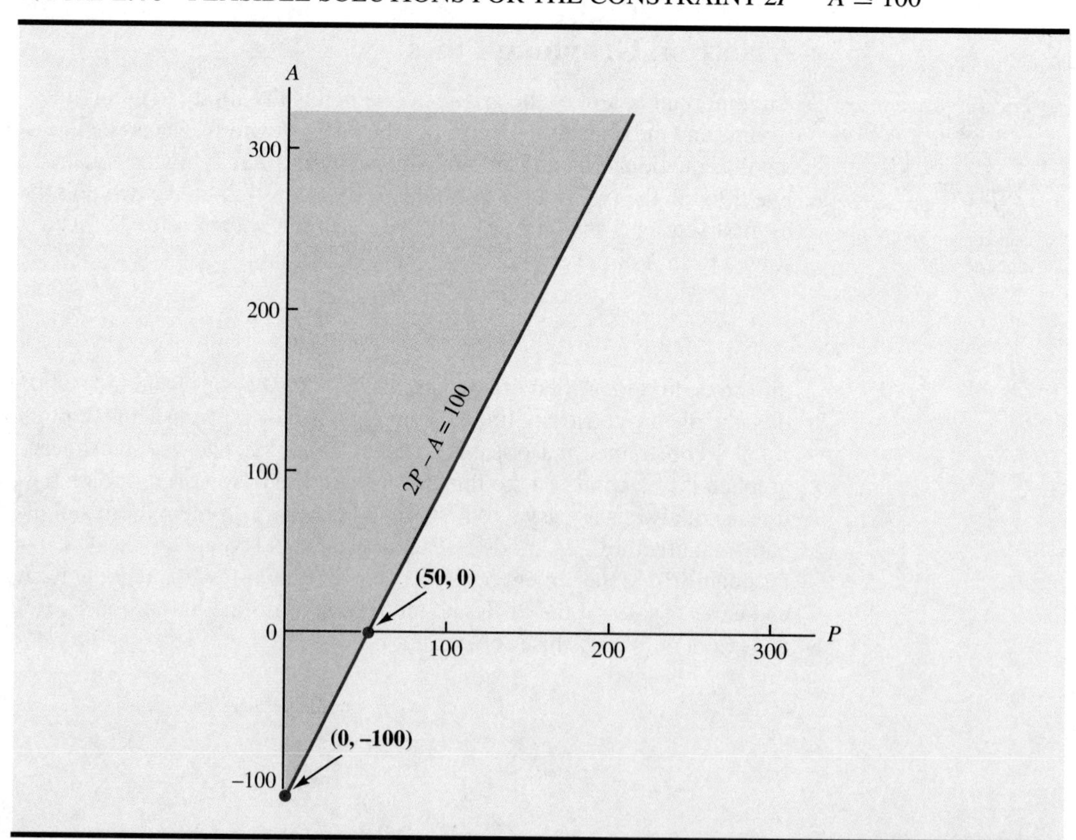

Can you graph a constraint line when the origin is on the constraint line? Try Problem 5.

To find all solutions satisfying the constraint as an equality, we first set $R = 0$ and solve for T. This result shows that the origin ($T = 0$, $R = 0$) is on the constraint line. Setting $T = 0$ and solving for R provides the same point. However, we can obtain a second point on the line by setting T equal to any value other than zero and then solving for R. For instance, setting $T = 100$ and solving for R, we find that the point ($T = 100$, $R = 100$) is on the line. With the two points ($R = 0$, $T = 0$) and ($R = 100$, $T = 100$), the constraint line $R - T = 0$ and the feasible solutions for $R - T \geq 0$ can be plotted as shown in Figure 2.11.

Summary of the Graphical Solution Procedure for Maximization Problems

For additional practice in using the graphical solution procedure, try Problem 22(b), 22(c), and 22(d).

As we have seen, the graphical solution procedure is a method for solving two-variable linear programming problems such as the Par, Inc., problem. The steps of the graphical solution procedure for a maximization problem are summarized here:

1. Prepare a graph of the feasible solutions for each of the constraints.
2. Determine the feasible region by identifying the solutions that satisfy all the constraints simultaneously.
3. Draw an objective function line showing the values of the decision variables that yield a specified value of the objective function.
4. Move parallel objective function lines toward larger objective function values until further movement would take the line completely outside the feasible region.
5. Any feasible solution on the objective function line with the largest value is an optimal solution.

FIGURE 2.11 FEASIBLE SOLUTIONS FOR THE CONSTRAINT $R - T \geq 0$

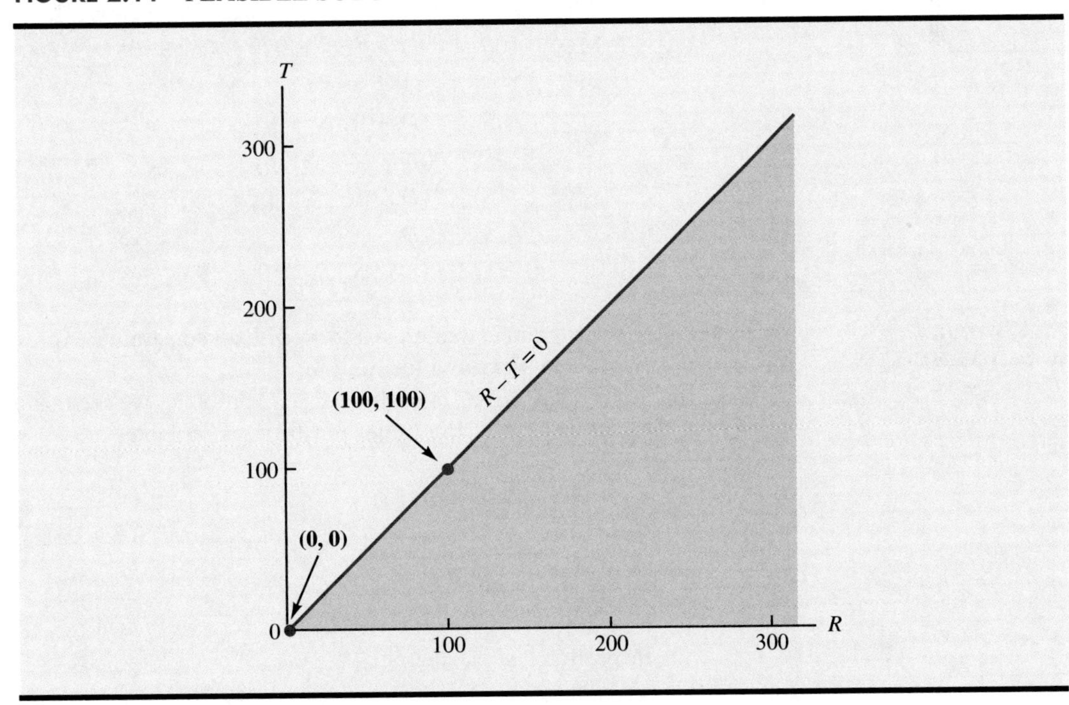

Slack Variables

In addition to the optimal solution and its associated profit contribution, Par's management will probably want information about the production time requirements for each production operation. We can determine this information by substituting the optimal solution values ($S = 540$, $D = 252$) into the constraints of the linear program.

Constraint	Hours Required for $S = 540$ and $D = 252$	Hours Available	Unused Hours
Cutting and dyeing	$\frac{7}{10}(540) + 1(252) = 630$	630	0
Sewing	$\frac{1}{2}(540) + \frac{5}{6}(252) = 480$	600	120
Finishing	$1(540) + \frac{2}{3}(252) = 708$	708	0
Inspection and packaging	$\frac{1}{10}(540) + \frac{1}{4}(252) = 117$	135	18

Thus, the complete solution tells management that the production of 540 standard bags and 252 deluxe bags will require all available cutting and dyeing time (630 hours) and all available finishing time (708 hours), while $600 - 480 = 120$ hours of sewing time and $135 - 117 = 18$ hours of inspection and packaging time will remain unused. The 120 hours of unused sewing time and 18 hours of unused inspection and packaging time are referred to as *slack* for the two departments. In linear programming terminology, any unused capacity for a $\leq$ constraint is referred to as the *slack* associated with the constraint.

Can you identify the slack associated with a constraint? Try Problem 22(e).

Often variables, called **slack variables,** are added to the formulation of a linear programming problem to represent the slack, or idle capacity. Unused capacity makes no contribution to profit; thus, slack variables have coefficients of zero in the objective function. After the addition of four slack variables, denoted S_1, S_2, S_3, and S_4, the mathematical model of the Par, Inc., problem becomes

$$\begin{aligned}
\text{Max} \quad & 10S + 9D + 0S_1 + 0S_2 + 0S_3 + 0S_4 \\
\text{s.t.} \quad & \\
& \tfrac{7}{10}S + 1D + 1S_1 = 630 \\
& \tfrac{1}{2}S + \tfrac{5}{6}D + 1S_2 = 600 \\
& 1S + \tfrac{2}{3}D + 1S_3 = 708 \\
& \tfrac{1}{10}S + \tfrac{1}{4}D + 1S_4 = 135 \\
& S, D, S_1, S_2, S_3, S_4 \geq 0
\end{aligned}$$

Can you write a linear program in standard form? Try Problem 18.

Whenever a linear program is written in a form with all constraints expressed as equalities, it is said to be written in **standard form.**

Referring to the standard form of the Par, Inc., problem, we see that at the optimal solution ($S = 540$ and $D = 252$), the values for the slack variables are

Constraint	Value of Slack Variable
Cutting and dyeing	$S_1 = 0$
Sewing	$S_2 = 120$
Finishing	$S_3 = 0$
Inspection and packaging	$S_4 = 18$

Could we have used the graphical solution to provide some of this information? The answer is yes. By finding the optimal solution point on Figure 2.5, we can see that the cutting and dyeing and the finishing constraints restrict, or *bind,* the feasible region at this point. Thus, this solution requires the use of all available time for these two operations. In other words, the graph shows us that the cutting and dyeing and the finishing departments will have zero slack. On the other hand, the sewing and the inspection and packaging constraints are not binding the feasible region at the optimal solution, which means we can expect some unused time or slack for these two operations.

As a final comment on the graphical analysis of this problem, we call your attention to the sewing capacity constraint as shown in Figure 2.5. Note, in particular, that this constraint did not affect the feasible region. That is, the feasible region would be the same whether the sewing capacity constraint were included or not, which tells us that there is enough sewing time available to accommodate any production level that can be achieved by the other three departments. The sewing constraint does not affect the feasible region and thus cannot affect the optimal solution; it is called a **redundant constraint.**

NOTES AND COMMENTS

1. In the standard-form representation of a linear programming model, the objective function coefficients for slack variables are zero. This zero coefficient implies that slack variables, which represent unused resources, do not affect the value of the objective function. However, in some applications, unused resources can be sold and contribute to profit. In such cases, the corresponding slack variables become decision variables representing the amount of unused resources to be sold. For each of these variables, a nonzero coefficient in the objective function would reflect the profit associated with selling a unit of the corresponding resource.
2. Redundant constraints do not affect the feasible region; as a result, they can be removed from a linear programming model without affecting the optimal solution. However, if the linear programming model is to be resolved later, changes in some of the data might make a previously redundant constraint a binding constraint. Thus, we recommend keeping all constraints in the linear programming model even though at some point in time one or more of the constraints may be redundant.

2.3 EXTREME POINTS AND THE OPTIMAL SOLUTION

Suppose that the profit contribution for Par's standard golf bag is reduced from $10 to $5 per bag, while the profit contribution for the deluxe golf bag and all the constraints remain unchanged. The complete linear programming model of this new problem is identical to the mathematical model in Section 2.1, except for the revised objective function:

$$\text{Max } 5S + 9D$$

How does this change in the objective function affect the optimal solution to the Par, Inc., problem? Figure 2.12 shows the graphical solution of this new problem with the revised objective function. Note that without any change in the constraints, the feasible region does not change. However, the profit lines have been altered to reflect the new objective function.

By moving the profit line in a parallel manner toward higher profit values, we find the optimal solution as shown in Figure 2.12. The values of the decision variables at this point are $S = 300$ and $D = 420$. The reduced profit contribution for the standard bag caused a change in the optimal solution. In fact, as you may have suspected, we are cutting back the

FIGURE 2.12 OPTIMAL SOLUTION FOR THE PAR, INC., PROBLEM WITH AN OBJECTIVE FUNCTION OF $5S + 9D$

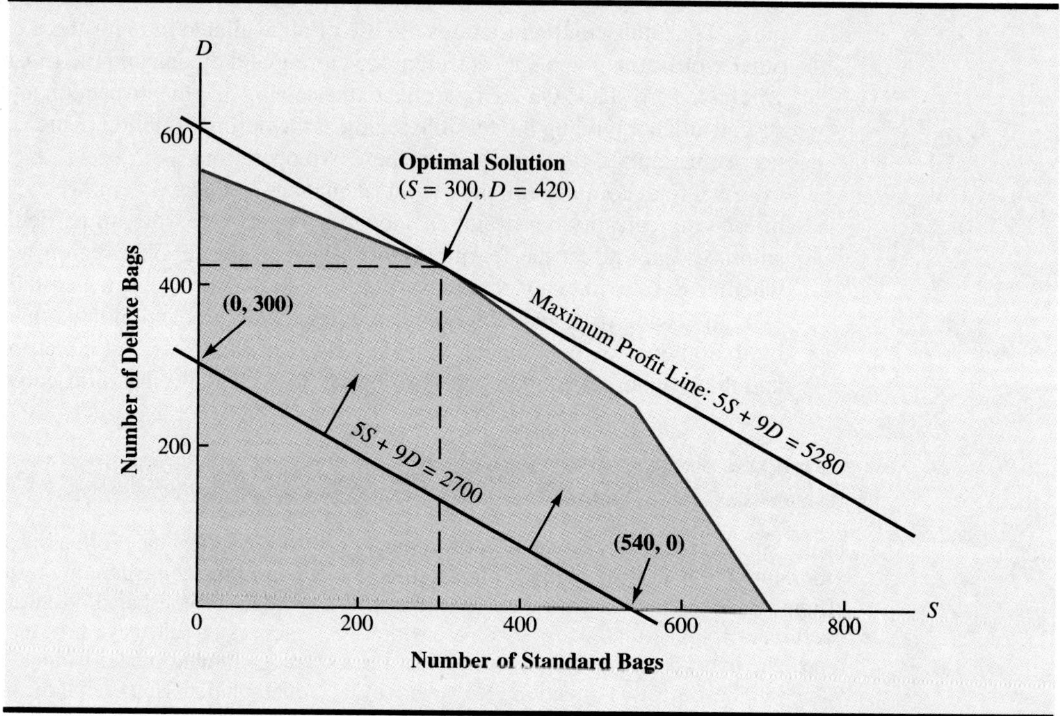

production of the lower-profit standard bags and increasing the production of the higher-profit deluxe bags.

What observations can you make about the location of the optimal solutions in the two linear programming problems solved thus far? Look closely at the graphical solutions in Figures 2.9 and 2.12. Notice that the optimal solutions occur at one of the vertices or "corners" of the feasible region. In linear programming terminology, these vertices are referred to as the **extreme points** of the feasible region. The Par, Inc., feasible region has five vertices, or five extreme points (see Figure 2.13). We can now formally state our observation about the location of optimal solutions as follows:

For additional practice in identifying the extreme points of the feasible region and determining the optimal solution by computing and comparing the objective function value at each extreme point, try Problem 14.

> The optimal solution to a linear program can be found at an extreme point of the feasible region.[2]

This property means that if you are looking for the optimal solution to a linear program, you do not have to evaluate all feasible solution points. In fact, you have to consider *only* the feasible solutions that occur at the extreme points of the feasible region. Thus, for the Par, Inc., problem, instead of computing and comparing the profit contributions for all feasible solutions, we can find the optimal solution by evaluating the five extreme-point solu-

[2]We will discuss in Section 2.6 the two special cases (infeasibility and unboundedness) in linear programming that have no optimal solution, and for which this statement does not apply.

FIGURE 2.13 THE FIVE EXTREME POINTS OF THE FEASIBLE REGION FOR THE PAR, INC., PROBLEM

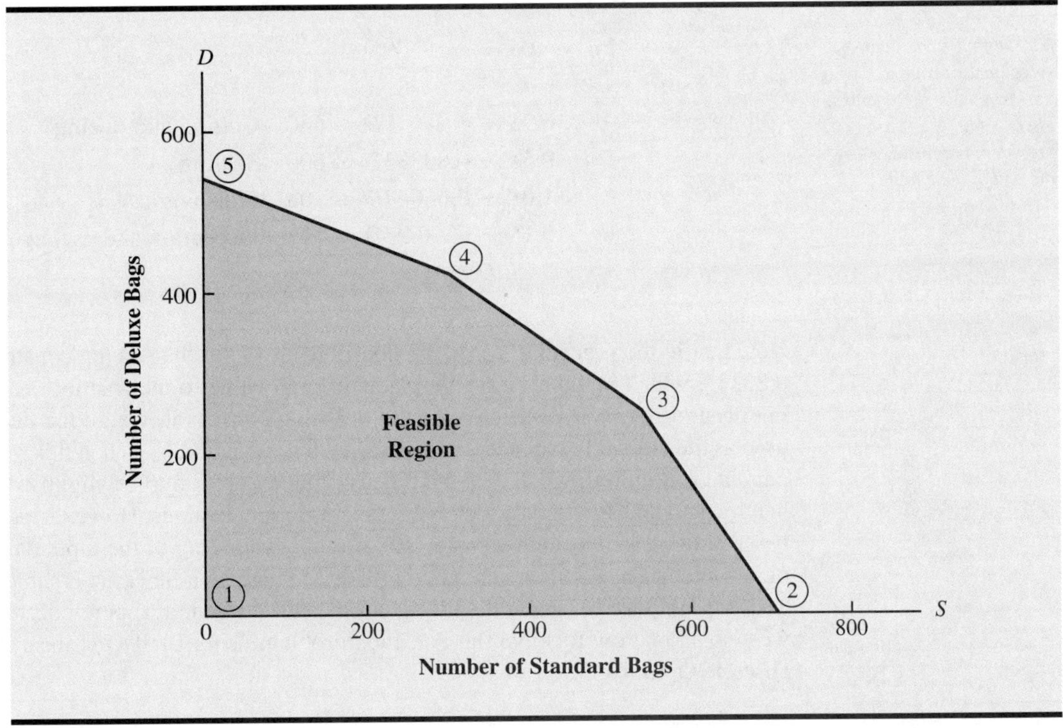

tions and selecting the one that provides the largest profit contribution. Actually, the graphical solution procedure is nothing more than a convenient way of identifying an optimal extreme point for two-variable problems.

2.4 COMPUTER SOLUTION OF THE PAR, INC., PROBLEM

In January 1952 the first successful computer solution of a linear programming problem was performed on the SEAC (Standards Eastern Automatic Computer). The SEAC, the first digital computer built by the National Bureau of Standards under U.S. Air Force sponsorship, had a 512-word memory and magnetic tape for external storage.

Computer programs designed to solve linear programming problems are now widely available. Most companies and universities have access to these computer programs. After a short period of familiarization with the specific features of the package, users are able to solve linear programming problems with few difficulties. Problems involving thousands of variables and thousands of constraints are now routinely solved with computer packages. Most large linear programs can be solved with just a few minutes of computer time; small linear programs usually require only a few seconds.

More recently, with the virtual explosion of software for personal computers, a large number of user-friendly computer programs that can solve linear programs became available. These programs, developed by academicians and small software companies, are almost all easy to use. Most of these programs are designed to solve smaller linear programs (a few hundred variables). But, some can be used to solve problems involving thousands of variables and constraints. Linear programming solvers are now part of many spreadsheet packages. In Appendix 2.3, we show how to use the solver available with Microsoft Excel.

The Management Scientist, a software package developed by the authors of this text, contains a linear programming module. Let us demonstrate its use by solving the Par, Inc., problem introduced in Section 2.1. Because computer input must utilize decimal rather than fractional data values, we restate the linear program with decimal coefficients:

Instructions on how to solve linear programs using The Management Scientist, LINDO, and Excel are provided in appendixes at the end of the chapter.

$$
\begin{array}{lrcrl}
\text{Max} & 10S & + & 9D & \\
\text{s.t.} & & & & \\
& 0.7S & + & 1D \leq 630 & \text{Cutting and dyeing} \\
& 0.5S & + & 0.83333D \leq 600 & \text{Sewing} \\
& 1.0S & + & 0.66667D \leq 708 & \text{Finishing} \\
& 0.1S & + & 0.25D \leq 135 & \text{Inspection and packaging} \\
& & S, D \geq 0 & &
\end{array}
$$

Note that in the preceding form, the coefficient of D in the sewing constraint is written as 0.83333, which is the closest five-place decimal value to the fraction ⅚. A similar rounding occurs for the D coefficient in the finishing constraint, where the decimal 0.66667 is used as the closest five-place decimal value to the fraction ⅔. When this rounding of the input data is required, we may expect the computer solution to be slightly different from the hand-calculated solution based on the exact fractional values. However, as you will see, the two solutions are extremely close, and the slight rounding of the input data causes no serious problem. The solution generated by The Management Scientist is shown in Figure 2.14. The steps required to generate this solution are described in Appendix 2.1. In Appendix 2.2 we also show how to solve the Par, Inc., problem using LINDO (Linear, INteractive, and Discrete Optimizer).

Interpretation of Computer Output

Let us look more closely at The Management Scientist output in Figure 2.14 and interpret the computer solution provided for the Par, Inc., problem. First, note the number 7667.99417, which appears to the right of Objective Function Value. Rounding this value, we can conclude that the optimal solution to this problem will provide a profit of $7668. Directly below the objective function value, we find the values of the decision variables at the optimal solution. After rounding we have $S = 540$ standard bags and $D = 252$ deluxe bags as the optimal production quantities.

The information in the Reduced Costs column indicates how much the objective function coefficient of each decision variable would have to improve[3] before it would be possible for that variable to assume a positive value in the optimal solution. If a decision variable is already positive in the optimal solution, its reduced cost is zero. For the Par, Inc., problem, the optimal solution is $S = 540$ and $D = 252$. Both variables already have positive values; therefore, their corresponding reduced costs are zero. In Chapter 3 we will interpret the reduced cost for a decision variable that does not have a positive value in the optimal solution.

Immediately following the optimal S and D values and the reduced cost information, the computer output provides information about the status of the constraints. Recall that the Par, Inc., problem had four less-than-or-equal-to constraints corresponding to the hours available in each of four production departments. The information shown in the Slack/

[3]For a maximization problem, improve means get bigger; for a minimization problem, improve means get smaller.

FIGURE 2.14 THE MANAGEMENT SCIENTIST SOLUTION FOR THE PAR, INC., PROBLEM

```
Objective Function Value =              7667.99417

     Variable              Value              Reduced Costs
   --------------    ---------------      -----------------
         S               539.99842                 0.00000
         D               252.00110                 0.00000

    Constraint         Slack/Surplus           Dual Prices
   --------------    ---------------      -----------------
         1                 0.00000                 4.37496
         2               120.00071                 0.00000
         3                 0.00000                 6.93753
         4                17.99988                 0.00000

OBJECTIVE COEFFICIENT RANGES

  Variable       Lower Limit       Current Value      Upper Limit
 ------------  ---------------   ---------------   ---------------
     S              6.30000          10.00000          13.49993
     D              6.66670           9.00000          14.28571

RIGHT HAND SIDE RANGES

  Constraint     Lower Limit       Current Value      Upper Limit
 ------------  ---------------   ---------------   ---------------
       1          495.60000         630.00000         682.36316
       2          479.99929         600.00000    No Upper Limit
       3          580.00140         708.00000         900.00000
       4          117.00012         135.00000    No Upper Limit
```

EXCELfile
Par

Surplus column provides the value of the slack variable for each of the departments. This information (after rounding) is summarized here:

Constraint Number	Constraint Name	Slack
1	Cutting and dyeing	0
2	Sewing	120
3	Finishing	0
4	Inspection and packaging	18

From this information, we see that the binding constraints (the cutting and dyeing and the finishing constraints) have zero slack at the optimal solution. The sewing department has 120 hours of slack or unused capacity, and the inspection and packaging department has 18 hours of slack or unused capacity.

The rest of the output in Figure 2.14 can be used to determine how a change in a coefficient of the objective function or a change in the right-hand-side value of a constraint will affect the optimal solution. We will discuss the use of this information in Chapter 3 when we study the topic of sensitivity analysis.

NOTES AND COMMENTS

Linear programming solvers are now a standard feature of most spreadsheet packages. Excel, Lotus 1-2-3, and Quattro Pro all come with built-in solvers capable of solving optimization problems, including linear programs. The solver in each of these spreadsheet packages was developed by Frontline Systems and provides a similar user interface. In Appendix 2.3 we show how spreadsheets can be used to solve linear programs by using Excel to solve the Par, Inc., problem.

2.5 A SIMPLE MINIMIZATION PROBLEM

M&D Chemicals produces two products that are sold as raw materials to companies manufacturing bath soaps and laundry detergents. Based on an analysis of current inventory levels and potential demand for the coming month, M&D's management specified that the combined production for products A and B must total at least 350 gallons. Separately, a major customer's order for 125 gallons of product A must also be satisfied. Product A requires 2 hours of processing time per gallon and product B requires 1 hour of processing time per gallon. For the coming month, 600 hours of processing time are available. M&D's objective is to satisfy these requirements at a minimum total production cost. Production costs are $2 per gallon for product A and $3 per gallon for product B.

To find the minimum-cost production schedule, we will formulate the M&D Chemicals problem as a linear program. Following a procedure similar to the one used for the Par, Inc., problem, we first define the decision variables and the objective function for the problem. Let

$$A = \text{number of gallons of product A}$$
$$B = \text{number of gallons of product B}$$

With production costs at $2 per gallon for product A and $3 per gallon for product B, the objective function that corresponds to the minimization of the total production cost can be written as

$$\text{Min } 2A + 3B$$

Next consider the constraints placed on the M&D Chemicals problem. To satisfy the major customer's demand for 125 gallons of product A, we know A must be at least 125. Thus, we write the constraint

$$1A \geq 125$$

For the combined production for both products, which must total at least 350 gallons, we can write the constraint

$$1A + 1B \geq 350$$

Finally, for the limitation of 600 hours on available processing time, we add the constraint

$$2A + 1B \leq 600$$

After adding the nonnegativity constraints ($A, B \geq 0$), we arrive at the following linear program for the M&D Chemicals problem:

$$\begin{aligned}
\text{Min} \quad & 2A + 3B \\
\text{s.t.} \quad & \\
& 1A \qquad\quad \geq 125 \quad \text{Demand for product A} \\
& 1A + 1B \geq 350 \quad \text{Total production} \\
& 2A + 1B \leq 600 \quad \text{Processing time} \\
& A, B \geq 0
\end{aligned}$$

Because the linear programming model has only two decision variables, the graphical solution procedure can be used to find the optimal production quantities. The graphical solution procedure for this problem, just as in the Par problem, requires us to first graph the constraint lines to find the feasible region. By graphing each constraint line separately and then checking points on either side of the constraint line, the feasible solutions for each constraint can be identified. By combining the feasible solutions for each constraint on the same graph, we obtain the feasible region shown in Figure 2.15.

FIGURE 2.15 THE FEASIBLE REGION FOR THE M&D CHEMICALS PROBLEM

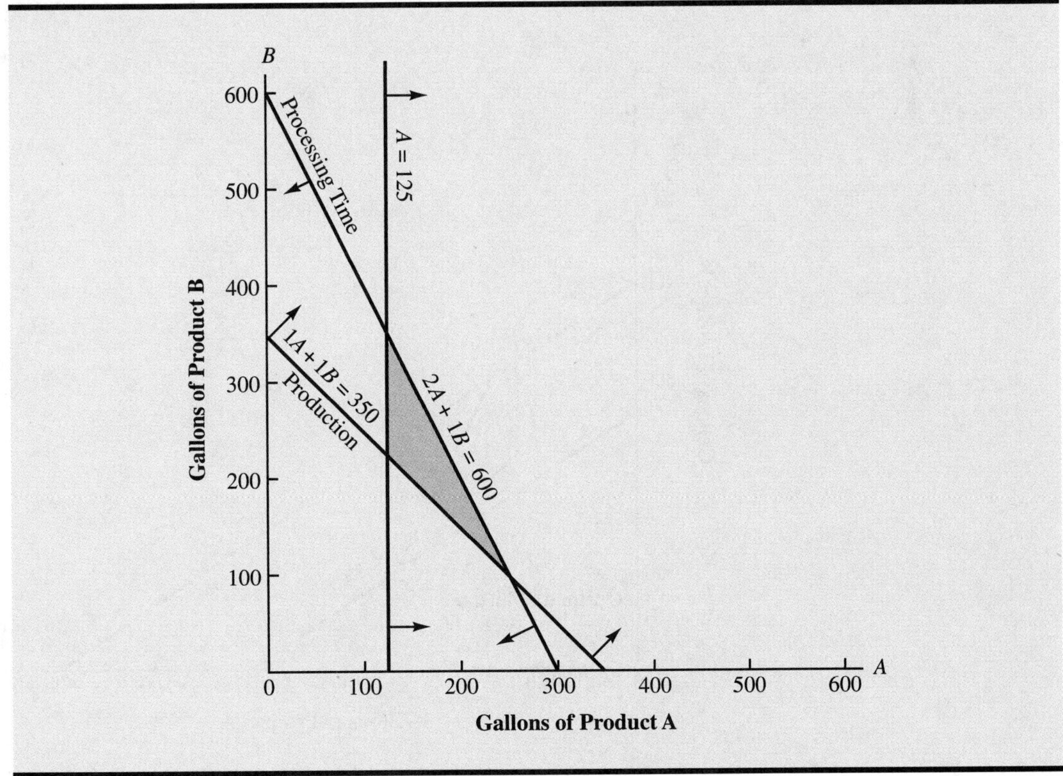

To find the minimum-cost solution, we now draw the objective function line corresponding to a particular total cost value. For example, we might start by drawing the line $2A + 3B = 1200$. This line is shown in Figure 2.16. Clearly some points in the feasible region would provide a total cost of \$1200. To find the values of A and B that provide smaller total cost values, we move the objective function line in a lower left direction until, if we moved it any farther, it would be entirely outside the feasible region. Note that the objective function line $2A + 3B = 800$ intersects the feasible region at the extreme point $A = 250$ and $B = 100$. This extreme point provides the minimum-cost solution with an objective function value of 800. From Figures 2.15 and 2.16, we can see that the total production constraint and the processing time constraint are binding. Just as in every linear programming problem, the optimal solution occurs at an extreme point of the feasible region.

Summary of the Graphical Solution Procedure for Minimization Problems

Can you use the graphical solution procedure to determine the optimal solution for a minimization problem? Try Problem 29.

The steps of the graphical solution procedure for a minimization problem are summarized here:

1. Prepare a graph of the feasible solutions for each of the constraints.
2. Determine the feasible region by identifying the solutions that satisfy all the constraints simultaneously.
3. Draw an objective function line showing the values of the decision variables that yield a specified value of the objective function.

FIGURE 2.16 GRAPHICAL SOLUTION FOR THE M&D CHEMICALS PROBLEM

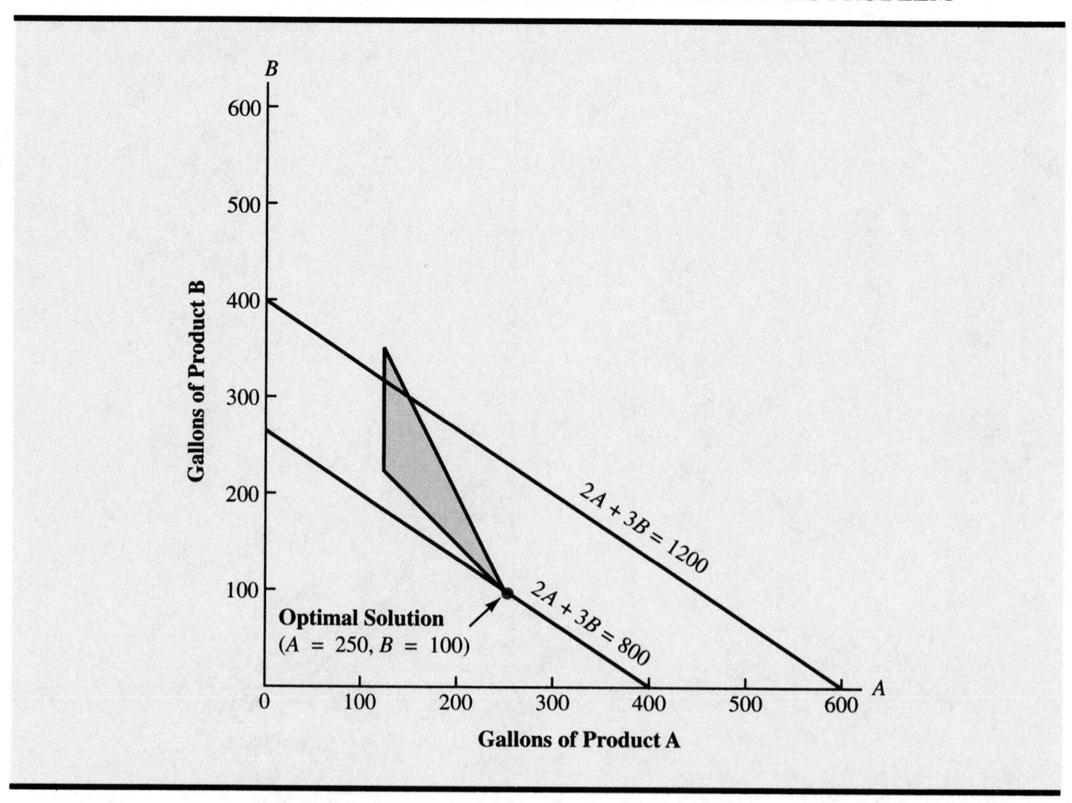

4. Move parallel objective function lines toward smaller objective function values until further movement would take the line completely outside the feasible region.
5. Any feasible solution on the objective function line with the smallest value is an optimal solution.

Surplus Variables

The optimal solution to the M&D Chemicals problem shows that the desired total production of $A + B = 350$ gallons has been achieved by using all available processing time of $2A + 1B = 2(250) + 1(100) = 600$ hours. In addition, note that the constraint requiring that product A demand be met has been satisfied with $A = 250$ gallons. In fact, the production of product A exceeds its minimum level by $250 - 125 = 125$ gallons. This excess production for product A is referred to as *surplus*. In linear programming terminology, any excess quantity corresponding to a $\geq$ constraint is referred to as surplus.

Recall that with a $\leq$ constraint, a slack variable can be added to the left-hand side of the inequality to convert the constraint to equality form. With a $\geq$ constraint, a **surplus variable** can be subtracted from the left-hand side of the inequality to convert the constraint to equality form. Just as with slack variables, surplus variables are given a coefficient of zero in the objective function because they have no effect on its value. After including two surplus variables, S_1 and S_2, for the $\geq$ constraints and one slack variable, S_3, for the $\leq$ constraint, the linear programming model of the M&D Chemicals problem becomes

$$\begin{aligned}
\text{Min} \quad & 2A + 3B + 0S_1 + 0S_2 + 0S_3 \\
\text{s.t.} \quad & \\
& 1A \qquad - 1S_1 \qquad\qquad = 125 \\
& 1A + 1B \qquad - 1S_2 \qquad = 350 \\
& 2A + 1B \qquad\qquad + 1S_3 = 600 \\
& A, B, S_1, S_2, S_3 \geq 0
\end{aligned}$$

Try Problem 33 to test your ability to use slack and surplus variables to write a linear program in standard form.

All the constraints are now equalities. Hence, the preceding formulation is the standard-form representation of the M&D Chemicals problem. At the optimal solution of $A = 250$ and $B = 100$, the values of the surplus and slack variables are as follows:

Constraint	Value of Surplus or Slack Variables
Demand for product A	$S_1 = 125$
Total production	$S_2 = 0$
Processing time	$S_3 = 0$

Refer to Figures 2.15 and 2.16. Note that the zero surplus and slack variables are associated with the constraints that are binding at the optimal solution—that is, the total production and processing time constraints. The surplus of 125 units is associated with the nonbinding constraint on the demand for product A.

In the Par, Inc., problem all the constraints were of the $\leq$ type, and in the M&D Chemicals problem the constraints were a mixture of $\geq$ and $\leq$ types. The number and types of constraints encountered in a particular linear programming problem depend on the specific conditions existing in the problem. Linear programming problems may have some $\leq$ constraints, some $\geq$ constraints, and some $=$ constraints. For an equality constraint, feasible solutions must lie directly on the constraint line.

Try Problem 32 to practice solving a linear program with all three constraint forms.

An example of a linear program with two decision variables, G and H, and all three constraint forms is given here:

$$\begin{aligned} \text{Min} \quad & 2G + 2H \\ \text{s.t.} \quad & \\ & 1G + 3H \leq 12 \\ & 3G + 1H \geq 13 \\ & 1G - 1H = 3 \\ & G, H \geq 0 \end{aligned}$$

The standard-form representation of this problem is

$$\begin{aligned} \text{Min} \quad & 2G + 2H + 0S_1 + 0S_2 \\ \text{s.t.} \quad & \\ & 1G + 3H + 1S_1 \qquad = 12 \\ & 3G + 1H \qquad - 1S_2 = 13 \\ & 1G - 1H \qquad\qquad = 3 \\ & G, H, S_1, S_2 \geq 0 \end{aligned}$$

The standard form requires a slack variable for the $\leq$ constraint and a surplus variable for the $\geq$ constraint. However, neither a slack nor a surplus variable is required for the third constraint since it is already in equality form.

When solving linear programs graphically, it is not necessary to write the problem in its standard form. Nevertheless, you should be able to compute the values of the slack and surplus variables and understand what they mean, because the values of slack and surplus variables are included in the computer solution of linear programs. In Chapter 5 we will introduce an algebraic solution procedure, the simplex method, which can be used to find optimal extreme-point solutions for linear programming problems with as many as several thousand decision variables. The mathematical steps of the simplex method involve solving simultaneous equations that represent the constraints of the linear program. Thus, in setting up a linear program for solution by the simplex method, we must have one linear equation for each constraint in the problem; therefore, the problem must be in its standard form.

A final point: The standard form of the linear programming problem is equivalent to the original formulation of the problem. That is, the optimal solution to any linear programming problem is the same as the optimal solution to the standard form of the problem. The standard form has not changed the basic problem; it has only changed how we write the constraints for the problem.

Computer Solution of the M&D Chemicals Problem

The solution obtained using The Management Scientist is presented in Figure 2.17. The computer output shows that the minimum-cost solution yields an objective function value of \$800. The values of the decision variables show that 250 gallons of product A and 100 gallons of product B provide the minimum-cost solution.

The Slack/Surplus column shows that the $\geq$ constraint corresponding to the demand for product A (see constraint 1) has a surplus of 125 units. This column tells us that production of product A in the optimal solution exceeds demand by 125 gallons. The Slack/Surplus values are zero for the total production requirement (constraint 2) and the processing time limitation (constraint 3), which indicates that these constraints are binding at the

FIGURE 2.17 THE MANAGEMENT SCIENTIST SOLUTION FOR THE M&D CHEMICALS PROBLEM

```
Objective Function Value =                 800.000

      Variable                 Value               Reduced Costs
   --------------        ---------------        -----------------
          A                    250.000                      0.000
          B                    100.000                      0.000

      Constraint            Slack/Surplus            Dual Prices
   --------------        ---------------        -----------------
          1                    125.000                      0.000
          2                      0.000                     -4.000
          3                      0.000                      1.000

OBJECTIVE COEFFICIENT RANGES

  Variable         Lower Limit        Current Value        Upper Limit
 ------------    ---------------    ---------------    ---------------
       A         No Lower Limit               2.000              3.000
       B                  2.000               3.000     No Upper Limit

RIGHT HAND SIDE RANGES

 Constraint        Lower Limit        Current Value        Upper Limit
 ------------    ---------------    ---------------    ---------------
       1         No Lower Limit             125.000            250.000
       2                300.000             350.000            475.000
       3                475.000             600.000            700.000
```

EXCELfile
M&D

optimal solution. We will discuss the rest of the computer output that appears in Figure 2.17 in Chapter 3 when we study the topic of sensitivity analysis.

2.6 SPECIAL CASES

In this section we discuss three special situations that can arise when we attempt to solve linear programming problems.

Alternative Optimal Solutions

From the discussion of the graphical solution procedure, we know that optimal solutions can be found at the extreme points of the feasible region. Now let us consider the special case in which the optimal objective function line coincides with one of the binding constraint lines on the boundary of the feasible region. We will see that this situation can lead to the case of **alternative optimal solutions;** in such cases, more than one solution provides the optimal value for the objective function.

To illustrate the case of alternative optimal solutions, we return to the Par, Inc., problem. However, let us assume that the profit for the standard golf bag (S) has been decreased to \$6.30. The revised objective function becomes $6.3S + 9D$. The graphical solution of this problem is shown in Figure 2.18. Note that the optimal solution still occurs at an extreme point. In fact, it occurs at two extreme points: extreme point (4) ($S = 300$, $D = 420$) and extreme point (3) ($S = 540$, $D = 252$).

The objective function values at these two extreme points are identical; that is,

$$6.3S + 9D = 6.3(300) + 9(420) = 5670$$

and

$$6.3S + 9D = 6.3(540) + 9(252) = 5670$$

Furthermore, any point on the line connecting the two optimal extreme points also provides an optimal solution. For example, the solution point ($S = 420$, $D = 336$), which is halfway between the two extreme points, also provides the optimal objective function value of

$$6.3S + 9D = 6.3(420) + 9(336) = 5670$$

A linear programming problem with alternative optimal solutions is generally a good situation for the manager or decision maker. It means that several combinations of the decision variables are optimal and that the manager can select the most desirable optimal so-

FIGURE 2.18 PAR, INC., PROBLEM WITH AN OBJECTIVE FUNCTION OF $6.3S + 9D$ (ALTERNATIVE OPTIMAL SOLUTIONS)

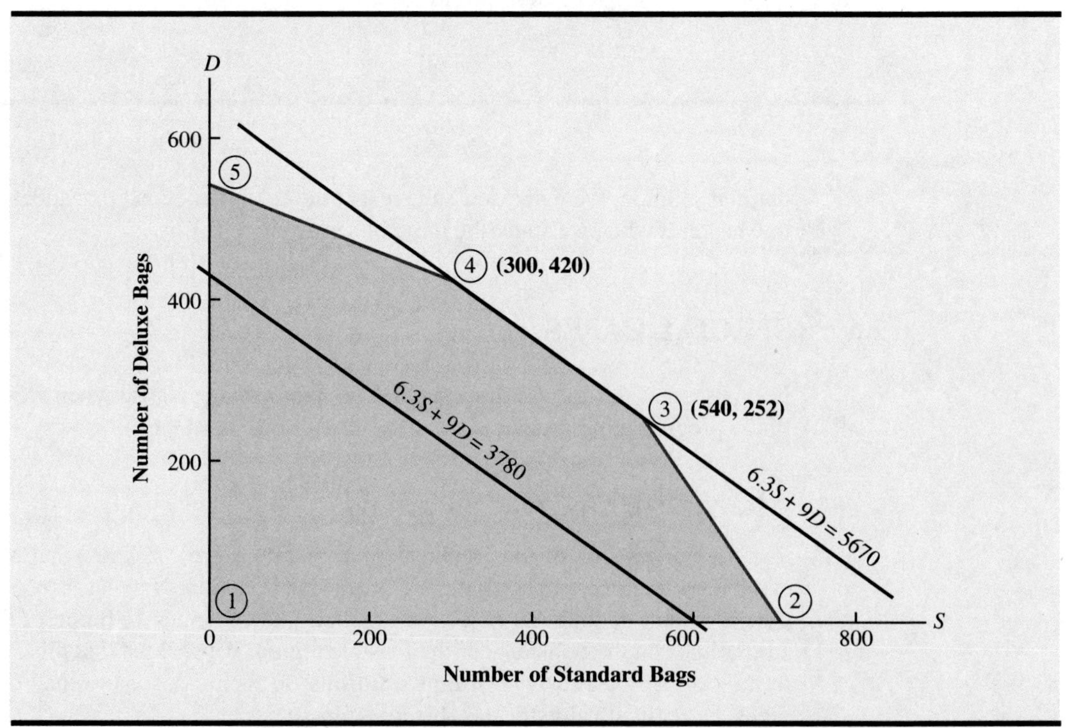

lution. Unfortunately, determining whether a problem has alternative optimal solutions is not a simple matter.

Infeasibility

Problems with no feasible solution do arise in practice, most often because management's expectations are too high or because too many restrictions have been placed on the problem.

Infeasibility means that no solution to the linear programming problem satisfies all the constraints, including the nonnegativity conditions. Graphically, infeasibility means that a feasible region does not exist; that is, no points satisfy all the constraints and the nonnegativity conditions simultaneously. To illustrate this situation, let us look again at the problem faced by Par, Inc.

Suppose that management had specified that at least 500 of the standard bags and at least 360 of the deluxe bags must be manufactured. The graph of the solution region may now be constructed to reflect these new requirements (see Figure 2.19). The shaded area in the lower left-hand portion of the graph depicts those points satisfying the departmental constraints on the availability of time. The shaded area in the upper right-hand portion depicts those points satisfying the minimum production requirements of 500 standard and 360 deluxe bags. But no points satisfy both sets of constraints. Thus, we see that if management imposes these minimum production requirements, no feasible region exists for the problem.

How should we interpret infeasibility in terms of this current problem? First, we should tell management that given the resources available (i.e., production time for cutting and dyeing, sewing, finishing, and inspection and packaging), it is not possible to make 500 standard bags and 360 deluxe bags. Moreover, we can tell management exactly how much of each resource must be expended to make it possible to manufacture 500 standard and 360 deluxe

FIGURE 2.19 NO FEASIBLE REGION FOR THE PAR, INC., PROBLEM WITH MINIMUM PRODUCTION REQUIREMENTS OF 500 STANDARD AND 360 DELUXE BAGS

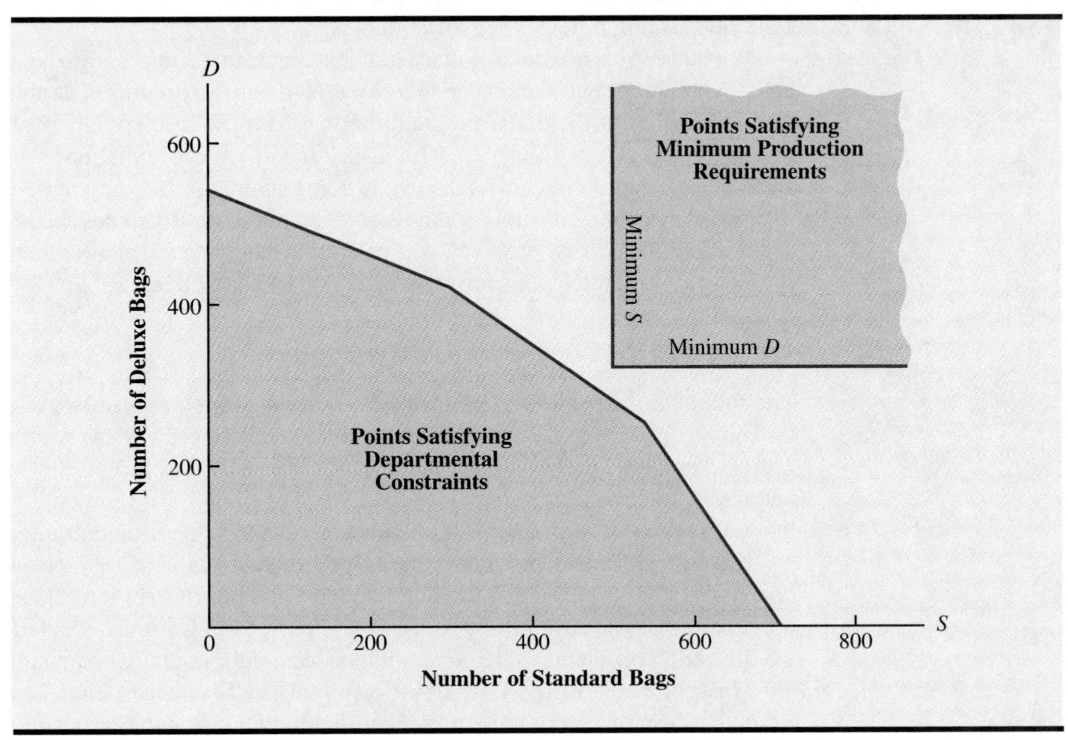

TABLE 2.2 RESOURCES NEEDED TO MANUFACTURE 500 STANDARD BAGS AND 360 DELUXE BAGS

Operation	Minimum Required Resources (hours)	Available Resources (hours)	Additional Resources Needed (hours)
Cutting and dyeing	$\frac{7}{10}(500) + 1(360) = 710$	630	80
Sewing	$\frac{1}{2}(500) + \frac{5}{6}(360) = 550$	600	None
Finishing	$1(500) + \frac{2}{3}(360) = 740$	708	32
Inspection and packaging	$\frac{1}{10}(500) + \frac{1}{4}(360) = 140$	135	5

bags. Table 2.2 shows the minimum amounts of resources that must be available, the amounts currently available, and additional amounts that would be required to accomplish this level of production. Thus, we need 80 more hours for cutting and dyeing, 32 more hours for finishing, and 5 more hours for inspection and packaging to meet management's minimum production requirements.

If, after reviewing this information, management still wants to manufacture 500 standard and 360 deluxe bags, additional resources must be provided. Perhaps by hiring another person to work in the cutting and dyeing department, transferring a person from elsewhere in the plant to work part-time in the finishing department, or having the sewing people help out periodically with the inspection and packaging, the resource requirements can be met. As you can see, many possibilities are available for corrective management action, once we discover the lack of a feasible solution. The important thing to realize is that linear programming analysis can help determine whether management's plans are feasible. By analyzing the problem using linear programming, we are often able to point out infeasible conditions and initiate corrective action.

Whenever you attempt to solve a problem that is infeasible using The Management Scientist, you will obtain a message that says "No Feasible Solution." In this case you know that no solution to the linear programming problem will satisfy all constraints, including the nonnegativity conditions. Careful inspection of your formulation is necessary to try to identify why the problem is infeasible. In some situations, the only reasonable approach is to drop one or more constraints and resolve the problem. If you are able to find an optimal solution for this revised problem, you will know that the constraint(s) that were omitted, in conjunction with the others, are causing the problem to be infeasible.

Unbounded

The solution to a maximization linear programming problem is **unbounded** if the value of the solution may be made infinitely large without violating any of the constraints; for a minimization problem, the solution is unbounded if the value may be made infinitely small. This condition might be termed *managerial utopia;* for example, if this condition were to occur in a profit maximization problem, the manager could achieve an unlimited profit.

However, in linear programming models of real problems, the occurrence of an unbounded solution means that the problem has been improperly formulated. We know it is not possible to increase profits indefinitely. Therefore, we must conclude that if a profit maximization problem results in an unbounded solution, the mathematical model doesn't represent the real-world problem sufficiently. Usually, what has happened is that a constraint has been inadvertently omitted during problem formulation.

As an illustration, consider the following linear program with two decision variables, X and Y.

$$\begin{aligned}
\text{Max} \quad & 20X + 10Y \\
\text{s.t.} \quad & \\
& 1X \qquad \geq 2 \\
& \qquad 1Y \leq 5 \\
& X, Y \geq 0
\end{aligned}$$

In Figure 2.20 we have graphed the feasible region associated with this problem. Note that we can only indicate part of the feasible region since the feasible region extends indefinitely in the direction of the X axis. Looking at the objective function lines in Figure 2.20, we see that the solution to this problem may be made as large as we desire. That is, no matter what solution we pick, we will always be able to reach some feasible solution with a larger value. Thus, we say that the solution to this linear program is *unbounded.*

FIGURE 2.20 EXAMPLE OF AN UNBOUNDED PROBLEM

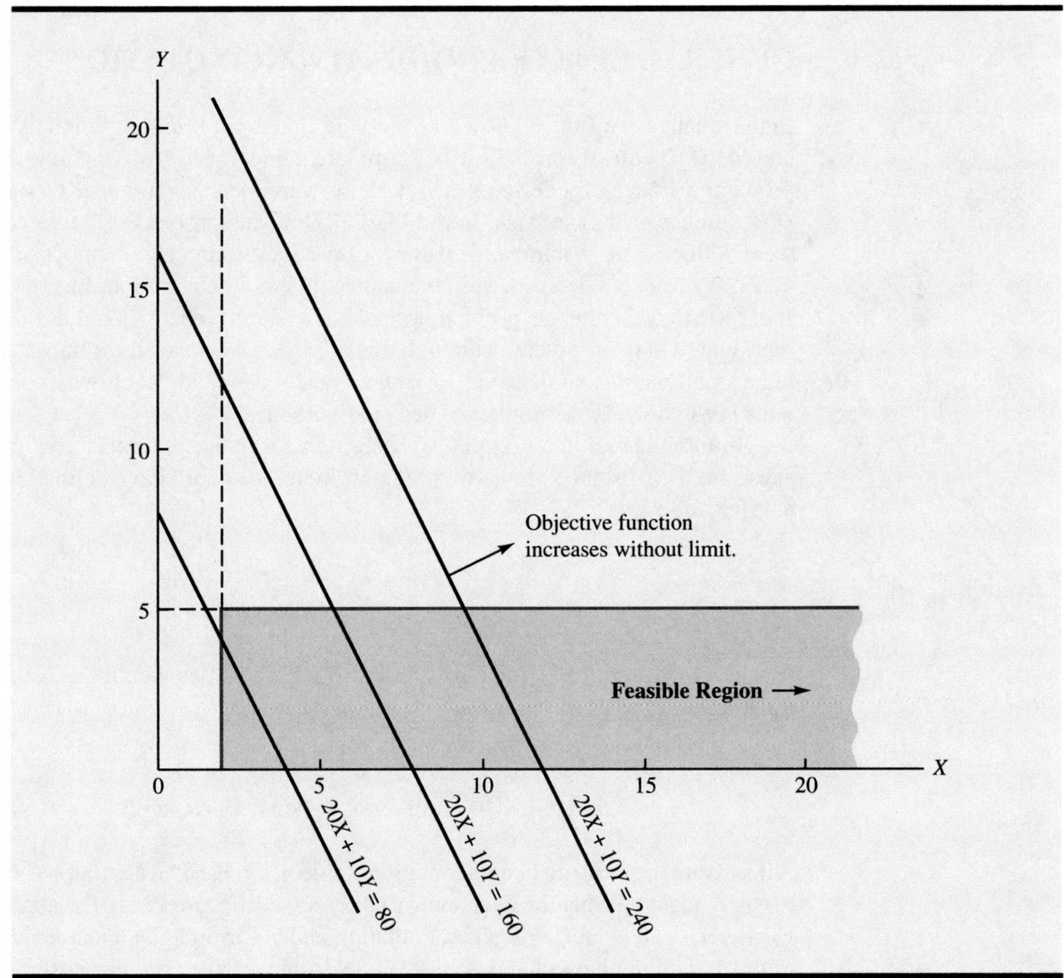

Can you recognize whether a linear program involves alternative optimal solutions, infeasibility, or is unbounded? Try Problems 40 and 41.

Whenever you attempt to solve a problem that is unbounded using The Management Scientist, you will obtain a message that says, "Problem is Unbounded." Because unbounded solutions cannot occur in real problems, the first thing you should do is to review your model to determine whether you have incorrectly formulated the problem. In many cases, this error is the result of inadvertently omitting a constraint during problem formulation.

NOTES AND COMMENTS

1. Infeasibility is independent of the objective function. It exists because the constraints are so restrictive that there is no feasible region for the linear programming model. Thus, when you encounter infeasibility, making changes in the coefficients of the objective function will not help; the problem will remain infeasible.
2. The occurrence of an unbounded solution is often the result of a missing constraint. However, a change in the objective function may cause a previously unbounded problem to become bounded with an optimal solution. For example, the graph in Figure 2.20 shows an unbounded solution for the objective function Max $20X + 10Y$. However, changing the objective function to Max $-20X - 10Y$ will provide the optimal solution $X = 2$ and $Y = 0$ even though no changes have been made in the constraints.

2.7 GENERAL LINEAR PROGRAMMING NOTATION

In this chapter we showed how to formulate linear programming models for the Par, Inc., and M&D Chemicals problems. To formulate a linear programming model of the Par, Inc., problem we began by defining two decision variables: S = number of standard bags, and D = number of deluxe bags. In the M&D Chemicals problem, the two decision variables were defined as A = number of gallons of product A, and B = number of gallons of product B. We selected decision-variable names of S and D in the Par, Inc., problem and A and B in the M&D Chemicals problem to make it easier to recall what these decision variables represented in the problem. Although this approach works well for linear programs involving a small number of decision variables, it can become difficult when dealing with problems involving a large number of decision variables.

A more general notation that is often used for linear programs uses the letter x with a subscript. For instance, in the Par, Inc., problem, we could have defined the decision variables as follows:

$$x_1 = \text{number of standard bags}$$
$$x_2 = \text{number of deluxe bags}$$

In the M&D Chemicals problem, the same variable names would be used, but their definitions would change:

$$x_1 = \text{number of gallons of product A}$$
$$x_2 = \text{number of gallons of product B}$$

A disadvantage of using general notation for decision variables is that we are no longer able to easily identify what the decision variables actually represent in the mathematical model. However, the advantage of general notation is that formulating a mathematical model for a problem that involves a large number of decision variables is much easier. For instance, for a linear programming model with three decision variables, we would use variable names of x_1, x_2, and x_3; for a problem with four decision variables, we would use variable names of x_1, x_2, x_3, and x_4, and so on. Clearly, if a problem involved 1000 decision variables, trying to identify 1000 unique names would be difficult. However, using the general linear programming notation, the decision variables would be defined as $x_1, x_2, x_3, \ldots, x_{1000}$.

To illustrate the graphical solution procedure for a linear program written using general linear programming notation, consider the following mathematical model for a maximization problem involving two decision variables:

$$
\begin{aligned}
\text{Max} \quad & 3x_1 + 2x_2 \\
\text{s.t.} \quad & \\
& 2x_1 + 2x_2 \leq 8 \\
& 1x_1 + 0.5x_2 \leq 3 \\
& x_1, x_2 \geq 0
\end{aligned}
$$

We must first develop a graph that displays the possible solutions (x_1 and x_2 values) for the problem. The usual convention is to plot values of x_1 along the horizontal axis and values of x_2 along the vertical axis. Figure 2.21 shows the graphical solution for this two-variable problem. Note that for this problem the optimal solution is $x_1 = 2$ and $x_2 = 2$, with an objective function value of 10.

Using general linear programming notation, we can write the standard form of the preceding linear program as follows:

$$
\begin{aligned}
\text{Max} \quad & 3x_1 + 2x_2 + 0s_1 + 0s_2 \\
\text{s.t.} \quad & \\
& 2x_1 + 2x_2 + 1s_1 = 8 \\
& 1x_1 + 0.5x_2 + 1s_2 = 3 \\
& x_1, x_2, s_1, s_2 \geq 0
\end{aligned}
$$

Thus, at the optimal solution $x_1 = 2$ and $x_2 = 2$; the values of the slack variables are $s_1 = s_2 = 0$.

SUMMARY

We formulated linear programming models for two problems: the Par, Inc., maximization problem and the M&D Chemicals minimization problem. For both problems we showed how a graphical solution procedure and The Management Scientist software package can be used to identify an optimal solution. In formulating a mathematical model of these problems, we developed a general definition of a linear programming model.

A linear programming model is a mathematical model that has

1. a linear objective function that is to be maximized or minimized,
2. a set of linear constraints, and
3. variables that are all restricted to nonnegative values.

Slack variables may be used to write less-than-or-equal-to constraints in equality form and surplus variables may be used to write greater-than-or-equal-to constraints in equality form. The value of a slack variable can usually be interpreted as the amount of unused resource, while the value of a surplus variable indicates the amount over and above some

FIGURE 2.21 GRAPHICAL SOLUTION OF A TWO-VARIABLE LINEAR PROGRAM WITH GENERAL NOTATION

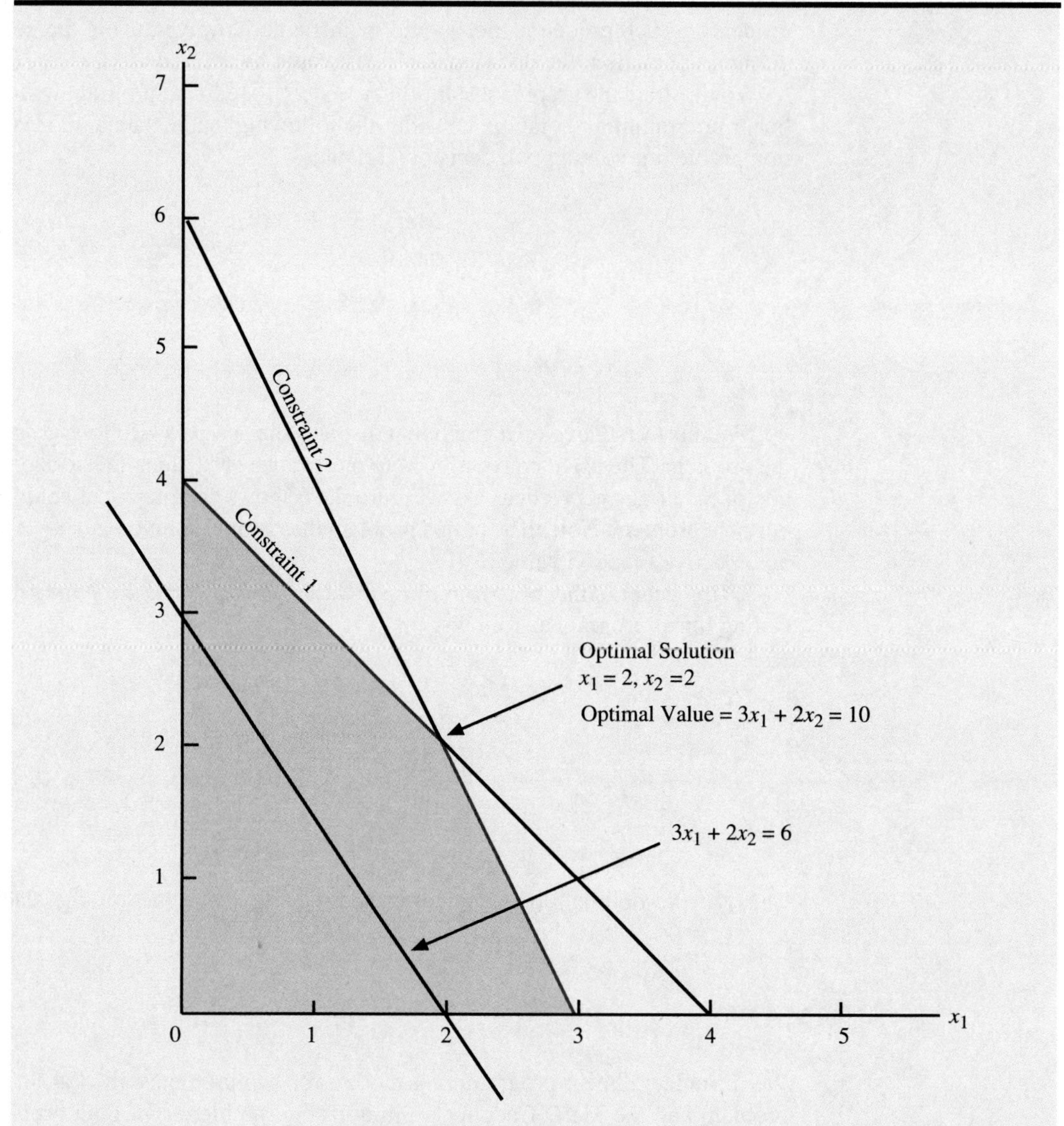

stated minimum requirement. When all constraints have been written as equalities, the linear program has been written in its standard form.

If the solution to a linear program is infeasible or unbounded, no optimal solution to the problem can be found. In the case of infeasibility, no feasible solutions are possible; whereas, in the case of an unbounded solution, the objective function can be made infinitely large for a maximization problem and infinitely small for a minimization problem. In the case of alternative optimal solutions, two or more optimal extreme points exist, and all the points on the line segment connecting them are also optimal.

This chapter concludes with a section showing how to write a linear program using general linear programming notation. The Management Science in Action, Using Linear Programming for Traffic Control, provides just one of many examples of the widespread use of linear programming. In the next two chapters we will see many more applications of linear programming.

MANAGEMENT SCIENCE IN ACTION

USING LINEAR PROGRAMMING FOR TRAFFIC CONTROL*

The Hanshin Expressway was the first urban toll expressway in Osaka, Japan. Although in 1964 its length was only 2.3 kilometers, today it is a large-scale urban expressway network of 200 kilometers. The Hanshin Expressway provides service for the Hanshin (Osaka-Kobe) area, the second-most populated area in Japan. An average of 828,000 vehicles use the expressway each day, with daily traffic sometimes exceeding 1 million vehicles. In 1990, the Hanshin Expressway Public Corporation started using an automated traffic control system in order to maximize the number of vehicles flowing into the expressway network.

The automated traffic control system relies on two control methods: (1) limiting the number of cars that enter the expressway at each entrance ramp; and (2) providing drivers with up-to-date and accurate traffic information, including expected travel times and information about accidents. The approach used to limit the number of vehicles depends upon whether the expressway is in a normal or steady state of operation, or whether some type of unusual event, such as an accident or a breakdown, has occurred.

In the first phase of the steady-state case, the Hanshin system uses a linear programming model to maximize the total number of vehicles entering the system, while preventing traffic congestion and adverse effects on surrounding road networks. The data that drive the linear programming model are collected from detectors installed every 500 meters along the expressway and at all entrance and exit ramps. Every five minutes the real-time data collected from the detectors are used to update the model coefficients, and a new linear program computes the maximum number of vehicles the expressway can accommodate.

The automated traffic control system has been successful. According to surveys, traffic control decreased the length of congested portions of the expressway by 30 percent and the duration by 20 percent. It proved to be extremely cost effective, and drivers consider it an indispensable service.

*Based on T. Yoshino, T. Sasaki, and T. Hasegawa, "The Traffic-Control System on the Hanshin Expressway," *Interfaces* (January/February 1995): 94–108.

GLOSSARY

Constraint An equation or inequality that rules out certain combinations of decision variables as feasible solutions.

Problem formulation The process of translating the verbal statement of a problem into a mathematical statement called the *mathematical model.*

Decision variable A controllable input for a linear programming model.

Nonnegativity constraints A set of constraints that requires all variables to be nonnegative.

Mathematical model A representation of a problem where the objective and all constraint conditions are described by mathematical expressions.

Linear programming model A mathematical model with a linear objective function, a set of linear constraints, and nonnegative variables.

Linear program Another term for linear programming model.

Linear functions Mathematical expressions in which the variables appear in separate terms and are raised to the first power.

Feasible solution A solution that satisfies all the constraints.

Feasible region The set of all feasible solutions.

Slack variable A variable added to the left-hand side of a less-than-or-equal-to constraint to convert the constraint into an equality. The value of this variable can usually be interpreted as the amount of unused resource.

Standard form A linear program in which all the constraints are written as equalities. The optimal solution of the standard form of a linear program is the same as the optimal solution of the original formulation of the linear program.

Redundant constraint A constraint that does not affect the feasible region. If a constraint is redundant, it can be removed from the problem without affecting the feasible region.

Extreme point Graphically speaking, extreme points are the feasible solution points occurring at the vertices or "corners" of the feasible region. With two-variable problems, extreme points are determined by the intersection of the constraint lines.

Surplus variable A variable subtracted from the left-hand side of a greater-than-or-equal-to constraint to convert the constraint into an equality. The value of this variable can usually be interpreted as the amount over and above some required minimum level.

Alternative optimal solutions The case in which more than one solution provides the optimal value for the objective function.

Infeasibility The situation in which no solution to the linear programming problem satisfies all the constraints.

Unbounded If the value of the solution may be made infinitely large in a maximization linear programming problem or infinitely small in a minimization problem without violating any of the constraints, the problem is said to be unbounded.

PROBLEMS

1. Which of the following mathematical relationships could be found in a linear programming model, and which could not? For the relationships that are unacceptable for linear programs, state why.
   a. $-1x_1 + 2x_2 - 1x_3 \leq 70$
   b. $2x_1 - 2x_3 = 50$
   c. $1x_1 - 2x_2^2 + 4x_3 \leq 10$
   d. $3\sqrt{x_1} + 2x_2 - 1x_3 \geq 15$
   e. $1x_1 + 1x_2 + 1x_3 = 6$
   f. $2x_1 + 5x_2 + 1x_1x_2 \leq 25$

2. Find the feasible solution points for the following constraints:
   a. $4x_1 + 2x_2 \leq 16$
   b. $4x_1 + 2x_2 \geq 16$
   c. $4x_1 + 2x_2 = 16$
3. Show a separate graph of the constraint lines and feasible solutions for each of the following constraints:
   a. $3x_1 + 2x_2 \leq 18$
   b. $12x_1 + 8x_2 \geq 480$
   c. $5x_1 + 10x_2 = 200$

4. Show a separate graph of the constraint lines and feasible solutions for each of the following constraints:
   a. $3x_1 - 4x_2 \geq 60$
   b. $-6x_1 + 5x_2 \leq 60$
   c. $5x_1 - 2x_2 \leq 0$
5. Show a separate graph of the constraint lines and feasible solutions for each of the following constraints:
   a. $x_1 \geq 0.25\,(x_1 + x_2)$
   b. $x_2 \leq 0.10\,(x_1 + x_2)$
   c. $x_1 \leq 0.50\,(x_1 + x_2)$

SELF test

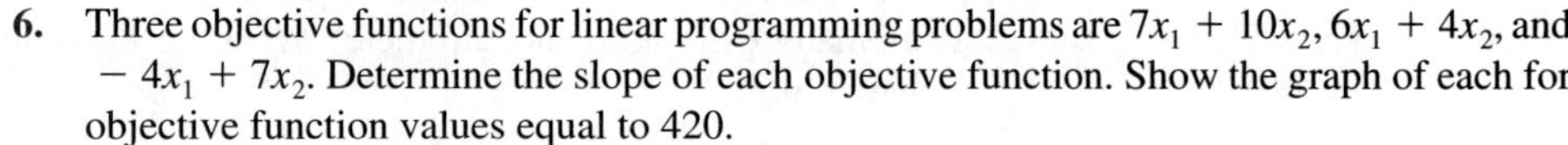

6. Three objective functions for linear programming problems are $7x_1 + 10x_2$, $6x_1 + 4x_2$, and $-4x_1 + 7x_2$. Determine the slope of each objective function. Show the graph of each for objective function values equal to 420.

SELF test

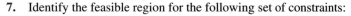

7. Identify the feasible region for the following set of constraints:

$$
\begin{aligned}
\tfrac{1}{2}x_1 + \tfrac{1}{4}x_2 &\geq 30 \\
1x_1 + 5x_2 &\geq 250 \\
\tfrac{1}{4}x_1 + \tfrac{1}{2}x_2 &\leq 50 \\
x_1, x_2 &\geq 0
\end{aligned}
$$

8. Identify the feasible region for the following set of constraints:

$$
\begin{aligned}
2x_1 - 1x_2 &\leq 0 \\
-1x_1 + 1.5x_2 &\leq 200 \\
x_1, x_2 &\geq 0
\end{aligned}
$$

9. Identify the feasible region for the following set of constraints:

$$
\begin{aligned}
3x_1 - 2x_2 &\geq 0 \\
2x_1 - 1x_2 &\leq 200 \\
1x_1 &\leq 150 \\
x_1, x_2 &\geq 0
\end{aligned}
$$

10. For the linear program

$$
\begin{aligned}
\text{Max} \quad & 2x_1 + 3x_2 \\
\text{s.t.} \quad & \\
& 1x_1 + 2x_2 \leq 6 \\
& 5x_1 + 3x_2 \leq 15 \\
& x_1, x_2 \geq 0
\end{aligned}
$$

find the optimal solution using the graphical solution procedure. What is the value of the objective function at the optimal solution?

11. Solve the following linear program using the graphical solution procedure.

$$
\begin{aligned}
\text{Max} \quad & 5x_1 + 5x_2 \\
\text{s.t.} \quad & \\
& 1x_1 \leq 100 \\
& 1x_2 \leq 80 \\
& 2x_1 + 4x_2 \leq 400 \\
& x_1, x_2 \geq 0
\end{aligned}
$$

12. Consider the following linear programming model:

$$\begin{aligned}\text{Max} \quad & 3x_1 + 3x_2 \\ \text{s.t.} \quad & \\ & 2x_1 + 4x_2 \leq 12 \\ & 6x_1 + 4x_2 \leq 24 \\ & x_1, x_2 \geq 0\end{aligned}$$

a. Find the optimal solution using the graphical solution procedure.
b. If the objective function is changed to $2x_1 + 6x_2$, what will the optimal solution be?
c. How many extreme points are there? What are the values of x_1 and x_2 at each extreme point?

13. Consider the following linear program:

$$\begin{aligned}\text{Max} \quad & 3x_1 + 2x_2 \\ \text{s.t.} \quad & \\ & 2x_1 + 2x_2 \leq 8 \\ & 3x_1 + 2x_2 \leq 12 \\ & 1x_1 + 0.5x_2 \leq 3 \\ & x_1, x_2 \geq 0\end{aligned}$$

a. Find the optimal solution using the graphical solution procedure. What is the value of the objective function?
b. Does this linear program have a redundant constraint? If so, what is it? Does the solution change if the redundant constraint is removed from the model? Explain.

14. Consider the following linear program:

$$\begin{aligned}\text{Max} \quad & 1x_1 + 2x_2 \\ \text{s.t.} \quad & \\ & 1x_1 \leq 5 \\ & 1x_2 \leq 4 \\ & 2x_1 + 2x_2 = 12 \\ & x_1, x_2 \geq 0\end{aligned}$$

a. Show the feasible region.
b. What are the extreme points of the feasible region?
c. Find the optimal solution using the graphical procedure.

15. Refer to the Par, Inc., problem described in Section 2.1. Suppose that Par's management encounters each of the following situations:

a. The accounting department revises its estimate of the profit contribution for the deluxe bag to \$18 per bag.
b. A new low-cost material is available for the standard bag, and the profit contribution per standard bag can be increased to \$20 per bag. (Assume the profit contribution of the deluxe bag is the original \$9 value.)
c. New sewing equipment is available that would increase the sewing operation capacity to 750 hours. (Assume $10S + 9D$ is the appropriate objective function.)

If each of these conditions is encountered separately, what are the optimal solution and the total profit contribution for each situation?

16. Refer to the feasible region for the Par, Inc., problem in Figure 2.13.
    a. Develop an objective function that will make extreme point ⑤ the optimal extreme point.
    b. What is the optimal solution using the objective function you selected in part (a)?
    c. What are the values of the slack variables associated with this solution?

17. Write the following linear program in standard form:

$$\begin{aligned} \text{Max} \quad & 5x_1 + 2x_2 + 8x_3 \\ \text{s.t.} \quad & \\ & 1x_1 + 2x_2 + \tfrac{1}{2}x_3 \le 420 \\ & 2x_1 + 3x_2 - 1x_3 \le 610 \\ & 6x_1 - 1x_2 + 3x_3 \le 125 \\ & x_1, x_2, x_3 \ge 0 \end{aligned}$$

18. For the linear program

$$\begin{aligned} \text{Max} \quad & 4x_1 + 1x_2 \\ \text{s.t.} \quad & \\ & 10x_1 + 2x_2 \le 30 \\ & 3x_1 + 2x_2 \le 12 \\ & 2x_1 + 2x_2 \le 10 \\ & x_1, x_2 \ge 0 \end{aligned}$$

    a. Write this linear program in standard form.
    b. Find the optimal solution using the graphical solution procedure.
    c. What are the values of the three slack variables at the optimal solution?

19. Given the linear program

$$\begin{aligned} \text{Max} \quad & 3x_1 + 4x_2 \\ \text{s.t.} \quad & \\ & -1x_1 + 2x_2 \le 8 \\ & 1x_1 + 2x_2 \le 12 \\ & 2x_1 + 1x_2 \le 16 \\ & x_1, x_2 \ge 0 \end{aligned}$$

    a. Write the linear program in standard form.
    b. Find the optimal solution using the graphical solution procedure.
    c. What are the values of the three slack variables at the optimal solution?

20. Embassy Motorcycles (EM) manufactures two lightweight motorcycles designed for easy handling and safety. The EZ-Rider model has a new engine and a low profile that make it easy to balance. The Lady-Sport model is slightly larger, uses a more traditional engine, and is specifically designed to appeal to women riders. Embassy produces the engines for both models at its Des Moines, Iowa, plant. Each EZ-Rider engine requires 6 hours of manufacturing time and each Lady-Sport engine requires 3 hours of manufacturing time. The Des Moines plant has 2100 hours of engine manufacturing time available for the next production period. Embassy's motorcycle frame supplier can supply as many EZ-Rider frames as needed. However, the Lady-Sport frame is more complex and the supplier can provide only up to 280 Lady-Sport frames for the next production period. Final assembly and testing requires 2 hours for each EZ-Rider model and 2.5 hours for each Lady-Sport

model. A maximum of 1000 hours of assembly and testing time are available for the next production period. The company's accounting department projects a profit contribution of $2400 for each EZ-Rider produced and $1800 for each Lady-Sport produced.

a. Formulate a linear programming model that can be used to determine the number of units of each model that should be produced in order to maximize the total contribution to profit.

b. Find the optimal solution using the graphical solution procedure.

c. Which constraints are binding?

21. RMC, Inc., is a small firm that produces a variety of chemical products. In a particular production process, three raw materials are blended (mixed together) to produce two products: a fuel additive and a solvent base. Each ton of fuel additive is a mixture of $\frac{2}{5}$ ton of material 1 and $\frac{3}{5}$ of material 3. A ton of solvent base is a mixture of $\frac{1}{2}$ ton of material 1, $\frac{1}{5}$ ton of material 2, and $\frac{3}{10}$ ton of material 3. After deducting relevant costs, the profit contribution is $40 for every ton of fuel additive produced and $30 for every ton of solvent base produced.

RMC's production is constrained by a limited availability of the three raw materials. For the current production period, RMC has available the following quantities of each raw material:

Raw Material	Amount Available for Production
Material 1	20 tons
Material 2	5 tons
Material 3	21 tons

Assuming that RMC is interested in maximizing the total profit contribution, answer the following:

a. What is the linear programming model for this problem?

b. Find the optimal solution using the graphical solution procedure. How many tons of each product should be produced, and what is the projected total profit contribution?

c. Is there any unused material? If so, how much?

d. Are there any redundant constraints? If so, which ones?

22. Kelson Sporting Equipment, Inc., makes two different types of baseball gloves: a regular model and a catcher's model. The firm has 900 hours of production time available in its cutting and sewing department, 300 hours available in its finishing department, and 100 hours available in its packaging and shipping department. The production time requirements and the profit contribution per glove are given in the following table.

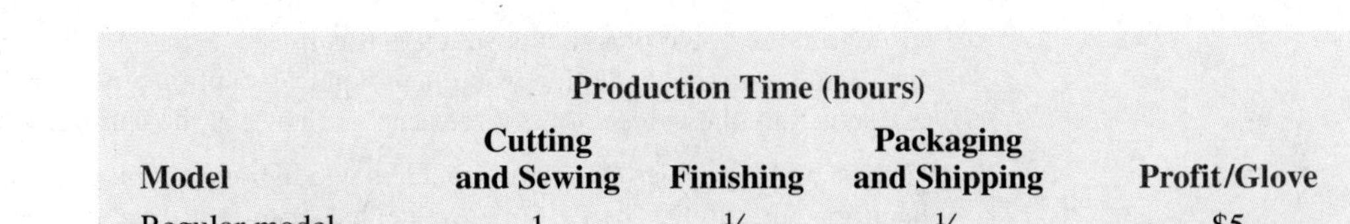

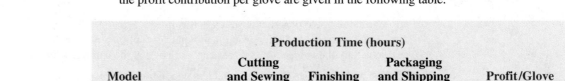

	Production Time (hours)			
Model	**Cutting and Sewing**	**Finishing**	**Packaging and Shipping**	**Profit/Glove**
Regular model	1	$\frac{1}{2}$	$\frac{1}{8}$	$5
Catcher's model	$\frac{3}{2}$	$\frac{1}{3}$	$\frac{1}{4}$	$8

Assuming that the company is interested in maximizing the total profit contribution, answer the following:

a. What is the linear programming model for this problem?

b. Find the optimal solution using the graphical solution procedure. How many gloves of each model should Kelson manufacture?

c. What is the total profit contribution Kelson can earn with the listed production quantities?

d. How many hours of production time will be scheduled in each department?
e. What is the slack time in each department?

23. George Johnson recently inherited a large sum of money; he wants to use a portion of this money to set up a trust fund for his two children. The trust fund has two investment options: (1) a bond fund and (2) a stock fund. The projected returns over the life of the investments are 6% for the bond fund and 10% for the stock fund. Whatever portion of the inheritance he finally decides to commit to the trust fund, he wants to invest at least 30% of that amount in the bond fund. In addition, he wants to select a mix that will enable him to obtain a total return of at least 7.5%.
a. Formulate a linear programming model that can be used to determine the percentage that should be allocated to each of the possible investment alternatives.
b. Find the optimal solution using the graphical solution procedure.

24. The Sea Wharf Restaurant would like to determine the best way to allocate a monthly advertising budget of $1000 between newspaper advertising and radio advertising. Management has decided that at least 25% of the budget must be spent on each type of media, and that the amount of money spent on local newspaper advertising must be at least twice the amount spent on radio advertising. A marketing consultant has developed an index that measures audience exposure per dollar of advertising on a scale from 0 to 100, with higher values implying greater audience exposure. If the value of the index for local newspaper advertising is 50 and the value of the index for spot radio advertising is 80, how should the restaurant allocate its advertising budget in order to maximize the value of total audience exposure?
a. Formulate a linear programming model that can be used to determine how the restaurant should allocate its advertising budget in order to maximize the value of total audience exposure.
b. Find the optimal solution using the graphical solution procedure.

25. Blair & Rosen, Inc. (B&R), is a brokerage firm that specializes in investment portfolios designed to meet the specific risk tolerances of its clients. A client who contacted B&R this past week has a maximum of $50,000 to invest. B&R's investment advisor has decided to recommend a portfolio consisting of two investment funds: an Internet fund and a Blue Chip fund. The Internet fund has a projected annual return of 12%, while the Blue Chip fund has a projected annual return of 9%. The investment advisor requires that at most $35,000 of the client's funds should be invested in the Internet fund. B&R services include a risk rating for each investment alternative. The Internet fund, which is the more risky of the two investment alternatives, has a risk rating of 6 per thousand dollars invested. The Blue Chip fund has a risk rating of 4 per thousand dollars invested. For example, if $10,000 is invested in each of the two investment funds, B&R's risk rating for the portfolio would be 6(10) + 4(10) = 100. Finally, B&R has developed a questionnaire to measure each client's risk tolerance. Based on the responses, each client is classified as a conservative, moderate, or aggressive investor. Suppose that the questionnaire results have classified the current client as a moderate investor. B&R recommends that a client who is a moderate investor limit his or her portfolio to a maximum risk rating of 240.
a. What is the recommended investment portfolio for this client? What is the annual return for the portfolio?
b. Suppose that a second client with $50,000 to invest has been classified as an aggressive investor. B&R recommends that the maximum portfolio risk rating for an aggressive investor is 320. What is the recommended investment portfolio for this aggressive investor? Discuss what happens to the portfolio under the aggressive investor strategy.
c. Suppose that a third client with $50,000 to invest has been classified as a conservative investor. B&R recommends that the maximum portfolio risk rating for a conservative investor is 160. Develop the recommended investment portfolio for the conservative investor. Discuss the interpretation of the slack variable for the total investment fund constraint.

26. Tom's, Inc., produces various Mexican food products and sells them to Western Foods, a chain of grocery stores located in Texas and New Mexico. Tom's, Inc., makes two salsa products: Western Foods Salsa and Mexico City Salsa. Essentially, the two products have different blends of whole tomatoes, tomato sauce, and tomato paste. The Western Foods Salsa is a blend of 50% whole tomatoes, 30% tomato sauce, and 20% tomato paste. The Mexico City Salsa, which has a thicker and chunkier consistency, consists of 70% whole tomatoes, 10% tomato sauce, and 20% tomato paste. Each jar of salsa produced weighs 10 ounces. For the current production period Tom's, Inc., can purchase up to 280 pounds of whole tomatoes, 130 pounds of tomato sauce, and 100 pounds of tomato paste; the price per pound for these ingredients is $0.96, $0.64, and $0.56, respectively. The cost of the spices and the other ingredients is approximately $0.10 per jar. Tom's, Inc., buys empty glass jars for $0.02 each, and labeling and filling costs are estimated to be $0.03 for each jar of salsa produced. Tom's contract with Western Foods results in sales revenue of $1.64 for each jar of Western Foods Salsa and $1.93 for each jar of Mexico City Salsa.

a. Develop a linear programming model that will enable Tom's to determine the mix of salsa products that will maximize the total profit contribution.

b. Find the optimal solution.

27. AutoIgnite produces electronic ignition systems for automobiles at a plant in Cleveland, Ohio. Each ignition system is assembled from two components produced at AutoIgnite's plants in Buffalo, New York, and Dayton, Ohio. The Buffalo plant can produce 2000 units of component 1, 1000 units of component 2, or any combination of the two components each day. For instance, 60% of Buffalo's production time could be used to produce component 1 and 40% of Buffalo's production time could be used to produce component 2; in this case, the Buffalo plant would be able to produce 0.6(2000) = 1200 units of component 1 each day and 0.4(1000) = 400 units of component 2 each day. The Dayton plant can produce 600 units of component 1, 1400 units of component 2, or any combination of the two components each day. At the end of each day, the component production at Buffalo and Dayton is sent to Cleveland for assembly of the ignition systems on the following work day.

a. Formulate a linear programming model that can be used to develop a daily production schedule for the Buffalo and Dayton plants that will maximize daily production of ignition systems at Cleveland.

b. Find the optimal solution.

28. A financial advisor at Diehl Investments identified two companies that are likely candidates for a takeover in the near future. Eastern Cable is a leading manufacturer of flexible cable systems used in the construction industry and ComSwitch is a new firm specializing in digital switching systems. Eastern Cable is currently trading for $40 per share and ComSwitch is currently trading for $25 per share. If the takeovers occur, the financial advisor estimates that the price of Eastern Cable will go to $55 per share and ComSwitch will go to $43 per share. At this point in time, the financial advisor identified ComSwitch as the higher risk alternative. Assume that a client who indicated a willingness to invest a maximum of $50,000 in the two companies wants to invest at least $15,000 in Eastern Cable and at least $10,000 in ComSwitch. Because of the higher risk associated with ComSwitch, the financial advisor recommends that at most $25,000 should be invested in ComSwitch.

a. Formulate a linear programming model that can be used to determine the number of shares of Eastern Cable and the number of shares of ComSwitch that will meet the investment constraints and maximize the total return for the investment.

b. Graph the feasible region.

c. Determine the coordinates of each extreme point.

d. Find the optimal solution.

29. Consider the following linear program:

$$
\begin{aligned}
\text{Min} \quad & 3x_1 + 4x_2 \\
\text{s.t.} \quad & \\
& 1x_1 + 3x_2 \geq 6 \\
& 1x_1 + 1x_2 \geq 4 \\
& x_1, x_2 \geq 0
\end{aligned}
$$

Identify the feasible region and find the optimal solution using the graphical solution procedure. What is the value of the objective function?

30. Identify the three extreme-point solutions for the M&D Chemicals problem (see Section 2.5). Identify the value of the objective function and the values of the slack and surplus variables at each extreme point.

31. Consider the following linear programming model:

$$
\begin{aligned}
\text{Min} \quad & x_1 + 2x_2 \\
\text{s.t.} \quad & \\
& x_1 + 4x_2 \leq 21 \\
& 2x_1 + x_2 \geq 7 \\
& 3x_1 + 1.5x_2 \leq 21 \\
& -2x_1 + 6x_2 \geq 0 \\
& x_1, x_2 \geq 0
\end{aligned}
$$

a. Find the optimal solution using the graphical solution procedure and the value of the objective function.
b. Determine the amount of slack or surplus for each constraint.
c. Suppose the objective function is changed to max $5x_1 + 2x_2$. Find the optimal solution and the value of the objective function.

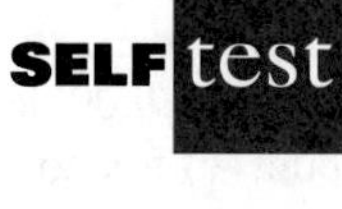

32. Consider the following linear program:

$$
\begin{aligned}
\text{Min} \quad & 2x_1 + 2x_2 \\
\text{s.t.} \quad & \\
& 1x_1 + 3x_2 \leq 12 \\
& 3x_1 + 1x_2 \geq 13 \\
& 1x_1 - 1x_2 = 3 \\
& x_1, x_2 \geq 0
\end{aligned}
$$

a. Show the feasible region.
b. What are the extreme points of the feasible region?
c. Find the optimal solution using the graphical solution procedure.

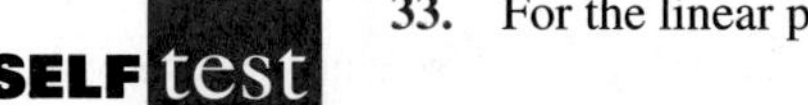

33. For the linear program

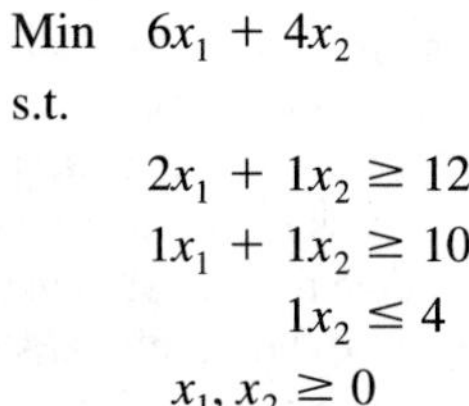

$$
\begin{aligned}
\text{Min} \quad & 6x_1 + 4x_2 \\
\text{s.t.} \quad & \\
& 2x_1 + 1x_2 \geq 12 \\
& 1x_1 + 1x_2 \geq 10 \\
& 1x_2 \leq 4 \\
& x_1, x_2 \geq 0
\end{aligned}
$$

a. Write the linear program in standard form.
b. Find the optimal solution using the graphical solution procedure.
c. What are the values of the slack and surplus variables?

34. As part of a quality improvement initiative, Consolidated Electronics employees complete a three-day training program on teaming and a two-day training program on problem solving. The manager of quality improvement requested that at least 8 training programs on teaming and at least 10 training programs on problem solving be offered during the next six months. In addition, senior-level management specified that at least 25 training programs must be offered during this period. Consolidated Electronics uses a consultant to teach the training programs. During the next six months, the consultant has 84 days of training time available. Each training program on teaming costs \$10,000 and each training program on problem solving costs \$8,000.
   a. Formulate a linear programming model that can be used to determine the number of training programs on teaming and the number of training programs on problem solving that should be offered in order to minimize total cost.
   b. Graph the feasible region.
   c. Determine the coordinates of each extreme point.
   d. Solve for the minimum-cost solution.

35. The New England Cheese Company produces two cheese spreads by blending mild cheddar cheese with extra sharp cheddar cheese. The cheese spreads are packaged in 12-ounce containers, which are then sold to distributors throughout the Northeast. The Regular blend contains 80% mild cheddar and 20% extra sharp, and the Zesty blend contains 60% mild cheddar and 40% extra sharp. This year, a local dairy cooperative offered to provide up to 8100 pounds of mild cheddar cheese for \$1.20 per pound and up to 3000 pounds of extra sharp cheddar cheese for \$1.40 per pound. The cost to blend and package the cheese spreads, excluding the cost of the cheese, is \$0.20 per container. If each container of Regular is sold for \$1.95 and each container of Zesty is sold for \$2.20, how many containers of Regular and Zesty should New England Cheese produce?

36. Applied Technology, Inc. (ATI), produces bicycle frames using two fiberglass materials that improve the strength-to-weight ratio of the frames. The cost of the standard grade material is \$7.50 per yard and the cost of the professional grade material is \$9.00 per yard. The standard and professional grade materials contain different amounts of fiberglass, carbon fiber, and Kevlar as shown in the following table.

	Standard Grade	**Professional Grade**
Fiberglass	84%	58%
Carbon fiber	10%	30%
Kevlar	6%	12%

ATI signed a contract with a bicycle manufacturer to produce a new frame with a carbon fiber content of least 20% and a Kevlar content of not greater than 10%. To meet the required weight specification, a total of 30 yards of material must be used for each frame.
   a. Formulate a linear program to determine the number of yards of each grade of fiberglass material that ATI should use in each frame in order to minimize total cost. Define the decision variables and indicate the purpose of each constraint.
   b. Use the graphical solution procedure to determine the feasible region. What are the coordinates of the extreme points?
   c. Compute the total cost at each extreme point. What is the optimal solution?

d. The distributor of the fiberglass material is currently overstocked with the professional grade material. To reduce inventory, the distributor offered ATI the opportunity to purchase the professional grade for $8 per yard. Will the optimal solution change?

e. Suppose that the distributor further lowers the price of the professional grade material to $7.40 per yard. Will the optimal solution change? What effect would an even lower price for the professional grade material have on the optimal solution? Explain.

37. Innis Investments manages funds for a number of companies and wealthy clients. The investment strategy is tailored to each client's needs. For a new client, Innis has been authorized to invest up to $1.2 million in two investment funds: a stock fund and a money market fund. Each unit of the stock fund costs $50 and provides an annual rate of return of 10%; each unit of the money market fund costs $100 and provides an annual rate of return of 4%.

The client wants to minimize risk subject to the requirement that the annual income from the investment be at least $60,000. According to Innis's risk measurement system, each unit invested in the stock fund has a risk index of 8, and each unit invested in the money market fund has a risk index of 3; the higher risk index associated with the stock fund simply indicates that it is the riskier investment. Innis's client also specified that at least $300,000 be invested in the money market fund.

a. Determine how many units of each fund Innis should purchase for the client to minimize the total risk index for the portfolio.

b. How much annual income will this investment strategy generate?

c. Suppose the client desires to maximize annual return. How should the funds be invested?

38. Photo Chemicals produces two types of photographic developing fluids. Both products cost Photo Chemicals $1 per gallon to produce. Based on an analysis of current inventory levels and outstanding orders for the next month, Photo Chemicals' management specified that at least 30 gallons of product 1 and at least 20 gallons of product 2 must be produced during the next two weeks. Management also stated that an existing inventory of highly perishable raw material required in the production of both fluids must be used within the next two weeks. The current inventory of the perishable raw material is 80 pounds. More of this raw material can be ordered if necessary, but any of the current inventory that is not used within the next two weeks will spoil—hence, the management requirement that at least 80 pounds be used in the next two weeks. Furthermore, it is known that product 1 requires 1 pound of this perishable raw material per gallon and product 2 requires 2 pounds of the raw material per gallon. Because Photo Chemicals' objective is to keep its production costs at the minimum possible level, the firm's management is looking for a minimum-cost production plan that uses all the 80 pounds of perishable raw material and provides at least 30 gallons of product 1 and at least 20 gallons of product 2. What is the minimum-cost solution?

39. Southern Oil Company produces two grades of gasoline: regular and premium. The profit contributions are $0.30 per gallon for regular gasoline and $0.50 per gallon for premium gasoline. Each gallon of regular gasoline contains 0.3 gallons of grade A crude oil and each gallon of premium gasoline contains 0.6 gallons of grade A crude oil. For the next production period, Southern has 18,000 gallons of grade A crude oil available. The refinery used to produce the gasolines has a production capacity of 50,000 gallons for the next production period. Southern Oil's distributors indicated that demand for the premium gasoline for the next production period will be at most 20,000 gallons.

a. Formulate a linear programming model that can be used to determine the number of gallons of regular gasoline and the number of gallons of premium gasoline that should be produced in order to maximize total profit contribution.

b. What is the optimal solution?

c. What are the values and interpretations of the slack variables?

d. What are the binding constraints?

40. Does the following linear program involve infeasibility, unbounded, and/or alternative optimal solutions? Explain.

$$\begin{aligned} \text{Max} \quad & 4x_1 + 8x_2 \\ \text{s.t.} \quad & \\ & 2x_1 + 2x_2 \leq 10 \\ & -1x_1 + 1x_2 \geq 8 \\ & x_1, x_2 \geq 0 \end{aligned}$$

41. Does the following linear program involve infeasibility, unbounded, and/or alternative optimal solutions? Explain.

$$\begin{aligned} \text{Max} \quad & 1x_1 + 1x_2 \\ \text{s.t.} \quad & \\ & 8x_1 + 6x_2 \geq 24 \\ & 4x_1 + 6x_2 \geq -12 \\ & 2x_2 \geq 4 \\ & x_1, x_2 \geq 0 \end{aligned}$$

42. Consider the following linear program:

$$\begin{aligned} \text{Max} \quad & 1x_1 + 1x_2 \\ \text{s.t.} \quad & \\ & 5x_1 + 3x_2 \leq 15 \\ & 3x_1 + 5x_2 \leq 15 \\ & x_1, x_2 \geq 0 \end{aligned}$$

a. Find the optimal solution.
b. Suppose that the objective function is changed to $1x_1 + 2x_2$. Find the new optimal solution.
c. By adjusting the coefficient of x_2 in the objective function, develop a new objective function that will make the solutions found in parts (a) and (b) alternative optimal solutions.

43. Consider the following linear program:

$$\begin{aligned} \text{Max} \quad & 1x_1 - 2x_2 \\ \text{s.t.} \quad & \\ & -4x_1 + 3x_2 \leq 3 \\ & 1x_1 - 1x_2 \leq 3 \\ & x_1, x_2 \geq 0 \end{aligned}$$

a. Graph the feasible region for the problem.
b. Is the feasible region unbounded? Explain.
c. Find the optimal solution.
d. Does an unbounded feasible region imply that the optimal solution to the linear program will be unbounded?

44. The manager of a small independent grocery store is trying to determine the best use of her shelf space for soft drinks. The store carries national and generic brands and currently has 200 square feet of shelf space available. The manager wants to allocate at least 60% of the space to the national brands and, regardless of the profitability, allocate at least 10% of the space to the generic brands. How many square feet of space should the manager allocate to the national brands and the generic brands if

a. The national brands are more profitable than the generic brands?
b. Both brands are equally profitable?
c. The generic brands are more profitable than the national brands?

45. Discuss what happens to the M&D Chemicals problem (see Section 2.5) if the cost per gallon for product A is increased to $3.00 per gallon. What would you recommend? Explain.

46. For the M&D Chemicals problem in Section 2.5, discuss the effect of management's requiring total production of 500 gallons for the two products. List two or three actions M&D should consider to correct the situation you encounter.

47. Reconsider the RMC situation in Problem 21.
    a. Identify all the extreme points of the feasible region.
    b. Suppose RMC discovers a way to increase the profit of its solvent base to $60 per ton. Does this profit increase change the optimal solution? If so, how?
    c. Suppose the profit for the solvent base is $50 per ton. What is the optimal solution now? Comment on any special characteristics that may exist with this profit for the solvent base.

48. Reconsider the RMC situation in Problem 21. Suppose that management adds the requirements that at least 30 tons of fuel additive and at least 15 tons of solvent base must be produced.
    a. Graph the constraints for this revised RMC problem. What happens to the feasible region? Explain.
    b. If no feasible solutions can be found, explain what is needed to produce 30 tons of fuel additive and 15 tons of solvent base.

49. PharmaPlus operates a chain of 30 pharmacies. The pharmacies are staffed by licensed pharmacists and pharmacy technicians. The company currently employs 85 full-time equivalent pharmacists (combination of full time and part time) and 175 full-time equivalent technicians. Each spring management reviews current staffing levels and makes hiring plans for the year. A recent forecast of the prescription load for the next year shows that at least 250 full-time equivalent employees (pharmacists and technicians) will be required to staff the pharmacies. The personnel department expects 10 pharmacists and 30 technicians to leave over the next year. To accommodate the expected attrition and prepare for future growth, management stated that at least 15 new pharmacists must be hired. In addition, PharmaPlus's new service quality guidelines specify no more than two technicians per licensed pharmacist. The average salary for licensed pharmacists is $40 per hour and the average salary for technicians is $10 per hour.
    a. Determine a minimum-cost staffing plan for PharmaPlus. How many pharmacists and technicians are needed?
    b. Given current staffing levels and expected attrition, how many new hires (if any) must be made to reach the level recommended in part (a)? What will be the impact on the payroll?

50. Expedition Outfitters manufactures a variety of specialty clothing for hiking, skiing, and mountain climbing. They decided to begin production on two new parkas designed for use in extremely cold weather. The names selected for the two models are the Mount Everest Parka and the Rocky Mountain Parka. Their manufacturing plant has 120 hours of cutting time and 120 hours of sewing time available for producing these two parkas. Each Mount Everest Parka requires 30 minutes of cutting time and 45 minutes of sewing time, and each Rocky Mountain Parka requires 20 minutes of cutting time and 15 minutes of sewing time. The labor and material cost is $150 for each Mount Everest Parka and $50 for each Rocky

Mountain Parka, and the retail prices through the firm's mail order catalog are $250 for the Mount Everest Parka and $200 for the Rocky Mountain Parka. Because management believes that the Mount Everest Parka is a unique coat that will enhance the image of the firm, they have specified that at least 20% of the total production must consist of this model. Assuming that Expedition Outfitters can sell as many coats of each type as they can produce, how many units of each model should they manufacture to maximize the total profit contribution?

51. English Motors, Ltd. (EML), developed a new all-wheel-drive sports utility vehicle. As part of the marketing campaign, EML developed a videotape sales presentation to send to both owners of current EML four-wheel-drive vehicles as well as to owners of four-wheel-drive sports utility vehicles offered by competitors; EML refers to these two target markets as the current customer market and the new customer market. Individuals who receive the new promotion video will also receive a coupon for a test drive of the new EML model for one weekend. A key factor in the success of the new promotion is the response rate, the percentage of individuals who receive the new promotion and test drive the new model. EML estimates that the response rate for the current customer market is 25% and the response rate for the new customer market is 20%. For the customers who test drive the new model the sales rate is the percentage of individuals who make a purchase. Marketing research studies indicate that the sales rate is 12% for the current customer market and 20% for the new customer market. The cost for each promotion, excluding the test drive costs, are $4 for each promotion sent to the current customer market and $6 for each promotion sent to the new customer market. Management also specified that a minimum of 30,000 current customers should test drive the new model and a minimum of 10,000 new customers should test drive the new model. In addition, the number of current customers who test drive the new vehicle must be at least twice the number of new customers who test drive the new vehicle. If the marketing budget, excluding test drive costs, is $1,200,000, how many promotions should be sent to each group of customers in order to maximize total sales?

52. Creative Sports Design (CSD) manufactures a standard-size tennis racket and an oversize tennis racket. The firm's rackets are extremely light due to the use of a magnesium-graphite alloy that was invented by the firm's founder. Each standard-size racket uses 0.125 kilograms of the alloy and each oversize racket uses 0.4 kilograms; over the next two-week production period only 80 kilograms of the alloy are available. Each standard-size racket uses 10 minutes of manufacturing time and each oversize racket uses 12 minutes. The profit contributions are $10 for each standard-size racket and $15 for each oversize racket, and 40 hours of manufacturing time are available each week. Management specified that at least 20% of the total production must be the standard-size racket. How many tennis rackets of each type should CSD manufacture over the next two weeks to maximize the total profit contribution? Assume that because of the unique nature of their products, CSD can sell as many rackets as they can produce.

53. Management of High Tech Services (HTS) would like to develop a model that will help allocate their technicians' time between service calls to regular contract customers and new customers. A maximum of 80 hours of technician time is available over the two-week planning period. To satisfy cash flow requirements, at least $800 in revenue (per technician) must be generated during the two-week period. Technician time for regular customers generates $25 per hour. However, technician time for new customers only generates an average of $8 per hour because in many cases a new customer contact does not provide billable services. To ensure that new customer contacts are being maintained, the technician time spent on new customer contacts must be at least 60% of the time spent on regular customer contacts. Given these revenue and policy requirements, HTS would like to determine how to allocate technician time between regular customers and new customers so that the total number of customers contacted during the two-week period will be maximized. Technicians require an average of 50 minutes for each regular customer contact and 1 hour for each new customer contact.

a. Develop a linear programming model that will enable HTS to allocate technician time between regular customers and new customers.

b. Find the optimal solution.

54. Jackson Hole Manufacturing is a small manufacturer of plastic products used in the automotive and computer industries. One of its major contracts is with a large computer company and involves the production of plastic printer cases for the computer company's portable printers. The printer cases are produced on two injection molding machines. The M-100 machine has a production capacity of 25 printer cases per hour, and the M-200 machine has a production capacity of 40 cases per hour. Both machines use the same chemical material to produce the printer cases; the M-100 uses 40 pounds of the raw material per hour and the M-200 uses 50 pounds per hour. The computer company asked Jackson Hole to produce as many of the cases during the upcoming week as possible and has said that it will pay $18 for each case Jackson Hole can deliver. However, next week is a regularly scheduled vacation period for most of Jackson Hole's production employees; during this time, annual maintenance is performed for all equipment in the plant. Because of the downtime for maintenance, the M-100 will be available for no more than 15 hours, and the M-200 will be available for no more than 10 hours. However, because of the high setup cost involved with both machines, management has a requirement that, if production is scheduled on either machine, the machine must be operated for at least 5 hours. The supplier of the chemical material used in the production process informed Jackson Hole that a maximum of 1000 pounds of the chemical material will be available for next week's production; the cost for this raw material is $6 per pound. In addition to the raw material cost, Jackson Hole estimates that the hourly cost of operating the M-100 and the M-200 are $50 and $75, respectively.

a. Formulate a linear programming model that can be used to maximize the contribution to profit.

b. Find the optimal solution.

Case Problem 1 WORKLOAD BALANCING

Digital Imaging (DI) produces photo printers for both the professional and consumer markets. The DI consumer division recently introduced two photo printers that provide color prints rivaling those produced by a professional processing lab. The DI-910 model can produce a 4″ × 6″ borderless print in approximately 37 seconds. The more sophisticated and faster DI-950 can even produce a 13″ × 19″ borderless print. Financial projections show profit contributions of $42 for each DI-910 and $87 for each DI-950.

The printers are assembled, tested, and packaged at DI's plant located in New Bern, North Carolina. This plant is highly automated and uses two manufacturing lines to produce the printers. Line 1 performs the assembly operation with times of 3 minutes per DI-910 printer and 6 minutes per DI-950 printer. Line 2 performs both the testing and packaging operations. Times are 4 minutes per DI-910 printer and 2 minutes per DI-950 printer. The shorter time for the DI-950 printer is a result of its faster print speed. Both manufacturing lines are in operation one 8-hour shift per day.

Managerial Report

Perform an analysis for Digital Imaging in order to determine how many units of each printer to produce. Prepare a report to DI's president presenting your findings and recommendations. Include (but do not limit your discussion to) a consideration of the following:

1. The recommended number of units of each printer to produce to maximize the total contribution to profit for an 8-hour shift. What reasons might management have for not implementing your recommendation?
2. Suppose that management also states that the number of DI-910 printers produced must be at least as great as the number of DI-950 units produced. Assuming that the objective is to maximize the total contribution to profit for an 8-hour shift, how many units of each printer should be produced?
3. Does the solution you developed in part (2) balance the total time spent on line 1 and the total time spent on line 2? Why might this balance or lack of it be a concern to management?
4. Management requested an expansion of the model in part (2) that would provide a better balance between the total time on line 1 and the total time on line 2. Management wants to limit the difference between the total time on line 1 and the total time on line 2 to 30 minutes or less. If the objective is still to maximize the total contribution to profit, how many units of each printer should be produced? What effect does this workload balancing have on total profit in part (2)?
5. Suppose that in part (1) management specified the objective of maximizing the total number of printers produced each shift rather than total profit contribution. With this objective, how many units of each printer should be produced per shift? What effect does this objective have on total profit and workload balancing?

For each solution that you develop include a copy of your linear programming model and graphical solution in the appendix to your report.

Case Problem 2 PRODUCTION STRATEGY

Better Fitness, Inc. (BFI), manufactures exercise equipment at its plant in Freeport, Long Island. It recently designed two universal weight machines for the home exercise market. Both machines use BFI-patented technology that provides the user with an extremely wide range of motion capability for each type of exercise performed. Until now, such capabilities have been available only on expensive weight machines used primarily by physical therapists.

At a recent trade show, demonstrations of the machines resulted in significant dealer interest. In fact, the number of orders that BFI received at the trade show far exceeded its manufacturing capabilities for the current production period. As a result, management decided to begin production of the two machines. The two machines, which BFI named the BodyPlus 100 and the BodyPlus 200, require different amounts of resources to produce.

The BodyPlus 100 consists of a frame unit, a press station, and a pec-dec station. Each frame produced uses 4 hours of machining and welding time and 2 hours of painting and finishing time. Each press station requires 2 hours of machining and welding time and 1 hour of painting and finishing time, and each pec-dec station uses 2 hours of machining and welding time and 2 hours of painting and finishing time. In addition, 2 hours are spent assembling, testing, and packaging each BodyPlus 100. The raw material costs are $450 for each frame, $300 for each press station, and $250 for each pec-dec station; packaging costs are estimated to be $50 per unit.

The BodyPlus 200 consists of a frame unit, a press station, a pec-dec station, and a leg-press station. Each frame produced uses 5 hours of machining and welding time and 4 hours of painting and finishing time. Each press station requires 3 hours machining and welding time and 2 hours of painting and finishing time, each pec-dec station uses 2 hours of machining and welding time and 2 hours of painting and finishing time, and each leg-press station requires 2 hours of machining and welding time and 2 hours of painting and finishing time. In addition, 2 hours are spent assembling, testing, and packaging each BodyPlus 200. The raw material costs are $650 for each frame, $400 for each press station, $250 for each pec-dec station, and $200 for each leg-press station; packaging costs are estimated to be $75 per unit.

For the next production period, management estimates that 600 hours of machining and welding time, 450 hours of painting and finishing time, and 140 hours of assembly, testing, and packaging time will be available. Current labor costs are $20 per hour for machining and welding time, $15 per hour for painting and finishing time, and $12 per hour for assembly, testing, and packaging time. The market in which the two machines must compete suggests a retail price of $2400 for the BodyPlus 100 and $3500 for the BodyPlus 200, although some flexibility may be available to BFI because of the unique capabilities of the new machines. Authorized BFI dealers can purchase machines for 70 percent of the suggested retail price.

BFI's president believes that the unique capabilities of the BodyPlus 200 can help position BFI as one of the leaders in high-end exercise equipment. Consequently, he has stated that the number of units of the BodyPlus 200 produced must be at least 25 percent of the total production.

Managerial Report

Analyze the production problem at Better Fitness, Inc., and prepare a report for BFI's president presenting your findings and recommendations. Include (but do not limit your discussion to) a consideration of the following items:

1. What is the recommended number of BodyPlus 100 and BodyPlus 200 machines to produce?
2. How does the requirement that the number of units of the BodyPlus 200 produced be at least 25 percent of the total production affect profits?
3. Where should efforts be expended in order to increase profits?

Include a copy of your linear programming model and graphical solution in an appendix to your report.

Case Problem 3 HART VENTURE CAPITAL

Hart Venture Capital (HVC) specializes in providing venture capital for software development and Internet applications. Currently HVC has two investment opportunities: (1) Security Systems, a firm that needs additional capital to develop an Internet security software package; (2) Market Analysis, a market research company that needs additional capital to develop a software package for conducting customer satisfaction surveys. In exchange for Security Systems stock, the firm has asked HVC to provide $600,000 in year 1, $600,000 in year 2, and $250,000 in year 3 over the coming three-year period. In exchange for their stock, Market Analysis has asked HVC to provide $500,000 in year 1, $350,000 in year 2, and $400,000 in year 3 over the same three-year period. HVC believes that both investment opportunities are worth pursuing. However, because of other investments, they are willing to commit at most $800,000 for both projects in the first year, at most $700,000 in the second year, and $500,000 in the third year.

HVC's financial analysis team reviewed both projects and recommended that the company's objective should be to maximize the net present value of the total investment in Security Systems and Market Analysis. The net present value takes into account the estimated value of the stock at the end of the three-year period as well as the capital outflows that are necessary during each of the three years. Using an 8% rate of return, HVC's financial analysis team estimates that 100 percent funding of the Security Systems project has a net present value of $1,800,000 and 100 percent funding of the Market Analysis project has a net present value of $1,600,000.

HVC has the option to fund any percentage of the Security Systems and Market Analysis projects. For example, if HVC decides to fund 40% of the Security Systems project, investments of 0.40($600,000) = $240,000 would be required in year 1, 0.40($600,000) = $240,000 would be required in year 2, and 0.40($250,000) = $100,000 would be required in year 3. In this case, the net present value of the Security Systems project would be 0.40($1,800,000) = $720,000. The investment amounts and the net present value for partial funding of the Market Analysis project would be computed in the same manner.

Managerial Report

Perform an analysis of HVC's investment problem and prepare a report that presents your findings and recommendations. Include (but do not limit your discussion to) a consideration of the following items:

1. What is the recommended percentage of each project that HVC should fund and the net present value of the total investment?
2. What capital allocation plan for Security Systems and Market Analysis for the coming three-year period and the total HVC investment each year would you recommend?
3. What effect, if any, would HVC's willingness to commit an additional $100,000 during the first year have on the recommended percentage of each project that HVC should fund?
4. What would the capital allocation plan look like if an additional $100,000 is made available?
5. What is your recommendation as to whether HVC should commit the additional $100,000 in the first year?

Provide model details and relevant computer output in a report appendix.

Appendix 2.1 SOLVING LINEAR PROGRAMS WITH THE MANAGEMENT SCIENTIST

In this appendix we describe how The Management Scientist software package can be used to solve the Par, Inc., linear programming problem. After starting The Management Scientist, execute the following steps.

Step 1. Select the **Linear Programming** module
Step 2. Select the **File** menu
Choose **New**
Step 3. When the **Problem Features** dialog box appears:
Enter 2 in the **Number of Decision Variables** box
Enter 4 in the **Number of Constraints** box

Select Maximize in the **Optimization Type** box
Click **OK**

Step 4. When the data input worksheet appears (see Figure 2.22):
Change **Variable Names** from X1 and X2 to S and D, respectively.
Enter the **Objective Function Coefficients**
For each constraint:
Enter the **Coefficients**
Enter the **Relation** ($<$, $=$, $>$)
Enter the **Right-Hand-Side** value

The Management Scientist interprets the $<$ symbol as $\leq$ and the $>$ symbol as $\geq$.

Step 5. Select the **Solution** menu
Choose **Solve**

The user entries in the data input worksheet are shown in Figure 2.22. The output from The Management Scientist is shown in Figure 2.14. When entering the problem data, zero coefficients do not have to be entered. The original problem can be edited or changed by selecting the **Edit** menu. Finally, printed output can be obtained by selecting the **Solution** menu and then selecting the **Print** option.

Appendix 2.2 SOLVING LINEAR PROGRAMS WITH LINDO

LINDO (Linear, INteractive, and Discrete Optimizer) was developed by Linus E. Schrage at the University of Chicago. In this appendix we describe how to use LINDO to solve the Par, Inc., problem.

When you start LINDO, two windows are immediately displayed. The outer window labeled "LINDO" contains all the command menus and the command toolbar. The smaller window labeled "<untitled>" is the model window. This window is used to enter and edit the linear programming model that you want to solve. The first item you must enter into the model window is the objective function. Thus, for the Par problem, enter MAX $10S + 9D$. To indicate that the objective function has been completely entered and that the model constraints will follow, press the enter key and type the words SUBJECT TO (or just the letters ST). Next, after pressing the enter key to move to a new line, enter the first Par, Inc., constraint $0.7S + 1D < 630$. Note that LINDO interprets the $<$ symbol as $\leq$. Then, after pressing the enter key, enter the second constraint $0.5S + 0.83333D < 600$. Press the enter key again and enter the third constraint $1S + 0.66667D < 708$. Then, press the enter key again

FIGURE 2.22 DATA INPUT WORKSHEET FOR THE PAR, INC., PROBLEM

Optimization Type: Max

	Objective Function	
Variable Names:	S	D
Coefficients:	10	9

	Constraints			
Subject To:	S	D	Relation(<,=,>)	Right-Hand-Side
Constraint 1	0.7	1	<	630
Constraint 2	0.5	0.83333	<	600
Constraint 3	1	0.66667	<	708
Constraint 4	0.1	0.25	<	135

and enter the fourth and final constraint, $0.1S + 0.25D < 135$. Finally, after pressing the enter key, type END to signal LINDO that the model input is complete. The model window will now contain the following model:

Max $10S + 9D$
ST
$0.7S + 1D < 630$
$0.5S + 0.83333D < 600$
$1S + 0.66667D < 708$
$0.1S + 0.250D < 135$
END

If you make an error entering the model, you can correct it at any time by simply positioning the cursor where you made the error and entering the necessary corrections.

To solve the model, you must select the Solve command from the Solve menu, or press the Solve button on the LINDO toolbar. If LINDO does not find any errors in the model input, it will begin to solve the model. As part of the solution process, LINDO displays a Status Window that can be used to monitor the progress of the solver. When the solver is finished, LINDO will ask whether you want to do range (sensitivity) analysis. If you select the YES button and close the Status Window, LINDO displays the complete solution to the Par, Inc., problem on a new window titled "Reports Window." The output that appears in the Reports Window is shown in Figure 2.23.

The first section of the output shown in Figure 2.23 is self-explanatory. For example, we see that the optimal solution is $S = 540$ and $D = 252$, the value of the optimal solution is 7668, and the slack variables for the four constraints are 0, 120, 0, and 18. The rest of the output in Figure 2.23 can be used to determine how a change in a coefficient of the objective function or a change in the right-hand-side value of a constraint will affect the optimal solution. We will discuss the use of this information in Chapter 3 when we study the topic of sensitivity analysis.

Appendix 2.3 SOLVING LINEAR PROGRAMS WITH EXCEL

In this appendix, we will use an Excel worksheet to solve the Par, Inc., linear programming problem. We will enter the problem data for the Par problem in the top part of the worksheet and develop the linear programming model in the bottom part of the worksheet.

Formulation

Whenever we formulate a worksheet model of a linear program, we perform the following steps:

Step 1. Enter the problem data in the top part of the worksheet
Step 2. Specify cell locations for the decision variables
Step 3. Select a cell and enter a formula for computing the value of the objective function
Step 4. Select a cell and enter a formula for computing the left-hand side of each constraint
Step 5. Select a cell and enter a formula for computing the right-hand side of each constraint

FIGURE 2.23 PAR, INC., SOLUTION USING LINDO

```
Objective Function Value

     1)        7667.994

     Variable                 Value                 Reduced Costs
   --------------        ---------------        -----------------
          S                 539.998413                   0.000000
          D                 252.001114                   0.000000

        Row               Slack/Surplus              Dual Prices
   --------------        ---------------        -----------------
          2)                  0.000000                   4.374956
          3)                120.000717                   0.000000
          4)                  0.000000                   6.937531
          5)                 17.999882                   0.000000

NO. ITERATIONS = 2

OBJ COEFFICIENT RANGES

                    Current             Allowable            Allowable
  Variable           Coef               Increase             Decrease
------------    ---------------     ---------------     ---------------
        S           10.000000            3.499932             3.700000
        D            9.000000            5.285714             2.3333009

RIGHT HAND SIDE RANGES

                    Current             Allowable            Allowable
    Row              RHS                Increase             Decrease
------------    ---------------     ---------------     ---------------
        2          630.000000           52.363155           134.400009
        3          600.000000            Infinity           120.000717
        4          708.000000          192.000000           127.998589
        5          135.000000            Infinity            17.999882
```

The formula worksheet that we developed for the Par, Inc., problem using these five steps is shown in Figure 2.24. Note that the worksheet consists of two sections: a data section and a model section. The four components of the model are screened, and the cells reserved for the decision variables are enclosed in a boldface box. Figure 2.24 is called a formula worksheet because it displays the formulas that we have entered and not the values computed from those formulas. In a moment we will see how Excel's Solver is used to find the optimal solution to the Par problem. But first, let's review each of the preceding steps as they apply to the Par problem.

Step 1. Enter the problem data in the top part of the worksheet.
Cells B5:C8 show the production requirements per unit for each product.
Cells B9:C9 show the profit contribution per unit for the two products.
Cells D5:D8 show the number of hours available in each department.

FIGURE 2.24 FORMULA WORKSHEET FOR THE PAR, INC., PROBLEM

	A	B	C	D	E
1	**Par, Inc.**				
2					
3		**Production Time**			
4	**Operation**	**Standard**	**Deluxe**	**Time Available**	
5	Cutting and Dyeing	0.7	1	630	
6	Sewing	0.5	0.83333	600	
7	Finishing	1	0.66667	708	
8	Inspection and Packaging	0.1	0.25	135	
9	**Profit Per Bag**	10	9		
10					
11					
12	**Model**				
13					
14		**Decision Variables**			
15		**Standard**	**Deluxe**		
16	**Bags Produced**				
17					
18	**Maximize Total Profit**	=B9*B16+C9*C16			
19					
20	**Constraints**	**Hours Used (LHS)**		**Hours Available (RHS)**	
21	Cutting and Dyeing	=B5*B16+C5*C16	<=	=D5	
22	Sewing	=B6*B16+C6*C16	<=	=D6	
23	Finishing	=B7*B16+C7*C16	<=	=D7	
24	Inspection and Packaging	=B8*B16+C8*C16	<=	=D8	
25					

Step 2. Specify cell locations for the decision variables.
Cell B16 will contain the number of standard bags produced, and cell C16 will contain the number of deluxe bags produced.

Step 3. Select a cell and enter a formula for computing the value of the objective function.
Cell B18: =B9*B16+C9*C16

Step 4. Select a cell and enter a formula for computing the left-hand side of each constraint.
With four constraints, we have
Cell B21: =B5*B16+C5*C16
Cell B22: =B6*B16+C6*C16
Cell B23: =B7*B16+C7*C16
Cell B24: =B8*B16+C8*C16

Step 5. Select a cell and enter a formula for computing the right-hand side of each constraint.
With four constraints, we have
Cell D21: =D5
Cell D22: =D6
Cell D23: =D7
Cell D24: =D8

Note that descriptive labels make the model section of the worksheet easier to read and understand. For example, we added "Standard," "Deluxe," and "Bags Produced" in rows 15 and 16 so that the values of the decision variables appearing in cells B16 and C16 can be easily interpreted. In addition, we entered "Maximize Total Profit" in cell A18 to indicate that the value of the objective function appearing in cell B18 is the maximum profit contribution. In the constraint section of the worksheet we added the constraint names as well as the "<=" symbols to show the relationship that exists between the left-hand side and the right-hand side of each constraint. Although these descriptive labels are not necessary to use Excel Solver to find a solution to the Par, Inc., problem, the labels make it easier for the user to understand and interpret the optimal solution.

Excel Solution

The standard Excel Solver developed by Frontline Systems can be used to solve all of the linear programming problems presented in this text. However, the CD that accompanies this text includes a more powerful version referred to as Premium Solver for Education. When first started, Premium Solver looks and behaves exactly like the standard Excel Solver. But, when the "Premium" button in the main Solver Parameters dialog box is selected, this version provides a variety of new features, including an online user's guide. The Premium Solver for Education has the same problem size limits as the standard Excel Solver: 200 decision variables and 100 constraints. We recommend that you install the new version and use the "Premium" mode option when developing and solving spreadsheet models of linear programs.

The following steps describe how Frontline Systems' Premium Solver for Education can be used to obtain the optimal solution to the Par, Inc., problem.

Step 1. Select the **Tools** menu
Step 2. Select the **Solver** option
Step 3. When the **Solver Parameters** dialog box appears (see Figure 2.25):
Enter B18 into the **Set Cell** box
Select the **Equal To: Max** option
Enter B16:C16 into the **By Changing Variable Cells** box
Select **Add**

FIGURE 2.25 SOLVER PARAMETERS DIALOG BOX FOR THE PAR, INC., PROBLEM

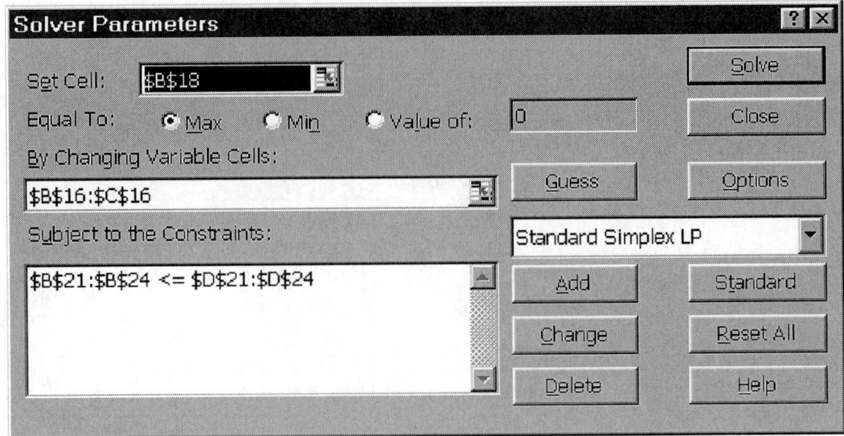

Step 4. When the **Add Constraint** dialog box appears:
Enter B21:B24 in the **Cell Reference** box
Select <=
Enter D21:D24 into the **Constraint** box
Click **OK**

Step 5. When the **Solver Parameters** dialog box reappears:
Choose **Options**

If the Standard button and Standard Simplex LP option do not appear, click the Premium button and select the Standard Simplex LP option.

Step 6. When the **Solver Options** dialog box appears:
Select **Assume Non-Negative**
Click **OK**

Step 7. When the **Solver Parameters** dialog box appears:
Choose **Solve**

Step 8. When the **Solver Results** dialog box appears:
Select **Keep Solver Solution**
Click **OK**

Figure 2.25 shows the completed **Solver Parameters** dialog box, and Figure 2.26 shows the optimal solution in the worksheet. Note that after rounding, the optimal solution of 540 standard bags and 252 deluxe bags is the same as we obtained using the graphical so-

FIGURE 2.26 EXCEL SOLUTION FOR THE PAR, INC., PROBLEM

EXCELfile
Par

	A	B	C	D	E
1	**Par, Inc.**				
2					
3		**Production Time**			
4	**Operation**	**Standard**	**Deluxe**	**Time Available**	
5	Cutting and Dyeing	0.7	1	630	
6	Sewing	0.5	0.83333	600	
7	Finishing	1	0.66667	708	
8	Inspection and Packaging	0.1	0.25	135	
9	**Profit Per Bag**	10	9		
10					
11					
12	**Model**				
13					
14		**Decision Variables**			
15		**Standard**	**Deluxe**		
16	**Bags Produced**	539.99842	252.00110		
17					
18	**Maximize Total Profit**	7668			
19					
20	**Constraints**	**Hours Used (LHS)**		**Hours Available (RHS)**	
21	Cutting and Dyeing	630	<=	630	
22	Sewing	479.99929	<=	600	
23	Finishing	708	<=	708	
24	Inspection and Packaging	117.00012	<=	135	
25					

lution procedure. In addition to the output information shown in Figure 2.26, Solver has an option to provide sensitivity analysis information. We discuss sensitivity analysis in Chapter 3.

In Step 6 we selected the **Assume Non-Negative** option in the **Solver Options** dialog box to avoid having to enter nonnegativity constraints for the decision variables. In general, whenever we want to solve a linear programming model in which the decision variables are all restricted to be nonnegative, we will select this option. In addition, in Step 4 we entered all four less-than-or-equal-to constraints simultaneously by entering B21:B24 into the **Cell Reference** box, selecting <=, and entering D21:D24 into the **Constraint** box. Alternatively, we could have entered the four constraints one at a time.

CHAPTER 3

Linear Programming: Sensitivity Analysis and Interpretation of Solution

CONTENTS

Sensitivity analysis is the study of how the changes in the coefficients of a linear program affect the optimal solution. Using sensitivity analysis, we can answer questions such as the following:

1. How will a change *in a coefficient of the objective function* affect the optimal solution?
2. How will a change in the *right-hand-side value for a constraint* affect the optimal solution?

Because sensitivity analysis is concerned with how these changes affect the optimal solution, the analysis does not begin until the optimal solution to the original linear programming problem has been obtained. For that reason, sensitivity analysis is often referred to as *postoptimality analysis.*

Our approach to sensitivity analysis parallels the approach used to introduce linear programming in Chapter 2. We begin by showing how a graphical method can be used to perform sensitivity analysis for linear programming problems with two decision variables. Then, we show how The Management Scientist provides sensitivity analysis information.

Finally, we extend the discussion of problem formulation started in Chapter 7 by formulating and solving three larger linear programming problems. In discussing the solution for each of these problems, we focus on managerial interpretation of the optimal solution and sensitivity analysis information.

Sensitivity analysis and the interpretation of the optimal solution are important aspects of applying linear programming. The Management Science in Action, Assigning Products to Worldwide Facilities at Eastman Kodak, shows some of the sensitivity analysis and interpretation issues encountered at Kodak in determining the optimal product assignments. Later in the chapter other Management Science in Action articles illustrate how Performance Analysis Corporation uses sensitivity analysis as part of an evaluation model for a chain of fast-food outlets, how the Nutrition Coordinating Center of the University of Minnesota uses a linear programming model to estimate the nutrient amounts in new food products, and how Duncan Industries Limited's linear programming model for tea distribution convinced management of the benefits of using quantitative analysis techniques to support the decision-making process.

MANAGEMENT SCIENCE IN ACTION

ASSIGNING PRODUCTS TO WORLDWIDE FACILITIES AT EASTMAN KODAK*

One of the major planning issues at Eastman Kodak involves the determination of what products should be manufactured at Kodak's facilities located throughout the world. The assignment of products to facilities is called the "world load." In determining the world load, Kodak faces a number of interesting trade-offs. For instance, not all manufacturing facilities are equally efficient for all products, and the margins by which some facilities are better varies from product to product. In addition to manufacturing costs, the transportation costs and the effects of duty and duty drawbacks can significantly affect the allocation decision.

To assist in determining the world load, Kodak developed a linear programming model that accounts for the physical nature of the distribution problem and the various costs (manufacturing, transportation, and duties) involved. The model's objective is to minimize the total cost subject to constraints such as satisfying demand and capacity constraints for each facility.

The linear programming model is a static representation of the problem situation, and the real world is always changing. Thus, the linear programming model must be used in a dynamic way. For instance, when demand expectations change, the model can be used to determine the effect the change will have on the world load. Suppose

(*continued*)

that the currency of country A rises compared to the currency of country B. How should the world load be modified? In addition to using the linear programming model in a "how-to-react" mode, the model is useful in a more active mode by considering questions such as the following: Is it worthwhile for facility F to spend *d* dollars to lower the unit manufacturing cost of product P from *x* to *y*? The linear programming model helps Kodak evaluate the overall effect of possible changes at any facility.

In the final analysis, managers recognize that they cannot use the model by simply turning it on, reading the results, and executing the solution. The model's recommendation combined with managerial judgment provide the final decision.

*Based on information provided by Greg Sampson of Eastman Kodak.

3.1 INTRODUCTION TO SENSITIVITY ANALYSIS

Sensitivity analysis is important to decision makers because real-world problems exist in a changing environment. Prices of raw materials change, product demand changes, companies purchase new machinery, stock prices fluctuate, employee turnover occurs, and so on. If a linear programming model has been used in such an environment, we can expect some of the coefficients to change over time. We will then want to determine how these changes affect the optimal solution to the original linear programming problem. Sensitivity analysis provides us with the information needed to respond to such changes without requiring the complete solution of a revised linear program.

Recall the Par, Inc., problem:

$$
\begin{aligned}
\text{Max} \quad & 10S + 9D \\
\text{s.t.} \quad & \\
& \tfrac{7}{10}S + 1D \le 630 \quad \text{Cutting and dyeing} \\
& \tfrac{1}{2}S + \tfrac{5}{6}D \le 600 \quad \text{Sewing} \\
& 1S + \tfrac{2}{3}D \le 708 \quad \text{Finishing} \\
& \tfrac{1}{10}S + \tfrac{1}{4}D \le 135 \quad \text{Inspection and packaging} \\
& S, D \ge 0
\end{aligned}
$$

The optimal solution, $S = 540$ standard bags and $D = 252$ deluxe bags, was based on profit contribution figures of \$10 per standard bag and \$9 per deluxe bag. Suppose we later learn that a price reduction causes the profit contribution for the standard bag to fall from \$10 to \$8.50. Sensitivity analysis can be used to determine whether the production schedule calling for 540 standard bags and 252 deluxe bags is still best. If it is, solving a modified linear programming problem with $8.50S + 9D$ as the new objective function will not be necessary.

Sensitivity analysis can also be used to determine which coefficients in a linear programming model are crucial. For example, suppose that management believes the \$9 profit contribution for the deluxe bag is only a rough estimate of the profit contribution that will actually be obtained. If sensitivity analysis shows that 540 standard bags and 252 deluxe bags will be the optimal solution as long as the profit contribution for the deluxe bag is between \$6.67 and \$14.29, management should feel comfortable with the \$9 per bag estimate and the recommended production quantities. However, if sensitivity analysis shows that 540 standard bags and 252 deluxe bags will be the optimal solution only if the profit contribution for the deluxe bags is between \$8.90 and \$9.25, management may want to review the accuracy of the \$9 per bag estimate. Management would especially want to consider how the optimal production quantities should be revised if the profit contribution per deluxe bag were to drop.

Another aspect of sensitivity analysis concerns changes in the right-hand-side values of the constraints. Recall that in the Par, Inc., problem the optimal solution used all available time in the cutting and dyeing department and the finishing department. What would happen to the optimal solution and total profit contribution if Par could obtain additional quantities of either of these resources? Sensitivity analysis can help determine how much each additional hour of production time is worth and how many hours can be added before diminishing returns set in.

3.2 GRAPHICAL SENSITIVITY ANALYSIS

For linear programming problems with two decision variables, graphical solution methods can be used to perform sensitivity analysis on the objective function coefficients and the right-hand-side values for the constraints.

Objective Function Coefficients

Let us consider how changes in the objective function coefficients might affect the optimal solution to the Par, Inc., problem. The current contribution to profit is $10 per unit for the standard bag and $9 per unit for the deluxe bag. It seems obvious that an increase in the profit contribution for one of the bags might lead management to increase production of that bag, and a decrease in the profit contribution for one of the bags might lead management to decrease production of that bag. It is not as obvious, however, how much the profit contribution would have to change before management would want to change the production quantities.

The current optimal solution to this problem calls for producing 540 standard golf bags and 252 deluxe golf bags. The **range of optimality** for each objective function coefficient provides the range of values over which the current solution will remain optimal. Managerial attention needs to be focused on those objective function coefficients that have a narrow range of optimality and coefficients near the end points of the range. With these coefficients, a small change can necessitate modifying the optimal solution. Let us now compute the ranges of optimality for this problem.

Figure 3.1 shows the graphical solution. A careful inspection of this graph shows that as long as the slope of the objective function line is between the slope of line A (which coincides with the cutting and dyeing constraint line) and the slope of line B (which coincides with the finishing constraint line), extreme point ③ with $S = 540$ and $D = 252$ will be optimal. Changing an objective function coefficient for S or D will cause the slope of the objective function line to change. In Figure 3.1 we see that such changes cause the objective function line to rotate around extreme point ③. However, as long as the objective function line stays within the shaded region, extreme point ③ will remain optimal.

Rotating the objective function line *counterclockwise* causes the slope to become less negative, and the slope increases. When the objective function line rotates counterclockwise (slope increased) enough to coincide with line A, we obtain alternative optimal solutions between extreme points ③ and ④. Any further counterclockwise rotation of the objective function line will cause extreme point ③ to be nonoptimal. Hence, the slope of line A provides an upper limit for the slope of the objective function line.

The slope of the objective function line usually is negative; hence, rotating the objective function line clockwise makes the line steeper even though the slope is getting smaller (more negative).

Rotating the objective function line *clockwise* causes the slope to become more negative, and the slope decreases. When the objective function line rotates clockwise (slope decreases) enough to coincide with line B, we obtain alternative optimal solutions between extreme points ③ and ②. Any further clockwise rotation of the objective function line will cause extreme point ③ to be nonoptimal. Hence, the slope of line B provides a lower limit for the slope of the objective function line.

FIGURE 3.1 GRAPHICAL SOLUTION OF PAR, INC., PROBLEM WITH SLOPE OF OBJECTIVE FUNCTION LINE BETWEEN SLOPES OF LINES A AND B; EXTREME POINT ③ IS OPTIMAL

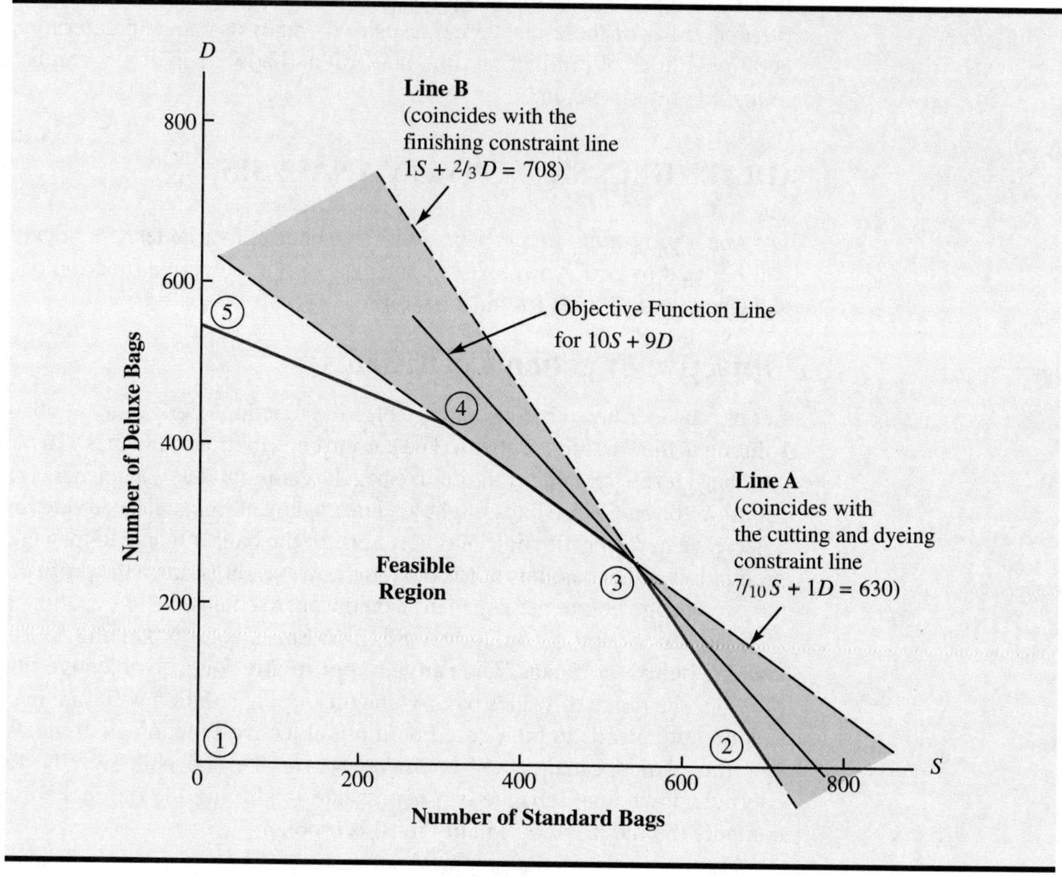

Thus, extreme point ③ will be the optimal solution as long as

$$\text{Slope of line B} \leq \text{slope of the objective function line} \leq \text{slope of line A}$$

In Figure 3.1 we see that the equation for line A, the cutting and dyeing constraint line, is as follows:

$$\tfrac{7}{10}S + 1D = 630$$

By solving this equation for D, we can write the equation for line A in its slope-intercept form, which yields

$$D = -\tfrac{7}{10}S + 630$$

↑ Slope of line A ↑ Intercept of line A on D axis

Thus, the slope for line A is $-\tfrac{7}{10}$, and its intercept on the D axis is 630.

The equation for line B in Figure 3.1 is

$$1S + \tfrac{2}{3}D = 708$$

Solving for D provides the slope-intercept form for line B. Doing so yields

$$\tfrac{2}{3}D = -1S + 708$$
$$D = -\tfrac{3}{2}S + 1062$$

Thus, the slope of line B is $-\tfrac{3}{2}$, and its intercept on the D axis is 1062.

Now that the slopes of lines A and B have been computed, we see that for extreme point ③ to remain optimal we must have

$$-\tfrac{3}{2} \leq \text{slope of objective function} \leq -\tfrac{7}{10} \qquad (3.1)$$

Let us now consider the general form of the slope of the objective function line. Let C_S denote the profit of a standard bag, C_D denote the profit of a deluxe bag, and P denote the value of the objective function. Using this notation, the objective function line can be written as

$$P = C_S S + C_D D$$

Writing this equation in slope-intercept form, we obtain

$$C_D D = -C_S S + P$$

and

$$D = -\frac{C_S}{C_D} S + \frac{P}{C_D}$$

Thus, we see that the slope of the objective function line is given by $-C_S/C_D$. Substituting $-C_S/C_D$ into expression (3.1), we see that extreme point ③ will be optimal as long as the following expression is satisfied:

$$-\tfrac{3}{2} \leq -\frac{C_S}{C_D} \leq -\tfrac{7}{10} \qquad (3.2)$$

To compute the range of optimality for the standard-bag profit contribution, we hold the profit contribution for the deluxe bag fixed at its initial value $C_D = 9$. Doing so in expression (3.2), we obtain

$$-\tfrac{3}{2} \leq -\frac{C_S}{9} \leq -\tfrac{7}{10}$$

From the left-hand inequality, we have

$$-\tfrac{3}{2} \leq -\frac{C_S}{9} \quad \text{or} \quad \tfrac{3}{2} \geq \frac{C_S}{9}$$

Thus,

$$\tfrac{27}{2} \geq C_S \quad \text{or} \quad C_S \leq \tfrac{27}{2} = 13.5$$

From the right-hand inequality, we have

$$-\frac{C_S}{9} \leq -\tfrac{7}{10} \quad \text{or} \quad \frac{C_S}{9} \geq \tfrac{7}{10}$$

Thus,

$$C_S \geq \tfrac{63}{10} \quad \text{or} \quad C_S \geq 6.3$$

Can you compute the range of optimality using the graphical solution procedure? Try Problem 3.

Combining the calculated limits for C_S provides the following range of optimality for the standard-bag profit contribution:

$$6.3 \leq C_S \leq 13.5$$

In the original problem for Par, Inc., the standard bag had a profit contribution of \$10. The resulting optimal solution was 540 standard bags and 252 deluxe bags. The range of optimality for C_S tells Par's management that, with other coefficients unchanged, the profit contribution for the standard bag can be anywhere between \$6.30 and \$13.50 and the production quantities of 540 standard bags and 252 deluxe bags will remain optimal. Note, however, that even though the production quantities will not change, the total profit contribution (value of objective function) will change due to the change in profit contribution per standard bag.

These computations can be repeated, holding the profit contribution for standard bags constant at $C_S = 10$. In this case, the range of optimality for the deluxe-bag profit contribution can be determined. Check to see that this range is $6.67 \leq C_D \leq 14.29$.

In cases where the rotation of the objective function line about an optimal extreme point causes the objective function line to become *vertical,* there will be either no upper limit or no lower limit for the slope as it appears in the form of expression (3.2). To show how this special situation can occur, suppose that the objective function for the Par, Inc., problem is $18C_S + 9C_D$; in this case, extreme point ② in Figure 3.2 provides the optimal solution. Rotating the objective function line counterclockwise around extreme point ② provides an upper limit for the slope when the objective function line coincides with line B. We showed previously that the slope of line B is $-\tfrac{3}{2}$, so the upper limit for the slope of the objective function line must be $-\tfrac{3}{2}$. However, rotating the objective function line clockwise results in the slope becoming more and more negative, approaching a value of minus infinity as the objective function line becomes vertical; in this case, the slope of the objective function has no lower limit. Using the upper limit of $-\tfrac{3}{2}$, we can write

$$-\frac{C_S}{C_D} \leq -\tfrac{3}{2}$$

Slope of the objective function line

FIGURE 3.2 GRAPHICAL SOLUTION OF PAR, INC., PROBLEM WITH AN OBJECTIVE FUNCTION OF $18S + 9D$; OPTIMAL SOLUTION AT EXTREME POINT ②

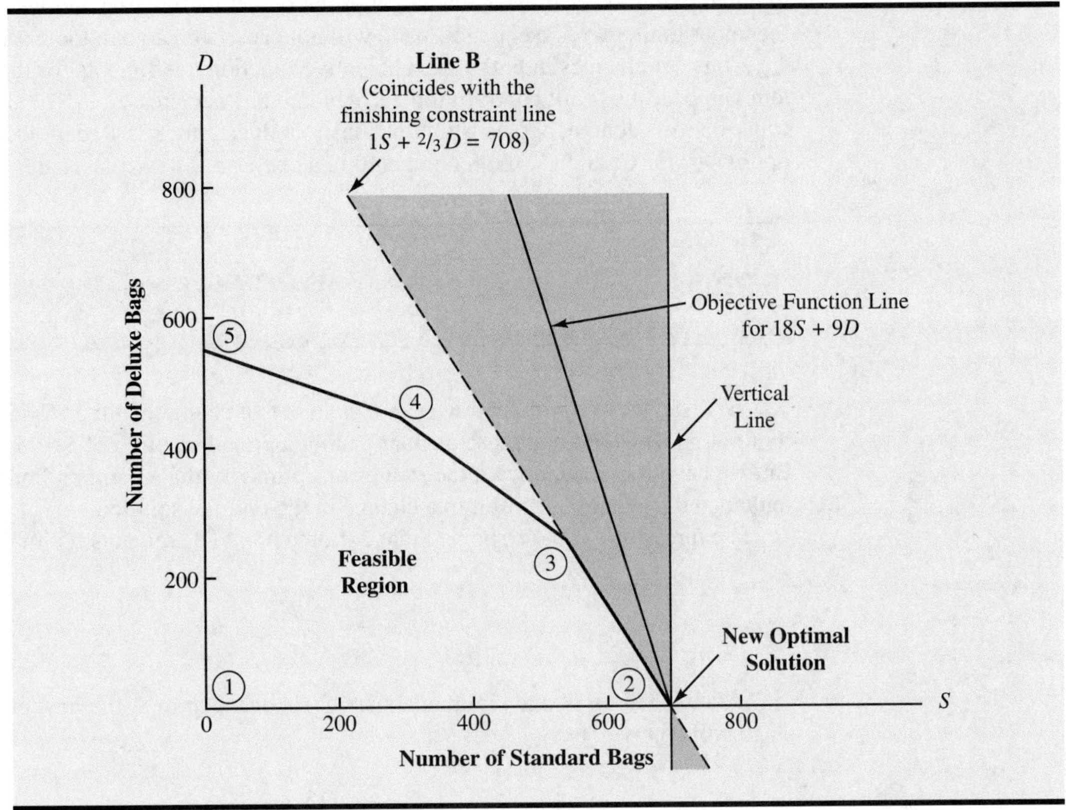

Following the previous procedure of holding C_D constant at its original value, $C_D = 9$, we have

$$-\frac{C_S}{9} \leq -3/2 \qquad \text{or} \qquad \frac{C_S}{9} \geq 3/2$$

Solving for C_S provides the following result:

$$C_S \geq 27/2 = 13.5$$

In reviewing Figure 3.2 we note that extreme point ② remains optimal for all values of C_S above 13.5. Thus, we obtain the following range of optimality for C_S at extreme point ②:

$$13.5 \leq C_S < \infty$$

Simultaneous Changes. The range of optimality for objective function coefficients is only applicable for changes made to one coefficient at a time. All other coefficients are assumed to be fixed at their initial values. If two or more objective function coefficients are changed simultaneously, further analysis is necessary to determine whether the optimal solution will change. However, when solving two-variable problems graphically, expression (3.2) suggests an easy way to determine whether simultaneous changes in both objective function coefficients will cause a change in the optimal solution. Simply compute the slope of the objective function ($-C_S/C_D$) for the new coefficient values. If this ratio is greater than or equal to the lower limit on the slope of the objective function and less than or equal to the upper limit, then the changes made will not cause a change in the optimal solution.

Consider changes in both of the objective function coefficients for the Par, Inc., problem. Suppose the profit contribution per standard bag is increased to \$13 and the profit contribution per deluxe bag is simultaneously reduced to \$8. Recall that the ranges of optimality for C_S and C_D (both computed in a one-at-a-time manner) are

$$6.3 \leq C_S \leq 13.5 \tag{3.3}$$

$$6.67 \leq C_D \leq 14.29 \tag{3.4}$$

For these ranges of optimality, we can conclude that changing either C_S to \$13 or C_D to \$8 (but not both) would not cause a change in the optimal solution of $S = 540$ and $D = 252$. But we cannot conclude from the ranges of optimality that changing both coefficients simultaneously would not result in a change in the optimal solution.

In expression (3.2) we showed that extreme point ③ remains optimal as long as

$$-3/2 \leq -\frac{C_S}{C_D} \leq -7/10$$

If C_S is changed to 13 and simultaneously C_D is changed to 8, the new objective function slope will be given by

$$-\frac{C_S}{C_D} = -\frac{13}{8} = -1.625$$

Because this value is less than the lower limit of $-3/2$, the current solution of $S = 540$ and $D = 252$ will no longer be optimal. By resolving the problem with $C_S = 13$ and $C_D = 8$ we will find that extreme point ② is the new optimal solution.

Looking at the ranges of optimality, we concluded that changing either C_S to \$13 or C_D to \$8 (but not both) would not cause a change in the optimal solution. But in recomputing the slope of the objective function with simultaneous changes for both C_S and C_D, we saw that the optimal solution did change. This result emphasizes the fact that a range of optimality, by itself, can only be used to draw a conclusion about changes made to *one objective function coefficient at a time.*

Right-Hand Sides

Let us now consider how a change in the right-hand side for a constraint may affect the feasible region and perhaps cause a change in the optimal solution to the problem. To illustrate this aspect of sensitivity analysis, let us consider what happens if an additional 10 hours of production time become available in the cutting and dyeing department of Par, Inc. The right-hand side of the cutting and dyeing constraint is changed from 630 to 640, and the constraint is rewritten as

$$7/10 S + 1D \leq 640$$

By obtaining an additional 10 hours of cutting and dyeing time, we expand the feasible region for the problem, as shown in Figure 3.3. With an enlarged feasible region, we now want to determine whether one of the new feasible solutions provides an improvement in the value of the objective function. Application of the graphical solution procedure to the problem with the enlarged feasible region shows that the extreme point with $S = 527.5$ and $D = 270.75$ now provides the optimal solution. The new value for the objective function is $10(527.5) + 9(270.75) = \$7711.75$, with an increase in profit of $\$7711.75 - \$7668.00 = \$43.75$. Thus, the increased profit occurs at a rate of $43.75/10 hours = $4.375 per hour added.

The *improvement* in the value of the optimal solution per unit increase in the right-hand side of the constraint is called the **dual price.** Here, the dual price for the cutting and dyeing constraint is $4.375; in other words, if we increase the right-hand side of the cutting and dyeing constraint by 1 hour, the value of the objective function will improve by $4.375. Conversely, if the right-hand side of the cutting and dyeing constraint were to decrease by 1 hour, the objective function would get worse by $4.375. The dual price can generally be used to determine what will happen to the value of the objective function when we make a one-unit change in the right-hand side of a constraint.

Can you compute and interpret the dual price for a constraint? Try Problem 4.

We caution here that the value of the dual price may be applicable only for small changes in the right-hand side. As more and more resources are obtained and the right-hand-side

FIGURE 3.3 EFFECT OF A 10-UNIT CHANGE IN THE RIGHT-HAND SIDE OF THE CUTTING AND DYEING CONSTRAINT

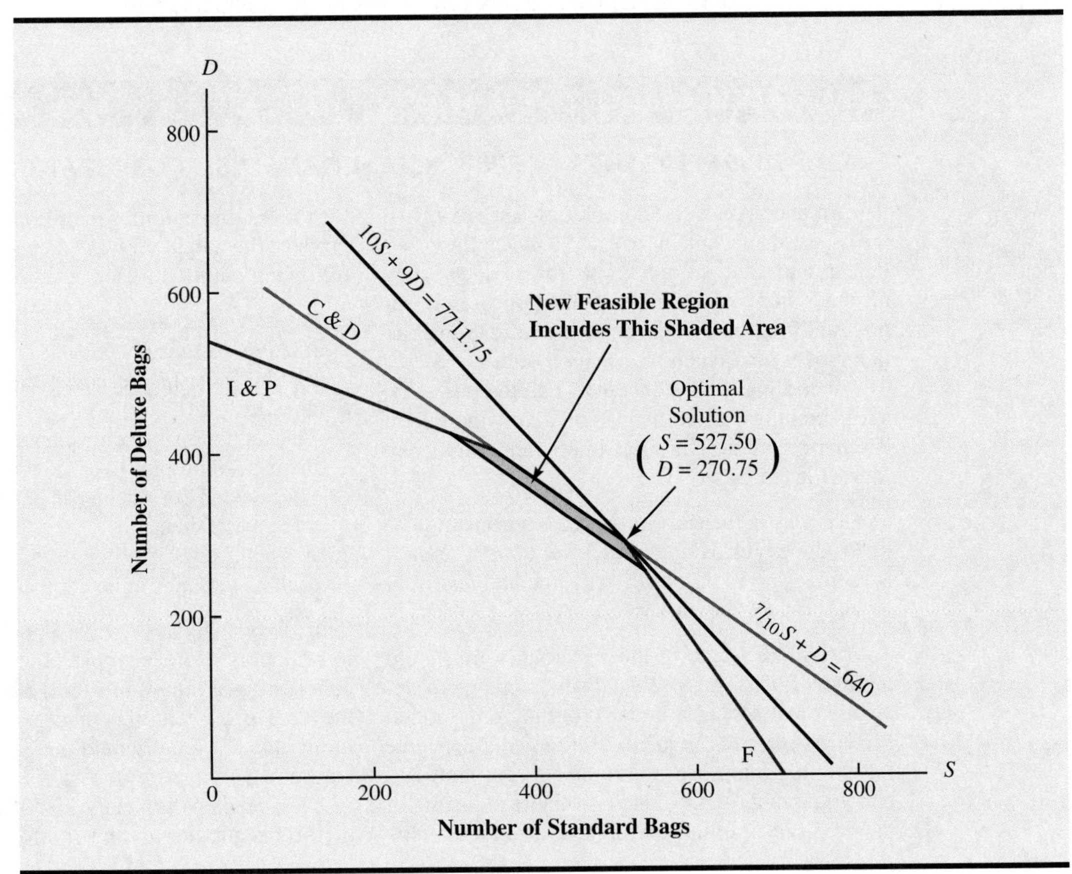

value continues to increase, other constraints will become binding and limit the change in the value of the objective function. For example, in the problem for Par, Inc., we would eventually reach a point where more cutting and dyeing time would be of no value; it would occur at the point where the cutting and dyeing constraint becomes nonbinding. At this point, the dual price would equal zero. In the next section we will show how to determine the range of values for a right-hand side over which the dual price will accurately predict the improvement in the objective function. Finally, we note that the dual price for any nonbinding constraint will be zero because an increase in the right-hand side of such a constraint will affect only the value of the slack or surplus variable for that constraint.

To illustrate the correct interpretation of dual prices for a minimization problem, suppose we had solved a problem involving the minimization of total cost and that the value of the optimal solution was \$100. Furthermore, suppose that the dual price for a particular constraint was −\$10. The *negative dual price* tells us that the objective function *will not improve* if the value of the right-hand side is increased by one unit. Thus, if the right-hand side of this constraint is increased by one unit, the value of the objective function will get worse by the amount of \$10. Becoming worse in a minimization problem means an increase in the total cost. In this case, the value of the objective function will become \$110 if the right-hand side is increased by one unit. Conversely, a decrease in the right-hand side of one unit will decrease the total cost by \$10.

The Management Science in Action, Evaluating Efficiency at Performance Analysis Corporation, illustrates the use of dual prices as part of an evaluation model for a chain of fast-food outlets. This type of model will be studied in more detail in the next chapter when we discuss an application referred to as data envelopment analysis.

MANAGEMENT SCIENCE IN ACTION

EVALUATING EFFICIENCY AT PERFORMANCE ANALYSIS CORPORATION*

Performance Analysis Corporation specializes in the use of management science to design more efficient and effective operations for a wide variety of chain stores. One such application uses linear programming methodology to provide an evaluation model for a chain of fast-food outlets.

According to the concept of Pareto optimality, a restaurant in a given chain is relatively inefficient if other restaurants in the same chain exhibit the following characteristics:

1. Operates in the same or worse environment.
2. Produces at least the same level of *all* outputs.
3. Utilizes no more of *any* resource and *less* of at least one of the resources.

To determine which of the restaurants are Pareto inefficient, Performance Analysis Corporation developed and solved a linear programming model. Model constraints involve requirements concerning the minimum acceptable levels of output and conditions imposed by uncontrollable elements in the environment, and the objective function calls for the minimization of the resources necessary to produce the output. Solving the model produces the following output for each restaurant:

1. A score that assesses the level of so-called relative technical efficiency achieved by the particular restaurant over the time period in question.
2. The reduction in controllable resources or the increase of outputs over the time period in question needed for an inefficient restaurant to be rated as efficient.
3. A peer group of other restaurants with which each restaurant can be compared in the future.

Sensitivity analysis provides important managerial information. For example, for each constraint concerning a minimum acceptable output level, the dual price tells the manager how much one more unit of output would increase the efficiency measure.

The analysis typically identifies 40% to 50% of the restaurants as underperforming, given the previously stated conditions concerning the inputs available and outputs produced. Performance Analysis Corporation finds that if all the relative inefficiencies identified are eliminated simultaneously, corporate profits typically increase approximately 5% to 10%. This increase is truly substantial given the large scale of operations involved.

*Based on information provided by Richard C. Morey of Performance Analysis Corporation.

NOTES AND COMMENTS

1. If two objective function coefficients change simultaneously, both may move outside their respective ranges of optimality and not affect the optimal solution. For instance, in a two-variable linear program, the slope of the objective function will not change at all if both coefficients are changed by the same percentage.
2. Some texts associate the term *shadow price* with each constraint. The concept of a shadow price is closely related to the concept of a dual price. The shadow price associated with a constraint is the *change* in the value of the optimal solution per unit increase in the right-hand side of the constraint. In general, the dual price and the shadow price are the *same* for all *maximization* linear programs. In *minimization* linear programs, the shadow price is the *negative* of the corresponding dual price.

3.3 SENSITIVITY ANALYSIS: COMPUTER SOLUTION

In Section 2.4 we showed how The Management Scientist can be used to solve the Par, Inc., linear program. Recall that in order to use The Management Scientist, we must use decimal rather than fractional values. The Par, Inc., problem with decimal coefficients is restated here:

$$\begin{array}{llll}
\text{Max} & 10S + 9D & & \\
\text{s.t.} & & & \\
& 0.7S + 1D & \leq 630 & \text{Cutting and dyeing} \\
& 0.5S + 0.83333D & \leq 600 & \text{Sewing} \\
& 1.0S + 0.66667D & \leq 708 & \text{Finishing} \\
& 0.1S + 0.25D & \leq 135 & \text{Inspection and packaging} \\
& S, D \geq 0 & &
\end{array}$$

Let us demonstrate the use of The Management Scientist in performing sensitivity analysis by considering the solution to the Par, Inc., linear program shown in Figure 3.4.

Interpretation of Computer Output

In Section 2.4 we discussed the output in the top portion of Figure 3.4. Thus, after rounding, we see that the optimal solution is $S = 540$ standard bags and $D = 252$ deluxe bags; the value of the optimal solution is $7668. As we discussed in Section 2.4, the **reduced costs** indicate how much the objective function coefficient of each decision variable would have to improve before that variable could assume a positive value in the optimal solution. For the Par, Inc., problem, both variables already have positive values, and thus their corresponding reduced costs are zero. In Section 3.4 we will interpret the reduced cost for a decision variable that does not have a positive value in the optimal solution.

FIGURE 3.4 THE MANAGEMENT SCIENTIST SOLUTION FOR THE PAR, INC., PROBLEM

EXCELfile
Par

```
Objective Function Value =          7667.99463

     Variable                 Value                 Reduced Costs
  --------------        ---------------           -----------------
          S                539.99841                    0.00000
          D                252.00113                    0.00000

    Constraint            Slack/Surplus              Dual Prices
  --------------        ---------------           -----------------
           1                 0.00000                    4.37496
           2               120.00070                    0.00000
           3                 0.00000                    6.93753
           4                17.99988                    0.00000

OBJECTIVE COEFFICIENT RANGES

  Variable         Lower Limit       Current Value       Upper Limit
------------     ---------------   ---------------   ---------------
      S                 6.30000          10.00000          13.49993
      D                 6.66670           9.00000          14.28572

RIGHT HAND SIDE RANGES

 Constraint        Lower Limit       Current Value       Upper Limit
------------     ---------------   ---------------   ---------------
       1              495.59998         630.00000         682.36316
       2              479.99930         600.00000    No Upper Limit
       3              580.00146         708.00000         900.00000
       4              117.00012         135.00000    No Upper Limit
```

Immediately following the optimal S and D values and the reduced cost information, the computer output provides information about the constraints. Recall that the Par, Inc., problem had four less-than-or-equal-to constraints corresponding to the hours available in each of four production departments. The information shown in the Slack/Surplus column provides the value of the slack variable for each of the departments. This information (after rounding) is summarized here:

Constraint Number	Constraint Name	Slack
1	Cutting and dyeing	0
2	Sewing	120
3	Finishing	0
4	Inspection and packaging	18

From this information, we see that the binding constraints (the cutting and dyeing and the finishing constraints) have zero slack at the optimal solution. The sewing department has

120 hours of slack, or unused capacity, and the inspection and packaging department has 18 hours of slack or unused capacity.

The Dual Prices column contains information about the marginal value of each of the four resources at the optimal solution. In Section 3.2 we defined the *dual price* as follows.

> The dual price associated with a constraint is the *improvement* in the value of the solution per unit increase in the right-hand side of the constraint.

Try Problem 11 to test your ability to use computer output to determine the optimal solution and to interpret the values of the dual prices.

Thus, the nonzero dual prices of 4.37496 for constraint 1 (cutting and dyeing constraint) and 6.93753 for constraint 3 (finishing constraint) tell us that an additional hour of cutting and dyeing time improves (increases) the value of the optimal solution by $4.37 and an additional hour of finishing time improves (increases) the value of the optimal solution by $6.94. Thus, if the cutting and dyeing time were increased from 630 to 631 hours, with all other coefficients in the problem remaining the same, Par's profit would be increased by $4.37 from $7668 to $7668 + $4.37 = $7672.37. A similar interpretation for the finishing constraint implies that an increase from 708 to 709 hours of available finishing time, with all other coefficients in the problem remaining the same, would increase Par's profit to $7668 + $6.94 = $7674.94. Because the sewing and the inspection and packaging constraints both have slack or unused capacity available, the dual prices of zero show that additional hours of these two resources will not improve the value of the objective function.

Referring again to the computer output in Figure 3.4, we see that after providing the constraint information on slack/surplus variables and dual prices, The Management Scientist provides ranges for the objective function coefficients and the right-hand sides of the constraints.

Considering the information provided under the computer output heading labeled OBJECTIVE COEFFICIENT RANGES, we see that variable S, which has a current profit coefficient of 10, has the following *range of optimality* for C_S:

$$6.30 \leq C_S \leq 13.50$$

Therefore, as long as the profit contribution associated with the standard bag is between $6.30 and $13.50, the production of $S = 540$ standard bags and $D = 252$ deluxe bags will remain the optimal solution. Note that the range of optimality is the same as obtained by performing graphical sensitivity analysis for C_S in Section 3.2.

Using the objective function coefficient range information for deluxe bags, we see that The Management Scientist computed the following range of optimality:

$$6.67 \leq C_D \leq 14.29$$

This result tells us that as long as the profit contribution associated with the deluxe bag is between $6.67 and $14.29, the production of $S = 540$ standard bags and $D = 252$ deluxe bags will remain the optimal solution.

Try Problem 12 to test your ability to use computer output to determine the ranges of optimality and the ranges of feasibility.

The final section of the computer output (RIGHT HAND SIDE RANGES) provides the limits within which the dual prices are applicable. As long as the constraint right-hand side is between the lower and upper limit values, the associated dual price gives the improvement in the value of the optimal solution per unit increase in the right-hand side. For example, let us consider the cutting and dyeing constraint with a current right-hand-side value of 630. Because the dual price for this constraint is $4.37, we can conclude that additional hours will increase the objective function by $4.37 per hour. It is also true that a reduction in the hours available will reduce the value of the objective function by $4.37 per hour. From the range information given, we see that the dual price of $4.37 is valid for increases up to 682.36316 and decreases down to 495.59998. A similar interpretation for the finishing constraint's right-hand side (constraint 3) shows that the dual price of $6.94 is applicable for increases up to 900 hours and decreases down to 580.00146 hours.

As mentioned, the right-hand-side ranges provide limits within which the dual prices are applicable. For changes outside the range, the problem must be resolved to find the new optimal solution and the new dual price. We shall call the range over which the dual price is applicable the **range of feasibility.** The ranges of feasibility for the Par, Inc., problem are summarized here:

Constraint	Min RHS	Max RHS
Cutting and dyeing	495.6	682.4
Sewing	480.0	No upper limit
Finishing	580.0	900.0
Inspection and packaging	117.0	No upper limit

As long as the values of the right-hand sides are within these ranges, the dual prices shown on the computer output will not change. Right-hand-side values outside these limits will result in changes in the dual price information.

Simultaneous Changes

The sensitivity analysis information in computer output is based on the assumption that only one coefficient changes; it is assumed that all other coefficients will remain as stated in the original problem. Thus, the ranges for the objective function coefficients and the constraint right-hand sides are only applicable for changes in a single coefficient. In many cases, however, we may be interested in what would happen if two or more coefficients are changed simultaneously. As we will demonstrate, some analysis of simultaneous changes is possible with the help of the **100 percent rule.**[1] We begin by showing how the 100 percent rule applies to simultaneous changes in the objective function coefficients.

Suppose that in the Par, Inc., problem the accounting department concluded that the original profit contributions of $10 and $9 for the standard and deluxe bags, respectively, were incorrectly computed; the correct values should have been $11.50 and $8.25. To determine what effect, if any, these simultaneous changes have on the optimal solution, we need to first define the terms *allowable increase* and *allowable decrease.* For an objective function coefficient, the allowable increase is the maximum amount the coefficient may increase without exceeding the upper limit of the range of optimality; the allowable decrease is the maximum amount the coefficient may decrease without dropping below the lower limit of the range of optimality.

From Figure 3.4 we see that the upper limit for the objective function coefficient of S is 13.49993; thus, the allowable increase is $3.49993 = 13.49993 - 10$. In terms of percentage change, the increase of $1.50 in the objective function coefficient (from 10 to 11.50) for the standard bags is $(1.50/3.49993)(100) = 42.86\%$ of the allowable increase. Given the

[1]See S. P. Bradley, A. C. Hax, and T. L. Magnanti, *Applied Mathematical Programming* (Reading, MA: Addison-Wesley, 1977).

lower limit of 6.66670 for D, the allowable decrease for D is 2.33330 = 9 − 6.66670. In terms of percentage change, the decrease of $0.75 in the objective function coefficient (from 9 to 8.25) for the deluxe bags is (0.75/2.33330)(100) = 32.14% of the allowable decrease. The sum of the percentage change of the allowable increase (42.86%) and the percentage change of the allowable decrease (32.14%) is 75.00%.

Let us now state the 100 percent rule as it applies to simultaneous changes in the objective function coefficients.

100 Percent Rule for Objective Function Coefficients

For all objective function coefficients that are changed, sum the percentages of the allowable increases and the allowable decreases represented by the changes. If the sum of the percentage changes does not exceed 100%, the optimal solution will not change.

Thus, because the sum of the two percentage changes in the objective function coefficients for the Par, Inc., problem is 75%, these simultaneous changes will not affect the optimal solution. Note, however, that although the optimal solution is still S = 539.99841 and D = 252.00113, the value of the optimal solution will change because the profit contribution for the standard bags has increased to $11.50 and the profit contribution of the deluxe bags has decreased to $8.25.

The 100 percent rule does not, however, say that the optimal solution will change if the sum of the percentage changes exceeds 100%. It is possible that the optimal solution will not change even though the sum of the percentage changes exceeds 100%. When the 100 percent rule is not satisfied, we must resolve the problem to determine what affect such changes will have on the optimal solution.

A similar version of the 100 percent rule also applies to simultaneous changes in the constraint right-hand sides.

100 Percent Rule for Constraint Right-Hand Sides

For all right-hand sides that are changed, sum the percentages of allowable increases and allowable decreases. If the sum of percentages does not exceed 100%, then the dual prices will not change.

Let us illustrate the 100 percent rule for constraint right-hand sides by considering simultaneous changes in the right-hand sides for the Par, Inc., problem. Suppose, for instance, that in this problem we could obtain 20 additional hours of cutting and dyeing time and 100 additional hours of finishing time. The allowable increase for cutting and dyeing time is 682.36316 − 630.0 = 52.36316, and the allowable increase for finishing time is 900.0 − 708.0 = 192.0 (see Figure 3.4). The 20 additional hours of cutting and dyeing time are (20/52.36316)(100) = 38.19% of the allowable increase in the constraint's right-hand side. The 100 additional hours of finishing time are (100/192)(100) = 52.08% of the allowable increase in the finishing time constraint's right-hand side. The sum of the percentage changes is 38.19% + 52.08% = 90.27%. The sum of the percentage changes does not exceed 100%; therefore, we can conclude that the dual prices are applicable and that the objective function will improve by (20)(4.37) + (100)(6.94) = 781.40.

Interpretation of Computer Output—A Second Example

As another example of interpreting computer output, let us reconsider the M&D Chemicals problem introduced in Section 2.5. M&D's objective was to find the minimum-cost production schedule for products A and B. The linear programming model for this problem is restated as follows, where A = number of gallons of product A and B = number of gallons of product B.

$$
\begin{array}{lll}
\text{Min} & 2A + 3B & \\
\text{s.t.} & & \\
 & 1A \qquad\quad \geq 125 & \text{Demand for product A} \\
 & 1A + 1B \geq 350 & \text{Total production} \\
 & 2A + 1B \leq 600 & \text{Processing time} \\
 & A, B \geq 0 &
\end{array}
$$

The solution obtained using The Management Scientist is presented in Figure 3.5. The computer output shows that the minimum-cost solution yields an objective function

FIGURE 3.5 THE MANAGEMENT SCIENTIST SOLUTION FOR THE M&D CHEMICALS PROBLEM

```
Objective Function Value =                800.000

     Variable              Value               Reduced Costs
  --------------      ---------------       -----------------
        A                   250.000                    0.000
        B                   100.000                    0.000

     Constraint          Slack/Surplus          Dual Prices
  --------------      ---------------       -----------------
          1                 125.000                    0.000
          2                   0.000                   -4.000
          3                   0.000                    1.000

OBJECTIVE COEFFICIENT RANGES

   Variable        Lower Limit      Current Value      Upper Limit
 ------------   ---------------  ---------------  ---------------
       A         No Lower Limit            2.000            3.000
       B                  2.000            3.000   No Upper Limit

RIGHT HAND SIDE RANGES

   Constraint      Lower Limit      Current Value      Upper Limit
 ------------   ---------------  ---------------  ---------------
       1         No Lower Limit          125.000          250.000
       2                300.000          350.000          475.000
       3                475.000          600.000          700.000
```

EXCELfile
M&D

value of \$800. The values of the decision variables show that 250 gallons of product A and 100 gallons of product B provide the minimum-cost production schedule.

The Slack/Surplus column shows that the ≥ constraint corresponding to the demand for product A (see constraint 1) has a surplus of 125 units. It tells us that production of product A in the optimal solution exceeds demand by 125 gallons. The Slack/Surplus values are zero for the total production requirement (constraint 2) and the processing time limitation (constraint 3), which indicates that these constraints are binding at the optimal solution.

The Dual Prices column again shows us the *improvement* in the value of the optimal solution per unit increase in the right-hand side of the constraint. Focusing first on the dual price of 1.00 for the processing time constraint (constraint 3), we see that if we can increase the processing time from 600 to 601 hours, the objective function value will *improve* by \$1. Because the objective is to minimize costs, improvement in this case means a lowering of costs. Thus, if 601 hours of processing time are available, the value of the optimal solution will improve to \$800 − \$1 = \$799. The RIGHT HAND SIDE RANGES section of the output shows that the upper limit for the processing time constraint (constraint 3) is 700 hours. Thus, the dual price of \$1 per unit would be applicable for every additional hour of processing time up to a total of 700 hours.

Let us again return to the Dual Prices section of the output and consider the dual price for the total production constraint (constraint 2). The *negative dual price* tells us that the value of the optimal solution *will not improve* if the value of the right-hand side is increased by one unit. In fact, the dual price of −4.00 tells us that if the right-hand side of the total production constraint is increased from 350 to 351 units, the value of the optimal solution will worsen by the amount of \$4. A worsening means an increase in cost, which also means the value of the optimal solution will become \$800 + \$4 = \$804 if the one-unit increase in the total production requirement is made.

Because the dual price refers to improvement in the value of the optimal solution per unit increase in the right-hand side, a constraint with a negative dual price should not have its right-hand side increased. In fact, if the dual price is negative, efforts should be made to reduce the right-hand side of the constraint. If the right-hand side of the total production constraint were decreased from 350 to 349 units, the dual price tells us the total cost could be lowered by \$4 to \$800 − \$4 = \$796.

Even though the dual price is the improvement in the value of the optimal solution per unit increase in the right-hand side of a constraint, the interpretation of an *improvement* in the value of an objective function depends on whether we are solving a maximization or a minimization problem. The dual price for a ≤ constraint will always be greater than or equal to zero because increasing the right-hand side cannot make the value of the objective function worse. Similarly, the dual price for a ≥ constraint will always be less than or equal to zero because increasing the right-hand side cannot improve the value of the optimal solution.

Finally, consider the right-hand-side ranges provided in Figure 3.5. The ranges of feasibility for the M&D Chemicals problem are summarized here:

Constraint	Min RHS	Max RHS
Demand for product A	No lower limit	250
Total production	300	475
Processing time	475	700

Try Problem 16 to test your ability to interpret the computer output for a minimization problem.

As long as the right-hand sides are within these ranges, the dual prices shown on the computer printout are applicable.

Cautionary Note on the Interpretation of Dual Prices

As stated previously, the dual price is the improvement in the value of the optimal solution per unit increase in the right-hand side of a constraint. When the right-hand side of the constraint represents the amount of a resource available, the associated dual price is often interpreted as the maximum amount one should be willing to pay for one additional unit of the resource. However, such an interpretation is not always correct. To see why, we need to understand the difference between sunk and relevant costs. A **sunk cost** is one that is not affected by the decision made. It will be incurred no matter what values the decision variables assume. A **relevant cost** is one that depends on the decision made. The amount of a relevant cost will vary depending on the values of the decision variables.

Let us reconsider the Par, Inc., problem. The amount of cutting and dyeing time available is 630 hours. The cost of the time available is a sunk cost if it must be paid regardless of the number of standard and deluxe golf bags produced. It would be a relevant cost if Par only had to pay for the number of hours of cutting and dyeing time actually used to produce golf bags. All relevant costs should be reflected in the objective function of a linear program. Sunk costs should not be reflected in the objective function. For Par, Inc., we have been assuming that the company must pay its employees' wages regardless of whether their time on the job is completely utilized. Therefore, the cost of the labor-hours resource for Par, Inc., is a sunk cost and has not been reflected in the objective function.

Only relevant costs should be included in the objective function.

When the cost of a resource is *sunk,* the dual price can be interpreted as the maximum amount the company should be willing to pay for one additional unit of the resource. When the cost of a resource used is relevant, the dual price can be interpreted as the amount by which the value of the resource exceeds its cost. Thus, when the resource cost is relevant, the dual price can be interpreted as the maximum premium over the normal cost that the company should be willing to pay for one unit of the resource.

NOTES AND COMMENTS

1. Computer software packages for solving linear programs are readily available. Most of these provide the optimal solution, dual or shadow price information, the range of optimality for the objective function coefficients, and the range of feasibility for the right-hand sides. The labels used for the ranges of optimality and feasibility may vary, but the meaning is the same as what we have described here.
2. Whenever one of the right-hand sides is at an end point of its range of feasibility, the dual and shadow prices only provide one-sided information. In this case, they only predict the change in the optimal value of the objective function for changes toward the interior of the range.
3. A condition called *degeneracy* can cause a subtle difference in how we interpret changes in the objective function coefficients beyond the end points of the range of optimality. Degeneracy occurs when the dual price equals zero for one of the binding constraints. Degeneracy does not affect the interpretation of changes toward the interior of the range of optimality. However, when degeneracy is present, changes beyond the end points of the range do not necessarily mean a different solution will be optimal. From a practical point of view, changes beyond the end points of the range of optimality necessitate resolving the problem.
4. The 100 percent rule permits an analysis of multiple changes in the right-hand sides or multiple changes in the objective function coefficients. But the 100 percent rule cannot be applied to changes in both objective function coefficients

and right-hand sides at the same time. In order to consider simultaneous changes for *both* right-hand-side values and objective function coefficients, the problem must be re-solved.

5. Managers are frequently called on to provide an economic justification for new technology. Often the new technology is developed, or purchased, in order to conserve resources. The dual price can be helpful in such cases because it can be used to determine the savings attributable to the new technology by showing the savings per unit of resource conserved.

3.4 MORE THAN TWO DECISION VARIABLES

The graphical solution procedure is useful only for linear programs involving two decision variables. Computer software packages are designed to handle linear programs involving large numbers of variables and constraints. In this section we discuss the formulation and computer solution for two linear programs with three decision variables. In doing so, we will show how to interpret the reduced-cost portion of the computer output and will also illustrate the interpretation of dual prices for constraints that involve percentages.

The Modified Par, Inc., Problem

The original Par, Inc., problem is restated as follows:

$$\begin{array}{llrl}
\text{Max} & 10S + 9D & & \\
\text{s.t.} & & & \\
& 0.7S + 1D \leq 630 & & \text{Cutting and dyeing} \\
& 0.5S + 0.83333D \leq 600 & & \text{Sewing} \\
& 1S + 0.66667D \leq 708 & & \text{Finishing} \\
& 0.1S + 0.25D \leq 135 & & \text{Inspection and packaging} \\
& S, D \geq 0 & &
\end{array}$$

Recall that S is the number of standard golf bags produced and D is the number of deluxe golf bags produced. Suppose that management is also considering producing a lightweight model designed specifically for golfers who prefer to carry their bags. The design department estimates that each new lightweight model will require 0.8 hours for cutting and dyeing, 1 hour for sewing, 1 hour for finishing, and 0.25 hours for inspection and packaging. Because of the unique capabilities designed into the new model, Par's management feels they will realize a profit contribution of \$12.85 for each lightweight model produced during the current production period.

Let us consider the modifications in the original linear programming model that are needed to incorporate the effect of this additional decision variable. We will let L denote the number of lightweight bags produced. After adding L to the objective function and to each of the four constraints, we obtain the following linear program for the modified problem:

$$\begin{array}{llrl}
\text{Max} & 10S + 9D + 12.85L & & \\
\text{s.t.} & & & \\
& 0.7S + 1D + 0.8L \leq 630 & & \text{Cutting and dyeing} \\
& 0.5S + 0.83333D + 1L \leq 630 & & \text{Sewing} \\
& 1S + 0.66667D + 1L \leq 708 & & \text{Finishing} \\
& 0.1S + 0.25D + 0.25L \leq 135 & & \text{Inspection and packaging} \\
& S, D, L \geq 0 & &
\end{array}$$

FIGURE 3.6 THE MANAGEMENT SCIENTIST SOLUTION FOR THE MODIFIED PAR, INC., PROBLEM

```
Objective Function Value =          8299.80078

      Variable             Value            Reduced Costs
   --------------     ---------------     -----------------
         S               280.00000             0.00000
         D                 0.00000             1.15003
         L               428.00000             0.00000

     Constraint        Slack/Surplus          Dual Prices
   --------------     ---------------     -----------------
         1                91.60001             0.00000
         2                32.00000             0.00000
         3                 0.00000             8.10000
         4                 0.00000            19.00000

OBJECTIVE COEFFICIENT RANGES

    Variable       Lower Limit      Current Value     Upper Limit
  ------------   ---------------   ---------------   ---------------
       S              5.14000          10.00000          12.07007
       D         No Lower Limit         9.00000          10.15003
       L             11.90907          12.85000          25.00000

RIGHT HAND SIDE RANGES

   Constraint      Lower Limit      Current Value     Upper Limit
  ------------   ---------------   ---------------   ---------------
       1            538.40002         630.00000     No Upper Limit
       2            568.00000         600.00000     No Upper Limit
       3            540.00000         708.00000         852.63159
       4             70.80000         135.00000         144.60001
```

Figure 3.6 shows the solution to the modified problem using The Management Scientist. We see that the optimal solution calls for the production of 280 standard bags, 0 deluxe bags, and 428 of the new lightweight bags; the value of the optimal solution after rounding is $8299.80.

Let us now look at the information contained in the Reduced Costs column. Recall that the reduced costs indicate how much each objective function coefficient would have to improve before the corresponding decision variable could assume a positive value in the optimal solution. As the computer output shows, the reduced costs for S and L are zero because the corresponding decision variables already have positive values in the optimal solution. The reduced cost of 1.15003 for decision variable D tells us that the profit contribution for the deluxe bag would have to increase to at least $9 + $1.15003 = $10.15003 before D *could*

FIGURE 3.7 THE MANAGEMENT SCIENTIST SOLUTION FOR THE MODIFIED PAR, INC., PROBLEM WITH THE COEFFICIENT OF *D* INCREASED BY $1.15003

```
Objective Function Value =              8299.80078

   Variable              Value              Reduced Costs
 --------------     ---------------     ------------------
        S               403.78317               0.00000
        D               222.81198               0.00000
        L               155.67476               0.00000

  Constraint          Slack/Surplus          Dual Prices
 --------------     ---------------     ------------------
        1                 0.00000               0.00000
        2                56.75776               0.00000
        3                 0.00000               8.10000
        4                 0.00000              19.00000

OBJECTIVE COEFFICIENT RANGES

 Variable        Lower Limit       Current Value      Upper Limit
------------   ---------------   ---------------   ---------------
     S              10.00000          10.00000          12.51072
     D              10.15003          10.15003          15.40790
     L              10.65313          12.85000          12.85000

RIGHT HAND SIDE RANGES

 Constraint      Lower Limit       Current Value      Upper Limit
------------   ---------------   ---------------   ---------------
     1             538.40002         630.00000         682.36316
     2             543.24225         600.00000    No Upper Limit
     3             580.00140         708.00000         852.63159
     4             117.00012         135.00000         151.15410
```

assume a positive value in the optimal solution.[2] In other words, unless the profit contribution for *D* increases by at least $1.15 the value of *D* will remain at zero in the optimal solution.

Suppose we increase the coefficient of *D* by exactly $1.15003 and then resolve the problem using The Management Scientist. Figure 3.7 shows the new solution. Note that although *D* assumes a positive value in the new solution, the value of the optimal solution has not changed. In other words, increasing the profit contribution of *D* by *exactly* the amount of the reduced cost has resulted in alternative optimal solutions. Using a different

[2]In the case of degeneracy, a variable may not assume a positive value in the optimal solution even when the improvement in the profit contribution exceeds the value of the reduced cost. Our definition of reduced costs, stated as ". . . could assume a positive value . . . ," provides for such special cases. More advanced texts on mathematical programming discuss these special types of situations.

computer software package, you may not see D assume a positive value if you resolve the problem with an objective function coefficient of exactly 10.15003 for D—that is, the software package may show a different alternative optimal solution. However, if the profit contribution of D is increased by *more than* \$1.15003, then D will not remain at zero in the optimal solution.

We also note from Figure 3.6 that the dual prices for constraints 3 and 4 are 8.1 and 19, respectively, indicating that these two constraints are binding in the optimal solution. Thus, each additional hour in the finishing department would increase the value of the optimal solution by \$8.10 and each additional hour in the inspection and packaging department would increase the value of the optimal solution by \$19.00. Because of a slack of 91.6 hours in the cutting and dyeing department and 32 hours in the sewing department (see Figure 3.6), management might want to consider the possibility of utilizing these unused labor-hours in the finishing or inspection and packaging departments. For example, some of the employees in the cutting and dyeing department could be used to perform certain operations in either the finishing department or the inspection and packaging department. In the future, Par's management may want to explore the possibility of cross-training employees so that unused capacity in one department could be shifted to other departments. In the next chapter we will consider similar modeling situations.

Suppose that after reviewing the solution shown in Figure 3.6, management states that they will not consider any solution that does not include the production of some deluxe bags. Management then decides to add the requirement that the number of deluxe bags produced must be at least 30% of the number of standard bags produced. Writing this requirement using the decision variables S and D, we obtain

$$D \geq 0.3S$$

or

$$-0.3S + D \geq 0$$

Adding this new constraint to the modified Par, Inc., linear program and resolving the problem using The Management Scientist, we obtain the optimal solution shown in Figure 3.8.

Let us consider the interpretation of the dual price for constraint 5, the requirement that the number of deluxe bags produced must be at least 30% of the number of standard bags produced. The dual price of -1.38 indicates that a one-unit increase in the right-hand side of the constraint will lower profits by \$1.38. Thus, what the dual price of -1.38 is really telling us is what will happen to the value of the optimal solution if the constraint is changed to

$$D \geq 0.3S + 1$$

The correct interpretation of the dual price of -1.38 can now be stated as follows: If we are forced to produce one deluxe bag over and above the minimum 30% requirement, total profits will decrease by \$1.38. Conversely, if we relax the minimum 30% requirement by one bag ($D \geq 0.3S - 1$), total profits will increase by \$1.38.

The dual price for similar percentage (or ratio) constraints will not directly provide answers to questions concerning a percentage increase or decrease in the right-hand side of the constraint. For example, we might wonder what would happen to the value of the optimal solution if the number of deluxe bags has to be at least 31% of the number of standard bags. To answer such a question, we would resolve the problem using the constraint $-0.31S + D \geq 0$.

FIGURE 3.8 THE MANAGEMENT SCIENTIST SOLUTION FOR THE MODIFIED PAR, INC., PROBLEM WITH THE 30% DELUXE BAG REQUIREMENT

```
Objective Function Value =          8183.87793

    Variable              Value              Reduced Costs
  --------------     ---------------     -----------------
        S               335.99933                 0.00000
        D               100.79980                 0.00000
        L               304.80048                 0.00000

   Constraint          Slack/Surplus           Dual Prices
  --------------     ---------------     -----------------
         1               50.16031                 0.00000
         2               43.20037                 0.00000
         3                0.00000                 7.40998
         4                0.00000                21.76006
         5                0.00000                -1.38003

OBJECTIVE COEFFICIENT RANGES

  Variable        Lower Limit       Current Value       Upper Limit
 ------------   ---------------    ---------------    ---------------
     S                6.29500           10.00000           12.07007
     D               -3.35000            9.00000           10.15003
     L               11.90907           12.85000           18.14286

RIGHT HAND SIDE RANGES

  Constraint      Lower Limit       Current Value       Upper Limit
 ------------   ---------------    ---------------    ---------------
      1             579.83972          630.00000     No Upper Limit
      2             556.79962          600.00000     No Upper Limit
      3             540.00000          708.00000          765.00049
      4             103.24991          135.00000          147.00008
      5             -84.00000            0.00000          101.67704
```

Because percentage (or ratio) constraints frequently occur in linear programming models, let us consider another example. For instance, suppose that Par's management states that the number of lightweight bags produced may not exceed 20% of the total golf bag production. If the total production of golf bags is $S + D + L$, we can write this constraint as

$$L \leq 0.2(S + D + L)$$
$$L \leq 0.2S + 0.2D + 0.2L$$
$$-0.2S - 0.2D + 0.8L \leq 0$$

The solution obtained using The Management Scientist for the model that incorporates both the effects of this new percentage requirement and the previous requirement ($-0.3S + D \geq 0$) is shown in Figure 3.9. After rounding, the dual price corresponding to the new

FIGURE 3.9 THE MANAGEMENT SCIENTIST SOLUTION FOR THE MODIFIED PAR, INC., PROBLEM INCORPORATING THE 20% LIGHTWEIGHT BAG REQUIREMENT AND THE 30% DELUXE BAG REQUIREMENT

```
Objective Function Value =           8044.25488

     Variable                  Value                 Reduced Costs
  --------------         ---------------          ------------------
        S                     403.44730                     0.00000
        D                     222.20738                     0.00000
        L                     156.41367                     0.00000

    Constraint              Slack/Surplus              Dual Prices
  --------------         ---------------          ------------------
        1                       0.24859                     0.00000
        2                      56.69057                     0.00000
        3                       0.00000                     8.87330
        4                       0.00000                    13.05157
        5                     101.17319                     0.00000
        6                       0.00000                     0.89226

OBJECTIVE COEFFICIENT RANGES

  Variable        Lower Limit       Current Value        Upper Limit
------------   ---------------   ---------------   ---------------
      S                3.13800          10.00000          12.07007
      D                6.47670           9.00000          10.15003
      L               11.90907          12.85000    No Upper Limit

RIGHT HAND SIDE RANGES

 Constraint       Lower Limit       Current Value        Upper Limit
------------   ---------------   ---------------   ---------------
      1              629.75140         630.00000    No Upper Limit
      2              543.30945         600.00000    No Upper Limit
      3              396.00146         708.00000         708.69653
      4              118.96714         135.00000         135.08900
      5         No Lower Limit           0.00000         101.17319
      6               -0.77936           0.00000         156.48053
```

constraint (constraint 6) is 0.89. Thus, every additional lightweight bag we are allowed to produce over the current 20% limit will increase the value of the objective function by \$0.89; moreover, the right-hand-side range for this constraint shows that this interpretation is valid for increases of up to 156 units.

The Bluegrass Farms Problem

To provide additional practice in formulating and interpreting the computer solution for linear programs involving more than two decision variables, we consider a minimization problem involving three decision variables. Bluegrass Farms, located in Lexington, Kentucky, has been experimenting with a special diet for its racehorses. The feed components available for the diet are a standard horse feed product, a vitamin-enriched oat product, and a new vitamin and mineral feed additive. The nutritional values in units per pound and the costs for the three feed components are summarized in Table 3.1; for example, each pound of the standard feed component contains 0.8 unit of ingredient A, 1 unit of ingredient B, and 0.1 unit of ingredient C. The minimum daily diet requirements for each horse are three units of ingredient A, six units of ingredient B, and four units of ingredient C. In addition, to control the weight of the horses, the total daily feed for a horse should not exceed 6 pounds. Bluegrass Farms would like to determine the minimum-cost mix that will satisfy the daily diet requirements.

Formulation of the Bluegrass Farms Problem

To formulate a linear programming model for the Bluegrass Farms problem, we introduce the following three decision variables:

$$S = \text{number of pounds of the standard horse feed product}$$
$$E = \text{number of pounds of the enriched oat product}$$
$$A = \text{number of pounds of the vitamin and mineral feed additive}$$

Using the data in Table 3.1, the objective function for minimizing the total cost associated with the daily feed can be written as follows:

$$\min 0.25S + 0.50E + 3A$$

For a minimum daily requirement for ingredient A of three units, we obtain the constraint

$$0.8S + 0.2E \geq 3$$

The constraint for ingredient B is

$$1.0S + 1.5E + 3.0A \geq 6$$

and the constraint for ingredient C is

$$0.1S + 0.6E + 2.0A \geq 4$$

Finally, the constraint that restricts the mix to at most 6 pounds is

$$S + E + A \leq 6$$

TABLE 3.1 NUTRITIONAL VALUE AND COST DATA FOR THE BLUEGRASS FARMS PROBLEM

Feed Component	Standard	Enriched Oat	Additive
Ingredient A	0.8	0.2	0.0
Ingredient B	1.0	1.5	3.0
Ingredient C	0.1	0.6	2.0
Cost per pound	$0.25	$0.50	$3.00

Combining all the constraints with the nonnegativity requirements enables us to write the complete linear programming model for the Bluegrass Farms problem as follows:

$$
\begin{aligned}
\text{Min} \quad & 0.25S + 0.50E + 3A \\
\text{s.t.} \quad & \\
& 0.8S + 0.2E \geq 3 \quad \text{Ingredient A} \\
& 1.0S + 1.5E + 3.0A \geq 6 \quad \text{Ingredient B} \\
& 0.1S + 0.6E + 2.0A \geq 4 \quad \text{Ingredient C} \\
& S + E + A \leq 6 \quad \text{Weight} \\
& S, E, A \geq 0
\end{aligned}
$$

Computer Solution and Interpretation for the Bluegrass Farms Problem

The output obtained using The Management Scientist to solve the Bluegrass Farms problem is shown in Figure 3.10. After rounding, we see that the optimal solution calls for a daily diet consisting of 3.51 pounds of the standard horse feed product, 0.95 pound of the enriched oat product, and 1.54 pounds of the vitamin and mineral feed additive. Thus, with feed component costs of \$0.25, \$0.50, and \$3.00, the total cost of the optimal diet is

3.51 pounds @ \$0.25 per pound =	\$0.88
0.95 pounds @ \$0.50 per pound =	0.47
1.54 pounds @ \$3.00 per pound =	4.62
Total cost =	\$5.97

Note that after rounding, this result is the same as the objective function value in the computer output (Figure 3.10).

Looking at the Slack/Surplus section of the computer output, we find a value of 3.554 for constraint 2. Because constraint 2 is a greater-than-or-equal-to constraint, 3.554 is the surplus; the optimal solution exceeds the minimum daily diet requirement for ingredient B (six units) by 3.554 units. Because the surplus values for constraints 1 and 3 are both zero, we see that the optimal diet just meets the minimum requirements for ingredients A and C; moreover, a slack value of zero for constraint 4 shows that the optimal solution provides a total daily feed weight of 6 pounds.

The dual price (after rounding) for the ingredient A constraint (constraint 1) is -1.22. To interpret this value properly, we first look at the sign; it is negative, and therefore we know that increasing the right-hand side of constraint 1 will cause the solution value to worsen. In a minimization problem, "worsen" means that the total daily cost will increase, and therefore, a one-unit increase in the right-hand side of constraint 1 will increase the total cost of the daily diet by \$1.22. Conversely, it is also correct to conclude that a decrease of one unit in the right-hand side will decrease the total cost by \$1.22. Looking at the RIGHT HAND SIDE RANGES section of the computer output, we see that these interpretations are correct as long as the right-hand side is between 1.143 and 3.368.

Suppose that the Bluegrass management is willing to reconsider their position regarding the maximum weight of the daily diet. The dual price of 0.92 (after rounding) for constraint 4 shows that a one-unit increase in the right-hand side of constraint 4 will reduce total cost by \$0.92. The RIGHT HAND SIDE RANGES section of the output shows that this interpretation is correct for increases in the right-hand side up to a maximum of 8.478 pounds. Thus, the effect of increasing the right-hand side of constraint 4 from 6 to 8 pounds is a de-

FIGURE 3.10 THE MANAGEMENT SCIENTIST SOLUTION FOR THE BLUEGRASS FARMS PROBLEM

EXCELfile
Bluegrass

```
Objective Function Value =              5.973

   Variable            Value           Reduced Costs
 --------------   ---------------   ------------------
          S                3.514                0.000
          E                0.946                0.000
          A                1.541                0.000

  Constraint       Slack/Surplus          Dual Prices
 --------------   ---------------   ------------------
          1                0.000               -1.216
          2                3.554                0.000
          3                0.000               -1.959
          4                0.000                0.919

OBJECTIVE COEFFICIENT RANGES

  Variable      Lower Limit      Current Value      Upper Limit
------------  ---------------  ---------------  ---------------
     S                 -0.393            0.250   No Upper Limit
     E         No Lower Limit            0.500            0.925
     A                  1.522            3.000   No Upper Limit

RIGHT HAND SIDE RANGES

 Constraint     Lower Limit      Current Value      Upper Limit
------------  ---------------  ---------------  ---------------
     1                  1.143            3.000            3.368
     2         No Lower Limit            6.000            9.554
     3                  2.100            4.000            4.875
     4                  5.562            6.000            8.478
```

crease in the total daily cost of 2 × \$0.92 or \$1.84. Keep in mind that if this change were made, the feasible region would change, and we would obtain a new optimal solution.

The OBJECTIVE COEFFICIENT RANGES section of the computer output shows a lower limit of −0.393 for *S*. Clearly, in a real problem, the objective function coefficient of *S* (the cost of the standard horse feed product) cannot take on a negative value. So, from a practical point of view, we can think of the lower limit for the objective function coefficient of *S* as being zero. We can thus conclude that no matter how much the cost of the standard mix were to decrease, the optimal solution would not change. Even if Bluegrass Farms could obtain the standard horse feed product for free, the optimal solution would still specify a daily diet of 3.51 pounds of the standard horse feed product, 0.95 pound of the enriched oat product, and 1.54 pounds of the vitamin and mineral feed additive. However, any decrease in the per-unit cost of the standard feed would result in a decrease in the total cost for the optimal daily diet.

Note that the objective function coefficient values for S and A have no upper limit. Even if the cost of A were to increase, for example, from \$3.00 to \$13.00 per pound, the optimal solution would not change; the total cost of the solution, however, would increase by \$10 (the amount of the increase) times 1.541 or \$15.41. You must always keep in mind that the interpretations we have made using the sensitivity analysis information in the computer output are only appropriate if all other coefficients in the problem do not change. To consider simultaneous changes we must use the 100 percent rule or re-solve the problem after making the changes.

Linear programming has been successfully applied to a variety of applications involving food products and information. The Management Science in Action, Estimation of Food Nutrient Values, discusses how the Nutrition Coordinating Center of the University of Minnesota uses linear programming to help estimate the nutrient amounts in new food products.

MANAGEMENT SCIENCE IN ACTION

ESTIMATION OF FOOD NUTRIENT VALUES*

The Nutrition Coordinating Center (NCC) of the University of Minnesota maintains a food-composition database that is used by nutritionists and researchers throughout the world. Nutrient information provided by NCC is used to estimate the nutrient intake of individuals, to plan menus, to research links between diet and disease, and to meet regulatory requirements.

Nutrient intake calculations require data on an enormous number of food nutrient values. NCC's food composition database contains information on 93 different nutrients for each food product. With many new brand-name products introduced each year, NCC has the significant task of maintaining an accurate and timely database. The task is made more difficult by the fact that new brand-name products only provide data on a relatively small number of nutrients. Because of the high cost of chemically analyzing the new products, NCC uses a linear programming model to help estimate thousands of nutrient values per year.

The decision variables in the linear programming model are the amounts of each ingredient in a food product. The objective is to minimize the difference between the estimated nutrient values and the known nutrient values for the food product. Constraints are that ingredients must be in descending order by weight, ingredients must be within nutritionist-specified bounds, and the differences between the calculated nutrient values and the known nutrient values must be within specified tolerances.

In practice, an NCC nutritionist employs the linear programming model to derive estimates of the amounts of each ingredient in a new food product. Given these estimates, the nutritionist refines the estimates based on his or her knowledge of the product formulation and the food composition. Once the amounts of each ingredient are obtained, the amounts of each nutrient in the food product can be calculated. With approximately 1000 products evaluated each year, the time and cost savings provided by using linear programming to help estimate the nutrient values are significant.

*Based on Brian J. Westrich, Michael A. Altmann, and Sandra J. Potthoff, "Minnesota's Nutrition Coordinating Center Uses Mathematical Optimization to Estimate Food Nutrient Values," *Interfaces* (September/October 1998): 86–99.

3.5 THE ELECTRONIC COMMUNICATIONS PROBLEM

The Electronic Communications problem introduced in this section is a maximization problem involving four decision variables, two less-than-or-equal-to constraints, one equality constraint, and one greater-than-or-equal-to constraint. Our objective is to provide a summary of the process of formulating a mathematical model, using The Management Scientist to obtain an optimal solution, and interpreting the solution and sensitivity report information. In the next chapter we will continue to illustrate how linear programming can be applied by showing additional examples from the areas of marketing, finance, and production management. Your ability to formulate, solve, and interpret the solution to problems like the Electronic Communications problem is critical to understanding how more complex problems can be modeled using linear programming.

Electronic Communications manufactures portable radio systems that can be used for two-way communications. The company's new product, which has a range of up to 25 miles, is particularly suitable for use in a variety of business and personal applications. The distribution channels for the new radio are as follows:

1. Marine equipment distributors
2. Business equipment distributors
3. National chain of retail stores
4. Direct mail

Because of differing distribution and promotional costs, the profitability of the product will vary with the distribution channel. In addition, the advertising cost and the personal sales effort required will vary with the distribution channels. Table 3.2 summarizes the contribution to profit, advertising cost, and personal sales effort data pertaining to the Electronic Communications problem. The firm set the advertising budget at $5000, and a maximum of 1800 hours of salesforce time is available for allocation to the sales effort. Management also decided to produce exactly 600 units for the current production period. Finally, an ongoing contract with the national chain of retail stores requires that at least 150 units be distributed through this distribution channel.

Electronic Communications is now faced with the problem of establishing a strategy that will provide for the distribution of the radios in such a way that overall profitability of the new radio production will be maximized. Decisions must be made as to how many units should be allocated to each of the four distribution channels, as well as how to allocate the advertising budget and salesforce effort to each of the four distribution channels.

Problem Formulation

We will now write the objective function and the constraints for the Electronic Communications problem. For the objective function, we can write

Objective function: Maximize profit

TABLE 3.2 PROFIT, ADVERTISING COST, AND PERSONAL SALES TIME DATA FOR THE ELECTRONIC COMMUNICATIONS PROBLEM

Distribution Channel	Profit per Unit Sold ($)	Advertising Cost per Unit Sold ($)	Personal Sales Effort per Unit Sold (hours)
Marine distributors	90	10	2
Business distributors	84	8	3
National retail stores	70	9	3
Direct mail	60	15	None

Four constraints appear necessary for this problem. They are necessary because of (1) a limited advertising budget, (2) limited salesforce availability, (3) a production requirement, and (4) a retail stores distribution requirement.

Constraint 1 Advertising expenditures ≤ Budget
Constraint 2 Sales time used ≤ Time available
Constraint 3 Radios produced = Management requirement
Constraint 4 Retail distribution ≥ Contract requirement

These expressions provide descriptions of the objective function and the constraints. We are now ready to define the decision variables that will represent the decisions the manager must make.

For the Electronic Communications problem, we introduce the following four decision variables:

M = the number of units produced for the marine equipment distribution channel
B = the number of units produced for the business equipment distribution channel
R = the number of units produced for the national retail chain distribution channel
D = the number of units produced for the direct mail distribution channel

Using the data in Table 3.2, the objective function for maximizing the total contribution to profit associated with the radios can be written as follows:

$$\text{Max } 90M + 84B + 70R + 60D$$

Let us now develop a mathematical statement of the constraints for the problem. Because the advertising budget is set at \$5000, the constraint that limits the amount of advertising expenditure can be written as follows:

$$10M + 8B + 9R + 15D \leq 5000$$

Similarly, because the sales time is limited to 1800 hours, we obtain the constraint

$$2M + 3B + 3R \leq 1800$$

Management's decision to produce exactly 600 units during the current production period is expressed as

$$M + B + R + D = 600$$

Finally, to account for the fact that the number of units distributed by the national chain of retail stores must be at least 150, we add the constraint

$$R \geq 150$$

Combining all of the constraints with the nonnegativity requirements enables us to write the complete linear programming model for the Electronic Communications problem as follows:

$$
\begin{aligned}
\text{Max} \quad & 90M + 84B + 70R + 60D \\
\text{s.t.} \quad & \\
& 10M + 8B + 9R + 15D \le 5000 \quad \text{Advertising budget} \\
& 2M + 3B + 3R \le 1800 \quad \text{Salesforce availability} \\
& M + B + R + D = 600 \quad \text{Production level} \\
& R \ge 150 \quad \text{Retail stores requirement} \\
& M, B, R, D \ge 0
\end{aligned}
$$

Computer Solution and Interpretation

A portion of the output obtained using The Management Scientist to solve the Electronic Communications problem is shown in Figure 3.11. The Objective Function Value section shows that the optimal solution to the problem will provide a maximum profit of $48,450. The optimal values of the decision variables are given by $M = 25$, $B = 425$, $R = 150$, and $D = 0$. Thus, the optimal strategy for Electronic Communications is to concentrate on the business equipment distribution channel with $B = 425$ units. In addition, the firm should allocate 25 units to the marine distribution channel ($M = 25$) and meet its 150-unit commitment to the national retail chain store distribution channel ($R = 150$). With $D = 0$, the optimal solution indicates that the firm should not use the direct mail distribution channel.

Now consider the information contained in the Reduced Costs column. Recall that the reduced costs indicate how much each objective function coefficient would have to improve before the corresponding decision variable could assume a positive value in the optimal solution. As the computer output shows, the first three reduced costs are zero because the corresponding decision variables already have positive values in the optimal solution. However, the reduced cost of 45 for decision variable D tells us that the profit for the new radios distributed via the direct mail channel would have to increase from its current value of \$60 per unit to at least \$60 + \$45 = \$105 per unit before it would be profitable to use the direct mail distribution channel.

FIGURE 3.11 A PORTION OF THE MANAGEMENT SCIENTIST COMPUTER OUTPUT FOR THE ELECTRONIC COMMUNICATIONS PROBLEM

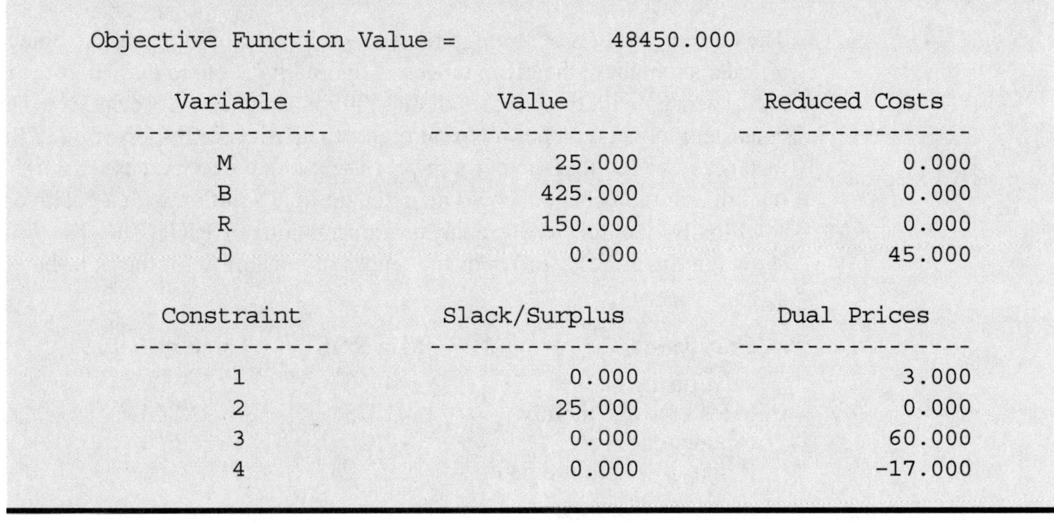

```
Objective Function Value =          48450.000

     Variable              Value             Reduced Costs
  --------------      ---------------      ----------------
         M                  25.000                 0.000
         B                 425.000                 0.000
         R                 150.000                 0.000
         D                   0.000                45.000

    Constraint          Slack/Surplus          Dual Prices
  --------------      ---------------      ----------------
         1                   0.000                 3.000
         2                  25.000                 0.000
         3                   0.000                60.000
         4                   0.000               -17.000
```

The computer output information for the slack/surplus variables and the dual prices is restated here:

Constraint Number	Constraint Name	Type of Constraint	Slack or Surplus	Dual Price
1	Advertising budget	$\leq$	0	3
2	Salesforce availability	$\leq$	25	0
3	Production level	$=$	0	60
4	Retail stores requirement	$\geq$	0	−17

The advertising budget constraint has a slack of zero, indicating that the entire budget of \$5000 has been used. The corresponding dual price of 3 tells us that an additional dollar added to the advertising budget will improve the objective function (increase the profit) by \$3. Thus, the possibility of increasing the advertising budget should be seriously considered by the firm. The slack of 25 hours for the salesforce availability constraint shows that the allocated 1800 hours of sales time are adequate to distribute the radios produced and that 25 hours of sales time will remain unused. Because the production level constraint is an equality constraint, the zero slack/surplus shown on the output is expected. However, the dual price of 60 associated with this constraint shows that if the firm were to consider increasing the production level for the radios, the value of the objective function, or profit, would improve at the rate of \$60 per radio produced. Finally, the surplus of zero associated with the retail store distribution channel commitment is a result of this constraint being binding. The negative dual price indicates that increasing the commitment from 150 to 151 units will actually decrease the profit by \$17. Thus, Electronic Communications may want to consider reducing its commitment to the retail store distribution channel. A *decrease* in the commitment will actually improve profit at the rate of \$17 per unit.

We now consider the additional sensitivity analysis information provided by the computer output shown in Figure 3.12. The ranges of optimality for the objective function coefficients are

$$84 \leq C_M < \text{No upper limit}$$
$$50 \leq C_B \leq 90$$
$$\text{No lower limit} < C_R \leq 87$$
$$\text{No lower limit} < C_D \leq 105$$

The current solution or strategy remains optimal, provided that the objective function coefficients remain in the given ranges of optimality. Note in particular the range of optimality associated with the direct mail distribution channel coefficient, C_D. This information is consistent with the earlier observation for the Reduced Costs portion of the output. In both instances, we see that the per-unit profit would have to increase to \$105 before the direct mail distribution channel could be in the optimal solution with a positive value.

Finally, the sensitivity analysis information on RIGHT HAND SIDE RANGES, as shown in Figure 3.12, provides the ranges of feasibility for the right-hand-side values.

Constraint	Min RHS	Current Value	Max RHS
Advertising budget	4950	5000	5850
Salesforce availability	1775	1800	No upper limit
Production level	515	600	603.57
Retail stores requirement	0	150	200

FIGURE 3.12 OBJECTIVE COEFFICIENT AND RIGHT-HAND-SIDE RANGES PROVIDED BY THE MANAGEMENT SCIENTIST FOR THE ELECTRONIC COMMUNICATIONS PROBLEM

```
OBJECTIVE COEFFICIENT RANGES

 Variable        Lower Limit      Current Value      Upper Limit
------------   ---------------   ---------------   ---------------
     M                 84.000            90.000    No Upper Limit
     B                 50.000            84.000            90.000
     R         No Lower Limit            70.000            87.000
     D         No Lower Limit            60.000           105.000

RIGHT HAND SIDE RANGES

 Constraint      Lower Limit      Current Value      Upper Limit
------------   ---------------   ---------------   ---------------
     1               4950.000          5000.000          5850.000
     2               1775.000          1800.000    No Upper Limit
     3                515.000           600.000           603.571
     4                  0.000           150.000           200.000
```

Try Problems 18 and 19 to test your ability at interpreting the computer output for problems involving more than two decision variables.

Several interpretations of these ranges are possible. In particular, recall that the dual price for the advertising budget enabled us to conclude that each \$1 increase in the budget would improve the profit by \$3. The range for the advertising budget shows that this statement about the value of increasing the budget is appropriate up to an advertising budget of \$5850. Increases above this level would not necessarily be beneficial. Also note that the dual price of -17 for the retail stores requirement suggested the desirability of reducing this commitment. The range of feasibility for this constraint shows that the commitment could be reduced to zero and the value of the reduction would be at the rate of \$17 per unit.

Again, the *sensitivity analysis* or *postoptimality analysis* provided by computer software packages for linear programming problems considers only *one change at a time,* with all other coefficients of the problem remaining as originally specified. As mentioned earlier, simultaneous changes can sometimes be analyzed without resolving the problem, provided that the cumulative changes are not large enough to violate the 100 percent rule.

Finally, recall that the complete solution to the Electronic Communications problem requested information not only on the number of units to be distributed over each channel, but also on the allocation of the advertising budget and the salesforce effort to each distribution channel. For the optimal solution of $M = 25$, $B = 425$, $R = 150$, and $D = 0$, we can simply evaluate each term in a given constraint to determine how much of the constraint resource is allocated to each distribution channel. For example, the advertising budget constraint of

$$10M + 8B + 9R + 15D \leq 5000$$

shows that $10M = 10(25) = \$250$, $8B = 8(425) = \$3400$, $9R = 9(150) = \$1350$, and $15D = 15(0) = \$0$. Thus, the advertising budget allocations are, respectively, \$250, \$3400, \$1350, and \$0 for each of the four distribution channels. Making similar calculations for the salesforce constraint results in the managerial summary of the Electronic Communications optimal solution as shown in Table 3.3.

TABLE 3.3 PROFIT-MAXIMIZING STRATEGY FOR THE ELECTRONIC COMMUNICATIONS PROBLEM

Distribution Channel	Volume	Advertising Allocation	Salesforce Allocation (hours)
Marine distributors	25	$ 250	50
Business distributors	425	3400	1275
National retail stores	150	1350	450
Direct mail	0	0	0
Totals	600	$5000	1775
Projected total profit = $48,450			

SUMMARY

We began the chapter with a discussion of sensitivity analysis: the study of how changes in the coefficients of a linear program affect the optimal solution. First, we showed how a graphical method can be used to determine how a change in one of the objective function coefficients or a change in the right-hand-side value for a constraint will affect the optimal solution to the problem. Because graphical sensitivity analysis is limited to linear programs with two decision variables, we showed how The Management Scientist can be used to produce a sensitivity report containing the same information.

We continued our discussion of problem formulation, sensitivity analysis, and the interpretation of the solution by introducing several modifications of the Par, Inc., problem. They involved an additional decision variable and several types of percentage, or ratio, constraints. Then, in order to provide additional practice in formulating and interpreting the solution for linear programs involving more than two decision variables, we introduced the Bluegrass Farms problem, a minimization problem involving three decision variables. In the last section we summarized all the work to date using the Electronic Communications problem, a maximization problem with four decision variables, two less-than-or-equal-to constraints, one equality constraint, and one greater-than-or-equal-to constraint.

The Management Science in Action, Tea Production and Distribution in India, illustrates the diversity of problems in which linear programming can be applied and the importance of sensitivity analysis. In the next chapter we will see many more applications of linear programming.

MANAGEMENT SCIENCE IN ACTION

TEA PRODUCTION AND DISTRIBUTION IN INDIA*

In India, one of the largest tea producers in the world, approximately $1 billion of tea packets and loose tea are sold. Duncan Industries Limited (DIL), the third largest producer of tea in the Indian tea market, sells about $37.5 million of tea, almost all of which is sold in packets.

DIL has 16 tea gardens, three blending units, six packing units, and 22 depots. Tea from the gardens is sent to blending units, which then mix various grades of tea to produce blends such as Sargam, Double Diamond, and Runglee Rungliot. The blended tea is transported to packing units, where it is placed in packets of different sizes and shapes to produce about 120 different product lines. For example, one line is Sargam tea packed in 500-gram cartons, another line is Double Diamond packed in 100-gram pouches, and so on. The tea is then shipped to the depots that supply 11,500 distributors through whom the needs of approximately 325,000 retailers are satisfied.

For the coming month, sales managers provide estimates of the demand for each line of tea at each depot. Using these estimates, a team of senior managers would determine the amounts of loose tea of each blend to ship to each packing unit, the quantity of each line of tea to be packed at each packing unit, and the amounts of packed tea of each line to be transported from each packing unit to the various depots. This process requires two to three days each month and often results in stockouts of lines in demand at specific depots.

Consequently, a linear programming model involving approximately 7000 decision variables and 1500 constraints was developed to minimize the company's freight cost while satisfying demand, supply, and all operational constraints. The model was tested on past data and showed that stockouts could be prevented at little or no additional cost. Moreover, the model was able to provide management with the ability to perform various what-if types of exercises, convincing them of the potential benefits of using management science techniques to support the decision-making process.

*Based on Nilotpal Chakravarti, "Tea Company Steeped in OR," *OR/MS Today* (April 2000).

GLOSSARY

Sensitivity analysis The study of how changes in the coefficients of a linear programming problem affect the optimal solution.

Range of optimality The range of values over which an objective function coefficient may vary without causing any change in the values of the decision variables in the optimal solution.

Dual price The improvement in the value of the objective function per unit increase in the right-hand side of a constraint.

Reduced cost The amount by which an objective function coefficient would have to improve (increase for a maximization problem, decrease for a minimization problem) before it would be possible for the corresponding variable to assume a positive value in the optimal solution.

Range of feasibility The range of values over which the dual price is applicable.

100 percent rule A rule indicating when simultaneous changes in two or more objective function coefficients will not cause a change in the optimal solution. It can also be applied to indicate when two or more right-hand-side changes will not cause a change in any of the dual prices.

Sunk cost A cost that is not affected by the decision made. It will be incurred no matter what values the decision variables assume.

Relevant cost A cost that depends upon the decision made. The amount of a relevant cost will vary depending on the values of the decision variables.

PROBLEMS

1. Recall the RMC problem (Chapter 2, Problem 21). Letting

$$F = \text{tons of fuel additive}$$
$$S = \text{tons of solvent base}$$

leads to the formulation

$$
\begin{aligned}
\text{Max} \quad & 40F + 30S \\
\text{s.t.} \quad & \\
& \tfrac{2}{5}F + \tfrac{1}{2}S \le 20 \quad \text{Material 1} \\
& \tfrac{1}{5}S \le 5 \quad \text{Material 2} \\
& \tfrac{3}{5}F + \tfrac{3}{10}S \le 21 \quad \text{Material 3} \\
& F, S \ge 0
\end{aligned}
$$

Use the graphical sensitivity analysis approach to determine the range of optimality for the objective function coefficients.

2. For Problem 1 use the graphical sensitivity approach to determine what happens if an additional 3 tons of material 3 become available. What is the corresponding dual price for the constraint?

3. Consider the following linear program:

$$
\begin{aligned}
\text{Max} \quad & 2x_1 + 3x_2 \\
\text{s.t.} \quad & \\
& x_1 + x_2 \le 10 \\
& 2x_1 + x_2 \ge 4 \\
& x_1 + 3x_2 \le 24 \\
& 2x_1 + x_2 \le 16 \\
& x_1, x_2 \ge 0
\end{aligned}
$$

a. Solve this problem using the graphical solution procedure.
b. Compute the range of optimality for the objective function coefficient of x_1.
c. Compute the range of optimality for the objective function coefficient of x_2.
d. Suppose the objective function coefficient of x_1 is increased from 2 to 2.5. What is the new optimal solution?
e. Suppose the objective function coefficient of x_2 is decreased from 3 to 1. What is the new optimal solution?

4. Refer to Problem 3. Compute the dual prices for constraints 1 and 2 and interpret them.

5. Consider the following linear program:

$$
\begin{aligned}
\text{Min} \quad & x_1 + x_2 \\
\text{s.t.} \quad & \\
& x_1 + 2x_2 \ge 7 \\
& 2x_1 + x_2 \ge 5 \\
& x_1 + 6x_2 \ge 11 \\
& x_1, x_2 \ge 0
\end{aligned}
$$

a. Solve this problem using the graphical solution procedure.
b. Compute the range of optimality for the objective function coefficient of x_1.
c. Compute the range of optimality for the objective function coefficient of x_2.
d. Suppose the objective function coefficient of x_1 is increased to 1.5. Find the new optimal solution.
e. Suppose the objective function coefficient of x_2 is decreased to $\tfrac{1}{3}$. Find the new optimal solution.

6. Refer to Problem 5. Compute and interpret the dual prices for the constraints.
7. Consider the following linear program:

$$\begin{aligned} \text{Max} \quad & 5x_1 + 7x_2 \\ \text{s.t.} \quad & \\ & 2x_1 + x_2 \geq 3 \\ & -x_1 + 5x_2 \geq 4 \\ & 2x_1 - 3x_2 \leq 6 \\ & 3x_1 + 2x_2 \leq 35 \\ & \tfrac{3}{7}x_1 + x_2 \leq 10 \\ & x_1, x_2 \geq 0 \end{aligned}$$

   a. Solve this problem using the graphical solution procedure.
   b. Compute the range of optimality for the objective function coefficient of x_1.
   c. Compute the range of optimality for the objective function coefficient of x_2.
   d. Suppose the objective function coefficient of x_1 is decreased to 2. What is the new optimal solution?
   e. Suppose the objective function coefficient of x_2 is increased to 10. What is the new optimal solution?

8. Refer to Problem 7. Suppose that the objective function coefficient of x_2 is reduced to 3.
   a. Re-solve using the graphical solution procedure.
   b. Compute the dual prices for constraints 2 and 3.

9. Refer again to Problem 3.
   a. Suppose the objective function coefficient of x_1 is increased to 3 and the objective function coefficient of x_2 is increased to 4. Find the new optimal solution.
   b. Suppose the objective function coefficient of x_1 is increased to 3 and the objective function coefficient of x_2 is decreased to 2. Find the new optimal solution.

10. Refer again to Problem 7.
   a. Suppose the objective function coefficient of x_1 is decreased to 4 and the objective function coefficient of x_2 is increased to 10. Find the new optimal solution.
   b. Suppose the objective function coefficient of x_1 is decreased to 4 and the objective function coefficient of x_2 is increased to 8. Find the new optimal solution.

11. Recall the Kelson Sporting Equipment problem (Chapter 2, Problem 22). Letting

$$\begin{aligned} R &= \text{number of regular gloves} \\ C &= \text{number of catcher's mitts} \end{aligned}$$

leads to the following formulation:

$$\begin{aligned} \text{Max} \quad & 5R + 8C \\ \text{s.t.} \quad & \\ & R + \tfrac{3}{2}C \leq 900 \quad \text{Cutting and sewing} \\ & \tfrac{1}{2}R + \tfrac{1}{3}C \leq 300 \quad \text{Finishing} \\ & \tfrac{1}{8}R + \tfrac{1}{4}C \leq 100 \quad \text{Packaging and shipping} \\ & R, C \geq 0 \end{aligned}$$

The computer solution obtained using The Management Scientist is shown in Figure 3.13.

FIGURE 3.13 THE MANAGEMENT SCIENTIST SOLUTION FOR THE KELSON SPORTING EQUIPMENT PROBLEM

```
Objective Function Value =              3700.00150

      Variable              Value               Reduced Costs
    --------------    ---------------       -----------------
            R              500.00150                  0.00000
            C              149.99925                  0.00000

     Constraint           Slack/Surplus          Dual Prices
    --------------    ---------------       -----------------
            1              174.99963                  0.00000
            2                0.00000                  2.99999
            3                0.00000                 28.00006

OBJECTIVE COEFFICIENT RANGES

  Variable       Lower Limit      Current Value      Upper Limit
 -----------   ---------------   ---------------   ---------------
      R             4.00000           5.00000          12.00012
      C             3.33330           8.00000          10.00000

RIGHT HAND SIDE RANGES

 Constraint      Lower Limit      Current Value      Upper Limit
 -----------   ---------------   ---------------   ---------------
      1           725.00037         900.00000     No Upper Limit
      2           133.33200         300.00000         400.00000
      3            75.00000         100.00000         134.99982
```

a. What is the optimal solution, and what is the value of the total profit contribution?
b. Which constraints are binding?
c. What are the dual prices for the resources? Interpret each.
d. If overtime can be scheduled in one of the departments, where would you recommend doing so?

12. Refer to the computer solution of the Kelson Sporting Equipment problem in Figure 3.13 (see Problem 11).
a. Compute the ranges of optimality for the objective function coefficients.
b. Interpret the ranges in part (a).
c. Interpret the range of feasibility for the right-hand sides.
d. How much will the value of the optimal solution improve if 20 extra hours of packaging and shipping time are made available?

13. Investment Advisors, Inc., is a brokerage firm that manages stock portfolios for a number of clients. A particular portfolio consists of U shares of U.S. Oil and H shares of Huber Steel. The annual return for U.S. Oil is \$3 per share and the annual return for Huber Steel is \$5 per share. U.S. oil sells for \$25 per share and Huber Steel sells for \$50 per share. The portfolio has \$80,000 to be invested. The portfolio risk index (0.50 per share of U.S. Oil and 0.25 per share of Huber Steel) has a maximum of 700. In addition, the portfolio is limited to a maximum of 1000 shares of U.S. Oil. The linear programming formation that will maximum the total annual return of the portfolio is as follows:

Max	$3U + 5H$	Maximize total annual return
s.t.		
	$25U + 50H \leq 80{,}000$	Funds available
	$0.50U + 0.25H \leq 700$	Risk maximum
	$1U \leq 1000$	U.S. Oil maximum
	$U, H \geq 0$	

The computer solution of this problem is shown in Figure 3.14.

a. What is the optimal solution, and what is the value of the total annual return?

b. Which constraints are binding? What is your interpretation of these constraints in terms of the problem?

c. What are the dual prices for the constraints? Interpret each.

d. Would it be beneficial to increase the maximum amount invested in U.S. Oil? Why or why not?

FIGURE 3.14 THE MANAGEMENT SCIENTIST SOLUTION FOR THE INVESTMENT ADVISORS PROBLEM

Objective Function Value = 8400.000

Variable	Value	Reduced Costs
U	800.000	0.000
H	1200.000	0.000

Constraint	Slack/Surplus	Dual Prices
1	0.000	0.093
2	0.000	1.333
3	200.000	0.000

OBJECTIVE COEFFICIENT RANGES

Variable	Lower Limit	Current Value	Upper Limit
U	2.500	3.000	10.000
H	1.500	5.000	6.000

RIGHT HAND SIDE RANGES

Constraint	Lower Limit	Current Value	Upper Limit
1	65000.000	80000.000	140000.000
2	400.000	700.000	775.000
3	800.000	1000.000	No Upper Limit

14. Refer to Figure 3.14, which shows the computer solution of Problem 13.

a. How much would the estimated per-share return for U.S. Oil have to increase before it would be beneficial to increase the investment in this stock?

b. How much would the estimated per-share return for Huber Steel have to decrease before it would be beneficial to reduce the investment in this stock?

c. How much would the total annual return be reduced if the U.S. Oil maximum were reduced to 900 shares?

15. Recall the Tom's, Inc., problem (Chapter 2, Problem 26). Letting

$$W = \text{jars of Western Foods Salsa}$$
$$M = \text{jars of Mexico City Salsa}$$

leads to the formulation:

$$\begin{aligned} \text{Max} \quad & 1W + 1.25M \\ \text{s.t.} \quad & \\ & 5W + 7M \leq 4480 \quad \text{Whole tomatoes} \\ & 3W + 1M \leq 2080 \quad \text{Tomato sauce} \\ & 2W + 2M \leq 1600 \quad \text{Tomato paste} \\ & W, M \geq 0 \end{aligned}$$

The Management Scientist solution is shown in Figure 3.15.

FIGURE 3.15 THE MANAGEMENT SCIENTIST SOLUTION FOR THE TOM'S, INC., PROBLEM

```
Objective Function Value =              860.000

   Variable                Value                Reduced Costs
 --------------       ---------------       -----------------
       W                   560.000                   0.000
       M                   240.000                   0.000

  Constraint           Slack/Surplus            Dual Prices
 --------------       ---------------       -----------------
       1                     0.000                   0.125
       2                   160.000                   0.000
       3                     0.000                   0.188

OBJECTIVE COEFFICIENT RANGES

  Variable      Lower Limit      Current Value      Upper Limit
 ------------  ---------------  ---------------  ---------------
     W               0.893             1.000             1.250
     M               1.000             1.250             1.400

RIGHT HAND SIDE RANGES

  Constraint    Lower Limit      Current Value      Upper Limit
 ------------  ---------------  ---------------  ---------------
     1            4320.000          4480.000          5600.000
     2            1920.000          2080.000    No Upper Limit
     3            1280.000          1600.000          1640.000
```

a. What is the optimal solution, and what are the optimal production quantities?
b. Specify the range of optimality for the objective function coefficients.
c. What are the dual prices for each constraint? Interpret each.
d. Identify the range of feasibility for each of the right-hand-side values.

16. Recall the Innis Investments problem (Chapter 2, Problem 37). Letting

S = units purchased in the stock fund
M = units purchased in the money market fund

leads to the following formulation:

$$\begin{aligned} \text{Min} \quad & 8S + 3M \\ \text{s.t.} \quad & \\ & 50S + 100M \leq 1{,}200{,}000 && \text{Funds available} \\ & 5S + 4M \geq 60{,}000 && \text{Annual income} \\ & M \geq 3000 && \text{Units in money market} \\ & S, M \geq 0 \end{aligned}$$

The computer solution is shown in Figure 3.16.

FIGURE 3.16 THE MANAGEMENT SCIENTIST SOLUTION FOR THE INNIS INVESTMENTS PROBLEM

```
Objective Function Value =              62000.000

     Variable              Value              Reduced Costs
  --------------      ---------------      -----------------
         S                 4000.000                  0.000
         M                10000.000                  0.000

     Constraint         Slack/Surplus           Dual Prices
  --------------      ---------------      -----------------
         1                    0.000                  0.057
         2                    0.000                 -2.167
         3                 7000.000                  0.000

OBJECTIVE COEFFICIENT RANGES

  Variable      Lower Limit       Current Value      Upper Limit
------------  ---------------    ---------------   ---------------
     S                 3.750             8.000      No Upper Limit
     M        No Lower Limit             3.000               6.400

RIGHT HAND SIDE RANGES

 Constraint     Lower Limit       Current Value      Upper Limit
------------  ---------------    ---------------   ---------------
     1            780000.000        1200000.000        1500000.000
     2             48000.000          60000.000         102000.000
     3        No Lower Limit           3000.000          10000.000
```

a. What is the optimal solution, and what is the minimum total risk?
b. Specify the range of optimality for the objective function coefficients.
c. How much annual income will be earned by the portfolio?
d. What is the rate of return for the portfolio?
e. What is the dual price for the funds available constraint?
f. What is the marginal rate of return on extra funds added to the portfolio?

17. Refer to Problem 16 and the computer solution shown in Figure 3.16.
a. Suppose the risk index for the stock fund (the value of C_S) increases from its current value of 8 to 12. How does the optimal solution change, if at all?
b. Suppose the risk index for the money market fund (the value of C_M) increases from its current value of 3 to 3.5. How does the optimal solution change, if at all?
c. Suppose C_S increases to 12 and C_M increases to 3.3. How does the optimal solution change, if at all?

18. Quality Air Conditioning manufactures three home air conditioners: an economy model, a standard model, and a deluxe model. The profits per unit are \$63, \$95, and \$135, respectively. The production requirements per unit are as follows:

	Number of Fans	Number of Cooling Coils	Manufacturing Time (hours)
Economy	1	1	8
Standard	1	2	12
Deluxe	1	4	14

For the coming production period, the company has 200 fan motors, 320 cooling coils and 2400 hours of manufacturing time available. How many economy models (E), standard models (S), and deluxe models (D) should the company produce in order to maximize profit? The linear programming model for the problem is as follows:

$$\text{Max} \quad 63E + 95S + 135D$$

s.t.

$$\begin{aligned} 1E + 1S + 1D &\leq 200 && \text{Fan motors} \\ 1E + 2S + 4D &\leq 320 && \text{Cooling coils} \\ 8E + 12S + 14D &\leq 2400 && \text{Manufacturing time} \\ E, S, D &\geq 0 \end{aligned}$$

The computer solution using The Management Scientist is shown in Figure 3.17.
a. What is the optimal solution, and what is the value of the objective function?
b. Which constraints are binding?
c. Which constraint shows extra capacity? How much?
d. If the profit for the deluxe model were increased to \$150 per unit, would the optimal solution change? Use the information in Figure 3.17 to answer this question.

19. Refer to the computer solution of Problem 18 in Figure 3.17.
a. Identify the range of optimality for each objective function coefficient.
b. Suppose the profit for the economy model is increased by \$6 per unit, the profit for the standard model is decreased by \$2 per unit, and the profit for the deluxe model is increased by \$4 per unit. What will the new optimal solution be?
c. Identify the range of feasibility for the right-hand-side values.
d. If the number of fan motors available for production is increased by 100, will the dual price for that constraint change? Explain.

FIGURE 3.17 THE MANAGEMENT SCIENTIST SOLUTION FOR THE QUALITY AIR CONDITIONING PROBLEM

```
Objective Function Value =          16440.000

     Variable              Value              Reduced Costs
  --------------      ---------------      -----------------
          E                 80.000                 0.000
          S                120.000                 0.000
          D                  0.000                24.000

    Constraint          Slack/Surplus          Dual Prices
  --------------      ---------------      -----------------
          1                  0.000                31.000
          2                  0.000                32.000
          3                320.000                 0.000

OBJECTIVE COEFFICIENT RANGES

  Variable        Lower Limit       Current Value      Upper Limit
 ------------   ---------------   ---------------   ---------------
       E                47.500            63.000            75.000
       S                87.000            95.000           126.000
       D        No Lower Limit           135.000           159.000

RIGHT HAND SIDE RANGES

  Constraint      Lower Limit       Current Value      Upper Limit
 ------------   ---------------   ---------------   ---------------
       1               160.000           200.000           280.000
       2               200.000           320.000           400.000
       3              2080.000          2400.000    No Upper Limit
```

20. Digital Controls, Inc. (DCI), manufactures two models of a radar gun used by police to monitor the speed of automobiles. Model A has an accuracy of plus or minus 1 mile per hour, whereas the smaller model B has an accuracy of plus or minus 3 miles per hour. For the next week, the company has orders for 100 units of model A and 150 units of model B. Although DCI purchases all the electronic components used in both models, the plastic cases for both models are manufactured at a DCI plant in Newark, New Jersey. Each model A case requires 4 minutes of injection-molding time and 6 minutes of assembly time. Each model B case requires 3 minutes of injection-molding time and 8 minutes of assembly time. For next week, the Newark plant has 600 minutes of injection-molding time available and 1080 minutes of assembly time available. The manufacturing cost is $10 per case for model A and $6 per case for model B. Depending upon demand and the time available at the Newark plant, DCI occasionally purchases cases for one or both models from an outside supplier in order to fill customer orders that could not be filled otherwise. The purchase cost is $14 for each model A case and $9 for each model B case. Management wants to develop a minimum-cost plan that will determine how many cases of each model should be produced at the Newark plant and how many cases of each model should be purchased. The following decision variables were used to formulate a linear programming model for this problem:

$$
\begin{aligned}
AM &= \text{number of cases of model A manufactured} \\
BM &= \text{number of cases of model B manufactured} \\
AP &= \text{number of cases of model A purchased} \\
BP &= \text{number of cases of model B purchased}
\end{aligned}
$$

The linear programming model that can be used to solve this problem is as follows:

$$
\begin{array}{llll}
\text{Min} & 10AM + 6BM + 14AP + 9BP & & \\
\text{s.t.} & & & \\
& 1AM + \quad\quad + 1AP + \quad\quad & = 100 & \text{Demand for model A} \\
& \quad\quad 1BM + \quad\quad\quad 1BP & = 150 & \text{Demand for model B} \\
& 4AM + 3BM & \leq 600 & \text{Injection-molding time} \\
& 6AM + 8BM & \leq 1080 & \text{Assembly time} \\
& AM, BM, AP, BP \geq 0 & &
\end{array}
$$

The computer solution developed using The Management Scientist is shown in Figure 3.18.

a. What is the optimal solution, and what is the optimal value of the objective function?
b. Which constraints are binding?
c. What are the dual prices? Interpret each.
d. If you could change the right-hand side of one constraint by one unit, which one would you choose? Why?

21. Refer to the computer solution of Problem 20 in Figure 3.18.

a. Interpret the ranges of optimality for the objective function coefficients.
b. Suppose that the manufacturing cost increases to \$11.20 per case for model A. What is the new optimal solution?
c. Suppose that the manufacturing cost increases to \$11.20 per case for model A and the manufacturing cost for model B decreases to \$5 per unit. Would the optimal solution change? Use the 100 percent rule and discuss.

22. Tucker Inc. produces high-quality suits and sport coats for men. Each suit requires 1.2 hours of cutting time and 0.7 hours of sewing time, uses 6 yards of material, and provides a profit contribution of \$190. Each sport coat requires 0.8 hours of cutting time and 0.6 hours of sewing time, uses 4 yards of material, and provides a profit contribution of \$150. For the coming week, 200 hours of cutting time, 180 hours of sewing time, and 1200 yards of fabric are available. Additional cutting and sewing time can be obtained by scheduling overtime for these operations. Each hour of overtime for the cutting operation increases the hourly cost by \$15, and each hour of overtime for the sewing operation increases the hourly cost by \$10. A maximum of 100 hours of overtime can be scheduled. Marketing requirements specify a minimum production of 100 suits and 75 sport coats. Let

$$
\begin{aligned}
S &= \text{number of suits produced} \\
SC &= \text{number of sport coats produced} \\
D1 &= \text{hours of overtime for the cutting operation} \\
D2 &= \text{hours of overtime for the sewing operation}
\end{aligned}
$$

FIGURE 3.18 THE MANAGEMENT SCIENTIST SOLUTION FOR THE DIGITAL CONTROLS, INC., PROBLEM

```
Objective Function Value =              2170.000

    Variable              Value              Reduced Costs
  --------------     ---------------      -----------------
       AM                  100.000                   0.000
       BM                   60.000                   0.000
       AP                    0.000                   1.750
       BP                   90.000                   0.000

   Constraint          Slack/Surplus           Dual Prices
  --------------     ---------------      -----------------
       1                     0.000                 -12.250
       2                     0.000                  -9.000
       3                    20.000                   0.000
       4                     0.000                   0.375

OBJECTIVE COEFFICIENT RANGES

  Variable       Lower Limit       Current Value       Upper Limit
------------   ---------------   ---------------   ---------------
     AM        No Lower Limit             10.000            11.750
     BM                 3.667              6.000             9.000
     AP                12.250             14.000    No Upper Limit
     BP                 6.000              9.000            11.333

RIGHT HAND SIDE RANGES

 Constraint      Lower Limit       Current Value       Upper Limit
------------   ---------------   ---------------   ---------------
     1                  0.000            100.000           111.429
     2                 60.000            150.000    No Upper Limit
     3                580.000            600.000    No Upper Limit
     4                600.000           1080.000          1133.333
```

The computer solution developed using The Management Scientist is shown in Figure 3.19.

a. What is the optimal solution, and what is the total profit? What is the plan for the use of overtime?
b. A price increase for suits is being considered that would result in a profit contribution of \$210 per suit. If this price increase is undertaken, how will the optimal solution change?
c. Discuss the need for additional material during the coming week. If a rush order for material can be placed at the usual price plus an extra \$8 per yard for handling, would you recommend the company consider placing a rush order for material? What is the maximum price Tucker would be willing to pay for an additional yard of material? How many additional yards of material should Tucker consider ordering?
d. Suppose the minimum production requirement for suits is lowered to 75. Would this change help or hurt profit? Explain.

FIGURE 3.19 THE MANAGEMENT SCIENTIST SOLUTION FOR THE TUCKER INC. PROBLEM

```
Objective Function Value =          40900.000

     Variable              Value              Reduced Costs
   --------------    ---------------    -----------------
          S                 100.000                0.000
          SC                150.000                0.000
          D1                 40.000                0.000
          D2                  0.000               10.000

    Constraint          Slack/Surplus          Dual Prices
   --------------    ---------------    -----------------
          1                   0.000               15.000
          2                  20.000                0.000
          3                   0.000               34.500
          4                  60.000                0.000
          5                   0.000              -35.000
          6                  75.000                0.000

OBJECTIVE COEFFICIENT RANGES

  Variable       Lower Limit       Current Value      Upper Limit
 ------------  ---------------   ---------------   ---------------
      S         No Lower Limit          190.000           225.000
      SC               126.667          150.000    No Upper Limit
      D1              -187.500          -15.000             0.000
      D2        No Lower Limit          -10.000             0.000

RIGHT HAND SIDE RANGES

  Constraint     Lower Limit       Current Value      Upper Limit
 ------------  ---------------   ---------------   ---------------
      1                140.000          200.000           240.000
      2                160.000          180.000    No Upper Limit
      3               1000.000         1200.000          1333.333
      4                 40.000          100.000    No Upper Limit
      5                  0.000          100.000           150.000
      6         No Lower Limit           75.000           150.000
```

23. Round Tree Manor is a hotel that has two types of rooms with three rental classes: Super Saver, Deluxe, and Business. The profit per night for each type of room and rental class is as follows:

		Rental Class		
		Super Saver	**Deluxe**	**Business**
Room	**Type I**	$30	$35	—
	Type II	$20	$30	$40

Type I rooms do not have Internet access and are not available for the Business rental class.

Round Tree's management makes a forecast of the demand by rental class for each night in the future. A linear programming model developed to maximize profit is used to determine how many reservations to accept for each rental class. The demand forecast for a particular night is 130 rentals in the Super Saver class, 60 rentals in the Deluxe class, and 50 rentals in the Business class. Round Tree has 100 Type I rooms and 120 Type II rooms.

a. Use linear programming to determine how many reservations to accept in each rental class and how the reservations should be allocated to room types. Is the demand by any rental class not satisfied? Explain.
b. How many reservations can be accommodated in each rental class?
c. Management is considering offering a free breakfast to anyone upgrading from a Super Saver reservation to Deluxe class. If the cost of the breakfast to Round Tree is $5, should this incentive be offered?
d. With a little work, an unused office area could be converted to a rental room. If the conversion cost is the same for both types of rooms, would you recommend converting the office to a Type I or a Type II room? Why?
e. Could the linear programming model be modified to plan for the allocation of rental demand for the next night? What information would be needed and how would the model change?

24. Adirondack Savings Bank (ASB) has $1 million in new funds that must be allocated to home loans, personal loans, and automobile loans. The annual rates of return for the three types of loans are 7% for home loans, 12% for personal loans, and 9% for automobile loans. The bank's planning committee decided that at least 40% of the new funds must be allocated to home loans. In addition, the planning committee specified that the amount allocated to personal loans cannot exceed 60% of the amount allocated to automobile loans.
 a. Formulate a linear programming model that can be used to determine the amount of funds ASB should allocate to each type of loan in order to maximize the total annual return for the new funds.
 b. How much should be allocated to each type of loan? What is the total annual return? What is the annual percentage return?
 c. If the interest rate on home loans increased to 9%, would the amount allocated to each type of loan change? Explain.
 d. Suppose the total amount of new funds available was increased by $10,000. What effect would this change have on the total annual return? Explain.
 e. Assume that ASB has the original $1 million in new funds available and that the planning committee agreed to relax by 1% the requirement that at least 40% of the new funds must be allocated to home loans. How much would the annual return change? How much would the annual percentage return change?

25. Better Products, Inc., manufactures three products on two machines. In a typical week, 40 hours are available on each machine. The profit contribution and production time in hours per unit follow:

Category	Product 1	Product 2	Product 3
Profit/unit	$30	$50	$20
Machine 1 time/unit	0.5	2.0	0.75
Machine 2 time/unit	1.0	1.0	0.5

Two operators are required for machine 1; thus, 2 hours of labor must be scheduled for each hour of machine 1 time. Only one operator is required for machine 2. A maximum of

100 labor-hours is available for assignment to the machines during the coming week. Other production requirements are that product 1 cannot account for more than 50% of the units produced and that product 3 must account for at least 20% of the units produced.

a. How many units of each product should be produced to maximize the total profit contribution? What is the projected weekly profit associated with your solution?
b. How many hours of production time will be scheduled on each machine?
c. What is the value of an additional hour of labor?
d. Assume that labor capacity can be increased to 120 hours. Would you be interested in using the additional 20 hours available for this resource? Develop the optimal product mix assuming the extra hours are made available.

26. Industrial Designs has been awarded a contract to design a label for a new wine produced by Lake View Winery. The company estimates that 150 hours will be required to complete the project. Three of the firm's graphics designers are available for assignment to this project: Lisa, a senior designer and team leader; David, a senior designer; and Sarah, a junior designer. Because Lisa has worked on several projects for Lake View Winery, management has specified that Lisa must be assigned at least 40% of the total number of hours that are assigned to the two senior designers. To provide label-designing experience, Sarah must be assigned at least 15% of the total project time. However, the number of hours assigned to Sarah must not exceed 25% of the total number of hours that are assigned to the two senior designers. Due to other project commitments, Lisa has a maximum of 50 hours available to work on this project. Hourly wage rates are $30 for Lisa, $25 for David, and $18 for Sarah.

a. Formulate a linear program that can be used to determine the number of hours each graphic designer should be assigned to the project in order to minimize total cost.
b. How many hours should each graphic designer be assigned to the project? What is the total cost?
c. Suppose Lisa could be assigned more than 50 hours. What effect would this change have on the optimal solution? Explain.
d. If Sarah were not required to work a minimum number of hours on this project, would the optimal solution change? Explain.

27. Vollmer Manufacturing makes three components for sale to refrigeration companies. The components are processed on two machines: a shaper and a grinder. The times (in minutes) required on each machine are as follows:

	Machine	
Component	**Shaper**	**Grinder**
1	6	4
2	4	5
3	4	2

The shaper is available for 120 hours, and the grinder is available for 110 hours. No more than 200 units of component 3 can be sold, but up to 1000 units of each of the other components can be sold. The company already has orders for 600 units of component 1 that must be satisfied. The profit contributions for components 1, 2, and 3 are $8, $6, and $9, respectively.

a. Formulate a linear programming model and solve for the recommended production quantities.
b. What are the ranges of optimality for the profit contributions of the three components? Interpret these ranges for company management.

c. What are the ranges of feasibility for the right-hand sides? Interpret these ranges for company management.
d. If more time could be made available on the grinder, how much would it be worth?
e. If more units of component 3 can be sold by reducing the sales price by $4, should the company reduce the price?

28. National Insurance Associates carries an investment portfolio of stocks, bonds, and other investment alternatives. Currently $200,000 of funds are available and must be considered for new investment opportunities. The four stock options National is considering and the relevant financial data are as follows:

	Stock			
	A	B	C	D
Price per share	$100	$50	$80	$40
Annual rate of return	0.12	0.08	0.06	0.10
Risk measure per dollar invested	0.10	0.07	0.05	0.08

The risk measure indicates the relative uncertainty associated with the stock in terms of its realizing the projected annual return; higher values indicate greater risk. The risk measures are provided by the firm's top financial advisor.

National's top management has stipulated the following investment guidelines: the annual rate of return for the portfolio must be at least 9% and no one stock can account for more than 50% of the total dollar investment.

a. Use linear programming to develop an investment portfolio that minimizes risk.
b. If the firm ignores risk and uses a maximum return-on-investment strategy, what is the investment portfolio?
c. What is the dollar difference between the portfolios in parts (a) and (b)? Why might the company prefer the solution developed in part (a)?

29. Georgia Cabinets manufactures kitchen cabinets that are sold to local dealers throughout the Southeast. The company has a large backlog of orders for oak and cherry cabinets and has decided to contract with three smaller cabinetmakers to do the final finishing operation. For the three cabinetmakers, the number of hours required to complete all the oak cabinets, the number of hours required to complete all the cherry cabinets, the number of hours available for the final finishing operation, and the cost per hour to perform the work are shown here.

	Cabinetmaker 1	Cabinetmaker 2	Cabinetmaker 3
Hours required to complete all the oak cabinets	50	42	30
Hours required to complete all the cherry cabinets	60	48	35
Hours available	40	30	35
Cost per hour	$36	$42	$55

For example, Cabinetmaker 1 estimates it will take 50 hours to complete all the oak cabinets and 60 hours to complete all the cherry cabinets. However, Cabinetmaker 1 only has

40 hours available for the final finishing operation. Thus, Cabinetmaker 1 can only complete 40/50 = 0.80 or 80% of the oak cabinets if it worked only on oak cabinets. Similarly, Cabinetmaker 1 can only complete 40/60 = 0.67 or 67% of the cherry cabinets if it worked only on cherry cabinets.

a. Formulate a linear programming model that can be used to determine the percentage of the oak cabinets and the percentage of the cherry cabinets that should be assigned to each of the three cabinetmakers in order to minimize the total cost of completing both projects.

b. Solve the model formulated in part (a). What percentage of the oak cabinets and what percentage of the cherry cabinets should be assigned to each cabinetmaker? What is the total cost of completing both projects?

c. If Cabinetmaker 1 has additional hours available, would the optimal solution change? Explain.

d. If Cabinetmaker 2 has additional hours available, would the optimal solution change? Explain.

e. Suppose Cabinetmaker 2 reduced its cost to $38 per hour. What effect would this change have on the optimal solution? Explain.

30. Benson Electronics manufactures three components used to produce cellular telephones and other communication devices. In a given production period, demand for the three components may exceed Benson's manufacturing capacity. In this case, the company meets demand by purchasing the components from another manufacturer at an increased cost per unit. Benson's manufacturing cost per unit and purchasing cost per unit for the three components are as follows:

Source	Component 1	Component 2	Component 3
Manufacture	$4.50	$5.00	$2.75
Purchase	$6.50	$8.80	$7.00

Manufacturing times in minutes per unit for Benson's three departments are as follows:

Department	Component 1	Component 2	Component 3
Production	2	3	4
Assembly	1	1.5	3
Testing and packaging	1.5	2	5

For instance, each unit of component 1 that Benson manufactures requires 2 minutes of production time, 1 minute of assembly time, and 1.5 minutes of testing and packaging time. For the next production period, Benson has capacities of 360 hours in the production department, 250 hours in the assembly department, and 300 hours in the testing and packaging department.

a. Formulate a linear programming model that can be used to determine how many units of each component to manufacture and how many units of each component to purchase. Assume that component demands that must be satisfied are 6000 units for component 1, 4000 units for component 2, and 3500 units for component 3. The objective is to minimize the total manufacturing and purchasing costs.

b. What is the optimal solution? How many units of each component should be manufactured and how many units of each component should be purchased?

c. Which departments are limiting Benson's manufacturing quantities? Use the dual price to determine the value of an *extra hour* in each of these departments.

d. Suppose that Benson had to obtain one additional unit of component 2. Discuss what the dual price for the component 2 constraint tells us about the cost to obtain the additional unit.

31. Golf Shafts, Inc. (GSI), produces graphite shafts for several manufacturers of golf clubs. Two GSI manufacturing facilities, one located in San Diego and the other in Tampa, have the capability to produce shafts in varying degrees of stiffness, ranging from regular models used primarily by average golfers to extra stiff models used primarily by low-handicap and professional golfers. GSI just received a contract for the production of 200,000 regular shafts and 75,000 stiff shafts. Both plants are currently producing shafts for previous orders, which means that neither plant has sufficient capacity by itself to fill the new order. The San Diego plant can produce up to a total of 120,000 shafts and the Tampa plant can produce up to a total of 180,000 shafts. Because of equipment differences at each of the plants and differing labor costs, the per-unit production costs vary as shown here:

	San Diego Cost	**Tampa Cost**
Regular shaft	\$5.25	\$4.95
Stiff shaft	\$5.45	\$5.70

a. Formulate a linear programming model to determine how GSI should schedule production for the new order in order to minimize the total production cost.

b. Solve the model that you developed in part (a).

c. Suppose that some of the previous orders at the Tampa plant could be rescheduled in order to free up additional capacity for the new order. Would this option be worthwhile? Explain.

d. Suppose that the cost to produce a stiff shaft in Tampa had been incorrectly computed, and that the correct cost is \$5.30 per shaft. What effect, if any, would this change have on the optimal solution developed in part (b)? What effect would it have on total production cost?

32. The Pfeiffer Company manages approximately \$15 million for clients. For each client, Pfeiffer chooses a mix of three investment vehicles: a growth stock fund, an income fund, and a money market fund. Each client has different investment objectives and different tolerances for risk. To accommodate these differences, Pfeiffer places limits on the percentage of each portfolio that may be invested in the three funds and assigns a portfolio risk index to each client.

Here's how the system works for Dennis Hartmann, one of Pfeiffer's clients. Based on an evaluation of Hartmann's risk tolerance, Pfeiffer has assigned Hartmann's portfolio a risk index of 0.05. Furthermore, to maintain diversity, the fraction of Hartmann's portfolio invested in the growth and income funds must be at least 10% for each, and at least 20% must be in the money market fund.

The risk ratings for the growth, income, and money market funds are 0.10, 0.05, and 0.01, respectively. A portfolio risk index is computed as a weighted average of the risk ratings for the three funds where the weights are the fraction of the portfolio invested in each of the funds. Hartmann has given Pfeiffer \$300,000 to manage. Pfeiffer is currently forecasting a yield of 20% on the growth fund, 10% on the income fund, and 6% on the money market fund.

a. Develop a linear programming model to determine the best mix of investments for Hartmann's portfolio.

b. Solve the model you developed in part (a).

c. How much may the yields on the three funds vary before it will be necessary for Pfeiffer to modify Hartmann's portfolio?

d. If Hartmann were more risk tolerant, how much of a yield increase could he expect? For instance, what if his portfolio risk index is increased to 0.06?

e. If Pfeiffer revised the yield estimate for the growth fund downward to 0.10, how would you recommend modifying Hartmann's portfolio?

f. What information must Pfeiffer maintain on each client in order to use this system to manage client portfolios?

g. On a weekly basis Pfeiffer revises the yield estimates for the three funds. Suppose Pfeiffer has 50 clients. Describe how you would envision Pfeiffer making weekly modifications in each client's portfolio and allocating the total funds managed among the three investment funds.

33. La Jolla Beverage Products is considering producing a wine cooler that would be a blend of a white wine, a rosé wine, and fruit juice. To meet taste specifications, the wine cooler must consist of at least 50% white wine, at least 20% and no more than 30% rosé, and exactly 20% fruit juice. La Jolla purchases the wine from local wineries and the fruit juice from a processing plant in San Francisco. For the current production period, 10,000 gallons of white wine and 8000 gallons of rosé wine can be purchased; there is no limit on the amount of fruit juice that can be ordered. The costs for the wine are $1.00 per gallon for the white and $1.50 per gallon for the rosé; the fruit juice can be purchased for $0.50 per gallon. La Jolla Beverage Products can sell all of the wine cooler they can produce for $2.50 per gallon.

a. Is the cost of the wine and fruit juice a sunk cost or a relevant cost in this situation? Explain.

b. Formulate a linear program to determine the blend of the three ingredients that will maximize the total profit contribution. Solve the linear program to determine the number of gallons of each ingredient La Jolla should purchase and the total profit contribution they will realize from this blend.

c. If La Jolla could obtain additional amounts of the white wine, should they do so? If so, how much should they be willing to pay for each additional gallon, and how many additional gallons would they want to purchase?

d. If La Jolla Beverage Products could obtain additional amounts of the rosé wine, should they do so? If so, how much should they be willing to pay for each additional gallon, and how many additional gallons would they want to purchase?

e. Interpret the dual price for the constraint corresponding to the requirement that the wine cooler must contain at least 50% white wine. What is your advice to management given this dual price?

f. Interpret the dual price for the constraint corresponding to the requirement that the wine cooler must contain exactly 20% fruit juice. What is your advice to management given this dual price?

34. The program manager for Channel 10 would like to determine the best way to allocate the time for the 11:00–11:30 evening news broadcast. Specifically, she would like to determine the number of minutes of broadcast time to devote to local news, national news, weather, and sports. Over the 30-minute broadcast, 10 minutes are set aside for advertising. The station's broadcast policy states that at least 15% of the time available should be devoted to local news coverage; the time devoted to local news or national news must be at least 50% of the total broadcast time; the time devoted to the weather segment must be less than or equal to the time devoted to the sports segment; the time devoted to the sports segment should be no longer than the total time spent on the local and national news; and at least 20% of the time should be devoted to the weather segment. The production costs per minute are $300 for local news, $200 for national news, $100 for weather, and $100 for sports.

a. Formulate and solve a linear program that can determine how the 20 available minutes should be used to minimize the total cost of producing the program.

b. Interpret the dual price for the constraint corresponding to the available time. What advice would you give the station manager given this dual price?

c. Interpret the dual price for the constraint corresponding to the requirement that at least 15% of the available time should be devoted to local coverage. What advice would you give the station manager given this dual price?

d. Interpret the dual price for the constraint corresponding to the requirement that the time devoted to the local and the national news must be at least 50% of the total broadcast time. What advice would you give the station manager given this dual price?

e. Interpret the dual price for the constraint corresponding to the requirement that the time devoted to the weather segment must be less than or equal to the time devoted to the sports segment. What advice would you give the station manager given this dual price?

35. Gulf Coast Electronics is ready to award contracts for printing their annual report. For the past several years, the four-color annual report has been printed by Johnson Printing and Lakeside Litho. A new firm, Benson Printing, has inquired into the possibility of doing a portion of the printing. The quality and service level provided by Lakeside Litho has been extremely high; in fact, only 0.5% of their reports have had to be discarded because of quality problems. Johnson Printing has also had a high quality level historically, producing an average of only 1% unacceptable reports. Because Gulf Coast Electronics lacks any experience with Benson Printing, they estimate their defective rate to be 10%. Gulf Coast would like to determine how many reports should be printed by each firm to obtain 75,000 acceptable-quality reports. To ensure that Benson Printing will receive some of the contract, management specified that the number of reports awarded to Benson Printing must be at least 10% of the volume given to Johnson Printing. In addition, the total volume assigned to Benson Printing, Johnson Printing, and Lakeside Litho should not exceed 30,000, 50,000, and 50,000 copies, respectively. Because of their long-term relationship with Lakeside Litho, management also specified that at least 30,000 reports should be awarded to Lakeside Litho. The cost per copy is $2.45 for Benson Printing, $2.50 for Johnson Printing, and $2.75 for Lakeside Litho.

a. Formulate and solve a linear program for determining how many copies should be assigned to each printing firm to minimize the total cost of obtaining 75,000 acceptable-quality reports.

b. Suppose that the quality level for Benson Printing is much better than estimated. What effect, if any, would this quality level have?

c. Suppose that management is willing to reconsider their requirement that Lakeside Litho be awarded at least 30,000 reports. What effect, if any, would this consideration have?

Case Problem 1 PRODUCT MIX

TJ's, Inc., makes three nut mixes for sale to grocery chains located in the Southeast. The three mixes, referred to as the Regular Mix, the Deluxe Mix, and the Holiday Mix, are made by mixing different percentages of five types of nuts.

In preparation for the fall season, TJ's has just purchased the following shipments of nuts at the prices shown:

Type of Nut	Shipment Amount (pounds)	Cost per Shipment ($)
Almond	6000	7500
Brazil	7500	7125
Filbert	7500	6750
Pecan	6000	7200
Walnut	7500	7875

The Regular Mix consists of 15% almonds, 25% Brazil nuts, 25% filberts, 10% pecans, and 25% walnuts. The Deluxe Mix consists of 20% of each type of nut, and the Holiday Mix consists of 25% almonds, 15% Brazil nuts, 15% filberts, 25% pecans, and 20% walnuts.

TJ's accountant analyzed the cost of packaging materials, sales price per pound, and so forth, and determined that the profit contribution per pound is $1.65 for the Regular Mix, $2.00 for the Deluxe Mix, and $2.25 for the Holiday Mix. These figures do not include the cost of specific types of nuts in the different mixes because that cost can vary greatly in the commodity markets.

Customer orders already received are summarized here:

Type of Mix	Orders (pounds)
Regular	10,000
Deluxe	3,000
Holiday	5,000

Because demand is running high, it is expected that TJ's will receive many more orders than can be satisfied.

TJ's is committed to using the available nuts to maximize profit over the fall season; nuts not used will be given to a local charity. Even if it is not profitable to do so, TJ's president indicated that the orders already received must be satisfied.

Managerial Report

Perform an analysis of TJ's product-mix problem, and prepare a report for TJ's president that summarizes your findings. Be sure to include information and analysis on the following:

1. The cost per pound of the nuts included in the Regular, Deluxe, and Holiday mixes
2. The optimal product mix and the total profit contribution
3. Recommendations regarding how the total profit contribution can be increased if additional quantities of nuts can be purchased
4. A recommendation as to whether TJ's should purchase an additional 1000 pounds of almonds for $1000 from a supplier who overbought
5. Recommendations on how profit contribution could be increased (if at all) if TJ's does not satisfy all existing orders

Case Problem 2 INVESTMENT STRATEGY

J. D. Williams, Inc., is an investment advisory firm that manages more than $120 million in funds for its numerous clients. The company uses an asset allocation model that recommends the portion of each client's portfolio to be invested in a growth stock fund, an income fund, and a money market fund. To maintain diversity in each client's portfolio, the firm places limits on the percentage of each portfolio that may be invested in each of the three funds. General guidelines indicate that the amount invested in the growth fund must be between 20% and 40% of the total portfolio value. Similar percentages for the other two funds stipulate that between 20% and 50% of the total portfolio value must be in the income fund and at least 30% of the total portfolio value must be in the money market fund.

In addition, the company attempts to assess the risk tolerance of each client and adjust the portfolio to meet the needs of the individual investor. For example, Williams just contracted with a new client who has $800,000 to invest. Based on an evaluation of the client's risk tolerance, Williams assigned a maximum risk index of 0.05 for the client. The firm's risk indicators show the risk of the growth fund at 0.10, the income fund at 0.07, and the money market fund at 0.01. An overall portfolio risk index is computed as a weighted average of the risk rating for the three funds where the weights are the fraction of the client's portfolio invested in each of the funds.

Additionally, Williams is currently forecasting annual yields of 18% for the growth fund, 12.5% for the income fund, and 7.5% for the money market fund. Based on the information provided, how should the new client be advised to allocate the $800,000 among the growth, income, and money market funds? Develop a linear programming model that will provide the maximum yield for the portfolio. Use your model to develop a managerial report.

Managerial Report

1. Recommend how much of the $800,000 should be invested in each of the three funds. What is the annual yield you anticipate for the investment recommendation?
2. Assume that the client's risk index could be increased to 0.055. How much would the yield increase and how would the investment recommendation change?
3. Refer again to the original situation where the client's risk index was assessed to be 0.05. How would your investment recommendation change if the annual yield for the growth fund were revised downward to 16% or even to 14%?
4. Assume that the client expressed some concern about having too much money in the growth fund. How would the original recommendation change if the amount invested in the growth fund is not allowed to exceed the amount invested in the income fund?
5. The asset allocation model you developed may be useful in modifying the portfolios for all of the firm's clients whenever the anticipated yields for the three funds are periodically revised. What is your recommendation as to whether use of this model is possible?

Case Problem 3 TRUCK LEASING STRATEGY

Reep Construction recently won a contract for the excavation and site preparation of a new rest area on the Pennsylvania Turnpike. In preparing his bid for the job, Bob Reep, founder and president of Reep Construction, estimated that it would take four months to perform the work and that 10, 12, 14, and 8 trucks would be needed in months 1 through 4, respectively.

The firm currently has 20 trucks of the type needed to perform the work on the new project. These trucks were obtained last year when Bob signed a long-term lease with PennState Leasing. Although most of these trucks are currently being used on existing jobs, Bob estimates that one truck will be available for use on the new project in month 1, two trucks will be available in month 2, three trucks will be available in month 3, and one truck will be available in month 4. Thus, to complete the project, Bob will have to lease additional trucks.

The long-term leasing contract with PennState has a monthly cost of $600 per truck. Reep Construction pays its truck drivers $20 an hour, and daily fuel costs are approximately $100 per truck. All maintenance costs are paid by PennState Leasing. For planning purposes, Bob estimates that each truck used on the new project will be operating eight hours a day, five days a week for approximately four weeks each month.

Bob does not believe that current business conditions justify committing the firm to additional long-term leases. In discussing the short-term leasing possibilities with PennState Leasing, Bob learned that he can obtain short-term leases of 1–4 months. Short-term leases differ from long-term leases in that the short-term leasing plans include the cost of both a truck and a driver. Maintenance costs for short-term leases also are paid by PennState Leasing. The following costs for each of the four months cover the lease of a truck and driver.

Length of Lease	Cost per Month ($)
1	4000
2	3700
3	3225
4	3040

Bob Reep would like to acquire a lease that would minimize the cost of meeting the monthly trucking requirements for his new project, but he also takes great pride in the fact that his company has never laid off employees. Bob is committed to maintaining his no-layoff policy; that is, he will use his own drivers even if costs are higher.

Managerial Report

Perform an analysis of Reep Construction's leasing problem and prepare a report for Bob Reep that summarizes your findings. Be sure to include information on and analysis of the following items.

1. The optimal leasing plan
2. The costs associated with the optimal leasing plan
3. The cost for Reep Construction to maintain its current policy of no layoffs

Appendix 3.1 SENSITIVITY ANALYSIS WITH EXCEL

In Appendix 2.3 we showed how Excel Solver can be used to solve a linear program by using it to solve the Par, Inc., problem. Let us now see how it can be used to provide sensitivity analysis.

When Excel Solver finds the optimal solution to a linear program, the **Solver Results** dialog box (see Figure 3.20) will appear on the screen. If only the solution is desired you simply click **OK.** To obtain the optimal solution and the sensitivity analysis output, you must select **Sensitivity** in the **Reports** box before clicking **OK;** the sensitivity report is created on another worksheet in the same Excel workbook. Using this procedure for the Par problem, we obtained the optimal solution shown in Figure 3.21 and the sensitivity report shown in Figure 3.22.

Interpretation of Excel Sensitivity Report

In the Adjustable Cells section of the Sensitivity Report, the column labeled Final Value contains the optimal values of the decision variables. For the Par, Inc., problem the optimal solution is 540 standard bags and 252 deluxe bags. Next, let us consider the values in the Reduced Cost column. In Excel, the value of a nonzero reduced cost indicates how much the value of the objective function would change* if the corresponding variable was increased by one unit. For the Par, Inc., problem, the reduced costs for both decision variables are zero; they are at their optimal values.

To the right of the Reduced Cost column in Figure 3.22, we find three columns labeled Objective Coefficient, Allowable Increase, and Allowable Decrease. Note that for the standard bag decision variable, the objective function coefficient value is 10, the allowable

*This definition of reduced cost is slightly different from (but equivalent to) the one in the glossary. Excel's solution algorithm permits variables in solution at their upper bound to have a nonzero reduced cost.

FIGURE 3.20 EXCEL SOLVER RESULTS DIALOG BOX

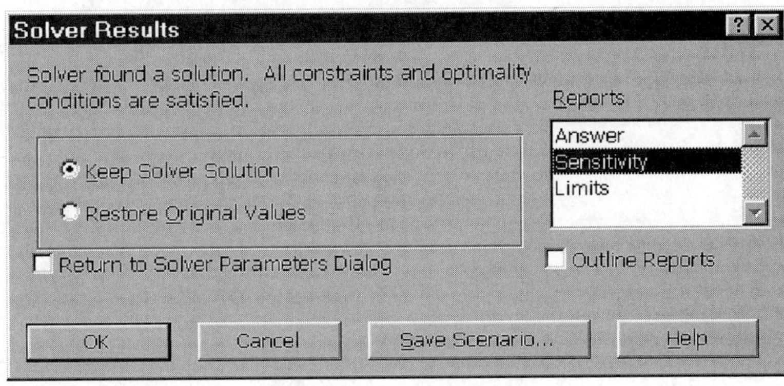

FIGURE 3.21 EXCEL SOLUTION FOR THE PAR, INC., PROBLEM

	A	B	C	D	E
1	**Par, Inc.**				
2					
3		**Production Time**			
4	**Operation**	**Standard**	**Deluxe**	**Time Available**	
5	Cutting and Dyeing	0.7	1	630	
6	Sewing	0.5	0.83333	600	
7	Finishing	1	0.66667	708	
8	Inspection and Packaging	0.1	0.25	135	
9	**Profit Per Bag**	10	9		
10					
11					
12	**Model**				
13					
14		**Decision Variables**			
15		**Standard**	**Deluxe**		
16	**Bags Produced**	539.99842	252.00110		
17					
18	**Maximize Total Profit**	7668			
19					
20	**Constraints**	**Hours Used (LHS)**		**Hours Available (RHS)**	
21	Cutting and Dyeing	630	<=	630	
22	Sewing	479.99929	<=	600	
23	Finishing	708	<=	708	
24	Inspection and Packaging	117.00012	<=	135	
25					

FIGURE 3.22 EXCEL SENSITIVITY REPORT FOR THE PAR, INC., PROBLEM

Adjustable Cells

Cell	Name	Final Value	Reduced Cost	Objective Coefficient	Allowable Increase	Allowable Decrease
$B$16	Bags Produced Standard	539.99842	0.00000	10	3.49993	3.7
$C$16	Bags Produced Deluxe	252.00110	0.00000	9	5.28571	2.3333

Constraints

Cell	Name	Final Value	Shadow Price	Constraint R.H. Side	Allowable Increase	Allowable Decrease
$B$21	Cutting and Dyeing Hours Used (LHS)	630	4.37496	630	52.36316	134.4
$B$22	Sewing Hours Used (LHS)	479.99929	0.00000	600	1E+30	120.00071
$B$23	Finishing Hours Used (LHS)	708	6.93753	708	192	127.9986
$B$24	Inspection and Packaging Hours Used (LHS)	117.00012	0.00000	135	1E+30	17.99988

increase is 3.5, and the allowable decrease is 3.7. Adding 3.5 to and subtracting 3.7 from the current coefficient of 10 provides the range of optimality for C_S.

$$6.3 \leq C_S \leq 13.5$$

Similarly, the range of optimality for C_D is

$$6.67 \leq C_D \leq 14.29$$

Next, consider the information in the Constraints section of the report. The entries in the Final Value column are the number of hours needed in each department to produce the optimal production quantities of 540 standard bags and 252 deluxe bags. Thus, at the optimal solution, 630 hours of cutting and dyeing time, 480 hours of sewing time, 708 hours of finishing time, and 117 hours of inspection and packaging time are required. The values in the Constraint R.H. Side column are just the original right-hand-side values: 630 hours of cutting and dyeing time, 600 hours of sewing time, 708 hours of finishing time, and 135 hours of inspection and packaging time. Note that for the Par, Inc., problem, the values of the slack variables for each constraint are simply the differences between the entries in the Constraint R.H. Side column and the corresponding entries in the Final Value column.

The entries in the Shadow Price column provide the *shadow price* for each constraint. The shadow price is the *change* in the value of the solution per unit increase in the right-hand side of the constraint. The Management Scientist uses the term *dual price* to describe the *improvement* in the value of the solution per unit increase in the right-hand side of a constraint. The shadow price and dual price are the same for maximization problems because improvement is an increase in value. For minimization problems, improvement is a decrease in value; thus, for minimization problems, the shadow price and dual price have opposite signs.

The last two columns of the Sensitivity Report contain the range of feasibility information for the constraint right-hand sides. For example, consider the cutting and dyeing constraint with an allowable increase value of 52.4 and an allowable decrease value of 134.4. The values in the Allowable Increase and Allowable Decrease columns indicate that the shadow price of $4.375 is valid for increases up to 52.4 hours and decreases to 134.4 hours. Thus, the shadow price of $4.375 is applicable for increases up to 630 + 52.4 = 682.4 and decreases down to 630 − 134.4 = 495.6 hours.

In summary, the range of feasibility information provides the limits where the shadow prices are applicable. For changes outside the range, the problem must be resolved to find the new optimal solution and the new shadow price.

CHAPTER 4

Linear Programming Applications

CONTENTS

Linear programming has proven to be one of the most successful quantitative approaches to decision making. Applications have been reported in almost every industry. Problems studied include production scheduling, media selection, financial planning, capital budgeting, transportation, distribution system design, product mix, staffing, and blending.

The wide variety of Management Science in Actions presented in Chapters 2 and 3 illustrated the use of linear programming as a flexible problem-solving tool. The Management Science in Action, A Marketing Planning Model at Marathon Oil Company, provides another example of the use of linear programming by showing how Marathon uses a large-scale linear programming model to solve a wide variety of planning problems. Later in the chapter other Management Science in Action features illustrate how GE Capital uses linear programming for optimal lease structuring, how the Kellogg Company uses a large-scale linear programming model to integrate production, distribution, and inventory planning, and how National Car Rental uses linear programming to manage rental car capacity, pricing, and reservations.

In this chapter we present a variety of applications, including several from the traditional business areas of marketing, finance, and operations management. Modeling, computer solution, and interpretation of output are emphasized. A mathematical model is developed for each problem studied, and solutions obtained using The Management Scientist are presented for most of the applications. In the chapter appendix we illustrate the use of Excel Solver by solving a financial planning problem.

MANAGEMENT SCIENCE IN ACTION

A MARKETING PLANNING MODEL AT MARATHON OIL COMPANY*

Marathon Oil Company has four refineries within the United States, operates 50 light products terminals, and has product demand at more than 95 locations. The Supply and Transportation Division faces the problem of determining which refinery should supply which terminal and, at the same time, determining which products should be transported via pipeline, barge, or tanker to minimize cost. Product demand must be satisfied, and the supply capability of each refinery must not be exceeded. To help solve this difficult problem, Marathon Oil developed a marketing planning model.

The marketing planning model is a large-scale linear programming model that takes into account sales not only at Marathon product terminals but also at all exchange locations. An exchange contract is an agreement with other oil product marketers that involves exchanging or trading Marathon's products for theirs at different locations. All pipelines, barges, and tankers within Marathon's marketing area are also represented in the linear programming model. The objective of the model is to minimize the cost of meeting a given demand structure, taking into account sales price, pipeline tariffs, exchange contract costs, product demand, terminal operating costs, refining costs, and product purchases.

The marketing planning model is used to solve a wide variety of planning problems that vary from evaluating gasoline blending economics to analyzing the economics of a new terminal or pipeline. With daily sales of about 10 million gallons of refined light product, a savings of even one-thousandth of a cent per gallon can result in significant long-term savings. At the same time, what may appear to be a savings in one area, such as refining or transportation, may actually add to overall costs when the effects are fully realized throughout the system. The marketing planning model allows a simultaneous examination of this total effect.

*Based on information provided by Robert W. Wernert at Marathon Oil Company, Findlay, Ohio.

4.1 MARKETING APPLICATIONS

Applications of linear programming in marketing are numerous. In this section we discuss applications in media selection and marketing research.

Media Selection

In Section 2.1 we provided some general guidelines for modeling linear programming problems. You may want to review Section 2.1 before proceeding with the linear programming applications in this chapter.

Media selection applications of linear programming are designed to help marketing managers allocate a fixed advertising budget to various advertising media. Potential media include newspapers, magazines, radio, television, and direct mail. In these applications, the objective is to maximize reach, frequency, and quality of exposure. Restrictions on the allowable allocation usually arise during consideration of company policy, contract requirements, and media availability. In the application that follows, we illustrate how a media selection problem might be formulated and solved using a linear programming model.

Relax-and-Enjoy Lake Development Corporation is developing a lakeside community at a privately owned lake. The primary market for the lakeside lots and homes includes all middle- and upper-income families within approximately 100 miles of the development. Relax-and-Enjoy employed the advertising firm of Boone, Phillips, and Jackson (BP&J) to design the promotional campaign.

After considering possible advertising media and the market to be covered, BP&J recommended that the first month's advertising be restricted to five media. At the end of the month, BP&J will then reevaluate its strategy based on the month's results. BP&J collected data on the number of potential customers reached, the cost per advertisement, the maximum number of times each medium is available, and the exposure quality rating for each of the five media. The quality rating is measured in terms of an exposure quality unit, a measure of the relative value of one advertisement in each of the media. This measure, based on BP&J's experience in the advertising business, takes into account factors such as audience demographics (age, income, and education of the audience reached), image presented, and quality of the advertisement. The information collected is presented in Table 4.1.

Relax-and-Enjoy provided BP&J with an advertising budget of $30,000 for the first month's campaign. In addition, Relax-and-Enjoy imposed the following restrictions on how BP&J may allocate these funds: At least 10 television commercials must be used, at least 50,000 potential customers must be reached, and no more than $18,000 may be spent on television advertisements. What advertising media selection plan should be recommended?

TABLE 4.1 ADVERTISING MEDIA ALTERNATIVES FOR THE RELAX-AND-ENJOY LAKE DEVELOPMENT CORPORATION

Advertising Media	Number of Potential Customers Reached	Cost ($) per Advertisement	Maximum Times Available per Month*	Exposure Quality Units
1. Daytime TV (1 min), station WKLA	1000	1500	15	65
2. Evening TV (30 sec), station WKLA	2000	3000	10	90
3. Daily newspaper (full page), *The Morning Journal*	1500	400	25	40
4. Sunday newspaper magazine (½ page color), *The Sunday Press*	2500	1000	4	60
5. Radio, 8:00 A.M. or 5:00 P.M. news (30 sec), station KNOP	300	100	30	20

*The maximum number of times the medium is available is either the maximum number of times the advertising medium occurs (e.g., four Sundays per month or the maximum number of times BP&J recommends that the medium be used).

The decision to be made is how many times to use each medium. We begin by defining the decision variables:

$$
\begin{aligned}
DTV &= \text{number of times daytime TV is used}\\
ETV &= \text{number of times evening TV is used}\\
DN &= \text{number of times daily newspaper is used}\\
SN &= \text{number of times Sunday newspaper is used}\\
R &= \text{number of times radio is used}
\end{aligned}
$$

The data on quality of exposure in Table 4.1 show that each daytime TV (DTV) advertisement is rated at 65 exposure quality units. Thus, an advertising plan with DTV advertisements will provide a total of $65DTV$ exposure quality units. Continuing with the data in Table 4.1, we find evening TV (ETV) rated at 90 exposure quality units, daily newspaper (DN) rated at 40 exposure quality units, Sunday newspaper (SN) rated at 60 exposure quality units, and radio (R) rated at 20 exposure quality units. With the objective of maximizing the total exposure quality units for the overall media selection plan, the objective function becomes

$$\text{Max} \quad 65DTV + 90ETV + 40DN + 60SN + 20R \qquad \text{Exposure quality}$$

Care must be taken to ensure the linear programming model accurately reflects the real problem. Always review your formulation thoroughly before attempting to solve the model.

We now formulate the constraints for the model from the information given:

$$
\begin{array}{llllll}
DTV & & & & & \le 15 \\
 & ETV & & & & \le 10 \\
 & & DN & & & < 25 \\
 & & & SN & & \le 4 \\
 & & & & R & \le 30 \\
1500DTV + & 3000ETV + & 400DN + & 1000SN + & 100R & \le 30{,}000 \\
DTV + & ETV & & & & \ge 10 \\
1500DTV + & 3000ETV & & & & \le 18{,}000 \\
1000DTV + & 2000ETV + & 1500DN + & 2500SN + & 300R & \ge 50{,}000 \\
DTV, ETV, DN, SN, R \ge 0 & & & & &
\end{array}
$$

(The first five constraints: Availability of media; $\le 30{,}000$: Budget; the next two: Television restrictions; $\ge 50{,}000$: Customers reached.)

Problem 1 provides practice at formulating a similar media selection model.

The optimal solution to this five-variable, nine-constraint linear programming model is shown in Figure 4.1; a summary is presented in Table 4.2.

The optimal solution calls for advertisements to be distributed among daytime TV, daily newspaper, Sunday newspaper, and radio. The maximum number of exposure quality units is 2370, and the total number of customers reached is 61,500. The Reduced Costs column in Figure 4.1 indicates that the number of exposure quality units for evening TV would have to increase by at least 65 before this media alternative could appear in the optimal solution. Note that the budget constraint (constraint 6) has a dual price of 0.060. Therefore, a \$1.00 increase in the advertising budget will lead to an increase of 0.06 exposure quality units. The dual price of -25.000 for constraint 7 indicates that reducing the number of television commercials by 1 will increase the exposure quality of the advertising plan by 25 units. Thus, Relax-and-Enjoy should consider reducing the requirement of having at least 10 television commercials.

More complex media selection models may include considerations such as the reduced exposure quality value for repeat media usage, cost discounts for repeat media usage, audience overlap by different media, and/or timing recommendations for the advertisements.

A possible shortcoming of this model is that, even if the exposure quality measure were not subject to error, it offers no guarantee that maximization of total exposure quality will lead to a maximization of profit or of sales (a common surrogate for profit). However, this issue is not a shortcoming of linear programming; rather, it is a shortcoming of the use of exposure quality as a criterion. If we could directly measure the effect of an advertisement on profit, we could use total profit as the objective to be maximized.

FIGURE 4.1 THE MANAGEMENT SCIENTIST SOLUTION FOR THE RELAX-AND-ENJOY LAKE DEVELOPMENT CORPORATION PROBLEM

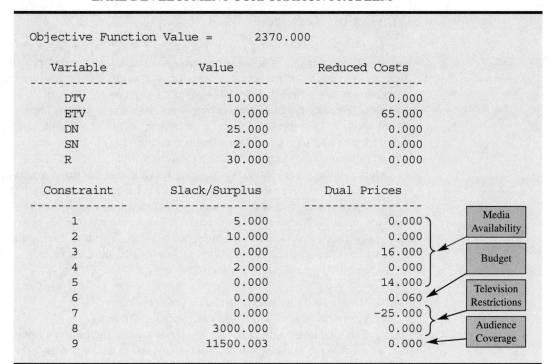

```
Objective Function Value =      2370.000

  Variable            Value           Reduced Costs
--------------   ---------------   -----------------
    DTV                10.000               0.000
    ETV                 0.000              65.000
    DN                 25.000               0.000
    SN                  2.000               0.000
    R                  30.000               0.000

 Constraint       Slack/Surplus        Dual Prices
--------------   ---------------   -----------------
     1                  5.000               0.000
     2                 10.000               0.000
     3                  0.000              16.000
     4                  2.000               0.000
     5                  0.000              14.000
     6                  0.000               0.060
     7                  0.000             -25.000
     8               3000.000               0.000
     9              11500.003               0.000
```


EXCELfile
Relax

TABLE 4.2 ADVERTISING PLAN FOR THE RELAX-AND-ENJOY LAKE DEVELOPMENT CORPORATION

Media	Frequency	Budget
Daytime TV	10	$15,000
Daily newspaper	25	10,000
Sunday newspaper	2	2,000
Radio	30	3,000
		$30,000

Exposure quality units = 2370
Total customers reached = 61,500

NOTES AND COMMENTS

1. The media selection model required subjective evaluations of the exposure quality for the media alternatives. Marketing managers may have substantial data concerning exposure quality, but the final coefficients used in the objective function may also include considerations based primarily on managerial judgment. Judgment is an acceptable way of obtaining input for a linear programming model.
2. The media selection model presented in this section uses exposure quality as the objective function and places a constraint on the number of customers reached. An alternative formulation of this problem would be to use the number of customers reached as the objective function and add a constraint indicating the minimum total exposure quality required for the media plan.

Marketing Research

An organization conducts marketing research to learn about consumer characteristics, attitudes, and preferences. Marketing research firms that specialize in providing such information often do the actual research for client organizations. Typical services offered by a marketing research firm include designing the study, conducting market surveys, analyzing the data collected, and providing summary reports and recommendations for the client. In the research design phase, targets or quotas may be established for the number and types of respondents to be surveyed. The marketing research firm's objective is to conduct the survey so as to meet the client's needs at a minimum cost.

Market Survey, Inc. (MSI), specializes in evaluating consumer reaction to new products, services, and advertising campaigns. A client firm requested MSI's assistance in ascertaining consumer reaction to a recently marketed household product. During meetings with the client, MSI agreed to conduct door-to-door personal interviews to obtain responses from households with children and households without children. In addition, MSI agreed to conduct both day and evening interviews. Specifically, the client's contract called for MSI to conduct 1000 interviews under the following quota guidelines.

1. Interview at least 400 households with children.
2. Interview at least 400 households without children.
3. The total number of households interviewed during the evening must be at least as great as the number of households interviewed during the day.
4. At least 40 percent of the interviews for households with children must be conducted during the evening.
5. At least 60 percent of the interviews for households without children must be conducted during the evening.

Because the interviews for households with children take additional interviewer time and because evening interviewers are paid more than daytime interviewers, the cost varies with the type of interview. Based on previous research studies, estimates of the interview costs are as follows:

	Interview Cost	
Household	**Day**	**Evening**
Children	\$20	\$25
No children	\$18	\$20

What is the household, time-of-day interview plan that will satisfy the contract requirements at a minimum total interviewing cost?

In formulating the linear programming model for the MSI problem, we utilize the following decision-variable notation:

DC = the number of daytime interviews of households with children
EC = the number of evening interviews of households with children
DNC = the number of daytime interviews of households without children
ENC = the number of evening interviews of households without children

We begin the linear programming model formulation by using the cost-per-interview data to develop the objective function:

$$\text{Min} \quad 20DC + 25EC + 18DNC + 20ENC$$

The constraint requiring a total of 1000 interviews is

$$DC + EC + DNC + ENC = 1000$$

The five specifications concerning the types of interviews are as follows.

- Households with children:

$$DC + EC \geq 400$$

- Households without children:

$$DNC + ENC \geq 400$$

- At least as many evening interviews as day interviews:

$$EC + ENC \geq DC + DNC$$

  The usual format for linear programming model formulation and computer input places all decision variables on the left side of the inequality and a constant (possibly zero) on the right side. Thus, we rewrite this constraint as

$$-DC + EC - DNC + ENC \geq 0$$

- At least 40 percent of interviews of households with children during the evening:

$$EC \geq 0.4(DC + EC) \quad \text{or} \quad -0.4DC + 0.6EC \geq 0$$

- At least 60 percent of interviews of households without children during the evening:

$$ENC \geq 0.6(DNC + ENC) \quad \text{or} \quad -0.6DNC + 0.4ENC \geq 0$$

When we add the nonnegativity requirements, the four-variable and six-constraint linear programming model becomes

$$
\begin{array}{llrl}
\text{Min} & 20DC + 25EC + 18DNC + 20ENC & & \\
\text{s.t.} & & & \\
& DC + EC + DNC + ENC = 1000 & & \text{Total interviews} \\
& DC + EC \geq 400 & & \text{Households with children} \\
& DNC + ENC \geq 400 & & \text{Households without children} \\
& -DC + EC - DNC + ENC \geq 0 & & \text{Evening interviews} \\
& -0.4DC + 0.6EC \geq 0 & & \text{Evening interviews in households with children} \\
& -0.6DNC + 0.4ENC \geq 0 & & \text{Evening interviews in households without children} \\
& DC, EC, DNC, ENC \geq 0 & &
\end{array}
$$

The optimal solution to this linear program is shown in Figure 4.2. The solution reveals that the minimum cost of $20,320 occurs with the following interview schedule.

	Number of Interviews		
Household	**Day**	**Evening**	**Totals**
Children	240	160	400
No children	240	360	600
Totals	480	520	1000

Hence, 480 interviews will be scheduled during the day and 520 during the evening. Households with children will be covered by 400 interviews, and households without children will be covered by 600 interviews.

Selected sensitivity analysis information from Figure 4.2 shows a dual price of −19.200 for constraint 1. In other words, the value of the optimal solution will get worse (the total interviewing cost will increase) by $19.20 if the number of interviews is increased from 1000 to 1001. Thus, $19.20 is the incremental cost of obtaining additional interviews. It also is the savings that could be realized by reducing the number of interviews from 1000 to 999.

The surplus variable, with a value of 200.000, for constraint 3 shows that 200 more households without children will be interviewed than required. Similarly, the surplus variable, with a value of 40.000, for constraint 4 shows that the number of evening interviews exceeds the number of daytime interviews by 40. The zero values for the surplus variables in constraints 5 and 6 indicate that the more expensive evening interviews are being held at a minimum. Indeed, the dual price of −5.000 for constraint 5 indicates that if one more household (with children) than the minimum requirement must be interviewed during the evening, the total interviewing cost will go up by $5.00. Similarly, constraint 6 shows that

FIGURE 4.2 THE MANAGEMENT SCIENTIST SOLUTION FOR THE MARKET SURVEY PROBLEM

```
Objective Function Value =          20320.000

     Variable              Value              Reduced Costs
  --------------     ---------------        -----------------
       DC                 240.000                   0.000
       EC                 160.000                   0.000
       DNC                240.000                   0.000
       ENC                360.000                   0.000

    Constraint         Slack/Surplus           Dual Prices
  --------------     ---------------        -----------------
       1                    0.000                 -19.200
       2                    0.000                  -2.800
       3                  200.000                   0.000
       4                   40.000                   0.000
       5                    0.000                  -5.000
       6                    0.000                  -2.000
```

requiring one more household (without children) to be interviewed during the evening will increase costs by $2.00.

4.2 FINANCIAL APPLICATIONS

In finance, linear programming can be applied in problem situations involving capital budgeting, make-or-buy decisions, asset allocation, portfolio selection, financial planning, and many more. In this section, we describe a portfolio selection problem and a problem involving funding of an early retirement program.

Portfolio Selection

Portfolio selection problems involve situations in which a financial manager must select specific investments—for example, stocks and bonds—from a variety of investment alternatives. Managers of mutual funds, credit unions, insurance companies, and banks frequently encounter this type of problem. The objective function for portfolio selection problems usually is maximization of expected return or minimization of risk. The constraints usually take the form of restrictions on the type of permissible investments, state laws, company policy, maximum permissible risk, and so on. Problems of this type have been formulated and solved using a variety of mathematical programming techniques. In this section we formulate and solve a portfolio selection problem as a linear program.

Consider the case of Welte Mutual Funds, Inc., located in New York City. Welte just obtained $100,000 by converting industrial bonds to cash and is now looking for other investment opportunities for these funds. Based on Welte's current investments, the firm's top financial analyst recommends that all new investments be made in the oil industry, steel industry, or in government bonds. Specifically, the analyst identified five investment opportunities and projected their annual rates of return. The investments and rates of return are shown in Table 4.3.

Management of Welte imposed the following investment guidelines.

1. Neither industry (oil or steel) should receive more than $50,000.
2. Government bonds should be at least 25 percent of the steel industry investments.
3. The investment in Pacific Oil, the high-return but high-risk investment, cannot be more than 60 percent of the total oil industry investment.

What portfolio recommendations—investments and amounts—should be made for the available $100,000? Given the objective of maximizing projected return subject to the budgetary and managerially imposed constraints, we can answer this question by formulating

TABLE 4.3 INVESTMENT OPPORTUNITIES FOR WELTE MUTUAL FUNDS

Investment	Projected Rate of Return (%)
Atlantic Oil	7.3
Pacific Oil	10.3
Midwest Steel	6.4
Huber Steel	7.5
Government bonds	4.5

and solving a linear programming model of the problem. The solution will provide investment recommendations for the management of Welte Mutual Funds.

Let

$$\begin{aligned} A &= \text{dollars invested in Atlantic Oil} \\ P &= \text{dollars invested in Pacific Oil} \\ M &= \text{dollars invested in Midwest Steel} \\ H &= \text{dollars invested in Huber Steel} \\ G &= \text{dollars invested in government bonds} \end{aligned}$$

Using the projected rates of return shown in Table 4.3, we write the objective function for maximizing the total return for the portfolio as

$$\text{Max} \quad 0.073A + 0.103P + 0.064M + 0.075H + 0.045G$$

The constraint specifying investment of the available \$100,000 is

$$A + P + M + H + G = 100{,}000$$

The requirements that neither the oil nor the steel industry should receive more than \$50,000 are

$$\begin{aligned} A + P &\le 50{,}000 \\ M + H &\le 50{,}000 \end{aligned}$$

The requirement that government bonds be at least 25 percent of the steel industry investment is expressed as

$$G \ge 0.25(M + H) \qquad \text{or} \qquad -0.25M - 0.25H + G \ge 0$$

Finally, the constraint that Pacific Oil cannot be more than 60 percent of the total oil industry investment is

$$P \le 0.60(A + P) \qquad \text{or} \qquad -0.60A + 0.40P \le 0$$

By adding the nonnegativity restrictions, we obtain the complete linear programming model for the Welte Mutual Funds investment problem:

$$\begin{array}{llllllll}
\text{Max} & 0.073A + 0.103P + 0.064M + 0.075H + 0.045G & & & & & & \\
\text{s.t.} & & & & & & & \\
& A + & P + & M + & H + & G = & 100{,}000 & \text{Available funds} \\
& A + & P & & & \le & 50{,}000 & \text{Oil industry maximum} \\
& & & M + & H & \le & 50{,}000 & \text{Steel industry maximum} \\
& & & -\ 0.25M - & 0.25H + & G \ge & 0 & \text{Government bonds minimum} \\
& -0.6A + & 0.4P & & & \le & 0 & \text{Pacific Oil restriction} \\
& A, P, M, H, G \ge 0 & & & & & &
\end{array}$$

FIGURE 4.3 THE MANAGEMENT SCIENTIST SOLUTION FOR THE WELTE MUTUAL FUNDS PROBLEM

```
Objective Function Value =          8000.000

     Variable              Value               Reduced Costs
  --------------      ---------------        ----------------
         A               20000.000                 0.000
         P               30000.000                 0.000
         M                   0.000                 0.011
         H               40000.000                 0.000
         G               10000.000                 0.000

    Constraint          Slack/Surplus           Dual Prices
  --------------      ---------------        ----------------
         1                   0.000                 0.069
         2                   0.000                 0.022
         3               10000.000                 0.000
         4                   0.000                -0.024
         5                   0.000                 0.030
```

EXCELfile
Welte

The optimal solution to this linear program is shown in Figure 4.3. Table 4.4 shows how the funds are divided among the securities. Note that the optimal solution indicates that the portfolio should be diversified among all the investment opportunities except Midwest Steel. The projected annual return for this portfolio is $8000, which is an overall return of 8 percent.

The optimal solution shows the dual price for constraint 3 is zero. The reason is that the steel industry maximum isn't a binding constraint; increases in the steel industry limit of $50,000 will not improve the value of the optimal solution. Indeed, the slack variable for this constraint shows that the current steel industry investment is $10,000 below its limit of $50,000. The dual prices for the other constraints are nonzero, indicating that these constraints are binding.

The dual price for the available funds constraint provides information on the rate of return from additional investment funds.

The dual price of 0.069 for constraint 1 shows that the value of the optimal solution can be increased by 0.069 if one more dollar can be made available for the portfolio investment. If more funds can be obtained at a cost of less than 6.9 percent, management should consider

TABLE 4.4 OPTIMAL PORTFOLIO SELECTION FOR WELTE MUTUAL FUNDS

Investment	Amount	Expected Annual Return
Atlantic Oil	$ 20,000	$1460
Pacific Oil	30,000	3090
Huber Steel	40,000	3000
Government bonds	10,000	450
Totals	$100,000	$8000

Expected annual return of $8000
Overall rate of return = 8%

obtaining them. However, if a return in excess of 6.9 percent can be obtained by investing funds elsewhere (other than in these five securities), management should question the wisdom of investing the entire \$100,000 in this portfolio.

Similar interpretations can be given to the other dual prices. Note that the dual price for constraint 4 is negative at −0.024. This result indicates that increasing the value on the right-hand side of the constraint by one unit can be expected to worsen the value of the optimal solution by 0.024. In terms of the optimal portfolio, then, if Welte invests one more dollar in government bonds (beyond the minimum requirement), the total return will decrease by \$0.024. To see why this decrease occurs, note again from the dual price for constraint 1 that the marginal return on the funds invested in the portfolio is 6.9 percent (the average return is 8 percent). The rate of return on government bonds is 4.5 percent. Thus, the cost of investing one more dollar in government bonds is the difference between the marginal return on the portfolio and the marginal return on government bonds: $6.9\% - 4.5\% = 2.4\%$.

Practice formulating a variation of the Welte problem by working Problem 9.

Note that the optimal solution shows that Midwest Steel should not be included in the portfolio ($M = 0$). The associated reduced cost for M of 0.011 tells us that the objective function coefficient for Midwest Steel would have to increase by 0.011 before considering the Midwest Steel investment alternative would be advisable. With such an increase the Midwest Steel return would be $0.064 + 0.011 = 0.075$, making this investment just as desirable as the currently used Huber Steel investment alternative.

Finally, a simple modification of the Welte linear programming model permits determining the fraction of available funds invested in each security. That is, we divide each of the right-hand-side values by 100,000. Then the optimal values for the variables will give the fraction of funds that should be invested in each security for a portfolio of any size.

NOTES AND COMMENTS

1. The optimal solution to the Welte Mutual Funds problem indicates that \$20,000 is to be spent on the Atlantic Oil stock. If Atlantic Oil sells for \$75 per share, we would have to purchase exactly 266⅔ shares in order to spend exactly \$20,000. The difficulty of purchasing fractional shares is usually handled by purchasing the largest possible integer number of shares with the allotted funds (e.g., 266 shares of Atlantic Oil). This approach guarantees that the budget constraint will not be violated. This approach, of course, introduces the possibility that the solution will no longer be optimal, but the danger is slight if a large number of securities are involved. In cases where the analyst believes that the decision variables *must* have integer values, the problem must be formulated as an integer linear programming model. Integer linear programming is the topic of Chapter 8.
2. Financial portfolio theory stresses obtaining a proper balance between risk and return. In the Welte problem, we explicitly considered return in the objective function. Risk is controlled by choosing constraints that ensure diversity among oil and steel stocks and a balance between government bonds and the steel industry investment.

Financial Planning

Linear programming has been used for a variety of financial planning applications. The Management Science in Action, Optimal Lease Structuring at GE Capital, describes how linear programming is used to optimize the structure of a leveraged lease.

Hewlitt Corporation established an early retirement program as part of its corporate restructuring. At the close of the voluntary sign-up period, 68 employees had elected early

MANAGEMENT SCIENCE IN ACTION

OPTIMAL LEASE STRUCTURING AT GE CAPITAL*

GE Capital is a $70 billion subsidiary of General Electric. As one of the nation's largest and most diverse financial services companies, GE Capital arranges leases in both domestic and international markets, including leases for telecommunications; data processing; construction; and fleets of cars, trucks, and commercial aircraft. To help allocate and schedule the rental and debt payments of a leveraged lease, GE Capital analysts developed an optimization model, which is available as an optional component of the company's lease analysis proprietary software.

Leveraged leases are designed to provide financing for assets with economic lives of at least five years, which require large capital outlays. A leveraged lease represents an agreement among the lessor (the owner of the asset), the lessee (the user of the asset), and the lender who provides a nonrecourse loan of 50% to 80% of the lessor's purchase price. In a nonrecourse loan, the lenders cannot turn to the lessor for repayment in the event of default. As the lessor in such arrangements, GE Capital is able to claim ownership and realize income tax benefits such as depreciation and interest deductions. These deductions usually produce tax losses during the early years of the lease, which reduces the total tax liability. Approximately 85% of all financial leases in the United States are leveraged leases.

In its simplest form, the leveraged lease structuring problem can be formulated as a linear program. The linear program models the after-tax cash flow for the lessor, taking into consideration rental receipts, borrowing and repaying of the loan, and income taxes. Constraints are formulated to ensure compliance with IRS guidelines and to enable customizing of leases to meet lessee and lessor requirements. The objective function can be entered in a custom fashion or selected from a predefined list. Typically, the objective is to minimize the lessee's cost, expressed as the net present value of rental payments, or to maximize the lessor's after-tax yield.

GE Capital developed an optimization approach that could be applied to single-investor lease structuring. In a study with the department most involved with these transactions, the optimization approach yielded substantial benefits. The approach helped GE Capital win some single-investor transactions ranging in size from $1 million to $20 million.

*Based on C. J. Litty, "Optimal Lease Structuring at GE Capital," *Interfaces* (May/June 1994): 34–45.

---

retirement. As a result of these early retirements, the company incurs the following obligations over the next eight years.

Year	1	2	3	4	5	6	7	8
Cash Requirement	430	210	222	231	240	195	225	255

The cash requirements (in thousands of dollars) are due at the beginning of each year.

The corporate treasurer must determine how much money must be set aside today to meet the eight yearly financial obligations as they come due. The financing plan for the retirement program includes investments in government bonds as well as savings. The investments in government bonds are limited to three choices:

Bond	**Price**	**Rate (%)**	**Years to Maturity**
1	$1150	8.875	5
2	1000	5.500	6
3	1350	11.750	7

The government bonds have a par value of \$1000, which means that even with different prices each bond pays \$1000 at maturity. The rates shown are based on the par value. For purposes of planning, the treasurer assumed that any funds not invested in bonds will be placed in savings and earn interest at an annual rate of 4 percent.

We define the decision variables as follows:

F = total dollars required to meet the retirement plan's eight-year obligation
B_1 = units of bond 1 purchased at the beginning of year 1
B_2 = units of bond 2 purchased at the beginning of year 1
B_3 = units of bond 3 purchased at the beginning of year 1
S_i = amount placed in savings at the beginning of year i for $i = 1, \ldots, 8$

The objective function is to minimize the total dollars needed to meet the retirement plan's eight-year obligation, or

$$\text{Min } F$$

A key feature of this type of financial planning problem is that a constraint must be formulated for each year of the planning horizon. In general, each constraint takes the form:

$$\begin{pmatrix}\text{Funds available at}\\\text{the beginning of the year}\end{pmatrix} - \begin{pmatrix}\text{Funds invested in bonds}\\\text{and placed in savings}\end{pmatrix} = \begin{pmatrix}\text{Cash obligation for}\\\text{the current year}\end{pmatrix}$$

The funds available at the beginning of year 1 is given by F. With a current price of \$1150 for bond 1 and investments expressed in thousands of dollars, the total investment for B_1 units of bond 1 would be $1.15B_1$. Similarly, the total investment in bonds 2 and 3 would be $1B_2$ and $1.35B_3$, respectively. The investment in savings for year 1 is S_1. Using these results and the first-year obligation of 430, we obtain the constraint for year 1:

$$F - 1.15B_1 - 1B_2 - 1.35B_3 - S_1 = 430 \quad \text{Year 1}$$

We do not consider future investments in bonds because the future price of bonds depends on interest rates and cannot be known in advance.

Investments in bonds can take place only in this first year, and the bonds will be held until maturity.

The funds available at the beginning of year 2 include the investment returns of 8.875 percent on the par value of bond 1, 5.5 percent on the par value of bond 2, 11.75 percent on the par value of bond 3, and 4 percent on savings. The new amount to be invested in savings for year 2 is S_2. With an obligation of 210, the constraint for year 2 is

$$0.08875B_1 + 0.055B_2 + 0.1175B_3 + 1.04S_1 - S_2 = 210 \quad \text{Year 2}$$

Similarly, the constraints for years 3 to 8 are

$$\begin{aligned}
0.08875B_1 + 0.055B_2 + 0.1175B_3 + 1.04S_2 - S_3 &= 222 \quad \text{Year 3}\\
0.08875B_1 + 0.055B_2 + 0.1175B_3 + 1.04S_3 - S_4 &= 231 \quad \text{Year 4}\\
0.08875B_1 + 0.055B_2 + 0.1175B_3 + 1.04S_4 - S_5 &= 240 \quad \text{Year 5}\\
1.08875B_1 + 0.055B_2 + 0.1175B_3 + 1.04S_5 - S_6 &= 195 \quad \text{Year 6}\\
1.055B_2 + 0.1175B_3 + 1.04S_6 - S_7 &= 225 \quad \text{Year 7}\\
1.1175B_3 + 1.04S_7 - S_8 &= 255 \quad \text{Year 8}
\end{aligned}$$

Note that the constraint for year 6 shows that funds available from bond 1 are $1.08875B_1$. The coefficient of 1.08875 reflects the fact that bond 1 matures at the end of year 5. As a result, the par value plus the interest from bond 1 during year 5 is available at the beginning of year 6. Also, because bond 1 matures in year 5 and becomes available for use at the beginning of year 6, the variable B_1 does not appear in the constraints for years 7 and 8. Note the similar interpretation for bond 2, which matures at the end of year 6 and has the par value plus interest available at the beginning of year 7. In addition, bond 3 matures at the end of year 7 and has the par value plus interest available at the beginning of year 8.

Finally, note that a variable S_8 appears in the constraint for year 8. The retirement fund obligation will be completed at the beginning of year 8, so we anticipate that S_8 will be zero and no funds will be put into savings. However, the formulation includes S_8 in the event that the bond income plus interest from the savings in year 7 exceed the 255 cash requirement for year 8. Thus, S_8 is a surplus variable that shows any funds remaining after the eight-year cash requirements have been satisfied.

The optimal solution to this 12-variable, 8-constraint linear program is shown in Figure 4.4. With an objective function value of 1728.79385, the total investment required to meet the retirement plan's eight-year obligation is $1,728,794. Using the current prices of

FIGURE 4.4 THE MANAGEMENT SCIENTIST SOLUTION FOR THE HEWLITT CORPORATION CASH REQUIREMENTS PROBLEM

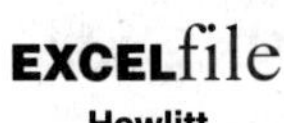
Hewlitt

```
Objective Function Value =          1728.79385

       Variable              Value              Reduced Costs
    --------------      ---------------      -----------------
            F              1728.79385                  0.00000
           B1               144.98815                  0.00000
           B2               187.85585                  0.00000
           B3               228.18792                  0.00000
           S1               636.14794                  0.00000
           S2               501.60571                  0.00000
           S3               349.68179                  0.00000
           S4               182.68091                  0.00000
           S5                 0.00000                  0.06403
           S6                 0.00000                  0.01261
           S7                 0.00000                  0.02132
           S8                 0.00000                  0.67084

      Constraint         Slack/Surplus            Dual Prices
    --------------      ---------------      -----------------
            1                 0.00000                 -1.00000
            2                 0.00000                 -0.96154
            3                 0.00000                 -0.92456
            4                 0.00000                 -0.88900
            5                 0.00000                 -0.85480
            6                 0.00000                 -0.76036
            7                 0.00000                 -0.71899
            8                 0.00000                 -0.67084
```

\$1150, \$1000, and \$1350 for each of the bonds respectively, we can summarize the initial investments in the three bonds as follows:

Bond	Units Purchased	Investment Amount
1	$B_1 = 144.988$	\$1150(144.988) = \$166,736
2	$B_2 = 187.856$	\$1000(187.856) = \$187,856
3	$B_3 = 228.188$	\$1350(228.188) = \$308,054

The solution also shows that \$636,148 (see S_1) will be placed in savings at the beginning of the first year. By starting with \$1,728,794, the company can make the specified bond and savings investments and have enough left over to meet the retirement program's first-year cash requirement of \$430,000.

The optimal solution in Figure 4.4 shows that the decision variables S_1, S_2, S_3, and S_4 all are greater than zero, indicating investments in savings are required in each of the first four years. However, interest from the bonds plus the bond maturity incomes will be sufficient to cover the retirement program's cash requirements in years 5 through 8.

In this application, the dual price can be thought of as the negative of the present value of each dollar in the cash requirement. For example, each dollar that must be paid in year 8 has a present value of \$0.67084.

The dual prices have an interesting interpretation in this application. Each right-hand-side value corresponds to the payment that must be made in that year. Note that the dual prices are negative, indicating that reducing the payment in any year would be beneficial because the total funds required for the retirement program's obligation would be less. Also note that the dual prices show that reductions are more beneficial in the early years, with decreasing benefits in subsequent years. As a result, Hewlitt would benefit by reducing cash requirements in the early years even if it had to make equivalently larger cash payments in later years.

NOTES AND COMMENTS

1. The optimal solution for the Hewlitt Corporation problem shows fractional numbers of government bonds at 144.988, 187.856, and 228.188 units, respectively. However, fractional bond units usually are not available. If we were conservative and rounded up to 145, 188, and 229 units, respectively, the total funds required for the eight-year retirement program obligation would be approximately \$1254 more than the total funds indicated by the objective function. Because of the magnitude of the funds involved, rounding up probably would provide a workable solution. If an optimal integer solution were required, the methods of integer linear programming covered in Chapter 8 would have to be used.
2. We implicitly assumed that interest from the government bonds is paid annually. Investments such as treasury notes actually provide interest payments every six months. In such cases, the model can be reformulated with six-month periods, with interest and/or cash payments occurring every six months.

4.3 PRODUCTION MANAGEMENT APPLICATIONS

Linear programming applications developed for production and operations management include scheduling, staffing, inventory control, and capacity planning. In this section we describe examples with make-or-buy decisions, production scheduling, and workforce assignments.

A Make-or-Buy Decision

We illustrate the use of a linear programming model to determine how much of each of several component parts a company should manufacture and how much it should purchase from an outside supplier. Such a decision is referred to as a make-or-buy decision.

The Janders Company markets various business and engineering products. Currently, Janders is preparing to introduce two new calculators: one for the business market called the Financial Manager and one for the engineering market called the Technician. Each calculator has three components: a base, an electronic cartridge, and a faceplate or top. The same base is used for both calculators, but the cartridges and tops are different. All components can be manufactured by the company or purchased from outside suppliers. The manufacturing costs and purchase prices for the components are summarized in Table 4.5.

Company forecasters indicate that 3000 Financial Manager calculators and 2000 Technician calculators will be needed. However, manufacturing capacity is limited. The company has 200 hours of regular manufacturing time and 50 hours of overtime that can be scheduled for the calculators. Overtime involves a premium at the additional cost of $9 per hour. Table 4.6 shows manufacturing times (in minutes) for the components.

The problem for Janders is to determine how many units of each component to manufacture and how many units of each component to purchase. We define the decision variables as follows:

$$\begin{aligned}
BM &= \text{number of bases manufactured} \\
BP &= \text{number of bases purchased} \\
FCM &= \text{number of Financial cartridges manufactured} \\
FCP &= \text{number of Financial cartridges purchased} \\
TCM &= \text{number of Technician cartridges manufactured} \\
TCP &= \text{number of Technician cartridges purchased} \\
FTM &= \text{number of Financial tops manufactured} \\
FTP &= \text{number of Financial tops purchased} \\
TTM &= \text{number of Technician tops manufactured} \\
TTP &= \text{number of Technician tops purchased}
\end{aligned}$$

TABLE 4.5 MANUFACTURING COSTS AND PURCHASE PRICES FOR JANDERS CALCULATOR COMPONENTS

	Cost per Unit	
Component	**Manufacture (regular time)**	**Purchase**
Base	$0.50	$0.60
Financial cartridge	$3.75	$4.00
Technician cartridge	$3.30	$3.90
Financial top	$0.60	$0.65
Technician top	$0.75	$0.78

TABLE 4.6 MANUFACTURING TIMES IN MINUTES PER UNIT FOR JANDERS CALCULATOR COMPONENTS

Component	Manufacturing Time
Base	1.0
Financial cartridge	3.0
Technician cartridge	2.5
Financial top	1.0
Technician top	1.5

One additional decision variable is needed to determine the hours of overtime that must be scheduled:

$$OT = \text{number of hours of overtime to be scheduled}$$

The objective function is to minimize the total cost, including manufacturing costs, purchase costs, and overtime costs. Using the cost-per-unit data in Table 4.5 and the overtime premium cost rate of \$9 per hour, we write the objective function as

$$\begin{aligned} \text{Min} \quad & 0.5BM + 0.6BP + 3.75FCM + 4FCP + 3.3TCM + 3.9TCP + 0.6FTM \\ & + 0.65FTP + 0.75TTM + 0.78TTP + 9OT \end{aligned}$$

The first five constraints specify the number of each component needed to satisfy the demand for 3000 Financial Manager calculators and 2000 Technician calculators. A total of 5000 base components are needed, with the number of other components depending on the demand for the particular calculator. The five demand constraints are

$$\begin{aligned} BM + BP &= 5000 \quad \text{Bases} \\ FCM + FCP &= 3000 \quad \text{Financial cartridges} \\ TCM + TCP &= 2000 \quad \text{Technician cartridges} \\ FTM + FTP &= 3000 \quad \text{Financial tops} \\ TTM + TTP &= 2000 \quad \text{Technician tops} \end{aligned}$$

Two constraints are needed to guarantee that manufacturing capacities for regular time and overtime cannot be exceeded. The first constraint limits overtime capacity to 50 hours, or

$$OT \leq 50$$

The same units of measure must be used for both the left-hand side and right-hand side of the constraint. In this case, minutes are used.

The second constraint states that the total manufacturing time required for all components must be less than or equal to the total manufacturing capacity, including regular time plus overtime. The manufacturing times for the components are expressed in minutes, so we state the total manufacturing capacity constraint in minutes, with the 200 hours of regular time capacity becoming 60(200) = 12,000 minutes. The actual overtime required is unknown at this point, so we write the overtime as $60OT$ minutes. Using the manufacturing times from Table 4.6, we have

$$BM + 3FCM + 2.5TCM + FTM + 1.5TTM \leq 12{,}000 + 60OT$$

Moving the decision variable for overtime to the left-hand side of the constraint provides the manufacturing capacity constraint:

$$BM + 3FCM + 2.5TCM + FTM + 1.5TTM - 60OT \leq 12{,}000$$

The complete formulation of the Janders make-or-buy problem with all decision variables greater than or equal to zero is

$$\begin{aligned}\text{Min}\quad & 0.5BM + 0.6BP + 3.75FCM + 4FCP + 3.3TCM + 3.9TCP \\ & + 0.6FTM + 0.65FTP + 0.75TTM + 0.78TTP + 9OT\end{aligned}$$

s.t.

$$\begin{array}{llllllrl}
BM & & & & & + BP = & 5000 & \text{Bases} \\
& FCM & & & & + FCP = & 3000 & \text{Financial cartridges} \\
& & TCM & & & + TCP = & 2000 & \text{Technician cartridges} \\
& & & FTM & & + FTP = & 3000 & \text{Financial tops} \\
& & & & TTM & + TTP = & 2000 & \text{Technician tops} \\
& & & & & OT \leq & 50 & \text{Overtime hours} \\
\multicolumn{6}{l}{BM + 3FCM + 2.5TCM + FTM + 1.5TTM - 60OT \leq} & 12{,}000 & \text{Manufacturing capacity}
\end{array}$$

The optimal solution to this 11-variable, 7-constraint linear program is shown in Figure 4.5. The optimal solution indicates that all 5000 bases (*BM*), 667 Financial Manager cartridges (*FCM*), and 2000 Technician cartridges (*TCM*) should be manufactured. The remaining 2333 Financial Manager cartridges (*FCP*), all the Financial Manager tops (*FTP*), and all Technician tops (*TTP*) should be purchased. No overtime manufacturing is necessary, and the total cost associated with the optimal make-or-buy plan is $24,443.33.

Sensitivity analysis provides some additional information about the unused overtime capacity. The Reduced Costs column shows that the overtime (*OT*) premium would have to decrease by $4 per hour before overtime production should be considered. That is, if the overtime premium is $9 − $4 = $5 or less, Janders may want to replace some of the purchased components with components manufactured on overtime.

The dual price for the manufacturing capacity constraint 7 is 0.083. This price indicates that an additional hour of manufacturing capacity is worth $0.083 per minute or ($0.083)(60) = $5 per hour. The right-hand-side range for constraint 7 shows that this conclusion is valid until the amount of regular time increases to 19,000 minutes, or 316.7 hours.

Sensitivity analysis also indicates that a change in prices charged by the outside suppliers can affect the optimal solution. For instance, the objective coefficient range for *BP* is 0.583 to no upper limit. If the purchase price for bases remains at $0.583 or more, the number of bases purchased (*BP*) will remain at zero. However, if the purchase price drops below $0.583, Janders should begin to purchase rather than manufacture the base component. Similar sensitivity analysis conclusions about the purchase price ranges can be drawn for the other components.

FIGURE 4.5 THE MANAGEMENT SCIENTIST SOLUTION FOR THE JANDERS MAKE-OR-BUY PROBLEM

EXCELfile
Janders

Objective Function Value = 24443.333

Variable	Value	Reduced Costs
BM	5000.000	0.000
BP	0.000	0.017
FCM	666.667	0.000
FCP	2333.333	0.000
TCM	2000.000	0.000
TCP	0.000	0.392
FTM	0.000	0.033
FTP	3000.000	0.000
TTM	0.000	0.095
TTP	2000.000	0.000
OT	0.000	4.000

Constraint	Slack/Surplus	Dual Prices
1	0.000	-0.583
2	0.000	-4.000
3	0.000	-3.508
4	0.000	-0.650
5	0.000	-0.780
6	50.000	0.000
7	0.000	0.083

OBJECTIVE COEFFICIENT RANGES

Variable	Lower Limit	Current Value	Upper Limit
BM	No Lower Limit	0.500	0.517
BP	0.583	0.600	No Upper Limit
FCM	3.700	3.750	3.850
FCP	3.900	4.000	4.050
TCM	No Lower Limit	3.300	3.692
TCP	3.508	3.900	No Upper Limit
FTM	0.567	0.600	No Upper Limit
FTP	No Lower Limit	0.650	0.683
TTM	0.655	0.750	No Upper Limit
TTP	No Lower Limit	0.780	0.875
OT	5.000	9.000	No Upper Limit

RIGHT HAND SIDE RANGES

Constraint	Lower Limit	Current Value	Upper Limit
1	0.000	5000.000	7000.000
2	666.667	3000.000	No Upper Limit
3	0.000	2000.000	2800.000
4	0.000	3000.000	No Upper Limit
5	0.000	2000.000	No Upper Limit
6	0.000	50.000	No Upper Limit
7	10000.000	12000.000	19000.000

NOTES AND COMMENTS

The proper interpretation of the dual price for manufacturing capacity (constraint 7) in the Janders problem is that an additional hour of manufacturing capacity is worth ($0.083)(60) = $5 per hour. Thus, the company should be willing to pay a premium of $5 per hour over and above the current regular time cost per hour, which is already included in the manufacturing cost of the product. Thus, if the regular time cost is $18 per hour, Janders should be willing to pay up to $18 + $5 = $23 per hour to obtain additional labor capacity.

Production Scheduling

One of the most important applications of linear programming deals with multiperiod planning such as production scheduling. The solution to a production scheduling problem enables the manager to establish an efficient low-cost production schedule for one or more products over several time periods (weeks or months). Essentially, a production scheduling problem can be viewed as a product-mix problem for each of several periods in the future. The manager must determine the production levels that will allow the company to meet product demand requirements, given limitations on production capacity, labor capacity, and storage space, while minimizing total production costs.

One advantage of using linear programming for production scheduling problems is that they recur. A production schedule must be established for the current month, then again for the next month, for the month after that, and so on. When looking at the problem each month, the production manager will find that, although demand for the products has changed, production times, production capacities, storage space limitations, and so on are roughly the same. Thus, the production manager is basically resolving the same problem handled in previous months, and a general linear programming model of the production scheduling procedure may be frequently applied. Once the model has been formulated, the manager can simply supply the data—demand, capacities, and so on—for the given production period and use the linear programming model repeatedly to develop the production schedule.

Let us consider the case of the Bollinger Electronics Company, which produces two different electronic components for a major airplane engine manufacturer. The airplane engine manufacturer notifies the Bollinger sales office each quarter of its monthly requirements for components for each of the next three months. The monthly requirements for the components may vary considerably, depending on the type of engine the airplane engine manufacturer is producing. The order shown in Table 4.7 has just been received for the next three-month period.

After the order is processed, a demand statement is sent to the production control department. The production control department must then develop a three-month production plan for the components. In arriving at the desired schedule, the production manager will want to identify the following:

1. Total production cost
2. Inventory holding cost
3. Change-in-production-level costs

In the remainder of this section, we show how to formulate a linear programming model of the production and inventory process for Bollinger Electronics to minimize the total cost.

To develop the model, we let x_{im} denote the production volume in units for product i in month m. Here $i = 1, 2$, and $m = 1, 2, 3$; $i = 1$ refers to component 322A, $i = 2$ refers to component 802B, $m = 1$ refers to April, $m = 2$ refers to May, and $m = 3$ refers to June. The

TABLE 4.7 THREE-MONTH DEMAND SCHEDULE FOR BOLLINGER ELECTRONICS COMPANY

Component	April	May	June
322A	1000	3000	5000
802B	1000	500	3000

purpose of the double subscript is to provide a more descriptive notation. We could simply use x_6 to represent the number of units of product 2 produced in month 3, but x_{23} is more descriptive, identifying directly the product and month represented by the variable.

If component 322A costs $20 per unit produced and component 802B costs $10 per unit produced, the total production cost part of the objective function is

$$\text{Total production cost} = 20x_{11} + 20x_{12} + 20x_{13} + 10x_{21} + 10x_{22} + 10x_{23}$$

Because the production cost per unit is the same each month, we don't need to include the production costs in the objective function; that is, regardless of the production schedule selected, the total production cost will remain the same. In other words, production costs are not relevant costs for the production scheduling decision under consideration. In cases in which the production cost per unit is expected to change each month, the variable production costs per unit per month must be included in the objective function. The solution for the Bollinger Electronics problem will be the same whether these costs are included, therefore we included them so that the value of the linear programming objective function will include all the costs associated with the problem.

To incorporate the relevant inventory holding costs into the model, we let s_{im} denote the inventory level for product i at the end of month m. Bollinger determined that on a monthly basis inventory holding costs are 1.5 percent of the cost of the product; that is, (0.015)($20) = $0.30 per unit for component 322A and (0.015)($10) = $0.15 per unit for component 802B. A common assumption made in using the linear programming approach to production scheduling is that monthly ending inventories are an acceptable approximation to the average inventory levels throughout the month. Making this assumption, we write the inventory holding cost portion of the objective function as

$$\text{Inventory holding cost} = 0.30s_{11} + 0.30s_{12} + 0.30s_{13} + 0.15s_{21} + 0.15s_{22} + 0.15s_{23}$$

To incorporate the costs of fluctuations in production levels from month to month, we need to define two additional variables:

I_m = increase in the total production level necessary during month m
D_m = decrease in the total production level necessary during month m

After estimating the effects of employee layoffs, turnovers, reassignment training costs, and other costs associated with fluctuating production levels, Bollinger estimates that the cost associated with increasing the production level for any month is $0.50 per unit increase. A similar cost associated with decreasing the production level for any month is $0.20 per unit. Thus, we write the third portion of the objective function as

$$\begin{aligned}\text{Change-in-production-level costs} = {} & 0.50I_1 + 0.50I_2 + 0.50I_3 \\ & + 0.20D_1 + 0.20D_2 + 0.20D_3\end{aligned}$$

Note that the cost associated with changes in production level is a function of the change in the total number of units produced in month m compared to the total number of units produced in month $m - 1$. In other production scheduling applications, fluctuations in production level might be measured in terms of machine hours or labor-hours required rather than in terms of the total number of units produced.

Combining all three costs, the complete objective function becomes

$$\begin{aligned}\text{Min} \quad & 20x_{11} + 20x_{12} + 20x_{13} + 10x_{21} + 10x_{22} + 10x_{23} + 0.30s_{11} \\ & + 0.30s_{12} + 0.30s_{13} + 0.15s_{21} + 0.50s_{22} + 0.15s_{23} + 0.50I_1 \\ & + 0.50I_2 + 0.50I_3 + 0.20D_1 + 0.20D_2 + 0.20D_3\end{aligned}$$

We now consider the constraints. First, we must guarantee that the schedule meets customer demand. Because the units shipped can come from the current month's production or from inventory carried over from previous months, the demand requirement takes the form

$$\begin{pmatrix}\text{Ending} \\ \text{inventory} \\ \text{from previous} \\ \text{month}\end{pmatrix} + \begin{pmatrix}\text{Current} \\ \text{production}\end{pmatrix} - \begin{pmatrix}\text{Ending} \\ \text{inventory} \\ \text{for this} \\ \text{month}\end{pmatrix} = \begin{pmatrix}\text{This month's} \\ \text{demand}\end{pmatrix}$$

Suppose that the inventories at the beginning of the three-month scheduling period were 500 units for component 322A and 200 units for component 802B. The demand for both products in the first month (April) was 1000 units, so the constraints for meeting demand in the first month become

$$\begin{aligned}500 + x_{11} - s_{11} &= 1000 \\ 200 + x_{21} - s_{21} &= 1000\end{aligned}$$

Moving the constants to the right-hand side, we have

$$\begin{aligned}x_{11} - s_{11} &= 500 \\ x_{21} - s_{21} &= 800\end{aligned}$$

Similarly, we need demand constraints for both products in the second and third months. We write them as follows.

Month 2

$$\begin{aligned}s_{11} + x_{12} - s_{12} &= 3000 \\ s_{21} + x_{22} - s_{22} &= 500\end{aligned}$$

Month 3

$$\begin{aligned}s_{12} + x_{13} - s_{13} &= 5000 \\ s_{22} + x_{23} - s_{23} &= 3000\end{aligned}$$

If the company specifies a minimum inventory level at the end of the three-month period of at least 400 units of component 322A and at least 200 units of component 802B, we can add the constraints

$$\begin{aligned}s_{13} &\geq 400 \\ s_{23} &\geq 200\end{aligned}$$

TABLE 4.8 MACHINE, LABOR, AND STORAGE CAPACITIES FOR BOLLINGER ELECTRONICS

Month	Machine Capacity (hours)	Labor Capacity (hours)	Storage Capacity (square feet)
April	400	300	10,000
May	500	300	10,000
June	600	300	10,000

Suppose that we have the additional information on machine, labor, and storage capacity shown in Table 4.8. Machine, labor, and storage space requirements are given in Table 4.9. To reflect these limitations, the following constraints are necessary.

Machine Capacity

$$0.10x_{11} + 0.08x_{21} \leq 400 \quad \text{Month 1}$$
$$0.10x_{12} + 0.08x_{22} \leq 500 \quad \text{Month 2}$$
$$0.10x_{13} + 0.08x_{23} \leq 600 \quad \text{Month 3}$$

Labor Capacity

$$0.05x_{11} + 0.07x_{21} \leq 300 \quad \text{Month 1}$$
$$0.05x_{12} + 0.07x_{22} \leq 300 \quad \text{Month 2}$$
$$0.05x_{13} + 0.07x_{23} \leq 300 \quad \text{Month 3}$$

Storage Capacity

$$2s_{11} + 3s_{21} \leq 10{,}000 \quad \text{Month 1}$$
$$2s_{12} + 3s_{22} \leq 10{,}000 \quad \text{Month 2}$$
$$2s_{13} + 3s_{23} \leq 10{,}000 \quad \text{Month 3}$$

One final set of constraints must be added to guarantee that I_m and D_m will reflect the increase or decrease in the total production level for month m. Suppose that the production levels for March, the month before the start of the current production scheduling period, had been 1500 units of component 322A and 1000 units of component 802B for a total production level of 1500 + 1000 = 2500 units. We can find the amount of the change in production for April from the relationship

$$\text{April production} - \text{March production} = \text{Change}$$

TABLE 4.9 MACHINE, LABOR, AND STORAGE REQUIREMENTS FOR COMPONENTS 322A AND 802B

Component	Machine (hours/unit)	Labor (hours/unit)	Storage (square feet/unit)
322A	0.10	0.05	2
802B	0.08	0.07	3

Using the April production variables, x_{11} and x_{21}, and the March production of 2500 units, we have

$$(x_{11} + x_{21}) - 2500 = \text{Change}$$

Note that the change can be positive or negative. A positive change reflects an increase in the total production level, and a negative change reflects a decrease in the total production level. We can use the increase in production for April, I_1, and the decrease in production for April, D_1, to specify the constraint for the change in total production for the month of April:

$$(x_{11} + x_{21}) - 2500 = I_1 - D_1$$

Of course, we cannot have an increase in production and a decrease in production during the same one-month period; thus, either, I_1 or D_1 will be zero. If April requires 3000 units of production, $I_1 = 500$ and $D_1 = 0$. If April requires 2200 units of production, $I_1 = 0$ and $D_1 = 300$. This approach of denoting the change in production level as the difference between two nonnegative variables, I_1 and D_1, permits both positive and negative changes in the total production level. If a single variable (say, c_m) had been used to represent the change in production level, only positive changes would be possible because of the nonnegativity requirement.

Using the same approach in May and June (always subtracting the previous month's total production from the current month's total production), we obtain the constraints for the second and third months of the production scheduling period:

$$(x_{12} + x_{22}) - (x_{11} + x_{21}) = I_2 - D_2$$
$$(x_{13} + x_{23}) - (x_{12} + x_{22}) = I_3 - D_3$$

Placing the variables on the left-hand side and the constants on the right-hand side yields the complete set of what are commonly referred to as production-smoothing constraints:

Problem 19 involves a production scheduling application with labor-smoothing constraints.

$$\begin{aligned} x_{11} + x_{21} \qquad\qquad\qquad\qquad\qquad\qquad - I_1 + D_1 &= 2500 \\ -x_{11} - x_{21} + x_{12} + x_{22} \qquad\qquad\qquad - I_2 + D_2 &= 0 \\ -x_{12} - x_{22} + x_{13} + x_{23} - I_3 + D_3 &= 0 \end{aligned}$$

Linear programming models for production scheduling are often very large. Thousands of decision variables and constraints are necessary when the problem involves numerous products, machines, and time periods. Data collection for large-scale models can be more time-consuming than either the formulation of the model or the development of the computer solution.

The initially rather small, two-product, three-month scheduling problem has now developed into an 18-variable, 20-constraint linear programming problem. Note that in this problem we were concerned only with one type of machine process, one type of labor, and one type of storage area. Actual production scheduling problems usually involve several machine types, several labor grades, and/or several storage areas, requiring large-scale linear programs. For instance, a problem involving 100 products over a 12-month period could have more than 1000 variables and constraints.

Figure 4.6 shows the optimal solution to the Bollinger Electronics production scheduling problem. Table 4.10 contains a portion of the managerial report based on the optimal solution.

Consider the monthly variation in the production and inventory schedule shown in Table 4.10. Recall that the inventory cost for component 802B is one-half the inventory cost for component 322A. Therefore, as might be expected, component 802B is produced heavily in the first month (April) and then held in inventory for the demand that will occur in future months. Component 322A tends to be produced when needed, and only small amounts are carried in inventory.

FIGURE 4.6 THE MANAGEMENT SCIENTIST SOLUTION FOR THE BOLLINGER ELECTRONICS PROBLEM

EXCELfile
Bollinger

Objective Function Value = 225295.000

Variable	Value	Reduced Costs
X11	500.000	0.000
X12	3200.000	0.000
X13	5200.000	0.000
X21	2500.000	0.000
X22	2000.000	0.000
X23	0.000	0.128
S11	0.000	0.172
S12	200.000	0.000
S13	400.000	0.000
S21	1700.000	0.000
S22	3200.000	0.000
S23	200.000	0.000
I1	500.000	0.000
I2	2200.000	0.000
I3	0.000	0.072
D1	0.000	0.700
D2	0.000	0.700
D3	0.000	0.628

Constraint	Slack/Surplus	Dual Prices
1	0.000	-20.000
2	0.000	-10.000
3	0.000	-20.128
4	0.000	-10.150
5	0.000	-20.428
6	0.000	-10.300
7	0.000	-20.728
8	0.000	-10.450
9	150.000	0.000
10	20.000	0.000
11	80.000	0.000
12	100.000	0.000
13	0.000	1.111
14	40.000	0.000
15	4900.000	0.000
16	0.000	0.000
17	8600.000	0.000
18	0.000	0.500
19	0.000	0.500
20	0.000	0.428

TABLE 4.10 MINIMUM COST PRODUCTION SCHEDULE INFORMATION FOR THE BOLLINGER ELECTRONICS PROBLEM

Activity	April	May	June
Production			
Component 322A	500	3200	5200
Component 802B	2500	2000	0
Totals	3000	5200	5200
Ending inventory			
Component 322A	0	200	400
Component 802B	1700	3200	200
Machine usage			
Scheduled hours	250	480	520
Slack capacity hours	150	20	80
Labor usage			
Scheduled hours	200	300	260
Slack capacity hours	100	0	40
Storage usage			
Scheduled storage	5100	10,000	1400
Slack capacity	4900	0	8600
Total production, inventory, and production-smoothing cost = $225,295			

The costs of increasing and decreasing the total production volume tend to smooth the monthly variations. In fact, the minimum-cost schedule calls for a 500-unit increase in total production in April and a 2200-unit increase in total production in May. The May production level of 5200 units is then maintained during June.

The machine usage section of the report shows ample machine capacity in all three months. However, labor capacity is at full utilization (slack = 0 for constraint 13 in Figure 4.6) in the month of May. The dual price shows that an additional hour of labor capacity in May will improve the value of the optimal solution (lower cost) by approximately $1.11.

A linear programming model of a two-product, three-month production system can provide valuable information in terms of identifying a minimum-cost production schedule. In larger production systems, where the number of variables and constraints is too large to track manually, linear programming models can provide a significant advantage in developing cost-saving production schedules. The Management Science in Action, Optimizing Production, Inventory, and Distribution at the Kellogg Company, illustrates the use of a large-scale multiperiod linear program for production planning and distribution.

MANAGEMENT SCIENCE IN ACTION

OPTIMIZING PRODUCTION, INVENTORY, AND DISTRIBUTION AT THE KELLOGG COMPANY*

The Kellogg Company is the largest cereal producer in the world and a leading producer of convenience foods, such as Kellogg's Pop-Tarts and Nutri-Grain cereal bars. Kellogg produces more than 40 different cereals at plants in 19 countries, on six continents. The company markets its

(continued)

products in more than 160 countries and employs more than 15,600 people in its worldwide organization. In the cereal business alone, Kellogg coordinates the production of about 80 products using a total of approximately 90 production lines and 180 packaging lines.

Kellogg has a long history of using linear programming for production planning and distribution. The Kellogg Planning System (KPS) is a large-scale, multiperiod linear program. The operational version of KPS makes production, packaging, inventory, and distribution decisions on a weekly basis. The primary objective of the system is to minimize the total cost of meeting estimated demand; constraints involve processing line capacities, packaging line capacities, and satisfying safety stock requirements.

A tactical version of KPS helps to establish plant budgets and make capacity-expansion and consolidation decisions on a monthly basis. The tactical version was recently used to guide a consolidation of production capacity that resulted in projected savings of $35 to $40 million per year. Because of the success Kellogg has had using KPS in their North American operations, the company is now introducing KPS into Latin America, and is studying the development of a global KPS model.

*Based on G. Brown, J. Keegan, B. Vigus, and K. Wood, "The Kellogg Company Optimizes Production, Inventory, and Distribution," *Interfaces* (November/December 2001): 1–15.

Workforce Assignment

Workforce assignment problems frequently occur when production managers must make decisions involving staffing requirements for a given planning period. Workforce assignments often have some flexibility, and at least some personnel can be assigned to more than one department or work center. Such is the case when employees have been cross-trained on two or more jobs or, for instance, when sales personnel can be transferred between stores. In the following application, we show how linear programming can be used to determine not only an optimal product mix, but also an optimal workforce assignment.

McCormick Manufacturing Company produces two products with contributions to profit per unit of $10 and $9, respectively. The labor requirements per unit produced and the total hours of labor available from personnel assigned to each of four departments are shown in Table 4.11. Assuming that the number of hours available in each department is fixed, we can formulate McCormick's problem as a standard product-mix linear program with the following decision variables:

$$P_1 = \text{units of product 1}$$
$$P_2 = \text{units of product 2}$$

TABLE 4.11 DEPARTMENTAL LABOR-HOURS PER UNIT AND TOTAL HOURS AVAILABLE FOR THE McCORMICK MANUFACTURING COMPANY

	Labor-Hours per Unit		
Department	**Product 1**	**Product 2**	**Total Hours Available**
1	0.65	0.95	6500
2	0.45	0.85	6000
3	1.00	0.70	7000
4	0.15	0.30	1400

The linear program is

$$
\begin{aligned}
\text{Max} \quad & 10P_1 + 9P_2 \\
\text{s.t.} \quad & \\
& 0.65P_1 + 0.95P_2 \le 6500 \\
& 0.45P_1 + 0.85P_2 \le 6000 \\
& 1.00P_1 + 0.70P_2 \le 7000 \\
& 0.15P_1 + 0.30P_2 \le 1400 \\
& P_1, P_2 \ge 0
\end{aligned}
$$

The optimal solution to the linear programming model is shown in Figure 4.7. After rounding, it calls for 5744 units of product 1, 1795 units of product 2, and a total profit of \$73,590. With this optimal solution, departments 3 and 4 are operating at capacity, and departments 1 and 2 have a slack of approximately 1062 and 1890 hours, respectively. We would anticipate that the product mix would change and that the total profit would increase if the workforce assignment could be revised so that the slack, or unused hours, in departments 1 and 2 could be transferred to the departments currently working at capacity. However, the production manager may be uncertain as to how the workforce should be reallocated among the four departments. Let us expand the linear programming model to include decision variables that will help determine the optimal workforce assignment in addition to the profit-maximizing product mix.

Suppose that McCormick has a cross-training program that enables some employees to be transferred between departments. By taking advantage of the cross-training skills, a limited number of employees and labor-hours may be transferred from one department to another. For example, suppose that the cross-training permits transfers as shown in Table 4.12. Row 1 of this table shows that some employees assigned to department 1 have cross-training skills that permit them to be transferred to department 2 or 3. The right-hand column shows that, for the current production planning period, a maximum of 400 hours can

FIGURE 4.7 THE MANAGEMENT SCIENTIST SOLUTION FOR THE McCORMICK MANUFACTURING COMPANY PROBLEM WITH NO WORKFORCE TRANSFERS PERMITTED

```
Objective Function Value =              73589.744

     Variable             Value              Reduced Costs
  --------------     ---------------      -----------------
        P1               5743.590                  0.000
        P2               1794.872                  0.000

    Constraint         Slack/Surplus          Dual Prices
  --------------     ---------------      -----------------
        1                1061.538                  0.000
        2                1889.744                  0.000
        3                   0.000                  8.462
        4                   0.000                 10.256
```

TABLE 4.12 CROSS-TRAINING ABILITY AND CAPACITY INFORMATION

From Department	Cross-Training Transfers Permitted to Department 1	2	3	4	Maximum Hours Transferable
1	—	yes	yes	—	400
2	—	—	yes	yes	800
3	—	—	—	yes	100
4	yes	yes	—	—	200

be transferred from department 1. Similar cross-training transfer capabilities and capacities are shown for departments 2, 3, and 4.

When workforce assignments are flexible, we do not automatically know how many hours of labor should be assigned to or be transferred from each department. We need to add decision variables to the linear programming model to account for such changes.

$$b_i = \text{the labor-hours allocated to department } i \text{ for } i = 1, 2, 3, \text{ and } 4$$
$$t_{ij} = \text{the labor-hours transferred from department } i \text{ to department } j$$

The right-hand sides are now treated as decision variables.

With the addition of decision variables b_1, b_2, b_3, and b_4, we write the capacity restrictions for the four departments as follows:

$$\begin{aligned}
0.65P_1 + 0.95P_2 &\le b_1 \\
0.45P_1 + 0.85P_2 &\le b_2 \\
1.00P_1 + 0.70P_2 &\le b_3 \\
0.15P_1 + 0.30P_2 &\le b_4
\end{aligned}$$

Since b_1, b_2, b_3, and b_4 are now decision variables, we follow the standard practice of placing these variables on the left side of the inequalities, and the first four constraints of the linear programming model become

$$\begin{aligned}
0.65P_1 + 0.95P_2 - b_1 \qquad\qquad\qquad &\le 0 \\
0.45P_1 + 0.85P_2 \qquad - b_2 \qquad\qquad &\le 0 \\
1.00P_1 + 0.70P_2 \qquad\qquad - b_3 \qquad &\le 0 \\
0.15P_1 + 0.30P_2 \qquad\qquad\qquad - b_4 &\le 0
\end{aligned}$$

The labor-hours ultimately allocated to each department must be determined by a series of labor balance equations, or constraints, that include the number of hours initially assigned to each department plus the number of hours transferred into the department minus the number of hours transferred out of the department. Using department 1 as an example, we determine the workforce allocation as follows:

$$b_1 = \begin{pmatrix}\text{Hours} \\ \text{initially in} \\ \text{department 1}\end{pmatrix} + \begin{pmatrix}\text{Hours} \\ \text{transferred into} \\ \text{department 1}\end{pmatrix} - \begin{pmatrix}\text{Hours} \\ \text{transferred out of} \\ \text{department 1}\end{pmatrix}$$

Table 4.11 shows 6500 hours initially assigned to department 1. We use the transfer decision variables t_{i1} to denote transfers into department 1 and t_{1j} to denote transfers from department 1. Table 4.12 shows that the cross-training capabilities involving department 1 are restricted to transfers from department 4 (variable t_{41}) and transfers to either department 2 or department 3 (variables t_{12} and t_{13}). Thus, we can express the total workforce allocation for department 1 as

$$b_1 = 6500 + t_{41} - t_{12} - t_{13}$$

Moving the decision variables for the workforce transfers to the left-hand side, we have the labor balance equation or constraint

$$b_1 - t_{41} + t_{12} + t_{13} = 6500$$

This form of constraint will be needed for each of the four departments. Thus, the following labor balance constraints for departments 2, 3, and 4 would be added to the model.

$$\begin{aligned} b_2 - t_{12} - t_{42} + t_{23} + t_{24} &= 6000 \\ b_3 - t_{13} - t_{23} + t_{34} \quad\quad &= 7000 \\ b_4 - t_{24} - t_{34} + t_{41} + t_{42} &= 1400 \end{aligned}$$

Finally, Table 4.12 shows the number of hours that may be transferred from each department is limited, indicating that a transfer capacity constraint must be added for each of the four departments. The additional constraints are

$$\begin{aligned} t_{12} + t_{13} &\leq 400 \\ t_{23} + t_{24} &\leq 800 \\ t_{34} \quad\quad &\leq 100 \\ t_{41} + t_{42} &\leq 200 \end{aligned}$$

The complete linear programming model has two product decision variables (P_1 and P_2), four department workforce assignment variables (b_1, b_2, b_3, and b_4), seven transfer variables (t_{12}, t_{13}, t_{23}, t_{24}, t_{34}, t_{41}, and t_{42}), and 12 constraints. Figure 4.8 shows the optimal solution to this linear program.

Variations in the workforce assignment model could be used in situations such as allocating raw material resources to products, allocating machine time to products, and allocating salesforce time to stores or sales territories.

McCormick's profit can be increased by \$84,011 − \$73,590 = \$10,421 by taking advantage of cross-training and workforce transfers. The optimal product mix of 6825 units of product 1 and 1751 units of product 2 can be achieved if $t_{13} = 400$ hours are transferred from department 1 to department 3; $t_{23} = 651$ hours are transferred from department 2 to department 3; and $t_{24} = 149$ hours are transferred from department 2 to department 4. The resulting workforce assignments for departments 1–4 would provide 6100, 5200, 8051, and 1549 hours, respectively.

If a manager has the flexibility to assign personnel to different departments, reduced workforce idle time, improved workforce utilization, and improved profit should result. The linear programming model in this section automatically assigns employees and labor-hours to the departments in the most profitable manner.

4.4 BLENDING PROBLEMS

Blending problems arise whenever a manager must decide how to blend two or more resources to produce one or more products. In these situations, the resources contain one or more essential ingredients that must be blended into final products that will contain specific

FIGURE 4.8 THE MANAGEMENT SCIENTIST SOLUTION FOR THE McCORMICK MANUFACTURING COMPANY PROBLEM

EXCELfile
McCormick

```
Objective Function Value =          84011.299

      Variable              Value              Reduced Costs
   --------------      ---------------      -----------------
        P1                 6824.859                 0.000
        P2                 1751.412                 0.000
        B1                 6100.000                 0.000
        B2                 5200.000                 0.000
        B3                 8050.847                 0.000
        B4                 1549.153                 0.000
        T12                   0.000                 8.249
        T13                 400.000                 0.000
        T23                 650.847                 0.000
        T24                 149.153                 0.000
        T34                   0.000                 0.000
        T41                   0.000                 7.458
        T42                   0.000                 8.249

     Constraint          Slack/Surplus          Dual Prices
   --------------      ---------------      -----------------
          1                   0.000                 0.791
          2                 640.113                 0.000
          3                   0.000                 8.249
          4                   0.000                 8.249
          5                   0.000                 0.791
          6                   0.000                 0.000
          7                   0.000                 8.249
          8                   0.000                 8.249
          9                   0.000                 7.458
         10                   0.000                 8.249
         11                 100.000                 0.000
         12                 200.000                 0.000
```

percentages of each. In most of these applications, then, management must decide how much of each resource to purchase to satisfy product specifications and product demands at minimum cost.

Blending problems occur frequently in the petroleum industry (e.g., blending crude oil to produce different octane gasolines), chemical industry (e.g., blending chemicals to produce fertilizers and weed killers), and food industry (e.g., blending ingredients to produce soft drinks and soups). In this section we illustrate how to apply linear programming to a blending problem in the petroleum industry.

The Grand Strand Oil Company produces regular and premium gasoline for independent service stations in the southeastern United States. The Grand Strand refinery manufactures the gasoline products by blending three petroleum components. The gasolines are sold at different prices, and the petroleum components have different costs. The firm wants to determine how to mix or blend the three components into the two gasoline products and maximize profits.

Data available show that regular gasoline can be sold for $1.00 per gallon and premium gasoline for $1.08 per gallon. For the current production planning period, Grand Strand can obtain the three petroleum components at the cost per gallon and in the quantities shown in Table 4.13.

Product specifications for the regular and premium gasolines restrict the amounts of each component that can be used in each gasoline product. Table 4.14 lists the product specifications. Current commitments to distributors require Grand Strand to produce at least 10,000 gallons of regular gasoline.

The Grand Strand blending problem is to determine how many gallons of each component should be used in the regular gasoline blend and how many should be used in the premium gasoline blend. The optimal blending solution should maximize the firm's profit, subject to the constraints on the available petroleum supplies shown in Table 4.13, the product specifications shown in Table 4.14, and the required 10,000 gallons of regular gasoline.

We define the decision variables as

$$\begin{aligned} x_{ij} = {} & \text{gallons of component } i \text{ used in gasoline } j, \\ & \text{where } i = 1, 2, \text{ or } 3 \text{ for components 1, 2, or 3,} \\ & \text{and } j = r \text{ if regular or } j = p \text{ if premium} \end{aligned}$$

The six decision variables are

$$\begin{aligned} x_{1r} &= \text{gallons of component 1 in regular gasoline} \\ x_{2r} &= \text{gallons of component 2 in regular gasoline} \\ x_{3r} &= \text{gallons of component 3 in regular gasoline} \\ x_{1p} &= \text{gallons of component 1 in premium gasoline} \\ x_{2p} &= \text{gallons of component 2 in premium gasoline} \\ x_{3p} &= \text{gallons of component 3 in premium gasoline} \end{aligned}$$

The total number of gallons of each type of gasoline produced is the sum of the number of gallons produced using each of the three petroleum components.

Total Gallons Produced

$$\begin{aligned} \text{Regular gasoline} &= x_{1r} + x_{2r} + x_{3r} \\ \text{Premium gasoline} &= x_{1p} + x_{2p} + x_{3p} \end{aligned}$$

TABLE 4.13 PETROLEUM COST AND SUPPLY FOR THE GRAND STRAND BLENDING PROBLEM

Petroleum Component	Cost/Gallon	Maximum Available
1	$0.50	5,000 gallons
2	$0.60	10,000 gallons
3	$0.84	10,000 gallons

TABLE 4.14 PRODUCT SPECIFICATIONS FOR THE GRAND STRAND BLENDING PROBLEM

Product	Specifications
Regular gasoline	At most 30% component 1
	At least 40% component 2
	At most 20% component 3
Premium gasoline	At least 25% component 1
	At most 40% component 2
	At least 30% component 3

The total gallons of each petroleum component are computed in a similar fashion.

Total Petroleum Component Use

$$\begin{aligned}\text{Component 1} &= x_{1r} + x_{1p}\\ \text{Component 2} &= x_{2r} + x_{2p}\\ \text{Component 3} &= x_{3r} + x_{3p}\end{aligned}$$

We develop the objective function of maximizing the profit contribution by identifying the difference between the total revenue from both gasolines and the total cost of the three petroleum components. By multiplying the \$1.00 per gallon price by the total gallons of regular gasoline, the \$1.08 per gallon price by the total gallons of premium gasoline, and the component cost per gallon figures in Table 4.13 by the total gallons of each component used, we obtain the objective function:

$$\begin{aligned}\text{Max}\quad & 1.00(x_{1r} + x_{2r} + x_{3r}) + 1.08(x_{1p} + x_{2p} + x_{3p})\\ & - 0.50(x_{1r} + x_{1p}) - 0.60(x_{2r} + x_{2p}) - 0.84(x_{3r} + x_{3p})\end{aligned}$$

When we combine terms, the objective function becomes

$$\text{Max}\quad 0.50x_{1r} + 0.40x_{2r} + 0.16x_{3r} + 0.58x_{1p} + 0.48x_{2p} + 0.24x_{3p}$$

The limitations on the availability of the three petroleum components are

$$\begin{aligned}x_{1r} + x_{1p} &\leq 5{,}000 \quad \text{Component 1}\\ x_{2r} + x_{2p} &\leq 10{,}000 \quad \text{Component 2}\\ x_{3r} + x_{3p} &\leq 10{,}000 \quad \text{Component 3}\end{aligned}$$

Six constraints are now required to meet the product specifications stated in Table 4.14. The first specification states that component 1 can account for no more than 30 percent of the total gallons of regular gasoline produced. That is,

$$x_{1r} \leq 0.30(x_{1r} + x_{2r} + x_{3r})$$

Rewriting this constraint with the variables on the left-hand side and a constant on the right-hand side yields

$$0.70x_{1r} - 0.30x_{2r} - 0.30x_{3r} \leq 0$$

The second product specification listed in Table 4.14 becomes

$$x_{2r} \geq 0.40(x_{1r} + x_{2r} + x_{3r})$$

and thus

$$-0.40x_{1r} + 0.60x_{2r} - 0.40x_{3r} \geq 0$$

Similarly, we write the four remaining blending specifications listed in Table 4.14 as

$$\begin{aligned}
-0.20x_{1r} - 0.20x_{2r} + 0.80x_{3r} &\leq 0 \\
+0.75x_{1p} - 0.25x_{2p} - 0.25x_{3p} &\geq 0 \\
-0.40x_{1p} + 0.60x_{2p} - 0.40x_{3p} &\leq 0 \\
-0.30x_{1p} - 0.30x_{2p} + 0.70x_{3p} &\geq 0
\end{aligned}$$

The constraint for at least 10,000 gallons of regular gasoline is

$$x_{1r} + x_{2r} + x_{3r} \geq 10{,}000$$

The complete linear programming model with six decision variables and 10 constraints is

$$\begin{array}{ll}
\text{Max} & 0.50x_{1r} + 0.40x_{2r} + 0.16x_{3r} + 0.58x_{1p} + 0.48x_{2p} + 0.24x_{3p} \\
\text{s.t.} & \\
& x_{1r} + x_{1p} \leq 5{,}000 \\
& x_{2r} + x_{2p} \leq 10{,}000 \\
& x_{3r} + x_{3p} \leq 10{,}000 \\
& 0.70x_{1r} - 0.30x_{2r} - 0.30x_{3r} \leq 0 \\
& -0.40x_{1r} + 0.60x_{2r} - 0.40x_{3r} \geq 0 \\
& -0.20x_{1r} - 0.20x_{2r} + 0.80x_{3r} \leq 0 \\
& 0.75x_{1p} - 0.25x_{2p} - 0.25x_{3p} \geq 0 \\
& -0.40x_{1p} + 0.60x_{2p} - 0.40x_{3p} \leq 0 \\
& -0.30x_{1p} - 0.30x_{2p} + 0.70x_{3p} \geq 0 \\
& x_{1r} + x_{2r} + x_{3r} \geq 10{,}000 \\
& x_{1r}, x_{2r}, x_{3r}, x_{1p}, x_{2p}, x_{3p} \geq 0
\end{array}$$

Try Problem 15 as another example of a blending model.

The optimal solution to the Grand Strand blending problem is shown in Figure 4.9. The optimal solution, which provides a profit of \$9300, is summarized in Table 4.15. The optimal blending strategy shows that 10,000 gallons of regular gasoline should be produced. The regular gasoline will be manufactured as a blend of 8000 gallons of component 2 and 2000 gallons of component 3. The 15,000 gallons of premium gasoline will be manufactured as a blend of 5000 gallons of component 1, 2000 gallons of component 2, and 8000 gallons of component 3.

FIGURE 4.9 THE MANAGEMENT SCIENTIST SOLUTION FOR THE GRAND STRAND BLENDING PROBLEM

EXCELfile
Grand

```
Objective Function Value =              9300.000

      Variable              Value             Reduced Costs
   --------------     ---------------     -----------------
         X1R                  0.000                 0.000
         X2R               8000.000                 0.000
         X3R               2000.000                 0.000
         X1P               5000.000                 0.000
         X2P               2000.000                 0.000
         X3P               8000.000                 0.000

     Constraint         Slack/Surplus          Dual Prices
   --------------     ---------------     -----------------
          1                   0.000                 0.580
          2                   0.000                 0.480
          3                   0.000                 0.240
          4                3000.000                 0.000
          5                4000.000                 0.000
          6                   0.000                 0.000
          7                1250.000                 0.000
          8                4000.000                 0.000
          9                3500.000                 0.000
         10                   0.000                -0.080
```

The interpretation of the slack and surplus variables associated with the product specification constraints (constraints 4–9) in Figure 4.9 needs some clarification. If the constraint is a ≤ constraint, the value of the slack variable can be interpreted as the gallons of component use below the maximum amount of the component use specified by the constraint. For example, the slack of 3000.000 for constraint 4 shows that component 1 use is 3000 gallons below the maximum amount of component 1 that could have been used in the production of 10,000 gallons of regular gasoline. If the product specification constraint is a ≥ constraint, a surplus variable shows the gallons of component use above the minimum amount of component use specified by the blending constraint. For example, the surplus of 4000.000 for constraint 5 shows that component 2 use is 4000 gallons above the minimum amount of component 2 that must be used in the production of 10,000 gallons of regular gasoline.

TABLE 4.15 GRAND STRAND GASOLINE BLENDING SOLUTION

	Gallons of Component (percentage)			
Gasoline	**Component 1**	**Component 2**	**Component 3**	**Total**
Regular	0 (0%)	8000 (80%)	2000 (20%)	10,000
Premium	5000 (33⅓%)	2000 (13⅓%)	8000 (53⅓%)	15,000

NOTES AND COMMENTS

A convenient way to define the decision variables in a blending problem is to use a matrix in which the rows correspond to the raw materials and the columns correspond to the final products. For example, in the Grand Strand blending problem, we could define the decision variables as follows:

		Final Products	
		Regular Gasoline	**Premium Gasoline**
Raw Materials	**Component 1**	x_{1r}	x_{1p}
	Component 2	x_{2r}	x_{2p}
	Component 3	x_{3r}	x_{3p}

This approach has two advantages: (1) it provides a systematic way to define the decision variables for any blending problem; and (2) it provides a visual image of the decision variables in terms of how they are related to the raw materials, products, and each other.

4.5 DATA ENVELOPMENT ANALYSIS

Data envelopment analysis (DEA) is an application of linear programming used to measure the relative efficiency of operating units with the same goals and objectives. For example, DEA has been used within individual fast-food outlets in the same chain. In this case, the goal of DEA was to identify the inefficient outlets that should be targeted for further study and, if necessary, corrective action. Other applications of DEA have measured the relative efficiencies of hospitals, banks, courts, schools, and so on. In these applications, the performance of each institution or organization was measured relative to the performance of all operating units in the same system. The Management Science in Action, Efficiency of Bank Branches, describes how a large nationally known bank used DEA to determine which branches were operating inefficiently.

MANAGEMENT SCIENCE IN ACTION

EFFICIENCY OF BANK BRANCHES*

Management of a large, nationally known bank wanted to improve operations at the branch level. A total of 182 branch banks located in four major cities were selected for the study. Data envelopment analysis (DEA) was used to determine which branches were operating inefficiently.

The DEA model compared the actual operating results of each branch with those of all other branches. A less-productive branch was one that required more resources to produce the same output as the best-performing branches. The best-performing branches are identified by a DEA efficiency rating of 100% ($E = 1.00$). The inefficient or less-productive branches are identified by an efficiency rating less than 100% ($E < 1.00$).

The inputs used for each branch were the number of teller full-time equivalents, the number of nonteller personnel full-time equivalents, the number of parking spaces, the number of ATMs, and the advertising expense per customer. The outputs were the amount of loans (direct, indirect, commercial, and equity), the amount of deposits (checking, savings, and CDs), the average number of accounts per customer, and the customer satisfaction score based on a quarterly customer survey. Data were collected over six consecutive quarters to determine how the branches were operating over time.

(*continued*)

The solution to the DEA linear programming model showed that 92 of the 182 branches were fully efficient. Only five branches fell below the 70% efficiency level, and approximately 25% of the branches had efficiency ratings between 80% to 89%. DEA identified the specific branches that were relatively inefficient and provided insights as to how these branches could improve productivity. Focusing on the less-productive branches, the bank was able to identify ways to reduce the input resources required without significantly reducing the volume and quality of service. In addition, the DEA analysis provided management with a better understanding of the factors that contribute most to the efficiency of the branch banks.

*Based on B. Golany and J. E. Storbeck, "A Data Envelopment Analysis of the Operational Efficiency of Bank Branches," *Interfaces* (May/June 1999): 14–26.

The operating units of most organizations have multiple inputs such as staff size, salaries, hours of operation, and advertising budget, as well as multiple outputs such as profit, market share, and growth rate. In these situations, it is often difficult for a manager to determine which operating units are inefficient in converting their multiple inputs into multiple outputs. This particular area is where data envelopment analysis has proven to be a helpful managerial tool. We illustrate the application of data envelopment analysis by evaluating the performance of a group of four hospitals.

Evaluating the Performance of Hospitals

The hospital administrators at General Hospital, University Hospital, County Hospital, and State Hospital have been meeting to discuss ways in which they can help one another improve the performance at each of their hospitals. A consultant suggested that they consider using DEA to measure the performance of each hospital relative to the performance of all four hospitals. In discussing how this evaluation could be done, the following three input measures and four output measures were identified:

Input Measures

1. The number of full-time equivalent (FTE) nonphysician personnel
2. The amount spent on supplies
3. The number of bed-days available

Output Measures

Problem 26 asks you to formulate and solve a linear program to assess the relative efficiency of General Hospital.

1. Patient-days of service under Medicare
2. Patient-days of service not under Medicare
3. Number of nurses trained
4. Number of interns trained

Summaries of the input and output measures for a one-year period at each of the four hospitals are shown in Tables 4.16 and 4.17. Let us show how DEA can use these data to identify relatively inefficient hospitals.

Overview of the DEA Approach

In this application of DEA, a linear programming model will be developed for each hospital whose efficiency is to be evaluated. To illustrate the modeling process, we will formulate a linear program that can be used to determine the relative efficiency of County Hospital.

First, using a linear programming model, we construct a **hypothetical composite,** in this case a composite hospital, based on the outputs and inputs for all operating units with

TABLE 4.16 ANNUAL RESOURCES CONSUMED (INPUTS) BY THE FOUR HOSPITALS

	Hospital			
Input Measure	**General**	**University**	**County**	**State**
Full-time equivalent nonphysicians	285.20	162.30	275.70	210.40
Supply expense ($1000s)	123.80	128.70	348.50	154.10
Bed-days available (1000s)	106.72	64.21	104.10	104.04

the same goals. For each of the four hospitals' output measures, the output for the composite hospital is determined by computing a weighted average of the corresponding outputs for all four hospitals. For each of the three input measures, the input for the composite hospital is determined by using the same weights to compute a weighted average of the corresponding inputs for all four hospitals. Constraints in the linear programming model require all outputs for the composite hospital to be *greater than or equal to* the outputs of County Hospital, the hospital being evaluated. If the inputs for the composite unit can be shown to be *less than* the inputs for County Hospital, the composite hospital is shown to have the same, or more, output for *less input.* In this case, the model shows that the composite hospital is more efficient than County Hospital. In other words, the hospital being evaluated is *less efficient* than the composite hospital. Because the composite hospital is based on all four hospitals, the hospital being evaluated can be judged *relatively inefficient* when compared to the other hospitals in the group.

DEA Linear Programming Model

To determine the weight that each hospital will have in computing the outputs and inputs for the composite hospital, we use the following decision variables:

wg = weight applied to inputs and outputs for General Hospital
wu = weight applied to inputs and outputs for University Hospital
wc = weight applied to inputs and outputs for County Hospital
ws = weight applied to inputs and outputs for State Hospital

The DEA approach requires that the sum of these weights equal 1. Thus, the first constraint is

$$wg + wu + wc + ws = 1$$

TABLE 4.17 ANNUAL SERVICES PROVIDED (OUTPUTS) BY THE FOUR HOSPITALS

	Hospital			
Output Measure	**General**	**University**	**County**	**State**
Medicare patient-days (1000s)	48.14	34.62	36.72	33.16
Non-Medicare patient-days (1000s)	43.10	27.11	45.98	56.46
Nurses trained	253	148	175	160
Interns trained	41	27	23	84

In general, every DEA linear programming model will include a constraint that requires the weights for the operating units to sum to 1.

As we stated previously, for each output measure, the output for the composite hospital is determined by computing a weighted average of the corresponding outputs for all four hospitals. For instance, for output measure 1, the number of patient days of service under Medicare, the output for the composite hospital is

$$\begin{matrix}\text{Medicare patient-days} \\ \text{for Composite Hospital}\end{matrix} = \begin{pmatrix}\text{Medicare patient-days} \\ \text{for General Hospital}\end{pmatrix} wg + \begin{pmatrix}\text{Medicare patient-days} \\ \text{for University Hospital}\end{pmatrix} wu$$
$$+ \begin{pmatrix}\text{Medicare patient-days} \\ \text{for County Hospital}\end{pmatrix} wc + \begin{pmatrix}\text{Medicare patient-days} \\ \text{for State Hospital}\end{pmatrix} ws$$

Substituting the number of medicare patient-days for each hospital as shown in Table 4.17, we obtain the following expression:

$$\begin{matrix}\text{Medicare patient-days} \\ \text{for Composite Hospital}\end{matrix} = 48.14wg + 34.62wu + 36.72wc + 33.16ws$$

The other output measures for the composite hospital are computed in a similar fashion. Figure 4.10 provides a summary of the results.

For each of the four output measures, we need to write a constraint that requires the output for the composite hospital to be greater than or equal to the output for County Hospital. Thus, the general form of the output constraints is

$$\begin{matrix}\text{Output for the} \\ \text{Composite Hospital}\end{matrix} \geq \begin{matrix}\text{Output for} \\ \text{County Hospital}\end{matrix}$$

FIGURE 4.10 RELATIONSHIP BETWEEN THE OUTPUT MEASURES FOR THE FOUR HOSPITALS AND THE OUTPUT MEASURES FOR THE COMPOSITE HOSPITAL

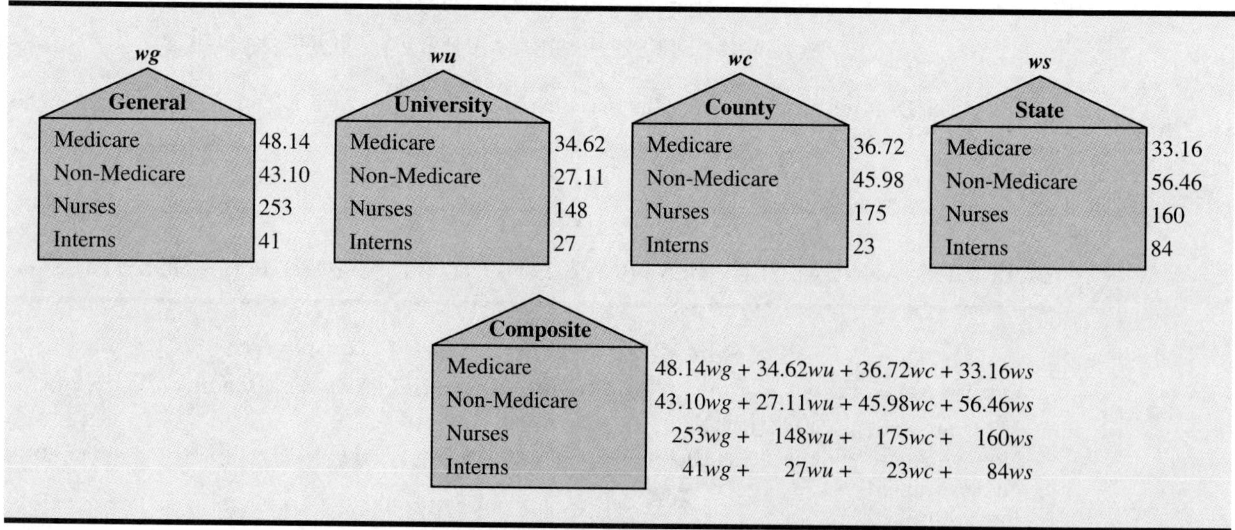

Because the number of Medicare patient-days for County Hospital is 36.72, the output constraint corresponding to the number of Medicare patient-days is

$$48.14wg + 34.62wu + 36.72wc + 33.16ws \geq 36.72$$

In a similar fashion, we formulated a constraint for each of the other three output measures, with the results as shown:

$$\begin{aligned} 43.10wg + 27.11wu + 45.98wc + 56.46ws &\geq 45.98 \quad \text{Non-Medicare} \\ 253wg + 148wu + 175wc + 160ws &\geq 175 \quad \text{Nurses} \\ 41wg + 27wu + 23wc + 84ws &\geq 23 \quad \text{Interns} \end{aligned}$$

The four output constraints require the linear programming solution to provide weights that will make each output measure for the composite hospital greater than or equal to the corresponding output measure for County Hospital. Thus, if a solution satisfying the output constraints can be found, the composite hospital will have produced at least as much of each output as County Hospital.

Next, we need to consider the constraints needed to model the relationship between the inputs for the composite hospital and the resources available to the composite hospital. A constraint is required for each of the three input measures. The general form for the input constraints is as follows:

$$\begin{matrix}\text{Input for the} \\ \text{Composite Hospital}\end{matrix} \leq \begin{matrix}\text{Resources available to} \\ \text{the Composite Hospital}\end{matrix}$$

For each input measure, the input for the composite hospital is a weighted average of the corresponding input for each of the four hospitals. Thus, for input measure 1, the number of full-time equivalent nonphysicians, the input for the composite hospital is

$$\begin{aligned} \begin{matrix}\text{FTE nonphysicians} \\ \text{for Composite Hospital}\end{matrix} &= \begin{pmatrix}\text{FTE nonphysicians} \\ \text{for General Hospital}\end{pmatrix} wg + \begin{pmatrix}\text{FTE nonphysicians} \\ \text{for University Hospital}\end{pmatrix} wu \\ &+ \begin{pmatrix}\text{FTE nonphysicians} \\ \text{for County Hospital}\end{pmatrix} wc + \begin{pmatrix}\text{FTE nonphysicians} \\ \text{for State Hospital}\end{pmatrix} ws \end{aligned}$$

Substituting the values for the number of full-time equivalent nonphysicians for each hospital as shown in Table 4.16, we obtain the following expression for the number of full-time equivalent nonphysicians for the composite hospital:

$$285.20wg + 162.30wu + 275.70wc + 210.40ws$$

The logic of a DEA model is to determine whether a hypothetical composite facility can achieve the same or more output while requiring less input. If more output with less input can be achieved, the facility being evaluated is judged to be relatively inefficient.

In a similar manner, we can write expressions for each of the other two input measures as shown in Figure 4.11.

To complete the formulation of the input constraints, we must write expressions for the right-hand-side values for each constraint. First, note that the right-hand-side values are the resources available to the composite hospital. In the DEA approach, these right-hand-side values are a percentage of the input values for County Hospital. Thus, we must introduce the following decision variables:

E = the fraction of County Hospital's input available to the composite hospital

FIGURE 4.11 RELATIONSHIP BETWEEN THE INPUT MEASURES FOR THE FOUR HOSPITALS AND THE INPUT MEASURES FOR THE COMPOSITE HOSPITAL

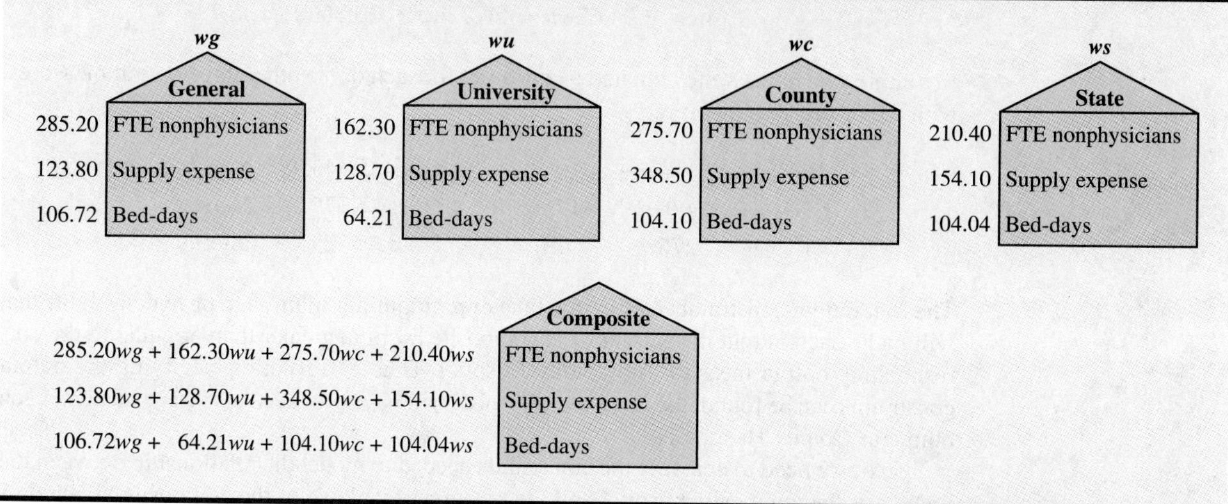

To illustrate the important role that E plays in the DEA approach, we show how to write the expression for the number of FTE nonphysicians available to the composite hospital. Table 4.16 shows that the number of FTE nonphysicians used by County Hospital was 275.70; thus, $275.70E$ is the number of FTE nonphysicians available to the composite hospital. If $E = 1$, the number of FTE nonphysicians available to the composite hospital is 275.70, the same as the number of FTE nonphysicians used by County Hospital. However, if E is greater than 1, the composite hospital would have available proportionally more nonphysicians, while if E is less than 1, the composite hospital would have available proportionally fewer FTE nonphysicians. Because of the effect that E has in determining the resources available to the composite hospital, E is referred to as the **efficiency index.**

We can now write the input constraint corresponding to the number of FTE nonphysicians available to the composite hospital:

$$285.20wg + 162.30wu + 275.70wc + 210.40ws \leq 275.70E$$

In a similar manner, we can write the input constraints for the supplies and bed-days available to the composite hospital. First, using the data in Table 4.16, we note that for each of these resources, the amount that is available to the composite hospital is $348.50E$ and $104.10E$, respectively. Thus, the input constraints for the supplies and bed-days are written as follows:

$$\begin{aligned} 123.80wg + 128.70wu + 348.50wc + 154.10ws &\leq 348.50E \quad \text{Supplies} \\ 106.72wg + 64.21wu + 104.10wc + 104.04ws &\leq 104.10E \quad \text{Bed-days} \end{aligned}$$

If a solution with $E < 1$ can be found, the composite hospital does not need as many resources as County Hospital needs to produce the same level of output.

The objective function for the DEA model is to minimize the value of E, which is equivalent to minimizing the input resources available to the composite hospital. Thus, the objective function is written as

$$\text{Min } E$$

The objective function in a DEA model is always Min E. The facility being evaluated (County Hospital in this example) can be judged relatively inefficient if the optimal solution provides E less than 1, indicating that the composite facility requires less in input resources.

The DEA efficiency conclusion is based on the optimal objective function value for E. The decision rule is as follows:

If $E = 1$, the composite hospital requires *as much input* as County Hospital does. There is no evidence that County Hospital is inefficient.

If $E < 1$, the composite hospital requires *less input* to obtain the output achieved by County Hospital. The composite hospital is more efficient; thus, County Hospital can be judged relatively inefficient.

The DEA linear programming model for the efficiency evaluation of County Hospital has five decision variables and eight constraints. The complete model is rewritten as follows:

$$
\begin{aligned}
\text{Min} \quad & E \\
\text{s.t.} \quad & \\
& wg + wu + wc + ws = 1 \\
& 48.14wg + 34.62wu + 36.72wc + 33.16ws \geq 36.72 \\
& 43.10wg + 27.11wu + 45.98wc + 56.46ws \geq 45.98 \\
& 253wg + 148wu + 175wc + 160ws \geq 175 \\
& 41wg + 27wu + 23wc + 84ws \geq 23 \\
& -275.70E + 285.20wg + 162.30wu + 275.70wc + 210.40ws \leq 0 \\
& -348.50E + 123.80wg + 128.70wu + 348.50wc + 154.10ws \leq 0 \\
& -104.10E + 106.72wg + 64.21wu + 104.10wc + 104.04ws \leq 0 \\
& E, wg, wu, wc, ws \geq 0
\end{aligned}
$$

Note that in this formulation of the model, we moved the terms involving E to the left side of the three input constraints because E is a decision variable.

The optimal solution is shown in Figure 4.12. We first note that the value of the objective function shows that the efficiency score for County Hospital is 0.905. This score tells us that the composite hospital can obtain at least the level of each output that County Hospital obtains by having available no more than 90.5 percent of the input resources required by County Hospital. Thus, the composite hospital is more efficient, and the DEA analysis identified County Hospital as being relatively inefficient.

From the solution in Figure 4.12, we see that the composite hospital is formed from the weighted average of General Hospital ($wg = 0.212$), University Hospital ($wu = 0.260$), and State Hospital ($ws = 0.527$). Each input and output of the composite hospital is determined by the same weighted average of the inputs and outputs of these three hospitals.

The Slack/Surplus column provides some additional information about the efficiency of County Hospital compared to the composite hospital. Specifically, the composite hospital has at least as much of each output as County Hospital has (constraints 2–5) and provides 1.6 more nurses trained (surplus for constraint 4) and 37 more interns trained (surplus for constraint 5). The slack of zero from constraint 8 shows that the composite hospital uses approximately 90.5 percent of the bed-days used by County Hospital. The slack values for constraints 6 and 7 show that less than 90.5 percent of the FTE nonphysician and the supplies expense resources used at County Hospital are used by the composite hospital.

Clearly, the composite hospital is more efficient than County Hospital, and we are justified in concluding that County Hospital is relatively inefficient compared to the other

FIGURE 4.12 THE MANAGEMENT SCIENTIST SOLUTION FOR THE COUNTY HOSPITAL DATA ENVELOPMENT ANALYSIS PROBLEM

```
Objective Function Value =          0.905

   Variable            Value           Reduced Costs
--------------    ---------------    -----------------
         E              0.905               0.000
        WG              0.212               0.000
        WU              0.260               0.000
        WC              0.000               0.095
        WS              0.527               0.000

  Constraint        Slack/Surplus        Dual Prices
--------------    ---------------    -----------------
         1              0.000               0.239
         2              0.000              -0.014
         3              0.000              -0.014
         4              1.615               0.000
         5             37.027               0.000
         6             35.824               0.000
         7            174.422               0.000
         8              0.000               0.010
```

hospitals in the group. Given the results of the DEA analysis, hospital administrators should examine operations to determine how County Hospital resources can be more effectively utilized.

Summary of the DEA Approach

To use data envelopment analysis to measure the relative efficiency of County Hospital, we used a linear programming model to construct a hypothetical composite hospital based on the outputs and inputs for the four hospitals in the problem. The approach to solving other types of problems using DEA is similar. For each operating unit that we want to measure the efficiency of, we must formulate and solve a linear programming model similar to the linear program we solved to measure the relative efficiency of County Hospital. The following step-by-step procedure should help you in formulating a linear programming model for other types of DEA applications. Note that the operating unit that we want to measure the relative efficiency of is referred to as the *j*th operating unit.

Step 1. Define decision variables or weights (one for each operating unit) that can be used to determine the inputs and outputs for the composite operating unit.

Step 2. Write a constraint that requires the weights to sum to 1.

Step 3. For each output measure, write a constraint that requires the output for the composite operating unit to be greater than or equal to the corresponding output for the *j*th operating unit.

Step 4. Define a decision variable, E, which determines the fraction of the jth operating unit's input available to the composite operating unit.

Step 5. For each input measure, write a constraint that requires the input for the composite operating unit to be less than or equal to the resources available to the composite operating unit.

Step 6. Write the objective function as Min E.

NOTES AND COMMENTS

1. Remember that the goal of data envelopment analysis is to identify operating units that are relatively inefficient. The method *does not* necessarily identify the operating units that are *relatively efficient.* Just because the efficiency index is $E = 1$, we cannot conclude that the unit being analyzed is relatively efficient. Indeed, any unit that has the largest output on any one of the output measures cannot be judged relatively inefficient.
2. It is possible for DEA to show all but one unit to be relatively inefficient. Such would be the case if a unit producing the most of every output also consumes the least of every input. Such cases are extremely rare in practice.
3. In applying data envelopment analysis to problems involving a large group of operating units, practitioners have found that roughly 50% of the operating units can be identified as inefficient. Comparing each relatively inefficient unit to the units contributing to the composite unit may be helpful in understanding how the operation of each relatively inefficient unit can be improved.

4.6 REVENUE MANAGEMENT

Revenue management involves managing the short-term demand for a fixed perishable inventory in order to maximize the revenue potential for an organization. The methodology, originally developed for American Airlines, was first used to determine how many airline flight seats to sell at an early reservation discount fare and how many airline flight seats to sell at a full fare. By making the optimal decision for the number of discount-fare seats and the number of full-fare seats on each flight, the airline is able to increase its average number of passengers per flight and maximize the total revenue generated by the combined sale of discount-fare and full-fare seats. Today, all major airlines use some form of revenue management.

Given the success of revenue management in the airline industry, it was not long before other industries began using revenue management. Modem systems have been expanded to include pricing strategies, overbooking policies, short-term supply decisions, and the management of nonperishable assets. Application areas now include hotels, apartment rentals, car rentals, cruise lines, and golf courses. The Management Science in Action, Revenue Management at National Car Rental, discusses how National Car Rental implemented revenue management.

The development of a revenue management system can be expensive and time-consuming, but the potential payoffs can be substantial. For instance, the revenue management system used at American Airlines generates nearly $1 billion in annual incremental revenue. To illustrate the fundamentals of revenue management, we will use a linear

MANAGEMENT SCIENCE IN ACTION

REVENUE MANAGEMENT AT NATIONAL CAR RENTAL*

During its recovery from a near liquidation in the mid-1990s, National Car Rental developed a revenue management system that uses linear programming and other analytical models to help manage rental car capacity, pricing, and reservations. The goal of the revenue management system is to develop procedures that identify unrealized revenue opportunities, improve utilization, and ultimately increase revenue for the company.

Management science models play a key role in revenue management at National. For instance, a linear programming model is used for length-of-rent control. An overbooking model identifies optimal overbooking levels subject to service level constraints, and a planned upgrade algorithm allows cars in a higher-priced class to be used to satisfy excess demand for cars in a lower-priced class.

Another model generates length-of-rent categories for each arrival day, which maximizes revenue. Pricing models are used to manage revenue by segmenting the market between business and leisure travel. For example, fares are adjusted to account for the fact that leisure travelers are willing to commit further in advance than business travelers and are willing to stay over a weekend.

The implementation of the revenue management system is credited with returning National Car Rental to profitability. In the first year of use, revenue management resulted in increased revenues of $56 million.

*Based on M. K. Geraghty and Ernest Johnson, "Revenue Management Saves National Car Rental," *Interfaces* 27, no. 1 (January/February 1997): 107–127.

---

programming model to develop a revenue management plan for Leisure Air, a regional airline that provides service for Pittsburgh, Newark, Charlotte, Myrtle Beach, and Orlando.

Leisure Air has two Boeing 737-400 airplanes, one based in Pittsburgh and the other in Newark. Both airplanes have a coach section with a 132-seat capacity. Each morning the Pittsburgh-based plane flies to Orlando with a stopover in Charlotte, and the Newark-based plane flies to Myrtle Beach, also with a stopover in Charlotte. At the end of the day, both planes return to their home bases. To keep the size of the problem reasonable we restrict our attention to the Pittsburgh–Charlotte, Charlotte–Orlando, Newark–Charlotte, and Charlotte–Myrtle Beach flight legs for the morning flights. Figure 4.13 illustrates the logistics of the Leisure Air problem situation.

Leisure Air uses two fare classes: a discount-fare Q class and a full-fare Y class. Reservations using the discount-fare Q class must be made 14 days in advance and must include a Saturday night stay in the destination city. Reservations using the full-fare Y class may be made anytime, with no penalty for changing the reservation at a later date. To determine the itinerary and fare alternatives that Leisure Air can offer its customers, we must consider not only the origin and the destination of each flight, but also the fare class. For instance, possible products include Pittsburgh to Charlotte using Q class, Newark to Orlando using Q class, Charlotte to Myrtle Beach using Y class, and so on. Each product is referred to as an origin-destination-itinerary fare (ODIF). For May 5, Leisure Air established fares and developed forecasts of customer demand for each of 16 ODIFs. These data are shown in Table 4.18.

Suppose that on April 4 a customer calls the Leisure Air reservation office and requests a Q class seat on the May 5 flight from Pittsburgh to Myrtle Beach. Should Leisure Air accept the reservation? The difficulty in making this decision is that even though Leisure Air may have seats available, the company may not want to accept this reservation at the Q class

FIGURE 4.13 LOGISTICS OF THE LEISURE AIR PROBLEM

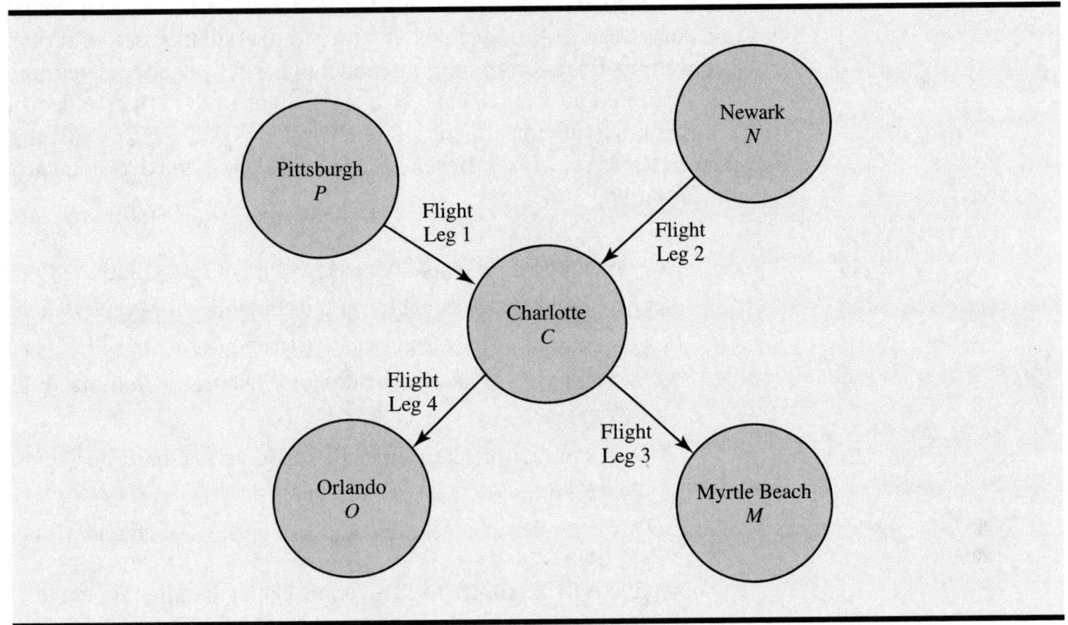

TABLE 4.18 FARE AND DEMAND DATA FOR 16 LEISURE AIR ORIGIN-DESTINATION-ITINERARY FARES (ODIFs)

ODIF	Origin	Destination	Fare Class	ODIF Code	Fare	Forecasted Demand
1	Pittsburgh	Charlotte	Q	PCQ	$178	33
2	Pittsburgh	Myrtle Beach	Q	PMQ	268	44
3	Pittsburgh	Orlando	Q	POQ	228	45
4	Pittsburgh	Charlotte	Y	PCY	380	16
5	Pittsburgh	Myrtle Beach	Y	PMY	456	6
6	Pittsburgh	Orlando	Y	POY	560	11
7	Newark	Charlotte	Q	NCQ	199	26
8	Newark	Myrtle Beach	Q	NMQ	249	56
9	Newark	Orlando	Q	NOQ	349	39
10	Newark	Charlotte	Y	NCY	385	15
11	Newark	Myrtle Beach	Y	NMY	444	7
12	Newark	Orlando	Y	NOY	580	9
13	Charlotte	Myrtle Beach	Q	CMQ	179	64
14	Charlotte	Myrtle Beach	Y	CMY	380	8
15	Charlotte	Orlando	Q	COQ	224	46
16	Charlotte	Orlando	Y	COY	582	10

fare of \$268, especially if it is possible to sell the same reservation later at the Y class fare of \$456. Thus, determining how many Q and Y class seats to make available are important decisions that Leisure Air must take in order to operate its reservation system.

To develop a linear programming model that can be used to determine how many seats Leisure Air should allocate to each fare class we need to define 16 decision variables, one for each origin-destination-itinerary fare alternative. Using P for Pittsburgh, N for Newark, C for Charlotte, M for Myrtle Beach, and O for Orlando, the decision variables take the following form:

$$
\begin{aligned}
PCQ &= \text{number of seats allocated to Pittsburgh–Charlotte Q class} \\
PMQ &= \text{number of seats allocated to Pittsburgh–Myrtle Beach Q class} \\
POQ &= \text{number of seats allocated to Pittsburgh–Orlando Q class} \\
PCY &= \text{number of seats allocated to Pittsburgh–Charlotte Y class} \\
&\vdots \\
NCQ &= \text{number of seats allocated to Newark–Charlotte Q class} \\
&\vdots \\
COY &= \text{number of seats allocated to Charlotte–Orlando Y class}
\end{aligned}
$$

The objective is to maximize total revenue. Using the fares shown in Table 4.18, we can write the objective function for the linear programming model as follows:

$$
\begin{aligned}
\text{Max} \quad & 178PCQ + 268PMQ + 228POQ + 380PCY + 456PMY + 560POY \\
& + 199NCQ + 249NMQ + 349NOQ + 385NCY + 444NMY \\
& + 580NOY + 179CMQ + 380CMY + 224COQ + 582COY
\end{aligned}
$$

Next we must write the constraints. We need two types of constraints: capacity and demand. We begin with the capacity constraints.

Consider the Pittsburgh–Charlotte flight leg in Figure 4.13. The Boeing 737-400 airplane has a 132-seat capacity. Three possible final destinations for passengers on this flight (Charlotte, Myrtle Beach, or Orlando) and two fare classes (Q and Y) provide six ODIF alternatives: (1) Pittsburgh–Charlotte Q class; (2) Pittsburgh–Myrtle Beach Q class; (3) Pittsburgh–Orlando Q class; (4) Pittsburgh–Charlotte Y class; (5) Pittsburgh–Myrtle Beach Y class; and (6) Pittsburgh–Orlando Y class. Thus, the number of seats allocated to the Pittsburgh–Charlotte flight leg is $PCQ + PMQ + POQ + PCY + PMY + POY$. With the capacity of 132 seats, the capacity constraint is as follows:

$$PCQ + PMQ + POQ + PCY + PMY + POY \leq 132 \quad \text{Pittsburgh–Charlotte}$$

The capacity constraints for the Newark–Charlotte, Charlotte–Myrtle Beach, and Charlotte–Orlando flight legs are developed in a similar manner. These three constraints are as follows:

$$
\begin{aligned}
NCQ + NMQ + NOQ + NCY + NMY + NOY &\leq 132 \quad \text{Newark–Charlotte} \\
PMQ + PMY + NMQ + NMY + CMQ + CMY &\leq 132 \quad \text{Charlotte–Myrtle Beach} \\
POQ + POY + NOQ + NOY + COQ + COY &\leq 132 \quad \text{Charlotte–Orlando}
\end{aligned}
$$

The demand constraints limit the number of seats for each ODIF based on the forecasted demand. Using the demand forecasts in Table 4.18, 16 demand constraints must be added to the model. The first four demand constraints are as follows:

$$\begin{aligned} PCQ &\le 33 \quad \text{Pittsburgh–Charlotte Q class} \\ PMQ &\le 44 \quad \text{Pittsburgh–Myrtle Beach Q class} \\ POQ &\le 45 \quad \text{Pittsburgh–Orlando Q class} \\ PCY &\le 16 \quad \text{Pittsburgh–Charlotte Y class} \end{aligned}$$

The complete linear programming model with 16 decision variables, 4 capacity constraints, and 16 demand constraints is as follows.

$$\begin{aligned} \text{Max} \quad & 178PCQ + 268PMQ + 228POQ + 380PCY + 456PMY + 560POY \\ & + 199NCQ + 249NMQ + 349NOQ + 385NCY + 444NMY \\ & + 580NOY + 179CMQ + 380CMY + 224COQ + 582COY \end{aligned}$$

s.t.

$$\begin{aligned} PCQ + PMQ + POQ + PCY + PMY + POY &\le 132 \quad \text{Pittsburgh–Charlotte} \\ NCQ + NMQ + NOQ + NCY + NMY + NOY &\le 132 \quad \text{Newark–Charlotte} \\ PMQ + PMY + NMQ + NMY + CMQ + CMY &\le 132 \quad \text{Charlotte–Myrtle Beach} \\ POQ + POY + NOQ + NOY + COQ + COY &\le 132 \quad \text{Charlotte–Orlando} \end{aligned}$$

$$\left.\begin{aligned} PCQ &\le 33 \\ PMQ &\le 44 \\ POQ &\le 45 \\ PCY &\le 16 \\ PMY &\le 6 \\ POY &\le 11 \\ NCQ &\le 26 \\ NMQ &\le 56 \\ NOQ &\le 39 \\ NCY &\le 15 \\ NMY &\le 7 \\ NOY &\le 9 \\ CMQ &\le 64 \\ CMY &\le 8 \\ COQ &\le 46 \\ COY &\le 10 \end{aligned}\right\} \text{Demand Constraints}$$

$$PCQ, PMQ, POQ, PCY, \ldots, COY \ge 0$$

The optimal solution to the Leisure Air revenue management problem is shown in Figure 4.14. The value of the optimal solution is \$103,103. The optimal solution shows that $PCQ = 33$, $PMQ = 44$, $POQ = 22$, $PCY = 16$, and so on. Thus, to maximize revenue Leisure Air should allocate 33 Q class seats to Pittsburgh–Charlotte, 44 Q class seats to Pittsburgh–Myrtle Beach, 22 Q class seats to Pittsburgh–Orlando, 16 Y class seats to Pittsburgh–Charlotte, and so on.

Over time, reservations will come into the system and the number of remaining seats available for each ODIF will decrease. For example, the optimal solution allocated 44 Q class seats to Pittsburgh–Myrtle Beach. Suppose that two weeks prior to the departure date of May 5, all 44 seats have been sold. Now, suppose that a new customer calls the Leisure Air reservation office and requests a Q class seat for the Pittsburgh–Myrtle Beach flight. Should Leisure Air accept the new reservation even though it exceeds the original 44-seat

FIGURE 4.14 THE MANAGEMENT SCIENTIST SOLUTION FOR THE LEISURE AIR REVENUE MANAGEMENT PROBLEM

EXCELfile
Leisure

Objective Function Value = 103103.000

Variable	Value	Reduced Costs
PCQ	33.000	0.000
PMQ	44.000	0.000
POQ	22.000	0.000
PCY	16.000	0.000
PMY	6.000	0.000
POY	11.000	0.000
NCQ	26.000	0.000
NMQ	36.000	0.000
NOQ	39.000	0.000
NCY	15.000	0.000
NMY	7.000	0.000
NOY	9.000	0.000
CMQ	31.000	0.000
CMY	8.000	0.000
COQ	41.000	0.000
COY	10.000	0.000

Constraint	Slack/Surplus	Dual Prices
1	0.000	4.000
2	0.000	70.000
3	0.000	179.000
4	0.000	224.000
5	0.000	174.000
6	0.000	85.000
7	23.000	0.000
8	0.000	376.000
9	0.000	273.000
10	0.000	332.000
11	0.000	129.000
12	20.000	0.000
13	0.000	55.000
14	0.000	315.000
15	0.000	195.000
16	0.000	286.000
17	33.000	0.000
18	0.000	201.000
19	5.000	0.000
20	0.000	358.000

allocation? The dual price for the Pittsburgh–Myrtle Beach Q class demand constraint will provide information that will help a Leisure Air reservation agent make this decision.

Dual prices tell reservation agents the additional revenue associated with overbooking each ODIF.

Constraint 6, $PMQ \leq 44$, restricts the number of Q class seats that can be allocated to Pittsburgh–Myrtle Beach to 44 seats. In Figure 4.14 we see that the dual price for constraint 6 is \$85. The dual price tells us that if one more Q class seat was available from Pittsburgh to Myrtle Beach, revenue would improve by \$85. This increase in revenue is referred to as the bid price for this origin-destination-itinerary fare. In general, the bid price for an ODIF tells a Leisure Air reservation agent the value of one additional reservation once a particular ODIF has been sold out.

By looking at the dual prices for the demand constraints in Figure 4.14, we see that the highest dual price (bid price) is \$376 for constraint 8, $PCY \leq 16$. This constraint corresponds to the Pittsburgh–Charlotte Y class itinerary. Thus, if all 16 seats allocated to this itinerary have been sold, accepting another reservation will provide additional revenue of \$376. Given this revenue contribution, a reservation agent would most likely accept the additional reservation even if it resulted in an overbooking of the flight. Other dual prices for the demand constraints show a bid price of \$358 for constraint 20 (COY) and a bid price of \$332 for constraint 10 (POY). Thus, accepting additional reservations for the Charlotte–Orlando Y class and the Pittsburgh–Orlando Y class itineraries is a good choice for increasing revenue.

A revenue management system like the one at Leisure Air must be flexible and adjust to the ever-changing reservation status. Conceptually, each time a reservation is accepted for an origin-destination-itinerary fare that is at its capacity, the linear programming model should be updated and resolved to obtain new seat allocations along with the revised bid price information. In practice, updating the allocations on a real-time basis is not practical because of the large number of itineraries involved. However, the bid prices from a current solution and some simple decision rules enable reservation agents to make decisions that improve the revenue for the firm. Then, on a periodic basis such as once a day or once a week, the entire linear programming model can be updated and resolved to generate new seat allocations and revised bid price information.

SUMMARY

In this chapter we presented a broad range of applications that demonstrate how to use linear programming to assist in the decision-making process. We formulated and solved problems from marketing, finance, and production management, and illustrated how linear programming can be applied to blending problems and data envelopment analysis.

Many of the illustrations presented in this chapter are scaled-down versions of actual situations in which linear programming has been applied. In real-world applications, the problem may not be so concisely stated, the data for the problem may not be as readily available, and the problem most likely will involve numerous decision variables and/or constraints. However, a thorough study of the applications in this chapter is a good place to begin in applying linear programming to real problems.

GLOSSARY

Data envelopment analysis (DEA) A linear programming application used to measure the relative efficiency of operating units with the same goals and objectives.

Hypothetical composite A weighted average of outputs and inputs of all operating units with similar goals.

Efficiency index Percentage of an individual operating unit's resources that are available to the composite operating unit.

PROBLEMS

Note: The following problems have been designed to give you an understanding and appreciation of the broad range of problems that can be formulated as linear programs. You should be able to formulate a linear programming model for each of the problems. However, you will need access to a linear programming computer package to develop the solutions and make the requested interpretations.

1. The Westchester Chamber of Commerce periodically sponsors public service seminars and programs. Currently, promotional plans are under way for this year's program. Advertising alternatives include television, radio, and newspaper. Audience estimates, costs, and maximum media usage limitations are as shown.

Constraint	Television	Radio	Newspaper
Audience per advertisement	100,000	18,000	40,000
Cost per advertisement	$2000	$300	$600
Maximum media usage	10	20	10

To ensure a balanced use of advertising media, radio advertisements must not exceed 50% of the total number of advertisements authorized. In addition, television should account for at least 10% of the total number of advertisements authorized.

a. If the promotional budget is limited to $18,200, how many commercial messages should be run on each medium to maximize total audience contact? What is the allocation of the budget among the three media, and what is the total audience reached?

b. By how much would audience contact increase if an extra $100 were allocated to the promotional budget?

2. The management of Hartman Company is trying to determine the amount of each of two products to produce over the coming planning period. The following information concerns labor availability, labor utilization, and product profitability.

	Product (hours/unit)		Labor-Hours
Department	1	2	Available
A	1.00	0.35	100
B	0.30	0.20	36
C	0.20	0.50	50
Profit contribution/unit	$30.00	$15.00	

a. Develop a linear programming model of the Hartman Company problem. Solve the model to determine the optimal production quantities of products 1 and 2.

b. In computing the profit contribution per unit, management doesn't deduct labor costs because they are considered fixed for the upcoming planning period. However, suppose that overtime can be scheduled in some of the departments. Which departments would you recommend scheduling for overtime? How much would you be willing to pay per hour of overtime in each department?

c. Suppose that 10, 6, and 8 hours of overtime may be scheduled in departments A, B, and C, respectively. The cost per hour of overtime is $18 in department A, $22.50 in department B, and $12 in department C. Formulate a linear programming model that can be used to determine the optimal production quantities if overtime is made available. What are the optimal production quantities, and what is the revised total contribution to profit? How much overtime do you recommend using in each department? What is the increase in the total contribution to profit if overtime is used?

3. The employee credit union at State University is planning the allocation of funds for the coming year. The credit union makes four types of loans to its members. In addition, the credit union invests in risk-free securities to stabilize income. The various revenue-producing investments together with annual rates of return are as follows:

Type of Loan/Investment	Annual Rate of Return (%)
Automobile loans	8
Furniture loans	10
Other secured loans	11
Signature loans	12
Risk-free securities	9

The credit union will have $2,000,000 available for investment during the coming year. State laws and credit union policies impose the following restrictions on the composition of the loans and investments.

- Risk-free securities may not exceed 30% of the total funds available for investment.
- Signature loans may not exceed 10% of the funds invested in all loans (automobile, furniture, other secured, and signature loans).
- Furniture loans plus other secured loans may not exceed the automobile loans.
- Other secured loans plus signature loans may not exceed the funds invested in risk-free securities.

How should the $2,000,000 be allocated to each of the loan/investment alternatives to maximize total annual return? What is the projected total annual return?

4. Hilltop Coffee manufactures a coffee product by blending three types of coffee beans. The cost per pound and the available pounds of each bean are as follows:

Bean	Cost per Pound	Available Pounds
1	$0.50	500
2	$0.70	600
3	$0.45	400

Consumer tests with coffee products were used to provide ratings on a scale of 0–100, with higher ratings indicating higher quality. Product quality standards for the blended coffee require a consumer rating for aroma to be at least 75 and a consumer rating for taste to be at least 80. The individual ratings of the aroma and taste for coffee made from 100% of each bean are as follows.

Bean	Aroma Rating	Taste Rating
1	75	86
2	85	88
3	60	75

Assume that the aroma and taste attributes of the coffee blend will be a weighted average of the attributes of the beans used in the blend.

a. What is the minimum-cost blend that will meet the quality standards and provide 1000 pounds of the blended coffee product?

b. What is the cost per pound for the coffee blend?

c. Determine the aroma and taste ratings for the coffee blend.

d. If additional coffee were to be produced, what would be the expected cost per pound?

5. Ajax Fuels, Inc., is developing a new additive for airplane fuels. The additive is a mixture of three ingredients: A, B, and C. For proper performance, the total amount of additive (amount of A + amount of B + amount of C) must be at least 10 ounces per gallon of fuel. However, because of safety reasons, the amount of additive must not exceed 15 ounces per gallon of fuel. The mix or blend of the three ingredients is critical. At least 1 ounce of ingredient A must be used for every ounce of ingredient B. The amount of ingredient C must be at least one-half the amount of ingredient A. If the costs per ounce for ingredients A, B, and C are \$0.10, \$0.03, and \$0.09, respectively, find the minimum-cost mixture of A, B, and C for each gallon of airplane fuel.

6. G. Kunz and Sons, Inc., manufactures two products used in the heavy equipment industry. Both products require manufacturing operations in two departments. The following are the production time (in hours) and profit contribution figures for the two products.

		Labor-Hours	
Product	Profit per Unit	Dept. A	Dept. B
1	\$25	6	12
2	\$20	8	10

For the coming production period, Kunz has available a total of 900 hours of labor that can be allocated to either of the two departments. Find the production plan and labor allocation (hours assigned in each department) that will maximize the total contribution to profit.

7. As part of the settlement for a class action lawsuit, Hoxworth Corporation must provide sufficient cash to make the following annual payments (in thousands of dollars).

Year	1	2	3	4	5	6
Payment	190	215	240	285	315	460

The annual payments must be made at the beginning of each year. The judge will approve an amount that, along with earnings on its investment, will cover the annual payments. Investment of the funds will be limited to savings (at 4% annually) and government securities, at prices and rates currently quoted in *The Wall Street Journal.*

Hoxworth wants to develop a plan for making the annual payments by investing in the following securities (par value = \$1000). Funds not invested in these securities will be placed in savings.

Security	Current Price	Rate (%)	Years to Maturity
1	\$1055	6.750	3
2	\$1000	5.125	4

Assume that interest is paid annually. The plan will be submitted to the judge and, if approved, Hoxworth will be required to pay a trustee the amount that will be required to fund the plan.

a. Use linear programming to find the minimum cash settlement necessary to fund the annual payments.

b. Use the dual price to determine how much more Hoxworth should be willing to pay now to reduce the payment at the beginning of year 6 to \$400,000.

c. Use the dual price to determine how much more Hoxworth should be willing to pay to reduce the year 1 payment to \$150,000.

d. Suppose that the annual payments are to be made at the end of each year. Reformulate the model to accommodate this change. How much would Hoxworth save if this change could be negotiated?

8. The Clark County Sheriff's Department schedules police officers for 8-hour shifts. The beginning times for the shifts are 8:00 A.M., noon, 4:00 P.M., 8:00 P.M., midnight, and 4:00 A.M. An officer beginning a shift at one of these times works for the next 8 hours. During normal weekday operations, the number of officers needed varies depending on the time of day. The department staffing guidelines require the following minimum number of officers on duty:

Time of Day	Minimum Officers on Duty
8:00 A.M.–Noon	5
Noon–4:00 P.M.	6
4:00 P.M.–8:00 P.M.	10
8:00 P.M.–Midnight	7
Midnight–4:00 A.M.	4
4:00 A.M.–8:00 A.M.	6

Determine the number of police officers that should be scheduled to begin the 8-hour shifts at each of the six times (8:00 A.M., noon, 4:00 P.M., 8:00 P.M., midnight, and 4:00 A.M.) to minimize the total number of officers required. (*Hint:* Let x_1 = the number of officers beginning work at 8:00 A.M., x_2 = the number of officers beginning work at noon, and so on.)

9. Reconsider the Welte Mutual Funds problem from Section 4.2. Define your decision variables as the fraction of funds invested in each security. Also, modify the constraints limiting investments in the oil and steel industries as follows: No more than 50% of the total funds invested in stock (oil and steel) may be invested in the oil industry, and no more than 50% of the funds invested in stock (oil and steel) may be invested in the steel industry.

a. Solve the revised linear programming model. What fraction of the portfolio should be invested in each type of security?

b. How much should be invested in each type of security?

c. What are the total earnings for the portfolio?

d. What is the marginal rate of return on the portfolio? That is, how much more could be earned by investing one more dollar in the portfolio?

10. An investment advisor at Shore Financial Services wants to develop a model that can be used to allocate investment funds among four alternatives: stocks, bonds, mutual funds, and cash. For the coming investment period, the company developed estimates of the annual rate of return and the associated risk for each alternative. Risk is measured using an index between 0 and 1, with higher risk values denoting more volatility and thus more uncertainty.

Investment	Annual Rate of Return (%)	Risk
Stocks	10	0.8
Bonds	3	0.2
Mutual funds	4	0.3
Cash	1	0.0

Because cash is held in a money market fund, the annual return is lower, but it carries essentially no risk. The objective is to determine the portion of funds allocated to each investment alternative in order to maximize the total annual return for the portfolio subject to the risk level the client is willing to tolerate.

Total risk is the sum of the risk for all investment alternatives. For instance, if 40% of a client's funds are invested in stocks, 30% in bonds, 20% in mutual funds, and 10% in cash, the total risk for the portfolio would be $0.40(0.8) + 0.30(0.2) + 0.20(0.3) + 0.10(0.0) = 0.44$. An investment advisor will meet with each client to discuss the client's investment objectives and to determine a maximum total risk value for the client. A maximum total risk value of less than 0.3 would be assigned to a conservative investor; a maximum total risk value of between 0.3 and 0.5 would be assigned to a moderate tolerance to risk; and a maximum total risk value greater than 0.5 would be assigned to a more aggressive investor.

Shore Financial Services specified additional guidelines that must be applied to all clients. The guidelines are as follows:

- No more than 75% of the total investment may be in stocks.
- The amount invested in mutual funds must be at least as much as invested in bonds.
- The amount of cash must be at least 10%, but no more than 30% of the total investment funds.

a. Suppose the maximum risk value for a particular client is 0.4. What is the optimal allocation of investment funds among stocks, bonds, mutual funds, and cash? What is the annual rate of return and the total risk for the optimal portfolio?

b. Suppose the maximum risk value for a more conservative client is 0.18. What is the optimal allocation of investment funds for this client? What is the annual rate of return and the total risk for the optimal portfolio?

c. Another more aggressive client has a maximum risk value of 0.7. What is the optimal allocation of investment funds for this client? What is the annual rate of return and the total risk for the optimal portfolio?

d. Refer to the solution for the more aggressive client in part (c). Would this client be interested in having the investment advisor increase the maximum percentage allowed in stocks or decrease the requirement that the amount of cash must be at least 10% of the funds invested? Explain.

e. What is the advantage of defining the decision variables as is done in this model rather than stating the amount to be invested and expressing the decision variables directly in dollar amounts?

11. Edwards Manufacturing Company purchases two component parts from three different suppliers. The suppliers have limited capacity, and no one supplier can meet all the company's needs. In addition, the suppliers charge different prices for the components. Component price data (in price per unit) are as follows:

	Supplier		
Component	**1**	**2**	**3**
1	$12	$13	$14
2	$10	$11	$10

Each supplier has a limited capacity in terms of the total number of components it can supply. However, as long as Edwards provides sufficient advance orders, each supplier can devote its capacity to component 1, component 2, or any combination of the two components, if the total number of units ordered is within its capacity. Supplier capacities are as follows.

Supplier	1	2	3
Capacity	600	1000	800

If the Edwards production plan for the next period includes 1000 units of component 1 and 800 units of component 2, what purchases do you recommend? That is, how many units of each component should be ordered from each supplier? What is the total purchase cost for the components?

12. The Atlantic Seafood Company (ASC) is a buyer and distributor of seafood products that are sold to restaurants and specialty seafood outlets throughout the Northeast. ASC has a frozen storage facility in New York City that serves as the primary distribution point for all products. One of the ASC products is frozen large black tiger shrimp, which are sized at 16–20 pieces per pound. Each Saturday ASC can purchase more tiger shrimp or sell the tiger shrimp at the existing New York City warehouse market price. The ASC goal is to buy tiger shrimp at a low weekly price and sell it later at a higher price. ASC currently has 20,000 pounds of tiger shrimp in storage. Space is available to store a maximum of 100,000 pounds of tiger shrimp each week. In addition, ASC developed the following estimates of tiger shrimp prices for the next four weeks:

Week	Price/lb.
1	$6.00
2	$6.20
3	$6.65
4	$5.55

ASC would like to determine the optimal buying-storing-selling strategy for the next four weeks. The cost to store a pound of shrimp for one week is $0.15, and to account for unforeseen changes in supply or demand, management also indicated that 25,000 pounds of tiger shrimp must be in storage at the end of week 4. Determine the optimal buying-storing-selling strategy for ASC. What is the projected four-week profit?

13. Romans Food Market, located in Saratoga, New York, carries a variety of specialty foods from around the world. Two of the store's leading products use the Romans Food Market name: Romans Regular Coffee and Romans DeCaf Coffee. These coffees are blends of Brazilian Natural and Colombian Mild coffee beans, which are purchased from a

distributor located in New York City. Because Romans purchases large quantities, the coffee beans may be purchased on an as-needed basis for a price 10% higher than the market price the distributor pays for the beans. The current market price is \$0.47 per pound for Brazilian Natural and \$0.62 per pound for Colombian Mild. The compositions of each coffee blend are as follows:

	Blend	
Bean	**Regular**	**DeCaf**
Brazilian Natural	75%	40%
Colombian Mild	25%	60%

Romans sells the Regular blend for \$3.60 per pound and the DeCaf blend for \$4.40 per pound. Romans would like to place an order for the Brazilian and Colombian coffee beans that will enable the production of 1000 pounds of Roman Regular coffee and 500 pounds of Roman DeCaf coffee. The production cost is \$0.80 per pound for the Regular blend. Because of the extra steps required to produce DeCaf, the production cost for the DeCaf blend is \$1.05 per pound. Packaging costs for both products are \$0.25 per pound. Formulate a linear programming model that can be used to determine the pounds of Brazilian Natural and Colombian Mild that will maximize the total contribution to profit. What is the optimal solution and what is the contribution to profit?

14. The production manager for the Classic Boat Corporation must determine how many units of the Classic 21 model to produce over the next four quarters. The company has a beginning inventory of 100 Classic 21 boats, and demand for the four quarters is 2000 units in quarter 1, 4000 units in quarter 2, 3000 units in quarter 3, and 1500 units in quarter 4. The firm has limited production capacity in each quarter. That is, up to 4000 units can be produced in quarter 1, 3000 units in quarter 2, 2000 units in quarter 3, and 4000 units in quarter 4. Each boat held in inventory in quarters 1 and 2 incurs an inventory holding cost of \$250 per unit; the holding cost for quarters 3 and 4 is \$300 per unit. The production costs for the first quarter are \$10,000 per unit; these costs are expected to increase by 10% each quarter because of increases in labor and material costs. Management specified that the ending inventory for quarter 4 must be at least 500 boats.
    a. Formulate a linear programming model that can be used to determine the production schedule that will minimize the total cost of meeting demand in each quarter subject to the production capacities in each quarter and also to the required ending inventory in quarter 4.
    b. Solve the linear program formulated in part (a). Then develop a table that will show for each quarter the number of units to manufacture, the ending inventory, and the costs incurred.
    c. Interpret each of the dual prices corresponding to the constraints developed to meet demand in each quarter. Based on these dual prices what advice would you give the production manager?
    d. Interpret each of the dual prices corresponding to the production capacity in each quarter. Based on each of these dual prices what advice would you give the production manager?

15. Seastrand Oil Company produces two grades of gasoline: regular and high octane. Both gasolines are produced by blending two types of crude oil. Although both types of crude oil contain the two important ingredients required to produce both gasolines, the percentage of important ingredients in each type of crude oil differs, as does the cost per gallon. The percentage of ingredients A and B in each type of crude oil and the cost per gallon are shown.

Crude Oil	Cost	Ingredient A	Ingredient B	
1	$0.10	20%	60%	← Crude oil 1 is 60% ingredient B
2	$0.15	50%	30%	

Each gallon of regular gasoline must contain at least 40% of ingredient A, whereas each gallon of high octane can contain at most 50% of ingredient B. Daily demand for regular and high-octane gasoline is 800,000 and 500,000 gallons, respectively. How many gallons of each type of crude oil should be used in the two gasolines to satisfy daily demand at a minimum cost?

16. The Ferguson Paper Company produces rolls of paper for use in adding machines, desk calculators, and cash registers. The rolls, which are 200 feet long, are produced in widths of 1½, 2½, and 3½ inches. The production process provides 200-foot rolls in 10-inch widths only. The firm must therefore cut the rolls to the desired final product sizes. The seven cutting alternatives and the amount of waste generated by each are as follows.

Cutting Alternative	Number of Rolls 1½ in.	2½ in.	3½ in.	Waste (inches)
1	6	0	0	1
2	0	4	0	0
3	2	0	2	0
4	0	1	2	½
5	1	3	0	1
6	1	2	1	0
7	4	0	1	½

The minimum requirements for the three products are

Roll Width (inches)	1½	2½	3½
Units	1000	2000	4000

a. If the company wants to minimize the number of 10-inch rolls that must be manufactured, how many 10-inch rolls will be processed on each cutting alternative? How many rolls are required, and what is the total waste (inches)?

b. If the company wants to minimize the waste generated, how many 10-inch units will be processed on each cutting alternative? How many rolls are required, and what is the total waste (inches)?

c. What are the differences in parts (a) and (b) to this problem? In this case, which objective do you prefer? Explain. What types of situations would make the other objective more desirable?

17. Frandec Company manufactures, assembles, and rebuilds material handling equipment used in warehouses and distribution centers. One product, called a Liftmaster, is assembled from four components: a frame, a motor, two supports, and a metal strap. Frandec's production schedule calls for 5000 Liftmasters to be made next month. Frandec purchases the motors from an outside supplier, but the frames, supports, and straps may either be

manufactured by the company or purchased from an outside supplier. Manufacturing and purchase costs per unit are shown.

Component	Manufacturing Cost	Purchase Cost
Frame	$38.00	$51.00
Support	$11.50	$15.00
Strap	$ 6.50	$ 7.50

Three departments are involved in the production of these components. The time (in minutes per unit) required to process each component in each department and the available capacity (in hours) for the three departments are as follows.

	Department		
Component	**Cutting**	**Milling**	**Shaping**
Frame	3.5	2.2	3.1
Support	1.3	1.7	2.6
Strap	0.8	—	1.7
Capacity (hours)	350	420	680

a. Formulate and solve a linear programming model for this make-or-buy application. How many of each component should be manufactured and how many should be purchased?
b. What is the total cost of the manufacturing and purchasing plan?
c. How many hours of production time are used in each department?
d. How much should Frandec be willing to pay for an additional hour of time in the shaping department?
e. Another manufacturer has offered to sell frames to Frandec for $45 each. Could Frandec improve its position by pursuing this opportunity? Why or why not?

18. The Two-Rivers Oil Company near Pittsburgh transports gasoline to its distributors by truck. The company recently contracted to supply gasoline distributors in southern Ohio, and it has $600,000 available to spend on the necessary expansion of its fleet of gasoline tank trucks. Three models of gasoline tank trucks are available.

Truck Model	Capacity (gallons)	Purchase Cost	Monthly Operating Cost, Including Depreciation
Super Tanker	5000	$67,000	$550
Regular Line	2500	$55,000	$425
Econo-Tanker	1000	$46,000	$350

The company estimates that the monthly demand for the region will be 550,000 gallons of gasoline. Because of the size and speed differences of the trucks, the number of deliveries or round trips possible per month for each truck model will vary. Trip capacities are estimated at 15 trips per month for the Super Tanker, 20 trips per month for the Regular Line, and 25 trips per month for the Econo-Tanker. Based on maintenance and driver availability, the firm does not want to add more than 15 new vehicles to its fleet. In addition, the company has decided to purchase at least three of the new Econo-Tankers for use on short-run, low-demand routes. As a final constraint, the company does not want more than half the new models to be Super Tankers.

a. If the company wishes to satisfy the gasoline demand with a minimum monthly operating expense, how many models of each truck should be purchased?

b. If the company did not require at least three Econo-Tankers and did not limit the number of Super Tankers to at most half the new models, how many models of each truck should be purchased?

19. The Silver Star Bicycle Company will be manufacturing both men's and women's models for its Easy-Pedal 10-speed bicycles during the next two months. Management wants to develop a production schedule indicating how many bicycles of each model should be produced in each month. Current demand forecasts call for 150 men's and 125 women's models to be shipped during the first month and 200 men's and 150 women's models to be shipped during the second month. Additional data are shown.

Model	Production Costs	Labor Requirements (hours) Manufacturing	Assembly	Current Inventory
Men's	$120	2.0	1.5	20
Women's	$ 90	1.6	1.0	30

Last month the company used a total of 1000 hours of labor. The company's labor relations policy will not allow the combined total hours of labor (manufacturing plus assembly) to increase or decrease by more than 100 hours from month to month. In addition, the company charges monthly inventory at the rate of 2% of the production cost based on the inventory levels at the end of the month. The company would like to have at least 25 units of each model in inventory at the end of the two months.

a. Establish a production schedule that minimizes production and inventory costs and satisfies the labor-smoothing, demand, and inventory requirements. What inventories will be maintained and what are the monthly labor requirements?

b. If the company changed the constraints so that monthly labor increases and decreases could not exceed 50 hours, what would happen to the production schedule? How much will the cost increase? What would you recommend?

20. Filtron Corporation produces filtration containers used in water treatment systems. Although business has been growing, the demand each month varies considerably. As a result, the company utilizes a mix of part-time and full-time employees to meet production demands. Although this approach provides Filtron with great flexibility, it resulted in increased costs and morale problems among employees. For instance, if Filtron needs to increase production from one month to the next, additional part-time employees have to be hired and trained, and costs go up. If Filtron has to decrease production, the workforce has to be reduced and Filtron incurs additional costs in terms of unemployment benefits and decreased morale. Best estimates are that increasing the number of units produced from one month to the next will increase production costs by $1.25 per unit, and that decreasing the number of units produced will increase production costs by $1.00 per unit. In February Filtron produced 10,000 filtration containers but only sold 7500 units; 2500 units are currently in inventory. The sales forecasts for March, April, and May are for 12,000 units, 8,000 units, and 15,000 units, respectively. In addition, Filtron has the capacity to store up to 3000 filtration containers at the end of any month. Management would like to determine the number of units to be produced in March, April, and May that will minimize the total cost of the monthly production increases and decreases.

21. Greenville Cabinets received a contract to produce speaker cabinets for a major speaker manufacturer. The contract calls for the production of 3300 bookshelf speakers and 4100 floor speakers over the next two months, with the following delivery schedule.

Model	Month 1	Month 2
Bookshelf	2100	1200
Floor	1500	2600

Greenville estimates that the production time for each bookshelf model is 0.7 hour and the production time for each floor model is 1 hour. The raw material costs are $10 for each bookshelf model and $12 for each floor model. Labor costs are $22 per hour using regular production time and $33 using overtime. Greenville has up to 2400 hours of regular production time available each month and up to 1000 additional hours of overtime available each month. If production for either cabinet exceeds demand in month 1, the cabinets can be stored at a cost of $5 per cabinet. For each product, determine the number of units that should be manufactured each month on regular time and on overtime to minimize total production and storage costs.

22. TriCity Manufacturing (TCM) makes Styrofoam cups, plates, and sandwich and meal containers. Next week's schedule calls for the production of 80,000 small sandwich containers, 80,000 large sandwich containers, and 65,000 meal containers. To make these containers, Styrofoam sheets are melted and formed into final products using three machines: M1, M2, and M3. Machine M1 can process Styrofoam sheets with a maximum width of 12 inches. The width capacity of machine M2 is 16 inches, and the width capacity of machine M3 is 20 inches. The small sandwich containers require 10-inch-wide Styrofoam sheets; thus, these containers can be produced on each of the three machines. The large sandwich containers require 12-inch-wide sheets; thus, these containers can also be produced on each of the three machines. However, the meal containers require 16-inch-wide Styrofoam sheets, so the meal containers cannot be produced on machine M1. Waste is incurred in the production of all three containers because Styrofoam is lost in the heating and forming process as well as in the final trimming of the product. The amount of waste generated varies depending upon the container produced and the machine used. The following table shows the waste in square inches for each machine and product combination. The waste material is recycled for future use.

Machine	Small Sandwich	Large Sandwich	Meal
M1	20	15	—
M2	24	28	18
M3	32	35	36

Production rates also depend upon the container produced and the machine used. The following table shows the production rates in units per minute for each machine and product combination. Machine capacities are limited for the next week. Time available is 35 hours for machine M1, 35 hours for machine M2, and 40 hours for machine M3.

Machine	Small Sandwich	Large Sandwich	Meal
M1	30	25	—
M2	45	40	30
M3	60	52	44

a. Costs associated with reprocessing the waste material have been increasing. Thus, TCM would like to minimize the amount of waste generated in meeting next week's production schedule. Formulate a linear programming model that can be used to determine the best production schedule.

b. Solve the linear program formulated in part (a) to determine the production schedule. How much waste is generated? Which machines, if any, have idle capacity?

23. EZ-Windows, Inc., manufactures replacement windows for the home remodeling business. In January, the company produced 15,000 windows and ended the month with 9000 windows in inventory. EZ-Windows management team would like to develop a production schedule for the next three months. A smooth production schedule is obviously desirable because it maintains the current workforce and provides a similar month-to-month operation. However, given the sales forecasts, the production capacities, and the storage capabilities as shown, the management team does not think a smooth production schedule with the same production quantity each month possible.

	February	March	April
Sales forecast	15,000	16,500	20,000
Production capacity	14,000	14,000	18,000
Storage capacity	6,000	6,000	6,000

The company's cost accounting department estimates that increasing production by one window from one month to the next will increase total costs by $1.00 for each unit increase in the production level. In addition, decreasing production by one unit from one month to the next will increase total costs by $0.65 for each unit decrease in the production level. Ignoring production and inventory carrying costs, formulate and solve a linear programming model that will minimize the cost of changing production levels while still satisfying the monthly sales forecasts.

24. Morton Financial must decide on the percentage of available funds to commit to each of two investments, referred to as A and B, over the next four periods. The following table shows the amount of new funds available for each of the four periods, as well as the cash expenditure required for each investment (negative values) or the cash income from the investment (positive values). The data shown (in thousands of dollars) reflect the amount of expenditure or income if 100% of the funds available in any period are invested in either A or B. For example, if Morton decides to invest 100% of the funds available in any period in investment A, it will incur cash expenditures of $1000 in period 1, $800 in period 2, $200 in period 3, and income of $200 in period 4. Note, however, if Morton made the decision to invest 80% in investment A, the cash expenditures or income would be 80% of the values shown.

Period	New Investment Funds Available	Investment A	Investment B
1	1500	−1000	−800
2	400	−800	−500
3	500	−200	−300
4	100	200	300

The amount of funds available in any period is the sum of the new investment funds for the period, the new loan funds, the savings from the previous period, the cash income from investment A, and the cash income from investment B. The funds available in any period can be used to pay the loan and interest from the previous period, placed in savings, used to pay the cash expenditures for investment A, or used to pay the cash expenditures for investment B.

Assume an interest rate of 10% per period for savings and an interest rate of 18% per period on borrowed funds. Let

$$S(t) = \text{the savings for period } t$$
$$L(t) = \text{the new loan funds for period } t$$

Then, in any period t, the savings income from the previous period is $1.1S(t - 1)$ and the loan and interest expenditure from the previous period is $1.18L(t - 1)$.

At the end of period 4, investment A is expected to have a cash value of \$3200 (assuming a 100% investment in A), and investment B is expected to have a cash value of \$2500 (assuming a 100% investment in B). Additional income and expenses at the end of period 4 will be income from savings in period 4 less the repayment of the period 4 loan plus interest.

Suppose that the decision variables are defined as

$$x_1 = \text{the proportion of investment A undertaken}$$
$$x_2 = \text{the proportion of investment B undertaken}$$

For example, if $x_1 = 0.5$, \$500 would be invested in investment A during the first period, and all remaining cash flows and ending investment A values would be multiplied by 0.5. The same holds for investment B. The model must include constraints $x_1 \leq 1$ and $x_2 \leq 1$ to make sure that no more than 100% of the investments can be undertaken.

If no more than \$200 can be borrowed in any period, determine the proportions of investments A and B and the amount of savings and borrowing in each period that will maximize the cash value for the firm at the end of the four periods.

25. Western Family Steakhouse offers a variety of low-cost meals and quick service. Other than management, the steakhouse operates with two full-time employees who work 8 hours per day. The rest of the employees are part-time employees who are scheduled for 4-hour shifts during peak meal times. On Saturdays the steakhouse is open from 11:00 A.M. to 10:00 P.M. Management wants to develop a schedule for part-time employees that will minimize labor costs and still provide excellent customer service. The average wage rate for the part-time employees is \$7.60 per hour. The total number of full-time and part-time employees needed varies with the time of day as shown.

Time	Total Number of Employees Needed
11:00 A.M.–Noon	9
Noon–1:00 P.M.	9
1:00 P.M.–2:00 P.M.	9
2:00 P.M.–3:00 P.M.	3
3:00 P.M.–4:00 P.M.	3
4:00 P.M.–5:00 P.M.	3
5:00 P.M.–6:00 P.M.	6
6:00 P.M.–7:00 P.M.	12
7:00 P.M.–8:00 P.M.	12
8:00 P.M.–9:00 P.M.	7
9:00 P.M.–10:00 P.M.	7

One full-time employee comes on duty at 11:00 A.M., works 4 hours, takes an hour off, and returns for another 4 hours. The other full-time employee comes to work at 1:00 P.M. and works the same 4-hours-on, 1-hour-off, 4-hours-on pattern.

a. Develop a minimum-cost schedule for part-time employees.

b. What is the total payroll for the part-time employees? How many part-time shifts are needed? Use the surplus variables to comment on the desirability of scheduling at least some of the part-time employees for 3-hour shifts.

c. Assume that part-time employees can be assigned either a 3-hour or 4-hour shift. Develop a minimum-cost schedule for the part-time employees. How many part-time shifts are needed, and what is the cost savings compared to the previous schedule?

26. In Section 4.5 data envelopment analysis was used to evaluate the relative efficiencies of four hospitals. Data for three input measures and four output measures were provided in Tables 4.16 and 4.17.

a. Use these data to develop a linear programming model that could be used to evaluate the performance of General Hospital.

b. The following optimal solution was obtained using The Management Scientist. Does the solution indicate that General Hospital is relatively inefficient?

Objective Function Value = 1.000

Variable	Value	Reduced Costs
E	1.000	0.000
WG	1.000	0.000
WU	0.000	0.000
WC	0.000	0.331
WS	0.000	0.215

c. Explain which hospital or hospitals make up the composite unit used to evaluate General Hospital and why.

27. Data envelopment analysis can measure the relative efficiency of a group of hospitals. The following data from a particular study involving seven teaching hospitals include three input measures and four output measures.

	Input Measures		
Hospital	Full-Time Equivalent Nonphysicians	Supply Expense (1000s)	Bed-Days Available (1000s)
A	310.0	134.60	116.00
B	278.5	114.30	106.80
C	165.6	131.30	65.52
D	250.0	316.00	94.40
E	206.4	151.20	102.10
F	384.0	217.00	153.70
G	530.1	770.80	215.00

	Output Measures			
Hospital	Patient-Days (65 or older) (1000s)	Patient-Days (under 65) (1000s)	Nurses Trained	Interns Trained
A	55.31	49.52	291	47
B	37.64	55.63	156	3
C	32.91	25.77	141	26
D	33.53	41.99	160	21
E	32.48	55.30	157	82
F	48.78	81.92	285	92
G	58.41	119.70	111	89

a. Formulate a linear programming model so that data envelopment analysis can be used to evaluate the performance of hospital D.
b. Solve the model.
c. Is hospital D relatively inefficient? What is the interpretation of the value of the objective function?
d. How many patient-days of each type are produced by the composite hospital?
e. Which hospitals would you recommend hospital D consider emulating to improve the efficiency of its operation?

28. Refer again to the data presented in Problem 27.

a. Formulate a linear programming model that can be used to perform data envelopment analysis for hospital E.
b. Solve the model.
c. Is hospital E relatively inefficient? What is the interpretation of the value of the objective function?
d. Which hospitals are involved in making up the composite hospital? Can you make a general statement about which hospitals will make up the composite unit associated with a unit that is not inefficient?

29. The Ranch House, Inc., operates five fast-food restaurants. Input measures for the restaurants include weekly hours of operation, full-time equivalent staff, and weekly supply expenses. Output measures of performance include average weekly contribution to profit, market share, and annual growth rate. Data for the input and output measures are shown in the following tables.

		Input Measures	
Restaurant	**Hours of Operation**	**FTE Staff**	**Supplies ($)**
Bardstown	96	16	850
Clarksville	110	22	1400
Jeffersonville	100	18	1200
New Albany	125	25	1500
St. Matthews	120	24	1600

		Output Measures	
Restaurant	**Weekly Profit**	**Market Share (%)**	**Growth Rate (%)**
Bardstown	$3800	25	8.0
Clarksville	$4600	32	8.5
Jeffersonville	$4400	35	8.0
New Albany	$6500	30	10.0
St. Matthews	$6000	28	9.0

a. Develop a linear programming model that can be used to evaluate the performance of the Clarksville Ranch House restaurant.
b. Solve the model.
c. Is the Clarksville Ranch House restaurant relatively inefficient? Discuss.
d. Where does the composite restaurant have more output than the Clarksville restaurant? How much less of each input resource does the composite restaurant require when compared to the Clarksville restaurant?
e. What other restaurants should be studied to find suggested ways for the Clarksville restaurant to improve its efficiency?

30. Reconsider the Leisure Airlines problem from Section 4.6. The demand forecasts shown in Table 4.18 represent Leisure Air's best estimates of demand. But, because demand cannot be forecasted perfectly, the number of seats actually sold for each origin-destination-itinerary fare (ODIF) may turn out to be smaller or larger than forecasted. Suppose that Leisure Air believes that economic conditions have improved and that their original forecast may be too low. To account for this possibility, Leisure Air is considering switching the Boeing 737-400 airplanes that are based in Pittsburgh and Newark with Boeing 757-200 airplanes that Leisure Air has available in other markets. The Boeing 757-200 airplane has a seating capacity of 158 in the coach section.

a. Because of scheduling conflicts in other markets, suppose that Leisure Air is only able to obtain one Boeing 757-200. Should the larger plane be based in Pittsburgh or in Newark? Explain.
b. Based upon your answer in part (a), determine a new allocation for the ODIFs. Briefly summarize the major differences between the new allocation using one Boeing 757-200 and the original allocation summarized in Figure 4.14.
c. Suppose that two Boeing 757-200 airplanes are available. Determine a new allocation for the ODIF's using the two larger airplanes. Briefly summarize the major differences between the new allocation using two Boeing 757-200 airplanes and the original allocation shown in Figure 4.14.
d. Consider the new solution obtained in part (b). Which ODIF has the highest bid price? What is the interpretation for this bid price?

31. Reconsider the Leisure Airlines problem from Section 4.6. Suppose that as of May 1 the following number of seats have been sold.

ODIF	1	2	3	4	5	6	7	8	9	10	11	12	13	14	15	16
Seats Sold	25	44	18	12	5	9	20	33	37	11	5	8	27	6	35	7

 a. Determine how many seats are still available for sale on each flight leg.
 b. Using the original demand forecasted for each ODIF, determine the remaining demand for each ODIF.
 c. Revise the linear programming model presented in Section 4.6 to account for the number of seats currently sold and a demand of one additional seat for the Pittsburgh–Myrtle Beach Q class ODIF. Resolve the linear programming model to determine a new allocation schedule for the ODIFs.

32. Hanson Inn is a 96-room hotel located near the airport and convention center in Louisville, Kentucky. When a convention or a special event is in town, Hanson increases its normal room rates and takes reservations based on a revenue management system. The Classic Corvette Owners Association scheduled its annual convention in Louisville for the first weekend in June. Hanson Inn agreed to make at least 50% of its rooms available for convention attendees at a special convention rate in order to be listed as a recommended hotel for the convention. Although the majority of attendees at the annual meeting typically requests a Friday and Saturday two-night package, some attendees may select a Friday night only or a Saturday night only reservation. Customers not attending the convention may also request a Friday and Saturday two-night package, or make a Friday night only or Saturday night only reservation. Thus, six types of reservations are possible: Convention customers/two-night package; convention customers/Friday night only; convention customers/Saturday night only; regular customers/two-night package; regular customers/Friday night only; and regular customers/Saturday night only. The cost for each type of reservation is shown here.

	Two-Night Package	Friday Night Only	Saturday Night Only
Convention	\$225	\$123	\$130
Regular	\$295	\$146	\$152

The anticipated demand for each type of reservation is as follows:

	Two-Night Package	Friday Night Only	Saturday Night Only
Convention	40	20	15
Regular	20	30	25

Hanson Inn would like to determine how many rooms to make available for each type of reservation in order to maximize total revenue.

 a. Define the decision variables and state the objective function.
 b. Formulate a linear programming model for this revenue management application.
 c. What is the optimal allocation and the anticipated total revenue?
 d. Suppose that one week before the convention, the number of regular customers/Saturday night only rooms that were made available sell out. If another nonconvention customer calls and requests a Saturday only room, what is the value of accepting this additional reservation?

Case Problem 1 PLANNING AN ADVERTISING CAMPAIGN

The Flamingo Grill is an upscale restaurant located in St. Petersburg, Florida. To help plan an advertising campaign for the coming season, Flamingo's management team hired the advertising firm of Haskell & Johnson (HJ). The management team requested HJ's recommendation concerning how the advertising budget should be distributed across television, radio, and newspaper advertisements. The budget has been set at $279,000.

In a meeting with Flamingo's management team, HJ consultants provided the following information about the industry exposure effectiveness rating per ad, their estimate of the number of potential new customers reached per ad, and the cost for each ad.

Advertising Media	Exposure Rating per Ad	New Customers per Ad	Cost per Ad
Television	90	4000	$10,000
Radio	25	2000	$ 3,000
Newspaper	10	1000	$ 1,000

The exposure rating is viewed as a measure of the value of the ad to both existing customers and potential new customers. It is a function of such things as image, message recall, visual and audio appeal, and so on. As expected, the more expensive television advertisement has the highest exposure effectiveness rating along with the greatest potential for reaching new customers.

At this point, the HJ consultants pointed out that the data concerning exposure and reach were only applicable to the first few ads in each media. For television, HJ stated that the exposure rating of 90 and the 4000 new customers reached per ad were reliable for the first 10 television ads. After 10 ads, the benefit is expected to decline. For planning purposes, HJ recommended reducing the exposure rating to 55 and the estimate of the potential new customers reached to 1500 for any television ads beyond 10. For radio ads, the preceding data are reliable up to a maximum of 15 ads. Beyond 15 ads, the exposure rating declines to 20 and number of new customers reached declines to 1200 per ad. Similarly, for newspaper ads, the preceding data are reliable up to a maximum of 20; the exposure rating declines to 5 and the potential number of new customers reached declines to 800 for additional ads.

Flamingo's management team accepted maximizing the total exposure rating, across all media, as the objective of the advertising campaign. Because of management's concern with attracting new customers, management stated that the advertising campaign must reach at least 100,000 new customers. To balance the advertising campaign and make use of all advertising media, Flamingo's management team also adopted the following guidelines.

- Use at least twice as many radio advertisements as television advertisements.
- Use no more than 20 television advertisements.
- The television budget should be at least $140,000.
- The radio advertising budget is restricted to a maximum of $99,000.
- The newspaper budget is to be at least $30,000.

HJ agreed to work with these guidelines and provide a recommendation as to how the $279,000 advertising budget should be allocated among television, radio, and newspaper advertising.

Managerial Report

Develop a model that can be used to determine the advertising budget allocation for the Flamingo Grill. Include a discussion of the following in your report.

1. A schedule showing the recommended number of television, radio, and newspaper advertisements and the budget allocation for each media. Show the total exposure and indicate the total number of potential new customers reached.
2. How would the total exposure change if an additional $10,000 were added to the advertising budget?
3. A discussion of the ranges for the objective function coefficients. What do the ranges indicate about how sensitive the recommended solution is to HJ's exposure rating coefficients?
4. After reviewing HJ's recommendation, the Flamingo's management team asked how the recommendation would change if the objective of the advertising campaign was to maximize the number of potential new customers reached. Develop the media schedule under this objective.
5. Compare the recommendations from parts 1 and 4. What is your recommendation for the Flamingo Grill's advertising campaign?

Case Problem 2 PHOENIX COMPUTER

Phoenix Computer manufactures and sells personal computers directly to customers. Orders are accepted by phone and through the company's Web site. Phoenix will be introducing several new laptop models over the next few months and management recognizes a need to develop technical support personnel to specialize in the new laptop systems. One option being considered is to hire new employees and put them through a three-month training program. Another option is to put current customer service specialists through a two-month training program on the new laptop models. Phoenix estimates that the need for laptop specialists will grow from 0 to 100 during the months of May through September as follows: May—20; June—30; July—85; August—85; and September—100. After September, Phoenix expects that maintaining a staff of 100 laptop specialists will be sufficient.

The annual salary for a new employee is estimated to be $27,000 whether the person is hired to enter the training program or to replace a current employee who is entering the training program. The annual salary for the current Phoenix employees who are being considered for the training program is approximately $36,000. The cost of the three-month training program is $1500 per person, and the cost of the two-month training program is $1000 per person. Note that the length of the training program means that a lag will occur between the time when a new person is hired and the time a new laptop specialist is available. The number of current employees who will be available for training is limited. Phoenix estimates that the following numbers can be made available in the coming months: March—15; April—20; May—0; June—5; and July—10. The training center has the capacity to start new three-month and two-month training classes each month; however, the total number of students (new and current employees) that begin training each month cannot exceed 25.

Phoenix needs to determine the number of new hires that should begin the three-month training program each month and the number of current employees that should begin the two-month training program each month. The objective is to satisfy staffing needs during May through September at the lowest possible total cost; that is, minimize the incremental salary cost and the total training cost.

It is currently January, and Phoenix Computer would like to develop a plan for hiring new employees and determining the mix of new hires and current employees to place in the training program.

Managerial Report

Perform an analysis of the Phoenix Computer problem and prepare a report that summarizes your findings. Be sure to include information on and analysis of the following items.

1. The incremental salary and training cost associated with hiring a new employee and training him/her to be a laptop specialist.
2. The incremental salary and training cost associated with putting a current employee through the training program. (Don't forget that a replacement must be hired when the current employee enters the program.)
3. Recommendations regarding the hiring and training plan that will minimize the salary and training costs over the February through August period as well as answers to these questions: What is the total cost of providing technical support for the new laptop models? How much higher will monthly payroll costs be in September than in January?

Case Problem 3 TEXTILE MILL SCHEDULING

The Scottsville Textile Mill* produces five different fabrics. Each fabric can be woven on one or more of the mill's 38 looms. The sales department's forecast of demand for the next month is shown in Table 4.19, along with data on the selling price per yard, variable cost per yard, and purchase price per yard. The mill operates 24 hours a day and is scheduled for 30 days during the coming month.

The mill has two types of looms: dobbie and regular. The dobbie looms are more versatile and can be used for all five fabrics. The regular looms can produce only three of the fabrics. The mill has a total of 38 looms: 8 are dobbie and 30 are regular. The rate of production for each fabric on each type of loom is given in Table 4.20. The time required to change over from producing one fabric to another is negligible and does not have to be considered.

The Scottsville Textile Mill satisfies all demand with either its own fabric or fabric purchased from another mill. Fabrics that cannot be woven at the Scottsville Mill because of limited loom capacity will be purchased from another mill. The purchase price of each fabric is also shown in Table 4.19.

TABLE 4.19 MONTHLY DEMAND, SELLING PRICE, VARIABLE COST, AND PURCHASE PRICE DATA FOR SCOTTSVILLE TEXTILE MILL FABRICS

Fabric	Demand (yards)	Selling Price ($/yard)	Variable Cost ($/yard)	Purchase Price ($/yard)
1	16,500	0.99	0.66	0.80
2	22,000	0.86	0.55	0.70
3	62,000	1.10	0.49	0.60
4	7,500	1.24	0.51	0.70
5	62,000	0.70	0.50	0.70

*This case is based on the Calhoun Textile Mill Case by Jeffrey D. Camm, P. M. Dearing, and Suresh K. Tadisnia, 1987.

TABLE 4.20 LOOM PRODUCTION RATES FOR THE SCOTTSVILLE TEXTILE MILL

	Loom Rate (yards/hour)	
Fabric	**Dobbie**	**Regular**
1	4.63	—
2	4.63	—
3	5.23	5.23
4	5.23	5.23
5	4.17	4.17

Note: Fabrics 1 and 2 can be manufactured only on the dobbie loom.

Managerial Report

Develop a model that can be used to schedule production for the Scottsville Textile Mill, and at the same time, determine how many yards of each fabric must be purchased from another mill. Include a discussion and analysis of the following items in your report.

1. The final production schedule and loom assignments for each fabric
2. The projected total contribution to profit
3. A discussion of the value of additional loom time (The mill is considering purchasing a ninth dobbie loom. What is your estimate of the monthly profit contribution of this additional loom?)
4. A discussion of the objective coefficients ranges
5. A discussion of how the objective of minimizing total costs would provide a different model than the objective of maximizing total profit contribution. (How would the interpretation of the objective coefficients ranges differ for these two models?)

Case Problem 4 WORKFORCE SCHEDULING

Davis Instruments has two manufacturing plants located in Atlanta, Georgia. Product demand varies considerably from month to month, causing Davis extreme difficulty in workforce scheduling. Recently Davis started hiring temporary workers supplied by WorkForce Unlimited, a company that specializes in providing temporary employees for firms in the greater Atlanta area. WorkForce Unlimited offered to provide temporary employees under three contract options that differ in terms of the length of employment and the cost. The three options are summarized:

Option	Length of Employment	Cost
1	One month	$2000
2	Two months	$4800
3	Three months	$7500

The longer contract periods are more expensive because WorkForce Unlimited experiences greater difficulty finding temporary workers who are willing to commit to longer work assignments.

Over the next six months, Davis projects the following needs for additional employees.

Month	January	February	March	April	May	June
Employees Needed	10	23	19	26	20	14

Each month, Davis can hire as many temporary employees as needed under each of the three options. For instance, if Davis hires five employees in January under Option 2, WorkForce Unlimited will supply Davis with five temporary workers who will work two months: January and February. For these workers, Davis will have to pay 5($4800) = $24,000. Because of some merger negotiations under way, Davis does not want to commit to any contractual obligations for temporary employees that extend beyond June.

Davis's quality control program requires each temporary employee to receive training at the time of hire. The training program is required even if the person worked for Davis Instruments in the past. Davis estimates that the cost of training is $875 each time a temporary employee is hired. Thus, if a temporary employee is hired for one month, Davis will incur a training cost of $875, but will incur no additional training cost if the employee is on a two- or three-month contract.

Managerial Report

Develop a model that can be used to determine the number of temporary employees Davis should hire each month under each contract plan in order to meet the projected needs at a minimum total cost. Include the following items in your report:

1. A schedule that shows the number of temporary employees that Davis should hire each month for each contract option.
2. A summary table that shows the number of temporary employees that Davis should hire under each contract option, the associated contract cost for each option, and the associated training cost for each option. Provide summary totals showing the total number of temporary employees hired, total contract costs, and total training costs.
3. If the cost to train each temporary employee could be reduced to $700 per month, what effect would this change have on the hiring plan? Explain. Discuss the implications that this effect on the hiring plan has for identifying methods for reducing training costs. How much of a reduction in training costs would be required to change the hiring plan based on a training cost of $875 per temporary employee?
4. Suppose that Davis hired 10 full-time employees at the beginning of January in order to satisfy part of the labor requirements over the next six months. If Davis can hire full-time employees for $16.50 per hour, including fringe benefits, what effect would it have on total labor and training costs over the six-month period as compared to hiring only temporary employees? Assume that full-time and temporary employees both work approximately 160 hours per month. Provide a recommendation regarding the decision to hire additional full-time employees.

Case Problem 5 CINERGY COAL ALLOCATION*

Cinergy Corporation manufactures and distributes electricity for customers located in Indiana, Kentucky, and Ohio. The company spends $725 to $750 million each year for the fuel needed to operate its coal-fired and gas-fired power plants; 92 percent to 95 percent of the fuel used is coal. Cinergy uses 10 coal-burning generating plants: five located inland and five located on the Ohio River. Some plants have more than one generating unit. As the seventh-largest coal-burning utility in the United States, Cinergy uses 28–29 million tons of coal per year at a cost of approximately $2 million every day.

The company purchases coal using fixed-tonnage or variable-tonnage contracts from mines in Indiana (49 percent), West Virginia (20 percent), Ohio (12 percent), Kentucky (11 percent), Illinois (5 percent), and Pennsylvania (3 percent). The company must purchase all of the coal contracted for on fixed-tonnage contracts, but on variable-tonnage contracts it can purchase varying amounts up to the limit specified in the contract. The coal is shipped from the mines to Cinergy's generating facilities in Ohio, Kentucky, and Indiana. The cost of coal varies from $19 to $35 per ton and transportation/delivery charges range from $1.50 to $5.00 per ton.

A model is used to determine the megawatt-hours (mWh) of electricity that each generating unit is expected to produce and to provide a measure of each generating unit's efficiency, referred to as the heat rate. The heat rate is the total BTUs required to produce 1 kilowatt-hour (kWh) of electrical power.

Coal Allocation Model

Cinergy uses a linear programming model, called the coal allocation model, to allocate coal to its generating facilities. The objective of the coal allocation model is to determine the lowest-cost method for purchasing and distributing coal to the generating units. The supply/availability of the coal is determined by the contracts with the various mines, and the demand for coal at the generating units is determined indirectly by the megawatt-hours of electricity each unit must produce.

The cost to process coal, called the add-on cost, depends upon the characteristics of the coal (moisture content, ash content, BTU content, sulfur content, and grindability) and the efficiency of the generating unit. The add-on cost plus the transportation cost are added to the purchase cost of the coal to determine the total cost to purchase and use the coal.

Current Problem

Cinergy signed three fixed-tonnage contracts and four variable-tonnage contracts. The company would like to determine the least-cost way to allocate the coal available through these contracts to five generating units. The relevant data for the three fixed-tonnage contracts are as follows:

Supplier	Number of Tons Contracted For	Cost ($/ton)	BTUs/lb
RAG	350,000	22	13,000
Peabody Coal Sales	300,000	26	13,300
American Coal Sales	275,000	22	12,600

For example, the contract signed with RAG requires Cinergy to purchase 350,000 tons of coal at a price of $22 per ton; each pound of this particular coal provides 13,000 BTUs.

The data for the four variable-tonnage contracts follow:

*The authors are indebted to Thomas Mason and David Bossee of Cinergy Corp. for their contribution to this case problem.

Supplier	Number of Tons Available	Cost ($/ton)	BTUs/lb
Consol, Inc.	200,000	32	12,250
Cyprus Amax	175,000	35	12,000
Addington Mining	200,000	31	12,000
Waterloo	180,000	33	11,300

For example, the contract with Consol, Inc., enables Cinergy to purchase up to 200,000 tons of coal at a cost of $32 per ton; each pound of this coal provides 12,250 BTUs.

The number of megawatt-hours of electricity that each generating unit must produce and the heat rate provided are as follows:

Generating Unit	Electricity Produced (mWh)	Heat Rate (BTUs per kWh)
Miami Fort Unit 5	550,000	10,500
Miami Fort Unit 7	500,000	10,200
Beckjord Unit 1	650,000	10,100
East Bend Unit 2	750,000	10,000
Zimmer Unit 1	1,100,000	10,000

For example, Miami Fort Unit 5 must produce 550,000 megawatt-hours of electricity, and 10,500 BTUs are needed to produce each kilowatt-hour.

The transportation cost and the add-on cost in dollars per ton are shown here:

	Transportation Cost ($/ton)				
Supplier	Miami Fort Unit 5	Miami Fort Unit 7	Beckjord Unit 1	East Bend Unit 2	Zimmer Unit 1
RAG	5.00	5.00	4.75	5.00	4.75
Peabody	3.75	3.75	3.50	3.75	3.50
American	3.00	3.00	2.75	3.00	2.75
Consol	3.25	3.25	2.85	3.25	2.85
Cyprus	5.00	5.00	4.75	5.00	4.75
Addington	2.25	2.25	2.00	2.25	2.00
Waterloo	2.00	2.00	1.60	2.00	1.60

	Add-On Cost ($/ton)				
Supplier	Miami Fort Unit 5	Miami Fort Unit 7	Beckjord Unit 1	East Bend Unit 2	Zimmer Unit 1
RAG	10.00	10.00	10.00	5.00	6.00
Peabody	10.00	10.00	11.00	6.00	7.00
American	13.00	13.00	15.00	9.00	9.00
Consol	10.00	10.00	11.00	7.00	7.00
Cyprus	10.00	10.00	10.00	5.00	6.00
Addington	5.00	5.00	6.00	4.00	4.00
Waterloo	11.00	11.00	11.00	7.00	9.00

Managerial Report

Prepare a report that summarizes your recommendations regarding Cinergy's coal allocation problem. Be sure to include information and analysis for the following issues.

1. Determine how much coal to purchase from each of the mining companies and how it should be allocated to the generating units. What is the cost to purchase, deliver, and process the coal?
2. Compute the average cost of coal in cents per million BTUs for each generating unit (a measure of the cost of fuel for the generating units).
3. Compute the average number of BTUs per pound of coal received at each generating unit (a measure of the energy efficiency of the coal received at each unit).
4. Suppose that Cinergy can purchase an additional 80,000 tons of coal from American Coal Sales as an "all or nothing deal" for $30 per ton. Should Cinergy purchase the additional 80,000 tons of coal?
5. Suppose that Cinergy learns that the energy content of the coal from Cyprus Amax is actually 13,000 BTUs per pound. Should Cinergy revise its procurement plan?
6. Cinergy has learned from its trading group that Cinergy can sell 50,000 megawatt-hours of electricity over the grid (to other electricity suppliers) at a price of $30 per megawatt-hour. Should Cinergy sell the electricity? If so, which generating units should produce the additional electricity?

Appendix 4.1 EXCEL SOLUTION OF HEWLITT CORPORATION FINANCIAL PLANNING PROBLEM

In Appendix 2.3 we showed how Excel could be used to solve the RMC linear programming problem. To illustrate the use of Excel in solving a more complex linear programming problem, we show the solution to the Hewlitt Corporation financial planning problem presented in Section 4.2.

The spreadsheet formulation and solution of the Hewlitt Corporation problem are shown in Figure 4.15. As described in Appendix 2.1, our practice is to put the data required for the problem in the top part of the spreadsheet and build the model in the bottom part of the spreadsheet. The model consists of a set of cells for the decision variables, a cell for the objective function, a set of cells for the left-hand-side functions, and a set of cells for the right-hand sides of the constraints. The cells for each of these model components are screened; the cells for the decision variables are also enclosed by a boldface line. Descriptive labels are used to make the spreadsheet easy to read.

Formulation

The data and descriptive labels are contained in cells A1:G12. The screened cells in the bottom portion of the spreadsheet contain the key elements of the model required by the Excel Solver.

Decision Variables Cells A17:L17 are reserved for the decision variables. The optimal values (rounded to three places), are shown to be $F = 1728.794$, $B_1 = 144.988$, $B_2 = 187.856$, $B_3 = 228.188$, $S_1 = 636.148$, $S_2 = 501.606$, $S_3 = 349.682$, $S_4 = 182.681$, and $S_5 = S_6 = S_7 = S_8 = 0$.

FIGURE 4.15 EXCEL SOLUTION FOR THE HEWLITT CORPORATION PROBLEM

EXCELfile
Hewlitt

	A	B	C	D	E	F	G	H	I	J	K	L
1	**Hewlitt Corporation Cash Requirements**											
2												
3		**Cash**										
4	**Year**	**Rqmt.**				**Bond**						
5	1	430			1	2	3					
6	2	210		**Price ($1000)**	1.15	1	1.35					
7	3	222		**Rate**	0.08875	0.055	0.1175					
8	4	231		**Years to Maturity**	5	6	7					
9	5	240										
10	6	195		**Annual Savings Multiple**		1.04						
11	7	225										
12	8	255										
13												
14	**Model**											
15												
16	F	B1	B2	B3	S1	S2	S3	S4	S5	S6	S7	S8
17	1728.794	144.988	187.856	228.188	636.148	501.606	349.682	182.681	0	0	0	0
18												
19					**Cash Flow**		**Net Cash**		**Cash**			
20	**Min Funds**	1728.794		**Constraints**	In	Out	**Flow**		**Rqmt.**			
21				Year 1	1728.79	1298.79	430	=	430			
22				Year 2	711.606	501.606	210	=	210			
23				Year 3	571.682	349.682	222	=	222			
24				Year 4	413.681	182.681	231	=	231			
25				Year 5	240	0	240	=	240			
26				Year 6	195	0	195	=	195			
27				Year 7	225	0	225	=	225			
28				Year 8	255	0	255	=	255			
29												

Objective Function The formula =A17 has been placed into cell B20 to reflect the total funds required. It is simply the value of the decision variable, *F*. The total funds required by the optimal solution is shown to be $1,728,794.

Left-Hand Sides The left-hand sides for the eight constraints represent the annual net cash flow. They are placed into cells G21:G28.

Cell G21 = E21 − F21 (Copy to G22:G28)

For this problem, some of the left-hand-side cells reference other cells that contain formulas. These referenced cells provide Hewlitt's cash flow in and cash flow out for each of the eight years.* The cells and their formulas are as follows:

Cell E21 =A17

Cell E22 =SUMPRODUCT($E$7:$G$7,$B$17:$D$17)+$F$10*E17

Cell E23 =SUMPRODUCT($E$7:$G$7,$B$17:$D$17)+$F$10*F17

Cell E24 =SUMPRODUCT($E$7:$G$7,$B$17:$D$17)+$F$10*G17

*The cash flow in is the sum of the positive terms in each constraint equation in the mathematical model, and the cash flow out is the sum of the negative terms in each constraint equation.

Cell E25 =SUMPRODUCT($E$7:$G$7,$B$17:$D$17)+$F$10*H17
Cell E26 =(1+E7)*B17+F7*C17+G7*D17+F10*I17
Cell E27 =(1+F7)*C17+G7*D17+F10*J17
Cell E28 =(1+G7)*D17+F10*K17
Cell F21 =SUMPRODUCT(E6:G6,B17:D17)+E17
Cell F22 =F17
Cell F23 =G17
Cell F24 =H17
Cell F25 =I17
Cell F26 =J17
Cell F27 =K17
Cell F28 =L17

Right-Hand Sides The right-hand sides for the eight constraints represent the annual cash requirements. They are placed into cells I21:I28.
Cell I21 = B5 (Copy to I22:I28)

Excel Solution

We are now ready to use the information in the spreadsheet to determine the optimal solution to the Hewlitt Corporation problem. The following steps describe how to use Excel to obtain the optimal solution.

Step 1. Select the **Tools** menu
Step 2. Select the **Solver** option
Step 3. When the **Solver Parameters** dialog box appears:
Enter B20 in the **Set Cell** box
Select the **Equal to: Min** option
Enter A17:L17 in the **By Changing Cells** box
Choose **Add**
Step 4. When the **Add Constraint** dialog box appears:
Enter G21:G28 in the **Cell Reference** box
Select =
Enter I21:I28 in the **Constraint** box
Click **OK**
Step 5. When the **Solver Parameters** dialog box appears:
Choose **Options**
Step 6. When the **Solver Options** dialog box appears:
Select **Assume Non-Negative**
Click **OK**
Step 7. When the **Solver Parameters** dialog box appears:
Choose **Solve**
Step 8. When the **Solver Results** dialog box appears:
Select **Keep Solver Solution**
Select **Sensitivity** in the **Reports** box
Click **OK**

The **Solver Parameters** dialog box is shown in Figure 4.16. The optimal solution is shown in Figure 4.15; the accompanying sensitivity report is shown in Figure 4.17.

FIGURE 4.16 SOLVER PARAMETERS DIALOG BOX FOR THE HEWLITT CORPORATION PROBLEM

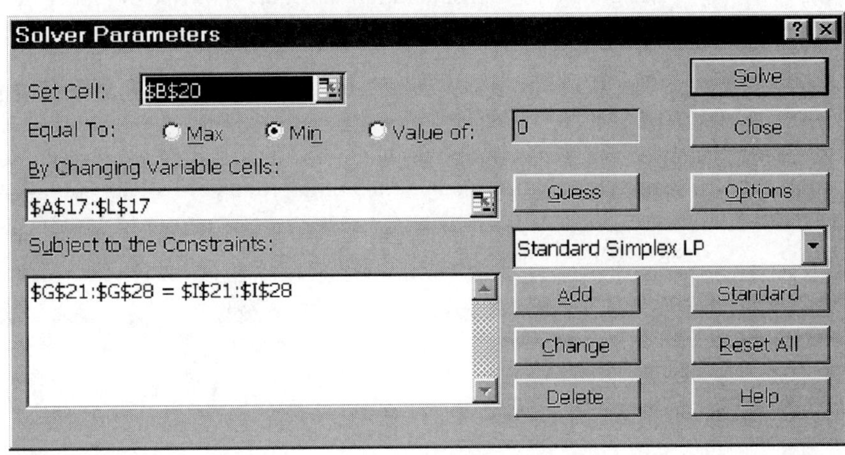

FIGURE 4.17 EXCEL'S SENSITIVITY REPORT FOR THE HEWLITT CORPORATION PROBLEM

Adjustable Cells

Cell	Name	Final Value	Reduced Cost	Objective Coefficient	Allowable Increase	Allowable Decrease
$A$17	F	1728.793855	0	1	1E+30	1
$B$17	B1	144.9881496	0	0	0.067026339	0.013026775
$C$17	B2	187.8558478	0	0	0.012795531	0.020273774
$D$17	B3	228.1879195	0	0	0.022906851	0.749663022
$E$17	S1	636.1479438	0	0	0.109559907	0.05507386
$F$17	S2	501.605712	0	0	0.143307365	0.056948823
$G$17	S3	349.681791	0	0	0.210854199	0.059039182
$H$17	S4	182.680913	0	0	0.413598622	0.061382404
$I$17	S5	0	0.064025159	0	1E+30	0.064025159
$J$17	S6	0	0.012613604	0	1E+30	0.012613604
$K$17	S7	0	0.021318233	0	1E+30	0.021318233
$L$17	S8	0	0.670839393	0	1E+30	0.670839393

Constraints

Cell	Name	Final Value	Shadow Price	Constraint R.H. Side	Allowable Increase	Allowable Decrease
$G$21	Year 1 Flow	430	1	430	1E+30	1728.793855
$G$22	Year 2 Flow	210	0.961538462	210	1E+30	661.5938616
$G$23	Year 3 Flow	222	0.924556213	222	1E+30	521.6699405
$G$24	Year 4 Flow	231	0.888996359	231	1E+30	363.6690626
$G$25	Year 5 Flow	240	0.854804191	240	1E+30	189.9881496
$G$26	Year 6 Flow	195	0.760364454	195	2149.927647	157.8558478
$G$27	Year 7 Flow	225	0.718991202	225	3027.962172	198.1879195
$G$28	Year 8 Flow	255	0.670839393	255	1583.881915	255

Discussion

Figures 4.15 and 4.17 contain essentially the same information as that provided by The Management Scientist solution in Figure 4.4. Recall that the Excel sensitivity report uses the term *shadow price* to describe the *change* in value of the solution per unit increase in the right-hand side of a constraint. The Management Scientist and LINDO use the term *dual price* to describe the *improvement* in value of the solution per unit increase in the right-hand side of a constraint. For maximization problems, the shadow price and dual price are the same; for minimization problems, the shadow price and dual price have opposite signs. Because the Hewlitt financial planning problem involves minimization, the shadow prices in the Excel sensitivity report (Figure 4.17) are the negative of the dual prices in The Management Scientist solution (Figure 4.4).

CHAPTER 5

Linear Programming: The Simplex Method

CONTENTS

In Chapter 2 we showed how the graphical solution procedure can be used to solve linear programming problems involving two decision variables. However, most linear programming problems are too large to be solved graphically, and an algebraic solution procedure must be employed. The most widely used algebraic procedure for solving linear programming problems is called the **simplex method.**[1] Computer programs based on this method can routinely solve linear programming problems with thousands of variables and constraints. The Management Science in Action, Fleet Assignment at Delta Air Lines, describes solving a linear program involving 60,000 variables and 40,000 constraints on a daily basis.

MANAGEMENT SCIENCE IN ACTION

FLEET ASSIGNMENT AT DELTA AIR LINES*

Delta Air Lines uses linear and integer programming in its Coldstart project to solve its fleet assignment problem. The problem is to match aircraft to flight legs and fill seats with paying passengers. Airline profitability depends on being able to assign the right size of aircraft to the right leg at the right time of day. An airline seat is a perishable commodity; once a flight takes off with an empty seat the profit potential of that seat is gone forever. Primary objectives of the fleet assignment model are to minimize operating costs and lost passenger revenue. Constraints are aircraft availability, balancing arrivals and departures at airports, and maintenance requirements.

The successful implementation of the Coldstart model for assigning fleet types to flight legs shows the size of linear programs that can be solved today. The typical size of the daily Coldstart model is about 60,000 variables and 40,000 constraints. The first step in solving the fleet assignment problem is to solve the model as a linear program. The model developers report successfully solving these problems on a daily basis and contend that use of the Coldstart model will save Delta Air Lines $300 million over the next three years.

*Based on R. Subramanian, R. P. Scheff, Jr., J. D. Quillinan, D. S. Wiper, and R. E. Marsten, "Coldstart: Fleet Assignment at Delta Air Lines," *Interfaces* (January/February 1994): 104–120.

5.1 AN ALGEBRAIC OVERVIEW OF THE SIMPLEX METHOD

Let us introduce the problem we will use to demonstrate the simplex method. HighTech Industries imports electronic components that are used to assemble two different models of personal computers. One model is called the Deskpro, and the other model is called the Portable. HighTech's management is currently interested in developing a weekly production schedule for both products.

The Deskpro generates a profit contribution of $50 per unit, and the Portable generates a profit contribution of $40 per unit. For next week's production, a maximum of 150 hours of assembly time can be made available. Each unit of the Deskpro requires 3 hours of assembly time, and each unit of the Portable requires 5 hours of assembly time. In addition, HighTech currently has only 20 Portable display components in inventory; thus, no more than 20 units of the Portable may be assembled. Finally, only 300 square feet of warehouse space can be made available for new production. Assembly of each Deskpro requires 8 square feet of warehouse space; similarly, each Portable requires 5 square feet.

[1]Several computer codes also employ what are called interior point solution procedures. They work well on many large problems, but the simplex method is still the most widely used solution procedure.

To develop a linear programming model for the HighTech problem, we will use the following decision variables:

$$x_1 = \text{number of units of the Deskpro}$$
$$x_2 = \text{number of units of the Portable}$$

The complete mathematical model for this problem is presented here.

$$\begin{aligned}
\text{Max} \quad & 50x_1 + 40x_2 \\
\text{s.t.} \quad & \\
& 3x_1 + 5x_2 \leq 150 \quad \text{Assembly time} \\
& 1x_2 \leq 20 \quad \text{Portable display} \\
& 8x_1 + 5x_2 \leq 300 \quad \text{Warehouse capacity} \\
& x_1, x_2 \geq 0
\end{aligned}$$

Adding a slack variable to each of the constraints permits us to write the problem in standard form.

$$\text{Max} \quad 50x_1 + 40x_2 + 0s_1 + 0s_2 + 0s_3 \tag{5.1}$$
s.t.
$$3x_1 + 5x_2 + 1s_1 = 150 \tag{5.2}$$
$$1x_2 + 1s_2 = 20 \tag{5.3}$$
$$8x_1 + 5x_2 + 1s_3 = 300 \tag{5.4}$$
$$x_1, x_2, s_1, s_2, s_3 \geq 0 \tag{5.5}$$

The simplex method was developed by George Dantzig while working for the U.S. Air Force. It was first published in 1949.

Algebraic Properties of the Simplex Method

Constraint equations (5.2) to (5.4) form a system of three simultaneous linear equations with five variables. Whenever a system of simultaneous linear equations has more variables than equations, we can expect an infinite number of solutions. The simplex method can be viewed as an algebraic procedure for finding the best solution to such a system of equations. In the preceding example, the best solution is the solution to equations (5.2) to (5.4) that maximizes the objective function (5.1) and satisfies the nonnegativity conditions given by (5.5).

Determining a Basic Solution

For the HighTech Industries constraint equations, which have more variables (five) than equations (three), the simplex method finds solutions for these equations by assigning zero values to two of the variables and then solving for the values of the remaining three variables. For example, if we set $x_2 = 0$ and $s_1 = 0$, the system of constraint equations becomes

$$3x_1 = 150 \tag{5.6}$$
$$1s_2 = 20 \tag{5.7}$$
$$8x_1 + 1s_3 = 300 \tag{5.8}$$

Using equation (5.6) to solve for x_1, we have

$$3x_1 = 150$$

and hence $x_1 = 150/3 = 50$. Equation (5.7) provides $s_2 = 20$. Finally, substituting $x_1 = 50$ into equation (5.8) results in

$$8(50) + 1s_3 = 300$$

Solving for s_3, we obtain $s_3 = -100$.

A basic solution is obtained by setting two of the five variables equal to zero and solving the three equations simultaneously for the values of the other three variables. Mathematically, we are guaranteed a solution only if the resulting three equations are linearly independent. Fortunately, the simplex method is designed to guarantee that a solution exists for the basic variables at each iteration.

Thus, we obtain the following solution to the three-equation, five-variable set of linear equations:

$$\begin{aligned} x_1 &= 50 \\ x_2 &= 0 \\ s_1 &= 0 \\ s_2 &= 20 \\ s_3 &= -100 \end{aligned}$$

This solution is referred to as a **basic solution** for the HighTech linear programming problem. To state a general procedure for determining a basic solution, we must consider a standard-form linear programming problem consisting of n variables and m linear equations, where n is greater than m.

Basic Solution

To determine a basic solution, set $n - m$ of the variables equal to zero, and solve the m linear constraint equations for the remaining m variables.[2]

In terms of the HighTech problem, a basic solution can be obtained by setting any two variables equal to zero and then solving the system of three linear equations for the remaining three variables. We shall refer to the $n - m$ variables set equal to zero as the **nonbasic variables** and the remaining m variables as the **basic variables.** Thus, in the preceding example, x_2 and s_1 are the nonbasic variables, and x_1, s_2, and s_3 are the basic variables.

Basic Feasible Solution

A basic solution can be either feasible or infeasible. A **basic feasible solution** is a basic solution that also satisfies the nonnegativity conditions. The basic solution found by setting x_2 and s_1 equal to zero and then solving for x_1, s_2, and s_3 is not a basic feasible solution because $s_3 = -100$. However, suppose that we had chosen to make x_1 and x_2 nonbasic variables by setting $x_1 = 0$ and $x_2 = 0$. Solving for the corresponding basic solution is easy because with $x_1 = x_2 = 0$, the three constraint equations reduce to

$$\begin{aligned} 1s_1 \qquad\qquad &= 150 \\ 1s_2 \qquad &= 20 \\ 1s_3 &= 300 \end{aligned}$$

[2]In some cases, a unique solution cannot be found for a system of m equations and n variables. However, these cases will never be encountered when using the simplex method.

The complete solution with $x_1 = 0$ and $x_2 = 0$ is

$$\begin{aligned} x_1 &= 0 \\ x_2 &= 0 \\ s_1 &= 150 \\ s_2 &= 20 \\ s_3 &= 300 \end{aligned}$$

This solution is a basic feasible solution because all of the variables satisfy the nonnegativity conditions.

The following graph shows all the constraint equations and basic solutions for the HighTech problem. Circled points ①–⑤ are basic feasible solutions; circled points ⑥–⑨ are basic solutions that are not feasible. The basic solution found by setting $x_2 = 0$ and $s_1 = 0$ corresponds to point ⑨; the basic feasible solution found by setting $x_1 = 0$ and $x_2 = 0$ corresponds to point ① in the feasible region.

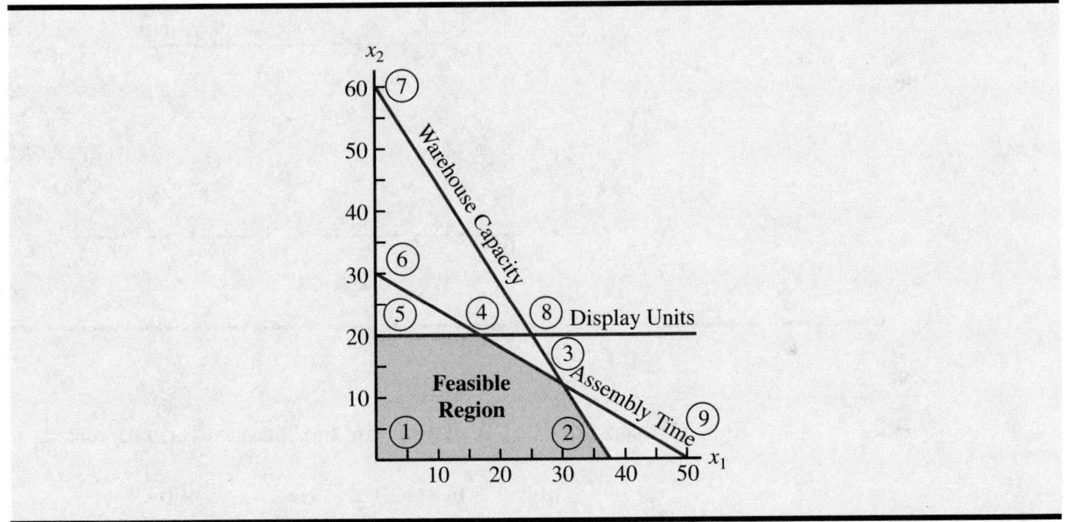

Can you find basic and basic feasible solutions to a system of equations at this point? Try Problem 1.

The graph in Figure 5.1 shows only the basic feasible solutions for the HighTech problem; note that each of these solutions is an extreme point of the feasible region. In Chapter 2 we showed that the optimal solution to a linear programming problem can be found at an extreme point. Because every extreme point corresponds to a basic feasible solution, we can now conclude that the HighTech problem does have an optimal basic feasible solution.[3] The simplex method is an iterative procedure for moving from one basic feasible solution (extreme point) to another until the optimal solution is reached.

5.2 TABLEAU FORM

A basic feasible solution to the system of m linear constraint equations and n variables is required as a starting point for the simplex method. The purpose of tableau form is to provide an initial basic feasible solution.

[3]We are only considering cases that have an optimal solution. That is, cases of infeasibility and unboundedness will have no optimal solution, so no optimal basic feasible solution is possible.

FIGURE 5.1 FEASIBLE REGION AND EXTREME POINTS FOR THE HIGHTECH INDUSTRIES PROBLEM

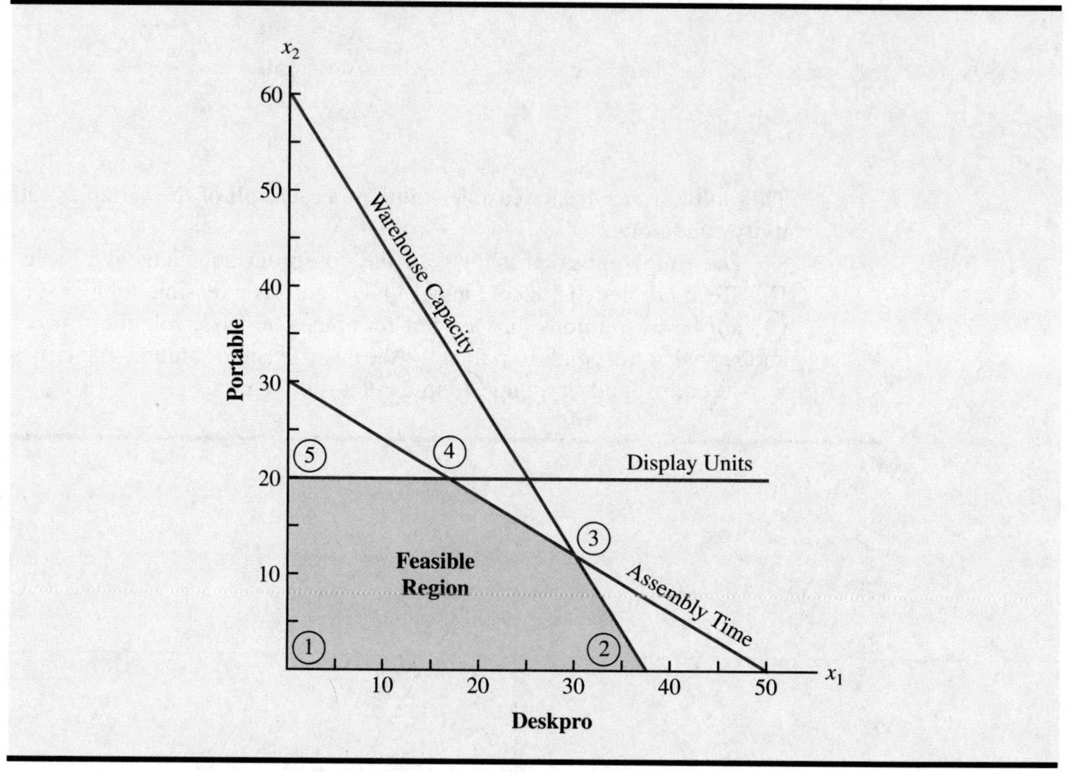

Recall that for the HighTech problem, the standard-form representation is

$$\begin{aligned}
\text{Max} \quad & 50x_1 + 40x_2 + 0s_1 + 0s_2 + 0s_3 \\
\text{s.t.} \quad & \\
& 3x_1 + 5x_2 + 1s_1 \qquad\qquad\quad = 150 \\
& \qquad\quad 1x_2 \qquad + 1s_2 \qquad\quad = 20 \\
& 8x_1 + 5x_2 \qquad\qquad\quad + 1s_3 = 300 \\
& x_1, x_2, s_1, s_2, s_3 \geq 0
\end{aligned}$$

When a linear programming problem with all less-than-or-equal-to constraints is written in standard form, it is easy to find a basic feasible solution. We simply set the decision variables equal to zero and solve for the values of the slack variables. Note that this procedure sets the values of the slack variables equal to the right-hand-side values of the constraint equations. For the HighTech problem, we obtain $x_1 = 0$, $x_2 = 0$, $s_1 = 150$, $s_2 = 20$, and $s_3 = 300$ as the initial basic feasible solution.

If we study the standard-form representation of the HighTech constraint equations closely, we can identify two properties that make it possible to find an initial basic feasible solution. The first property requires that the following conditions be satisfied:

a. For each constraint equation, the coefficient of one of the m basic variables in that equation must be 1, and the coefficients for all the remaining basic variables in that equation must be 0.
b. The coefficient for each basic variable must be 1 in only one constraint equation.

When these conditions are satisfied, exactly one basic variable with a coefficient of 1 is associated with each constraint equation, and for each of the m constraint equations, it is a different basic variable. Thus, if the $n - m$ nonbasic variables are set equal to zero, the values of the basic variables are the values of the right-hand sides of the constraint equations.

For linear programs with less-than-or-equal-to constraints, the slack variables provide the initial basic feasible solution identified in tableau form.

The second property that enables us to find a basic feasible solution requires the values of the right-hand sides of the constraint equations be nonnegative. This nonnegativity ensures that the basic solution obtained by setting the basic variables equal to the values of the right-hand sides will be feasible.

If a linear programming problem satisfies these two properties, it is said to be in **tableau form.** Thus, we see that the standard-form representation of the HighTech problem is already in tableau form. In fact, standard form and tableau form for linear programs that have all less-than-or-equal-to constraints and nonnegative right-hand-side values are the same. Later in this chapter we will show how to set up the tableau form for linear programming problems where the standard form and the tableau form are not the same.

In the HighTech problem, tableau form and standard form are the same, which is true for all LPs with only less-than-or-equal-to constraints and nonnegative right-hand sides.

To summarize, the following three steps are necessary to prepare a linear programming problem for solution using the simplex method:

Step 1. Formulate the problem.
Step 2. Set up the standard form by adding slack and/or subtracting surplus variables.
Step 3. Set up the tableau form.

5.3 SETTING UP THE INITIAL SIMPLEX TABLEAU

After a linear programming problem has been converted to tableau form, we have an initial basic feasible solution that can be used to begin the simplex method. To provide a convenient means for performing the calculations required by the simplex method, we will first develop what is referred to as the initial **simplex tableau.**

Part of the initial simplex tableau is a table containing all the coefficients shown in the tableau form of a linear program. If we adopt the general notation

$$c_j = \text{objective function coefficient for variable } j$$
$$b_i = \text{right-hand-side value for constraint } i$$
$$a_{ij} = \text{coefficient associated with variable } j \text{ in constraint } i$$

we can show this portion of the initial simplex tableau as follows:

c_1	c_2	$\ldots c_n$	
a_{11}	a_{12}	$\ldots a_{1n}$	b_1
a_{21}	a_{22}	$\ldots a_{2n}$	b_2
.	.	....	.
.	.	....	.
a_{m1}	a_{m2}	$\ldots a_{mn}$	b_m

Thus, for the HighTech problem we obtain the following partial initial simplex tableau:

50	40	0	0	0	
3	5	1	0	0	**150**
0	1	0	1	0	**20**
8	5	0	0	1	**300**

Later we may want to refer to the objective function coefficients, all the right-hand-side values, or all the coefficients in the constraints as a group. For such groupings, we will find the following general notation helpful:

c row = row of objective function coefficients
b column = column of right-hand-side values of the constraint equations
A matrix = *m* rows and *n* columns of coefficients of the variables in the constraint equations

Using this notation, we can show these portions of the initial simplex tableau as follows:

c row	
A matrix	*b* column

To practice setting up the portion of the simplex tableau corresponding to the objective function and constraints at this point, try Problem 4.

To help us recall that each of the columns contains the coefficients for one of the variables, we write the variable associated with each column directly above the column. By adding the variables we obtain

x_1	x_2	s_1	s_2	s_3	
50	40	0	0	0	
3	5	1	0	0	**150**
0	1	0	1	0	**20**
8	5	0	0	1	**300**

This portion of the initial simplex tableau contains the tableau-form representation of the problem; thus, it is easy to identify the initial basic feasible solution. First, we note that for each basic variable, a corresponding column has a 1 in the only nonzero position. Such columns are known as **unit columns** or **unit vectors.** Second, a row of the tableau is associated with each basic variable. This row has a 1 in the unit column corresponding to the basic variable. The value of each basic variable is then given by the b_i value in the row associated with the basic variable. In the example, row 1 is associated with basic variable s_1 because this row has a 1 in the unit column corresponding to s_1. Thus, the value of s_1 is given by the right-hand-side value b_1: $s_1 = b_1 = 150$. In a similar fashion, $s_2 = b_2 = 20$, and $s_3 = b_3 = 300$.

To move from an initial basic feasible solution to a better basic feasible solution, the simplex method must generate a new basic feasible solution that yields a better value for the objective function. To do so requires changing the set of basic variables: we select one of the current nonbasic variables to be made basic and one of the current basic variables to be made nonbasic.

For computational convenience, we will add two new columns to the simplex tableau. One column is labeled "*Basis*" and the other column is labeled "c_B." In the *Basis* column, we list the current basic variables, and in the c_B column, we list the corresponding objective function coefficient for each of the basic variables. For the HighTech problem, this results in the following:

		x_1	x_2	s_1	s_2	s_3	
Basis	c_B	50	40	0	0	0	
s_1	0	3	5	1	0	0	**150**
s_2	0	0	1	0	1	0	**20**
s_3	0	8	5	0	0	1	**300**

Note that in the column labeled *Basis,* s_1 is listed as the first basic variable because its value is given by the right-hand-side value for the first equation. With s_2 listed second and s_3 listed third, the *Basis* column and right-hand-side values show the initial basic feasible solution has $s_1 = 150$, $s_2 = 20$, and $s_3 = 300$.

Can we improve the value of the objective function by moving to a new basic feasible solution? To find out whether it is possible, we add two rows to the bottom of the tableau. The first row, labeled z_j, represents the decrease in the value of the objective function that will result if one unit of the variable corresponding to the jth column of the A matrix is brought into the basis. The second row, labeled $c_j - z_j$, represents the net change in the value of the objective function if one unit of the variable corresponding to the jth column of the A matrix is brought into the solution. We refer to the $c_j - z_j$ row as the **net evaluation row.**

Let us first see how the entries in the z_j row are computed. Suppose that we consider increasing the value of the nonbasic variable x_1 by one unit—that is, from $x_1 = 0$ to $x_1 = 1$. In order to make this change and at the same time continue to satisfy the constraint equations, the values of some of the other variables will have to be changed. As we will show, the simplex method requires that the necessary changes be made to basic variables only. For example, in the first constraint we have

$$3x_1 + 5x_2 + 1s_1 = 150$$

The current basic variable in this constraint equation is s_1. Assuming that x_2 remains a nonbasic variable with a value of 0, if x_1 is increased in value by 1, then s_1 must be decreased by 3 for the constraint to be satisfied. Similarly, if we were to increase the value of x_1 by 1 (and keep $x_2 = 0$), we can see from the second and third equations that although s_2 would not decrease, s_3 would decrease by 8.

From analyzing all the constraint equations, we see that the coefficients in the x_1 column indicate the amount of decrease in the current basic variables when the nonbasic variable x_1 is increased from 0 to 1. In general, all the column coefficients can be interpreted this way. For instance, if we make x_2 a basic variable at a value of 1, s_1 will decrease by 5, s_2 will decrease by 1, and s_3 will decrease by 5.

Recall that the values in the c_B column of the simplex tableau are the objective function coefficients for the current basic variables. Hence, to compute the values in the z_j row (the decrease in value of the objective function when x_j is increased by one), we form the sum of the products obtained by multiplying the elements in the c_B column by the corresponding elements in the jth column of the A matrix. Doing these calculations we obtain

$$\begin{aligned} z_1 &= 0(3) + 0(0) + 0(8) = 0 \\ z_2 &= 0(5) + 0(1) + 0(5) = 0 \\ z_3 &= 0(1) + 0(0) + 0(0) = 0 \\ z_4 &= 0(0) + 0(1) + 0(0) = 0 \\ z_5 &= 0(0) + 0(0) + 0(1) = 0 \end{aligned}$$

Because the objective function coefficient of x_1 is $c_1 = 50$, the value of $c_1 - z_1$ is $50 - 0 = 50$. Then the net result of bringing one unit of x_1 into the current basis will be an increase in profit of \$50. Hence, in the net evaluation row corresponding to x_1, we enter 50. In the same manner, we can calculate the $c_j - z_j$ values for the remaining variables. The result is the following initial simplex tableau:

The simplex tableau is nothing more than a table that helps keep track of the simplex method calculations. Reconstructing the original problem can be accomplished from the initial simplex tableau.

		x_1	x_2	s_1	s_2	s_3	
Basis	c_B	50	40	0	0	0	
s_1	0	3	5	1	0	0	**150**
s_2	0	0	1	0	1	0	**20**
s_3	0	8	5	0	0	1	**300**
z_j		0	0	0	0	0	**0**
$c_j - z_j$		50	40	0	0	0	↑ Value of the Objective Function

In this tableau we also see a boldfaced 0 in the z_j row in the last column. This zero is the value of the objective function associated with the current basic feasible solution. It was computed by multiplying the objective function coefficients in the c_B column by the corresponding values of the basic variables shown in the last column of the tableau—that is, $0(150) + 0(20) + 0(300) = 0$.

Try Problem 5(a) for practice in setting up the complete initial simplex tableau for a problem with less-than-or-equal-to constraints.

The initial simplex tableau is now complete. It shows that the initial basic feasible solution ($x_1 = 0, x_2 = 0, s_1 = 150, s_2 = 20$, and $s_3 = 300$) has an objective function value, or profit, of \$0. In addition, the $c_j - z_j$ or net evaluation row has values that will guide us in improving the solution by moving to a better basic feasible solution.

5.4 IMPROVING THE SOLUTION

From the net evaluation row, we see that each unit of the Deskpro (x_1) increases the value of the objective function by 50 and each unit of the Portable (x_2) increases the value of the objective function by 40. Because x_1 causes the largest per-unit increase, we choose it as the variable to bring into the basis. We must next determine which of the current basic variables to make nonbasic.

In discussing how to compute the z_j values, we noted that each of the coefficients in the x_1 column indicates the amount of decrease in the corresponding basic variable that would result from increasing x_1 by one unit. Considering the first row, we see that every unit of the Deskpro produced will use 3 hours of assembly time, reducing s_1 by 3. In the current solution, $s_1 = 150$ and $x_1 = 0$. Thus—considering this row only—the maximum possible value of x_1 can be calculated by solving

$$3x_1 = 150$$

which provides

$$x_1 = 50$$

If x_1 is 50 (and x_2 remains a nonbasic variable with a value of 0), s_1 will have to be reduced to zero in order to satisfy the first constraint:

$$3x_1 + 5x_2 + 1s_1 = 150$$

Considering the second row, $0x_1 + 1x_2 + 1s_2 = 20$, we see that the coefficient of x_1 is 0. Thus, increasing x_1 will not have any effect on s_2; that is, increasing x_1 cannot drive the basic variable in the second row (s_2) to zero. Indeed, increases in x_1 will leave s_2 unchanged.

Finally, with 8 as the coefficient of x_1 in the third row, every unit that we increase x_1 will cause a decrease of eight units in s_3. Because the value of s_3 is currently 300, we can solve

$$8x_1 = 300$$

to find the maximum possible increase in x_1 before s_3 will become nonbasic at a value of zero; thus, we see that x_1 cannot be any larger than $300/8 = 37.5$.

Considering the three rows (constraints) simultaneously, we see that row 3 is the most restrictive. That is, producing 37.5 units of the Deskpro will force the corresponding slack variable to become nonbasic at a value of $s_3 = 0$.

In making the decision to produce as many Deskpro units as possible, we must change the set of variables in the basic feasible solution, which means obtaining a new basis. The simplex method moves from one basic feasible solution to another by selecting a nonbasic variable to replace one of the current basic variables. This process of moving from one basic feasible solution to another is called an **iteration.** We now summarize the rules for selecting a nonbasic variable to be made basic and for selecting a current basic variable to be made nonbasic.

Criterion for Entering a New Variable into the Basis

Look at the net evaluation row ($c_j - z_j$), and select the variable to enter the basis that will cause the largest per-unit improvement in the value of the objective function. In the case of a tie, follow the convention of selecting the variable to enter the basis that corresponds to the leftmost of the columns.

To determine which basic variable will become nonbasic, only the positive coefficients in the incoming column correspond to basic variables that will decrease in value when the new basic variable enters.

Criterion for Removing a Variable from the Current Basis (Minimum Ratio Test)

Suppose the incoming basic variable corresponds to column j in the A portion of the simplex tableau. For each row i, compute the ratio b_i/a_{ij} for each a_{ij} greater than zero. The basic variable that will be removed from the basis corresponds to the minimum of these ratios. In case of a tie, we follow the convention of selecting the variable that corresponds to the uppermost of the tied rows.

To illustrate the computations involved, we add an extra column to the right of the tableau showing the b_i/a_{ij} ratios.

Basis	c_B	x_1 50	x_2 40	s_1 0	s_2 0	s_3 0		$\frac{b_i}{a_{i1}}$
s_1	0	3	5	1	0	0	**150**	$\frac{150}{3} = 50$
s_2	0	0	1	0	1	0	**20**	—
s_3	0	(8)	5	0	0	1	**300**	$\frac{300}{8} = 37.5$
	z_j	0	0	0	0	0	**0**	
	$c_j - z_j$	50	40	0	0	0		

We see that $c_1 - z_1 = 50$ is the largest positive value in the $c_j - z_j$ row. Hence, x_1 is selected to become the new basic variable. Checking the ratios b_i/a_{i1} for values of a_{i1} greater than zero, we see that $b_3/a_{31} = 300/8 = 37.5$ is the minimum of these ratios. Thus, the current basic variable associated with row 3 (s_3) is the variable selected to leave the basis. In the tableau we have circled $a_{31} = 8$ to indicate that the variable corresponding to the first column is to enter the basis and that the basic variable corresponding to the third row is to leave the basis. Adopting the usual linear programming terminology, we refer to this circled element as the **pivot element.** The column and the row containing the pivot element are called the **pivot column** and the **pivot row,** respectively.

The circled value is the pivot element; the corresponding column and row are called the pivot column and pivot row.

To improve the current solution of $x_1 = 0, x_2 = 0, s_1 = 150, s_2 = 20$, and $s_3 = 300$, we should increase x_1 to 37.5. The production of 37.5 units of the Deskpro results in a profit of $50(37.5) = 1875$. In producing 37.5 units of the Deskpro, s_3 will be reduced to zero. Hence, x_1 will become the new basic variable, replacing s_3 in the previous basis.

5.5 CALCULATING THE NEXT TABLEAU

We now want to update the simplex tableau in such a fashion that the column associated with the new basic variable is a unit column; in this way its value will be given by the right-hand-side value of the corresponding row. We would like the column in the new tableau corresponding to x_1 to look just like the column corresponding to s_3 in the original tableau, so our goal is to make the column in the A matrix corresponding to x_1 appear as

$$\begin{matrix} 0 \\ 0 \\ 1 \end{matrix}$$

The way in which we transform the simplex tableau so that it still represents an equivalent system of constraint equations is to use the following **elementary row operations.**

Elementary Row Operations

1. Multiply any row (equation) by a nonzero number.
2. Replace any row (equation) by the result of adding or subtracting a multiple of another row (equation) to it.

The application of these elementary row operations to a system of simultaneous linear equations will not change the solution to the system of equations; however, the elementary row operations will change the coefficients of the variables and the values of the right-hand sides.

The objective in performing elementary row operations is to transform the system of constraint equations into a form that makes it easy to identify the new basic feasible solution. Consequently, we must perform the elementary row operations in such a manner that we transform the column for the variable entering the basis into a unit column. We emphasize that the feasible solutions to the original constraint equations are the same as the feasible solutions to the modified constraint equations obtained by performing elementary row operations. However, many of the numerical values in the simplex tableau will change as the result of performing these row operations. Thus, the present method of referring to elements in the simplex tableau may lead to confusion.

Until now we made no distinction between the A matrix and b column coefficients in the tableau form of the problem and the corresponding coefficients in the simplex tableau. Indeed, we showed that the initial simplex tableau is formed by properly placing the a_{ij}, c_j, and b_i elements as given in the tableau form of the problem into the simplex tableau. To avoid confusion in subsequent simplex tableaus, we will refer to the portion of the simplex tableau that initially contained the a_{ij} values with the symbol $\bar{A}$, and the portion of the tableau that initially contained the b_i values with the symbol $\bar{b}$. In terms of the simplex tableau, elements in $\bar{A}$ will be denoted by $\bar{a}_{ij}$, and elements in $\bar{b}$ will be denoted by $\bar{b}_i$. In subsequent simplex tableaus, elementary row operations will change the tableau elements. The overbar notation should avoid any confusion when we wish to distinguish between (1) the original constraint coefficient values a_{ij} and right-hand-side values b_i of the tableau form, and (2) the simplex tableau elements $\bar{a}_{ij}$ and $\bar{b}_i$.

Now let us see how elementary row operations are used to create the next simplex tableau for the HighTech problem. Recall that the goal is to transform the column in the $\bar{A}$ portion of the simplex tableau corresponding to x_1 to a unit column; that is,

$$\begin{aligned}\bar{a}_{11} &= 0\\ \bar{a}_{21} &= 0\\ \bar{a}_{31} &= 1\end{aligned}$$

To set $\bar{a}_{31} = 1$, we perform the first elementary row operation by multiplying the pivot row (row 3) by $\frac{1}{8}$ to obtain the equivalent equation

$$\tfrac{1}{8}(8x_1 + 5x_2 + 0s_1 + 0s_2 + 1s_3) = \tfrac{1}{8}(300)$$

or

$$1x_1 + \tfrac{5}{8}x_2 + 0s_1 + 0s_2 + \tfrac{1}{8}s_3 = \tfrac{75}{2} \tag{5.9}$$

We refer to equation (5.9) in the updated simplex tableau as the *new pivot row.*

To set $\bar{a}_{11} = 0$, we perform the second elementary row operation by first multiplying the new pivot row by 3 to obtain the equivalent equation

$$3(1x_1 + \tfrac{5}{8}x_2 + 0s_1 + 0s_2 + \tfrac{1}{8}s_3) = 3(\tfrac{75}{2})$$

or

$$3x_1 + {}^{15}\!/_8 x_2 + 0s_1 + 0s_2 + {}^{3}\!/_8 s_3 = {}^{225}\!/_2 \tag{5.10}$$

Subtracting equation (5.10) from the equation represented by row 1 of the simplex tableau completes the application of the second elementary row operation; thus, after dropping the terms with zero coefficients, we obtain

$$(3x_1 + 5x_2 + 1s_1) - (3x_1 + {}^{15}\!/_8 x_2 + {}^{3}\!/_8 s_3) = 150 - {}^{225}\!/_2$$

or

$$0x_1 + {}^{25}\!/_8 x_2 + 1s_1 - {}^{3}\!/_8 s_3 = {}^{75}\!/_2 \tag{5.11}$$

Because $\bar{a}_{21} = 0$, no row operations need be performed on the second row of the simplex tableau. Replacing rows 1 and 3 with the coefficients in equations (5.11) and (5.9), respectively, we obtain the new simplex tableau

		x_1	x_2	s_1	s_2	s_3	
Basis	c_B	50	40	0	0	0	
s_1	0	0	$^{25}/_8$	1	0	$-^{3}/_8$	$^{75}/_2$
s_2	0	0	1	0	1	0	**20**
x_1	50	1	$^{5}/_8$	0	0	$^{1}/_8$	$^{75}/_2$
z_j							**1875**
$c_j - z_j$							

Assigning zero values to the nonbasic variables x_2 and s_3 permits us to identify the following new basic feasible solution:

$$s_1 = {}^{75}\!/_2$$
$$s_2 = 20$$
$$x_1 = {}^{75}\!/_2$$

This solution is also provided by the last column in the new simplex tableau. The profit associated with this solution is obtained by multiplying the solution values for the basic variables as given in the $\bar{b}$ column by their corresponding objective function coefficients as given in the c_B column; that is,

$$0({}^{75}\!/_2) + 0(20) + 50({}^{75}\!/_2) = 1875$$

Interpreting the Results of an Iteration

In our example, the initial basic feasible solution was

$$\begin{aligned} x_1 &= 0 \\ x_2 &= 0 \\ s_1 &= 150 \\ s_2 &= 20 \\ s_3 &= 300 \end{aligned}$$

with a corresponding profit of \$0. One iteration of the simplex method moved us to another basic feasible solution with an objective function value of \$1875. This new basic feasible solution is

$$\begin{aligned} x_1 &= 75/2 \\ x_2 &= 0 \\ s_1 &= 75/2 \\ s_2 &= 20 \\ s_3 &= 0 \end{aligned}$$

The first iteration moves us from the origin in Figure 5.2 to extreme point 2.

In Figure 5.2 we see that the initial basic feasible solution corresponds to extreme point ①. The first iteration moved us in the direction of the greatest increase per unit in profit—that is, along the x_1 axis. We moved away from extreme point ① in the x_1 direction until we could not move farther without violating one of the constraints. The tableau we obtained after one iteration provides the basic feasible solution corresponding to extreme point ②.

We note from Figure 5.2 that at extreme point ② the warehouse capacity constraint is binding with $s_3 = 0$ and that the other two constraints contain slack. From the simplex tableau, we see that the amount of slack for these two constraints is given by $s_1 = 75/2$ and $s_2 = 20$.

Moving Toward a Better Solution

To see whether a better basic feasible solution can be found, we need to calculate the z_j and $c_j - z_j$ rows for the new simplex tableau. Recall that the elements in the z_j row are the sum of the products obtained by multiplying the elements in the c_B column of the simplex tableau by the corresponding elements in the columns of the $\bar{A}$ matrix. Thus, we obtain

$$\begin{aligned} z_1 &= 0(0) + 0(0) + 50(1) = 50 \\ z_2 &= 0(25/8) + 0(1) + 50(5/8) = 250/8 \\ z_3 &= 0(1) + 0(0) + 50(0) = 0 \\ z_4 &= 0(0) + 0(1) + 50(0) = 0 \\ z_5 &= 0(-3/8) + 0(0) + 50(1/8) = 50/8 \end{aligned}$$

FIGURE 5.2 FEASIBLE REGION AND EXTREME POINTS FOR THE HIGHTECH INDUSTRIES PROBLEM

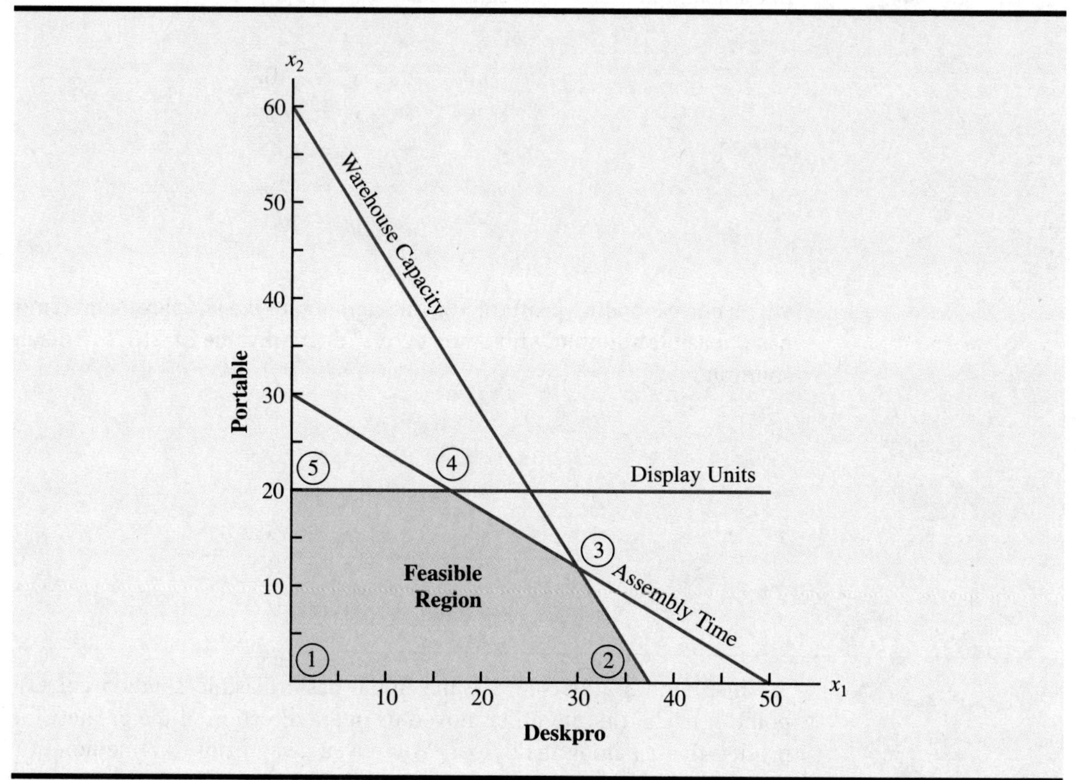

Subtracting z_j from c_j to compute the new net evaluation row, we obtain the following simplex tableau:

Basis	c_B	x_1	x_2	s_1	s_2	s_3	
		50	40	0	0	0	
s_1	0	0	$^{25}/_8$	1	0	$-^{3}/_8$	$^{75}/_2$
s_2	0	0	1	0	1	0	**20**
x_1	50	1	$^{5}/_8$	0	0	$^{1}/_8$	$^{75}/_2$
z_j		50	$^{250}/_8$	0	0	$^{50}/_8$	**1875**
$c_j - z_j$		0	$^{70}/_8$	0	0	$-^{50}/_8$	

Let us now analyze the $c_j - z_j$ row to see whether we can introduce a new variable into the basis and continue to improve the value of the objective function. Using the rule for determining which variable should enter the basis next, we select x_2 because it has the highest positive coefficient in the $c_j - z_j$ row.

To determine which variable will be removed from the basis when x_2 enters, we must compute for each row i the ratio $\bar{b}_i/\bar{a}_{i2}$ (remember, though, that we should compute this ratio only if $\bar{a}_{i2}$ is greater than zero); then we select the variable to leave the basis that corresponds to the minimum ratio. As before, we will show these ratios in an extra column of the simplex tableau:

		x_1	x_2	s_1	s_2	s_3		$\frac{\bar{b}_i}{\bar{a}_{i2}}$
Basis	c_B	50	40	0	0	0		
s_1	0	0	$^{25}/_8$ (circled)	1	0	$-^3/_8$	**$^{75}/_2$**	$\frac{^{75}/_2}{^{25}/_8} = 12$
s_2	0	0	1	0	1	0	**20**	$\frac{20}{1} = 20$
x_1	50	1	$^5/_8$	0	0	$^1/_8$	**$^{75}/_2$**	$\frac{^{75}/_2}{^5/_8} = 60$
z_j		50	$^{250}/_8$	0	0	$^{50}/_8$	**1875**	
$c_j - z_j$		0	$^{70}/_8$	0	0	$-^{50}/_8$		

With 12 as the minimum ratio, s_1 will leave the basis. The pivot element is $\bar{a}_{12} = {}^{25}/_8$, which is circled in the preceding tableau. The nonbasic variable x_2 must now be made a basic variable in row 1. This requirement means that we must perform the elementary row operations that will convert the x_2 column into a unit column with a 1 in row 1; that is, we will have to transform the second column in the tableau to the form

$$\begin{matrix} 1 \\ 0 \\ 0 \end{matrix}$$

We can make this change by performing the following elementary row operations:

Step 1. Multiply every element in row 1 (the pivot row) by $^8/_{25}$ in order to make $\bar{a}_{12} = 1$.
Step 2. Subtract the new row 1 (the new pivot row) from row 2 to make $\bar{a}_{22} = 0$.
Step 3. Multiply the new pivot row by $^5/_8$, and subtract the result from row 3 to make $\bar{a}_{32} = 0$.

The new simplex tableau resulting from these row operations is as follows:

		x_1	x_2	s_1	s_2	s_3	
Basis	c_B	50	40	0	0	0	
x_2	40	0	1	$^8/_{25}$	0	$-^3/_{25}$	**12**
s_2	0	0	0	$-^8/_{25}$	1	$^3/_{25}$	**8**
x_1	50	1	0	$-^5/_{25}$	0	$^5/_{25}$	**30**
z_j		50	40	$^{14}/_5$	0	$^{26}/_5$	**1980**
$c_j - z_j$		0	0	$-^{14}/_5$	0	$-^{26}/_5$	

Note that the values of the basic variables are $x_2 = 12$, $s_2 = 8$, and $x_1 = 30$, and the corresponding profit is $40(12) + 0(8) + 50(30) = 1980$.

We must now determine whether to bring any other variable into the basis and thereby move to another basic feasible solution. Looking at the net evaluation row, we see that every element is zero or negative. Because $c_j - z_j$ is less than or equal to zero for both of the nonbasic variables s_1 and s_3, any attempt to bring a nonbasic variable into the basis at this point will result in a lowering of the current value of the objective function. Hence, this tableau represents the optimal solution. In general, the simplex method uses the following criterion to determine when the optimal solution has been obtained.

Optimality Criterion

The optimal solution to a linear programming problem has been reached when all of the entries in the net evaluation row ($c_j - z_j$) are zero or negative. In such cases, the optimal solution is the current basic feasible solution.

Referring to Figure 5.2, we can see graphically the process that the simplex method used to determine an optimal solution. The initial basic feasible solution corresponds to the origin ($x_1 = 0$, $x_2 = 0$, $s_1 = 150$, $s_2 = 20$, $s_3 = 300$). The first iteration caused x_1 to enter the basis and s_3 to leave. The second basic feasible solution corresponds to extreme point ② ($x_1 = 75/2$, $x_2 = 0$, $s_1 = 75/2$, $s_2 = 20$, $s_3 = 0$). At the next iteration, x_2 entered the basis and s_1 left. This iteration brought us to extreme point ③ and the optimal solution ($x_1 = 30$, $x_2 = 12$, $s_1 = 0$, $s_2 = 8$, $s_3 = 0$).

For the HighTech problem with only two decision variables, we had a choice of using the graphical or simplex method. For problems with more than two variables, we shall always use the simplex method.

Interpreting the Optimal Solution

Using the final simplex tableau, we find the optimal solution to the HighTech problem consists of the basic variables x_1, x_2, and s_2 and nonbasic variables s_1 and s_3 with:

$$\begin{aligned} x_1 &= 30 \\ x_2 &= 12 \\ s_1 &= 0 \\ s_2 &= 8 \\ s_3 &= 0 \end{aligned}$$

The value of the objective function is \$1980. If management wants to maximize the total profit contribution, HighTech should produce 30 units of the Deskpro and 12 units of the Portable. When $s_2 = 8$, management should note that there will be eight unused Portable display units. Moreover, because $s_1 = 0$ and $s_3 = 0$, no slack is associated with the assembly time constraint and the warehouse capacity constraint; in other words, these constraints are both binding. Consequently, if it is possible to obtain additional assembly time and/or additional warehouse space, management should consider doing so.

Figure 5.3 shows the computer solution to the HighTech problem using The Management Scientist software package. The optimal solution with $x_1 = 30$ and $x_2 = 12$ is shown to have an objective function value of \$1980. The values of the slack variables complete the optimal solution with $s_1 = 0$, $s_2 = 8$, and $s_3 = 0$. The values in the Reduced Costs column are from the net evaluation row of the final simplex tableau. Note that the $c_j - z_j$ values in columns corresponding to x_1 and x_2 are both 0. The dual prices are the z_j values for the three slack variables in the final simplex tableau. Referring to the final tableau, we see that the dual price for constraint 1 is the z_j value corresponding to s_1 where $14/5 = 2.8$. Similarly, the dual price for constraint 2 is 0, and the dual price for constraint 3 is $26/5 = 5.2$. The use of the simplex method to compute dual prices will be discussed further when we cover sensitivity analysis in Chapter 6.

FIGURE 5.3 THE MANAGEMENT SCIENTIST SOLUTION FOR THE HIGHTECH INDUSTRIES PROBLEM

```
OPTIMAL SOLUTION

Objective Function Value =               1980.000

      Variable               Value            Reduced Costs
   --------------      ---------------      -----------------
         X1                    30.000                  0.000
         X2                    12.000                  0.000

     Constraint          Slack/Surplus          Dual Prices
   --------------      ---------------      -----------------
          1                     0.000                  2.800
          2                     8.000                  0.000
          3                     0.000                  5.200
```

Summary of the Simplex Method

Let us now summarize the steps followed to solve a linear program using the simplex method. We assume that the problem has all less-than-or-equal-to constraints and involves maximization.

Step 1. Formulate a linear programming model of the problem.

Step 2. Add slack variables to each constraint to obtain standard form. This also provides the tableau form necessary to identify an initial basic feasible solution for problems involving all less-than-or-equal-to constraints with nonnegative right-hand-side values.

Step 3. Set up the initial simplex tableau.

Step 4. Choose the nonbasic variable with the largest entry in the net evaluation row to bring into the basis. This variable identifies the pivot column: the column associated with the incoming variable.

Step 5. Choose as the pivot row that row with the smallest ratio of $\bar{b}_i/\bar{a}_{ij}$ for $\bar{a}_{ij} > 0$ where j is the pivot column. This pivot row is the row of the variable leaving the basis when variable j enters.

Step 6. Perform the necessary elementary row operations to convert the column for the incoming variable to a unit column with a 1 in the pivot row.

   a. Divide each element of the pivot row by the pivot element (the element in the pivot row and pivot column).

   b. Obtain zeroes in all other positions of the pivot column by adding or subtracting an appropriate multiple of the new pivot row. Once the row operations have been completed, the value of the new basic feasible solution can be read from the $\bar{b}$ column of the tableau.

Step 7. Test for optimality. If $c_j - z_j \leq 0$ for all columns, the solution is optimal. If not, return to step 4.

To test your ability to solve a problem employing the simplex method, try Problem 6.

The steps are basically the same for problems with equality and greater-than-or-equal-to constraints except that setting up tableau form requires a little more work. We discuss what is involved in Section 5.6. The modification necessary for minimization problems is covered in Section 5.7.

NOTES AND COMMENTS

The entries in the net evaluation row provide the reduced costs that appear in the computer solution to a linear program. Recall that in Chapter 3 we defined the reduced cost as the amount by which an objective function coefficient would have to improve before it would be possible for the corresponding variable to assume a positive value in the optimal solution. In general, the reduced costs are the absolute values of the entries in the net evaluation row.

5.6 TABLEAU FORM: THE GENERAL CASE

This section explains how to get started with the simplex method for problems with greater-than-or-equal-to and equality constraints.

When a linear program contains all less-than-or-equal-to constraints with nonnegative right-hand-side values, it is easy to set up the tableau form; we simply add a slack variable to each constraint. However, obtaining tableau form is somewhat more complex if the linear program contains greater-than-or-equal-to constraints, equality constraints, and/or negative right-hand-side values. In this section we describe how to develop tableau form for each of these situations and also how to solve linear programs involving equality and greater-than-or-equal-to constraints using the simplex method.

Greater-Than-or-Equal-to Constraints

Suppose that in the HighTech Industries problem, management wanted to ensure that the combined total production for both models would be at least 25 units. This requirement means that the following constraint must be added to the current linear program:

$$1x_1 + 1x_2 \geq 25$$

Adding this constraint results in the following modified problem:

$$\begin{aligned}
\text{Max} \quad & 50x_1 + 40x_2 \\
\text{s.t.} \quad & \\
& 3x_1 + 5x_2 \leq 150 \quad \text{Assembly time} \\
& \qquad\; 1x_2 \leq 20 \quad \text{Portable display} \\
& 8x_1 + 5x_2 \leq 300 \quad \text{Warehouse space} \\
& 1x_1 + 1x_2 \geq 25 \quad \text{Minimum total production} \\
& x_1, x_2 \geq 0
\end{aligned}$$

First, we use three slack variables and one surplus variable to write the problem in standard form. This provides the following:

$$\begin{aligned}
\text{Max} \quad & 50x_1 + 40x_2 + 0s_1 + 0s_2 + 0s_3 + 0s_4 \\
\text{s.t.} \quad & \\
& 3x_1 + 5x_2 + 1s_1 = 150 && (5.12) \\
& 1x_2 + 1s_2 = 20 && (5.13) \\
& 8x_1 + 5x_2 + 1s_3 = 300 && (5.14) \\
& 1x_1 + 1x_2 - 1s_4 = 25 && (5.15) \\
& x_1, x_2, s_1, s_2, s_3, s_4 \geq 0
\end{aligned}$$

Now let us consider how we obtain an initial basic feasible solution to start the simplex method. Previously, we set $x_1 = 0$ and $x_2 = 0$ and selected the slack variables as the initial basic variables. The extension of this notion to the modified HighTech problem would suggest setting $x_1 = 0$ and $x_2 = 0$ and selecting the slack and surplus variables as the initial basic variables. Doing so results in the basic solution

$$\begin{aligned} x_1 &= 0 \\ x_2 &= 0 \\ s_1 &= 150 \\ s_2 &= 20 \\ s_3 &= 300 \\ s_4 &= -25 \end{aligned}$$

Clearly this solution is not a basic feasible solution because $s_4 = -25$ violates the nonnegativity requirement. The difficulty is that the standard form and the tableau form are not equivalent when the problem contains greater-than-or-equal-to constraints.

Artificial variables are appropriately named; they have no physical meaning in the real problem.

To set up the tableau form, we shall resort to a mathematical "trick" that will enable us to find an initial basic feasible solution in terms of the slack variables s_1, s_2, and s_3 and a new variable we shall denote a_4. The new variable constitutes the mathematical trick. Variable a_4 really has nothing to do with the HighTech problem; it merely enables us to set up the tableau form and thus obtain an initial basic feasible solution. This new variable, which has been artificially created to start the simplex method, is referred to as an **artificial variable.**

The notation for artificial variables is similar to the notation used to refer to the elements of the A matrix. To avoid any confusion between the two, recall that the elements of the A matrix (constraint coefficients) always have two subscripts, whereas artificial variables have only one subscript.

With the addition of an artificial variable, we can convert the standard form of the problem into tableau form. We add artificial variable a_4 to constraint equation (5.15) to obtain the following representation of the system of equations in tableau form:

$$\begin{aligned} 3x_1 + 5x_2 + 1s_1 \qquad\qquad\qquad\qquad &= 150 \\ 1x_2 \qquad + 1s_2 \qquad\qquad\qquad &= 20 \\ 8x_1 + 5x_2 \qquad\qquad + 1s_3 \qquad\qquad &= 300 \\ 1x_1 + 1x_2 \qquad\qquad\qquad - 1s_4 + 1a_4 &= 25 \end{aligned}$$

Note that the subscript on the artificial variable identifies the constraint with which it is associated. Thus, a_4 is the artificial variable associated with the fourth constraint.

Because the variables s_1, s_2, s_3, and a_4 each appear in a different constraint with a coefficient of 1, and the right-hand-side values are nonnegative, both requirements of the tableau form have been satisfied. We can now obtain an initial basic feasible solution by setting $x_1 = x_2 = s_4 = 0$. The complete solution is

$$\begin{aligned} x_1 &= 0 \\ x_2 &= 0 \\ s_1 &= 150 \\ s_2 &= 20 \\ s_3 &= 300 \\ s_4 &= 0 \\ a_4 &= 25 \end{aligned}$$

Is this solution feasible in terms of the real HighTech problem? No, it is not. It does not satisfy the constraint 4 combined total production requirement of 25 units. We must make an important distinction between a basic feasible solution for the tableau form and a feasible solution for the real problem. A basic feasible solution for the tableau form of a linear programming problem is not always a feasible solution for the real problem.

A basic feasible solution containing one or more artificial variables at positive values is not feasible for the real problem.

The reason for creating the tableau form is to obtain the initial basic feasible solution that is required to start the simplex method. Thus, we see that whenever it is necessary to introduce artificial variables, the initial simplex solution will not in general be feasible for the real problem. This situation is not as difficult as it might seem, however, because the only time we must have a feasible solution for the real problem is at the last iteration of the simplex method. Thus, devising a way to guarantee that any artificial variable would be eliminated from the basic feasible solution before the optimal solution is reached would eliminate the difficulty.

The way in which we guarantee that artificial variables will be eliminated before the optimal solution is reached is to assign each artificial variable a very large cost in the objective function. For example, in the modified HighTech problem, we could assign a very large negative number as the profit coefficient for artificial variable a_4. Hence, if this variable is in the basis, it will substantially reduce profits. As a result, this variable will be eliminated from the basis as soon as possible, which is precisely what we want to happen.

As an alternative to picking a large negative number such as $-100{,}000$ for the profit coefficient, we will denote the profit coefficient of each artificial variable by $-M$. Here it is assumed that M represents a very large number—in other words, a number of large magnitude and hence, the letter M. This notation will make it easier to keep track of the elements of the simplex tableau that depend on the profit coefficients of the artificial variables. Using $-M$ as the profit coefficient for artificial variable a_4 in the modified HighTech problem, we can write the objective function for the tableau form of the problem as follows:

$$\text{Max} \quad 50x_1 + 40x_2 + 0s_1 + 0s_2 + 0s_3 + 0s_4 - Ma_4$$

The initial simplex tableau for the problem is shown here.

		x_1	x_2	s_1	s_2	s_3	s_4	a_4	
Basis	c_B	50	40	0	0	0	0	$-M$	
s_1	0	3	5	1	0	0	0	0	**150**
s_2	0	0	1	0	1	0	0	0	**20**
s_3	0	8	5	0	0	1	0	0	**300**
a_4	$-M$	(1)	1	0	0	0	-1	1	**25**
z_j		$-M$	$-M$	0	0	0	M	$-M$	**$-25M$**
$c_j - z_j$		$50 + M$	$40 + M$	0	0	0	$-M$	0	

This tableau corresponds to the solution $s_1 = 150$, $s_2 = 20$, $s_3 = 300$, $a_4 = 25$, and $x_1 = x_2 = s_4 = 0$. In terms of the simplex tableau, this solution is a basic feasible solution because all the variables are greater than or equal to zero, and $n - m = 7 - 4 = 3$ of the variables are equal to zero.

Since $c_1 - z_1 = 50 + M$ is the largest value in the net evaluation row, we see that x_1 will become a basic variable during the first iteration of the simplex method. Further calculations with the simplex method show that x_1 will replace a_4 in the basic solution. The following simplex tableau is the result of the first iteration.

Result of Iteration 1

		x_1	x_2	s_1	s_2	s_3	s_4	a_4	
Basis	c_B	50	40	0	0	0	0	$-M$	
s_1	0	0	2	1	0	0	3	-3	**75**
s_2	0	0	1	0	1	0	0	0	**20**
s_3	0	0	-3	0	0	1	8	-8	**100**
x_1	50	1	1	0	0	0	-1	1	**25**
z_j		50	50	0	0	0	-50	50	**1250**
$c_j - z_j$		0	-10	0	0	0	50	$-M - 50$	

When the artificial variable $a_4 = 0$, we have a situation in which the basic feasible solution contained in the simplex tableau is also a feasible solution to the real HighTech problem. In addition, because a_4 is an artificial variable that was added simply to obtain an initial basic feasible solution, we can now drop its associated column from the simplex tableau. Indeed, whenever artificial variables are used, they can be dropped from the simplex tableau as soon as they have been eliminated from the basic feasible solution.

When artificial variables are required to obtain an initial basic feasible solution, the iterations required to eliminate the artificial variables are referred to as **phase I** of the simplex method. When all the artificial variables have been eliminated from the basis, phase I is complete, and a basic feasible solution to the real problem has been obtained. Thus, by dropping the column associated with a_4 from the current tableau, we obtain the following simplex tableau at the end of phase I.

		x_1	x_2	s_1	s_2	s_3	s_4	
Basis	c_B	50	40	0	0	0	0	
s_1	0	0	2	1	0	0	3	**75**
s_2	0	0	1	0	1	0	0	**20**
s_3	0	0	-3	0	0	1	(8)	**100**
x_1	50	1	1	0	0	0	-1	**25**
z_j		50	50	0	0	0	-50	**1250**
$c_j - z_j$		0	-10	0	0	0	50	

We are now ready to begin phase II of the simplex method. This phase simply continues the simplex method computations after all artificial variables have been removed. At the next iteration, variable s_4 with $c_j - z_j = 50$ is entered into the solution and variable s_3 is eliminated. The simplex tableau after this iteration is:

		x_1	x_2	s_1	s_2	s_3	s_4	
Basis	c_B	50	40	0	0	0	0	
s_1	0	0	($25/8$)	1	0	$-3/8$	0	**$75/2$**
s_2	0	0	1	0	1	0	0	**20**
s_4	0	0	$-3/8$	0	0	$1/8$	1	**$25/2$**
x_1	50	1	$5/8$	0	0	$1/8$	0	**$75/2$**
z_j		50	$250/8$	0	0	$50/8$	0	**1875**
$c_j - z_j$		0	$70/8$	0	0	$-50/8$	0	

One more iteration is required. This time x_2 comes into the solution, and s_1 is eliminated. After performing this iteration, the following simplex tableau shows that the optimal solution has been reached.

		x_1	x_2	s_1	s_2	s_3	s_4	
Basis	c_B	50	40	0	0	0	0	
x_2	40	0	1	$8/25$	0	$-3/25$	0	**12**
s_2	0	0	0	$-8/25$	1	$3/25$	0	**8**
s_4	0	0	0	$3/25$	0	$2/25$	1	**17**
x_1	50	1	0	$-5/25$	0	$5/25$	0	**30**
z_j		50	40	$14/5$	0	$26/5$	0	**1980**
$c_j - z_j$		0	0	$-14/5$	0	$-26/5$	0	

It turns out that the optimal solution to the modified HighTech problem is the same as the solution for the original problem. However, the simplex method required more iterations to reach this extreme point, because an extra iteration was needed to eliminate the artificial variable (a_4) in phase I.

Fortunately, once we obtain an initial simplex tableau using artificial variables, we need not concern ourselves with whether the basic solution at a particular iteration is feasible for the real problem. We need only follow the rules for the simplex method. If we reach the optimality criterion (all $c_j - z_j \leq 0$) and all the artificial variables have been eliminated from the solution, then we have found the optimal solution. On the other hand, if we reach the optimality criterion and one or more of the artificial variables remain in solution at a positive value, then there is no feasible solution to the problem. This special case will be discussed further in Section 5.8.

Equality Constraints

When an equality constraint occurs in a linear programming problem, we need to add an artificial variable to obtain tableau form and an initial basic feasible solution. For example, if constraint 1 is

$$6x_1 + 4x_2 - 5x_3 = 30$$

we would simply add an artificial variable a_1 to create a basic feasible solution in the initial simplex tableau. With the artificial variable, the constraint equation becomes

$$6x_1 + 4x_2 - 5x_3 + 1a_1 = 30$$

Now a_1 can be selected as the basic variable for this row, and its value is given by the right-hand side. Once we have created tableau form by adding an artificial variable to each equality constraint, the simplex method proceeds exactly as before.

Eliminating Negative Right-Hand-Side Values

One of the properties of the tableau form of a linear program is that the values on the right-hand sides of the constraints have to be nonnegative. In formulating a linear programming problem, we may find one or more of the constraints have negative right-hand-side values. To see how this situation might happen, suppose that the management of HighTech has specified that the number of units of the Portable model, x_2, has to be less than or equal to the number of units of the Deskpro model, x_1, after setting aside five units of the Deskpro for internal company use. We could formulate this constraint as

$$x_2 \leq x_1 - 5 \tag{5.16}$$

Subtracting x_1 from both sides of the inequality places both variables on the left-hand side of the inequality. Thus,

$$-x_1 + x_2 \leq -5 \tag{5.17}$$

Because this constraint has a negative right-hand-side value, we can develop an equivalent constraint with a nonnegative right-hand-side value by multiplying both sides of the constraint by -1. In doing so, we recognize that multiplying an inequality constraint by -1 changes the direction of the inequality.

Thus, to convert inequality (5.17) to an equivalent constraint with a nonnegative right-hand-side value, we multiply by -1 to obtain

$$x_1 - x_2 \geq 5 \tag{5.18}$$

We now have an acceptable nonnegative right-hand-side value. Tableau form for this constraint can now be obtained by subtracting a surplus variable and adding an artificial variable.

For a greater-than-or-equal-to constraint, multiplying by -1 creates an equivalent less-than-or-equal-to constraint. For example, suppose we had the following greater-than-or-equal-to constraint:

$$6x_1 + 3x_2 - 4x_3 \geq -20$$

Multiplying by -1 to obtain an equivalent constraint with a nonnegative right-hand-side value leads to the following less-than-or-equal-to constraint

$$-6x_1 - 3x_2 + 4x_3 \leq 20$$

Tableau form can be created for this constraint by adding a slack variable.

For an equality constraint with a negative right-hand-side value, we simply multiply by -1 to obtain an equivalent constraint with a nonnegative right-hand-side value. An artificial variable can then be added to create the tableau form.

Summary of the Steps to Create Tableau Form

Step 1. If the original formulation of the linear programming problem contains one or more constraints with negative right-hand-side values, multiply each of these constraints by -1. Multiplying by -1 will change the direction of the inequalities. This step will provide an equivalent linear program with nonnegative right-hand-side values.

Step 2. For $\leq$ constraints, add a slack variable to obtain an equality constraint. The coefficient of the slack variable in the objective function is assigned a value of zero. It provides the tableau form for the constraint, and the slack variable becomes one of the basic variables in the initial basic feasible solution.

Step 3. For $\geq$ constraints, subtract a surplus variable to obtain an equality constraint, and then add an artificial variable to obtain the tableau form. The coefficient of the surplus variable in the objective function is assigned a value of zero. The coefficient of the artificial variable in the objective function is assigned a value of $-M$. The artificial variable becomes one of the basic variables in the initial basic feasible solution.

Step 4. For equality constraints, add an artificial variable to obtain the tableau form. The coefficient of the artificial variable in the objective function is assigned a value of $-M$. The artificial variable becomes one of the basic variables in the initial basic feasible solution.

To obtain some practice in applying these steps, convert the following example problem into tableau form, and then set up the initial simplex tableau:

$$\begin{aligned}
\text{Max} \quad & 6x_1 + 3x_2 + 4x_3 + 1x_4 \\
\text{s.t.} \quad & \\
& -2x_1 - \tfrac{1}{2}x_2 + 1x_3 - 6x_4 = -60 \\
& 1x_1 + 1x_3 + \tfrac{2}{3}x_4 \leq 20 \\
& -1x_2 - 5x_3 \leq -50 \\
& x_1, x_2, x_3, x_4 \geq 0
\end{aligned}$$

To eliminate the negative right-hand-side values in constraints 1 and 3, we apply step 1. Multiplying both constraints by -1, we obtain the following equivalent linear program:

$$\begin{aligned}
\text{Max} \quad & 6x_1 + 3x_2 + 4x_3 + 1x_4 \\
\text{s.t.} \quad & \\
& 2x_1 + \tfrac{1}{2}x_2 - 1x_3 + 6x_4 = 60 \\
& 1x_1 + 1x_3 + \tfrac{2}{3}x_4 \leq 20 \\
& 1x_2 + 5x_3 \geq 50 \\
& x_1, x_2, x_3, x_4 \geq 0
\end{aligned}$$

Note that the direction of the $\leq$ inequality in constraint 3 has been reversed as a result of multiplying the constraint by -1. By applying step 4 for constraint 1, step 2 for constraint 2, and step 3 for constraint 3, we obtain the following tableau form:

$$
\begin{aligned}
\text{Max} \quad & 6x_1 + 3x_2 + 4x_3 + 1x_4 + 0s_2 + 0s_3 - Ma_1 - Ma_3 \\
\text{s.t.} \quad & \\
& 2x_1 + \tfrac{1}{2}x_2 - 1x_3 + 6x_4 \qquad + 1a_1 = 60 \\
& 1x_1 \qquad + 1x_3 + \tfrac{2}{3}x_4 + 1s_2 = 20 \\
& \qquad 1x_2 + 5x_3 \qquad - 1s_3 \qquad + 1a_3 = 50 \\
& x_1, x_2, x_3, x_4, s_2, s_3, a_1, a_3 \geq 0
\end{aligned}
$$

The initial simplex tableau corresponding to this tableau form is

		x_1	x_2	x_3	x_4	s_2	s_3	a_1	a_3	
Basis	c_B	6	3	4	1	0	0	$-M$	$-M$	
a_1	$-M$	2	½	-1	(6)	0	0	1	0	**60**
s_2	0	1	0	1	⅔	1	0	0	0	**20**
a_3	$-M$	0	1	5	0	0	-1	0	1	**50**
	z_j	$-2M$	$-\tfrac{3}{2}M$	$-4M$	$-6M$	0	M	$-M$	$-M$	$\mathbf{-110M}$
	$c_j - z_j$	$6 + 2M$	$3 + \tfrac{3}{2}M$	$4 + 4M$	$1 + 6M$	0	$-M$	0	0	

For practice setting up tableau form and developing the initial simplex tableau for problems with any constraint form, try Problem 15.

Note that we have circled the pivot element indicating that x_4 will enter and a_1 will leave the basis at the first iteration.

NOTES AND COMMENTS

We have shown how to convert constraints with negative right-hand sides to equivalent constraints with positive right-hand sides. Actually, nothing is wrong with formulating a linear program and including negative right-hand sides. But if you want to use the ordinary simplex method to solve the linear program, you must first alter the constraints to eliminate the negative right-hand sides.

5.7 SOLVING A MINIMIZATION PROBLEM

We can use the simplex method to solve a minimization problem in two ways. The first approach requires that we change the rule used to introduce a variable into the basis. Recall that in the maximization case, we select the variable with the largest positive $c_j - z_j$ as the variable to introduce next into the basis, because the value of $c_j - z_j$ tells us the amount the objective function will increase if one unit of the variable in column j is brought into solution. To solve the minimization problem, we simply reverse this rule. That is, we select the variable with the most negative $c_j - z_j$ as the one to introduce next. Of course, this approach means the stopping rule for the optimal solution will also have to be changed. Using this approach to solve a minimization problem, we would stop when every value in the net evaluation row is zero or positive.

The second approach to solving a minimization problem is the one we shall employ in this book. It is based on the fact that any minimization problem can be converted to an equivalent maximization problem by multiplying the objective function by -1. Solving the resulting maximization problem will provide the optimal solution to the minimization problem.

In keeping with the general notation of this chapter, we are using x_1 and x_2 to represent units of product A and product B.

Let us illustrate this second approach by using the simplex method to solve the M&D Chemicals problem introduced in Chapter 2. Recall that in this problem, management wanted to minimize the cost of producing two products subject to a demand constraint for product A, a minimum total production quantity requirement, and a constraint on available processing time. The mathematical statement of the M&D Chemicals problem is shown here.

$$\begin{aligned} \text{Min} \quad & 2x_1 + 3x_2 \\ \text{s.t.} \quad & \\ & 1x_1 \geq 125 \quad \text{Demand for product A} \\ & 1x_1 + 1x_2 \geq 350 \quad \text{Total production} \\ & 2x_1 + 1x_2 \leq 600 \quad \text{Processing time} \\ & x_1, x_2 \geq 0 \end{aligned}$$

We convert a minimization problem to a maximization problem by multiplying the objective function by −1.

To solve this problem using the simplex method, we first multiply the objective function by −1 to convert the minimization problem into the following equivalent maximization problem:

$$\begin{aligned} \text{Max} \quad & -2x_1 - 3x_2 \\ \text{s.t.} \quad & \\ & 1x_1 \geq 125 \quad \text{Demand for product A} \\ & 1x_1 + 1x_2 \geq 350 \quad \text{Total production} \\ & 2x_1 + 1x_2 \leq 600 \quad \text{Processing time} \\ & x_1, x_2 \geq 0 \end{aligned}$$

The tableau form for this problem is as follows:

$$\begin{aligned} \text{Max} \quad & -2x_1 - 3x_2 + 0s_1 + 0s_2 + 0s_3 - Ma_1 - Ma_2 \\ \text{s.t.} \quad & \\ & 1x_1 - 1s_1 + 1a_1 = 125 \\ & 1x_1 + 1x_2 - 1s_2 + 1a_2 = 350 \\ & 2x_1 + 1x_2 + 1s_3 = 600 \\ & x_1, x_2, s_1, s_2, s_3, a_1, a_2 \geq 0 \end{aligned}$$

The initial simplex tableau is shown here:

		x_1	x_2	s_1	s_2	s_3	a_1	a_2	
Basis	c_B	−2	−3	0	0	0	−M	−M	
a_1	−M	(1)	0	−1	0	0	1	0	**125**
a_2	−M	1	1	0	−1	0	0	1	**350**
s_3	0	2	1	0	0	1	0	0	**600**
	z_j	−2M	−M	M	M	0	−M	−M	**−475M**
	$c_j - z_j$	−2 + 2M	−3 + M	−M	−M	0	0	0	

At the first iteration, x_1 is brought into the basis and a_1 is removed. After dropping the a_1 column from the tableau, the result of the first iteration is as follows:

		x_1	x_2	s_1	s_2	s_3	a_2	
Basis	c_B	-2	-3	0	0	0	$-M$	
x_1	-2	1	0	-1	0	0	0	**125**
a_2	$-M$	0	1	1	-1	0	1	**225**
s_3	0	0	1	②	0	1	0	**350**
z_j		-2	$-M$	$2 - M$	M	0	$-M$	**$-250 - 225M$**
$c_j - z_j$		0	$-3 + M$	$-2 + M$	$-M$	0	0	

Continuing with two more iterations of the simplex method provides the following final simplex tableau:

		x_1	x_2	s_1	s_2	s_3	
Basis	c_B	-2	-3	0	0	0	
x_1	-2	1	0	0	1	1	**250**
x_2	-3	0	1	0	-2	-1	**100**
s_1	0	0	0	1	1	1	**125**
z_j		-2	-3	0	4	1	**-800**
$c_j - z_j$		0	0	0	-4	-1	

The value of the objective function -800 must be multiplied by -1 to obtain the value of the objective function for the original minimization problem. Thus, the minimum total cost of the optimal solution is \$800.

Try Problem 17 for practice solving a minimization problem with the simplex method.

In the next section we discuss some important special cases that may occur when trying to solve any linear programming problem. We will only consider the case for maximization problems, recognizing that all minimization problems can be converted into an equivalent maximization problem by multiplying the objective function by -1.

5.8 SPECIAL CASES

In Chapter 2 we discussed how infeasibility, unboundedness, and alternative optimal solutions could occur when solving linear programming problems using the graphical solution procedure. These special cases can also arise when using the simplex method. In addition, a special case referred to as *degeneracy* can theoretically cause difficulties for the simplex method. In this section we show how these special cases can be recognized and handled when the simplex method is used.

Infeasibility

Infeasibility occurs whenever no solution to the linear program can be found that satisfies all the constraints, including the nonnegativity constraints. Let us now see how infeasibility is recognized when the simplex method is used.

In Section 5.6, when discussing artificial variables, we mentioned that infeasibility can be recognized when the optimality criterion indicates that an optimal solution has been obtained and one or more of the artificial variables remain in the solution at a positive value. As an illustration of this situation, let us consider another modification of the HighTech Industries problem. Suppose management imposed a minimum combined total production requirement of 50 units. The revised problem formulation is shown as follows.

$$\begin{aligned} \text{Max} \quad & 50x_1 + 40x_2 \\ \text{s.t.} \quad & \\ & 3x_1 + 5x_2 \leq 150 \quad \text{Assembly time} \\ & \qquad\; 1x_2 \leq 20 \quad \text{Portable display} \\ & 8x_1 + 5x_2 \leq 300 \quad \text{Warehouse space} \\ & 1x_1 + 1x_2 \geq 50 \quad \text{Minimum total production} \\ & x_1, x_2 \geq 0 \end{aligned}$$

Two iterations of the simplex method will provide the following tableau:

		x_1	x_2	s_1	s_2	s_3	s_4	a_4	
Basis	c_B	50	40	0	0	0	0	$-M$	
x_2	40	0	1	$8/25$	0	$-3/25$	0	0	**12**
s_2	0	0	0	$-8/25$	1	$3/25$	0	0	**8**
x_1	50	1	0	$-5/25$	0	$5/25$	0	0	**30**
a_4	$-M$	0	0	$-3/25$	0	$-2/25$	-1	1	**8**
z_j		50	40	$\frac{70 + 3M}{25}$	0	$\frac{130 + 2M}{25}$	M	$-M$	**1980 − 8M**
$c_j - z_j$		0	0	$\frac{-70 - 3M}{25}$	0	$\frac{-130 - 2M}{25}$	$-M$	0	

If an artificial variable is positive, the solution is not feasible for the real problem.

Note that $c_j - z_j \leq 0$ for all the variables; therefore, according to the optimality criterion, it should be the optimal solution. But this solution is *not feasible* for the modified HighTech problem because the artificial variable $a_4 = 8$ appears in the solution. The solution $x_1 = 30$ and $x_2 = 12$ results in a combined total production of 42 units instead of the constraint 4 requirement of at least 50 units. The fact that the artificial variable is in solution at a value of $a_4 = 8$ tells us that the final solution violates the fourth constraint $(1x_1 + 1x_2 \geq 50)$ by eight units.

If management is interested in knowing which of the first three constraints is preventing us from satisfying the total production requirement, a partial answer can be obtained from the final simplex tableau. Note that $s_2 = 8$, but that s_1 and s_3 are zero. This tells us that the assembly time and warehouse capacity constraints are binding. Because not enough assembly time and warehouse space are available, we cannot satisfy the minimum combined total production requirement.

The management implications here are that additional assembly time and/or warehouse space must be made available to satisfy the total production requirement. If more time and/or space cannot be made available, management will have to relax the total production requirement by at least eight units.

Try Problem 23 to practice recognizing when there is no feasible solution to a problem using the simplex method.

In summary, a linear program is infeasible if no solution satisfies all the constraints simultaneously. We *recognize infeasibility when one or more of the artificial variables remain in the final solution at a positive value.* In closing, we note that linear programming problems with all ≤ constraints and nonnegative right-hand sides will always have a feasible solution. Because it is not necessary to introduce artificial variables to set up the initial simplex tableau for these types of problems, the final solution cannot possibly contain an artificial variable.

Unboundedness

Usually a constraint has been overlooked if unboundedness occurs.

For maximization problems, we say that a linear program is unbounded if the value of the solution may be made infinitely large without violating any constraints. Thus, when unboundedness occurs, we can generally look for an error in the formulation of the problem.

The coefficients in the column of the $\bar{A}$ matrix associated with the incoming variable indicate how much each of the current basic variables will decrease if one unit of the incoming variable is brought into solution. Suppose then, that for a particular linear programming problem, we reach a point where the rule for determining which variable should enter the basis results in the decision to enter variable x_2. Assume that for this variable, $c_2 - z_2 = 5$, and that all $\bar{a}_{i2}$ in column 2 are ≤ 0. Thus, each unit of x_2 brought into solution increases the objective function by five units. Furthermore, because $\bar{a}_{i2} \leq 0$ for all i, none of the current basic variables will be driven to zero, no matter how many units of x_2 we introduce. Thus, we can introduce an infinite amount of x_2 into solution and still maintain feasibility. Because each unit of x_2 increases the objective function by 5, we will have an unbounded solution. Hence, *the way we recognize the unbounded situation is that all the* $\bar{a}_{ij}$ *are less than or equal to zero in the column associated with the incoming variable.*

To illustrate this concept, let us consider the following example of an unbounded problem.

$$\begin{aligned} \text{Max} \quad & 20x_1 + 10x_2 \\ \text{s.t.} \quad & 1x_1 \qquad\quad \geq 2 \\ & \qquad\quad 1x_2 \leq 5 \\ & x_1, x_2 \geq 0 \end{aligned}$$

We subtract a surplus variable s_1 from the first constraint equation and add a slack variable s_2 to the second constraint equation to obtain the standard-form representation. We then add an artificial variable a_1 to the first constraint equation to obtain the tableau form. In the initial simplex tableau the basic variables are a_1 and s_2. After bringing in x_1 and removing a_1 at the first iteration, the simplex tableau is as follows:

		x_1	x_2	s_1	s_2	
Basis	c_B	20	10	0	0	
x_1	20	1	0	−1	0	**2**
s_2	0	0	1	0	1	**5**
	z_j	20	0	−20	0	**40**
	$c_j - z_j$	0	10	20	0	

Because s_1 has the largest positive $c_j - z_j$, we know we can increase the value of the objective function most rapidly by bringing s_1 into the basis. But $\bar{a}_{13} = -1$ and $\bar{a}_{23} = 0$; hence, we cannot form the ratio $\bar{b}_i/\bar{a}_{i3}$ for any $\bar{a}_{i3} > 0$ because no values of $\bar{a}_{i3}$ are greater than zero.

This result indicates that the solution to the linear program is unbounded because each unit of s_1 that is brought into solution provides one extra unit of x_1 (since $\bar{a}_{13} = -1$) and drives zero units of s_2 out of solution (since $\bar{a}_{23} = 0$). Because s_1 is a surplus variable and can be interpreted as the amount of x_1 over the minimum amount required, the simplex tableau indicates we can introduce as much of s_1 as we desire without violating any constraints; the interpretation is that we can make as much as we want above the minimum amount of x_1 required. Because the objective function coefficient associated with x_1 is positive, there will be no upper bound on the value of the objective function.

In summary, a maximization linear program is unbounded if it is possible to make the value of the optimal solution as large as desired without violating any of the constraints. When employing the simplex method, an unbounded linear program exists if *at some iteration, the simplex method tells us to introduce variable j into the solution and all the $\bar{a}_{ij}$ are less than or equal to zero in the jth column.*

Try Problem 25 for another example of an unbounded problem.

We emphasize that the case of an unbounded solution will never occur in real cost minimization or profit maximization problems because it is not possible to reduce costs to minus infinity or to increase profits to plus infinity. Thus, if we encounter an unbounded solution to a linear programming problem, we should carefully reexamine the formulation of the problem to determine whether a formulation error has occurred.

Alternative Optimal Solutions

A linear program with two or more optimal solutions is said to have alternative optimal solutions. When using the simplex method, we cannot recognize that a linear program has alternative optimal solutions until the final simplex tableau is reached. Then if the linear program has alternative optimal solutions, $c_j - z_j$ will equal zero for one or more nonbasic variables.

To illustrate the case of alternative optimal solutions when using the simplex method, consider changing the objective function for the HighTech problem from $50x_1 + 40x_2$ to $30x_1 + 50x_2$; in doing so, we obtain the revised linear program:

$$\begin{aligned} \text{Max} \quad & 30x_1 + 50x_2 \\ \text{s.t.} \quad & \\ & 3x_1 + 5x_2 \le 150 \\ & \qquad\;\; 1x_2 \le 20 \\ & 8x_1 + 5x_2 \le 300 \\ & x_1, x_2 \ge 0 \end{aligned}$$

The final simplex tableau for this problem is shown here:

		x_1	x_2	s_1	s_2	s_3	
Basis	c_B	30	50	0	0	0	
x_2	50	0	1	0	1	0	**20**
s_3	0	0	0	$-8/3$	$25/3$	1	**200/3**
x_1	30	1	0	$1/3$	$-5/3$	0	**50/3**
	z_j	30	50	10	0	0	**1500**
	$c_j - z_j$	0	0	-10	0	0	

All values in the net evaluation row are less than or equal to zero, indicating that an optimal solution has been found. This solution is given by $x_1 = 50/3$, $x_2 = 20$, $s_1 = 0$, $s_2 = 0$, and $s_3 = 200/3$. The value of the objective function is 1500.

In looking at the net evaluation row in the optimal simplex tableau, we see that the $c_j - z_j$ value for nonbasic variable s_2 is equal to zero. It indicates that the linear program may have alternative optimal solutions. In other words, because the net evaluation row entry for s_2 is zero, we can introduce s_2 into the basis without changing the value of the solution. The tableau obtained after introducing s_2 follows:

		x_1	x_2	s_1	s_2	s_3	
Basis	c_B	30	50	0	0	0	
x_2	50	0	1	$8/25$	0	$-3/25$	**12**
s_2	0	0	0	$-8/25$	1	$3/25$	**8**
x_1	30	1	0	$-5/25$	0	$5/25$	**30**
z_j		30	50	10	0	0	**1500**
$c_j - z_j$		0	0	−10	0	0	

Try Problem 24 for another example of alternative optimal solutions.

As shown, we have a different basic feasible solution: $x_1 = 30$, $x_2 = 12$, $s_1 = 0$, $s_2 = 8$, and $s_3 = 0$. However, this new solution is also optimal because $c_j - z_j \leq 0$ for all j. Another way to confirm that this solution is still optimal is to note that the value of the solution has remained equal to 1500.

In summary, *when using the simplex method, we can recognize the possibility of alternative optimal solutions if $c_j - z_j$ equals zero for one or more of the nonbasic variables in the final simplex tableau.*

Degeneracy

A linear program is said to be degenerate if one or more of the basic variables have a value of zero. **Degeneracy** does not cause any particular difficulties for the graphical solution procedure; however, degeneracy can theoretically cause difficulties when the simplex method is used to solve a linear programming problem.

To see how a degenerate linear program could occur, consider a change in the right-hand-side value of the assembly time constraint for the HighTech problem. For example, what if the number of hours available had been 175 instead of 150? The modified linear program is shown here.

$$
\begin{aligned}
\text{Max} \quad & 50x_1 + 40x_2 \\
\text{s.t.} \quad & \\
& 3x_1 + 5x_2 \leq 175 \quad \text{Assembly time increased to 175 hours} \\
& \qquad\;\; 1x_2 \leq 20 \quad \text{Portable display} \\
& 8x_1 + 5x_2 \leq 300 \quad \text{Warehouse space} \\
& x_1, x_2 \geq 0
\end{aligned}
$$

The simplex tableau after one iteration is as follows:

Basis	c_B	x_1 50	x_2 40	s_1 0	s_2 0	s_3 0	
s_1	0	0	$25/8$	1	0	$-3/8$	**$125/2$**
s_2	0	0	1	0	1	0	**20**
x_1	50	1	$5/8$	0	0	$1/8$	**$75/2$**
z_j		50	$250/8$	0	0	$50/8$	**1875**
$c_j - z_j$		0	$70/8$	0	0	$-50/8$	

The entries in the net evaluation row indicate that x_2 should enter the basis. By calculating the appropriate ratios to determine the pivot row, we obtain

$$\frac{\bar{b}_1}{\bar{a}_{12}} = \frac{125/2}{25/8} = 20$$

$$\frac{\bar{b}_2}{\bar{a}_{22}} = \frac{20}{1} = 20$$

$$\frac{\bar{b}_3}{\bar{a}_{32}} = \frac{75/2}{5/8} = 60$$

We see that the first and second rows tie, which indicates that we will have a degenerate basic feasible solution at the next iteration. Recall that in the case of a tie, we follow the convention of selecting the uppermost row as the pivot row. Here, it means that s_1 will leave the basis. But from the tie for the minimum ratio we see that the basic variable in row 2, s_2, will also be driven to zero. Because it does not leave the basis, we will have a basic variable with a value of zero after performing this iteration. The simplex tableau after this iteration is as follows:

Basis	c_B	x_1 50	x_2 40	s_1 0	s_2 0	s_3 0	
x_2	40	0	1	$8/25$	0	$-3/25$	**20**
s_2	0	0	0	$-8/25$	1	$3/25$	**0**
x_1	50	1	0	$-5/25$	0	$5/25$	**25**
z_j		50	40	$70/25$	0	$130/25$	**2050**
$c_j - z_j$		0	0	$-70/25$	0	$-130/25$	

As expected, we have a basic feasible solution with one of the basic variables, s_2, equal to zero. Whenever we have a tie in the minimum $\bar{b}_i/\bar{a}_{ij}$ ratio, the next tableau will always have a basic variable equal to zero. Because we are at the optimal solution in the preceding case, we do not care that s_2 is in solution at a zero value. However, if degeneracy occurs at some iteration prior to reaching the optimal solution, it is theoretically possible for the simplex method to cycle; that is, the procedure could possibly alternate between the same set of nonoptimal basic feasible solutions and never reach the optimal solution. Cycling has not proven to be a significant difficulty in practice. Therefore, we do not recommend introducing any special steps into the simplex method to eliminate the possibility that degeneracy will occur. If while performing the iterations of the simplex algorithm a tie occurs for the minimum $\bar{b}_i/\bar{a}_{ij}$ ratio, then we recommend simply selecting the upper row as the pivot row.

NOTES AND COMMENTS

1. We stated that infeasibility is recognized when the stopping rule is encountered but one or more artificial variables are in solution at a positive value. This requirement does not necessarily mean that all artificial variables must be nonbasic to have a feasible solution. An artificial variable could be in solution at a zero value.
2. An unbounded feasible region must exist for a problem to be unbounded, but it does not guarantee that a problem will be unbounded. A minimization problem may be bounded whereas a maximization problem with the same feasible region is unbounded.

SUMMARY

In this chapter the simplex method was introduced as an algebraic procedure for solving linear programming problems. Although the simplex method can be used to solve small linear programs by hand calculations, it becomes too cumbersome as problems get larger. As a result, a computer software package must be used to solve large linear programs in any reasonable length of time. The computational procedures of most computer software packages are based on the simplex method.

We described how developing the tableau form of a linear program is a necessary step in preparing a linear programming problem for solution using the simplex method, including how to convert greater-than-or-equal-to constraints, equality constraints, and constraints with negative right-hand-side values into tableau form.

For linear programs with greater-than-or-equal-to constraints and/or equality constraints, artificial variables are used to obtain tableau form. An objective function coefficient of $-M$, where M is a very large number, is assigned to each artificial variable. If there is a feasible solution to the real problem, all artificial variables will be driven out of solution (or to zero) before the simplex method reaches its optimality criterion. The iterations required to remove the artificial variables from solution constitute what is called phase I of the simplex method.

Two techniques were mentioned for solving minimization problems. The first approach involved changing the rule for introducing a variable into solution and changing the optimality criterion. The second approach involved multiplying the objective function by -1 to obtain an equivalent maximization problem. With this change, any minimization problem can be solved using the steps required for a maximization problem, but the value of the optimal solution must be multiplied by -1 to obtain the optimal value of the original minimization problem.

As a review of the material in this chapter we now present a detailed step-by-step procedure for solving linear programs using the simplex method.

Step 1. Formulate a linear programming model of the problem.

Step 2. Define an equivalent linear program by performing the following operations:

a. Multiply each constraint with a negative right-hand-side value by -1, and change the direction of the constraint inequality.

b. For a minimization problem, convert the problem to an equivalent maximization problem by multiplying the objective function by -1.

Step 3. Set up the standard form of the linear program by adding appropriate slack and surplus variables.

Step 4. Set up the tableau form of the linear program to obtain an initial basic feasible solution. All linear programs must be set up this way before the initial simplex tableau can be obtained.

Step 5. Set up the initial simplex tableau to keep track of the calculations required by the simplex method.

Step 6. Choose the nonbasic variable with the largest $c_j - z_j$ to bring into the basis. The column associated with that variable is the pivot column.

Step 7. Choose as the pivot row that row with the smallest ratio of $\bar{b}_i/\bar{a}_{ij}$ for $\bar{a}_{ij} > 0$. This ratio is used to determine which variable will leave the basis when variable j enters the basis. This ratio also indicates how many units of variable j can be introduced into solution before the basic variable in the ith row equals zero.

Step 8. Perform the necessary elementary row operations to convert the pivot column to a unit column.

a. Divide each element in the pivot row by the pivot element. The result is a new pivot row containing a 1 in the pivot column.

b. Obtain zeroes in all other positions of the pivot column by adding or subtracting an appropriate multiple of the new pivot row.

Step 9. Test for optimality. If $c_j - z_j \leq 0$ for all columns, we have the optimal solution. If not, return to step 6.

In Section 5.8 we discussed how the special cases of infeasibility, unboundedness, alternative optimal solutions, and degeneracy can occur when solving linear programming problems with the simplex method.

GLOSSARY

Simplex method An algebraic procedure for solving linear programming problems. The simplex method uses elementary row operations to iterate from one basic feasible solution (extreme point) to another until the optimal solution is reached.

Basic solution Given a linear program in standard form, with n variables and m constraints, a basic solution is obtained by setting $n - m$ of the variables equal to zero and solving the constraint equations for the values of the other m variables. If a unique solution exists, it is a basic solution.

Nonbasic variable One of $n - m$ variables set equal to zero in a basic solution.

Basic variable One of the m variables not required to equal zero in a basic solution.

Basic feasible solution A basic solution that is also feasible; that is, it satisfies the nonnegativity constraints. A basic feasible solution corresponds to an extreme point.

Tableau form The form in which a linear program must be written before setting up the initial simplex tableau. When a linear program is written in tableau form, its A matrix contains m unit columns corresponding to the basic variables, and the values of these basic variables are given by the values in the b column. A further requirement is that the entries in the b column be greater than or equal to zero.

Simplex tableau A table used to keep track of the calculations required by the simplex method.

Unit column or unit vector A vector or column of a matrix that has a zero in every position except one. In the nonzero position there is a 1. There is a unit column in the simplex tableau for each basic variable.

Basis The set of variables that are not restricted to equal zero in the current basic solution. The variables that make up the basis are termed basic variables, and the remaining variables are called nonbasic variables.

Net evaluation row The row in the simplex tableau that contains the value of $c_j - z_j$ for every variable (column).

Iteration The process of moving from one basic feasible solution to another.

Pivot element The element of the simplex tableau that is in both the pivot row and the pivot column.

Pivot column The column in the simplex tableau corresponding to the nonbasic variable that is about to be introduced into solution.

Pivot row The row in the simplex tableau corresponding to the basic variable that will leave the solution.

Elementary row operations Operations that may be performed on a system of simultaneous equations without changing the solution to the system of equations.

Artificial variable A variable that has no physical meaning in terms of the original linear programming problem, but serves merely to enable a basic feasible solution to be created for starting the simplex method. Artificial variables are assigned an objective function coefficient of $-M$, where M is a very large number.

Phase I When artificial variables are present in the initial simplex tableau, phase I refers to the iterations of the simplex method that are required to eliminate the artificial variables. At the end of phase I, the basic feasible solution in the simplex tableau is also feasible for the real problem.

Degeneracy When one or more of the basic variables has a value of zero.

PROBLEMS

1. Consider the following system of linear equations:

$$
\begin{aligned}
3x_1 + x_2 \qquad &= 6 \\
2x_1 + 4x_2 + x_3 &= 12
\end{aligned}
$$

a. Find the basic solution with $x_1 = 0$.
b. Find the basic solution with $x_2 = 0$.
c. Find the basic solution with $x_3 = 0$.
d. Which of the preceding solutions would be basic feasible solutions for a linear program?

2. Consider the following linear program:

$$
\begin{aligned}
\text{Max} \quad & x_1 + 2x_2 \\
\text{s.t.} \quad & \\
& x_1 + 5x_2 \leq 10 \\
& 2x_1 + 6x_2 \leq 16 \\
& x_1, x_2 \geq 0
\end{aligned}
$$

a. Write the problem in standard form.
b. How many variables will be set equal to zero in a basic solution for this problem?
c. Find all the basic solutions, and indicate which are also feasible.
d. Find the optimal solution by computing the value of each basic feasible solution.

3. Consider the following linear program:

$$
\begin{aligned}
\text{Max} \quad & 5x_1 + 9x_2 \\
\text{s.t.} \quad & \\
& \tfrac{1}{2}x_1 + 1x_2 \leq 8 \\
& 1x_1 + 1x_2 \geq 10 \\
& \tfrac{1}{4}x_1 + \tfrac{3}{2}x_2 \geq 6 \\
& x_1, x_2 \geq 0
\end{aligned}
$$

a. Write the problem in standard form.
b. How many variables will be set equal to zero in a basic solution for this problem? Explain.
c. Find the basic solution that corresponds to s_1 and s_2 equal to zero.
d. Find the basic solution that corresponds to x_1 and s_3 equal to zero.
e. Are your solutions for parts (c) and (d) basic feasible solutions? Extreme-point solutions? Explain.
f. Use the graphical approach to identify the solutions found in parts (c) and (d). Do the graphical results agree with your answer to part (e)? Explain.

SELF test

4. Consider the following linear programming problem:

$$
\begin{aligned}
\text{Max} \quad & 60x_1 + 90x_2 \\
\text{s.t.} \quad & \\
& 15x_1 + 45x_2 \leq 90 \\
& 5x_1 + 5x_2 \leq 20 \\
& x_1, x_2 \geq 0
\end{aligned}
$$

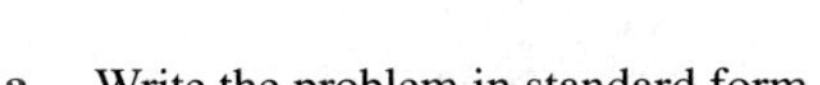

a. Write the problem in standard form.
b. Develop the portion of the simplex tableau involving the objective function coefficients, the coefficients of the variables in the constraints, and the constants for the right-hand sides.

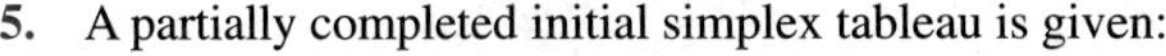

5. A partially completed initial simplex tableau is given:

		x_1	x_2	s_1	s_2	
Basis	c_B	5	9	0	0	
s_1	0	10	9	1	0	**90**
s_2	0	−5	3	0	1	**15**
z_j						
$c_j - z_j$						

a. Complete the initial tableau.
b. Which variable would be brought into solution at the first iteration?
c. Write the original linear program.

6. The following partial initial simplex tableau is given:

		x_1	x_2	x_3	s_1	s_2	s_3	
Basis	c_B	5	20	25	0	0	0	
		2	1	0	1	0	0	**40**
		0	2	1	0	1	0	**30**
		3	0	$-\frac{1}{2}$	0	0	1	**15**
z_j								
$c_j - z_j$								

a. Complete the initial tableau.
b. Write the problem in tableau form.
c. What is the initial basis? Does this basis correspond to the origin? Explain.
d. What is the value of the objective function at this initial solution?
e. For the next iteration, which variable should enter the basis, and which variable should leave the basis?
f. How many units of the entering variable will be in the next solution? Before making this first iteration, what do you think will be the value of the objective function after the first iteration?
g. Find the optimal solution using the simplex method.

7. Solve the following linear program using the graphical approach:

$$\begin{aligned} \text{Max} \quad & 4x_1 + 5x_2 \\ \text{s.t.} \quad & \\ & 2x_1 + 2x_2 \leq 20 \\ & 3x_1 + 7x_2 \leq 42 \\ & x_1, x_2 \geq 0 \end{aligned}$$

Put the linear program in tableau form, and solve using the simplex method. Show the sequence of extreme points generated by the simplex method on your graph.

8. Recall the problem for Par, Inc., introduced in Section 2.1. The mathematical model for this problem is restated as follows:

$$\begin{aligned} \text{Max} \quad & 10x_1 + 9x_2 \\ \text{s.t.} \quad & \\ & \tfrac{7}{10}x_1 + 1x_2 \leq 630 \quad \text{Cutting and dyeing} \\ & \tfrac{1}{2}x_1 + \tfrac{5}{6}x_2 \leq 600 \quad \text{Sewing} \\ & 1x_1 + \tfrac{2}{3}x_2 \leq 708 \quad \text{Finishing} \\ & \tfrac{1}{10}x_1 + \tfrac{1}{4}x_2 \leq 135 \quad \text{Inspection and packaging} \\ & x_1, x_2 \geq 0 \end{aligned}$$

where

x_1 = number of standard bags produced
x_2 = number of deluxe bags produced

a. Use the simplex method to determine how many bags of each model Par should manufacture.
b. What is the profit Par can earn with these production quantities?

c. How many hours of production time will be scheduled for each operation?
d. What is the slack time in each operation?

9. Solve the RMC problem (Chapter 2, Problem 21) using the simplex method. At each iteration, locate the basic feasible solution found by the simplex method on the graph of the feasible region. The problem formulation is shown here:

$$\begin{aligned} \text{Max} \quad & 40x_1 + 30x_2 \\ \text{s.t.} \quad & \\ & \tfrac{2}{5}x_1 + \tfrac{1}{2}x_2 \le 20 \quad \text{Material 1} \\ & \tfrac{1}{5}x_2 \le 5 \quad \text{Material 2} \\ & \tfrac{3}{5}x_1 + \tfrac{3}{10}x_2 \le 21 \quad \text{Material 3} \\ & x_1, x_2 \ge 0 \end{aligned}$$

where

x_1 = tons of fuel additive produced
x_2 = tons of solvent base produced

10. Solve the following linear program:

$$\begin{aligned} \text{Max} \quad & 5x_1 + 5x_2 + 24x_3 \\ \text{s.t.} \quad & \\ & 15x_1 + 4x_2 + 12x_3 \le 2800 \\ & 15x_1 + 8x_2 \le 6000 \\ & x_1 + 8x_3 \le 1200 \\ & x_1, x_2, x_3 \ge 0 \end{aligned}$$

11. Solve the following linear program using both the graphical and the simplex methods:

$$\begin{aligned} \text{Max} \quad & 2x_1 + 8x_2 \\ \text{s.t.} \quad & \\ & 3x_1 + 9x_2 \le 45 \\ & 2x_1 + 1x_2 \ge 12 \\ & x_1, x_2 \ge 0 \end{aligned}$$

Show graphically how the simplex method moves from one basic feasible solution to another. Find the coordinates of all extreme points of the feasible region.

12. Suppose a company manufactures three products from two raw materials. The amount of raw material in each unit of each product is given.

Raw Material	Product A	Product B	Product C
I	7 lb	6 lb	3 lb
II	5 lb	4 lb	2 lb

If the company has available 100 pounds of material I and 200 pounds of material II, and if the profits for the three products are \$20, \$20, and \$15, respectively, how much of each product should be produced to maximize profits?

13. Liva's Lumber, Inc., manufactures three types of plywood. The following table summarizes the production hours per unit in each of three production operations and other data for the problem.

	Operations (hours)			
Plywood	**I**	**II**	**III**	**Profit/Unit**
Grade A	2	2	4	$40
Grade B	5	5	2	$30
Grade X	10	3	2	$20
Maximum time available	900	400	600	

How many units of each grade of lumber should be produced?

14. Ye Olde Cording Winery in Peoria, Illinois, makes three kinds of authentic German wine: Heidelberg Sweet, Heidelberg Regular, and Deutschland Extra Dry. The raw materials, labor, and profit for a gallon of each of these wines are summarized here:

Wine	**Grade A Grapes (bushels)**	**Grade B Grapes (bushels)**	**Sugar (pounds)**	**Labor (hours)**	**Profit/ Gallon**
Heidelberg Sweet	1	1	2	2	$1.00
Heidelberg Regular	2	0	1	3	$1.20
Deutschland Extra Dry	0	2	0	1	$2.00

If the winery has 150 bushels of grade A grapes, 150 bushels of grade B grapes, 80 pounds of sugar, and 225 labor-hours available during the next week, what product mix of wines will maximize the company's profit?

a. Solve using the simplex method.
b. Interpret all slack variables.
c. An increase in which resources could improve the company's profit?

15. Set up the tableau form for the following linear program (do not attempt to solve):

$$
\begin{aligned}
\text{Max} \quad & 4x_1 + 2x_2 - 3x_3 + 5x_4 \\
\text{s.t.} \quad & \\
& 2x_1 - 1x_2 + 1x_3 + 2x_4 \geq 50 \\
& 3x_1 \qquad\quad - 1x_3 + 2x_4 \leq 80 \\
& 1x_1 + 1x_2 \qquad\quad + 1x_4 = 60 \\
& x_1, x_2, x_3, x_4 \geq 0
\end{aligned}
$$

16. Set up the tableau form for the following linear program (do not attempt to solve):

$$
\begin{aligned}
\text{Min} \quad & 4x_1 + 5x_2 + 3x_3 \\
\text{s.t.} \quad & \\
& 4x_1 \qquad\quad + 2x_3 \geq 20 \\
& \qquad 1x_2 - 1x_3 \leq -8 \\
& 1x_1 - 2x_2 \qquad\quad = -5 \\
& 2x_1 + 1x_2 + 1x_3 \leq 12 \\
& x_1, x_2, x_3 \geq 0
\end{aligned}
$$

17. Solve the following linear program:

$$
\begin{aligned}
\text{Min} \quad & 3x_1 + 4x_2 + 8x_3 \\
\text{s.t.} \quad & \\
& 4x_1 + 2x_2 \qquad\quad \geq 12 \\
& \qquad\quad 4x_2 + 8x_3 \geq 16 \\
& x_1, x_2, x_3 \geq 0
\end{aligned}
$$

18. Solve the following linear program:

$$
\begin{aligned}
\text{Min} \quad & 84x_1 + 4x_2 + 30x_3 \\
\text{s.t.} \quad & \\
& 8x_1 + 1x_2 + 3x_3 \leq 240 \\
& 16x_1 + 1x_2 + 7x_3 \geq 480 \\
& 8x_1 - 1x_2 + 4x_3 \geq 160 \\
& x_1, x_2, x_3 \geq 0
\end{aligned}
$$

19. Captain John's Yachts, Inc., located in Fort Lauderdale, Florida, rents three types of oceangoing boats: sailboats, cabin cruisers, and Captain John's favorite, the luxury yachts. Captain John advertises his boats with his famous "you rent—we pilot" slogan, which means that the company supplies the captain and crew for each rented boat. Each rented boat has one captain, of course, but the crew sizes (deck hands, galley hands, etc.) differ. The crew requirements, in addition to a captain, are one for sailboats, two for cabin cruisers, and three for yachts. Ten employees are captains, and an additional 18 employees fill the various crew positions. Currently, Captain John has rental requests for all of his boats: four sailboats, eight cabin cruisers, and three luxury yachts. If Captain John's daily profit contribution is \$50 for sailboats, \$70 for cruisers, and \$100 for luxury yachts, how many boats of each type should he rent?

20. The Our-Bags-Don't-Break (OBDB) plastic bag company manufactures three plastic refuse bags for home use: a 20-gallon garbage bag, a 30-gallon garbage bag, and a 33-gallon leaf-and-grass bag. Using purchased plastic material, three operations are required to produce each end product: cutting, sealing, and packaging. The production time required to process each type of bag in every operation and the maximum production time available for each operation are shown (note that the production time figures in this table are per box of each type of bag).

	Production Time (seconds/box)		
Type of Bag	**Cutting**	**Sealing**	**Packaging**
20 gallons	2	2	3
30 gallons	3	2	4
33 gallons	3	3	5
Time available	2 hours	3 hours	4 hours

If OBDB's profit contribution is \$0.10 for each box of 20-gallon bags produced, \$0.15 for each box of 30-gallon bags, and \$0.20 for each box of 33-gallon bags, what is the optimal product mix?

21. Kirkman Brothers ice cream parlors sell three different flavors of Dairy Sweet ice milk: chocolate, vanilla, and banana. Due to extremely hot weather and a high demand for its products, Kirkman has run short of its supply of ingredients: milk, sugar, and cream. Hence,

Kirkman will not be able to fill all the orders received from its retail outlets, the ice cream parlors. Due to these circumstances, Kirkman decided to make the most profitable amounts of the three flavors, given the constraints on supply of the basic ingredients. The company will then ration the ice milk to the retail outlets.

Kirkman collected the following data on profitability of the various flavors, availability of supplies, and amounts required for each flavor.

		Usage/Gallon		
Flavor	**Profit/ Gallon**	**Milk (gallons)**	**Sugar (pounds)**	**Cream (gallons)**
Chocolate	\$1.00	0.45	0.50	0.10
Vanilla	\$0.90	0.50	0.40	0.15
Banana	\$0.95	0.40	0.40	0.20
Maximum available		200	150	60

Determine the optimal product mix for Kirkman Brothers. What additional resources could be used profitably?

22. Uforia Corporation sells two brands of perfume: Incentive and Temptation No. 1. Uforia sells exclusively through department stores and employs a three-person sales staff to call on its customers. The amount of time necessary for each sales representative to sell one case of each product varies with experience and ability. Data on the average time for each of Uforia's three sales representatives is presented here.

	Average Sales Time per Case (minutes)	
Salesperson	**Incentive**	**Temptation No. 1**
John	10	15
Brenda	15	10
Red	12	6

Each sales representative spends approximately 80 hours per month in the actual selling of these two products. Cases of Incentive and Temptation No. 1 sell at profits of \$30 and \$25, respectively. How many cases of each perfume should each person sell during the next month to maximize the firm's profits? (Hint: Let x_1 = number of cases of Incentive sold by John, x_2 = number of cases of Temptation No. 1 sold by John, x_3 = number of cases of Incentive sold by Brenda, and so on.)

Note: In Problems 23–29, we provide examples of linear programs that result in one or more of the following situations:

- Optimal solution
- Infeasible solution
- Unbounded solution
- Alternative optimal solutions
- Degenerate solution

For each linear program, determine the solution situation that exists, and indicate how you identified each situation using the simplex method. For the problems with alternative optimal solutions, calculate at least two optimal solutions.

23.

$$\begin{aligned} \text{Max} \quad & 4x_1 + 8x_2 \\ \text{s.t.} \quad & \\ & 2x_1 + 2x_2 \leq 10 \\ & -1x_1 + 1x_2 \geq 8 \\ & x_1, x_2 \geq 0 \end{aligned}$$

SELF test

24.

$$\begin{aligned} \text{Min} \quad & 3x_1 + 3x_2 \\ \text{s.t.} \quad & \\ & 2x_1 + 0.5x_2 \geq 10 \\ & 2x_1 \geq 4 \\ & 4x_1 + 4x_2 \geq 32 \\ & x_1, x_2 \geq 0 \end{aligned}$$

SELF test

25.

$$\begin{aligned} \text{Min} \quad & 1x_1 + 1x_2 \\ \text{s.t.} \quad & \\ & 8x_1 + 6x_2 \geq 24 \\ & 4x_1 + 6x_2 \geq -12 \\ & 2x_2 \geq 4 \\ & x_1, x_2 \geq 0 \end{aligned}$$

26.

$$\begin{aligned} \text{Max} \quad & 2x_1 + 1x_2 + 1x_3 \\ \text{s.t.} \quad & \\ & 4x_1 + 2x_2 + 2x_3 \geq 4 \\ & 2x_1 + 4x_2 \leq 20 \\ & 4x_1 + 8x_2 + 2x_3 \leq 16 \\ & x_1, x_2, x_3 \geq 0 \end{aligned}$$

27.

$$\begin{aligned} \text{Max} \quad & 2x_1 + 4x_2 \\ \text{s.t.} \quad & \\ & 1x_1 + \tfrac{1}{2}x_2 \leq 10 \\ & 1x_1 + 1x_2 = 12 \\ & 1x_1 + \tfrac{3}{2}x_2 \leq 18 \\ & x_1, x_2 \geq 0 \end{aligned}$$

28.

$$\begin{aligned} \text{Min} \quad & -4x_1 + 5x_2 + 5x_3 \\ \text{s.t.} \quad & \\ & 1x_2 + 1x_3 \geq 2 \\ & -1x_1 + 1x_2 + 1x_3 \geq 1 \\ & -1x_3 \geq 1 \\ & x_1, x_2, x_3 \geq 0 \end{aligned}$$

29. Solve the following linear program and identify any alternative optimal solutions.

$$\begin{aligned} \text{Max} \quad & 120x_1 + 80x_2 + 14x_3 \\ \text{s.t.} \quad & \\ & 4x_1 + 8x_2 + x_3 \leq 200 \\ & 2x_2 + 1x_3 \leq 300 \\ & 32x_1 + 4x_2 + 2x_3 = 400 \\ & x_1, x_2, x_3 \geq 0 \end{aligned}$$

30. Supersport Footballs, Inc., manufactures three kinds of footballs: an All-Pro model, a College model, and a High School model. All three footballs require operations in the following departments: cutting and dyeing, sewing, and inspection and packaging. The production times and maximum production availabilities are shown here.

	Production Time (minutes)		
Model	**Cutting and Dyeing**	**Sewing**	**Inspection and Packaging**
All-Pro	12	15	3
College	10	15	4
High School	8	12	2
Time available	300 hours	200 hours	100 hours

Current orders indicate that at least 1000 All-Pro footballs must be manufactured.

a. If Supersport realizes a profit contribution of \$3 for each All-Pro model, \$5 for each College model, and \$4 for each High School model, how many footballs of each type should be produced? What occurs in the solution of this problem? Why?

b. If Supersport can increase sewing time to 300 hours and inspection and packaging time to 150 hours by using overtime, what is your recommendation?

CHAPTER 6

Simplex-Based Sensitivity Analysis and Duality

CONTENTS

In Chapter 3 we defined sensitivity analysis as the study of how the changes in the coefficients of a linear program affect the optimal solution. In this chapter we discuss how sensitivity analysis information such as the ranges for the objective function coefficients, dual prices, and the ranges for the right-hand-side values can be obtained from the final simplex tableau. The topic of duality is also introduced. We will see that associated with every linear programming problem is a dual problem that has an interesting economic interpretation.

6.1 SENSITIVITY ANALYSIS WITH THE SIMPLEX TABLEAU

The usual sensitivity analysis for linear programs involves computing ranges for the objective function coefficients and the right-hand-side values, as well as the dual prices.

Objective Function Coefficients

Sensitivity analysis for an objective function coefficient involves placing a range on the coefficient's value. We call this range the **range of optimality.** As long as the actual value of the objective function coefficient is within the range of optimality, *the current basic feasible solution will remain optimal.* The range of optimality for a basic variable defines the objective function coefficient values for which that variable will remain part of the current optimal basic feasible solution. The range of optimality for a nonbasic variable defines the objective function coefficient values for which that variable will remain nonbasic.

In computing the range of optimality for an objective function coefficient, all other coefficients in the problem are assumed to remain at their original values; in other words, *only one coefficient is allowed to change at a time.* To illustrate the process of computing ranges for objective function coefficients, recall the HighTech Industries problem introduced in Chapter 5. The linear program for this problem is restated as follows:

$$
\begin{aligned}
\text{Max}\quad & 50x_1 + 40x_2 \\
\text{s.t.}\quad & \\
& 3x_1 + 5x_2 \le 150 \quad \text{Assembly time} \\
& \phantom{3x_1 +{}} 1x_2 \le 20 \quad \text{Portable display} \\
& 8x_1 + 5x_2 \le 300 \quad \text{Warehouse capacity} \\
& x_1, x_2 \ge 0
\end{aligned}
$$

where

$$
\begin{aligned}
x_1 &= \text{number of units of the Deskpro} \\
x_2 &= \text{number of units of the Portable}
\end{aligned}
$$

The final simplex tableau for the HighTech problem is as follows.

		x_1	x_2	s_1	s_2	s_3	
Basis	c_B	50	40	0	0	0	
x_2	40	0	1	$8/25$	0	$-3/25$	**12**
s_2	0	0	0	$-8/25$	1	$3/25$	**8**
x_1	50	1	0	$-5/25$	0	$5/25$	**30**
z_j		50	40	$14/5$	0	$26/5$	**1980**
$c_j - z_j$		0	0	$-14/5$	0	$-26/5$	

Recall that when the simplex method is used to solve a linear program, an optimal solution is recognized when all entries in the net evaluation row ($c_j - z_j$) are ≤ 0. Because the preceding simplex tableau satisfies this criterion, the solution shown is optimal. However, if a change in one of the objective function coefficients were to cause one or more of the $c_j - z_j$ values to become positive, then the current solution would no longer be optimal; in such a case, one or more additional simplex iterations would be necessary to find the new optimal solution. *The range of optimality for an objective function coefficient is determined by those coefficient values that maintain*

$$c_j - z_j \leq 0 \tag{6.1}$$

for all values of j.

Let us illustrate this approach by computing the range of optimality for c_1, the profit contribution per unit of the Deskpro. Using c_1 (instead of 50) as the objective function coefficient of x_1, the final simplex tableau is as follows:

		x_1	x_2	s_1	s_2	s_3	
Basis	c_B	c_1	40	0	0	0	
x_2	40	0	1	$8/25$	0	$-3/25$	**12**
s_2	0	0	0	$-8/25$	1	$3/25$	**8**
x_1	c_1	1	0	$-5/25$	0	$5/25$	**30**
z_j		c_1	40	$\frac{64 - c_1}{5}$	0	$\frac{c_1 - 24}{5}$	$\mathbf{480 + 30c_1}$
$c_j - z_j$		0	0	$\frac{c_1 - 64}{5}$	0	$\frac{24 - c_1}{5}$	

Changing an objective function coefficient will result in changes in the z_j and $c_j - z_j$ rows, but not in the variable values.

Note that this tableau is the same as the previous optimal tableau except that c_1 replaces 50. Thus, we have a c_1 in the objective function coefficient row and the c_B column, and the z_j and $c_j - z_j$ rows have been recomputed using c_1 instead of 50. The current solution will remain optimal as long as the value of c_1 results in all $c_j - z_j \leq 0$. Hence, from the column for s_1 we must have

$$\frac{c_1 - 64}{5} \leq 0$$

and from the column for s_3, we must have

$$\frac{24 - c_1}{5} \leq 0$$

Using the first inequality, we obtain

$$c_1 - 64 \leq 0$$

or

$$c_1 \leq 64 \tag{6.2}$$

Similarly, from the second inequality, we obtain

$$24 - c_1 \leq 0$$

or

$$24 \leq c_1 \tag{6.3}$$

Because c_1 must satisfy both inequalities (6.2) and (6.3), the range of optimality for c_1 is given by

$$24 \leq c_1 \leq 64 \tag{6.4}$$

To see how management of HighTech can make use of this sensitivity analysis information, suppose an increase in material costs reduces the profit contribution per unit for the Deskpro to \$30. The range of optimality indicates that the current solution ($x_1 = 30$, $x_2 = 12$, $s_1 = 0$, $s_2 = 8$, $s_3 = 0$) is still optimal. To verify this solution, let us recompute the final simplex tableau after reducing the value of c_1 to 30.

We have simply set $c_1 = 30$ everywhere it appears in the previous tableau.

		x_1	x_2	s_1	s_2	s_3	
Basis	c_B	30	40	0	0	0	
x_2	40	0	1	$8/25$	0	$-3/25$	**12**
s_2	0	0	0	$-8/25$	1	$3/25$	**8**
x_1	30	1	0	$-5/25$	0	$5/25$	**30**
	z_j	30	40	$34/5$	0	$6/5$	**1380**
	$c_j - z_j$	0	0	$-34/5$	0	$-6/5$	

Because $c_j - z_j \leq 0$ for all variables, the solution with $x_1 = 30, x_2 = 12, s_1 = 0, s_2 = 8$, and $s_3 = 0$ is still optimal. That is, the optimal solution with $c_1 = 30$ is the same as the optimal solution with $c_1 = 50$. Note, however, that the decrease in profit contribution per unit of the Deskpro has caused a reduction in total profit from \$1980 to \$1380.

What if the profit contribution per unit were reduced even further—say, to \$20? Referring to the range of optimality for c_1 given by expression (6.4), we see that $c_1 = 20$ is outside the range; thus, we know that a change this large will cause a new basis to be optimal. To verify this new basis, we have modified the final simplex tableau by replacing c_1 by 20.

		x_1	x_2	s_1	s_2	s_3	
Basis	c_B	20	40	0	0	0	
x_2	40	0	1	$8/25$	0	$-3/25$	**12**
s_2	0	0	0	$-8/25$	1	$3/25$	**8**
x_1	20	1	0	$-5/25$	0	$5/25$	**30**
z_j		20	40	$44/5$	0	$-4/5$	**1080**
$c_j - z_j$		0	0	$-44/5$	0	$4/5$	

As expected, the current solution ($x_1 = 30$, $x_2 = 12$, $s_1 = 0$, $s_2 = 8$, and $s_3 = 0$) is no longer optimal because the entry in the s_3 column of the net evaluation row is greater than zero. This result implies that at least one more simplex iteration must be performed to reach the optimal solution. Continue to perform the simplex iterations in the previous tableau to verify that the new optimal solution will require the production of 16⅔ units of the Deskpro and 20 units of the Portable.

At the endpoints of the range, the corresponding variable is a candidate for entering the basis if it is currently out or for leaving the basis if it is currently in.

The procedure we used to compute the range of optimality for c_1 can be used for any basic variable. The procedure for computing the range of optimality for nonbasic variables is even easier because a change in the objective function coefficient for a nonbasic variable causes only the corresponding $c_j - z_j$ entry to change in the final simplex tableau. To illustrate the approach, we show the following final simplex tableau for the original HighTech problem after replacing 0, the objective function coefficient for s_1, with the coefficient c_{s_1}:

		x_1	x_2	s_1	s_2	s_3	
Basis	c_B	50	40	c_{s_1}	0	0	
x_2	40	0	1	$8/25$	0	$-3/25$	**12**
s_2	0	0	0	$-8/25$	1	$3/25$	**8**
x_1	50	1	0	$-5/25$	0	$5/25$	**30**
z_j		50	40	$14/5$	0	$26/5$	**1980**
$c_j - z_j$		0	0	$c_{s_1} - 14/5$	0	$-26/5$	

Note that the only changes in the tableau are in the s_1 column. In applying inequality (6.1) to compute the range of optimality, we get

$$c_{s_1} - 14/5 \leq 0$$

and hence

$$c_{s_1} \leq 14/5$$

Therefore, as long as the objective function coefficient for s_1 is less than or equal to $14/5$, the current solution will be optimal. With no lower bound on how much the coefficient may be decreased, we write the range of optimality for c_{s_1} as

$$c_{s_1} \leq 14/5$$

The same approach works for all nonbasic variables. In a maximization problem, the range of optimality has no lower limit, and the upper limit is given by z_j. Thus, the range of optimality for the objective function coefficient of any nonbasic variable is given by

$$c_j \leq z_j \tag{6.5}$$

Let us summarize the steps necessary to compute the range of optimality for objective function coefficients. In stating the following steps, we assume that computing the range of optimality for c_k, the coefficient of x_k, in a maximization problem is the desired goal. Keep in mind that x_k in this context may refer to one of the original decision variables, a slack variable, or a surplus variable.

Steps to Compute the Range of Optimality

Step 1. Replace the numerical value of the objective function coefficient for x_k with c_k everywhere it appears in the final simplex tableau.

Step 2. Recompute $c_j - z_j$ for each nonbasic variable (if x_k is a nonbasic variable, it is only necessary to recompute $c_k - z_k$).

Step 3. Requiring that $c_j - z_j \leq 0$, solve each inequality for any upper or lower bounds on c_k. If two or more upper bounds are found for c_k, the smallest of these is the upper bound on the range of optimality. If two or more lower bounds are found, the largest of these is the lower bound on the range of optimality.

Step 4. If the original problem is a minimization problem that was converted to a maximization problem in order to apply the simplex method, multiply the inequalities obtained in step 3 by -1, and change the direction of the inequalities to obtain the ranges of optimality for the original minimization problem.

Can you compute the range of optimality for objective function coefficients by working with the final simplex tableau? Try Problem 1.

By using the range of optimality to determine whether a change in an objective function coefficient is large enough to cause a change in the optimal solution, we can often avoid the process of formulating and solving a modified linear programming problem.

Right-Hand-Side Values

In many linear programming problems, we can interpret the right-hand-side values (the b_i's) as the resources available. For instance, in the HighTech Industries problem, the right-hand side of constraint 1 represents the available assembly time, the right-hand side of constraint 2 represents the available Portable displays, and the right-hand side of constraint 3 represents the available warehouse space. Dual prices provide information on the value of additional resources in these cases; the ranges over which these dual prices are valid are given by the ranges for the right-hand-side values.

Dual Prices. In Chapter 3 we stated that the improvement in the value of the optimal solution per unit increase in a constraint's right-hand-side value is called a **dual price.**[1] When the simplex method is used to solve a linear programming problem, the values of the dual

[1]The closely related term *shadow price* is used by some authors. The shadow price is the same as the dual price for maximization problems; for minimization problems, the dual and shadow prices are equal in absolute value but have opposite signs. LINDO/PC and The Management Scientist provide dual prices as part of the computer output. Some software packages, such as Excel Solver, provide shadow prices.

prices are easy to obtain. They are found in the z_j row of the final simplex tableau. To illustrate this point, the final simplex tableau for the HighTech problem is again shown.

		x_1	x_2	s_1	s_2	s_3	
Basis	c_B	50	40	0	0	0	
x_2	40	0	1	$8/25$	0	$-3/25$	**12**
s_2	0	0	0	$-8/25$	1	$3/25$	**8**
x_1	50	1	0	$-5/25$	0	$5/25$	**30**
z_j		50	40	$14/5$	0	$26/5$	**1980**
$c_j - z_j$		0	0	$-14/5$	0	$-26/5$	

The z_j values for the three slack variables are $14/5$, 0, and $26/5$, respectively. Thus, the dual prices for the assembly time constraint, Portable display constraint, and warehouse capacity constraint are, respectively, $14/5 = \$2.80$, 0.00, and $26/5 = \$5.20$. The dual price of \$5.20 shows that more warehouse space will have the biggest positive impact on HighTech's profit.

To see why the z_j values for the slack variables in the final simplex tableau are the dual prices, let us first consider the case for slack variables that are part of the optimal basic feasible solution. Each of these slack variables will have a z_j value of zero, implying a dual price of zero for the corresponding constraint. For example, consider slack variable s_2, a basic variable in the HighTech problem. Because $s_2 = 8$ in the optimal solution, HighTech will have eight Portable display units unused. Consequently, how much would management of HighTech Industries be willing to pay to obtain additional Portable display units? Clearly the answer is nothing because at the optimal solution HighTech has an excess of this particular component. Additional amounts of this resource are of no value to the company, and, consequently, the dual price for this constraint is zero. In general, if a slack variable is a basic variable in the optimal solution, the value of z_j—and hence, the dual price of the corresponding resource—is zero.

Consider now the nonbasic slack variables—for example, s_1. In the previous subsection we determined that the current solution will remain optimal as long as the objective function coefficient for s_1 (denoted c_{s_1}) stays in the following range:

$$c_{s_1} \leq 14/5$$

It implies that the variable s_1 should not be increased from its current value of zero unless it is worth more than $14/5 = \$2.80$ to do so. We can conclude then that \$2.80 is the marginal value to HighTech of 1 hour of assembly time used in the production of Deskpro and Portable computers. Thus, if additional time can be obtained, HighTech should be willing to pay up to \$2.80 per hour for it. A similar interpretation can be given to the z_j value for each of the nonbasic slack variables.

With a greater-than-or-equal-to constraint, the value of the dual price will be less than or equal to zero because a one-unit increase in the value of the right-hand side cannot be helpful; a one-unit increase makes it more difficult to satisfy the constraint. For a maximization problem, then, the optimal value can be expected to decrease when the right-hand side of a greater-than-or-equal-to constraint is increased. The dual price gives the amount of the expected improvement—a negative number, since we expect a decrease. As a result, the dual price for a greater-than-or-equal-to constraint is given by the negative of the z_j entry for the corresponding surplus variable in the optimal simplex tableau.

Finally, it is possible to compute dual prices for equality constraints. They are given by the z_j values for the corresponding artificial variables. We will not develop this case in detail here because we have recommended dropping each artificial variable column from the simplex tableau as soon as the corresponding artificial variable leaves the basis.

To summarize, when the simplex method is used to solve a linear programming problem, the dual prices for the constraints are contained in the final simplex tableau. Table 6.1 summarizes the rules for determining the dual prices for the various constraint types in a maximization problem solved by the simplex method.

Try Problem 3, parts (a), (b), and (c), for practice in finding dual prices from the optimal simplex tableau.

Recall that we convert a minimization problem to a maximization problem by multiplying the objective function by -1 before using the simplex method. Nevertheless, the dual price is given by the same z_j values because improvement for a minimization problem is a decrease in the optimal value.

To illustrate the approach for computing dual prices for a minimization problem, recall the M&D Chemicals problem that we solved in Section 5.7 as an equivalent maximization problem by multiplying the objective function by -1. The linear programming model for this problem and the final simplex tableau are restated as follows, with x_1 and x_2 representing manufacturing quantities of products A and B, respectively.

$$\begin{aligned}
\text{Min} \quad & 2x_1 + 3x_2 \\
\text{s.t.} \quad & \\
& 1x_1 \qquad\quad \geq 125 \quad \text{Demand for product A} \\
& 1x_1 + 1x_2 \geq 350 \quad \text{Total production} \\
& 2x_1 + 1x_2 \leq 600 \quad \text{Processing time} \\
& x_1, x_2 \geq 0
\end{aligned}$$

		x_1	x_2	s_1	s_2	s_3	
Basis	c_B	-2	-3	0	0	0	
x_1	-2	1	0	0	1	1	**250**
x_2	-3	0	1	0	-2	-1	**100**
s_1	0	0	0	1	1	1	**125**
	z_j	-2	-3	0	4	1	**−800**
	$c_j - z_j$	0	0	0	-4	-1	

Following the rules in Table 6.1 for identifying the dual price for each constraint type, the dual prices for the constraints in the M&D Chemicals problem are given in Table 6.2.

TABLE 6.1 TABLEAU LOCATION OF DUAL PRICE BY CONSTRAINT TYPE

Constraint Type	Dual Price Given by
$\leq$	z_j value for the slack variable associated with the constraint
$\geq$	Negative of the z_j value for the surplus variable associated with the constraint
$=$	z_j value for the artificial variable associated with the constraint

TABLE 6.2 DUAL PRICES FOR M&D CHEMICALS PROBLEM

Constraint	Constraint Type	Dual Price
Demand for product A	$\geq$	0
Total production	$\geq$	−4
Processing time	$\leq$	1

Constraint 1 is not binding, and its dual price is zero. The dual price for constraint 2 shows that the marginal cost of increasing the total production requirement is \$4 per unit. Finally, the dual price of one for the third constraint shows that the per-unit value of additional processing time is \$1.

A change in b_i does not affect optimality ($c_j - z_j$ is unchanged), but it does affect feasibility. One of the current basic variables may become negative.

Range of Feasibility. As we have just seen, the z_j row in the final simplex tableau can be used to determine the dual price and, as a result, predict the change in the value of the objective function corresponding to a unit change in a b_i. This interpretation is only valid, however, as long as the change in b_i is not large enough to make the current basic solution infeasible. Thus, we will be interested in calculating a range of values over which a particular b_i can vary without any of the current basic variables becoming infeasible (i.e., less than zero). This range of values will be referred to as the **range of feasibility.**

To demonstrate the effect of changing a b_i, consider increasing the amount of assembly time available in the HighTech problem from 150 to 160 hours. Will the current basis still yield a feasible solution? If so, given the dual price of \$2.80 for the assembly time constraint, we can expect an increase in the value of the solution of 10(2.80) = 28. The final simplex tableau corresponding to an increase in the assembly time of 10 hours is shown here.

		x_1	x_2	s_1	s_2	s_3	
Basis	c_B	50	40	0	0	0	
x_2	40	0	1	$8/25$	0	$-3/25$	**15.2**
s_2	0	0	0	$-8/25$	1	$3/25$	**4.8**
x_1	50	1	0	$-5/25$	0	$5/25$	**28.0**
	z_j	50	40	$14/5$	0	$26/5$	**2008**
	$c_j - z_j$	0	0	$-14/5$	0	$-26/5$	

The same basis, consisting of the basic variables x_2, s_2, and x_1, is feasible because all the basic variables are nonnegative. Note also that, just as we predicted using the dual price, the value of the optimal solution has increased by 10(\$2.80) = \$28, from \$1980 to \$2008.

You may wonder whether we had to re-solve the problem completely to find this new solution. The answer is no! The only changes in the final simplex tableau (as compared with the final simplex tableau with $b_1 = 150$) are the differences in the values of the basic variables and the value of the objective function. That is, only the last column of the simplex tableau changed. The entries in this new last column of the simplex tableau were obtained by adding 10 times the first four entries in the s_1 column to the last column in the previous tableau:

$$\begin{matrix} & \text{Old solution} & \text{Change in } b_1 & s_1 \text{ column} & & \text{New solution} \\ & \downarrow & \downarrow & \downarrow & & \downarrow \\ \text{New solution} = & \begin{bmatrix} 12 \\ 8 \\ 30 \\ \hline 1980 \end{bmatrix} & + 10 & \begin{bmatrix} 8/25 \\ -8/25 \\ -5/25 \\ \hline 14/5 \end{bmatrix} & = & \begin{bmatrix} 15.2 \\ 4.8 \\ 28.0 \\ \hline 2008 \end{bmatrix} \end{matrix}$$

Let us now consider why this procedure can be used to find the new solution. First, recall that each of the coefficients in the s_1 column indicates the amount of decrease in a basic variable that would result from increasing s_1 by one unit. In other words, these coefficients tell us how many units of each of the current basic variables will be driven out of solution if one unit of variable s_1 is brought into solution. Bringing one unit of s_1 into solution, however, is the same as reducing the availability of assembly time (decreasing b_1) by one unit; increasing b_1, the available assembly time, by one unit has just the opposite effect. Therefore, the entries in the s_1 column can also be interpreted as the changes in the values of the current basic variables corresponding to a one-unit increase in b_1.

To practice finding the new solution after a change in a right-hand side without re-solving the problem when the same basis remains feasible, try Problem 3, parts (d) and (e).

The change in the value of the objective function corresponding to a one-unit increase in b_1 is given by the value of z_j in that column (the dual price). In the foregoing case, the availability of assembly time increased by 10 units; thus, we multiplied the first four entries in the s_1 column by 10 to obtain the change in the value of the basic variables and the optimal value.

How do we know when a change in b_1 is so large that the current basis will become infeasible? We shall first answer this question specifically for the HighTech Industries problem and then state the general procedure for less-than-or-equal-to constraints. The approach taken with greater-than-or-equal-to and equality constraints will then be discussed.

We begin by showing how to compute upper and lower bounds for the maximum amount that b_1 can be changed before the current optimal basis becomes infeasible. We have seen how to find the new basic feasible solution values given a 10-unit increase in b_1. In general, given a change in b_1 of Δb_1, the new values for the basic variables in the HighTech problem are given by

$$\begin{bmatrix} x_2 \\ s_2 \\ x_1 \end{bmatrix} = \begin{bmatrix} 12 \\ 8 \\ 30 \end{bmatrix} + \Delta b_1 \begin{bmatrix} 8/25 \\ -8/25 \\ -5/25 \end{bmatrix} = \begin{bmatrix} 12 + 8/25\Delta b_1 \\ 8 - 8/25\Delta b_1 \\ 30 - 5/25\Delta b_1 \end{bmatrix} \tag{6.6}$$

As long as the new value of each basic variable remains nonnegative, the current basis will remain feasible and therefore optimal. We can keep the basic variables nonnegative by limiting the change in b_1 (i.e., Δb_1) so that we satisfy each of the following conditions:

$$12 + 8/25\Delta b_1 \geq 0 \tag{6.7}$$

$$8 - 8/25\Delta b_1 \geq 0 \tag{6.8}$$

$$30 - 5/25\Delta b_1 \geq 0 \tag{6.9}$$

The left-hand sides of these inequalities represent the new values of the basic variables after b_1 has been changed by Δb_1.

Solving for Δb_1 in inequalities (6.7), (6.8), and (6.9), we obtain

$$\begin{aligned}\Delta b_1 &\geq (25/8)(-12) = -37.5\\ \Delta b_1 &\leq (-25/8)(-8) = 25\\ \Delta b_1 &\leq (-25/5)(-30) = 150\end{aligned}$$

Because all three inequalities must be satisfied, the most restrictive limits on b_1 must be satisfied for all the current basic variables to remain nonnegative. Therefore, Δb_1 must satisfy

$$-37.5 \leq \Delta b_1 \leq 25 \qquad (6.10)$$

The initial amount of assembly time available was 150 hours. Therefore, $b_1 = 150 + \Delta b_1$, where b_1 is the amount of assembly time available. We add 150 to each of the three terms in expression (6.10) to obtain

$$150 - 37.5 \leq 150 + \Delta b_1 \leq 150 + 25 \qquad (6.11)$$

Replacing $150 + \Delta b_1$ with b_1, we obtain the range of feasibility for b_1:

$$112.5 \leq b_1 \leq 175$$

This range of feasibility for b_1 indicates that as long as the available assembly time is between 112.5 and 175 hours, the current optimal basis will remain feasible, which is why we call this range the range of feasibility.

Because the dual price for b_1 (assembly time) is $14/5$, we know profit can be increased by \$2.80 by obtaining an additional hour of assembly time. Suppose then that we increase b_1 by 25; that is, we increase b_1 to the upper limit of its range of feasibility, 175. The profit will increase to \$1980 + (\$2.80)25 = \$2050, and the values of the optimal basic variables become

$$\begin{aligned}x_2 &= 12 + 25(8/25) = 20\\ s_2 &= 8 + 25(-8/25) = 0\\ x_1 &= 30 + 25(-5/25) = 25\end{aligned}$$

What happened to the solution? The increased assembly time caused a revision in the optimal production plan. HighTech should produce more of the Portable and less of the Deskpro. Overall, the profit will be increased by (\$2.80)(25) = \$70. Note that although the optimal solution changed, the basic variables that were optimal before are still optimal.

The procedure for determining the range of feasibility has been illustrated with the assembly time constraint. The procedure for calculating the range of feasibility for the right-hand side of any less-than-or-equal-to constraint is the same. The first step for a general constraint i is to calculate the range of values for b_i that satisfies the following inequalities.

$$\begin{bmatrix} \bar{b}_1 \\ \bar{b}_2 \\ \cdot \\ \cdot \\ \cdot \\ \bar{b}_m \end{bmatrix} + \Delta b_i \begin{bmatrix} \bar{a}_{1j} \\ \bar{a}_{2j} \\ \cdot \\ \cdot \\ \cdot \\ \bar{a}_{mj} \end{bmatrix} \geq \begin{bmatrix} 0 \\ 0 \\ \cdot \\ \cdot \\ \cdot \\ 0 \end{bmatrix} \tag{6.12}$$

Current solution (last column of the final simplex tableau)

Column of the final simplex tableau corresponding to the slack variable associated with constraint i

The inequalities are used to identify lower and upper limits on Δb_i. The range of feasibility can then be established by the maximum of the lower limits and the minimum of the upper limits.

Similar arguments can be used to develop a procedure for determining the range of feasibility for the right-hand-side value of a greater-than-or-equal-to constraint. Essentially the procedure is the same, with the column corresponding to the surplus variable associated with the constraint playing the central role. For a general greater-than-or-equal-to constraint i, we first calculate the range of values for Δb_i that satisfy the inequalities shown in inequality (6.13).

$$\begin{bmatrix} \bar{b}_1 \\ \bar{b}_2 \\ \cdot \\ \cdot \\ \cdot \\ \bar{b}_m \end{bmatrix} - \Delta b_i \begin{bmatrix} \bar{a}_{1j} \\ \bar{a}_{2j} \\ \cdot \\ \cdot \\ \cdot \\ \bar{a}_{mj} \end{bmatrix} \geq \begin{bmatrix} 0 \\ 0 \\ \cdot \\ \cdot \\ \cdot \\ 0 \end{bmatrix} \tag{6.13}$$

Current solution (last column of the final simplex tableau)

Column of the final simplex tableau corresponding to the surplus variable associated with constraint i

Once again, these inequalities establish lower and upper limits on Δb_i. Given these limits, the range of feasibility is easily determined.

Try Problem 4 to make sure you can compute the range of feasibility by working with the final simplex tableau.

A range of feasibility for the right-hand side of an equality constraint can also be computed. To do so for equality constraint i, one could use the column of the final simplex tableau corresponding to the artificial variable associated with constraint i in equation (6.12). Because we have suggested dropping the artificial variable columns from the simplex tableau as soon as the artificial variable becomes nonbasic, these columns will not be available in the final tableau. Thus, more involved calculations are required to compute a range of feasibility for equality constraints. Details may be found in more advanced texts.

Changes that force b_i outside its range of feasibility are normally accompanied by changes in the dual prices.

As long as the change in a right-hand-side value is such that b_i stays within its range of feasibility, the same basis will remain feasible and optimal. Changes that force b_i outside its range of feasibility will force us to resolve the problem to find the new optimal solution consisting of a different set of basic variables. (More advanced linear programming texts show how it can be done without completely resolving the problem.) In any case, the calculation of the range of feasibility for each b_i is valuable management information and should be included as part of the management report on any linear programming project. The range of feasibility is typically made available as part of the computer solution to the problem.

Simultaneous Changes

In reviewing the procedures for developing the range of optimality and the range of feasibility, we note that only one coefficient at a time was permitted to vary. Our statements concerning changes within these ranges were made with the understanding that no other coefficients are permitted to change. However, sometimes we can make the same statements when either two or more objective function coefficients or two or more right-hand sides are varied simultaneously. When the simultaneous changes satisfy the 100 percent rule, the same statements are applicable. The 100 percent rule was explained in Chapter 3, but we will briefly review it here.

Let us define allowable increase as the amount a coefficient can be increased before reaching the upper limit of its range, and allowable decrease as the amount a coefficient can be decreased before reaching the lower limit of its range. Now suppose simultaneous changes are made in two or more objective function coefficients. For each coefficient changed, we compute the percentage of the allowable increase, or allowable decrease, represented by the change. If the sum of the percentages for all changes does not exceed 100 percent, we say that the 100 percent rule is satisfied and that the simultaneous changes will not cause a change in the optimal solution. However, just as with a single objective function coefficient change, the value of the solution will change because of the change in the coefficients.

Similarly, if two or more changes in constraint right-hand-side values are made, we again compute the percentage of allowable increase or allowable decrease represented by each change. If the sum of the percentages for all changes does not exceed 100 percent, we say that the 100 percent rule is satisfied. The dual prices are then valid for determining the change in value of the objective function associated with the right-hand-side changes.

NOTES AND COMMENTS

1. Sometimes, interpreting dual prices and choosing the appropriate sign can be confusing. It often helps to think of this process as follows. Relaxing a $\geq$ constraint means decreasing its right-hand side, and relaxing a $\leq$ constraint means increasing its right-hand side. Relaxing a constraint permits improvement in value; restricting a constraint (decreasing the right-hand side of a $\leq$ constraint or increasing the right-hand side of a $\geq$ constraint) has the opposite effect. In every case, the absolute value of the dual price gives the improvement in the optimal value associated with relaxing the constraint.
2. The Notes and Comments in Chapter 3 concerning sensitivity analysis are also applicable here. In particular, recall that the 100 percent rule cannot be applied to simultaneous changes in the objective function *and* the right-hand sides; it applies only to simultaneous changes in one or the other. Also note that this rule *does not* mean that simultaneous changes that do not satisfy the rule will necessarily cause a change in the solution. For instance, any proportional change in *all* the objective function coefficients will leave the optimal solution unchanged, and any proportional change in *all* the right-hand sides will leave the dual prices unchanged.

6.2 DUALITY

Every linear programming problem has an associated linear programming problem called the **dual problem.** Referring to the original formulation of the linear programming problem as the **primal problem,** we will see how the primal can be converted into its corresponding dual. Then we will solve the dual linear programming problem and interpret the results. A fundamental property of the primal-dual relationship is that the optimal solution to either the primal or the dual problem also provides the optimal solution to the other. In cases where the primal and the dual problems differ in terms of computational difficulty, we can choose the easier problem to solve.

Let us return to the HighTech Industries problem. The original formulation—the primal problem—is as follows:

$$
\begin{aligned}
\text{Max} \quad & 50x_1 + 40x_2 \\
\text{s.t.} \quad & \\
& 3x_1 + 5x_2 \leq 150 \quad \text{Assembly time} \\
& 1x_2 \leq 20 \quad \text{Portable display} \\
& 8x_1 + 5x_2 \leq 300 \quad \text{Warehouse space} \\
& x_1, x_2 \geq 0
\end{aligned}
$$

A maximization problem with all less-than-or-equal-to constraints and nonnegativity requirements for the variables is said to be in **canonical form.** For a maximization problem in canonical form, such as the HighTech Industries problem, the conversion to the associated dual linear program is relatively easy. Let us state the dual of the HighTech problem and then identify the steps taken to make the primal-dual conversion. The HighTech dual problem is as follows:

$$
\begin{aligned}
\text{Min} \quad & 150u_1 + 20u_2 + 300u_3 \\
\text{s.t.} \quad & \\
& 3u_1 \qquad\quad + 8u_3 \geq 50 \\
& 5u_1 + 1u_2 + 5u_3 \geq 40 \\
& u_1, u_2, u_3 \geq 0
\end{aligned}
$$

This **canonical form for a minimization problem** is a minimization problem with all greater-than-or-equal-to constraints and nonnegativity requirements for the variables. Thus, the dual of a maximization problem in canonical form is a minimization problem in canonical form. The variables u_1, u_2, and u_3 are referred to as **dual variables.**

With the preceding example in mind, we make the following general statements about the *dual of a maximization problem in canonical form.*

1. The dual is a minimization problem in canonical form.
2. When the primal has n decision variables ($n = 2$ in the HighTech problem), the dual will have n constraints. The first constraint of the dual is associated with variable x_1 in the primal, the second constraint in the dual is associated with variable x_2 in the primal, and so on.
3. When the primal has m constraints ($m = 3$ in the HighTech problem), the dual will have m decision variables. Dual variable u_1 is associated with the first primal constraint, dual variable u_2 is associated with the second primal constraint, and so on.

4. The right-hand sides of the primal constraints become the objective function coefficients in the dual.
5. The objective function coefficients of the primal become the right-hand sides of the dual constraints.
6. The constraint coefficients of the *i*th primal variable become the coefficients in the *i*th constraint of the dual.

Try part (a) of Problem 17 for practice in finding the dual of a maximization problem in canonical form.

These six statements are the general requirements that must be satisfied when converting a maximization problem in canonical form to its associated dual: a minimization problem in canonical form. Even though these requirements may seem cumbersome at first, practice with a few simple problems will show that the primal-dual conversion process is relatively easy to implement.

We have formulated the HighTech dual linear programming problem, so let us now proceed to solve it. With three variables in the dual, we will use the simplex method. After subtracting surplus variables s_1 and s_2 to obtain the standard form, adding artificial variables a_1 and a_2 to obtain the tableau form, and multiplying the objective function by -1 to convert the dual problem to an equivalent maximization problem, we arrive at the following initial simplex tableau.

		u_1	u_2	u_3	s_1	s_2	a_1	a_2	
Basis	c_B	-150	-20	-300	0	0	$-M$	$-M$	
a_1	$-M$	3	0	(8)	-1	0	1	0	**50**
a_2	$-M$	5	1	5	0	-1	0	1	**40**
z_j		$-8M$	$-M$	$-13M$	M	M	$-M$	$-M$	$\mathbf{-90M}$
$c_j - z_j$		$-150 + 8M$	$-20 + M$	$-300 + 13M$	$-M$	$-M$	0	0	

At the first iteration, u_3 is brought into the basis, and a_1 is removed. At the second iteration, u_1 is brought into the basis, and a_2 is removed. At this point, the simplex tableau appears as follows.

		u_1	u_2	u_3	s_1	s_2	
Basis	c_B	-150	-20	-300	0	0	
u_3	-300	0	$-3/25$	1	$-5/25$	$3/25$	**26/5**
u_1	-150	1	$8/25$	0	$5/25$	$-8/25$	**14/5**
z_j		-150	-12	-300	30	12	**−1980**
$c_j - z_j$		0	-8	0	-30	-12	

Because all the entries in the net evaluation row are less than or equal to zero, the optimal solution has been reached; it is $u_1 = 14/5$, $u_2 = 0$, $u_3 = 26/5$, $s_1 = 0$, and $s_2 = 0$. We have been maximizing the negative of the dual objective function; therefore, the value of the objective function for the optimal dual solution must be $-(-1980) = 1980$.

The final simplex tableau for the original HighTech Industries problem is shown here.

		x_1	x_2	s_1	s_2	s_3	
Basis	c_B	50	40	0	0	0	
x_2	40	0	1	$8/25$	0	$-3/25$	**12**
s_2	0	0	0	$-8/25$	1	$3/25$	**8**
x_1	50	1	0	$-5/25$	0	$5/25$	**30**
z_j		50	40	$14/5$	0	$26/5$	**1980**
$c_j - z_j$		0	0	$-14/5$	0	$-26/5$	

The optimal solution to the primal problem is $x_1 = 30, x_2 = 12, s_1 = 0, s_2 = 8$, and $s_3 = 0$. The optimal value of the objective function is 1980.

What observation can we make about the relationship between the optimal value of the objective function in the primal and the optimal value in the dual for the HighTech problem? The optimal value of the objective function is the same (1980) for both. This relationship is true for all primal and dual linear programming problems and is stated as property 1.

Property 1

If the dual problem has an optimal solution, the primal problem has an optimal solution, and vice versa. Furthermore, the values of the optimal solutions to the dual and primal problems are equal.

This property tells us that if we solved only the dual problem, we would know that HighTech could make a maximum of $1980.

Economic Interpretation of the Dual Variables

Before making further observations about the relationship between the primal and the dual solutions, let us consider the meaning or interpretation of the dual variables u_1, u_2, and u_3. Remember that in setting up the dual problem, each dual variable is associated with one of the constraints in the primal. Specifically, u_1 is associated with the assembly time constraint, u_2 with the Portable display constraint, and u_3 with the warehouse space constraint.

To understand and interpret these dual variables, let us return to property 1 of the primal-dual relationship, which stated that the objective function values for the primal and dual problems must be equal. At the optimal solution, the primal objective function results in

$$50x_1 + 40x_2 = 1980 \tag{6.14}$$

while the dual objective function is

$$150u_1 + 20u_2 + 300u_3 = 1980 \tag{6.15}$$

Using equation (6.14), let us restrict our interest to the interpretation of the primal objective function. With x_1 and x_2 as the number of units of the Deskpro and the Portable that are assembled respectively, we have

$$\begin{pmatrix}\text{Dollar value}\\ \text{per unit of}\\ \text{Deskpro}\end{pmatrix}\begin{pmatrix}\text{Number of}\\ \text{units of}\\ \text{Deskpro}\end{pmatrix} + \begin{pmatrix}\text{Dollar value}\\ \text{per unit of}\\ \text{Portable}\end{pmatrix}\begin{pmatrix}\text{Number of}\\ \text{units of}\\ \text{Portable}\end{pmatrix} = \begin{matrix}\text{Total dollar}\\ \text{value of}\\ \text{production}\end{matrix}$$

From equation (6.15), we see that the coefficients of the dual objective function (150, 20, and 300) can be interpreted as the number of units of resources available. Thus, because the primal and dual objective functions are equal at optimality, we have

$$\begin{pmatrix}\text{Units of}\\ \text{resource}\\ 1\end{pmatrix}u_1 + \begin{pmatrix}\text{Units of}\\ \text{resource}\\ 2\end{pmatrix}u_2 + \begin{pmatrix}\text{Units of}\\ \text{resource}\\ 3\end{pmatrix}u_3 = \begin{matrix}\text{Total dollar value}\\ \text{of production}\end{matrix}$$

Thus, we see that the dual variables must carry the interpretations of being the value per unit of resource. For the HighTech problem,

$$\begin{aligned} u_1 &= \text{dollar value per hour of assembly time}\\ u_2 &= \text{dollar value per unit of the Portable display}\\ u_3 &= \text{dollar value per square foot of warehouse space}\end{aligned}$$

Have we attempted to identify the value of these resources previously? Recall that in Section 6.1, when we considered sensitivity analysis of the right-hand sides, we identified the value of an additional unit of each resource. These values were called dual prices and are helpful to the decision maker in determining whether additional units of the resources should be made available.

The analysis in Section 6.1 led to the following dual prices for the resources in the HighTech problem.

Resource	Value per Additional Unit (dual price)
Assembly time	\$2.80
Portable display	\$0.00
Warehouse space	\$5.20

The dual variables are the shadow prices, but in a maximization problem, they also equal the dual prices. For a minimization problem, the dual prices are the negative of the dual variables.

Let us now return to the optimal solution for the HighTech dual problem. The values of the dual variables at the optimal solution are $u_1 = 14/5 = 2.80$, $u_2 = 0$, and $u_3 = 26/5 = 5.20$. For this maximization problem, the values of the dual variables and the dual prices are the same. For a minimization problem, the dual prices and the dual variables are the same in absolute value but have opposite signs. Thus, the optimal values of the dual variables identify the dual prices of each additional resource or input unit at the optimal solution.

In light of the preceding discussion, the following interpretation of the primal and dual problems can be made when the primal is a product-mix problem.

Primal Problem. Given a per-unit value of each product, determine how much of each should be produced to maximize the value of the total production. Constraints require the amount of each resource used to be less than or equal to the amount available.

Dual Problem. Given the availability of each resource, determine the per-unit value such that the total value of the resources used is minimized. Constraints require the resource value per unit be greater than or equal to the value of each unit of output.

Using the Dual to Identify the Primal Solution

At the beginning of this section, we mentioned that an important feature of the primal-dual relationship is that when an optimal solution is reached, the value of the optimal solution for the primal problem is the same as the value of the optimal solution for the dual problem; see property 1. However, the question remains: If we solve only the dual problem, can we identify the optimal values for the primal variables?

Recall that in Section 6.1 we showed that when a primal problem is solved by the simplex method, the optimal values of the primal variables appear in the right-most column of the final tableau, and the dual prices (values of the dual variables) are found in the z_j row. The final simplex tableau of the dual problem provides the optimal values of the dual variables, and therefore the values of the primal variables should be found in the z_j row of the optimal dual tableau. This result is, in fact, the case and is formally stated as property 2.

Property 2

Given the simplex tableau corresponding to the optimal dual solution, the optimal values of the primal decision variables are given by the z_j entries for the surplus variables; furthermore, the optimal values of the primal slack variables are given by the negative of the $c_j - z_j$ entries for the u_j variables.

To test your ability to find the primal solution from the optimal simplex tableau for the dual and interpret the dual variables, try parts (b) and (c) of Problem 17.

This property enables us to use the final simplex tableau for the dual of the HighTech problem to determine the optimal primal solution of $x_1 = 30$ units of the Deskpro and $x_2 = 12$ units of the Portable. These optimal values of x_1 and x_2, as well as the values for all primal slack variables, are given in the z_j and $c_j - z_j$ rows of the final simplex tableau of the dual problem, which is shown again here.

		u_1	u_2	u_3	s_1	s_2	
Basis	c_B	−150	−20	−300	0	0	
u_3	−300	0	−3/25	1	−5/25	3/25	**26/5**
u_1	−150	1	8/25	0	5/25	−8/25	**14/5**
	z_j	−150	−12	−300	30	12	**−1980**
	$c_j - z_j$	0	−8	0	−30	−12	

Finding the Dual of Any Primal Problem

The HighTech Industries primal problem provided a good introduction to the concept of duality because it was formulated as a maximization problem in canonical form. For this form of primal problem, we demonstrated that conversion to the dual problem is rather easy. If the primal problem is a minimization problem in canonical form, then the dual is a maximization problem in canonical form. Therefore, finding the dual of a minimization problem in canonical form is also easy. Consider the following linear program in canonical form for a minimization problem:

$$\begin{aligned} \text{Min} \quad & 6x_1 + 2x_2 \\ \text{s.t.} \quad & \\ & 5x_1 - 1x_2 \geq 13 \\ & 3x_1 + 7x_2 \geq 9 \\ & x_1, x_2 \geq 0 \end{aligned}$$

The dual is the following maximization problem in canonical form:

$$\begin{aligned} \text{Max} \quad & 13u_1 + 9u_2 \\ \text{s.t.} \quad & \\ & 5u_1 + 3u_2 \leq 6 \\ & -1u_1 + 7u_2 \leq 2 \\ & u_1, u_2 \geq 0 \end{aligned}$$

Try Problem 18 for practice in finding the dual of a minimization problem in canonical form.

Although we could state a special set of rules for converting each type of primal problem into its associated dual, we believe it is easier to first convert any primal problem into an equivalent problem in canonical form. Then, we follow the procedures already established for finding the dual of a maximization or minimization problem in canonical form.

Let us illustrate the procedure for finding the dual of any linear programming problem by finding the dual of the following minimization problem:

$$\begin{aligned} \text{Min} \quad & 2x_1 - 3x_2 \\ \text{s.t.} \quad & \\ & 1x_1 + 2x_2 \leq 12 \\ & 4x_1 - 2x_2 \geq 3 \\ & 6x_1 - 1x_2 = 10 \\ & x_1, x_2 \geq 0 \end{aligned}$$

For this minimization problem, we obtain the canonical form by converting all constraints to greater-than-or-equal-to form. The necessary steps are as follows:

Step 1. Convert the first constraint to greater-than-or-equal-to form by multiplying both sides of the inequality by (-1). Doing so yields

$$-x_1 - 2x_2 \geq -12$$

Step 2. Constraint 3 is an equality constraint. For an equality constraint, we first create two inequalities: one with $\leq$ form, the other with $\geq$ form. Doing so yields

$$\begin{aligned} 6x_1 - 1x_2 &\geq 10 \\ 6x_1 - 1x_2 &\leq 10 \end{aligned}$$

Then, we multiply the $\leq$ constraint by (-1) to get two $\geq$ constraints.

$$\begin{aligned} 6x_1 - 1x_2 &\geq 10 \\ -6x_1 + 1x_2 &\geq -10 \end{aligned}$$

Now the original primal problem has been restated in the following equivalent form:

$$\begin{aligned} \text{Min} \quad & 2x_1 - 3x_2 \\ \text{s.t.} \quad & \\ & -1x_1 - 2x_2 \geq -12 \\ & 4x_1 - 2x_2 \geq 3 \\ & 6x_1 - 1x_2 \geq 10 \\ & -6x_1 + 1x_2 \geq -10 \\ & x_1, x_2 \geq 0 \end{aligned}$$

With the primal problem now in canonical form for a minimization problem, we can easily convert to the dual problem using the primal-dual procedure presented earlier in this section. The dual becomes[2]

$$\begin{aligned} \text{Max} \quad & -12u_1 + 3u_2 + 10u_3' - 10u_3'' \\ \text{s.t.} \quad & \\ & -1u_1 + 4u_2 + 6u_3' - 6u_3'' \leq 2 \\ & -2u_1 - 2u_2 - 1u_3' + 1u_3'' \leq -3 \\ & u_1, u_2, u_3', u_3'' \geq 0 \end{aligned}$$

Can you write the dual of any linear programming problem? Try Problem 19.

The equality constraint required two $\geq$ constraints, so we denoted the dual variables associated with these constraints as u_3' and u_3''. This notation reminds us that u_3' and u_3'' both refer to the third constraint in the initial primal problem. Because two dual variables are associated with an equality constraint, the interpretation of the dual variable must be modified slightly. The dual variable for the equality constraint $6x_1 - 1x_2 = 10$ is given by the value of $u_3' - u_3''$ in the optimal solution to the dual. Hence, the dual variable for an equality constraint can be negative.

SUMMARY

In this chapter we showed how sensitivity analysis can be performed using the information in the final simplex tableau. This sensitivity analysis includes computing the range of optimality for objective function coefficients, dual prices, and the range of feasibility for the right-hand sides. Sensitivity information is routinely made available as part of the solution report provided by most linear programming computer packages.

We stress here that sensitivity analysis is based on the assumption that only one coefficient is allowed to change at a time; all other coefficients are assumed to remain at their original values. It is possible to do some limited sensitivity analysis on the effect of changing more than one coefficient at a time; the 100 percent rule was mentioned as being useful in this context.

In studying duality, we saw how the original linear programming problem, called the primal, can be converted into its associated dual linear programming problem. Solving either the primal or the dual provides the solution to the other. We learned that the value of the dual variable identifies the economic contribution or value of additional resources in the primal problem.

[2]Note that the right-hand side of the second constraint is negative. Thus, we must multiply both sides of the constraint by -1 to obtain a positive value for the right-hand side before attempting to solve the problem with the simplex method.

GLOSSARY

Range of optimality The range of values over which an objective function coefficient may vary without causing any change in the optimal solution (i.e., the values of all the variables will remain the same, but the value of the objective function may change).

Dual price The improvement in value of the optimal solution per unit increase in a constraint's right-hand-side value.

Range of feasibility The range of values over which a b_i may vary without causing the current basic solution to become infeasible. The values of the variables in the solution will change, but the same variables will remain basic. The dual prices for constraints do not change within these ranges.

Dual problem A linear programming problem related to the primal problem. Solution of the dual also provides the solution to the primal.

Primal problem The original formulation of a linear programming problem.

Canonical form for a maximization problem A maximization problem with all less-than-or-equal-to constraints and nonnegativity requirements for the decision variables.

Canonical form for a minimization problem A minimization problem with all greater-than-or-equal-to constraints and nonnegativity requirements for the decision variables.

Dual variable The variable in a dual linear programming problem. Its optimal value provides the dual price for the associated primal resource.

PROBLEMS

1. Consider the following linear programming problem.

$$\begin{aligned} \text{Max} \quad & 5x_1 + 6x_2 + 4x_3 \\ \text{s.t.} \quad & \\ & 3x_1 + 4x_2 + 2x_3 \leq 120 \\ & x_1 + 2x_2 + x_3 \leq 50 \\ & x_1 + 2x_2 + 3x_3 \geq 30 \\ & x_1, x_2, x_3 \geq 0 \end{aligned}$$

The optimal simplex tableau is

		x_1	x_2	x_3	s_1	s_2	s_3	
Basic	c_B	5	6	4	0	0	0	
s_3	0	0	4	0	−2	7	1	**80**
x_3	4	0	2	1	−1	3	0	**30**
x_1	5	1	0	0	1	−2	0	**20**
z_j		5	8	4	1	2	0	**220**
$c_j - z_j$		0	−2	0	−1	−2	0	

a. Compute the range of optimality for c_1.
b. Compute the range of optimality for c_2.
c. Compute the range of optimality for c_{s_1}.

2. For the HighTech problem, we found the range of optimality for c_1, the profit contribution per unit of the Deskpro. The final simplex tableau is given in Section 6.1. Find the following:
   a. The range of optimality for c_2.
   b. The range of optimality for c_{s_2}.
   c. The range of optimality for c_{s_3}.
   d. Suppose the per-unit profit contribution of the Portable (c_2) dropped to \$35. How would the optimal solution change? What is the new value for total profit?

SELF test

3. Refer to the problem formulation and optimal simplex tableau given in Problem 1.
   a. Find the dual price for the first constraint.
   b. Find the dual price for the second constraint.
   c. Find the dual price for the third constraint.
   d. Suppose the right-hand side of the first constraint is increased from 120 to 125. Find the new optimal solution and its value.
   e. Suppose the right-hand side of the first constraint is decreased from 120 to 110. Find the new optimal solution and its value.

4. Refer again to the problem formulation and optimal simplex tableau given in Problem 1.
   a. Find the range of feasibility for b_1.
   b. Find the range of feasibility for b_2.
   c. Find the range of feasibility for b_3.

5. For the HighTech problem, we found the range of feasibility for b_1, the assembly time available (see Section 6.1).
   a. Find the range of feasibility for b_2.
   b. Find the range of feasibility for b_3.
   c. How much will HighTech's profit increase if there is a 20-square-foot increase in the amount of warehouse space available (b_3)?

6. Recall the Par, Inc., problem introduced in Chapter 2. The linear program for this problem is

$$
\begin{aligned}
\text{Max} \quad & 10x_1 + 9x_2 \\
\text{s.t.} \quad & \\
& \tfrac{7}{10}x_1 + 1x_2 \le 630 \quad \text{Cutting and dyeing time} \\
& \tfrac{1}{2}x_1 + \tfrac{5}{6}x_2 \le 600 \quad \text{Sewing time} \\
& 1x_1 + \tfrac{2}{3}x_2 \le 708 \quad \text{Finishing time} \\
& \tfrac{1}{10}x_1 + \tfrac{1}{4}x_2 \le 135 \quad \text{Inspection and packaging time} \\
& x_1, x_2 \ge 0
\end{aligned}
$$

where

x_1 = number of standard bags produced
x_2 = number of deluxe bags produced

The final simplex tableau is

		x_1	x_2	s_1	s_2	s_3	s_4	
Basis	c_B	10	9	0	0	0	0	
x_2	9	0	1	$30/16$	0	$-21/16$	0	**252**
s_2	0	0	0	$-15/16$	1	$5/32$	0	**120**
x_1	10	1	0	$-20/16$	0	$30/16$	0	**540**
s_4	0	0	0	$-11/32$	0	$9/64$	1	**18**
z_j		10	9	$70/16$	0	$111/16$	0	**7668**
$c_j - z_j$		0	0	$-70/16$	0	$-111/16$	0	

a. Calculate the range of optimality for the profit contribution of the standard bag.
b. Calculate the range of optimality for the profit contribution of the deluxe bag.
c. If the profit contribution per deluxe bag drops to \$7 per unit, how will the optimal solution be affected?
d. What unit profit contribution would be necessary for the deluxe bag before Par, Inc., would consider changing its current production plan?
e. If the profit contribution of the deluxe bags can be increased to \$15 per unit, what is the optimal production plan? State what you think will happen before you compute the new optimal solution.

7. For the Par, Inc., problem (Problem 6):
   a. Calculate the range of feasibility for b_1 (cutting and dyeing capacity).
   b. Calculate the range of feasibility for b_2 (sewing capacity).
   c. Calculate the range of feasibility for b_3 (finishing capacity).
   d. Calculate the range of feasibility for b_4 (inspection and packaging capacity).
   e. Which of these four departments would you be interested in scheduling for overtime? Explain.
8. a. Calculate the final simplex tableau for the Par, Inc., problem (Problem 6) after increasing b_1 from 630 to $682\frac{4}{11}$.
   b. Would the current basis be optimal if b_1 were increased further? If not, what would be the new optimal basis?
9. For the Par, Inc., problem (Problem 6):
   a. How much would profit increase if an additional 30 hours became available in the cutting and dyeing department (i.e., if b_1 were increased from 630 to 660)?
   b. How much would profit decrease if 40 hours were removed from the sewing department?
   c. How much would profit decrease if, because of an employee accident, only 570 hours instead of 630 were available in the cutting and dyeing department?
10. The following are additional conditions encountered by Par, Inc. (Problem 6).
   a. Suppose because of some new machinery Par, Inc., was able to make a small reduction in the amount of time it took to do the cutting and dyeing (constraint 1) for a standard bag. What effect would this reduction have on the objective function?
   b. Management believes that by buying a new sewing machine, the sewing time for standard bags can be reduced from ½ to ⅓ hour. Do you think this machine would be a good investment? Why?
11. Recall the RMC problem (Chapter 2, Problem 21). Letting

$$x_1 = \text{tons of fuel additive produced}$$
$$x_2 = \text{tons of solvent base produced}$$

leads to the following formulation of the RMC problem:

$$
\begin{aligned}
\text{Max} \quad & 40x_1 + 30x_2 \\
\text{s.t.} \quad & \\
& \tfrac{2}{5}x_1 + \tfrac{1}{2}x_2 \le 20 \quad \text{Material 1} \\
& \tfrac{1}{5}x_2 \le 5 \quad \text{Material 2} \\
& \tfrac{3}{5}x_1 + \tfrac{3}{10}x_2 \le 21 \quad \text{Material 3} \\
& x_1, x_2 \ge 0
\end{aligned}
$$

The final simplex tableau is shown here.

		x_1	x_2	s_1	s_2	s_3	
Basis	c_B	40	30	0	0	0	
x_2	30	0	1	$10/3$	0	$-20/9$	**20**
s_2	0	0	0	$-2/3$	1	$4/9$	**1**
x_1	40	1	0	$-5/3$	0	$25/9$	**25**
z_j		40	30	$100/3$	0	$400/9$	**1600**
$c_j - z_j$		0	0	$-100/3$	0	$-400/9$	

a. Compute the ranges of optimality for c_1 and c_2.

b. Suppose that because of an increase in production costs, the profit per ton on the fuel additive is reduced to \$30 per ton. What effect will this change have on the optimal solution?

c. What is the dual price for the material 1 constraint? What is the interpretation?

d. If RMC had an opportunity to purchase additional materials, which material would be the most valuable? How much should the company be willing to pay for this material?

12. Refer to Problem 11.

a. Compute the range of feasibility for b_1 (material 1 availability).

b. Compute the range of feasibility for b_2 (material 2 availability).

c. Compute the range of feasibility for b_3 (material 3 availability).

d. What is the dual price for material 3? Over what range of values for b_3 is this dual price valid?

13. Consider the following linear program:

$$
\begin{aligned}
\text{Max} \quad & 3x_1 + 1x_2 + 5x_3 + 3x_4 \\
\text{s.t.} \quad & \\
& 3x_1 + 1x_2 + 2x_3 = 30 \\
& 2x_1 + 1x_2 + 3x_3 + 1x_4 \ge 15 \\
& 2x_2 + 3x_4 \le 25 \\
& x_1, x_2, x_3, x_4 \ge 0
\end{aligned}
$$

a. Find the optimal solution.

b. Calculate the range of optimality for c_3.

c. What would be the effect of a four-unit decrease in c_3 (from 5 to 1) on the optimal solution and the value of that solution?

d. Calculate the range of optimality for c_2.

e. What would be the effect of a three-unit increase in c_2 (from 1 to 4) on the optimal solution and the value of that solution?

14. Consider the final simplex tableau shown here.

		x_1	x_2	x_3	x_4	s_1	s_2	s_3	
Basis	c_B	4	6	3	1	0	0	0	
x_3	3	$3/60$	0	1	$1/2$	$3/10$	0	$-6/30$	**125**
s_2	0	$195/60$	0	0	$-1/2$	$-5/10$	1	-1	**425**
x_2	6	$39/60$	1	0	$1/2$	$-1/10$	0	$12/30$	**25**
z_j		$81/20$	6	3	$9/2$	$3/10$	0	$54/30$	**525**
$c_j - z_j$		$-1/20$	0	0	$-7/2$	$-3/10$	0	$-54/30$	

The original right-hand-side values were $b_1 = 550$, $b_2 = 700$, and $b_3 = 200$.

a. Calculate the range of feasibility for b_1.

b. Calculate the range of feasibility for b_2.

c. Calculate the range of feasibility for b_3.

15. Consider the following linear program:

$$\begin{aligned} \text{Max} \quad & 15x_1 + 30x_2 + 20x_3 \\ \text{s.t.} \quad & \\ & 1x_1 \qquad\quad\; + 1x_3 \le 4 \\ & 0.5x_1 + 2x_2 + 1x_3 \le 3 \\ & 1x_1 + 1x_2 + 2x_3 \le 6 \\ & x_1, x_2, x_3 \ge 0 \end{aligned}$$

Solve using the simplex method, and answer the following questions:

a. What is the optimal solution?

b. What is the value of the objective function?

c. Which constraints are binding?

d. How much slack is available in the nonbinding constraints?

e. What are the dual prices associated with the three constraints? Which right-hand-side value would have the greatest effect on the value of the objective function if it could be changed?

f. Develop the appropriate ranges for the coefficients of the objective function. What is your interpretation of these ranges?

g. Develop and interpret the ranges of feasibility for the right-hand-side values.

16. Recall the Innis Investments problem (Chapter 2, Problem 37). Letting

x_1 = units purchased in the stock fund
x_2 = units purchased in the money market fund

leads to the following formulation:

$$\begin{aligned} \text{Min} \quad & 8x_1 + 3x_2 && \text{Total risk} \\ \text{s.t.} \quad & \\ & 50x_1 + 100x_2 \le 1{,}200{,}000 && \text{Funds available} \\ & 5x_1 + 4x_2 \ge 60{,}000 && \text{Annual income} \\ & 1x_2 \ge 3{,}000 && \text{Minimum units in money market} \\ & x_1, x_2 \ge 0 \end{aligned}$$

a. Solve this problem using the simplex method.
b. The value of the optimal solution is a measure of the riskiness of the portfolio. What effect will increasing the annual income requirement have on the riskiness of the portfolio?
c. Find the range of feasibility for b_2.
d. How will the optimal solution and its value change if the annual income requirement is increased from \$60,000 to \$65,000?
e. How will the optimal solution and its value change if the risk measure for the stock fund is increased from 8 to 9?

17. Suppose that in a product-mix problem x_1, x_2, x_3, and x_4 indicate the units of products 1, 2, 3, and 4, respectively, and we have

$$\begin{aligned}
\text{Max} \quad & 4x_1 + 6x_2 + 3x_3 + 1x_4 \\
\text{s.t.} \quad & \\
& 1.5x_1 + 2x_2 + 4x_3 + 3x_4 \leq 550 \quad \text{Machine A hours} \\
& 4x_1 + 1x_2 + 2x_3 + 1x_4 \leq 700 \quad \text{Machine B hours} \\
& 2x_1 + 3x_2 + 1x_3 + 2x_4 \leq 200 \quad \text{Machine C hours} \\
& x_1, x_2, x_3, x_4 \geq 0
\end{aligned}$$

a. Formulate the dual to this problem.
b. Solve the dual. Use the dual solution to show that the profit-maximizing product mix is $x_1 = 0$, $x_2 = 25$, $x_3 = 125$, and $x_4 = 0$.
c. Use the dual variables to identify the machine or machines that are producing at maximum capacity. If the manager can select one machine for additional production capacity, which machine should have priority? Why?

18. Find the dual for the following linear program:

$$\begin{aligned}
\text{Min} \quad & 2800x_1 + 6000x_2 + 1200x_3 \\
\text{s.t.} \quad & \\
& 15x_1 + 15x_2 + 1x_3 \geq 5 \\
& 4x_1 + 8x_2 \geq 5 \\
& 12x_1 + 8x_3 \geq 24 \\
& x_1, x_2, x_3 \geq 0
\end{aligned}$$

19. Write the following primal problem in canonical form, and find its dual.

$$\begin{aligned}
\text{Max} \quad & 3x_1 + 1x_2 + 5x_3 + 3x_4 \\
\text{s.t.} \quad & \\
& 3x_1 + 1x_2 + 2x_3 = 30 \\
& 2x_1 + 1x_2 + 3x_3 + 1x_4 \geq 15 \\
& 2x_2 + 3x_4 \leq 25 \\
& x_1, x_2, x_3, x_4 \geq 0
\end{aligned}$$

20. Photo Chemicals produces two types of photograph-developing fluids at a cost of \$1.00 per gallon. Let

$$\begin{aligned}
x_1 &= \text{gallons of product 1} \\
x_2 &= \text{gallons of product 2}
\end{aligned}$$

Photo Chemicals management requires that at least 30 gallons of product 1 and at least 20 gallons of product 2 be produced. They also require that at least 80 pounds of a perishable raw material be used in production. A linear programming formulation of the problem is as follows:

$$\begin{array}{lrl}
\text{Min} & 1x_1 + 1x_2 & \\
\text{s.t.} & & \\
& 1x_1 \qquad \geq 30 & \text{Minimum product 1} \\
& 1x_2 \geq 20 & \text{Minimum product 2} \\
& 1x_1 + 2x_2 \geq 80 & \text{Minimum raw material} \\
& x_1, x_2 \geq 0 &
\end{array}$$

a. Write the dual problem.
b. Solve the dual problem. Use the dual solution to show that the optimal production plan is $x_1 = 30$ and $x_2 = 25$.
c. The third constraint involves a management request that the current 80 pounds of a perishable raw material be used. However, after learning that the optimal solution calls for an excess production of five units of product 2, management is reconsidering the raw material requirement. Specifically, you have been asked to identify the cost effect if this constraint is relaxed. Use the dual variable to indicate the change in the cost if only 79 pounds of raw material have to be used.

21. Consider the following linear programming problem:

$$\begin{array}{lrl}
\text{Min} & 4x_1 + \quad 3x_2 + 6x_3 & \\
\text{s.t.} & & \\
& 1x_1 + 0.5x_2 + 1x_3 \geq 15 & \\
& 2x_2 + 1x_3 \geq 30 & \\
& 1x_1 + \quad 1x_2 + 2x_3 \geq 20 & \\
& x_1, x_2, x_3 \geq 0 &
\end{array}$$

a. Write the dual problem.
b. Solve the dual.
c. Use the dual solution to identify the optimal solution to the original primal problem.
d. Verify the optimal values for the primal and dual problems are equal.

22. A sales representative who sells two products is trying to determine the number of sales calls that should be made during the next month to promote each product. Based on past experience, representatives earn an average $10 commission for every call on product 1 and a $5 commission for every call on product 2. The company requires at least 20 calls per month for each product and not more than 100 calls per month on any one product. In addition, the sales representative spends about 3 hours on each call for product 1 and 1 hour on each call for product 2. If 175 selling hours are available next month, how many calls should be made for each of the two products to maximize the commission?
a. Formulate a linear program for this problem.
b. Formulate and solve the dual problem.
c. Use the final simplex tableau for the dual problem to determine the optimal number of calls for the products. What is the maximum commission?
d. Interpret the values of the dual variables.

23. Consider the linear program

$$
\begin{aligned}
\text{Max} \quad & 3x_1 + 2x_2 \\
\text{s.t.} \quad & \\
& 1x_1 + 2x_2 \le 8 \\
& 2x_1 + 1x_2 \le 10 \\
& x_1, x_2 \ge 0
\end{aligned}
$$

a. Solve this problem using the simplex method. Keep a record of the value of the objective function at each extreme point.
b. Formulate and solve the dual of this problem using the graphical procedure.
c. Compute the value of the dual objective function for each extreme-point solution of the dual problem.
d. Compare the values of the objective function for each primal and dual extreme-point solution.
e. Can a dual feasible solution yield a value less than a primal feasible solution? Can you state a result concerning bounds on the value of the primal solution provided by any feasible solution to the dual problem?

24. Suppose the optimal solution to a three-variable linear programming problem has $x_1 = 10$, $x_2 = 30$, and $x_3 = 15$. It is later discovered that the following two constraints were inadvertently omitted when formulating the problem.

$$
\begin{aligned}
6x_1 + 4x_2 - 1x_3 &\le 170 \\
\tfrac{1}{4}x_1 + 1x_2 \qquad &\ge 25
\end{aligned}
$$

Find the new optimal solution if possible. If it is not possible, state why it is not possible.

CHAPTER 7

Transportation, Assignment, and Transshipment Problems

CONTENTS

Transportation, assignment, and transshipment problems belong to a special class of linear programming problems called *network flow problems.* A separate chapter is devoted to these problems because of the many applications of the transportation, assignment, and transshipment models. Some are described in the chapter's Management Science in Action features. The U.S. Marine Corps uses a transportation model to mobilize troops in the event of a world crisis or war. Heery International uses an assignment model to assign construction managers to projects. Procter & Gamble used a transshipment model as a tool in redesigning its North American product distribution system. Because of the special mathematical structure of network flow problems, even large problems involving thousands of variables can often be solved in a few seconds of computer time.

We approach the network flow problems by illustrating each problem with a specific application. We first develop a graphical representation, called a *network,* of the problem and then show how each can be formulated and solved as a linear program.

An applications-oriented introduction to the transportation, assignment, and transshipment problems can be obtained by covering Sections 7.1–7.4. Sections 7.5 and 7.6, involving special-purpose algorithms, are optional and can be skipped without loss of continuity.

7.1 TRANSPORTATION PROBLEM: A NETWORK MODEL AND A LINEAR PROGRAMMING FORMULATION

The **transportation problem** arises frequently in planning for the distribution of goods and services from several supply locations to several demand locations. Typically, the quantity of goods available at each supply location (origin) is limited, and the quantity of goods needed at each of several demand locations (destinations) is known. The usual objective in a transportation problem is to minimize the cost of shipping goods from the origins to the destinations.

Let us illustrate by considering a transportation problem faced by Foster Generators. This problem involves the transportation of a product from three plants to four distribution centers. Foster Generators has plants in Cleveland, Ohio; Bedford, Indiana; and York, Pennsylvania. Production capacities over the next three-month planning period for one particular type of generator are as follows:

Origin	Plant	Three-Month Production Capacity (units)
1	Cleveland	5000
2	Bedford	6000
3	York	2500
		Total 13,500

The firm distributes its generators through four regional distribution centers located in Boston, Chicago, St. Louis, and Lexington; the three-month forecast of demand for the distribution centers is as follows:

Destination	Distribution Center	Three-Month Demand Forecast (units)
1	Boston	6000
2	Chicago	4000
3	St. Louis	2000
4	Lexington	1500
		Total 13,500

Management would like to determine how much of its production should be shipped from each plant to each distribution center. Figure 7.1 shows graphically the 12 distribution routes Foster can use. Such a graph is called a **network;** the circles are referred to as **nodes** and the lines connecting the nodes as **arcs.** Each origin or destination is represented by a node, and each possible shipping route is represented by an arc. The amount of the supply is written next to each origin node, and the amount of the demand is written next to each destination node. The goods shipped from the origins to the destinations represent the flow in the network. Note that the direction of flow (from origin to destination) is indicated by the arrows.

Try Problem 1 for practice in developing a network model of a transportation problem.

For Foster's transportation problem, the objective is to determine the routes to be used and the quantity to be shipped via each route that will provide the minimum total transportation cost. The cost for each unit shipped on each route is given in Table 7.1 and is shown on each arc in Figure 7.1.

FIGURE 7.1 THE NETWORK REPRESENTATION OF THE FOSTER GENERATORS TRANSPORTATION PROBLEM

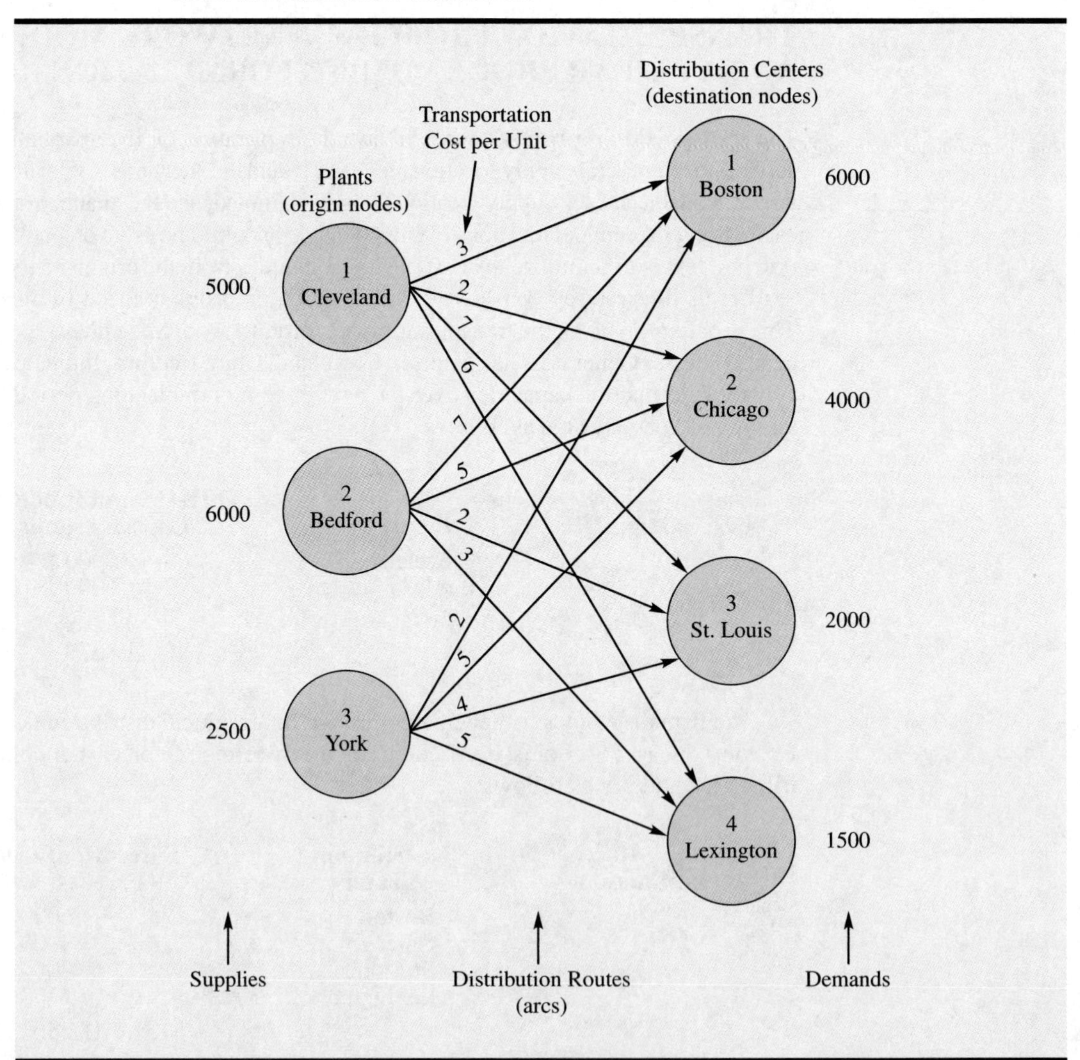

A linear programming model can be used to solve this transportation problem. We will use double-subscripted decision variables, with x_{11} denoting the number of units shipped from origin 1 (Cleveland) to destination 1 (Boston), x_{12} denoting the number of units shipped from origin 1 (Cleveland) to destination 2 (Chicago), and so on. In general, the decision variables for a transportation problem having m origins and n destinations are written as follows:

The first subscript identifies the "from" node of the corresponding arc and the second subscript identifies the "to" node of the arc.

$$x_{ij} = \text{number of units shipped from origin } i \text{ to destination } j$$
$$\text{where } i = 1, 2, 3, \ldots, m, \text{ and } j = 1, 2, \ldots, n$$

Because the objective of the transportation problem is to minimize the total transportation cost, we can use the cost data in Table 7.1 or on the arcs in Figure 7.1 to develop the following cost expressions:

$$\begin{aligned} &\text{Transportation costs for} \\ &\text{units shipped from Cleveland} = 3x_{11} + 2x_{12} + 7x_{13} + 6x_{14} \\ &\text{Transportation costs for} \\ &\text{units shipped from Bedford} \quad = 7x_{21} + 5x_{22} + 2x_{23} + 3x_{24} \\ &\text{Transportation costs for} \\ &\text{units shipped from York} \qquad = 2x_{31} + 5x_{32} + 4x_{33} + 5x_{34} \end{aligned}$$

The sum of these expressions provides the objective function showing the total transportation cost for Foster Generators.

Transportation problems need constraints because each origin has a limited supply and each destination has a specific demand. We will consider the supply constraints first. The capacity at the Cleveland plant is 5000 units. With the total number of units shipped from the Cleveland plant expressed as $x_{11} + x_{12} + x_{13} + x_{14}$, the supply constraint for the Cleveland plant is

$$x_{11} + x_{12} + x_{13} + x_{14} \leq 5000 \quad \text{Cleveland supply}$$

With three origins (plants), the Foster transportation problem has three supply constraints. Given the capacity of 6000 units at the Bedford plant and 2500 units at the York plant, the two additional supply constraints are

$$\begin{aligned} x_{21} + x_{22} + x_{23} + x_{24} &\leq 6000 \quad \text{Bedford supply} \\ x_{31} + x_{32} + x_{33} + x_{34} &\leq 2500 \quad \text{York supply} \end{aligned}$$

TABLE 7.1 TRANSPORTATION COST PER UNIT FOR THE FOSTER GENERATORS TRANSPORTATION PROBLEM

	Destination			
Origin	**Boston**	**Chicago**	**St. Louis**	**Lexington**
Cleveland	3	2	7	6
Bedford	7	5	2	3
York	2	5	4	5

With the four distribution centers as the destinations, four demand constraints are needed to ensure that destination demands will be satisfied:

To obtain a feasible solution, the total supply must be greater than or equal to the total demand.

$$\begin{aligned} x_{11} + x_{21} + x_{31} &= 6000 \quad \text{Boston demand} \\ x_{12} + x_{22} + x_{32} &= 4000 \quad \text{Chicago demand} \\ x_{13} + x_{23} + x_{33} &= 2000 \quad \text{St. Louis demand} \\ x_{14} + x_{24} + x_{34} &= 1500 \quad \text{Lexington demand} \end{aligned}$$

Combining the objective function and constraints into one model provides a 12-variable, 7-constraint linear programming formulation of the Foster Generators transportation problem:

$$\text{Min} \quad 3x_{11} + 2x_{12} + 7x_{13} + 6x_{14} + 7x_{21} + 5x_{22} + 2x_{23} + 3x_{24} + 2x_{31} + 5x_{32} + 4x_{33} + 5x_{34}$$

s.t.

$$\begin{aligned} x_{11} + x_{12} + x_{13} + x_{14} &\le 5000 \\ x_{21} + x_{22} + x_{23} + x_{24} &\le 6000 \\ x_{31} + x_{32} + x_{33} + x_{34} &\le 2500 \\ x_{11} + x_{21} + x_{31} &= 6000 \\ x_{12} + x_{22} + x_{32} &= 4000 \\ x_{13} + x_{23} + x_{33} &= 2000 \\ x_{14} + x_{24} + x_{34} &= 1500 \end{aligned}$$

$$x_{ij} \ge 0 \qquad \text{for } i = 1, 2, 3; j = 1, 2, 3, 4$$

Comparing the linear programming formulation to the network in Figure 7.1 leads to several observations. All the information needed for the linear programming formulation is on the network. Each node requires one constraint and each arc requires one variable. The sum of the variables corresponding to arcs from an origin node must be less than or equal to the origin's supply, and the sum of the variables corresponding to the arcs into a destination node must be equal to the destination's demand.

Try Problem 2 to test your ability to formulate and solve a linear programming model of a transportation problem.

We solved the Foster Generators problem with the linear programming module of The Management Scientist. The computer solution (see Figure 7.2) shows that the minimum total transportation cost is $39,500. The values for the decision variables show the optimal amounts to ship over each route. For example, with $x_{11} = 3500$, 3500 units should be shipped from Cleveland to Boston, and with $x_{12} = 1500$, 1500 units should be shipped from Cleveland to Chicago. Other values of the decision variables indicate the remaining shipping quantities and routes. Table 7.2 shows the minimum-cost transportation schedule, and Figure 7.3 summarizes the optimal solution on the network.

Problem Variations

The Foster Generators problem illustrates use of the basic transportation model. Variations of the basic transportation model may involve one or more of the following situations:

1. Total supply not equal to total demand
2. Maximization objective function
3. Route capacities or route minimums
4. Unacceptable routes

With slight modifications in the linear programming model, we can easily accommodate these situations.

FIGURE 7.2 THE MANAGEMENT SCIENTIST SOLUTION FOR THE FOSTER GENERATORS TRANSPORTATION PROBLEM

EXCELfile
Foster

```
Objective Function Value =            39500.000

      Variable              Value              Reduced Costs
   --------------      ---------------      ----------------
        X11                3500.000                 0.000
        X12                1500.000                 0.000
        X13                   0.000                 8.000
        X14                   0.000                 6.000
        X21                   0.000                 1.000
        X22                2500.000                 0.000
        X23                2000.000                 0.000
        X24                1500.000                 0.000
        X31                2500.000                 0.000
        X32                   0.000                 4.000
        X33                   0.000                 6.000
        X34                   0.000                 6.000
```

Total Supply Not Equal to Total Demand. Often *the total supply is not equal to the total demand.* If total supply exceeds total demand, no modification in the linear programming formulation is necessary. Excess supply will appear as slack in the linear programming solution. Slack for any particular origin can be interpreted as the unused supply or amount not shipped from the origin.

Whenever total supply is less than total demand, the model does not determine how the unsatisfied demand is handled (e.g., backorders). The manager must handle this aspect of the problem.

If total supply is less than total demand, the linear programming model of a transportation problem will not have a feasible solution. In this case, we modify the network representation by adding a *dummy origin* with a supply equal to the difference between the total demand and the total supply. With the addition of the dummy origin, and an arc from the dummy origin to each destination, the linear programming model will have a feasible solution. A zero cost per unit is assigned to each arc leaving the dummy origin so that the value of the optimal solution for the revised problem will represent the shipping cost for the units actually shipped (no shipments actually will be made from the dummy origin). When the

TABLE 7.2 OPTIMAL SOLUTION TO THE FOSTER GENERATORS TRANSPORTATION PROBLEM

Route				
From	**To**	**Units Shipped**	**Cost per Unit**	**Total Cost**
Cleveland	Boston	3500	$3	$10,500
Cleveland	Chicago	1500	$2	3,000
Bedford	Chicago	2500	$5	12,500
Bedford	St. Louis	2000	$2	4,000
Bedford	Lexington	1500	$3	4,500
York	Boston	2500	$2	5,000
				$39,500

FIGURE 7.3 OPTIMAL SOLUTION TO THE FOSTER GENERATORS TRANSPORTATION PROBLEM

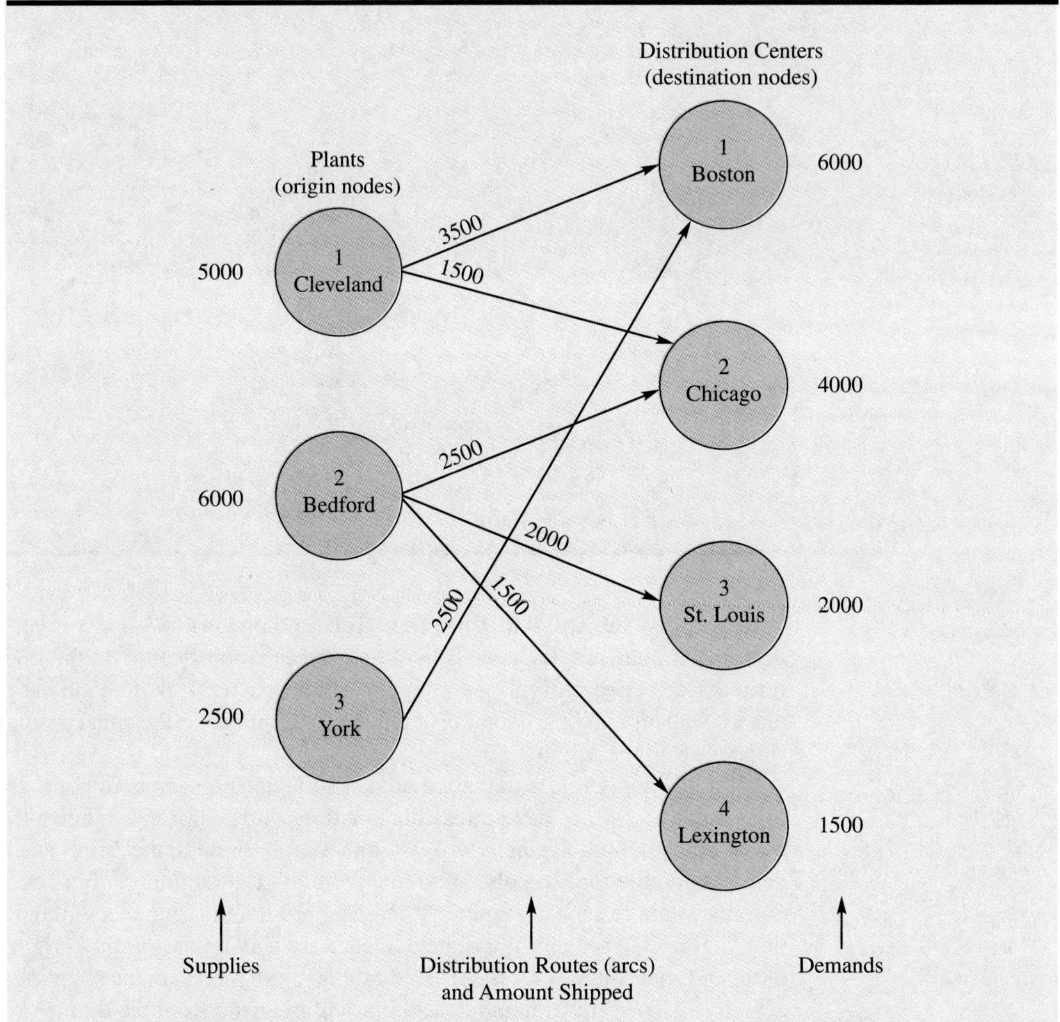

optimal solution is implemented, the destinations showing shipments being received from the dummy origin will be the destinations experiencing a shortfall or unsatisfied demand.

Try Problem 8 to test your ability to handle a case where demand is greater than supply with a maximization objective.

Maximization Objective Function. In some transportation problems, the objective is to find a solution that maximizes profit or revenue. Using the values for profit or revenue per unit as coefficients in the objective function, we simply solve a maximization rather than a minimization linear program. This change does not affect the constraints.

Route Capacities and/or Route Minimums. The linear programming formulation of the transportation problem also can accommodate capacities and/or minimum quantities for one or more of the routes. For example, suppose that in the Foster Generators problem the York–Boston route (origin 3 to destination 1) had a capacity of 1000 units because of limited space availability on its normal mode of transportation. With x_{31} denoting the amount shipped from York to Boston, the route capacity constraint for the York–Boston route would be

$$x_{31} \leq 1000$$

Similarly, route minimums can be specified. For example,

$$x_{22} \geq 2000$$

would guarantee that a previously committed order for a Bedford–Chicago delivery of at least 2000 units would be maintained in the optimal solution.

Unacceptable Routes. Finally, establishing a route from every origin to every destination may not be possible. To handle this situation, we simply drop the corresponding arc from the network and remove the corresponding variable from the linear programming formulation. For example, if the Cleveland–St. Louis route were unacceptable or unusable, the arc from Cleveland to St. Louis could be dropped in Figure 7.1, and x_{13} could be removed from the linear programming formulation. Solving the resulting 11-variable, 7-constraint model would provide the optimal solution while guaranteeing that the Cleveland–St. Louis route is not used.

A General Linear Programming Model of the Transportation Problem

To show the general linear programming model of the transportation problem, we use the notation:

$$\begin{aligned} i &= \text{index for origins, } i = 1, 2, \ldots, m \\ j &= \text{index for destinations, } j = 1, 2, \ldots, n \\ x_{ij} &= \text{number of units shipped from origin } i \text{ to destination } j \\ c_{ij} &= \text{cost per unit of shipping from origin } i \text{ to destination } j \\ s_i &= \text{supply or capacity in units at origin } i \\ d_j &= \text{demand in units at destination } j \end{aligned}$$

The general linear programming model of the m-origin, n-destination transportation problem is

$$\begin{aligned} \text{Min} \quad & \sum_{i=1}^{m}\sum_{j=1}^{n} c_{ij}x_{ij} \\ \text{s.t.} \quad & \\ & \sum_{j=1}^{n} x_{ij} \leq s_i \qquad i = 1, 2, \ldots, m \quad \text{Supply} \\ & \sum_{i=1}^{m} x_{ij} = d_j \qquad j = 1, 2, \ldots, n \quad \text{Demand} \\ & x_{ij} \geq 0 \qquad \text{for all } i \text{ and } j \end{aligned}$$

As mentioned previously, we can add constraints of the form $x_{ij} \leq L_{ij}$ if the route from origin i to destination j has capacity L_{ij}. A transportation problem that includes constraints of this type is called a **capacitated transportation problem.** Similarly, we can add route minimum constraints of the form $x_{ij} \geq M_{ij}$ if the route from origin i to destination j must handle at least M_{ij} units.

NOTES AND COMMENTS

1. Transportation problems encountered in practice usually lead to large linear programs. Transportation problems with 100 origins and 100 destinations are not unusual. Such a problem would involve (100)(100) = 10,000 variables.
2. To handle a situation in which some routes may be unacceptable, we stated that you could drop the corresponding arc from the network and remove the corresponding variable from the linear programming formulation. Another approach often used is to assign an extremely large objective function cost coefficient to any unacceptable arc. If the problem has already been formulated, another option is to add a constraint to the formulation that sets the variable you want to remove equal to zero.
3. The optimal solution to a transportation model will consist of integer values for the decision variables as long as all supply and demand values are integers. The reason is the special mathematical structure of the linear programming model. Each variable appears in exactly one supply and one demand constraint, and all coefficients in the constraint equations are 1s and 0s.
4. Although many transportation problems involve minimizing the cost of transporting goods between locations, many other applications of the transportation model exist. The Management Science in Action, Marine Corps Mobilization, illustrates the use of a transportation model to send Marine Corps officers to billets.

MANAGEMENT SCIENCE IN ACTION

MARINE CORPS MOBILIZATION*

The U.S. Marine Corps has developed a network model for mobilizing its officers in the event of a world crisis or war. The problem is to send officers to billets (duty assignments) as quickly as possible. The model developed to solve this problem is a transportation model much like the ones discussed in this chapter, only much larger. The origins or supply nodes represent the officers available, and the destinations or demand nodes represent the billets. A realistic implementation might involve as many as 40,000 officers and 25,000 billets. If all officer-to-billets arc combinations are permitted, the transportation problem would have 1 billion arcs. To reduce the problem size, officers with similar qualifications are aggregated into the same supply node and similar duty assignments are aggregated into the same demand nodes. Using this approach and methods for eliminating infeasible arcs, the Marine Corps has solved problems involving 27,000 officers and 10,000 billets in 10 seconds on a personal computer.

Excellent results in sending officers of appropriate grade and job qualifications to the desired billets have been obtained. In a crisis, the availability and use of this system can make the difference between an appropriate response and disaster. The prior system required 2–4 days to produce a complete mobilization plan and provided a lower quality match between officer qualifications and billet needs. The Marine Corps is now using the mobilization model to enhance its peacetime capability.

*Based on D. O. Bausch, G. G. Brown, D. R. Hundley, S. H. Rapp, and R. E. Rosenthal, "Mobilizing Marine Corps Officers," *Interfaces* (July/August 1991): 26–38.

7.2 ASSIGNMENT PROBLEM: THE NETWORK MODEL AND A LINEAR PROGRAMMING FORMULATION

The **assignment problem** arises in a variety of decision-making situations; typical assignment problems involve assigning jobs to machines, agents to tasks, sales personnel to sales territories, contracts to bidders, and so on. A distinguishing feature of the assignment problem is that *one* agent is assigned to *one and only one* task. Specifically, we look for the set of assignments that will optimize a stated objective, such as minimize cost, minimize time, or maximize profit.

To illustrate the assignment problem, let us consider the case of Fowle Marketing Research, which has just received requests for market research studies from three new clients. The company faces the task of assigning a project leader (agent) to each client (task). Currently, three individuals have no other commitments and are available for the project leader assignments. Fowle's management realizes, however, that the time required to complete each study will depend on the experience and ability of the project leader assigned. The three projects have approximately the same priority, and the company wants to assign project leaders to minimize the total number of days required to complete all three projects. If a project leader is to be assigned to one client only, what assignments should be made?

To answer the assignment question, Fowle's management must first consider all possible project leader–client assignments and then estimate the corresponding project completion times. With three project leaders and three clients, nine assignment alternatives are possible. The alternatives and the estimated project completion times in days are summarized in Table 7.3.

Try part (a) of Problem 12 for practice in developing a network model for an assignment problem.

Figure 7.4 shows the network representation of Fowle's assignment problem. The nodes correspond to the project leaders and clients, and the arcs represent the possible assignments of project leaders to clients. The supply at each origin node and the demand at each destination node are 1; the cost of assigning a project leader to a client is the time it takes that project leader to complete the client's task. Note the similarity between the network models of the assignment problem (Figure 7.4) and the transportation problem (Figure 7.1). The assignment problem is a special case of the transportation problem in which all supply and demand values equal 1 and the amount shipped over each arc is either 0 or 1.

Because the assignment problem is a special case of the transportation problem, a linear programming formulation can be developed. Again, we need a constraint for each node and a variable for each arc. As in the transportation problem, we use double-subscripted decision variables, with x_{11} denoting the assignment of project leader 1 (Terry) to client 1, x_{12} denoting the assignment of project leader 1 (Terry) to client 2, and so on. Thus, we define the decision variables for Fowle's assignment problem as

$$x_{ij} = \begin{cases} 1 \text{ if project leader } i \text{ is assigned to client } j \\ 0 \text{ otherwise} \end{cases}$$
$$\text{where } i = 1, 2, 3; j = 1, 2, 3$$

Using this notation and the completion time data in Table 7.3, we develop completion time expressions:

$$\begin{aligned} \text{Days required for Terry's assignment} &= 10x_{11} + 15x_{12} + 9x_{13} \\ \text{Days required for Carle's assignment} &= 9x_{21} + 18x_{22} + 5x_{23} \\ \text{Days required for McClymonds's assignment} &= 6x_{31} + 14x_{32} + 3x_{33} \end{aligned}$$

TABLE 7.3 ESTIMATED PROJECT COMPLETION TIMES (DAYS) FOR THE FOWLE MARKETING RESEARCH ASSIGNMENT PROBLEM

		Client	
Project Leader	**1**	**2**	**3**
1. Terry	10	15	9
2. Carle	9	18	5
3. McClymonds	6	14	3

FIGURE 7.4 A NETWORK MODEL OF THE FOWLE MARKETING RESEARCH ASSIGNMENT PROBLEM

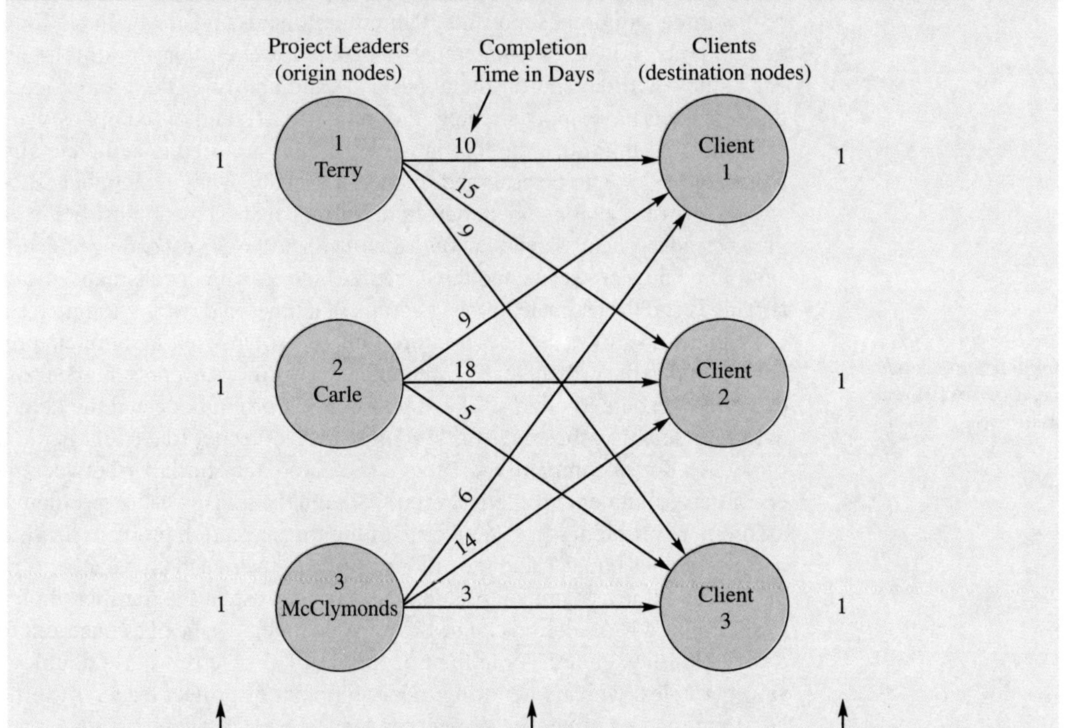

The sum of the completion times for the three project leaders will provide the total days required to complete the three assignments. Thus, the objective function is

$$\text{Min} \quad 10x_{11} + 15x_{12} + 9x_{13} + 9x_{21} + 18x_{22} + 5x_{23} + 6x_{31} + 14x_{32} + 3x_{33}$$

The constraints for the assignment problem reflect the conditions that each project leader can be assigned to at most one client and that each client must have one assigned project leader. These constraints are written as follows:

Because the number of project leaders equals the number of clients, all the constraints could be written as equalities. But when the number of project leaders exceeds the number of clients, less-than-or-equal-to constraints must be used for the project leader constraints.

$$\begin{aligned}
x_{11} + x_{12} + x_{13} &\le 1 \quad \text{Terry's assignment} \\
x_{21} + x_{22} + x_{23} &\le 1 \quad \text{Carle's assignment} \\
x_{31} + x_{32} + x_{33} &\le 1 \quad \text{McClymonds's assignment} \\
x_{11} + x_{21} + x_{31} &= 1 \quad \text{Client 1} \\
x_{12} + x_{22} + x_{32} &= 1 \quad \text{Client 2} \\
x_{13} + x_{23} + x_{33} &= 1 \quad \text{Client 3}
\end{aligned}$$

Note that one constraint matches up with each node in Figure 7.4.

FIGURE 7.5 THE MANAGEMENT SCIENTIST SOLUTION FOR THE FOWLE MARKETING RESEARCH ASSIGNMENT PROBLEM

EXCELfile
Fowle

```
Objective Function Value =          26.000

     Variable              Value              Reduced Costs
  --------------      ---------------      -----------------
        X11                0.000                    0.000
        X12                1.000                    0.000
        X13                0.000                    3.000
        X21                0.000                    0.000
        X22                0.000                    4.000
        X23                1.000                    0.000
        X31                1.000                    0.000
        X32                0.000                    3.000
        X33                0.000                    1.000
```

Can you formulate and solve a linear programming model for an assignment problem? Try part (b) of Problem 12.

Combining the objective function and constraints into one model provides the following nine-variable, six-constraint linear programming model of the Fowle Marketing Research assignment problem.

$$
\begin{aligned}
\text{Min}\quad & 10x_{11} + 15x_{12} + 9x_{13} + 9x_{21} + 18x_{22} + 5x_{23} + 6x_{31} + 14x_{32} + 3x_{33} \\
\text{s.t.}\quad & \\
& x_{11} + x_{12} + x_{13} \le 1 \\
& x_{21} + x_{22} + x_{23} \le 1 \\
& x_{31} + x_{32} + x_{33} \le 1 \\
& x_{11} + x_{21} + x_{31} = 1 \\
& x_{12} + x_{22} + x_{32} = 1 \\
& x_{13} + x_{23} + x_{33} = 1 \\
& x_{ij} \ge 0 \quad \text{for } i = 1, 2, 3;\ j = 1, 2, 3
\end{aligned}
$$

Figure 7.5 shows the computer solution for this model. Terry is assigned to client 2 ($x_{12} = 1$), Carle is assigned to client 3 ($x_{23} = 1$), and McClymonds is assigned to client 1 ($x_{31} = 1$). The total completion time required is 26 days. This solution is summarized in Table 7.4.

TABLE 7.4 OPTIMAL PROJECT LEADER ASSIGNMENTS FOR THE FOWLE MARKETING RESEARCH PROBLEM

Project Leader	Assigned Client		Days
Terry	2		15
Carle	3		5
McClymonds	1		6
		Total	26

Problem Variations

Because the assignment problem can be viewed as a special case of the transportation problem, the problem variations that may arise in an assignment problem parallel those for the transportation problem. Specifically, we can handle the following:

1. Total number of agents (supply) not equal to the total number of tasks (demand)
2. A maximization objective function
3. Unacceptable assignments

The situation in which the number of agents does not equal the number of tasks is analogous to total supply not equaling total demand in a transportation problem. If the number of agents exceeds the number of tasks, the extra agents simply remain unassigned in the linear programming model. If the number of tasks exceeds the number of agents, the linear programming model will not have a feasible solution. In this situation, a simple modification is to add enough dummy agents to equalize the number of agents and the number of tasks. For instance, in the Fowle problem we might have had five clients (tasks) and only three project leaders (agents). By adding two dummy project leaders, we can create a new assignment problem with the number of project leaders equal to the number of clients. The objective function coefficients for the assignment of dummy project leaders would be zero so that the value of the optimal solution would represent the total number of days required by the assignments actually made (no assignments will actually be made to the clients receiving dummy project leaders).

If the assignment alternatives are evaluated in terms of revenue or profit rather than time or cost, the linear programming formulation can be solved as a maximization rather than a minimization problem. In addition, if one or more assignments are unacceptable, the corresponding decision variable can be removed from the linear programming formulation. This scenario could happen, for example, if an agent did not have the experience necessary for one or more of the tasks.

A General Linear Programming Model of the Assignment Problem

The general assignment problem involves m agents and n tasks. If we let $x_{ij} = 1$ or 0 according to whether agent i is assigned to task j, and if c_{ij} denotes the cost of assigning agent i to task j, we can write the general assignment model as

$$\text{Min} \quad \sum_{i=1}^{m}\sum_{j=1}^{n} c_{ij}x_{ij}$$

s.t.

$$\sum_{j=1}^{n} x_{ij} \leq 1 \qquad i = 1, 2, \ldots, m \quad \text{Agents}$$

$$\sum_{i=1}^{m} x_{ij} = 1 \qquad j = 1, 2, \ldots, n \quad \text{Tasks}$$

$$x_{ij} \geq 0 \qquad \text{for all } i \text{ and } j$$

Multiple Assignments

At the beginning of this section, we indicated that a distinguishing feature of the assignment problem is that *one* agent is assigned to *one and only one* task. In generalizations of the assignment problem where one agent can be assigned to two or more tasks, the linear programming formulation of the problem can be easily modified. For example, let us assume that in the Fowle Marketing Research problem Terry could be assigned up to two clients; in this case, the constraint representing Terry's assignment would be $x_{11} + x_{12} + x_{13} \leq 2$. In general, if a_i denotes the upper limit for the number of tasks to which agent i can be assigned, we write the agent constraints as

If some tasks require more than one agent, the linear programming formulation can also accommodate the situation. Use the number of agents required as the right-hand side of the appropriate task constraint.

$$\sum_{j=1}^{n} x_{ij} \leq a_i \qquad i = 1, 2, \ldots, m$$

Thus, we see that one advantage of formulating and solving assignment problems as linear programs is that special cases such as the situation involving multiple assignments can be easily handled.

NOTES AND COMMENTS

1. As noted, the assignment model is a special case of the transportation model. We stated in the notes and comments at the end of the preceding section that the optimal solution to the transportation problem will consist of integer values for the decision variables as long as the supplies and demands are integers. For the assignment problem, all supplies and demands equal 1; thus, the optimal solution must be integer valued and the integer values must be 0 or 1.
2. Combining the method for handling multiple assignments with the notion of a dummy agent provides another means of dealing with situations when the number of tasks exceeds the number of agents. That is, we add one dummy agent, but provide the dummy agent with the capability to handle multiple tasks. The number of tasks the dummy agent can handle is equal to the difference between the number of tasks and the number of agents.
3. The Management Science in Action, Heery International, describes how managers are assigned to construction projects. The application involves multiple assignments.

MANAGEMENT SCIENCE IN ACTION

HEERY INTERNATIONAL*

Heery International contracts with the State of Tennessee and others for a variety of construction projects including higher education facilities, hotels, and park facilities. At any particular time, Heery typically has more than 100 ongoing projects. Each of these projects must be assigned a single manager. With seven managers available, it means that more than 700 = 7(100) assignments are possible. Assisted by an outside consultant, Heery International has developed a mathematical model for assigning construction managers to projects.

The assignment problem developed by Heery uses 0/1 decision variables for each manager/project pair, just as in the assignment problem discussed previously. The goal in assigning managers is to balance the workload among managers and, at the same time, to minimize travel cost from the manager's home to the construction site. Thus, an objective function coefficient for each possible assignment was developed that combined project intensity (a function of the size of the project budget) with the travel distance from the manager's home to the construction site. The objective function calls for minimizing the sum over all possible assignments of the product of these coefficients with the assignment variables.

With more construction projects than managers, it was necessary to consider a variation of the standard assignment problem involving multiple assignments. Of the two sets of constraints, one set enforces the requirement that each project receive one and only one manager. The other set of constraints limits the number of assignments each manager can accept by placing an upper bound on the total intensity that is acceptable over all projects assigned.

(*continued*)

Heery International has implemented this assignment model with considerable success. According to Emory F. Redden, a Heery vice president, "The optimization model . . . has been very helpful for assigning managers to projects. . . . We have been satisfied with the assignments chosen at the Nashville office. . . . We look forward to using the model in our Atlanta office and elsewhere in the Heery organization."

*Based on Larry J. LeBlanc, Dale Randels, Jr., and T. K. Swann, "Heery International's Spreadsheet Optimization Model for Assigning Managers to Construction Projects," *Interfaces* (November/December 2000): 95–106.

7.3 TRANSSHIPMENT PROBLEM: THE NETWORK MODEL AND A LINEAR PROGRAMMING FORMULATION

The **transshipment problem** is an extension of the transportation problem in which intermediate nodes, referred to as *transshipment nodes,* are added to account for locations such as warehouses. In this more general type of distribution problem, shipments may be made between any pair of the three general types of nodes: origin nodes, transshipment nodes, and destination nodes. For example, the transshipment problem permits shipments of goods from origins to transshipment nodes and on to destinations, from one origin to another origin, from one transshipment location to another, from one destination location to another, and directly from origins to destinations.

As was true for the transportation problem, the supply available at each origin is limited and the demand at each destination is specified. The objective in the transshipment problem is to determine how many units should be shipped over each arc in the network so that all destination demands are satisfied with the minimum possible transportation cost.

Try part (a) of Problem 23 for practice in developing a network representation of a transshipment problem.

Let us consider the transshipment problem faced by Ryan Electronics. Ryan is an electronics company with production facilities in Denver and Atlanta. Components produced at either facility may be shipped to either of the firm's regional warehouses, which are located in Kansas City and Louisville. From the regional warehouses, the firm supplies retail outlets in Detroit, Miami, Dallas, and New Orleans. The transportation cost per unit for each distribution route is shown in Table 7.5 and on the arcs of the network model depicted in Figure 7.6. The key features of the problem are shown in the network model in Figure 7.6. Note that the supply at each origin and demand at each destination are shown in the left and right margins, respectively. Nodes 1 and 2 are the origin nodes; nodes 3 and 4 are the transshipment nodes; and nodes 5, 6, 7, and 8 are the destination nodes.

TABLE 7.5 TRANSPORTATION COSTS PER UNIT FOR THE RYAN ELECTRONICS TRANSSHIPMENT PROBLEM

	Warehouse	
Plant	**Kansas City**	**Louisville**
Denver	2	3
Atlanta	3	1

	Retail Outlet			
Warehouse	**Detroit**	**Miami**	**Dallas**	**New Orleans**
Kansas City	2	6	3	6
Louisville	4	4	6	5

FIGURE 7.6 NETWORK REPRESENTATION OF THE RYAN ELECTRONICS TRANSSHIPMENT PROBLEM

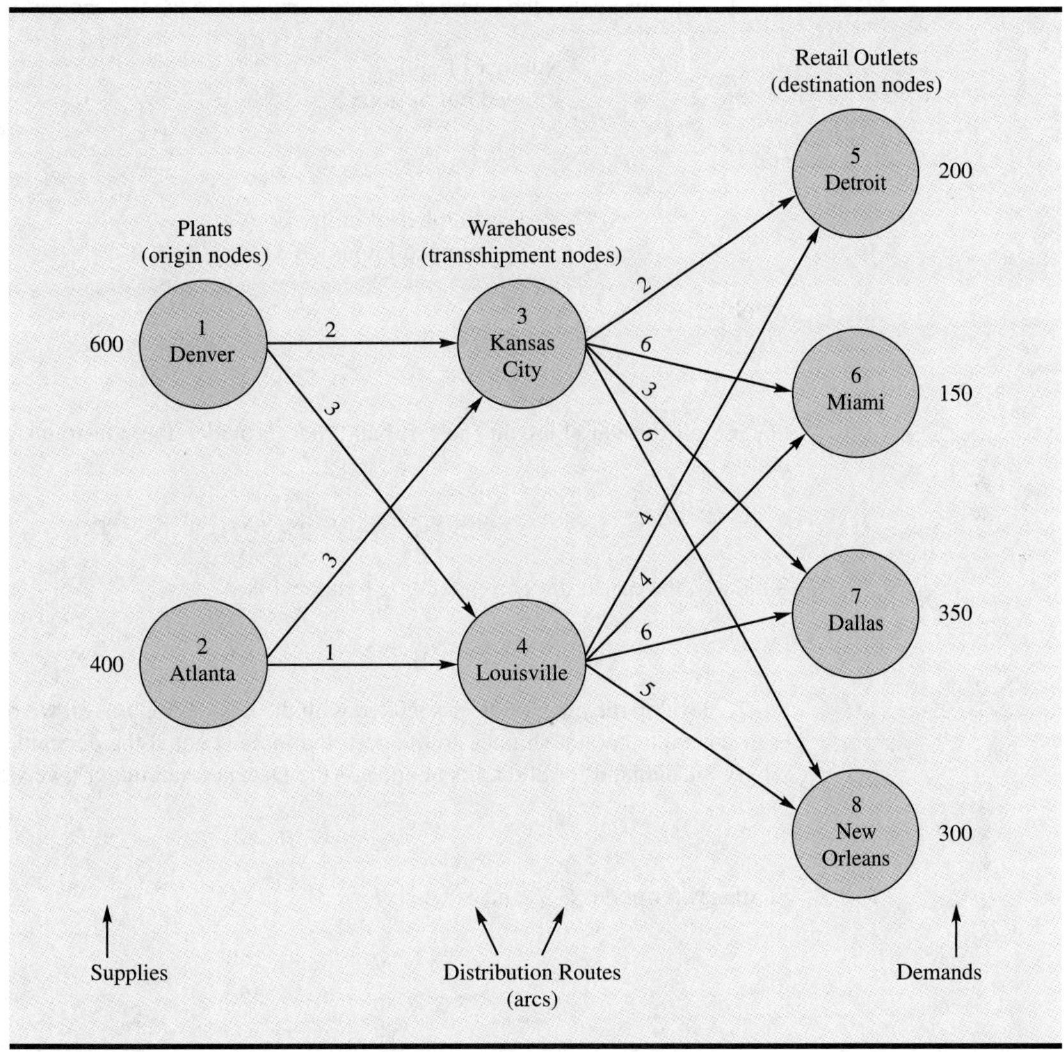

As with the transportation and assignment problems, we can formulate a linear programming model of the transshipment problem from a network representation. Again, we need a constraint for each node and a variable for each arc. Let x_{ij} denote the number of units shipped from node i to node j. For example, x_{13} denotes the number of units shipped from the Denver plant to the Kansas City warehouse, x_{14} denotes the number of units shipped from the Denver plant to the Louisville warehouse, and so on. If the supply at the Denver plant is 600 units, the amount shipped from the Denver plant must be less than or equal to 600. Mathematically, we write this supply constraint as

$$x_{13} + x_{14} \leq 600$$

Similarly, for the Atlanta plant we have

$$x_{23} + x_{24} \leq 400$$

We now consider how to write the constraints corresponding to the two transshipment nodes. For node 3 (the Kansas City warehouse), we must guarantee that the number of units shipped out must equal the number of units shipped into the warehouse. Because

$$\text{Number of units shipped out of node 3} = x_{35} + x_{36} + x_{37} + x_{38}$$

and

$$\text{Number of units shipped into node 3} = x_{13} + x_{23}$$

we obtain

$$x_{35} + x_{36} + x_{37} + x_{38} = x_{13} + x_{23}$$

Placing all the variables on the left-hand side provides the constraint corresponding to node 3 as

$$-x_{13} - x_{23} + x_{35} + x_{36} + x_{37} + x_{38} = 0$$

Similarly, the constraint corresponding to node 4 is

$$-x_{14} - x_{24} + x_{45} + x_{46} + x_{47} + x_{48} = 0$$

To develop the constraints associated with the destination nodes, we recognize that for each node the amount shipped to the destination must equal the demand. For example, to satisfy the demand for 200 units at node 5 (the Detroit retail outlet), we write

$$x_{35} + x_{45} = 200$$

Similarly, for nodes 6, 7, and 8, we have

$$x_{36} + x_{46} = 150$$
$$x_{37} + x_{47} = 350$$
$$x_{38} + x_{48} = 300$$

As usual, the objective function reflects the total shipping cost over the 12 shipping routes. Combining the objective function and constraints leads to a 12-variable, 8-constraint linear programming model of the Ryan Electronics transshipment problem (see Figure 7.7). We used the linear programming module of The Management Scientist to obtain the optimal solution. Figure 7.8 shows the computer output, and Table 7.6 summarizes the optimal solution.

Try parts (b) and (c) of Problem 23 for practice in developing the linear programming model and solving a transshipment problem.

As mentioned at the beginning of this section, in the transshipment problem arcs may connect any pair of nodes. All such shipping patterns are possible in a transshipment problem. We still require only one constraint per node, but the constraint must include a variable for every arc entering or leaving the node. For origin nodes, the sum of the shipments out minus the sum of the shipments in must be less than or equal to the origin supply. For destination nodes, the sum of the shipments in minus the sum of the shipments out must equal demand. For transshipment nodes, the sum of the shipments out must equal the sum of the shipments in, as before.

For an illustration of this more general type of transshipment problem, let us modify the Ryan Electronics problem. Suppose that it is possible to ship directly from Atlanta to

FIGURE 7.7 LINEAR PROGRAMMING FORMULATION OF THE RYAN ELECTRONICS TRANSSHIPMENT PROBLEM

$$\begin{aligned}
\text{Min } & 2x_{13} + 3x_{14} + 3x_{23} + 1x_{24} + 2x_{35} + 6x_{36} + 3x_{37} + 6x_{38} + 4x_{45} + 4x_{46} + 6x_{47} + 5x_{48} \\
\text{s.t.} & \\
& x_{13} + x_{14} \le 600 \\
& x_{23} + x_{24} \le 400 \\
& -x_{13} - x_{23} + x_{35} + x_{36} + x_{37} + x_{38} = 0 \\
& -x_{14} - x_{24} + x_{45} + x_{46} + x_{47} + x_{48} = 0 \\
& x_{35} + x_{45} = 200 \\
& x_{36} + x_{46} = 150 \\
& x_{37} + x_{47} = 350 \\
& x_{38} + x_{48} = 300 \\
& x_{ij} \ge 0 \text{ for all } i \text{ and } j
\end{aligned}$$

Origin node constraints (first two constraints); Transshipment node constraints (third and fourth); Destination node constraints (last four).

New Orleans at \$4 per unit and from Dallas to New Orleans at \$1 per unit. The network model corresponding to this modified Ryan Electronics problem is shown in Figure 7.9, the linear programming formulation is shown in Figure 7.10, and the computer solution is shown in Figure 7.11.

Try Problem 24 for practice working with transshipment problems with this more general structure.

In Figure 7.9 we added two new arcs to the network model. Thus, two new variables are necessary in the linear programming formulation. Figure 7.10 shows that the new variables x_{28} and x_{78} appear in the objective function and in the constraints corresponding to the nodes to which the new arcs are connected. Figure 7.11 shows that the value of the optimal solution has been reduced \$600 by adding the two new shipping routes; $x_{28} = 250$ units are being shipped directly from Atlanta to New Orleans, and $x_{78} = 50$ units are being shipped from Dallas to New Orleans.

FIGURE 7.8 THE MANAGEMENT SCIENTIST SOLUTION FOR THE RYAN ELECTRONICS TRANSSHIPMENT PROBLEM

EXCELfile
Ryan

Objective Function Value = 5200.000

Variable	Value	Reduced Costs
X13	550.000	0.000
X14	50.000	0.000
X23	0.000	3.000
X24	400.000	0.000
X35	200.000	0.000
X36	0.000	1.000
X37	350.000	0.000
X38	0.000	0.000
X45	0.000	3.000
X46	150.000	0.000
X47	0.000	4.000
X48	300.000	0.000

TABLE 7.6 OPTIMAL SOLUTION TO THE RYAN ELECTRONICS TRANSSHIPMENT PROBLEM

Route			Cost	
From	To	Units Shipped	per Unit	Total Cost
Denver	Kansas City	550	$2	$1100
Denver	Louisville	50	$3	150
Atlanta	Louisville	400	$1	400
Kansas City	Detroit	200	$2	400
Kansas City	Dallas	350	$3	1050
Louisville	Miami	150	$4	600
Louisville	New Orleans	300	$5	1500
				$5200

FIGURE 7.9 NETWORK REPRESENTATION OF THE MODIFIED RYAN ELECTRONICS TRANSSHIPMENT PROBLEM

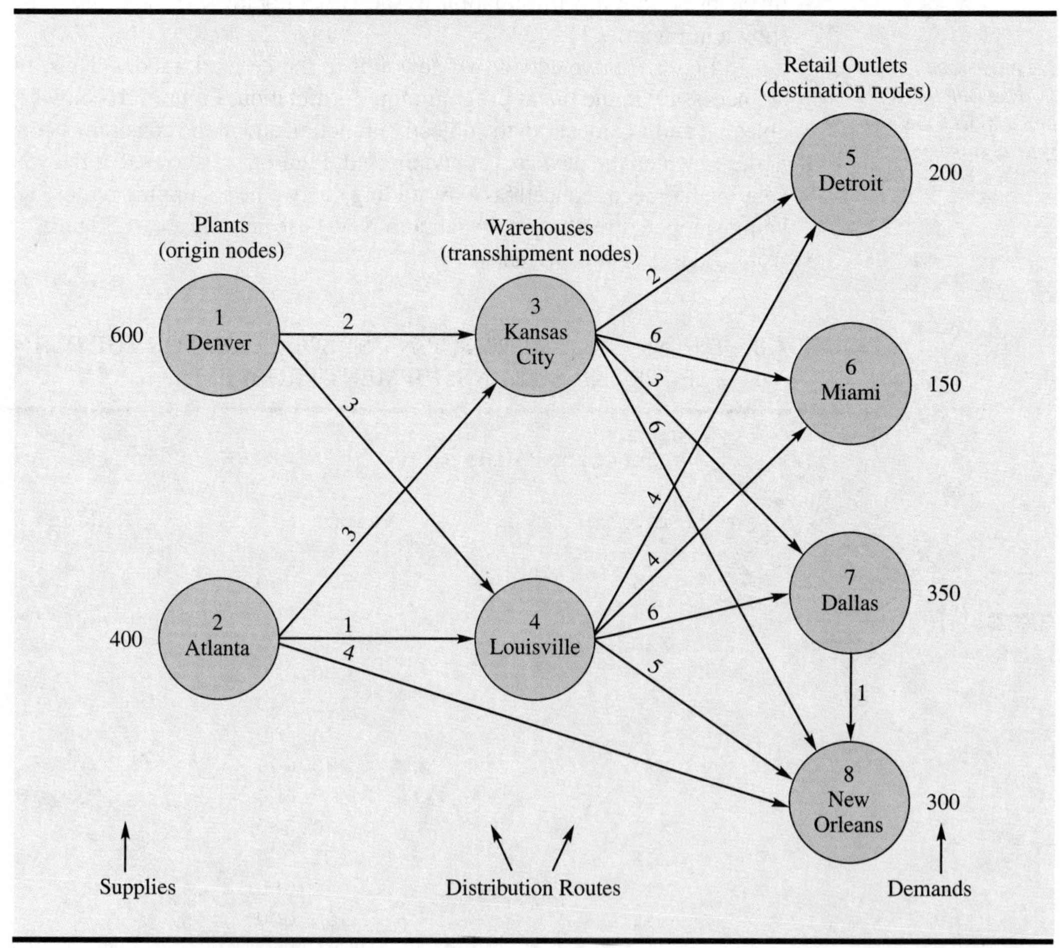

FIGURE 7.10 LINEAR PROGRAMMING FORMULATION OF THE MODIFIED RYAN ELECTRONICS TRANSSHIPMENT PROBLEM

$$
\begin{aligned}
\text{Min}\quad & 2x_{13} + 3x_{14} + 3x_{23} + 1x_{24} + 2x_{35} + 6x_{36} + 3x_{37} + 6x_{38} + 4x_{45} + 4x_{46} + 6x_{47} + 5x_{48} + 4x_{28} + 1x_{78} \\
\text{s.t.}\quad & \\
& x_{13} + x_{14} \le 600 \\
& x_{23} + x_{24} + x_{28} \le 400 \quad \text{(Origin node constraints)} \\
& -x_{13} - x_{23} + x_{35} + x_{36} + x_{37} + x_{38} = 0 \\
& -x_{14} - x_{24} + x_{45} + x_{46} + x_{47} + x_{48} = 0 \quad \text{(Transshipment node constraints)} \\
& x_{35} + x_{45} = 200 \\
& x_{36} + x_{46} = 150 \\
& x_{37} + x_{47} - x_{78} = 350 \\
& x_{38} + x_{48} + x_{28} + x_{78} = 300 \quad \text{(Destination node constraints)} \\
& x_{ij} \ge 0 \text{ for all } i \text{ and } j
\end{aligned}
$$

Problem Variations

As with transportation and assignment problems, transshipment problems may be formulated with several variations, including the following:

1. Total supply not equal to total demand
2. Maximization objective function
3. Route capacities or route minimums
4. Unacceptable routes

FIGURE 7.11 THE MANAGEMENT SCIENTIST SOLUTION FOR THE MODIFIED RYAN ELECTRONICS TRANSSHIPMENT PROBLEM

Objective Function Value = 4600.000

Variable	Value	Reduced Costs
X13	600.000	0.000
X14	0.000	0.000
X23	0.000	3.000
X24	150.000	0.000
X35	200.000	0.000
X36	0.000	1.000
X37	400.000	0.000
X38	0.000	2.000
X45	0.000	3.000
X46	150.000	0.000
X47	0.000	4.000
X48	0.000	2.000
X28	250.000	0.000
X78	50.000	0.000

The linear programming model modifications required to accommodate these variations are identical to the modifications required for the transportation problem described in Section 7.1. When we add one or more constraints of the form $x_{ij} \le L_{ij}$ to show that the route from node i to node j has capacity L_{ij}, we refer to the transshipment problem as a **capacitated transshipment problem.**

A General Linear Programming Model of the Transshipment Problem

The general linear programming model of the transshipment problem is

$$\text{Min} \quad \sum_{\text{all arcs}} c_{ij} x_{ij}$$

s.t.

$$\sum_{\text{arcs out}} x_{ij} - \sum_{\text{arcs in}} x_{ij} \le s_i \qquad \text{Origin nodes } i$$

$$\sum_{\text{arcs out}} x_{ij} - \sum_{\text{arcs in}} x_{ij} = 0 \qquad \text{Transshipment nodes}$$

$$\sum_{\text{arcs in}} x_{ij} - \sum_{\text{arcs out}} x_{ij} = d_j \qquad \text{Destination nodes } j$$

$$x_{ij} \ge 0 \text{ for all } i \text{ and } j$$

where

x_{ij} = number of units shipped from node i to node j
c_{ij} = cost per unit of shipping from node i to node j
s_i = supply at origin node i
d_j = demand at destination node j

NOTES AND COMMENTS

1. The Management Science in Action, Product Sourcing Heuristic at Procter & Gamble, describes how Procter & Gamble used a transshipment model to redesign its North American distribution system.
2. In more advanced treatments of linear programming and network flow problems, the capacitated transshipment problem is called the pure network flow problem. Efficient special-purpose solution procedures are available for network flow problems and their special cases.
3. In the general linear programming formulation of the transshipment problem, the constraints for the destination nodes are often written as

$$\sum_{\text{arcs out}} x_{ij} - \sum_{\text{arcs in}} x_{ij} = -d_j$$

The advantage of writing the constraints this way is that the left-hand side of each constraint then represents the flow out of the node minus the flow in. But such constraints would then have to be multiplied by -1 to obtain nonnegative right-hand sides before the problem could be solved by many linear programming codes.

MANAGEMENT SCIENCE IN ACTION

PRODUCT SOURCING HEURISTIC AT PROCTER & GAMBLE*

A few years ago Procter & Gamble (P&G) embarked on a major strategic planning initiative called the North American Product Sourcing Study. P&G wanted to consolidate its product sources and optimize its distribution system design throughout North America. A decision support system used to aid in this project was called the Product Sourcing Heuristic (PSH) and was based on a transshipment model much like the ones described in this chapter.

In a preprocessing phase, the many P&G products were aggregated into groups that shared the same technology and could be made at the same plant. The PSH employing the transshipment model was then used by product strategy teams responsible for developing product sourcing options for these product groups. The various plants that could produce the product group were the source nodes, the company's regional distribution centers were the transshipment nodes, and P&G's customer zones were the destinations. Direct shipments to customer zones as well as shipments through distribution centers were employed.

The product strategy teams used the heuristic interactively to explore a variety of questions concerning product sourcing and distribution. For instance, the team might be interested in the impact of closing two of five plants and consolidating production in the three remaining plants. The Product Sourcing Heuristic would then delete the source nodes corresponding to the two closed plants, make any capacity modifications necessary to the sources corresponding to the remaining three plants, and resolve the transshipment problem. The product strategy team could then examine the new solution, make some more modifications, solve again, and so on.

The Product Sourcing Heuristic was viewed as a valuable decision support system by all who used it. When P&G implemented the results of the study, it realized annual savings in the $200 million range. The PSH proved so successful in North America that P&G used it in other markets around the world.

*Based on information provided by Franz Dill and Tom Chorman of Procter & Gamble.

7.4 A PRODUCTION AND INVENTORY APPLICATION

The introduction to the transportation and transshipment problems in Sections 7.1 and 7.3 involved applications for the shipment of goods from several supply locations or origins to several demand sites or destinations. Although the shipment of goods is the subject of many transportation and transshipment problems, transportation and/or transshipment models can be developed for applications that have nothing to do with the physical shipment of goods from origins to destinations. In this section we show how to use a transshipment model to solve a production scheduling and inventory problem.

Contois Carpets is a small manufacturer of carpeting for home and office installations. Production capacity, demand, production cost per square yard, and inventory holding cost per square yard for the next four quarters are shown in Table 7.7. Note that production capacity, demand, and production costs vary by quarter, whereas the cost of carrying inventory from one quarter to the next is constant at $0.25 per square yard. Contois wants to determine how many square yards of carpeting to manufacture each quarter to minimize the total production and inventory cost for the four-quarter period.

The fact that the network shows flows into and out of demand nodes is what makes the model a transshipment model.

We begin by developing a network representation of the problem. First, we create four nodes corresponding to the production in each quarter and four nodes corresponding to the demand in each quarter. Each production node is connected by an outgoing arc to the demand node for the same period. The flow on the arc represents the number of square yards of carpet manufactured for the period. For each demand node, an outgoing arc represents the amount of inventory (square yards of carpet) carried over to the demand node for the next period. Figure 7.12 shows

TABLE 7.7 PRODUCTION, DEMAND, AND COST ESTIMATES FOR CONTOIS CARPETS

Quarter	Production Capacity (square yards)	Demand (square yards)	Production Cost ($/square yard)	Inventory Cost ($/square yard)
1	600	400	2	0.25
2	300	500	5	0.25
3	500	400	3	0.25
4	400	400	3	0.25

FIGURE 7.12 NETWORK REPRESENTATION OF THE CONTOIS CARPETS PROBLEM

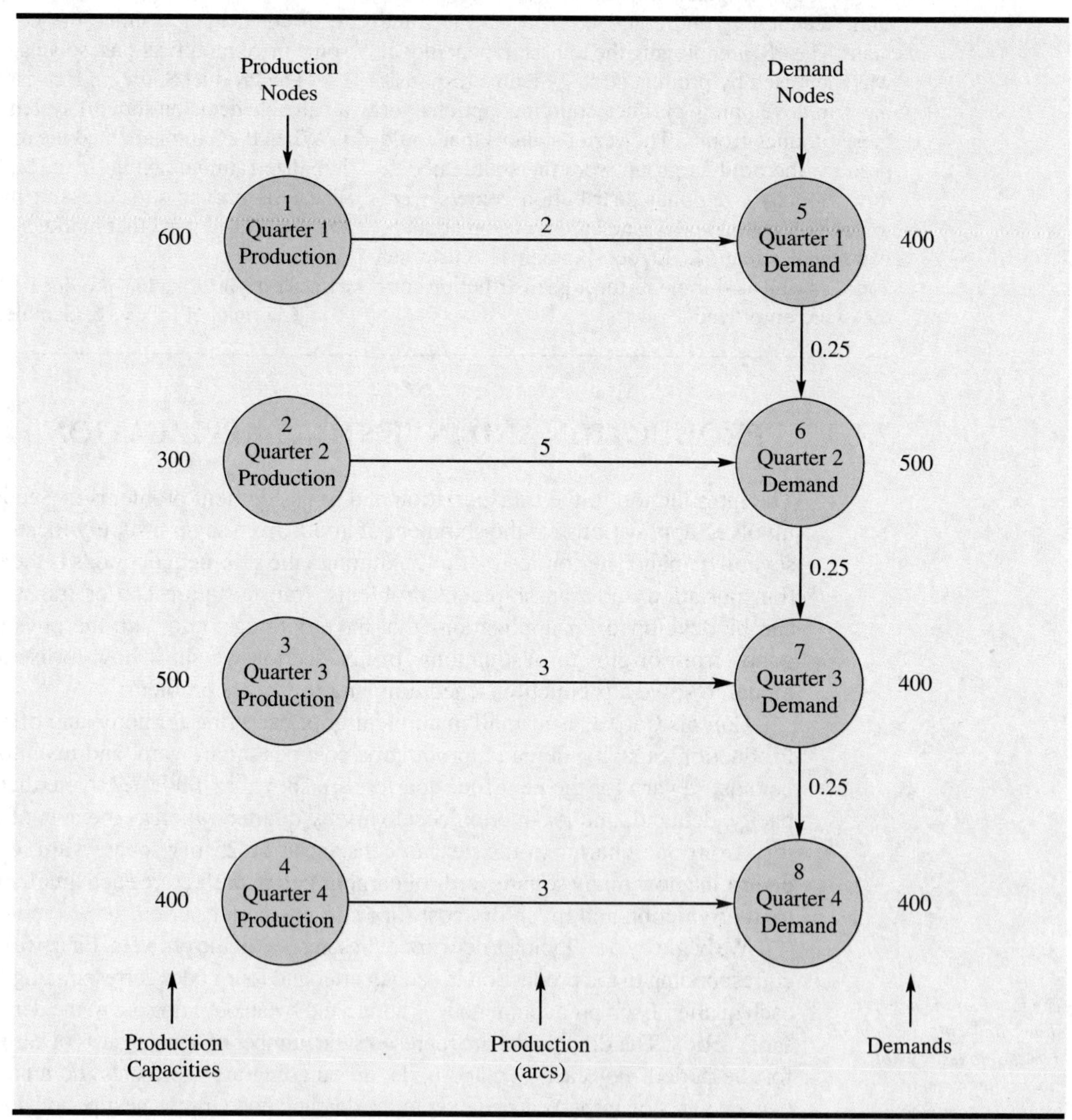

the network model. Note that nodes 1–4 represent the production for each quarter and that nodes 5–8 represent the demand for each quarter. The quarterly production capacities are shown in the left margin, and the quarterly demands are shown in the right margin.

The objective is to determine a production scheduling and inventory policy that will minimize the total production and inventory cost for the four quarters. Constraints involve production capacity and demand in each quarter. As usual, a linear programming model can be developed from the network by establishing a constraint for each node and a variable for each arc.

Let x_{15} denote the number of square yards of carpet manufactured in quarter 1. The capacity of the facility is 600 square yards in quarter 1, so the production capacity constraint is

$$x_{15} \leq 600$$

Using similar decision variables, we obtain the production capacities for quarters 2–4:

$$\begin{aligned} x_{26} &\leq 300 \\ x_{37} &\leq 500 \\ x_{48} &\leq 400 \end{aligned}$$

We now consider the development of the constraints for each of the demand nodes. For node 5, one arc enters the node, which represents the number of square yards of carpet produced in quarter 1, and one arc leaves the node, which represents the number of square yards of carpet that will not be sold in quarter 1 and will be carried over for possible sale in quarter 2. In general, for each quarter the beginning inventory plus the production minus the ending inventory must equal demand. However, for quarter 1 there is no beginning inventory; thus, the constraint for node 5 is

$$x_{15} - x_{56} = 400$$

The constraints associated with the demand nodes in quarters 2, 3, and 4 are

$$\begin{aligned} x_{56} + x_{26} - x_{67} &= 500 \\ x_{67} + x_{37} - x_{78} &= 400 \\ x_{78} + x_{48} &= 400 \end{aligned}$$

Note that the constraint for node 8 (fourth-quarter demand) involves only two variables because no provision is made for holding inventory for a fifth quarter.

The objective is to minimize total production and inventory cost, so we write the objective function as

$$\text{Min} \quad 2x_{15} + 5x_{26} + 3x_{37} + 3x_{48} + 0.25x_{56} + 0.25x_{67} + 0.25x_{78}$$

The complete linear programming formulation of the Contois Carpets problem is

$$\begin{array}{llllllllll} \text{Min} & 2x_{15} + 5x_{26} + 3x_{37} + 3x_{48} + 0.25x_{56} + 0.25x_{67} + 0.25x_{78} \\ \text{s.t.} \\ & x_{15} & & & & & & & \leq 600 \\ & & x_{26} & & & & & & \leq 300 \\ & & & x_{37} & & & & & \leq 500 \\ & & & & x_{48} & & & & \leq 400 \\ & x_{15} & & & & - x_{56} & & & = 400 \\ & & x_{26} & & & + x_{56} & - x_{67} & & = 500 \\ & & & x_{37} & & & + x_{67} & - x_{78} & = 400 \\ & & & & x_{48} & & & + x_{78} & = 400 \\ & x_{ij} \geq 0 & \text{for all } i \text{ and } j \end{array}$$

FIGURE 7.13 THE MANAGEMENT SCIENTIST SOLUTION FOR THE CONTOIS CARPETS PROBLEM

EXCELfile
Contois

```
Objective Function Value =              5150.000

      Variable              Value            Reduced Costs
    --------------     ---------------    -----------------
         X15                600.000                0.000
         X26                300.000                0.000
         X37                400.000                0.000
         X48                400.000                0.000
         X56                200.000                0.000
         X67                  0.000                2.250
         X78                  0.000                0.000
```

We used the linear programming module of The Management Scientist to solve the Contois Carpets problem. Figure 7.13 shows the results: Contois Carpets should manufacture 600 square yards of carpet in quarter 1, 300 square yards in quarter 2, 400 square yards in quarter 3, and 400 square yards in quarter 4. Note also that 200 square yards will be carried over from quarter 1 to quarter 2. The total production and inventory cost is $5150.

NOTES AND COMMENTS

1. Often the same problem can be modeled in different ways. In this section we modeled the Contois Carpets problem as a transshipment problem. It also can be modeled as a transportation problem. In Problem 39 at the end of the chapter, we ask you to develop such a model.
2. In the network model we developed for the transshipment problem, the amount leaving the starting node for an arc is always equal to the amount entering the ending node for that arc. An extension of such a network model is the case where a gain or a loss occurs as an arc is traversed. The amount entering the destination node may be greater or smaller than the amount leaving the origin node. For instance, if cash is the commodity flowing across an arc, the cash earns interest from one period to the next. Thus, the amount of cash entering the next period is greater than the amount leaving the previous period by the amount of interest earned. Networks with gains or losses are treated in more advanced texts on network flow programming.

7.5 TRANSPORTATION SIMPLEX METHOD: A SPECIAL-PURPOSE SOLUTION PROCEDURE (OPTIONAL)

Solving transportation problems with a general-purpose linear programming code is fine for small to medium-sized problems. However, these problems often grow very large (a problem with 100 origins and 1000 destinations would have 100,000 variables), and more efficient solution procedures may be needed. The network structure of the transportation problem has enabled management scientists to develop special-purpose solution procedures that greatly simplify the computations.

In Section 7.1 we introduced the Foster Generators transportation problem and showed how to formulate and solve it as a linear program. The linear programming formulation involved 12 variables and 7 constraints. In this section we describe a special-purpose solution procedure, called the **transportation simplex method,** that takes advantage of the network structure of the transportation problem and makes possible the solution of large transportation problems efficiently on a computer and small transportation problems by hand.

The transportation simplex method, like the simplex method for linear programs, is a two-phase procedure; it involves first finding an initial feasible solution and then proceeding iteratively to make improvements in the solution until an optimal solution is reached. To summarize the data conveniently and to keep track of the calculations, we utilize a **transportation tableau.** The transportation tableau for the Foster Generators problem is presented in Table 7.8.

Note that the 12 *cells* in the tableau correspond to the 12 arcs shown in Figure 7.1; that is, each cell corresponds to the route from one origin to one destination. Thus, each cell in the transportation tableau corresponds to a variable in the linear programming formulation. The entries in the right-hand margin of the tableau indicate the supply at each origin, and the entries in the bottom margin indicate the demand at each destination. Each row corresponds to a supply node, and each column corresponds to a demand node in the network model of the problem. The number of rows plus the number of columns equals the number of constraints in the linear programming formulation of the problem. The entries in the upper right-hand corner of each cell show the transportation cost per unit shipped over the corresponding route. Note also that for the Foster Generators problem total supply equals total demand. The transportation simplex method can be applied only to a balanced problem (total supply = total demand); if a problem is not balanced, a dummy origin or dummy destination must be added. The use of dummy origins and destinations will be discussed later in this section.

TABLE 7.8 TRANSPORTATION TABLEAU FOR THE FOSTER GENERATORS TRANSPORTATION PROBLEM

	Destination				
Origin	Boston	Chicago	St. Louis	Lexington	**Origin Supply**
Cleveland	3	2	7	6	5,000
Bedford	7	5	2	3	6,000
York	2	5	4	5	2,500
Destination Demand	6000	4000	2000	1500	13,500

Cell corresponding to shipments from Bedford to Boston

Total supply and total demand

Phase I: Finding an Initial Feasible Solution

The first phase of the transportation simplex method involves finding an initial feasible solution. Such a solution provides arc flows that satisfy each demand constraint without shipping more from any origin node than the supply available. The procedures most often used to find an initial feasible solution to a transportation problem are called heuristics. A **heuristic** is a commonsense procedure for quickly finding a solution to a problem.

Several heuristics have been developed to find an initial feasible solution to a transportation problem. Although some heuristics can find an initial feasible solution quickly, often the solution they find is not especially good in terms of minimizing total cost. Other heuristics may not find an initial feasible solution as quickly, but the solution they find is often good in terms of minimizing total cost. The heuristic we describe for finding an initial feasible solution to a transportation problem is called the **minimum cost method.** This heuristic strikes a compromise between finding a feasible solution quickly and finding a feasible solution that is close to the optimal solution.

We begin by allocating as much flow as possible to the minimum cost arc. In Table 7.8 we see that the Cleveland–Chicago, Bedford–St. Louis, and York–Boston routes each qualifies as the minimum cost arc because they each have a transportation cost of $2 per unit. When ties between arcs occur, we follow the convention of selecting the arc to which the most flow can be allocated. In this case it corresponds to shipping 4000 units from Cleveland to Chicago, so we write 4000 in the Cleveland–Chicago cell of the transportation tableau. This selection reduces the supply at Cleveland from 5000 to 1000; hence, we cross out the 5000-unit supply value and replace it with the reduced value of 1000. In addition, allocating 4000 units to this arc satisfies the demand at Chicago, so we reduce the Chicago demand to zero and eliminate the corresponding column from further consideration by drawing a line through it. The transportation tableau now appears as shown in Table 7.9.

TABLE 7.9 TRANSPORTATION TABLEAU AFTER ONE ITERATION OF THE MINIMUM COST METHOD

	Boston	Chicago	St. Louis	Lexington	**Supply**
Cleveland	3	2 4000	7	6	1000 ~~5000~~
Bedford	7	5	2	3	6000
York	2	5	4	5	2500
Demand	6000	~~4000~~ 0	2000	1500	

Now we look at the reduced tableau consisting of all unlined cells to identify the next minimum cost arc. The routes between the Bedford–St. Louis and York–Boston tie with transportation cost of $2 per unit. More units of flow can be allocated to the York–Boston route, so we choose it for the next allocation. This step results in an allocation of 2500 units over the York–Boston route. To update the tableau, we reduce the Boston demand by 2500 units to 3500, reduce the York supply to zero, and eliminate this row from further consideration by lining through it. Continuing the process results in an allocation of 2000 units over the Bedford–St. Louis route and the elimination of the St. Louis column because its demand goes to zero. The transportation tableau obtained after carrying out the second and third iterations is shown in Table 7.10.

We now have two arcs that qualify for the minimum cost arc with a value of 3: Cleveland–Boston and Bedford–Lexington. We can allocate a flow of 1000 units to the Cleveland–Boston route and a flow of 1500 to the Bedford–Lexington route, so we allocate 1500 units to the Bedford–Lexington route. Doing so results in a demand of zero at Lexington and eliminates this column. The next minimum cost allocation is 1000 over the Cleveland–Boston route. After we make these two allocations, the transportation tableau appears as shown in Table 7.11.

The only remaining unlined cell is Bedford–Boston. Allocating 2500 units to the corresponding arc uses up the remaining supply at Bedford and satisfies all the demand at Boston. The resulting tableau is shown in Table 7.12.

This solution is feasible because all the demand is satisfied and all the supply is used. The total transportation cost resulting from this initial feasible solution is calculated in Table 7.13. Phase I of the transportation simplex method is now complete; we have an initial feasible solution. The total transportation cost associated with this solution is $42,000.

TABLE 7.10 TRANSPORTATION TABLEAU AFTER THREE ITERATIONS OF THE MINIMUM COST METHOD

	Boston	Chicago	St. Louis	Lexington	**Supply**
Cleveland	[3]	[2] 4000	[7]	[6]	1000 ~~5000~~
Bedford	[7]	[5]	[2] 2000	[3]	4000 ~~6000~~
York	[2] ~~2500~~	[5]	[4]	[5]	0 ~~2500~~
Demand	~~6000~~ 3500	~~4000~~ 0	~~2000~~ 0	1500	

TABLE 7.11 TRANSPORTATION TABLEAU AFTER FIVE ITERATIONS OF THE MINIMUM COST METHOD

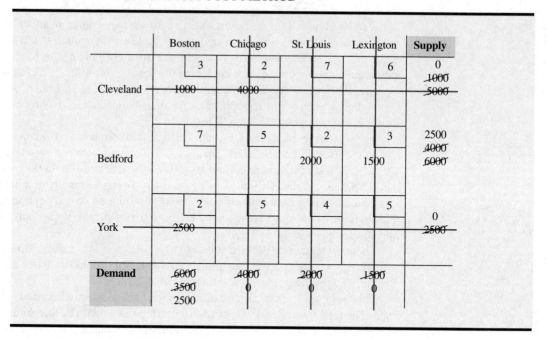

	Boston	Chicago	St. Louis	Lexington	**Supply**
Cleveland	3 1000	2 4000	7	6	0 ~~1000~~ ~~5000~~
Bedford	7	5	2 2000	3 1500	2500 ~~4000~~ ~~6000~~
York	2 2500	5	4	5	0 ~~2500~~
Demand	~~6000~~ ~~3500~~ 2500	~~4000~~ 0	~~2000~~ 0	~~1500~~ 0	

TABLE 7.12 FINAL TABLEAU SHOWING THE INITIAL FEASIBLE SOLUTION OBTAINED USING THE MINIMUM COST METHOD

	Boston	Chicago	St. Louis	Lexington	**Supply**
Cleveland	3 1000	2 4000	7	6	0 ~~1000~~ ~~5000~~
Bedford	7 2500	5	2 2000	3 1500	0 ~~2500~~ ~~4000~~ ~~6000~~
York	2 2500	5	4	5	0 ~~2500~~
Demand	~~6000~~ ~~3500~~ ~~2500~~ 0	~~4000~~ 0	~~2000~~ 0	~~1500~~ 0	

Summary of the Minimum Cost Method. Before applying phase II of the transportation simplex method, let us summarize the steps for obtaining an initial feasible solution using the minimum cost method.

Step 1. Identify the cell in the transportation tableau with the lowest cost, and allocate as much flow as possible to this cell. In case of a tie, choose the cell corresponding to the arc over which the most units can be shipped. If ties still exist, choose any of the tied cells.

Step 2. Reduce the row supply and the column demand by the amount of flow allocated to the cell identified in step 1.

To test your ability to use the minimum cost method to find an initial feasible solution, try part (a) of Problem 34.

Step 3. If *all* row supplies and column demands have been exhausted, then stop; the allocations made will provide an initial feasible solution. Otherwise, continue with step 4.

Step 4. If the row supply is now zero, eliminate the row from further consideration by drawing a line through it. If the column demand is now zero, eliminate the column by drawing a line through it.

Step 5. Continue with step 1 for all unlined rows and columns.

Phase II: Iterating to the Optimal Solution

Phase II of the transportation simplex method is a procedure for iterating from the initial feasible solution identified in phase I to the optimal solution. Recall that each cell in the transportation tableau corresponds to an arc (route) in the network model of the transportation problem. The first step at each iteration of phase II is to identify an incoming arc. The **incoming arc** is the currently unused route (unoccupied cell) where making a flow allocation will cause the largest per-unit reduction in total cost. Flow is then assigned to the incoming arc, and the amounts being shipped over all other arcs to which flow had previously been assigned (occupied cells) are adjusted as necessary to maintain a feasible solution. In the process of adjusting the flow assigned to the occupied cells, we identify and drop an **outgoing arc** from the solution. Thus, at each iteration in phase II, we bring a currently unused arc (unoccupied cell) into the solution, and remove an arc to which flow had previously been assigned (occupied cell) from the solution.

To show how phase II of the transportation simplex method works, we must explain how to identify the incoming arc (cell), how to make the adjustments to the other occupied cells when flow is allocated to the incoming arc, and how to identify the outgoing arc (cell). We first consider identifying the incoming arc.

TABLE 7.13 TOTAL COST OF THE INITIAL FEASIBLE SOLUTION OBTAINED USING THE MINIMUM COST METHOD

Route		Units	Cost	
From	**To**	**Shipped**	**per Unit**	**Total Cost**
Cleveland	Boston	1000	$3	$ 3,000
Cleveland	Chicago	4000	$2	8,000
Bedford	Boston	2500	$7	17,500
Bedford	St. Louis	2000	$2	4,000
Bedford	Lexington	1500	$3	4,500
York	Boston	2500	$2	5,000
				$42,000

As mentioned, the incoming arc is the one that will cause the largest reduction per unit in the total cost of the current solution. To identify this arc, we must compute for each unused arc the amount by which total cost will be reduced by shipping one unit over that arc. The *mo*dified *di*stribution or **MODI method** is a way to make this computation.

The MODI method requires that we define an index u_i for each row of the tableau and an index v_j for each column of the tableau. Computing these row and column indexes requires that the cost coefficient for each occupied cell equal $u_i + v_j$. Thus, since c_{ij} is the cost per unit from origin i to destination j, $u_i + v_j = c_{ij}$ for each occupied cell. Let us return to the initial feasible solution for the Foster Generators problem, which we found using the minimum cost method (see Table 7.14), and use the MODI method to identify the incoming arc.

Requiring that $u_i + v_j = c_{ij}$ for all the occupied cells in the initial feasible solution leads to a system of six equations and seven indexes, or variables:

Occupied Cell	$u_i + v_j = c_{ij}$
Cleveland–Boston	$u_1 + v_1 = 3$
Cleveland–Chicago	$u_1 + v_2 = 2$
Bedford–Boston	$u_2 + v_1 = 7$
Bedford–St. Louis	$u_2 + v_3 = 2$
Bedford–Lexington	$u_2 + v_4 = 3$
York–Boston	$u_3 + v_1 = 2$

With one more index (variable) than equation in this system, we can freely pick a value for one of the indexes and then solve for the others. We will always choose $u_1 = 0$ and then solve for the values of the other indexes. Setting $u_1 = 0$, we obtain

$$\begin{aligned} 0 + v_1 &= 3 \\ 0 + v_2 &= 2 \\ u_2 + v_1 &= 7 \\ u_2 + v_3 &= 2 \\ u_2 + v_4 &= 3 \\ u_3 + v_1 &= 2 \end{aligned}$$

Solving these equations leads to the following values for u_1, u_2, u_3, v_1, v_2, v_3, and v_4:

$$\begin{aligned} u_1 &= 0 \qquad & v_1 &= 3 \\ u_2 &= 4 \qquad & v_2 &= 2 \\ u_3 &= -1 \qquad & v_3 &= -2 \\ & & v_4 &= -1 \end{aligned}$$

Management scientists have shown that for each *unoccupied* cell, $e_{ij} = c_{ij} - u_i - v_j$ provides the change in total cost per unit that will be obtained by allocating one unit of flow to the corresponding arc. Thus, we will call e_{ij} the **net evaluation index.** Because of the way u_i and v_j are computed, the net evaluation index for each occupied cell equals zero.

Rewriting the tableau containing the initial feasible solution for the Foster Generators problem and replacing the previous marginal information with the values of u_i and v_j, we obtain Table 7.15. We computed the net evaluation index (e_{ij}) for each unoccupied cell, which is the circled number in the cell. Thus, shipping one unit over the route from origin 1 to destination 3 (Cleveland–St. Louis) will increase total cost by \$9; shipping one unit from

TABLE 7.14 INITIAL FEASIBLE SOLUTION TO THE FOSTER GENERATORS PROBLEM

	Boston	Chicago	St. Louis	Lexington	**Supply**
Cleveland	cost 3: 1000	cost 2: 4000	cost 7	cost 6	5000
Bedford	cost 7: 2500	cost 5	cost 2: 2000	cost 3: 1500	6000
York	cost 2: 2500	cost 5	cost 4	cost 5	2500
Demand	6000	4000	2000	1500	

origin 1 to destination 4 (Cleveland–Lexington) will increase total cost by $7; shipping one unit from origin 2 to destination 2 (Bedford–Chicago) will decrease total cost by $1; and so on.

On the basis of the net evaluation indexes, the best arc in terms of cost reduction (a net evaluation index of −1) is associated with the Bedford–Chicago route (origin 2–destination 2); thus, the cell in row 2 and column 2 is chosen as the incoming cell. Total cost decreases by $1 for every unit of flow assigned to this arc. The question now is: How

TABLE 7.15 NET EVALUATION INDEXES FOR THE INITIAL FEASIBLE SOLUTION TO THE FOSTER GENERATORS PROBLEM COMPUTED USING THE MODI METHOD

u_i \ v_j	3	2	−2	−1
0	cost 3: 1000	cost 2: 4000	cost 7: (9)	cost 6: (7)
4	cost 7: 2500	cost 5: (−1)	cost 2: 2000	cost 3: 1500
−1	cost 2: 2500	cost 5: (4)	cost 4: (7)	cost 5: (7)

much flow should we assign to this arc? Because the total cost decreases by \$1 per unit assigned, we want to allocate the maximum possible flow. To find that maximum, we must recognize that, to maintain feasibility, each unit of flow assigned to this arc will require adjustments in the flow over the other currently used arcs. The **stepping-stone method** can be used to determine the adjustments necessary and to identify an outgoing arc.

The Stepping-Stone Method. Suppose that we allocate one unit of flow to the incoming arc (the Bedford–Chicago route). To maintain feasibility—that is, not exceed the number of units to be shipped to Chicago—we would have to reduce the flow assigned to the Cleveland–Chicago arc to 3999. But then we would have to increase the flow on the Cleveland–Boston arc to 1001 so that the total Cleveland supply of 5000 units could be shipped. Finally, we would have to reduce the flow on the Bedford–Boston arc by 1 to satisfy the Boston demand exactly. Table 7.16 summarizes this cycle of adjustments.

The cycle of adjustments needed in making an allocation to the Bedford–Chicago cell required changes in four cells: the incoming cell (Bedford–Chicago) and three currently occupied cells. We can view these four cells as forming a stepping-stone path in the tableau, where the corners of the path are currently occupied cells. The idea behind the stepping-stone name is to view the tableau as a pond with the occupied cells as stones sticking up in it. To identify the stepping-stone path for an incoming cell, we start at the incoming cell and move horizontally and vertically using occupied cells as the stones at the corners of the path; the objective is to step from stone to stone and return to the incoming cell where we started. To focus attention on which occupied cells are part of the stepping-stone path, we draw each occupied cell in the stepping-stone path as a cylinder, which should reinforce the image of these cells as stones sticking up in the pond. Table 7.17 depicts the stepping-stone path associated with the incoming arc of the Bedford–Chicago route.

In Table 7.17 we placed a plus sign (+) or a minus sign (−) in each occupied cell on the stepping-stone path. A plus sign indicates that the allocation to that cell will increase by the same amount we allocate to the incoming cell. A minus sign indicates that the alloca-

TABLE 7.16 CYCLE OF ADJUSTMENTS IN OCCUPIED CELLS NECESSARY TO MAINTAIN FEASIBILITY WHEN SHIPPING ONE UNIT FROM BEDFORD TO CHICAGO

	Boston	Chicago	St. Louis	Lexington	**Supply**
Cleveland	3 1001 ~~1000~~	2 3999 ~~4000~~	7	6	5000
Bedford	7 2499 ~~2500~~	5 1	2 2000	3 1500	6000
York	2 2500	5	4	5	2500
Demand	6000	4000	2000	1500	

TABLE 7.17 STEPPING-STONE PATH WITH THE BEDFORD–CHICAGO ROUTE AS THE INCOMING ARC

	Boston	Chicago	St. Louis	Lexington	**Supply**
Cleveland	+ 3 1000	− 2 4000	7	6	5000
Bedford	− 7 2500	5	2 2000	3 1500	6000
York	2 2500	5	4	5	2500
Demand	6000	4000	2000	1500	

An occupied cell not on the stepping-stone path

An unoccupied cell

An occupied cell on the stepping-stone path

tion to that cell will decrease by the amount allocated to the incoming cell. Thus, to determine the maximum amount that may be allocated to the incoming cell, we simply look to the cells on the stepping-stone path identified with a minus sign. Because no arc can have a negative flow, the minus-sign cell with the *smallest amount* allocated to it will determine the maximum amount that can be allocated to the incoming cell. After allocating this maximum amount to the incoming cell, we then make all the adjustments necessary on the stepping-stone path to maintain feasibility. The incoming cell becomes an occupied cell, and the outgoing cell is dropped from the current solution.

In the Foster Generators problem, the Bedford–Boston and Cleveland–Chicago cells are the ones where the allocation will decrease (the ones with a minus sign) as flow is allocated to the incoming arc (Bedford–Chicago). The 2500 units currently assigned to Bedford–Boston is less than the 4000 units assigned to Cleveland–Chicago, so we identify Bedford–Boston as the outgoing arc. We then obtain the new solution by allocating 2500 units to the Bedford–Chicago arc, making the appropriate adjustments on the stepping-stone path and dropping Bedford–Boston from the solution (its allocation has been driven to zero). Table 7.18 shows the tableau associated with the new solution. Note that the only changes from the previous tableau are located on the stepping-stone path originating in the Bedford–Chicago cell.

We now try to improve on the current solution. Again, the first step is to apply the MODI method to find the best incoming arc, so we recompute the row and column indexes by requiring that $u_i + v_j = c_{ij}$ for all occupied cells. The values of u_i and v_j can easily be computed directly on the tableau. Recall that we begin the MODI method by setting $u_1 = 0$. Thus, for the two occupied cells in row 1 of the table, $v_j = c_{1j}$; as a result, $v_1 = 3$ and $v_2 = 2$.

TABLE 7.18 NEW SOLUTION AFTER ONE ITERATION IN PHASE II OF THE TRANSPORTATION SIMPLEX METHOD

	Boston	Chicago	St. Louis	Lexington	Supply
Cleveland	[3] 3500	[2] 1500	[7]	[6]	5000
Bedford	[7]	[5] 2500	[2] 2000	[3] 1500	6000
York	[2] 2500	[5]	[4]	[5]	2500
Demand	6000	4000	2000	1500	

Moving down the column associated with each newly computed column index, we compute the row index associated with each occupied cell in that column by subtracting v_j from c_{ij}. Doing so for the newly found column indexes, v_1 and v_2, we find that $u_3 = 2 - 3 = -1$ and that $u_2 = 5 - 2 = 3$. Next, we use these row indexes to compute the column indexes for occupied cells in the associated rows, obtaining $v_3 = 2 - 3 = -1$ and $v_4 = 3 - 3 = 0$. Table 7.19 shows these new row and column indexes.

TABLE 7.19 MODI EVALUATION OF EACH CELL IN SOLUTION

u_i \ v_j	3	2	−1	0
0	[3] 3500	[2] 1500	[7] (8)	[6] (6)
3	[7] (1)	[5] 2500	[2] 2000	[3] 1500
−1	[2] 2500	[5] (4)	[4] (6)	[5] (6)

Also shown in Table 7.19 are the net changes (the circled numbers) in the value of the solution that will result from allocating one unit to each unoccupied cell. Recall that these are the net evaluation indexes given by $e_{ij} = c_{ij} - u_i - v_j$. Note that the net evaluation index for every unoccupied cell is now greater than or equal to zero. This condition shows that if current unoccupied cells are used, the cost will actually increase. Without an arc to which flow can be assigned to decrease the total cost, we have reached the optimal solution. Table 7.20 summarizes the optimal solution and shows its total cost. As expected, this solution is exactly the same as the one obtained using the linear programming solution approach (Figure 7.2).

Maintaining $m + n - 1$ Occupied Cells. Recall that m represents the number of origins and n represents the number of destinations. A solution to a transportation problem that has less than $m + n - 1$ cells with positive allocations is said to be **degenerate.** The solution to the Foster Generators problem is not degenerate; six cells are occupied and $m + n - 1 = 3 + 4 - 1 = 6$. The problem with degeneracy is that $m + n - 1$ occupied cells are required by the MODI method to compute all the row and column indexes. When degeneracy occurs, we must artificially create an occupied cell in order to compute the row and column indexes. Let us illustrate how degeneracy could occur and how to deal with it.

Table 7.21 shows the initial feasible solution obtained using the minimum cost method for a transportation problem involving $m = 3$ origins and $n = 3$ destinations. To use the MODI method for this problem, we must have $m + n - 1 = 3 + 3 - 1 = 5$ occupied cells. Since the initial feasible solution has only four occupied cells, the solution is degenerate.

Suppose that we try to use the MODI method to compute row and column indexes to begin phase II for this problem. Setting $u_1 = 0$ and computing the column indexes for each occupied cell in row 1, we obtain $v_1 = 3$ and $v_2 = 6$ (see Table 7.21). Continuing, we then compute the row indexes for all occupied cells in columns 1 and 2. Doing so yields $u_2 = 5 - 6 = -1$. At this point, we cannot compute any more row and column indexes because no cells in columns 1 and 2 of row 3 and no cells in rows 1 or 2 of column 3 are occupied.

To compute all the row and column indexes when fewer than $m + n - 1$ cells are occupied, we must create one or more "artificially" occupied cells with a flow of zero. In Table 7.21 we must create one artificially occupied cell to have five occupied cells. Any currently unoccupied cell can be made an artificially occupied cell if doing so makes it possible to compute the remaining row and column indexes. For instance, treating the cell in row 2 and column 3 of Table 7.21 as an artificially occupied cell will enable us to compute v_3 and u_3, but placing it in row 2 and column 1 will not.

TABLE 7.20 OPTIMAL SOLUTION TO THE FOSTER GENERATORS TRANSPORTATION PROBLEM

Route		Units	Cost	
From	**To**	**Shipped**	**per Unit**	**Total Cost**
Cleveland	Boston	3500	\$3	\$10,500
Cleveland	Chicago	1500	\$2	3,000
Bedford	Chicago	2500	\$5	12,500
Bedford	St. Louis	2000	\$2	4,000
Bedford	Lexington	1500	\$3	4,500
York	Boston	2500	\$2	5,000
				\$39,500

TABLE 7.21 TRANSPORTATION TABLEAU WITH A DEGENERATE INITIAL FEASIBLE SOLUTION

u_i \ v_j	3	6		Supply
0	[3] 35	[6] 25	[7]	60
–1	[8]	[5] 30	[7]	30
	[4]	[9]	[11] 30	30
Demand	35	55	30	

As we previously stated, whenever an artificially occupied cell is created, we assign a flow of zero to the corresponding arc. Table 7.22 shows the results of creating an artificially occupied cell in row 2 and column 3 of Table 7.21. Creation of the artificially occupied cell results in five occupied cells, so we can now compute the remaining row and column indexes. Using the row 2 index ($u_2 = -1$) and the artificially occupied cell in row 2, we compute the column index for column 3; thus, $v_3 = c_{23} - u_2 = 7 - (-1) = 8$. Then, using the column 3 index ($v_3 = 8$) and the occupied cell in row 3 and column 3 of the tableau, we compute the row 3 index: $u_3 = c_{33} - v_3 = 11 - 8 = 3$. Table 7.22 shows the complete set of row and column indexes and the net evaluation index for each unoccupied cell.

Reviewing the net evaluation indexes in Table 7.22, we identify the cell in row 3 and column 1 (net evaluation index $= -2$) as the incoming cell. The stepping-stone path and the adjustments necessary to maintain feasibility are shown in Table 7.23. Note that the stepping-stone path can be more complex than the simple one obtained for the incoming cell in the Foster Generators problem. The path in Table 7.23 requires adjustments in all five occupied cells to maintain feasibility. Again, the plus- and minus-sign labels simply show where increases and decreases in the allocation will occur as units of flow are added to the incoming cell. The smallest flow in a decreasing cell is a tie between the cell in row 2 and column 2 and the cell in row 3 and column 3.

Because the smallest amount in a decreasing cell is 30, the allocation we make to the incoming cell is 30 units. However, when 30 units are allocated to the incoming cell and the appropriate adjustments are made to the occupied cells on the stepping-stone path, the allocation to two cells goes to zero (row 2, column 2 and row 3, column 3). We may choose either one as the outgoing cell, but not both. One will be treated as unoccupied; the other will become an artificially occupied cell with a flow of zero allocated to it. The reason we cannot let both become unoccupied cells is that doing so would lead to a degenerate solution, and as before, we could not use the MODI method to compute the row and column

TABLE 7.22 TRANSPORTATION TABLEAU WITH AN ARTIFICIAL CELL IN ROW 2 AND COLUMN 3

u_i \ v_j	3	6	8	Supply
0	[3] 35	[6] 25	[7] (−1)	60
−1	[8] (6)	[5] 30	[7] 0	30
3	[4] (−2)	[9] (0)	[11] 30	30
Demand	35	55	30	

Artificially occupied cell (the cell in row −1, column 3 with value 0)

TABLE 7.23 STEPPING-STONE PATH FOR THE INCOMING CELL IN ROW 3 AND COLUMN 1

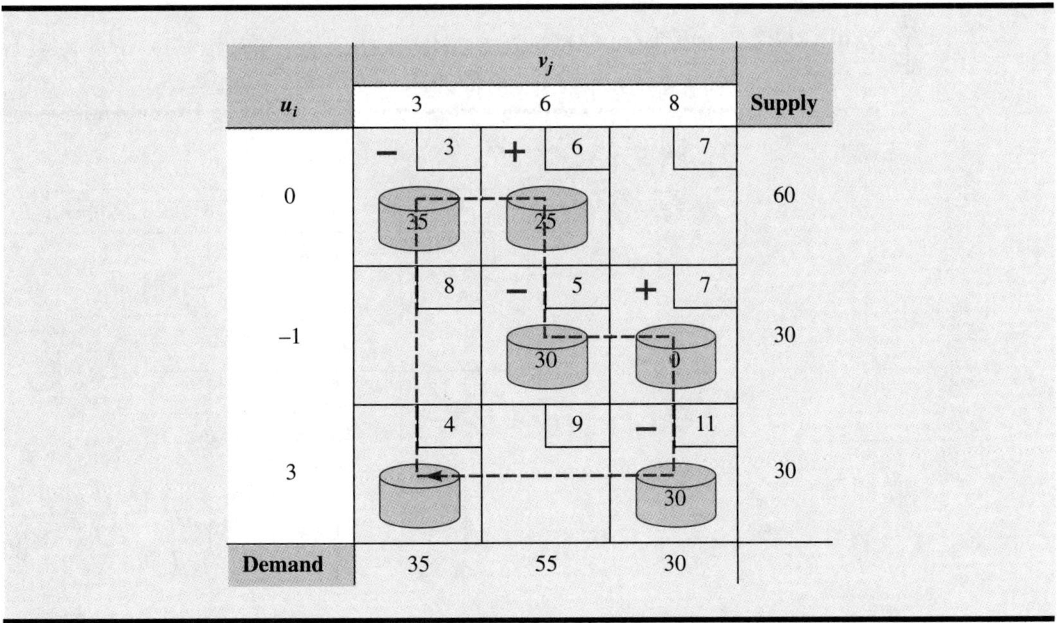

u_i \ v_j	3	6	8	Supply
0	− [3] 35	+ [6] 25	[7]	60
−1	[8]	− [5] 30	+ [7] 0	30
3	[4]	[9]	− [11] 30	30
Demand	35	55	30	

indexes for the next iteration. When ties occur in choosing the outgoing cell, we can choose any one of the tied cells as the artificially occupied cell and then use the MODI method to recompute the row and column indexes. As long as no more than one cell is dropped at each iteration, the MODI method will work.

The solution obtained after allocating 30 units to the incoming cell in row 3 and column 1 and making the appropriate adjustments on the stepping-stone path leads to the tableau shown in Table 7.24. Note that we treated the cell in row 2 and column 2 as the artificially occupied cell. After computing the new row and column indexes, we see that the cell in row 1 and column 3 will be the next incoming cell. Each unit allocated to this cell will further decrease the value of the solution by 1. The stepping-stone path associated with this incoming cell is shown in Table 7.25. The cell in row 2 and column 3 is the outgoing cell; the tableau after this iteration is shown in Table 7.26. Note that we have found the optimal solution and that, even though several earlier iterations were degenerate, the final solution is not degenerate.

Summary of the Transportation Simplex Method

The transportation simplex method is a special-purpose solution procedure applicable to any network model having the special structure of the transportation problem. It is actually a clever implementation of the general simplex method for linear programming that takes advantage of the special mathematical structure of the transportation problem; but because of the special structure, the transportation simplex method is hundreds of times faster than the general simplex method.

Try part (b) of Problem 34 for practice using the transportation simplex method.

To apply the transportation simplex method, you must have a transportation problem with total supply equal to total demand; thus, for some problems you may need to add a dummy origin or dummy destination to put the problem in this form. The transportation simplex method takes the problem in this form and applies a two-phase solution procedure. In

TABLE 7.24 NEW ROW AND COLUMN INDEXES OBTAINED AFTER ALLOCATING 30 UNITS TO THE INCOMING CELL

	v_j			
u_i	3	6	8	**Supply**
0	[3] 5	[6] 55	[7] (−1)	60
−1	[8] (6)	[5] 0	[7] 30	30
1	[4] 30	[9] (2)	[11] (2)	30
Demand	35	55	30	

TABLE 7.25 STEPPING-STONE PATH ASSOCIATED WITH THE INCOMING CELL IN ROW 1 AND COLUMN 3

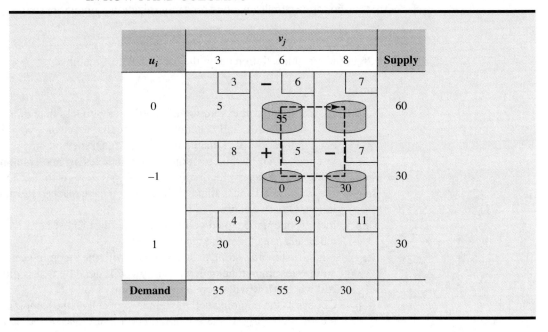

u_i \ v_j	3	6	8	Supply
0	[3] 5	[6] − 55	[7]	60
−1	[8]	[5] + 0	[7] − 30	30
1	[4] 30	[9]	[11]	30
Demand	35	55	30	

TABLE 7.26 OPTIMAL SOLUTION TO A PROBLEM WITH A DEGENERATE INITIAL FEASIBLE SOLUTION

u_i \ v_j	3	6	7	Supply
0	[3] 5	[6] 25	[7] 30	60
−1	[8] (6)	[5] 30	[7] (1)	30
1	[4] 30	[9] (2)	[11] (3)	30
Demand	35	55	30	

phase I, apply the minimum cost method to find an initial feasible solution. In phase II, begin with the initial feasible solution and iterate until you reach an optimal solution. The steps of the transportation simplex method for a minimization problem are summarized as follows.

Phase I

Find an initial feasible solution using the minimum cost method.

Phase II

Step 1. If the initial feasible solution is degenerate with less than $m + n - 1$ occupied cells, add an artificially occupied cell or cells so that $m + n - 1$ occupied cells exist in locations that enable use of the MODI method.

Step 2. Use the MODI method to compute row indexes, u_i, and column indexes, v_j.

Step 3. Compute the net evaluation index $e_{ij} = c_{ij} - u_i - v_j$ for each unoccupied cell.

Step 4. If $e_{ij} \geq 0$ for all unoccupied cells, stop; you have reached the minimum cost solution. Otherwise, proceed to step 5.

Step 5. Identify the unoccupied cell with the smallest (most negative) net evaluation index and select it as the incoming cell.

Step 6. Find the stepping-stone path associated with the incoming cell. Label each cell on the stepping-stone path whose flow will increase with a plus sign and each cell whose flow will decrease with a minus sign.

Step 7. Choose as the outgoing cell the minus-sign cell on the stepping-stone path with the smallest flow. If there is a tie, choose any one of the tied cells. The tied cells that are not chosen will be artificially occupied with a flow of zero at the next iteration.

Step 8. Allocate to the incoming cell the amount of flow currently given to the outgoing cell; make the appropriate adjustments to all cells on the stepping-stone path, and continue with step 2.

Problem Variations

The following problem variations can be handled, with slight adaptations, by the transportation simplex method:

1. Total supply not equal to total demand
2. Maximization objective function
3. Unacceptable routes

The case where the total supply is not equal to the total demand can be handled easily by the transportation simplex method if we first introduce a dummy origin or a dummy destination. If total supply is greater than total demand, we introduce a **dummy destination** with demand equal to the excess of supply over demand. Similarly, if total demand is greater than total supply, we introduce a **dummy origin** with supply equal to the excess of demand over supply. In either case, the use of a dummy destination or a dummy origin will equalize total supply and total demand so that we can use the transportation simplex method. When a dummy destination or origin is present, we assign cost coefficients of zero to every arc into a dummy destination and to every arc out of a dummy origin. The reason is that no shipments will actually be made from a dummy origin or to a dummy destination when the solution is implemented and thus a zero cost per unit is appropriate.

The transportation simplex method also can be used to solve maximization problems. The only modification necessary involves the selection of an incoming cell. Instead of picking the cell with the smallest or most negative e_{ij} value, we pick that cell for which e_{ij} is largest. That is, we pick the cell that will cause the largest increase per unit in the objective function. If $e_{ij} \leq 0$ for all unoccupied cells, we stop; the maximization solution has been reached.

To handle unacceptable routes in a minimization problem, infeasible arcs must carry an extremely high cost, denoted M, to keep them out of the solution. Thus, if we have a route (arc) from an origin to a destination that for some reason cannot be used, we simply assign this arc a cost per unit of M, and it will not enter the solution. Unacceptable arcs would be assigned a profit per unit of $-M$ in a maximization problem.

NOTES AND COMMENTS

1. Research devoted to developing efficient special-purpose solution procedures for network problems has shown that the transportation simplex method is one of the best. It is used in the transportation and assignment modules of The Management Scientist software package. A simple extension of this method also can be used to solve transshipment problems.
2. As we previously noted, each cell in the transportation tableau corresponds to an arc (route) in the network model of the problem and a variable in the linear programming formulation. Phase II of the transportation simplex method is thus the same as phase II of the simplex method for linear programming. At each iteration, one variable is brought into solution and another variable is dropped from solution. The reason the method works so much better for transportation problems is that the special mathematical structure of the constraint equations means that only addition and subtraction operations are necessary. We can implement the entire procedure in a transportation tableau that has one row for each origin and one column for each destination. A simplex tableau for such a problem would require a row for each origin, a row for each destination, and a column for each arc; thus, the simplex tableau would be much larger.

7.6 ASSIGNMENT PROBLEM: A SPECIAL-PURPOSE SOLUTION PROCEDURE (OPTIONAL)

As mentioned previously, the assignment problem is a special case of the transportation problem. Thus, the transportation simplex method can be used to solve the assignment problem. However, the assignment problem has an even more special structure: All supplies and demands equal 1. Because of this additional special structure, special-purpose solution procedures have been specifically designed to solve the assignment problem; one such procedure is called the **Hungarian method.** In this section we will show how the Hungarian method can be used to solve the Fowle Marketing Research problem.

Recall that the Fowle problem (see Section 7.2) involved assigning project leaders to clients; three project leaders were available and three research projects were to be completed for three clients. Fowle's assignment alternatives and estimated project completion times in days are restated in Table 7.27.

The Hungarian method involves what is called *matrix reduction.* Subtracting and adding appropriate values in the matrix yields an optimal solution to the assignment problem. Three major steps are associated with the procedure. Step 1 involves row and column reduction.

Step 1. Reduce the initial matrix by subtracting the smallest element in each row from every element in that row. Then, using the row-reduced matrix, subtract the smallest element in each column from every element in that column.

TABLE 7.27 ESTIMATED PROJECT COMPLETION TIMES (DAYS) FOR THE FOWLE ASSIGNMENT PROBLEM

	Client		
Project Leader	**1**	**2**	**3**
Terry	10	15	9
Carle	9	18	5
McClymonds	6	14	3

Thus, we first reduce the matrix in Table 7.27 by subtracting the minimum value in each row from each element in the row. With the minimum values of 9 for row 1, 5 for row 2, and 3 for row 3, the row-reduced matrix becomes

	1	**2**	**3**
Terry	1	6	0
Carle	4	13	0
McClymonds	3	11	0

The assignment problem represented by this reduced matrix is equivalent to the original assignment problem in the sense that the same solution will be optimal. To understand why, first note that the row 1 minimum element, 9, has been subtracted from every element in the first row. Terry must still be assigned to one of the clients, so the only change is that in this revised problem the time for any assignment will be 9 days less. Similarly, Carle and McClymonds are shown with completion times requiring 5 and 3 fewer days, respectively.

Continuing with step 1 in the matrix reduction process, we now subtract the minimum element in each column of the row-reduced matrix from every element in the column. This operation also leads to an equivalent assignment problem; that is, the same solution will still be optimal, but the times required to complete each project are reduced. With the minimum values of 1 for column 1, 6 for column 2, and 0 for column 3, the reduced matrix becomes

	1	**2**	**3**
Terry	0	0	0
Carle	3	7	0
McClymonds	2	5	0

The goal of the Hungarian method is to continue reducing the matrix until the value of one of the solutions is zero—that is, until an assignment of project leaders to clients can be made that, in terms of the reduced matrix, requires a total time expenditure of zero days. Then, as long as there are no negative elements in the matrix, the zero-valued solution will be optimal. The way in which we perform this further reduction and recognize when we have reached an optimal solution is described in the following two steps.

Step 2. Find the minimum number of straight lines that must be drawn through the rows and the columns of the current matrix so that all the zeros in the matrix will be covered. If the minimum number of straight lines is the same as the number of rows (or equivalently, columns), an optimal assignment with a value of zero can be made. If the minimum number of lines is less than the number of rows, go to step 3.

Applying step 2, we see that the minimum number of lines required to cover all the zeros is 2. Thus, we must continue to step 3.

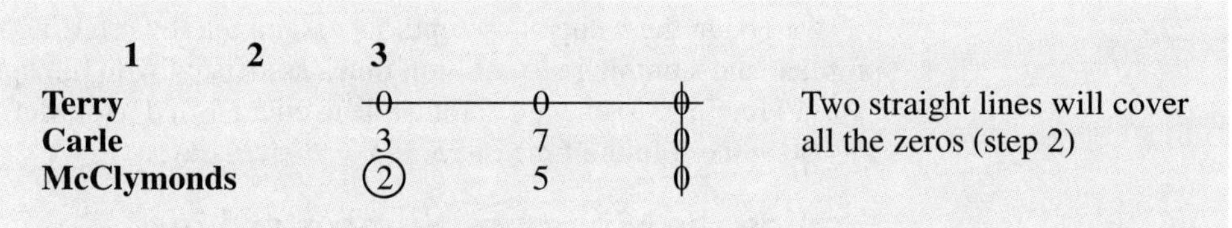

	1	**2**	**3**
Terry	0	0	0
Carle	3	7	0
McClymonds	2	5	0

Two straight lines will cover all the zeros (step 2)

Step 3. Subtract the value of the smallest unlined element from every unlined element, and add this same value to every element at the intersection of two lines. All other elements remain unchanged. Return to step 2, and continue until the minimum number of lines necessary to cover all the zeros in the matrix is equal to the number of rows.

The minimum unlined element is 2. In the preceding matrix we circled this element. Subtracting 2 from all unlined elements and adding 2 to the intersection element for Terry and client 3 produces the new matrix:

	1	**2**	**3**
Terry	0	0	2
Carle	1	5	0
McClymonds	0	3	0

Returning to step 2, we find that the minimum number of straight lines required to cover all the zeros in the current matrix is 3. The following matrix illustrates the step 2 calculations.

	1	**2**	**3**
Terry	0	0	2
Carle	1	5	0
McClymonds	0	3	0

Three lines must be drawn to cover all zeros; therefore, the optimal solution has been reached

According to step 2, then, it must be possible to find an assignment with a value of zero. To do so we first locate any row or column that contains only one zero. If all have more than one zero, we choose the row or column with the fewest zeros. We draw a square around a zero in the chosen row or column, indicating an assignment, and eliminate that row and column from further consideration. Row 2 has only one zero in the Fowle problem, so we assign Carle to client 3 and eliminate row 2 and column 3 from further consideration. McClymonds must then be assigned to client 1 (the only remaining zero in row 3) and, finally, Terry to client 2. The solution to the Fowle problem, in terms of the reduced matrix, requires a time expenditure of zero days, as follows:

	1	2	3
Terry	0	[0]	2
Carle	1	5	[0]
McClymonds	[0]	3	0

We obtain the value of the optimal assignment by referring to the original assignment problem and summing the solution times associated with the optimal assignment—in this case, 15 for Terry to client 2, 5 for Carle to client 3, and 6 for McClymonds to client 1. Thus, we obtain the solution time of $15 + 5 + 6 = 26$ days.

Finding the Minimum Number of Lines

Sometimes it is not obvious how the lines should be drawn through rows and columns of the matrix in order to cover all the zeros with the smallest number of lines. In these cases, the following heuristic works well. Choose any row or column with a single zero. If it is a row, draw a line through the column the zero is in; if it is a column, draw a line through the row the zero is in. Continue in this fashion until you cover all the zeros.

Can you solve an assignment problem using the Hungarian method? Try Problem 40.

If you make the mistake of drawing too many lines to cover the zeros in the reduced matrix and thus conclude incorrectly that you have reached an optimal solution, you will be unable to identify a zero-value assignment. Thus, if you think you have reached the optimal solution, but cannot find a set of zero-value assignments, go back to the preceding step and check to see whether you can cover all the zeros with fewer lines.

Problem Variations

We now discuss how to handle the following problem variations with the Hungarian method:

1. Number of agents not equal to number of tasks
2. Maximization objective function
3. Unacceptable assignments

Number of Agents Not Equal to Number of Tasks. The Hungarian method requires that the number of rows (agents) equal the number of columns (tasks). Suppose that in the Fowle problem four project leaders (agents) had been available for assignment to the three new clients (tasks). Fowle still faces the same basic problem, namely, which project leaders should be assigned to which clients to minimize the total days required. Table 7.28 shows the project completion time estimates with a fourth project leader.

We know how to apply the Hungarian method when the number of rows and the number of columns are equal. We can apply the same procedure if we can add a new client. If we do not have another client, we simply add a *dummy column,* or a dummy client. This dummy client is nonexistent, so the project leader assigned to the dummy client in the optimal assignment solution, in effect, will be the unassigned project leader.

What project completion time estimates should we show in this new dummy column? The dummy client assignment will not actually take place, which means that a zero project completion time for all project leaders seems logical. Table 7.29 shows the Fowle assignment problem with a dummy client, labeled D. (Problem 42 at the end of the chapter asks you to use the Hungarian method to determine the optimal solution to this problem.)

TABLE 7.28 ESTIMATED PROJECT COMPLETION TIME (DAYS) FOR THE FOWLE ASSIGNMENT PROBLEM WITH FOUR PROJECT LEADERS

	Client		
Project Leader	**1**	**2**	**3**
Terry	10	15	9
Carle	9	18	5
McClymonds	6	14	3
Higley	8	16	6

Note that if we had considered the case of four new clients and only three project leaders, we would have had to add a *dummy row* (dummy project leader) in order to apply the Hungarian method. The client receiving the dummy leader would not actually be assigned a project leader immediately and would have to wait until one becomes available. To obtain a problem form compatible with the solution algorithm, adding several dummy rows or dummy columns, but never both, may be necessary.

Maximization Objective. To illustrate how maximization assignment problems can be handled, let us consider the problem facing management of Salisbury Discounts, Inc. Suppose that Salisbury Discounts has just leased a new store and is attempting to determine where various departments should be located within the store. The store manager has four locations that have not yet been assigned a department and is considering five departments that might occupy the four locations. The departments under consideration are shoes, toys, auto parts, housewares, and videos. After a careful study of the layout of the remainder of the store, the store manager has made estimates of the expected annual profit for each department in each location. These estimates are presented in Table 7.30.

This assignment problem requires a maximization objective. However, the problem also involves more rows than columns. Thus, we must first add a dummy column, corresponding to a dummy or fictitious location, in order to apply the Hungarian method. After adding a dummy column, we obtain the 5×5 Salisbury Discounts, Inc., assignment problem shown in Table 7.31.

We can obtain an equivalent minimization assignment problem by converting all the elements in the matrix to **opportunity losses.** We do so by subtracting every element in each column from the largest element in the column. Finding the assignment that minimizes opportunity loss leads to the same solution that maximizes the value of the assignment in the

TABLE 7.29 ESTIMATED PROJECT COMPLETION TIME (DAYS) FOR THE FOWLE ASSIGNMENT PROBLEM WITH A DUMMY CLIENT

	Client			Dummy client
Project Leader	**1**	**2**	**3**	**D**
Terry	10	15	9	0
Carle	9	18	5	0
McClymonds	6	14	3	0
Higley	8	16	6	0

TABLE 7.30 ESTIMATED ANNUAL PROFIT ($1000s) FOR EACH DEPARTMENT-LOCATION COMBINATION

	Location			
Department	**1**	**2**	**3**	**4**
Shoe	10	6	12	8
Toy	15	18	5	11
Auto parts	17	10	13	16
Housewares	14	12	13	10
Video	14	16	6	12

TABLE 7.31 ESTIMATED ANNUAL PROFIT ($1000s) FOR EACH DEPARTMENT-LOCATION COMBINATION, INCLUDING A DUMMY LOCATION

	Location				Dummy location
Department	**1**	**2**	**3**	**4**	**5**
Shoe	10	6	12	8	0
Toy	15	18	5	11	0
Auto parts	17	10	13	16	0
Housewares	14	12	13	10	0
Video	14	16	6	12	0

original problem. Thus, any maximization assignment problem can be converted to a minimization problem by converting the assignment matrix to one in which the elements represent opportunity losses. Hence, we begin the solution to this maximization assignment problem by developing an assignment matrix in which each element represents the opportunity loss for not making the "best" assignment. Table 7.32 presents the opportunity losses.

The opportunity loss from putting the shoe department in location 1 is $7000. That is, if we put the shoe department, instead of the best department (auto parts), in that location, we forgo the opportunity to make an additional $7000 in profit. The opportunity loss associated with putting the toy department in location 2 is zero because it yields the highest profit in that location. What about the opportunity losses associated with the dummy column? The

TABLE 7.32 OPPORTUNITY LOSS ($1000s) FOR EACH DEPARTMENT-LOCATION COMBINATION

	Location				Dummy location
Department	**1**	**2**	**3**	**4**	**5**
Shoe	7	12	1	8	0
Toy	2	0	8	5	0
Auto parts	0	8	0	0	0
Housewares	3	6	0	6	0
Video	3	2	7	4	0

assignment of a department to this dummy location means that the department will not be assigned a store location in the optimal solution. All departments earn the same amount from this dummy location, zero, making the opportunity loss for each department zero.

Try Problem 43 for practice in using the Hungarian method for a maximization problem.

Using steps 1, 2, and 3 of the Hungarian method on Table 7.32 will minimize opportunity loss and determine the maximum profit assignment.

Unacceptable Assignments. As an illustration of how we can handle unacceptable assignments, suppose that in the Salisbury Discounts, Inc., assignment problem the store manager believed that the toy department should not be considered for location 2 and that the auto parts department should not be considered for location 4. Essentially the store manager is saying that, based on other considerations, such as size of the area, adjacent departments, and so on, these two assignments are unacceptable alternatives.

Using the same approach for the assignment problem as we did for the transportation problem, we define a value of M for unacceptable minimization assignments and a value of $-M$ for unacceptable maximization assignments, where M is an arbitrarily large value. In fact, we assume M to be so large that M plus or minus any value is still extremely large. Thus, an M-valued cell in an assignment matrix retains its M value throughout the matrix reduction calculations. An M-valued cell can never be zero, so it can never be an assignment in the final solution.

Problem 44 at the end of this chapter asks you to solve this assignment problem.

The Salisbury Discounts, Inc., assignment problem with the two unacceptable assignments is shown in Table 7.33. When this assignment matrix is converted to an opportunity loss matrix, the $-M$ profit value will be changed to M.

SUMMARY

In this chapter we introduced transportation, assignment, and transshipment problems. All three types of problems belong to the special category of linear programs called *network flow problems.* The network model of a transportation problem consists of nodes representing a set of origins and a set of destinations. In the basic model, an arc is used to represent the route from each origin to each destination. Each origin has a supply and each destination has a demand. The problem is to determine the optimal amount to ship from each origin to each destination.

The assignment model is a special case of the transportation model in which all supply and all demand values are equal to 1. We represent each agent as an origin node and each task as a destination node. The transshipment model is an extension of the transportation model to distribution problems involving transfer points referred to as transshipment nodes. In this more general model, we allow arcs between any pair of nodes. A variation of the transshipment

TABLE 7.33 ESTIMATED PROFIT FOR THE SALISBURY DEPARTMENT-LOCATION COMBINATIONS

	Location				
Department	**1**	**2**	**3**	**4**	**5**
Shoe	10	6	12	8	0
Toy	15	$-M$	5	11	0
Auto parts	17	10	13	$-M$	0
Housewares	14	12	13	10	0
Video	14	16	6	12	0

problem allows for placing capacities on the arcs. This variation, called the *capacitated transshipment problem,* is also known in the network flow literature as the pure network problem.

We showed how each of these network flow problems could be modeled as a linear program, and we solved each using a general-purpose linear programming computer package. However, many practical applications of network flow models lead to large problems for which general-purpose linear programming codes are not efficient. The transportation simplex method was presented as an efficient special-purpose solution procedure for solving transportation problems. The procedure, and its extension to the transshipment problem, is hundreds of times faster than the general-purpose simplex method for large transportation and transshipment problems. The Hungarian method was presented as a special-purpose solution procedure for assignment problems.

In network flow problems, the optimal solution will be integral as long as all supplies and demands are integral. Therefore, when solving any transportation, assignment, or transshipment problem in which the supplies and demands are integral, we can expect to obtain an integer-valued solution.

GLOSSARY

Transportation problem A network flow problem that often involves minimizing the cost of shipping goods from a set of origins to a set of destinations; it can be formulated and solved as a linear program by including a variable for each arc and a constraint for each node.

Network A graphical representation of a problem consisting of numbered circles (nodes) interconnected by a series of lines (arcs); arrowheads on the arcs show the direction of flow. Transportation, assignment, and transshipment problems are network flow problems.

Nodes The intersection or junction points of a network.

Arcs The lines connecting the nodes in a network.

Capacitated transportation problem A variation of the basic transportation problem in which some or all of the arcs are subject to capacity constraints.

Assignment problem A network flow problem that often involves the assignment of agents to tasks; it can be formulated as a linear program and is a special case of the transportation problem.

Transshipment problem An extension of the transportation problem to distribution problems involving transfer points and possible shipments between any pair of nodes.

Capacitated transshipment problem A variation of the transshipment problem that involves constraints on the capacities of some or all of the arcs.

Transportation simplex method A special-purpose solution procedure for the transportation problem.

Transportation tableau A table representing a transportation problem in which each cell corresponds to a variable, or arc.

Heuristic A commonsense procedure for quickly finding a solution to a problem. Heuristics are used to find initial feasible solutions for the transportation simplex method and in other applications.

Minimum cost method A heuristic used to find an initial feasible solution to a transportation problem; it is easy to use and usually provides a good (but no optimal) solution.

Incoming arc The unused arc (represented by an unoccupied cell in the transportation tableau) to which flow is assigned during an iteration of the transportation simplex method.

Outgoing arc The arc corresponding to an occupied cell that is dropped from solution during an iteration of the transportation simplex method.

MODI method A procedure in which a modified distribution method determines the incoming arc in the transportation simplex method.

Net evaluation index The per-unit change in the objective function associated with assigning flow to an unused arc in the transportation simplex method.

Stepping-stone method Using a sequence or path of occupied cells to identify flow adjustments necessary when flow is assigned to an unused arc in the transportation simplex method. This identifies the outgoing arc.

Degenerate solution A solution to a transportation problem in which fewer than $m + n - 1$ arcs (cells) have positive flow; m is the number of origins and n is the number of destinations.

Dummy destination A destination added to a transportation problem to make the total supply equal to the total demand. The demand assigned to the dummy destination is the difference between the total supply and the total demand.

Dummy origin An origin added to a transportation problem in order to make the total supply equal to the total demand. The supply assigned to the dummy origin is the difference between the total demand and the total supply.

Hungarian method A special-purpose solution procedure for solving an assignment problem.

Opportunity loss For each cell in an assignment matrix, the difference between the largest value in the column and the value in the cell. The entries in the cells of an assignment matrix must be converted to opportunity losses to solve maximization problems using the Hungarian method.

PROBLEMS

Note: For Problems 1–32 a variety of solution methods can be used. In many cases, we ask you to formulate and solve the problem as a linear program. Where the solution method is not specified, you may also use the transportation or assignment modules of The Management Scientist or some other software package. Problems 33–45 are intended to be solved using the special-purpose algorithms of Sections 7.5 and 7.6. These special-purpose algorithms could also be used for many of the first 32 problems.

1. A company imports goods at two ports: Philadelphia and New Orleans. Shipments of one of its products are made to customers in Atlanta, Dallas, Columbus, and Boston. For the next planning period, the supplies at each port, customer demands, and the shipping costs per case from each port to each customer are as follows:

	Customers				
Port	**Atlanta**	**Dallas**	**Columbus**	**Boston**	**Port Supply**
Philadelphia	2	6	6	2	5000
New Orleans	1	2	5	7	3000
Demand	1400	3200	2000	1400	

Develop a network model of the distribution system for this problem.

2. Consider the following network representation of a transportation problem:

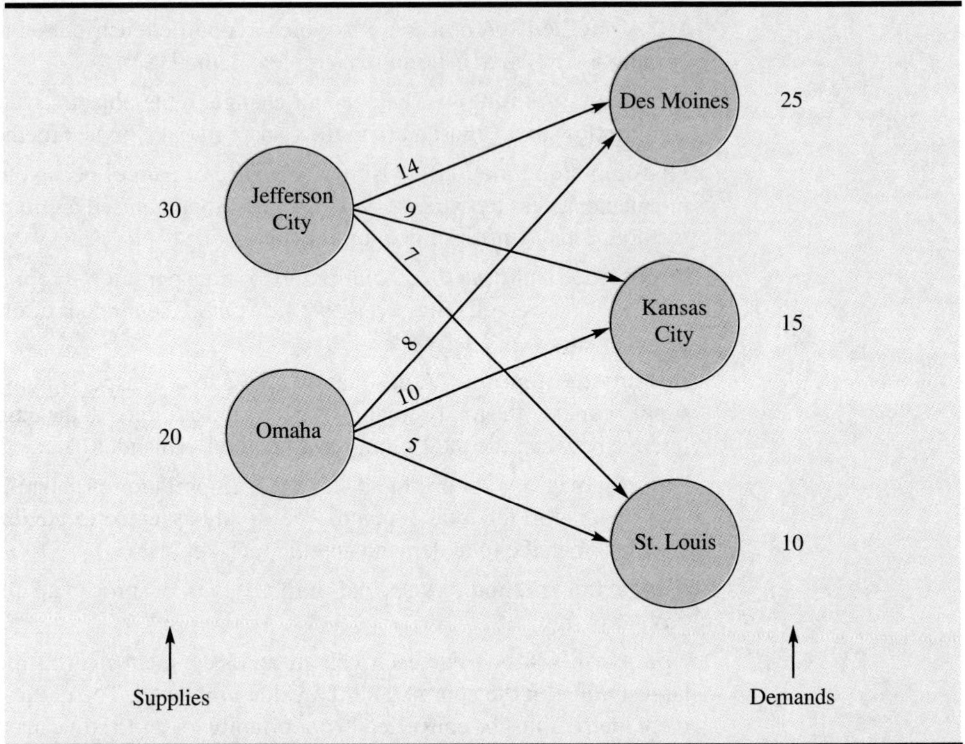

The supplies, demands, and transportation costs per unit are shown on the network.

a. Develop a linear programming model for this problem; be sure to define the variables in your model.

b. Solve the linear program to determine the optimal solution.

3. Reconsider the distribution system described in Problem 1.

a. Develop a linear programming model for minimizing transportation costs.

b. Solve the linear program to determine the minimum cost shipping schedule.

4. A product is produced at three plants and shipped to three warehouses (the transportation costs per unit are shown in the following table).

	Warehouse			
Plant	W_1	W_2	W_3	**Plant Capacity**
P_1	20	16	24	300
P_2	10	10	8	500
P_3	12	18	10	100
Warehouse demand	200	400	300	

a. Show a network representation of the problem.

b. Develop a linear programming model for minimizing transportation costs; solve this model to determine the minimum cost solution.

c. Suppose that the entries in the table represent profit per unit produced at plant i and sold to warehouse j. How does the model change from that in part (b)?

5. Tri-County Utilities, Inc., supplies natural gas to customers in a three-county area. The company purchases natural gas from two companies: Southern Gas and Northwest Gas. Demand forecasts for the coming winter season are Hamilton County, 400 units; Butler County, 200 units; and Clermont County, 300 units. Contracts to provide the following quantities have been written: Southern Gas, 500 units; and Northwest Gas, 400 units. Distribution costs for the counties vary, depending upon the location of the suppliers. The distribution costs per unit (in $1000s) are as follows:

		To	
From	**Hamilton**	**Butler**	**Clermont**
Southern Gas	10	20	15
Northwest Gas	12	15	18

a. Develop a network representation of this problem.
b. Develop a linear programming model that can be used to determine the plan that will minimize total distribution costs.
c. Describe the distribution plan and show the total distribution cost.
d. Recent residential and industrial growth in Butler County has the potential for increasing demand by as much as 100 units. Which supplier should Tri-County contract with to supply the additional capacity?

6. Arnoff Enterprises manufactures the central processing unit (CPU) for a line of personal computers. The CPUs are manufactured in Seattle, Columbus, and New York and shipped to warehouses in Pittsburgh, Mobile, Denver, Los Angeles, and Washington, D.C., for further distribution. The following transportation tableau shows the number of CPUs available at each plant and the number of CPUs required by each warehouse. The shipping costs (dollars per unit) are also shown in each cell.

	Warehouse					
Plant	Pittsburgh	Mobile	Denver	Los Angeles	Washington	**CPUs Available**
Seattle	10	20	5	9	10	9000
Columbus	2	10	8	30	6	4000
New York	1	20	7	10	4	8000
CPUs Required	3000	5000	4000	6000	3000	21,000

a. Develop a network representation of this problem.
b. Determine the amount that should be shipped from each plant to each warehouse to minimize the total shipping cost.
c. The Pittsburgh warehouse has just increased its order by 1000 units, and Arnoff has authorized the Columbus plant to increase its production by 1000 units. Will this change lead to an increase or decrease in total shipping costs? Solve for the new optimal solution.

7. Premier Consulting has two consultants, Avery and Baker, who can be scheduled to work for clients up to a maximum of 160 hours each over the next four weeks. A third consultant, Campbell, has some administrative assignments already planned and is available for clients up to a maximum of 140 hours over the next four weeks. The company has four clients with projects in process. The estimated hourly requirements for each of the clients over the four-week period are

Client	Hours
A	180
B	75
C	100
D	85

Hourly rates vary for the consultant-client combination and are based on several factors, including project type and the consultant's experience. The rates (dollars per hour) for each consultant-client combination are

Consultant	Client A	Client B	Client C	Client D
Avery	100	125	115	100
Baker	120	135	115	120
Campbell	155	150	140	130

a. Develop a network representation of the problem.
b. Formulate the problem as a linear program, with the optimal solution providing the hours each consultant should be scheduled for each client in order to maximize the consulting firm's billings. What is the schedule and what is the total billing?
c. New information shows that Avery doesn't have the experience to be scheduled for client B. If this consulting assignment is not permitted, what impact does it have on total billings? What is the revised schedule?

8. Klein Chemicals, Inc., produces a special oil-base material that is currently in short supply. Four of Klein's customers have already placed orders that together exceed the combined capacity of Klein's two plants. Klein's management faces the problem of deciding how many units it should supply to each customer. Because the four customers are in different industries, different prices can be charged based on the various industry pricing structures. However, slightly different production costs at the two plants and varying transportation costs between the plants and customers make a "sell to the highest bidder" strategy questionable. After considering price, production costs, and transportation costs, Klein has established the following profit per unit for each plant-customer alternative.

	Customer			
Plant	D_1	D_2	D_3	D_4
Clifton Springs	\$32	\$34	\$32	\$40
Danville	\$34	\$30	\$28	\$38

The plant capacities and customer orders are as follows:

Plant Capacity (units)		Distributor Orders (units)
Clifton Springs	5000	D_1 2000
		D_2 5000
Danville	3000	D_3 3000
		D_4 2000

How many units should each plant produce for each customer to maximize profits? Which customer demands will not be met? Show your network model and linear programming formulation.

9. Sound Electronics, Inc., produces a battery-operated tape recorder at plants located in Martinsville, North Carolina; Plymouth, New York; and Franklin, Missouri. The unit transportation cost for shipments from the three plants to distribution centers in Chicago, Dallas, and New York are as follows:

	To		
From	**Chicago**	**Dallas**	**New York**
Martinsville	1.45	1.60	1.40
Plymouth	1.10	2.25	0.60
Franklin	1.20	1.20	1.80

After considering transportation costs, management has decided that under no circumstances will it use the Plymouth-Dallas route. The plant capacities and distributor orders for the next month are as follows:

Plant	Capacity (units)
Martinsville	400
Plymouth	600
Franklin	300

Distributor	Orders (units)
Chicago	400
Dallas	400
New York	400

Because of different wage scales at the three plants, the unit production cost varies from plant to plant. Assuming the costs are \$29.50 per unit at Martinsville, \$31.20 per unit at Plymouth, and \$30.35 per unit at Franklin, find the production and distribution plan that minimizes production and transportation costs.

10. The Ace Manufacturing Company has orders for three similar products:

Product	Orders (units)
A	2000
B	500
C	1200

Three machines are available for the manufacturing operations. All three machines can produce all the products at the same production rate. However, due to varying defect percentages of each product on each machine, the unit costs of the products vary depending on the machine used. Machine capacities for the next week, and the unit costs, are as follows:

Machine	Capacity (units)
1	1500
2	1500
3	1000

	Product		
Machine	A	B	C
1	\$1.00	\$1.20	\$0.90
2	\$1.30	\$1.40	\$1.20
3	\$1.10	\$1.00	\$1.20

Formulate and solve a linear programming model that can be used to develop the minimum cost production schedule for the products and machines.

11. Forbelt Corporation has a one-year contract to supply motors for all refrigerators produced by the Ice Age Corporation. Ice Age manufactures the refrigerators at four locations around the country: Boston, Dallas, Los Angeles, and St. Paul. Plans call for the following number (in thousands) of refrigerators to be produced at each location.

Boston	50
Dallas	70
Los Angeles	60
St. Paul	80

Forbelt has three plants that are capable of producing the motors. The plants and production capacities (in thousands) are

Denver	100
Atlanta	100
Chicago	150

Because of varying production and transportation costs, the profit that Forbelt earns on each lot of 1000 units depends on which plant produced the lot and which destination it was shipped to. The following table gives the accounting department estimates of the profit per unit (shipments will be made in lots of 1000 units).

	Shipped To			
Produced At	**Boston**	**Dallas**	**Los Angeles**	**St. Paul**
Denver	7	11	8	13
Atlanta	20	17	12	10
Chicago	8	18	13	16

With profit maximization as a criterion, Forbelt wants to determine how many motors should be produced at each plant and how many motors should be shipped from each plant to each destination.

a. Develop a network representation of this problem.

b. Find the optimal solution.

12. Scott and Associates, Inc., is an accounting firm that has three new clients. Project leaders will be assigned to the three clients. Based on the different backgrounds and experiences of the leaders, the various leader-client assignments differ in terms of projected completion times. The possible assignments and the estimated completion times in days are

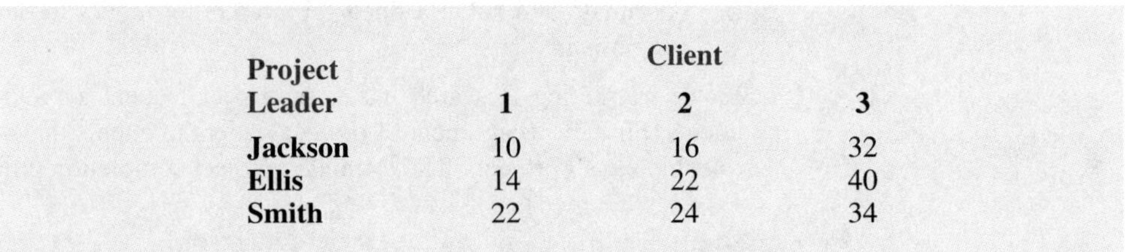

Project Leader	Client 1	2	3
Jackson	10	16	32
Ellis	14	22	40
Smith	22	24	34

a. Develop a network representation of this problem.

b. Formulate the problem as a linear program, and solve. What is the total time required?

13. Assume that in Problem 12 an additional employee is available for possible assignment. The following table shows the assignment alternatives and the estimated completion times.

Project Leader	Client 1	2	3
Jackson	10	16	32
Ellis	14	22	40
Smith	22	24	34
Burton	14	18	36

a. What is the optimal assignment?

b. How did the assignment change compared to the best assignment possible in Problem 12? Were any savings associated with considering Burton as one of the possible project leaders?

c. Which project leader remains unassigned?

14. CarpetPlus sells and installs floor covering for commercial buildings. Brad Sweeney, a CarpetPlus account executive, was just awarded the contract for five jobs. Brad must now assign a CarpetPlus installation crew to each of the five jobs. Because the commission Brad will earn depends on the profit CarpetPlus makes, Brad would like to determine an assignment that will minimize total installation costs. Currently, five installation crews are available for assignment. Each crew is identified by a color code, which aids in tracking of job progress on a large white board. The following table shows the costs (in hundreds of dollars) for each crew to complete each of the five jobs.

		Job				
		1	**2**	**3**	**4**	**5**
Crew	**Red**	30	44	38	47	31
	White	25	32	45	44	25
	Blue	23	40	37	39	29
	Green	26	38	37	45	28
	Brown	26	34	44	43	28

a. Develop a network representation of the problem.

b. Formulate and solve a linear programming model to determine the minimum cost assignment.

15. Fowle Marketing Research has four project leaders available for assignment to three clients. Find the assignment of project leaders to clients that will minimize the total time to complete all projects. The estimated project completion times in days are as follows:

Project Leader	Client 1	Client 2	Client 3
Terry	10	15	9
Carle	9	18	5
McClymonds	6	14	3
Higley	8	16	6

16. **a.** Develop a network representation of the Salisbury Discount, Inc., department-location assignment problem using the estimated annual profit data provided in Table 7.30.

b. Formulate a linear programming model, and solve for the department-location assignment that maximizes profit.

17. Consider the Salisbury Discount, Inc., assignment problem with two unacceptable assignments (see Table 7.33).

a. Develop a network representation of the problem.

b. Formulate and solve a linear programming model.

18. The U.S. Cable Company uses a distribution system with five distribution centers and eight customer zones. Each customer zone is assigned a sole source supplier and receives all of its cable products from the same distribution center. In an effort to balance demand and workload at the distribution centers, the company's vice president of logistics specified that distribution centers may not be assigned more than three customer zones. The following table shows the five distribution centers and cost of supplying each customer zone ($1000s).

	Customer Zones							
Distribution Centers	**Los Angeles**	**Chicago**	**Columbus**	**Atlanta**	**Newark**	**Kansas City**	**Denver**	**Dallas**
Plano	70	47	22	53	98	21	27	13
Nashville	75	38	19	58	90	34	40	26
Flagstaff	15	78	37	82	111	40	29	32
Springfield	60	23	8	39	82	36	32	45
Boulder	45	40	29	75	86	25	11	37

a. Determine the assignment of customer zones to distribution centers that will minimize cost.

b. Which distribution centers, if any, are not used?

c. Suppose that each distribution center is limited to a maximum of two customer zones. How does this constraint change the assignment and the cost of supplying customer zones?

19. Mayfax Distributors, Inc., has four sales territories, each of which must be assigned a sales representative. From past experience the firm's sales manager has estimated the annual sales volume ($1000s) for each sales representative in each sales territory. Find the territory assignments that will maximize sales.

	Sales Territory			
Sales Representative	**A**	**B**	**C**	**D**
Washington	44	80	52	60
Benson	60	56	40	72
Fredricks	36	60	48	48
Hodson	52	76	36	40

20. The department head of a management science department at a major midwestern university will be scheduling faculty to teach courses during the coming autumn term. Four core courses need to be covered. The four courses are at the UG, MBA, MS, and Ph.D. levels. Four professors will be assigned to the courses, with each professor receiving one of the courses. Student evaluations of professors are available from previous terms. Based on a rating scale of 4 (excellent), 3 (good), 2 (average), 1 (fair), and 0 (poor), the average student evaluations for each professor are shown. Professor D does not have a Ph.D. and cannot be assigned to teach the Ph.D.-level course. If the department head makes teaching assignments based on maximizing the student evaluation ratings over all four courses, what staffing assignments should be made?

	Course			
Professor	**UG**	**MBA**	**MS**	**Ph.D.**
A	2.8	2.2	3.3	3.0
B	3.2	3.0	3.6	3.6
C	3.3	3.2	3.5	3.5
D	3.2	2.8	2.5	—

21. A market research firm has three clients who have each requested that the firm conduct a sample survey. Four available statisticians can be assigned to these three projects; however, all four statisticians are busy, and therefore each can handle only one of the clients. The following data show the number of hours required for each statistician to complete each job; the differences in time are based on experience and ability of the statisticians.

	Client		
Statistician	**A**	**B**	**C**
1	150	210	270
2	170	230	220
3	180	230	225
4	160	240	230

a. Formulate and solve a linear programming model for this problem.
b. Suppose that the time it takes statistician 4 to complete the job for client A is increased from 160 to 165 hours. What effect will this change have on the solution?
c. Suppose that the time it takes statistician 4 to complete the job for client A is decreased to 140 hours. What effect will this change have on the solution?
d. Suppose that the time it takes statistician 3 to complete the job for client B increases to 250 hours. What effect will this change have on the solution?

22. Hatcher Enterprises uses a chemical called Rbase in production operations at five divisions. Only six suppliers of Rbase meet Hatcher's quality control standards. All six of the suppliers can produce Rbase in sufficient quantities to accommodate the needs of each division. The quantity of Rbase needed by each of Hatcher's divisions and the price per gallon charged by each supplier are as follows:

Division	Demand (1000s of gallons)
1	40
2	45
3	50
4	35
5	45

Supplier	Price per Gallon ($)
1	12.60
2	14.00
3	10.20
4	14.20
5	12.00
6	13.00

The cost per gallon ($) for shipping from each supplier to each division is provided in the following table.

	Supplier					
Division	**1**	**2**	**3**	**4**	**5**	**6**
1	2.75	2.50	3.15	2.80	2.75	2.75
2	0.80	0.20	5.40	1.20	3.40	1.00
3	4.70	2.60	5.30	2.80	6.00	5.60
4	2.60	1.80	4.40	2.40	5.00	2.80
5	3.40	0.40	5.00	1.20	2.60	3.60

Hatcher believes in spreading its business among suppliers so that the company will be less affected by supplier problems (e.g., labor strikes or resource availability). Company policy requires that each division have a separate supplier.

a. For each supplier-division combination, compute the total cost of supplying the division's demand.

b. Determine the optimal assignment of supplier to divisions.

23. The distribution system for the Herman Company consists of three plants, two warehouses, and four customers. Plant capacities and shipping costs ($) from each plant to each warehouse are

	Warehouse		
Plant	**1**	**2**	**Capacity**
1	4	7	450
2	8	5	600
3	5	6	380

Customer demand and shipping costs per unit (in $) from each warehouse to each customer are

	Customer			
Warehouse	**1**	**2**	**3**	**4**
1	6	4	8	4
2	3	6	7	7
Demand	300	300	300	400

a. Develop a network model of this problem.

b. Formulate a linear programming model of the problem.

c. Find the optimal shipping plan.

24. Refer to Problem 23. Suppose that shipments between the two warehouses are permitted at $2 per unit and that direct shipments can be made from plant 3 to customer 4 at a cost of $7 per unit.

a. Develop a network model of this problem.

b. Formulate a linear programming model of this problem.

c. Find the optimal shipping plan.

25. CARD, Cleveland Area Rapid Delivery, operates a delivery service in the Cleveland metropolitan area. Most of CARD's business involves rapid delivery of documents and parcels between offices during the business day. CARD promotes its ability to make fast and on-time deliveries anywhere in the metropolitan area. When a customer calls with a delivery request, CARD quotes a guaranteed delivery time. The following network shows the routes between seven pickup and delivery locations. The numbers above each arc indicate the travel time in minutes between the two locations.

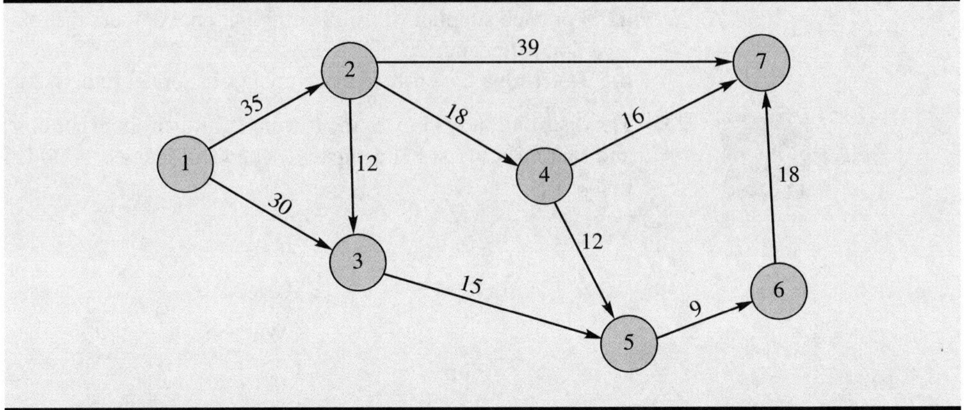

a. Develop a linear programming model of a transshipment problem that can be used to find the minimum time required to make a delivery from location 1 to location 7.
b. How long does it take to make a delivery from location 1 to location 7?
c. Assume that it is now 1:00 P.M. CARD has just received a request for a pickup at location 1, and the closest CARD courier is 8 minutes away from location 1. If CARD provides a 20% safety margin in guaranteeing a delivery time, what is the guaranteed delivery time if the package picked up at location 1 is to be delivered to location 7?

26. Adirondack Paper Mills, Inc., has paper plants in Augusta, Maine, and Tupper Lake, New York. Warehouse facilities are located in Albany, New York, and Portsmouth, New Hampshire. Distributors are located in Boston, New York, and Philadelphia. The plant capacities and distributor demands for the next month are as follows:

Plant	Capacity (units)
Augusta	300
Tupper Lake	100

Distributor	Demand (units)
Boston	150
New York	100
Philadelphia	150

The unit transportation costs ($) for shipments from the two plants to the two warehouses and from the two warehouses to the three distributors are as follows:

	Warehouse	
Plant	**Albany**	**Portsmouth**
Augusta	7	5
Tupper Lake	3	4

		Distributor	
Warehouse	**Boston**	**New York**	**Philadelphia**
Albany	8	5	7
Portsmouth	5	6	10

a. Draw the network representation of the Adirondack Paper Mills problem.
b. Formulate the Adirondack Paper Mills problem as a linear programming problem.
c. Determine the minimum cost shipping schedule for the problem.

27. Consider a transshipment problem consisting of three origin nodes, two transshipment nodes, and four destination nodes. The supplies at the origin nodes and the demands at the destination nodes are as follows:

Origin	Supply
1	400
2	450
3	350

Destination	Demand
1	200
2	500
3	300
4	200

The shipping costs per unit ($) are provided in the following table.

From		To					
		Transshipment		Destination			
		1	2	1	2	3	4
Origin	1	6	8	—	—	—	—
	2	8	12	—	—	—	—
	3	10	5	—	—	—	—
Transshipment	1	—	—	9	7	6	10
	2	—	—	7	9	6	8

a. Draw the network representation of this problem.
b. Formulate the appropriate linear programming problem.
c. Solve for the optimal solution.

28. The Moore & Harman Company is in the business of buying and selling grain. An important aspect of the company's business is arranging for the purchased grain to be shipped to customers. If the company can keep freight costs low, profitability will be improved.

The company purchased three rail cars of grain at Muncie, Indiana; six rail cars at Brazil, Indiana; and five rail cars at Xenia, Ohio. Twelve carloads of grain are already sold. The locations and the amount sold at each location are as follows:

Location	Number of Rail Car Loads
Macon, GA	2
Greenwood, SC	4
Concord, SC	3
Chatham, NC	3

All shipments must be routed through either Louisville or Cincinnati. Shown are the shipping costs per bushel (in cents) from the origins to Louisville and Cincinnati and the costs per bushel to ship from Louisville and Cincinnati to the destinations.

	To	
From	**Louisville**	**Cincinnati**
Muncie	8	6 ← Cost per bushel from Muncie to Cincinnati is 6¢
Brazil	3	8
Xenia	9	3

	To			
From	**Macon**	**Greenwood**	**Concord**	**Chatham**
Louisville	44	34	34	32
Cincinnati	57	35	28	24

Cost per bushel from Cincinnati to Greenwood is 35¢

Determine a shipping schedule that will minimize the freight costs necessary to satisfy demand. Which (if any) rail cars of grain must be held at the origin until buyers can be found?

29. A rental car company has an imbalance of cars at seven of its locations. The following network shows the locations of concern (the nodes) and the cost to move a car between locations. A positive number by a node indicates an excess supply at the node, and a negative number indicates an excess demand.

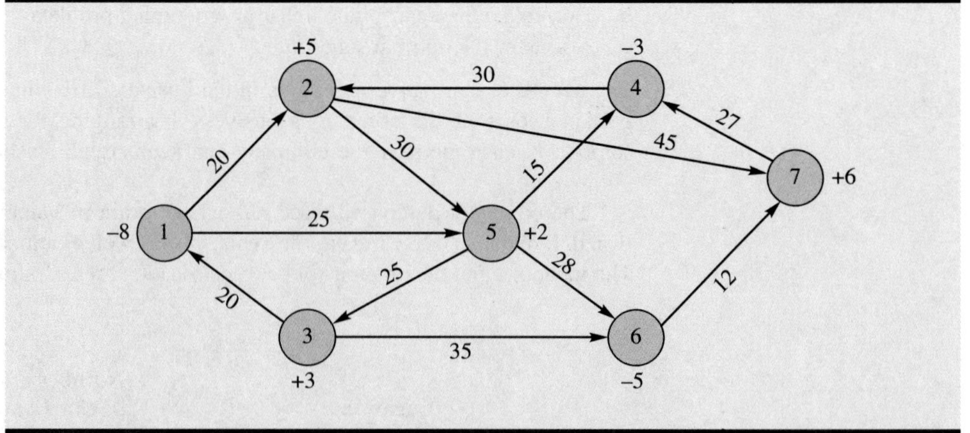

a. Develop a linear programming model for restoring the proper balance at the locations.

b. Solve the model formulated in part (a) to determine how the cars should be redistributed among the locations.

30. The following linear programming formulation is for a transshipment problem.

$$\text{Min} \quad 11x_{13} + 12x_{14} + 10x_{21} + 8x_{34} + 10x_{35} + 11x_{42} + 9x_{45} + 12x_{52}$$

s.t.

$$\begin{aligned}
x_{13} + x_{14} - x_{21} & \leq 5 \\
x_{21} - x_{42} - x_{52} & \leq 3 \\
x_{13} - x_{34} - x_{35} & = 6 \\
-x_{14} - x_{34} + x_{42} + x_{45} & \leq 2 \\
x_{35} + x_{45} - x_{52} & = 4
\end{aligned}$$

$$x_{ij} \geq 0 \quad \text{for all } i, j$$

Show the network representation of this problem.

31. Refer to the Contois Carpets problem for which the network representation is shown in Figure 7.12. Suppose that Contois has a beginning inventory of 50 square yards of carpet and requires an inventory of 100 square yards at the end of quarter 4.

a. Develop a network representation of this modified problem.

b. Develop a linear programming model, and solve for the optimal solution.

32. Sanders Fishing Supply of Naples, Florida, manufactures a variety of fishing equipment, which it sells throughout the United States. For the next three months, Sanders estimates demand for a particular product at 150, 250, and 300 units, respectively. Sanders can supply this demand by producing on regular time or overtime. Because of other commitments and anticipated cost increases in month 3, the production capacities in units and the production costs per unit are as follows:

Production	Capacity (units)	Cost per Unit
Month 1—Regular	275	$ 50
Month 1—Overtime	100	80
Month 2—Regular	200	50
Month 2—Overtime	50	80
Month 3—Regular	100	60
Month 3—Overtime	50	100

Inventory may be carried from one month to the next, but the cost is $20 per unit per month. For example, regular production from month 1 used to meet demand in month 2 would cost Sanders $50 + $20 = $70 per unit. This same month 1 production used to meet demand in month 3 would cost Sanders $50 + 2($20) = $90 per unit.

a. Develop a network representation of this production scheduling problem as a transportation problem. (*Hint:* Use six origin nodes; the supply for origin node 1 is the maximum that can be produced in month 1 on regular time, and so on.)

b. Develop a linear programming model that can be used to schedule regular and overtime production for each of the three months.

c. What is the production schedule, how many units are carried in inventory each month, and what is the total cost?

d. Is there any unused production capacity? If so, where?

Note: The remaining problems involve the use of the special-purpose algorithms described in Sections 7.5 and 7.6 for solving transportation and assignment problems.

33. Consider the following transportation tableau with four origins and four destinations.

Origin	Destination				Supply
	D_1	D_2	D_3	D_4	
O_1	[5] 25	[7]	[10] 50	[5]	75
O_2	[6]	[5]	[8] 100	[2] 75	175
O_3	[6] 100	[6]	[12]	[7]	100
O_4	[8]	[5] 100	[14]	[4] 50	150
Demand	125	100	150	125	

a. Use the MODI method to determine whether this solution provides the minimum transportation cost. If it is not the minimum cost solution, find that solution. If it is the minimum cost solution, what is the total transportation cost?

b. Does an alternative optimal solution exit? Explain. If so, find the alternative optimal solution. What is the total transportation cost associated with this solution?

34. Consider the following minimum cost transportation problem.

Origin	Destination			Supply
	Los Angeles	San Francisco	San Diego	
San Jose	[4]	[10]	[6]	100
Las Vegas	[8]	[16]	[6]	300
Tucson	[14]	[18]	[10]	300
Demand	200	300	200	700

a. Use the minimum cost method to find an initial feasible solution.
b. Use the transportation simplex method to find an optimal solution.
c. How would the optimal solution change if you must ship 100 units on the Tucson–San Diego route?
d. Because of road construction, the Las Vegas–San Diego route is now unacceptable. Resolve the initial problem.

35. Refer to Problem 2.
a. Set up the transportation tableau for the problem.
b. Use the minimum cost method to find an initial feasible solution.

36. Refer to Problem 4. Use the transportation simplex method to find an optimal solution.

37. Consider the following minimum cost transportation problem.

Origin	Destination D_1	D_2	D_3	Supply
O_1	6	8	8	250
O_2	18	12	14	150
O_3	8	12	10	100
Demand	150	200	150	

a. Use the minimum cost method to find an initial feasible solution.
b. Use the transportation simplex method to find an optimal solution.
c. Using your solution to part (b), identify an alternative optimal solution.

38. Use the per-unit cost changes for each unoccupied cell shown in Table 7.15 to do the following:
a. Consider the arc connecting Bedford and Chicago as a candidate for the incoming arc. Allocate 1 unit of flow, and make the necessary adjustments on the stepping-stone path to maintain feasibility. Compute the value of the new solution, and show that the change in value is exactly what has been indicated by the cost change per unit obtained using the MODI method.
b. Repeat part (a) for the arc connecting York and Lexington.

39. Refer again to the Contois Carpets problem for which the network representation is shown in Figure 7.12. This problem can also be formulated and solved as a transportation problem.
a. Develop a network representation of it as a transportation problem. (*Hint:* Eliminate the inventory arcs, and add arcs showing that quarterly production can be used to satisfy demand in the current quarter and all future quarters.)
b. Solve the problem using the transportation simplex method.

40. Refer to Problem 12. Using the Hungarian method, obtain the optimal solution.

41. Refer to Problem 14. Use the Hungarian method to obtain the optimal solution.

42. Refer to Problem 15. Use the Hungarian method to obtain the optimal solution.

SELF test

43. Use the Hungarian method to solve the Salisbury Discount, Inc., problem by using the profit data in Table 7.30.

44. Use the Hungarian method to solve the Salisbury Discount, Inc., problem as described in Problem 17.

45. Refer to Problem 19. Use the Hungarian method to find an optimal solution.

Case Problem DISTRIBUTION SYSTEM DESIGN

The Darby Company manufactures and distributes meters used to measure electric power consumption. The company started with a small production plant in El Paso and gradually built a customer base throughout Texas. A distribution center was established in Ft. Worth, Texas, and later, as business expanded to the north, a second distribution center was established in Santa Fe, New Mexico.

The El Paso plant was expanded when the company began marketing its meters in Arizona, California, Nevada, and Utah. With the growth of the West Coast business, the Darby Company opened a third distribution center in Las Vegas and just two years ago opened a second production plant in San Bernardino, California.

Manufacturing costs differ between the company's production plants. The cost of each meter produced at the El Paso plant is \$10.50. The San Bernardino plant utilizes newer and more efficient equipment; as a result, manufacturing costs are \$0.50 per meter less than at the El Paso plant.

The company's rapid growth meant that not much attention was paid to the efficiency of the distribution system. Darby's management decided it is now time to address this issue. The cost of shipping a meter from each of the two plants to each of the three distribution centers is shown in Table 7.34.

The quarterly production capacity is 30,000 meters at the older El Paso plant and 20,000 meters at the San Bernardino plant. Note that no shipments are allowed from the San Bernardino plant to the Ft. Worth distribution center.

The company serves nine customer zones from the three distribution centers. The forecast of the number of meters needed in each customer zone for the next quarter is shown in Table 7.35.

The cost per unit of shipping from each distribution center to each customer zone is given in Table 7.36; note that some of the distribution centers cannot serve certain customer zones.

TABLE 7.34 SHIPPING COST PER UNIT FROM PRODUCTION PLANTS TO DISTRIBUTION CENTERS (\$)

	Distribution Center		
Plant	**Ft. Worth**	**Santa Fe**	**Las Vegas**
El Paso	3.20	2.20	4.20
San Bernardino	—	3.90	1.20

TABLE 7.35 QUARTERLY DEMAND FORECAST

Customer Zone	Demand (meters)
Dallas	6300
San Antonio	4880
Wichita	2130
Kansas City	1210
Denver	6120
Salt Lake City	4830
Phoenix	2750
Los Angeles	8580
San Diego	4460

In the current distribution system, demand at the Dallas, San Antonio, Wichita, and Kansas City customer zones is satisfied by shipments from the Ft. Worth distribution center. In a similar manner, the Denver, Salt Lake City, and Phoenix customer zones are served by the Santa Fe distribution center, and the Los Angeles and San Diego customer zones are served by the Las Vegas distribution center. To determine how many units to ship from each plant, the quarterly customer demand forecasts are aggregated at the distribution centers, and a transportation model is used to minimize the cost of shipping from the production plants to the distribution centers.

Managerial Report

You are called in to make recommendations for improving the distribution system. Your report should address, but not be limited to, the following issues.

1. If the company does not change its current distribution strategy, what will its manufacturing and distribution costs be for the following quarter?
2. Suppose that the company is willing to consider dropping the distribution center limitations; that is, customers could be served by any of the distribution centers for which costs are available. Can costs be reduced? By how much?
3. The company wants to explore the possibility of satisfying some of the customer demand directly from the production plants. In particular, the shipping cost is \$0.30 per unit from San Bernardino to Los Angeles and \$0.70 from San Bernardino to San Diego. The cost for direct shipments from El Paso to San Antonio is \$3.50 per

TABLE 7.36 SHIPPING COST FROM THE DISTRIBUTION CENTERS TO THE CUSTOMER ZONES (\$)

	Customer Zone								
Distribution Center	Dallas	San Antonio	Wichita	Kansas City	Denver	Salt Lake City	Phoenix	Los Angeles	San Diego
Ft. Worth	0.3	2.1	3.1	4.4	6.0	—	—	—	—
Santa Fe	5.2	5.4	4.5	6.0	2.7	4.7	3.4	3.3	2.7
Las Vegas	—	—	—	—	5.4	3.3	2.4	2.1	2.5

unit. Can distribution costs be further reduced by considering these direct plant-customer shipments?

4. Over the next five years, Darby is anticipating moderate growth (5000 meters) to the North and West. Would you recommend that they consider plant expansion at this time?

Appendix 7.1 EXCEL SOLUTION OF TRANSPORTATION, ASSIGNMENT, AND TRANSSHIPMENT PROBLEMS

In this appendix we show how Excel Solver can be used to solve transportation, assignment, and transshipment problems. We start with the Foster Generators transportation problem (see Section 7.1).

Transportation Problem

The first step is to enter the data for the transportation costs, the origin supplies, and the destination demands in the top portion of the worksheet. Then the linear programming model is developed in the bottom portion of the worksheet. As with all linear programs the worksheet model has four key elements: the decision variables, the objective function, the constraint left-hand sides, and the constraint right-hand sides. For a transportation problem, the decision variables are the amounts shipped from each origin to each destination; the objective function is the total transportation cost; the left-hand sides are the number of units shipped from each origin and the number of units shipped into each destination; and the right-hand sides are the origin supplies and the destination demands.

The formulation and solution of the Foster Generators problem are shown in Figure 7.14. The data are in the top portion of the worksheet. The model appears in the bottom portion of the worksheet; the key elements are screened.

Formulation

The data and descriptive labels are contained in cells A1:F8. The transportation costs are in cells B5:E7. The origin supplies are in cells F5:F7, and the destination demands are in cells B8:E8. The key elements of the model required by the Excel Solver are the decision variables, the objective function, the constraint left-hand sides, and the constraint right-hand sides. These cells are screened in the bottom portion of the worksheet.

Decision Variables — Cells B17:E19 are reserved for the decision variables. The optimal values are shown to be $x_{11} = 3500$, $x_{12} = 1500$, $x_{22} = 2500$, $x_{23} = 2000$, $x_{24} = 1500$, and $x_{41} = 2500$. All other decision variables equal zero indicating nothing will be shipped over the corresponding routes.

Objective Function — The formula =SUMPRODUCT(B5:E7,B17:E19) has been placed into cell C13 to compute the cost of the solution. The minimum cost solution is shown to have a value of $39,500.

Left-Hand Sides — Cells F17:F19 contain the left-hand sides for the supply constraints, and cells B20:E20 contain the left-hand sides for the demand constraints.

Cell F17 = SUM(B17:E17) (Copy to F18:F19)
Cell B20 = SUM(B17:B19) (Copy to C20:E20)

FIGURE 7.14 EXCEL SOLUTION OF THE FOSTER GENERATORS PROBLEM

EXCELfile
Foster

	A	B	C	D	E	F	G	H	I
1	**Foster Generators**								
2									
3			**Destination**						
4	**Origin**	Boston	Chicago	St. Louis	Lexington	**Supply**			
5	Cleveland	3	2	7	6	5000			
6	Bedford	7	5	2	3	6000			
7	York	2	5	4	5	2500			
8	**Demand**	6000	4000	2000	1500				
9									
10									
11	**Model**								
12									
13		**Min Cost**	39500						
14									
15			**Destination**						
16	**Origin**	Boston	Chicago	St. Louis	Lexington	**Total**			
17	Cleveland	3500	1500	0	0	5000	<=	5000	
18	Bedford	0	2500	2000	1500	6000	<=	6000	
19	York	2500	0	0	0	2500	<=	2500	
20	**Total**	6000	4000	2000	1500				
21		=	=	=	=				
22		6000	4000	2000	1500				
23									

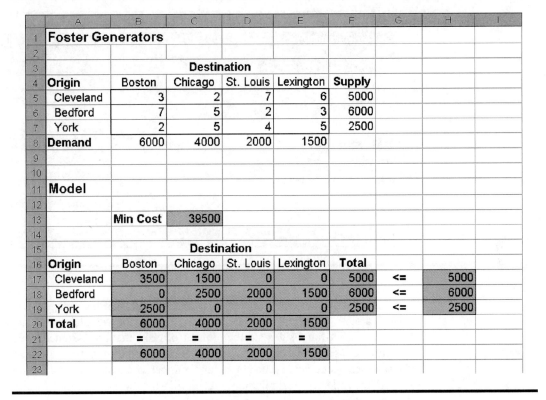

Right-Hand Sides Cells H17:H19 contain the right-hand sides for the supply constraints, and cells B22:E22 contain the right-hand sides for the demand constraints.

Cell H17 = F5 (Copy to H18:H19)
Cell B22 = B8 (Copy to C22:E22)

Excel Solution

The solution shown in Figure 7.14 can be obtained by selecting **Solver** from the **Tools** menu, entering the proper values into the **Solver Parameters** dialog box, selecting **Standard Simplex LP,** and specifying the option **Assume Non-Negative.** Then click **Solve.** The information entered into the **Solver Parameters** dialog box is shown in Figure 7.15.

Assignment Problem

The first step is to enter the data for the assignment costs in the top portion of the worksheet. Even though the assignment model is a special case of the transportation model, it is not necessary to enter values for origin supplies and destination demands because they are always equal to one.

The linear programming model is developed in the bottom portion of the worksheet. As with all linear programs the model has four key elements: the decision variables, the objective function, the constraint left-hand sides, and the constraint right-hand sides. For an

FIGURE 7.15 SOLVER PARAMETERS DIALOG BOX FOR THE FOSTER GENERATORS PROBLEM

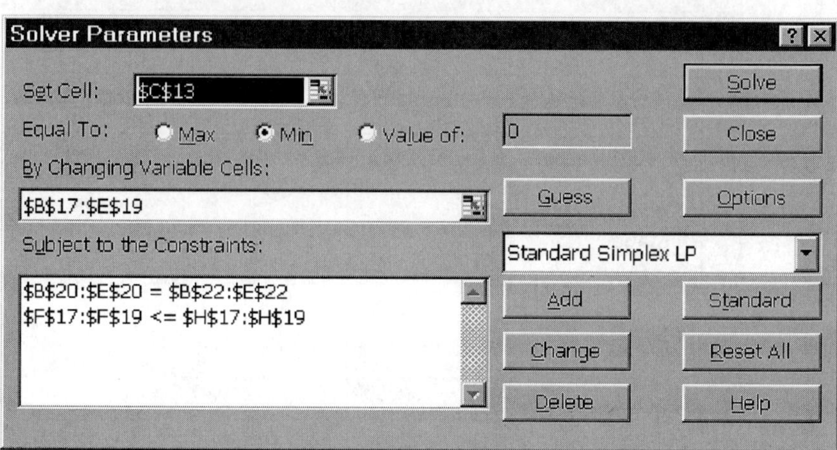

assignment problem the decision variables indicate whether an agent is assigned to a task (with a 1 for yes or 0 for no); the objective function is the total cost of all assignments; the constraint left-hand sides are the number of tasks that are assigned to each agent and the number of agents that are assigned to each task; and the right-hand sides are the number of tasks each agent can handle (1) and the number of agents each task requires (1).

The worksheet formulation and solution for the Fowle Marketing Research Problem (see Section 7.2) are shown in Figure 7.16.

Formulation

The data and descriptive labels are contained in cells A1:D7. Note that we have not inserted supply and demand values because they are always equal to 1 in an assignment problem. The model appears in the bottom portion of the worksheet with the key elements screened.

Decision Variables — Cells B16:D18 are reserved for the decision variables. The optimal values are shown to be $x_{12} = 1$, $x_{23} = 1$, and $x_{31} = 1$ with all other variables = 0.

Objective Function — The formula =SUMPRODUCT(B5:D7,B16:D18) has been placed into cell C12 to compute the number of days required to complete all the jobs. The minimum time solution has a value of 26 days.

Left-Hand Sides — Cells E16:E18 contain the left-hand sides of the constraints for the number of clients each project leader can handle. Cells B19:D19 contain the left-hand sides of the constraints requiring that each client must be assigned a project leader.

Cell E16 =SUM(B16:D16) (Copy to E17:E18)
Cell B19 =SUM(B16:B18) (Copy to C19:D19)

Right-Hand Sides — Cells G16:G18 contain the right-hand sides for the project leader constraints and cells B21:D21 contain the right-hand sides for the client constraints. All right-hand side cell values are 1.

FIGURE 7.16 EXCEL SOLUTION OF THE FOWLE MARKETING RESEARCH PROBLEM

	A	B	C	D	E	F	G	H
1	**Fowle Marketing Research**							
2								
3			**Client**					
4	**Project Leader**	1	2	3				
5	Terry	10	15	9				
6	Carle	9	18	5				
7	McClymonds	6	14	3				
8								
9								
10	**Model**							
11								
12		Min Time	26					
13								
14			**Client**					
15	**Project Leader**	1	2	3	**Total**			
16	Terry	0	1	0	1	<=	1	
17	Carle	0	0	1	1	<=	1	
18	McClymonds	1	0	0	1	<=	1	
19	**Total**	1	1	1				
20		=	=	=				
21		1	1	1				
22								

EXCELfile
Fowle

Excel Solution

The solution shown in Figure 7.16 can be obtained by selecting **Solver** from the **Tools** menu, entering the proper values into the **Solver Parameters** dialog box, selecting **Standard Simplex LP**, and specifying the option **Assume Non-Negative.** Then click **Solve.** The information entered into the **Solver Parameters** dialog box is shown in Figure 7.17.

Transshipment Problem

The worksheet model we present for the transshipment problem can be used for all the network flow problems (transportation, assignment, and transshipment) in this chapter. We organize the worksheet into two sections: an arc section and a node section. Let us illustrate by showing the worksheet formulation and solution of the Ryan Electronics transshipment problem (see Section 7.3). Refer to Figure 7.18 as we describe the steps involved. The key elements are screened.

Formulation

The arc section uses cells A3:D16. For each arc, the start node and end node are identified in cells A5:B16. The arc costs are identified in cells C5:C16, and cells D5:D16 are reserved for the values of the decision variables (the amount shipped over the arcs).

FIGURE 7.17 SOLVER PARAMETERS DIALOG BOX FOR THE FOWLE MARKETING RESEARCH PROBLEM

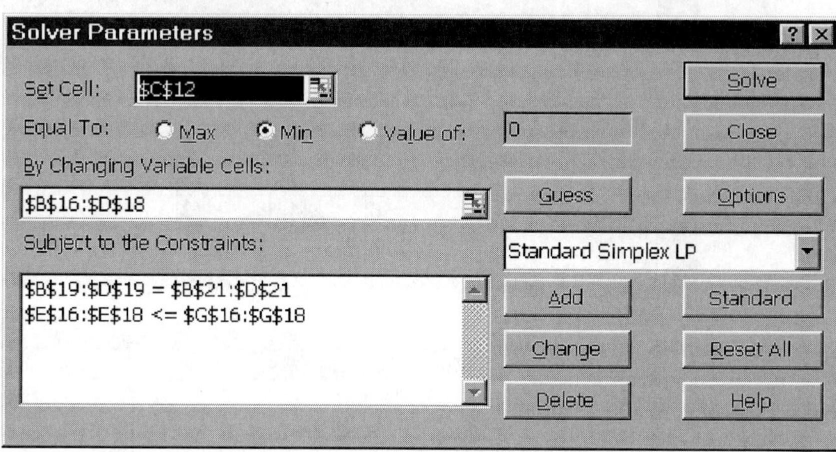

The node section uses cells F5:K14. Each of the nodes is identified in cells F7:F14. The following formulas are entered into cells G7:H14 to represent the flow out and the flow in for each node.

Units shipped in:	Cell G9	=D5+D7
	Cell G10	=D6+D8
	Cell G11	=D9+D13
	Cell G12	=D10+D14
	Cell G13	=D11+D15
	Cell G14	=D12+D16

FIGURE 7.18 EXCEL SOLUTION FOR THE RYAN ELECTRONICS PROBLEM

	A	B	C	D	E	F	G	H	I	J	K
1	**Ryan Electronics Transshipment**										
2											
3	**Arc**			**Units**							
4	**Start Node**	**End Node**	**Cost**	**Shipped**							
5	Denver	Kansas City	2	550			**Units Shipped**		**Net**		
6	Denver	Louisville	3	50		**Node**	In	Out	**Shipments**		**Supply**
7	Atlanta	Kansas City	3	0		Denver		600	600	<=	600
8	Atlanta	Louisville	1	400		Atlanta		400	400	<=	400
9	Kansas City	Detroit	2	200		Kansas City	550	550	0	=	0
10	Kansas City	Miami	6	0		Louisville	450	450	0	=	0
11	Kansas City	Dallas	3	350		Detroit	200		-200	=	-200
12	Kansas City	New Orleans	6	0		Miami	150		-150	=	-150
13	Louisville	Detroit	4	0		Dallas	350		-350	=	-350
14	Louisville	Miami	4	150		New Orleans	300		-300	=	-300
15	Louisville	Dallas	6	0							
16	Louisville	New Orleans	5	300							
17											
18								**Total Cost**	5200		
19											

Units shipped out:	Cell H7	=SUM(D5:D6)
	Cell H8	=SUM(D7:D8)
	Cell H9	=SUM(D9:D12)
	Cell H10	=SUM(D13:D16)

The net shipments in cells I7:I14 are the flows out minus the flows in for each node. For supply nodes, the flow out will exceed the flow in resulting in positive net shipments. For demand nodes, the flow out will be less than the flow in resulting in negative net shipments. The "net" supply appears in cells K7:K14. Note that the net supply is negative for demand nodes.

As in previous worksheet formulations, we screened the key elements required by the Excel Solver.

Decision Variables: Cells D5:D16 are reserved for the decision variables. The optimal number of units to ship over each arc is shown.

Objective Function: The formula =SUMPRODUCT(C5:C16,D5:D16) is placed into cell I18 to show the total cost associated with the solution. As shown, the minimum total cost is $5200.

Left-Hand Sides: The left-hand sides of the constraints represent the net shipments for each node. Cells I7:I14 are reserved for these constraints.

Cell I7 =H7-G7 (Copy to I8:I14)

Right-Hand Sides: The right-hand sides of the constraints represent the supply at each node. Cells K7:K14 are reserved for these values. (Note the negative supply at the four demand nodes.)

Excel Solution

The solution can be obtained by selecting **Solver** from the **Tools** menu, entering the proper values into the **Solver Parameters** dialog box, selecting **Standard Simplex LP,** and specifying the option **Assume Non-Negative.** Then click **Solve.** The information entered into the **Solver Parameters** dialog box is shown in Figure 7.19.

FIGURE 7.19 SOLVER PARAMETERS DIALOG BOX FOR THE RYAN ELECTRONICS PROBLEM

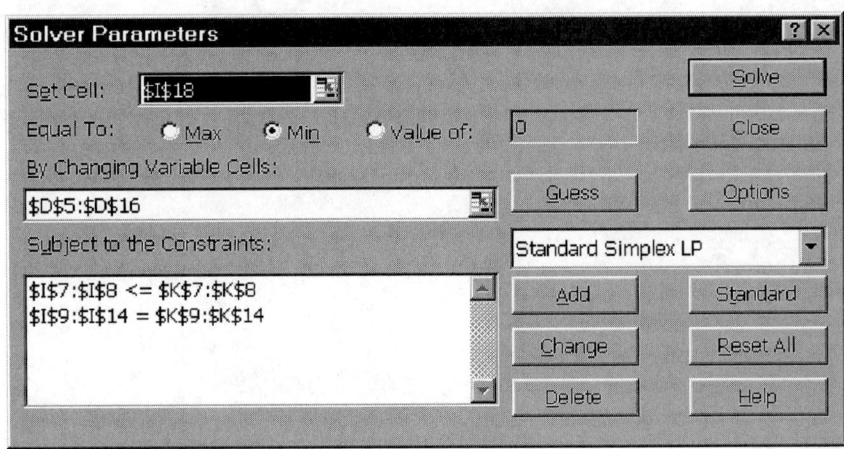

CHAPTER 8

Integer Linear Programming

CONTENTS

In this chapter we discuss a class of problems that are modeled as linear programs with the additional requirement that one or more variables must be integer. Such problems are called **integer linear programs.** If all variables must be integer, we have an all-integer linear program. If some, but not all, variables must be integer, we have a mixed-integer linear program. In many applications of integer linear programming, one or more integer variables are required to equal either 0 or 1. Such variables are called 0-1 or *binary variables.* If all variables are 0-1 variables, we have a 0-1 integer linear program.

Integer variables—especially 0-1 variables—provide substantial modeling flexibility. As a result, the number of applications that can be addressed with linear programming methodology is expanded. For instance, the Management Science in Action, Crew Scheduling at Air New Zealand, describes how that airline company employs 0-1 integer programming models to schedule its pilots and flight attendants. Later Management Science in Actions describe how Valley Metal Containers uses a mixed-integer program for scheduling aluminum can production for Coors beer, and how a mixed-integer programming model developed by Bellcore helps its clients save money using business volume discounts. Many other applications of integer programming are described throughout the chapter.

The objective of this chapter is to provide an applications-oriented introduction to integer linear programming. First, we discuss the different types of integer linear programming models. Then we show the formulation, graphical solution, and computer solution of an all-integer linear program. In Section 8.3, we discuss five applications of integer linear programming that make use of 0-1 variables: capital budgeting, fixed cost, distribution system design, bank location, and market share optimization problems. In Section 8.4, we provide additional illustrations of the modeling flexibility provided by 0-1 variables. A chapter appendix illustrates the use of Excel for solving integer programs.

The cost of the added modeling flexibility provided by integer programming is that problems involving integer variables are often much more difficult to solve. A linear programming problem with several thousand continuous variables can be solved with any of several commercial linear programming solvers. However, an all-integer linear programming problem with less than 100 variables can be extremely difficult to solve. Experienced management scientists can help identify the types of integer linear programs that are easy, or at least reasonable, to solve. Commercial computer software packages, such as MPSX-MIP®, OSL®, CPLEX®, and LINDO, have extensive integer programming capability. The Management Scientist and spreadsheet packages, such as Excel, have the capability for solving smaller integer linear programs.

MANAGEMENT SCIENCE IN ACTION

CREW SCHEDULING AT AIR NEW ZEALAND*

As noted in Chapter 1, airlines make extensive use of management science (see Management Science in Action, Revenue Management at American Airlines). Air New Zealand is the largest national and international airline based in New Zealand. Over the past 15 years, Air New Zealand developed integer programming models for crew scheduling.

Air New Zealand finalizes flight schedules at least 12 weeks in advance of when the flights are to take place. At that point the process of assigning crews to implement the flight schedule begins. The crew-scheduling problem involves staffing the flight schedule with pilots and flight attendants. It is solved in two phases. In the first phase, tours of duty (ToD) are generated that will permit constructing sequences of flights for pilots and flight attendants that will allow the airline's flight schedule to be implemented. A tour of duty is a one-day or multiday alternating sequence of duty periods (flight legs, training, etc.) and rest periods (layovers).

(*continued*)

In the ToD problem, no consideration is given to which individual crew members will perform the tours of duty. In the second phase, individual crew members are assigned to the tours of duty, which is called the rostering problem.

Air New Zealand employs integer programming models to solve both the ToD problem and the rostering problem. In the integer programming model of the ToD problem, each variable is a 0-1 variable that corresponds to a possible tour of duty that could be flown by a crew member (e.g., pilot or flight attendant). Each constraint corresponds to a particular flight and ensures that the flight is included in exactly one tour of duty. The cost of variable j reflects the cost of operating the jth tour of duty, and the objective is to minimize total cost. Air New Zealand solves a separate ToD problem for each crew type (pilot type or flight attendant type).

In the rostering problem, the tours of duty from the solution to the ToD problem are used to construct lines of work (LoW) for each crew member. In the integer programming model of the rostering problem, a 0-1 variable represents the possible LoWs for each crew member. A separate constraint for each crew member guarantees that each will be assigned a single LoW. Other constraints correspond to the ToDs that must be covered by any feasible solution to the rostering problem.

The crew-scheduling optimizers developed by Air New Zealand showed a significant impact on profitability. Over the 15 years it took to develop these systems, the estimated development costs were approximately NZ$2 million. The estimated savings are NZ$15.6 million per year. In 1999 the savings from employing these integer programming models represented 11% of Air New Zealand's net operating profit. In addition to the direct dollar savings, the optimization systems provided many intangible benefits such as higher-quality solutions in less time, less dependence on a small number of highly skilled schedulers, flexibility to accommodate small changes in the schedule, and a guarantee that the airline satisfies legislative and contractual rules.

*Based on E. Rod Butchers et al., "Optimized Crew Scheduling at Air New Zealand," *Interfaces* (January/February 2001): 30–56.

NOTES AND COMMENTS

1. Because integer linear programs are harder to solve than linear programs, one should not try to solve a problem as an integer program if simply rounding the linear programming solution is adequate. In many linear programming problems, such as those in previous chapters, rounding has little economic consequence on the objective function, and feasibility is not an issue. But, in problems such as determining how many jet engines to manufacture, the consequences of rounding can be substantial and integer programming methodology should be employed.
2. Some linear programming problems have a special structure, which guarantees that the variables will have integer values. The assignment, transportation, and transshipment problems of Chapter 7 have such structures. If the supply and the demand for transportation and transshipment problems are integer, the optimal linear programming solution will provide integer amounts shipped. For the assignment problem, the optimal linear programming solution will consist of 0s and 1s. So, for these specially structured problems, linear programming methodology can be used to find optimal integer solutions. Integer linear programming algorithms are not necessary.

8.1 TYPES OF INTEGER LINEAR PROGRAMMING MODELS

The only difference between the problems studied in this chapter and the ones studied in earlier chapters on linear programming is that one or more variables are required to be integer. If all variables are required to be integer, we have an **all-integer linear program.** The following is a two-variable, all-integer linear programming model.

$$
\begin{aligned}
\text{Max} \quad & 2x_1 + 3x_2 \\
\text{s.t.} \quad & \\
& 3x_1 + 3x_2 \le 12 \\
& \tfrac{2}{3}x_1 + 1x_2 \le 4 \\
& 1x_1 + 2x_2 \le 6 \\
& x_1, x_2 \ge 0 \text{ and integer}
\end{aligned}
$$

If we drop the phrase "and integer" from the last line of this model, we have the familiar two-variable linear program. The linear program that results from dropping the integer requirements is called the **LP Relaxation** of the integer linear program.

If some, but not necessarily all, variables are required to be integer, we have a **mixed-integer linear program.** The following is a two-variable, mixed-integer linear program.

$$
\begin{aligned}
\text{Max} \quad & 3x_1 + 4x_2 \\
\text{s.t.} \quad & \\
& -1x_1 + 2x_2 \le 8 \\
& 1x_1 + 2x_2 \le 12 \\
& 2x_1 + 1x_2 \le 16 \\
& x_1, x_2 \ge 0 \textit{ and } x_2 \text{ integer}
\end{aligned}
$$

We obtain the LP Relaxation of this mixed-integer linear program by dropping the requirement that x_2 be integer.

In some applications, the integer variables may only take on the values 0 or 1. Then we have a **0-1 linear integer program.** As we see later in the chapter, 0-1 variables provide additional modeling capability. The Management Science in Action, Aluminum Can Production at Valley Metal Container, describes how a mixed-integer linear program involving 0-1 integer variables is used to schedule production of aluminum beer cans for Coors breweries. The 0-1 variables are used to model production line changeovers; the continuous variables model production quantities.

MANAGEMENT SCIENCE IN ACTION

ALUMINUM CAN PRODUCTION AT VALLEY METAL CONTAINER*

Valley Metal Container (VMC) produces cans for the seven brands of beer produced by the Coors breweries: Coors Extra Gold, Coors Light, Coors Original, Keystone Ale, Keystone Ice, Keystone Light, and Keystone Premium. VMC produces these cans on six production lines and stores them in three separate inventory storage areas from which they are shipped on to the Coors breweries in Golden, Colorado; Memphis, Tennessee; and Shenandoah, Virginia.

Two important issues face production scheduling at the VMC facility. First, each time a production line must be changed over from producing one type of can to another (label change), it takes time to get the color just right for the new label. As a result, downtime is incurred and scrap is generated. Second, proper scheduling can reduce the amount of inventory that must be transferred from long-term to short-term storage. Thus, two costs are critical in determining the best production schedule at the VMC facility: the label-change cost and the cost of transferring inventory from one type of storage to another. To determine a production schedule that will minimize these two costs, VMC developed a mixed-integer linear programming model of its production process.

The model's objective function calls for minimizing the sum of the weekly cost of changing labels

(continued)

and the cost of transferring inventory from long-term to short-term storage. Binary (0-1) variables are used to represent a label change in the production process. Continuous variables are used to represent the size of the production run for each type of label on each line during each shift; analogous variables are used to represent inventories for each type of can produced. Additional continuous variables are used to represent the amount of inventory transferred to short-term storage during the week.

The VMC production scheduling problem is solved weekly using a personal computer. Excel worksheets are used for input data preparation and for storing the output report. The GAMS mathematical programming system is used to solve the mixed-integer linear program. Susan Schultz, manager of Logistics for Coors Container Operations, reports that using the system resulted in documented annual savings of $169,230.

*Based on Elena Katok and Dennis Ott, "Using Mixed-Integer Programming to Reduce Label Changes in the Coors Aluminum Can Plant," *Interfaces* (March/April 2000): 1–12.

8.2 GRAPHICAL AND COMPUTER SOLUTIONS FOR AN ALL-INTEGER LINEAR PROGRAM

Eastborne Realty has $2 million available for the purchase of new rental property. After an initial screening, Eastborne reduced the investment alternatives to townhouses and apartment buildings. Each townhouse can be purchased for $282,000, and five are available. Each apartment building can be purchased for $400,000, and the developer will construct as many buildings as Eastborne wants to purchase.

Eastborne's property manager can devote up to 140 hours per month to these new properties; each townhouse is expected to require 4 hours per month, and each apartment building is expected to require 40 hours per month. The annual cash flow, after deducting mortgage payments and operating expenses, is estimated to be $10,000 per townhouse and $15,000 per apartment building. Eastborne's owner would like to determine the number of townhouses and the number of apartment buildings to purchase to maximize annual cash flow.

We begin by defining the decision variables as follows:

$$T = \text{number of townhouses}$$
$$A = \text{number of apartment buildings}$$

The objective function for cash flow ($1000s) is

$$\text{Max} \quad 10T + 15A$$

Three constraints must be satisfied:

$$\begin{aligned} 282T + 400A &\leq 2000 \quad \text{Funds available (\$1000s)} \\ 4T + 40A &\leq 140 \quad \text{Manager's time (hours)} \\ T &\leq 5 \quad \text{Townhouses available} \end{aligned}$$

The variables T and A must be nonnegative. In addition, the purchase of a fractional number of townhouses and/or a fractional number of apartment buildings is unacceptable. Thus, T and A must be integer. The model for the Eastborne Realty problem is the following all-integer linear program.

$$\begin{aligned} \text{Max} \quad & 10T + 15A \\ \text{s.t.} \quad & \\ & 282T + 400A \leq 2000 \\ & 4T + 40A \leq 140 \\ & T \leq 5 \\ & T, A \geq 0 \text{ and integer} \end{aligned}$$

Graphical Solution of the LP Relaxation

Suppose that we drop the integer requirements for T and A and solve the LP Relaxation of the Eastborne Realty problem. Using the graphical solution procedure, as presented in Chapter 2, the optimal linear programming solution is shown in Figure 8.1. It is $T = 2.479$ townhouses and $A = 3.252$ apartment buildings. The optimal value of the objective function is 73.574, which indicates an annual cash flow of $73,574. Unfortunately, Eastborne cannot purchase fractional numbers of townhouses and apartment buildings; further analysis is necessary.

FIGURE 8.1 GRAPHICAL SOLUTION TO THE LP RELAXATION OF THE EASTBORNE REALTY PROBLEM

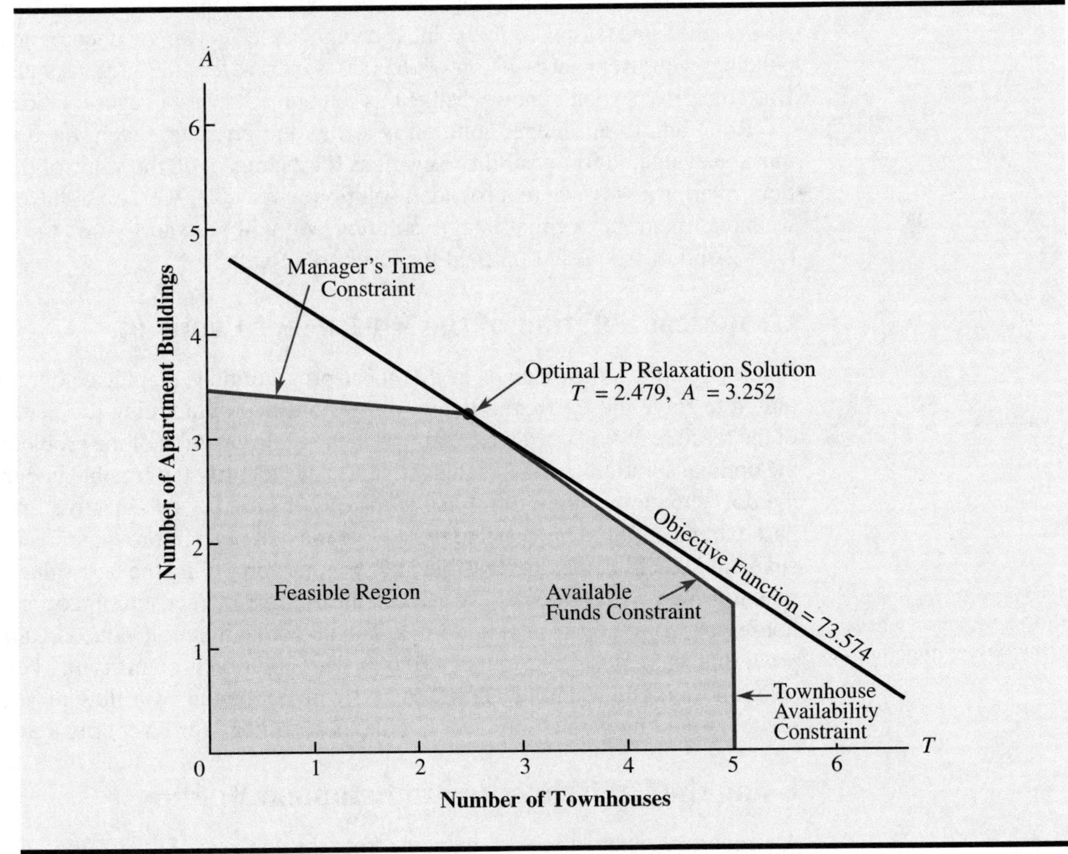

Rounding to Obtain an Integer Solution

In many cases, a noninteger solution can be rounded to obtain an acceptable integer solution. For instance, a linear programming solution to a production scheduling problem might call for the production of 15,132.4 cases of breakfast cereal. The rounded integer solution of 15,132 cases would probably have minimal impact on the value of the objective function and the feasibility of the solution. Rounding would be a sensible approach. Indeed, whenever rounding has a minimal impact on the objective function and constraints, most managers find it acceptable. A near-optimal solution is fine.

However, rounding may not always be a good strategy. When the decision variables take on small values that have a major impact on the value of the objective function or feasibility, an optimal integer solution is needed. Let us return to the Eastborne Realty problem and examine the impact of rounding. The optimal solution to the LP Relaxation for Eastborne Realty resulted in $T = 2.479$ townhouses and $A = 3.252$ apartment buildings. Because each townhouse costs \$282,000 and each apartment building costs \$400,000, rounding to an integer solution can be expected to have a significant economic impact on the problem.

If a problem has only less-than-or-equal-to constraints with positive coefficients for the variables, rounding down will always provide a feasible integer solution.

Suppose that we round the solution to the LP Relaxation to obtain the integer solution $T = 2$ and $A = 3$, with an objective function value of $10(2) + 15(3) = 65$. The annual cash flow of \$65,000 is substantially less than the annual cash flow of \$73,574 provided by the solution to the LP Relaxation. Do other rounding possibilities exist? Exploring other rounding alternatives shows that the integer solution $T = 3$ and $A = 3$ is infeasible because it requires more funds than the \$2,000,000 Eastborne has available. The rounded solution of $T = 2$ and $A = 4$ is also infeasible for the same reason. At this point, rounding has led to two townhouses and three apartment buildings with an annual cash flow of \$65,000 as the best feasible integer solution to the problem. Unfortunately, we don't know whether this solution is the best integer solution to the problem.

Rounding to an integer solution is a trial-and-error approach. Each rounded solution must be evaluated for feasibility as well as for its impact on the value of the objective function. Even in cases where a rounded solution is feasible, we do not have a guarantee that we have found the optimal integer solution. We will see shortly that the rounded solution ($T = 2$ and $A = 3$) is not optimal for Eastborne Realty.

Graphical Solution of the All-Integer Problem

Figure 8.2 shows the changes in the linear programming graphical solution procedure required to solve the Eastborne Realty integer linear programming problem. First, the graph of the feasible region is drawn exactly as in the LP Relaxation of the problem. Then, because the optimal solution must have integer values, we identify the feasible integer solutions with the dots shown in Figure 8.2. Finally, instead of moving the objective function line to the best extreme point in the feasible region, we move it in an improving direction as far as possible until reaching the dot (feasible integer point) providing the best value for the objective function. Viewing Figure 8.2, we see that the optimal integer solution occurs at $T = 4$ townhouses and $A = 2$ apartment buildings. The objective function value is $10(4) + 15(2) = 70$ providing an annual cash flow of \$70,000. This solution is significantly better than the best solution found by rounding: $T = 2$, $A = 3$ with an annual cash flow of \$65,000. Thus, we see that rounding would not have been the best strategy for Eastborne Realty.

Try Problem 2 for practice with the graphical solution of an integer program.

Using the LP Relaxation to Establish Bounds

An important observation can be made from the analysis of the Eastborne Realty problem. It has to do with the relationship between the value of the optimal integer solution and the value of the optimal solution to the LP Relaxation.

For integer linear programs involving maximization, the value of the optimal solution to the LP Relaxation provides an upper bound on the value of the optimal integer solution. For integer linear programs involving minimization, the value of the optimal solution to the LP Relaxation provides a lower bound on the value of the optimal integer solution.

This observation is valid for the Eastborne Realty problem. The value of the optimal integer solution is \$70,000, and the value of the optimal solution to the LP Relaxation is \$73,574. Thus, we know from the LP Relaxation solution that the upper bound for the value of the objective function is \$73,574.

Try Problem 5 for the graphical solution of a mixed-integer program.

The bounding property of the LP Relaxation allows us to conclude that if, by chance, the solution to an LP Relaxation turns out to be an integer solution, it is also optimal for the integer linear program. This bounding property can also be helpful in determining whether a rounded solution is "good enough." If a rounded LP Relaxation solution is feasible and provides a value of the objective function that is "almost as good as" the value of the objective function for the LP Relaxation, we know the rounded solution is a near-optimal integer solution. In this case, we can avoid having to solve the problem as an integer linear program.

FIGURE 8.2 GRAPHICAL SOLUTION OF THE EASTBORNE REALTY INTEGER PROBLEM

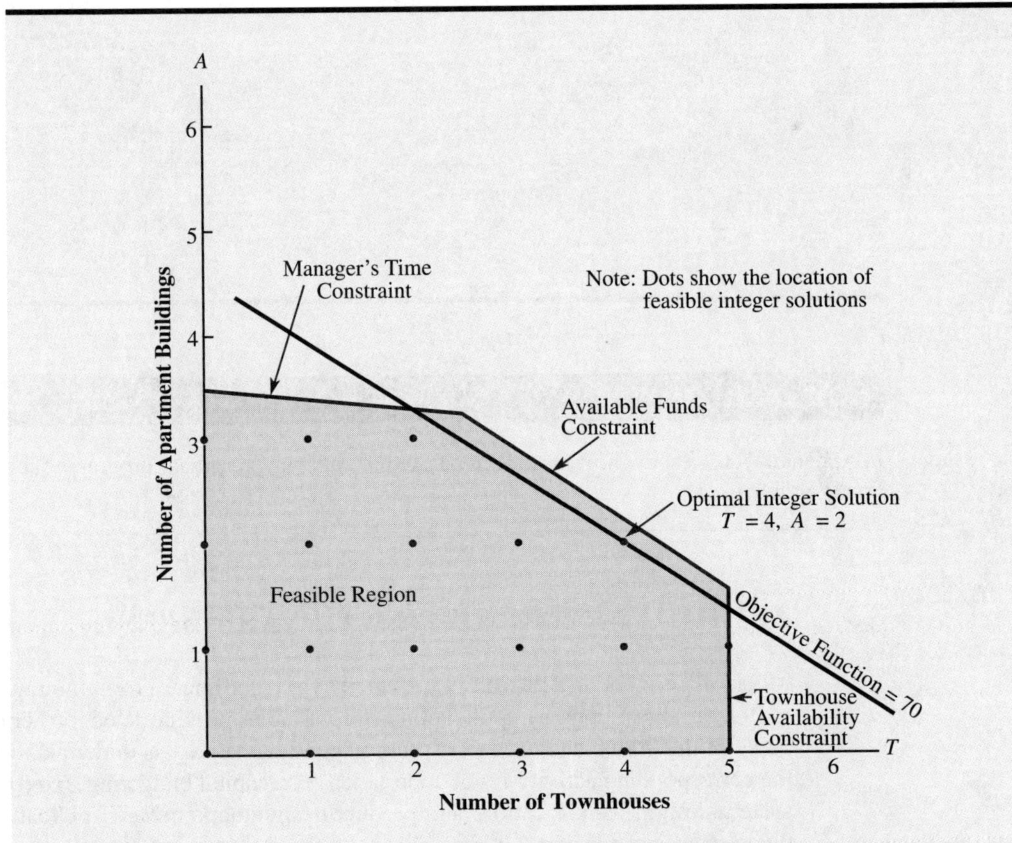

Computer Solution

As mentioned earlier, commercial software packages that can solve integer linear programs are widely available. Generally, these packages are reliable for problems having up to approximately 100 integer variables and may be used to solve specially structured problems with several thousand integer variables.

The Management Scientist can be used to solve most of the integer linear programs in this chapter. To use The Management Scientist to solve the Eastborne Realty problem, the data input worksheet is completed in the same way as for any linear program (see Appendix 2.1). Then after instructing the computer to solve the problem, the user will be asked to indicate which of the variables are integer. Specifying both T and A as integers provides the optimal integer solution shown in Figure 8.3. The solution of $T = 4$ townhouses and $A = 2$ apartment buildings has a maximum annual cash flow of $70,000. The values of the slack variables tell us that the optimal solution has $72,000 of available funds unused, 44 hours of the manager's time still available, and 1 of the available townhouses not purchased.

FIGURE 8.3 THE MANAGEMENT SCIENTIST SOLUTION FOR THE EASTBORNE REALTY PROBLEM

EXCELfile
Eastborne

```
Objective Function Value =    70.000

    Variable              Value
 --------------      ---------------
        T                     4.000
        A                     2.000

   Constraint           Slack/Surplus
 --------------      ---------------
        1                    72.000
        2                    44.000
        3                     1.000
```

NOTES AND COMMENTS

In Appendix 8.1 we show how Excel can be used to solve integer linear programs such as the Eastborne Realty problem.

8.3 APPLICATIONS INVOLVING 0-1 VARIABLES

Much of the modeling flexibility provided by integer linear programming is due to the use of 0-1 variables. In many applications, 0-1 variables provide selections or choices with the value of the variable equal to 1 if a corresponding activity is undertaken and equal to 0 if the corresponding activity is not undertaken. The capital budgeting, fixed cost, distribution system design, bank location, and product design/market share applications presented in this section make use of 0-1 variables.

Capital Budgeting

The Ice-Cold Refrigerator Company is considering investing in several projects that have varying capital requirements over the next four years. Faced with limited capital each year, management would like to select the most profitable projects. The estimated net present value for each project,[1] the capital requirements, and the available capital over the four-year period are shown in Table 8.1.

The four 0-1 decision variables are as follows:

$$P = 1 \text{ if the plant expansion project is accepted; 0 if rejected}$$
$$W = 1 \text{ if the warehouse expansion project is accepted; 0 if rejected}$$
$$M = 1 \text{ if the new machinery project is accepted; 0 if rejected}$$
$$R = 1 \text{ if the new product research project is accepted; 0 if rejected}$$

In a **capital budgeting problem,** the company's objective function is to maximize the net present value of the capital budgeting projects. This problem has four constraints: one for the funds available in each of the next four years.

A 0-1 integer linear programming model with dollars in thousands is as follows:

$$
\begin{aligned}
\text{Max} \quad & 90P + 40W + 10M + 37R \\
\text{s.t.} \quad & \\
& 15P + 10W + 10M + 15R \leq 40 \quad \text{(Year 1 capital available)} \\
& 20P + 15W + 10R \leq 50 \quad \text{(Year 2 capital available)} \\
& 20P + 20W + 10R \leq 40 \quad \text{(Year 3 capital available)} \\
& 15P + 5W + 4M + 10R \leq 35 \quad \text{(Year 4 capital available)} \\
& P, W, M, R = 0, 1
\end{aligned}
$$

The integer programming solution from The Management Scientist is shown in Figure 8.4. The optimal solution is $P = 1, W = 1, M = 1, R = 0$, with a total estimated net present value of $140,000. Thus, the company should fund the plant expansion, the warehouse expansion, and the new machinery projects. The new product research project should be put on hold unless additional capital funds become available. The values of the slack variables (see

TABLE 8.1 PROJECT NET PRESENT VALUE, CAPITAL REQUIREMENTS, AND AVAILABLE CAPITAL FOR THE ICE-COLD REFRIGERATOR COMPANY

	Project				
	Plant Expansion	**Warehouse Expansion**	**New Machinery**	**New Product Research**	**Total Capital Available**
Present Value	$90,000	$40,000	$10,000	$37,000	
Year 1 Cap Rqmt	$15,000	$10,000	$10,000	$15,000	$40,000
Year 2 Cap Rqmt	$20,000	$15,000		$10,000	$50,000
Year 3 Cap Rqmt	$20,000	$20,000		$10,000	$40,000
Year 4 Cap Rqmt	$15,000	$ 5,000	$ 4,000	$10,000	$35,000

[1]The estimated net present value is the net cash flow discounted back to the beginning of year 1.

FIGURE 8.4 THE MANAGEMENT SCIENTIST SOLUTION FOR THE ICE-COLD REFRIGERATOR COMPANY PROBLEM

EXCELfile
Ice-Cold

```
Objective Function Value =  140.000

    Variable             Value
 --------------     ---------------
        P                 1.000
        W                 1.000
        M                 1.000
        R                 0.000

   Constraint         Slack/Surplus
 --------------     ---------------
        1                 5.000
        2                15.000
        3                 0.000
        4                11.000
```

Figure 8.4) show that the company will have $5,000 remaining in year 1, $15,000 remaining in year 2, and $11,000 remaining in year 4. Checking the capital requirements for the new product research project, we see that enough funds are available for this project in year 2 and year 4. However, the company would have to find additional capital funds of $10,000 in year 1 and $10,000 in year 3 to fund the new product research project.

Fixed Cost

In many applications, the cost of production has two components: a setup cost, which is a fixed cost, and a variable cost, which is directly related to the production quantity. The use of 0-1 variables makes including the setup cost possible in a model for a production application.

As an example of a **fixed cost problem,** consider the RMC problem. Three raw materials are used to produce three products: a fuel additive, a solvent base, and a carpet cleaning fluid. The following decision variables are used.

$$F = \text{tons of fuel additive produced}$$
$$S = \text{tons of solvent base produced}$$
$$C = \text{tons of carpet cleaning fluid produced}$$

The profit contributions are $40 per ton for the fuel additive, $30 per ton for the solvent base, and $50 per ton for the carpet cleaning fluid. Each ton of fuel additive is a blend of 0.4 tons of material 1 and 0.6 tons of material 3. Each ton of solvent base requires 0.5 tons of material 1, 0.2 tons of material 2, and 0.3 tons of material 3. Each ton of carpet cleaning fluid is a blend of 0.6 tons of material 1, 0.1 tons of material 2, and 0.3 tons of material 3. RMC has 20 tons of material 1, 5 tons of material 2, and 21 tons of material 3 and is interested in determining the optimal production quantities for the upcoming planning period.

A linear programming model of the RMC problem is shown.

$$\begin{aligned} \text{Max} \quad & 40F + 30S + 50C \\ \text{s.t.} \quad & \\ & 0.4F + 0.5S + 0.6C \leq 20 \quad \text{Material 1} \\ & \qquad\quad 0.2S + 0.1C \leq 5 \quad \text{Material 2} \\ & 0.6F + 0.3S + 0.3C \leq 21 \quad \text{Material 3} \\ & F, S, C \geq 0 \end{aligned}$$

Using the linear programming module of The Management Scientist, we obtained an optimal solution consisting of 27.5 tons of fuel additive, 0 tons of solvent base, and 15 tons of carpet cleaning fluid, with a value of $1850, as shown in Figure 8.5.

This linear programming formulation of the RMC problem does not include a fixed cost for production setup of the products. Suppose that the following data are available concerning the setup cost and the maximum production quantity for each of the three products.

Product	Setup Cost	Maximum Production
Fuel additive	$200	50 tons
Solvent base	$ 50	25 tons
Carpet cleaning fluid	$400	40 tons

The modeling flexibility provided by 0-1 variables can now be used to incorporate the fixed setup costs into the production model. The 0-1 variables are defined as follows:

$$\begin{aligned} SF &= 1 \text{ if the fuel additive is produced; 0 if not} \\ SS &= 1 \text{ if the solvent base is produced; 0 if not} \\ SC &= 1 \text{ if the carpet cleaning fluid is produced; 0 if not} \end{aligned}$$

Using these setup variables, the total setup cost is

$$200SF + 50SS + 400SC$$

We can now rewrite the objective function to include the setup cost. Thus, the net profit objective function becomes

$$\text{Max} \quad 40F + 30S + 50C - 200SF - 50SS - 400SC$$

FIGURE 8.5 THE MANAGEMENT SCIENTIST SOLUTION TO THE RMC PROBLEM

```
Objective Function Value =  1850.00

   Variable              Value              Reduced Costs
 --------------     ---------------     ------------------
        F                27.500                 0.000
        S                 0.000                12.500
        C                15.000                 0.000
```

Next, we must write production capacity constraints so that if a setup variable equals 0, production of the corresponding product is not permitted and, if a setup variable equals 1, production is permitted up to the maximum quantity. For the fuel additive, we do so by adding the following constraint:

$$F \leq 50SF$$

Note that, with this constraint present, production of the fuel additive is not permitted when $SF = 0$. When $SF = 1$, production of up to 50 tons of fuel additive is permitted. We can think of the setup variable as a switch. When it is off ($SF = 0$), production is not permitted; when it is on ($SF = 1$), production is permitted.

Similar production capacity constraints, using 0-1 variables, are added for the solvent base and carpet cleaning products

$$S \leq 25SS$$
$$C \leq 40SC$$

Moving all the variables to the left-hand side of the constraints provides the following fixed cost model for the RMC problem.

$$
\begin{array}{llr}
\text{Max} & 40F + 30S + 50C - 200SF - 50SS - 400SC & \\
\text{s.t.} & & \\
& 0.4F + 0.5S + 0.6C \leq 20 & \text{Material 1} \\
& 0.2S + 0.1C \leq 5 & \text{Material 2} \\
& 0.6F + 0.3S + 0.3C \leq 21 & \text{Material 3} \\
& F - 50SF \leq 0 & \text{Maximum } F \\
& S - 25SS \leq 0 & \text{Maximum } S \\
& C - 40SC \leq 0 & \text{Maximum } C \\
& F, S, C \geq 0;\ SF, SS, SC = 0, 1 &
\end{array}
$$

We solved the RMC problem with setup costs using The Management Scientist. As shown in Figure 8.6, the optimal solution shows 25 tons of fuel additive and 20 tons of solvent base. The value of the objective function after deducting the setup cost is \$1350. The setup cost for the fuel additive and the solvent base is \$200 + \$50 = \$250. The optimal solution shows $SC = 0$, which indicates that the more expensive \$400 setup cost for the carpet cleaning fluid should be avoided. Thus the carpet cleaning fluid is not produced.

The Management Science in Action, Aluminum Can Production at Valley Metal Containers (see Section 8.1), employs 0-1 fixed cost variables for production line changeovers.

The key to developing a fixed cost model is the introduction of a 0-1 variable for each fixed cost and the specification of an upper bound for the corresponding production variable. For a production quantity x, a constraint of the form $x \leq My$ can then be used to allow production when the setup variable $y = 1$ and not to allow production when the setup variable $y = 0$. The value of the maximum production quantity M should be large enough to allow for all reasonable levels of production. But research has shown that choosing values of M excessively large will slow the solution procedure.

Distribution System Design

The Martin-Beck Company operates a plant in St. Louis with an annual capacity of 30,000 units. Product is shipped to regional distribution centers located in Boston, Atlanta, and Houston. Because of an anticipated increase in demand, Martin-Beck plans to increase capacity by constructing a new plant in one or more of the following cities: Detroit, Toledo,

FIGURE 8.6 THE MANAGEMENT SCIENTIST SOLUTION TO THE RMC PROBLEM WITH SETUP COSTS

```
Objective Function Value = 1350.000

      Variable              Value
   --------------      ---------------
         F                   25.000
         S                   20.000
         C                    0.000
         SF                   1.000
         SS                   1.000
         SC                   0.000
```

EXCELfile
RMC Setup

Denver, or Kansas City. The estimated annual fixed cost and the annual capacity for the four proposed plants are as follows:

Proposed Plant	Annual Fixed Cost	Annual Capacity
Detroit	$175,000	10,000
Toledo	$300,000	20,000
Denver	$375,000	30,000
Kansas City	$500,000	40,000

The company's long-range planning group developed forecasts of the anticipated annual demand at the distribution centers as follows:

Distribution Center	Annual Demand
Boston	30,000
Atlanta	20,000
Houston	20,000

The shipping cost per unit from each plant to each distribution center is shown in Table 8.2. A network representation of the potential Martin-Beck distribution system is shown in

TABLE 8.2 SHIPPING COST PER UNIT FOR THE MARTIN-BECK DISTRIBUTION SYSTEM

	Distribution Centers		
Plant Site	**Boston**	**Atlanta**	**Houston**
Detroit	5	2	3
Toledo	4	3	4
Denver	9	7	5
Kansas City	10	4	2
St. Louis	8	4	3

Figure 8.7. Each potential plant location is shown; capacities and demands are shown in thousands of units. This network representation is for a transportation problem with a plant at St. Louis and at all four proposed sites. However, the decision has not yet been made as to which new plant or plants will be constructed.

Let us now show how 0-1 variables can be used in this **distribution system design problem** to develop a model for choosing the best plant locations and for determining how much to ship from each plant to each distribution center. We can use the following 0-1 variables to represent the plant construction decision.

$$y_1 = 1 \text{ if a plant is constructed in Detroit; 0 if not}$$
$$y_2 = 1 \text{ if a plant is constructed in Toledo; 0 if not}$$
$$y_3 = 1 \text{ if a plant is constructed in Denver; 0 if not}$$
$$y_4 = 1 \text{ if a plant is constructed in Kansas City; 0 if not}$$

The variables representing the amount shipped from each plant site to each distribution center are defined just as for a transportation problem.

$$x_{ij} = \text{the units shipped in thousands from plant } i \text{ to distribution center } j$$
$$i = 1, 2, 3, 4, 5 \quad \text{and} \quad j = 1, 2, 3$$

Using the shipping cost data in Table 8.2, the annual transportation cost in thousands of dollars is written

$$5x_{11} + 2x_{12} + 3x_{13} + 4x_{21} + 3x_{22} + 4x_{23} + 9x_{31} + 7x_{32} + 5x_{33}$$
$$+ 10x_{41} + 4x_{42} + 2x_{43} + 8x_{51} + 4x_{52} + 3x_{53}$$

The annual fixed cost of operating the new plant or plants in thousands of dollars is written as

$$175y_1 + 300y_2 + 375y_3 + 500y_4$$

Note that the 0-1 variables are defined so that the annual fixed cost of operating the new plants is only calculated for the plant or plants that are actually constructed (i.e., $y_i = 1$). If a plant is not constructed, $y_i = 0$ and the corresponding annual fixed cost is \$0.

The Martin-Beck objective function is the sum of the annual transportation cost plus the annual fixed cost of operating the newly constructed plants.

Now let us consider the capacity constraints at the four proposed plants. Using Detroit as an example, we write the following constraint:

$$x_{11} + x_{12} + x_{13} \le 10y_1$$

If the Detroit plant is constructed, $y_1 = 1$ and the total amount shipped from Detroit to the three distribution centers must be less than or equal to Detroit's 10,000-unit capacity. If the Detroit plant is not constructed, $y_1 = 0$ will result in a 0 capacity at Detroit. In this case, the variables corresponding to the shipments from Detroit must all equal zero: $x_{11} = 0$, $x_{12} = 0$, and $x_{13} = 0$. By placing all variables on the left-hand side of the constraints, we have the following Detroit capacity constraint:

$$x_{11} + x_{12} + x_{13} - 10y_1 \le 0 \quad \text{Detroit capacity}$$

FIGURE 8.7 THE NETWORK REPRESENTATION OF THE MARTIN-BECK COMPANY DISTRIBUTION SYSTEM PROBLEM

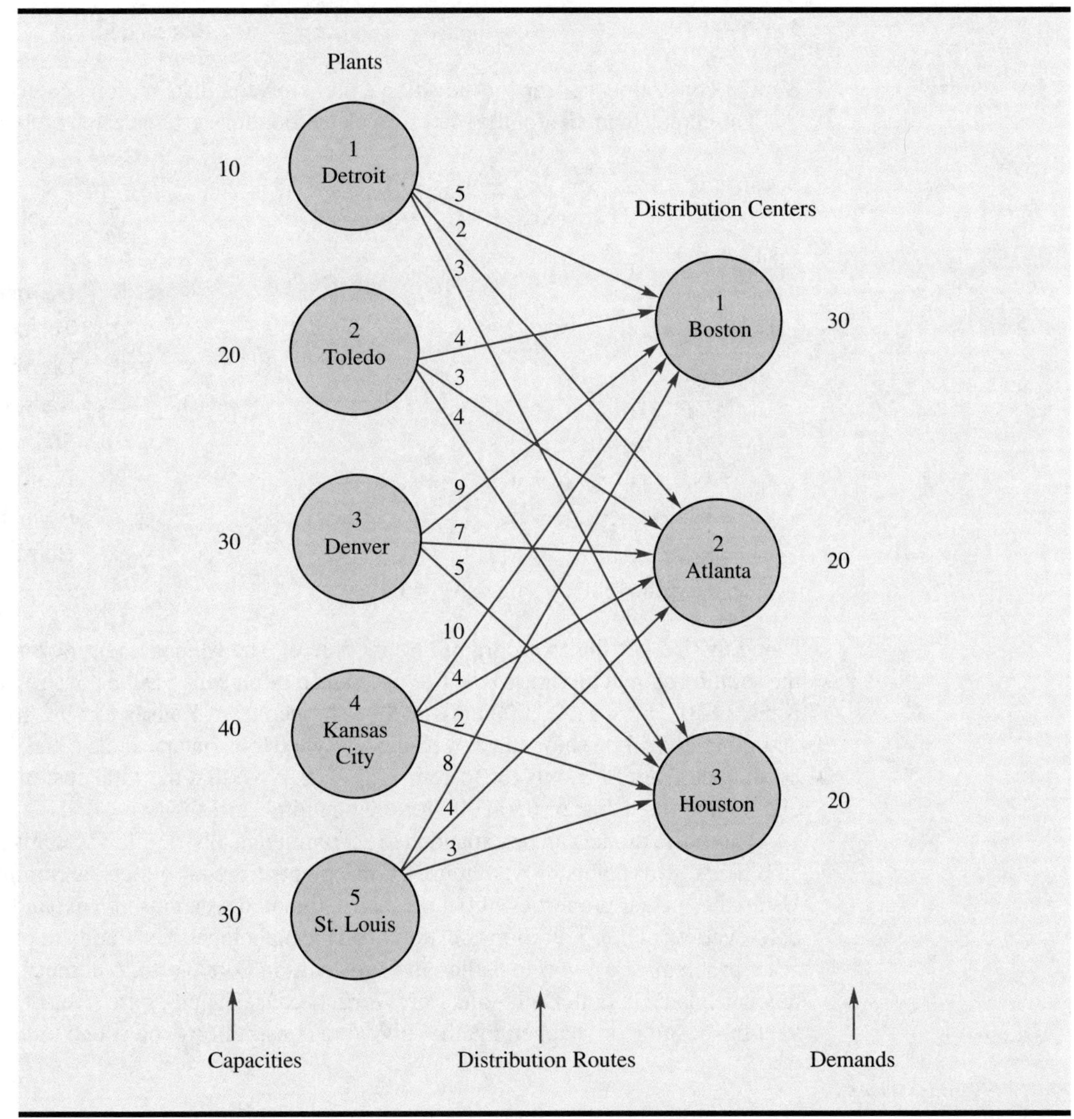

In a similar fashion, the capacity constraint for the proposed plant in Toledo can be written

$$x_{21} + x_{22} + x_{23} - 20y_2 \leq 0 \quad \text{Toledo capacity}$$

Similar constraints can be written for the proposed plants in Denver and Kansas City. Note that because a plant already exists in St. Louis, we do not define a 0-1 variable for this plant. Its capacity constraint can be written as follows:

$$x_{51} + x_{52} + x_{53} \leq 30 \quad \text{St. Louis capacity}$$

Three demand constraints will be needed, one for each of the three distribution centers. The demand constraint for the Boston distribution center with units in thousands is written as

$$x_{11} + x_{21} + x_{31} + x_{41} + x_{51} = 30 \quad \text{Boston demand}$$

Similar constraints appear for the Atlanta and Houston distribution centers.

The complete model for the Martin-Beck distribution system design problem is as follows:

$$\begin{aligned} \text{Min}\ \ & 5x_{11} + 2x_{12} + 3x_{13} + 4x_{21} + 3x_{22} + 4x_{23} + 9x_{31} + 7x_{32} + 5x_{33} + 10x_{41} + 4x_{42} \\ & + 2x_{43} + 8x_{51} + 4x_{52} + 3x_{53} + 175y_1 + 300y_2 + 375y_3 + 500y_4 \end{aligned}$$

s.t.

$$\begin{array}{lllll} x_{11} + x_{12} + x_{13} & - 10y_1 & & \leq 0 & \text{Detroit capacity} \\ x_{21} + x_{22} + x_{23} & - 20y_2 & & \leq 0 & \text{Toledo capacity} \\ x_{31} + x_{32} + x_{33} & - 30y_3 & & \leq 0 & \text{Denver capacity} \\ x_{41} + x_{42} + x_{43} & - 40y_4 & & \leq 0 & \text{Kansas City capacity} \\ x_{51} + x_{52} + x_{53} & & & \leq 30 & \text{St. Louis capacity} \\ x_{11} + x_{21} + x_{31} + x_{41} + x_{51} & & & = 30 & \text{Boston demand} \\ x_{12} + x_{22} + x_{32} + x_{42} + x_{52} & & & = 20 & \text{Atlanta demand} \\ x_{13} + x_{23} + x_{33} + x_{43} + x_{53} & & & = 20 & \text{Houston demand} \end{array}$$

$x_{ij} \geq 0$ for all i and j; $y_1, y_2, y_3, y_4 = 0, 1$

Using the integer linear programming module of The Management Scientist, we obtained the solution shown in Figure 8.8. The optimal solution calls for the construction of a plant in Kansas City ($y_4 = 1$); 20,000 units will be shipped from Kansas City to Atlanta ($x_{42} = 20$), 20,000 units will be shipped from Kansas City to Houston ($x_{43} = 20$), and 30,000 units will be shipped from St. Louis to Boston ($x_{51} = 30$). Note that the total cost of this solution including the fixed cost of \$500,000 for the plant in Kansas City is \$860,000.

This basic model can be expanded to accommodate distribution systems involving direct shipments from plants to warehouses, from plants to retail outlets, and multiple products.[2] Using the special properties of 0-1 variables, the model can also be expanded to accommodate a variety of configuration constraints on the plant locations. For example, suppose in another problem, site 1 was in Dallas and site 2 was in Fort Worth. A company might not want to locate plants in both Dallas and Fort Worth because the cities are so close together. To prevent this result from happening, the following constraint can be added to the model:

Problem 13, which is based on the Martin-Beck distribution system problem, provides additional practice involving 0-1 variables.

$$y_1 + y_2 \leq 1$$

This constraint allows either y_1 or y_2 to equal 1, but not both. If we had written the constraints as an equality, it would require that a plant be located in either Dallas or Fort Worth.

Bank Location

The long-range planning department for the Ohio Trust Company is considering expanding its operation into a 20-county region in northeastern Ohio (see Figure 8.9). Currently, Ohio Trust does not have a principal place of business in any of the 20 counties. According to the

[2] For computational reasons, it is usually preferable to replace the m plant capacity constraints with mn shipping route capacity constraints of the form $x_{ij} \leq \text{Min}\ \{s_i, d_j\}\ y_i$ for $i = 1, \ldots, m$, and $j = 1, \ldots, n$. The coefficient for y_i in each of these constraints is the smaller of the origin capacity (s_i) or the destination demand (d_j). These additional constraints often cause the solution of the LP Relaxation to be integer.

FIGURE 8.8 THE MANAGEMENT SCIENTIST SOLUTION FOR THE MARTIN-BECK COMPANY DISTRIBUTION SYSTEM PROBLEM

EXCELfile
Martin-Beck

```
OPTIMAL SOLUTION

Objective Function Value =  860.000

      Variable              Value
   --------------      ---------------
        X11                  0.000
        X12                  0.000
        X13                  0.000
        X21                  0.000
        X22                  0.000
        X23                  0.000
        X31                  0.000
        X32                  0.000
        X33                  0.000
        X41                  0.000
        X42                 20.000
        X43                 20.000
        X51                 30.000
        X52                  0.000
        X53                  0.000
        Y1                   0.000
        Y2                   0.000
        Y3                   0.000
        Y4                   1.000

     Constraint          Slack/Surplus
   --------------      ---------------
        1                    0.000
        2                    0.000
        3                    0.000
        4                    0.000
        5                    0.000
        6                    0.000
        7                    0.000
        8                    0.000
```

banking laws in Ohio, if a bank establishes a principal place of business (PPB) in any county, branch banks can be established in that county and in any adjacent county. However, to establish a new principal place of business, Ohio Trust must either obtain approval for a new bank from the state's superintendent of banks or purchase an existing bank.

Table 8.3 lists the 20 counties in the region and adjacent counties. For example, Ashtabula County is adjacent to Lake, Geauga, and Trumbull counties; Lake County is adjacent to Ashtabula, Cuyahoga, and Geauga counties; and so on.

As an initial step in its planning, Ohio Trust would like to determine the minimum number of PPBs necessary to do business throughout the 20-county region. A 0-1 integer

FIGURE 8.9 THE 20-COUNTY REGION IN NORTHEASTERN OHIO

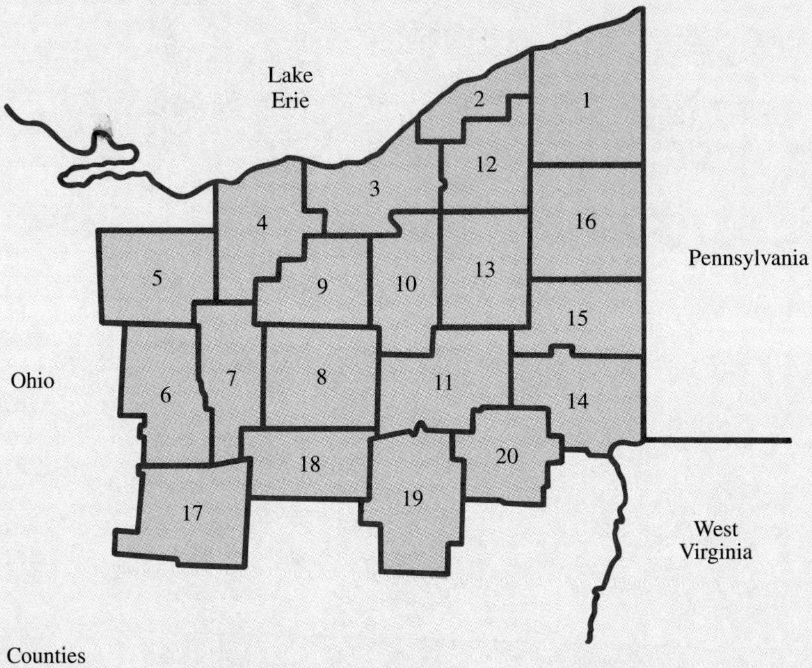

Counties

1. Ashtabula
2. Lake
3. Cuyahoga
4. Lorain
5. Huron
6. Richland
7. Ashland
8. Wayne
9. Medina
10. Summit
11. Stark
12. Geauga
13. Portage
14. Columbiana
15. Mahoning
16. Trumbull
17. Knox
18. Holmes
19. Tuscarawas
20. Carroll

programming model can be used to solve this **location problem** for Ohio Trust. We define the variables as

$$x_i = 1 \text{ if a PPB is established in county } i\text{; 0 otherwise}$$

To minimize the number of PPBs needed, we write the objective function as

$$\text{Min} \quad x_1 + x_2 + \cdots + x_{20}$$

The bank may locate branches in a county if the county contains a PPB or is adjacent to another county with a PPB. Thus, the linear program will need one constraint for each county. For example, the constraint for Ashtabula County is

$$x_1 + x_2 + x_{12} + x_{16} \geq 1 \quad \text{Ashtabula}$$

Note that satisfaction of this constraint ensures that a PPB will be placed in Ashtabula County *or* in one or more of the adjacent counties. This constraint thus guarantees that Ohio Trust will be able to place branch banks in Ashtabula County.

TABLE 8.3 COUNTIES IN THE OHIO TRUST EXPANSION REGION

Counties Under Consideration	Adjacent Counties (by Number)
1. Ashtabula	2, 12, 16
2. Lake	1, 3, 12
3. Cuyahoga	2, 4, 9, 10, 12, 13
4. Lorain	3, 5, 7, 9
5. Huron	4, 6, 7
6. Richland	5, 7, 17
7. Ashland	4, 5, 6, 8, 9, 17, 18
8. Wayne	7, 9, 10, 11, 18
9. Medina	3, 4, 7, 8, 10
10. Summit	3, 8, 9, 11, 12, 13
11. Stark	8, 10, 13, 14, 15, 18, 19, 20
12. Geauga	1, 2, 3, 10, 13, 16
13. Portage	3, 10, 11, 12, 15, 16
14. Columbiana	11, 15, 20
15. Mahoning	11, 13, 14, 16
16. Trumbull	1, 12, 13, 15
17. Knox	6, 7, 18
18. Holmes	7, 8, 11, 17, 19
19. Tuscarawas	11, 18, 20
20. Carroll	11, 14, 19

The complete statement of the bank location problem is

$$
\begin{array}{llr}
\text{Min} & x_1 + x_2 + \quad \cdots \quad + x_{20} & \\
\text{s.t.} & & \\
& x_1 + x_2 \qquad + x_{12} + x_{16} \geq 1 & \text{Ashtabula} \\
& x_1 + x_2 + x_3 + x_{12} \qquad \geq 1 & \text{Lake} \\
& \vdots & \vdots \\
& x_{11} + x_{14} + x_{19} + x_{20} \geq 1 & \text{Carroll} \\
& x_i = 0, 1 \quad i = 1, 2, \ldots, 20 &
\end{array}
$$

We used The Management Scientist to solve this 20-variable, 20-constraint problem formulation. In Figure 8.10 we show a portion of the computer output. Note that the variable names correspond to the first four letters in the name of each county. Using the output, we see that the optimal solution calls for principal places of business in Ashland, Stark, and Geauga counties. With PPBs in these three counties, Ohio Trust can place branch banks in all 20 counties (see Figure 8.11). All other decision variables have an optimal value of zero, indicating that a PPB should not be placed in these counties. Clearly the integer programming model could be enlarged to allow for expansion into a larger area or throughout the entire state.

FIGURE 8.10 THE MANAGEMENT SCIENTIST SOLUTION FOR THE OHIO TRUST PPB LOCATION PROBLEM

EXCELfile
Ohio Trust

```
OPTIMAL SOLUTION

Objective Function Value = 3.000

    Variable              Value
--------------      ---------------
     ASHT                    0.000
     LAKE                    0.000
     CUYA                    0.000
     LORA                    0.000
     HURO                    0.000
     RICH                    0.000
     ASHL                    1.000
     WAYN                    0.000
     MEDI                    0.000
     SUMM                    0.000
     STAR                    1.000
     GEAU                    1.000
     PORT                    0.000
     COLU                    0.000
     MAHO                    0.000
     TRUM                    0.000
     KNOX                    0.000
     HOLM                    0.000
     TUSC                    0.000
     CARR                    0.000
```

Product Design and Market Share Optimization

Conjoint analysis is a market research technique that can be used to learn how prospective buyers of a product value the product's attributes. In this section we will show how the results of conjoint analysis can be used in an integer programming model of a **product design and market share optimization problem.** We illustrate the approach by considering a problem facing Salem Foods, a major producer of frozen foods.

Salem Foods is planning to enter the frozen pizza market. Currently, two existing brands, Antonio's and King's, have the major share of the market. In trying to develop a sausage pizza that will capture a significant share of the market, Salem determined that the four most important attributes when consumers purchase a frozen sausage pizza are crust, cheese, sauce, and sausage flavor. The crust attribute has two levels (thin and thick); the cheese attribute has two levels (mozzarella and blend); the sauce attribute has two levels (smooth and chunky); and the sausage flavor attribute has three levels (mild, medium, and hot).

In a typical conjoint analysis, a sample of consumers is asked to express their preference for specially prepared pizzas with chosen levels for the attributes. Then regression analysis is used to determine the part-worth for each of the attribute levels. In essence, the part-worth is the utility value that a consumer attaches to each level of each attribute. A discussion of how to use regression analysis to compute the part-worths is beyond the scope

FIGURE 8.11 PRINCIPAL PLACE OF BUSINESS COUNTIES FOR OHIO TRUST

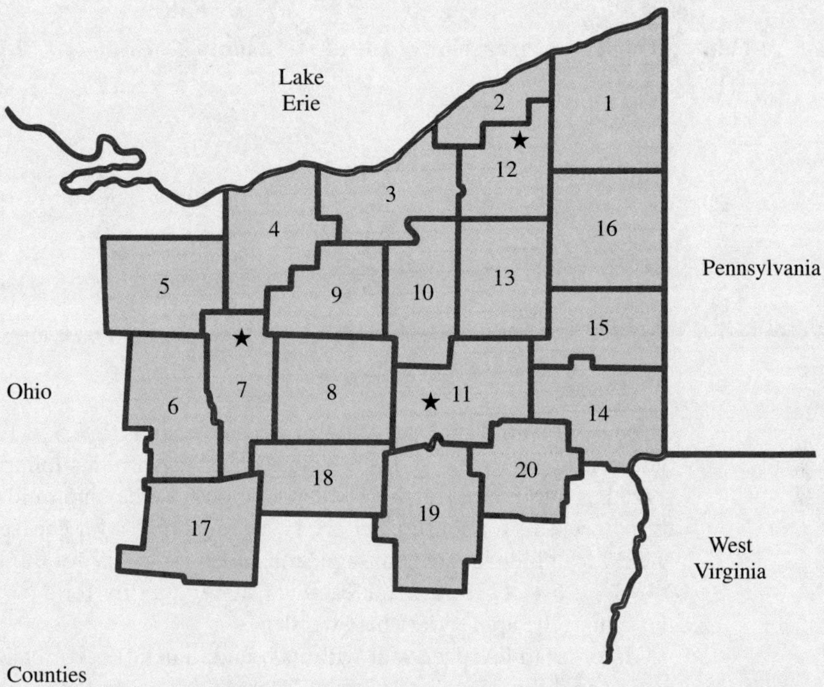

Lake Erie

Pennsylvania

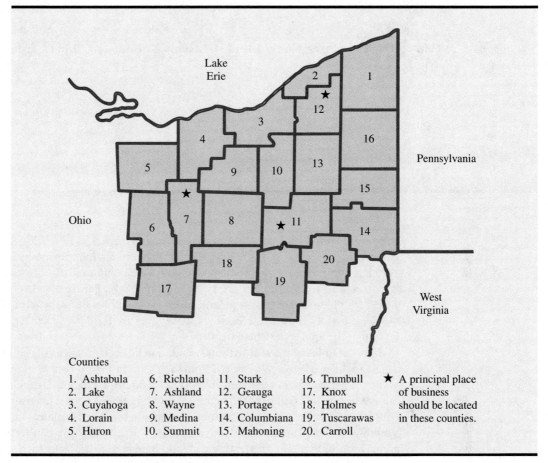

Ohio

West Virginia

Counties

1. Ashtabula	6. Richland	11. Stark	16. Trumbull	★ A principal place
2. Lake	7. Ashland	12. Geauga	17. Knox	of business
3. Cuyahoga	8. Wayne	13. Portage	18. Holmes	should be located
4. Lorain	9. Medina	14. Columbiana	19. Tuscarawas	in these counties.
5. Huron	10. Summit	15. Mahoning	20. Carroll	

of this text, but we will show how the part-worths can be used to determine the overall value a consumer attaches to a particular pizza.

Table 8.4 shows the part-worths for each level of each attribute provided by a sample of eight potential Salem customers who are currently buying either King's or Antonio's pizza. For consumer 1 the part-worths for the crust attribute are 11 for thin crust and 2 for thick crust, indicating a preference for thin crust. For the cheese attribute, the part-worths are 6 for the mozzarella cheese and 7 for the cheese blend; thus, consumer 1 has a slight preference for the cheese blend. From the other part-worths, we see that consumer 1 shows a strong preference for the chunky sauce over the smooth sauce (17 to 3) and has a slight preference for the medium-flavored sausage. Note that consumer 2 shows a preference for the thin crust, the cheese blend, the chunky sauce, and mild-flavored sausage. The part-worths for the others consumers are interpreted in a similar manner.

The part-worths can be used to determine the overall value (utility) each consumer attaches to a particular type of pizza. For instance, consumer 1's current favorite pizza is the Antonio's brand, which has a thick crust, mozzarella cheese, chunky sauce, and medium-flavored sausage. We can determine consumer 1's utility for this particular type of pizza using the part-worths in Table 8.4. For consumer 1 the part-worths are 2 for thick crust, 6 for mozzarella cheese, 17 for chunky sauce, and 27 for medium-flavored sausage. Thus,

TABLE 8.4 PART-WORTHS FOR THE SALEM FOODS PROBLEM

	Crust		Cheese		Sauce		Sausage Flavor		
Consumer	**Thin**	**Thick**	**Mozzarella**	**Blend**	**Smooth**	**Chunky**	**Mild**	**Medium**	**Hot**
1	11	2	6	7	3	17	26	27	8
2	11	7	15	17	16	26	14	1	10
3	7	5	8	14	16	7	29	16	19
4	13	20	20	17	17	14	25	29	10
5	2	8	6	11	30	20	15	5	12
6	12	17	11	9	2	30	22	12	20
7	9	19	12	16	16	25	30	23	19
8	5	9	4	14	23	16	16	30	3

consumer 1's utility for the Antonio's brand pizza is 2 + 6 + 17 + 27 = 52. We can compute consumer 1's utility for a King's brand pizza in a similar manner. The King's brand pizza has a thin crust, a cheese blend, smooth sauce, and mild-flavored sausage. Because the part-worths for consumer 1 are 11 for thin crust, 7 for cheese blend, 3 for smooth sauce, and 26 for mild-flavored sausage, consumer 1's utility for the King's brand pizza is 11 + 7 + 3 + 26 = 47. In general, each consumer's utility for a particular type of pizza is just the sum of the appropriate part-worths.

In order to be successful with its brand, Salem Foods realizes that it must entice consumers in the marketplace to switch from their current favorite brand of pizza to the Salem product. That is, Salem must design a pizza (choose the type of crust, cheese, sauce, and sausage flavor) that will have the highest utility for enough people to ensure sufficient sales to justify making the product. Assuming the sample of eight consumers in the current study is representative of the marketplace for frozen sausage pizza, we can formulate and solve an integer programming model that can help Salem come up with such a design. In marketing literature, the problem being solved is called the *share of choices* problem.

The decision variables are defined as follows:

l_{ij} = 1 if Salem chooses level i for attribute j; 0 otherwise
y_k = 1 if consumer k chooses the Salem brand; 0 otherwise

The objective is to choose the levels of each attribute that will maximize the number of consumers preferring the Salem brand pizza. Because the number of customers preferring the Salem brand pizza is just the sum of the y_k variables, the objective function is

$$\text{Max} \quad y_1 + y_2 + \cdots + y_8$$

One constraint is needed for each consumer in the sample. To illustrate how the constraints are formulated, let us consider the constraint corresponding to consumer 1. For consumer 1, the utility of a particular type of pizza can be expressed as the sum of the part-worths:

$$\text{Utility for Consumer 1} = 11l_{11} + 2l_{21} + 6l_{12} + 7l_{22} + 3l_{13} + 17l_{23} + 26l_{14} + 27l_{24} + 8l_{34}$$

In order for consumer 1 to prefer the Salem pizza, the utility for the Salem pizza must be greater than the utility for consumer 1's current favorite. Recall that consumer 1's current favorite brand of pizza is Antonio's, with a utility of 52. Thus, consumer 1 will only purchase the Salem brand if the levels of the attributes for the Salem brand are chosen such that

$$11l_{11} + 2l_{21} + 6l_{12} + 7l_{22} + 3l_{13} + 17l_{23} + 26l_{14} + 27l_{24} + 8l_{34} > 52$$

Given the definitions of the y_k decision variables, we want $y_1 = 1$ when the consumer prefers the Salem brand and $y_1 = 0$ when the consumer does not prefer the Salem brand. Thus, we write the constraint for consumer 1 as follows:

$$11l_{11} + 2l_{21} + 6l_{12} + 7l_{22} + 3l_{13} + 17l_{23} + 26l_{14} + 27l_{24} + 8l_{34} \geq 1 + 52y_1$$

With this constraint, y_1 cannot equal 1 unless the utility for the Salem design (the left-hand side of the constraint) exceeds the utility for consumer 1's current favorite by at least 1. Because the objective function is to maximize the sum of the y_k variables, the optimization will seek a product design that will allow as many y_k as possible to equal 1.

Placing all the decision variables on the left-hand side of the constraint enables us to rewrite constraint 1 as follows:

$$11l_{11} + 2l_{21} + 6l_{12} + 7l_{22} + 3l_{13} + 17l_{23} + 26l_{14} + 27l_{24} + 8l_{34} - 52y_1 \geq 1$$

A similar constraint is written for each consumer in the sample. The coefficients for the l_{ij} variables in the utility functions are taken from Table 8.4 and the coefficients for the y_k variables are obtained by computing the overall utility of the consumer's current favorite brand of pizza. The following constraints correspond to the eight consumers in the study.

Antonio's brand is the current favorite pizza for consumers 1, 4, 6, 7, and 8. King's brand is the current favorite pizza for consumers 2, 3, and 5.

$$\begin{aligned}
11l_{11} + 2l_{21} + 6l_{12} + 7l_{22} + 3l_{13} + 17l_{23} + 26l_{14} + 27l_{24} + 8l_{34} - 52y_1 &\geq 1\\
11l_{11} + 7l_{21} + 15l_{12} + 17l_{22} + 16l_{13} + 26l_{23} + 14l_{14} + 1l_{24} + 10l_{34} - 58y_2 &\geq 1\\
7l_{11} + 5l_{21} + 8l_{12} + 14l_{22} + 16l_{13} + 7l_{23} + 29l_{14} + 16l_{24} + 19l_{34} - 66y_3 &\geq 1\\
13l_{11} + 20l_{21} + 20l_{12} + 17l_{22} + 17l_{13} + 14l_{23} + 25l_{14} + 29l_{24} + 10l_{34} - 83y_4 &\geq 1\\
2l_{11} + 8l_{21} + 6l_{12} + 11l_{22} + 30l_{13} + 20l_{23} + 15l_{14} + 5l_{24} + 12l_{34} - 58y_5 &\geq 1\\
12l_{11} + 17l_{21} + 11l_{12} + 9l_{22} + 2l_{13} + 30l_{23} + 22l_{14} + 12l_{24} + 20l_{34} - 70y_6 &\geq 1\\
9l_{11} + 19l_{21} + 12l_{12} + 16l_{22} + 16l_{13} + 25l_{23} + 30l_{14} + 23l_{24} + 19l_{34} - 79y_7 &\geq 1\\
5l_{11} + 9l_{21} + 4l_{12} + 14l_{22} + 23l_{13} + 16l_{23} + 16l_{14} + 30l_{24} + 3l_{34} - 59y_8 &\geq 1
\end{aligned}$$

Four more constraints must be added, one for each attribute. These constraints are necessary to ensure that one and only one level is selected for each attribute. For attribute 1 (crust), we must add the constraint

$$l_{11} + l_{21} = 1$$

Because l_{11} and l_{21} are both 0-1 variables, this constraint requires that one of the two variables equals 1 and the other equals 0. The following three constraints ensure that one and only one level is selected for each of the other three attributes.

$$\begin{aligned}
l_{12} + l_{22} &= 1\\
l_{13} + l_{23} &= 1\\
l_{14} + l_{24} + l_{34} &= 1
\end{aligned}$$

EXCELfile
Salem

The optimal solution (obtained using LINDO)[3] to this 17-variable, 12-constraint integer linear program is $l_{11} = l_{22} = l_{23} = l_{14} = 1$ and $y_1 = y_2 = y_6 = y_7 = 1$. The value of the optimal solution is 4, indicating that if Salem makes this type of pizza it will be preferable to the current favorite for four of the eight consumers. With $l_{11} = l_{22} = l_{23} = l_{14} = 1$, the pizza design that obtains the largest market share for Salem has a thin crust, a cheese blend, a chunky sauce, and mild-flavored sausage. Note also that with $y_1 = y_2 = y_6 = y_7 = 1$, consumers 1, 2, 6, and 7 will prefer the Salem pizza. With this information Salem may choose to market this type of pizza.

NOTES AND COMMENTS

1. Most practical applications of integer linear programming involve only 0-1 integer variables. Indeed, some mixed-integer computer codes are designed to handle only integer variables with binary values. However, if a clever mathematical trick is employed, these codes can still be used for problems involving general integer variables. The trick is called *binary expansion* and requires that an upper bound be established for each integer variable. More advanced texts on integer programming show how it can be done.
2. The Management Science in Action, Analyzing Price Quotations at Bellcore, describes how 0-1 variables can be used in a model designed to take advantage of business volume discounts. Bellcore clients have saved millions of dollars by using a mixed-integer programming model.
3. General-purpose mixed-integer linear programming codes and some spreadsheet packages can be used for linear programming problems, all-integer problems, and problems involving some continuous and some integer variables. General-purpose codes are seldom the fastest for solving problems with special structure (such as the transportation, assignment, and transshipment problems); however, unless the problems are very large, speed is usually not a critical issue. Thus, most practitioners prefer to use one general-purpose computer package that can be used on a variety of problems rather than to maintain a variety of computer programs designed for special problems.

MANAGEMENT SCIENCE IN ACTION

ANALYZING PRICE QUOTATIONS AT BELLCORE*

Bellcore was formed in 1984 to provide various support services for the regional Bell operating telephone companies. To reduce the cost of buying goods and services, Bellcore client companies are increasingly requesting business volume discounts from suppliers in place of traditional quantity discounts. With traditional quantity discounts, the price of each item purchased is discounted on the basis of the amount of the item purchased. Business volume discounts differ from single-item quantity discounts in that the supplier discounts the price of each item by a percentage that is based on the total dollar volume of business over all items awarded to the supplier; whatever this percentage, it remains the same for each item. In general, a firm can realize lower overall purchasing costs with business volume discounts and a supplier can increase total revenues by obtaining a large volume of that firm's business. However, business volume discounts greatly increase the complexity of the procurement process because the discount obtained depends on the purchase quantities and prices of all products purchased.

To assist Bellcore client companies in using business volume discounts, Bellcore developed the procurement decision support system (PDSS),

[3]We noted at the beginning of this chapter that some fairly small integer programs can be difficult to solve. The combinatorial structure of the share of choices problem in this section makes it too difficult for The Management Scientist. We have solved the Salem Foods problem using LINDO. The Excel solution to this problem is contained on the CD that accompanies this text.

a PC-based decision support program that uses a mixed-integer programming model to minimize the total cost of purchases. The model uses 0-1 integer variables to model the discount categories applicable to the problem and includes a variety of constraints involving factors such as supplier capacity and limits on the dollar amount awarded to a supplier. Since 1990, one Bellcore client company reported two savings, one of $4.5 million and another of $15 million; these figures represent approximately 10% on the cost of purchases. Another client company realized a reduction of approximately 80% in the cost of analyzing quotations, and users generally believe that PDSS is a useful tool in identifying opportunities in negotiations with suppliers.

*Based on P. Katz, A. Sadrian, and P. Tendick, "Telephone Companies Analyze Price Quotations with Bellcore's PDSS Software," *Interfaces* (January/February 1994): 50–63.

8.4 MODELING FLEXIBILITY PROVIDED BY 0-1 INTEGER VARIABLES

In Section 8.3 we presented four applications involving 0-1 integer variables. In this section we continue the discussion of the use of 0-1 integer variables in modeling. First, we show how 0-1 integer variables can be used to model multiple-choice and mutually exclusive constraints. Then, we show how 0-1 integer variables can be used to model situations in which k projects out of a set of n projects must be selected, as well as situations in which the acceptance of one project is conditional on the acceptance of another. We close the section with a cautionary note on the role of sensitivity analysis in integer linear programming.

Multiple-Choice and Mutually Exclusive Constraints

Recall the Ice-Cold Refrigerator capital budgeting problem introduced in Section 8.3. The decision variables were defined as

P = 1 if the plant expansion project is accepted; 0 if rejected
W = 1 if the warehouse expansion project is accepted; 0 if rejected
M = 1 if the new machinery project is accepted; 0 if rejected
R = 1 if the new product research project is accepted; 0 if rejected

Suppose that, instead of one warehouse expansion project, the Ice-Cold Refrigerator Company actually has three warehouse expansion projects under consideration. One of the warehouses *must* be expanded because of increasing product demand, but new demand isn't sufficient to make expansion of more than one warehouse necessary. The following variable definitions and **multiple-choice constraint** could be incorporated into the previous 0-1 integer linear programming model to reflect this situation. Let

W_1 = 1 if the original warehouse expansion project is accepted; 0 if rejected
W_2 = 1 if the second warehouse expansion project is accepted; 0 if rejected
W_3 = 1 if the third warehouse expansion project is accepted; 0 if rejected

The following multiple-choice constraint reflects the requirement that exactly one of these projects must be selected:

$$W_1 + W_2 + W_3 = 1$$

If W_1, W_2, and W_3 are allowed to assume only the values 0 or 1, then one and only one of these projects will be selected from among the three choices.

If the requirement that one warehouse must be expanded did not exist, the multiple-choice constraint could be modified as follows:

$$W_1 + W_2 + W_3 \leq 1$$

This modification allows for the case of no warehouse expansion ($W_1 = W_2 = W_3 = 0$) but does not permit more than one warehouse to be expanded. This type of constraint is often called a **mutually exclusive constraint.**

k Out of *n* Alternatives Constraint

An extension of the notion of a multiple-choice constraint can be used to model situations in which *k out of a set of n* projects must be selected—a ***k* out of *n* alternatives constraint.** Suppose that W_1, W_2, W_3, W_4, and W_5 represent five potential warehouse expansion projects and that two of the five projects must be accepted. The constraint that satisfies this new requirement is

$$W_1 + W_2 + W_3 + W_4 + W_5 = 2$$

If no more than two of the projects are to be selected, we would use the following less-than-or-equal-to constraint:

$$W_1 + W_2 + W_3 + W_4 + W_5 \leq 2$$

Again, each of these variables must be restricted to 0-1 values.

Conditional and Corequisite Constraints

Sometimes the acceptance of one project is conditional on the acceptance of another. For example, suppose for the Ice-Cold Refrigerator Company that the warehouse expansion project was conditional on the plant expansion project. That is, management will not consider expanding the warehouse unless the plant is expanded. With P representing plant expansion and W representing warehouse expansion, a **conditional constraint** could be introduced to enforce this requirement:

$$W \leq P$$

Both P and W must be 0 or 1; whenever P is 0, W will be forced to 0. When P is 1, W is also allowed to be 1; thus, both the plant and the warehouse can be expanded. However, we note that the preceding constraint does not force the warehouse expansion project (W) to be accepted if the plant expansion project (P) is accepted.

If the warehouse expansion project had to be accepted whenever the plant expansion project was, and vice versa, we would say that P and W represented **corequisite constraint** projects. To model such a situation, we simply write the preceding constraint as an equality:

$$W = P$$

Try Problem 7 for practice with the modeling flexibility provided by 0-1 variables.

The constraint forces P and W to take on the same value.

The Management Science in Action, Customer Order Allocation Model at Ketron, describes how the modeling flexibility provided by 0-1 variables helped Ketron build a customer order allocation model for a sporting goods company.

MANAGEMENT SCIENCE IN ACTION

CUSTOMER ORDER ALLOCATION MODEL AT KETRON*

Ketron Management Science provides consulting services for the design and implementation of mathematical programming applications. One such application involved the development of a mixed-integer programming model of the customer order allocation problem for a major sporting goods company. The sporting goods company markets approximately 300 products and has about 30 sources of supply (factory and warehouse locations). The problem is to determine how best to allocate customer orders to the various sources of supply such that the total manufacturing cost for the products ordered is minimized. Figure 8.12 provides a graphical representation of this problem. Note in the figure that each customer can receive shipments from only a few of the various sources of supply. For example, we see that customer 1 may be supplied by source A or B, customer 2 may be supplied only by source A, and so on.

The sporting equipment company classifies each customer order as either a "guaranteed" or "secondary" order. Guaranteed orders are single-source orders in that they must be filled by a single supplier to ensure that the complete order will be delivered to the customer at one time. This single-source requirement necessitates the use of 0-1 integer variables in the model. Approximately 80% of the company's orders are guaranteed orders. Secondary orders can be split among the various sources of supply. These orders are made by customers restocking inventory, and receiving partial shipments from different sources at different times is not a problem. The 0-1 variables are used to represent the assignment of a guaranteed order to a supplier and continuous variables are used to represent the secondary orders.

Constraints for the problem involve raw material capacities, manufacturing capacities, and individual product capacities. A fairly typical problem has about 800 constraints, 2000 0-1 assignment variables, and 500 continuous variables associated with the secondary orders. The customer order allocation problem is solved periodically as orders are received. In a typical period, between 20 and 40 customers are to be supplied. Because most customers require several products, usually between 600 and 800 orders must be assigned to the sources of supply.

*Based on information provided by J. A. Tomlin of Ketron Management Science.

FIGURE 8.12 GRAPHICAL REPRESENTATION OF THE CUSTOMER ORDER ALLOCATION PROBLEM

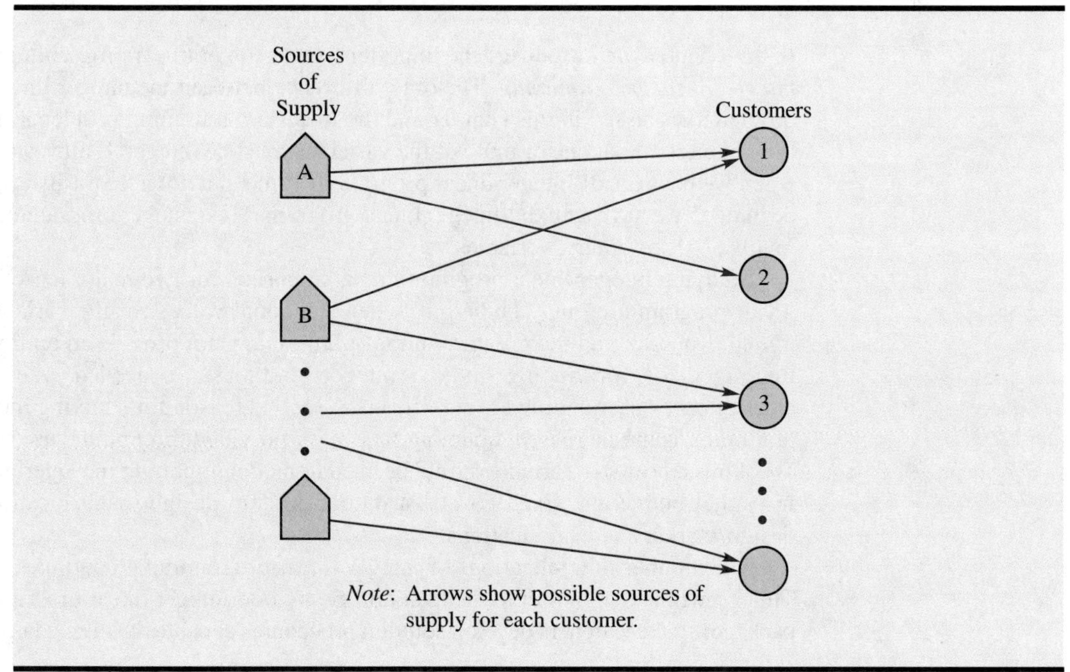

A Cautionary Note About Sensitivity Analysis

Sensitivity analysis often is more crucial for integer linear programming problems than for linear programming problems. A small change in one of the coefficients in the constraints can cause a relatively large change in the value of the optimal solution. To understand why, consider the following integer programming model of a simple capital budgeting problem involving four projects and a budgetary constraint for a single time period:

$$\begin{aligned} \text{Max} \quad & 40x_1 + 60x_2 + 70x_3 + 160x_4 \\ \text{s.t.} \quad & \\ & 16x_1 + 35x_2 + 45x_3 + 85x_4 \leq 100 \\ & x_1, x_2, x_3, x_4 = 0, 1 \end{aligned}$$

Dual prices cannot be used for integer programming sensitivity analysis because they are designed for linear programs. Multiple computer runs usually are necessary for sensitivity analysis of integer linear programs.

We can obtain the optimal solution to this problem by enumerating the alternatives. It is $x_1 = 1$, $x_2 = 1$, $x_3 = 1$, and $x_4 = 0$, with an objective function value of \$170. However, note that if the budget available is increased by \$1 (from \$100 to \$101), the optimal solution changes to $x_1 = 1$, $x_2 = 0$, $x_3 = 0$, and $x_4 = 1$, with an objective function value of \$200. That is, one additional dollar in the budget would lead to a \$30 increase in the return. Surely management, when faced with such a situation, would increase the budget by \$1. Because of the extreme sensitivity of the value of the optimal solution to the constraint coefficients, practitioners usually recommend resolving the integer linear program several times with slight variations in the coefficients before attempting to choose the best solution for implementation.

SUMMARY

In this chapter, we introduced the important extension of linear programming referred to as *integer linear programming.* The only difference between the integer linear programming problems discussed in this chapter and the linear programming problems studied in previous chapters is that one or more of the variables must be integer. If all variables must be integer, we have an all-integer linear program. If some, but not necessarily all, variables must be integer, we have a mixed-integer linear program. Most integer programming applications involve 0-1, or binary, variables.

Studying integer linear programming is important for two major reasons. First, integer linear programming may be helpful when fractional values for the variables are not permitted. Rounding a linear programming solution may not provide an optimal integer solution; methods for finding optimal integer solutions are needed when the economic consequences of rounding are significant. A second reason for studying integer linear programming is the increased modeling flexibility provided through the use of 0-1 variables. We showed how 0-1 variables could be used to model important managerial considerations in capital budgeting, fixed cost, distribution system design, bank location, and product design/market share applications.

The number of applications of integer linear programming continues to grow rapidly. This growth is due in part to the availability of good integer linear programming software packages. As researchers develop solution procedures capable of solving larger integer linear programs and as computer speed increases, a continuation of the growth of integer programming applications is expected.

GLOSSARY

Integer linear program A linear program with the additional requirement that one or more of the variables must be integer.

All-integer linear program An integer linear program in which all variables are required to be integer.

LP Relaxation The linear program that results from dropping the integer requirements for the variables in an integer linear program.

Mixed-integer linear program An integer linear program in which some, but not necessarily all, variables are required to be integer.

0-1 integer linear program An all-integer or mixed-integer linear program in which the integer variables are only permitted to assume the values 0 or 1. Also called *binary integer program.*

Capital budgeting problem A 0-1 integer programming problem that involves choosing which projects or activities provide the best investment return.

Fixed cost problem A 0-1 mixed-integer programming problem in which the binary variables represent whether an activity, such as a production run, is undertaken (variable = 1) or not (variable = 0).

Distribution system design problem A mixed-integer linear program in which the binary integer variables usually represent sites selected for warehouses or plants and continuous variables represent the amount shipped over arcs in the distribution network.

Location problem A 0-1 integer programming problem in which the objective is to select the best locations to meet a stated objective. Variations of this problem (see the bank location problem in Section 8.3) are known as covering problems.

Product design and market share optimization problem Sometimes called the share of choices problem, it involves choosing a product design that maximizes the number of consumers preferring it.

Multiple-choice constraint A constraint requiring that the sum of two or more 0-1 variables equal 1. Thus, any feasible solution makes a choice of which variable to set equal to 1.

Mutually exclusive constraint A constraint requiring that the sum of two or more 0-1 variables be less than or equal to 1. Thus, if one of the variables equals 1, the others must equal 0. However, all variables could equal 0.

***k* out of *n* alternatives constraint** An extension of the multiple-choice constraint. This constraint requires that the sum of *n* 0-1 variables equal *k*.

Conditional constraint A constraint involving 0-1 variables that does not allow certain variables to equal 1 unless certain other variables are equal to 1.

Corequisite constraint A constraint requiring that two 0-1 variables be equal. Thus, they are both in or out of solution together.

PROBLEMS

1. Indicate which of the following is an all-integer linear program and which is a mixed-integer linear program. Write the LP Relaxation for the problem but do not attempt to solve.

   a. Max $30x_1 + 25x_2$

   s.t.

   $$3x_1 + 1.5x_2 \leq 400$$
   $$1.5x_1 + 2x_2 \leq 250$$
   $$1x_1 + 1x_2 \leq 150$$
   $$x_1, x_2 \geq 0 \text{ and } x_2 \text{ integer}$$

   b. Min $3x_1 + 4x_2$

   s.t.

   $$2x_1 + 4x_2 \geq 8$$
   $$2x_1 + 6x_2 \geq 12$$
   $$x_1, x_2 \geq 0 \text{ and integer}$$

2. Consider the following all-integer linear program.

   Max $5x_1 + 8x_2$

   s.t.

   $$6x_1 + 5x_2 \leq 30$$
   $$9x_1 + 4x_2 \leq 36$$
   $$1x_1 + 2x_2 \leq 10$$
   $$x_1, x_2 \geq 0 \text{ and integer}$$

   a. Graph the constraints for this problem. Use dots to indicate all feasible integer solutions.
   b. Find the optimal solution to the LP Relaxation. Round down to find a feasible integer solution.
   c. Find the optimal integer solution. Is it the same as the solution obtained in part (b) by rounding down?

3. Consider the following all-integer linear program.

   Max $1x_1 + 1x_2$

   s.t.

   $$4x_1 + 6x_2 \leq 22$$
   $$1x_1 + 5x_2 \leq 15$$
   $$2x_1 + 1x_2 \leq 9$$
   $$x_1, x_2 \geq 0 \text{ and integer}$$

   a. Graph the constraints for this problem. Use dots to indicate all feasible integer solutions.
   b. Solve the LP Relaxation of this problem.
   c. Find the optimal integer solution.

4. Consider the following all-integer linear program.

   Max $10x_1 + 3x_2$

   s.t.

   $$6x_1 + 7x_2 \leq 40$$
   $$3x_1 + 1x_2 \leq 11$$
   $$x_1, x_2 \geq 0 \text{ and integer}$$

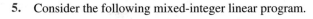

a. Formulate and solve the LP Relaxation of the problem. Solve it graphically, and round down to find a feasible solution. Specify an upper bound on the value of the optimal solution.
b. Solve the integer linear program graphically. Compare the value of this solution with the solution obtained in part (a).
c. Suppose the objective function changes to Max $3x_1 + 6x_2$. Repeat parts (a) and (b).

5. Consider the following mixed-integer linear program.

$$
\begin{aligned}
\text{Max} \quad & 2x_1 + 3x_2 \\
\text{s.t.} \quad & \\
& 4x_1 + 9x_2 \leq 36 \\
& 7x_1 + 5x_2 \leq 35 \\
& x_1, x_2 \geq 0 \text{ and } x_1 \text{ integer}
\end{aligned}
$$

a. Graph the constraints for this problem. Indicate on your graph all feasible mixed-integer solutions.
b. Find the optimal solution to the LP Relaxation. Round the value of x_1 down to find a feasible mixed-integer solution. Is this solution optimal? Why or why not?
c. Find the optimal solution for the mixed-integer linear program.

6. Consider the following mixed-integer linear program.

$$
\begin{aligned}
\text{Max} \quad & 1x_1 + 1x_2 \\
\text{s.t.} \quad & \\
& 7x_1 + 9x_2 \leq 63 \\
& 9x_1 + 5x_2 \leq 45 \\
& 3x_1 + 1x_2 \leq 12 \\
& x_1, x_2 \geq 0 \text{ and } x_2 \text{ integer}
\end{aligned}
$$

a. Graph the constraints for this problem. Indicate on your graph all feasible mixed-integer solutions.
b. Find the optimal solution to the LP Relaxation. Round the value of x_2 down to find a feasible mixed-integer solution. Specify upper and lower bounds on the value of the optimal solution to the mixed-integer linear program.
c. Find the optimal solution to the mixed-integer linear program.

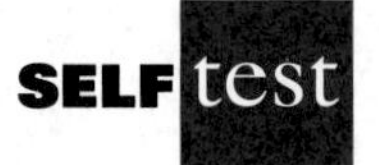

7. The following questions refer to a capital budgeting problem with six projects represented by 0-1 variables x_1, x_2, x_3, x_4, x_5, and x_6.
a. Write a constraint modeling a situation in which two of the projects 1, 3, 5, and 6 must be undertaken.
b. Write a constraint modeling a situation in which, if projects 3 and 5 must be undertaken, they must be undertaken simultaneously.
c. Write a constraint modeling a situation in which project 1 or 4 must be undertaken, but not both.
d. Write constraints modeling a situation where project 4 cannot be undertaken unless projects 1 and 3 also are undertaken.
e. Revise the requirement in part (d) to accommodate the case in which, when projects 1 and 3 are undertaken, project 4 also must be undertaken.

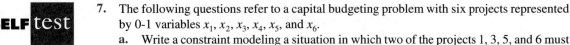

8. Spencer Enterprises must choose among a series of new investment alternatives. The potential investment alternatives, the net present value of the future stream of returns, the capital requirements, and the available capital funds over the next three years are summarized as follows:

Alternative	Net Present Value ($)	Capital Requirements ($)		
		Year 1	**Year 2**	**Year 3**
Limited warehouse expansion	4,000	3,000	1,000	4,000
Extensive warehouse expansion	6,000	2,500	3,500	3,500
Test market new product	10,500	6,000	4,000	5,000
Advertising campaign	4,000	2,000	1,500	1,800
Basic research	8,000	5,000	1,000	4,000
Purchase new equipment	3,000	1,000	500	900
Capital funds available		10,500	7,000	8,750

a. Develop and solve an integer programming model for maximizing the net present value.
b. Assume that only one of the warehouse expansion projects can be implemented. Modify your model of part (a).
c. Suppose that, if test marketing of the new product is carried out, the advertising campaign also must be conducted. Modify your formulation of part (b) to reflect this new situation.

9. Hawkins Manufacturing Company produces connecting rods for 4- and 6-cylinder automobile engines using the same production line. The cost required to set up the production line to produce the 4-cylinder connecting rods is $2000, and the cost required to set up the production line for the 6-cylinder connecting rods is $3500. Manufacturing costs are $15 for each 4-cylinder connecting rod and $18 for each 6-cylinder connecting rod. Hawkins makes a decision at the end of each week as to which product will be manufactured the following week. If a production changeover is necessary from one week to the next, the weekend is used to reconfigure the production line. Once the line has been set up, the weekly production capacities are 6000 6-cylinder connecting rods and 8000 4-cylinder connecting rods. Let

x_4 = the number of 4-cylinder connecting rods produced next week
x_6 = the number of 6-cylinder connecting rods produced next week
s_4 = 1 if the production line is set up to produce the 4-cylinder connecting rods; 0 if otherwise
s_6 = 1 if the production line is set up to produce the 6-cylinder connecting rods; 0 if otherwise

a. Using the decision variables x_4 and s_4, write a constraint that limits next week's production of the 4-cylinder connecting rods to either 0 or 8000 units.
b. Using the decision variables x_6 and s_6, write a constraint that limits next week's production of the 6-cylinder connecting rods to either 0 or 6000 units.
c. Write three constraints that, taken together, limit the production of connecting rods for next week.
d. Write an objective function for minimizing the cost of production for next week.

10. Grave City is considering the relocation of several police substations to obtain better enforcement in high-crime areas. The locations under consideration together with the areas that can be covered from these locations are given in the following table.

Potential Locations for Substations	Areas Covered
A	1, 5, 7
B	1, 2, 5, 7
C	1, 3, 5
D	2, 4, 5
E	3, 4, 6
F	4, 5, 6
G	1, 5, 6, 7

a. Formulate an integer programming model that could be used to find the minimum number of locations necessary to provide coverage to all areas.
b. Solve the problem in part (a).

11. Hart Manufacturing makes three products. Each product requires manufacturing operations in three departments: A, B, and C. The labor-hour requirements, by department, are as follows:

Department	Product 1	Product 2	Product 3
A	1.50	3.00	2.00
B	2.00	1.00	2.50
C	0.25	0.25	0.25

During the next production period, the labor-hours available are 450 in department A, 350 in department B, and 50 in department C. The profit contributions per unit are $25 for product 1, $28 for product 2, and $30 for product 3.

a. Formulate a linear programming model for maximizing total profit contribution.
b. Solve the linear program formulated in part (a). How much of each product should be produced, and what is the projected total profit contribution?
c. After evaluating the solution obtained in part (b), one of the production supervisors noted that production setup costs had not been taken into account. She noted that setup costs are $400 for product 1, $550 for product 2, and $600 for product 3. If the solution developed in part (b) is to be used, what is the total profit contribution after taking into account the setup costs?
d. Management realized that the optimal product mix, taking setup costs into account, might be different from the one recommended in part (b). Formulate a mixed-integer linear program that takes setup costs into account. Management also stated that we should not consider making more than 175 units of product 1, 150 units of product 2, or 140 units of product 3.
e. Solve the mixed-integer linear program formulated in part (d). How much of each product should be produced, and what is the projected total profit contribution? Compare this profit contribution to that obtained in part (c).

12. Yates Company supplies road salt to county highway departments. The company has three trucks, and the dispatcher is trying to schedule tomorrow's deliveries to Polk, Dallas, and Jasper counties. Two trucks have 15-ton capacities, and the third truck has a 30-ton capacity. Based on these truck capacities, two counties will receive 15 tons and the third will receive 30 tons of road salt. The dispatcher wants to determine how much to ship to each county. Let

$$x_1 = \text{amount shipped to Polk County}$$
$$x_2 = \text{amount shipped to Dallas County}$$
$$x_3 = \text{amount shipped to Jasper County}$$

and

$$y_i = \begin{cases} 1 \text{ if the 30-ton truck is assigned to county } i \\ 0 \text{ otherwise} \end{cases}$$

a. Use these variable definitions and write constraints that appropriately restrict the amount shipped to each county.

b. The cost of assigning the 30-ton truck to the three counties is $100 to Polk, $85 to Dallas, and $50 to Jasper. Formulate and solve a mixed-integer linear program to determine how much to ship to each county.

13. Recall the Martin-Beck Company distribution system problem in Section 8.3.

a. Modify the formulation shown in Section 8.3 to account for the policy restriction that one plant, but not two, must be located either in Detroit or in Toledo.

b. Modify the formulation shown in Section 8.3 to account for the policy restriction that no more than two plants can be located in Denver, Kansas City, and St. Louis.

14. An automobile manufacturer has five outdated plants: one each in Michigan, Ohio, and California and two in New York. Management is considering modernizing these plants to manufacture engine blocks and transmissions for a new model car. The cost to modernize each plant and the manufacturing capacity after modernization are as follows:

Plant	Cost ($ millions)	Engine Blocks (1000s)	Transmissions (1000s)
Michigan	25	500	300
New York	35	800	400
New York	35	400	800
Ohio	40	900	600
California	20	200	300

The projected needs are for total capacities of 900,000 engine blocks and 900,000 transmissions. Management wants to determine which plants to modernize to meet projected manufacturing needs and, at the same time, minimize the total cost of modernization.

a. Develop a table that lists every possible option available to management. As part of your table, indicate the total engine block capacity and transmission capacity for each possible option, whether the option is feasible based on the projected needs, and the total modernization cost for each option.

b. Based on your analysis in part (a), what recommendation would you provide management?

c. Formulate a 0-1 integer programming model that could be used to determine the optimal solution to the modernization question facing management.
d. Solve the model formulated in part (c) to provide a recommendation for management.

15. CHB, Inc., is a bank holding company that is evaluating the potential for expanding into a 13-county region in the southwestern part of the state. State law permits establishing branches in any county that is adjacent to a county in which a PPB (principal place of business) is located. The following map shows the 13-county region with the population of each county indicated.

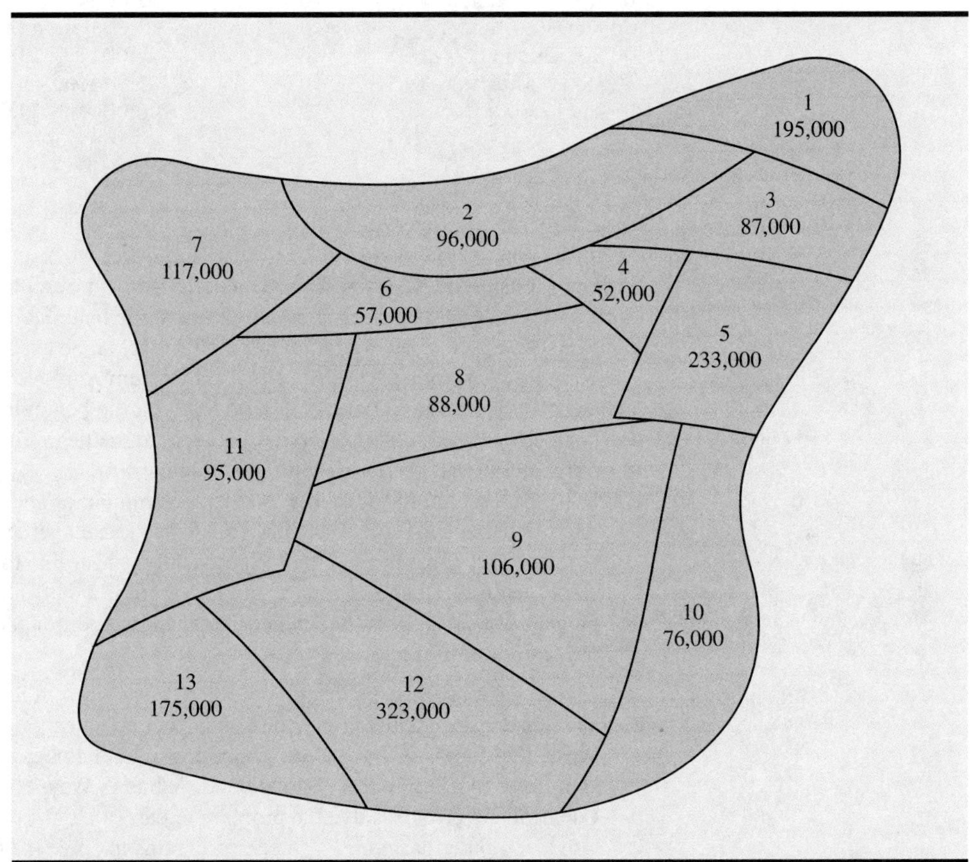

a. Assume that only one PPB can be established in the region. Where should it be located to maximize the population served? (*Hint:* Review the Ohio Trust formulation in Section 8.3. Consider minimizing the population not served, and introduce variable $y_i = 1$ if it is not possible to establish a branch in county i, and $y_i = 0$ otherwise.)
b. Suppose that two PPBs can be established in the region. Where should they be located to maximize the population served?
c. Management learned that a bank located in county 5 is considering selling. If CHB purchases this bank, the requisite PPB will be established in county 5, and a base for beginning expansion in the region will also be established. What advice would you give the management of CHB?

16. The Northshore Bank is working to develop an efficient work schedule for full-time and part-time tellers. The schedule must provide for efficient operation of the bank including adequate customer service, employee breaks, and so on. On Fridays the bank is open from 9:00 A.M. to 7:00 P.M. The number of tellers necessary to provide adequate customer service during each hour of operation is summarized here.

Time	Number of Tellers	Time	Number of Tellers
9:00 A.M.–10:00 A.M.	6	2:00 P.M.–3:00 P.M.	6
10:00 A.M.–11:00 A.M.	4	3:00 P.M.–4:00 P.M.	4
11:00 A.M.–Noon	8	4:00 P.M.–5:00 P.M.	7
Noon–1:00 P.M.	10	5:00 P.M.–6:00 P.M.	6
1:00 P.M.–2:00 P.M.	9	6:00 P.M.–7:00 P.M.	6

Each full-time employee starts on the hour and works a 4-hour shift, followed by 1 hour for lunch and then a 3-hour shift. Part-time employees work one 4-hour shift beginning on the hour. Considering salary and fringe benefits, full-time employees cost the bank $15 per hour ($105 a day), and part-time employees cost the bank $8 per hour ($32 per day).

a. Formulate an integer programming model that can be used to develop a schedule that will satisfy customer service needs at a minimum employee cost. (*Hint:* Let x_i = number of full-time employees coming on duty at the beginning of hour i and y_i = number of part-time employees coming on duty at the beginning of hour i.)
b. Solve the LP Relaxation of your model in part (a).
c. Solve for the optimal schedule of tellers. Comment on the solution.
d. After reviewing the solution to part (c), the bank manager realized that some additional requirements must be specified. Specifically, she wants to ensure that one full-time employee is on duty at all times and that there is a staff of at least five full-time employees. Revise your model to incorporate these additional requirements and solve for the optimal solution.

17. Refer to the Ohio Trust bank location problem introduced in Section 8.3. Table 8.3 shows the counties under consideration and the adjacent counties.
a. Write the complete integer programming model for expansion into the following counties only: Lorain, Huron, Richland, Ashland, Wayne, Medina, and Knox.
b. Use trial and error to solve the problem in part (a).
c. Use a computer program for integer programs to solve the problem.

18. Refer to the Salem Foods share of choices problem in Section 8.3 and address the following issues. It is rumored that King's is getting out of the frozen pizza business. If so, the major competitor for Salem Foods will be the Antonio's brand pizza.
a. Compute the overall utility for the Antonio's brand pizza for each of the consumers in Table 8.4.
b. Assume that Salem's only competitor is the Antonio's brand pizza. Formulate and solve the share of choices problem that will maximize market share. What is the best product design and what share of the market can be expected?

19. Burnside Marketing Research conducted a study for Barker Foods on some designs for a new dry cereal. Three attributes were found to be most influential in determining which cereal had the best taste: ratio of wheat to corn in the cereal flake, type of sweetener (sugar, honey, or artificial), and the presence or absence of flavor bits. Seven children participated in taste tests and provided the following part-worths for the attributes.

	Wheat/Corn		Sweetener			Flavor Bits	
Child	**Low**	**High**	**Sugar**	**Honey**	**Artificial**	**Present**	**Absent**
1	15	35	30	40	25	15	9
2	30	20	40	35	35	8	11
3	40	25	20	40	10	7	14
4	35	30	25	20	30	15	18
5	25	40	40	20	35	18	14
6	20	25	20	35	30	9	16
7	30	15	25	40	40	20	11

a. Suppose the overall utility (sum of part-worths) of the current favorite cereal is 75 for each child. What is the product design that will maximize the share of choices for the seven children in the sample?

b. Assume the overall utility of the current favorite cereal for children 1–4 is 70, and the overall utility of the current favorite cereal for children 5–7 is 80. What is the product design that will maximize the share of choices for the seven children in the sample?

20. Refer to Problem 14. Suppose that management determined that its cost estimates to modernize the New York plants were too low. Specifically, suppose that the actual cost is $40 million to modernize each plant.

a. What changes in your previous 0-1 integer linear programming model are needed to incorporate these changes in costs?

b. For these cost changes, what recommendations would you now provide management regarding the modernization plan?

c. Reconsider the solution obtained using the revised cost figures. Suppose that management decides that closing two plants in the same state is not acceptable. How could this policy restriction be added to your 0-1 integer programming model?

d. Based on the cost revision and the policy restriction presented in part (c), what recommendations would you now provide management regarding the modernization plan?

21. The Bayside Art Gallery is considering installing a video camera security system to reduce its insurance premiums. A diagram of the eight display rooms that Bayside uses for exhibitions is shown in Figure 8.13; the openings between the rooms are numbered 1–13. A security firm proposed that two-way cameras be installed at some room openings. Each camera has the ability to monitor the two rooms between which the camera is located. For example, if a camera were located at opening number 4, rooms 1 and 4 would be covered; if a camera were located at opening 11, rooms 7 and 8 would be covered; and so on. Management decided not to locate a camera system at the entrance to the display rooms. The objective is to provide security coverage for all eight rooms using the minimum number of two-way cameras.

a. Formulate a 0-1 integer linear programming model that will enable Bayside's management to determine the locations for the camera systems.

b. Solve the model formulated in part (a) to determine how many two-way cameras to purchase and where they should be located.

c. Suppose that management wants to provide additional security coverage for room 7. Specifically, management wants room 7 to be covered by two cameras. How would your model formulated in part (a) have to change to accommodate this policy restriction?

d. With the policy restriction specified in part (c), determine how many two-way camera systems will need to be purchased and where they will be located.

FIGURE 8.13 DIAGRAM OF DISPLAY ROOMS FOR BAYSIDE ART GALLERY

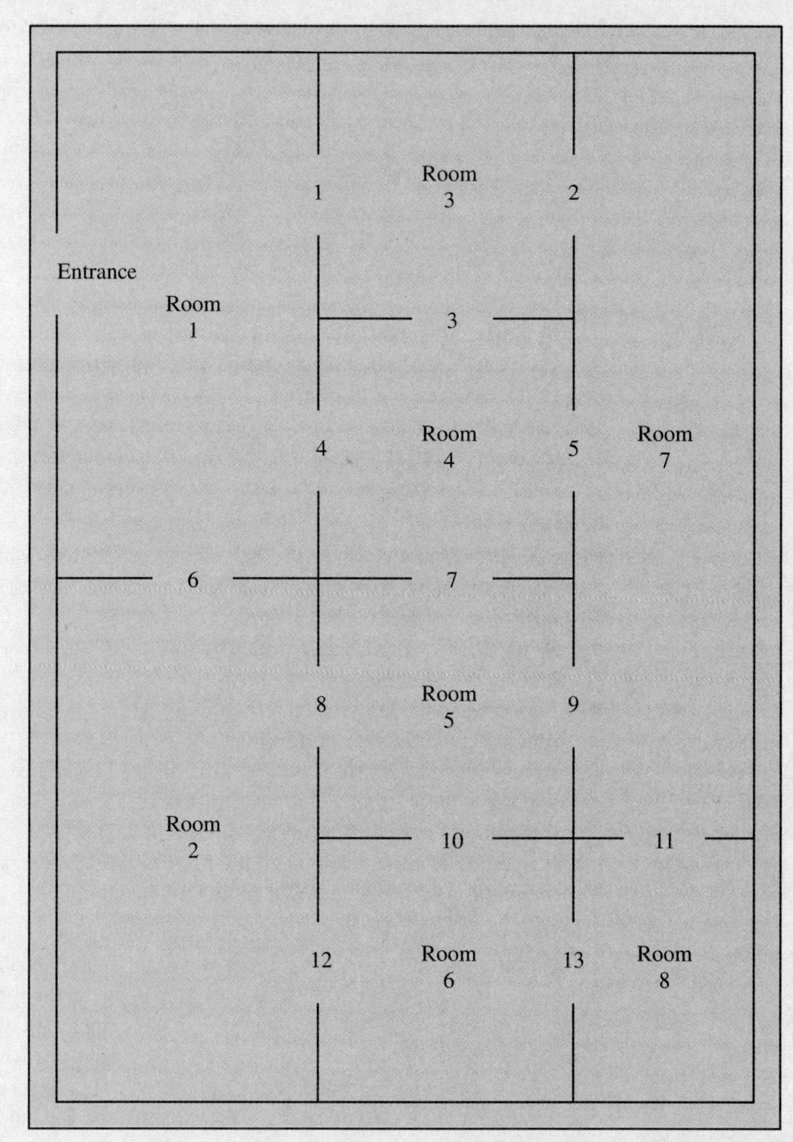

22. The Delta Group is a management consulting firm specializing in the health care industry. A team is being formed to study possible new markets, and a linear programming model has been developed for selecting team members. However, one constraint the president imposed is a team size of three, five, or seven members. The staff cannot figure out how to incorporate this requirement in the model. The current model requires that team members be selected from three departments and uses the following variable definitions.

x_1 = the number of employees selected from department 1
x_2 = the number of employees selected from department 2
x_3 = the number of employees selected from department 3

Show the staff how to write constraints that will ensure that the team will consist of three, five, or seven employees. The following integer variables should be helpful.

$$y_1 = \begin{cases} 1 & \text{if team size is 3} \\ 0 & \text{otherwise} \end{cases}$$

$$y_2 = \begin{cases} 1 & \text{if team size is 5} \\ 0 & \text{otherwise} \end{cases}$$

$$y_3 = \begin{cases} 1 & \text{if team size is 7} \\ 0 & \text{otherwise} \end{cases}$$

23. Roedel Electronics produces a variety of electrical components, including a remote controller for televisions and a remote controller for VCRs. Each controller consists of three subassemblies that are manufactured by Roedel: a base, a cartridge, and a keypad. Both controllers use the same base subassembly, but different cartridge and keypad subassemblies.

Roedel's sales forecast indicates that 7000 TV controllers and 5000 VCR controllers will be needed to satisfy demand during the upcoming Christmas season. Because only 500 hours of in-house manufacturing time are available, Roedel is considering purchasing some, or all, of the subassemblies from outside suppliers. If Roedel manufactures a subassembly in-house, it incurs a fixed setup cost as well as a variable manufacturing cost. The following table shows the setup cost, the manufacturing time per subassembly, the manufacturing cost per subassembly, and the cost to purchase each of the subassemblies from an outside supplier.

Subassembly	Setup Cost ($)	Manufacturing Time per Unit (min.)	Manufacturing Cost per Unit ($)	Purchase Cost per Unit ($)
Base	1000	0.9	0.40	0.65
TV cartridge	1200	2.2	2.90	3.45
VCR cartridge	1900	3.0	3.15	3.70
TV keypad	1500	0.8	0.30	0.50
VCR keypad	1500	1.0	0.55	0.70

a. Determine how many units of each subassembly Roedel should manufacture and how many units Roedel should purchase. What is the total manufacturing and purchase cost associated with your recommendation?

b. Suppose Roedel is considering purchasing new machinery to produce VCR cartridges. For the new machinery, the setup cost is $3000; the manufacturing time is 2.5 minutes per cartridge, and the manufacturing cost is $2.60 per cartridge. Assuming that the new machinery is purchased, determine how many units of each subassembly Roedel should manufacture and how many units of each subassembly Roedel should purchase. What is the total manufacturing and purchase cost associated with your recommendation? Do you think the new machinery should be purchased? Explain.

24. A mathematical programming system named SilverScreener uses a 0-1 integer programming model to help theater managers decide which movies to show on a weekly basis in a multiple-screen theater (*Interfaces,* May/June 2001). Suppose that management of Valley Cinemas would like to investigate the potential of using a similar scheduling system for their chain of multiple-screen theaters. Valley selected a small two-screen movie theater for the pilot testing and would like to develop an integer programming model to help schedule movies for the next four weeks. Six movies are available. The first week each movie is available, the last week each movie can be shown, and the maximum number of weeks that each movie can run are shown here.

Movie	First Week Available	Last Week Available	Max. Run (weeks)
1	1	2	2
2	1	3	2
3	1	1	2
4	2	4	2
5	3	6	3
6	3	5	3

The overall viewing schedule for the theater is composed of the individual schedules for each of the six movies. For each movie a schedule must be developed that specifies the week the movie starts and the number of consecutive weeks it will run. For instance, one possible schedule for movie 2 is for it to start in week 1 and run for two weeks. Theater policy requires that once a movie is started it must be shown in consecutive weeks. It cannot be stopped and restarted again. To represent the schedule possibilities for each movie, the following decision variables were developed:

$$x_{ijw} = \begin{cases} 1 & \text{if movie } i \text{ is scheduled to start in week } j \text{ and run for } w \text{ weeks} \\ 0 & \text{otherwise} \end{cases}$$

For example, $x_{532} = 1$ means that the schedule selected for movie 5 is to begin in week 3 and run for two weeks. For each movie, a separate variable is given for each possible schedule.

a. Three schedules are associated with movie 1. List the variables that represent these schedules.
b. Write a constraint requiring that only one schedule be selected for movie 1.
c. Write a constraint requiring that only one schedule be selected for movie 5.
d. What restricts the number of movies that can be shown in week 1? Write a constraint that restricts the number of movies selected for viewing in week 1.
e. Write a constraint that restricts the number of movies selected for viewing in week 3.

25. East Coast Trucking provides service from Boston to Miami using regional offices located in Boston, New York, Philadelphia, Baltimore, Washington, Richmond, Raleigh, Florence, Savannah, Jacksonville, and Tampa. The number of miles between each of the regional offices is provided in the following table.

	New York	Philadelphia	Baltimore	Washington	Richmond	Raleigh	Florence	Savannah	Jacksonville	Tampa	Miami
Boston	211	320	424	459	565	713	884	1056	1196	1399	1669
New York		109	213	248	354	502	673	845	985	1188	1458
Philadelphia			104	139	245	393	564	736	876	1079	1349
Baltimore				35	141	289	460	632	772	975	1245
Washington					106	254	425	597	737	940	1210
Richmond						148	319	491	631	834	1104
Raleigh							171	343	483	686	956
Florence								172	312	515	785
Savannah									140	343	613
Jacksonville										203	473
Tampa											270

The company's expansion plans involve constructing service facilities in some of the cities where a regional office is located. Each regional office must be within 400 miles of a service facility. For instance, if a service facility is constructed in Richmond, it can provide service to regional offices located in New York, Philadelphia, Baltimore, Washington, Richmond, Raleigh, and Florence. Management would like to determine the minimum number of service facilities needed and where they should be located.

a. Formulate an integer linear program that can be used to determine the minimum number of service facilities needed and their location.
b. Solve the linear program formulated in part (a). How many service facilities are required, and where should they be located?
c. Suppose that each service facility can only provide service to regional offices within 300 miles. How many service facilities are required, and where should they be located?

Case Problem 1 TEXTBOOK PUBLISHING

ASW Publishing, Inc., a small publisher of college textbooks, must make a decision regarding which books to publish next year. The books under consideration are listed in the following table, along with the projected three-year sales expected from each book.

Book Subject	Type of Book	Projected Sales ($1000s)
Business calculus	New	20
Finite mathematics	Revision	30
General statistics	New	15
Mathematical statistics	New	10
Business statistics	Revision	25
Finance	New	18
Financial accounting	New	25
Managerial accounting	Revision	50
English literature	New	20
German	New	30

The books listed as revisions are texts that ASW already has under contract; these texts are being considered for publication as new editions. The books that are listed as new have been reviewed by the company, but contracts have not yet been signed.

Three individuals in the company can be assigned to these projects, all of whom have varying amounts of time available; John has 60 days available, and Susan and Monica both have 40 days available. The days required by each person to complete each project are shown in the following table. For instance, if the business calculus book is published, it will require 30 days of John's time and 40 days of Susan's time. An "X" indicates that the person will not be used on the project. Note that at least two staff members will be assigned to each project except the finance book.

Book Subject	John	Susan	Monica
Business calculus	30	40	X
Finite mathematics	16	24	X
General statistics	24	X	30

(continued)

Book Subject	John	Susan	Monica
Mathematical statistics	20	X	24
Business statistics	10	X	16
Finance	X	X	14
Financial accounting	X	24	26
Managerial accounting	X	28	30
English literature	40	34	30
German	X	50	36

ASW will not publish more than two statistics books or more than one accounting text in a single year. In addition, management decided that one of the mathematics books (business calculus or finite math) must be published, but not both.

Managerial Report

Prepare a report for the managing editor of ASW that describes your findings and recommendations regarding the best publication strategy for next year. In carrying out your analysis, assume that the fixed costs and the sales revenues per unit are approximately equal for all books; management is interested primarily in maximizing the total unit sales volume.

The managing editor also asked that you include recommendations regarding the following possible changes.

1. If it would be advantageous to do so, Susan can be moved off another project to allow her to work 12 more days.
2. If it would be advantageous to do so, Monica can also be made available for another 10 days.
3. If one or more of the revisions could be postponed for another year, should they be? Clearly the company will risk losing market share by postponing a revision.

Include details of your analysis in an appendix to your report.

Case Problem 2 YEAGER NATIONAL BANK

Using aggressive mail promotion with low introductory interest rates, Yeager National Bank (YNB) built a large base of credit card customers throughout the continental United States. Currently, all customers send their regular payments to the bank's corporate office located in Charlotte, North Carolina. Daily collections from customers making their regular payments are substantial, with an average of approximately $600,000. YNB estimates that it makes about 15 percent on its funds and would like to ensure that customer payments are credited to the bank's account as soon as possible. For instance, if it takes five days for a customer's payment to be sent through the mail, processed, and credited to the bank's account, YNB has potentially lost five days' worth of interest income. Although the time needed for this collection process cannot be completely eliminated, reducing it can be beneficial given the large amounts of money involved.

Instead of having all its credit card customers send their payments to Charlotte, YNB is considering having customers send their payments to one or more regional collection centers, referred to in the banking industry as lockboxes. Four lockbox locations have been proposed: Phoenix, Salt Lake City, Atlanta, and Boston. To determine which lockboxes to open and where lockbox customers should send their payments, YNB divided its customer base into five geographical regions: Northwest, Southwest, Central, Northeast, and Southeast. Every customer in the same region will be instructed to send his or her payment to the same lockbox. The following table shows the average number of days it takes before a customer's payment is credited to the bank's account when the payment is sent from each of the regions to each of the potential lockboxes.

Customer Zone	Location of Lockbox				Daily Collection ($1000s)
	Phoenix	Salt Lake City	Atlanta	Boston	
Northwest	4	2	4	4	80
Southwest	2	3	4	6	90
Central	5	3	3	4	150
Northeast	5	4	3	2	180
Southeast	4	6	2	3	100

Managerial Report

Dave Wolff, the vice president for cash management, asked you to prepare a report containing your recommendations for the number of lockboxes and the best lockbox locations. Mr. Wolff is primarily concerned with minimizing lost interest income, but he wants you to also consider the effect of an annual fee charged for maintaining a lockbox at any location. Although the amount of the fee is unknown at this time, we can assume that the fees will be in the range of $20,000 to $30,000 per location. Once good potential locations have been selected, Mr. Wolff will inquire as to the annual fees.

Case Problem 3 PRODUCTION SCHEDULING WITH CHANGEOVER COSTS

Buckeye Manufacturing produces heads for engines used in the manufacture of trucks. The production line is highly complex, and it measures 900 feet in length. Two types of engine heads are produced on this line: the P-Head and the H-Head. The P-Head is used in heavy-duty trucks and the H-Head is used in smaller trucks. Because only one type of head can be produced at a time, the line is either set up to manufacture the P-Head or the H-Head, but not both. Changeovers are made over a weekend; costs are $500 in going from a setup for the P-Head to a setup for the H-Head, and vice versa. When set up for the P-Head, the maximum production rate is 100 units per week and when set up for the H-Head, the maximum production rate is 80 units per week.

Buckeye just shut down for the week after using the line to produce the P-Head. The manager wants to plan production and changeovers for the next eight weeks. Currently, Buckeye's inventory consists of 125 P-Heads and 143 H-Heads. Inventory carrying costs are charged at an annual rate of 19.5 percent of the value of inventory. The production cost for the P-Head is $225, and the production cost for the H-Head is $310. The objective in developing a production schedule is to minimize the sum of production cost, plus inventory carrying cost, plus changeover cost.

Buckeye received the following requirements schedule from its customer (an engine assembly plant) for the next nine weeks.

	Product Demand	
Week	P-Head	H-Head
1	55	38
2	55	38
3	44	30
4	0	0
5	45	48
6	45	48
7	36	58
8	35	57
9	35	58

Safety stock requirements are such that week-ending inventory must provide for at least 80 percent of the next week's demand.

Managerial Report

Prepare a report for Buckeye's management with a production and changeover schedule for the next eight weeks. Be sure to note how much of the total cost is due to production, how much is due to inventory, and how much is due to changeover.

Appendix 8.1 EXCEL SOLUTION OF INTEGER LINEAR PROGRAMS

Worksheet formulation and solution for integer linear programs are similar to that for linear programming problems. Actually the worksheet formulation is exactly the same, but some additional information must be provided when setting up the **Solver Parameters** and **Integer Options** dialog boxes. First, constraints must be added in the **Solver Parameters** dialog box to identify the integer variables. In addition, the value for **Tolerance** in the **Integer Options** dialog box may need to be adjusted to obtain a solution.

Let us demonstrate the Excel solution of an integer linear program by showing how Excel can be used to solve the Eastborne Realty problem. The worksheet with the optimal solution is shown in Figure 8.14. We will describe the key elements of the worksheet, describe how to obtain the solution, and then interpret the solution.

Formulation

The data and descriptive labels appear in cells A1:G7 of the worksheet in Figure 8.14. The screened cells in the lower portion of the worksheet contain the information required by the Excel Solver (decision variables, objective function, constraint left-hand sides, and constraint right-hand sides).

Decision Variables — Cells B17:C17 are reserved for the decision variables. The optimal solution is to purchase four townhouses and two apartment buildings.

Objective Function — The formula =SUMPRODUCT(B7:C7,B17:C17) has been placed into cell B13 to reflect the annual cash flow associated

FIGURE 8.14 EXCEL SOLUTION FOR THE EASTBORNE REALTY PROBLEM

	A	B	C	D	E	F	G	H
1	**Eastborne Realty Problem**							
2								
3		**Townhouse**	**Apt. Bldg.**					
4	**Price($1000s)**	282	400			**Funds Avl.($1000s)**	2000	
5	**Mgr. Time**	4	40			**Mgr. Time Avl.**	140	
6						**Townhouses Avl.**	5	
7	**Ann. Cash Flow ($1000s)**	10	15					
8								
9								
10	**Model**							
11								
12								
13	**Max Cash Flow**	70						
14					**Constraints**	**LHS**		**RHS**
15		**Number of**			Funds	1928	<=	2000
16		Townhouses	Apt. Bldgs.		Time	96	<=	140
17	**Purchase Plan**	4	2		Townhouses	4	<=	5
18								

EXCELfile
Eastborne

with the solution. The optimal solution provides an annual cash flow of $70,000.

Left-Hand Sides — The left-hand sides for the three constraints are placed into cells F15:F17.

Cell F15 =SUMPRODUCT (B4:C4, $B$17:$C$17)
(Copy to sell F16)

Cell F17 =B17

Right-Hand Sides — The right-hand sides for the three constraints are placed into cells H15:H17.

Cell H15 =G4 (Copy to cells H16:H17)

Excel Solution

Begin the solution procedure by selecting **Solver** from the **Tools** menu and entering the proper values into the **Solver Parameters** dialog box as shown in Figure 8.15. The first constraint shown is $B$17:$C$17 = integer. This constraint tells Solver that the decision variables in cell B17 and cell C17 must be integer. The integer requirement is created by using the **Add-Constraint** procedure. $B$17:$C17 is entered as the **Cell Reference** and **"int"** rather than <=, =, or => is selected as the form of the constraint. When **"int"** is selected, the term integer automatically appears as the right-hand side of the constraint. Figure 8.15 shows the additional information required to complete the **Solver Parameters** dialog box.

Next the **Options** button must be selected. The option **Assume Non-Negative** must be checked. Figure 8.16 shows the completed **Solver Options** dialog box for the Eastborne Realty problem. Clicking **OK** in the **Solver Options** dialog box and selecting **Solve** in the **Solver Parameters** dialog box will instruct Solver to compute the optimal integer solution.

FIGURE 8.15 SOLVER PARAMETERS DIALOG BOX FOR THE EASTBORNE REALTY PROBLEM

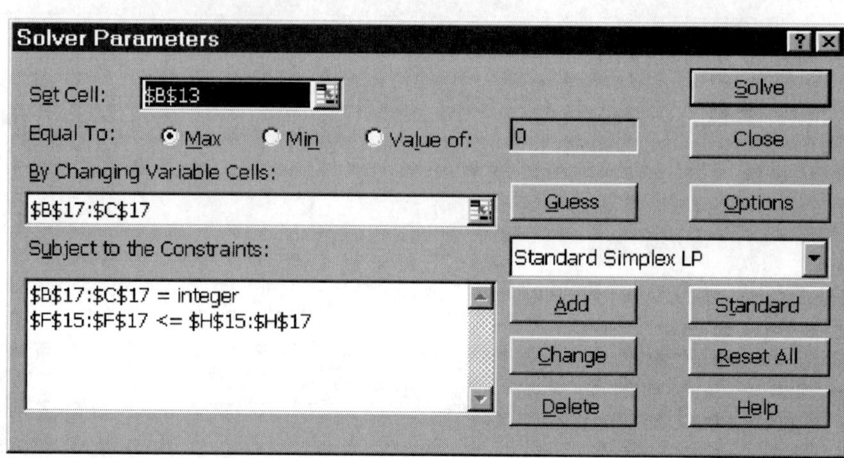

The worksheet in Figure 8.14 shows that the optimal solution is to purchase four townhouses and two apartment buildings. The annual cash flow is $70,000.

0-1 variables are identified with the "bin" designation in the Solver Parameters dialog box.

If binary variables are present in an integer linear programming problem, you must select the designation **"bin"** instead of **"int"** when setting up the constraints in the **Solver Parameters** dialog box.

The time required to obtain an optimal solution can be highly variable for integer linear programs. If an optimal solution cannot be found within a reasonable amount of time, the

FIGURE 8.16 SOLVER OPTIONS DIALOG BOX FOR THE EASTBORNE REALTY PROBLEM

Solver Options

Max Time: 100 seconds

Iterations: 100

Precision: 0.000001

Pivot Tol: 0.000001

Reduced Tol: 0.000001

☐ Show Iteration Results

☐ Use Automatic Scaling

☑ Assume Non-Negative

☐ Bypass Solver Reports

OK

Cancel

Integer Options...

Load Model...

Save Model...

Help

tolerance can be reset to 5 percent, or some higher value, so that the search procedure may stop when a near-optimal solution (within the tolerance of being optimal) has been found. To reset the tolerance, click on **Integer Options . . .** in the **Solver Options** dialog box (see Figure 8.16). Then, when the **Integer Options** dialog box appears (see Figure 8.17), enter the desired value in the **Tolerance** box. Figure 8.17 shows a 0 in the **Tolerance** box for the Eastborne Realty problem. In a more difficult problem, .05 could be entered to allow the solution procedure to stop with a solution within 5 percent of optimal.

FIGURE 8.17 INTEGER OPTIONS DIALOG BOX FOR THE EASTBORNE REALTY PROBLEM

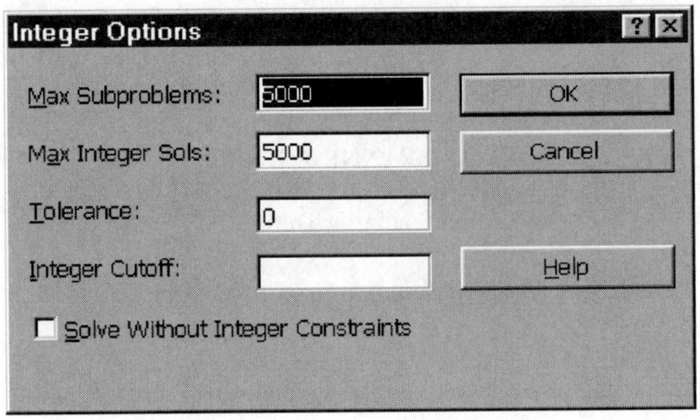

CHAPTER 9

Network Models

CONTENTS

Many managerial problems in areas such as transportation systems design, information systems design, and project scheduling have been successfully solved with the aid of network models and network analysis techniques. In Chapter 7 we showed how *networks* consisting of nodes and arcs can be used to provide graphical representations of transportation, assignment, and transshipment problems. In this chapter we present three additional network problems: the shortest-route problem, the minimal spanning tree problem, and the maximal flow problem. In each case, we will show how a network model can be developed and solved in order to provide an optimal solution to the problem. The Management Science in Action, Optimizing Restoration Capacity at AT&T, notes that AT&T solved shortest-route and maximal flow problems in designing their transmission network.

MANAGEMENT SCIENCE IN ACTION

OPTIMIZING RESTORATION CAPACITY AT AT&T*

AT&T is a global telecommunications company that provides long-distance voice and data, video, wireless, satellite, and Internet services. The company uses state-of-the-art switching and transmission equipment to provide service to more than 80 million customers. In the continental United States, AT&T's transmission network consists of more than 40,000 miles of fiber-optic cable. On peak days AT&T handles as many as 290 million calls of various types.

Power outages, natural disasters, cable cuts, and other events can disable a portion of the transmission network. When such events occur, spare capacity comprising the restoration network must be immediately employed so that service is not disrupted. Critical issues with respect to the restoration network are: How much capacity is necessary? and where should it be located? In 1997, AT&T assembled a RestNet team to address these issues.

To optimize restoration capacity, the RestNet team developed a large-scale linear programming model. One subproblem in their model involves determining the shortest route connecting an origin and destination whenever a failure occurs in a span of the transmission network. Another subproblem solves a maximal flow problem to find the best restoration paths from each switch to a disaster recovery switch.

The RestNet team was successful, and their work is an example of how valuable management science methodology is to companies. According to C. Michael Armstrong, chair and CEO, "Last year the work of the RestNet team allowed us to reduce capital spending by tens of millions of dollars."

*Based on Ken Ambs, Sebastian Cwilich, Mei Deng, David J. Houck, David F. Lynch, and Dicky Yan, "Optimizing Restoration Capacity in the AT&T Network," *Interfaces* (January/February 2000): 26–44.

9.1 SHORTEST-ROUTE PROBLEM

In this section we consider a network application in which the primary objective is to determine the **shortest route** or *path* between any pair of nodes in a network. Let us demonstrate the shortest-route problem by considering the situation facing the Gorman Construction Company. Gorman has several construction projects located throughout a three-county area. Construction sites are sometimes located as far as 50 miles from Gorman's main office. With multiple daily trips carrying personnel, equipment, and supplies to and from the construction locations, the costs associated with transportation activities are substantial. For any given construction site, the travel alternatives between the site and the office can be described by a network of roads, streets, and highways. The network shown in Figure 9.1 describes the travel alternatives to and from six of Gorman's newest construction sites. The circles or *nodes* of the network correspond to the site locations. The roads, streets, and highways appear as the *arcs* in the network. The distances between the sites are shown above the corresponding arcs. Gorman would like to determine the routes or paths that will minimize the total travel distance from the office to each site.

FIGURE 9.1 ROAD NETWORK FOR THE GORMAN COMPANY SHORTEST-ROUTE PROBLEM

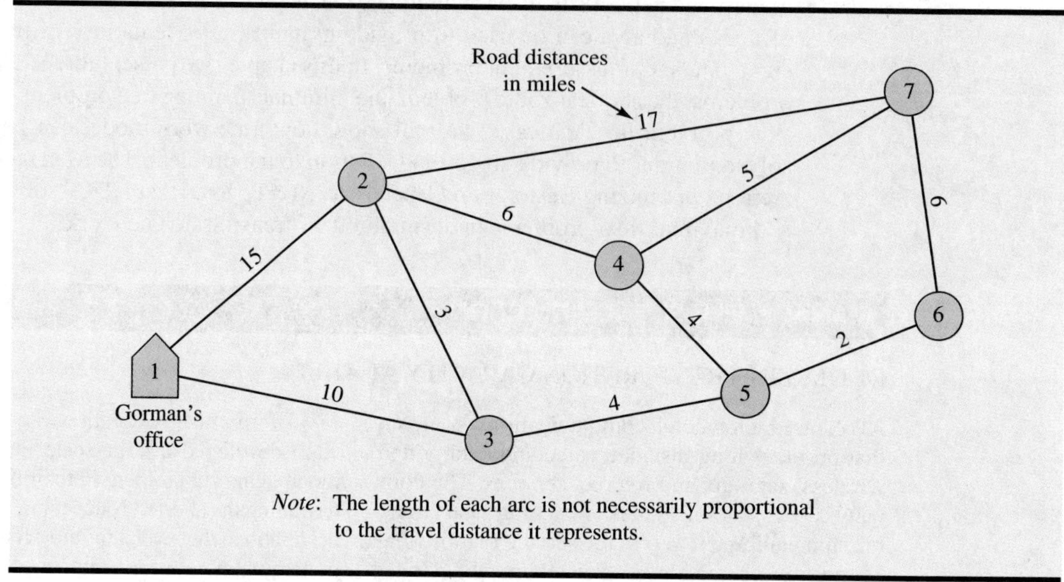

A Shortest-Route Algorithm

To solve Gorman's problem, we need to determine the shortest route from Gorman's office, node 1, to each of the other nodes in the network. The algorithm we present uses a labeling procedure to find the shortest distance from node 1 to each of the other nodes. As we perform the steps of the labeling procedure, we will identify a *label* consisting of two numbers enclosed in brackets for each node. The first number in the label for a particular node indicates the distance from node 1 to that node, while the second number indicates the preceding node on the route from node 1 to that node. We will show the label for each node directly above or below the node in the network. For example, a label for a particular node might appear as shown in Figure 9.2.

At any step of the labeling procedure, a node is said to be either labeled or unlabeled. A labeled node is any node for which we have identified a path from node 1 to that node, and an unlabeled node is any node for which a path has not yet been identified. A labeled node is also said to be either permanently or tentatively labeled. Whenever the algorithm has determined the *shortest* distance from node 1 to a particular node, the node is said to

FIGURE 9.2 AN EXAMPLE OF A NODE LABEL

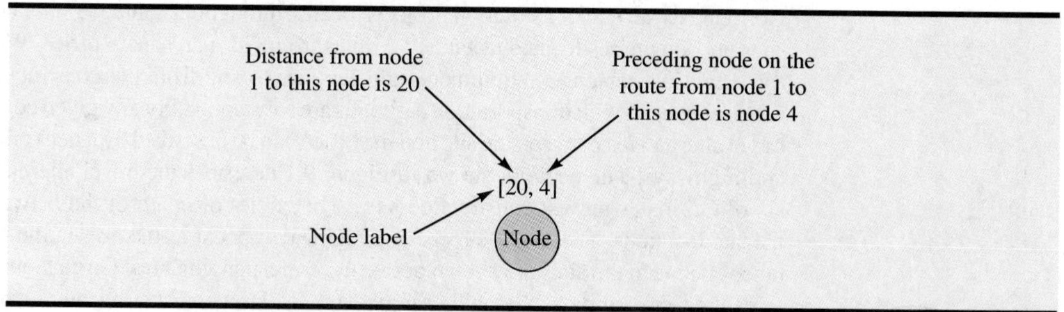

have a *permanent* label. If, however, the shortest distance from node 1 to a particular labeled node has not yet been determined, the node is said to have a *tentative* label. Now let us show how labels are computed and how the labeling process can be used to determine the shortest route to each of the nodes in the network.

We begin the labeling process by giving node 1 the permanent label [0,S]. The 0 indicates that the distance from node 1 to itself is zero and the S identifies node 1 as the starting node. To distinguish between tentatively and permanently labeled nodes, we use dark shading for all permanently labeled nodes in the network. In addition, an arrow indicates the permanently labeled node being investigated at each step of the labeling algorithm. The initial identification of Gorman's network is shown in Figure 9.3 when only node 1 is permanently labeled.

To perform the first step or iteration of the labeling procedure, we must consider every node that can be reached directly from node 1; hence, we look first at node 2 and then at node 3. We see that the direct distance from node 1 to node 2 is 15 miles. Thus, node 2 can be tentatively labeled [15,1], with the second number indicating that the preceding node on this route to node 2 is node 1. Next, we consider node 3 and find that the direct distance from node 1 to node 3 is 10 miles. Thus, the tentative label at node 3 is [10,1]. Figure 9.4 shows the results thus far with nodes 2 and 3 tentatively labeled.

Refer to Figure 9.4. We now consider all tentatively labeled nodes and identify the node with the smallest distance value in its label; thus, node 3 with a travel distance of 10 miles is selected. Could we get to node 3 following a shorter route? Because any other route to node 3 would require passing through other nodes, and because the distance from node 1 to all other nodes is greater than or equal to 10, a shorter route to node 3 cannot be found. Accordingly, node 3 is permanently labeled with a distance of 10 miles. Dark shading indicates that node 3 is a permanently labeled node and the arrow indicates that node 3 will be used to start the next step of the labeling process; the result of these steps is shown in Figure 9.5.

We proceed by considering all nodes that are not permanently labeled and that can be reached directly from node 3; these are nodes 2 and 5. Note that the direct distance is 3 miles from node 3 to node 2 and it is 4 miles from node 3 to node 5. Because node 3's permanent label indicates that the shortest distance to node 3 is 10 miles, we see that we can reach node 2 in 10 + 3 = 13 miles and node 5 in 10 + 4 = 14 miles. Thus, the tentative label at node 2 is revised to [13,3] to indicate that we have now found a route from node 1 to node 2

FIGURE 9.3 INITIAL NETWORK IDENTIFICATION FOR GORMAN'S SHORTEST-ROUTE PROBLEM

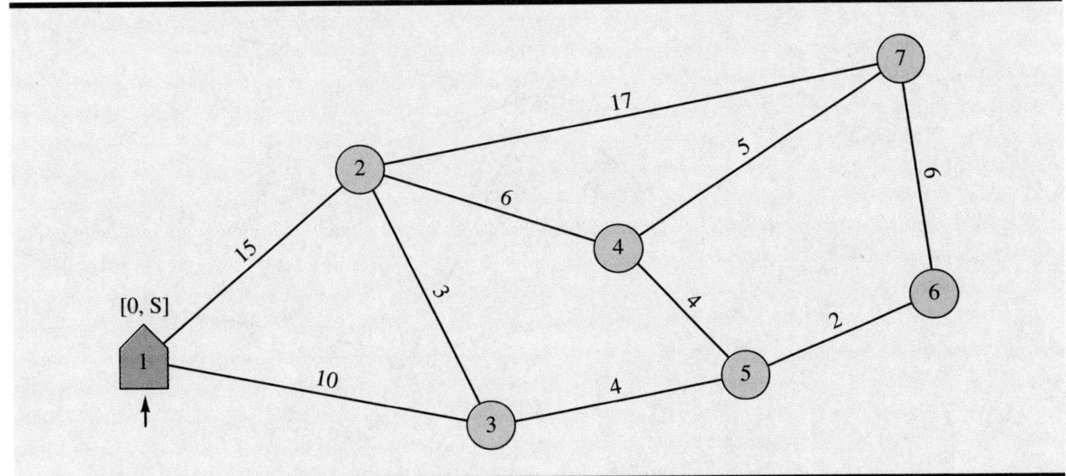

FIGURE 9.4 GORMAN'S NETWORK WITH TENTATIVE LABELS FOR NODES 2 AND 3

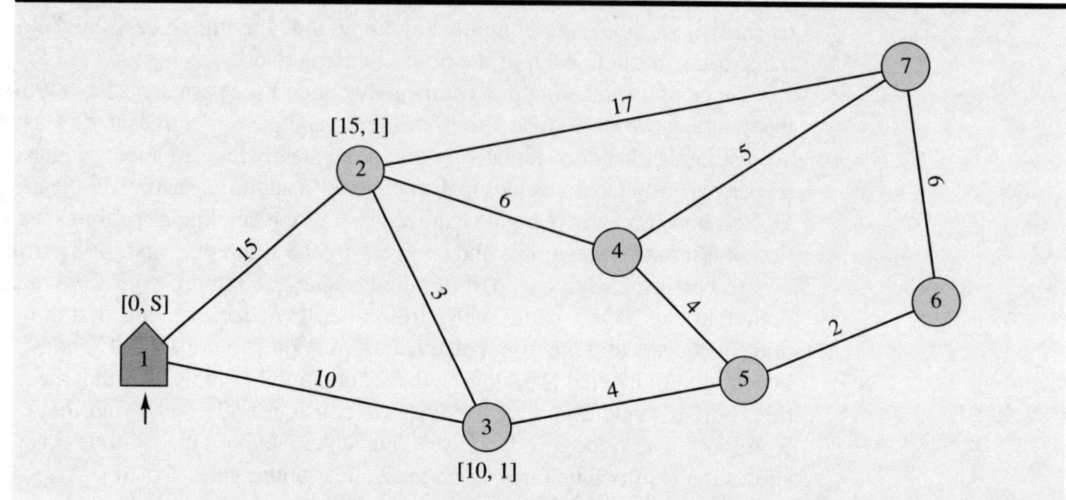

that has a distance of 13 miles and passes through node 3. The tentative label for node 5 is set to [14,3]. Figure 9.6 shows the network computations up to this point.

We next consider all tentatively labeled nodes in order to find the node with the smallest distance value in its label. From Figure 9.6 we see that this is node 2 with a distance of 13 miles. Node 2 is now permanently labeled because we know that it can be reached from node 1 in the shortest possible distance of 13 miles by going through node 3.

The next step or iteration begins at node 2, the most recently permanently labeled node. As before, we consider every nonpermanently labeled node that can be reached directly from node 2; that is, nodes 4 and 7. Starting with the distance value of 13 in the permanent

FIGURE 9.5 GORMAN'S NETWORK WITH NODE 3 IDENTIFIED AS A PERMANENTLY LABELED NODE

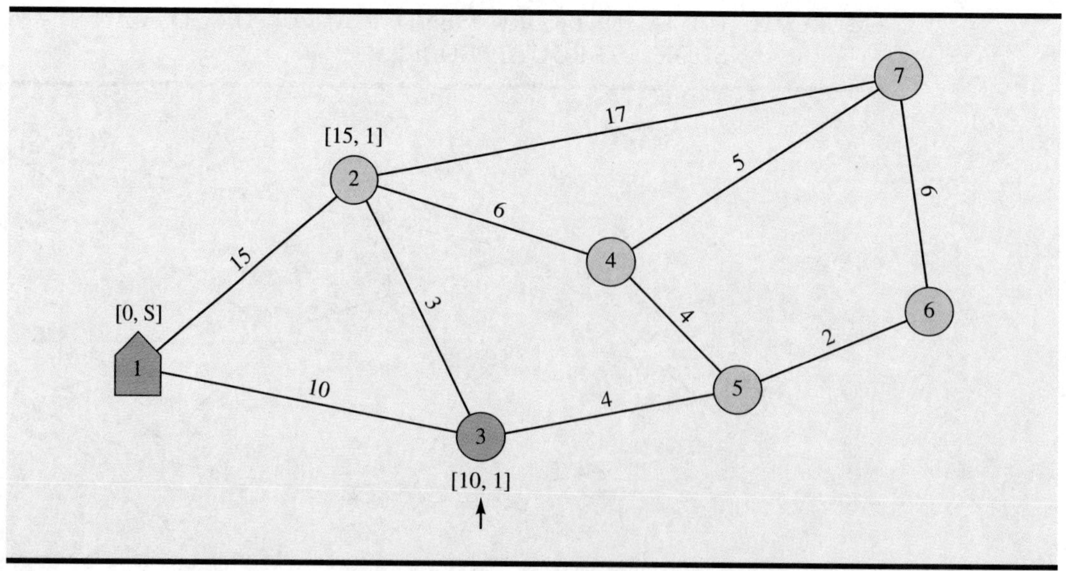

FIGURE 9.6 GORMAN'S NETWORK WITH NEW TENTATIVE LABELS FOR NODES 2 AND 5

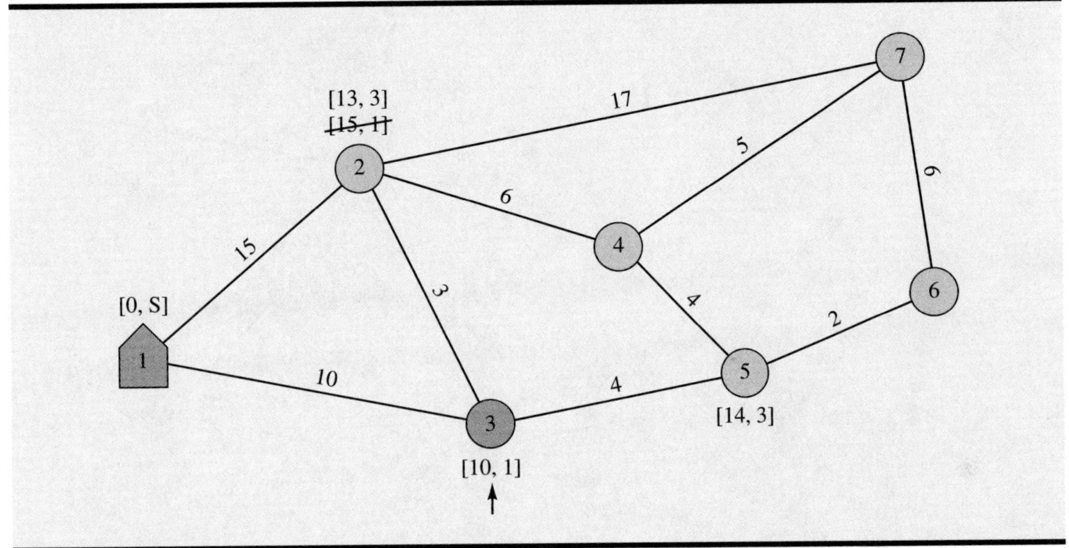

label at node 2 and adding the direct distance from node 2 to both nodes 4 and 7, we see that node 4 can be reached in 13 + 6 = 19 miles, while node 7 can be reached in 13 + 17 = 30 miles. Thus, the tentative labels at nodes 4 and 7 are as shown in Figure 9.7.

From among the tentatively labeled nodes (nodes 4, 5, and 7), we select the node with the smallest distance value and declare that node permanently labeled. Thus node 5, with a distance of 14, becomes the new permanently labeled node. From node 5, then, we consider all nonpermanently labeled nodes that can be reached directly from node 5. Thus, the tentative label on node 4 is revised, and node 6 is tentatively labeled. Figure 9.8 depicts these calculations.

FIGURE 9.7 GORMAN'S NETWORK WITH A PERMANENT LABEL AT NODE 2 AND NEW TENTATIVE LABELS FOR NODES 4 AND 7

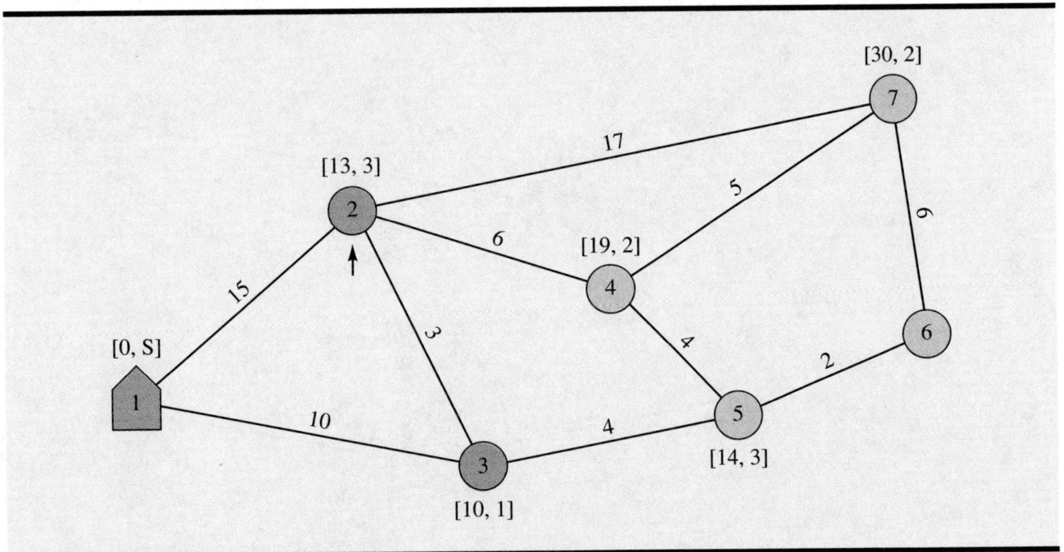

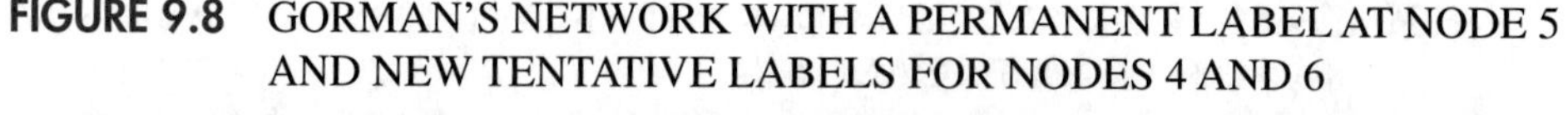

FIGURE 9.8 GORMAN'S NETWORK WITH A PERMANENT LABEL AT NODE 5 AND NEW TENTATIVE LABELS FOR NODES 4 AND 6

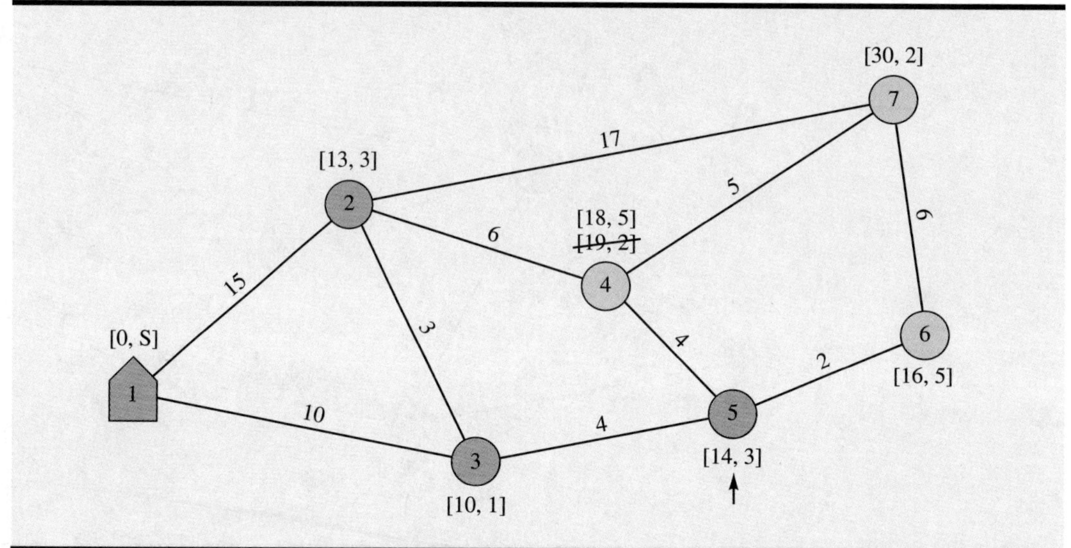

The smallest distance is again identified for the remaining tentatively labeled nodes, and this results in node 6 being permanently labeled. From node 6 we can determine a new tentative label with a distance value of 22 for node 7. After this step, the network appears as shown in Figure 9.9.

We now have only two remaining nonpermanently labeled nodes. Because the distance value at node 4 is smaller than that at node 7, node 4 becomes the new permanently labeled

FIGURE 9.9 GORMAN'S NETWORK WITH A PERMANENT LABEL AT NODE 6 AND A NEW TENTATIVE LABEL FOR NODE 7

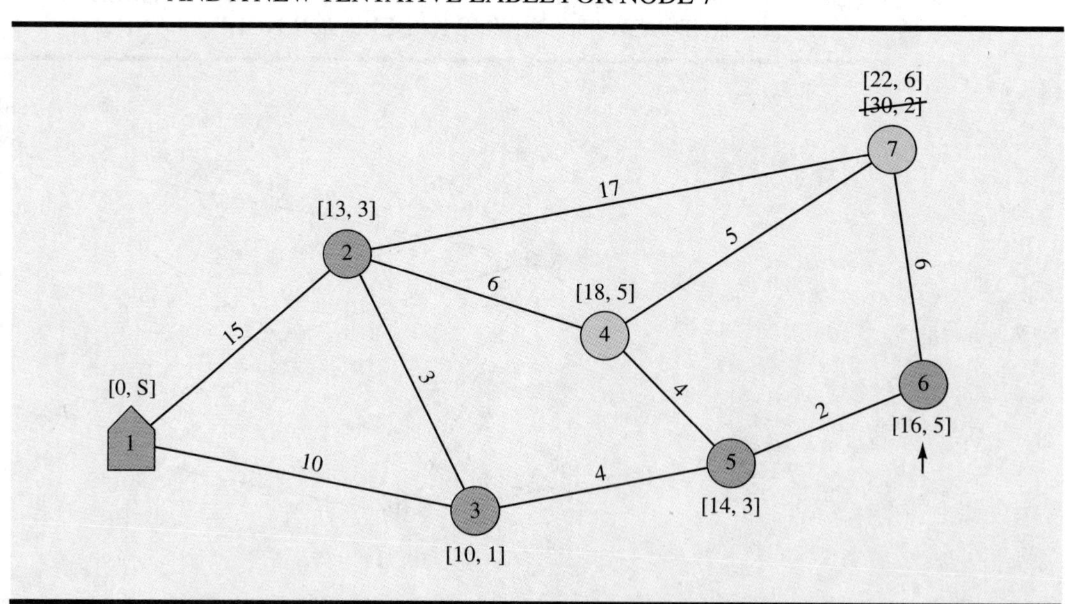

FIGURE 9.10 GORMAN'S NETWORK WITH A PERMANENT LABEL AT NODE 4

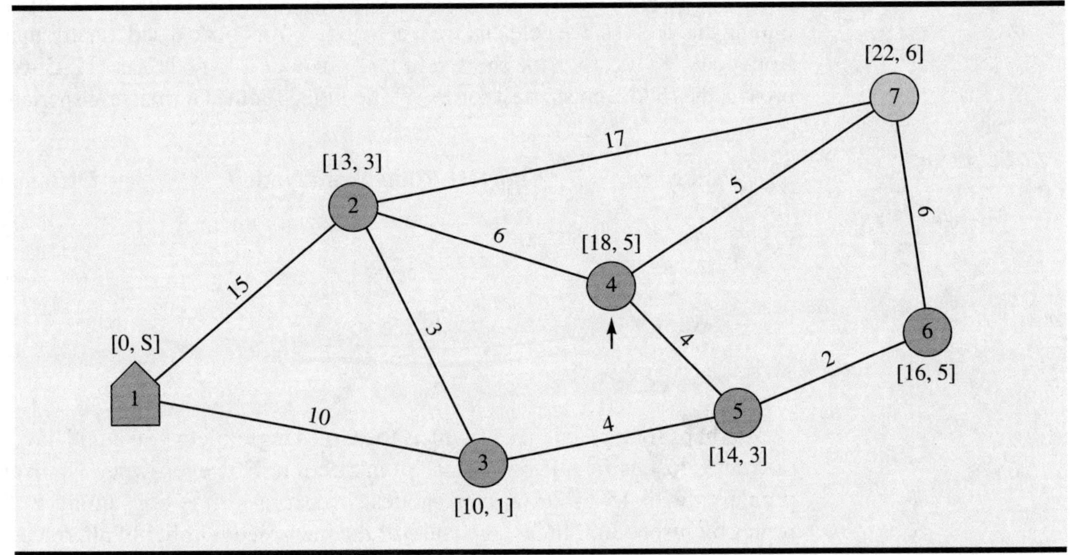

node. Because node 7 is the only nonpermanently labeled node that can be reached directly from node 4, we compare its distance value of 22 with the sum of the distance value at node 4 and the direct distance from node 4 to node 7, that is, 18 + 5 = 23. Because the [22,6] tentative label at node 7 is smaller, it remains unchanged. Figure 9.10 shows the network at this point.

Because node 7 is the only remaining node with a tentative label, it is now permanently labeled. Figure 9.11 shows the final network with all nodes permanently labeled.

We can now use the information in the permanent labels to find the shortest route from node 1 to each node in the network. For example, node 7's permanent label tells us the shortest distance from node 1 to node 7 is 22 miles. To find the particular route that enables us to reach

FIGURE 9.11 GORMAN'S NETWORK WITH ALL NODES PERMANENTLY LABELED

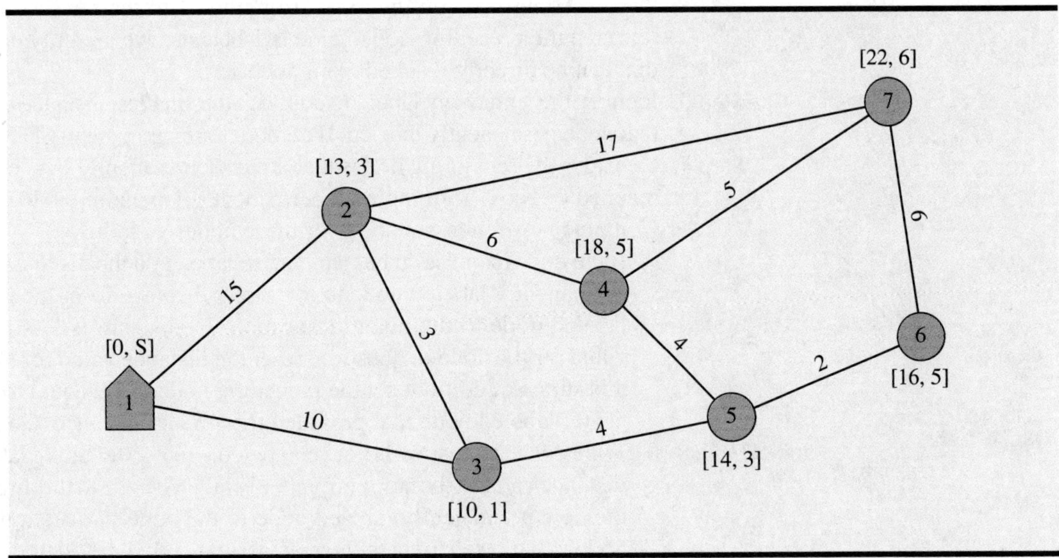

node 7 in 22 miles, we *start* at node 7 and work back to node 1. Node 7's label gives us the next direct link—node 6—and node 6's label indicates that node 5 is the next shortest-route link. Continuing this process, we note that we reach node 5 from node 3 and, finally, that we reach node 3 from node 1. Therefore, the shortest route from node 1 to node 7 is 1–3–5–6–7. Using this approach, the following shortest routes are identified for the Gorman transportation network:

Node	Shortest Route from Node 1	Distance in Miles
2	1–3–2	13
3	1–3	10
4	1–3–5–4	18
5	1–3–5	14
6	1–3–5–6	16
7	1–3–5–6–7	22

Perhaps for a problem as small as the Gorman problem you could have found the shortest routes just as fast, if not faster, by inspection. However, when we begin to investigate problems with 15 to 20 or more nodes, it becomes time-consuming to find the shortest routes by inspection. In fact, because of the increased number of alternate routes in a larger network, it is easy to miss one or more routes and come up with the wrong answer. Thus, for larger problems a systematic procedure such as the preceding labeling procedure is required. Even with the labeling method, we find that as the networks grow in size, it becomes necessary to implement the algorithm on a computer.

As we summarize the shortest-route algorithm, think of a network consisting of N nodes. The following procedure can be used to find the shortest route from node 1 to each of the other nodes in the network.

Step 1. Assign node 1 the permanent label [0,S]. The 0 indicates that the distance from node 1 to itself is zero and the S indicates that node 1 is the starting node.

Step 2. Compute tentative labels for the nodes that can be reached directly from node 1. The first number in each label is the direct distance from node 1 to the node in question; we refer to this portion of the label as the distance value. The second number in each label, which we refer to as the preceding node value, indicates the preceding node on the route from node 1 to the node in question; thus, in this step the preceding node value is 1 because we are only considering nodes that can be directly reached from node 1.

Step 3. Identify the tentatively labeled node with the smallest distance value, and declare that node permanently labeled. If all nodes are permanently labeled, go to step 5.

Step 4. Consider the remaining nodes that are not permanently labeled and that can be reached directly from the new permanently labeled node identified in step 3. Compute new tentative labels for these nodes as follows:

a. If the node in question has a tentative label, add the distance value at the new permanently labeled node to the direct distance from the new permanently labeled node to the node in question. If this sum is less than the distance value for the node in question, reset the distance value for this node equal to this sum; in addition, set the preceding node value equal to the new permanently labeled node that provided the smaller distance. Go to step 3.

b. If the node in question is not yet labeled, create a tentative label by adding the distance value at the new permanently labeled node to the direct distance from the new permanently labeled node to the node in question. The preceding node value is set equal to the new permanently labeled node. Go to step 3.

The shortest-route problem can also be formulated and solved as a transshipment problem. Simply set the supply at the start node and the demand at the end node equal to 1. However, unlike the labeling algorithm, this approach does not find the shortest route from the start node to every other node.

Step 5. The permanent labels identify both the shortest distance from node 1 to each node and the preceding node on the shortest route. The shortest route to a given node can be found by starting at the given node and moving backward to its preceding node. Continuing this backward movement through the network will provide the shortest route from node 1 to the node in question.

This algorithm will determine the shortest distance from node 1 to each of the other nodes in the network. Note that $N - 1$ iterations of the algorithm are required to find the shortest distance to all other nodes. If the shortest distance to every node is not needed, the algorithm can be stopped when those nodes of interest have been permanently labeled. The algorithm can also be easily modified to find the shortest distance from any node, say node k, to all other nodes in the network. To make such a change, we would merely begin by labeling node k with the permanent label [0,S]. Then by applying the steps of the algorithm, we can find the shortest route from node k to each of the other nodes in the network.

For practice in using the labeling algorithm to solve a shortest-route problem, try Problem 1.

The Management Scientist software package can be used to solve small shortest-route problems. Input for the program includes the number of nodes, the number of arcs, and the length of each arc. The output shown in Figure 9.12 provides the shortest route from node 1 to node 7 for the Gorman problem.

FIGURE 9.12 THE MANAGEMENT SCIENTIST SOLUTION FOR THE GORMAN SHORTEST-ROUTE PROBLEM

```
               ****  NETWORK DESCRIPTION  ****

                    7 NODES AND 10 ARCS

         ARC     START NODE     END NODE     DISTANCE
         ---     ----------     --------     --------
          1          1              2            15
          2          1              3            10
          3          2              3             3
          4          2              4             6
          5          2              7            17
          6          3              5             4
          7          4              5             4
          8          4              7             5
          9          5              6             2
         10          6              7             6

         THE SHORTEST ROUTE FROM NODE 1 TO NODE 7
         ***************************************

         START NODE        END NODE        DISTANCE
         ----------        --------        --------
              1                3               10
              3                5                4
              5                6                2
              6                7                6

                   TOTAL DISTANCE              22
```

NOTES AND COMMENTS

1. Many applications of the shortest-route algorithm involve criteria such as time or cost instead of distance. In these cases, the shortest-route algorithm provides the minimum-time or minimum-cost solution. However, since the shortest-route algorithm always identifies a minimum-value solution, it would not make sense to apply the algorithm to problems that involve a profit criterion.
2. In some applications, the value associated with an arc may be negative. For example, in situations where cost is the criterion, a negative arc value would denote a negative cost; in other words, a profit would be realized by traversing the arc. The shortest-route algorithm presented in this section can only be applied to networks with nonnegative arc values. More advanced texts discuss algorithms that can solve problems with negative arc values.

9.2 MINIMAL SPANNING TREE PROBLEM

In network terminology, the minimal spanning tree problem involves using the arcs of the network to reach *all* nodes of the network in such a fashion that the total length of all the arcs used is minimized. To better understand this problem, let us consider the communications system design problem encountered by a regional computer center.

The Southwestern Regional Computer Center must have special computer communications lines installed to connect five satellite users with a new central computer. The telephone company will install the new communications network. However, the installation is an expensive operation. To reduce costs, the center's management group wants the total length of the new communications lines to be as short as possible. Although the central computer could be connected directly to each user, it appears to be more economical to install a direct line to some users and let other users tap into the system by linking them with users already connected to the system. The determination of this minimal length communications system design is an example of the **minimal spanning tree** problem. The network for this problem with possible connection alternatives and distances is shown in Figure 9.13.

FIGURE 9.13 COMMUNICATIONS NETWORK FOR THE REGIONAL COMPUTER SYSTEM

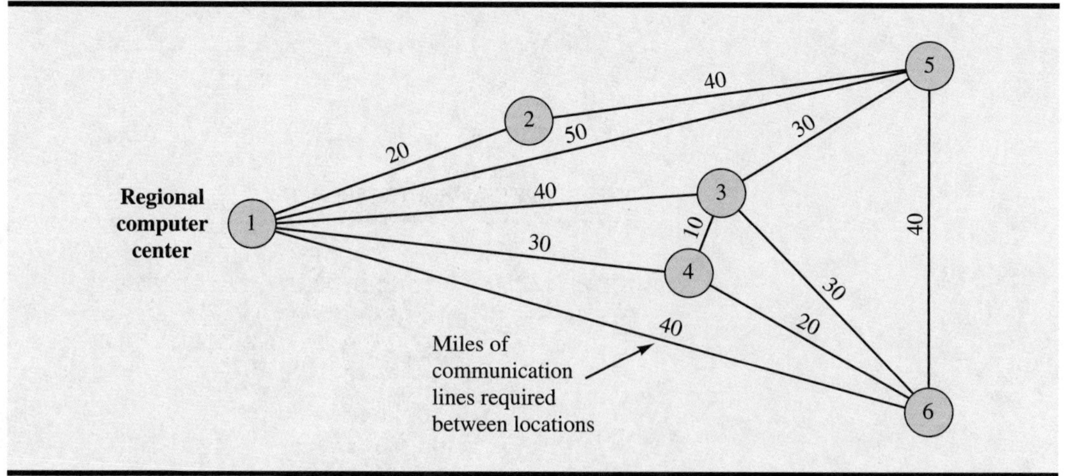

An algorithm that can be used to solve this network model is explained in the following subsection.

A Minimal Spanning Tree Algorithm

For a network consisting of N nodes, a spanning tree will consist of N − 1 arcs.

A **spanning tree** for an N-node network is a set of $N - 1$ arcs that connects every node to every other node. A minimal spanning tree provides this set of arcs at minimal total arc cost, distance, or some other measure. The network algorithm that can be used to solve the minimal spanning tree problem is simple. The steps of the algorithm are as follows:

Step 1. Arbitrarily begin at any node and connect it to the closest node in terms of the criterion being used (e.g., time, cost, or distance). The two nodes are referred to as *connected* nodes, and the remaining nodes are referred to as *unconnected* nodes.

Step 2. Identify the unconnected node that is closest to one of the connected nodes. Break ties arbitrarily if two or more nodes qualify as the closest node. Add this new node to the set of connected nodes. Repeat this step until all nodes have been connected.

This network algorithm is easily implemented by making the connection decisions directly on the network.

Referring to the communications network for the regional computer center and arbitrarily beginning at node 1, we find the closest node is node 2 with a distance of 20. Using a bold line to connect nodes 1 and 2, step 1 of the algorithm provides the following result:

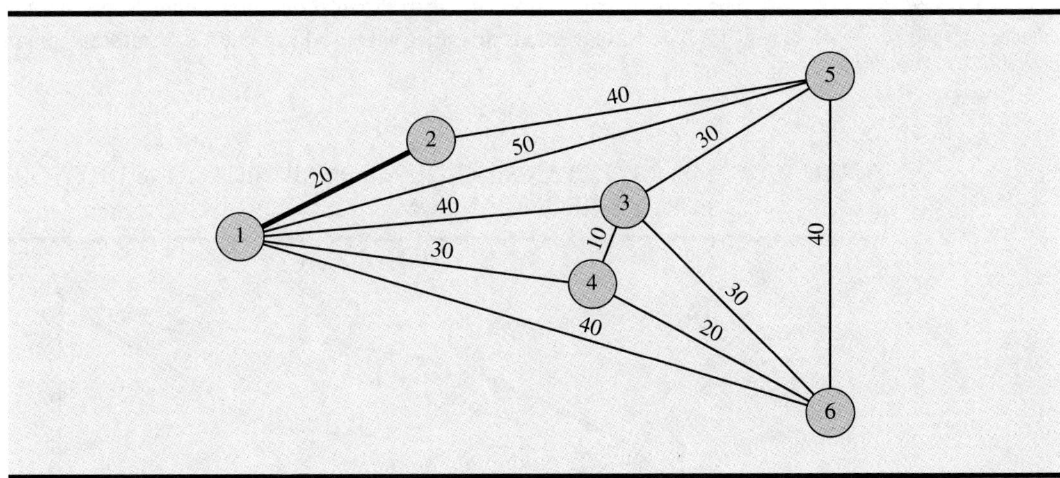

In step 2 of the algorithm, we find that the unconnected node closest to one of the connected nodes is node 4, with a distance of 30 miles from node 1. Adding node 4 to the set of connected nodes provides the following result:

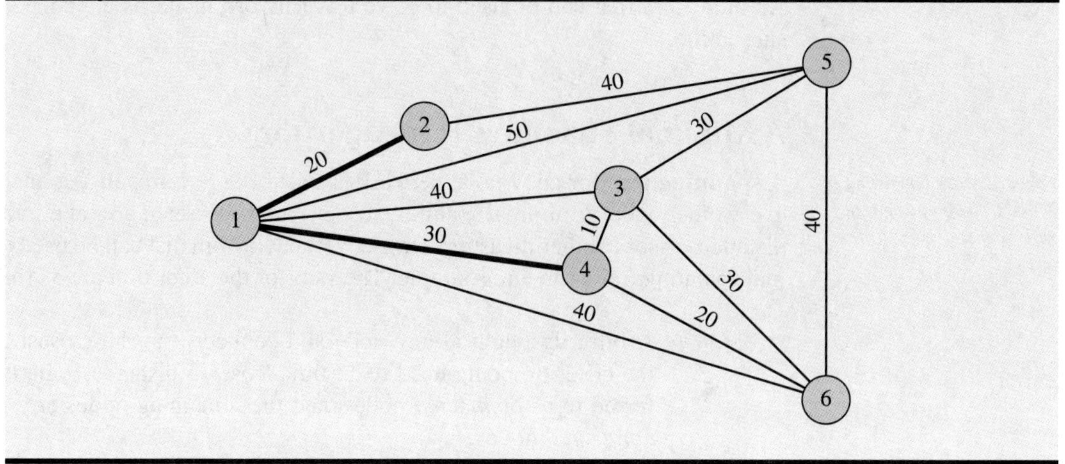

Repeating the step of always adding the closest unconnected node to the connected segment of the network provides the minimal spanning tree solution shown in Figure 9.14. Follow the steps of the algorithm, and see whether you obtain this solution. The minimal length of the spanning tree is given by the sum of the distances on the arcs forming the spanning tree. In this case, the total distance is 110 miles for the computer center's communications network. Note that while the computer center's network arcs were measured in distance, other network models may measure the arcs in terms of other criteria such as cost, time, and so on. In such cases, the minimal spanning tree algorithm will identify the optimal solution (minimal cost, minimal time, etc.) for the criterion being considered.

Can you now find a minimal spanning tree for a network? Try Problem 10.

The computer solution to the regional computer center's problem is shown in Figure 9.15. The Management Scientist was used to obtain the minimal spanning tree solution of 110 miles.

FIGURE 9.14 MINIMAL SPANNING TREE COMMUNICATIONS NETWORK FOR THE REGIONAL COMPUTER CENTER

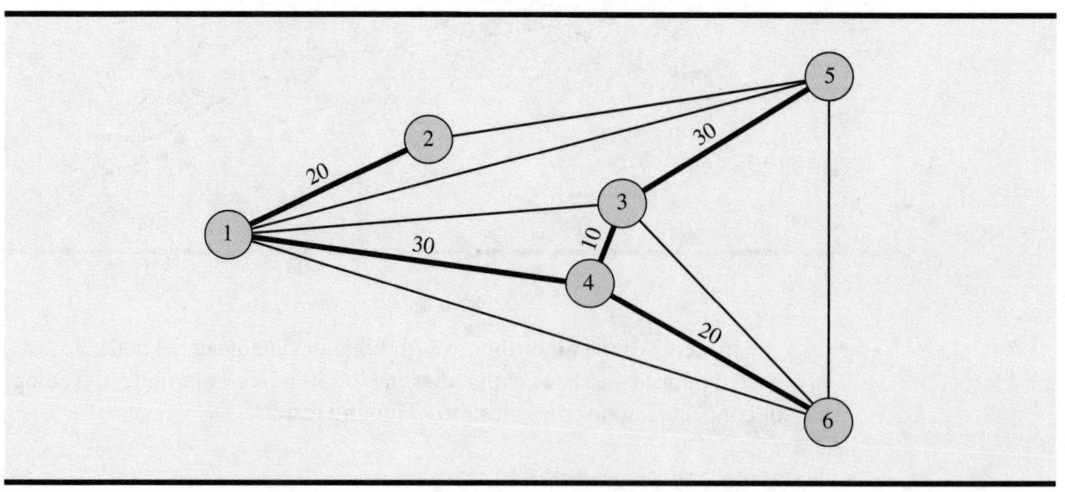

FIGURE 9.15 THE MANAGEMENT SCIENTIST SOLUTION FOR THE REGIONAL COMPUTER CENTER MINIMAL SPANNING TREE PROBLEM

```
                **** NETWORK DESCRIPTION ****

                    6 NODES AND 11 ARCS

        ARC    START NODE    END NODE    DISTANCE
        ---    ----------    --------    --------
         1         1            2           20
         2         1            3           40
         3         1            4           30
         4         1            5           50
         5         1            6           40
         6         2            5           40
         7         3            4           10
         8         3            5           30
         9         3            6           30
        10         4            6           20
        11         5            6           40

                  MINIMAL SPANNING TREE
                  *********************

        START NODE       END NODE        DISTANCE
        ----------       --------        --------
             1               2              20
             1               4              30
             4               3              10
             4               6              20
             3               5              30

                TOTAL LENGTH               110
```

NOTES AND COMMENTS

1. The Management Science in Action, EDS Designs a Communication Network, describes an interesting application of the minimal spanning tree algorithm.
2. The minimal spanning tree algorithm is considered a *greedy algorithm* because at each stage we can be "greedy" and take the best action available at that stage. Following this strategy at each successive stage will provide the overall optimal solution. Cases in which a greedy algorithm provides the optimal solution are rare. For many problems, however, greedy algorithms are excellent heuristics.

MANAGEMENT SCIENCE IN ACTION

EDS DESIGNS A COMMUNICATION NETWORK*

EDS, headquartered in Plano, Texas, is a global leader in information technology services. The company provides hardware, software, communications, and process solutions to many companies and governments around the world.

EDS designs communication systems and information networks for many of its customers. In one application, an EDS customer wanted to link together 64 locations for information flow and communications. Interactive transmission involving voice, video, and digital data had to be accommodated in the information flow between the various sites. The customer's locations included approximately 50 offices and information centers in the continental United States; they ranged from Connecticut to Florida to Michigan to Texas to California. Additional locations existed in Canada, Mexico, Hawaii, and Puerto Rico. A total of 64 locations formed the nodes of the information network.

EDS's task was to span the network by finding the most cost-effective way to link the 64 customer locations with each other and with existing EDS data centers. The arcs of the network represented communication links between pairs of nodes in the network. In cases where land communication lines were available, the arcs consisted of fiber-optic telephone lines. In other cases, the arcs represented satellite communication connections.

Using cost as the criterion, EDS developed the information network for the customer by solving a minimal spanning tree problem. The minimum cost network design made it possible for all customer locations to communicate with each other and with the existing EDS data centers.

*The authors are indebted to Greg A. Dennis of EDS for providing this application.

9.3 MAXIMAL FLOW PROBLEM

The objective in a **maximal flow** problem is to determine the maximum amount of flow (vehicles, messages, fluid, etc.) that can enter and exit a network system in a given period of time. In this problem, we attempt to transmit flow through all arcs of the network as efficiently as possible. The amount of flow is limited due to capacity restrictions on the various arcs of the network. For example, highway types limit vehicle flow in a transportation system, while pipe sizes limit oil flow in an oil distribution system. The maximum or upper limit on the flow in an arc is referred to as the **flow capacity** of the arc. Even though we do not specify capacities for the nodes, we do assume that the flow out of a node is equal to the flow into the node.

As an example of the maximal flow problem, consider the north-south interstate highway system passing through Cincinnati, Ohio. The north–south vehicle flow reaches a level of 15,000 vehicles per hour at peak times. Due to a summer highway maintenance program, which calls for the temporary closing of lanes and lower speed limits, a network of alternate routes through Cincinnati has been proposed by a transportation planning committee. The alternate routes include other highways as well as city streets. Because of differences in speed limits and traffic patterns, flow capacities vary, depending on the particular streets and roads used. The proposed network with arc flow capacities is shown in Figure 9.16.

The direction of flow for each arc is indicated, and the arc capacity is shown next to each arc. Note that most of the streets are one-way. However, a two-way street can be found between nodes 2 and 3 and between nodes 5 and 6. In both cases, the capacity is the same in each direction.

We will show how to develop a capacitated transshipment model (see Chapter 7) for the maximal flow problem. First, we will add an arc from node 7 back to node 1 to represent the total flow through the highway system. Figure 9.17 shows the modified network. The newly added arc shows no capacity; indeed, we will want to maximize the flow over that arc. Maximizing the flow over the arc from node 7 to node 1 is equivalent to maxi-

FIGURE 9.16 NETWORK OF HIGHWAY SYSTEM AND FLOW CAPACITIES (1000s/HOUR) FOR CINCINNATI

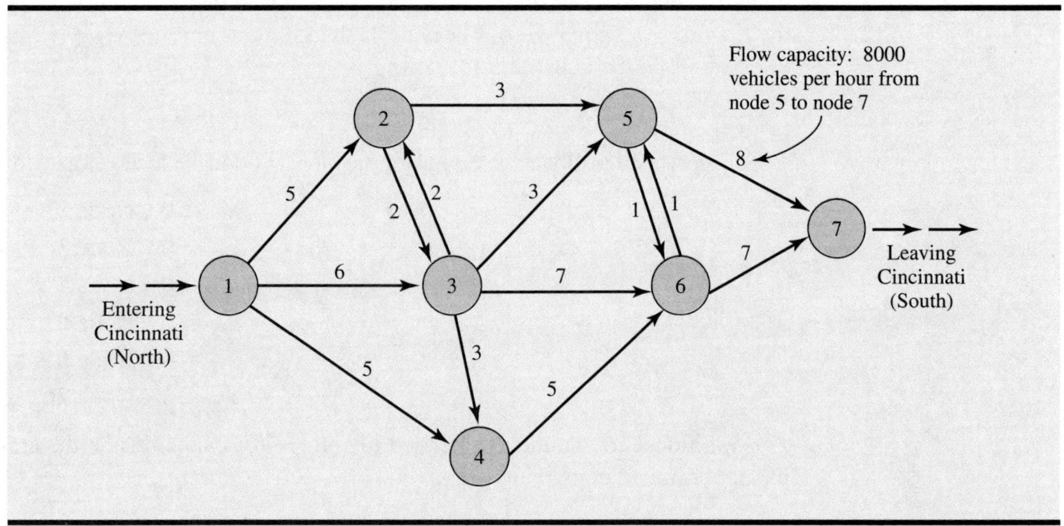

mizing the number of cars that can get through the north–south highway system passing through Cincinnati.

As we did in Chapter 7 we define our decision variables as follows:

$$x_{ij} = \text{amount of traffic flow from node } i \text{ to node } j$$

The objective function that maximizes the flow over the highway system is

$$\text{Max} \quad x_{71}$$

FIGURE 9.17 FLOW OVER ARC FROM NODE 7 TO NODE 1 TO REPRESENT TOTAL FLOW THROUGH THE CINCINNATI HIGHWAY SYSTEM

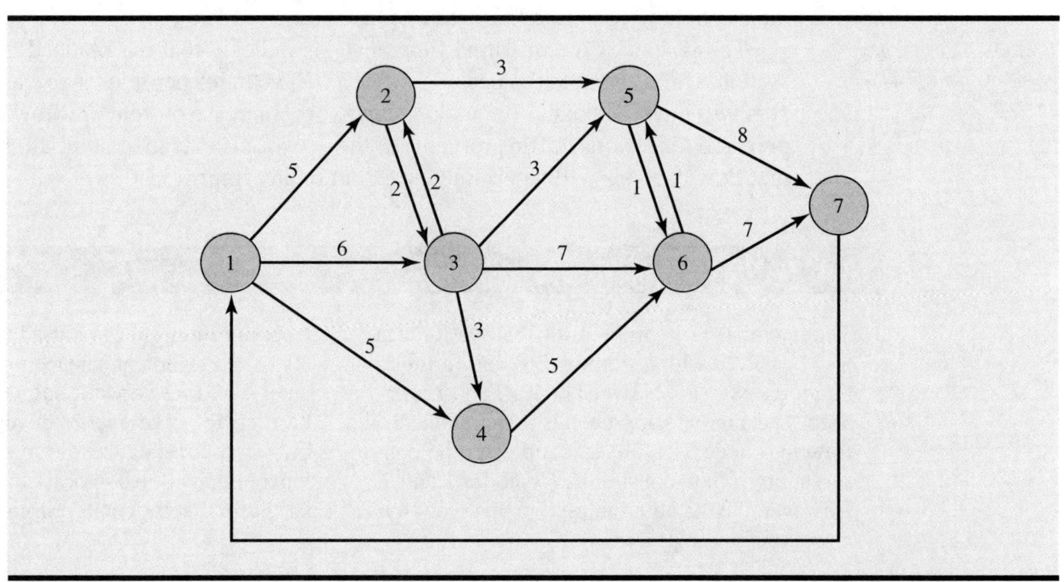

As with all transshipment problems, each arc generates a variable and each node generates a constraint. For each node, a conservation of flow constraint represents the requirement that the flow out must equal the flow in. Or, stated another way, the flow out minus the flow in must equal zero. For node 1, the flow out is $x_{12} + x_{13} + x_{14}$, and the flow in is x_{71}. Therefore, the constraint for node 1 is

$$x_{12} + x_{13} + x_{14} - x_{71} = 0$$

The conservation of flow constraints for the other six nodes are developed in a similar fashion.

$$
\begin{aligned}
x_{23} + x_{25} - x_{12} - x_{32} &= 0 \quad \text{Node 2} \\
x_{32} + x_{34} + x_{35} + x_{36} - x_{13} - x_{23} &= 0 \quad \text{Node 3} \\
x_{46} - x_{14} - x_{34} &= 0 \quad \text{Node 4} \\
x_{56} + x_{57} - x_{25} - x_{35} - x_{65} &= 0 \quad \text{Node 5} \\
x_{65} + x_{67} - x_{36} - x_{46} - x_{56} &= 0 \quad \text{Node 6} \\
x_{71} - x_{57} - x_{67} &= 0 \quad \text{Node 7}
\end{aligned}
$$

Additional constraints are needed to enforce the capacities on the arcs. These 14 simple upper-bound constraints are given.

$$
\begin{array}{llll}
x_{12} \le 5 & x_{13} \le 6 & x_{14} \le 5 & \\
x_{23} \le 2 & x_{25} \le 3 & & \\
x_{32} \le 2 & x_{34} \le 3 & x_{35} \le 3 & x_{36} \le 7 \\
x_{46} \le 5 & & & \\
x_{56} \le 1 & x_{57} \le 8 & & \\
x_{65} \le 1 & x_{67} \le 7 & &
\end{array}
$$

Note that the only arc without a capacity is the one we added out of node 7.

The Management Scientist solution to this 15-variable, 21-constraint linear programming problem is shown in Figure 9.18. We note that the value of the optimal solution is 14. This result implies that the maximal flow over the highway system is 14,000 vehicles. Figure 9.19 shows how the vehicle flow is routed through the original highway network. We note, for instance, that 5000 vehicles per hour are routed between nodes 1 and 2, 2000 vehicles per hour are routed between nodes 2 and 3, and so on.

Try Problem 15 for practice in solving a maximal flow problem.

The results of the maximal flow analysis indicate that the planned highway network system will not handle the peak flow of 15,000 vehicles per hour. The transportation planners will have to expand the highway network, increase current arc flow capacities, or be prepared for serious traffic problems. If the network is extended or modified, another maximal flow analysis will determine the extent of any improved flow.

NOTES AND COMMENTS

1. The maximal flow problem of this section can also be solved with a slightly different formulation if the extra arc between nodes 7 and 1 is not used. The alternate approach is to maximize the flow into node 7 ($x_{57} + x_{67}$) and drop the conservation of flow constraints for nodes 1 and 7. However, the formulation used in this section is most common in practice.
2. Network models can be used to describe a variety of management science problems. Unfortunately, no one network solution algorithm can be used to solve every network problem. It is important to recognize the specific type of problem being modeled in order to select the correct specialized solution algorithm.

FIGURE 9.18 THE MANAGEMENT SCIENTIST SOLUTION TO THE CINCINNATI HIGHWAY SYSTEM MAXIMAL FLOW PROBLEM

EXCELfile
Cincinnati

```
OPTIMAL SOLUTION

Objective Function Value = 14.000

    Variable            Value
  --------------    --------------
      X12                5.000
      X13                6.000
      X14                3.000
      X23                2.000
      X25                3.000
      X34                0.000
      X35                3.000
      X36                5.000
      X32                0.000
      X46                3.000
      X56                0.000
      X57                7.000
      X65                1.000
      X67                7.000
      X71               14.000
```

FIGURE 9.19 MAXIMAL FLOW PATTERN FOR THE CINCINNATI HIGHWAY SYSTEM NETWORK

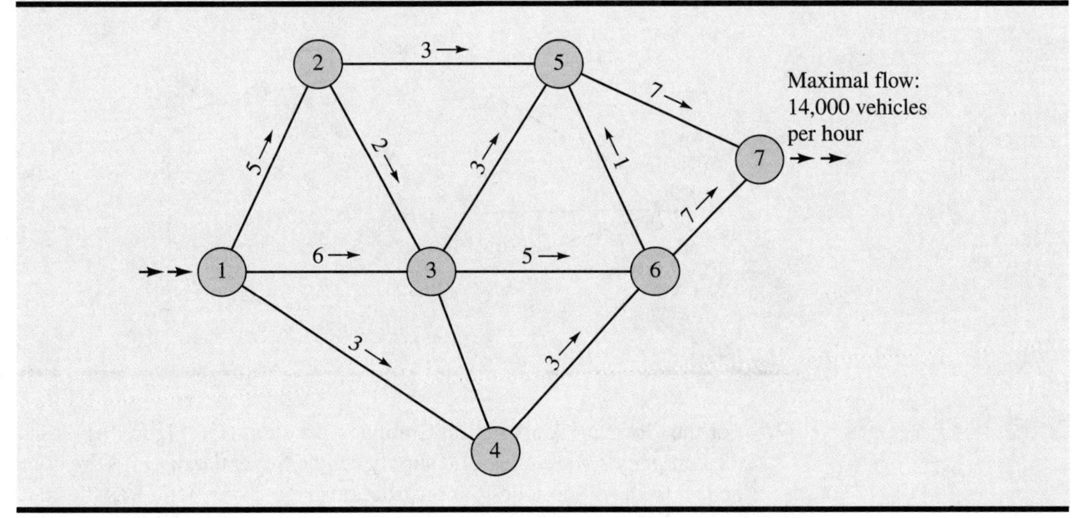

SUMMARY

In this chapter we extended the discussion of the use of network models in managerial decision making. We introduced the shortest-route, minimal spanning tree, and maximal flow problems and presented specialized solution algorithms for the shortest-route and minimal spanning tree problems. We showed how to formulate the maximal flow problem as a transshipment problem and solved it as a linear program. The key to success in network approaches to problem solving is in seeing how the problem can be represented as a network model. Some network formulations are obvious, but other problems may require substantial ingenuity to develop the appropriate network representation. In any case, once the network representation has been developed, specialized solution algorithms are available to solve the problem.

GLOSSARY

Shortest route Shortest path between two nodes in a network.

Minimal spanning tree The spanning tree with the minimum length.

Spanning tree A set of $N - 1$ arcs that connects every node in the network with all other nodes where N is the number of nodes.

Maximal flow The maximum amount of flow that can enter and exit a network system during a given period of time.

Flow capacity The maximum flow for an arc of the network. The flow capacity in one direction may not equal the flow capacity in the reverse direction.

PROBLEMS

1. Find the shortest route from node 1 to each of the other nodes in the transportation network shown.

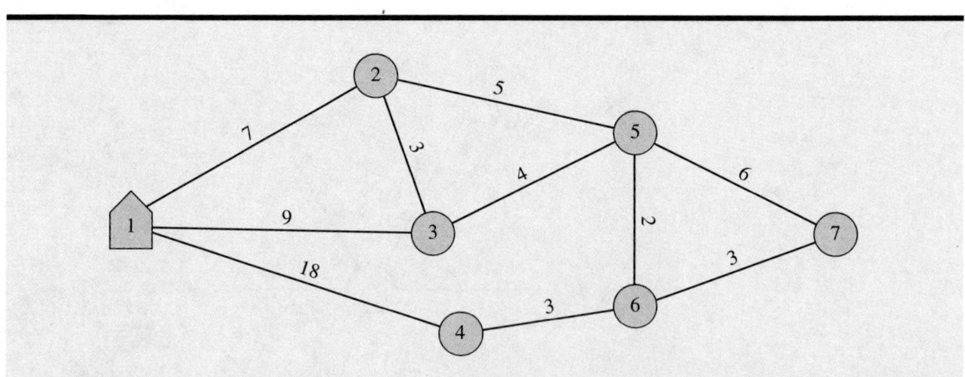

2. For the Gorman Construction Company problem (see Figure 9.1), assume that node 7 is the company's warehouse and supply center. Several daily trips are commonly made from node 7 to the other nodes or construction sites. Using node 7 as the starting node, find the shortest route from this node to each of the other nodes in the network.
3. In the original Gorman Construction Company problem, we found the shortest distance from the office (node 1) to each of the other nodes or construction sites. Because some of the roads are highways and others are city streets, the shortest-distance routes between the

office and the construction sites may not necessarily provide the quickest or shortest-time routes. Shown here is the Gorman road network with travel time values rather than distance values. Find the shortest route from Gorman's office to each of the construction sites if the objective is to minimize travel time rather than distance.

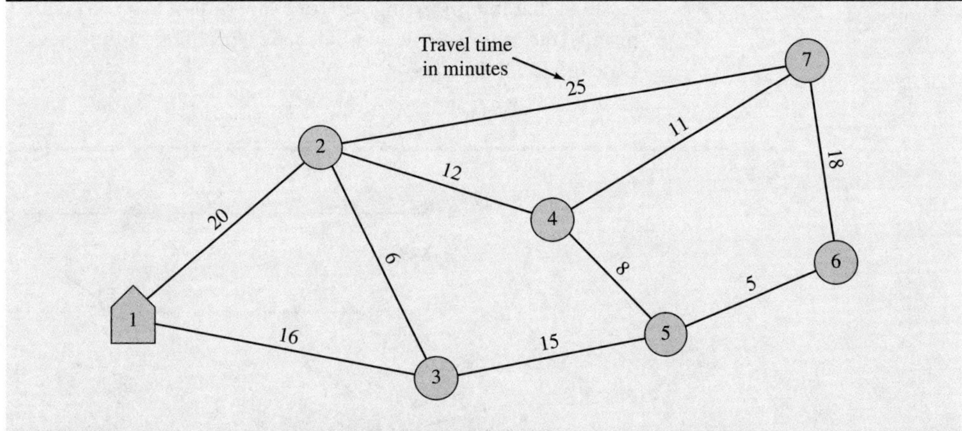

4. Find the shortest route between nodes 1 and 8 in the following network:

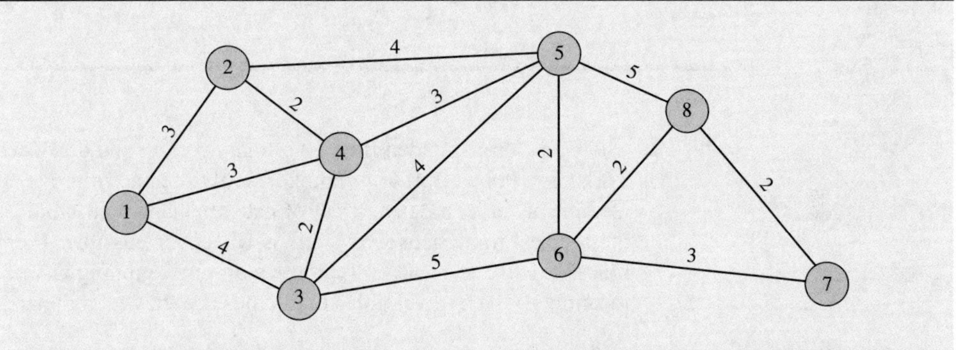

5. Find the shortest route between nodes 1 and 10 in the following network:

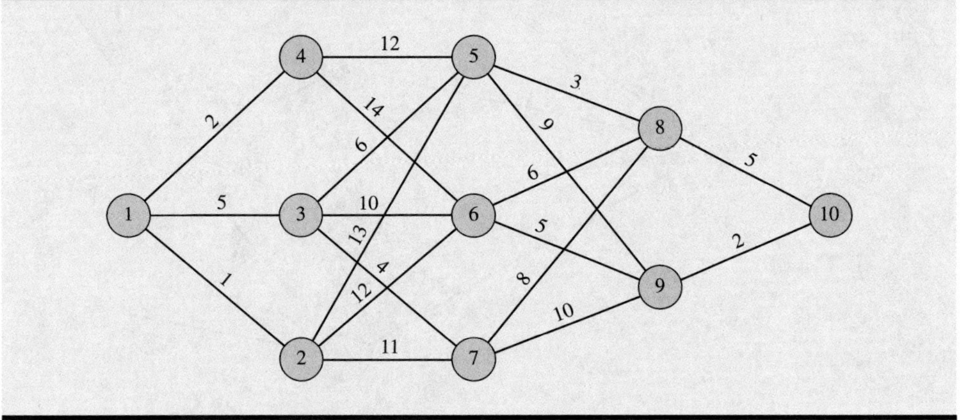

6. Morgan Trucking Company operates a special speedy pickup and delivery service between Chicago and 10 other cities located in a four-state area. When Morgan receives a request for service, it dispatches a truck from Chicago to the city requesting service as soon as possible. With both fast service and minimum travel costs as objectives for Morgan, it is important that the dispatched truck take the shortest route from Chicago to the specified city. Assume that the following network (not drawn to scale) with distances given in miles represents the highway network for this problem. Find the shortest-route distances from Chicago to all 10 cites.

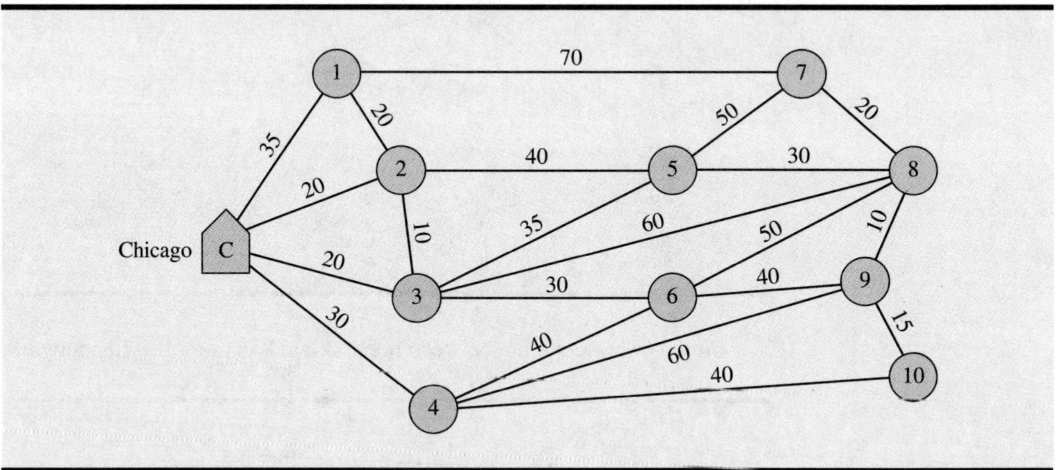

7. City Cab Company identified 10 primary pickup and drop locations for cab riders in New York City. In an effort to minimize travel time and improve customer service and the utilization of the company's fleet of cabs, management would like the cab drivers to take the shortest route between locations whenever possible. Using the following network of roads and streets, what is the route a driver beginning at location 1 should take to reach location 10? The travel times in minutes are shown on the arcs of the network.

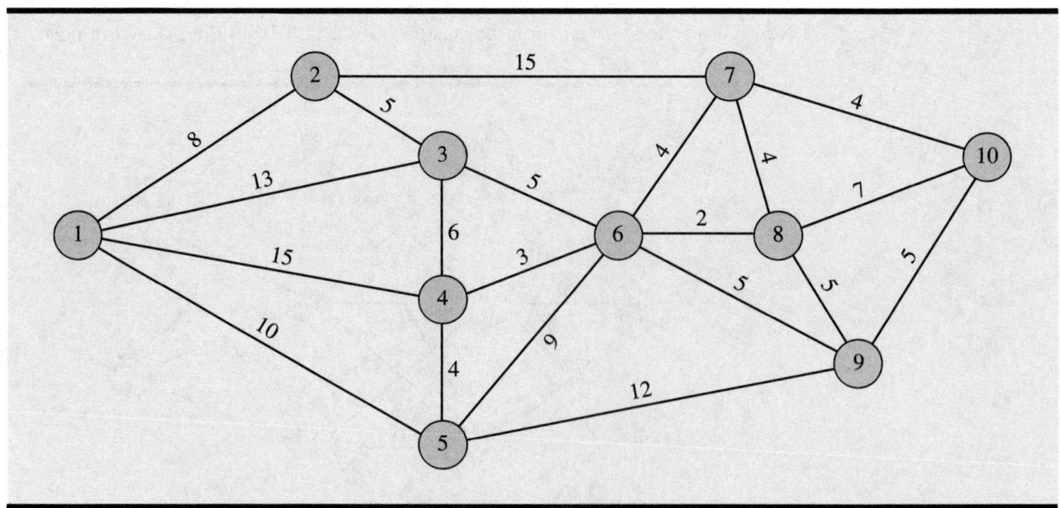

8. The Wisman Candy Company manufactures a variety of candy products. Company trucks are used to deliver local orders directly to retail outlets. When the business was small, the drivers of the trucks were free to take routes of their choice as they made the delivery rounds to the retail outlets. However, as the business has grown, transportation and delivery costs have become significant. In an effort to improve the efficiency of the delivery operation, Wisman's management would like to determine the shortest delivery routes between retail outlets. For example, the following network shows the roads that may be taken between a retail outlet at node 1 and a retail outlet at node 11. Determine the shortest route for a truck that is currently at node 1 and must make a delivery to node 11.

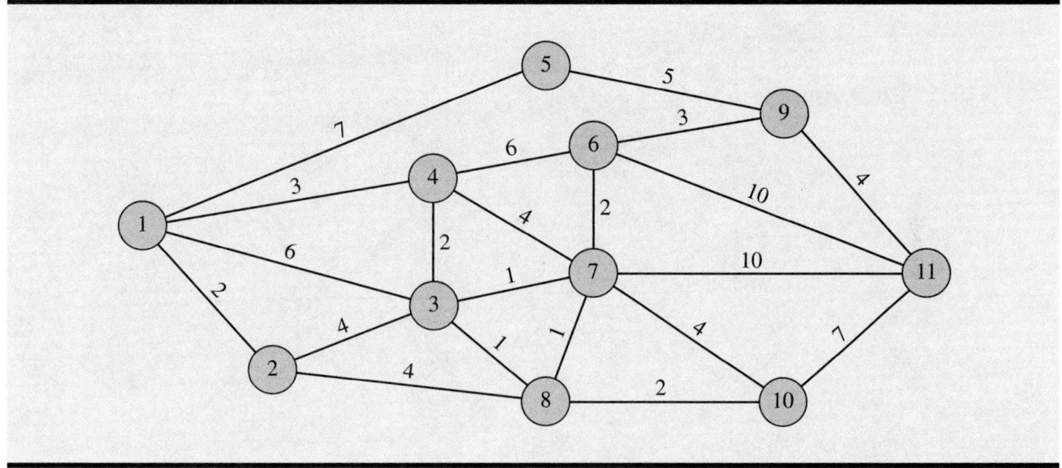

9. The five nodes in the following network represent points one year apart over a four-year period. Each node indicates a time when a decision is made to keep or replace a firm's computer equipment. If a decision is made to replace the equipment, a decision must also be made as to how long the new equipment will be used. The arc from node 0 to node 1 represents the decision to keep the current equipment one year and replace it at the end of the year. The arc from node 0 to node 2 represents the decision to keep the current equipment two years and replace it at the end of year 2. The numbers above the arcs indicate the total cost associated with the equipment replacement decisions. These costs include discounted purchase price, trade-in value, operating costs, and maintenance costs. Determine the minimum cost equipment replacement policy for the four-year period.

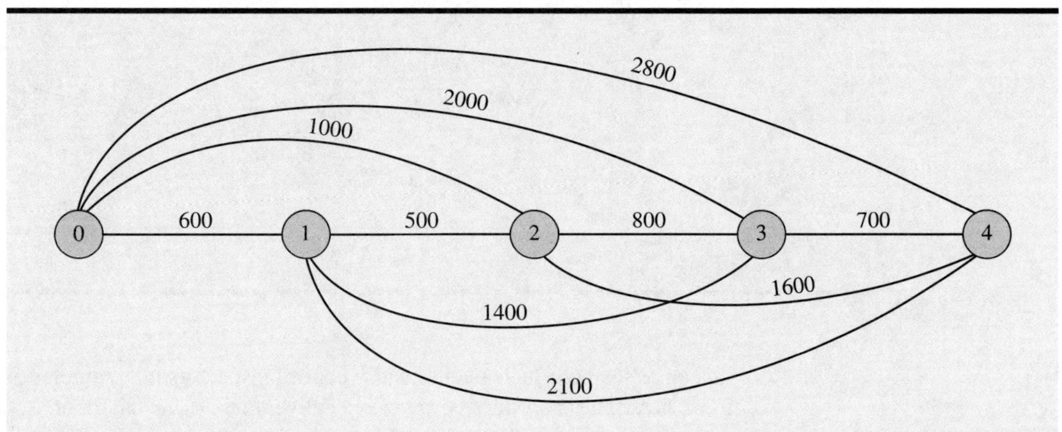

10. The State of Ohio recently purchased land for a new state park, and park planners identified the ideal locations for the lodge, cabins, picnic groves, boat dock, and scenic points of interest. These locations are represented by the nodes of the following network. The arcs of the network represent possible road connections in the park. If the state park designers want to minimize the total road miles that must be constructed in the park and still permit access to all facilities (nodes), which road connections should be constructed?

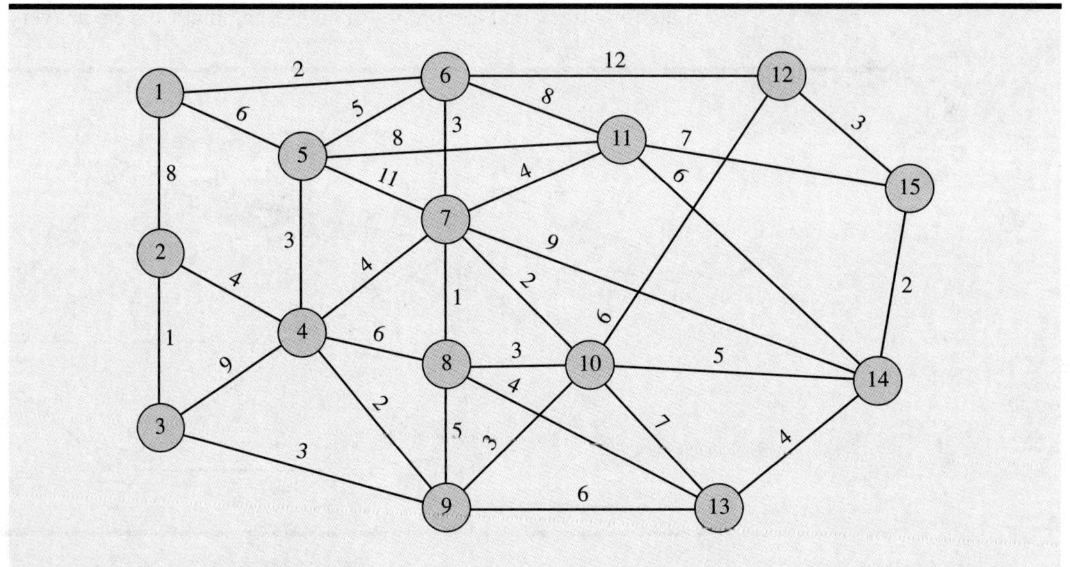

11. Develop the minimal spanning tree solution for the following emergency communication network.

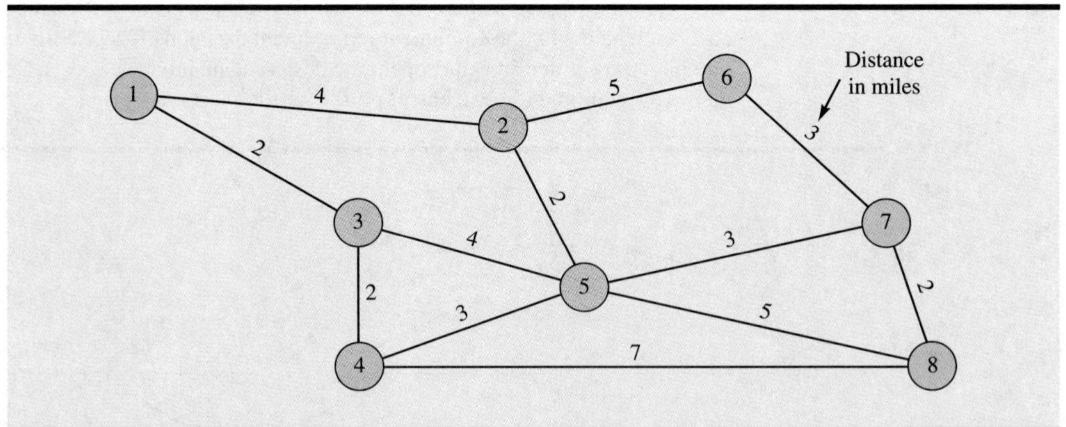

12. In a large soap products plant, quality control inspectors take samples of various products from the different production areas and deliver them to the lab for analysis. The inspection process is slow, and the inspectors spend substantial time transporting samples from the

production areas to the lab. The company is considering installing a pneumatic tube conveyor system that could transport the samples between the production areas and the lab. The following network shows the location of the lab and the production areas (nodes) where the samples must be collected. The arcs are the alternatives being considered for the conveyor system. What is the minimum total length and layout of the conveyor system that will enable all production areas to send samples to the lab?

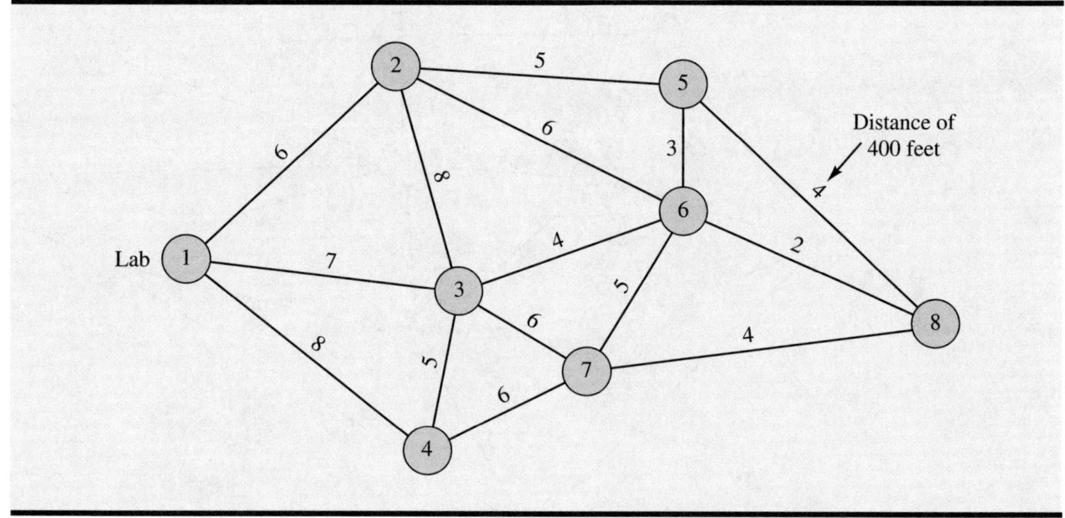

13. Midwest University is installing an electronic mail system. The following network shows the possible electronic connections among the offices. Distances between offices are shown in thousands of feet. Develop a design for the office communication system that will enable all offices to have access to the electronic mail service. Provide the design that minimizes the total length of connection among the eight offices.

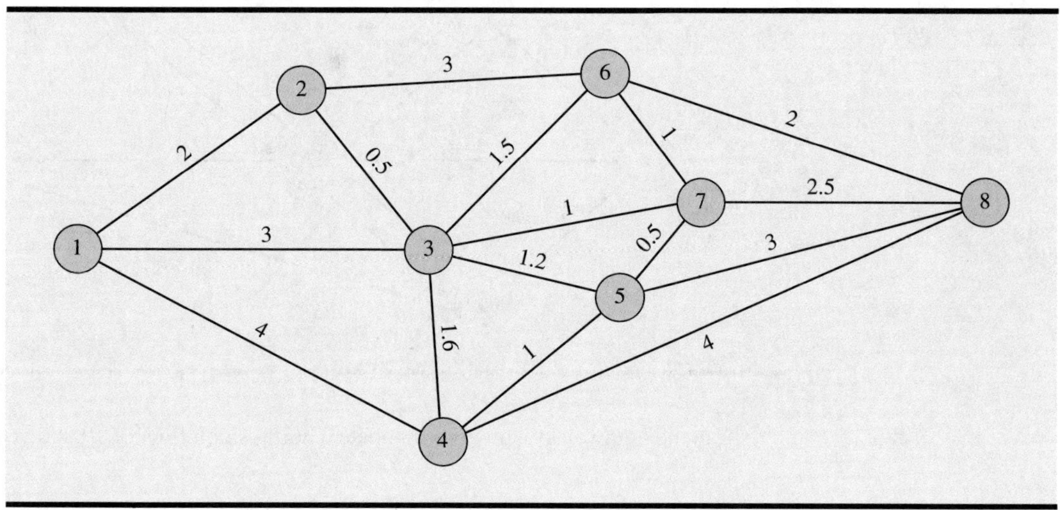

14. The Metrovision Cable Company just received approval to begin providing cable television service to a suburb of Memphis, Tennessee. The nodes of the following network show the distribution points that must be reached by the company's primary cable lines. The arcs of the network show the number of miles between the distribution points. Determine the solution that will enable the company to reach all distribution points with the minimum length of primary cable line.

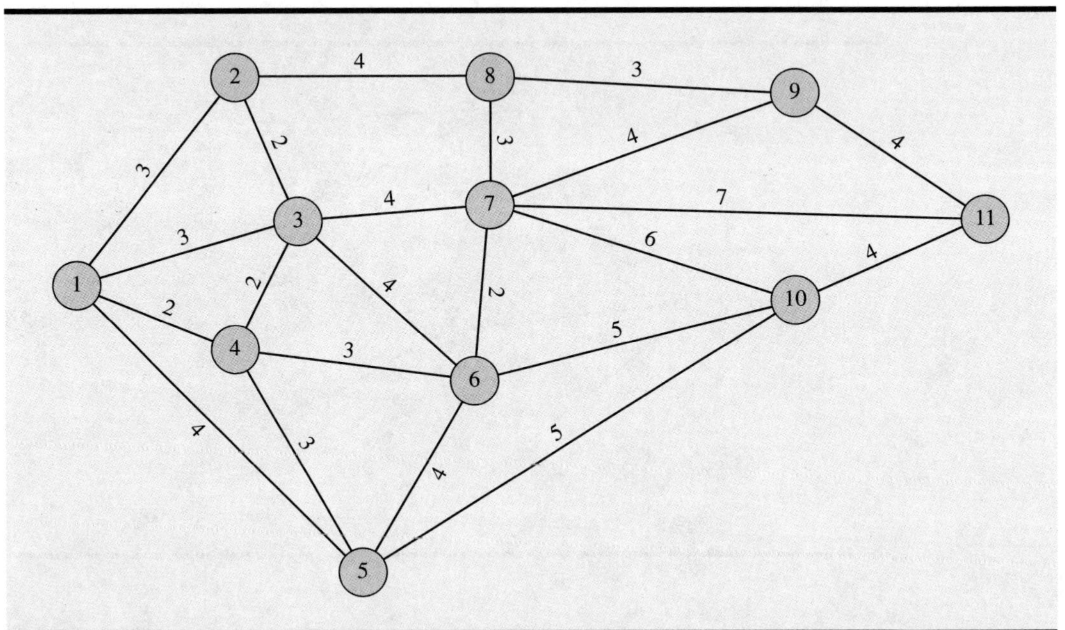

SELF test

15. The north–south highway system passing through Albany, New York, can accommodate the capacities shown.

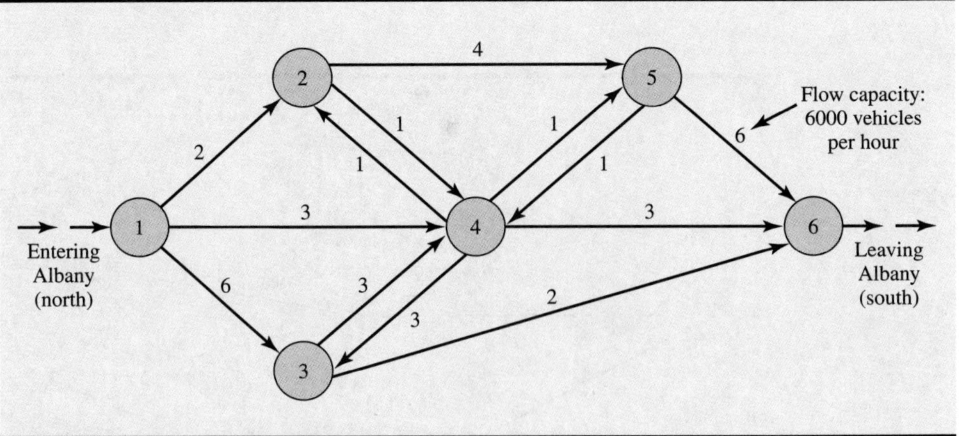

Can the highway system accommodate a north–south flow of 10,000 vehicles per hour?

16. If the Albany highway system described in Problem 15 has revised flow capacities as shown in the following network, what is the maximal flow in vehicles per hour through the system? How many vehicles per hour must travel over each road (arc) to obtain this maximal flow?

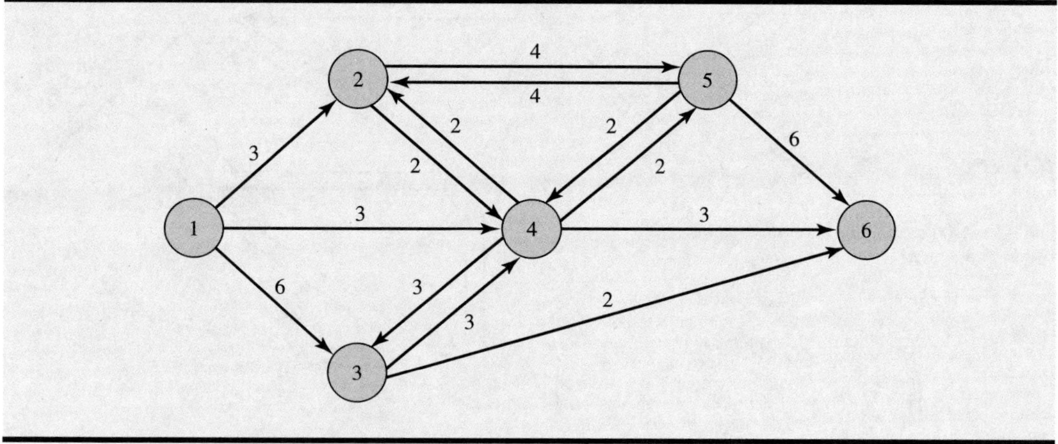

17. A long-distance telephone company uses a fiber-optic network to transmit phone calls and other information between locations. Calls are carried through cable lines and switching nodes. A portion of the company's transmission network is shown here. The numbers above each arc show the capacity in thousands of messages that can be transmitted over that branch of the network.

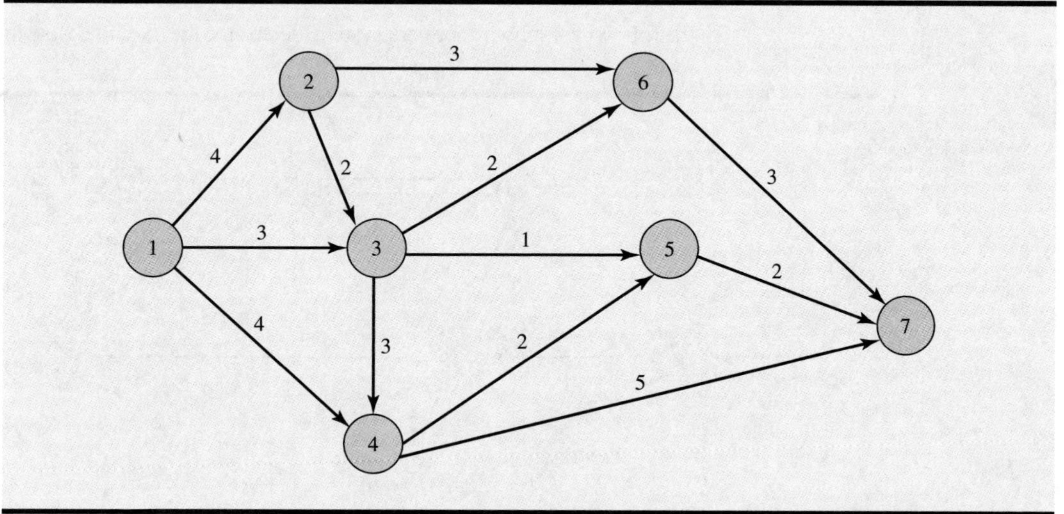

To keep up with the volume of information transmitted between origin and destination points, use the network to determine the maximum number of messages that may be sent from a city located at node 1 to a city located at node 7.

18. The High-Price Oil Company owns a pipeline network that is used to convey oil from its source to several storage locations. A portion of the network is as follows:

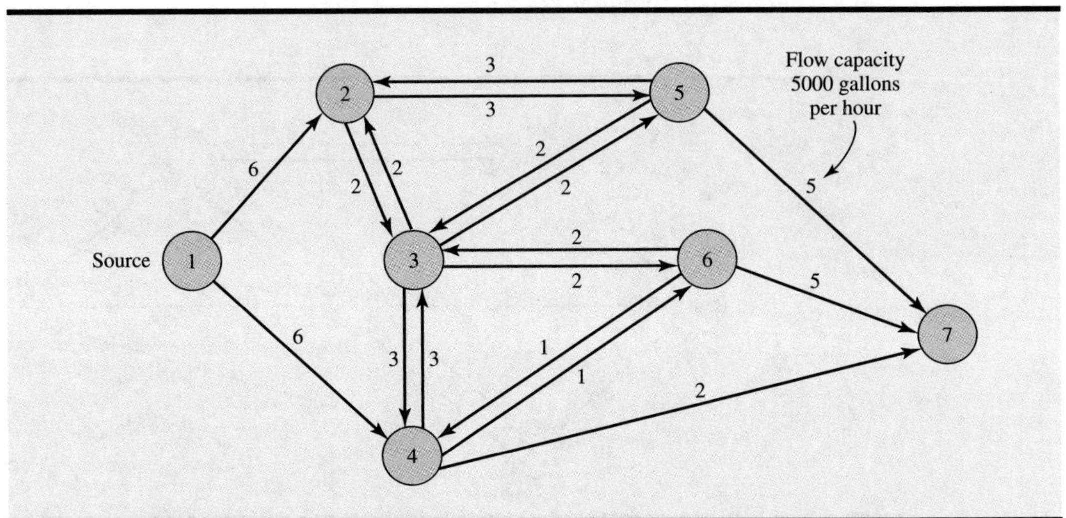

Due to the varying pipe sizes, the flow capacities vary. By selectively opening and closing sections of the pipeline network, the firm can supply any of the storage locations.

a. If the firm wants to fully utilize the system capacity to supply storage location 7, how long will it take to satisfy a location 7 demand of 100,000 gallons? What is the maximal flow for this pipeline system?

b. If a break occurs on line 2–3 and it is closed down, what is the maximal flow for the system? How long will it take to transmit 100,000 gallons to location 7?

19. For the following highway network system, determine the maximal flow in vehicles per hour.

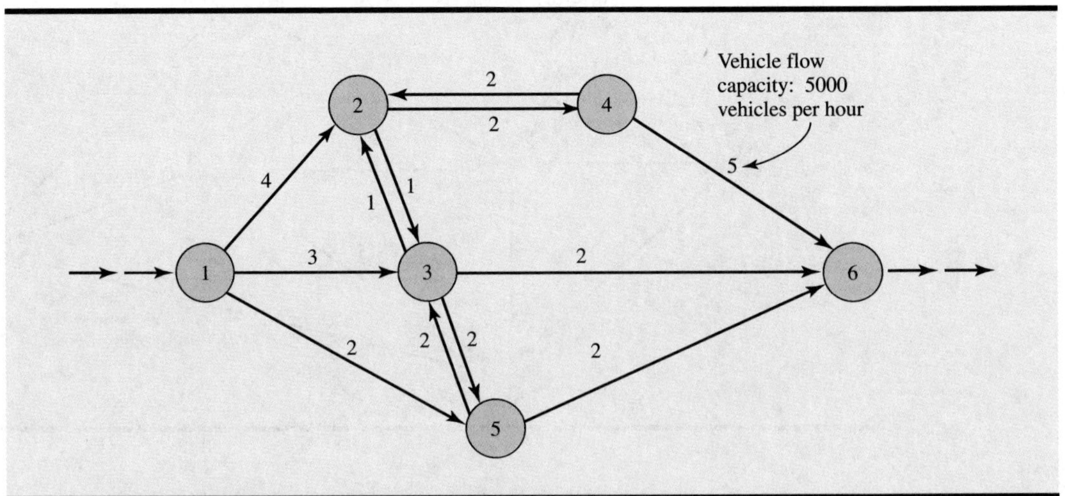

The highway commission is considering adding highway section 3–4 to permit a flow of 2000 vehicles per hour or, at an additional cost, a flow of 3000 vehicles per hour. What is your recommendation for the 3–4 arc of the network?

20. A chemical processing plant has a network of pipes that are used to transfer liquid chemical products from one part of the plant to another. The following pipe network has pipe flow capacities in gallons per minute as shown. What is the maximum flow capacity for the system if the company wishes to transfer as much liquid chemical as possible from location 1 to location 9? How much of the chemical will flow through the section of pipe from node 3 to node 5?

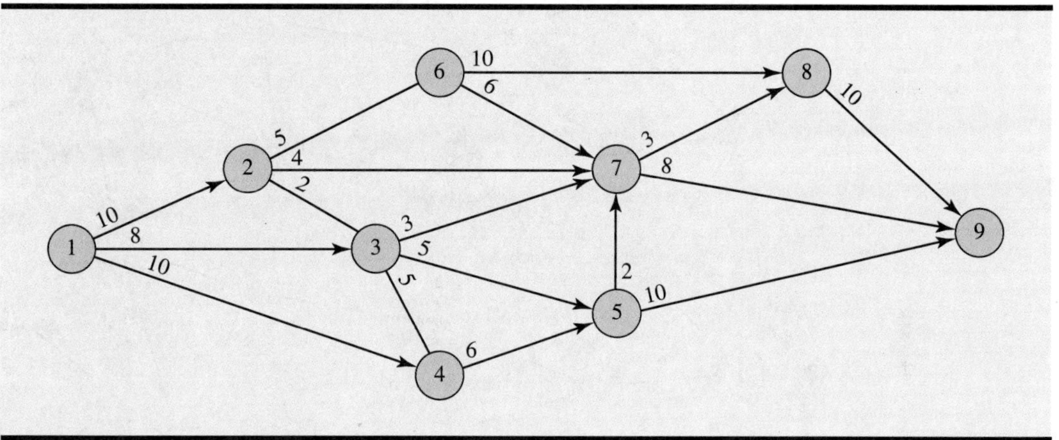

Case Problem AMBULANCE ROUTING

The city of Binghamton is served by two major hospitals: Western Medical and Binghamton General. Western Medical is located in the southwest part of the city, and Binghamton General is in the northeast.

Bob Jones, the hospital administrator at Western Medical, has been discussing the problem of scheduling and routing ambulances with Margaret Johnson, the hospital administrator at Binghamton General. Both administrators feel that some type of system needs to be developed to better coordinate the use of the ambulance services at the two hospitals so that together they can provide the fastest possible emergency service for the city.

A proposal being considered is for all ambulance service calls to be handled through a central dispatcher, who would assign a call to the hospital capable of providing the fastest service. In studying this proposal, a project team consisting of employees from both hospitals met and decided that the best approach would be to divide the city into 20 service zones. In the proposed configuration, Western Medical would be located in zone 1 and Binghamton General in zone 20. A map showing the placement of the 20 zones and the travel time (in minutes) between adjacent zones is provided in Figure 9.20.

According to the proposed operating procedure, incoming emergency calls would be identified by zone number, and an ambulance from the hospital closest to that zone would be assigned the service call. However, if all ambulances from the closest hospital were occupied with other emergencies, the service call would be assigned to the other hospital. Regardless of which hospital responded to the service call, the individual or individuals requiring the emergency service would be taken to the closest hospital.

To make the coordinated service as efficient as possible, the ambulance drivers must know in advance the quickest route to take to each zone, which hospital the individual or individuals in that zone should be taken to, and the quickest route to that hospital.

FIGURE 9.20 NETWORK FOR PROPOSED AMBULANCE SERVICE

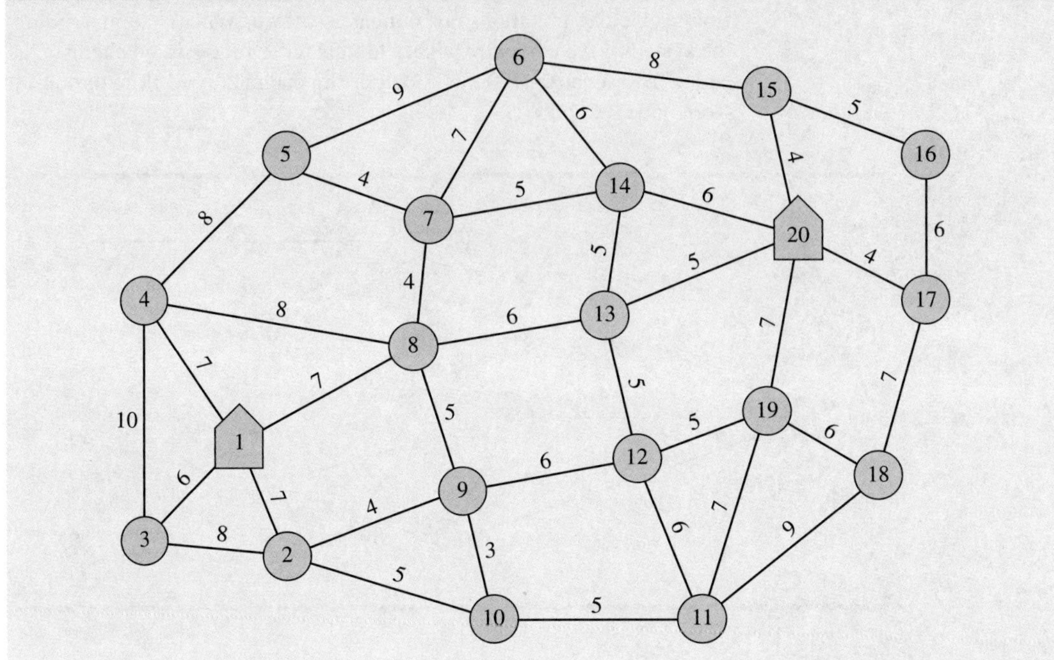

Managerial Report

Prepare a report for the two hospital administrators describing your analysis of the problem. Include in your report recommendations regarding the following items:

1. A chart for the dispatcher that identifies the primary hospital ambulance service for every zone in the city.
2. A chart for the Western Medical ambulance drivers that provides the minimum time routes from Western Medical to every zone in the city, including Binghamton General. Include a chart that tells Western Medical drivers which hospital the individuals should be taken to and the route that should be followed.
3. A chart for the Binghamton General ambulance drivers that provides the minimum time routes from Binghamton General to every zone in the city, including Western Medical. Include a chart that tells Binghamton General drivers which hospital the individuals should be taken to and the route that should be followed.
4. Include recommendations regarding how the system could be modified to take into account varying traffic conditions that occur throughout the day and changes in driving conditions resulting from temporary road construction projects.

CHAPTER 10

Project Scheduling: PERT/CPM

CONTENTS

In many situations, managers are responsible for planning, scheduling, and controlling projects that consist of numerous separate jobs or tasks performed by a variety of departments and individuals. Often these projects are so large or complex that the manager cannot possibly remember all the information pertaining to the plan, schedule, and progress of the project. In these situations the **program evaluation and review technique (PERT)** and the **critical path method (CPM)** have proven to be extremely valuable.

Henry L. Gantt developed the Gantt Chart as a graphical aid to scheduling jobs on machines in 1918. This application was the first of what has become known as project scheduling techniques.

PERT and CPM can be used to plan, schedule, and control a wide variety of projects:

1. Research and development of new products and processes
2. Construction of plants, buildings, and highways
3. Maintenance of large and complex equipment
4. Design and installation of new systems

In these types of projects, project managers must schedule and coordinate the various jobs or **activities** so that the entire project is completed on time. A complicating factor in carrying out this task is the interdependence of the activities; for example, some activities depend on the completion of other activities before they can be started. Because projects may have as many as several thousand activities, project managers look for procedures that will help them answer questions such as the following.

1. What is the total time to complete the project?
2. What are the scheduled start and finish dates for each specific activity?
3. Which activities are "critical" and must be completed *exactly* as scheduled to keep the project on schedule?
4. How long can "noncritical" activities be delayed before they cause an increase in the total project completion time?

PERT and CPM can help answer these questions.

PERT (Navy) and CPM (Du Pont and Remington Rand) differ because they were developed by different people working on different projects. Today, the best aspects of each have been combined to provide a valuable project scheduling technique.

Although PERT and CPM have the same general purpose and utilize much of the same terminology, the techniques were developed independently. PERT was developed in the late 1950s specifically for the Polaris missile project. Many activities associated with this project had never been attempted previously, so PERT was developed to handle uncertain activity times. CPM was developed primarily for industrial projects for which activity times were known. CPM offered the option of reducing activity times by adding more workers and/or resources, usually at an increased cost. Thus, a distinguishing feature of CPM was that it identified trade-offs between time and cost for various project activities.

Today's computerized versions of PERT and CPM combine the best features of both approaches. Thus, the distinction between the two techniques is no longer necessary. As a result, we refer to the project scheduling procedures covered in this chapter as PERT/CPM. We begin the discussion of PERT/CPM by considering a project for the expansion of the Western Hills Shopping Center. At the end of Section 10.1, we describe how the investment securities firm of Seasongood & Mayer used PERT/CPM to schedule a $31 million hospital revenue bond project.

10.1 PROJECT SCHEDULING WITH KNOWN ACTIVITY TIMES

The owner of the Western Hills Shopping Center is planning to modernize and expand the current 32-business shopping center complex. The project is expected to provide room for 8 to 10 new businesses. Financing has been arranged through a private investor. All that remains is for the owner of the shopping center to plan, schedule, and complete the expansion project. Let us show how PERT/CPM can help.

The effort that goes into identifying activities, determining interrelationships among activities, and estimating activity times is crucial to the success of PERT/CPM. A significant amount of time may be needed to complete this initial phase of the project scheduling process.

Immediate predecessor information determines whether activities can be completed in parallel (worked on simultaneously) or in series (one completed before another begins). Generally, the more series relationships present in a project, the more time will be required to complete the project.

A project network is extremely helpful in visualizing the interrelationships among the activities. No rules guide the conversion of a list of activities and immediate predecessor information into a project network. The process of constructing a project network generally improves with practice and experience.

The first step in the PERT/CPM scheduling process is to develop a list of the activities that make up the project. Table 10.1 shows the list of activities for the Western Hills Shopping Center expansion project. Nine activities are described and denoted A through I for later reference. Table 10.1 also shows the immediate predecessor(s) and the activity time (in weeks) for each activity. For a given activity, the **immediate predecessor** column identifies the activities that must be completed *immediately prior* to the start of that activity. Activities A and B do not have immediate predecessors and can be started as soon as the project begins; thus, a dash is written in the immediate predecessor column for these activities. The other entries in the immediate predecessor column show that activities C, D, and E cannot be started until activity A has been completed; activity F cannot be started until activity E has been completed; activity G cannot be started until both activities D and F have been completed; activity H cannot be started until both activities B and C have been completed; and, finally, activity I cannot be started until both activities G and H have been completed. The project is finished when activity I is completed.

The last column in Table 10.1 shows the number of weeks required to complete each activity. For example, activity A takes 5 weeks, activity B takes 6 weeks, and so on. The sum of activity times is 51. As a result, you may think that the total time required to complete the project is 51 weeks. However, as we show, two or more activities often may be scheduled concurrently, thus shortening the completion time for the project. Ultimately, PERT/CPM will provide a detailed activity schedule for completing the project in the shortest time possible.

Using the immediate predecessor information in Table 10.1, we can construct a graphical representation of the project, or the **project network.** Figure 10.1 depicts the project network for Western Hills Shopping Center. The activities correspond to the *nodes* of the network (drawn as rectangles) and the *arcs* (the lines with arrows) show the precedence relationships among the activities. In addition, nodes have been added to the network to denote the start and the finish of the project. A project network will help a manager visualize the activity relationships and provide a basis for carrying out the PERT/CPM computations.

The Concept of a Critical Path

To facilitate the PERT/CPM computations, we modified the project network as shown in Figure 10.2. Note that the upper left-hand corner of each node contains the corresponding activity letter. The activity time appears immediately below the letter.

TABLE 10.1 LIST OF ACTIVITIES FOR THE WESTERN HILLS SHOPPING CENTER PROJECT

Activity	Activity Description	Immediate Predecessor	Activity Time
A	Prepare architectural drawings	—	5
B	Identify potential new tenants	—	6
C	Develop prospectus for tenants	A	4
D	Select contractor	A	3
E	Prepare building permits	A	1
F	Obtain approval for building permits	E	4
G	Perform construction	D, F	14
H	Finalize contracts with tenants	B, C	12
I	Tenants move in	G, H	2
		Total	51

FIGURE 10.1 PROJECT NETWORK FOR THE WESTERN HILLS SHOPPING CENTER

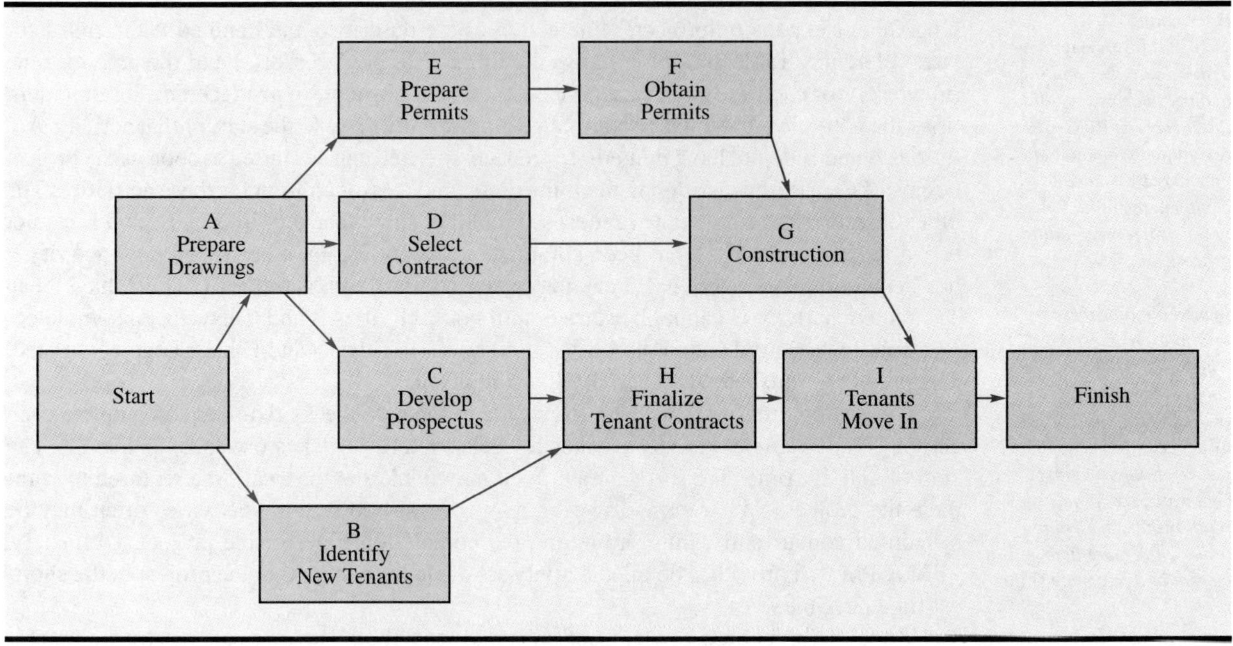

FIGURE 10.2 WESTERN HILLS SHOPPING CENTER PROJECT NETWORK WITH ACTIVITY TIMES

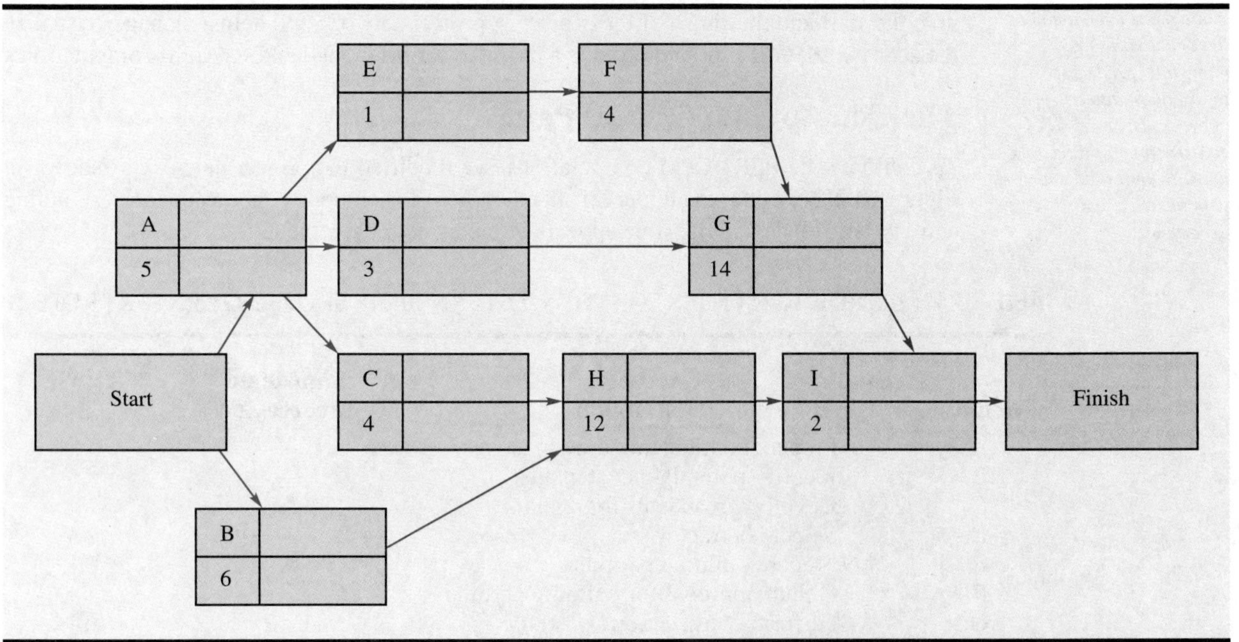

Problem 3 provides the immediate predecessor information for a project with seven activities and asks you to develop the project network.

For convenience, we use the convention of referencing activities with letters. Generally, we assign the letters in approximate order as we move from left to right through the project network.

To determine the project completion time, we have to analyze the network and identify what is called the **critical path** for the network. However, before doing so, we need to define the concept of a path through the network. A **path** is a sequence of connected nodes that leads from the Start node to the Finish node. For instance, one path for the network in Figure 10.2 is defined by the sequence of nodes A-E-F-G-I. By inspection, we see that other paths are possible, such as A-D-G-I, A-C-H-I, and B-H-I. All paths in the network must be traversed in order to complete the project, so we will look for the path that requires the most time. Because all other paths are shorter in duration, this *longest* path determines the total time required to complete the project. If activities on the longest path are delayed, the entire project will be delayed. Thus, the longest path is the *critical path.* Activities on the critical path are referred to as the **critical activities** for the project. The following discussion presents a step-by-step algorithm for finding the critical path in a project network.

Determining the Critical Path

We begin by finding the **earliest start time** and a **latest start time** for all activities in the network. Let

$$ES = \text{earliest start time for an activity}$$
$$EF = \text{earliest finish time for an activity}$$
$$t = \text{activity time}$$

The **earliest finish time** for any activity is

$$EF = ES + t \qquad (10.1)$$

Activity A can start as soon as the project starts, so we set the earliest start time for activity A equal to 0. With an activity time of 5 weeks, the earliest finish time for activity A is $EF = ES + t = 0 + 5 = 5$.

We will write the earliest start and earliest finish times in the node to the right of the activity letter. Using activity A as an example, we have

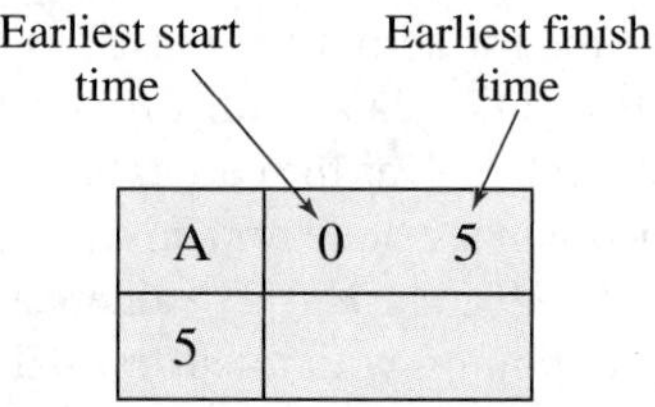

Because an activity cannot be started until *all* immediately preceding activities have been finished, the following rule can be used to determine the earliest start time for each activity.

The earliest start time for an activity is equal to the *largest* of the earliest finish times for all its immediate predecessors.

Let us apply the earliest start time rule to the portion of the network involving nodes A, B, C, and H, as shown in Figure 10.3. With an earliest start time of 0 and an activity time of 6 for activity B, we show $ES = 0$ and $EF = ES + t = 0 + 6 = 6$ in the node for activity B.

FIGURE 10.3 A PORTION OF THE WESTERN HILLS SHOPPING CENTER PROJECT NETWORK, SHOWING ACTIVITIES A, B, C, AND H

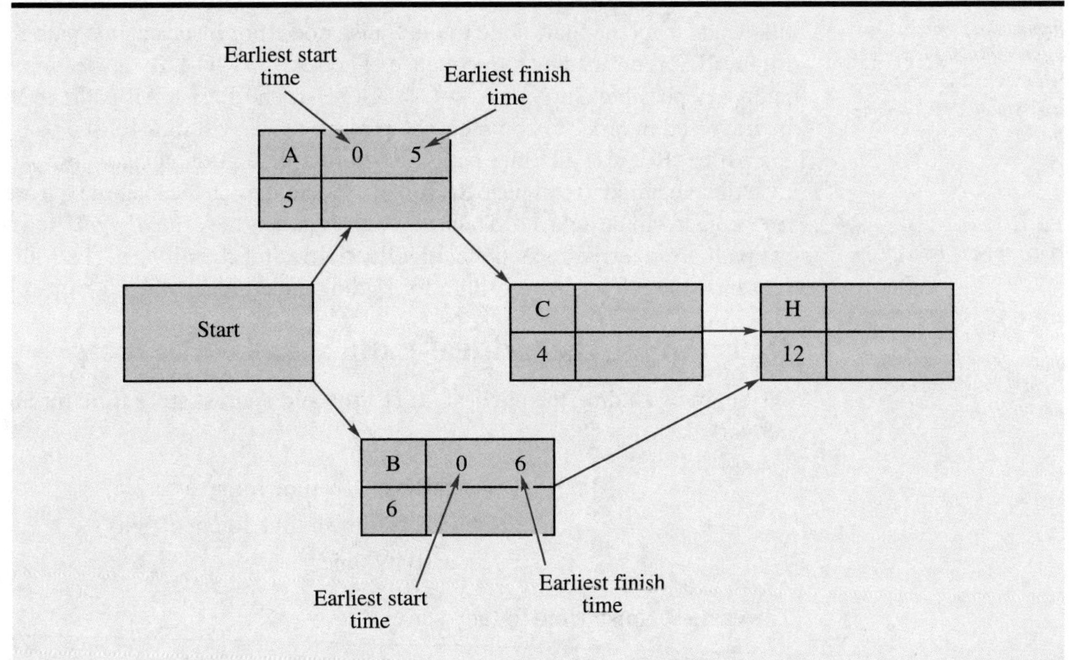

Looking at node C, we note that activity A is the only immediate predecessor for activity C. The earliest finish time for activity A is 5, so the earliest start time for activity C must be $ES = 5$. Thus, with an activity time of 4, the earliest finish time for activity C is $EF = ES + t = 5 + 4 = 9$. Both the earliest start time and the earliest finish time can be shown in the node for activity C (see Figure 10.4).

Continuing with Figure 10.4, we move on to activity H and apply the earliest start time rule for this activity. With both activities B and C as immediate predecessors, the earliest start time for activity H must be equal to the largest of the earliest finish times for activities B and C. Thus, with $EF = 6$ for activity B and $EF = 9$ for activity C, we select the largest value, 9, as the earliest start time for activity H ($ES = 9$). With an activity time of 12 as shown in the node for activity H, the earliest finish time is $EF = ES + t = 9 + 12 = 21$. The $ES = 9$ and $EF = 21$ values can now be entered in the node for activity H in Figure 10.4.

Continuing with this **forward pass** through the network, we can establish the earliest start times and the earliest finish times for all activities in the network. Figure 10.5 shows the Western Hills Shopping Center project network with the *ES* and *EF* values for each activity. Note that the earliest finish time for activity I, the last activity in the project, is 26 weeks. Therefore, we now know that the total completion time for the project is 26 weeks.

We now continue the algorithm for finding the critical path by making a **backward pass** through the network. Because the total completion time for the project is 26 weeks, we begin the backward pass with a **latest finish time** of 26 for activity I. Once the latest finish time for an activity is known, the *latest start time* for an activity can be computed as follows. Let

$$LS = \text{latest start time for an activity}$$
$$LF = \text{latest finish time for an activity}$$

FIGURE 10.4 DETERMINING THE EARLIEST START TIME FOR ACTIVITY H

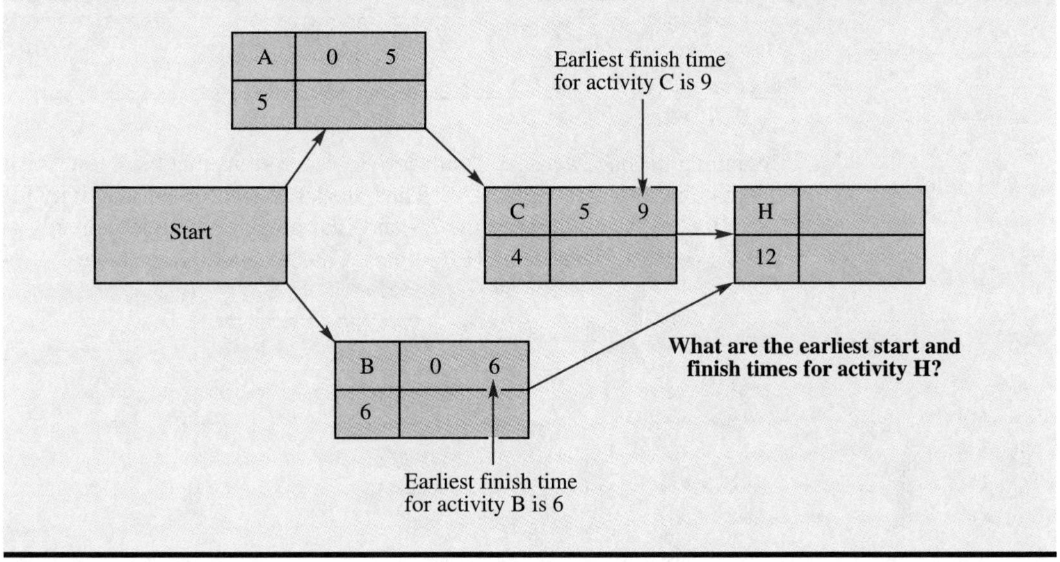

A 0 5
5
Earliest finish time for activity C is 9
Start
C 5 9
4
H
12
B 0 6
6
What are the earliest start and finish times for activity H?
Earliest finish time for activity B is 6

FIGURE 10.5 WESTERN HILLS SHOPPING CENTER PROJECT NETWORK WITH EARLIEST START AND EARLIEST FINISH TIMES SHOWN FOR ALL ACTIVITIES

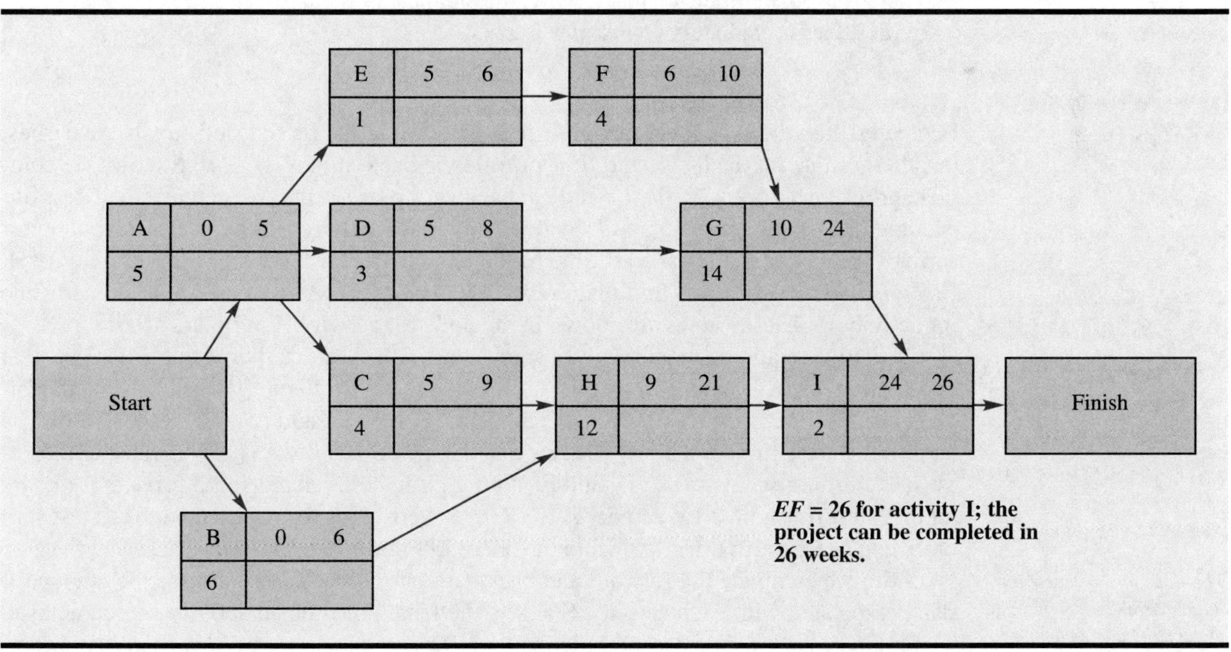

then

$$LS = LF - t \tag{10.2}$$

Beginning the backward pass with activity I, we know that the latest finish time is $LF = 26$ and that the activity time is $t = 2$. Thus, the latest start time for activity I is $LS = LF - t = 26 - 2 = 24$. We will write the LS and LF values in the node directly below the earliest start (ES) and earliest finish (EF) times. Thus, for node I, we have

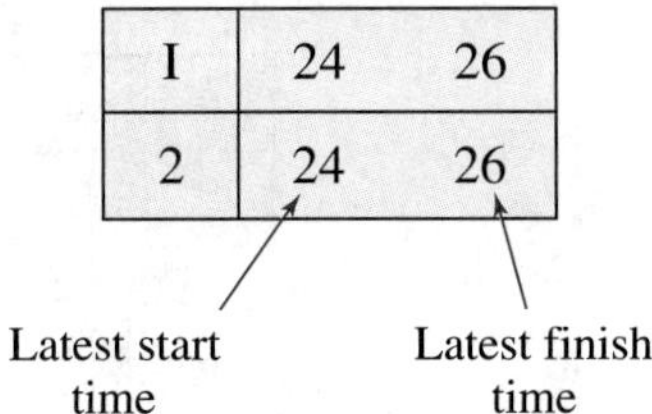

The following rule can be used to determine the latest finish time for each activity in the network.

The latest finish time for an activity is the smallest of the latest start times for all activities that immediately follow the activity.

Logically, this rule states that the latest time an activity can be finished equals the earliest (smallest) value for the latest start time of following activities. Figure 10.6 shows the complete project network with the LS and LF backward pass results. We can use the latest finish time rule to verify the LS and LF values shown for activity H. The latest finish time for activity H must be the latest start time for activity I. Thus, we set $LF = 24$ for activity H. Using equation (10.2), we find that $LS = LF - t = 24 - 12 = 12$ as the latest start time for activity H. These values are shown in the node for activity H in Figure 10.6.

Activity A requires a more involved application of the latest start time rule. First, note that three activities (C, D, and E) immediately follow activity A. Figure 10.6 shows that the latest start times for activities C, D, and E are $LS = 8$, $LS = 7$, and $LS = 5$, respectively. The latest finish time rule for activity A states that the LF for activity A is the smallest of the latest start times for activities C, D, and E. With the smallest value being 5 for activity E, we set the latest finish time for activity A to $LF = 5$. Verify this result and the other latest start times and latest finish times shown in the nodes in Figure 10.6.

The slack for each activity indicates the length of time the activity can be delayed without increasing the project completion time.

After we complete the forward and backward passes, we can determine the amount of slack associated with each activity. **Slack** is the length of time an activity can be delayed without increasing the project completion time. The amount of slack for an activity is computed as follows:

$$\text{Slack} = LS - ES = LF - EF \tag{10.3}$$

FIGURE 10.6 WESTERN HILLS SHOPPING CENTER PROJECT NETWORK WITH LATEST START AND LATEST FINISH TIMES SHOWN IN EACH NODE

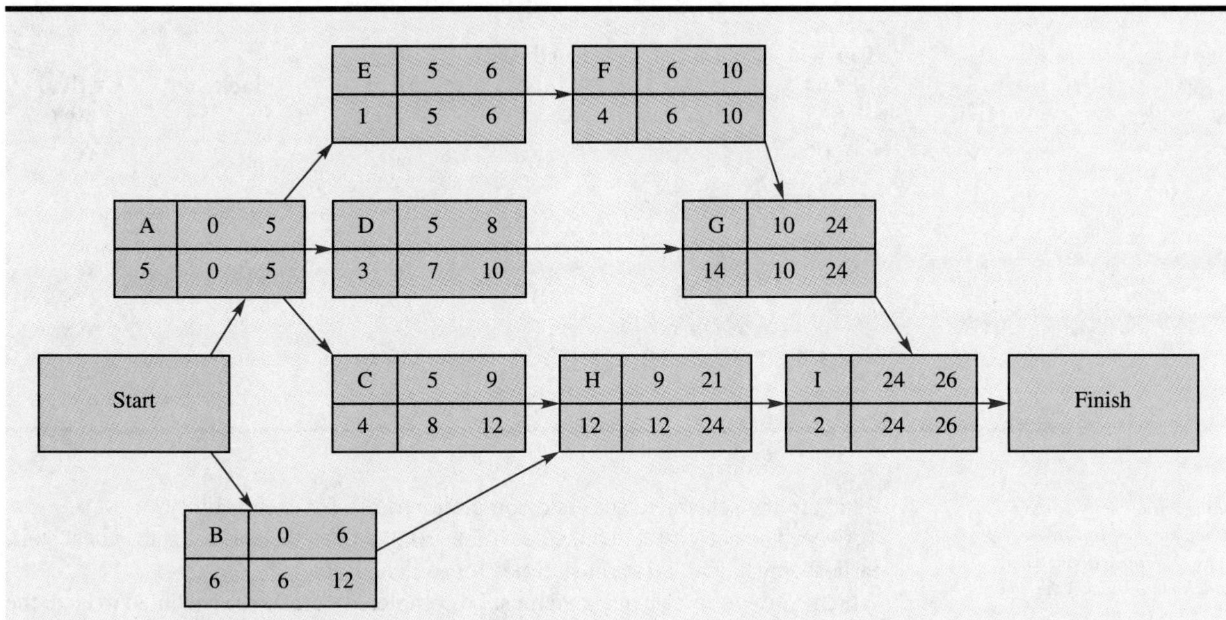

For example, the slack associated with activity C is $LS - ES = 8 - 5 = 3$ weeks. Hence, activity C can be delayed up to 3 weeks, and the entire project can still be completed in 26 weeks. In this sense, activity C is not critical to the completion of the entire project in 26 weeks. Next, we consider activity E. Using the information in Figure 10.6, we find that the slack is $LS - ES = 5 - 5 = 0$. Thus, activity E has zero, or no, slack. Thus, this activity cannot be delayed without increasing the completion time for the entire project. In other words, completing activity E exactly as scheduled is critical in terms of keeping the project on schedule. Thus, activity E is a critical activity. In general, the *critical activities* are the activities with zero slack.

One of the primary contributions of PERT/CPM is the identification of the critical activities. The project manager will want to monitor critical activities closely because a delay in any one of these activities will lengthen the project completion time.

The start and finish times shown in Figure 10.6 can be used to develop a detailed start time and finish time schedule for all activities. Putting this information in tabular form provides the activity schedule shown in Table 10.2. Note that the slack column shows that activities A, E, F, G, and I have zero slack. Hence, these activities are the critical activities for the project. The path formed by nodes A-E-F-G-I is the *critical path* in the Western Hills Shopping Center project network. The detailed schedule shown in Table 10.2 indicates the slack or delay that can be tolerated for the noncritical activities before these activities will increase project completion time.

The critical path algorithm is essentially a longest path algorithm. From the start node to the finish node, the critical path identifies the path that requires the most time.

Contributions of PERT/CPM

Previously, we stated that project managers look for procedures that will help answer important questions regarding the planning, scheduling, and controlling of projects. Let us reconsider these questions in light of the information that the critical path calculations have given us.

1. How long will the project take to complete?
   Answer: The project can be completed in 26 weeks if each activity is completed on schedule.

TABLE 10.2 ACTIVITY SCHEDULE FOR THE WESTERN HILLS SHOPPING CENTER PROJECT

Activity	Earliest Start (*ES*)	Latest Start (*LS*)	Earliest Finish (*EF*)	Latest Finish (*LF*)	Slack (*LS* − *ES*)	Critical Path?
A	0	0	5	5	0	Yes
B	0	6	6	12	6	
C	5	8	9	12	3	
D	5	7	8	10	2	
E	5	5	6	6	0	Yes
F	6	6	10	10	0	Yes
G	10	10	24	24	0	Yes
H	9	12	21	24	3	
I	24	24	26	26	0	Yes

If the total time required to complete the project is too long, judgment about where and how to shorten the time of critical activities must be exercised. If any activity times are altered, the critical path calculations should be repeated to determine the impact on the activity schedule and the impact on total project completion time. In Section 10.3 we show how to use linear programming to find the least-cost way to shorten the project completion time.

Software packages such as The Management Scientist perform the critical path calculations quickly and efficiently. The project manager can modify any aspect of the project and quickly determine how the modification affects the activity schedule and the total time required to complete the project.

2. What are the scheduled start and completion times for each activity?
   Answer: The activity schedule (see Table 10.2) shows the earliest start, latest start, earliest finish, and latest finish times for each activity.
3. Which activities are critical and must be completed *exactly* as scheduled to keep the project on schedule?
   Answer: A, E, F, G, and I are the critical activities.
4. How long can noncritical activities be delayed before they cause an increase in the completion time for the project?
   Answer: The activity schedule (see Table 10.2) shows the slack associated with each activity.

Such information is valuable in managing any project. Although larger projects usually increase the effort required to develop the immediate predecessor relationships and the activity time estimates, the procedure and contribution of PERT/CPM to larger projects are identical to those shown for the shopping center expansion project. The Management Science in Action, Hospital Revenue Bond at Seasongood & Mayer, describes a 23-activity project that introduced a $31 million hospital revenue bond. PERT/CPM identified the critical activities, the expected project completion time of 29 weeks, and the activity start times and finish times necessary to keep the entire project on schedule.

Finally, computer packages may be used to carry out the steps of the PERT/CPM procedure. Figure 10.7 shows the activity schedule for the shopping center expansion project developed by The Management Scientist software package. Input to the program included the activities, their immediate predecessors, and the expected activity times. Only a few minutes were required to input the information and generate the critical path and activity schedule.

Summary of the PERT/CPM Critical Path Procedure

Before leaving this section, let us summarize the PERT/CPM critical path procedure.

Step 1. Develop a list of the activities that make up the project.
Step 2. Determine the immediate predecessor(s) for each activity in the project.
Step 3. Estimate the completion time for each activity.
Step 4. Draw a project network depicting the activities and immediate predecessors listed in steps 1 and 2.

FIGURE 10.7 THE MANAGEMENT SCIENTIST ACTIVITY SCHEDULE FOR THE WESTERN HILLS SHOPPING CENTER PROJECT

```
                  ***    ACTIVITY SCHEDULE    ***

             EARLIEST  LATEST  EARLIEST  LATEST           CRITICAL
  ACTIVITY    START    START   FINISH    FINISH  SLACK   ACTIVITY
-------------------------------------------------------------------
     A          0        0        5        5       0       YES
     B          0        6        6       12       6
     C          5        8        9       12       3
     D          5        7        8       10       2
     E          5        5        6        6       0       YES
     F          6        6       10       10       0       YES
     G         10       10       24       24       0       YES
     H          9       12       21       24       3
     I         24       24       26       26       0       YES
-------------------------------------------------------------------

         CRITICAL PATH:   A-E-F-G-I

         PROJECT COMPLETION TIME = 26
```

Step 5. Use the project network and the activity time estimates to determine the earliest start and the earliest finish time for each activity by making a forward pass through the network. The earliest finish time for the last activity in the project identifies the total time required to complete the project.

Step 6. Use the project completion time identified in step 5 as the latest finish time for the last activity and make a backward pass through the network to identify the latest start and latest finish time for each activity.

Step 7. Use the difference between the latest start time and the earliest start time for each activity to determine the slack for each activity.

Step 8. Find the activities with zero slack; these are the critical activities.

Step 9. Use the information from steps 5 and 6 to develop the activity schedule for the project.

MANAGEMENT SCIENCE IN ACTION

HOSPITAL REVENUE BOND AT SEASONGOOD & MAYER

Seasongood & Mayer is an investment securities firm located in Cincinnati, Ohio. The firm engages in municipal financing including the underwriting of new issues of municipal bonds, acting as a market maker for previously issued bonds, and performing other investment banking services.

Seasongood & Mayer provided the underwriting for a $31 million issue of hospital facilities revenue bonds for Providence Hospital in Hamilton County, Ohio. The project of underwriting this municipal bond issue began with activities such as drafting the legal documents, drafting a description of the existing hospital facilities, and completing a feasibility study. A total of 23 activities

(*continued*)

defined the project that would be completed when the hospital signed the construction contract and then made the bond proceeds available. The immediate predecessor relationships for the activities and the activity times were developed by a project management team.

PERT/CPM analysis of the project network identified the 10 critical path activities. The analysis also provided the expected completion time of 29 weeks, or approximately seven months. The activity schedule showed the start time and finish time for each activity and provided the information necessary to monitor the project and keep it on schedule. PERT/ CPM was instrumental in helping Seasongood & Mayer obtain the financing for the project within the time specified in the construction bid.

NOTES AND COMMENTS

Suppose that, after analyzing a PERT/CPM network, the project manager finds that the project completion time is unacceptable (i.e., the project is going to take too long). In this case, the manager must take one or both of the following steps. First, review the original PERT/CPM network to see whether any immediate predecessor relationships can be modified so that at least some of the critical path activities can be done simultaneously. Second, consider adding resources to critical path activities in an attempt to shorten the critical path; we discuss this alternative, referred to as *crashing,* in Section 10.3.

10.2 PROJECT SCHEDULING WITH UNCERTAIN ACTIVITY TIMES

In this section we consider the details of project scheduling for a problem involving new-product research and development. Because many of the activities in this project have never been attempted, the project manager wants to account for uncertainties in the activity times. Let us show how project scheduling can be conducted with uncertain activity times.

The Daugherty Porta-Vac Project

The H. S. Daugherty Company has manufactured industrial vacuum cleaning systems for many years. Recently, a member of the company's new-product research team submitted a report suggesting that the company consider manufacturing a cordless vacuum cleaner. The new product, referred to as Porta-Vac, could contribute to Daugherty's expansion into the household market. Management hopes that it can be manufactured at a reasonable cost and that its portability and no-cord convenience will make it extremely attractive.

Accurate activity time estimates are important in the development of an activity schedule. When activity times are uncertain, the three time estimates—optimistic, most probable, and pessimistic—allow the project manager to take uncertainty into consideration in determining the critical path and the activity schedule. This approach was developed by the designers of PERT.

Daugherty's management wants to study the feasibility of manufacturing the Porta-Vac product. The feasibility study will recommend the action to be taken. To complete this study, information must be obtained from the firm's research and development (R&D), product testing, manufacturing, cost estimating, and market research groups. How long will this feasibility study take? In the following discussion, we show how to answer this question and provide an activity schedule for the project.

Again, the first step in the project scheduling process is to identify all activities that make up the project and then determine the immediate predecessor(s) for each activity. Table 10.3 shows these data for the Porta-Vac project.

The Porta-Vac project network is shown in Figure 10.8. Verify that the network does in fact maintain the immediate predecessor relationships shown in Table 10.3.

FIGURE 10.8 PORTA-VAC CORDLESS VACUUM CLEANER PROJECT NETWORK

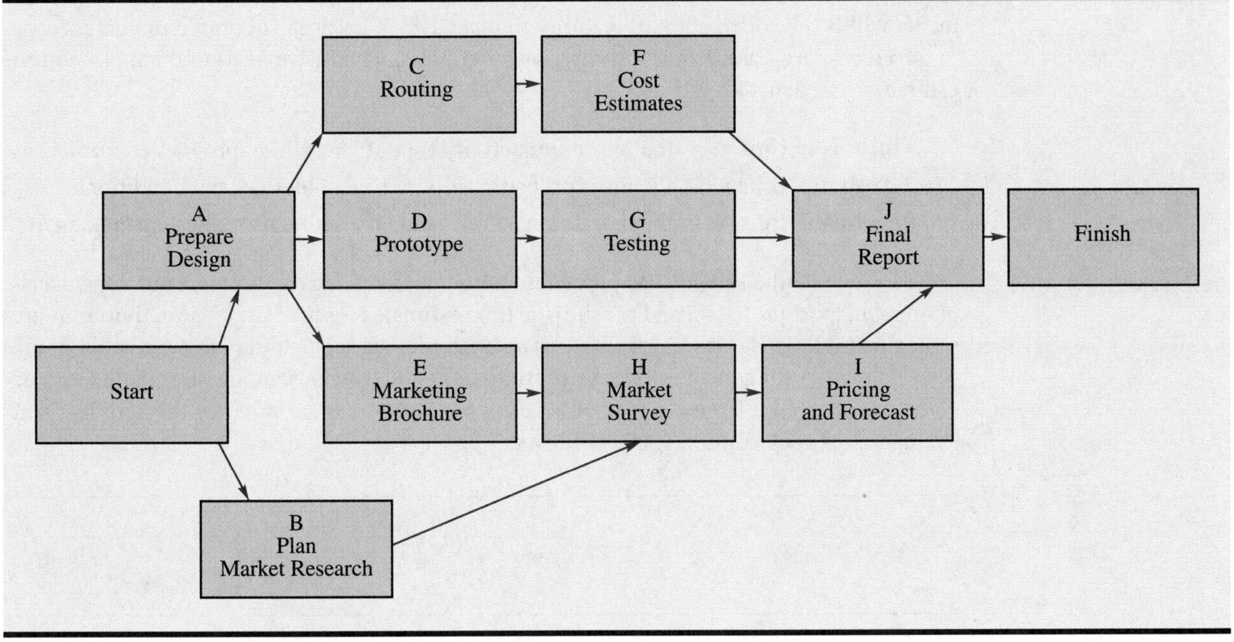

Uncertain Activity Times

Once we develop the project network, we will need information on the time required to complete each activity. This information is used in the calculation of the total time required to complete the project and in the scheduling of specific activities. For repeat projects, such as construction and maintenance projects, managers may have the experience and historical data necessary to provide accurate activity time estimates. However, for new or unique projects, estimating the time for each activity may be quite difficult. In fact, in many cases, activity times are uncertain and are best described by a range of possible values rather than

TABLE 10.3 ACTIVITY LIST FOR THE PORTA-VAC PROJECT

Activity	Description	Immediate Predecessor
A	Develop product design	—
B	Plan market research	—
C	Prepare routing (manufacturing engineering)	A
D	Build prototype model	A
E	Prepare marketing brochure	A
F	Prepare cost estimates (industrial engineering)	C
G	Do preliminary product testing	D
H	Complete market survey	B, E
I	Prepare pricing and forecast report	H
J	Prepare final report	F, G, I

by one specific time estimate. In these instances, the uncertain activity times are treated as random variables with associated probability distributions. As a result, probability statements will be provided about the ability to meet a specific project completion date.

To incorporate uncertain activity times into the analysis, we need to obtain three time estimates for each activity:

Optimistic time a = the minimum activity time if everything progresses ideally
Most probable time m = the most probable activity time under normal conditions
Pessimistic time b = the maximum activity time if significant delays are encountered

To illustrate the PERT/CPM procedure with uncertain activity times, let us consider the optimistic, most probable, and pessimistic time estimates for the Porta-Vac activities as presented in Table 10.4. Using activity A as an example, we see that the most probable time is 5 weeks with a range from 4 weeks (optimistic) to 12 weeks (pessimistic). If the activity could be repeated a large number of times, what is the average time for the activity? This average or **expected time** (t) is as follows:

$$t = \frac{a + 4m + b}{6} \tag{10.4}$$

For activity A we have an average or expected time of

$$t_{\text{A}} = \frac{4 + 4(5) + 12}{6} = \frac{36}{6} = 6 \text{ weeks}$$

With uncertain activity times, we can use the *variance* to describe the dispersion or variation in the activity time values. The variance of the activity time is given by the formula[1]

$$\sigma^2 = \left(\frac{b - a}{6}\right)^2 \tag{10.5}$$

The difference between the pessimistic (b) and optimistic (a) time estimates greatly affects the value of the variance. Large differences in these two values reflect a high degree of uncertainty in the activity time. Using equation (10.5), we obtain the measure of uncertainty—that is, the variance—of activity A, denoted σ_{A}^2:

$$\sigma_{\text{A}}^2 = \left(\frac{12 - 4}{6}\right)^2 = \left(\frac{8}{6}\right)^2 = 1.78$$

Equations (10.4) and (10.5) are based on the assumption that the activity time distribution can be described by a **beta probability distribution.**[2] With this assumption, the proba-

[1]The variance equation is based on the notion that a standard deviation is approximately $\frac{1}{6}$ of the difference between the extreme values of the distribution: $(b - a)/6$. The variance is the square of the standard deviation.

[2]The equations for t and σ^2 require additional assumptions about the parameters of the beta probability distribution. However, even when these additional assumptions are not made, the equations still provide good approximations of t and σ^2.

TABLE 10.4 OPTIMISTIC, MOST PROBABLE, AND PESSIMISTIC ACTIVITY TIME ESTIMATES (IN WEEKS) FOR THE PORTA-VAC PROJECT

Activity	Optimistic (*a*)	Most Probable (*m*)	Pessimistic (*b*)
A	4	5	12
B	1	1.5	5
C	2	3	4
D	3	4	11
E	2	3	4
F	1.5	2	2.5
G	1.5	3	4.5
H	2.5	3.5	7.5
I	1.5	2	2.5
J	1	2	3

When uncertain activity times are used, the critical path calculations will determine only the expected or average time to complete the project. The actual time required to complete the project may differ. However, for planning purposes, the expected time should be valuable information for the project manager.

bility distribution for the time to complete activity A is as shown in Figure 10.9. Using equations (10.4) and (10.5) and the data in Table 10.4, we calculated the expected times and variances for all Porta-Vac activities; the results are summarized in Table 10.5. The Porta-Vac project network with expected activity times is shown in Figure 10.10.

The Critical Path

When we have the project network and the expected activity times, we are ready to proceed with the critical path calculations necessary to determine the expected time required to complete the project and determine the activity schedule. In these calculations, we treat the expected activity times (Table 10.5) as the fixed length or known duration of each activity. As a result, we can use the critical path procedure introduced in Section 10.1 to find the critical

FIGURE 10.9 ACTIVITY TIME DISTRIBUTION FOR PRODUCT DESIGN (ACTIVITY A) FOR THE PORTA-VAC PROJECT

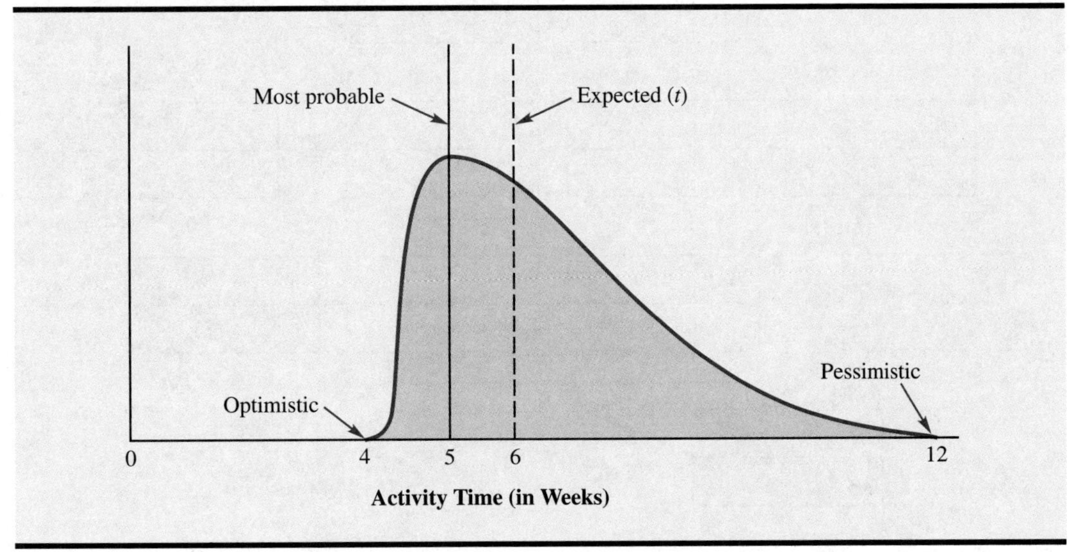

TABLE 10.5 EXPECTED TIMES AND VARIANCES FOR THE PORTA-VAC PROJECT ACTIVITIES

Activity	Expected Time (weeks)	Variance
A	6	1.78
B	2	0.44
C	3	0.11
D	5	1.78
E	3	0.11
F	2	0.03
G	3	0.25
H	4	0.69
I	2	0.03
J	2	0.11
Total	32	

Activities that have larger variances show a greater degree of uncertainty. The project manager should monitor the progress of any activity with a large variance even if the expected time does not identify the activity as a critical activity.

path for the Porta-Vac project. After the critical activities and the expected time to complete the project have been determined, we analyze the effect of the activity time variability.

Proceeding with a forward pass through the network shown in Figure 10.10, wc can establish the earliest start (*ES*) and earliest finish (*EF*) times for each activity. Figure 10.11 shows thc project network with the *ES* and *EF* values. Note that the earliest finish time for activity J, the last activity, is 17 weeks. Thus, the expected completion time for the project is 17 weeks. Next, we make a backward pass through the network. The backward pass provides the latest start (*LS*) and latest finish (*LF*) times shown in Figure 10.12.

FIGURE 10.10 PORTA-VAC PROJECT NETWORK WITH EXPECTED ACTIVITY TIMES

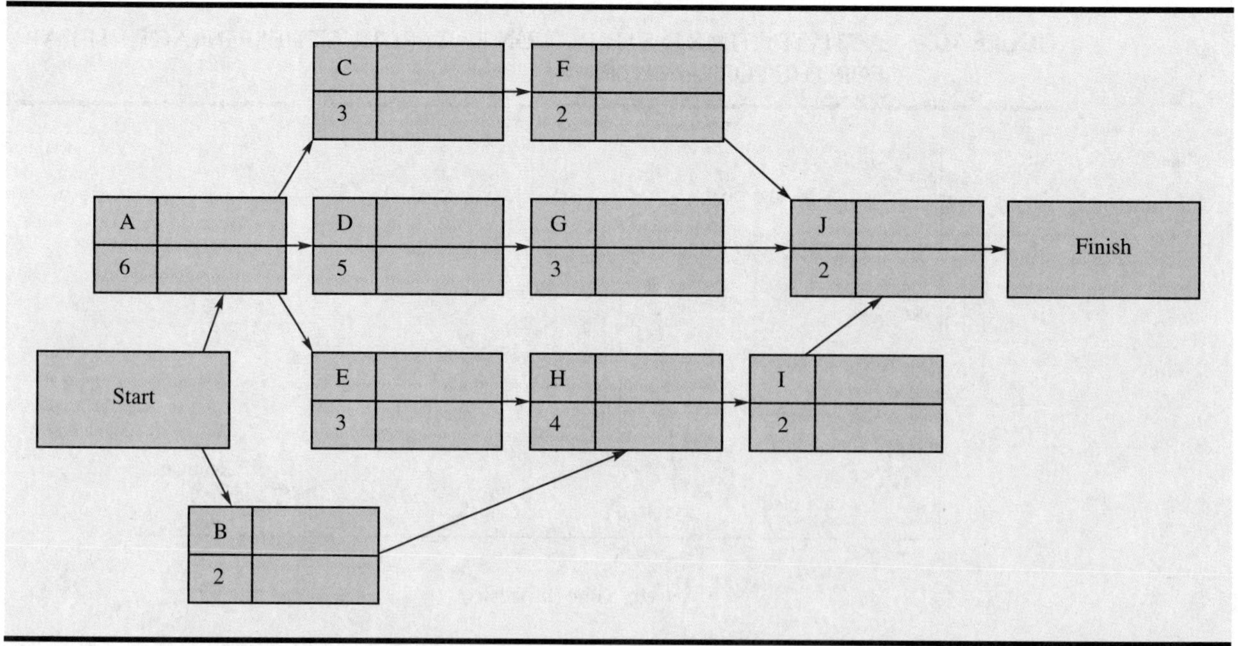

FIGURE 10.11 PORTA-VAC PROJECT NETWORK WITH EARLIEST START AND EARLIEST FINISH TIMES

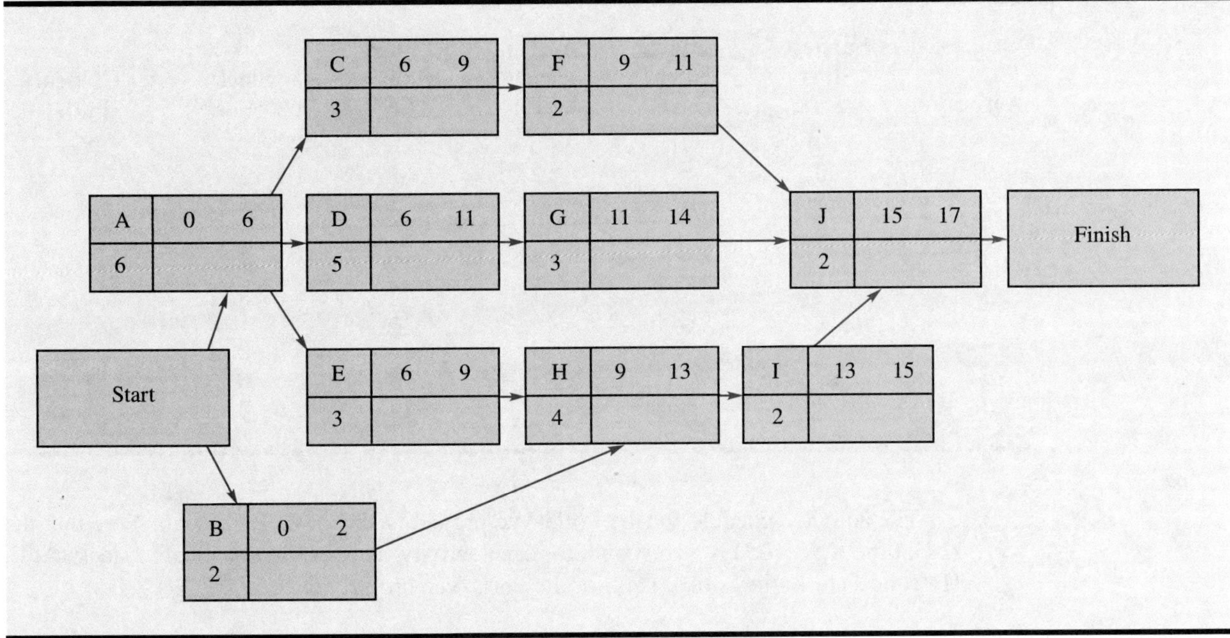

FIGURE 10.12 PORTA-VAC PROJECT NETWORK WITH LATEST START AND LATEST FINISH TIMES

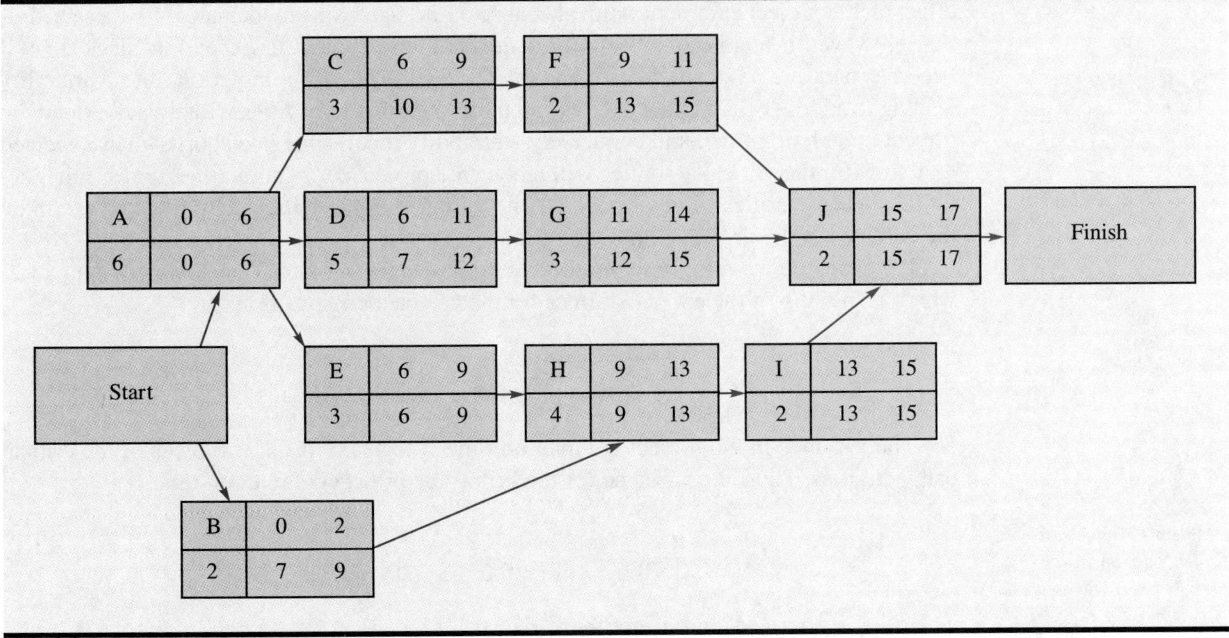

TABLE 10.6 ACTIVITY SCHEDULE FOR THE PORTA-VAC PROJECT

Activity	Earliest Start (*ES*)	Latest Start (*LS*)	Earliest Finish (*EF*)	Latest Finish (*LF*)	Slack (*LS* − *ES*)	Critical Path?
A	0	0	6	6	0	Yes
B	0	7	2	9	7	
C	6	10	9	13	4	
D	6	7	11	12	1	
E	6	6	9	9	0	Yes
F	9	13	11	15	4	
G	11	12	14	15	1	
H	9	9	13	13	0	Yes
I	13	13	15	15	0	Yes
J	15	15	17	17	0	Yes

The activity schedule for the Porta-Vac project is shown in Table 10.6. Note that the slack time (*LS* − *ES*) is also shown for each activity. The activities with zero slack (A, E, H, I, and J) form the critical path for the Porta-Vac project network.

Variability in Project Completion Time

We know that for the Porta-Vac project the critical path of A-E-H-I-J resulted in an expected total project completion time of 17 weeks. However, variation in critical activities can cause variation in the project completion time. Variation in noncritical activities ordinarily has no effect on the project completion time because of the slack time associated with these activities. However, if a noncritical activity is delayed long enough to expend its slack time, it becomes part of a new critical path and may affect the project completion time. Variability leading to a longer-than-expected total time for the critical activities will always extend the project completion time, and conversely, variability that results in a shorter-than-expected total time for the critical activities will reduce the project completion time, unless other activities become critical. Let us now use the variance in the critical activities to determine the variance in the project completion time.

Let T denote the total time required to complete the project. The expected value of T, which is the sum of the expected times for the critical activities is

$$\begin{aligned} E(T) &= t_A + t_E + t_H + t_I + t_J \\ &= 6 + 3 + 4 + 2 + 2 = 17 \text{ weeks} \end{aligned}$$

The variance in the project completion time is the sum of the variances of the critical path activities. Thus, the variance for the Porta-Vac project completion time is

Problem 10 involves a project with uncertain activity times and asks you to compute the expected completion time and the variance for the project.

$$\begin{aligned} \sigma^2 &= \sigma_A^2 + \sigma_E^2 + \sigma_H^2 + \sigma_I^2 + \sigma_J^2 \\ &= 1.78 + 0.11 + 0.69 + 0.03 + 0.11 = 2.72 \end{aligned}$$

where σ_A^2, σ_E^2, σ_H^2, σ_I^2, and σ_J^2 are the variances of the critical activities.

The formula for σ^2 is based on the assumption that the activity times are independent. If two or more activities are dependent, the formula provides only an approximation of the variance of the project completion time. The closer the activities are to being independent, the better the approximation.

Knowing that the standard deviation is the square root of the variance, we compute the standard deviation σ for the Porta-Vac project completion time as

$$\sigma = \sqrt{\sigma^2} = \sqrt{2.72} = 1.65$$

The normal distribution tends to be a better approximation of the distribution of total time for larger projects where the critical path has many activities.

Assuming that the distribution of the project completion time T follows a normal or bell-shaped distribution[3] allows us to draw the distribution shown in Figure 10.13. With this distribution, we can compute the probability of meeting a specified project completion date. For example, suppose that management allotted 20 weeks for the Porta-Vac project. What is the probability that we will meet the 20-week deadline? Using the normal probability distribution shown in Figure 10.14, we are asking for the probability that $T \leq 20$; this

FIGURE 10.13 NORMAL DISTRIBUTION OF THE PROJECT COMPLETION TIME FOR THE PORTA-VAC PROJECT

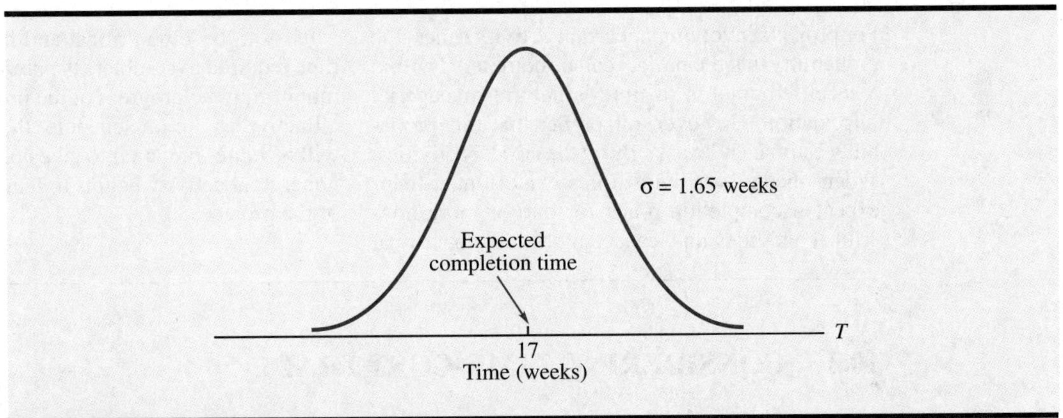

FIGURE 10.14 PROBABILITY THE PORTA-VAC PROJECT WILL MEET THE 20-WEEK DEADLINE

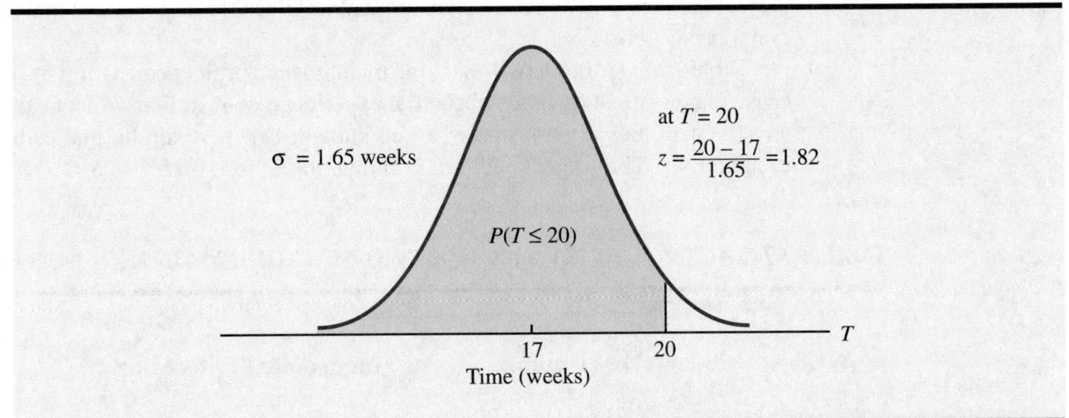

[3]Use of the normal distribution as an approximation is based on the central limit theorem, which indicates that the sum of independent random variables (activity times) follows a normal distribution as the number of random variables becomes large.

probability is shown graphically as the shaded area in the figure. The z value for the normal probability distribution at $T = 20$ is

$$z = \frac{20 - 17}{1.65} = 1.82$$

Using $z = 1.82$ and the table for the normal distribution (see Appendix A), we find that the probability of the project meeting the 20-week deadline is $0.4656 + 0.5000 = 0.9656$. Thus, even though activity time variability may cause the completion time to exceed 17 weeks, calculations indicate an excellent chance that the project will be completed before the 20-week deadline. Similar probability calculations can be made for other project deadline alternatives.

NOTES AND COMMENTS

For projects involving uncertain activity times, the probability that the project can be completed within a specified amount of time is helpful managerial information. However, remember that this probability estimate is based *only* on the critical activities. When uncertain activity times exist, longer-than-expected completion times for one or more noncritical activities may cause an original noncritical activity to become critical and hence increase the time required to complete the project. By frequently monitoring the progress of the project to make sure all activities are on schedule, the project manager will be better prepared to take corrective action if a noncritical activity begins to lengthen the duration of the project.

10.3 CONSIDERING TIME-COST TRADE-OFFS

Using more resources to reduce activity times was proposed by the developers of CPM. The shortening of activity times is referred to as crashing.

The original developers of CPM provided the project manager with the option of adding resources to selected activities to reduce project completion time. Added resources (such as more workers, overtime, and so on) generally increase project costs, so the decision to reduce activity times must take into consideration the additional cost involved. In effect, the project manager must make a decision that involves trading reduced activity time for additional project cost.

Table 10.7 defines a two-machine maintenance project consisting of five activities. Because management has had substantial experience with similar projects, the times for maintenance activities are considered to be known; hence, a single time estimate is given for each activity. The project network is shown in Figure 10.15.

TABLE 10.7 ACTIVITY LIST FOR THE TWO-MACHINE MAINTENANCE PROJECT

Activity	Description	Immediate Predecessor	Expected Time (days)
A	Overhaul machine I	—	7
B	Adjust machine I	A	3
C	Overhaul machine II	—	6
D	Adjust machine II	C	3
E	Test system	B, D	2

FIGURE 10.15 TWO-MACHINE MAINTENANCE PROJECT NETWORK

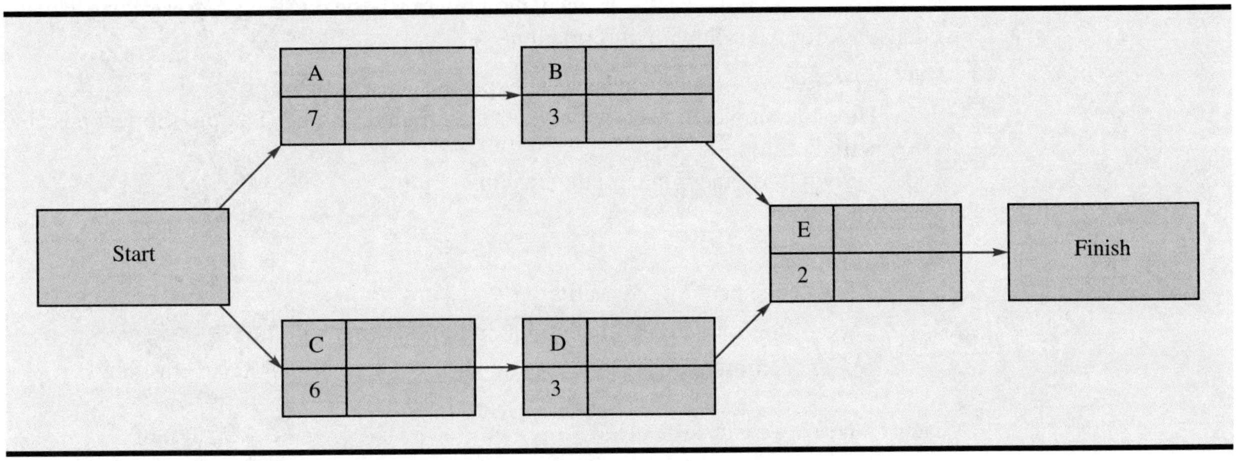

The procedure for making critical path calculations for the maintenance project network is the same one used to find the critical path in the networks for both the Western Hills Shopping Center expansion project and the Porta-Vac project. Making the forward pass and backward pass calculations for the network in Figure 10.15, we obtained the activity schedule shown in Table 10.8. The zero slack times, and thus the critical path, are associated with activities A-B-E. The length of the critical path, and thus the total time required to complete the project, is 12 days.

Crashing Activity Times

Now suppose that current production levels make completing the maintenance project within 10 days imperative. By looking at the length of the critical path of the network (12 days), we realize that meeting the desired project completion time is impossible unless we can shorten selected activity times. This shortening of activity times, which usually can be achieved by adding resources, is referred to as **crashing.** However, the added resources associated with crashing activity times usually result in added project costs, so we will want to identify the activities that cost the least to crash and then crash those activities only the amount necessary to meet the desired project completion time.

TABLE 10.8 ACTIVITY SCHEDULE FOR THE TWO-MACHINE MAINTENANCE PROJECT

Activity	Earliest Start (*ES*)	Latest Start (*LS*)	Earliest Finish (*EF*)	Latest Finish (*LF*)	Slack (*LS* − *ES*)	Critical Path?
A	0	0	7	7	0	Yes
B	7	7	10	10	0	Yes
C	0	1	6	7	1	
D	6	7	9	10	1	
E	10	10	12	12	0	Yes

To determine just where and how much to crash activity times, we need information on how much each activity can be crashed and how much the crashing process costs. Hence, we must ask for the following information:

1. Activity cost under the normal or expected activity time
2. Time to complete the activity under maximum crashing (i.e., the shortest possible activity time)
3. Activity cost under maximum crashing

Let

τ_i = expected time for activity i
τ_i' = time for activity i under maximum crashing
M_i = maximum possible reduction in time for activity i due to crashing

Given τ_i and τ_i', we can compute M_i:

$$M_i = \tau_i - \tau_i' \tag{10.6}$$

Next, let C_i denote the cost for activity i under the normal or expected activity time and C_i' denote the cost for activity i under maximum crashing. Thus, per unit of time (e.g., per day), the crashing cost K_i for each activity is given by

$$K_i = \frac{C_i' - C_i}{M_i} \tag{10.7}$$

For example, if the normal or expected time for activity A is 7 days at a cost of $C_A = \$500$ and the time under maximum crashing is 4 days at a cost of $C_A' = \$800$, equations (10.6) and (10.7) show that the maximum possible reduction in time for activity A is

$$M_A = 7 - 4 = 3 \text{ days}$$

with a crashing cost of

$$K_A = \frac{C_A' - C_A}{M_A} = \frac{800 - 500}{3} = \frac{300}{3} = \$100 \text{ per day}$$

We make the assumption that any portion or fraction of the activity crash time can be achieved for a corresponding portion of the activity crashing cost. For example, if we decided to crash activity A by only 1½ days, the added cost would be 1½($100) = $150, which results in a total activity cost of $500 + $150 = $650. Figure 10.16 shows the graph of the time-cost relationship for activity A. The complete normal and crash activity data for the two-machine maintenance project are given in Table 10.9.

Which activities should be crashed—and by how much—to meet the 10-day project completion deadline at minimum cost? Your first reaction to this question may be to consider crashing the critical activities—A, B, or E. Activity A has the lowest crashing cost per

FIGURE 10.16 TIME-COST RELATIONSHIP FOR ACTIVITY A

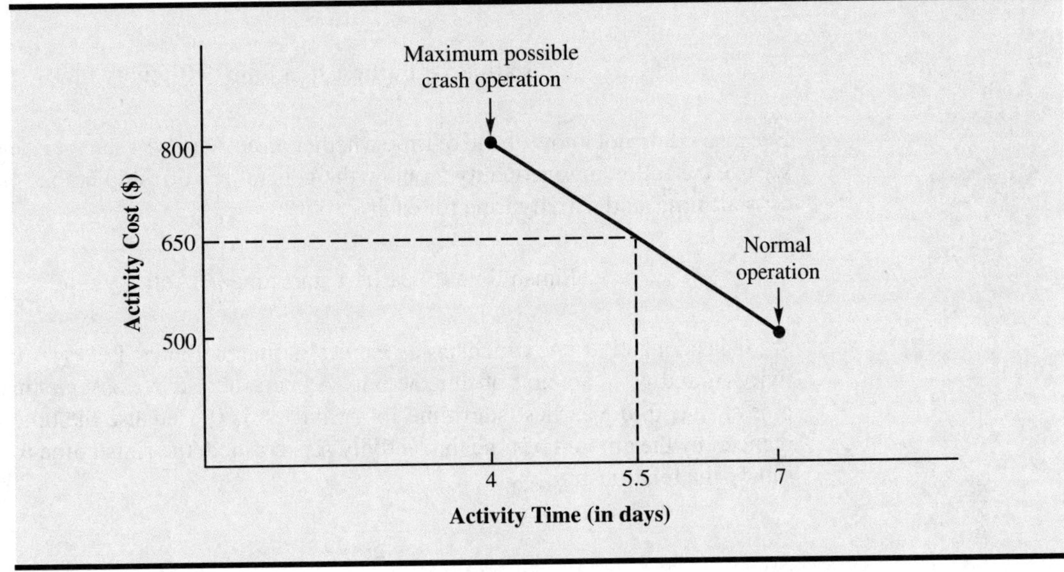

day of the three, and crashing this activity by 2 days will reduce the A-B-E path to the desired 10 days. Keep in mind, however, that as you crash the current critical activities, other paths may become critical. Thus, you will need to check the critical path in the revised network and perhaps either identify additional activities to crash or modify your initial crashing decision. For a small network, this trial-and-error approach can be used to make crashing decisions; in larger networks, however, a mathematical procedure is required to determine the optimal crashing decisions.

Linear Programming Model for Crashing

Let us describe how linear programming can be used to solve the network crashing problem. With PERT/CPM, we know that when an activity starts at its earliest start time, then

$$\text{Finish time} = \text{Earliest start time} + \text{Activity time}$$

TABLE 10.9 NORMAL AND CRASH ACTIVITY DATA FOR THE TWO-MACHINE MAINTENANCE PROJECT

Activity	Time (days) Normal	Time (days) Crash	Total Cost Normal (C_i)	Total Cost Crash (C'_i)	Maximum Reduction in Time (M_i)	Crash Cost per Day $\left(K_i = \frac{C'_i - C_i}{M_i}\right)$
A	7	4	\$ 500	\$ 800	3	\$100
B	3	2	200	350	1	150
C	6	4	500	900	2	200
D	3	1	200	500	2	150
E	2	1	300	550	1	250
			\$1700	\$3100		

However, if slack time is associated with an activity, then the activity need not start at its earliest start time. In this case, we may have

$$\text{Finish time} > \text{Earliest start time} + \text{Activity time}$$

Because we do not know ahead of time whether an activity will start at its earliest start time, we use the following inequality to show the general relationship among finish time, earliest start time, and activity time for each activity:

$$\text{Finish time} \geq \text{Earliest start time} + \text{Activity time}$$

Consider activity A, which has an expected time of 7 days. Let x_A = finish time for activity A, and y_A = amount of time activity A is crashed. If we assume that the project begins at time 0, the earliest start time for activity A is 0. Because the time for activity A is reduced by the amount of time that activity A is crashed, the finish time for activity A must satisfy the relationship

$$x_A \geq 0 + (7 - y_A)$$

Moving y_A to the left side,

$$x_A + y_A \geq 7$$

In general, let

$$\begin{aligned} x_i &= \text{the finish time for activity } i & i &= \text{A, B, C, D, E} \\ y_i &= \text{the amount of time activity } i \text{ is crashed} & i &= \text{A, B, C, D, E} \end{aligned}$$

If we follow the same approach that we used for activity A, the constraint corresponding to the finish time for activity C (expected time = 6 days) is

$$x_C \geq 0 + (6 - y_C) \quad \text{or} \quad x_C + y_C \geq 6$$

Continuing with the forward pass of the PERT/CPM procedure, we see that the earliest start time for activity B is x_A, the finish time for activity A. Thus, the constraint corresponding to the finish time for activity B is

$$x_B \geq x_A + (3 - y_B) \quad \text{or} \quad x_B + y_B - x_A \geq 3$$

Similarly, we obtain the constraint for the finish time for activity D:

$$x_D \geq x_C + (3 - y_D) \quad \text{or} \quad x_D + y_D - x_C \geq 3$$

Finally, we consider activity E. The earliest start time for activity E equals the *largest* of the finish times for activities B and D. Because the finish times for both activities B and D will be determined by the crashing procedure, we must write two constraints for activity E, one based on the finish time for activity B and one based upon the finish time for activity D:

$$x_E + y_E - x_B \geq 2 \quad \text{and} \quad x_E + y_E - x_D \geq 2$$

Recall that current production levels made completing the maintenance project within 10 days imperative. Thus, the constraint for the finish time for activity E is

$$x_E \leq 10$$

In addition, we must add the following five constraints corresponding to the maximum allowable crashing time for each activity:

$$y_A \leq 3, \qquad y_B \leq 1, \qquad y_C \leq 2, \qquad y_D \leq 2, \qquad \text{and} \qquad y_E \leq 1$$

As with all linear programs, we add the usual nonnegativity requirements for the decision variables.

All that remains is to develop an objective function for the model. Because the total project cost for a normal completion time is fixed at \$1700 (see Table 10.9), we can minimize the total project cost (normal cost plus crashing cost) by minimizing the total crashing costs. Thus, the linear programming objective function becomes

$$\text{Min} \quad 100y_A + 150y_B + 200y_C + 150y_D + 250y_E$$

Thus, to determine the optimal crashing for each of the activities, we must solve a 10-variable, 12-constraint linear programming model. The linear programming module of The Management Scientist provides the optimal solution of crashing activity A by 1 day and activity E by 1 day, with a total crashing cost of \$100 + \$250 = \$350. With the minimum cost crashing solution, the activity times are as follows:

Activity	**Time in Days**
A	6 (Crash 1 day)
B	3
C	6
D	3
E	1 (Crash 1 day)

The linear programming solution provided the revised activity times, but not the revised earliest start time, latest start time, and slack information. The revised activity times and the usual PERT/CPM procedure must be used to develop the activity schedule for the project.

NOTES AND COMMENTS

Note that the two-machine maintenance project network for the crashing illustration (see Figure 10.15) has only one activity, activity E, leading directly to the Finish node. As a result, the project completion time is equal to the completion time for activity E. Thus, the linear programming constraint requiring the project completion in 10 days or less could be written $x_E \leq 10$.

(continued)

If two or more activities lead directly to the Finish node of a project network, a slight modification is required in the linear programming model for crashing. Consider the portion of the project network shown here. In this case, we suggest creating an additional variable, x_{FIN}, which indicates the finish or completion time for the entire project. The fact that the project cannot be finished until both activities E and G are completed can be modeled by the two constraints

$$x_{\text{FIN}} \geq x_{\text{E}} \quad \text{or} \quad x_{\text{FIN}} - x_{\text{E}} \geq 0$$
$$x_{\text{FIN}} \geq x_{\text{G}} \quad \text{or} \quad x_{\text{FIN}} - x_{\text{G}} \geq 0$$

The constraint that the project must be finished by time T can be added as $x_{\text{FIN}} \leq \text{T}$. Problem 22 gives you practice with this type of project network.

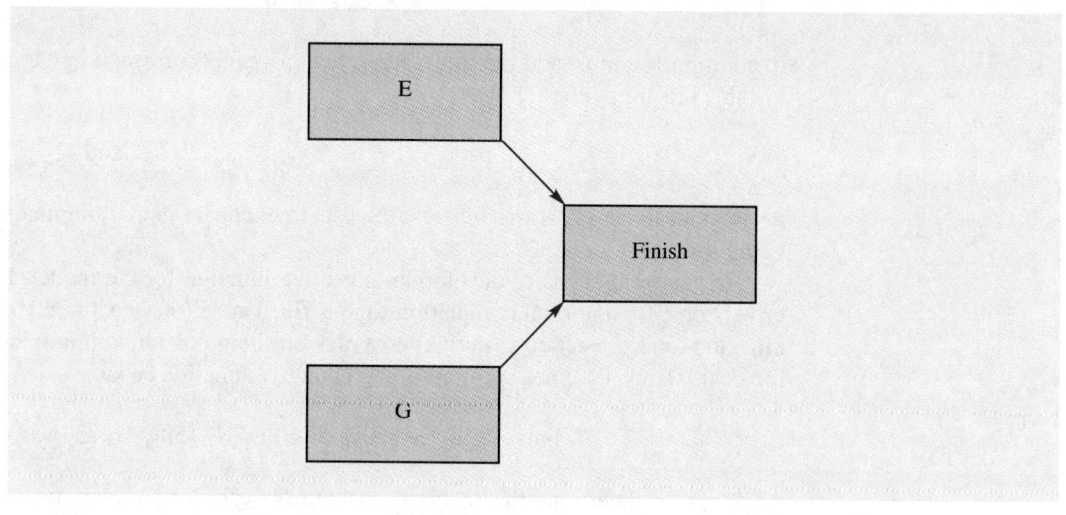

SUMMARY

In this chapter we showed how PERT/CPM can be used to plan, schedule, and control a wide variety of projects. The key to this approach to project scheduling is the development of a PERT/CPM project network that depicts the activities and their precedence relationships. From this project network and activity time estimates, the critical path for the network and the associated critical activities can be identified. In the process, an activity schedule showing the earliest start and earliest finish times, the latest start and latest finish times, and the slack for each activity can be identified.

We showed how we can include capabilities for handling variable or uncertain activity times and how to use this information to provide a probability statement about the chances the project can be completed in a specified period of time. We introduced crashing as a procedure for reducing activity times to meet project completion deadlines, and showed how a linear programming model can be used to determine the crashing decisions that will minimize the cost of reducing the project completion time.

GLOSSARY

Program evaluation and review technique (PERT) A network-based project scheduling procedure.

Critical path method (CPM) A network-based project scheduling procedure.

Activities Specific jobs or tasks that are components of a project. Activities are represented by nodes in a project network.

Immediate predecessors The activities that must be completed immediately prior to the start of a given activity.

Project network A graphical representation of a project that depicts the activities and shows the predecessor relationships among the activities.

Critical path The longest path in a project network.

Path A sequence of connected nodes that leads from the Start node to the Finish node.

Critical activities The activities on the critical path.

Earliest start time The earliest time an activity may begin.

Latest start time The latest time an activity may begin without increasing the project completion time.

Earliest finish time The earliest time an activity may be completed.

Forward pass Part of the PERT/CPM procedure that involves moving forward through the project network to determine the earliest start and earliest finish times for each activity.

Backward pass Part of the PERT/CPM procedure that involves moving backward through the network to determine the latest start and latest finish times for each activity.

Latest finish time The latest time an activity may be completed without increasing the project completion time.

Slack The length of time an activity can be delayed without affecting the project completion time.

Optimistic time The minimum activity time if everything progresses ideally.

Most probable time The most probable activity time under normal conditions.

Pessimistic time The maximum activity time if significant delays are encountered.

Expected time The average activity time.

Beta probability distribution A probability distribution used to describe activity times.

Crashing The shortening of activity times by adding resources and hence usually increasing cost.

PROBLEMS

1. The Mohawk Discount Store is designing a management training program for individuals at its corporate headquarters. The company wants to design the program so that trainees can complete it as quickly as possible. Important precedence relationships must be maintained between assignments or activities in the program. For example, a trainee cannot serve as an assistant to the store manager until the trainee has obtained experience in the credit department and at least one sales department. The following activities are the assignments that must be completed by each trainee in the program. Construct a project network for this problem. Do not perform any further analysis.

Activity	A	B	C	D	E	F	G	H
Immediate Predecessor	—	—	A	A, B	A, B	C	D, F	E, G

2. Bridge City Developers is coordinating the construction of an office complex. As part of the planning process, the company generated the following activity list. Draw a project network that can be used to assist in the scheduling of the project activities.

Activity	A	B	C	D	E	F	G	H	I	J
Immediate Predecessor	—	—	—	A, B	A, B	D	E	C	C	F, G, H, I

3. Construct a project network for the following project. The project is completed when activities F and G are both complete.

Activity	A	B	C	D	E	F	G
Immediate Predecessor	—	—	A	A	C, B	C, B	D, E

4. Assume that the project in Problem 3 has the following activity times (in months).

Activity	A	B	C	D	E	F	G
Time	4	6	2	6	3	3	5

a. Find the critical path.
b. The project must be completed in 1½ years. Do you anticipate difficulty in meeting the deadline? Explain.

5. Management Decision Systems (MDS) is a consulting company that specializes in the development of decision support systems. MDS obtained a contract to develop a computer system to assist the management of a large company in formulating its capital expenditure plan. The project leader developed the following list of activities and immediate predecessors. Construct a project network for this problem.

Activity	A	B	C	D	E	F	G	H	I	J
Immediate Predecessor	—	—	—	B	A	B	C, D	B, E	F, G	H

6. Consider the following project network and activity times (in weeks).

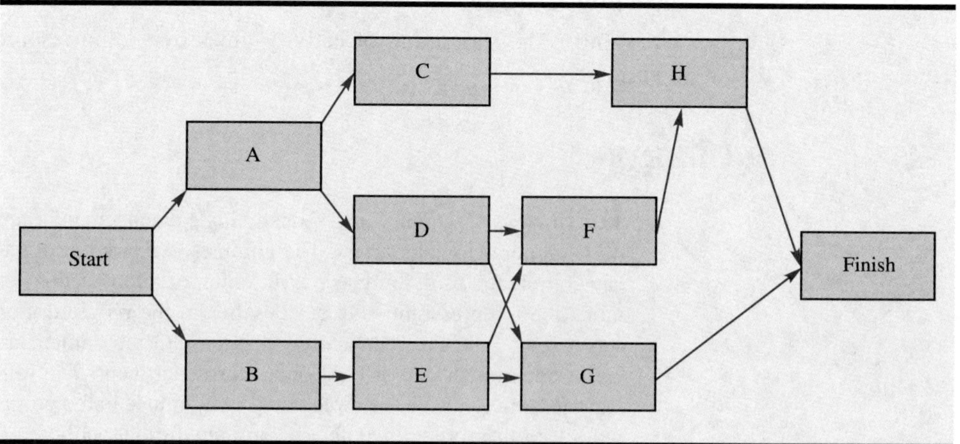

Activity	A	B	C	D	E	F	G	H
Time	5	3	7	6	7	3	10	8

a. Identify the critical path.
b. How much time will be needed to complete this project?
c. Can activity D be delayed without delaying the entire project? If so, by how many weeks?
d. Can activity C be delayed without delaying the entire project? If so, by how many weeks?
e. What is the schedule for activity E?

7. A project involving the installation of a computer system comprises eight activities. The following table lists immediate predecessors and activity times (in weeks).

Activity	Immediate Predecessor	Time
A	—	3
B	—	6
C	A	2
D	B, C	5
E	D	4
F	E	3
G	B, C	9
H	F, G	3

a. Draw a project network.
b. What are the critical activities?
c. What is the expected project completion time?

8. Colonial State College is considering building a new multipurpose athletic complex on campus. The complex would provide a new gymnasium for intercollegiate basketball games, expanded office space, classrooms, and intramural facilities. The following activities would have to be undertaken before construction can begin.

Activity	Description	Immediate Predecessor	Time (weeks)
A	Survey building site	—	6
B	Develop initial design	—	8
C	Obtain board approval	A, B	12
D	Select architect	C	4
E	Establish budget	C	6
F	Finalize design	D, E	15
G	Obtain financing	E	12
H	Hire contractor	F, G	8

a. Draw a project network.
b. Identify the critical path.
c. Develop the activity schedule for the project.
d. Does it appear reasonable that construction of the athletic complex could begin one year after the decision to begin the project with the site survey and initial design plans? What is the expected completion time for the project?

9. Hamilton County Parks is planning to develop a new park and recreational area on a recently purchased 100-acre tract. Project development activities include clearing playground and picnic areas, constructing roads, constructing a shelter house, purchasing picnic equipment, and so on. The following network and activity times (in weeks) are being used in the planning, scheduling, and controlling of this project.

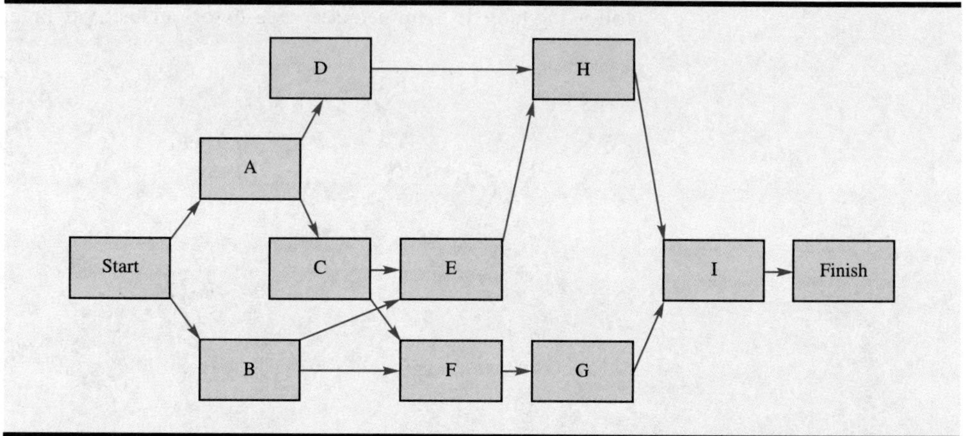

Activity	A	B	C	D	E	F	G	H	I
Time	9	6	6	3	0	3	2	6	3

a. What is the critical path for this network?
b. Show the activity schedule for this project.
c. The park commissioner would like to open the park to the public within six months from the time the work on the project is started. Does this opening date appear to be feasible? Explain.

10. The following estimates of activity times (in days) are available for a small project.

Activity	Optimistic	Most Probable	Pessimistic
A	4	5.0	6
B	8	9.0	10
C	7	7.5	11
D	7	9.0	10
E	6	7.0	9
F	5	6.0	7

a. Compute the expected activity completion times and the variance for each activity.
b. An analyst determined that the critical path consists of activities B-D-F. Compute the expected project completion time and the variance.

11. Building a backyard swimming pool consists of nine major activities. The activities and their immediate predecessors are shown. Develop the project network.

Activity	A	B	C	D	E	F	G	H	I
Immediate Predecessor	—	—	A, B	A, B	B	C	D	D, F	E, G, H

12. Assume that the activity time estimates (in days) for the swimming pool construction project in Problem 11 are as follows:

Activity	Optimistic	Most Probable	Pessimistic
A	3	5	6
B	2	4	6
C	5	6	7
D	7	9	10
E	2	4	6
F	1	2	3
G	5	8	10
H	6	8	10
I	3	4	5

a. What are the critical activities?
b. What is the expected time to complete the project?
c. What is the probability that the project can be completed in 25 or fewer days?

13. Suppose that the following estimates of activity times (in weeks) were provided for the network shown in Problem 6.

Activity	Optimistic	Most Probable	Pessimistic
A	4.0	5.0	6.0
B	2.5	3.0	3.5
C	6.0	7.0	8.0
D	5.0	5.5	9.0
E	5.0	7.0	9.0
F	2.0	3.0	4.0
G	8.0	10.0	12.0
H	6.0	7.0	14.0

What is the probability that the project will be completed
a. Within 21 weeks?
b. Within 22 weeks?
c. Within 25 weeks?

14. Consider the following project network.

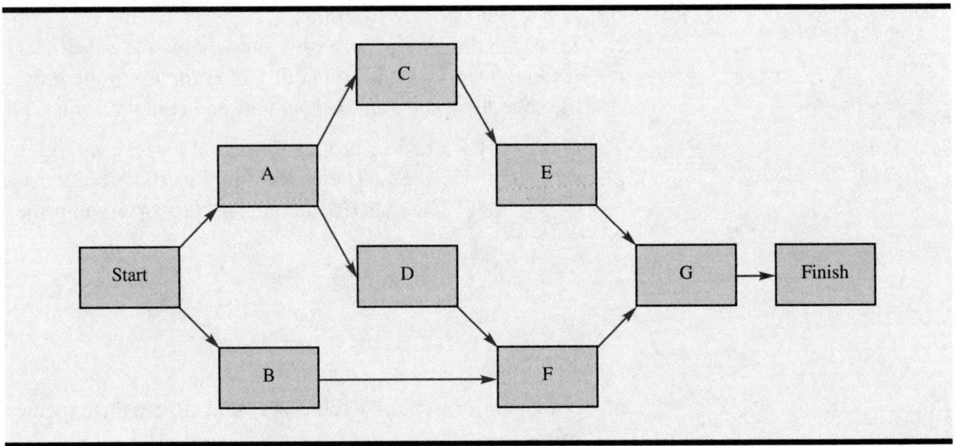

Estimates of the optimistic, most probable, and pessimistic times (in days) for the activities are

Activity	Optimistic	Most Probable	Pessimistic
A	5	6	7
B	5	12	13
C	6	8	10
D	4	10	10
E	5	6	13
F	7	7	10
G	4	7	10

a. Find the critical path.
b. How much slack time, if any, is in activity C?
c. Determine the expected project completion time and the variance.
d. Find the probability that the project will be completed in 30 or fewer days.

15. Doug Casey is in charge of planning and coordinating next spring's sales management training program for his company. Doug listed the following activity information for this project.

Activity	Description	Immediate Predecessor	Time (weeks) Optimistic	Most Probable	Pessimistic
A	Plan topic	—	1.5	2.0	2.5
B	Obtain speakers	A	2.0	2.5	6.0
C	List meeting locations	—	1.0	2.0	3.0
D	Select location	C	1.5	2.0	2.5
E	Finalize speaker travel plans	B, D	0.5	1.0	1.5
F	Make final check with speakers	E	1.0	2.0	3.0
G	Prepare and mail brochure	B, D	3.0	3.5	7.0
H	Take reservations	G	3.0	4.0	5.0
I	Handle last-minute details	F, H	1.5	2.0	2.5

a. Draw a project network.
b. Prepare an activity schedule.
c. What are the critical activities and what is the expected project completion time?
d. If Doug wants a 0.99 probability of completing the project on time, how far ahead of the scheduled meeting date should he begin working on the project?

16. The Daugherty Porta-Vac project discussed in Section 10.2 has an expected project completion time of 17 weeks. The probability that the project could be completed in 20 weeks or less is 0.9656. The noncritical paths in the Porta-Vac project network are

A-D-G-J

A-C-F-J

B-H-I-J

a. Use the information in Table 10.5 to compute the expected time and variance for each path shown.

b. Compute the probability that each path will be completed in the desired 20-week period.

c. Why is the computation of the probability of completing a project on time based on the analysis of the critical path? In what case, if any, would making the probability computation for a noncritical path be desirable?

17. The Porsche Shop, founded in 1985 by Dale Jensen, specializes in the restoration of vintage Porsche automobiles. One of Jensen's regular customers asked him to prepare an estimate for the restoration of a 1964 model 356SC Porsche. To estimate the time and cost to perform such a restoration, Jensen broke the restoration process into four separate activities: disassembly and initial preparation work (A), body restoration (B), engine restoration (C), and final assembly (D). Once activity A has been completed, activities B and C can be performed independently of each other; however, activity D can be started only if both activities B and C have been completed. Based on his inspection of the car, Jensen believes that the following time estimates (in days) are applicable.

Activity	Optimistic	Most Probable	Pessimistic
A	3	4	8
B	5	8	11
C	2	4	6
D	4	5	12

Jensen estimates that the parts needed to restore the body will cost $3000 and that the parts needed to restore the engine will cost $5000. His current labor costs are $400 a day.

a. Develop a project network.

b. What is the expected project completion time?

c. Jensen's business philosophy is based on making decisions using a best- and worst-case scenario. Develop cost estimates for completing the restoration based on both a best- and worst-case analysis. Assume that the total restoration cost is the sum of the labor cost plus the material cost.

d. If Jensen obtains the job with a bid that is based on the costs associated with an expected completion time, what is the probability that he will lose money on the job?

e. If Jensen obtains the job based on a bid of $16,800, what is the probability that he will lose money on the job?

18. The manager of the Oak Hills Swimming Club is planning the club's swimming team program. The first team practice is scheduled for May 1. The activities, their immediate predecessors, and the activity time estimates (in weeks) are as follows.

			Time (weeks)		
Activity	Description	Immediate Predecessor	Optimistic	Most Probable	Pessimistic
A	Meet with board	—	1	1	2
B	Hire coaches	A	4	6	8
C	Reserve pool	A	2	4	6
D	Announce program	B, C	1	2	3
E	Meet with coaches	B	2	3	4
F	Order team suits	A	1	2	3
G	Register swimmers	D	1	2	3
H	Collect fees	G	1	2	3
I	Plan first practice	E, H, F	1	1	1

a. Draw a project network.
b. Develop an activity schedule.
c. What are the critical activities, and what is the expected project completion time?
d. If the club manager plans to start the project on February 1, what is the probability the swimming program will be ready by the scheduled May 1 date (13 weeks)? Should the manager begin planning the swimming program before February 1?

19. The product development group at Landon Corporation has been working on a new computer software product that has the potential to capture a large market share. Through outside sources, Landon's management learned that a competitor is working to introduce a similar product. As a result, Landon's top management increased its pressure on the product development group. The group's leader turned to PERT/CPM as an aid to scheduling the activities remaining before the new product can be brought to the market. The project network is as follows.

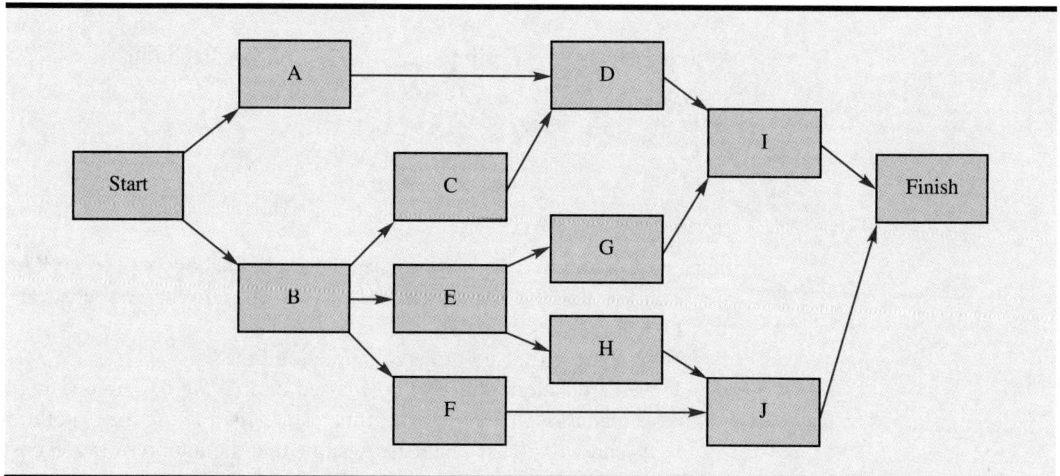

The activity time estimates (in weeks) are

Activity	Optimistic	Most Probable	Pessimistic
A	3.0	4.0	5.0
B	3.0	3.5	7.0
C	4.0	5.0	6.0
D	2.0	3.0	4.0
E	6.0	10.0	14.0
F	7.5	8.5	12.5
G	4.5	6.0	7.5
H	5.0	6.0	13.0
I	2.0	2.5	6.0
J	4.0	5.0	6.0

a. Develop an activity schedule for this project and identify the critical path activities.
b. What is the probability that the project will be completed so that Landon Corporation may introduce the new product within 25 weeks? Within 30 weeks?

20. Return to the computer installation project in Problem 7 and assume that the project has to be completed in 16 weeks. Crashing of the project is necessary. Use the following relevant information.

	Time (weeks)		Cost ($)	
Activity	**Normal**	**Crash**	**Normal**	**Crash**
A	3	1	900	1700
B	6	3	2000	4000
C	2	1	500	1000
D	5	3	1800	2400
E	4	3	1500	1850
F	3	1	3000	3900
G	9	4	8000	9800
H	3	2	1000	2000

a. Formulate a linear programming model that can be used to make the crashing decisions for this project.

b. Solve the linear programming model and make the minimum cost crashing decisions. What is the added cost of meeting the 16-week completion time?

c. Develop a complete activity schedule based on the crashed activity times.

21. Consider the following project network and activity times (in days).

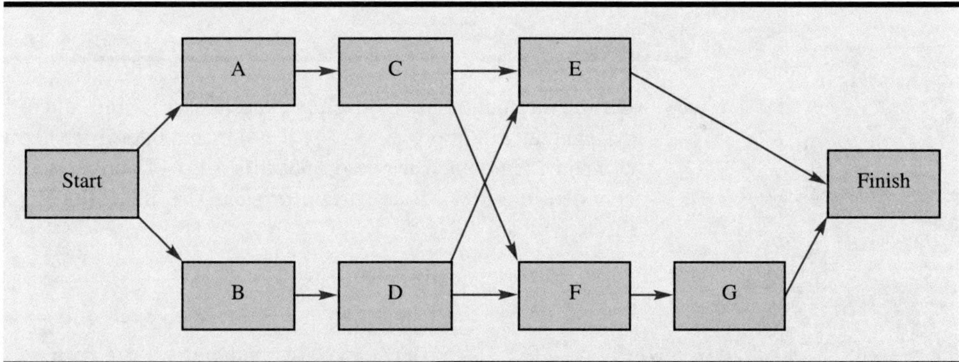

Activity	A	B	C	D	E	F	G
Time	3	2	5	5	6	2	2

The crashing data for this project are as follows.

	Time (days)		Cost ($)	
Activity	**Normal**	**Crash**	**Normal**	**Crash**
A	3	2	800	1400
B	2	1	1200	1900
C	5	3	2000	2800
D	5	3	1500	2300
E	6	4	1800	2800
F	2	1	600	1000
G	2	1	500	1000

a. Find the critical path and the expected project completion time.
b. What is the total project cost using the normal times?

22. Refer to Problem 21. Assume that management desires a 12-day project completion time.
a. Formulate a linear programming model that can be used to assist with the crashing decisions.
b. What activities should be crashed?
c. What is the total project cost for the 12-day completion time?

23. Consider the following project network. Note that the normal or expected activity times are denoted τ_i, i = A, B, . . . , I. Let x_i = the earliest finish time for activity i. Formulate a linear programming model that can be used to determine the length of the critical path.

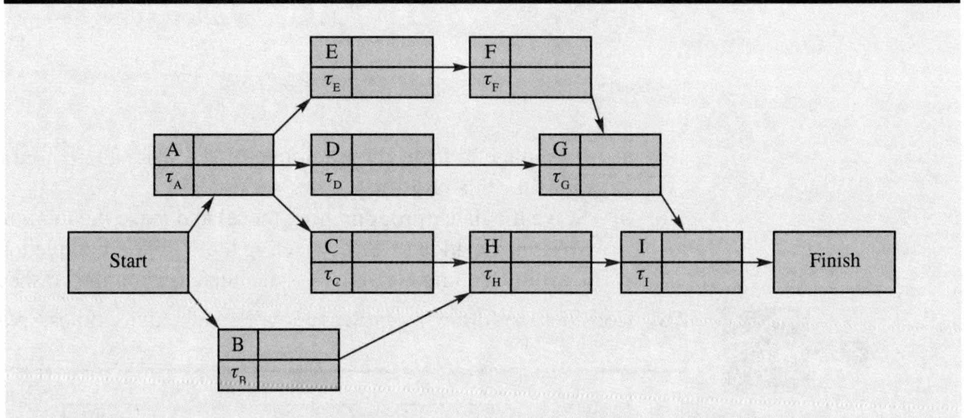

24. Office Automation, Inc., developed a proposal for introducing a new computerized office system that will improve word processing and interoffice communications for a particular company. Contained in the proposal is a list of activities that must be accomplished to complete the new office system project. Use the following relevant information about the activities.

Activity	Description	Immediate Predecessor	Time (weeks) Normal	Time (weeks) Crash	Cost ($1000s) Normal	Cost ($1000s) Crash
A	Plan needs	—	10	8	30	70
B	Order equipment	A	8	6	120	150
C	Install equipment	B	10	7	100	160
D	Set up training lab	A	7	6	40	50
E	Conduct training course	D	10	8	50	75
F	Test system	C, E	3	3	60	—

a. Develop a project network.
b. Develop an activity schedule.
c. What are the critical activities, and what is the expected project completion time?
d. Assume that the company wants to complete the project in six months or 26 weeks. What crashing decisions do you recommend to meet the desired completion time at the least possible cost? Work through the network and attempt to make the crashing decisions by inspection.
e. Develop an activity schedule for the crashed project.
f. What added project cost is required to meet the six-month completion time?

25. Because Landon Corporation (see Problem 19) is being pressured to complete the product development project at the earliest possible date, the project leader requested that the possibility of crashing the project be evaluated.
    a. Formulate a linear programming model that could be used in making the crashing decisions.
    b. What information would have to be provided before the linear programming model could be implemented?

Case Problem R. C. COLEMAN

R. C. Coleman distributes a variety of food products that are sold through grocery store and supermarket outlets. The company receives orders directly from the individual outlets, with a typical order requesting the delivery of several cases of anywhere from 20 to 50 different products. Under the company's current warehouse operation, warehouse clerks dispatch order-picking personnel to fill each order and have the goods moved to the warehouse shipping area. Because of the high labor costs and relatively low productivity of hand order-picking, management has decided to automate the warehouse operation by installing a computer-controlled order-picking system, along with a conveyor system for moving goods from storage to the warehouse shipping area.

R. C. Coleman's director of material management has been named the project manager in charge of the automated warehouse system. After consulting with members of the engineering staff and warehouse management personnel, the director compiled a list of activities associated with the project. The optimistic, most probable, and pessimistic times (in weeks) have also been provided for each activity.

Activity	Description	Immediate Predecessor
A	Determine equipment needs	—
B	Obtain vendor proposals	—
C	Select vendor	A, B
D	Order system	C
E	Design new warehouse layout	C
F	Design warehouse	E
G	Design computer interface	C
H	Interface computer	D, F, G
I	Install system	D, F
J	Train system operators	H
K	Test system	I, J

		Time	
Activity	Optimistic	Most Probable	Pessimistic
A	4	6	8
B	6	8	16
C	2	4	6
D	8	10	24

(continued)

Activity	Time		
	Optimistic	Most Probable	Pessimistic
E	7	10	13
F	4	6	8
G	4	6	20
H	4	6	8
I	4	6	14
J	3	4	5
K	2	4	6

Managerial Report

Develop a report that presents the activity schedule and expected project completion time for the warehouse expansion project. Include a project network in the report. In addition, take into consideration the following issues.

1. R. C. Coleman's top management established a required 40-week completion time for the project. Can this completion time be achieved? Include probability information in your discussion. What recommendations do you have if the 40-week completion time is required?
2. Suppose that management requests that activity times be shortened to provide an 80 percent chance of meeting the 40-week completion time. If the variance in the project completion time is the same as you found in part (1), how much should the expected project completion time be shortened to achieve the goal of an 80 percent chance of completion within 40 weeks?
3. Using the expected activity times as the normal times and the following crashing information, determine the activity crashing decisions and revised activity schedule for the warehouse expansion project.

Activity	Crashed Activity Time (weeks)	Cost ($)	
		Normal	Crashed
A	4	1,000	1,900
B	7	1,000	1,800
C	2	1,500	2,700
D	8	2,000	3,200
E	7	5,000	8,000
F	4	3,000	4,100
G	5	8,000	10,250
H	4	5,000	6,400
I	4	10,000	12,400
J	3	4,000	4,400
K	3	5,000	5,500

CHAPTER 11

Inventory Models

CONTENTS

Inventory refers to idle goods or materials held by an organization for use sometime in the future. Items carried in inventory include raw materials, purchased parts, components, subassemblies, work-in-process, finished goods, and supplies. Some reasons organizations maintain inventory include the difficulties in precisely predicting sales levels, production times, demand, and usage needs. Thus, inventory serves as a buffer against uncertain and fluctuating usage and keeps a supply of items available in case the items are needed by the organization or its customers. Even though inventory serves an important and essential role, the expense associated with financing and maintaining inventories is a substantial part of the cost of doing business. In large organizations, the cost associated with inventory can run into the millions of dollars.

In applications involving inventory, managers must answer two important questions.

1. *How much* should be ordered when the inventory is replenished?
2. *When* should the inventory be replenished?

Virtually every business uses some sort of inventory management model or system to address the preceding questions. Hewlett-Packard works with its retailers to help determine the retailer's inventory replenishment strategies for the printers and other HP products. IBM developed inventory management policies for a range of microelectronic parts that are used in IBM plants as well as sold to a number of outside customers. The Management Science in Action, Inventory Management at CVS Corporation, describes an inventory system used to determine order quantities in the drugstore industry.

The purpose of this chapter is to show how quantitative models can assist in making the how-much-to-order and when-to-order inventory decisions. We will first consider *deterministic* inventory models in which we assume that the rate of demand for the item is constant or nearly constant. Later we will consider *probabilistic* inventory models in which the demand for the item fluctuates and can be described only in probabilistic terms.

MANAGEMENT SCIENCE IN ACTION

INVENTORY MANAGEMENT AT CVS CORPORATION*

The inventory procedure described for the drugstore industry is discussed in detail in Section 11.7.

CVS is the largest drugstore chain in the United States with 4100 stores in 25 states. The primary inventory management area in the drugstore involves the numerous basic products that are carried in inventory on an everyday basis. For these items, the most important issue is the replenishment quantity or order size each time an order is placed. In most drugstore chains, basic products are ordered under a periodic review inventory system, with the review period being one week.

The weekly review system uses electronic ordering equipment that scans an order label affixed to the shelf directly below each item. Among other information on the label is the item's replenishment level or order-to-quantity. The store employee placing the order determines the weekly order quantity by counting the number of units of the product on the shelf and subtracting this quantity from the replenishment level. A computer program determines the replenishment quantity for each item in each individual store, based on each store's movement, rather than on the company movement. To minimize stockouts the replenishment quantity is set equal to the store's three-week demand or movement for the product.

*Based on information provided by Bob Carver. (The inventory system described was originally implemented in the CVS stores formerly known as SupeRx.)

11.1 ECONOMIC ORDER QUANTITY (EOQ) MODEL

The **economic order quantity (EOQ)** model is applicable when the demand for an item shows a constant, or nearly constant, rate and when the entire quantity ordered arrives in inventory at one point in time. The **constant demand rate** assumption means that the

The cost associated with developing and maintaining inventory is larger than many people think. Models such as the ones presented in this chapter can be used to develop cost-effective inventory management decisions.

same number of units is taken from inventory each period of time such as 5 units every day, 25 units every week, 100 units every four-week period, and so on.

To illustrate the EOQ model, let us consider the situation faced by the R & B Beverage Company. R & B Beverage is a distributor of beer, wine, and soft drink products. From a main warehouse located in Columbus, Ohio, R & B supplies nearly 1000 retail stores with beverage products. The beer inventory, which constitutes about 40 percent of the company's total inventory, averages approximately 50,000 cases. With an average cost per case of approximately $8, R & B estimates the value of its beer inventory to be $400,000.

The warehouse manager decided to conduct a detailed study of the inventory costs associated with Bub Beer, the number-one-selling R & B beer. The purpose of the study is to establish the how-much-to-order and the when-to-order decisions for Bub Beer that will result in the lowest possible total cost. As the first step in the study, the warehouse manager obtained the following demand data for the past 10 weeks:

One of the most criticized assumptions of the EOQ model is the constant demand rate. Obviously, the model would be inappropriate for items with widely fluctuating and variable demand rates. However, as this example shows, the EOQ model can provide a realistic approximation of the optimal order quantity when demand is relatively stable and occurs at a nearly constant rate.

Week	Demand (cases)
1	2000
2	2025
3	1950
4	2000
5	2100
6	2050
7	2000
8	1975
9	1900
10	2000
Total cases	20,000
Average cases per week	2000

Strictly speaking, these weekly demand figures do not show a constant demand rate. However, given the relatively low variability exhibited by the weekly demand, inventory planning with a constant demand rate of 2000 cases per week appears acceptable. In practice, you will find that the actual inventory situation seldom, if ever, satisfies the assumptions of the model exactly. Thus, in any particular application, the manager must determine whether the model assumptions are close enough to reality for the model to be useful. In this situation, because demand varies from a low of 1900 cases to a high of 2100 cases, the assumption of constant demand of 2000 cases per week appears to be a reasonable approximation.

The how-much-to-order decision involves selecting an order quantity that draws a compromise between (1) keeping small inventories and ordering frequently, and (2) keeping large inventories and ordering infrequently. The first alternative can result in undesirably high ordering costs, while the second alternative can result in undesirably high inventory holding costs. To find an optimal compromise between these conflicting alternatives, let us consider a mathematical model that shows the total cost as the sum of the holding cost and the ordering cost.[1]

---

[1]Even though analysts typically refer to "total cost" models for inventory systems, often these models describe only the total variable or total relevant costs for the decision being considered. Costs that are not affected by the how-much-to-order decision are considered fixed or constant and are not included in the model.

As with other quantitative models, accurate estimates of cost parameters are critical. In the EOQ model, estimates of both the inventory holding cost and the ordering cost are needed. Also see footnote 1, which refers to relevant costs.

Holding costs are the costs associated with maintaining or carrying a given level of inventory; these costs depend on the size of the inventory. The first holding cost to consider is the cost of financing the inventory investment. When a firm borrows money, it incurs an interest charge. If the firm uses its own money, it experiences an opportunity cost associated with not being able to use the money for other investments. In either case, an interest cost exists for the capital tied up in inventory. This **cost of capital** is usually expressed as a percentage of the amount invested. R & B estimates its cost of capital at an annual rate of 18 percent.

A number of other holding costs such as insurance, taxes, breakage, pilferage, and warehouse overhead also depend on the value of the inventory. R & B estimates these other costs at an annual rate of approximately 7 percent of the value of its inventory. Thus, the total holding cost for the R & B beer inventory is 18% + 7% = 25% of the value of the inventory. The cost of one case of Bub Beer is $8. With an annual holding cost rate of 25 percent, the cost of holding one case of Bub Beer in inventory for 1 year is 0.25($8) = $2.00.

The next step in the inventory analysis is to determine the **ordering cost.** This cost, which is considered fixed regardless of the order quantity, covers the preparation of the voucher, the processing of the order including payment, postage, telephone, transportation, invoice verification, receiving, and so on. For R & B Beverage, the largest portion of the ordering cost involves the salaries of the purchasers. An analysis of the purchasing process showed that a purchaser spends approximately 45 minutes preparing and processing an order for Bub Beer. With a wage rate and fringe benefit cost for purchasers of $20 per hour, the labor portion of the ordering cost is $15. Making allowances for paper, postage, telephone, transportation, and receiving costs at $17 per order, the manager estimates that the ordering cost is $32 per order. That is, R & B is paying $32 per order regardless of the quantity requested in the order.

The holding cost, ordering cost, and demand information are the three data items that must be known prior to the use of the EOQ model. After developing these data for the R & B problem, we can look at how they are used to develop a total cost model. We begin by defining Q as the order quantity. Thus, the how-much-to-order decision involves finding the value of Q that will minimize the sum of holding and ordering costs.

The inventory for Bub Beer will have a maximum value of Q units when an order of size Q is received from the supplier. R & B will then satisfy customer demand from inventory until the inventory is depleted, at which time another shipment of Q units will be received. Thus, assuming a constant demand, the graph of the inventory for Bub Beer is as shown in Figure 11.1. Note that the graph indicates an average inventory of $\frac{1}{2}Q$ for the period in question. This level should appear reasonable because the maximum inventory is Q, the minimum is zero, and the inventory declines at a constant rate over the period.

Figure 11.1 shows the inventory pattern during one order cycle of length T. As time goes on, this pattern will repeat. The complete inventory pattern is shown in Figure 11.2. If the average inventory during each cycle is $\frac{1}{2}Q$, the average inventory over any number of cycles is also $\frac{1}{2}Q$.

Most inventory cost models use an annual cost. Thus, demand should be expressed in units per year and inventory holding cost should be based on an annual rate.

The holding cost can be calculated using the average inventory. That is, we can calculate the holding cost by multiplying the average inventory by the cost of carrying one unit in inventory for the stated period. The period selected for the model is up to you; it could be one week, one month, one year, or more. However, because the holding cost for many industries and businesses is expressed as an *annual* percentage, most inventory models are developed on an *annual* cost basis.

FIGURE 11.1 INVENTORY FOR BUB BEER

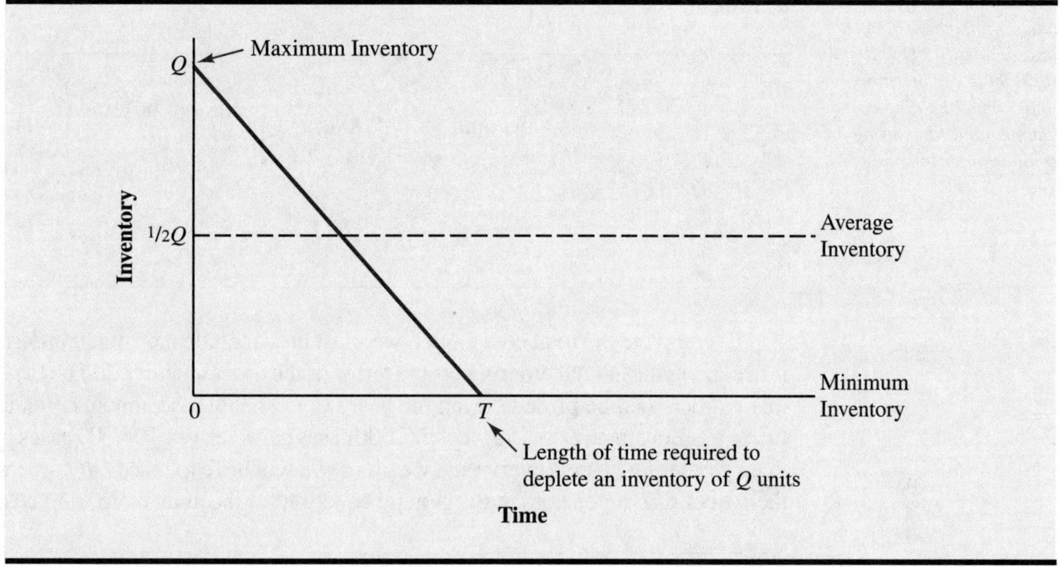

FIGURE 11.2 INVENTORY PATTERN FOR THE EOQ INVENTORY MODEL

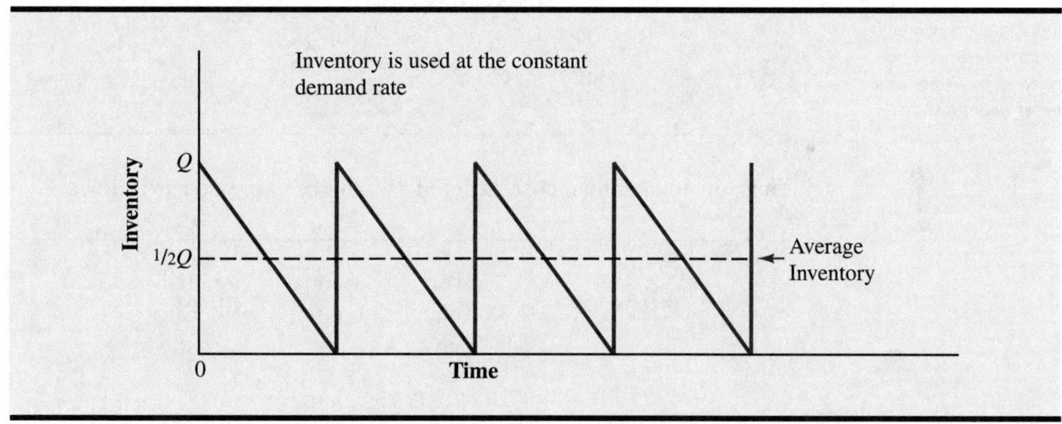

Let

$$
\begin{aligned}
I &= \text{annual holding cost rate} \\
C &= \text{unit cost of the inventory item} \\
C_{\text{h}} &= \text{annual cost of holding one unit in inventory}
\end{aligned}
$$

The annual cost of holding one unit in inventory is

$$C_{\text{h}} = IC \tag{11.1}$$

C_h is the cost of holding one unit in inventory for one year. Because smaller order quantities Q will result in lower inventory, total annual holding cost can be reduced by using smaller order quantities.

The general equation for the annual holding cost for the average inventory of ½Q units is as follows:

$$\begin{aligned}\text{Annual holding cost} &= \begin{pmatrix}\text{Average}\\ \text{inventory}\end{pmatrix}\begin{pmatrix}\text{Annual holding}\\ \text{cost}\\ \text{per unit}\end{pmatrix}\\ &= \frac{1}{2}QC_h \qquad (11.2)\end{aligned}$$

To complete the total cost model, we must now include the annual ordering cost. The goal is to express the annual ordering cost in terms of the order quantity Q. The first question is, How many orders will be placed during the year? Let D denote the annual demand for the product. For R & B Beverage, D = (52 weeks)(2000 cases per week) = 104,000 cases per year. We know that by ordering Q units every time we order, we will have to place D/Q orders per year. If C_o is the cost of placing one order, the general equation for the annual ordering cost is as follows:

C_o, the fixed cost per order, is independent of the amount ordered. For a given annual demand of D units, the total annual ordering cost can be reduced by using larger order quantities.

$$\begin{aligned}\text{Annual ordering cost} &= \begin{pmatrix}\text{Number of}\\ \text{orders}\\ \text{per year}\end{pmatrix}\begin{pmatrix}\text{Cost}\\ \text{per}\\ \text{order}\end{pmatrix}\\ &= \left(\frac{D}{Q}\right)C_o \qquad (11.3)\end{aligned}$$

Thus, the total annual cost, denoted TC, can be expressed as follows:

$$\begin{aligned}\text{Total annual cost} &= \text{Annual holding cost} + \text{Annual ordering cost}\\ TC &= \frac{1}{2}QC_h + \frac{D}{Q}C_o \qquad (11.4)\end{aligned}$$

Using the Bub Beer data [$C_h = IC = (0.25)(\$8) = \$2$, $C_o = \$32$, and $D = 104{,}000$], the total annual cost model is

$$TC = \frac{1}{2}Q(\$2) + \frac{104{,}000}{Q}(\$32) = Q + \frac{3{,}328{,}000}{Q}$$

The development of the total cost model goes a long way toward solving the inventory problem. We now are able to express the total annual cost as a function of *how much* should be ordered. The development of a realistic total cost model is perhaps the most important part of the application of quantitative methods to inventory decision making. Equation (11.4) is the general total cost equation for inventory situations in which the assumptions of the economic order quantity model are valid.

The How-Much-to-Order Decision

The next step is to find the order quantity Q that will minimize the total annual cost for Bub Beer. Using a trial-and-error approach, we can compute the total annual cost for several possible order quantities. As a starting point, let us consider $Q = 8000$. The total annual cost for Bub Beer is

$$TC = Q + \frac{3,328,000}{Q}$$
$$= 8000 + \frac{3,328,000}{8000} = \$8416$$

A trial order quantity of 5000 gives

$$TC = 5000 + \frac{3,328,000}{5000} = \$5666$$

The results of several other trial order quantities are shown in Table 11.1. It shows the lowest cost solution to be about 2000 cases. Graphs of the annual holding and ordering costs and total annual costs are shown in Figure 11.3.

The advantage of the trial-and-error approach is that it is rather easy to do and provides the total annual cost for a number of possible order quantity decisions. In this case, the minimum cost order quantity appears to be approximately 2000 cases. The disadvantage of this approach, however, is that it does not provide the exact minimum cost order quantity.

The EOQ formula determines the optimal order quantity by balancing the annual holding cost and the annual ordering cost.

In 1915 F. W. Harris derived the mathematical formula for the economic order quantity. It was the first application of quantitative methods to the area of inventory management.

Refer to Figure 11.3. The minimum total cost order quantity is denoted by an order size of Q^*. By using differential calculus, it can be shown (see Appendix 11.1) that the value of Q^* that minimizes the total annual cost is given by the formula

$$Q^* = \sqrt{\frac{2DC_o}{C_h}} \tag{11.5}$$

This formula is referred to as the *economic order quantity (EOQ) formula.*

TABLE 11.1 ANNUAL HOLDING, ORDERING, AND TOTAL COSTS FOR VARIOUS ORDER QUANTITIES OF BUB BEER

	Annual Cost		
Order Quantity	**Holding**	**Ordering**	**Total**
5000	\$5000	\$ 666	\$5666
4000	\$4000	\$ 832	\$4832
3000	\$3000	\$1109	\$4109
2000	\$2000	\$1664	\$3664
1000	\$1000	\$3328	\$4328

FIGURE 11.3 ANNUAL HOLDING, ORDERING, AND TOTAL COSTS FOR BUB BEER

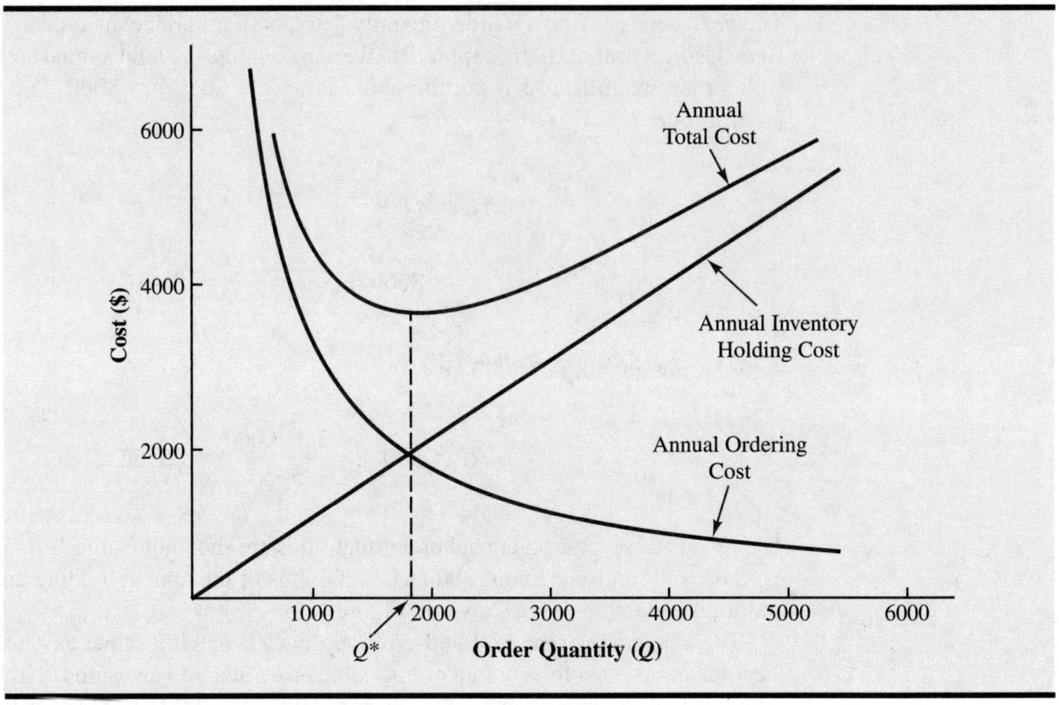

Using equation (11.5), the minimum total annual cost order quantity for Bub Beer is

$$Q^* = \sqrt{\frac{2(104{,}000)32}{2}} = 1824 \text{ cases}$$

Problem 2 at the end of the chapter asks you to show that equal holding and ordering costs is a property of the EOQ model.

The use of an order quantity of 1824 in equation (11.4) shows that the minimum cost inventory policy for Bub Beer has a total annual cost of \$3649. Note that $Q^* = 1824$ balances the holding and ordering costs. Check for yourself to see that these costs are equal.[2]

The When-to-Order Decision

The reorder point is expressed in terms of inventory position, the amount of inventory on hand plus the amount on order. Some people think that the reorder point is expressed in terms of inventory on hand. With short lead times, inventory position is usually the same as the inventory on hand. However, with long lead times, inventory position may be larger than inventory on hand.

Now that we know how much to order, we want to address the question of *when* to order. To answer this question, we need to introduce the concept of inventory position. The **inventory position** is defined as the amount of inventory on hand plus the amount of inventory on order. The when-to-order decision is expressed in terms of a **reorder point**—the inventory position at which a new order should be placed.

The manufacturer of Bub Beer guarantees a two-day delivery on any order placed by R & B Beverage. Hence, assuming R & B Beverage operates 250 days per year, the annual demand of 104,000 cases implies a daily demand of 104,000/250 = 416 cases. Thus, we expect (2 days)(416 cases per day) = 832 cases of Bub to be sold during the two days it takes a new order to reach the R & B warehouse. In inventory terminology, the two-day de-

[2]Actually, Q^* from equation (11.5) is 1824.28, but because we cannot order fractional cases of beer, a Q^* of 1824 is shown. This value of Q^* may cause a few cents deviation between the two costs. If Q^* is used at its exact value, the holding and ordering costs will be exactly the same.

livery period is referred to as the **lead time** for a new order, and the 832-case demand anticipated during this period is referred to as the **lead-time demand.** Thus, R & B should order a new shipment of Bub Beer from the manufacturer when the inventory reaches 832 cases. For inventory systems using the constant demand rate assumption and a fixed lead time, the reorder point is the same as the lead-time demand. For these systems, the general expression for the reorder point is as follows:

$$r = dm \tag{11.6}$$

where

r = reorder point
d = demand per day
m = lead time for a new order in days

The question of how frequently the order will be placed can now be answered. The period between orders is referred to as the **cycle time.** Previously in equation (11.2), we defined D/Q as the number of orders that will be placed in a year. Thus, $D/Q^* =$ 104,000/1824 = 57 is the number of orders R & B Beverage will place for Bub Beer each year. If R & B places 57 orders over 250 working days, it will order approximately every 250/57 = 4.39 working days. Thus, the cycle time is 4.39 working days. The general expression for a cycle time[3] of T days is given by

$$T = \frac{250}{D/Q^*} = \frac{250Q^*}{D} \tag{11.7}$$

Sensitivity Analysis for the EOQ Model

Even though substantial time may have been spent in arriving at the cost per order ($32) and the holding cost rate (25 percent), we should realize that these figures are at best good estimates. Thus, we may want to consider how much the recommended order quantity would change with different estimated ordering and holding costs. To determine the effects of various cost scenarios, we can calculate the recommended order quantity under several different cost conditions. Table 11.2 shows the minimum total cost order quantity for several cost possibilities. As you can see from the table, the value of Q^* appears relatively stable, even with some variations in the cost estimates. Based on these results, the best order quantity for Bub Beer is in the range of 1700–2000 cases. If operated properly, the total cost for the Bub Beer inventory system should be close to $3400–$3800 per year. We also note that little risk is associated with implementing the calculated order quantity of 1824. For example, if holding cost rate = 24%, C_o = $34, and the true optimal order quantity Q^* = 1919, R & B experiences only a $5 increase in the total annual cost; that is, $3690 − $3685 = $5, with Q = 1824.

From the preceding analysis, we would say that this EOQ model is insensitive to small variations or errors in the cost estimates. This insensitivity is a property of EOQ models in general,

[3]This general expression for cycle time is based on 250 working days per year. If the firm operated 300 working days per year and wanted to express cycle time in terms of working days, the cycle time would be given by $T = 300Q^*/D$.

TABLE 11.2 OPTIMAL ORDER QUANTITIES FOR SEVERAL COST POSSIBILITIES

Possible Inventory Holding Cost (%)	Possible Cost per Order	Optimal Order Quantity (Q^*)	Projected Total Annual Cost Using Q^*	Projected Total Annual Cost Using $Q = 1824$
24	$30	1803	$3461	$3462
24	34	1919	3685	3690
26	30	1732	3603	3607
26	34	1844	3835	3836

which indicates that if we have at least reasonable estimates of ordering cost and holding cost, we can expect to obtain a good approximation of the true minimum cost order quantity.

Excel Solution of the EOQ Model

Inventory models such as the EOQ model are easily implemented with the aid of worksheets. The Excel EOQ worksheet for Bub Beer is shown in Figure 11.4. The formula worksheet is in the background; the value worksheet is in the foreground. Data on annual demand, ordering cost, annual inventory holding cost rate, cost per unit, working days per

FIGURE 11.4 WORKSHEET FOR THE BUB BEER EOQ INVENTORY MODEL

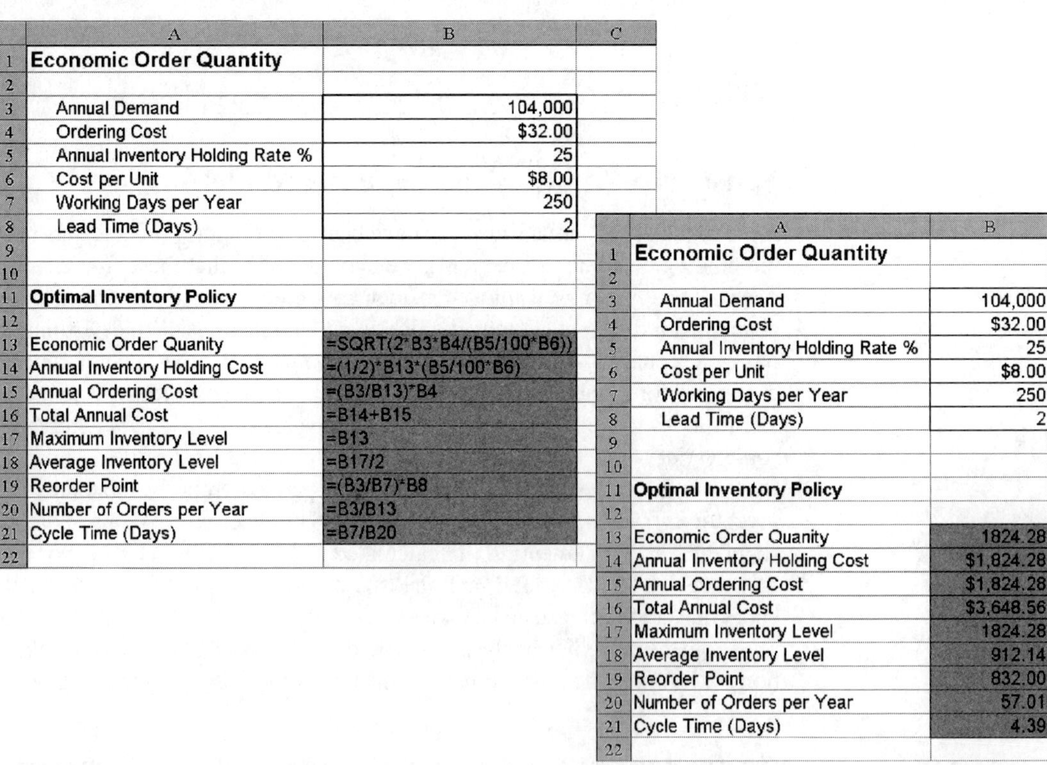

year, and lead time in days are input in cells B3 to B8. The appropriate EOQ model formulas, which determine the optimal inventory policy, are placed in cells B13 to B21. The value worksheet in the foreground shows the optimal economic order quantity 1824.28, the total annual cost $3,648.56, and a variety of additional information. If sensitivity analysis is desired, one or more of the input data values can be modified. The impact of any change or changes on the optimal inventory policy will then appear in the worksheet.

The Management Scientist software has an inventory module that can also be used to solve the inventory problems in this chapter.

The Excel worksheet in Figure 11.4 is a template that can be used for the EOQ model. This worksheet and similar Excel worksheets for the other inventory models presented in this chapter are available on the CD that accompanies this text.

You should carefully review the assumptions of the inventory model before applying it in an actual situation. Several inventory models discussed later in this chapter alter one or more of the assumptions of the EOQ model.

Summary of the EOQ Model Assumptions

To use the optimal order quantity and reorder point model described in this section, an analyst must make assumptions about how the inventory system operates. The EOQ model with its economic order quantity formula is based on some specific assumptions about the R & B inventory system. A summary of the assumptions for this model is provided in Table 11.3. Before using the EOQ formula, carefully review these assumptions to ensure that they are applicable to the inventory system being analyzed. If the assumptions are not reasonable, seek a different inventory model.

Various types of inventory systems are used in practice, and the inventory models presented in the following sections alter one or more of the EOQ model assumptions shown in Table 11.3. When the assumptions change, a different inventory model with different optimal operating policies becomes necessary.

TABLE 11.3 THE EOQ MODEL ASSUMPTIONS

1. Demand D is deterministic and occurs at a constant rate.
2. The order quantity Q is the same for each order. The inventory level increases by Q units each time an order is received.
3. The cost per order, C_o, is constant and does not depend on the quantity ordered.
4. The purchase cost per unit, C, is constant and does not depend on the quantity ordered.
5. The inventory holding cost per unit per time period, C_h, is constant. The total inventory holding cost depends on both C_h and the size of the inventory.
6. Shortages such as stock-outs or backorders are not permitted.
7. The lead time for an order is constant.
8. The inventory position is reviewed continuously. As a result, an order is placed as soon as the inventory position reaches the reorder point.

NOTES AND COMMENTS

With relatively long lead times, the lead-time demand and the resulting reorder point r, determined by equation (11.6), may exceed Q^*. If this condition occurs, at least one order will be outstanding when a new order is placed. For example, assume that Bub Beer has a lead time of $m = 6$ days. With a daily demand of $d = 432$ cases, equation (11.6) shows that the reorder point would be $r = dm = 6 \times 432 = 2592$ cases. Thus, a new order for Bub Beer should be placed whenever the inventory position (the amount of inventory on hand plus the amount of inventory on order) reaches 2592. With an order quantity of $Q = 2000$ cases, the inventory position of 2592 cases occurs when one order of 2000 cases is outstanding and $2592 - 2000 = 592$ cases are on hand.

11.2 ECONOMIC PRODUCTION LOT SIZE MODEL

The inventory model in this section alters assumption 2 of the EOQ model (see Table 11.3). The assumption concerning the arrival of Q units each time an order is received is changed to a constant production supply rate.

The inventory model presented in this section is similar to the EOQ model in that we are attempting to determine *how much* we should order and *when* the order should be placed. We again assume a constant demand rate. However, instead of assuming that the order arrives in a shipment of size Q^*, as in the EOQ model, we assume that units are supplied to inventory at a constant rate over several days or several weeks. The **constant supply rate** assumption implies that the same number of units is supplied to inventory each period of time (e.g., 10 units every day or 50 units every week). This model is designed for production situations in which, once an order is placed, production begins and a constant number of units is added to inventory each day until the production run has been completed.

If we have a production system that produces 50 units per day and we decide to schedule 10 days of production, we have a $50(10) = 500$-unit production lot size. The **lot size** is the number of units in an order. In general, if we let Q indicate the production lot size, the approach to the inventory decisions is similar to the EOQ model; that is, we build a holding and ordering cost model that expresses the total cost as a function of the production lot size. Then we attempt to find the production lot size that minimizes the total cost.

One other condition that should be mentioned at this time is that the model only applies to situations where the production rate is greater than the demand rate; the production system must be able to satisfy demand. For instance, if the constant demand rate is 400 units per day, the production rate must be at least 400 units per day to satisfy demand.

During the production run, demand reduces the inventory while production adds to inventory. Because we assume that the production rate exceeds the demand rate, each day during a production run we produce more units than are demanded. Thus, the excess production causes a gradual inventory buildup during the production period. When the production run is completed, the continuing demand causes the inventory to gradually decline until a new production run is started. The inventory pattern for this system is shown in Figure 11.5.

This model differs from the EOQ model in that a setup cost replaces the ordering cost and the saw-tooth inventory pattern shown in Figure 11.5 differs from the inventory pattern shown in Figure 11.2.

As in the EOQ model, we are now dealing with two costs, the holding cost and the ordering cost. Here the holding cost is identical to the definition in the EOQ model, but the interpretation of the ordering cost is slightly different. In fact, in a production situation the ordering cost is more correctly referred to as the production **setup cost.** This cost, which includes labor, material, and lost production costs incurred while preparing the production system for operation, is a fixed cost that occurs for every production run regardless of the production lot size.

FIGURE 11.5 INVENTORY PATTERN FOR THE PRODUCTION LOT SIZE INVENTORY MODEL

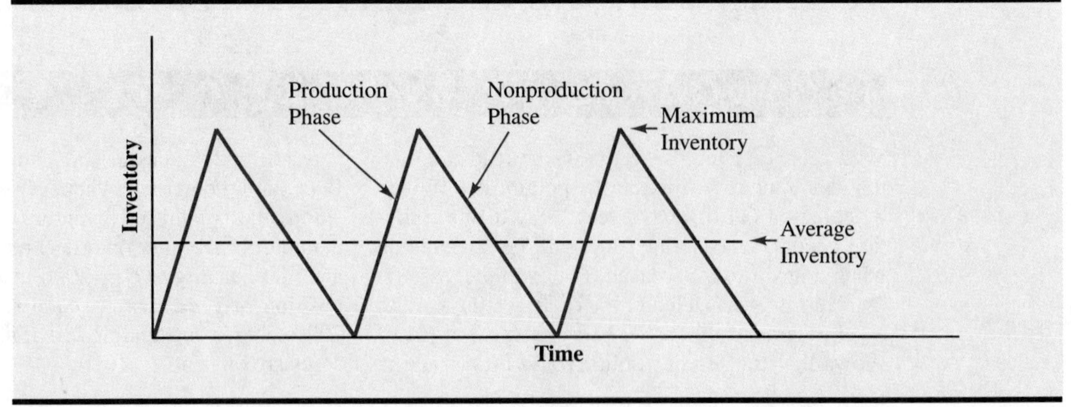

Total Cost Model

Let us begin building the production lot size model by writing the holding cost in terms of the production lot size Q. Again, the approach is to develop an expression for average inventory and then establish the holding costs associated with the average inventory. We use a one-year time period and an annual cost for the model.

In the EOQ model the average inventory is one-half the maximum inventory or ½Q. Figure 11.5 shows that for a production lot size model a constant inventory buildup rate occurs during the production run and a constant inventory depletion rate occurs during the nonproduction period; thus, the average inventory will be one-half the maximum inventory. However, in this inventory system the production lot size Q does not go into inventory at one point in time, and thus the inventory never reaches a level of Q units.

To show how we can compute the maximum inventory, let

$$d = \text{daily demand rate}$$
$$p = \text{daily production rate}$$
$$t = \text{number of days for a production run}$$

At this point, the logic of the production lot size model is easier to follow using a daily demand rate d and a daily production rate p. However, when the total annual cost model is eventually developed, we recommend that inputs to the model be expressed in terms of the annual demand rate D and the annual production rate P.

Because we are assuming that p will be larger than d, the daily inventory buildup rate during the production phase is $p - d$. If we run production for t days and place $p - d$ units in inventory each day, the inventory at the end of the production run will be $(p - d)t$. From Figure 11.5 we can see that the inventory at the end of the production run is also the maximum inventory. Thus

$$\text{Maximum inventory} = (p - d)t \tag{11.8}$$

If we know we are producing a production lot size of Q units at a daily production rate of p units, then $Q = pt$, and the length of the production run t must be

$$t = \frac{Q}{p} \text{ days} \tag{11.9}$$

Thus

$$\begin{aligned} \text{Maximum inventory} &= (p - d)t = (p - d)\left(\frac{Q}{p}\right) \\ &= \left(1 - \frac{d}{p}\right)Q \end{aligned} \tag{11.10}$$

The average inventory, which is one-half the maximum inventory, is given by

$$\text{Average inventory} = \frac{1}{2}\left(1 - \frac{d}{p}\right)Q \tag{11.11}$$

With an annual per unit holding cost of C_h, the general equation for annual holding cost is as follows:

$$\text{Annual holding cost} = \begin{pmatrix}\text{Average}\\ \text{inventory}\end{pmatrix}\begin{pmatrix}\text{Annual}\\ \text{cost}\\ \text{per unit}\end{pmatrix}$$

$$= \frac{1}{2}\left(1 - \frac{d}{p}\right)QC_h \qquad (11.12)$$

If D is the annual demand for the product and C_o is the setup cost for a production run, then the annual setup cost, which takes the place of the annual ordering cost in the EOQ model, is as follows:

$$\text{Annual setup cost} = \begin{pmatrix}\text{Number of production}\\ \text{runs per year}\end{pmatrix}\begin{pmatrix}\text{Setup cost}\\ \text{per run}\end{pmatrix}$$

$$= \frac{D}{Q}C_o \qquad (11.13)$$

Thus, the total annual cost (TC) model is

$$TC = \frac{1}{2}\left(1 - \frac{d}{p}\right)QC_h + \frac{D}{Q}C_o \qquad (11.14)$$

Suppose that a production facility operates 250 days per year. Then we can write daily demand d in terms of annual demand D as follows:

$$d = \frac{D}{250}$$

Now let P denote the annual production for the product if the product were produced every day. Then

$$P = 250p \qquad \text{and} \qquad p = \frac{P}{250}$$

Thus[4]

$$\frac{d}{p} = \frac{D/250}{P/250} = \frac{D}{P}$$

[4]The ratio $d/p = D/P$ holds regardless of the number of days of operation; 250 days is used here merely as an illustration.

Therefore, we can write the total annual cost model as follows:

$$TC = \frac{1}{2}\left(1 - \frac{D}{P}\right)QC_h + \frac{D}{Q}C_o \tag{11.15}$$

Equations (11.14) and (11.15) are equivalent. However, equation (11.15) may be used more frequently because an *annual* cost model tends to make the analyst think in terms of collecting *annual* demand data (D) and *annual* production data (P) rather than daily data.

Economic Production Lot Size

Given estimates of the holding cost (C_h), setup cost (C_o), annual demand rate (D), and annual production rate (P), we could use a trial-and-error approach to compute the total annual cost for various production lot sizes (Q). However, trial and error is not necessary; we can use the minimum cost formula for Q^* that has been developed using differential calculus (see Appendix 11.2). The equation is as follows:

$$Q^* = \sqrt{\frac{2DC_o}{(1 - D/P)C_h}} \tag{11.16}$$

As the production rate P approaches infinity, D/P approaches zero. In this case, equation (11.16) is equivalent to the EOQ model in equation (11.5).

EXCELfile
Lot Size

An Example Beauty Bar Soap is produced on a production line that has an annual capacity of 60,000 cases. The annual demand is estimated at 26,000 cases, with the demand rate essentially constant throughout the year. The cleaning, preparation, and setup of the production line cost approximately \$135. The manufacturing cost per case is \$4.50, and the annual holding cost is figured at a 24% rate. Thus, $C_h = IC = 0.24(\$4.50) = \$1.08$. What is the recommended production lot size?

Using equation (11.16), we have

$$Q^* = \sqrt{\frac{2(26{,}000)(135)}{(1 - 26{,}000/60{,}000)(1.08)}} = 3387$$

The total annual cost using equation (11.15) and $Q^* = 3387$ is \$2073.

Work Problem 13 as an example of an economic production lot size model.

Other relevant data include a five-day lead time to schedule and set up a production run and 250 working days per year. Thus, the lead-time demand of $(26{,}000/250)(5) = 520$ cases is the reorder point. The cycle time is the time between production runs. Using equation (11.7), the cycle time is $T = 250Q^*/D = [(250)(3387)]/26{,}000$, or 33 working days. Thus, we should plan a production run of 3387 units every 33 working days.

11.3 INVENTORY MODEL WITH PLANNED SHORTAGES

A **shortage** or **stock-out** is a demand that cannot be supplied. In many situations, shortages are undesirable and should be avoided if at all possible. However, in other cases it may be desirable—from an economic point of view—to plan for and allow shortages. In practice, these types of situations are most commonly found where the value of the inventory per unit is high and hence the holding cost is high. An example of this type of situation is a new car dealer's inventory. Often a specific car that a customer wants is not in stock. However, if the customer is willing to wait a few weeks, the dealer is usually able to order the car.

The assumptions of the EOQ model in Table 11.3 apply to this inventory model with the exception that shortages, referred to as backorders, are now permitted.

The model developed in this section takes into account a type of shortage known as a **backorder.** In a backorder situation, we assume that when a customer places an order and discovers that the supplier is out of stock, the customer waits until the new shipment arrives, and then the order is filled. Frequently, the waiting period in back-ordering situations is relatively short. Thus, by promising the customer top priority and immediate delivery when the goods become available, companies may be able to convince the customer to wait until the order arrives. In these cases, the backorder assumption is valid.

The backorder model that we develop is an extension of the EOQ model presented in Section 11.1. We use the EOQ model in which all goods arrive in inventory at one time and are subject to a constant demand rate. If we let S indicate the number of backorders that are accumulated when a new shipment of size Q is received, then the inventory system for the backorder case has the following characteristics:

- If S backorders exist when a new shipment of size Q arrives, then S backorders are shipped to the appropriate customers, and the remaining $Q - S$ units are placed in inventory. Therefore, $Q - S$ is the maximum inventory.
- The inventory cycle of T days is divided into two distinct phases: t_1 days when inventory is on hand and orders are filled as they occur, and t_2 days when stock-outs occur and all new orders are placed on backorder.

The inventory pattern for the inventory model with backorders, where negative inventory represents the number of backorders, is shown in Figure 11.6.

With the inventory pattern now defined, we can proceed with the basic step of all inventory models—namely, the development of a total cost model. For the inventory model with backorders, we encounter the usual holding costs and ordering costs. We also incur a backorder cost in terms of the labor and special delivery costs directly associated with the handling of the backorders. Another portion of the backorder cost accounts for the loss of goodwill because some customers will have to wait for their orders. Because the **goodwill cost** depends on how long a customer has to wait, it is customary to adopt the convention of expressing backorder cost in terms of the cost of having a unit on backorder for a stated period of time. This method of costing backorders on a time basis is similar to the method

FIGURE 11.6 INVENTORY PATTERN FOR AN INVENTORY MODEL WITH BACKORDERS

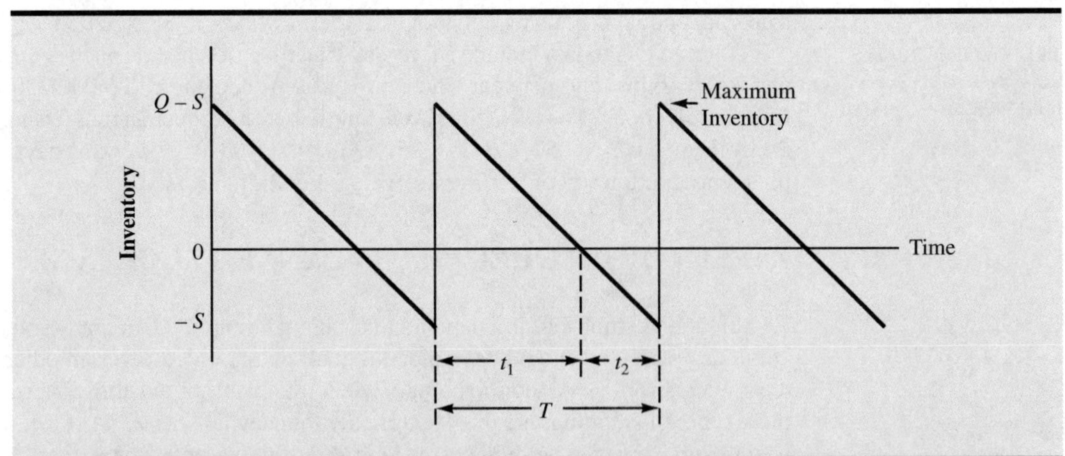

used to compute the inventory holding cost, and we can use it to compute a total annual cost of backorders once the average backorder level and the backorder cost per unit per period are known.

Let us begin the development of a total cost model by calculating the average inventory for a hypothetical problem. If we have an average inventory of two units for three days and no inventory on the fourth day, what is the average inventory over the four-day period? It is

$$\frac{2 \text{ units (3 days)} + 0 \text{ units (1 day)}}{4 \text{ days}} = \frac{6}{4} = 1.5 \text{ units}$$

Refer to Figure 11.6. You can see that this situation is what happens in the backorder model. With a maximum inventory of $Q - S$ units, the t_1 days we have inventory on hand will have an average inventory of $(Q - S)/2$. No inventory is carried for the t_2 days in which we experience backorders. Thus, over the total cycle time of $T = t_1 + t_2$ days, we can compute the average inventory as follows:

$$\text{Average inventory} = \frac{\frac{1}{2}(Q - S)t_1 + 0t_2}{t_1 + t_2} = \frac{\frac{1}{2}(Q - S)t_1}{T} \qquad (11.17)$$

Can we find other ways of expressing t_1 and T? Because we know that the maximum inventory is $Q - S$ and that d represents the constant daily demand, we have

$$t_1 = \frac{Q - S}{d} \text{ days} \qquad (11.18)$$

That is, the maximum inventory of $Q - S$ units will be used up in $(Q - S)/d$ days. Because Q units are ordered each cycle, we know the length of a cycle must be

$$T = \frac{Q}{d} \text{ days} \qquad (11.19)$$

Combining equations (11.18) and (11.19) with equation (11.17), we can compute the average inventory as follows:

$$\text{Average inventory} = \frac{\frac{1}{2}(Q - S)[(Q - S)/d]}{Q/d} = \frac{(Q - S)^2}{2Q} \qquad (11.20)$$

Thus, the average inventory is expressed in terms of two inventory decisions: how much we will order (Q) and the maximum number of backorders (S).

The formula for the annual number of orders placed using this model is identical to that for the EOQ model. With D representing the annual demand, we have

$$\text{Annual number of orders} = \frac{D}{Q} \tag{11.21}$$

The next step is to develop an expression for the average backorder level. Because we know the maximum for backorders is S, we can use the same logic we used to establish average inventory in finding the average number of backorders. We have an average number of backorders during the period t_2 of ½ the maximum number of backorders or ½S. We do not have any backorders during the t_1 days we have inventory, therefore we can calculate the average backorders in a manner similar to equation (11.17). Using this approach, we have

$$\text{Average backorders} = \frac{0t_1 + (S/2)t_2}{T} = \frac{(S/2)t_2}{T} \tag{11.22}$$

When we let the maximum number of backorders reach an amount S at a daily rate of d, the length of the backorder portion of the inventory cycle is

$$t_2 = \frac{S}{d} \tag{11.23}$$

Using equations (11.23) and (11.19) in equation (11.22), we have

$$\text{Average backorders} = \frac{(S/2)(S/d)}{Q/d} = \frac{S^2}{2Q} \tag{11.24}$$

Let

C_h = cost to maintain one unit in inventory for one year
C_o = cost per order
C_b = cost to maintain one unit on backorder for one year

The total annual cost (TC) for the inventory model with backorders becomes

$$TC = \frac{(Q - S)^2}{2Q} C_h + \frac{D}{Q} C_o + \frac{S^2}{2Q} C_b \tag{11.25}$$

Given C_h, C_o, and C_b and the annual demand D, differential calculus can be used to show that the minimum cost values for the order quantity Q^* and the planned backorders S^* are as follows:

$$Q^* = \sqrt{\frac{2DC_o}{C_h}\left(\frac{C_h + C_b}{C_b}\right)} \tag{11.26}$$

$$S^* = Q^*\left(\frac{C_h}{C_h + C_b}\right) \tag{11.27}$$

EXCELfile
Shortage

An Example. Suppose that the Higley Radio Components Company has a product for which the assumptions of the inventory model with backorders are valid. Information obtained by the company is as follows:

$$\begin{aligned} D &= 2000 \text{ units per year} \\ I &= 20\% \\ C &= \$50 \text{ per unit} \\ C_h &= IC = (0.20)(\$50) = \$10 \text{ per unit per year} \\ C_o &= \$25 \text{ per order} \end{aligned}$$

An inventory situation that incorporates backorder costs is considered in Problem 15.

The company is considering the possibility of allowing some backorders to occur for the product. The annual backorder cost is estimated to be \$30 per unit per year. Using equations (11.26) and (11.27), we have

The backorder cost C_b is one of the most difficult costs to estimate in inventory models. The reason is that it attempts to measure the cost associated with the loss of goodwill when a customer must wait for an order. Expressing this cost on an annual basis adds to the difficulty.

$$Q^* = \sqrt{\frac{2(2000)(25)}{10}\left(\frac{10 + 30}{20}\right)} = 115.47$$

and

$$S^* = 115\left(\frac{10}{10 + 30}\right) = 28.87$$

If this solution is implemented, the system will operate with the following properties:

$$\text{Maximum inventory} = Q - S = 115.47 - 28.87 = 86.6$$

$$\text{Cycle time} = T = \frac{Q}{D}(250) = \frac{115.47}{2000}(250) = 14.43 \text{ working days}$$

If backorders can be tolerated, the total cost including the back-ordering cost will be less than the total cost of the EOQ model. Some people think the model with backorders will have a greater cost because it includes a back-ordering cost in addition to the usual inventory holding and ordering costs. You can point out the fallacy in this thinking by noting that the backorder model leads to lower inventory and hence lower inventory holding costs.

The total annual cost is

$$\begin{aligned} \text{Holding cost} &= \frac{(86.6)^2}{2(115.47)}(10) = \$325 \\ \text{Ordering cost} &= \frac{2000}{115.47}(25) = \$433 \\ \text{Backorder cost} &= \frac{(28.87)^2}{2(115.47)}(30) = \$108 \\ \text{Total cost} &= \$866 \end{aligned}$$

If the company chooses to prohibit backorders and adopts the regular EOQ model, the recommended inventory decision would be

$$Q^* = \sqrt{\frac{2(2000)(25)}{10}} = \sqrt{10{,}000} = 100$$

This order quantity would result in a holding cost and an ordering cost of \$500 each or a total annual cost of \$1000. Thus, in this problem, allowing backorders is projecting a \$1000 − \$866 = \$134 or 13.4% savings in cost from the no-stock-out EOQ model. The preceding comparison and conclusion are based on the assumption that the backorder model with an annual cost per back-ordered unit of \$30 is a valid model for the actual inventory situation. If the company is concerned that stock-outs might lead to lost sales, then the savings might not be enough to warrant switching to an inventory policy that allowed for planned shortages.

NOTES AND COMMENTS

Equation (11.27) shows that the optimal number of planned backorders S^* is proportional to the ratio $C_h/(C_h + C_b)$, where C_h is the annual holding cost per unit and C_b is the annual backorder cost per unit. Whenever C_h increases, this ratio becomes larger, and the number of planned backorders increases. This relationship explains why items that have a high per-unit cost and a correspondingly high annual holding cost are more economically handled on a backorder basis. On the other hand, whenever the backorder cost C_b increases, the ratio becomes smaller, and the number of planned backorders decreases. Thus, the model provides the intuitive result that items with high back-ordering costs will be handled with few backorders. In fact, with high backorder costs, the backorder model and the EOQ model with no back-ordering allowed provide similar inventory policies.

11.4 QUANTITY DISCOUNTS FOR THE EOQ MODEL

In the quantity discount model, assumption 4 of the EOQ model in Table 11.3 is altered. The cost per unit varies depending on the quantity ordered.

Quantity discounts occur in numerous situations in which suppliers provide an incentive for large order quantities by offering a lower purchase cost when items are ordered in larger quantities. In this section we show how the EOQ model can be used when quantity discounts are available.

Assume that we have a product in which the basic EOQ model (see Table 11.3) is applicable. Instead of a fixed unit cost, the supplier quotes the following discount schedule.

Discount Category	Order Size	Discount (%)	Unit Cost
1	0 to 999	0	\$5.00
2	1000 to 2499	3	4.85
3	2500 and over	5	4.75

The 5 percent discount for the 2500-unit minimum order quantity looks tempting. However, realizing that higher order quantities result in higher inventory holding costs, we should prepare a thorough cost analysis before making a final ordering and inventory policy recommendation.

Suppose that the data and cost analyses show an annual holding cost rate of 20 percent, an ordering cost of \$49 per order, and an annual demand of 5000 units; what order quantity should we select? The following three-step procedure shows the calculations necessary to make this decision. In the preliminary calculations, we use Q_1 to indicate the order quantity for discount category 1, Q_2 for discount category 2, and Q_3 for discount category 3.

Step 1. For each discount category, compute a Q^* using the EOQ formula based on the unit cost associated with the discount category.

Recall that the EOQ model provides $Q^* = \sqrt{2DC_o/C_h}$, where $C_h = IC = (0.20)C$. With three discount categories providing three different unit costs C, we obtain

EXCELfile
Discount

$$Q_1^* = \sqrt{\frac{2(5000)49}{(0.20)(5.00)}} = 700$$

$$Q_2^* = \sqrt{\frac{2(5000)49}{(0.20)(4.85)}} = 711$$

$$Q_3^* = \sqrt{\frac{2(5000)49}{(0.20)(4.75)}} = 718$$

Because the only differences in the EOQ formulas come from slight differences in the holding cost, the economic order quantities resulting from this step will be approximately the same. However, these order quantities will usually not all be of the size necessary to qualify for the discount price assumed. In the preceding case, both Q_2^* and Q_3^* are insufficient order quantities to obtain their assumed discounted costs of \$4.85 and \$4.75, respectively. For those order quantities for which the assumed price cannot be obtained, the following procedure must be used.

Step 2. For the Q^* that is too small to qualify for the assumed discount price, adjust the order quantity upward to the nearest order quantity that will allow the product to be purchased at the assumed price.

In our example, this adjustment causes us to set

$$Q_2^* = 1000$$

and

$$Q_3^* = 2500$$

Problem 23 at the end of the chapter asks you to show that this property is true.

If a calculated Q^* for a given discount price is large enough to qualify for a bigger discount, that value of Q^* cannot lead to an optimal solution. Although the reason may not be obvious, it does turn out to be a property of the EOQ quantity discount model.

In the EOQ model with quantity discounts, the annual purchase cost must be included because purchase cost depends on the order quantity. Thus, it is a relevant cost.

In the previous inventory models considered, the annual purchase cost of the item was not included because it was constant and never affected by the inventory order policy decision. However, in the quantity discount model, the annual purchase cost depends on the order quantity and the associated unit cost. Thus, annual purchase cost (annual demand $D \times$ unit cost C) is included in the equation for total cost as shown here.

$$TC = \frac{Q}{2}C_h + \frac{D}{Q}C_o + DC \tag{11.28}$$

Using this total cost equation, we can determine the optimal order quantity for the EOQ discount model in step 3.

Step 3. For each order quantity resulting from steps 1 and 2, compute the total annual cost using the unit price from the appropriate discount category and equation (11.28). The order quantity yielding the minimum total annual cost is the optimal order quantity.

Problem 21 will give you practice in applying the EOQ model to situations with quantity discounts.

The step 3 calculations for the example problem are summarized in Table 11.4. As you can see, a decision to order 1000 units at the 3% discount rate yields the minimum cost solution. Even though the 2500-unit order quantity would result in a 5% discount, its excessive holding cost makes it the second-best solution. Figure 11.7 shows the total cost curve for each of the three discount categories. Note that $Q^* = 1000$ provides the minimum cost order quantity.

11.5 SINGLE-PERIOD INVENTORY MODEL WITH PROBABILISTIC DEMAND

This inventory model is the first in the chapter that explicitly treats probabilistic demand. Unlike the EOQ model, it is for a single period with unused inventory not carried over to future periods.

The inventory models discussed thus far were based on the assumption that the demand rate is constant and **deterministic** throughout the year. We developed minimum cost order quantity and reorder point policies based on this assumption. In situations in which the demand rate is not deterministic, other models treat demand as **probabilistic** and best described by a probability distribution. In this section we consider a **single-period inventory model** with probabilistic demand.

The single-period inventory model refers to inventory situations in which *one* order is placed for the product; at the end of the period, the product has either sold out, or a surplus of unsold items will be sold for a salvage value. The single-period inventory model is applicable in situations involving seasonal or perishable items that cannot be carried in inventory and sold in future periods. Seasonal clothing (such as bathing suits and winter coats) are typically handled in a single-period manner. In these situations, a buyer places one preseason order for each item and then experiences a stock-out or holds a clearance sale on the surplus stock at the end of the season. No items are carried in inventory and sold the following year. Newspapers are another example of a product that is ordered one time and is either sold or not sold during the single period. Although newspapers are ordered daily, they cannot be carried in inventory and sold in later periods. Thus, newspaper orders may be treated as a sequence of single-period models; that is, each day or period is separate, and a single-period inventory decision must be made each period (day). Because we order only once for the period, the only inventory decision we must make is *how much* of the product to order at the start of the period.

TABLE 11.4 TOTAL ANNUAL COST CALCULATIONS FOR THE EOQ MODEL WITH QUANTITY DISCOUNTS

Discount Category	Unit Cost	Order Quantity	Annual Cost			
			Holding	Ordering	Purchase	Total
1	$5.00	700	$ 350	$350	$25,000	$25,700
2	4.85	1000	$ 485	$245	$24,250	$24,980
3	4.75	2500	$1188	$ 98	$23,750	$25,036

FIGURE 11.7 TOTAL COST CURVES FOR THE THREE DISCOUNT CATEGORIES

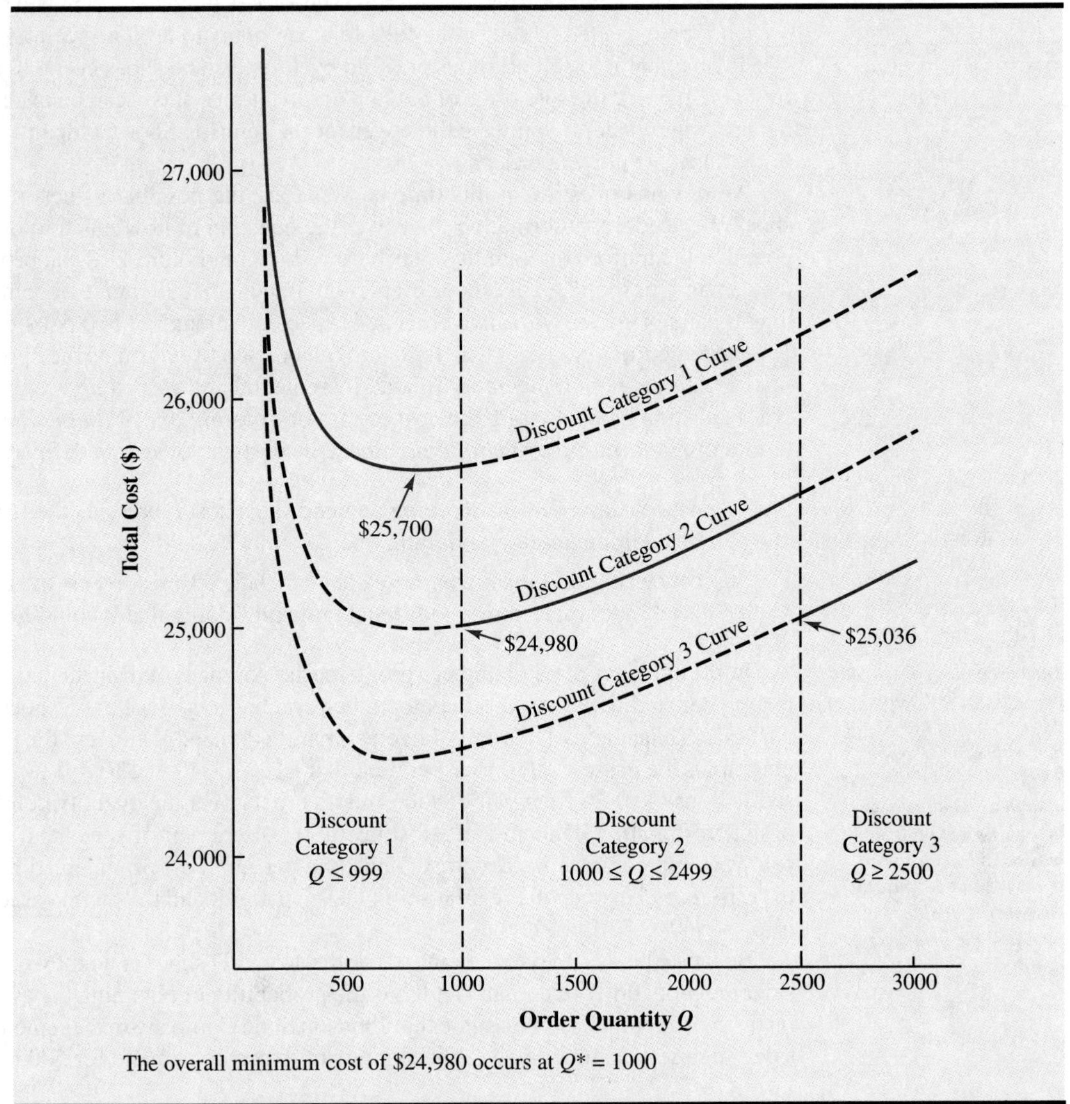

The overall minimum cost of \$24,980 occurs at $Q^* = 1000$

Obviously, if the demand were known for a single-period inventory situation, the solution would be easy; we would simply order the amount we knew would be demanded. However, in most single-period models, the exact demand is not known. In fact, forecasts may show that demand can have a wide variety of values. If we are going to analyze this type of inventory problem in a quantitative manner, we need information about the probabilities associated with the various demand values. Thus, the single-period model presented in this section is based on probabilistic demand.

Johnson Shoe Company

Let us consider a single-period inventory model that could be used to make a how-much-to-order decision for the Johnson Shoe Company. The buyer for the Johnson Shoe Company decided to order a men's shoe shown at a buyers' meeting in New York City. The shoe will be part of the company's spring-summer promotion and will be sold through nine retail stores in the Chicago area. Because the shoe is designed for spring and summer months, it cannot be expected to sell in the fall. Johnson plans to hold a special August clearance sale in an attempt to sell all shoes not sold by July 31. The shoes cost $40 a pair and retail for $60 a pair. At the sale price of $30 a pair, all surplus shoes can be expected to sell during the August sale. If you were the buyer for the Johnson Shoe Company, how many pairs of the shoes would you order?

An obvious question at this time is, What are the possible values of demand for the shoe? We need this information to answer the question of how much to order. Let us suppose that the uniform probability distribution shown in Figure 11.8 can be used to describe the demand for the size 10D shoes. In particular, note that the range of demand is from 350 to 650 pairs of shoes, with an average, or expected, demand of 500 pairs of shoes.

Incremental analysis is a method that can be used to determine the optimal order quantity for a single-period inventory model. Incremental analysis addresses the how-much-to-order question by comparing the cost or loss of *ordering one additional unit* with the cost or loss of *not ordering one additional unit.* The costs involved are defined as follows:

c_o = cost per unit of *overestimating* demand. This cost represents the loss of ordering one additional unit and finding that it cannot be sold.

c_u = cost per unit of *underestimating* demand. This cost represents the opportunity loss of not ordering one additional unit and finding that it could have been sold.

The cost of underestimating demand is usually harder to determine than the cost of overestimating demand. The reason is that the cost of underestimating demand includes a lost profit and may include a customer goodwill cost because the customer is unable to purchase the item when desired.

In the Johnson Shoe Company problem, the company will incur the cost of overestimating demand whenever it orders too much and has to sell the extra shoes during the August sale. Thus, the cost per unit of overestimating demand is equal to the purchase cost per unit minus the August sales price per unit; that is, $c_o = \$40 - \$30 = \$10$. Therefore, Johnson will lose $10 for each pair of shoes that it orders over the quantity demanded. The cost of underestimating demand is the lost profit because a pair of shoes that could have been sold was not available in inventory. Thus, the per-unit cost of underestimating demand is the difference between the regular selling price per unit and the purchase cost per unit; that is, $c_u = \$60 - \$40 = \$20$.

Because the exact level of demand for the size 10D shoes is unknown, we have to consider the probability of demand and thus the probability of obtaining the associated costs or losses. For example, let us assume that Johnson Shoe Company management wishes to consider an order quantity equal to the average or expected demand for 500 pairs of shoes. In

FIGURE 11.8 UNIFORM PROBABILITY DISTRIBUTION OF DEMAND FOR THE JOHNSON SHOE COMPANY PROBLEM

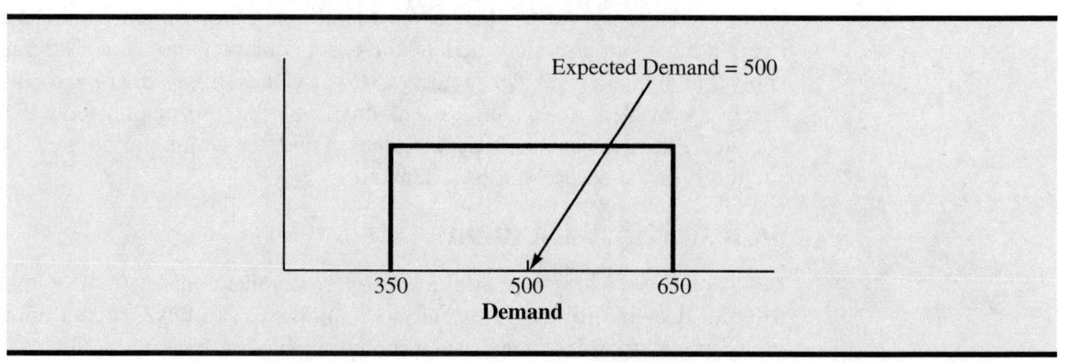

incremental analysis, we consider the possible losses associated with an order quantity of 501 (ordering one additional unit) and an order quantity of 500 (not ordering one additional unit). The order quantity alternatives and the possible losses are summarized here.

Order Quantity Alternatives	Loss Occurs If	Possible Loss	Probability Loss Occurs
$Q = 501$	Demand overestimated; the additional unit *cannot* be sold	$c_o = \$10$	$P(\text{demand} \leq 500)$
$Q = 500$	Demand underestimated; an additional unit *could have* been sold	$c_u = \$20$	$P(\text{demand} > 500)$

By looking at the demand probability distribution in Figure 11.8, we see that $P(\text{demand} \leq 500) = 0.50$ and that $P(\text{demand} > 500) = 0.50$. By multiplying the possible losses, $c_o = \$10$ and $c_u = \$20$, by the probability of obtaining the loss, we can compute the expected value of the loss, or simply the *expected loss* (EL), associated with the order quantity alternatives. Thus

$$\text{EL}(Q = 501) = c_o P(\text{demand} \leq 500) = \$10(0.50) = \$5$$
$$\text{EL}(Q = 500) = c_u P(\text{demand} > 500) = \$20(0.50) = \$10$$

Based on these expected losses, do you prefer an order quantity of 501 or 500 pairs of shoes? Because the expected loss is greater for $Q = 500$, and because we want to avoid this higher cost or loss, we should make $Q = 501$ the preferred decision. We could now consider incrementing the order quantity one additional unit to $Q = 502$ and repeating the expected loss calculations.

Although we could continue this unit-by-unit analysis, it would be time-consuming and cumbersome. We would have to evaluate $Q = 502$, $Q = 503$, $Q = 504$, and so on, until we found the value of Q where the expected loss of ordering one incremental unit is equal to the expected loss of not ordering one incremental unit; that is, the optimal order quantity Q^* occurs when the incremental analysis shows that

$$\text{EL}(Q^* + 1) = \text{EL}(Q^*) \tag{11.29}$$

When this relationship holds, increasing the order quantity by one additional unit has no economic advantage. Using the logic with which we computed the expected losses for the order quantities of 501 and 500, the general expressions for $\text{EL}(Q^* + 1)$ and $\text{EL}(Q^*)$ can be written

$$\text{EL}(Q^* + 1) = c_o P(\text{demand} \leq Q^*) \tag{11.30}$$
$$\text{EL}(Q^*) = c_u P(\text{demand} > Q^*) \tag{11.31}$$

Because we know from basic probability that

$$P(\text{demand} \leq Q^*) + P(\text{demand} > Q^*) = 1 \tag{11.32}$$

we can write

$$P(\text{demand} > Q^*) = 1 - P(\text{demand} \leq Q^*) \tag{11.33}$$

Using this expression, equation (11.31) can be rewritten as

$$\text{EL}(Q^*) = c_u[1 - P(\text{demand} \leq Q^*)] \tag{11.34}$$

Equations (11.30) and (11.34) can be used to show that $\text{EL}(Q^* + 1) = \text{EL}(Q^*)$ whenever

$$c_o P(\text{demand} \leq Q^*) = c_u[1 - P(\text{demand} \leq Q^*)] \tag{11.35}$$

Solving for $P(\text{demand} \leq Q^*)$, we have

$$P(\text{demand} \leq Q^*) = \frac{c_u}{c_u + c_o} \tag{11.36}$$

This expression provides the general condition for the optimal order quantity Q^* in the single-period inventory model.

In the Johnson Shoe Company problem $c_o = \$10$ and $c_u = \$20$. Thus, equation (11.36) shows that the optimal order size for Johnson shoes must satisfy the following condition:

$$P(\text{demand} \leq Q^*) = \frac{c_u}{c_u + c_o} = \frac{20}{20 + 10} = \frac{20}{30} = \frac{2}{3}$$

We can find the optimal order quantity Q^* by referring to the probability distribution shown in Figure 11.8 and finding the value of Q that will provide $P(\text{demand} \leq Q^*) = 2/3$. To find this solution, we note that in the uniform distribution the probability is evenly distributed over the entire range of 350–650 pairs of shoes. Thus, we can satisfy the expression for Q^* by moving two-thirds of the way from 350 to 650. Because this range is $650 - 350 = 300$, we move 200 units from 350 toward 650. Doing so provides the optimal order quantity of 550 pairs of shoes.

In summary, the key to establishing an optimal order quantity for single-period inventory models is to identify the probability distribution that describes the demand for the item and the costs of overestimation and underestimation. Then, using the information for the costs of overestimation and underestimation, equation (11.36) can be used to find the location of Q^* in the probability distribution.

Nationwide Car Rental

As another example of a single-period inventory model with probabilistic demand, consider the situation faced by Nationwide Car Rental. Nationwide must decide how many automobiles to have available at each car rental location at specific points in time throughout the year. Using the Myrtle Beach, South Carolina, location as an example, management would like to know the number of full-sized automobiles to have available for the Labor Day weekend. Based on previous experience, customer demand for full-sized automobiles for the Labor Day weekend has a normal distribution with a mean of 150 automobiles and a standard deviation of 14 automobiles.

The Nationwide Car Rental situation can benefit from use of a single-period inventory model. The company must establish the number of full-sized automobiles to have available prior to the weekend. Customer demand over the weekend will then result in either a stock-out or a surplus. Let us denote the number of full-sized automobiles available by Q. If Q is greater than customer demand, Nationwide will have a surplus of cars. The cost of a surplus is the cost of overestimating demand. This cost is set at \$80 per car, which reflects, in part, the opportunity cost of not having the car available for rent elsewhere.

If Q is less than customer demand, Nationwide will rent all available cars and experience a stock-out or shortage. A shortage results in an underestimation cost of \$200 per car. This figure reflects the cost due to lost profit and the lost goodwill of not having a car available for a customer. Given this information, how many full-sized automobiles should Nationwide make available for the Labor Day weekend?

Using the cost of underestimation, $c_u = \$200$, and the cost of overestimation, $c_o = \$80$, equation (11.36) indicates that the optimal order quantity must satisfy the following condition:

$$P(\text{demand} \leq Q^*) = \frac{c_u}{(c_u + c_o)} = \frac{200}{200 + 80} = 0.7143$$

We can use the normal probability distribution for demand as shown in Figure 11.9 to find the order quantity that satisfies the condition that $P(\text{demand} \leq Q^*) = 0.7143$. From Appendix A, we see that 0.7143 of the area in the left tail of the normal probability distribution

FIGURE 11.9 PROBABILITY DISTRIBUTION OF DEMAND FOR THE NATIONWIDE CAR RENTAL PROBLEM SHOWING THE LOCATION OF Q^*

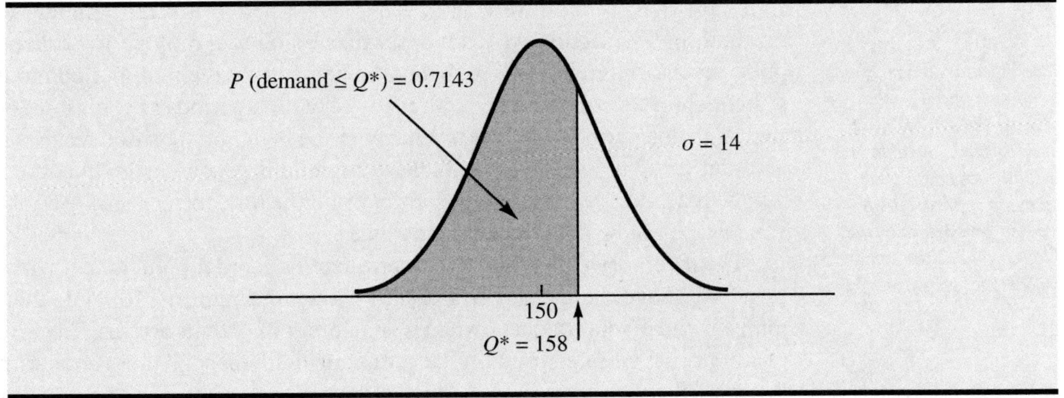

occurs at $z = 0.57$ standard deviations *above* the mean. With a mean demand of $\mu = 150$ automobiles and a standard deviation of $\sigma = 14$ automobiles, we have

EXCELfile
Single-Period

$$Q^* = \mu + 0.57\sigma$$
$$= 150 + 0.57(14) = 158$$

Thus, Nationwide Car Rental should plan to have 158 full-sized automobiles available in Myrtle Beach for the Labor Day weekend. Note that in this case the cost of overestimation is less than the cost of underestimation. Thus, Nationwide is willing to risk a higher probability of overestimating demand and hence a higher probability of a surplus. In fact, Nationwide's optimal order quantity has a 0.7143 probability of a surplus and a $1 - 0.7143 = 0.2857$ probability of a stock-out. As a result, the probability is 0.2857 that all 158 full-sized automobiles will be rented during the Labor Day weekend.

An example of a single-period inventory model with probabilistic demand described by a normal probability distribution is considered in Problem 25.

NOTES AND COMMENTS

1. In any probabilistic inventory model, the assumption about the probability distribution for demand is critical and can affect the recommended inventory decision. In the problems presented in this section, we used the uniform and the normal probability distributions to describe demand. In some situations, other probability distributions may be more appropriate. In using probabilistic inventory models, we must exercise care in selecting the probability distribution that most realistically describes demand.
2. In the single-period inventory model, the value of $c_u/(c_u + c_o)$ plays a critical role in selecting the order quantity [see equation (11.36)]. Whenever $c_u = c_o$, $c_u/(c_u + c_o)$ equals 0.50; in this case, we should select an order quantity corresponding to the median demand. With this choice, a stock-out is just as likely as a surplus because the two costs are equal. However, whenever $c_u < c_o$, a smaller order quantity will be recommended. In this case, the smaller order quantity will provide a higher probability of a stock-out; however, the more expensive cost of overestimating demand and having a surplus will tend to be avoided. Finally, whenever $c_u > c_o$, a larger order quantity will be recommended. In this case, the larger order quantity provides a lower probability of a stock-out in an attempt to avoid the more expensive cost of underestimating demand and experiencing a stock-out.

11.6 ORDER-QUANTITY, REORDER POINT MODEL WITH PROBABILISTIC DEMAND

In the previous section we considered a single-period inventory model with probabilistic demand. In this section we extend our discussion to a multiperiod order-quantity, reorder point inventory model with probabilistic demand. In the multiperiod model, the inventory system operates continuously with many repeating periods or cycles; inventory can be carried from one period to the next. Whenever the inventory position reaches the reorder point, an order for Q units is placed. Because demand is probabilistic, the time the reorder point will be reached, the time between orders, and the time the order of Q units will arrive in inventory cannot be determined in advance.

The inventory model in this section is based on the assumptions of the EOQ model shown in Table 11.3 with the exception that demand is probabilistic rather than deterministic. With probabilistic demand, occasional shortages may occur.

The inventory pattern for the order-quantity, reorder point model with probabilistic demand will have the general appearance shown in Figure 11.10. Note that the increases or jumps in the inventory occur whenever an order of Q units arrives. The inventory decreases at a nonconstant rate based on the probabilistic demand. A new order is placed whenever the reorder point is reached. At times, the order quantity of Q units will arrive before in-

FIGURE 11.10 INVENTORY PATTERN FOR AN ORDER-QUANTITY, REORDER POINT MODEL WITH PROBABILISTIC DEMAND

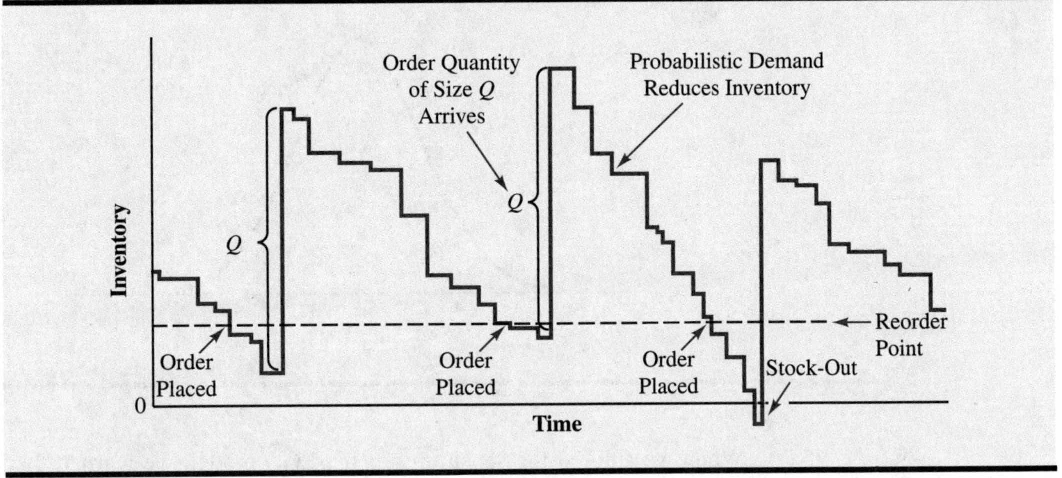

ventory reaches zero. However, at other times, higher demand will cause a stock-out before a new order is received. As with other order-quantity, reorder point models, the manager must determine the order quantity Q and the reorder point r for the inventory system.

The exact mathematical formulation of an order-quantity, reorder point inventory model with probabilistic demand is beyond the scope of this text. However, we present a procedure that can be used to obtain good, workable order quantity and reorder point inventory policies. The solution procedure can be expected to provide only an approximation of the optimal solution, but it can yield good solutions in many practical situations.

Let us consider the inventory problem of Dabco Industrial Lighting Distributors. Dabco purchases a special high-intensity lightbulb for industrial lighting systems from a well-known lightbulb manufacturer. Dabco would like a recommendation on how much to order and when to order so that a low-cost inventory policy can be maintained. Pertinent facts are that the ordering cost is \$12 per order, one bulb costs \$6, and Dabco uses a 20% annual holding cost rate for its inventory ($C_h = IC = 0.20 \times \$6 = \$1.20$). Dabco, which has more than 1000 customers, experiences a probabilistic demand; in fact, the number of units demanded varies considerably from day to day and from week to week. The lead time for a new order of lightbulbs is one week. Historical sales data indicate that demand during a one-week lead time can be described by a normal probability distribution with a mean of 154 lightbulbs and a standard deviation of 25 lightbulbs. The normal distribution of demand during the lead time is shown in Figure 11.11. Because the mean demand during one week is 154 units, Dabco can anticipate a mean or expected annual demand of 154 units per week × 52 weeks per year = 8008 units per year.

The How-Much-to-Order Decision

Although we are in a probabilistic demand situation, we have an estimate of the expected annual demand of 8008 units. We can apply the EOQ model from Section 11.1 as an approximation of the best order quantity, with the expected annual demand used for D. In Dabco's case

EXCELfile
Q Prob

$$Q^* = \sqrt{\frac{2DC_o}{C_h}} = \sqrt{\frac{2(8008)(12)}{(1.20)}} = 400 \text{ units}$$

FIGURE 11.11 LEAD-TIME DEMAND PROBABILITY DISTRIBUTION FOR DABCO LIGHTBULBS

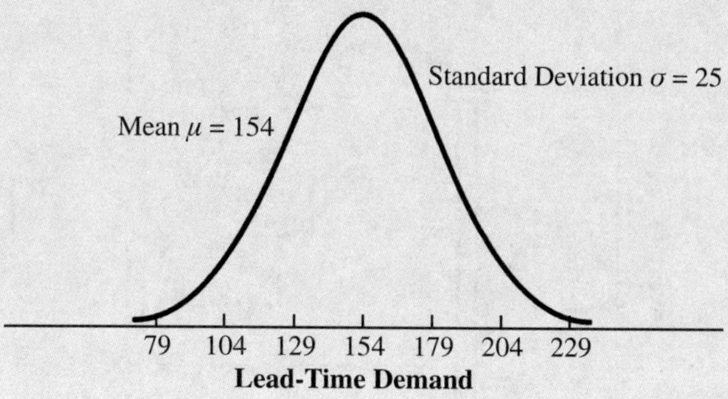

When we studied the sensitivity of the EOQ model, we learned that the total cost of operating an inventory system was relatively insensitive to order quantities that were in the neighborhood of Q^*. Using this knowledge, we expect 400 units per order to be a good approximation of the optimal order quantity. Even if annual demand were as low as 7000 units or as high as 9000 units, an order quantity of 400 units should be a relatively good low-cost order size. Thus, given our best estimate of annual demand at 8008 units, we will use $Q^* = 400$.

We have established the 400 unit order quantity by ignoring the fact that demand is probabilistic. Using $Q^* = 400$, Dabco can anticipate placing approximately $D/Q^* = 8008/400 = 20$ orders per year with an average of approximately $250/20 = 12.5$ working days between orders.

The When-to-Order Decision

The probability of a stock-out during any one inventory cycle is easiest to estimate by first determining the number of orders that are expected during the year. The inventory manager can usually state a willingness to allow perhaps one, two, or three stock-outs during the year. The allowable stock-outs per year divided by the number of orders per year will provide the desired probability of a stock-out.

We now want to establish a when-to-order decision rule or reorder point that will trigger the ordering process. With a mean lead-time demand of 154 units, you might first suggest a 154-unit reorder point. However, considering the probability of demand now becomes extremely important. If 154 is the mean lead-time demand, and if demand is symmetrically distributed about 154, then the lead-time demand will be more than 154 units roughly 50% of the time. When the demand during the one-week lead time exceeds 154 units, Dabco will experience a shortage or stock-out. Thus, using a reorder point of 154 units, approximately 50% of the time (10 of the 20 orders a year) Dabco will be short of bulbs before the new supply arrives. This shortage rate would most likely be viewed as unacceptable.

Refer to the **lead-time demand distribution** shown in Figure 11.11. Given this distribution, we can now determine how the reorder point r affects the probability of a stock-out. Because stock-outs occur whenever the demand during the lead time exceeds the reorder point, we can find the probability of a stock-out by using the lead-time demand distribution to compute the probability that demand will exceed r.

We could now approach the when-to-order problem by defining a cost per stock-out and then attempting to include this cost in a total cost equation. Alternatively, we can ask management to specify the average number of stock-outs that can be tolerated per year. If demand for a product is probabilistic, a manager who will never tolerate a stock-out is being somewhat unrealistic because attempting to avoid stock-outs completely will require high reorder points, high inventory, and an associated high holding cost.

Suppose in this case that Dabco management is willing to tolerate an average of one stock-out per year. Because Dabco places 20 orders per year, this decision implies that management is willing to allow demand during lead time to exceed the reorder point one time in 20, or 5% of the time. The reorder point r can be found by using the lead-time demand distribution to find the value of r with a 5% chance of having a lead-time demand that will exceed it. This situation is shown graphically in Figure 11.12.

From the standard normal probability distribution table in Appendix A, we see that the r value is 1.645 standard deviations above the mean. Therefore, for the assumed normal distribution for lead-time demand with $\mu = 154$ and $\sigma = 25$, the reorder point r is

$$r = 154 + 1.645(25) = 195$$

If a normal distribution is used for lead-time demand, the general equation for r is

$$r = \mu + z\sigma \tag{11.37}$$

where z is the number of standard deviations necessary to obtain the acceptable stock-out probability.

Thus, the recommended inventory decision is to order 400 units whenever the inventory reaches the reorder point of 195. Because the mean or expected demand during the lead time is 154 units, the 195 − 154 = 41 units serve as a **safety stock,** which absorbs higher-than-usual demand during the lead time. Roughly 95% of the time, the 195 units will be able to satisfy demand during the lead time. The anticipated annual cost for this system is as follows:

Holding cost, normal inventory	$(Q/2)C_h$ =	(400/2)(1.20) =	\$240
Holding cost, safety stock	$(41)C_h$ =	41(1.20) =	\$ 49
Ordering cost	$(D/Q)C_o$ =	(8008/400)12 =	\$240
		Total	\$529

If Dabco could assume that a known, constant demand rate of 8008 units per year existed for the lightbulbs, then $Q^* = 400$, $r = 154$, and a total annual cost of \$240 + \$240 = \$480

FIGURE 11.12 REORDER POINT r THAT ALLOWS A 5% CHANCE OF A STOCK-OUT FOR DABCO LIGHTBULBS

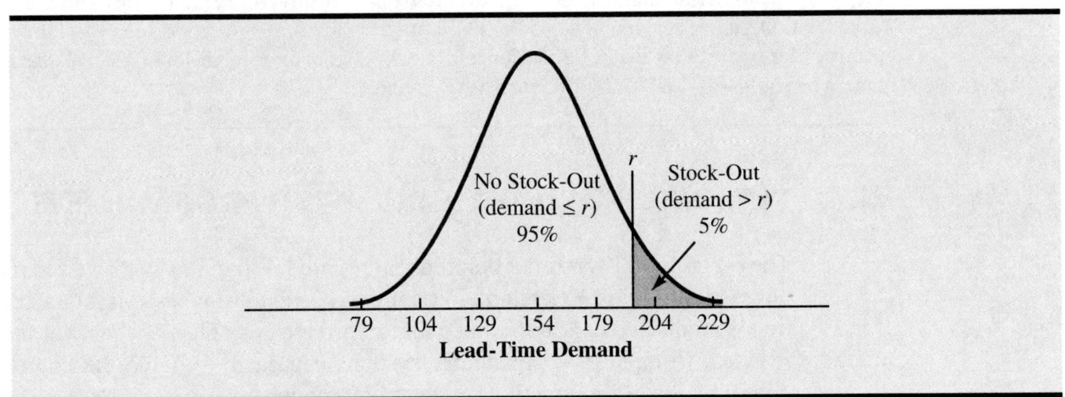

Try Problem 29 as an example of an order-quantity, reorder point model with probabilistic demand.

would be optimal. When demand is uncertain and can only be expressed in probabilistic terms, a larger total cost can be expected. The larger cost occurs in the form of larger holding costs because more inventory must be maintained to limit the number of stock-outs. For Dabco, this additional inventory or safety stock was 41 units, with an additional annual holding cost of $49. The Management Science in Action, Lowering Inventory Cost at Dutch Companies, describes how a warehouser in the Netherlands implemented an order-quantity, reorder point system with probabilistic demand.

MANAGEMENT SCIENCE IN ACTION

LOWERING INVENTORY COST AT DUTCH COMPANIES*

In the Netherlands, companies such as Philips, Rank Xerox, and Fokker have followed the trend of developing closer relations between the firm and its suppliers. As teamwork, coordination, and information sharing improve, opportunities are available for better cost control in the operation of inventory systems.

One Dutch public warehouser has a contract with its supplier under which the supplier routinely provides information regarding the status and schedule of upcoming production runs. The warehouser's inventory system operates as an order-quantity, reorder point system with probabilistic demand. When the order quantity Q has been determined, the warehouser selects the desired reorder point for the product. The distribution of the lead-time demand is essential in determining the reorder point. Usually, the lead-time demand distribution is approximated directly, taking into account both the probabilistic demand and the probabilistic length of the lead-time period.

The supplier's information concerning scheduled production runs provides the warehouser with a better understanding of the lead time involved for a product and the resulting lead-time demand distribution. With this information, the warehouse can modify the reorder point accordingly. Information sharing by the supplier thus enables the order-quantity, reorder point system to operate with a lower inventory holding cost.

*Based on F. A. van der Duyn Schouten, M. J. G. van Eijs, and R. M. J. Heuts, "The Value of Supplier Information to Improve Management of a Retailer's Inventory," *Decision Sciences* 25, no. 1 (January/February 1994): 1–14.

NOTES AND COMMENTS

The Dabco reorder point was based on a 5% probability of a stock-out during the lead-time period. Thus, on 95% of all order cycles Dabco will be able to satisfy customer demand without experiencing a stock-out. Defining *service level* as the percentage of all order cycles that do not experience a stock-out, we would say that Dabco has a 95% service level. However, other definitions of service level may include the percentage of all customer demand that can be satisfied from inventory. Thus, when an inventory manager expresses a desired service level, it is a good idea to clarify exactly what the manager means by the term *service level.*

11.7 PERIODIC REVIEW MODEL WITH PROBABILISTIC DEMAND

The order-quantity, reorder point inventory models previously discussed require a **continuous review inventory system.** In a continuous review inventory system, the inventory position is monitored continuously so that an order can be placed whenever the reorder point is reached. Computerized inventory systems can easily provide the continuous review required by the order-quantity, reorder point models.

Up to this point, we assumed that the inventory position is reviewed continuously so that an order can be placed as soon as the inventory position reaches the reorder point. The inventory model in this section assumes probabilistic demand and a periodic review of the inventory position.

An alternative to the continuous review system is the **periodic review inventory system.** With a periodic review system, the inventory is checked and reordering is done only at specified points in time. For example, inventory may be checked and orders placed on a weekly, biweekly, monthly, or some other periodic basis. When a firm or business handles multiple products, the periodic review system offers the advantage of requiring that orders for several items be placed at the same preset periodic review time. With this type of inventory system, the shipping and receiving of orders for multiple products are easily coordinated. Under the previously discussed order-quantity, reorder point systems, the reorder points for various products can be encountered at substantially different points in time, making the coordination of orders for multiple products more difficult.

To illustrate this system, let us consider Dollar Discounts, a firm with several retail stores that carry a wide variety of products for household use. The company operates its inventory system with a two-week periodic review. Under this system, a retail store manager may order any number of units of any product from the Dollar Discounts central warehouse every two weeks. Orders for all products going to a particular store are combined into one shipment. When making the order quantity decision for each product at a given review period, the store manager knows that a reorder for the product cannot be made until the next review period.

Assuming that the lead time is less than the length of the review period, an order placed at a review period will be received prior to the next review period. In this case, the how-much-to-order decision at any review period is determined using the following:

$$Q = M - H \tag{11.38}$$

where

Q = the order quality
M = the replenishment level
H = the inventory on hand at the review period

Because the demand is probabilistic, the inventory on hand at the review period, H, will vary. Thus, the order quantity that must be sufficient to bring the inventory position back to its maximum or replenishment level M can be expected to vary each period. For example, if the replenishment level for a particular product is 50 units, and the inventory on hand at the review period is $H = 12$ units, an order of $Q = M - H = 50 - 12 = 38$ units should be made. Thus, under the periodic review model, enough units are ordered each review period to bring the inventory position back up to the replenishment level.

A typical inventory pattern for a periodic review system with probabilistic demand is shown in Figure 11.13. Note that the time between periodic reviews is predetermined and fixed. The order quantity Q at each review period can vary and is shown to be the difference between the replenishment level and the inventory on hand. Finally, as with other probabilistic models, an unusually high demand can result in an occasional stock-out.

The decision variable in the periodic review model is the replenishment level M. To determine M, we could begin by developing a total cost model, including holding, ordering, and stock-out costs. Instead, we describe an approach that is often used in practice. In this approach, the objective is to determine a replenishment level that will meet a desired performance level, such as a reasonably low probability of stock-out or a reasonably low number of stock-outs per year.

FIGURE 11.13 INVENTORY PATTERN FOR PERIODIC REVIEW MODEL WITH PROBABILISTIC DEMAND

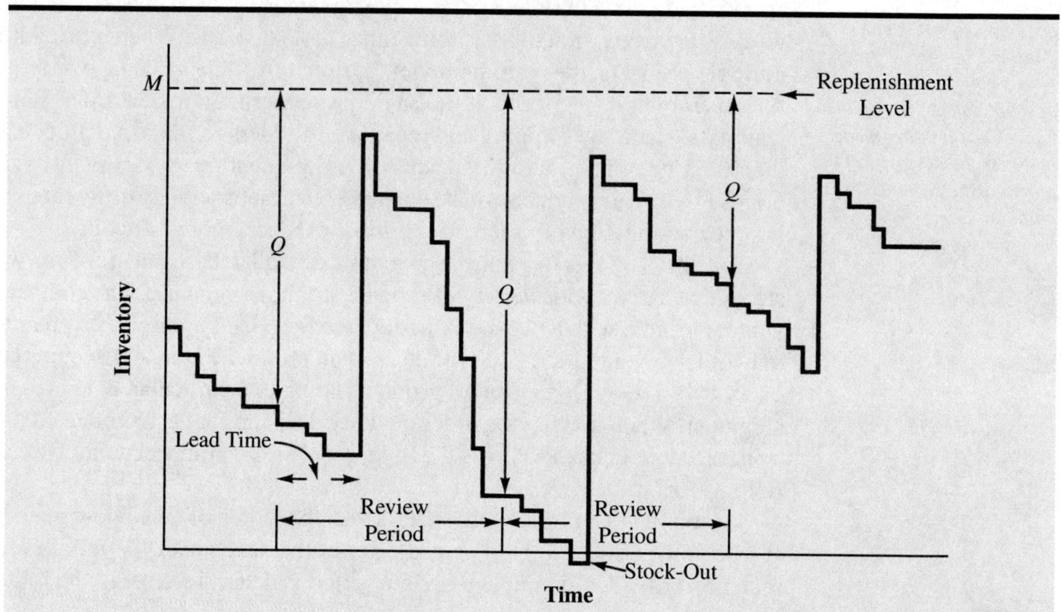

In the Dollar Discounts problem, we assume that management's objective is to determine the replenishment level with only a 1% chance of a stock-out. In the periodic review model, the order quantity at each review period must be sufficient to cover demand for the *review period plus the demand for the following lead time.* That is, the order quantity that brings the inventory position up to the replenishment level M must last until the order made at the next review period is received in inventory. The length of this time is equal to the review period plus the lead time. Figure 11.14 shows the normal probability distribution of demand during the review period plus the lead-time period for one of the Dollar Discounts products. The mean demand is 250 units, and the standard deviation of demand is 45 units. Given this situation, the logic used to establish M is similar to the logic used to establish

FIGURE 11.14 PROBABILITY DISTRIBUTION OF DEMAND DURING THE REVIEW PERIOD AND LEAD TIME FOR THE DOLLAR DISCOUNTS PROBLEM

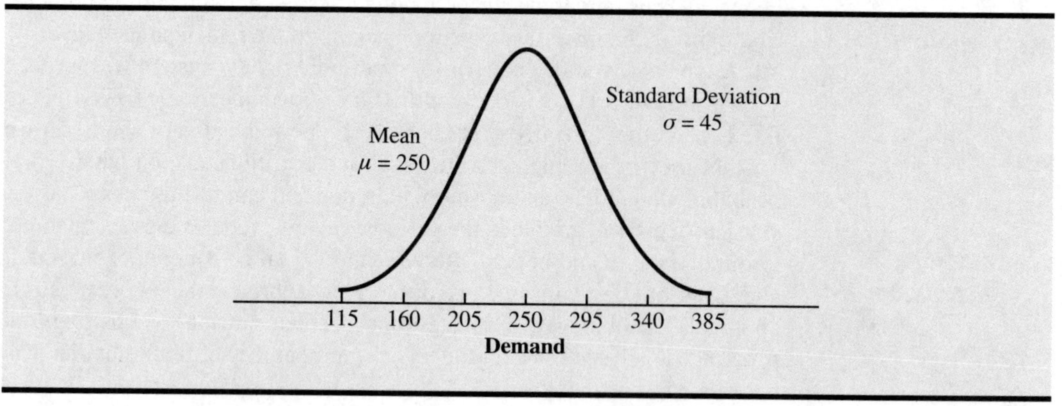

the reorder point in Section 11.6. Figure 11.15 shows the replenishment level M with a 1% chance that demand will exceed that replenishment level. In other words, Figure 11.15 shows the replenishment level that allows a 1% chance of a stock-out associated with the replenishment decision. Using the normal probability distribution table in Appendix A, we see that a value of M that is 2.33 standard deviations above the mean will allow stock-outs with a 1% probability. Therefore, for the assumed normal probability distribution with $\mu = 250$ and $\sigma = 45$, the replenishment level is determined by

EXCELfile
Periodic

$$M = 250 + 2.33(45) = 355$$

Problem 33 gives you practice in computing the replenishment level for a periodic review model with probabilistic demand.

Although other probability distributions can be used to express the demand during the review period plus the lead-time period, if the normal probability distribution is used, the general expression for M is

$$M = \mu + z\sigma \tag{11.39}$$

where z is the number of standard deviations necessary to obtain the acceptable stock-out probability.

Periodic review systems provide advantages of coordinated orders for multiple items. However, periodic review systems require larger safety stock levels than corresponding continuous review systems.

If demand had been deterministic rather than probabilistic, the replenishment level would have been the demand during the review period plus the demand during the lead-time period. In this case, the replenishment level would have been 250 units, and no stock-out would have occurred. However, with the probabilistic demand, we have seen that higher inventory is necessary to allow for uncertain demand and to control the probability of a stock-out. In the Dollar Discounts problem, 355 − 250 = 105 is the safety stock that is necessary to absorb any higher-than-usual demand during the review period plus the demand during the lead-time period. This safety stock limits the probability of a stock-out to 1%.

More Complex Periodic Review Models

The periodic review model just discussed is one approach to determining a replenishment level for the periodic review inventory system with probabilistic demand. More complex versions of the periodic review model incorporate a reorder point as another decision

FIGURE 11.15 REPLENISHMENT LEVEL M THAT ALLOWS A 1% CHANCE OF A STOCK-OUT FOR THE DOLLAR DISCOUNTS PROBLEM

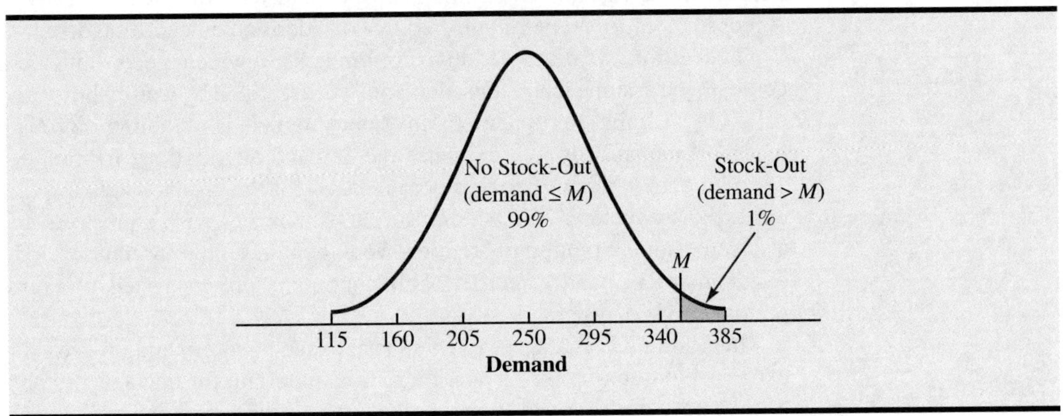

variable; that is, instead of ordering at every periodic review, a reorder point is established. If the inventory on hand at the periodic review is at or below the reorder point, a decision is made to order up to the replenishment level. However, if the inventory on hand at the periodic review is greater than the reorder level, such an order is not placed, and the system continues until the next periodic review. In this case, the cost of ordering is a relevant cost and can be included in a cost model along with holding and stock-out costs. Optimal policies can be reached based on minimizing the expected total cost. Situations with lead times longer than the review period add to the complexity of the model. The mathematical level required to treat these more extensive periodic review models is beyond the scope of this text.

NOTES AND COMMENTS

1. The periodic review model presented in this section is based on the assumption that the lead time for an order is less than the periodic review period. Most periodic review systems operate under this condition. However, the case in which the lead time is longer than the review period can be handled by defining H in equation (11.38) as the inventory position, where H includes the inventory on hand plus the inventory on order. In this case, the order quantity at any review period is the amount needed for the inventory on hand plus *all* outstanding orders needed to reach the replenishment level.
2. In the order-quantity, reorder point model discussed in Section 11.6, a continuous review was used to initiate an order whenever the reorder point was reached. The safety stock for this model was based on the probabilistic demand during the lead time. The periodic review model presented in this section also determined a recommended safety stock. However, because the inventory review was only periodic, the safety stock was based on the probabilistic demand during the *review period plus the lead-time period.* This longer period for the safety stock computation means that periodic review systems tend to require a larger safety stock than do continuous review systems.

SUMMARY

In this chapter we presented some of the approaches management scientists use to assist managers in establishing low-cost inventory policies. We first considered cases in which the demand rate for the product is constant. In analyzing these inventory systems, total cost models were developed, which included ordering costs, holding costs, and, in some cases, back-ordering costs. Then minimum cost formulas for the order quantity Q were presented. A reorder point r can be established by considering the lead-time demand.

In addition, we discussed inventory models in which a deterministic and constant rate could not be assumed, and thus, demand was described by a probability distribution. A critical issue with these probabilistic inventory models is obtaining a probability distribution that most realistically approximates the demand distribution. We first described a single-period model where only one order is placed for the product and, at the end of the period, either the product has sold out or a surplus remains of unsold products that will be sold for a salvage value. Solution procedures were then presented for multiperiod models based on either an order-quantity, reorder point, continuous review system or a replenishment-level, periodic review system.

In closing this chapter, we reemphasize that inventory and inventory systems can be an expensive phase of a firm's operation. It is important for managers to be aware of the cost of inventory systems and to make the best possible operating policy decisions for the inventory system. Inventory models, as presented in this chapter, can help managers to develop good inventory policies. The Management Science in Action, Multistage Inventory Planning at Deere & Company, provides another example of how computer-based inventory models can be used to provide optimal inventory policies and cost reductions.

MANAGEMENT SCIENCE IN ACTION

MULTISTAGE INVENTORY PLANNING AT DEERE & COMPANY*

Deere & Company's Commercial & Consumer Equipment (C&CE) Division, located in Raleigh, North Carolina, produces seasonal products such as lawn mowers and snow blowers. The seasonal aspect of demand requires the products to be built in advance. Because many of the products involve impulse purchases, the products must be available at dealerships when the customers walk in. Historically high inventory levels resulted in high inventory costs and an unacceptable return on assets. As a result, management concluded that C&CE needed an inventory planning system that would reduce the average finished goods inventory levels in company warehouses and dealer locations, and at the same time would ensure that stock-outs would not cause a negative impact on sales.

In order to optimize inventory levels, Deere moved from an aggregate inventory planning model to a series of individual product inventory models. This approach enabled Deere to determine optimal inventory levels for each product at each dealer, as well as optimal levels for each product at each plant and warehouse. The computerized system developed, known as SmartOps Multistage Inventory Planning and Optimization (MIPO), manages inventory for four C&CE Division plants, 21 dealers, and 150 products. Easily updated, MIPO provides target inventory levels for each product on a weekly basis. In addition, the system provides information about how optimal inventory levels are affected by lead times, forecast errors, and target service levels.

The inventory optimization system enabled the C&CE Division to meet its inventory reduction goals. C&CE management estimates that the company will continue to achieve annual cost savings from lower inventory carrying costs. Meanwhile, the dealers also benefit from lower warehouse expenses, as well as lower interest and insurance costs.

*Based on "Deere's New Software Achieves Inventory Reduction Goals," *Inventory Management Report* (March 2003): 2.

GLOSSARY

Economic order quantity (EOQ) The order quantity that minimizes the annual holding cost plus the annual ordering cost.

Constant demand rate An assumption of many inventory models that states that the same number of units are taken from inventory each period of time.

Holding cost The cost associated with maintaining an inventory investment, including the cost of the capital investment in the inventory, insurance, taxes, warehouse overhead, and so on. This cost may be stated as a percentage of the inventory investment or as a cost per unit.

Cost of capital The cost a firm incurs to obtain capital for investment. It may be stated as an annual percentage rate, and it is part of the holding cost associated with maintaining inventory.

Ordering cost The fixed cost (salaries, paper, transportation, etc.) associated with placing an order for an item.

Inventory position The inventory on hand plus the inventory on order.

Reorder point The inventory position at which a new order should be placed.

Lead time The time between the placing of an order and its receipt in the inventory system.

Lead-time demand The number of units demanded during the lead-time period.

Cycle time The length of time between the placing of two consecutive orders.

Constant supply rate A situation in which the inventory is built up at a constant rate over a period of time.

Lot size The order quantity in the production inventory model.

Setup cost The fixed cost (labor, materials, lost production) associated with preparing for a new production run.

Shortage or stock-out Demand that cannot be supplied from inventory.

Backorder The receipt of an order for a product when no units are in inventory. These backorders become shortages, which are eventually satisfied when a new supply of the product becomes available.

Goodwill cost A cost associated with a backorder, a lost sale, or any form of stock-out or unsatisfied demand. This cost may be used to reflect the loss of future profits because a customer experienced an unsatisfied demand.

Quantity discounts Discounts or lower unit costs offered by the manufacturer when a customer purchases larger quantities of the product.

Deterministic inventory model A model where demand is considered known and not subject to uncertainty.

Probabilistic inventory model A model where demand is not known exactly; probabilities must be associated with the possible values for demand.

Single-period inventory model An inventory model in which only one order is placed for the product, and at the end of the period either the item has sold out, or a surplus of unsold items will be sold for a salvage value.

Incremental analysis A method used to determine an optimal order quantity by comparing the cost of ordering an additional unit with the cost of not ordering an additional unit.

Lead-time demand distribution The distribution of demand that occurs during the lead-time period.

Safety stock Inventory maintained in order to reduce the number of stock-outs resulting from higher-than-expected demand.

Continuous review inventory system A system in which the inventory position is monitored or reviewed on a continuous basis so that a new order can be placed as soon as the reorder point is reached.

Periodic review inventory system A system in which the inventory position is checked or reviewed at predetermined periodic points in time. Reorders are placed only at periodic review points.

PROBLEMS

1. Suppose that the R & B Beverage Company has a soft drink product that shows a constant annual demand rate of 3600 cases. A case of the soft drink costs R & B \$3. Ordering costs are \$20 per order and holding costs are 25% of the value of the inventory. R & B has 250 working days per year, and the lead time is 5 days. Identify the following aspects of the inventory policy.

a. Economic order quantity

b. Reorder point

c. Cycle time
d. Total annual cost

2. A general property of the EOQ inventory model is that total inventory holding and total ordering costs are equal at the optimal solution. Use the data in Problem 1 to show that this result is true. Use equations (11.1), (11.2), and (11.3) to show that, in general, total holding costs and total ordering costs are equal whenever Q^* is used.

3. The reorder point [see equation (11.6)] is defined as the lead-time demand for an item. In cases of long lead times, the lead-time demand and thus the reorder point may exceed the economic order quantity Q^*. In such cases, the inventory position will not equal the inventory on hand when an order is placed, and the reorder point may be expressed in terms of either the inventory position or the inventory on hand. Consider the economic order quantity model with $D = 5000$, $C_o = \$32$, $C_h = \$2$, and 250 working days per year. Identify the reorder point in terms of the inventory position and in terms of the inventory on hand for each of the following lead times.
   a. 5 days
   b. 15 days
   c. 25 days
   d. 45 days

4. Westside Auto purchases a component used in the manufacture of automobile generators directly from the supplier. Westside's generator production operation, which is operated at a constant rate, will require 1000 components per month throughout the year (12,000 units annually). Assume that the ordering costs are \$25 per order, the unit cost is \$2.50 per component, and annual holding costs are 20% of the value of the inventory. Westside has 250 working days per year and a lead time of 5 days. Answer the following inventory policy questions.
   a. What is the EOQ for this component?
   b. What is the reorder point?
   c. What is the cycle time?
   d. What are the total annual holding and ordering costs associated with your recommended EOQ?

5. Suppose that Westside's management in Problem 4 likes the operational efficiency of ordering once each month and in quantities of 1000 units. How much more expensive would this policy be than your EOQ recommendation? Would you recommend in favor of the 1000-unit order quantity? Explain. What would the reorder point be if the 1000-unit quantity were acceptable?

6. Tele-Reco is a new specialty store that sells television sets, videotape recorders, video games, and other television-related products. A new Japanese-manufactured videotape recorder costs Tele-Reco \$600 per unit. Tele-Reco's annual holding cost rate is 22%. Ordering costs are estimated to be \$70 per order.
   a. If demand for the new videotape recorder is expected to be constant with a rate of 20 units per month, what is the recommended order quantity for the videotape recorder?
   b. What are the estimated annual inventory holding and ordering costs associated with this product?
   c. How many orders will be placed per year?
   d. With 250 working days per year, what is the cycle time for this product?

7. A large distributor of oil-well drilling equipment operated over the past two years with EOQ policies based on an annual holding cost rate of 22%. Under the EOQ policy, a particular product has been ordered with a $Q^* = 80$. A recent evaluation of holding costs shows that because of an increase in the interest rate associated with bank loans, the annual holding cost rate should be 27%.
   a. What is the new economic order quantity for the product?
   b. Develop a general expression showing how the economic order quantity changes when the annual holding cost rate is changed from I to I'.

8. Nation-Wide Bus Lines is proud of its six-week bus driver training program that it conducts for all new Nation-Wide drivers. As long as the class size remains less than or equal to 35, a six-week training program costs Nation-Wide \$22,000 for instructors, equipment, and so on. The Nation-Wide training program must provide the company with approximately five new drivers per month. After completing the training program, new drivers are paid \$1600 per month but do not work until a full-time driver position is open. Nation-Wide views the \$1600 per month paid to each idle new driver as a holding cost necessary to maintain a supply of newly trained drivers available for immediate service. Viewing new drivers as inventory-type units, how large should the training classes be to minimize Nation-Wide's total annual training and new driver idle-time costs? How many training classes should the company hold each year? What is the total annual cost associated with your recommendation?

9. Cress Electronic Products manufactures components used in the automotive industry. Cress purchases parts for use in its manufacturing operation from a variety of different suppliers. One particular supplier provides a part where the assumptions of the EOQ model are realistic. The annual demand is 5000 units, the ordering cost is \$80 per order, and the annual holding cost rate is 25%.
   a. If the cost of the part is \$20 per unit, what is the economic order quantity?
   b. Assume 250 days of operation per year. If the lead time for an order is 12 days, what is the reorder point?
   c. If the lead time for the part is seven weeks (35 days), what is the reorder point?
   d. What is the reorder point for part (c) if the reorder point is expressed in terms of the inventory on hand rather than the inventory position?

10. All-Star Bat Manufacturing, Inc., supplies baseball bats to major and minor league baseball teams. After an initial order in January, demand over the six-month baseball season is approximately constant at 1000 bats per month. Assuming that the bat production process can handle up to 4000 bats per month, the bat production setup costs are \$150 per setup, the production cost is \$10 per bat, and the holding costs have a monthly rate of 2%, what production lot size would you recommend to meet the demand during the baseball season? If All-Star operates 20 days per month, how often will the production process operate, and what is the length of a production run?

11. Assume that a production line operates such that the production lot size model of Section 11.2 is applicable. Given $D = 6400$ units per year, $C_o = \$100$, and $C_h = \$2$ per unit per year, compute the minimum cost production lot size for each of the following production rates:
   a. 8000 units per year
   b. 10,000 units per year
   c. 32,000 units per year
   d. 100,000 units per year

   Compute the EOQ recommended lot size using equation (11.5). What two observations can you make about the relationship between the EOQ model and the production lot size model?

12. Assume that you are reviewing the production lot size decision associated with a production operation where $P = 8000$ units per year, $D = 2000$ units per year, $C_o = \$300$, and $C_h = \$1.60$ per unit per year. Also assume that current practice calls for production runs of 500 units every three months. Would you recommend changing the current production lot size? Why or why not? How much could be saved by converting to your production lot size recommendation?

SELF test

13. Wilson Publishing Company produces books for the retail market. Demand for a current book is expected to occur at a constant annual rate of 7200 copies. The cost of one copy of the book is \$14.50. The holding cost is based on an 18% annual rate, and production setup costs are \$150 per setup. The equipment on which the book is produced has an annual pro-

duction volume of 25,000 copies. Wilson has 250 working days per year, and the lead time for a production run is 15 days. Use the production lot size model to compute the following values:

a. Minimum cost production lot size
b. Number of production runs per year
c. Cycle time
d. Length of a production run
e. Maximum inventory
f. Total annual cost
g. Reorder point

14. A well-known manufacturer of several brands of toothpaste uses the production lot size model to determine production quantities for its various products. The product known as Extra White is currently being produced in production lot sizes of 5000 units. The length of the production run for this quantity is 10 days. Because of a recent shortage of a particular raw material, the supplier of the material announced that a cost increase will be passed along to the manufacturer of Extra White. Current estimates are that the new raw material cost will increase the manufacturing cost of the toothpaste products by 23% per unit. What will be the effect of this price increase on the production lot sizes for Extra White?

15. Suppose that Westside Auto of Problem 4, with $D = 12{,}000$ units per year, $C_h = (2.50)(0.20) = \$0.50$, and $C_o = \$25$, decided to operate with a backorder inventory policy. Backorder costs are estimated to be \$5 per unit per year. Identify the following:

a. Minimum cost order quantity
b. Maximum number of backorders
c. Maximum inventory
d. Cycle time
e. Total annual cost

16. Assuming 250 days of operation per year and a lead time of 5 days, what is the reorder point for Westside Auto in Problem 15? Show the general formula for the reorder point for the EOQ model with backorders. In general, is the reorder point when backorders are allowed greater than or less than the reorder point when backorders are not allowed? Explain.

17. A manager of an inventory system believes that inventory models are important decision-making aids. Even though often using an EOQ policy, the manager never considered a backorder model because of the assumption that backorders were "bad" and should be avoided. However, with upper management's continued pressure for cost reduction, you have been asked to analyze the economics of a back-ordering policy for some products that can possibly be back ordered. For a specific product with $D = 800$ units per year, $C_o = \$150$, $C_h = \$3$, and $C_b = \$20$, what is the difference in total annual cost between the EOQ model and the planned shortage or backorder model? If the manager adds constraints that no more than 25% of the units can be back ordered and that no customer will have to wait more than 15 days for an order, should the backorder inventory policy be adopted? Assume 250 working days per year.

18. If the lead time for new orders is 20 days for the inventory system discussed in Problem 17, find the reorder point for both the EOQ and the backorder models.

19. The A&M Hobby Shop carries a line of radio-controlled model racing cars. Demand for the cars is assumed to be constant at a rate of 40 cars per month. The cars cost \$60 each, and ordering costs are approximately \$15 per order, regardless of the order size. The annual holding cost rate is 20%.

a. Determine the economic order quantity and total annual cost under the assumption that no backorders are permitted.
b. Using a \$45 per-unit per-year backorder cost, determine the minimum cost inventory policy and total annual cost for the model racing cars.

c. What is the maximum number of days a customer would have to wait for a backorder under the policy in part (b)? Assume that the Hobby Shop is open for business 300 days per year.
d. Would you recommend a no-backorder or a backorder inventory policy for this product? Explain.
e. If the lead time is six days, what is the reorder point for both the no-backorder and backorder inventory policies?

20. Assume that the following quantity discount schedule is appropriate. If annual demand is 120 units, ordering costs are \$20 per order, and the annual holding cost rate is 25%, what order quantity would you recommend?

Order Size	Discount (%)	Unit Cost
0 to 49	0	\$30.00
50 to 99	5	\$28.50
100 or more	10	\$27.00

21. Apply the EOQ model to the following quantity discount situation in which $D = 500$ units per year, $C_o = \$40$, and the annual holding cost rate is 20%. What order quantity do you recommend?

Discount Category	Order Size	Discount (%)	Unit Cost
1	0 to 99	0	\$10.00
2	100 or more	3	\$ 9.70

22. Keith Shoe Stores carries a basic black dress shoe for men that sells at an approximate constant rate of 500 pairs of shoes every three months. Keith's current buying policy is to order 500 pairs each time an order is placed. It costs Keith \$30 to place an order. The annual holding cost rate is 20%. With the order quantity of 500, Keith obtains the shoes at the lowest possible unit cost of \$28 per pair. Other quantity discounts offered by the manufacturer are as follows. What is the minimum cost order quantity for the shoes? What are the annual savings of your inventory policy over the policy currently being used by Keith?

Order Quantity	Price per Pair
0–99	\$36
100–199	\$32
200–299	\$30
300 or more	\$28

23. In the EOQ model with quantity discounts, we stated that if the Q^* for a price category is larger than necessary to qualify for the category price, the category cannot be optimal. Use the two discount categories in Problem 21 to show that this statement is true. That is, plot total cost curves for the two categories and show that if the category 2 minimum cost Q is an acceptable solution, we do not have to consider category 1.

24. The J&B Card Shop sells calendars depicting a different Colonial scene each month. The once-a-year order for each year's calendar arrives in September. From past experience, the September-to-July demand for the calendars can be approximated by a normal probability distribution with $\mu = 500$ and $\sigma = 120$. The calendars cost \$1.50 each, and J&B sells them for \$3 each.
   a. If J&B throws out all unsold calendars at the end of July (i.e., salvage value is zero), how many calendars should be ordered?
   b. If J&B reduces the calendar price to \$1 at the end of July and can sell all surplus calendars at this price, how many calendars should be ordered?

25. The Gilbert Air-Conditioning Company is considering the purchase of a special shipment of portable air conditioners manufactured in Japan. Each unit will cost Gilbert \$80, and it will be sold for \$125. Gilbert does not want to carry surplus air conditioners over until the following year. Thus, all surplus air conditioners will be sold to a wholesaler for \$50 per unit. Assume that the air conditioner demand follows a normal probability distribution with $\mu = 20$ and $\sigma = 8$.
   a. What is the recommended order quantity?
   b. What is the probability that Gilbert will sell all units it orders?

26. The Bridgeport city manager and the chief of police agreed on the size of the police force necessary for normal daily operations. However, they need assistance in determining the number of additional police officers needed to cover daily absences due to injuries, sickness, vacations, and personal leave. Records over the past three years show that the daily demand for additional police officers is normally distributed with a mean of 50 officers and a standard deviation of 10 officers. The cost of an additional police officer is based on the average pay rate of \$150 per day. If the daily demand for additional police officers exceeds the number of additional officers available, the excess demand will be covered by overtime at the pay rate of \$240 per day for each overtime officer.
   a. If the number of additional police officers available is greater than demand, the city will have to pay for more additional police officers than needed. What is the cost of overestimating demand?
   b. If the number of additional police officers available is less than demand, the city will have to use overtime to meet the demand. What is the cost of underestimating demand?
   c. What is the optimal number of additional police officers that should be included in the police force?
   d. On a typical day, what is the probability that overtime will be necessary?

27. A perishable dairy product is ordered daily at a particular supermarket. The product, which costs \$1.19 per unit, sells for \$1.65 per unit. If units are unsold at the end of the day, the supplier takes them back at a rebate of \$1 per unit. Assume that daily demand is approximately normally distributed with $\mu = 150$ and $\sigma = 30$.
   a. What is your recommended daily order quantity for the supermarket?
   b. What is the probability that the supermarket will sell all the units it orders?
   c. In problems such as these, why would the supplier offer a rebate as high as \$1? For example, why not offer a nominal rebate of, say, 25¢ per unit? What happens to the supermarket order quantity as the rebate is reduced?

28. A retail outlet sells a seasonal product for \$10 per unit. The cost of the product is \$8 per unit. All units not sold during the regular season are sold for half the retail price in an end-of-season clearance sale. Assume that demand for the product is uniformly distributed between 200 and 800.
   a. What is the recommended order quantity?
   b. What is the probability that at least some customers will ask to purchase the product after the outlet is sold out? That is, what is the probability of a stock-out using your order quantity in part (a)?

c. To keep customers happy and returning to the store later, the owner feels that stock-outs should be avoided if at all possible. What is your recommended order quantity if the owner is willing to tolerate a 0.15 probability of a stock-out?

d. Using your answer to part (c), what is the goodwill cost you are assigning to a stock-out?

29. Floyd Distributors, Inc., provides a variety of auto parts to small local garages. Floyd purchases parts from manufacturers according to the EOQ model and then ships the parts from a regional warehouse direct to its customers. For a particular type of muffler, Floyd's EOQ analysis recommends orders with $Q^* = 25$ to satisfy an annual demand of 200 mufflers. Floyd's has 250 working days per year, and the lead time averages 15 days.
    a. What is the reorder point if Floyd assumes a constant demand rate?
    b. Suppose that an analysis of Floyd's muffler demand shows that the lead-time demand follows a normal probability distribution with $\mu = 12$ and $\sigma = 2.5$. If Floyd's management can tolerate one stock-out per year, what is the revised reorder point?
    c. What is the safety stock for part (b)? If $C_h = \$5$/unit/year, what is the extra cost due to the uncertainty of demand?

30. For Floyd Distributors in Problem 29, we were given $Q^* = 25$, $D = 200$, $C_h = \$5$, and a normal lead-time demand distribution with $\mu = 12$ and $\sigma = 2.5$.
    a. What is Floyd's reorder point if the firm is willing to tolerate two stock-outs during the year?
    b. What is Floyd's reorder point if the firm wants to restrict the probability of a stock-out on any one cycle to at most 1%?
    c. What are the safety stock levels and the annual safety stock costs for the reorder points found in parts (a) and (b)?

31. A product with an annual demand of 1000 units has $C_o = \$25.50$ and $C_h = \$8$. The demand exhibits some variability such that the lead-time demand follows a normal probability distribution with $\mu = 25$ and $\sigma = 5$.
    a. What is the recommended order quantity?
    b. What are the reorder point and safety stock if the firm desires at most a 2% probability of stock-out on any given order cycle?
    c. If a manager sets the reorder point at 30, what is the probability of a stock-out on any given order cycle? How many times would you expect a stock-out during the year if this reorder point were used?

32. The B&S Novelty and Craft Shop in Bennington, Vermont, sells a variety of quality handmade items to tourists. B&S will sell 300 hand-carved miniature replicas of a Colonial soldier each year, but the demand pattern during the year is uncertain. The replicas sell for \$20 each, and B&S uses a 15% annual inventory holding cost rate. Ordering costs are \$5 per order, and demand during the lead time follows a normal probability distribution with $\mu = 15$ and $\sigma = 6$.
    a. What is the recommended order quantity?
    b. If B&S is willing to accept a stock-out roughly twice a year, what reorder point would you recommend? What is the probability that B&S will have a stock-out in any one order cycle?
    c. What are the safety stock and annual safety stock costs for this product?

33. A firm uses a one-week periodic review inventory system. A two-day lead time is needed for any order, and the firm is willing to tolerate an average of one stock-out per year.
    a. Using the firm's service guideline, what is the probability of a stock-out associated with each replenishment decision?
    b. What is the replenishment level if demand during the review period plus lead-time period is normally distributed with a mean of 60 units and a standard deviation of 12 units?
    c. What is the replenishment level if demand during the review period plus lead-time period is uniformly distributed between 35 and 85 units?

34. Foster Drugs, Inc., handles a variety of health and beauty aid products. A particular hair conditioner product costs Foster Drugs $2.95 per unit. The annual holding cost rate is 20%. An order-quantity, reorder point inventory model recommends an order quantity of 300 units per order.

a. Lead time is one week and the lead-time demand is normally distributed with a mean of 150 units and a standard deviation of 40 units. What is the reorder point if the firm is willing to tolerate a 1% chance of stock-out on any one cycle?

b. What safety stock and annual safety stock costs are associated with your recommendation in part (a)?

c. The order-quantity, reorder point model requires a continuous review system. Management is considering making a transition to a periodic review system in an attempt to coordinate ordering for many of its products. The demand during the proposed two-week review period and the one-week lead-time period is normally distributed with a mean of 450 units and a standard deviation of 70 units. What is the recommended replenishment level for this periodic review system if the firm is willing to tolerate the same 1% chance of stock-out associated with any replenishment decision?

d. What safety stock and annual safety stock costs are associated with your recommendation in part (c)?

e. Compare your answers to parts (b) and (d). The company is seriously considering the periodic review system. Would you support this decision? Explain.

f. Would you tend to favor the continuous review system for more expensive items? For example, assume that the product in the preceding example sold for $295 per unit. Explain.

35. Statewide Auto Parts uses a four-week periodic review system to reorder parts for its inventory stock. A one-week lead time is required to fill the order. Demand for one particular part during the five-week replenishment period is normally distributed with a mean of 18 units and a standard deviation of 6 units.

a. At a particular periodic review, 8 units are in inventory. The parts manager places an order for 16 units. What is the probability that this part will have a stock-out before an order that is placed at the next four-week review period arrives?

b. Assume that the company is willing to tolerate a 2.5% chance of a stock-out associated with a replenishment decision. How many parts should the manager have ordered in part (a)? What is the replenishment level for the four-week periodic review system?

36. Rose Office Supplies, Inc., which is open six days a week, uses a two-week periodic review for its store inventory. On alternating Monday mornings, the store manager fills out an order sheet requiring a shipment of various items from the company's warehouse. A particular three-ring notebook sells at an average rate of 16 notebooks per week. The standard deviation in sales is 5 notebooks per week. The lead time for a new shipment is three days. The mean lead-time demand is 8 notebooks with a standard deviation of 3.5.

a. What is the mean or expected demand during the review period plus the lead-time period?

b. Under the assumption of independent demand from week to week, the variances in demands are additive. Thus, the variance of the demand during the review period plus the lead-time period is equal to the variance of demand during the first week plus the variance of demand during the second week plus the variance of demand during the lead-time period. What is the variance of demand during the review period plus the lead-time period? What is the standard deviation of demand during the review period plus the lead-time period?

c. Assuming that demand has a normal probability distribution, what is the replenishment level that will provide an expected stock-out rate of one per year?

d. On Monday, March 22, 18 notebooks remain in inventory at the store. How many notebooks should the store manager order?

Case Problem 1 WAGNER FABRICATING COMPANY

Managers at Wagner Fabricating Company are reviewing the economic feasibility of manufacturing a part that it currently purchases from a supplier. Forecasted annual demand for the part is 3200 units. Wagner operates 250 days per year.

Wagner's financial analysts established a cost of capital of 14% for the use of funds for investments within the company. In addition, over the past year $600,000 was the average investment in the company's inventory. Accounting information shows that a total of $24,000 was spent on taxes and insurance related to the company's inventory. In addition, an estimated $9000 was lost due to inventory shrinkage, which included damaged goods as well as pilferage. A remaining $15,000 was spent on warehouse overhead, including utility expenses for heating and lighting.

An analysis of the purchasing operation shows that approximately two hours are required to process and coordinate an order for the part regardless of the quantity ordered. Purchasing salaries average $28 per hour, including employee benefits. In addition, a detailed analysis of 125 orders showed that $2375 was spent on telephone, paper, and postage directly related to the ordering process.

A one-week lead time is required to obtain the part from the supplier. An analysis of demand during the lead time shows it is approximately normally distributed with a mean of 64 units and a standard deviation of 10 units. Service level guidelines indicate that one stock-out per year is acceptable.

Currently, the company has a contract to purchase the part from a supplier at a cost of $18 per unit. However, over the past few months, the company's production capacity has been expanded. As a result, excess capacity is now available in certain production departments, and the company is considering the alternative of producing the parts itself.

Forecasted utilization of equipment shows that production capacity will be available for the part being considered. The production capacity is available at the rate of 1000 units per month, with up to five months of production time available. Management believes that with a two-week lead time, schedules can be arranged so that the part can be produced whenever needed. The demand during the two-week lead time is approximately normally distributed, with a mean of 128 units and a standard deviation of 20 units. Production costs are expected to be $17 per part.

A concern of management is that setup costs will be significant. The total cost of labor and lost production time is estimated to be $50 per hour, and a full eight-hour shift will be needed to set up the equipment for producing the part.

Managerial Report

Develop a report for management of Wagner Fabricating that will address the question of whether the company should continue to purchase the part from the supplier or begin to produce the part itself. Include the following factors in your report:

1. An analysis of the holding costs, including the appropriate annual holding cost rate
2. An analysis of ordering costs, including the appropriate cost per order from the supplier
3. An analysis of setup costs for the production operation
4. A development of the inventory policy for the following two alternatives:
   a. Ordering a fixed quantity Q from the supplier
   b. Ordering a fixed quantity Q from in-plant production
5. Include the following in the policies of parts 4(a) and 4(b):
   a. Optimal quantity Q^*
   b. Number of order or production runs per year

c. Cycle time
d. Reorder point
e. Amount of safety stock
f. Expected maximum inventory
g. Average inventory
h. Annual holding cost
i. Annual ordering cost
j. Annual cost of the units purchased or manufactured
k. Total annual cost of the purchase policy and the total annual cost of the production policy

6. Make a recommendation as to whether the company should purchase or manufacture the part. What savings are associated with your recommendation as compared with the other alternative?

Case Problem 2 RIVER CITY FIRE DEPARTMENT

The River City Fire Department (RCFD) fights fires and provides a variety of rescue operations in the River City metropolitan area. The RCFD staffs 13 ladder companies, 26 pumper companies, and several rescue units and ambulances. Normal staffing requires 186 firefighters to be on duty every day.

RCFD is organized with three firefighting units. Each unit works a full 24-hour day and then has two days (48 hours) off. For example, Unit 1 covers Monday, Unit 2 covers Tuesday, and Unit 3 covers Wednesday. Then Unit 1 returns on Thursday and so on. Over a three-week (21-day) scheduling period, each unit will be scheduled for seven days. On a rotational basis, firefighters within each unit are given one of the seven regularly scheduled days off. This day off is referred to as a Kelley day. Thus, over a three-week scheduling period, each firefighter in a unit works six of the seven scheduled unit days and gets one Kelley day off.

Determining the number of firefighters to be assigned to each unit includes the 186 firefighters who must be on duty plus the number of firefighters in the unit who are off for a Kelley day. Furthermore, each unit needs additional staffing to cover firefighter absences due to injury, sick leave, vacations, or personal time. This additional staffing involves finding the best mix of adding full-time firefighters to each unit and the selective use of overtime. If the number of absences on a particular day brings the number available firefighters below the required 186, firefighters who are currently off (e.g., on a Kelley day) must be scheduled to work overtime. Overtime is compensated at 1.55 times the regular pay rate.

Analysis of the records maintained over the last several years concerning the number of daily absences shows a normal probability distribution. A mean of 20 and a standard deviation of 5 provides a good approximation of the probability distribution for the number of daily absences.

Managerial Report

Develop a report that will enable Fire Chief O. E. Smith to determine the necessary numbers for the Fire Department. Include, at a minimum, the following items in your report.

1. Assuming no daily absences and taking into account the need to staff Kelley days, determine the base number of firefighters needed by each unit.
2. Using a minimum cost criterion, how many additional firefighters should be added to each unit in order to cover the daily absences? These extra daily needs will be

filled by the additional firefighters and, when necessary, the more expensive use of overtime by off-duty firefighters.

3. On a given day, what is the probability that Kelley-day firefighters will be called in to work overtime?
4. Based on the three-unit organization, how many firefighters should be assigned to each unit? What is the total number of full-time firefighters required for the River City Fire Department?

Appendix 11.1 DEVELOPMENT OF THE OPTIMAL ORDER QUANTITY (Q) FORMULA FOR THE EOQ MODEL

Given equation (11.4) as the total annual cost for the EOQ model,

$$TC = \frac{1}{2}QC_h + \frac{D}{Q}C_o \qquad (11.4)$$

we can find the order quantity Q that minimizes the total cost by setting the derivative, dTC/dQ, equal to zero and solving for Q^*.

$$\frac{dTC}{dQ} = \frac{1}{2}C_h - \frac{D}{Q^2}C_o = 0$$

$$\frac{1}{2}C_h = \frac{D}{Q^2}C_o$$

$$C_hQ^2 = 2DC_o$$

$$Q^2 = \frac{2DC_o}{C_h}$$

Hence,

$$Q^* = \sqrt{\frac{2DC_o}{C_h}} \qquad (11.5)$$

The second derivative is

$$\frac{d^2TC}{dQ^2} = \frac{2D}{Q^3}C_o$$

Because the value of the second derivative is greater than zero, Q^* from equation (11.5) is the minimum cost solution.

Appendix 11.2 DEVELOPMENT OF THE OPTIMAL LOT SIZE (Q^*) FORMULA FOR THE PRODUCTION LOT SIZE MODEL

Given equation (11.15) as the total annual cost for the production lot size model,

$$TC = \frac{1}{2}\left(1 - \frac{D}{P}\right)QC_h + \frac{D}{Q}C_o \qquad (11.15)$$

we can find the order quantity Q that minimizes the total cost by setting the derivative, dTC/dQ, equal to zero and solving for Q^*.

$$\frac{dTC}{dQ} = \frac{1}{2}\left(1 - \frac{D}{P}\right)C_h + \frac{D}{Q^2}C_o = 0$$

Solving for Q^*, we have

$$\frac{1}{2}\left(1 - \frac{D}{P}\right)C_h = \frac{D}{Q^2}C_o$$

$$\left(1 - \frac{D}{P}\right)C_h Q^2 = 2DC_o$$

$$Q^2 = \frac{2DC_o}{(1 - D/P)C_h}$$

Hence,

$$Q^* = \sqrt{\frac{2DC_o}{(1 - D/P)C_h}} \qquad (11.16)$$

The second derivative is

$$\frac{d^2TC}{dQ^2} = \frac{2DC_o}{Q^3}$$

Because the value of the second derivative is greater than zero, Q^* from equation (11.16) is a minimum cost solution.

CHAPTER 12

Waiting Line Models

CONTENTS

Recall the last time that you had to wait at a supermarket checkout counter, for a teller at your local bank, or to be served at a fast-food restaurant. In these and many other waiting line situations, the time spent waiting is undesirable. Adding more checkout clerks, bank tellers, or servers is not always the most economical strategy for improving service, so businesses need to determine ways to keep waiting times within tolerable limits.

Models have been developed to help managers understand and make better decisions concerning the operation of waiting lines. In management science terminology, a waiting line is also known as a **queue,** and the body of knowledge dealing with waiting lines is known as **queueing theory.** In the early 1900s, A. K. Erlang, a Danish telephone engineer, began a study of the congestion and waiting times occurring in the completion of telephone calls. Since then, queueing theory has grown far more sophisticated with applications in a wide variety of waiting line situations.

Waiting line models consist of mathematical formulas and relationships that can be used to determine the **operating characteristics** (performance measures) for a waiting line. Operating characteristics of interest include the following:

1. The probability that no units are in the system
2. The average number of units in the waiting line
3. The average number of units in the system (the number of units in the waiting line plus the number of units being served)
4. The average time a unit spends in the waiting line
5. The average time a unit spends in the system (the waiting time plus the service time)
6. The probability that an arriving unit has to wait for service

Managers who have such information are better able to make decisions that balance desirable service levels against the cost of providing the service.

The Management Science in Action, ATM Waiting Times at Citibank, describes how a waiting line model was used to help determine the number of automatic teller machines (ATMs) to place at New York City banking centers. A waiting line model prompted the creation of a new kind of line and a chief line director to implement first-come, first-served queue discipline at Whole Foods Market in the Chelsea neighborhood of New York City. In addition, a waiting line model helped the New Haven, Connecticut, fire department develop policies to improve response time for both fire and medical emergencies.

MANAGEMENT SCIENCE IN ACTION

ATM WAITING TIMES AT CITIBANK*

The waiting line model used at Citibank is discussed in Section 12.3.

The New York City franchise of U.S. Citibanking operates approximately 250 banking centers. Each center provides one or more automatic teller machines (ATMs) capable of performing a variety of banking transactions. At each center, a waiting line is formed by randomly arriving customers who seek service at one of the ATMs.

In order to make decisions on the number of ATMs to have at selected banking center locations, management needed information about potential waiting times and general customer service. Waiting line operating characteristics such as average number of customers in the waiting line, average time a customer spends waiting, and the probability that an arriving customer has to wait would help management determine the number of ATMs to recommend at each banking center.

For example, one busy Midtown Manhattan center had a peak arrival rate of 172 customers per hour. A multiple-channel waiting line model with six ATMs showed that 88% of the customers would have to wait, with an average wait time between

(continued)

six and seven minutes. This level of service was judged unacceptable. Expansion to seven ATMs was recommended for this location based on the waiting line model's projection of acceptable waiting times. Use of the waiting line model provided guidelines for making incremental ATM decisions at each banking center location.

*Based on information provided by Stacey Karter of Citibank.

12.1 STRUCTURE OF A WAITING LINE SYSTEM

To illustrate the basic features of a waiting line model, we consider the waiting line at the Burger Dome fast-food restaurant. Burger Dome sells hamburgers, cheeseburgers, french fries, soft drinks, and milk shakes, as well as a limited number of specialty items and dessert selections. Although Burger Dome would like to serve each customer immediately, at times more customers arrive than can be handled by the Burger Dome food service staff. Thus, customers wait in line to place and receive their orders.

Burger Dome is concerned that the methods currently used to serve customers are resulting in excessive waiting times. Management wants to conduct a waiting line study to help determine the best approach to reduce waiting times and improve service.

Single-Channel Waiting Line

In the current Burger Dome operation, a server takes a customer's order, determines the total cost of the order, takes the money from the customer, and then fills the order. Once the first customer's order is filled, the server takes the order of the next customer waiting for service. This operation is an example of a **single-channel waiting line.** Each customer entering the Burger Dome restaurant must pass through the *one* channel—one order-taking and order-filling station—to place an order, pay the bill, and receive the food. When more customers arrive than can be served immediately, they form a waiting line and wait for the order-taking and order-filling station to become available. A diagram of the Burger Dome single-channel waiting line is shown in Figure 12.1.

Distribution of Arrivals

Defining the arrival process for a waiting line involves determining the probability distribution for the number of arrivals in a given period of time. For many waiting line situations, the arrivals occur *randomly and independently* of other arrivals, and we cannot predict

FIGURE 12.1 THE BURGER DOME SINGLE-CHANNEL WAITING LINE

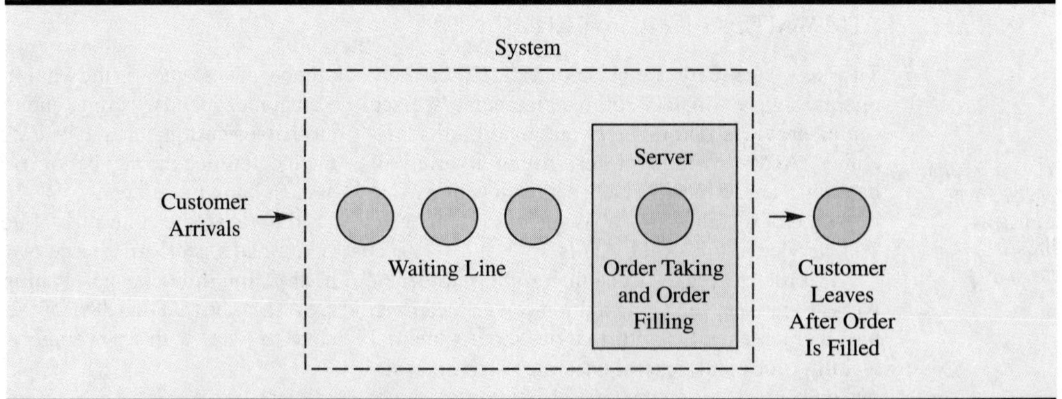

when an arrival will occur. In such cases, quantitative analysts have found that the **Poisson probability distribution** provides a good description of the arrival pattern.

The Poisson probability function provides the probability of x arrivals in a specific time period. The probability function is as follows.[1]

$$P(x) = \frac{\lambda^x e^{-\lambda}}{x!} \quad \text{for } x = 0, 1, 2, \ldots \tag{12.1}$$

where

$$x = \text{the number of arrivals in the time period}$$
$$\lambda = \text{the mean number of arrivals per time period}$$
$$e = 2.71828$$

Values of $e^{-\lambda}$ can be found using a calculator or by using Appendix B.

Suppose that Burger Dome analyzed data on customer arrivals and concluded that the mean arrival rate is 45 customers per hour. For a one-minute period, the mean arrival rate would be $\lambda = 45$ customers/60 minutes $= 0.75$ customers per minute. Thus, we can use the following Poisson probability function to compute the probability of x customer arrivals during a one-minute period:

$$P(x) = \frac{\lambda^x e^{-\lambda}}{x!} = \frac{0.75^x e^{-0.75}}{x!} \tag{12.2}$$

Thus, the probabilities of 0, 1, and 2 customer arrivals during a one-minute period are

$$P(0) = \frac{(0.75)^0 e^{-0.75}}{0!} = e^{-0.75} = 0.4724$$
$$P(1) = \frac{(0.75)^1 e^{-0.75}}{1!} = 0.75e^{-0.75} = 0.75(0.4724) = 0.3543$$
$$P(2) = \frac{(0.75)^2 e^{-0.75}}{2!} = \frac{(0.75)^2 e^{-0.75}}{2!} = \frac{(0.5625)(0.4724)}{2} = 0.1329$$

The probability of no customers in a one-minute period is 0.4724, the probability of one customer in a one-minute period is 0.3543, and the probability of two customers in a one-minute period is 0.1329. Table 12.1 shows the Poisson probabilities for customer arrivals during a one-minute period.

The waiting line models that will be presented in Sections 12.2 and 12.3 use the Poisson probability distribution to describe the customer arrivals at Burger Dome. In practice, you should record the actual number of arrivals per time period for several days or weeks and compare the frequency distribution of the observed number of arrivals to the Poisson

[1]The term $x!$, *x factorial,* is defined as $x! = x(x-1)(x-2)\ldots(2)(1)$. For example $4! = (4)(3)(2)(1) = 24$. For the special case of $x = 0$, $0! = 1$ by definition.

TABLE 12.1 POISSON PROBABILITIES FOR THE NUMBER OF CUSTOMER ARRIVALS AT A BURGER DOME RESTAURANT DURING A ONE-MINUTE PERIOD ($\lambda = 0.75$)

Number of Arrivals	Probability
0	0.4724
1	0.3543
2	0.1329
3	0.0332
4	0.0062
5 or more	0.0010

probability distribution to determine whether the Poisson probability distribution provides a reasonable approximation of the arrival distribution.

Distribution of Service Times

The service time is the time a customer spends at the service facility once the service has started. At Burger Dome, the service time starts when a customer begins to place the order with the food server and continues until the customer receives the order. Service times are rarely constant. At Burger Dome, the number of items ordered and the mix of items ordered vary considerably from one customer to the next. Small orders can be handled in a matter of seconds, but large orders may require more than two minutes.

Management scientists have found that if the probability distribution for the service time can be assumed to follow an **exponential probability distribution,** formulas are available for providing useful information about the operation of the waiting line. Using an exponential probability distribution, the probability that the service time will be less than or equal to a time of length t is

$$P(\text{service time} \leq t) = 1 - e^{-\mu t} \qquad (12.3)$$

where

A property of the exponential probability distribution is that there is a 0.6321 probability that the random variable takes on a value less than its mean. In waiting line applications, the exponential probability distribution indicates that approximately 63 percent of the service times are less than the mean service time and approximately 37 percent of the service times are greater than the mean service time.

μ = the mean number of units that can be served per time period
e = 2.71828

Suppose that Burger Dome studied the order-taking and order-filling process and found that the single food server can process an average of 60 customer orders per hour. On a one-minute basis, the mean service rate would be μ = 60 customers/60 minutes = 1 customer per minute. For example, with $\mu = 1$, we can use equation (12.3) to compute probabilities such as the probability an order can be processed in ½ minute or less, 1 minute or less, and 2 minutes or less. These computations are

$$P(\text{service time} \leq 0.5 \text{ min.}) = 1 - e^{-1(0.5)} = 1 - 0.6065 = 0.3935$$
$$P(\text{service time} \leq 1.0 \text{ min.}) = 1 - e^{-1(1.0)} = 1 - 0.3679 = 0.6321$$
$$P(\text{service time} \leq 2.0 \text{ min.}) = 1 - e^{-1(2.0)} = 1 - 0.1353 = 0.8647$$

Thus, we would conclude that there is a 0.3935 probability that an order can be processed in ½ minute or less, a 0.6321 probability that it can be processed in 1 minute or less, and a 0.8647 probability that it can be processed in 2 minutes or less.

In several waiting line models presented in this chapter, we assume that the probability distribution for the service time follows an exponential probability distribution. In practice, you should collect data on actual service times to determine whether the exponential probability distribution is a reasonable approximation of the service times for your application.

Queue Discipline

In describing a waiting line system, we must define the manner in which the waiting units are arranged for service. For the Burger Dome waiting line, and in general for most customer-oriented waiting lines, the units waiting for service are arranged on a **first-come, first-served** basis; this approach is referred to as an **FCFS** queue discipline. However, some situations call for different queue disciplines. For example, when people wait for an elevator, the last one on the elevator is often the first one to complete service (i.e., the first to leave the elevator). Other types of queue disciplines assign priorities to the waiting units and then serve the unit with the highest priority first. In this chapter we consider only waiting lines based on a first-come, first-served queue discipline. The Management Science in Action, The Serpentine Line and an FCFS Queue Discipline at Whole Foods Market, describes how an FCFS queue discipline is used at a supermarket.

MANAGEMENT SCIENCE IN ACTION

THE SERPENTINE LINE AND AN FCFS QUEUE DISCIPLINE AT WHOLE FOODS MARKET*

The Whole Foods Market in the Chelsea neighborhood of New York City employs a chief line director to implement a first-come, first-served (FCFS) queue discipline. In the early 1980s, Wendy's, American Airlines, and Chemical Bank were among the first to employ serpentine lines to implement an FCFS queue discipline. Such lines are commonplace today. We see them at banks, amusement parks, and fast-food outlets. The line is called *serpentine* because of the way it winds around. When a customer gets to the front of the line, the customer then goes to the first available server. People like serpentine lines because they prevent people who join the line later from being served ahead of an earlier arrival.

As popular as serpentine lines have become, supermarkets have not employed them because of a lack of space. At the typical supermarket, a separate line forms at each checkout counter. When ready to check out a person picks one of the checkout counters and stays in that line until receiving service. Sometimes a person joining another checkout line later will receive service first, which tends to upset people. Manhattan's Whole Foods Market solved this problem by creating a new kind of line and employing a chief line director to direct the first person in line to the next available checkout counter.

The waiting line at the Whole Foods Market is actually three parallel lines. Customers join the shortest line and follow a rotation when they reach the front of the line. For instance, if the first customer in line 1 is sent to a checkout counter, the next customer sent to a checkout counter is the first person in line 2, then the first person in line 3, and so on. This way an FCFS queue discipline is implemented without a long, winding serpentine line.

The Whole Foods Market's customers seem to really like the system and the line director, Bill Jones, has become something of a celebrity. Children point to him on the street and customers invite him over for dinner.

*Based on Ian Parker, "Mr. Next," *The New Yorker* (January 13, 2003).

Steady-State Operation

When the Burger Dome restaurant opens in the morning, no customers are in the restaurant. Gradually, activity builds up to a normal or steady state. The beginning or start-up period is referred to as the **transient period.** The transient period ends when the system reaches the normal or **steady-state operation.** Waiting line models describe the steady-state operating characteristics of a waiting line.

12.2 SINGLE-CHANNEL WAITING LINE MODEL WITH POISSON ARRIVALS AND EXPONENTIAL SERVICE TIMES

Waiting line models are often based on assumptions such as Poisson arrivals and exponential service times. When applying any waiting line model, data should be collected on the actual system to ensure that the assumptions of the model are reasonable.

In this section we present formulas that can be used to determine the steady-state operating characteristics for a single-channel waiting line. The formulas are applicable if the arrivals follow a Poisson probability distribution and the service times follow an exponential probability distribution. As these assumptions apply to the Burger Dome waiting line problem introduced in Section 12.1, we show how formulas can be used to determine Burger Dome's operating characteristics and thus provide management with helpful decision-making information.

The mathematical methodology used to derive the formulas for the operating characteristics of waiting lines is rather complex. However, our purpose in this chapter is not to provide the theoretical development of waiting line models, but rather to show how the formulas that have been developed can provide information about operating characteristics of the waiting line. Readers interested in the mathematical development of the formulas can consult the specialized texts listed in Appendix C at the end of the text.

Operating Characteristics

The following formulas can be used to compute the steady-state operating characteristics for a single-channel waiting line with Poisson arrivals and exponential service times, where

λ = the mean number of arrivals per time period (the mean arrival rate)
μ = the mean number of services per time period (the mean service rate)

Equations (12.4) through (12.10) do not provide formulas for optimal conditions. Rather, these equations provide information about the steady-state operating characteristics of a waiting line.

1. The probability that no units are in the system:

$$P_0 = 1 - \frac{\lambda}{\mu} \tag{12.4}$$

2. The average number of units in the waiting line:

$$L_q = \frac{\lambda^2}{\mu(\mu - \lambda)} \tag{12.5}$$

3. The average number of units in the system:

$$L = L_q + \frac{\lambda}{\mu} \tag{12.6}$$

4. The average time a unit spends in the waiting line:

$$W_q = \frac{L_q}{\lambda} \tag{12.7}$$

5. The average time a unit spends in the system:

$$W = W_q + \frac{1}{\mu} \tag{12.8}$$

6. The probability that an arriving unit has to wait for service:

$$P_w = \frac{\lambda}{\mu} \tag{12.9}$$

7. The probability of n units in the system:

$$P_n = \left(\frac{\lambda}{\mu}\right)^n P_0 \tag{12.10}$$

The values of the **mean arrival rate** λ and the **mean service rate** μ are clearly important components in determining the operating characteristics. Equation (12.9) shows that the ratio of the mean arrival rate to the mean service rate, λ/μ, provides the probability that an arriving unit has to wait because the service facility is in use. Hence, λ/μ often is referred to as the *utilization factor* for the service facility.

The operating characteristics presented in equations (12.4) through (12.10) are applicable only when the mean service rate μ is *greater than* the mean arrival rate λ—in other words, when $\lambda/\mu < 1$. If this condition does not exist, the waiting line will continue to grow without limit because the service facility does not have sufficient capacity to handle the arriving units. Thus, in using equations (12.4) through (12.10), we must have $\mu > \lambda$.

Operating Characteristics for the Burger Dome Problem

Recall that for the Burger Dome problem we had a mean arrival rate of $\lambda = 0.75$ customers per minute and a mean service rate of $\mu = 1$ customer per minute. Thus, with $\mu > \lambda$, equations (12.4) through (12.10) can be used to provide operating characteristics for the Burger Dome single-channel waiting line:

$$P_0 = 1 - \frac{\lambda}{\mu} = 1 - \frac{0.75}{1} = 0.25$$

$$L_q = \frac{\lambda^2}{\mu(\mu - \lambda)} = \frac{0.75^2}{1(1 - 0.75)} = 2.25 \text{ customers}$$

$$L = L_q = \frac{\lambda}{\mu} + 2.25 + \frac{0.75}{1} = 3 \text{ customers}$$

$$W_q = \frac{L_q}{\lambda} = \frac{2.25}{0.75} = 3 \text{ minutes}$$

$$W = W_q + \frac{1}{\mu} = 3 + \frac{1}{1} = 4 \text{ minutes}$$

$$P_w = \frac{\lambda}{\mu} = \frac{0.75}{1} = 0.75$$

Problem 5 asks you to compute the operating characteristics for a single-channel waiting line application.

Equation (12.10) can be used to determine the probability of any number of customers in the system. Applying it provides the probability information in Table 12.2.

Managers' Use of Waiting Line Models

The results of the single-channel waiting line for Burger Dome show several important things about the operation of the waiting line. In particular, customers wait an average of three minutes before beginning to place an order, which appears somewhat long for a business based on fast service. In addition, the facts that the average number of customers waiting in line is 2.25 and that 75 percent of the arriving customers have to wait for service are indicators that something should be done to improve the waiting line operation. Table 12.2 shows a 0.1335 probability that seven or more customers are in the Burger Dome system at one time. This condition indicates a fairly high probability that Burger Dome will experience some long waiting lines if it continues to use the single-channel operation.

If the operating characteristics are unsatisfactory in terms of meeting company standards for service, Burger Dome's management should consider alternative designs or plans for improving the waiting line operation.

Improving the Waiting Line Operation

Waiting line models often indicate where improvements in operating characteristics are desirable. However, the decision of how to modify the waiting line configuration to improve the operating characteristics must be based on the insights and creativity of the analyst.

TABLE 12.2 THE PROBABILITY OF n CUSTOMERS IN THE SYSTEM FOR THE BURGER DOME WAITING LINE PROBLEM

Number of Customers	Probability
0	0.2500
1	0.1875
2	0.1406
3	0.1055
4	0.0791
5	0.0593
6	0.0445
7 or more	0.1335

After reviewing the operating characteristics provided by the waiting line model, Burger Dome's management concluded that improvements designed to reduce waiting times are desirable. To make improvements in the waiting line operation, analysts often focus on ways to improve the service rate. Generally, service rate improvements are obtained by making either or both the following changes:

1. Increase the mean service rate μ by making a creative design change or by using new technology.
2. Add service channels so that more customers can be served simultaneously.

Assume that in considering alternative 1, Burger Dome's management decides to employ an order filler who will assist the order taker at the cash register. The customer begins the service process by placing the order with the order taker. As the order is placed, the order taker announces the order over an intercom system, and the order filler begins filling the order. When the order is completed, the order taker handles the money, while the order filler continues to fill the order. With this design, Burger Dome's management estimates the mean service rate can be increased from the current service rate of 60 customers per hour to 75 customers per hour. Thus, the mean service rate for the revised system is μ = 75 customers/60 minutes = 1.25 customers per minute. For $\lambda = 0.75$ customers per minute and $\mu = 1.25$ customers per minute, equations (12.4) through (12.10) can be used to provide the new operating characteristics for the Burger Dome waiting line. These operating characteristics are summarized in Table 12.3.

The information in Table 12.3 indicates that all operating characteristics have improved because of the increased service rate. In particular, the average time a customer spends in the waiting line has been reduced from 3 to 1.2 minutes and the average time a customer spends in the system has been reduced from 4 to 2 minutes. Are any other alternatives available that Burger Dome can use to increase the service rate? If so, and if the mean service rate μ can be identified for each alternative, equations (12.4) through (12.10) can be used to determine the revised operating characteristics and any improvements in the waiting line system. The added cost of any proposed change can be compared to the corresponding service improvements to help the manager determine whether the proposed service improvements are worthwhile.

Problem 11 asks you to determine whether a change in the mean service rate will meet the company's service guideline for its customers.

As mentioned previously, another option often available is to provide one or more additional service channels so that more than one customer may be served at the same time. The extension of the single-channel waiting line model to the multiple-channel waiting line model is the topic of the next section.

TABLE 12.3 OPERATING CHARACTERISTICS FOR THE BURGER DOME SYSTEM WITH THE MEAN SERVICE RATE INCREASED TO $\mu = 1.25$ CUSTOMERS PER MINUTE

Probability of no customers in the system	0.400
Average number of customers in the waiting line	0.900
Average number of customers in the system	1.500
Average time in the waiting line	1.200 minutes
Average time in the system	2.000 minutes
Probability that an arriving customer has to wait	0.600
Probability that seven or more customers are in the system	0.028

Excel Solution of Waiting Line Model

Waiting line models are easily implemented with the aid of worksheets. The Excel worksheet for the Burger Dome single-channel waiting line is shown in Figure 12.2. The formula worksheet is in the background; the value worksheet is in the foreground. The mean arrival rate and the mean service rate are entered in cells B7 and B8. The formulas for the waiting line's operating characteristics are placed in cells C13 to C18. The worksheet shows the same values for the operating characteristics that we obtained earlier. Modifications in the waiting line design can be evaluated by entering different mean arrival rates and/or mean service rates into cells B7 and B8. The new operating characteristics of the waiting line will be shown immediately.

The Management Scientist software also has a waiting line module that can be used to solve the waiting line problems in this chapter.

The Excel worksheet in Figure 12.2 is a template that can be used with any single-channel waiting line model with Poisson arrivals and exponential service times. This worksheet and similar Excel worksheets for the other waiting line models presented in this chapter are available on the CD that accompanies this text.

FIGURE 12.2 WORKSHEET FOR THE BURGER DOME SINGLE-CHANNEL WAITING LINE

EXCELfile
Single

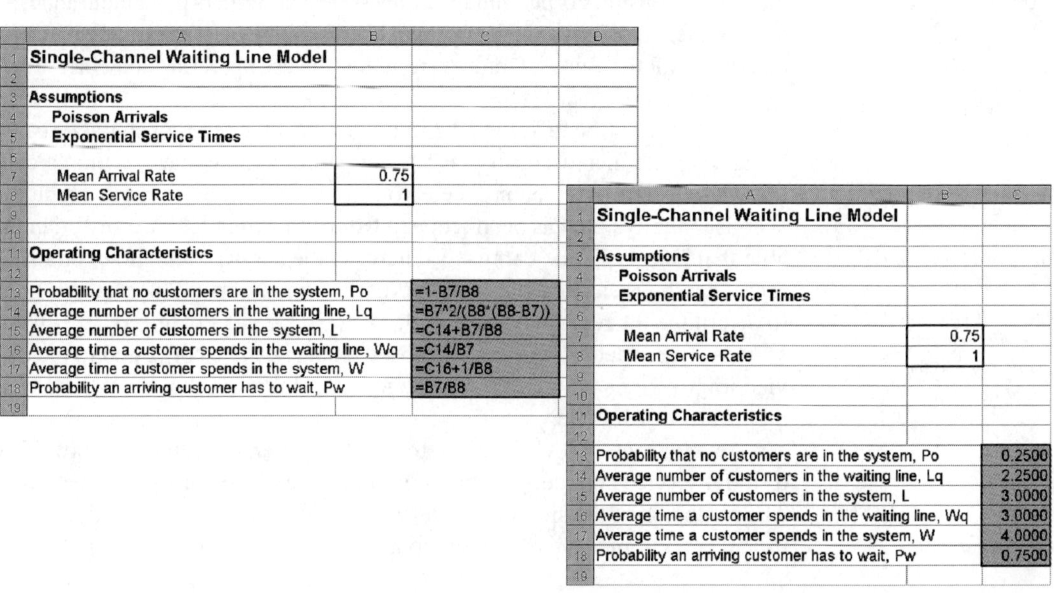

	A	B	C	D
1	**Single-Channel Waiting Line Model**			
2				
3	**Assumptions**			
4	**Poisson Arrivals**			
5	**Exponential Service Times**			
6				
7	Mean Arrival Rate	0.75		
8	Mean Service Rate	1		
9				
10				
11	**Operating Characteristics**			
12				
13	Probability that no customers are in the system, Po		=1-B7/B8	
14	Average number of customers in the waiting line, Lq		=B7^2/(B8*(B8-B7))	
15	Average number of customers in the system, L		=C14+B7/B8	
16	Average time a customer spends in the waiting line, Wq		=C14/B7	
17	Average time a customer spends in the system, W		=C16+1/B8	
18	Probability an arriving customer has to wait, Pw		=B7/B8	
19				

	A	B	C
1	**Single-Channel Waiting Line Model**		
2			
3	**Assumptions**		
4	**Poisson Arrivals**		
5	**Exponential Service Times**		
6			
7	Mean Arrival Rate	0.75	
8	Mean Service Rate	1	
9			
10			
11	**Operating Characteristics**		
12			
13	Probability that no customers are in the system, Po		0.2500
14	Average number of customers in the waiting line, Lq		2.2500
15	Average number of customers in the system, L		3.0000
16	Average time a customer spends in the waiting line, Wq		3.0000
17	Average time a customer spends in the system, W		4.0000
18	Probability an arriving customer has to wait, Pw		0.7500
19			

NOTES AND COMMENTS

1. The assumption that arrivals follow a Poisson probability distribution is equivalent to the assumption that the time between arrivals has an exponential probability distribution. For example, if the arrivals for a waiting line follow a Poisson probability distribution with a mean of 20 arrivals per hour, the time between arrivals will follow an exponential probability distribution, with a mean time between arrivals of $\frac{1}{20}$ or 0.05 hour.
2. Many individuals believe that whenever the mean service rate μ is greater than the mean arrival rate λ, the system should be able to handle or serve all arrivals. However, as the Burger

Dome example shows, the variability of arrival times and service times may result in long waiting times even when the mean service rate exceeds the mean arrival rate. A contribution of waiting line models is that they can point out undesirable waiting line operating characteristics even when the $\mu > \lambda$ condition appears satisfactory.

12.3 MULTIPLE-CHANNEL WAITING LINE MODEL WITH POISSON ARRIVALS AND EXPONENTIAL SERVICE TIMES

You may be familiar with multiple-channel systems that also have multiple waiting lines. The waiting line model in this section has multiple channels, but only a single waiting line. Operating characteristics for a multiple-channel system are better when a single waiting line, rather than multiple waiting lines, is used.

A **multiple-channel waiting line** consists of two or more service channels that are assumed to be identical in terms of service capability. In the multiple-channel system, arriving units wait in a single waiting line and then move to the first available channel to be served. The single-channel Burger Dome operation can be expanded to a two-channel system by opening a second service channel. Figure 12.3 shows a diagram of the Burger Dome two-channel waiting line.

In this section we present formulas that can be used to determine the steady-state operating characteristics for a multiple-channel waiting line. These formulas are applicable if the following conditions exist.

1. The arrivals follow a Poisson probability distribution.
2. The service time for each channel follows an exponential probability distribution.
3. The mean service rate μ is the same for each channel.
4. The arrivals wait in a single waiting line and then move to the first open channel for service.

Operating Characteristics

The following formulas can be used to compute the steady-state operating characteristics for multiple-channel waiting lines, where

$$\lambda = \text{the mean arrival rate for the system}$$
$$\mu = \text{the mean service rate for } each \text{ channel}$$
$$k = \text{the number of channels}$$

1. The probability that no units are in the system:

$$P_0 = \frac{1}{\displaystyle\sum_{n=0}^{k-1} \frac{(\lambda/\mu)^n}{n!} + \frac{(\lambda/\mu)^k}{k!}\left(\frac{k\mu}{k\mu - \lambda}\right)} \tag{12.11}$$

2. The average number of units in the waiting line:

$$L_q = \frac{(\lambda/\mu)^k \lambda\mu}{(k-1)!(k\mu - \lambda)^2} P_0 \tag{12.12}$$

FIGURE 12.3 THE BURGER DOME TWO-CHANNEL WAITING LINE

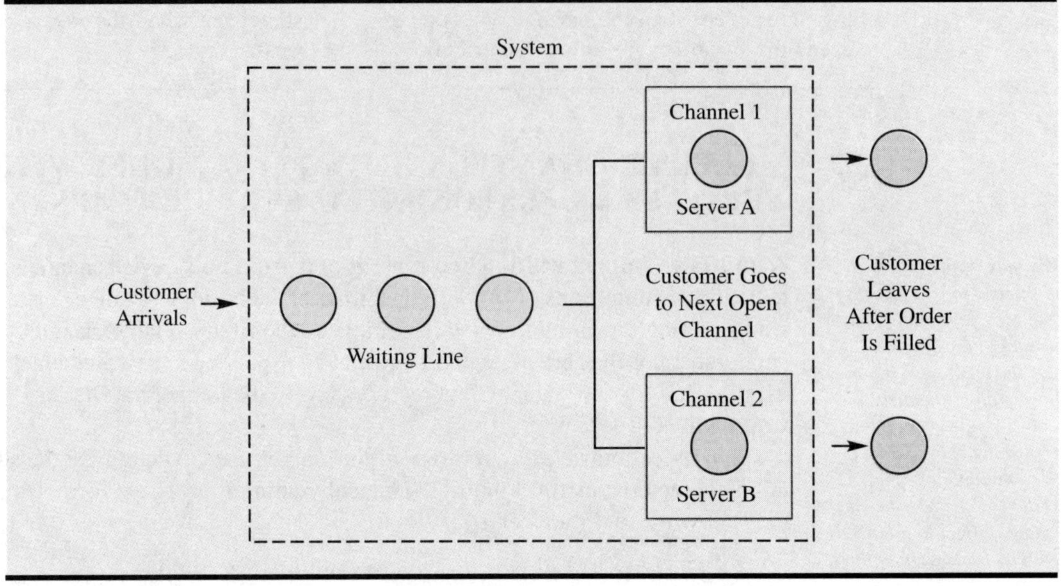

3. The average number of units in the system:

$$L = L_q + \frac{\lambda}{\mu} \tag{12.13}$$

4. The average time a unit spends in the waiting line:

$$W_q = \frac{L_q}{\lambda} \tag{12.14}$$

5. The average time a unit spends in the system:

$$W = W_q + \frac{1}{\mu} \tag{12.15}$$

6. The probability that an arriving unit has to wait for service:

$$P_w = \frac{1}{k!}\left(\frac{\lambda}{\mu}\right)^k\left(\frac{k\mu}{k\mu - \lambda}\right)P_0 \tag{12.16}$$

7. The probability of n units in the system:

$$P_n = \frac{(\lambda/\mu)^n}{n!} P_0 \quad \text{for } n \leq k \tag{12.17}$$

$$P_n = \frac{(\lambda/\mu)^n}{k!k^{(n-k)}} P_0 \quad \text{for } n > k \tag{12.18}$$

Because μ is the mean service rate for each channel, $k\mu$ is the mean service rate for the multiple-channel system. As was true for the single-channel waiting line model, the formulas for the operating characteristics of multiple-channel waiting lines can be applied only in situations where the mean service rate for the system is greater than the mean arrival rate for the system; in other words, the formulas are applicable only if $k\mu$ is greater than λ.

Some expressions for the operating characteristics of multiple-channel waiting lines are more complex than their single-channel counterparts. However, equations (12.11) through (12.18) provide the same information as provided by the single-channel model. To help simplify the use of the multiple-channel equations, Table 12.4 contains values of P_0 for selected values of λ/μ and k. The values provided in the table correspond to cases where $k\mu > \lambda$, and hence the service rate is sufficient to process all arrivals.

Operating Characteristics for the Burger Dome Problem

To illustrate the multiple-channel waiting line model, we return to the Burger Dome fast-food restaurant waiting line problem. Suppose that management wants to evaluate the desirability of opening a second order-processing station so that two customers can be served simultaneously. Assume a single waiting line with the first customer in line moving to the first available server. Let us evaluate the operating characteristics for this two-channel system.

We use equations (12.12) through (12.18) for the $k = 2$ channel system. For a mean arrival rate of $\lambda = 0.75$ customers per minute and mean service rate of $\mu = 1$ customer per minute for each channel, we obtain the operating characteristics:

EXCELfile
Multiple

$$P_0 = 0.4545 \quad \text{(from Table 12.4 with } \lambda/\mu = 0.75)$$

$$L_q = \frac{(0.75/1)^2(0.75)(1)}{(2-1)![2(1) - 0.75]^2}(0.4545) = 0.1227 \text{ customer}$$

$$L = L_q + \frac{\lambda}{\mu} = 0.1227 + \frac{0.75}{1} = 0.8727 \text{ customer}$$

$$W_q = \frac{L_q}{\lambda} = \frac{0.1227}{0.75} = 0.1636 \text{ minute}$$

$$W = W_q + \frac{1}{\mu} = 0.1636 + \frac{1}{1} = 1.1636 \text{ minutes}$$

$$P_w = \frac{1}{2!}\left(\frac{0.75}{1}\right)^2\left[\frac{2(1)}{2(1) - 0.75}\right](0.4545) = 0.2045$$

Try Problem 18 for practice in determining the operating characteristics for a two-channel waiting line.

Using equations (12.17) and (12.18), we can compute the probabilities of n customers in the system. The results from these computations are summarized in Table 12.5.

TABLE 12.4 VALUES OF P_0 FOR MULTIPLE-CHANNEL WAITING LINES WITH POISSON ARRIVALS AND EXPONENTIAL SERVICE TIMES

	Number of Channels (k)			
Ratio λ/μ	2	3	4	5
0.15	0.8605	0.8607	0.8607	0.8607
0.20	0.8182	0.8187	0.8187	0.8187
0.25	0.7778	0.7788	0.7788	0.7788
0.30	0.7391	0.7407	0.7408	0.7408
0.35	0.7021	0.7046	0.7047	0.7047
0.40	0.6667	0.6701	0.6703	0.6703
0.45	0.6327	0.6373	0.6376	0.6376
0.50	0.6000	0.6061	0.6065	0.6065
0.55	0.5686	0.5763	0.5769	0.5769
0.60	0.5385	0.5479	0.5487	0.5488
0.65	0.5094	0.5209	0.5219	0.5220
0.70	0.4815	0.4952	0.4965	0.4966
0.75	0.4545	0.4706	0.4722	0.4724
0.80	0.4286	0.4472	0.4491	0.4493
0.85	0.4035	0.4248	0.4271	0.4274
0.90	0.3793	0.4035	0.4062	0.4065
0.95	0.3559	0.3831	0.3863	0.3867
1.00	0.3333	0.3636	0.3673	0.3678
1.20	0.2500	0.2941	0.3002	0.3011
1.40	0.1765	0.2360	0.2449	0.2463
1.60	0.1111	0.1872	0.1993	0.2014
1.80	0.0526	0.1460	0.1616	0.1646
2.00		0.1111	0.1304	0.1343
2.20		0.0815	0.1046	0.1094
2.40		0.0562	0.0831	0.0889
2.60		0.0345	0.0651	0.0721
2.80		0.0160	0.0521	0.0581
3.00			0.0377	0.0466
3.20			0.0273	0.0372
3.40			0.0186	0.0293
3.60			0.0113	0.0228
3.80			0.0051	0.0174
4.00				0.0130
4.20				0.0093
4.40				0.0063
4.60				0.0038
4.80				0.0017

TABLE 12.5 THE PROBABILITY OF n CUSTOMERS IN THE SYSTEM FOR THE BURGER DOME TWO-CHANNEL WAITING LINE

Number of Customers	Probability
0	0.4545
1	0.3409
2	0.1278
3	0.0479
4	0.0180
5 or more	0.0109

We can now compare the steady-state operating characteristics of the two-channel system to the operating characteristics of the original single-channel system discussed in Section 12.2.

1. The average time a customer spends in the system (waiting time plus service time) is reduced from $W = 4$ minutes to $W = 1.1636$ minutes.
2. The average number of customers in the waiting line is reduced from $L_q = 2.25$ customers to $L_q = 0.1227$ customer.
3. The average time a customer spends in the waiting line is reduced from $W_q = 3$ minutes to $W_q = 0.1636$ minute.
4. The probability that a customer has to wait for service is reduced from $P_w = 0.75$ to $P_w = 0.2045$.

Clearly the two-channel system will significantly improve the operating characteristics of the waiting line. However, adding an order filler at each service station would further increase the mean service rate and improve the operating characteristics. The final decision regarding the staffing policy at Burger Dome rests with the Burger Dome management. The waiting line study simply provides the operating characteristics that can be anticipated under three configurations: a single-channel system with one employee, a single-channel system with two employees, and a two-channel system with an employee for each channel. After considering these results, what action would you recommend? In this case, Burger Dome adopted the following policy statement: For periods when customer arrivals are expected to average 45 customers per hour, Burger Dome will open two order-processing channels with one employee assigned to each.

By changing the mean arrival rate λ to reflect arrival rates at different times of the day, and then computing the operating characteristics, Burger Dome's management can establish guidelines and policies that tell the store managers when they should schedule service operations with a single channel, two channels, or perhaps even three or more channels.

NOTES AND COMMENTS

The multiple-channel waiting line model is based on a single waiting line. You may have also encountered situations where each of the k channels has its own waiting line. Management scientists have shown that the operating characteristics of multiple-channel systems are better if a single waiting line is used. People like them better also; no one who comes in after you can be served ahead of you. Thus, when possible, banks, airline reservation counters, food-service establishments, and other businesses frequently use a single waiting line for a multiple-channel system.

12.4 SOME GENERAL RELATIONSHIPS FOR WAITING LINE MODELS

In Sections 12.2 and 12.3 we presented formulas for computing the operating characteristics for single-channel and multiple-channel waiting lines with Poisson arrivals and exponential service times. The operating characteristics of interest included

$$L_q = \text{the average number of units in the waiting line}$$
$$L = \text{the average number of units in the system}$$
$$W_q = \text{the average time a unit spends in the waiting line}$$
$$W = \text{the average time a unit spends in the system}$$

John D. C. Little showed that several relationships exist among these four characteristics and that these relationships apply to a variety of different waiting line systems. Two of the relationships, referred to as *Little's flow equations,* are

$$L = \lambda W \qquad (12.19)$$
$$L_q = \lambda W_q \qquad (12.20)$$

Equation (12.19) shows that the average number of units in the system, L, can be found by multiplying the mean arrival rate, λ, by the average time a unit spends in the system, W. Equation (12.20) shows that the same relationship holds between the average number of units in the waiting line, L_q, and the average time a unit spends in the waiting line, W_q.

Using equation (12.20) and solving for W_q, we obtain

$$W_q = \frac{L_q}{\lambda} \qquad (12.21)$$

Equation (12.21) follows directly from Little's second flow equation. We used it for the single-channel waiting line model in Section 12.2 and the multiple-channel waiting line model in Section 12.3 [see equations (12.7) and (12.14)]. Once L_q is computed for either of these models, equation (12.21) can then be used to compute W_q.

Another general expression that applies to waiting line models is that the average time in the system, W, is equal to the average time in the waiting line, W_q, plus the average service time. For a system with a mean service rate μ, the mean service time is $1/\mu$. Thus, we have the general relationship

$$W = W_q + \frac{1}{\mu} \qquad (12.22)$$

Recall that we used equation (12.22) to provide the average time in the system for both the single- and multiple-channel waiting line models [see equations (12.8) and (12.15)].

The importance of Little's flow equations is that they apply to *any waiting line model* regardless of whether arrivals follow the Poisson probability distribution and regardless of

The advantage of Little's flow equations is that they show how operating characteristics L, L_q, W, and W_q are related in any waiting line system. Arrivals and service times do not have to follow specific probability distributions for the flow equations to be applicable.

The application of Little's flow equations is demonstrated in Problem 25.

whether service times follow the exponential probability distribution. For example, in a study of the grocery checkout counters at Murphy's Foodliner, an analyst concluded that arrivals follow the Poisson probability distribution with the mean arrival rate of 24 customers per hour or $\lambda = 24/60 = 0.40$ customers per minute. However, the analyst found that service times follow a normal probability distribution rather than an exponential probability distribution. The mean service rate was found to be 30 customers per hour or $\mu = 30/60 = 0.50$ customers per minute. A time study of actual customer waiting times showed that, on average, a customer spends 4.5 minutes in the system (waiting time plus checkout time); that is, $W = 4.5$. Using the waiting line relationships discussed in this section, we can now compute other operating characteristics for this waiting line.

First, using equation (12.22) and solving for W_q, we have

$$W_q = W - \frac{1}{\mu} = 4.5 - \frac{1}{0.50} = 2.5 \text{ minutes}$$

With both W and W_q known, we can use Little's flow equations, (12.19) and (12.20), to compute

$$L = \lambda W = 0.40(4.5) = 1.8 \text{ customers}$$
$$L_q = \lambda W_q = 0.40(2.5) = 1 \text{ customer}$$

The manager of Murphy's Foodliner can now review these operating characteristics to see whether action should be taken to improve the service and to reduce the waiting time and the length of the waiting line.

NOTES AND COMMENTS

In waiting line systems where the length of the waiting line is limited (e.g., a small waiting area), some arriving units will be blocked from joining the waiting line and will be lost. In this case, the blocked or lost arrivals will make the mean number of units entering the system something less than the mean arrival rate. By defining λ as the mean number of units *joining the system,* rather than the mean arrival rate, the relationships discussed in this section can be used to determine W, L, W_q, and L_q.

12.5 ECONOMIC ANALYSIS OF WAITING LINES

Frequently, decisions involving the design of waiting lines will be based on a subjective evaluation of the operating characteristics of the waiting line. For example, a manager may decide that an average waiting time of one minute or less and an average of two customers or fewer in the system are reasonable goals. The waiting line models presented in the preceding sections can be used to determine the number of channels that will meet the manager's waiting line performance goals.

On the other hand, a manager may want to identify the cost of operating the waiting line system and then base the decision regarding system design on a minimum hourly or daily operating cost. Before an economic analysis of a waiting line can be conducted, a total cost model, which includes the cost of waiting and the cost of service, must be developed.

To develop a total cost model for a waiting line, we begin by defining the notation to be used:

Waiting cost is based on average number of units in the system. It includes the time spent waiting in line plus the time spent being served.

$$\begin{aligned} c_w &= \text{the waiting cost per time period for each unit} \\ L &= \text{the average number of units in the system} \\ c_s &= \text{the service cost per time period for each channel} \\ k &= \text{the number of channels} \\ TC &= \text{the total cost per time period} \end{aligned}$$

The total cost is the sum of the waiting cost and the service cost; that is,

$$TC = c_w L + c_s k \tag{12.23}$$

Adding more channels always improves the operating characteristics of the waiting line and reduces the waiting cost. However, additional channels increase the service cost. An economic analysis of waiting lines attempts to find the number of channels that will minimize total cost by balancing the waiting cost and the service cost.

To conduct an economic analysis of a waiting line, we must obtain reasonable estimates of the waiting cost and the service cost. Of these two costs, the waiting cost is usually the more difficult to evaluate. In the Burger Dome restaurant problem, the waiting cost would be the cost per minute for a customer waiting for service. This cost is not a direct cost to Burger Dome. However, if Burger Dome ignores this cost and allows long waiting lines, customers ultimately will take their business elsewhere. Thus, Burger Dome will experience lost sales and, in effect, incur a cost.

The service cost is generally easier to determine. This cost is the relevant cost associated with operating each service channel. In the Burger Dome problem, this cost would include the server's wages, benefits, and any other direct costs associated with operating the service channel. At Burger Dome, this cost is estimated to be $7 per hour.

To demonstrate the use of equation (12.23), we assume that Burger Dome is willing to assign a cost of $10 per hour for customer waiting time. We use the average number of units in the system, L, as computed in Sections 12.2 and 12.3 to obtain the total hourly cost for the single-channel and two-channel systems:

Single-channel system ($L = 3$ customers)

$$\begin{aligned} TC &= c_w L + c_s k \\ &= 10(3) + 7(1) = \$37.00 \text{ per hour} \end{aligned}$$

Two-channel system ($L = 0.8727$ customer):

$$\begin{aligned} TC &= c_w L + c_s k \\ &= 10(0.8727) + 7(2) = \$22.73 \text{ per hour} \end{aligned}$$

Thus, based on the cost data provided by Burger Dome, the two-channel system provides the most economical operation.

Problem 21 tests your ability to conduct an economic analysis of proposed single-channel and two-channel waiting line systems.

Figure 12.4 shows the general shape of the cost curves in the economic analysis of waiting lines. The service cost increases as the number of channels is increased. However, with more channels, the service is better. As a result, waiting time and cost decrease as the number of channels is increased. The number of channels that will provide a good approximation of the minimum total cost design can be found by evaluating the total cost for several design alternatives.

FIGURE 12.4 THE GENERAL SHAPE OF WAITING COST, SERVICE COST, AND TOTAL COST CURVES IN WAITING LINE MODELS

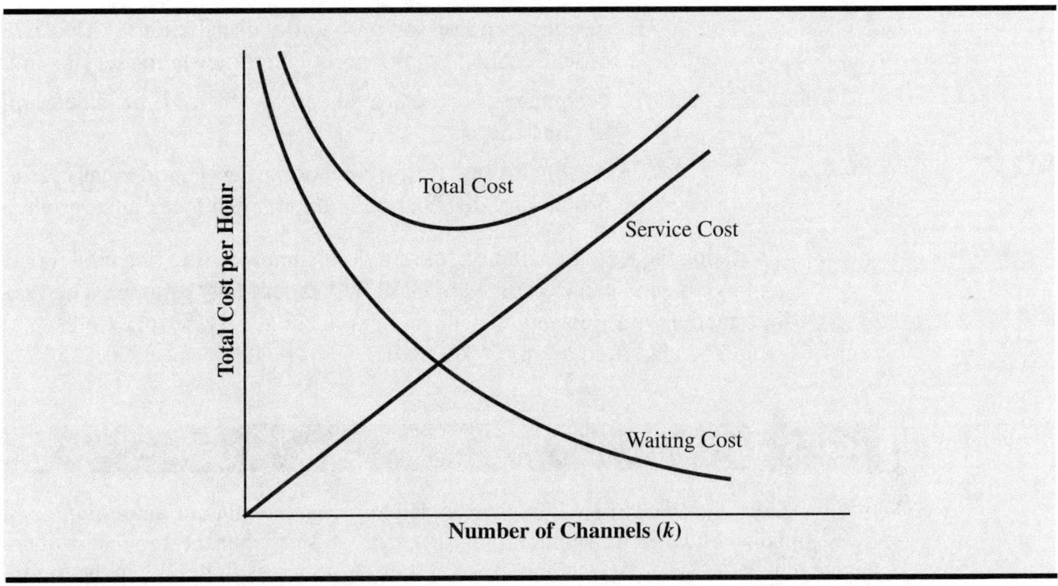

NOTES AND COMMENTS

1. In dealing with government agencies and utility companies, customers may not be able to take their business elsewhere. In these situations, no lost business occurs when long waiting times are encountered. This condition is one reason that service in such organizations may be poor and that customers in such situations may experience long waiting times.
2. In some instances, the organization providing the service also employs the units waiting for the service. For example, consider the case of a company that owns and operates the trucks used to deliver goods to and from its manufacturing plant. In addition to the costs associated with the trucks waiting to be loaded or unloaded, the firm also pays the wages of the truck loaders and unloaders who operate the service channel. In this case, the cost of having the trucks wait and the cost of operating the service channel are direct expenses to the firm. An economic analysis of the waiting line system is highly recommended for these types of situations.

12.6 OTHER WAITING LINE MODELS

D. G. Kendall suggested a notation that is helpful in classifying the wide variety of different waiting line models that have been developed. The three-symbol Kendall notation is as follows:

$$A/B/k$$

where

A denotes the probability distribution for the arrivals

B denotes the probability distribution for the service time

k denotes the number of channels

Depending on the letter appearing in the *A* or *B* position, a variety of waiting line systems can be described. The letters that are commonly used are as follows:

- *M* designates a Poisson probability distribution for the arrivals or an exponential probability distribution for service time
- *D* designates that the arrivals or the service time is deterministic or constant
- *G* designates that the arrivals or the service time has a general probability distribution with a known mean and variance

Using the Kendall notation, the single-channel waiting line model with Poisson arrivals and exponential service times is classified as an *M*/*M*/1 model. The two-channel waiting line model with Poisson arrivals and exponential service times presented in Section 12.3 would be classified as an *M*/*M*/2 model.

NOTES AND COMMENTS

In some cases, the Kendall notation is extended to five symbols. The fourth symbol indicates the largest number of units that can be in the system, and the fifth symbol indicates the size of the population. The fourth symbol is used in situations where the waiting line can hold a finite or maximum number of units, and the fifth symbol is necessary when the population of arriving units or customers is finite. When the fourth and fifth symbols of the Kendall notation are omitted, the waiting line system is assumed to have infinite capacity, and the population is assumed to be infinite.

12.7 SINGLE-CHANNEL WAITING LINE MODEL WITH POISSON ARRIVALS AND ARBITRARY SERVICE TIMES

Let us return to the single-channel waiting line model where arrivals are described by a Poisson probability distribution. However, we now assume that the probability distribution for the service times is not an exponential probability distribution. Thus, using the Kendall notation, the waiting line model that is appropriate is an *M*/*G*/1 model, where *G* denotes a general or unspecified probability distribution.

When providing input to the M/G/1 model, be consistent in terms of the time period. For example, if λ and μ are expressed in terms of the number of units per hour, the standard deviation of the service time should be expressed in hours. The example that follows uses minutes as the time period for the arrival and service data.

Operating Characteristics for the *M*/*G*/1 Model

The notation used to describe the operating characteristics for the *M*/*G*/1 model is

λ = the mean arrival rate

μ = the mean service rate

σ = the standard deviation of the service time

Some of the steady-state operating characteristics of the *M*/*G*/1 waiting line model are as follows:

1. The probability that no units are in the system:

$$P_0 = 1 - \frac{\lambda}{\mu} \tag{12.24}$$

2. The average number of units in the waiting line:

$$L_q = \frac{\lambda^2\sigma^2 + (\lambda/\mu)^2}{2(1 - \lambda/\mu)} \tag{12.25}$$

3. The average number of units in the system:

$$L = L_q + \frac{\lambda}{\mu} \tag{12.26}$$

4. The average time a unit spends in the waiting line:

$$W_q = \frac{L_q}{\lambda} \tag{12.27}$$

5. The average time a unit spends in the system:

$$W = W_q + \frac{1}{\mu} \tag{12.28}$$

6. The probability that an arriving unit has to wait for service:

$$P_w = \frac{\lambda}{\mu} \tag{12.29}$$

Note that the relationships for L, W_q, and W are the same as the relationships used for the waiting line models in Sections 12.2 and 12.3. They are given by Little's flow equations.

Problem 27 provides another application of a single-channel waiting line with Poisson arrivals and arbitrary service times.

An Example Retail sales at Hartlage's Seafood Supply are handled by one clerk. Customer arrivals are random, and the average arrival rate is 21 customers per hour or $\lambda = 21/60 = 0.35$ customers per minute. A study of the service process shows that the average or mean service time is 2 minutes per customer, with a standard deviation of $\sigma = 1.2$ minutes. The mean time of 2 minutes per customer shows that the clerk has a mean service rate of $\mu = \frac{1}{2} = 0.50$ customers per minute. The operating characteristics of this $M/G/1$ waiting line system are

EXCELfile
Single-Arbitrary

$$P_0 = 1 - \frac{\lambda}{\mu} = 1 - \frac{0.35}{0.50} = 0.30$$

$$L_q = \frac{(0.35)^2(1.2)^2 + (0.35/0.50)^2}{2(1 - 0.35/0.50)} = 1.1107 \text{ customers}$$

$$L = L_q + \frac{\lambda}{\mu} = 1.1107 + \frac{0.35}{0.50} = 1.8107 \text{ customers}$$

$$W_q = \frac{L_q}{\lambda} = \frac{1.1107}{0.35} = 3.1733 \text{ minutes}$$

$$W = W_q + \frac{1}{\mu} = 3.1733 + \frac{1}{0.50} = 5.1733 \text{ minutes}$$

$$P_w = \frac{\lambda}{\mu} = \frac{0.35}{0.50} = 0.70$$

Hartlage's manager can review these operating characteristics to determine whether scheduling a second clerk appears to be worthwhile.

Constant Service Times

We want to comment briefly on the single-channel waiting line model that assumes random arrivals but constant service times. Such a waiting line can occur in production and manufacturing environments where machine-controlled service times are constant. This waiting line is described by the *M*/*D*/1 model, with the *D* referring to the deterministic service times. With the *M*/*D*/1 model, the average number of units in the waiting line, L_q, can be found by using equation (12.25) with the condition that the standard deviation of the constant service time is $\sigma = 0$. Thus, the expression for the average number of units in the waiting line for the *M*/*D*/1 waiting line becomes

$$L_q = \frac{(\lambda/\mu)^2}{2(1 - \lambda/\mu)} \tag{12.30}$$

The other expressions presented earlier in this section can be used to determine additional operating characteristics of the *M*/*D*/1 system.

NOTES AND COMMENTS

Whenever the operating characteristics of a waiting line are unacceptable, managers often try to improve service by increasing the mean service rate μ. This approach is good, but equation (12.25) shows that the variation in the service times also affects the operating characteristics of the waiting line. Because the standard deviation of service times, σ, appears in the numerator of equation (12.25), a larger variation in service times results in a larger average number of units in the waiting line. Hence, another alternative for improving the service capabilities of a waiting line is to reduce the variation in the service times. Thus, even when the mean service rate of the service facility cannot be increased, a reduction in σ will reduce the average number of units in the waiting line and improve the other operating characteristics of the system.

12.8 MULTIPLE-CHANNEL MODEL WITH POISSON ARRIVALS, ARBITRARY SERVICE TIMES, AND NO WAITING LINE

An interesting variation of the waiting line models discussed so far involves a system in which no waiting is allowed. Arriving units or customers seek service from one of several service channels. If all channels are busy, arriving units are denied access to the system. In waiting line terminology, arrivals occurring when the system is full are **blocked** and are cleared from the system. Such customers may be lost or may attempt a return to the system later.

The specific model considered in this section is based on the following assumptions.

1. The system has k channels.
2. The arrivals follow a Poisson probability distribution, with mean arrival rate λ.
3. The service times for each channel may have any probability distribution.
4. The mean service rate μ is the same for each channel.
5. An arrival enters the system only if at least one channel is available. An arrival occurring when all channels are busy is blocked—that is, denied service and not allowed to enter the system.

With G denoting a general or unspecified probability distribution for service times, the appropriate model for this situation is referred to as an $M/G/k$ model with "blocked customers cleared." The question addressed in this type of situation is, How many channels or servers should be used?

A primary application of this model involves the design of telephone and other communication systems where the arrivals are the calls and the channels are the number of telephone or communication lines available. In such a system, the calls are made to one telephone number, with each call automatically switched to an open channel if possible. When all channels are busy, additional calls receive a busy signal and are denied access to the system.

Operating Characteristics for the *M/G/k* Model with Blocked Customers Cleared

We approach the problem of selecting the best number of channels by computing the steady-state probabilities that j of the k channels will be busy. These probabilities are

$$P_j = \frac{(\lambda/\mu)^j/j!}{\sum_{i=0}^{k}(\lambda/\mu)^i/i!} \tag{12.31}$$

where

λ = the mean arrival rate
μ = the mean service rate for each channel
k = the number of channels
P_j = the probability that j of the k channels are busy for $j = 0, 1, 2, \ldots, k$

With no waiting allowed, operating characteristics L_q and W_q considered in previous waiting line models are automatically zero regardless of the number of service channels. In this situation, the more important design consideration involves determining how the percentage of blocked customers is affected by the number of service channels.

The most important probability value is P_k, which is the probability that all k channels are busy. On a percentage basis, P_k indicates the percentage of arrivals that are blocked and denied access to the system.

Another operating characteristic of interest is the average number of units in the system; note that this number is equivalent to the average number of channels in use. Letting L denote the average number of units in the system, we have

$$L = \frac{\lambda}{\mu}(1 - P_k) \tag{12.32}$$

An Example Microdata Software, Inc., uses a telephone ordering system for its computer software products. Callers place orders with Microdata by using the company's 800 telephone number. Assume that calls to this telephone number arrive at an average rate of $\lambda =$ 12 calls per hour. The time required to process a telephone order varies considerably from order to order. However, each Microdata sales representative can be expected to handle an average of $\mu = 6$ calls per hour. Currently, the Microdata 800 telephone number has three internal lines or channels, each operated by a separate sales representative. Calls received on the 800 number are automatically transferred to an open line or channel if available.

Whenever all three lines are busy, callers receive a busy signal. In the past, Microdata's management assumed that callers receiving a busy signal would call back later. However, recent research on telephone ordering showed that a substantial number of callers who are denied access do not call back later. These lost calls represent lost revenues for the firm, so Microdata's management requested an analysis of the telephone ordering system. Specifically, management wanted to know the percentage of callers who get busy signals and are blocked from the system. If management's goal is to provide sufficient capacity to handle 90 percent of the callers, how many telephone lines and sales representatives should Microdata use?

We can demonstrate the use of equation (12.31) by computing P_3, the probability that all three of the currently available telephone lines will be in use and additional callers will be blocked:

EXCELfile
No Waiting

$$P_3 = \frac{(^{12}/_6)^3/3!}{(^{12}/_6)^0/0! + (^{12}/_6)^1/1! + (^{12}/_6)^2/2! + (^{12}/_6)^3/3!} = \frac{1.3333}{6.3333} = 0.2105$$

With $P_3 = 0.2105$, approximately 21 percent of the calls, or slightly more than one in five calls, are being blocked. Only 79 percent of the calls are being handled immediately by the three-line system.

Let us assume that Microdata expands to a four-line system. Then, the probability that all four channels will be in use and that callers will be blocked is

$$P_4 = \frac{(^{12}/_6)^4/4!}{(^{12}/_6)^0/0! + (^{12}/_6)^1/1! + (^{12}/_6)^2/2! + (^{12}/_6)^3/3! + (^{12}/_6)^4/4!} = \frac{0.667}{7} = 0.0952$$

With only 9.52 percent of the callers blocked, 90.48 percent of the callers will reach the Microdata sales representatives. Thus, Microdata should expand its order-processing operation to four lines to meet management's goal of providing sufficient capacity to handle at least 90 percent of the callers. The average number of calls in the four-line system and thus the average number of lines and sales representatives that will be busy is

Problem 30 provides practice in calculating probabilities for multiple-channel systems with no waiting line.

$$L = \frac{\lambda}{\mu}(1 - P_4) = \frac{12}{6}(1 - 0.0952) = 1.8095$$

Although an average of fewer than two lines will be busy, the four-line system is necessary to provide the capacity to handle at least 90 percent of the callers. We used equation (12.31) to calculate the probability that 0, 1, 2, 3, or 4 lines will be busy. These probabilities are summarized in Table 12.6.

As we discussed in Section 12.5, an economic analysis of waiting lines can be used to guide system design decisions. In the Microdata system, the cost of the additional line and additional sales representative should be relatively easy to establish. This cost can

TABLE 12.6 PROBABILITIES OF BUSY LINES FOR THE MICRODATA FOUR-LINE SYSTEM

Number of Busy Lines	Probability
0	0.1429
1	0.2857
2	0.2857
3	0.1905
4	0.0952

be balanced against the cost of the blocked calls. With 9.52 percent of the calls blocked and $\lambda = 12$ calls per hour, an eight-hour day will have an average of $8(12)(0.0952) = 9.1$ blocked calls. If Microdata can estimate the cost of possible lost sales, the cost of these blocked calls can be established. The economic analysis based on the service cost and the blocked-call cost can assist in determining the optimal number of lines for the system.

NOTES AND COMMENTS

Many of the operating characteristics considered in previous sections are not relevant for the *M/G/k* model with blocked customers cleared. In particular, the average time in the waiting line, W_q, and the average number of units in the waiting line, L_q, are no longer considered because waiting is not permitted in this type of system.

12.9 WAITING LINE MODELS WITH FINITE CALLING POPULATIONS

For the waiting line models introduced so far, the population of units or customers arriving for service has been considered to be unlimited. In technical terms, when no limit is placed on how many units may seek service, the model is said to have an **infinite calling population.** Under this assumption, the mean arrival rate λ remains constant regardless of how many units are in the waiting line system. This assumption of an infinite calling population is made in most waiting line models.

In other cases, the maximum number of units or customers that may seek service is assumed to be finite. In this situation, the mean arrival rate for the system changes, depending on the number of units in the waiting line, and the waiting line model is said to have a **finite calling population.** The formulas for the operating characteristics of the previous waiting line models must be modified to account for the effect of the finite calling population.

In previous waiting line models, the arrival rate was constant and independent of the number of units in the system. With a finite calling population, the arrival rate decreases as the number of units in the system increases because, with more units in the system, fewer units are available for arrivals.

The finite calling population model discussed in this section is based on the following assumptions.

1. The arrivals for *each unit* follow a Poisson probability distribution, with mean arrival rate λ.
2. The service times follow an exponential probability distribution, with mean service rate μ.
3. The population of units that may seek service is finite.

The mean arrival rate λ is defined differently for the finite calling population model. Specifically, λ is defined in terms of the mean arrival rate for each unit.

With a single channel, the waiting line model is referred to as an *M/M/*1 model with a finite calling population.

The mean arrival rate for the *M/M/*1 model with a finite calling population is defined in terms of how often *each unit* arrives or seeks service. This situation differs from that for previous waiting line models in which λ denoted the mean arrival rate for the system. With a finite calling population, the mean arrival rate for the system varies, depending on the number of units in the system. Instead of adjusting for the changing system arrival rate, in the finite calling population model λ indicates the mean arrival rate for each unit.

Operating Characteristics for the *M/M/*1 Model with a Finite Calling Population

The following formulas are used to determine the steady-state operating characteristics for an *M/M/*1 model with a finite calling population, where

$$\lambda = \text{the mean arrival rate for each unit}$$
$$\mu = \text{the mean service rate}$$
$$N = \text{the size of the population}$$

1. The probability that no units are in the system:

$$P_0 = \frac{1}{\displaystyle\sum_{n=0}^{N} \frac{N!}{(N-n)!}\left(\frac{\lambda}{\mu}\right)^n} \tag{12.33}$$

2. The average number of units in the waiting line:

$$L_q = N - \frac{\lambda + \mu}{\lambda}(1 - P_0) \tag{12.34}$$

3. The average number of units in the system:

$$L = L_q + (1 - P_0) \tag{12.35}$$

4. The average time a unit spends in the waiting line:

$$W_q = \frac{L_q}{(N - L)\lambda} \tag{12.36}$$

5. The average time a unit spends in the system:

$$W = W_q + \frac{1}{\mu} \tag{12.37}$$

6. The probability an arriving unit has to wait for service:

$$P_w = 1 - P_0 \tag{12.38}$$

7. The probability of n units in the system:

$$P_n = \frac{N!}{(N-n)!}\left(\frac{\lambda}{\mu}\right)^n P_0 \quad \text{for } n = 0, 1, \ldots, N \tag{12.39}$$

One of the primary applications of the *M/M/*1 model with a finite calling population is referred to as the *machine repair problem.* In this problem, a group of machines is considered to be the finite population of "customers" that may request repair service. Whenever a machine breaks down, an arrival occurs in the sense that a new repair request is initiated. If another machine breaks down before the repair work has been completed on the first machine, the second machine begins to form a "waiting line" for repair service. Additional breakdowns by other machines will add to the length of the waiting line. The assumption of first-come, first-served indicates that machines are repaired in the order they break down. The *M/M/*1 model shows that one person or one channel is available to perform the repair service. To return the machine to operation, each machine with a breakdown must be repaired by the single-channel operation.

An Example The Kolkmeyer Manufacturing Company uses a group of six identical machines; each machine operates an average of 20 hours between breakdowns. Thus, the mean arrival rate or request for repair service for each machine is $\lambda = 1/20 = 0.05$ per hour. With randomly occurring breakdowns, the Poisson probability distribution is used to describe the machine breakdown arrival process. One person from the maintenance department provides the single-channel repair service for the six machines. The exponentially distributed service times have a mean of two hours per machine or a mean service rate of $\mu = 1/2 = 0.50$ machines per hour.

With $\lambda = 0.05$ and $\mu = 0.50$, we use equations (12.33) through (12.38) to compute the operating characteristics for this system. Note that the use of equation (12.33) makes the computations involved somewhat cumbersome. Confirm for yourself that equation (12.33) provides the value of $P_0 = 0.4845$. The computations for the other operating characteristics are

$$L_q = 6 - \left(\frac{0.05 + 0.50}{0.05}\right)(1 - 0.4845) = 0.3297 \text{ machine}$$

$$L = 0.3295 + (1 - 0.4845) = 0.8451 \text{ machine}$$

$$W_q = \frac{0.3295}{(6 - 0.845)0.50} = 1.279 \text{ hours}$$

$$W = 1.279 + \frac{1}{0.50} = 3.279 \text{ hours}$$

$$P_w = 1 - P_0 = 1 - 0.4845 = 0.5155$$

Operating characteristics of an M/M/1 waiting line with a finite calling population are considered in Problem 34.

Finally, equation (12.39) can be used to compute the probabilities of any number of machines being in the repair system.

As with other waiting line models, the operating characteristics provide the manager with information about the operation of the waiting line. In this case, the fact that a machine breakdown waits an average of $W_q = 1.279$ hours before maintenance begins and the fact that more than 50 percent of the machine breakdowns must wait for service, $P_w = 0.5155$, indicates a two-channel system may be needed to improve the machine repair service.

An Excel worksheet template on the CD that accompanies this text or The Management Scientist software may be used to analyze the two-channel finite calling population model.

Computations of the operating characteristics of a multiple-channel finite calling population waiting line are more complex than those for the single-channel model. A computer solution is virtually mandatory in this case. The Excel worksheet for the Kolkmeyer two-channel machine repair system is shown in Figure 12.5. With two repair personnel, the average machine breakdown waiting time is reduced to $W_q = 0.0834$ hours or 5 minutes and only 10%, $P_w = 0.1036$, of the machine breakdowns wait for service. Thus, the two-channel system significantly improves the machine repair service operation. Ultimately, by considering the cost of machine downtime and the cost of the repair personnel, management can determine whether the improved service of the two-channel system is cost effective.

FIGURE 12.5 WORKSHEET FOR THE KOLKMEYER TWO-CHANNEL MACHINE REPAIR PROBLEM

EXCELfile
Finite

	A	B	C	D
1	**Waiting Line Model with a Finite Calling Population**			
2				
3	**Assumptions**			
4	**Poisson Arrivals**			
5	**Exponential Service Times**			
6	**Finite Calling Population**			
7				
8	Number of Channels	2		
9	Mean Arrival Rate	0.05		
10	Mean Service Rate	0.5		
11	Population Size	6		
12				
13				
14	**Operating Characteristics**			
15				
16	Probability that no machines are in the system, Po		0.5602	
17	Average number of machines in the waiting line, Lq		0.0227	
18	Average number of machines in the system, L		0.5661	
19	Average time a machine spends in the waiting line, Wq		0.0834	
20	Average time a machine spends in the system, W		2.0834	
21	Probability an arriving machine has to wait, Pw		0.1036	
22				

SUMMARY

In this chapter we presented a variety of waiting line models that have been developed to help managers make better decisions concerning the operation of waiting lines. For each model, we presented formulas that could be used to develop operating characteristics or performance measures for the system being studied. The operating characteristics presented include the following:

1. Probability that no units are in the system
2. Average number of units in the waiting line
3. Average number of units in the system
4. Average time a unit spends in the waiting line
5. Average time a unit spends in the system
6. Probability that arriving units will have to wait for service

We also showed how an economic analysis of the waiting line could be conducted by developing a total cost model that includes the cost associated with units waiting for service and the cost required to operate the service facility.

As many of the examples in this chapter show, the most obvious applications of waiting line models are situations in which customers arrive for service such as at a grocery checkout counter, bank, or restaurant. However, with a little creativity, waiting line models can be applied to many different situations such as telephone calls waiting for connections, mail orders waiting for processing, machines waiting for repairs, manufacturing jobs waiting to be processed, and money waiting to be spent or invested. The Management Science in Action, Improving Productivity at the New Haven Fire Department, describes an application in which a waiting line model helped improve emergency medical response time and also provided a significant savings in operating costs.

MANAGEMENT SCIENCE IN ACTION

IMPROVING PRODUCTIVITY AT THE NEW HAVEN FIRE DEPARTMENT*

The New Haven, Connecticut, Fire Department implemented a reorganization plan with cross-trained fire and medical personnel responding to both fire and medical emergencies. A waiting line model provided the basis for the reorganization by demonstrating that substantial improvements in emergency medical response time could be achieved with only a small reduction in fire protection. Annual savings were reported to be $1.4 million.

The model was based on Poisson arrivals and exponential service times for both fire and medical emergencies. It was used to estimate the average time that a person placing a call would have to wait for the appropriate emergency unit to arrive at the location. Waiting times were estimated by the model's prediction of the average travel time to reach each of the city's 28 census tracts.

The model was first applied to the original system of 16 fire units and 4 emergency medical units that operated independently. It was then applied to the proposed reorganization plan that involved cross-trained department personnel qualified to respond to both fire and medical emergencies. Results from the model demonstrated that average travel times could be reduced under the reorganization plan. Various facility location alternatives also were evaluated. When implemented, the reorganization plan reduced operating cost and improved public safety services.

*Based on A. J. Swersey, L. Goldring, and E. D. Geyer, "Improving Fire Department Productivity: Merging Fire and Emergency Medical Units in New Haven," *Interfaces* 23, no. 1 (January/February 1993): 109–129.

The complexity and diversity of waiting line systems found in practice often prevent an analyst from finding an existing waiting line model that fits the specific application being studied. Simulation, the topic discussed in Chapter 13, provides an approach to determining the operating characteristics of such waiting line systems.

GLOSSARY

Queue A waiting line.

Queueing theory The body of knowledge dealing with waiting lines.

Operating characteristics The performance measures for a waiting line including the probability that no units are in the system, the average number of units in the waiting line, the average waiting time, and so on.

Single-channel waiting line A waiting line with only one service facility.

Poisson probability distribution A probability distribution used to describe the arrival pattern for some waiting line models.

Exponential probability distribution A probability distribution used to describe the service time for some waiting line models.

First-come, first-served (FCFS) The queue discipline that serves waiting units on a first-come, first-served basis.

Transient period The start-up period for a waiting line, occurring before the waiting line reaches a normal or steady-state operation.

Steady-state operation The normal operation of the waiting line after it has gone through a start-up or transient period. The operating characteristics of waiting lines are computed for steady-state conditions.

Mean arrival rate The average number of customers or units arriving in a given period of time.

Mean service rate The average number of customers or units that can be served by one service facility in a given period of time.

Multiple-channel waiting line A waiting line with two or more parallel service facilities.

Blocked When arriving units cannot enter the waiting line because the system is full. Blocked units can occur when waiting lines are not allowed or when waiting lines have a finite capacity.

Infinite calling population The population of customers or units that may seek service has no specified upper limit.

Finite calling population The population of customers or units that may seek service has a fixed and finite value.

PROBLEMS

1. Willow Brook National Bank operates a drive-up teller window that allows customers to complete bank transactions without getting out of their cars. On weekday mornings, arrivals to the drive-up teller window occur at random, with a mean arrival rate of 24 customers per hour or 0.4 customer per minute.
   a. What is the mean or expected number of customers that will arrive in a five-minute period?

b. Assume that the Poisson probability distribution can be used to describe the arrival process. Use the mean arrival rate in part (a) and compute the probabilities that exactly 0, 1, 2, and 3 customers will arrive during a five-minute period.
c. Delays are expected if more than three customers arrive during any five-minute period. What is the probability that delays will occur?

2. In the Willow Brook National Bank waiting line system (see Problem 1), assume that the service times for the drive-up teller follow an exponential probability distribution with a mean service rate of 36 customers per hour or 0.6 customer per minute. Use the exponential probability distribution to answer the following questions.
   a. What is the probability the service time is one minute or less?
   b. What is the probability the service time is two minutes or less?
   c. What is the probability the service time is more than two minutes?

3. Use the single-channel drive-up bank teller operation referred to in Problems 1 and 2 to determine the following operating characteristics for the system.
   a. The probability that no customers are in the system
   b. The average number of customers waiting
   c. The average number of customers in the system
   d. The average time a customer spends waiting
   e. The average time a customer spends in the system
   f. The probability that arriving customers will have to wait for service

4. Use the single-channel drive-up bank teller operation referred to in Problems 1–3 to determine the probabilities of 0, 1, 2, and 3 customers in the system. What is the probability that more than three customers will be in the drive-up teller system at the same time?

5. The reference desk of a university library receives requests for assistance. Assume that a Poisson probability distribution with a mean rate of 10 requests per hour can be used to describe the arrival pattern and that service times follow an exponential probability distribution with a mean service rate of 12 requests per hour.
   a. What is the probability that no requests for assistance are in the system?
   b. What is the average number of requests that will be waiting for service?
   c. What is the average waiting time in minutes before service begins?
   d. What is the average time at the reference desk in minutes (waiting time plus service time)?
   e. What is the probability that a new arrival has to wait for service?

6. Movies Tonight is a typical video and DVD movie rental outlet for home viewing customers. During the weeknight evenings, customers arrive at Movies Tonight at the average rate of 1.25 customers per minute. The checkout clerk can serve an average of two customers per minute. Assume Poisson arrivals and exponential service times.
   a. What is the probability that no customers are in the system?
   b. What is the average number of customers waiting for service?
   c. What is the average time a customer waits for service to begin?
   d. What is the probability that an arriving customer will have to wait for service?
   e. Do the operating characteristics indicate that the one-clerk checkout system provides an acceptable level of service?

7. Speedy Oil provides a single-channel automobile oil change and lubrication service. New arrivals occur at the rate of 2.5 cars per hour and the mean service rate is 5 cars per hour. Assume that arrivals follow a Poisson probability distribution and that service times follow an exponential probability distribution.
   a. What is the average number of cars in the system?
   b. What is the average time that a car waits for the oil and lubrication service to begin?
   c. What is the average time a car spends in the system?
   d. What is the probability that an arrival has to wait for service?

8. For the Burger Dome single-channel waiting line in Section 12.2, assume that the arrival rate is increased to 1 customer per minute and that the mean service rate is increased to 1.25 customers per minute. Compute the following operating characteristics for the new system: P_0, L_q, L, W_q, W, and P_w. Does this system provide better or poorer service compared to the original system? Discuss any differences and the reason for these differences.

9. Marty's Barber Shop has one barber. Customers arrive at the rate of 2.2 customers per hour, and haircuts are given at the average rate of 5 per hour. Use the Poisson arrivals and exponential service times model to answer the following questions.
   a. What is the probability that no units are in the system?
   b. What is the probability that one customer is receiving a haircut and no one is waiting?
   c. What is the probability that one customer is receiving a haircut and one customer is waiting?
   d. What is the probability that one customer is receiving a haircut and two customers are waiting?
   e. What is the probability that more than two customers are waiting?
   f. What is the average time a customer waits for service?

10. Trosper Tire Company decided to hire a new mechanic to handle all tire changes for customers ordering a new set of tires. Two mechanics applied for the job. One mechanic has limited experience, can be hired for $14 per hour, and can service an average of three customers per hour. The other mechanic has several years of experience, can service an average of four customers per hour, but must be paid $20 per hour. Assume that customers arrive at the Trosper garage at the rate of two customers per hour.
   a. What are the waiting line operating characteristics using each mechanic, assuming Poisson arrivals and exponential service times?
   b. If the company assigns a customer waiting cost of $30 per hour, which mechanic provides the lower operating cost?

11. Agan Interior Design provides home and office decorating assistance to its customers. In normal operation, an average of 2.5 customers arrive each hour. One design consultant is available to answer customer questions and make product recommendations. The consultant averages 10 minutes with each customer.
   a. Compute the operating characteristics of the customer waiting line, assuming Poisson arrivals and exponential service times.
   b. Service goals dictate that an arriving customer should not wait for service more than an average of 5 minutes. Is this goal being met? If not, what action do you recommend?
   c. If the consultant can reduce the average time spent per customer to 8 minutes, what is the mean service rate? Will the service goal be met?

12. Pete's Market is a small local grocery store with only one checkout counter. Assume that shoppers arrive at the checkout lane according to a Poisson probability distribution, with a mean arrival rate of 15 customers per hour. The checkout service times follow an exponential probability distribution, with a mean service rate of 20 customers per hour.
   a. Compute the operating characteristics for this waiting line.
   b. If the manager's service goal is to limit the waiting time prior to beginning the checkout process to no more than five minutes, what recommendations would you provide regarding the current checkout system?

13. After reviewing the waiting line analysis of Problem 12, the manager of Pete's Market wants to consider one of the following alternatives for improving service. What alternative would you recommend? Justify your recommendation.
   a. Hire a second person to bag the groceries while the cash register operator is entering the cost data and collecting money from the customer. With this improved

single-channel operation, the mean service rate could be increased to 30 customers per hour.

b. Hire a second person to operate a second checkout counter. The two-channel operation would have a mean service rate of 20 customers per hour for each channel.

14. Ocala Software Systems operates a technical support center for its software customers. If customers have installation or use problems with Ocala software products, they may telephone the technical support center and obtain free consultation. Currently, Ocala operates its support center with one consultant. If the consultant is busy when a new customer call arrives, the customer hears a recorded message stating that all consultants are currently busy with other customers. The customer is then asked to hold and a consultant will provide assistance as soon as possible. The customer calls follow a Poisson probability distribution with a mean arrival rate of five calls per hour. On average, it takes 7.5 minutes for a consultant to answer a customer's questions. The service time follows an exponential probability distribution.
   a. What is the mean service rate in terms of customers per hour?
   b. What is the probability that no customers are in the system and the consultant is idle?
   c. What is the average number of customers waiting for a consultant?
   d. What is the average time a customer waits for a consultant?
   e. What is the probability that a customer will have to wait for a consultant?
   f. Ocala's customer service department recently received several letters from customers complaining about the difficulty in obtaining technical support. If Ocala's customer service guidelines state that no more than 35% of all customers should have to wait for technical support and that the average waiting time should be two minutes or less, does your waiting line analysis indicate that Ocala is or is not meeting its customer service guidelines? What action, if any, would you recommend?

15. To improve customer service, Ocala Software Systems (see Problem 14) wants to investigate the effect of using a second consultant at its technical support center. What effect would the additional consultant have on customer service? Would two technical consultants enable Ocala to meet its service guidelines with no more than 35% of all customers having to wait for technical support and an average customer waiting time of two minutes or less? Discuss.

16. The new Fore and Aft Marina is to be located on the Ohio River near Madison, Indiana. Assume that Fore and Aft decides to build a docking facility where one boat at a time can stop for gas and servicing. Assume that arrivals follow a Poisson probability distribution, with a mean of 5 boats per hour, and that service times follow an exponential probability distribution, with a mean of 10 boats per hour. Answer the following questions.
   a. What is the probability that no boats are in the system?
   b. What is the average number of boats that will be waiting for service?
   c. What is the average time a boat will spend waiting for service?
   d. What is the average time a boat will spend at the dock?
   e. If you were the manager of Fore and Aft Marina, would you be satisfied with the service level your system will be providing? Why or why not?

17. The manager of the Fore and Aft Marina in Problem 16 wants to investigate the possibility of enlarging the docking facility so that two boats can stop for gas and servicing simultaneously. Assume that the mean arrival rate is 5 boats per hour and that the mean service rate for each channel is 10 boats per hour.
   a. What is the probability that the boat dock will be idle?
   b. What is the average number of boats that will be waiting for service?
   c. What is the average time a boat will spend waiting for service?
   d. What is the average time a boat will spend at the dock?
   e. If you were the manager of Fore and Aft Marina, would you be satisfied with the service level your system will be providing? Why or why not?

18. Consider a two-channel waiting line with Poisson arrivals and exponential service times. The mean arrival rate is 14 units per hour, and the mean service rate is 10 units per hour for each channel.
    a. What is the probability that no units are in the system?
    b. What is the average number of units in the system?
    c. What is the average time a unit waits for service?
    d. What is the average time a unit is in the system?
    e. What is the probability of having to wait for service?
19. Refer to Problem 19. Assume that the system is expanded to a three-channel operation.
    a. Compute the operating characteristics for this waiting line system.
    b. If the service goal is to provide sufficient capacity so that no more than 25% of the customers have to wait for service, is the two- or three-channel system preferred?
20. A Florida coastal community experiences a population increase during the winter months with seasonal residents arriving from northern states and Canada. Staffing at a local post office is often in a state of change due to the relatively low volume of customers in the summer months and the relatively high volume of customers in the winter months. The mean service rate of a postal clerk is 0.75 customer per minute. The post office counter has a maximum of three work stations. The target maximum time a customer waits in the system is five minutes.
    a. For a particular Monday morning in November, the anticipated arrival rate is 1.2 customers per minute. What is the recommended staffing for this Monday morning? Show the operating characteristics of the waiting line.
    b. A new population growth study suggests that over the next two years the arrival rate at the postal office during the busy winter months can be expected to be 2.1 customers per minute. Use a waiting line analysis to make a recommendation to the post office manager.

21. Refer to the Agan Interior Design situation in Problem 11. Agan's management would like to evaluate two alternatives:
    - Use one consultant with an average service time of 8 minutes per customer.
    - Expand to two consultants, each of whom has an average service time of 10 minutes per customer.

    If the consultants are paid $16 per hour and the customer waiting time is valued at $25 per hour for waiting time prior to service, should Agan expand to the two-consultant system? Explain.
22. A fast-food franchise is considering operating a drive-up window food-service operation. Assume that customer arrivals follow a Poisson probability distribution, with a mean arrival rate of 24 cars per hour, and that service times follow an exponential probability distribution. Arriving customers place orders at an intercom station at the back of the parking lot and then drive to the service window to pay for and receive their orders. The following three service alternatives are being considered.
    - A single-channel operation in which one employee fills the order and takes the money from the customer. The average service time for this alternative is 2 minutes.
    - A single-channel operation in which one employee fills the order while a second employee takes the money from the customer. The average service time for this alternative is 1.25 minutes.
    - A two-channel operation with two service windows and two employees. The employee stationed at each window fills the order and takes the money for customers arriving at the window. The average service time for this alternative is 2 minutes for each channel.

    Answer the following questions and recommend an alternative design for the fast-food franchise.

a. What is the probability that no cars are in the system?
b. What is the average number of cars waiting for service?
c. What is the average number of cars in the system?
d. What is the average time a car waits for service?
e. What is the average time in the system?
f. What is the probability that an arriving car will have to wait for service?

23. The following cost information is available for the fast-food franchise in Problem 22.
- Customer waiting time is valued at $25 per hour to reflect the fact that waiting time is costly to the fast-food business.
- The cost of each employee is $6.50 per hour.
- To account for equipment and space, an additional cost of $20 per hour is attributable to each channel.

What is the lowest-cost design for the fast-food business?

24. Patients arrive at a dentist's office at a mean rate of 2.8 patients per hour. The dentist can treat patients at the mean rate of 3 patients per hour. A study of patient waiting times shows that, on average, a patient waits 30 minutes before seeing the dentist.
a. What are the mean arrival and treatment rates in terms of patients per minute?
b. What is the average number of patients in the waiting room?
c. If a patient arrives at 10:10 A.M., at what time is the patient expected to leave the office?

25. A study of the multiple-channel food-service operation at the Red Birds baseball park shows that the average time between the arrival of a customer at the food-service counter and his or her departure with a filled order is 10 minutes. During the game, customers arrive at the average rate of four per minute. The food-service operation requires an average of 2 minutes per customer order.
a. What is the mean service rate per channel in terms of customers per minute?
b. What is the average waiting time in the line prior to placing an order?
c. On average, how many customers are in the food-service system?

26. Manning Autos operates an automotive service counter. While completing the repair work, Manning mechanics arrive at the company's parts department counter at the mean rate of four per hour. The parts coordinator spends an average of 6 minutes with each mechanic, discussing the parts the mechanic needs and retrieving the parts from inventory.
a. Currently, Manning has one parts coordinator. On average, each mechanic waits 4 minutes before the parts coordinator is available to answer questions or retrieve parts from inventory. Find L_q, W, and L for this single-channel parts operation.
b. A trial period with a second parts coordinator showed that, on average, each mechanic waited only 1 minute before a parts coordinator was available. Find L_q, W, and L for this two-channel parts operation.
c. If the cost of each mechanic is $20 per hour and the cost of each parts coordinator is $12 per hour, is the one-channel or the two-channel system more economical?

27. Gubser Welding, Inc., operates a welding service for construction and automotive repair jobs. Assume that the arrival of jobs at the company's office can be described by a Poisson probability distribution with a mean arrival rate of two jobs per 8-hour day. The time required to complete the jobs follows a normal probability distribution with a mean time of 3.2 hours and a standard deviation of 2 hours. Answer the following questions, assuming that Gubser uses one welder to complete all jobs.
a. What is the mean arrival rate in jobs per hour?
b. What is the mean service rate in jobs per hour?
c. What is the average number of jobs waiting for service?
d. What is the average time a job waits before the welder can begin working on it?

e. What is the average number of hours between when a job is received and when it is completed?

f. What percentage of the time is Gubser's welder busy?

28. Jobs arrive randomly at a particular assembly plant; assume that the mean arrival rate is five jobs per hour. Service times (in minutes per job) do not follow the exponential probability distribution. Two proposed designs for the plant's assembly operation are shown.

	Service Time	
Design	**Mean**	**Standard Deviation**
A	6.0	3.0
B	6.25	0.6

a. What is the mean service rate in jobs per hour for each design?

b. For the mean service rates in part (a), what design appears to provide the best or fastest service rate?

c. What are the standard deviations of the service times in hours?

d. Use the *M/G/*1 model to compute the operating characteristics for each design.

e. Which design provides the best operating characteristics? Why?

29. The Robotics Manufacturing Company operates an equipment repair business where emergency jobs arrive randomly at the rate of three jobs per 8-hour day. The company's repair facility is a single-channel system operated by a repair technician. The service time varies with a mean repair time of 2 hours and a standard deviation of 1.5 hours. The company's cost of the repair operation is $28 per hour. In the economic analysis of the waiting line system, Robotics uses $35 per hour cost for customers waiting during the repair process.

a. What are the arrival rate and service rate in jobs per hour?

b. Show the operating characteristics including the total cost per hour.

c. The company is considering purchasing a computer-based equipment repair system that would enable a constant repair time of 2 hours. For practical purposes, the standard deviation is 0. Because of the computer-based system, the company's cost of the new operation would be $32 per hour. The firm's director of operations said no to the request for the new system because the hourly cost is $4 higher and the mean repair time is the same. Do you agree? What effect will the new system have on the waiting line characteristics of the repair service?

d. Does paying for the computer-based system to reduce the variation in service time make economic sense? How much will the new system save the company during a 40-hour work week?

30. A large insurance company maintains a central computing system that contains a variety of information about customer accounts. Insurance agents in a six-state area use telephone lines to access the customer information database. Currently, the company's central computer system allows three users to access the central computer simultaneously. Agents who attempt to use the system when it is full are denied access; no waiting is allowed. Management realizes that with its expanding business, more requests will be made to the central information system. Being denied access to the system is inefficient as well as annoying for agents. Access requests follow a Poisson probability distribution, with a mean of 42 calls per hour. The mean service rate per line is 20 calls per hour.

a. What is the probability that 0, 1, 2, and 3 access lines will be in use?

b. What is the probability that an agent will be denied access to the system?

c. What is the average number of access lines in use?

d. In planning for the future, management wants to be able to handle $\lambda = 50$ calls per hour; in addition, the probability that an agent will be denied access to the system should be no greater than the value computed in part (b). How many access lines should this system have?

31. Mid-West Publishing Company publishes college textbooks. The company operates an 800 telephone number whereby potential adopters can ask questions about forthcoming texts, request examination copies of texts, and place orders. Currently, two extension lines are used, with two representatives handling the telephone inquiries. Calls occurring when both extension lines are being used receive a busy signal; no waiting is allowed. Each representative can accommodate an average of 12 calls per hour. The mean arrival rate is 20 calls per hour.

a. How many extension lines should be used if the company wants to handle 90% of the calls immediately?

b. What is the average number of extension lines that will be busy if your recommendation in part (a) is used?

c. What percentage of calls receive a busy signal for the current telephone system with two extension lines?

32. City Cab, Inc., uses two dispatchers to handle requests for service and to dispatch the cabs. The telephone calls that are made to City Cab use a common telephone number. When both dispatchers are busy, the caller hears a busy signal; no waiting is allowed. Callers who receive a busy signal can call back later or call another cab service. Assume that the arrival of calls follows a Poisson probability distribution, with a mean of 40 calls per hour, and that each dispatcher can handle a mean of 30 calls per hour.

a. What percentage of time are both dispatchers idle?

b. What percentage of time are both dispatchers busy?

c. What is the probability callers will receive a busy signal if two, three, or four dispatchers are used?

d. If management wants no more than 12% of the callers to receive a busy signal, how many dispatchers should be used?

33. Kolkmeyer Manufacturing Company (see Section 12.9) is considering adding two machines to its manufacturing operation. This addition will bring the number of machines to eight. The president of Kolkmeyer asked for a study of the need to add a second employee to the repair operation. The mean arrival rate is 0.05 machine per hour for each machine, and the mean service rate for each individual assigned to the repair operation is 0.50 machine per hour.

a. Compute the operating characteristics if the company retains the single-employee repair operation.

b. Compute the operating characteristics if a second employee is added to the machine repair operation.

c. Each employee is paid \$20 per hour. Machine downtime is valued at \$80 per hour. From an economic point of view, should one or two employees handle the machine repair operation? Explain.

34. Five administrative assistants use an office copier. The average time between arrivals for each assistant is 40 minutes, which is equivalent to a mean arrival rate of $1/40 = 0.025$ arrival per minute. The mean time each assistant spends at the copier is 5 minutes, which is equivalent to a mean service rate of $\frac{1}{5} = 0.20$ user per minute. Use the *M/M/*1 model with a finite calling population to determine the following:

a. The probability that the copier is idle

b. The average number of administrative assistants in the waiting line

c. The average number of administrative assistants at the copier

d. The average time an assistant spends waiting for the copier
e. The average time an assistant spends at the copier
f. During an 8-hour day, how many minutes does an assistant spend at the copier? How much of this time is waiting time?
g. Should management consider purchasing a second copier? Explain.

35. Schips Department Store operates a fleet of 10 trucks. The trucks arrive at random times throughout the day at the store's truck dock to be loaded with new deliveries or to have incoming shipments from the regional warehouse unloaded. Each truck returns to the truck dock for service two times per 8-hour day. Thus, the mean arrival rate per truck is 0.25 trucks per hour. The mean service rate is 4 trucks per hour. Using the Poisson arrivals and exponential service times model with a finite calling population of 10 trucks, determine the following operating characteristics:
    a. The probability no trucks are at the truck dock
    b. The average number of trucks waiting for loading/unloading
    c. The average number of trucks in the truck dock area
    d. The average waiting time before loading/unloading begins
    e. The average waiting time in the system
    f. What is the hourly cost of operation if the cost is $50 per hour for each truck and $30 per hour for the truck dock?
    g. Consider a two-channel truck dock operation where the second channel could be operated for an additional $30 per hour. How much would the average number of trucks waiting for loading/unloading have to be reduced to make the two-channel truck dock economically feasible?
    h. Should the company consider expanding to the two-channel truck dock? Explain.

Case Problem 1 REGIONAL AIRLINES

Regional Airlines is establishing a new telephone system for handling flight reservations. During the 10:00 A.M. to 11:00 A.M. time period, calls to the reservation agent occur randomly at an average of one call every 3.75 minutes. Historical service time data show that a reservation agent spends an average of 3 minutes with each customer. The waiting line model assumptions of Poisson arrivals and exponential service times appear reasonable for the telephone reservation system.

Regional Airlines' management believes that offering an efficient telephone reservation system is an important part of establishing an image as a service-oriented airline. If the system is properly implemented, Regional Airlines will establish good customer relations, which in the long run will increase business. However, if the telephone reservation system is frequently overloaded and customers have difficulty contacting an agent, a negative customer reaction may lead to an eventual loss of business. The cost of a ticket reservation agent is $20 per hour. Thus, management wants to provide good service, but it does not want to incur the cost of overstaffing the telephone reservation operation by using more agents than necessary.

At a planning meeting, Regional's management team agreed that an acceptable customer service goal is to answer at least 85 percent of the incoming calls immediately. During the planning meeting, Regional's vice president of administration pointed out that the data show that the average service rate for an agent is faster than the average arrival rate of the telephone calls. The vice president's conclusion was that personnel costs could be minimized by using one agent and that the single agent should be able to handle the telephone reservations and still have some idle time. The vice president of marketing restated the importance of customer service and expressed support for at least two reservation agents.

The current telephone reservation system design does not allow callers to wait. Callers who attempt to reach a reservation agent when all agents are occupied receive a busy signal and are blocked from the system. A representative from the telephone company suggested that Regional Airlines consider an expanded system that accommodates waiting. In the expanded system, when a customer calls and all agents are busy, a recorded message tells the customer that the call is being held in the order received and that an agent will be available shortly. The customer can stay on the line and listen to background music while waiting for an agent. Regional's management will need more information before switching to the expanded system.

Managerial Report

Prepare a managerial report for Regional Airlines analyzing the telephone reservation system. Evaluate both the system that does not allow waiting and the expanded system that allows waiting. Include the following information in your report.

1. A detailed analysis of the operating characteristics of the reservation system with one agent as proposed by the vice president of administration. What is your recommendation concerning a single-agent system?
2. A detailed analysis of the operating characteristics of the reservation system based on your recommendation regarding the number of agents Regional should use.
3. What appear to be the advantages or disadvantages of the expanded system? Discuss the number of waiting callers the expanded system would need to accommodate.
4. The telephone arrival data presented are for the 10:00 A.M. to 11:00 A.M. time period; however, the arrival rate of incoming calls is expected to change from hour to hour. Describe how your waiting line analysis could be used to develop a ticket agent staffing plan that would enable the company to provide different levels of staffing for the ticket reservation system at different times during the day. Indicate the information that you would need to develop this staffing plan.

Case Problem 2 OFFICE EQUIPMENT, INC.

Office Equipment, Inc. (OEI), leases automatic mailing machines to business customers in Fort Wayne, Indiana. The company built its success on a reputation of providing timely maintenance and repair service. Each OEI service contract states that a service technician will arrive at a customer's business site within an average of three hours from the time that the customer notifies OEI of an equipment problem.

Currently, OEI has 10 customers with service contracts. One service technician is responsible for handling all service calls. A statistical analysis of historical service records indicates that a customer requests a service call at an average rate of one call per 50 hours of operation. If the service technician is available when a customer calls for service, it takes the technician an average of 1 hour of travel time to reach the customer's office and an average of 1.5 hours to complete the repair service. However, if the service technician is busy with another customer when a new customer calls for service, the technician completes the current service call and any other waiting service calls before responding to the new service call. In such cases, once the technician is free from all existing service commitments, the technician takes an average of 1 hour of travel time to reach the new customer's office and an average of 1.5 hours to complete the repair service. The cost of the service technician is $80 per hour. The downtime cost (wait time and service time) for customers is $100 per hour.

OEI is planning to expand its business. Within one year, OEI projects that it will have 20 customers, and within two years, OEI projects that it will have 30 customers. Although OEI is satisfied that one service technician can handle the 10 existing customers, management is concerned about the ability of one technician to meet the average three-hour service call guarantee when the OEI customer base expands. In a recent planning meeting, the marketing manager made a proposal to add a second service technician when OEI reaches 20 customers and to add a third service technician when OEI reaches 30 customers. Before making a final decision, management would like an analysis of OEI service capabilities. OEI is particularly interested in meeting the average three-hour waiting time guarantee at the lowest possible total cost.

Managerial Report

Develop a managerial report summarizing your analysis of the OEI service capabilities. Make recommendations regarding the number of technicians to be used when OEI reaches 20 customers and when OEI reaches 30 customers. Include a discussion of the following in your report.

1. What is the mean arrival rate for each customer per hour?
2. What is the mean service rate in terms of the number of customers per hour? Note that the average travel time of 1 hour becomes part of the service time because the time that the service technician is busy handling a service call includes the travel time plus the time required to complete the repair.
3. Waiting line models generally assume that the arriving customers are in the same location as the service facility. Discuss the OEI situation in light of the fact that a service technician travels an average of 1 hour to reach each customer. How should the travel time and the waiting time predicted by the waiting line model be combined to determine the total customer waiting time?
4. OEI is satisfied that one service technician can handle the 10 existing customers. Use a waiting line model to determine the following information:
   - Probability that no customers are in the system
   - Average number of customers in the waiting line
   - Average number of customers in the system
   - Average time a customer waits until the service technician arrives
   - Average time a customer waits until the machine is back in operation
   - Probability that a customer will have to wait more than one hour for the service technician to arrive
   - The number of hours a week the technician is not making service calls
   - The total cost per hour for the service operation

   Do you agree with OEI management that one technician can meet the average three-hour service call guarantee? Explain.
5. What is your recommendation for the number of service technicians to hire when OEI expands to 20 customers? Use the information that you developed in part (4) to justify your answer.
6. What is your recommendation for the number of service technicians to hire when OEI expands to 30 customers? Use the information that you developed in part (4) to justify your answer.
7. What are the annual savings of your recommendation in part (6) compared to the planning committee's proposal that 30 customers will require three service technicians? Assume 250 days of operation per year.

CHAPTER 13

Simulation

CONTENTS

Simulation is one of the most widely used quantitative approaches to decision making. It is a method for learning about a real system by experimenting with a model that represents the system. The simulation model contains the mathematical expressions and logical relationships that describe how to compute the value of the outputs given the values of the inputs. Any simulation model has two inputs: controllable inputs and probabilistic inputs. Figure 13.1 shows a conceptual diagram of a simulation model.

In conducting a **simulation experiment,** an analyst selects the value, or values, for the **controllable inputs.** Then values for the **probabilistic inputs** are randomly generated. The simulation model uses the values of the controllable inputs and the values of the probabilistic inputs to compute the value, or values, of the output. By conducting a series of experiments using a variety of values for the controllable inputs, the analyst learns how values of the controllable inputs affect or change the output of the simulation model. After reviewing the simulation results, the analyst is often able to make decision recommendations for the controllable inputs that will provide the desired output for the real system.

Simulation has been successfully applied in a variety of applications. The following examples are typical.

1. *New Product Development* The objective of this simulation is to determine the probability that a new product will be profitable. A model is developed relating profit (the output measure) to various probabilistic inputs such as demand, parts cost, and labor cost. The only controllable input is whether to introduce the product. A variety of possible values will be generated for the probabilistic inputs, and the resulting profit will be computed. We develop a simulation model for this type of application in Section 13.1.
2. *Airline Overbooking* The objective of this simulation is to determine the number of reservations an airline should accept for a particular flight. A simulation model is developed relating profit for the flight to a probabilistic input, the number of passengers with a reservation who show up and use their reservation, and a controllable input, the number of reservations accepted for the flight. For each selected value for the controllable input, a variety of possible values will be generated for the number of passengers who show up, and the resulting profit can be computed. Similar simulation models are applicable for hotel and car rental reservation systems.
3. *Inventory Policy* The objective of this simulation is to choose an inventory policy that will provide good customer service at a reasonable cost. A model is developed relating two output measures, total inventory cost and the service level, to probabilistic inputs, such as product demand and delivery lead time from vendors, and controllable inputs, such as the order quantity and the reorder point. For each setting of the controllable inputs, a variety of possible values would be generated for the probabilistic inputs, and the resulting cost and service levels would be computed.

FIGURE 13.1 DIAGRAM OF A SIMULATION MODEL

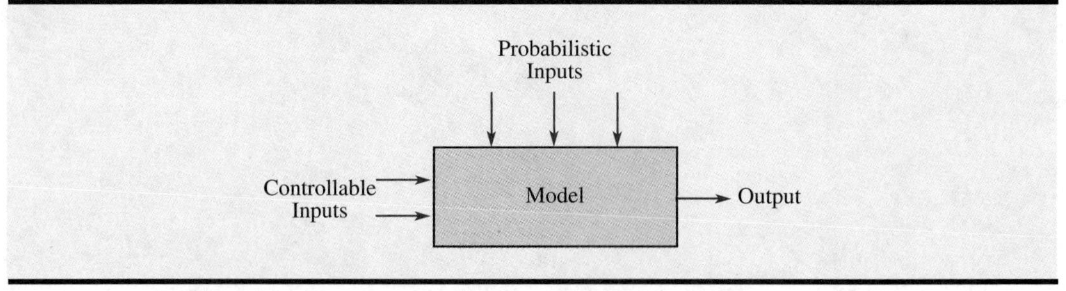

4. *Traffic Flow* The objective of this simulation is to determine the effect of installing a left turn signal on the flow of traffic through a busy intersection. A model is developed relating waiting time for vehicles to get through the intersection to probabilistic inputs such as the number of vehicle arrivals and the fraction that want to make a left turn, and controllable inputs such as the length of time the left turn signal is on. For each setting of the controllable inputs, values would be generated for the probabilistic inputs, and the resulting vehicle waiting times would be computed.
5. *Waiting Lines* The objective of this simulation is to determine the waiting times for customers at a bank's automated teller machine (ATM). A model is developed relating customer waiting times to probabilistic inputs such as customer arrivals and service times, and a controllable input, the number of ATM machines installed. For each value of the controllable input (the number of ATM machines), a variety of values would be generated for the probabilistic inputs and the customer waiting times would be computed. The Management Science in Action, Call Center Design, describes how simulation of a waiting line system at a call center helped the company balance the service to its customers with the cost of agents providing the service.

Simulation is not an optimization technique. It is a method that can be used to describe or predict how a system will operate given certain choices for the controllable inputs and randomly generated values for the probabilistic inputs. Management scientists often use

MANAGEMENT SCIENCE IN ACTION

CALL CENTER DESIGN*

A call center is a place where large volumes of calls are made to or received from current or potential customers. More than 60,000 call centers operate in the United States. Saltzman and Mehrotra describe how a simulation model helped make a strategic change in the design of the technical support call center for a major software company. The application used a waiting line simulation model to balance the service to customers calling for assistance with the cost of agents providing the service.

Historically, the software company provided free phone-in technical support, but over time service requests grew to the point where 80% of the callers were waiting between 5 and 10 minutes and abandonment rates were too high. On some days 40% of the callers hung up before receiving service. This service level was unacceptable. As a result, management considered instituting a Rapid Program in which customers would pay a fee for service, but would be guaranteed to receive service within one minute, or the service would be free. Nonpaying customers would continue receiving service but without a guarantee of short service times.

A simulation model was developed to help understand the impact of this new program on the waiting line characteristics of the call center. Data available were used to develop the arrival distribution, the service time distribution, and the probability distribution for abandonment. The key design variables considered were the number of agents (channels) and the percentage of callers subscribing to the Rapid Program. The model was developed using the Arena simulation package.

The simulation results helped the company decide to go ahead with the Rapid Program. Under most of the scenarios considered, the simulation model showed that 95% of the callers in the Rapid Program would receive service within one minute and that free service to the remaining customers could be maintained within acceptable limits. Within nine months, 10% of the software company's customers subscribed to the Rapid Program, generating $2 million in incremental revenue. The company viewed the simulation model as a vehicle for mitigating risk. The model helped evaluate the likely impact of the Rapid Program without experimenting with actual customers.

*Based on Robert M. Saltzman and Vijay Mehrotra, "A Call Center Uses Simulation to Drive Strategic Change," *Interfaces* (May/June 2001): 87–101.

simulation to determine values for the controllable inputs that are likely to lead to desirable system outputs. In this sense, simulation can be an effective tool in designing a system to provide good performance.

In this chapter we begin by showing how simulation can be used to study the financial risks associated with the development of a new product. We continue with illustrations showing how simulation can be used to establish an effective inventory policy and how simulation can be used to design waiting line systems. Other issues, such as verifying the simulation program, validating the model, and selecting a simulation software package, are discussed in Section 13.4.

13.1 RISK ANALYSIS

Risk analysis is the process of predicting the outcome of a decision in the face of uncertainty. In this section, we describe a problem that involves considerable uncertainty: the development of a new product. We first show how risk analysis can be conducted without using simulation; then, we show how a more comprehensive risk analysis can be conducted with the aid of simulation.

PortaCom Project

PortaCom manufactures personal computers and related equipment. PortaCom's product design group developed a prototype for a new high-quality portable printer. The new printer features an innovative design and has the potential to capture a significant share of the portable printer market. Preliminary marketing and financial analyses provided the following selling price, first-year administrative cost, and first-year advertising cost.

$$\begin{aligned} \text{Selling price} &= \$249 \text{ per unit} \\ \text{Administrative cost} &= \$400{,}000 \\ \text{Advertising cost} &= \$600{,}000 \end{aligned}$$

In the simulation model for the PortaCom problem, the preceding values are constants and are referred to as **parameters** of the model.

The cost of direct labor, the cost of parts, and the first-year demand for the printer are not known with certainty and are considered probabilistic inputs. At this stage of the planning process, PortaCom's best estimates of these inputs are $45 per unit for the direct labor cost, $90 per unit for the parts cost, and 15,000 units for the first-year demand. PortaCom would like an analysis of the first-year profit potential for the printer. Because of PortaCom's tight cash flow situation, management is particularly concerned about the potential for a loss.

What-If Analysis

One approach to risk analysis is called **what-if analysis.** A what-if analysis involves generating values for the probabilistic inputs (direct labor cost, parts cost, and first-year demand) and computing the resulting value for the output (profit). With a selling price of $249 per unit and administrative plus advertising costs equal to $400,000 + $600,000 = $1,000,000, the PortaCom profit model is

$$\text{Profit} = (\$249 - \text{Direct labor cost per unit} - \text{Parts cost per unit})(\text{Demand}) - \$1{,}000{,}000$$

Letting

$$c_1 = \text{direct labor cost per unit}$$
$$c_2 = \text{parts cost per unit}$$
$$x = \text{first-year demand}$$

the profit model for the first year can be written as follows:

$$\text{Profit} = (249 - c_1 - c_2)x - 1{,}000{,}000 \tag{13.1}$$

The PortaCom profit model can be depicted as shown in Figure 13.2.

Recall that PortaCom's best estimates of the direct labor cost per unit, the parts cost per unit, and first-year demand are \$45, \$90, and 15,000 units, respectively. These values constitute the **base-case scenario** for PortaCom. Substituting these values into equation (13.1) yields the following profit projection:

$$\text{Profit} = (249 - 45 - 90)(15{,}000) - 1{,}000{,}000 = 710{,}000$$

Thus, the base-case scenario leads to an anticipated profit of \$710,000.

In risk analysis we are concerned with both the probability of a loss and the magnitude of a loss. Although the base-case scenario looks appealing, PortaCom might be interested in what happens if the estimates of the direct labor cost per unit, parts cost per unit, and first-year demand do not turn out to be as expected under the base-case scenario. For instance, suppose that PortaCom believes that direct labor costs could range from \$43 to \$47 per unit, parts cost could range from \$80 to \$100 per unit, and first-year demand could range from 1500 to 28,500 units. Using these ranges, what-if analysis can be used to evaluate a **worst-case scenario** and a **best-case scenario.**

The worst-case value for the direct labor cost is \$47 (the highest value), the worst-case value for the parts cost is \$100 (the highest value), and the worst-case value for demand is 1500 units (the lowest value). Thus, in the worst-case scenario, $c_1 = 47$, $c_2 = 100$, and $x = 1500$. Substituting these values into equation (13.1) leads to the following profit projection:

$$\text{Profit} = (249 - 47 - 100)(1500) - 1{,}000{,}000 = -847{,}000$$

So, the worst-case scenario leads to a projected loss of \$847,000.

FIGURE 13.2 PORTACOM PROFIT MODEL

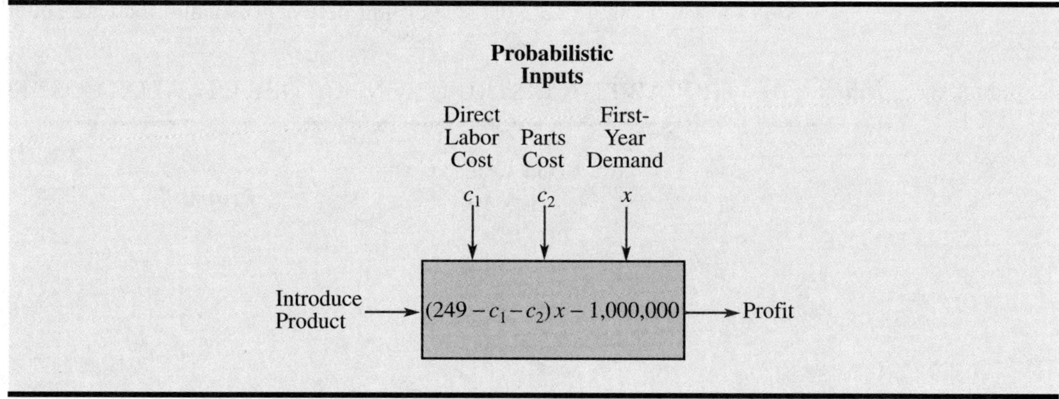

The best-case value for the direct labor cost is $43 (the lowest value), the best-case value for the parts cost is $80 (the lowest value), and the best-case value for demand is 28,500 units (the highest value). Substituting these values into equation (13.1) leads to the following profit projection:

Problem 2 will give you practice using what-if analysis.

$$\text{Profit} = (249 - 43 - 80)(28{,}500) - 1{,}000{,}000 = 2{,}591{,}000$$

So, the best-case scenario leads to a projected profit of $2,591,000.

At this point the what-if analysis provides the conclusion that profits can range from a loss of $847,000 to a profit of $2,591,000 with a base-case scenario value of $710,000. Although the base-case profit of $710,000 is possible, the what-if analysis indicates that either a substantial loss or a substantial profit is possible. Other scenarios that PortaCom might want to consider can also be evaluated. However, the difficulty with what-if analysis is that it does not indicate the likelihood of the various profit or loss values. In particular, we do not know anything about the *probability* of a loss.

Simulation

Using simulation to perform risk analysis for the PortaCom problem is like playing out many what-if scenarios by randomly generating values for the probabilistic inputs. The advantage of simulation is that it allows us to assess the probability of a profit and the probability of a loss.

Using the what-if approach to risk analysis, we selected values for the probabilistic inputs [direct labor cost per unit (c_1), parts cost per unit (c_2), and first-year demand (x)], and then computed the resulting profit. Applying simulation to the PortaCom problem requires generating values for the probabilistic inputs that are representative of what we might observe in practice. To generate such values, we must know the probability distribution for each probabilistic input. Further analysis by PortaCom led to the following probability distributions for the direct labor cost per unit, the parts cost per unit, and first-year demand:

One advantage of simulation is the ability to use probability distributions that are unique to the system being studied.

Direct Labor Cost PortaCom believes that the direct labor cost will range from $43 to $47 per unit and is described by the discrete probability distribution shown in Table 13.1. Thus, we see a 0.1 probability that the direct labor cost will be $43 per unit, a 0.2 probability that the direct labor cost will be $44 per unit, and so on. The highest probability of 0.4 is associated with a direct labor cost of $45 per unit.

Parts Cost This cost depends upon the general economy, the overall demand for parts, and the pricing policy of PortaCom's parts suppliers. PortaCom believes that the parts cost will range from $80 to $100 per unit and is described by the uniform probability distribution shown in Figure 13.3. Costs per unit between $80 and $100 are equally likely.

TABLE 13.1 PROBABILITY DISTRIBUTION FOR DIRECT LABOR COST PER UNIT

Direct Labor Cost per Unit	Probability
$43	0.1
$44	0.2
$45	0.4
$46	0.2
$47	0.1

FIGURE 13.3 UNIFORM PROBABILITY DISTRIBUTION FOR THE PARTS COST PER UNIT

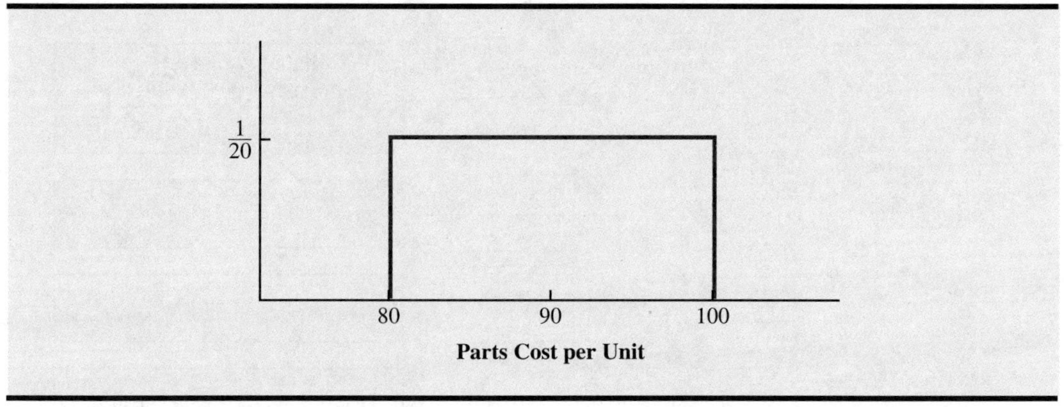

First-Year Demand PortaCom believes that first-year demand is described by the normal probability distribution shown in Figure 13.4. The mean or expected value of first-year demand is 15,000 units. The standard deviation of 4500 units describes the variability in the first-year demand.

A flowchart provides a graphical representation that helps describe the logic of the simulation model.

To simulate the PortaCom problem, we must generate values for the three probabilistic inputs and compute the resulting profit. Then, we generate another set of values for the probabilistic inputs, compute a second value for profit, and so on. We continue this process until we are satisfied that enough trials have been conducted to describe the probability distribution for profit. This process of generating probabilistic inputs and computing the value of the output is called *simulation*. The sequence of logical and mathematical operations required to conduct a simulation can be depicted with a flowchart. A flowchart for the PortaCom simulation is shown in Figure 13.5.

Following the logic described by the flowchart we see that the model parameters—selling price, administrative cost, and advertising cost—are \$249, \$400,000, and \$600,000, respectively. These values will remain fixed throughout the simulation.

The next three blocks depict the generation of values for the probabilistic inputs. First, a value for the direct labor cost (c_1) is generated. Then a value for the parts cost (c_2) is

FIGURE 13.4 NORMAL PROBABILITY DISTRIBUTION OF FIRST-YEAR DEMAND

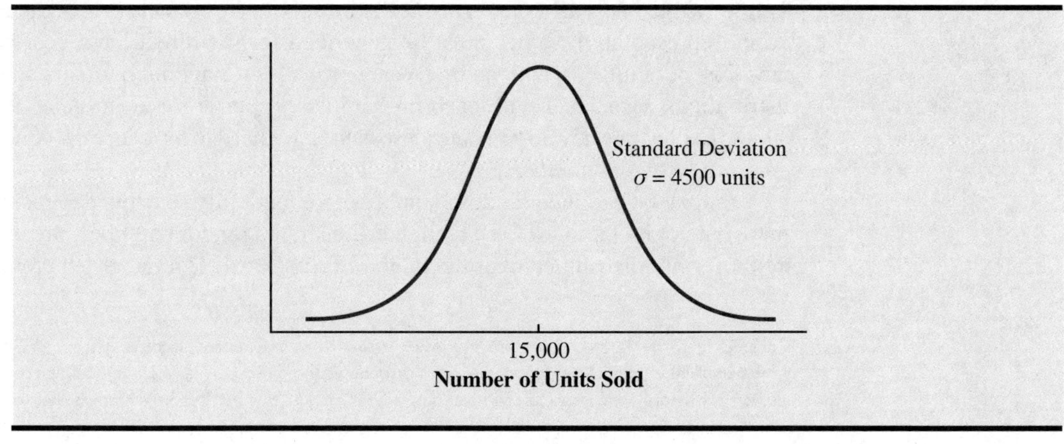

FIGURE 13.5 FLOWCHART FOR THE PORTACOM SIMULATION

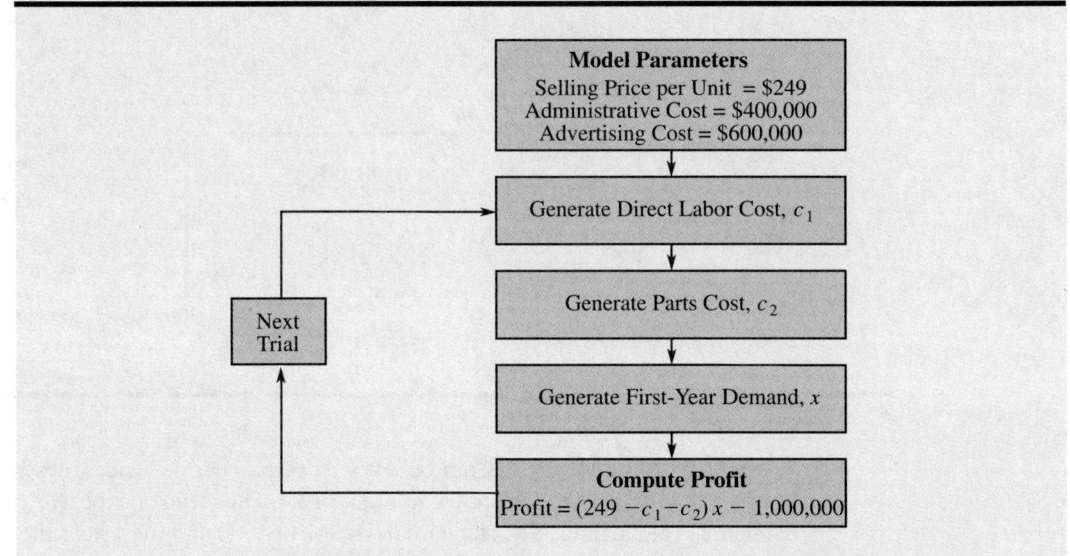

generated, followed by a value for the first-year demand (x). These probabilistic input values are combined using the profit model given by equation (13.1).

$$\text{Profit} = (249 - c_1 - c_2)x - 1{,}000{,}000$$

The computation of profit completes one trial of the simulation. We then return to the block where we generated the direct labor cost and begin another trial. This process is repeated until a satisfactory number of trials has been generated.

At the end of the simulation, output measures of interest can be developed. For example, we will be interested in computing the average profit and the probability of a loss. For the output measures to be meaningful, the values of the probabilistic inputs must be representative of what is likely to happen when the PortaCom printer is introduced into the market. An essential part of the simulation procedure is the ability to generate representative values for the probabilistic inputs. We now discuss how to generate these values.

Random Numbers and Generating Probabilistic Input Values In the PortaCom simulation, representative values must be generated for the direct labor cost per unit (c_1), the parts cost per unit (c_2), and the first-year demand (x). Random numbers and the probability distributions associated with each probabilistic input are used to generate representative values. To illustrate how to generate these values, we need to introduce the concept of *computer-generated random numbers.*

Computer-generated random numbers[1] are randomly selected decimal numbers from 0 up to, but not including, 1. The computer-generated random numbers are equally likely and are uniformly distributed over the interval from 0 to 1. Computer-generated random num-

[1]Computer-generated random numbers are called *pseudorandom numbers.* Because they are generated through the use of mathematical formulas, they are not technically random. The difference between random numbers and pseudorandom numbers is primarily philosophical, and we use the term *random numbers* regardless of whether they are generated by a computer.

Because random numbers are equally likely, quantitative analysts can assign ranges of random numbers to corresponding values of probabilistic inputs so that the probability of any input value to the simulation model is identical to the probability of its occurrence in the real system.

bers can be obtained using built-in functions available in computer simulation packages and spreadsheets. For instance, placing =RAND() in a cell of an Excel worksheet will result in a random number between 0 and 1 being placed into that cell.

Table 13.2 contains 500 random numbers generated using Excel. These numbers can be viewed as a random sample of 500 values from a uniform probability distribution over the interval from 0 to 1. Let us show how random numbers can be used to generate values for the PortaCom probability distributions. We begin by showing how to generate a value for the direct labor cost per unit. The approach described is applicable for generating values from any discrete probability distribution.

An interval of random numbers is assigned to each possible value of the direct labor cost in such a fashion that the probability of generating a random number in the interval is equal to the probability of the corresponding direct labor cost. Table 13.3 shows how this process is done. The interval of random numbers 0.0 but less than 0.1 is associated with a direct labor cost of $43, the interval of random numbers 0.1 but less than 0.3 is associated with a direct labor cost of $44, and so on. With this assignment of random number intervals to the possible values of the direct labor cost, the probability of generating a random number in any interval is equal to the probability of obtaining the corresponding value for the direct labor cost. Thus, to select a value for the direct labor cost, we generate a random number between 0 and 1. If the random number is 0.0 but less than 0.1, we set the direct labor cost equal to $43. If the random number is 0.1 but less than 0.3, we set the direct labor cost equal to $44, and so on.

Try Problem 5 for an opportunity to establish intervals of random numbers and simulate demand from a discrete probability distribution.

Each trial of the simulation requires a value for the direct labor cost. Suppose that on the first trial the random number is 0.9109. From Table 13.3, the simulated value for the direct labor cost is $47 per unit. Suppose that on the second trial the random number is 0.2841. From Table 13.3, the simulated value for the direct labor cost is $44 per unit. Table 13.4 shows the results obtained for the first 10 simulation trials.

Each trial in the simulation requires a value of the direct labor cost, parts cost, and first-year demand. Let us now turn to the issue of generating values for the parts cost. The probability distribution for the parts cost per unit is the uniform distribution shown in Figure 13.3. Because this random variable has a different probability distribution than direct labor cost, we use random numbers in a slightly different way to generate values for parts cost. With a uniform probability distribution, the following relationship between the random number and the associated value of the parts cost is used.

$$\text{Parts cost} = a + r(b - a) \tag{13.2}$$

where

$$\begin{aligned} r &= \text{random number between 0 and 1} \\ a &= \text{smallest value for parts cost} \\ b &= \text{largest value for parts cost} \end{aligned}$$

For PortaCom, the smallest value for the parts cost is $80, and the largest value is $100. Applying equation (13.2) with $a = 80$ and $b = 100$ leads to the following formula for generating the parts cost given a random number, r.

$$\text{Parts cost} = 80 + r(100 - 80) = 80 + r20 \tag{13.3}$$

TABLE 13.2 500 COMPUTER-GENERATED RANDOM NUMBERS

0.6953	0.5247	0.1368	0.9850	0.7467	0.3813	0.5827	0.7893	0.7169	0.8166
0.0082	0.9925	0.6874	0.2122	0.6885	0.2159	0.4299	0.3467	0.2186	0.1033
0.6799	0.1241	0.3056	0.5590	0.0423	0.6515	0.2750	0.8156	0.2871	0.4680
0.8898	0.1514	0.1826	0.0004	0.5259	0.2425	0.8421	0.9248	0.9155	0.9518
0.6515	0.5027	0.9290	0.5177	0.3134	0.9177	0.2605	0.6668	0.1167	0.7870
0.3976	0.7790	0.0035	0.0064	0.0441	0.3437	0.1248	0.5442	0.9800	0.1857
0.0642	0.4086	0.6078	0.2044	0.0484	0.4691	0.7058	0.8552	0.5029	0.3288
0.0377	0.5250	0.7774	0.2390	0.9121	0.5345	0.8178	0.8443	0.4154	0.2526
0.5739	0.5181	0.0234	0.7305	0.0376	0.5169	0.5679	0.5495	0.7872	0.5321
0.5827	0.0341	0.7482	0.6351	0.9146	0.4700	0.7869	0.1337	0.0702	0.4219
0.0508	0.7905	0.2932	0.4971	0.0225	0.4466	0.5118	0.1200	0.0200	0.5445
0.4757	0.1399	0.5668	0.9569	0.7255	0.4650	0.4084	0.3701	0.9446	0.8064
0.6805	0.9931	0.4166	0.1091	0.7730	0.0691	0.9411	0.3468	0.0014	0.7379
0.2603	0.7507	0.6414	0.9907	0.2699	0.4571	0.9254	0.2371	0.8664	0.9553
0.8143	0.7625	0.1708	0.1900	0.2781	0.2830	0.6877	0.0488	0.8635	0.3155
0.5681	0.7854	0.5016	0.9403	0.1078	0.5255	0.8727	0.3815	0.5541	0.9833
0.1501	0.9363	0.3858	0.3545	0.5448	0.0643	0.3167	0.6732	0.6283	0.2631
0.8806	0.7989	0.7484	0.8083	0.2701	0.5039	0.9439	0.1027	0.9677	0.4597
0.4582	0.7590	0.4393	0.4704	0.6903	0.3732	0.6587	0.8675	0.2905	0.3058
0.0785	0.1467	0.3880	0.5274	0.8723	0.7517	0.9905	0.8904	0.8177	0.6660
0.1158	0.6635	0.4992	0.9070	0.2975	0.5686	0.8495	0.1652	0.2039	0.2553
0.2762	0.7018	0.6782	0.4013	0.2224	0.4672	0.5753	0.6219	0.6871	0.9255
0.9382	0.6411	0.7984	0.0608	0.5945	0.3977	0.4570	0.9924	0.8398	0.8361
0.5102	0.7021	0.4353	0.3398	0.8038	0.2260	0.1250	0.1884	0.3432	0.1192
0.2354	0.7410	0.7089	0.2579	0.1358	0.8446	0.1648	0.3889	0.5620	0.6555
0.9082	0.7906	0.7589	0.8870	0.1189	0.7125	0.6324	0.1096	0.5155	0.3449
0.6936	0.0702	0.9716	0.0374	0.0683	0.2397	0.7753	0.2029	0.1464	0.8000
0.4042	0.8158	0.3623	0.6614	0.7954	0.7516	0.6518	0.3638	0.3107	0.2718
0.9410	0.2201	0.6348	0.0367	0.0311	0.0688	0.2346	0.3927	0.7327	0.9994
0.0917	0.2504	0.2878	0.1735	0.3872	0.6816	0.2731	0.3846	0.6621	0.8983
0.8532	0.4869	0.2685	0.6349	0.9364	0.3451	0.4998	0.2842	0.0643	0.6656
0.8980	0.0455	0.8314	0.8189	0.6783	0.8086	0.1386	0.4442	0.9941	0.6812
0.8412	0.8792	0.2025	0.9320	0.7656	0.3815	0.5302	0.8744	0.4584	0.3585
0.5688	0.8633	0.5818	0.0692	0.2543	0.5453	0.9955	0.1237	0.7535	0.5993
0.5006	0.1215	0.8102	0.1026	0.9251	0.6851	0.1559	0.1214	0.2628	0.9374
0.5748	0.4164	0.3427	0.2809	0.8064	0.5855	0.2229	0.2805	0.9139	0.9013
0.1100	0.0873	0.9407	0.8747	0.0496	0.4380	0.5847	0.4183	0.5929	0.4863
0.5802	0.7747	0.1285	0.0074	0.6252	0.7747	0.0112	0.3958	0.3285	0.5389
0.1019	0.6628	0.8998	0.1334	0.2798	0.7351	0.7330	0.6723	0.6924	0.3963
0.9909	0.8991	0.2298	0.2603	0.6921	0.5573	0.8191	0.0384	0.2954	0.0636
0.6292	0.4923	0.0276	0.6734	0.6562	0.4231	0.1980	0.6551	0.3716	0.0507
0.9430	0.2579	0.7933	0.0945	0.3192	0.3195	0.7772	0.4672	0.7070	0.5925
0.9938	0.7098	0.7964	0.7952	0.8947	0.1214	0.8454	0.8294	0.5394	0.9413
0.4690	0.1395	0.0930	0.3189	0.6972	0.7291	0.8513	0.9256	0.7478	0.8124
0.2028	0.3774	0.0485	0.7718	0.9656	0.2444	0.0304	0.1395	0.1577	0.8625
0.6141	0.4131	0.2006	0.2329	0.6182	0.5151	0.6300	0.9311	0.3837	0.7828
0.2757	0.8479	0.7880	0.8492	0.6859	0.8947	0.6246	0.1574	0.4936	0.8077
0.0561	0.0126	0.6531	0.0378	0.4975	0.1133	0.3572	0.0071	0.4555	0.7563
0.1419	0.4308	0.8073	0.4681	0.0481	0.2918	0.2975	0.0685	0.6384	0.0812
0.3125	0.0053	0.9209	0.9768	0.3584	0.0390	0.2161	0.6333	0.4391	0.6991

TABLE 13.3 RANDOM NUMBER INTERVALS FOR GENERATING VALUES OF DIRECT LABOR COST PER UNIT

Direct Labor Cost per Unit	Probability	Interval of Random Numbers
$43	0.1	0.0 but less than 0.1
$44	0.2	0.1 but less than 0.3
$45	0.4	0.3 but less than 0.7
$46	0.2	0.7 but less than 0.9
$47	0.1	0.9 but less than 1.0

Equation (13.3) generates a value for the parts cost. Suppose that a random number of 0.2680 is obtained. The value for the parts cost is

$$\text{Parts cost} = 80 + 0.2680(20) = 85.36 \text{ per unit}$$

Suppose that a random number of 0.5842 is generated on the next trial. The value for the parts cost is

$$\text{Parts cost} = 80 + 0.5842(20) = 91.68 \text{ per unit}$$

With appropriate choices of a and b, equation (13.2) can be used to generate values for any uniform probability distribution. Table 13.5 shows the generation of 10 values for the parts cost per unit.

Spreadsheet packages such as Excel have built-in functions that make simulations based on probability distributions such as the normal probability distribution relatively easy.

Finally, we need a random number procedure for generating the first-year demand. Because first-year demand is normally distributed with a mean of 15,000 units and a standard deviation of 4500 units (see Figure 13.4), we need a procedure for generating random values from a normal probability distribution. Because of the mathematical complexity, a detailed discussion of the procedure for generating random values from a normal probability distribution is omitted. However, computer simulation packages and spreadsheets include a built-in function that provides randomly generated values from a normal probability distribution. In most cases the user only needs to provide the mean and standard deviation of

TABLE 13.4 RANDOM GENERATION OF 10 VALUES FOR THE DIRECT LABOR COST PER UNIT

Trial	Random Number	Direct Labor Cost ($)
1	0.9109	47
2	0.2841	44
3	0.6531	45
4	0.0367	43
5	0.3451	45
6	0.2757	44
7	0.6859	45
8	0.6246	45
9	0.4936	45
10	0.8077	46

TABLE 13.5 RANDOM GENERATION OF 10 VALUES FOR THE PARTS COST PER UNIT

Trial	Random Number	Parts Cost ($)
1	0.2680	85.36
2	0.5842	91.68
3	0.6675	93.35
4	0.9280	98.56
5	0.4180	88.36
6	0.7342	94.68
7	0.4325	88.65
8	0.1186	82.37
9	0.6944	93.89
10	0.7869	95.74

the normal distribution. For example, using Excel the following formula can be placed into a cell to obtain a value for a probabilistic input that is normally distributed:

=NORMINV(RAND(),Mean,Standard Deviation)

Because the mean for the first-year demand in the PortaCom problem is 15,000 and the standard deviation is 4500, the Excel statement

=NORMINV(RAND(),15000,4500) (13.4)

will provide a normally distributed value for first-year demand. For example, if Excel's RAND() function generates the random number 0.7005, the Excel function shown in equation (13.4) will provide a first-year demand of 17,366 units. If RAND() generates the random number 0.3204, equation (13.4) will provide a first-year demand of 12,900. Table 13.6 shows the results for the first 10 randomly generated values for demand. Note that random numbers less than 0.5 generate first-year demand values below the mean and that random numbers greater than 0.5 generate first-year demand values greater than the mean.

TABLE 13.6 RANDOM GENERATION OF 10 VALUES FOR FIRST-YEAR DEMAND

Trial	Random Number	Demand
1	0.7005	17,366
2	0.3204	12,900
3	0.8968	20,686
4	0.1804	10,888
5	0.4346	14,259
6	0.9605	22,904
7	0.5646	15,732
8	0.7334	17,804
9	0.0216	5,902
10	0.3218	12,918

Running the Simulation Model Running the simulation model means implementing the sequence of logical and mathematical operations described in the flowchart in Figure 13.5. The model parameters are \$249 per unit for the selling price, \$400,000 for the administrative cost, and \$600,000 for the advertising cost. Each trial in the simulation involves randomly generating values for the probabilistic inputs (direct labor cost, parts cost, and first-year demand) and computing profit. The simulation is complete when a satisfactory number of trials have been conducted.

Let us compute the profit for the first trial assuming the following probabilistic inputs:

Direct labor cost:	$c_1 = 47$
Parts cost:	$c_2 = 85.36$
First-year demand:	$x = 17{,}366$

Referring to the flowchart in Figure 13.5, we see that the profit obtained is

$$\begin{aligned}\text{Profit} &= (249 - c_1 - c_2)x - 1{,}000{,}000 \\ &= (249 - 47 - 85.36)17{,}366 - 1{,}000{,}000 = 1{,}025{,}570\end{aligned}$$

The first row of Table 13.7 shows the result of this trial of the PortaCom simulation.

The simulated profit for the PortaCom printer if the direct labor cost is \$47 per unit, the parts cost is \$85.36 per unit, and first-year demand is 17,366 units is \$1,025,570. Of course, one simulation trial does not provide a complete understanding of the possible profit and loss. Because other values are possible for the probabilistic inputs, we can benefit from additional simulation trials.

Suppose that on a second simulation trial, random numbers of 0.2841, 0.5842, and 0.3204 are generated for the direct labor cost, the parts cost, and first-year demand, respectively. These random numbers will provide the probabilistic inputs of \$44 for the direct labor cost, \$91.68 for the parts cost, and 12,900 for first-year demand. These values provide a simulated profit of \$461,828 on the second simulation trial (see the second row of Table 13.7).

TABLE 13.7 PORTACOM SIMULATION RESULTS FOR 10 TRIALS

Trial	Direct Labor Cost per Unit (\$)	Parts Cost per Unit (\$)	Units Sold	Profit (\$)
1	47	85.36	17,366	1,025,570
2	44	91.68	12,900	461,828
3	45	93.35	20,686	1,288,906
4	43	98.56	10,888	169,807
5	45	88.36	14,259	648,911
6	44	94.68	22,904	1,526,769
7	45	88.65	15,732	814,686
8	45	82.37	17,804	1,165,501
9	45	93.89	5,902	−350,131
10	46	95.74	12,918	385,585
Total	449	912.64	151,359	7,137,432
Average	\$44.90	\$91.26	15,136	\$713,743

Repetition of the simulation process with different values for the probabilistic inputs is an essential part of any simulation. Through the repeated trials, management will begin to understand what might happen when the product is introduced into the real world. We have shown the results of 10 simulation trials in Table 13.7. For these 10 cases, we find a profit as high as $1,526,769 for the 6th trial and a loss of $350,131 for the 9th trial. Thus, we see both the possibility of a profit and a loss. Averages for the 10 trials are presented at the bottom of the table. We see that the average profit for the 10 trials is $713,743. The probability of a loss is 0.10, because one of the 10 trials (the 9th) resulted in a loss. We note also that the average values for labor cost, parts cost, and first-year demand are fairly close to their means of $45, $90, and 15,000, respectively.

Simulation of the PortaCom Problem

Using an Excel worksheet, we simulated the PortaCom project 500 times. The worksheet used to carry out the simulation is shown in Figure 13.6. Note that the simulation results for trials 6 through 495 have been hidden so that the results can be shown in a reasonably sized figure. If desired, the rows for these trials can be shown and the simulation results displayed for all 500 trials. The details of the Excel worksheet that provided the PortaCom simulation are described in Appendix 13.1.

Excel worksheets for all simulations presented in this chapter are available on the CD that accompanies this text.

The simulation summary statistics in Figure 13.6 provide information about the risk associated with PortaCom's new printer. The worst result obtained in a simulation of 500 trials is a loss of $785,234, and the best result is a profit of $2,367,058. The mean profit is $698,457. Fifty-one of the trials resulted in a loss; thus, the estimated probability of a loss is 51/500 = 0.1020.

Simulation studies enable an objective estimate of the probability of a loss, which is an important aspect of risk analysis.

A histogram of simulated profit values is shown in Figure 13.7. We note that the distribution of profit values is fairly symmetric with a large number of values in the range of $250,000 to $1,250,000. The probability of a large loss or a large gain is small. Only 3 trials resulted in a loss more than $500,000, and only 3 trials resulted in a profit greater than $2,000,000. However, the probability of a loss is significant. Forty-eight of the 500 trials resulted in a loss in the $0 to $500,000 range—almost 10 percent. The modal category, the one with the largest number of values, is the range of profits between $750,000 and $1,000,000.

In comparing the simulation approach to risk analysis to the what-if approach, we see that much more information is obtained by using simulation. With the what-if analysis, we learned that the base-case scenario projected a profit of $710,000. The worst-case scenario projected a loss of $847,000, and the best-case scenario projected a profit of $2,591,000. From the 500 trials of the simulation run, we see that the worst- and best-case scenarios, although possible, are unlikely. None of the 500 trials provided a loss as low as the worst-case or a profit as high as the best-case. Indeed, the advantage of simulation for risk analysis is the information it provides on the likely values of the output. We now know the probability of a loss, how the profit values are distributed over their range, and what profit values are most likely.

For practice working through a simulation problem, try Problems 9 and 14.

The simulation results help PortaCom's management better understand the profit/loss potential of the PortaCom portable printer. The 0.1020 probability of a loss may be acceptable to management given a probability of almost 0.80 (see Figure 13.7) that profit will exceed $250,000. On the other hand, PortaCom might want to conduct further market research before deciding whether to introduce the product. In any case, the simulation results should be helpful in reaching an appropriate decision. The Management Science in Action, Meeting Demand Levels at Pfizer, describes how a simulation model helped find ways to meet increasing demand for a product.

FIGURE 13.6 EXCEL WORKSHEET FOR THE PORTACOM PROBLEM

EXCELfile
PortaCom

	A	B	C	D	E	F
1	**PortaCom Risk Analysis**					
2						
3	Selling Price per Unit		$249			
4	Administrative Cost		$400,000			
5	Advertising Cost		$600,000			
6						
7	**Direct Labor Cost**			**Parts Cost (Uniform Distribution)**		
8	Lower	Upper		Smallest Value	$80	
9	Random No.	Random No.	Cost per Unit	Largest Value	$100	
10	0.0	0.1	$43			
11	0.1	0.3	$44			
12	0.3	0.7	$45	**Demand (Normal Distribution)**		
13	0.7	0.9	$46	Mean	15000	
14	0.9	1.0	$47	Std Deviation	4500	
15						
16						
17	**Simulation Trials**					
18						
19		Direct Labor	Parts	First-Year		
20	Trial	Cost Per Unit	Cost Per Unit	Demand	Profit	
21	1	47	$85.36	17,366	$1,025,570	
22	2	44	$91.68	12,900	$461,828	
23	3	45	$93.35	20,686	$1,288,906	
24	4	43	$98.56	10,888	$169,807	
25	5	45	$88.36	14,259	$648,911	
516	496	44	$98.67	8,730	($71,739)	
517	497	45	$94.38	19,257	$1,110,952	
518	498	44	$90.85	14,920	$703,118	
519	499	43	$90.37	13,471	$557,652	
520	500	46	$92.50	18,614	$1,056,847	
521						
522			**Summary Statistics**			
523			Mean Profit		$698,457	
524			Standard Deviation		$520,485	
525			Minimum Profit		($785,234)	
526			Maximum Profit		$2,367,058	
527			Number of Losses		51	
528			Probabilitiy of Loss		0.1020	
529						

FIGURE 13.7 HISTOGRAM OF SIMULATED PROFIT FOR 500 TRIALS OF THE PORTACOM SIMULATION

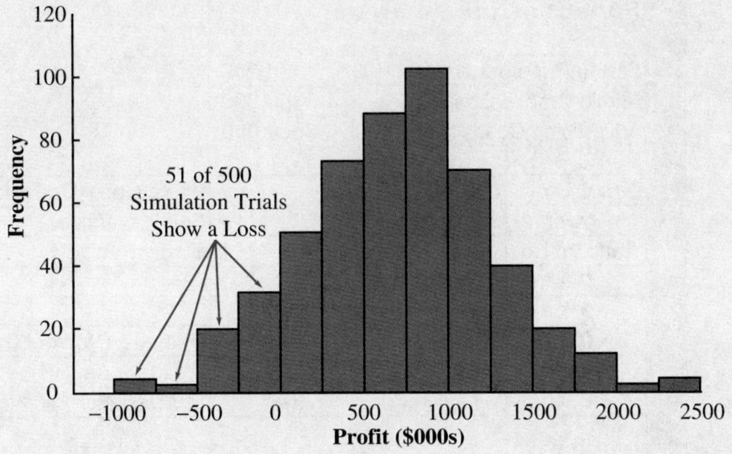

MANAGEMENT SCIENCE IN ACTION

MEETING DEMAND LEVELS AT PFIZER*

Pharmacia & Upjohn recently merged with Pfizer to create one of the world's largest pharmaceutical firms. Demand for one of Pharmacia & Upjohn's long-standing products remained stable for several years at a level easily satisfied by the company's manufacturing facility. However, changes in market conditions caused an increase in demand to a level beyond the current capacity. A simulation model of the production process was developed to explore ways to increase production to meet the new level of demand in a cost-effective manner.

Simulation results were used to help answer the following questions:

- What is the maximum throughput of the existing facility?
- How can the existing production process be modified to increase throughput?
- How much equipment must be added to the existing facility to meet the increased demand?
- What is the desired size and configuration of the new production process?

The simulation model was able to demonstrate that the existing facilities, with some operating policy improvements, were large enough to satisfy the increased demand for the next several years. Expansion to a new production facility was not necessary. The simulation model also helped determine the number of operators required as the production level increased in the future. This result helped ensure that the proper number of operators would be trained by the time they were needed. The simulation model also provided a way reprocessed material could be used to replace fresh raw materials, resulting in a savings of approximately $3 million per year.

*Based on information provided by David B. Magerlein, James M. Magerlein, and Michael J. Goodrich.

NOTES AND COMMENTS

1. The PortaCom simulation model is based on independent trials in which the results for one trial do not affect what happens in subsequent trials. Historically, this type of simulation study was referred to as a *Monte Carlo simulation.* The term *Monte Carlo simulation* was used because early practitioners of simulation saw similarities between the models they were developing and the gambling games played in the casinos of Monte Carlo. Today, many individuals interpret the term *Monte Carlo simulation* more broadly to mean any simulation that involves randomly generating values for the probabilistic inputs.
2. The probability distribution used to generate values for probabilistic inputs in a simulation model is often developed using historical data. For instance, suppose that an analysis of daily sales at a new car dealership for the past 50 days showed that on 2 days no cars were sold, on 5 days one car was sold, on 9 days two cars were sold, on 24 days three cars were sold, on 7 days four cars were sold, and on 3 days five cars were sold. We can estimate the probability distribution of daily demand using the relative frequencies for the observed data. An estimate of the probability that no cars are sold on a given day is 2/50 = 0.04, an estimate of the probability that one car is sold is 5/50 = 0.10, and so on. The estimated probability distribution of daily demand is as follows:

Daily Sales	0	1	2	3	4	5
Probability	0.04	0.10	0.18	0.48	0.14	0.06

Appendix 13.2 shows how to perform a simulation of the PortaCom problem using Crystal Ball.

3. Spreadsheet add-in packages such as @RISK® and Crystal Ball® have been developed to make spreadsheet simulation easier. For instance, using Crystal Ball we could simulate the PortaCom new product introduction by first entering the formulas showing the relationships between the probabilistic inputs and the output measure, profit. Then, a probability distribution type is selected for each probabilistic input from among a number of available choices. Crystal Ball will generate random values for each probabilistic input, compute the profit, and repeat the simulation for as many trials as specified. Graphical displays and a variety of descriptive statistics can be easily obtained.

13.2 INVENTORY SIMULATION

In this section we describe how simulation can be used to establish an inventory policy for a product that has an uncertain demand. The product is a home ventilation fan distributed by the Butler Electrical Supply Company. Each fan costs Butler \$75 and sells for \$125. Thus Butler realizes a gross profit of \$125 − \$75 = \$50 for each fan sold. Monthly demand for the fan is described by a normal probability distribution with a mean of 100 units and a standard deviation of 20 units.

Butler receives monthly deliveries from its supplier and replenishes its inventory to a level of Q at the beginning of each month. This beginning inventory level is referred to as the replenishment level. If monthly demand is less than the replenishment level, an inventory holding cost of \$15 is charged for each unit that is not sold. However, if monthly demand is greater than the replenishment level, a stock-out occurs and a shortage cost is incurred. Because Butler assigns a goodwill cost of \$30 for each customer turned away, a shortage cost of \$30 is charged for each unit of demand that cannot be satisfied. Management would like to use a simulation model to determine the average monthly net profit resulting from using a particular replenishment level. Management would also like information on the percentage of total demand that will be satisfied. This percentage is referred to as the *service level.*

The controllable input to the Butler simulation model is the replenishment level, Q. The probabilistic input is the monthly demand, D. The two output measures are the average monthly net profit and the service level. Computation of the service level requires that we keep track of the number of fans sold each month and the total demand for fans for each month. The service level will be computed at the end of the simulation run as the ratio of total units sold to total demand. A diagram of the relationship between the inputs and the outputs is shown in Figure 13.8.

When demand is less than or equal to the replenishment level ($D \leq Q$), D units are sold, and an inventory holding cost of \$15 is incurred for each of the $Q - D$ units that remain in inventory. Net profit for this case is computed as follows:

Case 1: $D \leq Q$

$$\begin{aligned} \text{Gross profit} &= \$50D \\ \text{Holding cost} &= \$15(Q - D) \\ \text{Net profit} &= \text{Gross profit} - \text{Holding cost} = \$50D - \$15(Q - D) \end{aligned} \tag{13.5}$$

When demand is greater than the replenishment level ($D >$ Q), Q fans are sold, and a shortage cost of \$30 is imposed for each of the $D - Q$ units of demand not satisfied. Net profit for this case is computed as follows:

Case 2: $D > Q$

$$\begin{aligned} \text{Gross profit} &= \$50Q \\ \text{Shortage cost} &= \$30(D - Q) \\ \text{Net profit} &= \text{Gross profit} - \text{Shortage cost} = \$50Q - \$30(D - Q) \end{aligned} \tag{13.6}$$

Figure 13.9 shows a flowchart that defines the sequence of logical and mathematical operations required to simulate the Butler inventory system. Each trial in the simulation represents one month of operation. The simulation is run for 300 months using a given replenishment level, Q. Then, the average profit and service level output measures are computed. Let us describe the steps involved in the simulation by illustrating the results for the first two months of a simulation run using a replenishment level of $Q = 100$.

The first block of the flowchart in Figure 13.9 sets the values of the model parameters: gross profit = \$50 per unit, holding cost = \$15 per unit, and shortage cost = \$30 per unit.

FIGURE 13.8 BUTLER INVENTORY SIMULATION MODEL

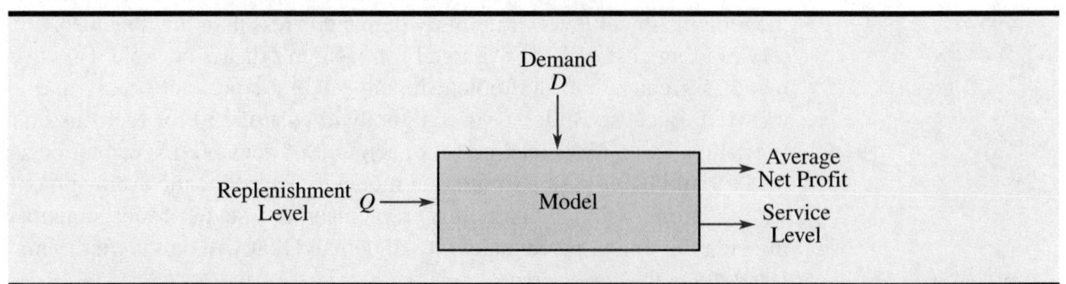

FIGURE 13.9 FLOWCHART FOR THE BUTLER INVENTORY SIMULATION

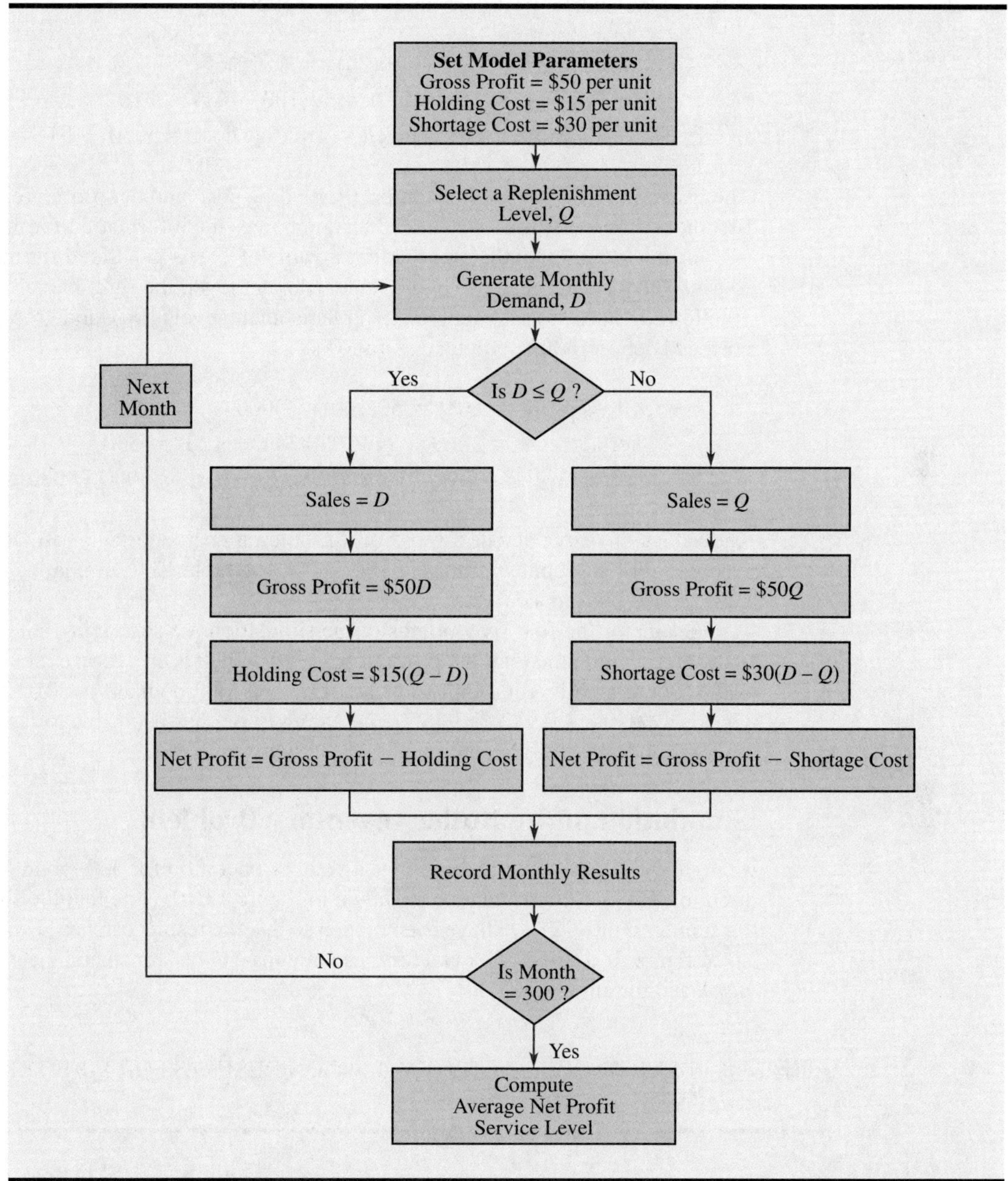

The next block shows that a replenishment level of Q is selected; in our illustration, $Q = 100$. Then, a value for monthly demand is generated. Because monthly demand is normally distributed with a mean of 100 units and a standard deviation of 20 units, we can use the Excel function =NORMINV(RAND(),100,20), as described in Section 13.1, to generate a value for monthly demand. Suppose that a value of $D = 79$ is generated on the first trial. This value of demand is then compared with the replenishment level, Q. With the replenishment level set at $Q = 100$, demand is less than the replenishment level, and the left branch of the flowchart is followed. Sales are set equal to demand (79), and gross profit, holding cost, and net profit are computed as follows:

$$\begin{aligned}\text{Gross profit} &= 50D = 50(79) = 3950\\ \text{Holding cost} &= 15(Q - D) = 15(100 - 79) = 315\\ \text{Net profit} &= \text{Gross profit} - \text{Holding cost} = 3950 - 315 = 3635\end{aligned}$$

The values of demand, sales, gross profit, holding cost, and net profit are recorded for the first month. The first row of Table 13.8 summarizes the information for this first trial.

For the second month, suppose that a value of 111 is generated for monthly demand. Because demand is greater than the replenishment level, the right branch of the flowchart is followed. Sales are set equal to the replenishment level (100), and gross profit, shortage cost, and net profit are computed as follows:

$$\begin{aligned}\text{Gross profit} &= 50Q = 50(100) = 5000\\ \text{Shortage cost} &= 30(D - Q) = 30(111 - 100) = 330\\ \text{Net profit} &= \text{Gross profit} - \text{Shortage cost} = 5000 - 330 = 4670\end{aligned}$$

The values of demand, sales, gross profit, holding cost, shortage cost, and net profit are recorded for the second month. The second row of Table 13.8 summarizes the information generated in the second trial.

Results for the first five months of the simulation are shown in Table 13.8. The totals show an accumulated total net profit of \$22,310, which is an average monthly net profit of \$22,310/5 = \$4462. Total unit sales are 472, and total demand is 501. Thus, the service level is 472/501 = 0.942, or 94.2%, indicating Butler has been able to satisfy 94.2 percent of demand during the five-month period.

Simulation of the Butler Inventory Problem

Using Excel, we simulated the Butler inventory operation for 300 months. The worksheet used to carry out the simulation is shown in Figure 13.10. Note that the simulation results for months 6 through 295 have been hidden so that the results can be shown in a reasonably sized figure. If desired, the rows for these months can be shown and the simulation results displayed for all 300 months.

TABLE 13.8 BUTLER INVENTORY SIMULATION RESULTS FOR FIVE TRIALS WITH $Q = 100$

Month	Demand	Sales	Gross Profit (\$)	Holding Cost (\$)	Shortage Cost (\$)	Net Profit (\$)
1	79	79	3,950	315	0	3,635
2	111	100	5,000	0	330	4,670
3	93	93	4,650	105	0	4,545
4	100	100	5,000	0	0	5,000
5	118	100	5,000	0	540	4,460
Totals	501	472	23,600	420	870	22,310
Average	100	94	\$4,720	\$ 84	\$174	\$4,462

FIGURE 13.10 EXCEL WORKSHEET FOR THE BUTLER INVENTORY PROBLEM

EXCELfile
Butler

	A	B	C	D	E	F	G	H
1	**Butler Inventory**							
2								
3	Gross Profit per Unit		$50					
4	Holding Cost per Unit		$15					
5	Shortage Cost per Unit		$30					
6								
7	**Replenishment Level**		100					
8								
9	**Demand (Normal Distribution)**							
10	Mean	100						
11	Std Deviation	20						
12								
13								
14	**Simulation**							
15								
16	Month	Demand	Sales	Gross Profit	Holding Cost	Shortage Cost	Net Profit	
17	1	79	79	$3,950	$315	$0	$3,635	
18	2	111	100	$5,000	$0	$330	$4,670	
19	3	93	93	$4,650	$105	$0	$4,545	
20	4	100	100	$5,000	$0	$0	$5,000	
21	5	118	100	$5,000	$0	$540	$4,460	
312	296	89	89	$4,450	$165	$0	$4,285	
313	297	91	91	$4,550	$135	$0	$4,415	
314	298	122	100	$5,000	$0	$660	$4,340	
315	299	93	93	$4,650	$105	$0	$4,545	
316	300	126	100	$5,000	$0	$780	$4,220	
317								
318	**Totals**	30,181	27,917		**Summary Statistics**			
319					Mean Profit		$4,293	
320					Standard Deviation		$658	
321					Minimum Profit		($206)	
322					Maximum Profit		$5,000	
323					Service Level		92.5%	
324								

The summary statistics in Figure 13.10 show what can be anticipated over 300 months if Butler operates its inventory system using a replenishment level of 100. The average net profit is $4293 per month. Because 27,917 units of the total demand of 30,181 units were satisfied, the service level is 27,917/30,181 = 92.5%. We are now ready to use the simulation model to consider other replenishment levels that may improve the net profit and the service level.

Simulation allows the user to consider different operating policies and changes to model parameters and then to observe the impact of the changes on output measures such as profit or service level.

At this point, we conducted a series of simulation experiments by repeating the Butler inventory simulation with replenishment levels of 110, 120, 130, and 140 units. The average monthly net profits and the service levels are shown in Table 13.9. The highest monthly net profit of $4575 occurs with a replenishment level of $Q = 120$. The associated service level is 98.6 percent. On the basis of these results, Butler selected a replenishment level of $Q = 120$.

Experimental simulation studies, such as this one for Butler's inventory policy, can help identify good operating policies and decisions. Butler's management used simulation to

TABLE 13.9 BUTLER INVENTORY SIMULATION RESULTS FOR 300 TRIALS

Replenishment Level	Average Net Profit ($)	Service Level (%)
100	4293	92.5
110	4524	96.5
120	4575	98.6
130	4519	99.6
140	4399	99.9

choose a replenishment level of 120 for its home ventilation fan. With the simulation model in place, management can also explore the sensitivity of this decision to some of the model parameters. For instance, we assigned a shortage cost of $30 for any customer demand not met. With this shortage cost, the replenishment level was $Q = 120$ and the service level was 98.6 percent. If management felt a more appropriate shortage cost was $10 per unit, running the simulation again using $10 as the shortage cost would be a simple matter.

Problem 18 gives you a chance to develop a different simulation model.

We mentioned earlier that simulation is not an optimization technique. Even though we used simulation to choose a replenishment level, it does not guarantee that this choice is optimal. All possible replenishment levels were not tested. Perhaps a manager would like to consider additional simulation runs with replenishment levels of $Q = 115$ and $Q = 125$ to search for an even better inventory policy. Also, we have no guarantee that with another set of 300 randomly generated demand values that the replenishment level with the highest profit would not change. However, with a large number of simulation trials, we should find a good and, at least, near optimal solution. The Management Science in Action, Petroleum Distribution in the Gulf of Mexico, describes a simulation application for 15 petroleum companies in the state of Florida.

MANAGEMENT SCIENCE IN ACTION

PETROLEUM DISTRIBUTION IN THE GULF OF MEXICO*

Domestic suppliers who operate oil refineries along the Gulf Coast are helping to satisfy Florida's increasing demand for refined petroleum products. Barge fleets, operated either by independent shipping companies or by the petroleum companies themselves, are used to transport more than 20 different petroleum products to 15 Florida petroleum companies. The petroleum products are loaded at refineries in Texas, Louisiana, and Mississippi and are discharged at tank terminals concentrated in Tampa, Port Everglades, and Jacksonville.

Barges operate under three types of contracts between the fleet operator and the client petroleum company:

- The client assumes total control of a barge and uses it for trips between its own refinery and one or more discharging ports.
- The client is guaranteed a certain volume will be moved during the contract period. Schedules vary considerably depending upon the customer's needs and the fleet operator's capabilities.
- The client hires a barge for a single trip.

A simulation model was developed to analyze the complex process of operating barge fleets in the Gulf of Mexico. An appropriate probability distribution was used to simulate requests for shipments by the petroleum companies. Additional probability distributions were used to simulate the travel times depending upon the size and type of barge. Using this information, the simulation model was used to track barge loading times, barge discharge times, barge utilization, and total cost.

Analysts used simulation runs with a variety of what-if scenarios to answer questions about the petroleum distribution system and to make recommendations for improving the efficiency of the operation. Simulation helped determine the following:

- The optimal trade-off between fleet utilization and on-time delivery
- The recommended fleet size
- The recommended barge capacities
- The best service contract structure to balance the trade-off between customer service and delivery cost

Implementation of the simulation-based recommendations demonstrated a significant improvement in the operation and a significant lowering of petroleum distribution costs.

*Based on E. D. Chajakis, "Sophisticated Crude Transportation," *OR/MS Today* (December 1997): 30–34.

13.3 WAITING LINE SIMULATION

The simulation models discussed thus far have been based on independent trials in which the results for one trial do not affect what happens in subsequent trials. In this sense, the system being modeled does not change or evolve over time. Simulation models such as these are referred to as **static simulation models.** In this section, we develop a simulation model of a waiting line system where the state of the system, including the number of customers in the waiting line and whether the service facility is busy or idle, changes or evolves over time. To incorporate time into the simulation model, we use a simulation clock to record the time that each customer arrives for service as well as the time that each customer completes service. Simulation models that must take into account how the system changes or evolves over time are referred to as **dynamic simulation models.** In situations where the arrivals and departures of customers are **events** that occur at *discrete* points in time, the simulation model is also referred to as a **discrete-event simulation model.**

In Chapter 12, we presented formulas that could be used to compute the steady-state operating characteristics of a waiting line, including the average waiting time, the average number of units in the waiting line, the probability of waiting, and so on. In most cases, the waiting line formulas were based on specific assumptions about the probability distribution for arrivals, the probability distribution for service times, the queue discipline, and so on. Simulation, as an alternative for studying waiting lines, is more flexible. In applications where the assumptions required by the waiting line formulas are not reasonable, simulation may be the only feasible approach to studying the waiting line system. In this section we discuss the simulation of the waiting line for the Hammondsport Savings Bank automated teller machine (ATM).

Hammondsport Savings Bank ATM Waiting Line

Hammondsport Savings Bank will open several new branch banks during the coming year. Each new branch is designed to have one automated teller machine (ATM). A concern is that during busy periods several customers may have to wait to use the ATM. This concern prompted the bank to undertake a study of the ATM waiting line system. The bank's vice president wants to determine whether one ATM will be sufficient. The bank established service guidelines for its ATM system stating that the average customer waiting time for an ATM should be one minute or less. Let us show how a simulation model can be used to study the ATM waiting line at a particular branch.

Customer Arrival Times

One probabilistic input to the ATM simulation model is the arrival times of customers who use the ATM. In waiting line simulations, arrival times are determined by randomly generating the time between two successive arrivals, referred to as the *interarrival time*. For the branch bank being studied, the customer interarrival times are assumed to be uniformly distributed between 0 and 5 minutes as shown in Figure 13.11. With r denoting a random number between 0 and 1, an interarrival time for two successive customers can be simulated by using the formula for generating values from a uniform probability distribution.

$$\text{Interarrival time} = a + r(b - a) \tag{13.7}$$

where

r = random number between 0 and 1
a = minimum interarrival time
b = maximum interarrival time

For the Hammondsport ATM system, the minimum interarrival time is $a = 0$ minutes, and the maximum interarrival time is $b = 5$ minutes; therefore, the formula for generating an interarrival time is

A uniform probability distribution of interarrival times is used here to illustrate the simulation computations. Actually, any interarrival time probability distribution can be assumed, and the logic of the waiting line simulation model will not change.

$$\text{Interarrival time} = 0 + r(5 - 0) = 5r \tag{13.8}$$

Assume that the simulation run begins at time = 0. A random number of $r = 0.2804$ generates an interarrival time of 5(0.2804) = 1.4 minutes for customer 1. Thus, customer 1 arrives 1.4 minutes after the simulation run begins. A second random number of $r = 0.2598$ generates an interarrival time of 5(0.2598) = 1.3 minutes, indicating that customer 2 arrives 1.3 minutes after customer 1. Thus, customer 2 arrives 1.4 + 1.3 = 2.7 minutes after the simulation begins. Continuing, a third random number of $r = 0.9802$ indicates that customer 3 arrives 4.9 minutes after customer 2, which is 7.6 minutes after the simulation begins.

FIGURE 13.11 UNIFORM PROBABILITY DISTRIBUTION OF INTERARRIVAL TIMES FOR THE ATM WAITING LINE SYSTEM

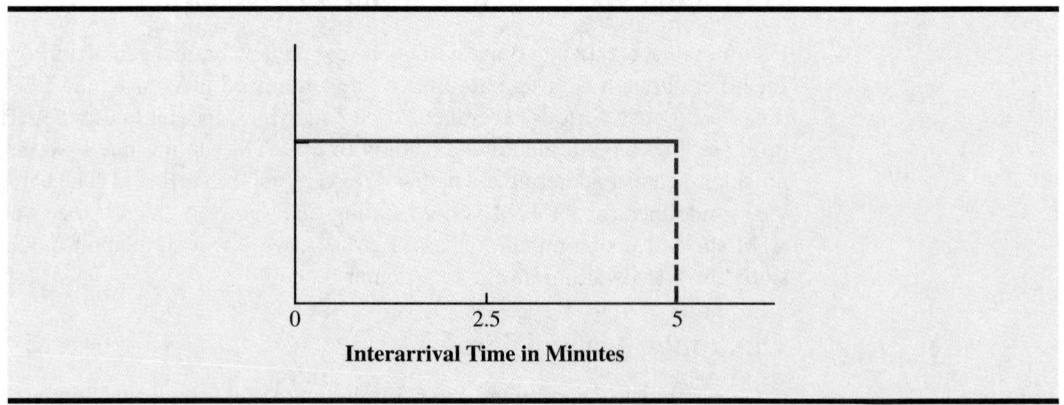

FIGURE 13.12 NORMAL PROBABILITY DISTRIBUTION OF SERVICE TIMES FOR THE ATM WAITING LINE SYSTEM

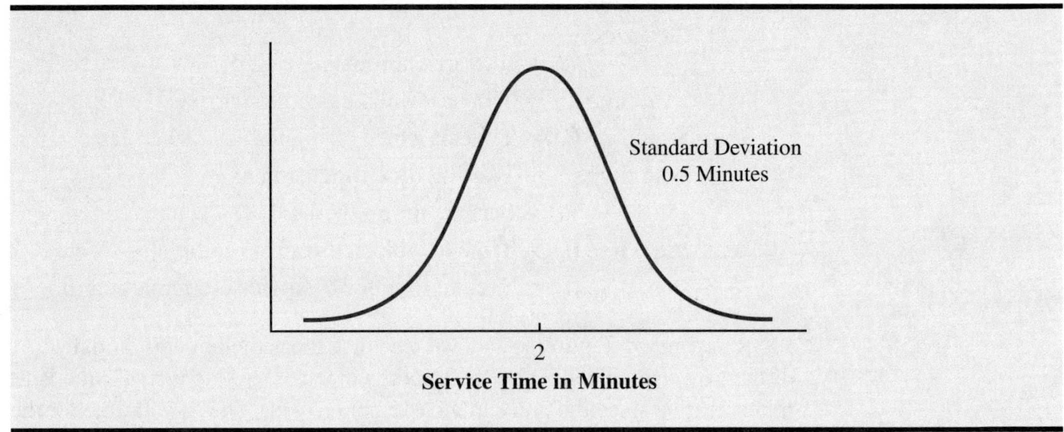

Customer Service Times

Another probabilistic input in the ATM simulation model is the service time, which is the time a customer spends using the ATM machine. Past data from similar ATMs indicate that a normal probability distribution with a mean of 2 minutes and a standard deviation of 0.5 minutes, as shown in Figure 13.12, can be used to describe service times. As discussed in Sections 13.1 and 13.2, values from a normal probability distribution with mean 2 and standard deviation 0.5 can be generated using the Excel function =NORMINV(RAND(),2,0.5). For example, the random number of 0.7257 generates a customer service time of 2.3 minutes.

Simulation Model

The probabilistic inputs to the Hammondsport Savings Bank ATM simulation model are the interarrival time and the service time. The controllable input is the number of ATMs used. The output will consist of various operating characteristics such as the probability of waiting, the average waiting time, the maximum waiting time, and so on. We show a diagram of the ATM simulation model in Figure 13.13.

FIGURE 13.13 HAMMONDSPORT SAVINGS BANK ATM SIMULATION MODEL

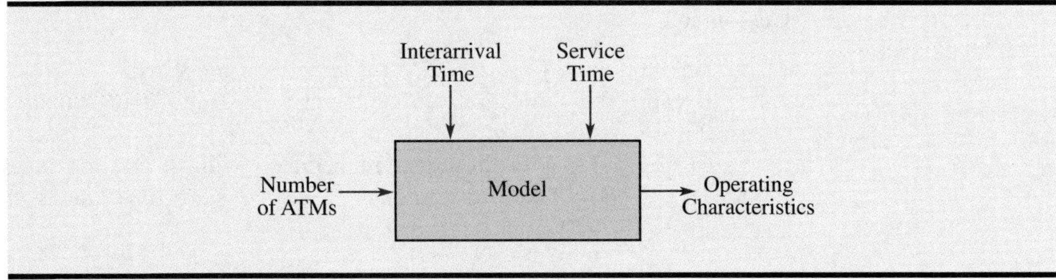

Figure 13.14 shows a flowchart that defines the sequence of logical and mathematical operations required to simulate the Hammondsport ATM system. The flowchart uses the following notation:

$$IAT = \text{Interarrival time generated}$$
$$\text{Arrival time } (i) = \text{Time at which customer } i \text{ arrives}$$
$$\text{Start time } (i) = \text{Time at which customer } i \text{ starts service}$$
$$\text{Wait time } (i) = \text{Waiting time for customer } i$$
$$ST = \text{Service time generated}$$
$$\text{Completion time } (i) = \text{Time at which customer } i \text{ completes service}$$
$$\text{System time } (i) = \text{System time for customer } i \text{ (completion time } - \text{ arrival time)}$$

Referring to Figure 13.14, we see that the simulation is initialized in the first block of the flowchart. Then a new customer is created. An interarrival time is generated to determine the time since the preceding customer arrived.[2] The arrival time for the new customer is then computed by adding the interarrival time to the arrival time of the preceding customer.

The decision rule for deciding whether the ATM is idle or busy is the most difficult aspect of the logic in a waiting line simulation model.

The arrival time for the new customer must be compared to the completion time of the preceding customer to determine whether the ATM is idle or busy. If the arrival time of the new customer is greater than the completion time of the preceding customer, the preceding customer will have finished service prior to the arrival of the new customer. In this case, the ATM will be idle, and the new customer can begin service immediately. The service start time for the new customer is equal to the arrival time of the new customer. However, if the arrival time for the new customer is not greater than the completion time of the preceding customer, the new customer arrived before the preceding customer finished service. In this case, the ATM is busy; the new customer must wait to use the ATM until the preceding customer completes service. The service start time for the new customer is equal to the completion time of the preceding customer.

Note that the time the new customer has to wait to use the ATM is the difference between the customer's service start time and the customer's arrival time. At this point, the customer is ready to use the ATM, and the simulation run continues with the generation of the customer's service time. The time at which the customer begins service plus the service time generated determine the customer's completion time. Finally, the total time the customer spends in the system is the difference between the customer's service completion time and the customer's arrival time. At this point, the computations are complete for the current customer, and the simulation continues with the next customer. The simulation is continued until a specified number of customers have been served by the ATM.

Simulation results for the first 10 customers are shown in Table 13.10. We discuss the computations for the first three customers to illustrate the logic of the simulation model and to show how the information in Table 13.10 was developed.

Customer 1

- An interarrival time of $IAT = 1.4$ minutes is generated.
- Because the simulation run begins at time 0, the arrival time for customer 1 is $0 + 1.4 = 1.4$ minutes.
- Customer 1 may begin service immediately with a start time of 1.4 minutes.
- The waiting time for customer 1 is the start time minus the arrival time: $1.4 - 1.4 = 0$ minutes.

[2]For the first customer, the interarrival time determines the time since the simulation started. Thus, the first interarrival time determines the time the first customer arrives.

FIGURE 13.14 FLOWCHART OF THE HAMMONDSPORT SAVINGS BANK ATM WAITING LINE SIMULATION

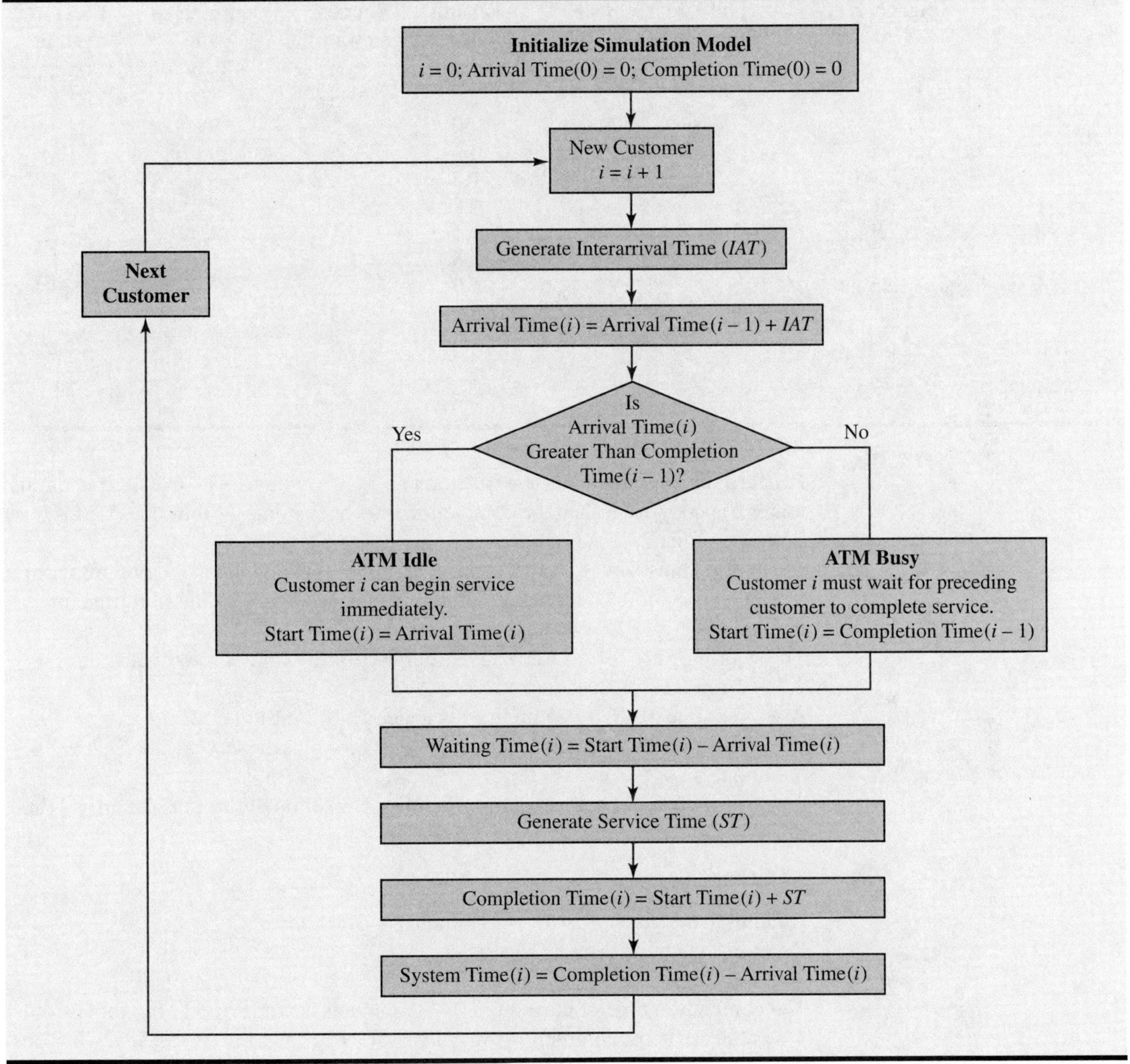

- A service time of $ST = 2.3$ minutes is generated for customer 1.
- The completion time for customer 1 is the start time plus the service time: $1.4 + 2.3 = 3.7$ minutes.
- The time in the system for customer 1 is the completion time minus the arrival time: $3.7 - 1.4 = 2.3$ minutes.

Customer 2

- An interarrival time of $IAT = 1.3$ minutes is generated.
- Because the arrival time of customer 1 is 1.4, the arrival time for customer 2 is $1.4 + 1.3 = 2.7$ minutes.

TABLE 13.10 SIMULATION RESULTS FOR 10 ATM CUSTOMERS

Customer	Interarrival Time	Arrival Time	Service Start Time	Waiting Time	Service Time	Completion Time	Time in System
1	1.4	1.4	1.4	0.0	2.3	3.7	2.3
2	1.3	2.7	3.7	1.0	1.5	5.2	2.5
3	4.9	7.6	7.6	0.0	2.2	9.8	2.2
4	3.5	11.1	11.1	0.0	2.5	13.6	2.5
5	0.7	11.8	13.6	1.8	1.8	15.4	3.6
6	2.8	14.6	15.4	0.8	2.4	17.8	3.2
7	2.1	16.7	17.8	1.1	2.1	19.9	3.2
8	0.6	17.3	19.9	2.6	1.8	21.7	4.4
9	2.5	19.8	21.7	1.9	2.0	23.7	3.9
10	1.9	21.7	23.7	2.0	2.3	26.0	4.3
Totals	21.7			11.2	20.9		32.1
Averages	2.17			1.12	2.09		3.21

- Because the completion time of customer 1 is 3.7 minutes, the arrival time of customer 2 is not greater than the completion time of customer 1; thus, the ATM is busy when customer 2 arrives.
- Customer 2 must wait for customer 1 to complete service before beginning service. Customer 1 completes service at 3.7 minutes, which becomes the start time for customer 2.
- The waiting time for customer 2 is the start time minus the arrival time: $3.7 - 2.7 = 1$ minute.
- A service time of $ST = 1.5$ minutes is generated for customer 2.
- The completion time for customer 2 is the start time plus the service time: $3.7 + 1.5 = 5.2$ minutes.
- The time in the system for customer 2 is the completion time minus the arrival time: $5.2 - 2.7 = 2.5$ minutes.

Customer 3

- An interarrival time of $IAT = 4.9$ minutes is generated.
- Because the arrival time of customer 2 was 2.7 minutes, the arrival time for customer 3 is $2.7 + 4.9 = 7.6$ minutes.
- The completion time of customer 2 is 5.2 minutes, so the arrival time for customer 3 is greater than the completion time of customer 2. Thus, the ATM is idle when customer 3 arrives.
- Customer 3 begins service immediately with a start time of 7.6 minutes.
- The waiting time for customer 3 is the start time minus the arrival time: $7.6 - 7.6 = 0$ minutes.
- A service time of $ST = 2.2$ minutes is generated for customer 3.
- The completion time for customer 3 is the start time plus the service time: $7.6 + 2.2 = 9.8$ minutes.
- The time in the system for customer 3 is the completion time minus the arrival time: $9.8 - 7.6 = 2.2$ minutes.

Using the totals in Table 13.10, we can compute an average waiting time for the 10 customers of $11.2/10 = 1.12$ minutes, and an average time in the system of $32.1/10 = 3.21$ minutes. Table 13.10 shows that seven of the 10 customers had to wait. The total time for the 10-customer simulation is given by the completion time of the 10th customer: 26.0 minutes. However, at this point, we realize that a simulation for 10 customers is much too short a period to draw any firm conclusions about the operation of the waiting line.

Simulation of the Hammondsport Savings Bank ATM Problem

Using an Excel worksheet, we simulated the operation of the Hammondsport ATM waiting line system for 1000 customers. The worksheet used to carry out the simulation is shown in Figure 13.15. Note that the simulation results for customers 6 through 995 have been hidden so that the results can be shown in a reasonably sized figure. If desired, the rows for these customers can be shown and the simulation results displayed for all 1000 customers.

FIGURE 13.15 EXCEL WORKSHEET FOR THE HAMMONDSPORT SAVINGS BANK WITH ONE ATM

Hammondsport1

	A	B	C	D	E	F	G	H
1	**Hammonsdsport Savings Bank with One ATM**							
2								
3	**Interarrival Times (Uniform Distribution)**							
4	Smallest Value	0						
5	Largest Value	5						
6								
7	**Service Times (Normal Distribution)**							
8	Mean	2						
9	Std Deviation	0.5						
10								
11								
12	**Simulation**							
13								
14		Interarrival	Arrival	Service	Waiting	Service	Completion	Time
15	Customer	Time	Time	Start Time	Time	Time	Time	in System
16	1	1.4	1.4	1.4	0.0	2.3	3.7	2.3
17	2	1.3	2.7	3.7	1.0	1.5	5.2	2.5
18	3	4.9	7.6	7.6	0.0	2.2	9.8	2.2
19	4	3.5	11.1	11.1	0.0	2.5	13.6	2.5
20	5	0.7	11.8	13.6	1.8	1.8	15.4	3.6
1011	996	0.5	2496.8	2498.1	1.3	0.6	2498.7	1.9
1012	997	0.2	2497.0	2498.7	1.7	2.0	2500.7	3.7
1013	998	2.7	2499.7	2500.7	1.0	1.8	2502.5	2.8
1014	999	3.7	2503.4	2503.4	0.0	2.4	2505.8	2.4
1015	1000	4.0	2507.4	2507.4	0.0	1.9	2509.3	1.9
1016								
1017		**Summary Statistics**						
1018		Number Waiting			549			
1019		Probability of Waiting			0.6100			
1020		Average Waiting Time			1.59			
1021		Maximum Waiting Time			13.5			
1022		Utilization of ATM			0.7860			
1023		Number Waiting > 1 Min			393			
1024		Probability of Waiting > 1 Min			0.4367			
1025								

Ultimately, summary statistics will be collected in order to describe the results of 1000 customers. Before collecting the summary statistics, let us point out that most simulation studies of dynamic systems focus on the operation of the system during its long-run or steady-state operation. To ensure that the effect of start-up conditions are not included in the steady-state calculations, a dynamic simulation model is usually run for a specified period without collecting any data about the operation of the system. The length of the start-up period can vary depending on the application. For the Hammondsport Savings Bank ATM simulation, we treated the results for the first 100 customers as the start-up period. Thus, the summary statistics shown in Figure 13.15 are for the 900 customers arriving during the steady-state period.

The summary statistics show that 549 of the 900 Hammondsport customers had to wait. This result provides a 549/900 = 0.61 probability that a customer will have to wait for service. In other words, approximately 61 percent of the customers will have to wait because the ATM is in use. The average waiting time is 1.59 minutes per customer with at least one customer waiting the maximum time of 13.5 minutes. The utilization rate of 0.7860 indicates that the ATM is in use 78.6 percent of the time. Finally, 393 of the 900 customers had to wait more than 1 minute (43.67 percent of all customers). A histogram of waiting times for the 900 customers is shown in Figure 13.16. This figure shows that 45 customers (5 percent) had a waiting time greater than 6 minutes.

The simulation supports the conclusion that the branch will have a busy ATM system. With an average customer wait time of 1.59 minutes, the branch does not satisfy the bank's customer service guideline. This branch is a good candidate for installation of a second ATM.

Simulation with Two ATMs

We extended the simulation model to the case of two ATMs. For the second ATM we also assume that the service time is normally distributed with a mean of 2 minutes and a standard deviation of 0.5 minutes. Table 13.11 shows the simulation results for the first 10 customers. In comparing the two-ATM system results in Table 13.11 with the single ATM simulation results shown in Table 13.10, we see that two additional columns are needed. These two columns show when each ATM becomes available for customer service. We assume that, when a new customer arrives, the customer will be served by the ATM that frees up first. When the simulation begins, the first customer is assigned to ATM 1.

FIGURE 13.16 HISTOGRAM SHOWING THE WAITING TIME FOR 900 ATM CUSTOMERS

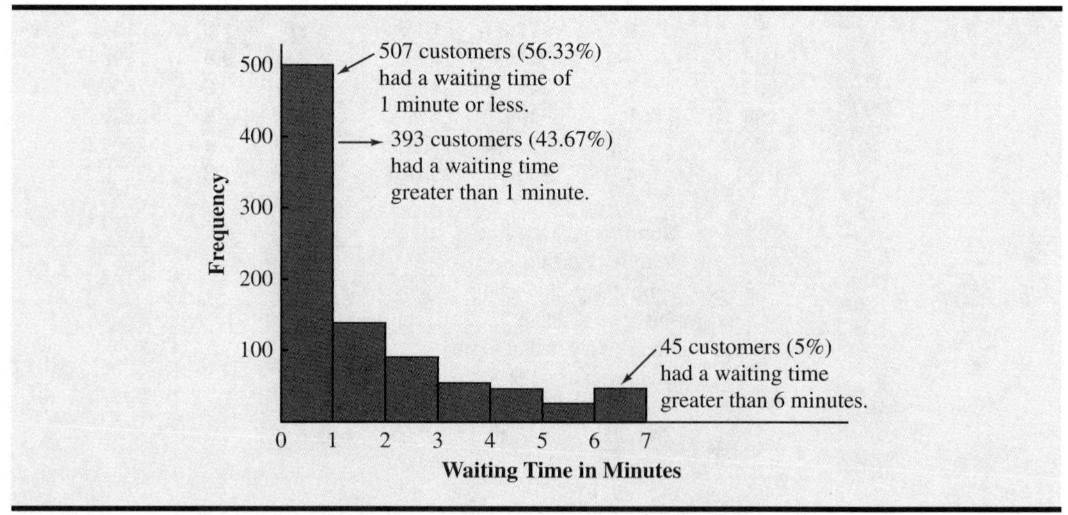

TABLE 13.11 SIMULATION RESULTS FOR 10 CUSTOMERS FOR A TWO-ATM SYSTEM

Customer	Interarrival Time	Arrival Time	Service Start Time	Waiting Time	Service Time	Completion Time	Time in System	Time Available ATM 1	Time Available ATM 2
1	1.7	1.7	1.7	0.0	2.1	3.8	2.1	3.8	0.0
2	0.7	2.4	2.4	0.0	2.0	4.4	2.0	3.8	4.4
3	2.0	4.4	4.4	0.0	1.4	5.8	1.4	5.8	4.4
4	0.1	4.5	4.5	0.0	0.9	5.4	0.9	5.8	5.4
5	4.6	9.1	9.1	0.0	2.2	11.3	2.2	5.8	11.3
6	1.3	10.4	10.4	0.0	1.6	12.0	1.6	12.0	11.3
7	0.6	11.0	11.3	0.3	1.7	13.0	2.0	12.0	13.0
8	0.3	11.3	12.0	0.7	2.2	14.2	2.9	14.2	13.0
9	3.4	14.7	14.7	0.0	2.9	17.6	2.9	14.2	17.6
10	0.1	14.8	14.8	0.0	2.8	17.6	2.8	17.6	17.6
Totals	14.8			1.0	19.8		20.8		
Averages	1.48			0.1	1.98		2.08		

Table 13.11 shows that customer 7 is the first customer who has to wait to use an ATM. We describe how customers 6, 7, and 8 are processed to show how the logic of the simulation run for two ATMs differs from that with a single ATM.

Customer 6

- An interarrival time of 1.3 minutes is generated, and customer 6 arrives 9.1 + 1.3 = 10.4 minutes into the simulation.
- From the customer 5 row, we see that ATM 1 frees up at 5.8 minutes, and ATM 2 will free up at 11.3 minutes into the simulation. Because ATM 1 is free, customer 6 does not wait and begins service on ATM 1 at the arrival time of 10.4 minutes.
- A service time of 1.6 minutes is generated for customer 6. So customer 6 has a completion time of 10.4 + 1.6 = 12.0 minutes.
- The time ATM 1 will next become available is set at 12.0 minutes; the time available for ATM 2 remains 11.3 minutes.

Customer 7

- An interarrival time of 0.6 minute is generated, and customer 7 arrives 10.4 + 0.6 = 11.0 minutes into the simulation.
- From the previous row, we see that ATM 1 will not be available until 12.0 minutes, and ATM 2 will not be available until 11.3 minutes. So customer 7 must wait to use an ATM. Because ATM 2 will free up first, customer 7 begins service on that machine at a start time of 11.3 minutes. With an arrival time of 11.0 and a service start time of 11.3, customer 7 experiences a waiting time of 11.3 − 11.0 = 0.3 minute.
- A service time of 1.7 minutes is generated leading to a completion time of 11.3 + 1.7 = 13.0 minutes.
- The time available for ATM 2 is updated to 13.0 minutes, and the time available for ATM 1 remains at 12.0 minutes.

Customer 8

- An interarrival time of 0.3 minute is generated, and customer 8 arrives 11.0 + 0.3 = 11.3 minutes into the simulation.
- From the previous row, we see that ATM 1 will be the first available. Thus, customer 8 starts service on ATM 1 at 12.0 minutes resulting in a waiting time of 12.0 − 11.3 = 0.7 minute.

- A service time of 2.2 minutes is generated resulting in a completion time of 12.0 + 2.2 = 14.2 minutes and a system time of 0.7 + 2.2 = 2.9 minutes.
- The time available for ATM 1 is updated to 14.2 minutes, and the time available for ATM 2 remains at 13.0 minutes.

From the totals in Table 13.11, we see that the average waiting time for these 10 customers is only 1.0/10 = 0.1 minute. Of course, a much longer simulation will be necessary before any conclusions can be drawn.

Simulation Results with Two ATMs

Worksheets for the Hammondsport one-ATM and two-ATM systems are available on the CD that accompanies this text.

The Excel worksheet that we used to conduct a simulation for 1000 customers using two ATMs is shown in Figure 13.17. Results for the first 100 customers were discarded to account for the start-up period. With two ATMs, the number of customers who had to wait was reduced from 549 to 78. This reduction provides a 78/900 = 0.0867 probability that a customer will have to wait for service when two ATMs are used. The two-ATM system also

FIGURE 13.17 EXCEL WORKSHEET FOR THE HAMMONDSPORT SAVINGS BANK WITH TWO ATMs

EXCELfile
Hammondsport2

	A	B	C	D	E	F	G	H	I	J	K
1	**Hammondsport Savings Bank with Two ATMs**										
2											
3	**Interarrival Times (Uniform Distribution)**										
4	Smallest Value	0									
5	Largest Value	5									
6											
7	**Service Times (Normal Distribution)**										
8	Mean	2									
9	Std Deviation	0.5									
10											
11											
12	**Simulation**										
13											
14		Interarrival	Arrival	Service	Waiting	Service	Completion	Time	Time Available		
15	Customer	Time	Time	Start Time	Time	Time	Time	in System	ATM 1	ATM 2	
16	1	1.7	1.7	1.7	0.0	2.1	3.8	2.1	3.8	0.0	
17	2	0.7	2.4	2.4	0.0	2.0	4.4	2.0	3.8	4.4	
18	3	2.0	4.4	4.4	0.0	1.4	5.8	1.4	5.8	4.4	
19	4	0.1	4.5	4.5	0.0	0.9	5.4	0.9	5.8	5.4	
20	5	4.6	9.1	9.1	0.0	2.2	11.3	2.2	5.8	11.3	
1011	996	3.3	2483.2	2483.2	0.0	2.2	2485.4	2.2	2485.4	2482.1	
1012	997	4.5	2487.7	2487.7	0.0	1.9	2489.6	1.9	2485.4	2489.6	
1013	998	3.8	2491.5	2491.5	0.0	3.2	2494.7	3.2	2494.7	2489.6	
1014	999	0.0	2491.5	2491.5	0.0	2.4	2493.9	2.4	2494.7	2493.9	
1015	1000	2.6	2494.1	2494.1	0.0	2.8	2496.9	2.8	2494.7	2496.9	
1016											
1017		**Summary Statistics**									
1018		Number Waiting			78						
1019		Probability of Waiting			0.0867						
1020		Average Waiting Time			0.07						
1021		Maximum Waiting Time			2.9						
1022		Utilization of ATMs			0.4084						
1023		Number Waiting > 1 Min			23						
1024		Probability of Waiting > 1 Min			0.0256						
1025											

reduced the average waiting time to 0.07 minute (4.2 seconds) per customer. The maximum waiting time was reduced from 13.5 to 2.9 minutes, and each ATM was in use 40.84 percent of the time. Finally, only 23 of the 900 customers had to wait more than 1 minute for an ATM to become available. Thus, only 2.56 percent of customers had to wait more than 1 minute. The simulation results provide evidence that Hammondsport Savings Bank needs to expand to the two-ATM system.

The simulation models that we developed can now be used to study the ATM operation at other branch banks. In each case, assumptions must be made about the appropriate interarrival time and service time probability distributions. However, once appropriate assumptions have been made, the same simulation models can be used to determine the operating characteristics of the ATM waiting line system. The Management Science in Action, Preboard Screening at Vancouver International Airport, describes another use of simulation for a queueing system.

MANAGEMENT SCIENCE IN ACTION

PREBOARD SCREENING AT VANCOUVER INTERNATIONAL AIRPORT*

Following the September 11, 2001, terrorist attacks in the United States, long lines at airport security checkpoints have become commonplace. In order to reduce passenger waiting time, the Vancouver International Airport Authority teamed up with students and faculty at the University of British Columbia's Centre for Operations Excellence (COE) to build a simulation model of the airport's preboard screening security checkpoints. The goal was to use the simulation model to help achieve acceptable service standards.

Prior to building the simulation model, students from the COE observed the flow of passengers through the screening process and collected data on the service time at each process step. In addition to service time data, passenger demand data provided input to the simulation model. Two triangular probability distributions were used to simulate passenger arrivals at the preboarding facilities. For flights to Canadian destinations a 90-40-20 triangle was used. This distribution assumes that, for each flight, the first passenger will arrive at the screening checkpoint 90 minutes before departure, the last passenger will arrive 20 minutes before departure, and the most likely arrival time is 40 minutes before departure. For international flights a 150-80-20 triangle was used.

Output statistics from the simulation model provided information concerning resource utilization, waiting line lengths and the time passengers spend in the system. The simulation model provided information concerning the number of personnel needed to process 90% of the passengers with a waiting time of 10 minutes or less. Ultimately the airport authority was able to design and staff the preboarding checkpoints in such a fashion that waiting times for 90% of the passengers were a maximum of 10 minutes.

*Based on Derek Atkins et al., "Right on Queue," *OR/MS Today* (April 2003): 26–29.

NOTES AND COMMENTS

1. The ATM waiting line model was based on uniformly distributed interarrival times and normally distributed service times. One advantage of simulation is its flexibility in accommodating a variety of different probability distributions. For instance, if we believe an exponential distribution is more appropriate for interarrival times, the ATM simulation could be repeated by simply changing the way the interarrival times are generated.
2. At the beginning of this section, we defined *discrete-event simulation* as involving a dynamic system that evolves over time. The simulation computations focus on the sequence of events as they occur at discrete points in time. In the ATM waiting line example, customer arrivals and the customer service completions

(*continued*)

were the discrete events. Referring to the arrival times and completion times in Table 13.10, we see that the first five discrete events for the ATM waiting line simulation were as follows:

Event	Time
Customer 1 arrives	1.4
Customer 2 arrives	2.7
Customer 1 finished	3.7
Customer 2 finished	5.2
Customer 3 arrives	7.6

3. We did not keep track of the number of customers in the ATM waiting line as we carried out the ATM simulation computations on a customer-by-customer basis. However, we can determine the average number of customers in the waiting line from other information in the simulation output. The following relationship is valid for any waiting line system:

$$\begin{array}{c}\text{Average number}\\ \text{in waiting line}\end{array} = \frac{\text{Total waiting time}}{\text{Total time of simulation}}$$

For the system with one ATM, the 100th customer completed service at 247.8 minutes into the simulation. Thus, the total time of the simulation for the next 900 customers was 2509.3 − 247.8 = 2261.5 minutes. The average waiting time was 1.59 minutes. During the simulation, the 900 customers had a total waiting time of 900(1.59) = 1431 minutes. Therefore, the average number of customers in the waiting line is

$$\begin{aligned}\begin{array}{c}\text{Average number}\\ \text{in waiting line}\end{array} &= 1431/2261.5\\ &= 0.63 \text{ customer}\end{aligned}$$

13.4 OTHER SIMULATION ISSUES

Because simulation is one of the most widely used quantitative analysis techniques, various software tools have been developed to help analysts implement a simulation model on a computer. In this section we comment on the software available and discuss some issues involved in verifying and validating a simulation model. We close the section with a discussion of some of the advantages and disadvantages of using simulation to study a real system.

Computer Implementation

The use of spreadsheets for simulation has grown rapidly in recent years, and third-party software vendors have developed spreadsheet add-ins that make building simulation models on a spreadsheet much easier. These add-in packages provide an easy facility for generating random values from a variety of probability distributions and provide a rich array of statistics describing the simulation output. Two popular spreadsheet add-ins are Crystal Ball from Decisioneering and @RISK from Palisade Corporation. Although spreadsheets can be a valuable tool for some simulation studies, they are generally limited to smaller, less complex systems.

With the growth of simulation applications, both users of simulation and software developers began to realize that computer simulations have many common features: model development, generating values from probability distributions, maintaining a record of what happens during the simulation, and recording and summarizing the simulation output. A variety of special-purpose simulation packages are available, including GPSS®, SIMSCRIPT®, SLAM®, and Arena®. These packages have built-in simulation clocks, simplified methods for generating probabilistic inputs, and procedures for collecting and summarizing the simulation output. Special-purpose simulation packages enable quantitative analysts to simplify the process of developing and implementing the simulation model. Indeed, Arena 6.0 was used to develop the simulation model described in the Management Science in Action, Preboard Screening at Vancouver International Airport.

Simulation models can also be developed using general-purpose computer programming languages such as BASIC, FORTRAN, PASCAL, C, and C++. The disadvantage of using these languages is that special simulation procedures are not built in. One command in a special-purpose simulation package often performs the computations and record-keeping tasks that would require several BASIC, FORTRAN, PASCAL, C, or C++ statements to duplicate. The advantage of using a general-purpose programming language is that they offer greater flexibility in terms of being able to model more complex systems.

The computational and record-keeping aspects of simulation models are assisted by special simulation software packages. The packages ease the tasks of developing a computer simulation model.

To decide which software to use, an analyst will have to consider the relative merits of a spreadsheet, a special-purpose simulation package, and a general-purpose computer programming language. The goal is to select the method that is easy to use while still providing an adequate representation of the system being studied.

Verification and Validation

An important aspect of any simulation study involves confirming that the simulation model accurately describes the real system. Inaccurate simulation models cannot be expected to provide worthwhile information. Thus, before using simulation results to draw conclusions about a real system, one must take steps to verify and validate the simulation model.

Verification is the process of determining that the computer procedure that performs the simulation calculations is logically correct. Verification is largely a debugging task to make sure that no errors are in the computer procedure that implements the simulation. In some cases, an analyst may compare computer results for a limited number of events with independent hand calculations. In other cases, tests may be performed to verify that the probabilistic inputs are being generated correctly and that the output from the simulation model seems reasonable. The verification step is not complete until the user develops a high degree of confidence that the computer procedure is error free.

Validation is the process of ensuring that the simulation model provides an accurate representation of a real system. Validation requires an agreement among analysts and managers that the logic and the assumptions used in the design of the simulation model accurately reflect how the real system operates. The first phase of the validation process is done prior to, or in conjunction with, the development of the computer procedure for the simulation process. Validation continues after the computer program has been developed with the analyst reviewing the simulation output to see whether the simulation results closely approximate the performance of the real system. If possible, the output of the simulation model is compared to the output of an existing real system to make sure that the simulation output closely approximates the performance of the real system. If this form of validation is not possible, an analyst can experiment with the simulation model and have one or more individuals experienced with the operation of the real system review the simulation output to determine whether it is a reasonable approximation of what would be obtained with the real system under similar conditions.

Verification and validation are not tasks to be taken lightly. They are key steps in any simulation study and are necessary to ensure that decisions and conclusions based on the simulation results are appropriate for the real system.

Advantages and Disadvantages of Using Simulation

The primary advantages of simulation are that it is easy to understand and that the methodology can be used to model and learn about the behavior of complex systems that would be difficult, if not impossible, to deal with analytically. Simulation models are flexible; they can be used to describe systems without requiring the assumptions that are often required by mathematical models. In general, the larger the number of probabilistic inputs a system has, the more likely that a simulation model will provide the best approach for studying the system. Another advantage of simulation is that a simulation model provides a convenient experimental laboratory for the real system. Changing assumptions or operating policies in the simulation model and rerunning it can provide results that help predict how such changes will affect the operation of the real system. Experimenting directly with a real system is often not feasible.

Using simulation, we can ask what-if questions and project how the real system will behave. Although simulation does not guarantee optimality, it will usually provide near-optimal solutions. In addition, simulation models often warn against poor decision strategies by projecting disastrous outcomes such as system failures, large financial losses, and so on.

Simulation is not without some disadvantages. For complex systems, the process of developing, verifying, and validating a simulation model can be time-consuming and expensive. In addition, each simulation run provides only a sample of how the real system will operate. As such, the summary of the simulation data provides only estimates or approximations about the real system. Consequently, simulation does not guarantee an optimal solution. Nonetheless, the danger of obtaining poor solutions is slight if the analyst exercises good judgment in developing the simulation model and if the simulation process is run long enough under a wide variety of conditions so that the analyst has sufficient data to predict how the real system will operate.

SUMMARY

Simulation is a method for learning about a real system by experimenting with a model that represents the system. Some of the reasons simulation is frequently used are

1. It can be used for a wide variety of practical problems.
2. The simulation approach is relatively easy to explain and understand. As a result, management confidence is increased, and acceptance of the results is more easily obtained.
3. Spreadsheet packages now provide another alternative for model implementation, and third-party vendors have developed add-ins that expand the capabilities of the spreadsheet packages.
4. Computer software developers have produced simulation packages that make it easier to develop and implement simulation models for more complex problems.

We first showed how simulation can be used for risk analysis by analyzing a situation involving the development of a new product: the PortaCom printer. We then showed how simulation can be used to select an inventory replenishment level that would provide both a good profit and a good customer service level. Finally, we developed a simulation model for the Hammondsport Savings Bank ATM waiting line system. This model is an example of a dynamic simulation model in which the state of the system changes or evolves over time.

Our approach was to develop a simulation model that contained both controllable inputs and probabilistic inputs. Procedures were developed for randomly generating values for the probabilistic inputs, and a flowchart was developed to show the sequence of logical and mathematical operations that describe the steps of the simulation process. Simulation results were obtained by running the simulation for a suitable number of trials or length of time. Simulation results were obtained and conclusions were drawn about the operation of the real system.

The Management Science in Action, Designing Manufacturing Systems at Mexico's Vilpac, describes how a simulation model assisted a truck manufacturing company in Mexico.

MANAGEMENT SCIENCE IN ACTION

DESIGNING MANUFACTURING SYSTEMS AT MEXICO'S VILPAC*

In increasing numbers, U.S. firms are joining diverse geographical and cultural partners in Western Europe, Asia, and Mexico to capitalize on each other's advantages and remain competitive in world markets. Mexico, the United States' third largest trading partner, offers a unique opportunity for integrating manufacturing operations. For example, Mexican and U.S. firms have been working together to turn the Mexican truck company, Vilpac, into a world-class manufacturing firm.

The selection of manufacturing configurations and the design of new plants at Vilpac are being guided by a simulation model of the firm's manufacturing operations. A network simulation language, SIMNET II®, has been used to model the manufacturing system that comprises some 95 machines and 1900 parts. Various simulation runs were used to validate the model. When applied to a plant that was producing 20 trucks per day, the simulation model accurately predicted production at 19.8 trucks per day.

The three interrelated modules of the simulation model include operations, corrective maintenance, and preventive maintenance. Various components of the model include capabilities for handling changes in customer demand, manufacturing cost, capacity, and work-in-process and inventory levels. Experimentation with the model investigated capacity requirements, product-mix effects, new products, inventory policies, product flow, setup times, production planning and control strategies, plant expansion, and new plant design. Tangible benefits include an increase in production of 260%, a reduction in work-in-process of 70%, and an increase in market share.

*Based on J. P. Nuno, D. L. Shunk, J. M. Padillo, and B. Beltran, "Mexico's Vilpac Truck Company Uses a CIM Implementation to Become a World Class Manufacturer," *Interfaces,* no. 1 (January/February 1993): 59–75.

GLOSSARY

Simulation A method for learning about a real system by experimenting with a model that represents the system.

Simulation experiment The generation of a sample of values for the probabilistic inputs of a simulation model and computing the resulting values of the model outputs.

Controllable input Input to a simulation model that is selected by the decision maker.

Probabilistic input Input to a simulation model that is subject to uncertainty. A probabilistic input is described by a probability distribution.

Risk analysis The process of predicting the outcome of a decision in the face of uncertainty.

Parameters Numerical values that appear in the mathematical relationships of a model. Parameters are considered known and remain constant over all trials of a simulation.

What-if analysis A trial-and-error approach to learning about the range of possible outputs for a model. Trial values are chosen for the model inputs (these are the what-ifs) and the value of the output(s) is computed.

Base-case scenario Determining the output given the most likely values for the probabilistic inputs of a model.

Worst-case scenario Determining the output given the worst values that can be expected for the probabilistic inputs of a model.

Best-case scenario Determining the output given the best values that can be expected for the probabilistic inputs of a model.

Static simulation model A simulation model used in situations where the state of the system at one point in time does not affect the state of the system at future points in time. Each trial of the simulation is independent.

Dynamic simulation model A simulation model used in situations where the state of the system affects how the system changes or evolves over time.

Event An instantaneous occurrence that changes the state of the system in a simulation model.

Discrete-event simulation model A simulation model that describes how a system evolves over time by using events that occur at discrete points in time.

Verification The process of determining that a computer program implements a simulation model as it is intended.

Validation The process of determining that a simulation model provides an accurate representation of a real system.

PROBLEMS

Note: Problems 1–12 are designed to give you practice in setting up a simulation model and demonstrating how random numbers can be used to generate values for the probabilistic inputs. These problems, which ask you to provide a small number of simulation trials, can be done with hand calculations. This approach should give you a good understanding of the simulation process, but the simulation results will not be sufficient for you to draw final conclusions or make decisions about the situation. Problems 13–24 are more realistic in that they ask you to generate simulation output(s) for a large number of trials and use the results to draw conclusions about the behavior of the system being studied. These problems require the use of a computer to carry out the simulation computations. The ability to use Excel or some other spreadsheet package will be necessary when you attempt Problems 13–24.

1. Consider the PortaCom project discussed in Section 13.1
   a. An engineer on the product development team believes that first-year sales for the new printer will be 20,000 units. Using estimates of $45 per unit for the direct labor cost and $90 per unit for the parts cost, what is the first-year profit using the engineer's sales estimate?
   b. The financial analyst on the product development team is more conservative, indicating that parts cost may well be $100 per unit. In addition, the analyst suggests that a sales volume of 10,000 units is more realistic. Using the most likely value of $45 per unit for the direct labor cost, what is the first-year profit using the financial analyst's estimates?
   c. Why is the simulation approach to risk analysis preferable to generating a variety of what-if scenarios such as those suggested by the engineer and the financial analyst?

2. The management of Madeira Manufacturing Company is considering the introduction of a new product. The fixed cost to begin the production of the product is $30,000. The variable cost for the product is expected to be between $16 and $24 with a most likely value of $20 per unit. The product will sell for $50 per unit. Demand for the product is expected to range from 300 to 2100 units, with 1200 units the most likely demand.
   a. Develop the profit model for this product.
   b. Provide the base-case, worst-case, and best-case analyses.
   c. Discuss why simulation would be desirable.
3. Use the random numbers 0.3753, 0.9218, 0.0336, 0.5145, and 0.7000 to generate five simulated values for the PortaCom direct labor cost per unit.

4. A retail store experiences the following probability distribution for sales of a product.

Sales (units)	0	1	2	3	4	5	6
Probability	0.08	0.12	0.28	0.24	0.14	0.10	0.04

a. Set up intervals of random numbers that can be used to simulate sales.
b. Random numbers generated for the first 10 days of a simulation are as follows: 0.4627, 0.8745, 0.4479, 0.6712, 0.4557, 0.8435, 0.2162, 0.1699, 0.1338, 0.2278. What is the sales value generated for each day?
c. What are the total sales over the 10-day period?

5. The price of a share of a particular stock listed on the New York Stock Exchange is currently \$39. The following probability distribution shows how the price per share is expected to change over a three-month period.

Stock Price Change (\$)	Probability
−2	0.05
−1	0.10
0	0.25
+1	0.20
+2	0.20
+3	0.10
+4	0.10

a. Set up intervals of random numbers that can be used to generate the change in stock price over a three-month period.
b. With the current price of \$39 per share and the random numbers 0.1091, 0.9407, 0.1941, and 0.8083, simulate the price per share for the next four 3-month periods. What is the ending simulated price per share?

6. The Statewide Auto Insurance Company developed the following probability distribution for automobile collision claims paid during the past year.

Payment(\$)	Probability
0	0.83
500	0.06
1,000	0.05
2,000	0.02
5,000	0.02
8,000	0.01
10,000	0.01

a. Set up intervals of random numbers that can be used to generate automobile collision claim payments.
b. Using the first 20 random numbers in column 4 of Table 13.2, simulate the payments for 20 policyholders. How many claims are paid and what is the total amount paid to the policyholders?

7. A variety of routine maintenance checks are made on commercial airplanes prior to each takeoff. A particular maintenance check of an airplane's landing gear requires between 10 and 18 minutes of a maintenance engineer's time. In fact, the exact time required is uniformly distributed over this interval. As part of a larger simulation model designed to

determine total on-ground maintenance time for an airplane, we will need to simulate the actual time required to perform this maintenance check on the airplane's landing gear. Using random numbers of 0.1567, 0.9823, 0.3419, 0.5572, and 0.7758, compute the time required for each of five simulated maintenance checks of the airplane's landing gear.

8. Baseball's World Series is a maximum of seven games, with the winner being the first team to win four games. Assume that the Atlanta Braves are in the World Series and that the first two games are to be played in Atlanta, the next three games at the opponent's ball park, and the last two games, if necessary, back in Atlanta. Taking into account the projected starting pitchers for each game and the homefield advantage, the probabilities of Atlanta winning each game are as follows:

Game	1	2	3	4	5	6	7
Probability of Win	0.60	0.55	0.48	0.45	0.48	0.55	0.50

a. Set up random number intervals that can be used to determine the winner of each game. Let the smaller random numbers indicate that Atlanta wins the game. For example, the random number interval "0.00 but less than 0.60" corresponds to Atlanta winning game 1.

b. Use the random numbers in column 6 of Table 13.2 beginning with 0.3813 to simulate the playing of the World Series. Do the Atlanta Braves win the series? How many games are played?

c. Discuss how repeated simulation trials could be used to estimate the overall probability of Atlanta winning the series as well as the most likely number of games in the series.

9. A project has four activities (A, B, C, and D) that must be performed sequentially. The probability distributions for the time required to complete each of the activities are as follows:

Activity	**Activity Time (weeks)**	**Probability**
A	5	0.25
	6	0.35
	7	0.25
	8	0.15
B	3	0.20
	5	0.55
	7	0.25
C	10	0.10
	12	0.25
	14	0.40
	16	0.20
	18	0.05
D	8	0.60
	10	0.40

a. Provide the base-case, worst-case, and best-case calculations for the time to complete the project.

b. Use the random numbers 0.1778, 0.9617, 0.6849, and 0.4503 to simulate the completion time of the project in weeks.

c. Discuss how simulation could be used to estimate the probability the project can be completed in 35 weeks or less.

10. The gambling game of roulette is played in casinos in Monte Carlo, Las Vegas, and elsewhere around the world. The roulette wheel has 38 slots: 18 red, 18 black, and 2 green. One of the simplest bets is betting on the color. If the color chosen comes up, the gambler wins an amount equal to the amount wagered. Assume a gambler will place a bet on the color red every time a new bet is placed. Also, assume the gambler is thinking of two betting strategies:

- Bet \$25. If the color red comes up, take \$25 off the table and let the original \$25 remain for the next spin of the wheel.
- Bet \$25. If the color red comes up, take \$0 off the table and let the original bet of \$25 plus the \$25 winnings ride on the next spin. If red comes up a second time, take \$75 off the table and let the original bet of \$25 remain for the next spin of the wheel.

a. What is the probability that a bet on the color red will win on each spin of the wheel?
b. What is the random number rule that will simulate a win or loss on each spin of the roulette wheel? Let red correspond to the lower random numbers.
c. Use the random numbers in column 3 of Table 13.2 to simulate the win or loss outcome for 20 plays. Begin with 0.1368 and read down the column. Using these same random numbers for both betting strategies, what are the total winnings of the 20 plays under each strategy?
d. Are you comfortable with reaching a conclusion based on your simulation results? Would additional simulation trials be beneficial?

11. Over a five-year period, the quarterly change in the price per share of common stock for a major oil company ranged from -8% to $+12\%$. A financial analyst wants to learn what can be expected for price appreciation of this stock over the next two years. Using the five-year history as a basis, the analyst is willing to assume the change in price for each quarter is uniformly distributed between -8% and 12%. Use simulation to provide information about the price per share for the stock over the coming two-year period (eight quarters).

a. Use two-digit random numbers from column 2 of Table 13.2, beginning with 0.52, 0.99, and so on, to simulate the quarterly price change for each of the eight quarters.
b. If the current price per share is \$80, what is the simulated price per share at the end of the two-year period?
c. Discuss how risk analysis would be helpful in identifying the risk associated with a two-year investment in this stock.

12. The management of Brinkley Corporation is interested in using simulation to estimate the profit per unit for a new product. Probability distributions for the purchase cost, the labor cost, and the transportation cost are as follows:

Purchase Cost (\$)	Probability	Labor Cost (\$)	Probability	Transportation Cost (\$)	Probability
10	0.25	20	0.10	3	0.75
11	0.45	22	0.25	5	0.25
12	0.30	24	0.35		
		25	0.30		

Assume that these are the only costs and that the selling price for the product will be \$45 per unit.

a. Provide the base-case, worst-case, and best-case calculations for the profit per unit.
b. Set up intervals of random numbers that can be used to randomly generate the three cost components.
c. Using the random numbers 0.3726, 0.5839, and 0.8275, calculate the profit per unit.

d. Using the random numbers 0.1862, 0.7466, and 0.6171, calculate the profit per unit.
e. Management believes the project may not be profitable if the profit per unit is less than \$5. Explain how simulation can be used to estimate the probability the profit per unit will be less than \$5.

13. Using the PortaCom Risk Analysis worksheet in Figure 13.6 and on the CD accompanying the text, develop your own worksheet for the PortaCom simulation model.
    a. Compute the mean profit, the minimum profit, and the maximum profit.
    b. What is your estimate of the probability of a loss?

14. Develop a worksheet simulation for the following problem. The management of Madeira Manufacturing Company is considering the introduction of a new product. The fixed cost to begin the production of the product is \$30,000. The variable cost for the product is uniformly distributed between \$16 and \$24 per unit. The product will sell for \$50 per unit. Demand for the product is best described by a normal probability distribution with a mean of 1200 units and a standard deviation of 300 units. Develop a spreadsheet simulation similar to Figure 13.6. Use 500 simulation trials to answer the following questions.
    a. What is the mean profit for the simulation?
    b. What is the probability the project will result in a loss?
    c. What is your recommendation concerning the introduction of the product?

15. Use a worksheet to simulate the rolling of dice. Use the VLOOKUP function as described in Appendix 13.1 to select the outcome for each die. Place the number for the first die in column B and the number for the second die in column C. Show the sum in column D. Repeat the simulation for 1000 rolls of the dice. What is your simulation estimate of the probability of rolling a 7?

16. Strassel Investors buys real estate, develops it, and resells it for a profit. A new property is available, and Bud Strassel, the president and owner of Strassel Investors, believes it can be sold for \$160,000. The current property owner asked for bids and stated that the property will be sold for the highest bid in excess of \$100,000. Two competitors will be submitting bids for the property. Strassel does not know what the competitors will bid, but he assumes for planning purposes that the amount bid by each competitor will be uniformly distributed between \$100,000 and \$150,000.
    a. Develop a worksheet that can be used to simulate the bids made by the two competitors. Strassel is considering a bid of \$130,000 for the property. Using a simulation of 1000 trials, what is the estimate of the probability Strassel will be able to obtain the property using a bid of \$130,000?
    b. How much does Strassel need to bid to be assured of obtaining the property? What is the profit associated with this bid?
    c. Use the simulation model to compute the profit for each trial of the simulation run. With maximization of profit as Strassel's objective, use simulation to evaluate Strassel's bid alternatives of \$130,000, \$140,000, or \$150,000. What is the recommended bid, and what is the expected profit?

17. Grear Tire Company has produced a new tire with an estimated mean lifetime mileage of 36,500 miles. Management also believes that the standard deviation is 5000 miles and that tire mileage is normally distributed. Use a worksheet to simulate the miles obtained for a sample of 500 tires.
    a. Use the Excel COUNTIF function to determine the number of tires that last longer than 40,000 miles. What is your estimate of the percentage of tires that will exceed 40,000 miles?
    b. Use COUNTIF to find the number of tires that obtain mileage less than 32,000 miles. Then, find the number with less than 30,000 miles and the number with less than 28,000 miles.
    c. If management would like to advertise a tire mileage guarantee such that approximately no more than 10% of the tires would obtain mileage low enough to qualify for the guarantee, what tire mileage considered in part (b) would you recommend for the guarantee?

18. A building contractor is preparing a bid on a new construction project. Two other contractors will be submitting bids for the same project. Based on past bidding practices, bids from the other contractors can be described by the following probability distributions:

Contractor	Probability Distribution of Bid
A	Uniform probability distribution between $600,000 and $800,000
B	Normal probability distribution with a mean bid of $700,000 and a standard deviation of $50,000

a. If the building contractor submits a bid of $750,000, what is the probability the building contractor will obtain the bid? Use a worksheet to simulate 1000 trials of the contract bidding process.

b. The building contractor is also considering bids of $775,000 and $785,000. If the building contractor would like to bid such that the probability of winning the bid is about 0.80, what bid would you recommend? Repeat the simulation process with bids of $775,000 and $785,000 to justify your recommendation.

19. Develop your own worksheet for the Butler inventory simulation model shown in Figure 13.10. Suppose that management prefers not to charge for loss of goodwill. Run the Butler inventory simulation model with replenishment levels of 110, 115, 120, and 125. What is your recommendation?

20. In preparing for the upcoming holiday season, Mandrell Toy Company designated a new doll called Freddy. The fixed cost to produce the doll is $100,000. The variable cost, which includes material, labor, and shipping costs, is $34 per doll. During the holiday selling season, Mandrell will sell the dolls for $42 each. If Mandrell overproduces the dolls, the excess dolls will be sold in January through a distributor who has agreed to pay Mandrell $10 per doll. Demand for new toys during the holiday selling season is extremely uncertain. Forecasts are for expected sales of 60,000 dolls with a standard deviation of 15,000. The normal probability distribution is assumed to be a good description of the demand.

a. Create a worksheet similar to the inventory worksheet in Figure 13.10. Include columns showing demand, sales, revenue from sales, amount of surplus, revenue from sales of surplus, total cost, and net profit. Use your worksheet to simulate the sales of the Freddy doll using a production quantity of 60,000 units. Using 500 simulation trials, what is the estimate of the mean profit associated with the production quantity of 60,000 dolls?

b. Before making a final decision on the production quantity, management wants an analysis of a more aggressive 70,000 unit production quantity and a more conservative 50,000 unit production quantity. Run your simulation with these two production quantities. What is the mean profit associated with each? What is your recommendation on the production of the Freddy doll?

c. Assuming that Mandrell's management adopts your recommendation, what is the probability of a stock-out and a shortage of the Freddy dolls during the holiday season?

21. South Central Airlines operates a commuter flight between Atlanta and Charlotte. The plane holds 30 passengers, and the airline makes a $100 profit on each passenger on the flight. When South Central takes 30 reservations for the flight, experience has shown that on average, two passengers do not show up. As a result, with 30 reservations, South Central is averaging 28 passengers with a profit of 28(100) = $2800 per flight. The airline operations office has asked for an evaluation of an overbooking strategy where they would accept 32 reservations even though the airplane holds only 30 passengers. The probability

distribution for the number of passengers showing up when 32 reservations are accepted is as follows.

Passengers Showing Up	Probability
28	0.05
29	0.25
30	0.50
31	0.15
32	0.05

The airline will receive a profit of \$100 for each passenger on the flight up to the capacity of 30 passengers. The airline will incur a cost for any passenger denied seating on the flight. This cost covers added expenses of rescheduling the passenger as well as loss of goodwill, estimated to be \$150 per passenger. Develop a worksheet model that will simulate the performance of the overbooking system. Simulate the number of passengers showing up for each of 500 flights by using the VLOOKUP function. Use the results to compute the profit for each flight.

a. Does your simulation recommend the overbooking strategy? What is the mean profit per flight if overbooking is implemented?

b. Explain how your simulation model could be used to evaluate other overbooking levels such as 31, 33, 34 and for recommending a best overbooking strategy.

22. Develop your own waiting line simulation model for the Hammondsport Savings Bank problem (see Figure 13.14). Assume that a new branch is expected to open with interarrival times uniformly distributed between 0 and 4 minutes. The service times at this branch are anticipated to be normal with a mean of 2 minutes and a standard deviation of 0.5 minute. Simulate the operation of this system for 600 customers using one ATM. What is your assessment of the ability to operate this branch with one ATM? What happens to the average waiting time for customers near the end of the simulation period?

23. The Burger Dome waiting line model in Section 12.1 studies the waiting time of customers at its fast-food restaurant. Burger Dome's single-channel waiting line system has a mean of 0.75 arrivals per minute and a service rate of 1 customer per minute.

a. Use a worksheet based on Figure 13.15 to simulate the operation of this waiting line. Assuming that customer arrivals follow a Poisson probability distribution, the interarrival times can be simulated with the cell formula $-(1/\lambda)$*LN(RAND()), where $\lambda = 0.75$. Assuming that the service time follows an exponential probability distribution, the service times can be simulated with the cell formula $-\mu$*LN(RAND()), where $\mu = 1$. Run the Burger Dome simulation for 500 customers. The analytical model in Chapter 12 indicates an average waiting time of 3 minutes per customer. What average waiting time does your simulation model show?

b. One advantage of using simulation is that a simulation model can be altered easily to reflect other assumptions about the probabilistic inputs. Assume that the service time is more accurately described by a normal probability distribution with a mean of 1 minute and a standard deviation of 0.2 minute. This distribution has less service time variability than the exponential probability distribution used in part (a). What is the impact of this change on the average waiting time?

24. Telephone calls come into an airline reservations office randomly at the mean rate of 15 calls per hour. The time between calls follows an exponential distribution with a mean of 4 minutes. When the two reservation agents are busy, a telephone message tells the caller that the call is important and to please wait on the line until the next reservation agent becomes available. The service time for each reservation agent is normally distributed with a mean of 4 minutes and a standard deviation of 1 minute. Use a two-channel waiting line simulation model to evaluate this waiting line system. Use the worksheet design shown in Figure 13.17. The cell formula =−4*LN(RAND()) can be used to generate the interarrival times. Simulate the operation of the telephone reservation system for 600 customers. Discard the first 100 customers, and collect data over the next 500 customers.

a. Compute the mean interarrival time and the mean service time. If your simulation model is operating correctly, both of these should have means of approximately 4 minutes.

b. What is the mean customer waiting time for this system?

c. Use the =COUNTIF function to determine the number of customers who have to wait for a reservation agent. What percentage of the customers have to wait?

Case Problem 1 TRI-STATE CORPORATION

What will your portfolio be worth in 10 years? In 20 years? When you stop working? The Human Resources Department at Tri-State Corporation was asked to develop a financial planning model that would help employees address these questions. Tom Gifford was asked to lead this effort and decided to begin by developing a financial plan for himself. Tom has a degree in business and, at the age of 25, is making $34,000 per year. After two years of contributions to his company's retirement program and the receipt of a small inheritance, Tom has accumulated a portfolio valued at $14,500. Tom plans to work 30 more years and hopes to accumulate a portfolio valued at $1,000,000. Can he do it?

Tom began with a few assumptions about his future salary, his new investment contributions, and his portfolio growth rate. He assumed 5 percent annual salary growth rate as reasonable and wanted to make new investment contributions at 4 percent of his salary. After some research on historical stock market performance, Tom decided that a 10 percent annual portfolio growth rate was reasonable. Using these assumptions, Tom developed the Excel worksheet shown in Figure 13.18. Tom's specific situation and his assumptions are in the top portion of the worksheet (cells D3:D8). The worksheet provides a financial plan for the next five years. In computing the portfolio earnings for a given year, Tom assumed that his new investment contribution would occur evenly throughout the year and thus half of the new investment could be included in the computation of the portfolio earnings for the year. Using Figure 13.18, we see that at age 29, Tom is projected to have a portfolio valued at $32,898.

Tom's plan was to use this worksheet as a template to develop financial plans for the company's employees. The assumptions in cells D3:D8 would be different for each employee, and rows would be added to the worksheet to reflect the number of years appropriate for each employee. After adding another 25 rows to the worksheet, Tom found that he could expect to have a portfolio of $627,937 after 30 years. Tom then took his results to show his boss, Kate Riegle.

Although Kate was pleased with Tom's progress, she voiced several criticisms. One of the criticisms was the assumption of a constant annual salary growth rate. She noted that most employees experience some variation in the annual salary growth rate from year to year. In addition, she pointed out that the constant annual portfolio growth rate was unrealistic and that the actual growth rate would vary considerably from year to year. She further suggested that a simulation model for the portfolio projection might allow Tom to account for the random variability in the salary growth rate and the portfolio growth rate.

After some research, Tom and Kate decided to assume that the annual salary growth rate would vary from 0 percent to 10 percent and that a uniform probability distribution would provide a realistic approximation. Tri-State's accounting firm suggested that the

FIGURE 13.18 FINANCIAL PLANNING WORKSHEET FOR TOM GIFFORD

	A	B	C	D	E	F	G	H
1	Financial Analysis - Portfolio Projection							
2								
3	Age			25				
4	Current Salary			$34,000				
5	Current Portfolio			$14,500				
6	Annual Salary Growth Rate			5%				
7	Annual Investment Rate			4%				
8	Annual Portfolio Growth Rate			10%				
9								
10			Beginning		New	Portfolio	Ending	
11	Year	Age	Portfolio	Salary	Investment	Earnings	Portfolio	
12	1	25	14,500	34,000	1,360	1,518	17,378	
13	2	26	17,378	35,700	1,428	1,809	20,615	
14	3	27	20,615	37,485	1,499	2,136	24,251	
15	4	28	24,251	39,359	1,574	2,504	28,329	
16	5	29	28,329	41,327	1,653	2,916	32,898	
17								

annual portfolio growth rate could be approximated by a normal probability distribution with a mean of 10 percent and a standard deviation of 5 percent. With this information, Tom set off to develop a simulation model that could be used by the company's employees for financial planning.

Managerial Report

Play the role of Tom Gifford and develop a simulation model for financial planning. Write a report for Tom's boss and, at a minimum, include the following:

1. Without considering the random variability in growth rates, extend the worksheet in Figure 13.18 to 30 years. Confirm that by using the constant annual salary growth rate and the constant annual portfolio growth rate, Tom can expect to have a 30-year portfolio of $627,937. What would Tom's annual investment rate have to increase to in order for his portfolio to reach a 30-year, $1,000,000 goal?
2. Incorporate the random variability of the annual salary growth rate and the annual portfolio growth rate into a simulation model. Assume that Tom is willing to use the annual investment rate that predicted a 30-year, $1,000,000 portfolio in part 1. Show how to simulate Tom's 30-year financial plan. Use results from the simulation model to comment on the uncertainty associated with Tom reaching the 30-year, $1,000,000 goal. Discuss the advantages of repeating the simulation numerous times.
3. What recommendations do you have for employees with a current profile similar to Tom's after seeing the impact of the uncertainty in the annual salary growth rate and the annual portfolio growth rate?
4. Assume that Tom is willing to consider working 35 years instead of 30 years. What is your assessment of this strategy if Tom's goal is to have a portfolio worth $1,000,000?
5. Discuss how the financial planning model developed for Tom Gifford can be used as a template to develop a financial plan for any of the company's employees.

Case Problem 2 HARBOR DUNES GOLF COURSE

Harbor Dunes Golf Course was recently honored as one of the top public golf courses in South Carolina. The course, situated on land that was once a rice plantation, offers some of the best views of saltwater marshes available in the Carolinas. Harbor Dunes targets the upper end of the golf market and in the peak spring golfing season, charges green fees of $160 per person and golf cart fees of $20 per person.

Harbor Dunes takes reservations for tee times for groups of four players (foursome) starting at 7:30 each morning. Foursomes start at the same time on both the front nine and the back nine of the course, with a new group teeing off every nine minutes. The process continues with new foursomes starting play on both the front and back nine at noon. To enable all players to complete 18 holes before darkness, the last two afternoon foursomes start their rounds at 1:21 P.M. Under this plan, Harbor Dunes can sell a maximum of 20 afternoon tee times.

Last year Harbor Dunes was able to sell every morning tee time available for every day of the spring golf season. The same result is anticipated for the coming year. Afternoon tee times, however, are generally more difficult to sell. An analysis of the sales data for last year enabled Harbor Dunes to develop the probability distribution of sales for the afternoon tee times as shown in Table 13.12. For the season, Harbor Dunes averaged selling approximately 14 of the 20 available afternoon tee times. The average income from afternoon green fees and cart fees has been $10,240. However, the average of six unused tee times per day resulted in lost revenue.

In an effort to increase the sale of afternoon tee times, Harbor Dunes is considering an idea popular at other golf courses. These courses offer foursomes that play in the morning the option to play another round of golf in the afternoon by paying a reduced fee for the afternoon round. Harbor Dunes is considering two replay options: (1) a green fee of $25 per player plus a cart fee of $20 per player; (2) a green fee of $50 per player plus a cart fee of $20 per player. For option 1, each foursome will generate additional revenues of $180; for option 2, each foursome will generate additional revenues of $280. The key in making a decision as to what option is best depends upon the number of groups that find the option attractive enough to take the replay offer. Working with a consultant who has expertise in statistics and the golf industry, Harbor Dunes developed probability distributions for the

TABLE 13.12 PROBABILITY DISTRIBUTION OF SALES FOR THE AFTERNOON TEE TIMES

Number of Tee Times Sold	Probability
8	0.01
9	0.04
10	0.06
11	0.08
12	0.10
13	0.11
14	0.12
15	0.15
16	0.10
17	0.09
18	0.07
19	0.05
20	0.02

TABLE 13.13 PROBABILITY DISTRIBUTIONS FOR THE NUMBER OF GROUPS REQUESTING A REPLAY

Option 1: $25 per person + Cart Fee		**Option 2: $50 per person + Cart Fee**	
Number of Foursomes Requesting a Replay	**Probability**	**Number of Foursomes Requesting a Replay**	**Probability**
0	0.01	0	0.06
1	0.03	1	0.09
2	0.05	2	0.12
3	0.05	3	0.17
4	0.11	4	0.20
5	0.15	5	0.13
6	0.17	6	0.11
7	0.15	7	0.07
8	0.13	8	0.05
9	0.09		
10	0.06		

number of foursomes requesting a replay for each of the two options. These probability distributions are shown in Table 13.13.

In offering these replay options, Harbor Dunes' first priority will be to sell full-price afternoon advance reservations. If the demand for replay tee times exceeds the number of afternoon tee times available, Harbor Dunes will post a notice that the course is full. In this case, any excess replay requests will not be accepted.

Managerial Report

Develop simulation models for both replay options using Crystal Ball. Run each simulation for 5000 trials. Prepare a report that will help management of Harbor Dunes Golf Course decide which replay option to implement for the upcoming spring golf season. In preparing your report be sure to include the following:

1. Statistical summaries of the revenue expected under each replay option.
2. Your recommendation as to the best replay option.
3. Assuming a 90-day spring golf season, what is the estimate of the added revenue using your recommendation?
4. Discuss any other recommendations you have that might improve the income for Harbor Dunes.

Case Problem 3 COUNTY BEVERAGE DRIVE-THRU

County Beverage Drive-Thru, Inc., operates a chain of beverage supply stores in Northern Illinois. Each store has a single service lane; cars enter at one end of the store and exit at the other end. Customers pick up soft drinks, beer, snacks, and party supplies without getting out of their cars. When a new customer arrives at the store, the customer waits until the preceding customer's order is complete and then drives into the store for service.

Typically, three employees operate each store during peak periods; two clerks take and fill orders, and a third clerk serves as cashier and store supervisor. County Beverage is considering a revised store design in which computerized order-taking and payment are integrated with specialized warehousing equipment. Management hopes that the new design will permit operating each store with one clerk. To determine whether the new design is beneficial, management decided to build a new store using the revised design.

County Beverage's new store will be located near a major shopping center. Based on experience at other locations, management believes that during the peak late afternoon and evening hours, the time between arrivals follows an exponential probability distribution with a mean of six minutes. These peak hours are the most critical time period for the company; most of their profit is generated during these peak hours.

An extensive study of times required to fill orders with a single clerk led to the following probability distribution of service times.

Service Time (minutes)	Probability
2	0.24
3	0.20
4	0.15
5	0.14
6	0.12
7	0.08
8	0.05
9	0.02
Total	1.00

In case customer waiting times prove too long with just a single clerk, County Beverage's management is considering two alternatives: add a second clerk to help with bagging, taking orders, and related tasks, or enlarge the drive-thru area so that two cars can be served at once (a two-channel system). With either of these options, two clerks will be needed. With the two-channel option, service times are expected to be the same for each channel. With the second clerk helping with a single channel, service times will be reduced. The following probability distribution describes service times given that option.

Service Time (minutes)	Probability
1	0.20
2	0.35
3	0.30
4	0.10
5	0.05
Total	1.00

County Beverage's management would like you to develop a spreadsheet simulation model of the new system and use it to compare the operation of the system using the following three designs:

Design	
A	One channel, one clerk
B	One channel, two clerks
C	Two channels, each with one clerk

Management is especially concerned with how long customers have to wait for service. Research has shown that 30 percent of the customers will wait no longer than 6 minutes and that 90 percent will wait no longer than 10 minutes. As a guideline, management requires the average waiting time to be less than 1.5 minutes.

Managerial Report

Prepare a report that discusses the general development of the spreadsheet simulation model, and make any recommendations that you have regarding the best store design and staffing plan for County Beverage. One additional consideration is that the design allowing for a two-channel system will cost an additional $10,000 to build.

1. List the information the spreadsheet simulation model should generate so that a decision can be made on the store design and the desired number of clerks.
2. Run the simulation for 1000 customers for each alternative considered. You may want to consider making more than one run with each alternative. [*Note:* Values from an exponential probability distribution with mean μ can be generated in Excel using the following function: $=-\mu$*LN(RAND()).]
3. Be sure to note the number of customers County Beverage is likely to lose due to long customer waiting times with each design alternative.

Appendix 13.1 SIMULATION WITH EXCEL

Excel enables small and moderate-sized simulation models to be implemented relatively easily and quickly. In this appendix we show the Excel worksheets for the three simulation models presented in the chapter.

The PortaCom Simulation Model

We simulated the PortaCom problem 500 times. The worksheet used to carry out the simulation is shown again in Figure 13.19. Note that the simulation results for trials 6 through 495 have been hidden so that the results can be shown in a reasonably sized figure. If desired, the rows for these trials can be shown and the simulation results displayed for all 500 trials. Let us describe the details of the Excel worksheet that provided the PortaCom simulation.

First, the PortaCom data are presented in the first 14 rows of the worksheet. The selling price per unit, administrative cost, and advertising cost parameters are entered directly into cells C3, C4, and C5. The discrete probability distribution for the direct labor cost per unit is shown in a tabular format. Note that the random number intervals are entered first followed by the corresponding cost per unit. For example, 0.0 in cell A10 and 0.1 in cell B10 show that a cost of $43 per unit will be assigned if the random number is in the interval 0.0 but less than 0.1. Thus, approximately 10 percent of the simulated direct labor costs will be $43 per unit. The uniform probability distribution with a smallest value of $80 in cell E8 and a largest value of $100 in cell E9 describes the parts cost per unit. Finally, a normal probability distribution with a mean of 15,000 units in cell E13 and a standard deviation of 4500 units in cell E14 describes the first-year demand distribution for the product. At this point we are ready to insert the Excel formulas that will carry out each simulation trial.

FIGURE 13.19 WORKSHEET FOR THE PORTACOM PROBLEM

EXCELfile
PortaCom

	A	B	C	D	E	F
1	**PortaCom Risk Analysis**					
2						
3	Selling Price per Unit		$249			
4	Administrative Cost		$400,000			
5	Advertising Cost		$600,000			
6						
7	**Direct Labor Cost**			**Parts Cost (Uniform Distribution)**		
8	Lower	Upper		Smallest Value	$80	
9	Random No.	Random No.	Cost per Unit	Largest Value	$100	
10	0.0	0.1	$43			
11	0.1	0.3	$44			
12	0.3	0.7	$45	**Demand (Normal Distribution)**		
13	0.7	0.9	$46	Mean	15000	
14	0.9	1.0	$47	Std Deviation	4500	
15						
16						
17	**Simulation Trials**					
18						
19		Direct Labor	Parts	First-Year		
20	Trial	Cost Per Unit	Cost Per Unit	Demand	Profit	
21	1	47	$85.36	17,366	$1,025,570	
22	2	44	$91.68	12,900	$461,828	
23	3	45	$93.35	20,686	$1,288,906	
24	4	43	$98.56	10,888	$169,807	
25	5	45	$88.36	14,259	$648,911	
516	496	44	$98.67	8,730	($71,739)	
517	497	45	$94.38	19,257	$1,110,952	
518	498	44	$90.85	14,920	$703,118	
519	499	43	$90.37	13,471	$557,652	
520	500	46	$92.50	18,614	$1,056,847	
521						
522			**Summary Statistics**			
523			Mean Profit		$698,457	
524			Standard Deviation		$520,485	
525			Minimum Profit		($785,234)	
526			Maximum Profit		$2,367,058	
527			Number of Losses		51	
528			Probabilitiy of Loss		0.1020	
529						

Simulation information for the first trial appears in row 21 of the worksheet. The cell formulas for row 21 are as follows:

Cell A21 Enter 1 for the first simulation trial

Cell B21 Simulate the direct labor cost per unit*
=VLOOKUP(RAND(),$A$10:$C$14,3)

Cell C21 Simulate the parts cost per unit (uniform distribution)
=$E$8+($E$9−$E$8)*RAND()

Cell D21 Simulate the first-year demand (normal distribution)
=NORMINV(RAND(),$E$13,$E$14)

Cell E21 The profit obtained for the first trial
=($C$3−B21−C21)*D21−$C$4−$C$5

Cells A21:E21 can be copied to A520:E520 in order to provide the 500 simulation trials.

Ultimately, summary statistics will be collected in order to describe the results of the 500 simulated trials. Using the standard Excel functions, the following summary statistics are computed for the 500 simulated profits appearing in cells E21 to E520.

Cell E523 The mean profit per trial = AVERAGE(E21:E520)

Cell E524 The standard deviation of profit – STDEV(E21:E520)

Cell E525 The minimum profit = MIN(E21:E520)

Cell E526 The maximum profit = MAX(E21:E520)

Cell E527 The count of the number of trials where a loss occurred
(i.e., profit < $0) = COUNTIF(E21:E520,"<0")

Cell E528 The percentage or probability of a loss based on the 500 trials = E527/500

The F9 key can be used to perform another complete simulation of PortaCom. In this case, the entire worksheet will be recalculated and a set of new simulation results will be provided. Any data summaries, measures, or functions that have been built into the worksheet earlier will be updated automatically.

The Butler Inventory Simulation Model

We simulated the Butler inventory operation for 300 months. The worksheet used to carry out the simulation is shown again in Figure 13.20. Note that the simulation results for months 6 through 295 have been hidden so that the results can be shown in a reasonably sized figure. If desired, the rows for these months can be shown and the simulation results displayed for all 300 months. Let us describe the details of the Excel worksheet that provided the Butler inventory simulation.

First, the Butler inventory data are presented in the first 11 rows of the worksheet. The gross profit per unit, holding cost per unit, and shortage cost per unit data are entered directly into cells C3, C4, and C5. The replenishment level is entered into cell C7, and the mean and standard deviation of the normal probability distribution for demand are entered into cells B10 and B11. At this point we are ready to insert Excel formulas that will carry out each simulation month or trial.

*The VLOOKUP function generates a random number using the RAND() function. Then, using the table defined by the region from cells $A$10 to $C$14, the function identifies the row containing the RAND() random number and assigns the corresponding direct labor cost per unit shown in column C.

FIGURE 13.20 WORKSHEET FOR THE BUTLER INVENTORY PROBLEM

EXCELfile
Butler

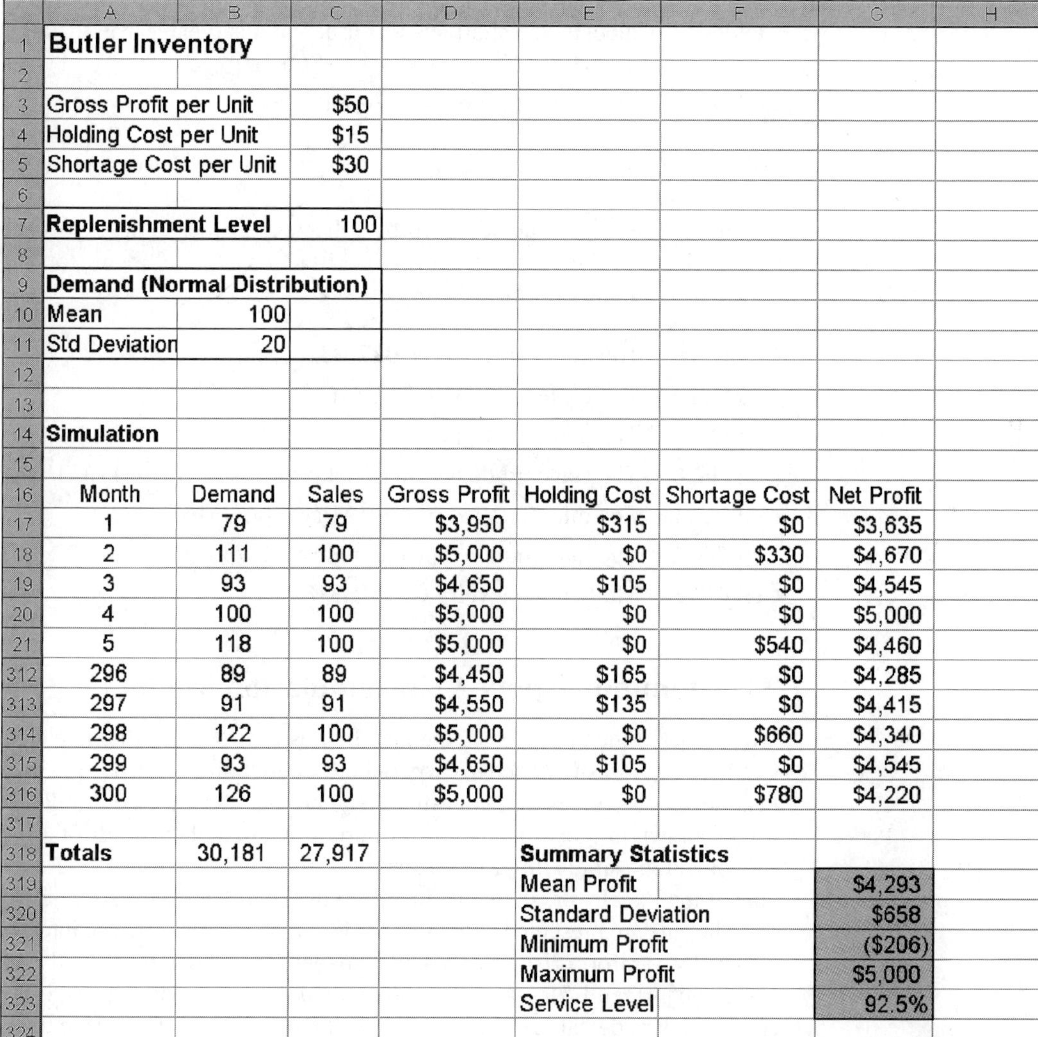

	A	B	C	D	E	F	G	H
1	**Butler Inventory**							
2								
3	Gross Profit per Unit		$50					
4	Holding Cost per Unit		$15					
5	Shortage Cost per Unit		$30					
6								
7	**Replenishment Level**		100					
8								
9	**Demand (Normal Distribution)**							
10	Mean	100						
11	Std Deviation	20						
12								
13								
14	**Simulation**							
15								
16	Month	Demand	Sales	Gross Profit	Holding Cost	Shortage Cost	Net Profit	
17	1	79	79	$3,950	$315	$0	$3,635	
18	2	111	100	$5,000	$0	$330	$4,670	
19	3	93	93	$4,650	$105	$0	$4,545	
20	4	100	100	$5,000	$0	$0	$5,000	
21	5	118	100	$5,000	$0	$540	$4,460	
312	296	89	89	$4,450	$165	$0	$4,285	
313	297	91	91	$4,550	$135	$0	$4,415	
314	298	122	100	$5,000	$0	$660	$4,340	
315	299	93	93	$4,650	$105	$0	$4,545	
316	300	126	100	$5,000	$0	$780	$4,220	
317								
318	**Totals**	30,181	27,917		**Summary Statistics**			
319					Mean Profit		$4,293	
320					Standard Deviation		$658	
321					Minimum Profit		($206)	
322					Maximum Profit		$5,000	
323					Service Level		92.5%	
324								

Simulation information for the first month or trial appears in row 17 of the worksheet. The cell formulas for row 17 are as follows:

Cell A17 Enter 1 for the first simulation month

Cell B17 Simulate demand (normal distribution)
=NORMINV(RAND(),$B$10,$B$11)

Next compute the sales, which is equal to demand (cell B17) if demand is less than or equal to the replenishment level, or is equal to the replenishment level (cell C7) if demand is greater than the replenishment level.

Cell C17 Compute sales =IF(B17<=$C$7,B17,$C$7)

Cell D17 Calculate gross profit =$C$3*C17

Cell E17 Calculate the holding cost if demand is less than or equal to the replenishment level =IF(B17<= $C$7,$C$4*($C$7−B17),0)

Cell F17 Calculate the shortage cost if demand is greater than the replenishment level =IF(B17>$C$7,$C$5*(B17−$C$7),0)

Cell G17 Calculate net profit =D17−E17−F17

Cells A17:G17 can be copied to cells A316:G316 in order to provide the 300 simulation months.

Finally, summary statistics will be collected in order to describe the results of the 300 simulated trials. Using the standard Excel functions, the following totals and summary statistics are computed for the 300 months.

Cell B318 Total demand =SUM(B17:B316)

Cell C319 Total sales =SUM(C17:C316)

Cell G319 The mean profit per month =AVERAGE(G17:G316)

Cell G320 The standard deviation of net profit =STDEV(G17:G316)

Cell G321 The minimum net profit =MIN(G17:G316)

Cell G322 The maximum net profit =MAX(G17:G316)

Cell G323 The service level =C318/B318

The Hammondsport ATM Simulation Model

We simulated the operation of the Hammondsport ATM waiting line system for 1000 customers. The worksheet used to carry out the simulation is shown again in Figure 13.21. Note that the simulation results for customers 6 through 995 have been hidden so that the results can be shown in a reasonably sized figure. If desired, the rows for these customers can be shown and the simulation results displayed for all 1000 customers. Let us describe the details of the Excel worksheet that provided the Hammondsport ATM simulation.

The data are presented in the first 9 rows of the worksheet. The interarrival times are described by a uniform distribution with a smallest time of 0 minutes (cell B4) and a largest time of 5 minutes (cell B5). A normal probability distribution with a mean of 2 minutes (cell B8) and a standard deviation of 0.5 minute (cell B9) describes the service time distribution.

Simulation information for the first customer appears in row 16 of the worksheet. The cell formulas for row 16 are as follows:

Cell A16 Enter 1 for the first customer

Cell B16 Simulate the interarrival time for customer 1 (uniform distribution) =$B$4+RAND()*($B$5−$B$4)

Cell C16 Compute the arrival time for customer 1 =B16

Cell D16 Compute the start time for customer 1 =C16

Cell E16 Compute the waiting time for customer 1 =D1−C16

Cell F16 Simulate the service time for customer 1 (normal distribution) =NORMINV(RAND(),$B$8,$B$9)

Cell G16 Compute the completion time for customer 1 =D16+F16

Cell H16 Compute the time in the system for customer 1 =G16−C16

FIGURE 13.21 WORKSHEET FOR THE HAMMONDSPORT SAVINGS BANK WITH ONE ATM

EXCELfile
Hammondsport1

	A	B	C	D	E	F	G	H
1	**Hammonsdsport Savings Bank with One ATM**							
2								
3	**Interarrival Times (Uniform Distribution)**							
4	Smallest Value	0						
5	Largest Value	5						
6								
7	**Service Times (Normal Distribution)**							
8	Mean	2						
9	Std Deviation	0.5						
10								
11								
12	**Simulation**							
13								
14		Interarrival	Arrival	Service	Waiting	Service	Completion	Time
15	Customer	Time	Time	Start Time	Time	Time	Time	in System
16	1	1.4	1.4	1.4	0.0	2.3	3.7	2.3
17	2	1.3	2.7	3.7	1.0	1.5	5.2	2.5
18	3	4.9	7.6	7.6	0.0	2.2	9.8	2.2
19	4	3.5	11.1	11.1	0.0	2.5	13.6	2.5
20	5	0.7	11.8	13.6	1.8	1.8	15.4	3.6
1011	996	0.5	2496.8	2498.1	1.3	0.6	2498.7	1.9
1012	997	0.2	2497.0	2498.7	1.7	2.0	2500.7	3.7
1013	998	2.7	2499.7	2500.7	1.0	1.8	2502.5	2.8
1014	999	3.7	2503.4	2503.4	0.0	2.4	2505.8	2.4
1015	1000	4.0	2507.4	2507.4	0.0	1.9	2509.3	1.9
1016								
1017		**Summary Statistics**						
1018		Number Waiting			549			
1019		Probability of Waiting			0.6100			
1020		Average Waiting Time			1.59			
1021		Maximum Waiting Time			13.5			
1022		Utilization of ATM			0.7860			
1023		Number Waiting > 1 Min			393			
1024		Probability of Waiting > 1 Min			0.4367			
1025								

Simulation information for the second customer appears in row 17 of the worksheet. The cell formulas for row 17 are as follows:

Cell A17 Enter 2 for the second customer

Cell B17 Simulate the interarrival time for customer 2 (uniform distribution)
=$B$4+RAND()*($B$5−$B$4)

Cell C17 Compute the arrival time for customer 2 =C16+B17

Cell D17 Compute the start time for customer 2 =IF(C17>G16,C17,G16)

Cell E17 Compute the waiting time for customer 2 =D17−C17

Cell F17 Simulate the service time for customer 2 (normal distribution)
=NORMINV(RAND(),$B$8,$B$9)

Cell G17 Compute the completion time for customer 2 =D17+F17

Cell H17 Compute the time in the system for customer 2 =G17−C17

Cells A17:H17 can be copied to cells A1015:H1015 in order to provide the 1000-customer simulation.

Ultimately, summary statistics will be collected in order to describe the results of 1000 customers. Before collecting the summary statistics, let us point out that most simulation studies of dynamic systems focus on the operation of the system during its long-run or steady-state operation. To ensure that the effect of start-up conditions are not included in the steady-state calculations, a dynamic simulation model is usually run for a specified period without collecting any data about the operation of the system. The length of the start-up period can vary depending on the application. For the Hammondsport Savings Bank ATM simulation, we treated the results for the first 100 customers as the start-up period. The simulation information for customer 100 appears in row 115 of the spreadsheet. Cell G115 shows that the completion time for the 100th customer is 247.8. Thus the length of the start-up period is 247.8 minutes.

Summary statistics are collected for the next 900 customers corresponding to rows 116 to 1015 of the spreadsheet. The following Excel formulas provided the summary statistics.

Cell E1018 Number of customers who had to wait (i.e., waiting time > 0)
=COUNTIF(E116:E1015,">0")

Cell E1019 Probability of waiting =E1018/900

Cell E1020 The average waiting time =AVERAGE(E116:E1015)

Cell E1021 The maximum waiting time =MAX(E116:E1015)

Cell E1022 The utilization of the ATM* =SUM(F116:F1015)/(G1015 − G115)

Cell E1023 The number of customers who had to wait more than 1 minute
=COUNTIF(E116:E1015,">1")

Cell E1024 Probability of waiting more than 1 minute =E1023/900

Appendix 13.2 SIMULATION OF THE PORTACOM PROBLEM USING CRYSTAL BALL

In Section 13.1 we used simulation to perform risk analysis for the PortaCom problem, and in Appendix 13.1 we showed how to construct the Excel worksheet that provided the simulation results. Developing the worksheet simulation for the PortaCom problem using the basic Excel package was relatively easy. The use of add-ins enable larger and more complex simulation problems to be easily analyzed using spreadsheets. In this appendix, we show how Crystal Ball, an add-in package, can be used to perform the PortaCom simulation. We will run the simulation for 1000 trials here. Instructions for installing and starting Crystal Ball are included with the Crystal Ball software.

*The proportion of time the ATM is in use is equal to the sum of the 900 customer service times in column F divided by the total elapsed time required for the 900 customers to complete service. This total elapsed time is the difference between the completion time of customer 1000 and the completion time of customer 100.

Formulating a Crystal Ball Model

We begin by entering the problem data into the top portion of the worksheet. For the PortaCom problem, we must enter the following data: selling price, administrative cost, advertising cost, probability distribution for the direct labor cost per unit, smallest and largest values for the parts cost per unit (uniform distribution), and the mean and standard deviation for first-year demand (normal distribution). These data with appropriate descriptive labels are shown in cells A1:E13 of Figure 13.22.

For the PortaCom problem, the Crystal Ball model contains the following two components: (1) cells for the probabilistic inputs (direct labor cost, parts cost, first-year demand), and (2) a cell containing a formula for computing the value of the simulation model output (profit). In Crystal Ball the cells that contain the values of the probabilistic inputs are called *assumption cells,* and the cells that contain the formulas for the model outputs are referred to as *forecast cells*. The PortaCom problem requires only one output (profit), and thus the Crystal Ball model only contains one forecast cell. In more complex simulation problems more than one forecast cell may be necessary.

The assumption cells may only contain simple numeric values. In this model-building stage, we entered PortaCom's best estimates of the direct labor cost ($45), the parts cost

FIGURE 13.22 CRYSTAL BALL WORKSHEET FOR THE PORTACOM PROBLEM

	A	B	C	D	E	F
1	**PortaCom Crystal Ball Risk Analysis**					
2						
3	Selling Price per Unit		$249			
4	Administrative Cost		$400,000			
5	Advertising Cost		$600,000			
6						
7		**Direct Labor**		**Parts Cost (Uniform Distribution)**		
8		Cost per Unit	Probability	Smallest Value	$80	
9		$43	0.1	Largest Value	$100	
10		$44	0.2			
11		$45	0.4	**Demand (Normal Distribution)**		
12		$46	0.2	Mean	15,000	
13		$47	0.1	Standard Dev	4,500	
14						
15						
16						
17	**Crystal Ball Model**					
18						
19			**Assumption**			
20			**Cells**			
21		**Direct Labor Cost**	$45			
22		**Parts Cost**	$90			
23		**Demand**	15,000			
24						
25			**Forecast**			
26			**Cell**			
27		**Profit**	$710,000			
28						

($90), and the first-year demand (15,000) into cells C21:C23, respectively. The forecast cells in a Crystal Ball model contain formulas that refer to one or more of the assumption cells. Because only one forecast cell in the PortaCom problem corresponds to profit, we entered the following formula into cell C27:

=(C3−C21−C22)*C23−C4−C5

The resulting value of $710,000 is the profit corresponding to the base-case scenario discussed in Section 13.1.

Defining and Entering Assumptions

We are now ready to define the probability distributions corresponding to each of the assumption cells. We begin by defining the probability distribution for the direct labor cost.

Step 1. Select cell C21
Step 2. Select the **Cell** menu
Step 3. Choose **Define Assumption**
Step 4. When the **Cell 21: Distribution Gallery** dialog box appears:
 Choose **Custom**
 Click **OK**
Step 5. When the **Cell C21: Custom Distribution** dialog box appears:
 Choose **Data**
 Enter B9:C13 in the **Cell Range** box
 Click **OK** to terminate the data entry process
 Click **OK**

The procedure for defining the probability distribution for the parts cost is similar.

Step 1. Select cell C22
Step 2. Select the **Cell** menu
Step 3. Choose **Define Assumption**
Step 4. When the **Cell C22: Distribution Gallery** dialog box appears:
 Choose **Uniform**
 Click **OK**
Step 5. When the **Cell C22: Uniform Distribution** dialog box appears:
 Enter =E8 in the **Min** box
 Enter =E9 in the **Max** box
 Click **OK**

Finally, we perform the following steps to define the probability distribution for first-year demand.

Step 1. Select cell C23
Step 2. Select the **Cell** menu
Step 3. Choose **Define Assumption**
Step 4. When the **Cell 23: Distribution Gallery** dialog box appears:
 Choose **Normal**
 Click **OK**
Step 5. When the **Cell C23: Normal Distribution** dialog box appears:
 Enter =E12 in the **Mean** box
 Enter =E13 in the **Std Dev** box
 Click **OK**

Defining Forecasts

After defining the assumption cells, we are ready to define the forecast cells. The following steps show how to do it for C27, the forecast cell for the PortaCom problem.

Step 1. Select cell C27
Step 2. Select the **Cell** menu
Step 3. Choose **Define Forecast**
Step 4. When the **Cell C27: Define Forecast** dialog box appears:
Enter Profit in the **Forecast Name** box
Click **OK**

The Define Forecast dialog box in step 4 allows you to change the forecast name and contains options for setting the forecast units, controlling the size of the forecast window, and determining when the forecast window is displayed.

Setting Run Preferences

We must now make the choices that determine how Crystal Ball runs the simulation. For the PortaCom simulation, we only need to specify the number of trials.

Step 1. Select the **Run** menu
Step 2. Choose **Run Preferences**
Step 3. When the **Run Preferences** dialog box appears:
Make sure **Trials** has been selected
Enter 1000 in the **Maximum Number of Trials** box
Click **OK**

Running the Simulation

Crystal Ball repeats three steps on each of the 1000 trials for the PortaCom simulation.

1. For each assumption cell, Crystal Ball generates a value at random according to the probability distribution defined.
2. Crystal Ball recalculates the value of the forecast cell (profit) corresponding to the values in the assumption cells.
3. The new profit value is added to the graph in the Forecast window.

The following steps describe how to begin the simulation.

Step 1. Select the **Run** menu
Step 2. Choose **Run**

When the run is complete, Crystal Ball displays 996 of the 1000 simulated values of profit in the frequency chart shown in Figure 13.23. Other types of charts and output can be displayed in the forecast window. For instance, the following steps describe how to display the descriptive statistics corresponding to this simulation.

Step 1. Select the **View** menu in the Forecast window (Figure 13.23)
Step 2. Choose **Statistics**

Figure 13.24 shows the forecast window with the descriptive statistics. Note that the worst result obtained in this simulation of 1000 trials is a loss of $1,374,699, and the best result is a profit of $2,202,019. The mean profit is $699,302. These values are similar to the results obtained in Section 13.1. The differences result from the different random numbers used in the two simulations and from the fact that we used 1000 trials with Crystal Ball. If you perform another simulation, your results will differ slightly.

FIGURE 13.23 CRYSTAL BALL FREQUENCY CHART FOR THE PORTACOM SIMULATION

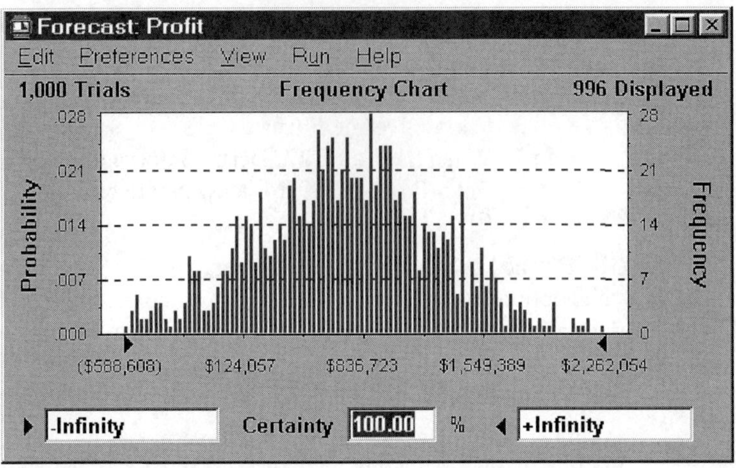

FIGURE 13.24 CRYSTAL BALL STATISTICS FOR THE PORTACOM SIMULATION

Forecast: Profit

Edit Preferences View Run Help

Cell C27 Statistics

Statistic	Value
Trials	1,000
Mean	$699,302
Median	$699,451
Mode	---
Standard Deviation	$527,255
Variance	$277,997,963,059
Skewness	-0.02
Kurtosis	2.97
Coeff. of Variability	0.75
Range Minimum	($1,374,699)
Range Maximum	$2,202,019
Range Width	$3,576,718
Mean Std. Error	$16,673.27

CHAPTER 14

Decision Analysis

CONTENTS

Decision analysis can be used to develop an optimal strategy when a decision maker is faced with several decision alternatives and an uncertain or risk-filled pattern of future events. For example, Ohio Edison used decision analysis to choose the best type of particulate control equipment for coal-fired generating units when it faced future uncertainties concerning sulfur content requirements, construction costs, and so on. The State of North Carolina used decision analysis in evaluating whether to implement a medical screening test to detect metabolic disorders in newborns. Thus, decision analysis repeatedly proves its value in decision making. The Management Science in Action, Decision Analysis at Eastman Kodak, describes how the use of decision analysis during the 1990s added approximately $1 billion in value.

Even when a careful decision analysis has been conducted, the uncertain future events make the final consequence uncertain. In some cases, the selected decision alternative may provide good or excellent results. In other cases, a relatively unlikely future event may occur causing the selected decision alternative to provide only fair or even poor results. The risk associated with any decision alternative is a direct result of the uncertainty associated with the final consequence. A good decision analysis includes risk analysis. Through risk analysis the decision maker is provided with probability information about the favorable as well as the unfavorable consequences that may occur.

MANAGEMENT SCIENCE IN ACTION

DECISION ANALYSIS AT EASTMAN KODAK*

Clemen and Kwit conducted a study to determine the value of decision analysis at the Eastman Kodak company. The study involved an analysis of 178 decision analysis projects over the 10-year period from 1990 to 1999. The projects involved a variety of applications including strategy development, vendor selection, process analysis, new-product brainstorming, product-portfolio selection, and emission-reduction analysis. These projects required 14,372 hours of analyst time and the involvement of many other individuals at Kodak over the 10-year period. The shortest projects took less than 20 hours, and the longest projects took almost a year to complete.

Most decision analysis projects are one-time activities, which makes it difficult to measure the value added to the corporation. Clemen and Kwit used detailed records that were available and some innovative approaches to develop estimates of the incremental dollar value generated by the decision analysis projects. Their conservative estimate of the average value per project was $6.65 million and their optimistic estimate of the average value per project was $16.35 million. Their analysis led to the conclusion that all projects taken together added more than $1 billion in value to Eastman Kodak. Using these estimates, Clemen and Kwit concluded that decision analysis returned substantial value to the company. Indeed, they concluded that the value added by the projects was at least 185 times the cost of the analysts' time.

In addition to the monetary benefits, the authors point out that decision analysis adds value by facilitating discussion among stakeholders, promoting careful thinking about strategies, providing a common language for discussing the elements of a decision problem, and speeding implementation by helping to build consensus among decision makers. In commenting on the value of decision analysis at Eastman Kodak, Nancy L. S. Sousa said, "As General Manager, New Businesses, VP Health Imaging, Eastman Kodak, I encourage all of the business planners to use the decision and risk principles and processes as part of evaluating new business opportunities. The processes have clearly led to better decisions about entry and exit of businesses."

Although measuring the value of a particular decision analysis project can be difficult, it would be difficult to dispute the success that decision analysis had at Kodak.

*Based on Robert T. Clemen and Robert C. Kwit, "The Value of Decision Analysis at Eastman Kodak Company, 1990–1999," *Interfaces* (September/October 2001): 74–92.

We begin the study of decision analysis by considering problems having reasonably few decision alternatives and reasonably few possible future events. Influence diagrams and payoff tables are introduced to provide a structure for the decision problem and to illustrate the fundamentals of decision analysis. We then introduce decision trees to show the sequential nature of decision problems. Decision trees are used to analyze more complex problems and to identify an optimal sequence of decisions, referred to as an optimal decision strategy. Sensitivity analysis shows how changes in various aspects of the problem affect the recommended decision alternative.

14.1 PROBLEM FORMULATION

The first step in the decision analysis process is problem formulation. We begin with a verbal statement of the problem. We then identify the decision alternatives, the uncertain future events, referred to as **chance events,** and the **consequences** associated with each decision alternative and each chance event outcome. Let us begin by considering a construction project of the Pittsburgh Development Corporation.

Pittsburgh Development Corporation (PDC) purchased land that will be the site of a new luxury condominium complex. The location provides a spectacular view of downtown Pittsburgh and the Golden Triangle where the Allegheny and Monongahela rivers meet to form the Ohio River. PDC plans to price the individual condominium units between $300,000 and $1,400,000.

PDC commissioned preliminary architectural drawings for three different-sized projects: one with 30 condominiums, one with 60 condominiums, and one with 90 condominiums. The financial success of the project depends upon the size of the condominium complex and the chance event concerning the demand for the condominiums. The statement of the PDC decision problem is to select the size of the new luxury condominium project that will lead to the largest profit given the uncertainty concerning the demand for the condominiums.

Given the statement of the problem, it is clear that the decision is to select the best size for the condominium complex. PDC has the following three decision alternatives:

$$d_1 = \text{a small complex with 30 condominiums}$$
$$d_2 = \text{a medium complex with 60 condominiums}$$
$$d_3 = \text{a large complex with 90 condominiums}$$

A factor in selecting the best decision alternative is the uncertainty associated with the chance event concerning the demand for the condominiums. When asked about the possible demand for the condominiums, PDC's president acknowledged a wide range of possibilities, but decided that it would be adequate to consider two possible chance event outcomes: a strong demand and a weak demand.

In decision analysis, the possible outcomes for a chance event are referred to as the **states of nature.** The states of nature are defined so that one and only one of the possible states of nature will occur. For the PDC problem, the chance event concerning the demand for the condominiums has two states of nature:

$$s_1 = \text{strong demand for the condominiums}$$
$$s_2 = \text{weak demand for the condominiums}$$

Management must first select a decision alternative (complex size), then a state of nature follows (demand for the condominiums), and finally a consequence will occur. In this case, the consequence is PDC's profit.

Influence Diagrams

An **influence diagram** is a graphical device that shows the relationships among the decisions, the chance events, and the consequences for a decision problem. The **nodes** in an influence diagram are used to represent the decisions, chance events, and consequences. Rectangles or squares are used to depict **decision nodes,** circles or ovals are used to depict **chance nodes,** and diamonds are used to depict consequence nodes. The lines connecting the nodes, referred to as *arcs,* show the direction of influence that the nodes have on one another. Figure 14.1 shows the influence diagram for the PDC problem. The complex size is the decision node, demand is the chance node, and profit is the consequence node. The arcs connecting the nodes show that both the complex size and the demand influence PDC's profit.

Payoff Tables

Given the three decision alternatives and the two states of nature, which complex size should PDC choose? To answer this question, PDC will need to know the consequence associated with each decision alternative and each state of nature. In decision analysis, we refer to the consequence resulting from a specific combination of a decision alternative and a state of nature as a **payoff.** A table showing payoffs for all combinations of decision alternatives and states of nature is a **payoff table.**

Payoffs can be expressed in terms of profit, cost, time, distance, or any other measure appropriate for the decision problem being analyzed.

Because PDC wants to select the complex size that provides the largest profit, profit is used as the consequence. The payoff table with profits expressed in millions of dollars is shown in Table 14.1. Note, for example, that if a medium complex is built and demand turns out to be strong, a profit of \$14 million will be realized. We will use the notation V_{ij} to denote the payoff associated with decision alternative i and state of nature j. Using Table 14.1, $V_{31} = 20$ indicates a payoff of \$20 million occurs if the decision is to build a large complex (d_3) and the strong demand state of nature (s_1) occurs. Similarly, $V_{32} = -9$ indicates a loss of \$9 million if the decision is to build a large complex (d_3) and the weak demand state of nature (s_2) occurs.

FIGURE 14.1 INFLUENCE DIAGRAM FOR THE PDC PROBLEM

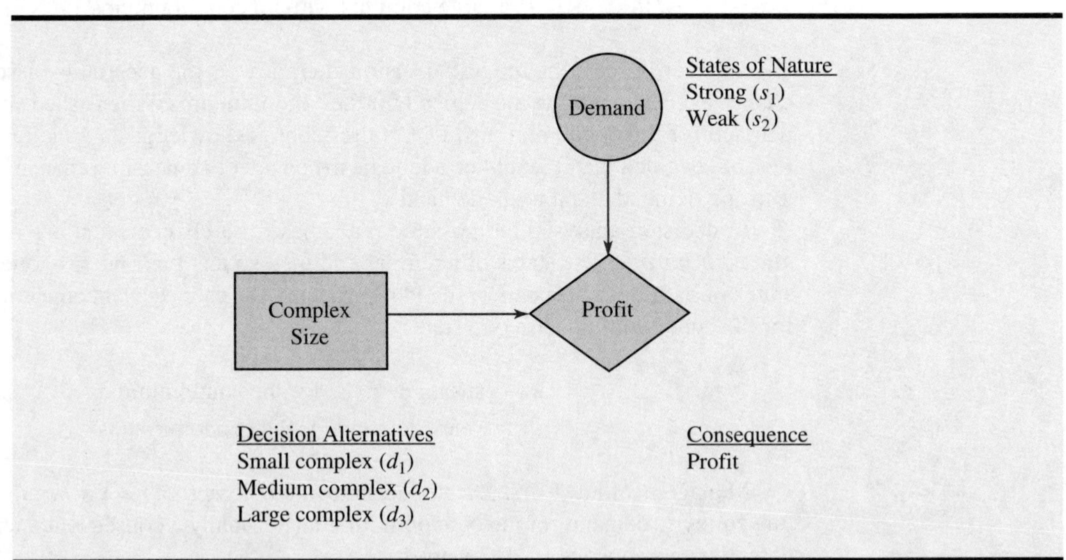

TABLE 14.1 PAYOFF TABLE FOR THE PDC CONDOMINIUM PROJECT (PAYOFFS IN \$ MILLION)

	State of Nature	
Decision Alternative	**Strong Demand s_1**	**Weak Demand s_2**
Small complex, d_1	8	7
Medium complex, d_2	14	5
Large complex, d_3	20	−9

Decision Trees

A **decision tree** provides a graphical representation of the decision-making process. Figure 14.2 presents a decision tree for the PDC problem. Note that the decision tree shows the natural or logical progression that will occur over time. First, PDC must make a decision regarding the size of the condominium complex (d_1, d_2, or d_3). Then, after the decision is implemented, either state of nature s_1 or s_2 will occur. The number at each end point of the tree indicates the payoff associated with a particular sequence. For example the topmost payoff of 8 indicates that an \$8 million profit is anticipated if PDC constructs a small condominium complex (d_1) and demand turns out to be strong (s_1). The next payoff of 7 indicates an anticipated profit of \$7 million if PDC constructs a small condominium complex (d_1) and demand turns out to be weak (s_2). Thus, the decision tree shows graphically the sequences of decision alternatives and states of nature that provide the six possible payoffs for PDC.

If you have a payoff table, you can develop a decision tree. Try Problem 1(a).

The decision tree in Figure 14.2 has four nodes, numbered 1–4. Squares are used to depict decision nodes and circles are used to depict chance nodes. Thus, node 1 is a decision node, and nodes 2, 3, and 4 are chance nodes. The **branches,** which connect the nodes, leaving

FIGURE 14.2 DECISION TREE FOR THE PDC CONDOMINIUM PROJECT (PAYOFFS IN \$ MILLION)

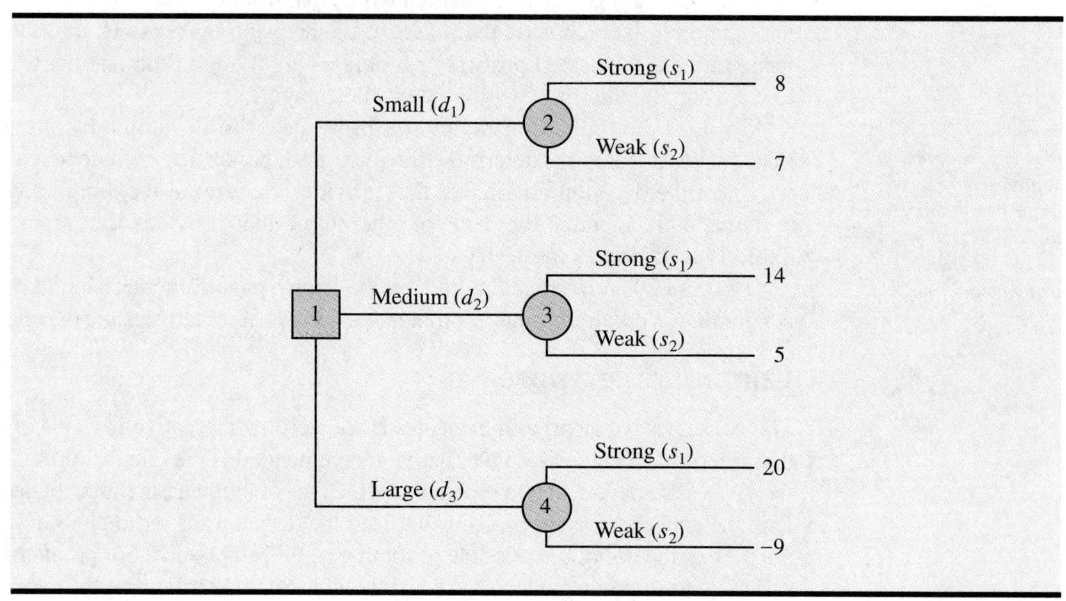

the decision node correspond to the decision alternatives. The branches leaving each chance node correspond to the states of nature. The payoffs are shown at the end of the states-of-nature branches. We now turn to the question: How can the decision maker use the information in the payoff table or the decision tree to select the best decision alternative? Several approaches may be used.

NOTES AND COMMENTS

1. Experts in problem solving agree that the first step in solving a complex problem is to decompose it into a series of smaller subproblems. Decision trees provide a useful way to show how a problem can be decomposed and the sequential nature of the decision process.
2. People often view the same problem from different perspectives. Thus, the discussion regarding the development of a decision tree may provide additional insight about the problem.

14.2 DECISION MAKING WITHOUT PROBABILITIES

Many people think of a good decision as one in which the consequence is good. However, in some instances, a good, well-thought-out decision may still lead to a bad or undesirable consequence.

In this section we consider approaches to decision making that do not require knowledge of the probabilities of the states of nature. These approaches are appropriate in situations in which the decision maker has little confidence in his or her ability to assess the probabilities, or in which a simple best-case and worst-case analysis is desirable. Because different approaches sometimes lead to different decision recommendations, the decision maker needs to understand the approaches available and then select the specific approach that, according to the decision maker's judgment, is the most appropriate.

Optimistic Approach

The **optimistic approach** evaluates each decision alternative in terms of the *best* payoff that can occur. The decision alternative that is recommended is the one that provides the best possible payoff. For a problem in which maximum profit is desired, as in the PDC problem, the optimistic approach would lead the decision maker to choose the alternative corresponding to the largest profit. For problems involving minimization, this approach leads to choosing the alternative with the smallest payoff.

For a maximization problem, the optimistic approach often is referred to as the maximax approach; for a minimization problem, the corresponding terminology is minimin.

To illustrate the optimistic approach, we use it to develop a recommendation for the PDC problem. First, we determine the maximum payoff for each decision alternative; then we select the decision alternative that provides the overall maximum payoff. These steps systematically identify the decision alternative that provides the largest possible profit. Table 14.2 illustrates these steps.

Because 20, corresponding to d_3, is the largest payoff, the decision to construct the large condominium complex is the recommended decision alternative using the optimistic approach.

Conservative Approach

The **conservative approach** evaluates each decision alternative in terms of the *worst* payoff that can occur. The decision alternative recommended is the one that provides the best of the worst possible payoffs. For a problem in which the output measure is profit, as in the PDC problem, the conservative approach would lead the decision maker to choose the alternative that maximizes the minimum possible profit that could be obtained. For problems involving minimization, this approach identifies the alternative that will minimize the maximum payoff.

TABLE 14.2 MAXIMUM PAYOFF FOR EACH PDC DECISION ALTERNATIVE

Decision Alternative	Maximum Payoff	
Small complex, d_1	8	
Medium complex, d_2	14	
Large complex, d_3	20	← Maximum of the maximum payoff values

For a maximization problem, the conservative approach is often referred to as the maximin approach; for a minimization problem, the corresponding terminology is minimax.

To illustrate the conservative approach, we use it to develop a recommendation for the PDC problem. First, we identify the minimum payoff for each of the decision alternatives; then we select the decision alternative that maximizes the minimum payoff. Table 14.3 illustrates these steps for the PDC problem.

Because 7, corresponding to d_1, yields the maximum of the minimum payoffs, the decision alternative of a small condominium complex is recommended. This decision approach is considered conservative because it identifies the worst possible payoffs and then recommends the decision alternative that avoids the possibility of extremely "bad" payoffs. In the conservative approach, PDC is guaranteed a profit of at least \$7 million. Although PDC may make more, it *cannot* make less than \$7 million.

Minimax Regret Approach

The **minimax regret approach** to decision making is neither purely optimistic nor purely conservative. Let us illustrate the minimax regret approach by showing how it can be used to select a decision alternative for the PDC problem.

Suppose that PDC constructs a small condominium complex (d_1) and demand turns out to be strong (s_1). Table 14.1 showed that the resulting profit for PDC would be \$8 million. However, given that the strong demand state of nature (s_1) has occurred, we realize that the decision to construct a large condominium complex (d_3), yielding a profit of \$20 million, would have been the best decision. The difference between the payoff for the best decision alternative (\$20 million) and the payoff for the decision to construct a small condominium complex (\$8 million) is the **opportunity loss,** or **regret,** associated with decision alternative d_1 when state of nature s_1 occurs; thus, for this case, the opportunity loss or regret is \$20 million − \$8 million = \$12 million. Similarly, if PDC makes the decision to construct a medium condominium complex (d_2) and the strong demand state of nature (s_1) occurs, the opportunity loss, or regret, associated with d_2 would be \$20 million − \$14 million = \$6 million.

In general the following expression represents the opportunity loss, or regret.

$$R_{ij} = |V_j^* - V_{ij}| \tag{14.1}$$

TABLE 14.3 MINIMUM PAYOFF FOR EACH PDC DECISION ALTERNATIVE

Decision Alternative	Minimum Payoff	
Small complex, d_1	7	← Maximum of the minimum payoff values
Medium complex, d_2	5	
Large complex, d_3	−9	

where

R_{ij} = the regret associated with decision alternative d_i and state of nature s_j
V_j^* = the payoff value[1] corresponding to the best decision for the state of nature s_j
V_{ij} = the payoff corresponding to decision alternative d_i and state of nature s_j

Note the role of the absolute value in equation (14.1). For minimization problems, the best payoff, V_j^*, is the smallest entry in column j. Because this value always is less than or equal to V_{ij}, the absolute value of the difference between V_j^* and V_{ij} ensures that the regret is always the magnitude of the difference.

Using equation (14.1) and the payoffs in Table 14.1, we can compute the regret associated with each combination of decision alternative d_i and state of nature s_j. Because the PDC problem is a maximization problem, V_j^* will be the largest entry in column j of the payoff table. Thus, to compute the regret, we simply subtract each entry in a column from the largest entry in the column. Table 14.4 shows the opportunity loss, or regret, table for the PDC problem.

The next step in applying the minimax regret approach is to list the maximum regret for each decision alternative; Table 14.5 shows the results for the PDC problem. Selecting the decision alternative with the *minimum* of the *maximum* regret values—hence, the name *minimax regret*—yields the minimax regret decision. For the PDC problem, the alternative to construct the medium condominium complex, with a corresponding maximum regret of \$6 million, is the recommended minimax regret decision.

For practice in developing a decision recommendation using the optimistic, conservative, and minimax regret approaches, try Problem 1(b).

Note that the three approaches discussed in this section provide different recommendations, which in itself isn't bad. It simply reflects the difference in decision-making philosophies that underlie the various approaches. Ultimately, the decision maker will have to

TABLE 14.4 OPPORTUNITY LOSS, OR REGRET, TABLE FOR THE PDC CONDOMINIUM PROJECT ($ MILLION)

	State of Nature	
Decision Alternative	**Strong Demand s_1**	**Weak Demand s_2**
Small complex, d_1	12	0
Medium complex, d_2	6	2
Large complex, d_3	0	16

TABLE 14.5 MAXIMUM REGRET FOR EACH PDC DECISION ALTERNATIVE

Decision Alternative	**Maximum Regret**	
Small complex, d_1	12	
Medium complex, d_2	6	← Minimum of the maximum regret
Large complex, d_3	16	

[1]In maximization problems, V_j^* will be the largest entry in column j of the payoff table. In minimization problems, V_j^* will be the smallest entry in column j of the payoff table.

choose the most appropriate approach and then make the final decision accordingly. The main criticism of the approaches discussed in this section is that they do not consider any information about the probabilities of the various states of nature. In the next section we discuss an approach that utilizes probability information in selecting a decision alternative.

14.3 DECISION MAKING WITH PROBABILITIES

In many decision-making situations, we can obtain probability assessments for the states of nature. When such probabilities are available, we can use the **expected value approach** to identify the best decision alternative. Let us first define the expected value of a decision alternative and then apply it to the PDC problem.

Let

$$N = \text{the number of states of nature}$$
$$P(s_j) = \text{the probability of state of nature } s_j$$

Because one and only one of the N states of nature can occur, the probabilities must satisfy two conditions:

$$P(s_j) \geq 0 \qquad \text{for all states of nature} \tag{14.2}$$

$$\sum_{j=1}^{N} P(s_j) = P(s_1) + P(s_2) + \cdots + P(s_N) = 1 \tag{14.3}$$

The **expected value (EV)** of decision alternative d_i is defined as follows:

$$\text{EV}(d_i) = \sum_{j=1}^{N} P(s_j)V_{ij} \tag{14.4}$$

In words, the expected value of a decision alternative is the sum of weighted payoffs for the decision alternative. The weight for a payoff is the probability of the associated state of nature and therefore the probability that the payoff will occur. Let us return to the PDC problem to see how the expected value approach can be applied.

PDC is optimistic about the potential for the luxury high-rise condominium complex. Suppose that this optimism leads to an initial subjective probability assessment of 0.8 that demand will be strong (s_1) and a corresponding probability of 0.2 that demand will be weak (s_2). Thus, $P(s_1) = 0.8$ and $P(s_2) = 0.2$. Using the payoff values in Table 14.1 and equation (14.4), we compute the expected value for each of the three decision alternatives as follows:

$$\text{EV}(d_1) = 0.8(8) + 0.2(7) = 7.8$$
$$\text{EV}(d_2) = 0.8(14) + 0.2(5) = 12.2$$
$$\text{EV}(d_3) = 0.8(20) + 0.2(-9) = 14.2$$

Thus, using the expected value approach, we find that the large condominium complex, with an expected value of \$14.2 million, is the recommended decision.

FIGURE 14.3 PDC DECISION TREE WITH STATE-OF-NATURE BRANCH PROBABILITIES

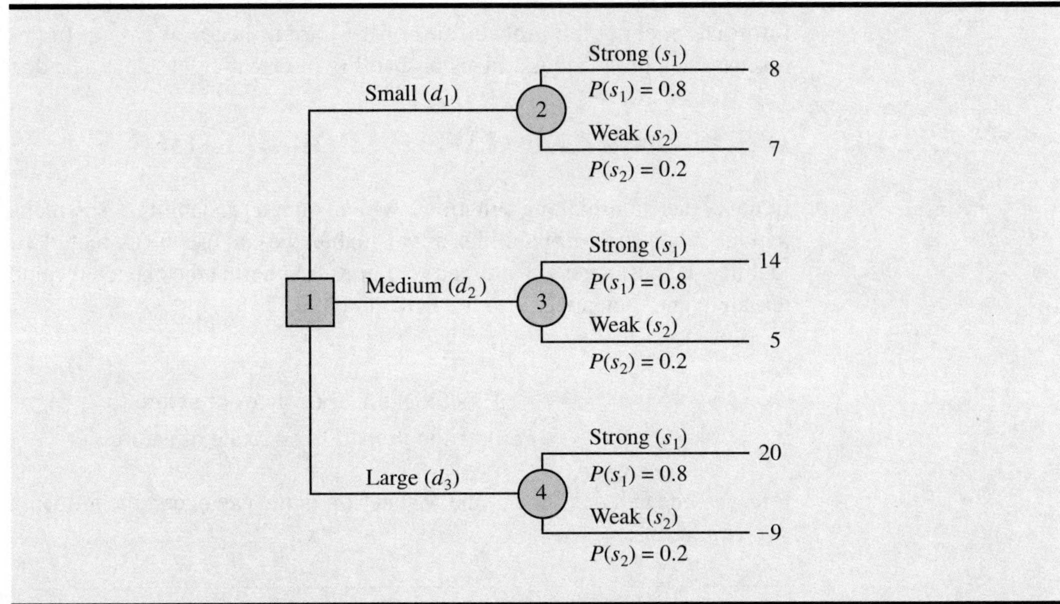

Can you now use the expected value approach to develop a decision recommendation? Try Problem 5.

The calculations required to identify the decision alternative with the best expected value can be conveniently carried out on a decision tree. Figure 14.3 shows the decision tree for the PDC problem with state-of-nature branch probabilities. Working backward through the decision tree, we first compute the expected value at each chance node. That is, at each chance node, we weight each possible payoff by its probability of occurrence. By doing so, we obtain the expected values for nodes 2, 3, and 4, as shown in Figure 14.4.

Because the decision maker controls the branch leaving decision node 1 and because we are trying to maximize the expected profit, the best decision alternative at node 1 is d_3.

FIGURE 14.4 APPLYING THE EXPECTED VALUE APPROACH USING A DECISION TREE

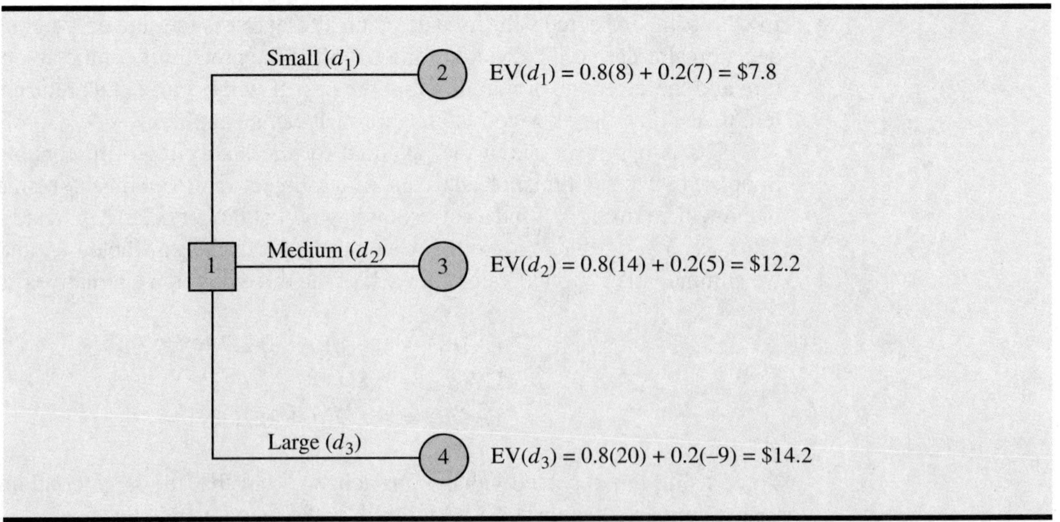

Thus, the decision tree analysis leads to a recommendation of d_3 with an expected value of \$14.2 million. Note that this recommendation is also obtained with the expected value approach in conjunction with the payoff table.

Computer software packages are available to help in constructing more complex decision trees. See Appendix 14.1.

Other decision problems may be substantially more complex than the PDC problem, but if a reasonable number of decision alternatives and states of nature are present, you can use the decision tree approach outlined here. First, draw a decision tree consisting of decision nodes, chance nodes, and branches that describe the sequential nature of the problem. If you use the expected value approach, the next step is to determine the probabilities for each of the states of nature and compute the expected value at each chance node. Then select the decision branch leading to the chance node with the best expected value. The decision alternative associated with this branch is the recommended decision.

The Management Science in Action, Controlling Particulate Emissions at Ohio Edison Company, describes how a decision tree was constructed to help choose the best technology to control particulate emissions.

Expected Value of Perfect Information

Suppose that PDC has the opportunity to conduct a market research study that would help evaluate buyer interest in the condominium project and provide information that management could use to improve the probability assessments for the states of nature. To determine the potential value of this information, we begin by supposing that the study could provide *perfect information* regarding the states of nature; that is, we assume for the moment that PDC could determine with certainty, prior to making a decision, which state of nature is going to occur. To make use of this perfect information, we will develop a decision strategy that PDC should follow once it knows which state of nature will occur. A decision strategy is simply a decision rule that specifies the decision alternative to be selected after new information becomes available.

To help determine the decision strategy for PDC, we reproduced PDC's payoff table as Table 14.6. Note that, if PDC knew for sure that state of nature s_1 would occur, the best decision alternative would be d_3, with a payoff of \$20 million. Similarly, if PDC knew for sure that state of nature s_2 would occur, the best decision alternative would be d_1, with a payoff of \$7 million. Thus, we can state PDC's optimal decision strategy when the perfect information becomes available as follows:

If s_1, select d_3 and receive a payoff of \$20 million.
If s_2, select d_1 and receive a payoff of \$7 million.

What is the expected value for this decision strategy? To compute the expected value with perfect information, we return to the original probabilities for the states of nature: $P(s_1) = 0.8$, and $P(s_2) = 0.2$. Thus, there is a 0.8 probability that the perfect information will indicate

TABLE 14.6 PAYOFF TABLE FOR THE PDC CONDOMINIUM PROJECT (\$ MILLION)

	State of Nature	
Decision Alternative	**Strong Demand s_1**	**Weak Demand s_2**
Small complex, d_1	8	7
Medium complex, d_2	14	5
Large complex, d_3	20	−9

state of nature s_1 and the resulting decision alternative d_3 will provide a $20 million profit. Similarly, with a 0.2 probability for state of nature s_2, the optimal decision alternative d_1 will provide a $7 million profit. Thus, from equation (14.4), the expected value of the decision strategy that uses perfect information is

$$0.8(20) + 0.2(7) = 17.4$$

We refer to the expected value of $17.4 million as the *expected value with perfect information* (EVwPI).

Earlier in this section we showed that the recommended decision using the expected value approach is decision alternative d_3, with an expected value of $14.2 million. Because this decision recommendation and expected value computation were made without the benefit of perfect information, $14.2 million is referred to as the *expected value without perfect information* (EVwoPI).

It would be worth $3.2 million for PDC to learn the level of market acceptance before selecting a decision alternative.

The expected value with perfect information is $17.4 million, and the expected value without perfect information is $14.2; therefore, the expected value of the perfect information (EVPI) is $17.4 − $14.2 = $3.2 million. In other words, $3.2 million represents the additional expected value that can be obtained if perfect information were available about the states of nature.

MANAGEMENT SCIENCE IN ACTION

CONTROLLING PARTICULATE EMISSIONS AT OHIO EDISON COMPANY*

Ohio Edison Company is an operating company of FirstEnergy Corporation. Ohio Edison and its subsidiary, Pennsylvania Power Company, provide electrical service to more than 1 million customers in central and northeastern Ohio and western Pennsylvania. Most of this electricity is generated by coal-fired power plants. To meet evolving air quality standards, Ohio Edison conducted a decision analysis to help them select the best particulate control equipment for three of its coal-fired generating units.

Preliminary studies narrowed the particulate control equipment choice to a decision between fabric filters and electrostatic precipitators. The decision was affected by a number of uncertainties: the uncertainty concerning the way air quality regulations might be interpreted, the uncertainty concerning sulfur content requirements for the coal to be burned, and the uncertainty concerning construction costs, among others. Because of the complexity of the problem, the uncertain events involved, and the importance of the choice, a comprehensive decision analysis was conducted.

The choice was based on minimizing the annual revenue requirements for the three large generating units over their remaining lifetime. These revenue requirements represented the monies that would have to be collected from the utility's customers to recover costs resulting from the choice made. A decision tree was constructed to represent the particulate control decision and its uncertainties and costs. A decision node was used to represent the two choices possible: fabric filters or electrostatic precipitators. Chance nodes were used to represent the uncertainties involved. Costs associated with the decision model were obtained from engineering calculations or estimates. Probabilities for the chance nodes were obtained from existing data or the subjective assessments of knowledgeable persons.

The result of the decision analysis led Ohio Edison to select the electrostatic precipitator technology for the three generating units. Had the decision analysis not been performed, the particulate control decision would have favored the fabric filter equipment. Decision analysis offered a means for effectively analyzing the uncertainties involved in the decision and led to a decision that yielded both lower expected revenue requirements and lower risk.

*Based on information provided by Thomas J. Madden and M. S. Hyrnick of Ohio Edison Company, Akron, Ohio.

Generally speaking, a market research study will not provide "perfect" information; however, if the market research study is a good one, the information gathered might be worth a sizable portion of the $3.2 million. Given the EVPI of $3.2 million, PDC might seriously consider a market survey as a way to obtain more information about the states of nature.

In general, the **expected value of perfect information (EVPI)** is computed as follows:

$$\text{EVPI} = |\text{EVwPI} - \text{EVwoPI}| \tag{14.5}$$

where

EVPI = expected value of perfect information
EVwPI = expected value *with* perfect information about the states of nature
EVwoPI = expected value *without* perfect information about the states of nature

For practice in determining the expected value of perfect information, try Problem 14.

Note the role of the absolute value in equation (14.5). For minimization problems the expected value with perfect information is always less than or equal to the expected value without perfect information. In this case, EVPI is the magnitude of the difference between EVwPI and EVwoPI, or the absolute value of the difference as shown in equation (14.5).

NOTES AND COMMENTS

We restate the *opportunity loss,* or *regret,* table for the PDC problem (see Table 14.4) as follows.

	State of Nature	
	Strong Demand	**Weak Demand**
Decision Alternative	s_1	s_2
Small complex, d_1	12	0
Medium complex, d_2	6	2
Large complex, d_3	0	16

Using $P(s_1)$, $P(s_2)$, and the opportunity loss values, we can compute the *expected opportunity loss* (EOL) for each decision alternative. With $P(s_1) = 0.8$ and $P(s_2) = 0.2$, the expected opportunity loss for each of the three decision alternatives is

$$\text{EOL}(d_1) = 0.8(12) + 0.2(0) = 9.6$$
$$\text{EOL}(d_2) = 0.8(6) + 0.2(2) = 5.2$$
$$\text{EOL}(d_3) = 0.8(0) + 0.2(16) = 3.2$$

Regardless of whether the decision analysis involves maximization or minimization, the *minimum* expected opportunity loss always provides the best decision alternative. Thus, with $\text{EOL}(d_3) = 3.2$, d_3 is the recommended decision. In addition, the minimum expected opportunity loss always is *equal to the expected value of perfect information.* That is, EOL(best decision) = EVPI; for the PDC problem, this value is $3.2 million.

14.4 RISK ANALYSIS AND SENSITIVITY ANALYSIS

Risk analysis helps the decision maker recognize the difference between the expected value of a decision alternative and the payoff that may actually occur. **Sensitivity analysis** also helps the decision maker by describing how changes in the state-of-nature probabilities and/or changes in the payoffs affect the recommended decision alternative.

Risk Analysis

A decision alternative and a state of nature combine to generate the payoff associated with a decision. The **risk profile** for a decision alternative shows the possible payoffs along with their associated probabilities.

Let us demonstrate risk analysis and the construction of a risk profile by returning to the PDC condominium construction project. Using the expected value approach, we identified the large condominium complex (d_3) as the best decision alternative. The expected value of \$14.2 million for d_3 is based on a 0.8 probability of obtaining a \$20 million profit and a 0.2 probability of obtaining a \$9 million loss. The 0.8 probability for the \$20 million payoff and the 0.2 probability for the −\$9 million payoff provide the risk profile for the large complex decision alternative. This risk profile is shown graphically in Figure 14.5.

Sometimes a review of the risk profile associated with an optimal decision alternative may cause the decision maker to choose another decision alternative even though the expected value of the other decision alternative is not as good. For example, the risk profile for the medium complex decision alternative (d_2) shows a 0.8 probability for a \$14 million payoff and 0.2 probability for a \$5 million payoff. Because no probability of a loss is associated with decision alternative d_2, the medium complex decision alternative would be judged less risky than the large complex decision alternative. As a result, a decision maker might prefer the less-risky medium complex decision alternative even though it has an expected value of \$2 million less than the large complex decision alternative.

Sensitivity Analysis

Sensitivity analysis can be used to determine how changes in the probabilities for the states of nature or changes in the payoffs affect the recommended decision alternative. In many cases, the probabilities for the states of nature and the payoffs are based on subjective assessments. Sensitivity analysis helps the decision maker understand which of these inputs are critical to the choice of the best decision alternative. If a small change in the value of one of the inputs causes a change in the recommended decision alternative, the solution to the decision analysis problem is sensitive to that particular input. Extra effort and care should be taken

FIGURE 14.5 RISK PROFILE FOR THE LARGE COMPLEX DECISION ALTERNATIVE FOR THE PDC CONDOMINIUM PROJECT

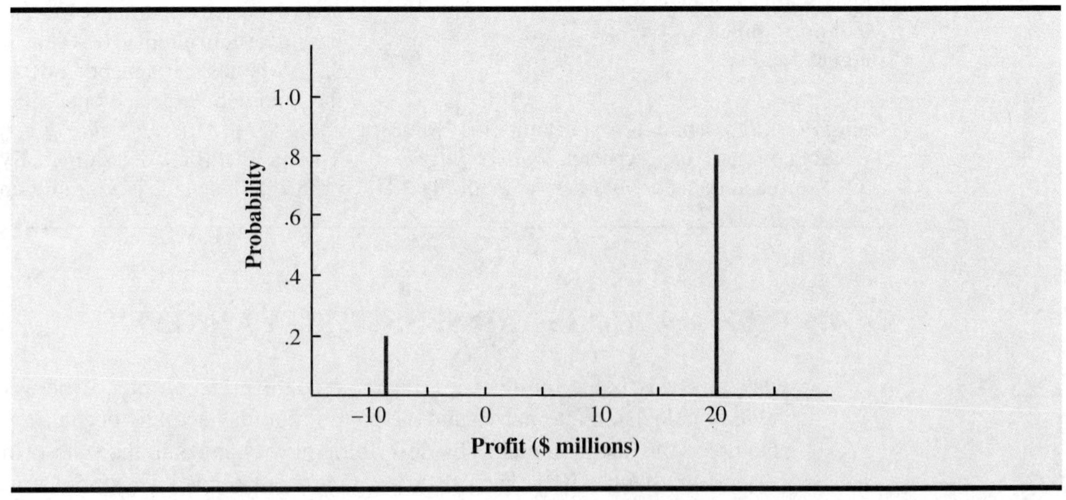

to make sure the input value is as accurate as possible. On the other hand, if a modest to large change in the value of one of the inputs does not cause a change in the recommended decision alternative, the solution to the decision analysis problem is not sensitive to that particular input. No extra time or effort would be needed to refine the estimated input value.

One approach to sensitivity analysis is to select different values for the probabilities of the states of nature and the payoffs and then resolve the decision analysis problem. If the recommended decision alternative changes, we know that the solution is sensitive to the changes made. For example, suppose that in the PDC problem the probability for a strong demand is revised to 0.2 and the probability for a weak demand is revised to 0.8. Would the recommended decision alternative change? Using $P(s_1) = 0.2$, $P(s_2) = 0.8$, and equation (14.4), the revised expected values for the three decision alternatives are

$$\begin{aligned} \text{EV}(d_1) &= 0.2(8) + 0.8(7) = 7.2 \\ \text{EV}(d_2) &= 0.2(14) + 0.8(5) = 6.8 \\ \text{EV}(d_3) &= 0.2(20) + 0.8(-9) = -3.2 \end{aligned}$$

With these probability assessments the recommended decision alternative is to construct a small condominium complex (d_1), with an expected value of $7.2 million. The probability of strong demand is only 0.2, so constructing the large condominium complex (d_3) is the least preferred alternative, with an expected value of −$3.2 million (a loss).

Computer software packages for decision analysis make it easy to calculate these revised scenarios.

Thus, when the probability of strong demand is large, PDC should build the large complex; when the probability of strong demand is small, PDC should build the small complex. Obviously, we could continue to modify the probabilities of the states of nature and learn even more about how changes in the probabilities affect the recommended decision alternative. The drawback to this approach is the numerous calculations required to evaluate the effect of several possible changes in the state-of-nature probabilities.

For the special case of two states of nature, a graphical procedure can be used to determine how changes for the probabilities of the states of nature affect the recommended decision alternative. To demonstrate this procedure, we let p denote the probability of state of nature s_1; that is, $P(s_1) = p$. With only two states of nature in the PDC problem, the probability of state of nature s_2 is

$$P(s_2) = 1 - P(s_1) = 1 - p$$

Using equation (14.4) and the payoff values in Table 14.1, we determine the expected value for decision alternative d_1 as follows:

$$\begin{aligned} \text{EV}(d_1) &= P(s_1)(8) + P(s_2)(7) \\ &= p(8) + (1 - p)(7) \\ &= 8p + 7 - 7p = p + 7 \end{aligned} \tag{14.6}$$

Repeating the expected value computations for decision alternatives d_2 and d_3, we obtain expressions for the expected value of each decision alternative as a function of p:

$$\text{EV}(d_2) = 9p + 5 \tag{14.7}$$

$$\text{EV}(d_3) = 29p - 9 \tag{14.8}$$

Thus, we have developed three equations that show the expected value of the three decision alternatives as a function of the probability of state of nature s_1.

We continue by developing a graph with values of p on the horizontal axis and the associated EVs on the vertical axis. Because equations (14.6), (14.7), and (14.8) are linear equations, the graph of each equation is a straight line. For each equation, then, we can obtain the line by identifying two points that satisfy the equation and drawing a line through the points. For instance, if we let $p = 0$ in equation (14.6), $\text{EV}(d_1) = 7$. Then, letting $p = 1$, $\text{EV}(d_1) = 8$. Connecting these two points, (0,7) and (1,8), provides the line labeled $\text{EV}(d_1)$ in Figure 14.6. Similarly, we obtain the lines labeled $\text{EV}(d_2)$ and $\text{EV}(d_3)$; these lines are the graphs of equations (14.7) and (14.8), respectively.

Figure 14.6 shows how the recommended decision changes as p, the probability of the strong demand state of nature (s_1), changes. Note that for small values of p, decision alternative d_1 (small complex) provides the largest expected value and is thus the recommended decision. When the value of p increases to a certain point, decision alternative d_2 (medium complex) provides the largest expected value and is the recommended decision. Finally, for large values of p, decision alternative d_3 (large complex) becomes the recommended decision.

The value of p for which the expected values of d_1 and d_2 are equal is the value of p corresponding to the intersection of the $\text{EV}(d_1)$ and the $\text{EV}(d_2)$ lines. To determine this value, we set $\text{EV}(d_1) = \text{EV}(d_2)$ and solve for the value of p:

$$\begin{aligned} p + 7 &= 9p + 5 \\ 8p &= 2 \\ p &= \frac{2}{8} = 0.25 \end{aligned}$$

Graphical sensitivity analysis shows how changes in the probabilities for the states of nature affect the recommended decision alternative. Try Problem 8.

Hence, when $p = 0.25$, decision alternatives d_1 and d_2 provide the same expected value. Repeating this calculation for the value of p corresponding to the intersection of the $\text{EV}(d_2)$ and $\text{EV}(d_3)$ lines, we obtain $p = 0.70$.

Using Figure 14.6, we can conclude that decision alternative d_1 provides the largest expected value for $p \leq 0.25$, decision alternative d_2 provides the largest expected value for $0.25 \leq p \leq 0.70$, and decision alternative d_3 provides the largest expected value for $p \geq 0.70$. Because p is the probability of state of nature s_1 and $(1 - p)$ is the probability of state of nature s_2, we now have the sensitivity analysis information that tells us how changes in the state-of-nature probabilities affect the recommended decision alternative.

Sensitivity analysis calculations can also be made for the values of the payoffs. In the original PDC problem, the expected values for the three decision alternatives were as follows: $\text{EV}(d_1) = 7.8$, $\text{EV}(d_2) = 12.2$, and $\text{EV}(d_3) = 14.2$. Decision alternative d_3 (large complex) was recommended. Note that decision alternative d_2 with $\text{EV}(d_2) = 12.2$ was the second best decision alternative. Decision alternative d_3 will remain the optimal decision alternative as long as $\text{EV}(d_3)$ is greater than or equal to the expected value of the second best decision alternative. Thus, decision alternative d_3 will remain the optimal decision alternative as long as

$$\text{EV}(d_3) \geq 12.2 \tag{14.9}$$

FIGURE 14.6 EXPECTED VALUE FOR THE PDC DECISION ALTERNATIVES AS A FUNCTION OF p

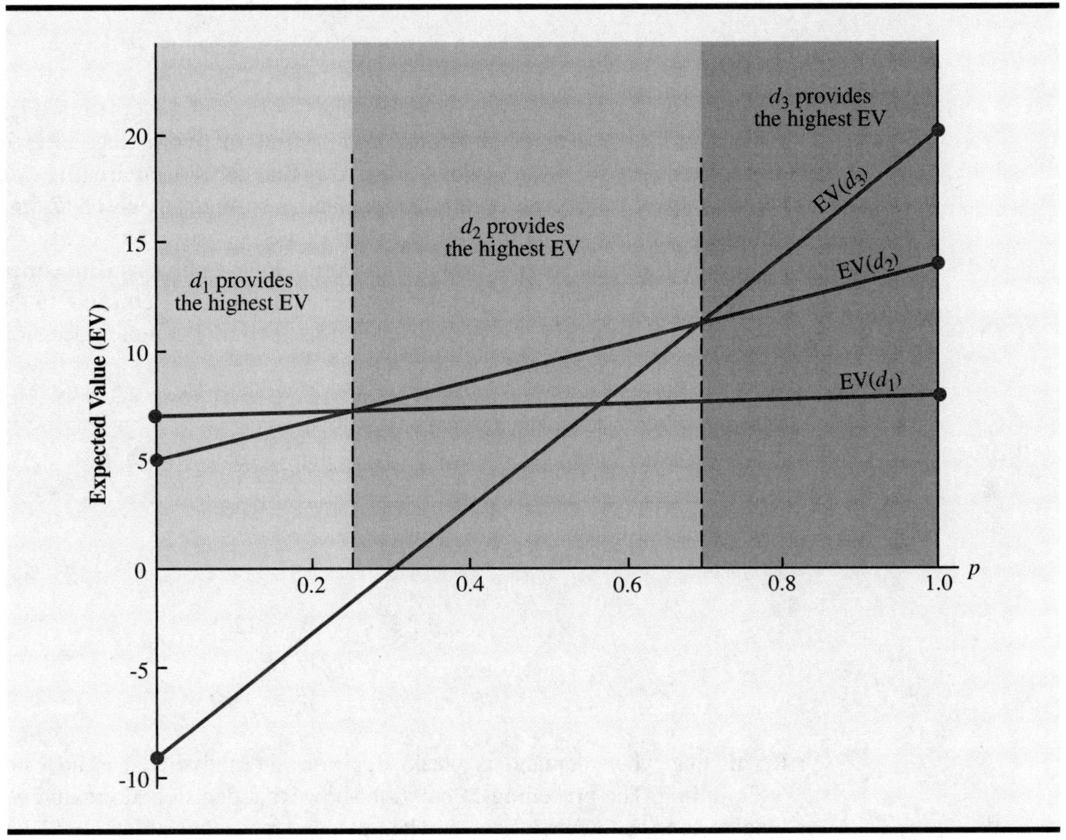

Let

S = the payoff of decision alternative d_3 when demand is strong
W = the payoff of decision alternative d_3 when demand is weak

Using $P(s_1) = 0.8$ and $P(s_2) = 0.2$, the general expression for EV(d_3) is

$$\text{EV}(d_3) = 0.8S + 0.2W \tag{14.10}$$

Assuming that the payoff for d_3 stays at its original value of $-\$9$ million when demand is weak, the large complex decision alternative will remain optimal as long as

$$\text{EV}(d_3) = 0.8S + 0.2(-9) \geq 12.2 \tag{14.11}$$

Solving for S, we have

$$\begin{aligned} 0.8S - 1.8 &\geq 12.2 \\ 0.8S &\geq 14 \\ S &\geq 17.5 \end{aligned}$$

Recall that when demand is strong, decision alternative d_3 has an estimated payoff of \$20 million. The preceding calculation shows that decision alternative d_3 will remain optimal as long as the payoff for d_3 when demand is strong is at least \$17.5 million.

Assuming that the payoff for d_3 when demand is strong stays at its original value of \$20 million, we can make a similar calculation to learn how sensitive the optimal solution is with regard to the payoff for d_3 when demand is weak. Returning to the expected value calculation of equation (14.10), we know that the large complex decision alternative will remain optimal as long as

$$\text{EV}(d_3) = 0.8(20) + 0.2W \geq 12.2 \tag{14.12}$$

Solving for W, we have

$$\begin{aligned} 16 + 0.2W &\geq 12.2 \\ 0.2W &\geq -3.8 \\ W &\geq -19 \end{aligned}$$

Recall that when demand is weak, decision alternative d_3 has an estimated payoff of −\$9 million. The preceding calculation shows that decision alternative d_3 will remain optimal as long as the payoff for d_3 when demand is weak is at least −\$19 million.

Sensitivity analysis can assist management in deciding whether more time and effort should be spent obtaining better estimates of payoffs and probabilities.

Based on this sensitivity analysis, we conclude that the payoffs for the large complex decision alternative (d_3) could vary considerably and d_3 would remain the recommended decision alternative. Thus, we conclude that the optimal solution for the PDC decision problem is not particularly sensitive to the payoffs for the large complex decision alternative. We note, however, that this sensitivity analysis has been conducted based on only one change at a time. That is, only one payoff was changed and the probabilities for the states of nature remained $P(s_1) = 0.8$ and $P(s_2) = 0.2$. Note that similar sensitivity analysis calculations can be made for the payoffs associated with the small complex decision alternative d_1 and the medium complex decision alternative d_2. However, in these cases, decision alternative d_3 remains optimal only if the changes in the payoffs for decision alternatives d_1 and d_2 meet the requirements that $\text{EV}(d_1) \leq 14.2$ and $\text{EV}(d_2) \leq 14.2$.

NOTES AND COMMENTS

1. Some decision analysis software automatically provide the risk profiles for the optimal decision alternative. These packages also allow the user to obtain the risk profiles for other decision alternatives. After comparing the risk profiles, a decision maker may decide to select a decision alternative with a good risk profile even though the expected value of the decision alternative is not as good as the optimal decision alternative.
2. A *tornado diagram*, a graphical display, is particularly helpful when several inputs combine to determine the value of the optimal solution. By

varying each input over its range of values, we obtain information about how each input affects the value of the optimal solution. To display this information, a bar is constructed for the input with the width of the bar showing how the input affects the value of the optimal solution. The widest bar corresponds to the input that is most sensitive. The bars are arranged in a graph with the widest bar at the top, resulting in a graph that has the appearance of a tornado.

14.5 DECISION ANALYSIS WITH SAMPLE INFORMATION

In applying the expected value approach, we showed how probability information about the states of nature affects the expected value calculations and thus the decision recommendation. Frequently, decision makers have preliminary or **prior probability** assessments for the states of nature that are the best probability values available at that time. However, to make the best possible decision, the decision maker may want to seek additional information about the states of nature. This new information can be used to revise or update the prior probabilities so that the final decision is based on more accurate probabilities for the states of nature. Most often, additional information is obtained through experiments designed to provide **sample information** about the states of nature. Raw material sampling, product testing, and market research studies are examples of experiments (or studies) that may enable management to revise or update the state-of-nature probabilities. These revised probabilities are called **posterior probabilities.**

Let us return to the PDC problem and assume that management is considering a six-month market research study designed to learn more about potential market acceptance of the PDC condominium project. Management anticipates that the market research study will provide one of the following two results:

1. Favorable report: A significant number of the individuals contacted express interest in purchasing a PDC condominium.
2. Unfavorable report: Very few of the individuals contacted express interest in purchasing a PDC condominium.

Influence Diagram

By introducing the possibility of conducting a market research study, the PDC problem becomes more complex. The influence diagram for the expanded PDC problem is shown in Figure 14.7. Note that the two decision nodes correspond to the research study and the complex-size decisions. The two chance nodes correspond to the research study results and demand for the condominiums. Finally, the consequence node is the profit. From the arcs of the influence diagram, we see that demand influences both the research study results and profit. Although demand is currently unknown to PDC, some level of demand for the condominiums already exists in the Pittsburgh area. If existing demand is strong, the research study is likely to find a significant number of individuals who express an interest in purchasing a condominium. However, if the existing demand is weak, the research study is more likely to find a significant number of individuals who express little interest in purchasing a condominium. In this sense, existing demand for the condominiums will influence the research study results, and clearly, demand will have an influence upon PDC's profit.

The arc from the research study decision node to the complex-size decision node indicates that the research study decision precedes the complex-size decision. No arc spans from the research study decision node to the research study results node, because the decision to conduct the research study does not actually influence the research study results. The decision to conduct the research study makes the research study results available, but

FIGURE 14.7 INFLUENCE DIAGRAM FOR THE PDC PROBLEM WITH SAMPLE INFORMATION

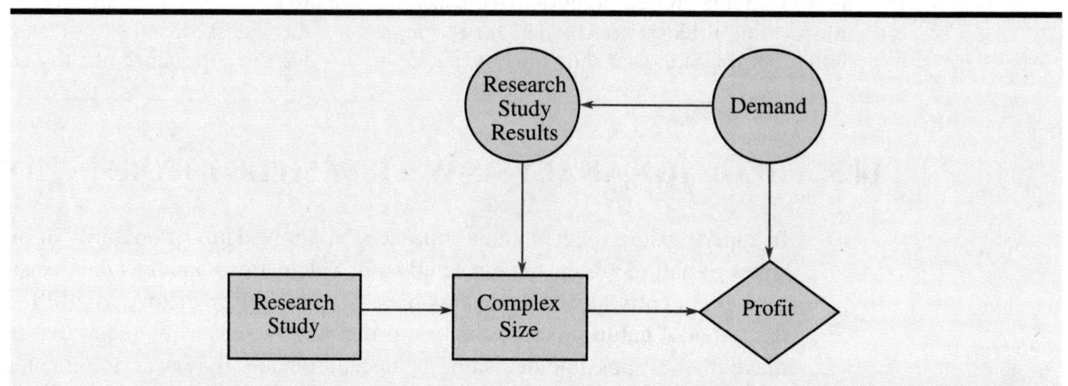

it does not influence the results of the research study. Finally, the complex-size node and the demand node both influence profit. Note that if a stated cost to conduct the research study were given, the decision to conduct the research study would also influence profit. In such a case, we would need to add an arc from the research study decision node to the profit node to show the influence that the research study cost would have on profit.

Decision Tree

The decision tree for the PDC problem with sample information shows the logical sequence for the decisions and the chance events in Figure 14.8.

First, PDC's management must decide whether the market research should be conducted. If it is conducted, PDC's management must be prepared to make a decision about the size of the condominium project if the market research report is favorable and, possibly, a different decision about the size of the condominium project if the market research report is unfavorable. In Figure 14.8, the squares are decision nodes and the circles are chance nodes. At each decision node, the branch of the tree that is taken is based on the decision made. At each chance node, the branch of the tree that is taken is based on probability or chance. For example, decision node 1 shows that PDC must first make the decision of whether to conduct the market research study. If the market research study is undertaken, chance node 2 indicates that both the favorable report branch and the unfavorable report branch are not under PDC's control and will be determined by chance. Node 3 is a decision node, indicating that PDC must make the decision to construct the small, medium, or large complex if the market research report is favorable. Node 4 is a decision node showing that PDC must make the decision to construct the small, medium, or large complex if the market research report is unfavorable. Node 5 is a decision node indicating that PDC must make the decision to construct the small, medium, or large complex if the market research is not undertaken. Nodes 6 to 14 are chance nodes indicating that the strong demand or weak demand state-of-nature branches will be determined by chance.

We explain in Section 14.6 how these probabilities can be developed.

Analysis of the decision tree and the choice of an optimal strategy requires that we know the branch probabilities corresponding to all chance nodes. PDC has developed the following branch probabilities.

If the market research study is undertaken

$$P(\text{Favorable report}) = 0.77$$
$$P(\text{Unfavorable report}) = 0.23$$

FIGURE 14.8 THE PDC DECISION TREE INCLUDING THE MARKET RESEARCH STUDY

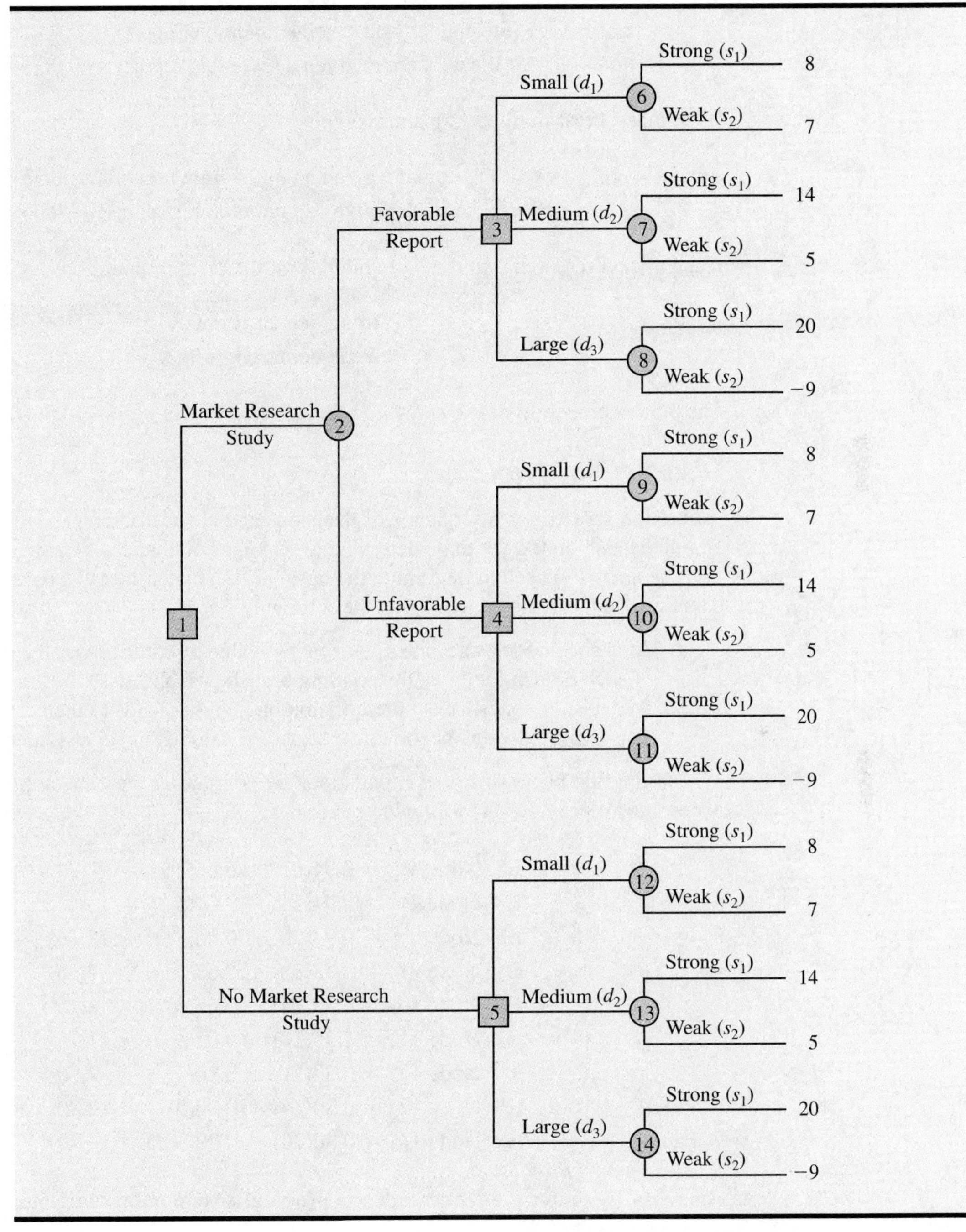

If the market research report is favorable

$$P(\text{Strong demand given a favorable report}) = 0.94$$
$$P(\text{Weak demand given a favorable report}) = 0.06$$

If the market research report is unfavorable

$$P(\text{Strong demand given an unfavorable report}) = 0.35$$
$$P(\text{Weak demand given an unfavorable report}) = 0.65$$

If the market research report is not undertaken, the prior probabilities are applicable.

$$P(\text{Strong demand}) = 0.80$$
$$P(\text{Weak demand}) = 0.20$$

The branch probabilities are shown on the decision tree in Figure 14.9.

Decision Strategy

A **decision strategy** is a sequence of decisions and chance outcomes where the decisions chosen depend on the yet to be determined outcomes of chance events.

The approach used to determine the optimal decision strategy is based on a backward pass through the decision tree using the following steps:

1. At chance nodes, compute the expected value by multiplying the payoff at the end of each branch by the corresponding branch probabilities.
2. At decision nodes, select the decision branch that leads to the best expected value. This expected value becomes the expected value at the decision node.

Starting the backward pass calculations by computing the expected values at chance nodes 6 to 14 provides the following results.

$$\begin{aligned}
\text{EV(Node 6)} &= 0.94(8) + 0.06(7) = 7.94 \\
\text{EV(Node 7)} &= 0.94(14) + 0.06(5) = 13.46 \\
\text{EV(Node 8)} &= 0.94(20) + 0.06(-9) = 18.26 \\
\text{EV(Node 9)} &= 0.35(8) + 0.65(7) = 7.35 \\
\text{EV(Node 10)} &= 0.35(14) + 0.65(5) = 8.15 \\
\text{EV(Node 11)} &= 0.35(20) + 0.65(-9) = 1.15 \\
\text{EV(Node 12)} &= 0.80(8) + 0.20(7) = 7.80 \\
\text{EV(Node 13)} &= 0.80(14) + 0.20(5) = 12.20 \\
\text{EV(Node 14)} &= 0.80(20) + 0.20(-9) = 14.20
\end{aligned}$$

Figure 14.10 shows the reduced decision tree after computing expected values at these chance nodes.

Next, move to decision nodes 3, 4, and 5. For each of these nodes, we select the decision alternative branch that leads to the best expected value. For example, at node 3 we have the choice of the small complex branch with EV(Node 6) = 7.94, the medium complex branch with EV(Node 7) = 13.46, and the large complex branch with EV(Node 8) = 18.26. Thus, we select the large complex decision alternative branch and the expected value at node 3 becomes EV(Node 3) = 18.26.

FIGURE 14.9 THE PDC DECISION TREE WITH BRANCH PROBABILITIES

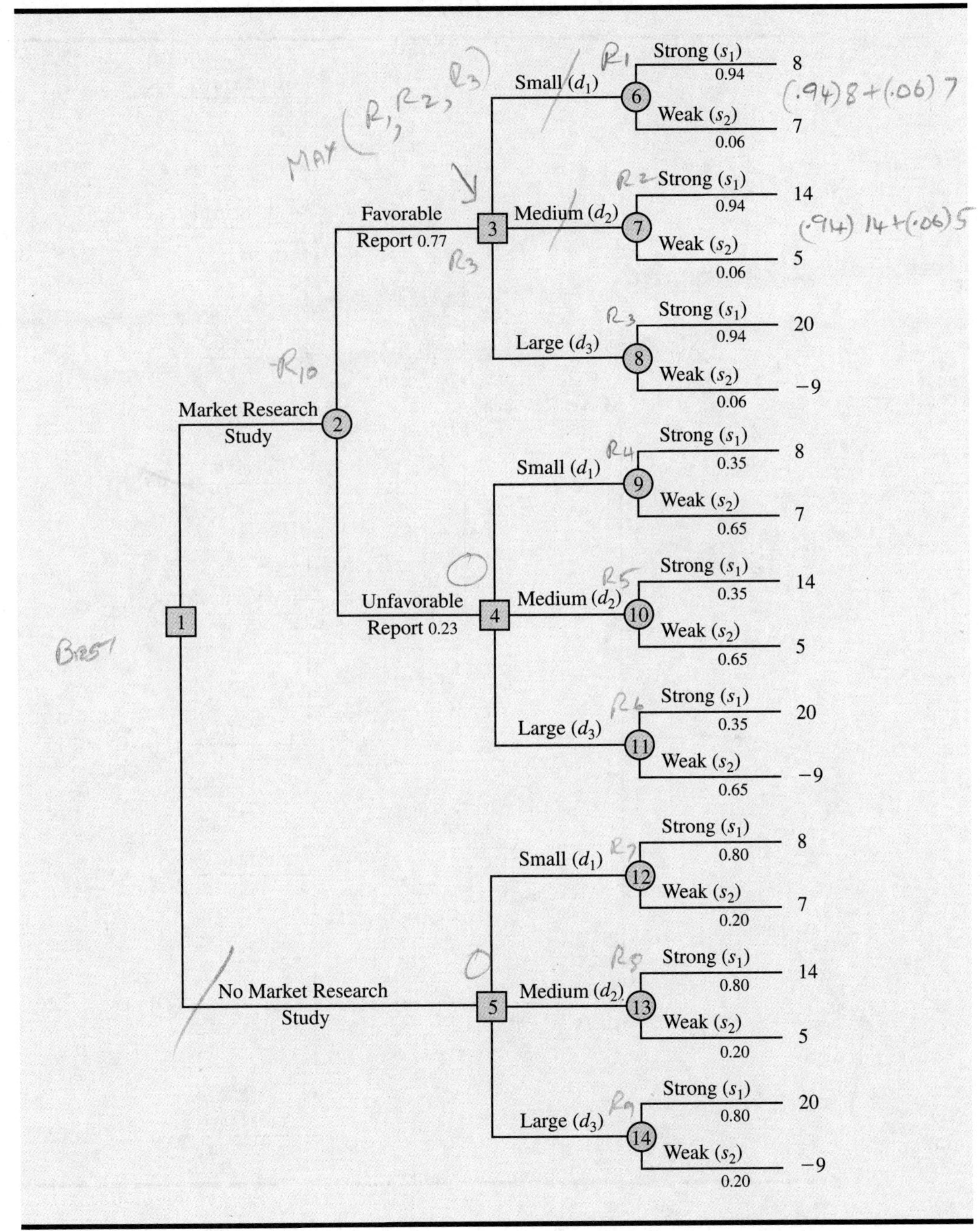

FIGURE 14.10 PDC DECISION TREE AFTER COMPUTING EXPECTED VALUES AT CHANCE NODES 6 TO 14

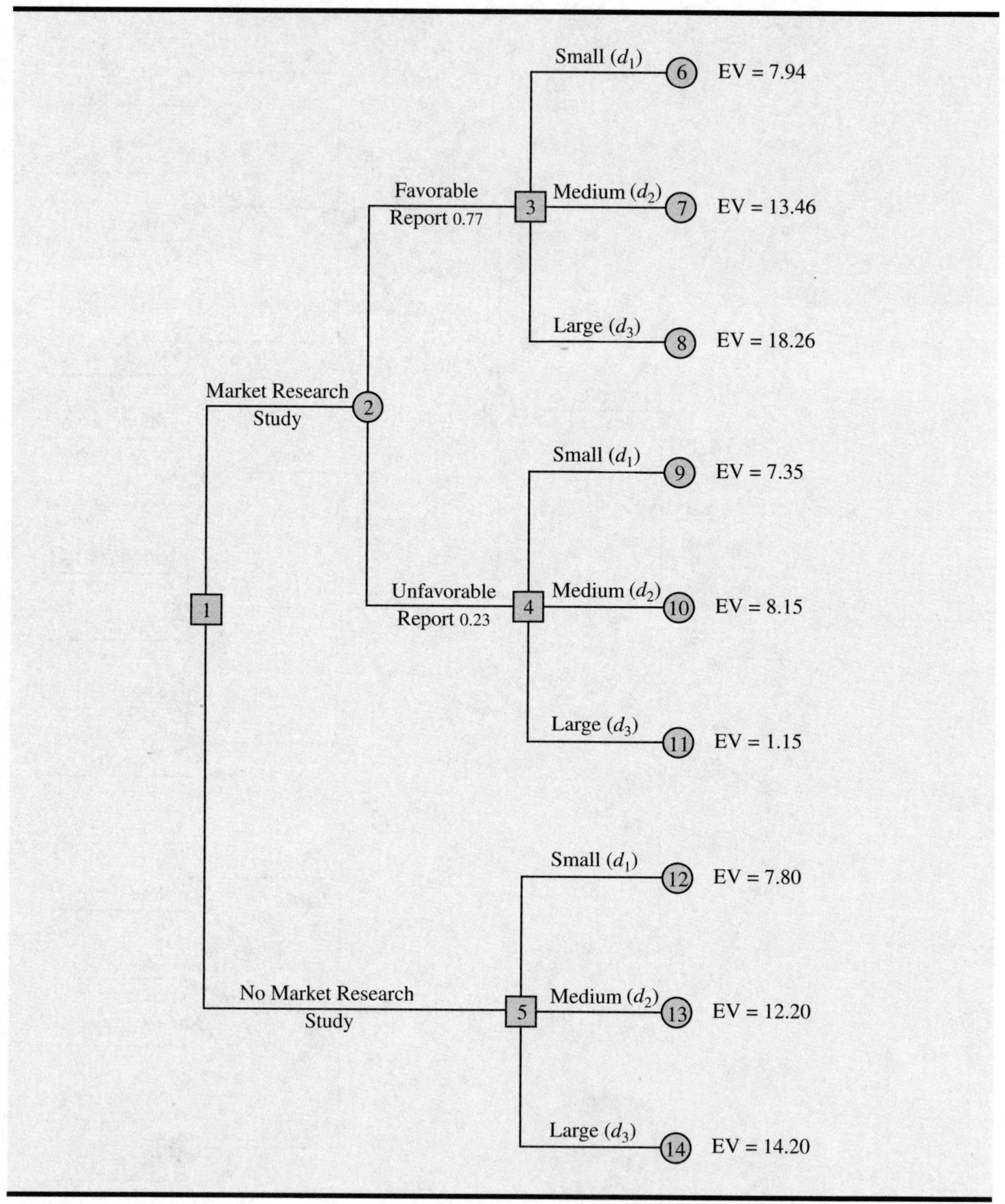

For node 4, we select the best expected value from nodes 9, 10, and 11. The best decision alternative is the medium complex branch that provides EV(Node 4) = 8.15. For node 5, we select the best expected value from nodes 12, 13, and 14. The best decision alternative is the large complex branch that provides EV(Node 5) = 14.20. Figure 14.11 shows the reduced decision tree after choosing the best decisions at nodes 3, 4, and 5.

The expected value at chance node 2 can now be computed as follows:

$$\begin{aligned} \text{EV(Node 2)} &= 0.77\text{EV(Node 3)} + 0.23\text{EV(Node 4)} \\ &= 0.77(18.26) + 0.23(8.15) = 15.93 \end{aligned}$$

This calculation reduces the decision tree to one involving only the two decision branches from node 1 (see Figure 14.12).

Finally, the decision can be made at decision node 1 by selecting the best expected values from nodes 2 and 5. This action leads to the decision alternative to conduct the market research study, which provides an overall expected value of 15.93.

FIGURE 14.11 PDC DECISION TREE AFTER CHOOSING BEST DECISIONS AT NODES 3, 4, AND 5

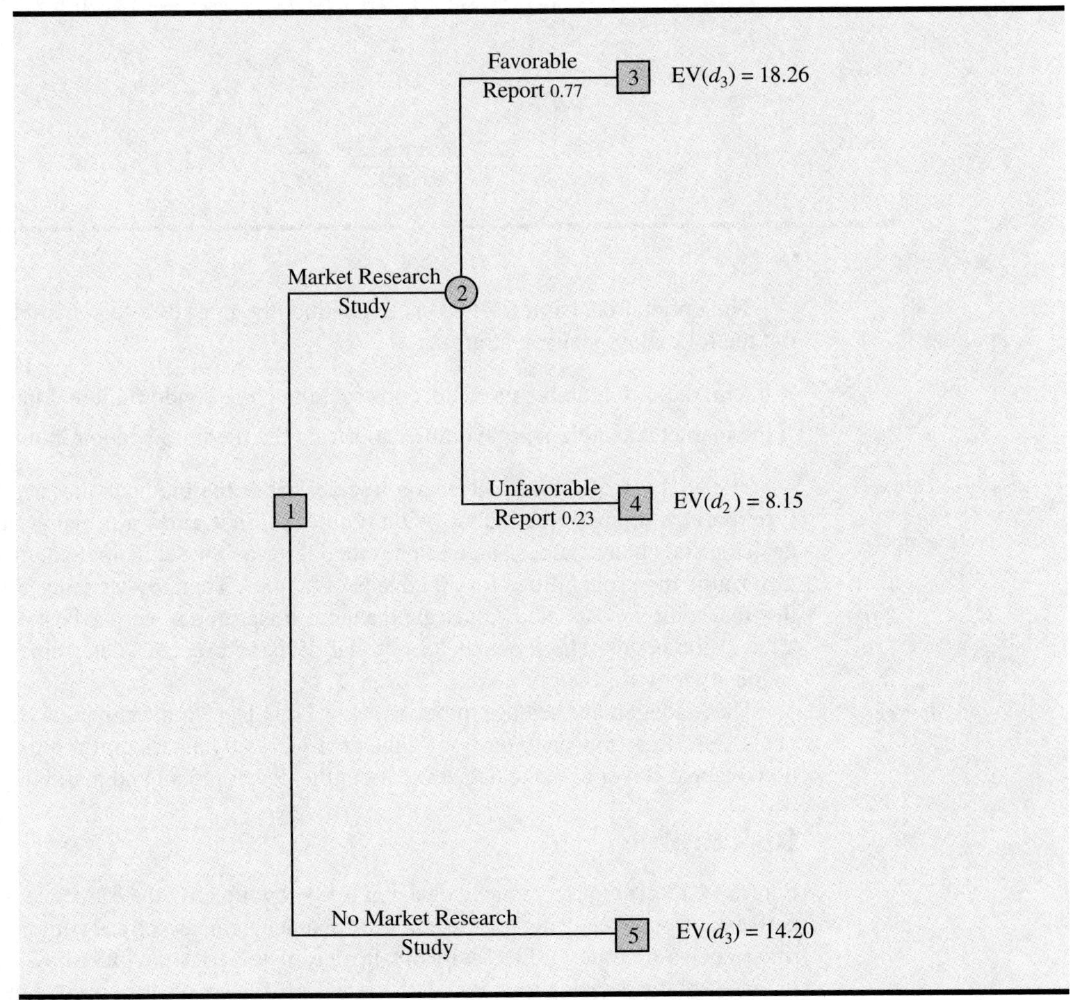

FIGURE 14.12 PDC DECISION TREE REDUCED TO TWO DECISION BRANCHES

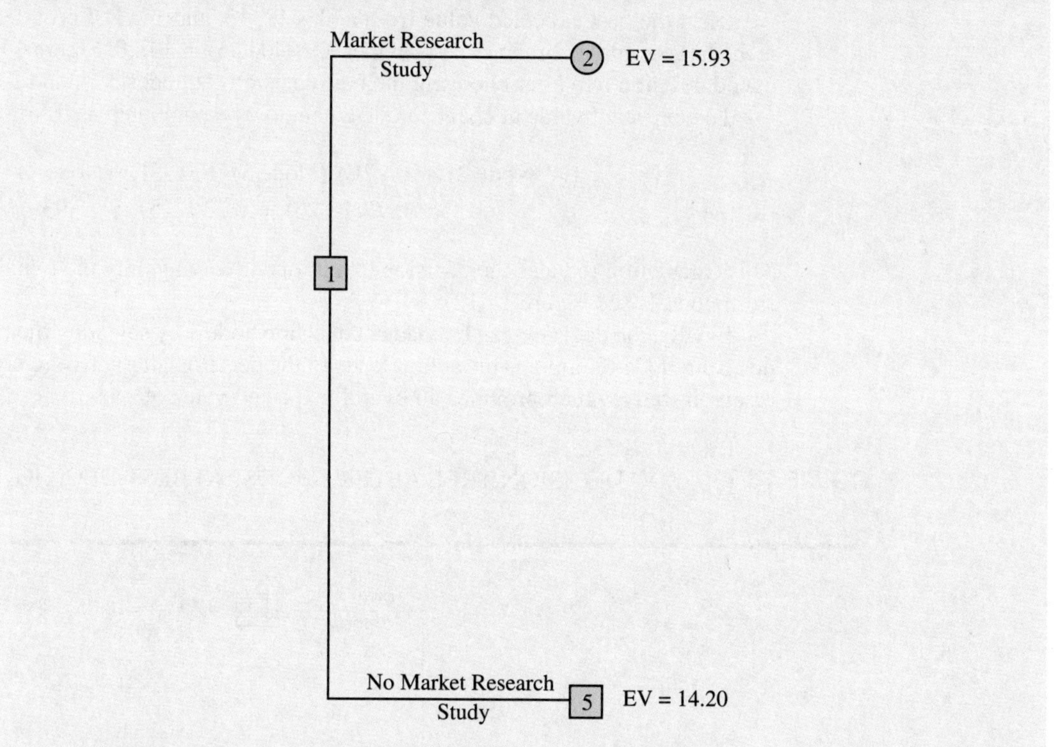

The optimal decision for PDC is to conduct the market research study and then carry out the following decision strategy:

If the market research is favorable, construct the large condominium complex.

If the market research is unfavorable, construct the medium condominium complex.

Problem 16 will test your ability to develop an optimal decision strategy.

The analysis of the PDC decision tree describes the methods that can be used to analyze more complex sequential decision problems. First, draw a decision tree consisting of decision and chance nodes and branches that describe the sequential nature of the problem. Determine the probabilities for all chance outcomes. Then, by working backward through the tree, compute expected values at all chance nodes and select the best decision branch at all decision nodes. The sequence of optimal decision branches determines the optimal decision strategy for the problem.

The Management Science in Action, New Drug Decision Analysis at Bayer Pharmaceuticals, describes how an extension of the decision analysis principles presented in this section enabled Bayer to make decisions about the development and marketing of a new drug.

Risk Profile

Figure 14.13 provides a reduced decision tree showing only the sequence of decision alternatives and chance events for the PDC optimal decision strategy. By implementing the optimal decision strategy, PDC will obtain one of the four payoffs shown at the terminal branches of the decision tree. Recall that a risk profile shows the possible payoffs with their

MANAGEMENT SCIENCE IN ACTION

NEW DRUG DECISION ANALYSIS AT BAYER PHARMACEUTICALS*

Drug development in the United States requires substantial investment and is very risky. It takes nearly 15 years to research and develop a new drug. The Bayer Biological Products (BP) group used decision analysis to evaluate the potential for a new blood-clot-busting drug. An influence diagram was used to describe the complex structure of the decision analysis process. Six key yes-or-no decision nodes were identified: (1) begin preclinical development, (2) begin testing in humans, (3) continue development into phase 3, (4) continue development into phase 4, (5) file a license application with the FDA, and (6) launch the new drug into the marketplace. More than 50 chance nodes appeared in the influence diagram. The chance nodes showed how uncertainties—related to factors such as direct labor costs, process development costs, market share, tax rate, and pricing—affected the outcome. Net present value provided the consequence and the decision-making criterion.

Probability assessments were made concerning both the technical risk and market risk at each stage of the process. The resulting sequential decision tree had 1955 possible paths that led to different net present value outcomes. Cost inputs, judgments of potential outcomes, and the assignment of probabilities helped evaluate the project's potential contribution. Sensitivity analysis was used to identify key variables that would require special attention by the project team and management during the drug development process. Application of decision analysis principles allowed Bayer to make good decisions about how to develop and market the new drug.

*Based on Jeffrey S. Stonebraker, "How Bayer Makes Decisions to Develop New Drugs," *Interfaces,* no. 6 (November/December 2002): 77–90.

FIGURE 14.13 PDC DECISION TREE SHOWING ONLY BRANCHES ASSOCIATED WITH OPTIMAL DECISION STRATEGY

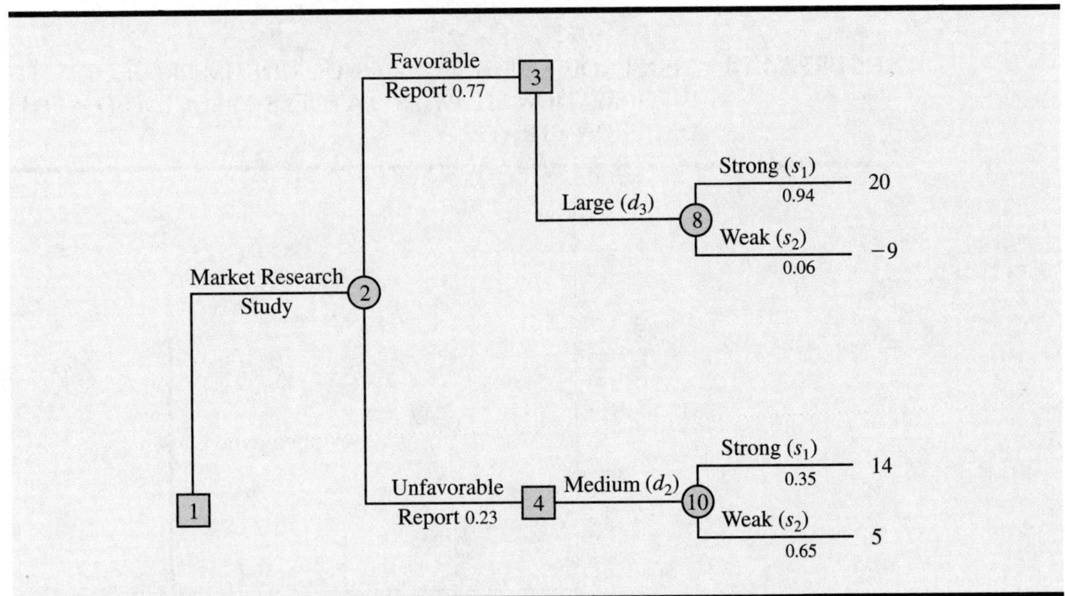

associated probabilities. Thus, in order to construct a risk profile for the optimal decision strategy we will need to compute the probability for each of the four payoffs.

Note that each payoff results from a sequence of branches leading from node 1 to the payoff. For instance, the payoff of \$20 million is obtained by following the upper branch from node 1, the upper branch from node 2, the lower branch from node 3, and the upper branch from node 8. The probability of following that sequence of branches can be found by multiplying the probabilities for the branches from the chance nodes in the sequence. Thus, the probability of the \$20 million payoff is $(0.77)(0.94) = 0.72$. Similarly, the probabilities for each of the other payoffs are obtained by multiplying the probabilities for the branches from the chance nodes leading to the payoffs. Doing so, we find the probability of the $-\$9$ million payoff is $(0.77)(0.06) = 0.05$; the probability of the \$14 million payoff is $(0.23)(0.35) = 0.08$; and the probability of the \$5 million payoff is $(0.23)(0.65) = 0.15$. The following table showing the probability distribution for the payoffs for the PDC optimal decision strategy is the tabular representation of the risk profile for the optimal decision strategy.

Payoff ($ Million)	**Probability**
−9	0.05
5	0.15
14	0.08
20	0.72
	1.00

Figure 14.14 provides a graphical representation of the risk profile. Comparing Figures 14.5 and 14.14, we see that the PDC risk profile is changed by the strategy to conduct the market research study. In fact, the use of the market research study has lowered the proba-

FIGURE 14.14 RISK PROFILE FOR PDC CONDOMINIUM PROJECT WITH SAMPLE INFORMATION SHOWING PAYOFFS ASSOCIATED WITH OPTIMAL DECISION STRATEGY

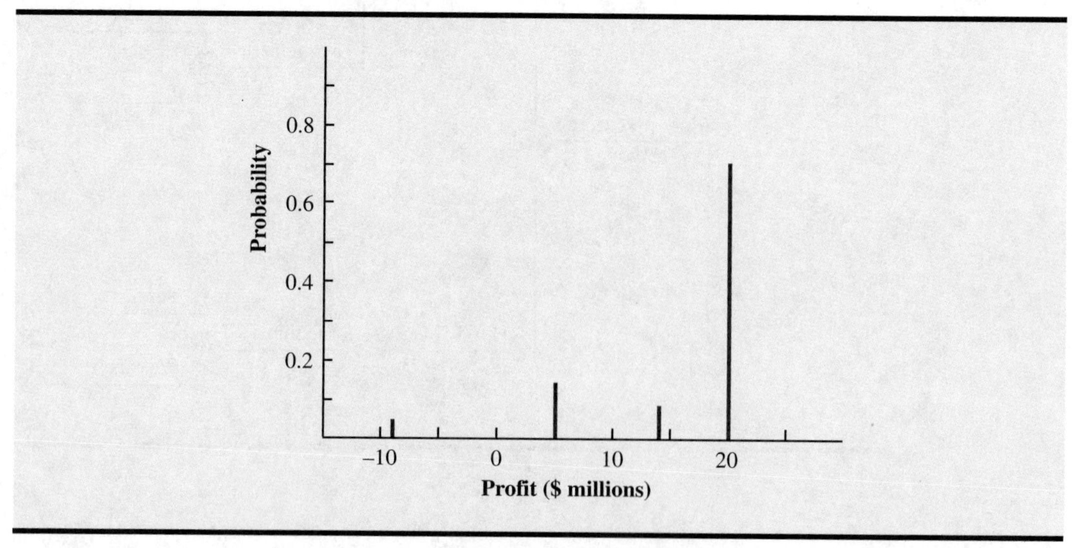

bility of the \$9 million loss from 0.20 to 0.05. PDC's management would most likely view that change as a significant reduction in the risk associated with the condominium project.

Expected Value of Sample Information

The EVSI = \$1.73 million suggests PDC should be willing to pay up to \$1.73 million to conduct the market research study.

In the PDC problem, the market research study is the sample information used to determine the optimal decision strategy. The expected value associated with the market research study is \$15.93. In Section 14.3 we showed that the best expected value if the market research study is *not* undertaken is \$14.20. Thus, we can conclude that the difference, \$15.93 − \$14.20 = \$1.73, is the **expected value of sample information (EVSI).** In other words, conducting the market research study adds \$1.73 million to the PDC expected value. In general, the expected value of sample information is as follows:

$$\text{EVSI} = |\text{EVwSI} - \text{EVwoSI}| \qquad (14.13)$$

where

$$\begin{aligned} \text{EVSI} &= \text{expected value of sample information} \\ \text{EVwSI} &= \text{expected value } \textit{with} \text{ sample information about the states of nature} \\ \text{EVwoSI} &= \text{expected value } \textit{without} \text{ sample information about the states of nature} \end{aligned}$$

Note the role of the absolute value in equation (14.13). For minimization problems the expected value with sample information is always less than or equal to the expected value without sample information. In this case, EVSI is the magnitude of the difference between EVwSI and EVwoSI; thus, by taking the absolute value of the difference as shown in equation (14.13), we can handle both the maximization and minimization cases with one equation.

Efficiency of Sample Information

In Section 14.3 we showed that the expected value of perfect information (EVPI) for the PDC problem is \$3.2 million. We never anticipated that the market research report would obtain perfect information, but we can use an **efficiency** measure to express the value of the market research information. With perfect information having an efficiency rating of 100 percent, the efficiency rating E for sample information is computed as follows.

$$\text{E} = \frac{\text{EVSI}}{\text{EVPI}} \times 100 \qquad (14.14)$$

For the PDC problem,

$$\text{E} = \frac{1.73}{3.2} \times 100 = 54.1\%$$

In other words, the information from the market research study is 54.1 percent as efficient as perfect information.

Low efficiency ratings for sample information might lead the decision maker to look for other types of information. However, high efficiency ratings indicate that the sample information is almost as good as perfect information and that additional sources of information would not yield significantly better results.

14.6 COMPUTING BRANCH PROBABILITIES

In Section 14.5 the branch probabilities for the PDC decision tree chance nodes were specified in the problem description. No computations were required to determine these probabilities. In this section we show how **Bayes' theorem** can be used to compute branch probabilities for decision trees.

The PDC decision tree is shown again in Figure 14.15. Let

$$F = \text{Favorable market research report}$$
$$U = \text{Unfavorable market research report}$$
$$s_1 = \text{Strong demand (state of nature 1)}$$
$$s_2 = \text{Weak demand (state of nature 2)}$$

At chance node 2, we need to know the branch probabilities $P(F)$ and $P(U)$. At chance nodes 6, 7, and 8, we need to know the branch probabilities $P(s_1 \mid F)$, the probability of state of nature 1 given a favorable market research report, and $P(s_2 \mid F)$, the probability of state of nature 2 given a favorable market research report. $P(s_1 \mid F)$ and $P(s_2 \mid F)$ are referred to as *posterior probabilities* because they are conditional probabilities based on the outcome of the sample information. At chance nodes 9, 10, and 11, we need to know the branch probabilities $P(s_1 \mid U)$ and $P(s_2 \mid U)$; note that these are also posterior probabilities, denoting the probabilities of the two states of nature *given* that the market research report is unfavorable. Finally, at chance nodes 12, 13, and 14, we need the probabilities for the states of nature, $P(s_1)$ and $P(s_2)$, if the market research study is not undertaken.

In making the probability computations, we need to know PDC's assessment of the probabilities for the two states of nature, $P(s_1)$ and $P(s_2)$, which are the prior probabilities as discussed earlier. In addition, we must know the **conditional probability** of the market research outcomes (the sample information) *given* each state of nature. For example, we need to know the conditional probability of a favorable market research report given that the state of nature is strong demand for the PDC project; note that this conditional probability of F given state of nature s_1 is written $P(F \mid s_1)$. To carry out the probability calculations, we will need conditional probabilities for all sample outcomes given all states of nature, that is, $P(F \mid s_1)$, $P(F \mid s_2)$, $P(U \mid s_1)$, and $P(U \mid s_2)$. In the PDC problem, we assume that the following assessments are available for these conditional probabilities.

	Market Research	
State of Nature	**Favorable, *F***	**Unfavorable, *U***
Strong demand, s_1	$P(F \mid s_1) = 0.90$	$P(U \mid s_1) = 0.10$
Weak demand, s_2	$P(F \mid s_2) = 0.25$	$P(U \mid s_2) = 0.75$

Note that the preceding probability assessments provide a reasonable degree of confidence in the market research study. If the true state of nature is s_1, the probability of a favorable market research report is 0.90, and the probability of an unfavorable market research report is 0.10. If the true state of nature is s_2, the probability of a favorable market research report is 0.25, and the probability of an unfavorable market research report is 0.75.

FIGURE 14.15 THE PDC DECISION TREE

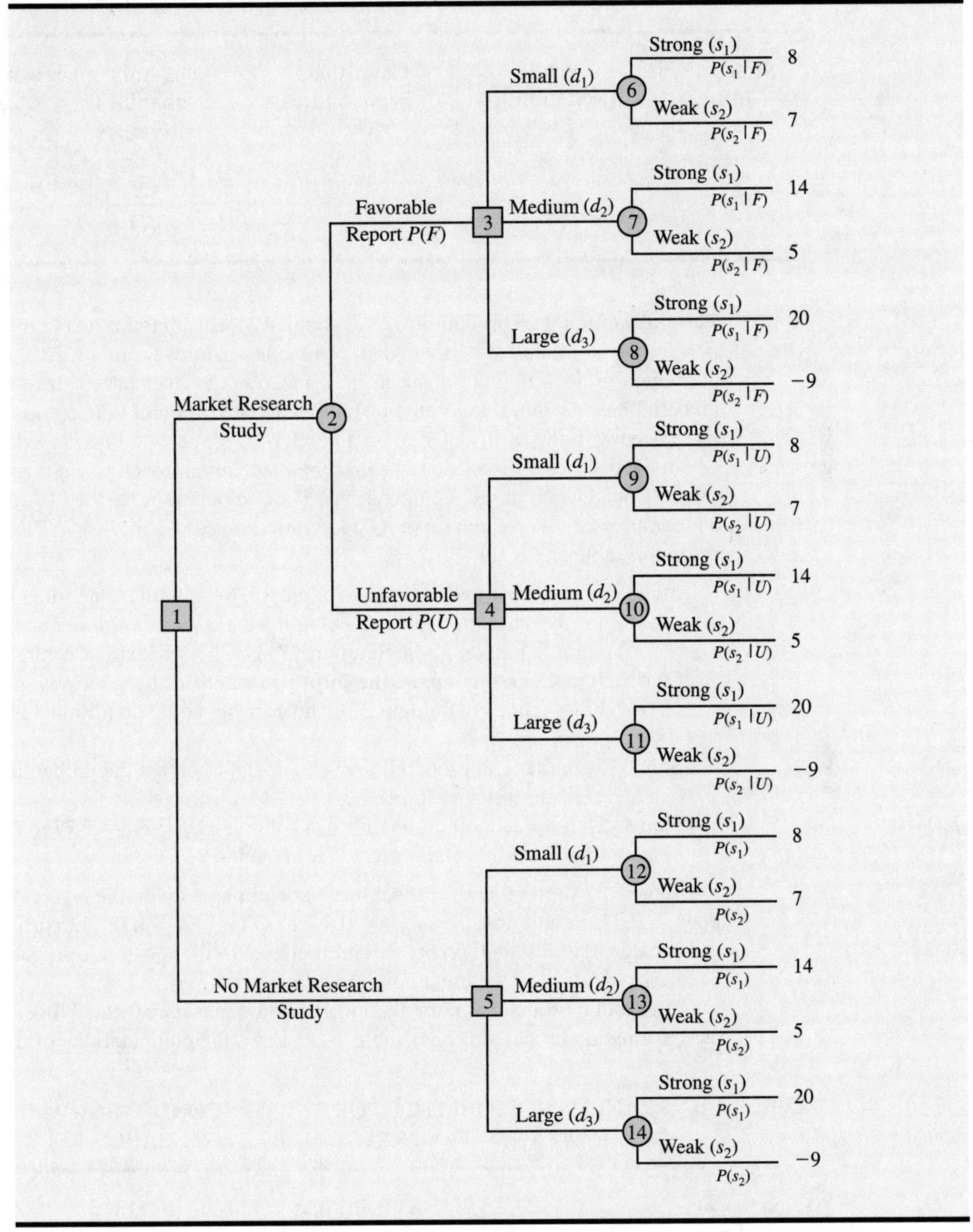

TABLE 14.7 BRANCH PROBABILITIES FOR THE PDC CONDOMINIUM PROJECT BASED ON A FAVORABLE MARKET RESEARCH REPORT

States of Nature s_j	Prior Probabilities $P(s_j)$	Conditional Probabilities $P(F \mid s_j)$	Joint Probabilities $P(F \cap s_j)$	Posterior Probabilities $P(s_j \mid F)$
s_1	0.8	0.90	0.72	0.94
s_2	0.2	0.25	0.05	0.06
	1.0		$P(F) = 0.77$	1.00

The reason for a 0.25 probability of a potentially misleading favorable market research report for state of nature s_2 is that when some potential buyers first hear about the new condominium project, their enthusiasm may lead them to overstate their real interest in it. A potential buyer's initial favorable response can change quickly to a "no thank you" when later faced with the reality of signing a purchase contract and making a down payment.

In the following discussion, we present a tabular approach as a convenient method for carrying out the probability computations. The computations for the PDC problem based on a favorable market research report (F) are summarized in Table 14.7. The steps used to develop this table are as follows.

Step 1. In column 1 enter the states of nature. In column 2 enter the *prior probabilities* for the states of nature. In column 3 enter the *conditional probabilities* of a favorable market research report (F) given each state of nature.

Step 2. In column 4 compute the **joint probabilities** by multiplying the prior probability values in column 2 by the corresponding conditional probability values in column 3.

Step 3. Sum the joint probabilities in column 4 to obtain the probability of a favorable market research report, $P(F)$.

Step 4. Divide each joint probability in column 4 by $P(F) = 0.77$ to obtain the revised or *posterior probabilities,* $P(s_1 \mid F)$ and $P(s_2 \mid F)$.

Table 14.7 shows that the probability of obtaining a favorable market research report is $P(F) = 0.77$. In addition, $P(s_1 \mid F) = 0.94$ and $P(s_2 \mid F) = 0.06$. In particular, note that a favorable market research report will prompt a revised or posterior probability of 0.94 that the market demand of the condominium will be strong, s_1.

The tabular probability computation procedure must be repeated for each possible sample information outcome. Thus, Table 14.8 shows the computations of the branch proba-

TABLE 14.8 BRANCH PROBABILITIES FOR THE PDC CONDOMINIUM PROJECT BASED ON AN UNFAVORABLE MARKET RESEARCH REPORT

States of Nature s_j	Prior Probabilities $P(s_j)$	Conditional Probabilities $P(U \mid s_j)$	Joint Probabilities $P(U \cap s_j)$	Posterior Probabilities $P(s_j \mid U)$
s_1	0.8	0.10	0.08	0.35
s_2	0.2	0.75	0.15	0.65
	1.0		$P(U) = 0.23$	1.00

bilities of the PDC problem based on an unfavorable market research report. Note that the probability of obtaining an unfavorable market research report is $P(U) = 0.23$. If an unfavorable report is obtained, the posterior probability of a strong market demand, s_1, is 0.35 and of a weak market demand, s_2, is 0.65. The branch probabilities from Tables 14.7 and 14.8 were shown on the PDC decision tree in Figure 14.9.

Problem 22 asks you to compute the posterior probabilities.

The discussion in this section shows an underlying relationship between the probabilities on the various branches in a decision tree. To assume different prior probabilities, $P(s_1)$ and $P(s_2)$, without determining how these changes would alter $P(F)$ and $P(U)$, as well as the posterior probabilities $P(s_1 \mid F)$, $P(s_2 \mid F)$, $P(s_1 \mid U)$, and $P(s_2 \mid U)$, would be inappropriate.

The Management Science in Action, Medical Screening Test at Duke University Medical Center, shows how posterior probability information and decision analysis helped management understand the risks and costs associated with a new screening procedure.

MANAGEMENT SCIENCE IN ACTION

MEDICAL SCREENING TEST AT DUKE UNIVERSITY MEDICAL CENTER*

A new medical screening test developed at the Duke University Medical Center involved using blood samples from newborns to screen for metabolic disorders. A positive test result indicated that a deficiency was present, while a negative test result indicated that a deficiency was not present. However, it was understood that the screening test was not a perfect predictor; that is, false-positive test results as well as false-negative test results were possible. A false-positive test result meant that the test detected a deficiency when in fact no deficiency was present. This case resulted in unnecessary further testing as well as unnecessary worry for the parents of the newborn. A false-negative test result meant that the test did not detect the presence of an existing deficiency. Using probability and decision analysis, a research team analyzed the role and value of the screening test.

A decision tree with six nodes, 13 branches, and eight outcomes was used to model the screening test procedure. A decision node with the decision branches Test and No Test was placed at the start of the decision tree. Chance nodes and branches were used to describe the possible sequences of a positive test result, a negative test result, a deficiency present, and a deficiency not present.

The particular deficiency in question was rare, occurring at a rate of one case for every 250,000 newborns. Thus, the prior probability of a deficiency was 1/250,000 = 0.000004. Based on judgments about the probabilities of false-positive and false-negative test results, Bayes' theorem was used to calculate the posterior probability that a newborn with a positive test result actually had a deficiency. This posterior probability was 0.074. Thus, while a positive test result increased the probability the newborn had a deficiency from 0.000004 to 0.074, the probability that the newborn had a deficiency was still relatively low (0.074). The probability information was helpful to doctors in reassuring worried parents that even though further testing was recommended, the chances were greater than 90% that a deficiency was not present. After the assignment of costs to the eight possible outcomes, decision analysis showed that the decision alternative to conduct the test provided the optimal decision strategy. The expected cost criterion established the expected cost to be approximately $6 per test.

Decision analysis helped provide a realistic understanding of the risks and costs associated with the screening test. In 1998, the test was given to every child born in the state of North Carolina.

*Based on James E. Smith and Robert L. Winkler, "Casey's Problem: Interpreting and Evaluating a New Test," *Interfaces* 29, no. 3 (May/June 1999): 63–76.

14.7 UTILITY AND DECISION MAKING

In the preceding sections of this chapter we expressed the payoffs in terms of monetary values. When probability information was available about the states of nature, we recommended selecting the decision alternative with the best expected monetary value. However, in some situations the decision alternative with the best expected monetary value may not be the most desirable decision.

By the most desirable decision we mean the one that is preferred by the decision maker after taking into account not only monetary value, but also other factors such as the risk associated with the outcomes. Examples of situations in which selecting the decision alternative with the best expected monetary value may not lead to the selection of the most preferred decision are numerous. One such example is the decision to buy house insurance. Clearly, buying insurance for a house does not provide a higher expected monetary value than not buying such insurance. Otherwise, insurance companies could not pay expenses and make a profit. Similarly, many people buy tickets for state lotteries even though the expected monetary value of such a decision is negative.

Should we conclude that persons or businesses that buy insurance or participate in lotteries do so because they are unable to determine which decision alternative leads to the best expected monetary value? On the contrary, we take the view that in these cases monetary value is not the sole measure of the true worth of the outcome to the decision maker.

We will see that in cases where expected monetary value does not lead to the most preferred decision alternative, expressing the value (or worth) of an outcome in terms of its *utility* will permit the use of *expected utility* to identify the most desirable decision.

The Meaning of Utility

Utility is a measure of the total worth of a particular outcome; it reflects the decision maker's attitude toward a collection of factors such as profit, loss, and risk. As an example of a case where utility can help in selecting the best decision alternative, let us consider the problem faced by Swofford, Inc., a relatively small real estate investment firm located in Atlanta, Georgia. Swofford currently has two investment opportunities that require approximately the same cash outlay. The cash requirements necessary prohibit Swofford from making more than one investment at this time. Consequently, three possible decision alternatives may be considered.

The three decision alternatives, denoted by d_1, d_2, and d_3, are as follows:

$$d_1 = \text{make investment A}$$
$$d_2 = \text{make investment B}$$
$$d_3 = \text{do not invest}$$

The monetary payoffs associated with the investment opportunities depend largely on what happens to the real estate market during the next six months. Real estate prices will go up, remain stable, or go down. Thus, the states of nature, denoted by s_1, s_2, and s_3, are as follows:

$$s_1 = \text{real estate prices go up}$$
$$s_2 = \text{real estate prices remain stable}$$
$$s_3 = \text{real estate prices go down}$$

Using the best information available, Swofford estimated the profits or payoffs associated with each decision alternative and state-of-nature combination. The resulting payoff table is shown in Table 14.9.

The best estimate of the probability that prices will go up is 0.3, the best estimate of the probability that prices will remain stable is 0.5, and the best estimate of the probability that

TABLE 14.9 PAYOFF TABLE FOR SWOFFORD, INC. (PROFIT IN $)

	State of Nature		
	Prices Up	**Prices Stable**	**Prices Down**
Decision Alternative	s_1	s_2	s_3
Investment A, d_1	30,000	20,000	−50,000
Investment B, d_2	50,000	−20,000	−30,000
Do not invest, d_3	0	0	0

real estate prices will go down is 0.2. Thus, the expected values for the three decision alternatives are

$$
\begin{aligned}
\text{EV}(d_1) &= 0.3(\$30{,}000) + 0.5(\$20{,}000) + 0.2(-\$50{,}000) = \$9{,}000 \\
\text{EV}(d_2) &= 0.3(\$50{,}000) + 0.5(-\$20{,}000) + 0.2(-\$30{,}000) = -\$1{,}000 \\
\text{EV}(d_3) &= 0.3(\$0) + 0.5(\$0) + 0.2(\$0) = \$0
\end{aligned}
$$

Using the expected value approach, the optimal decision is to select investment A, with an expected monetary value of $9000. Is this really the best decision alternative? Let us consider some other relevant factors that relate to Swofford's capability for absorbing the $50,000 loss if investment A is made and real estate prices go down.

It turns out that Swofford's financial position is weak. This fact was partly reflected in Swofford's ability to undertake, at most, one investment at the current time. More important, however, the firm's president feels that if the next investment results in substantial losses, Swofford's future will be in jeopardy. Although the expected value approach leads to a recommendation for d_1, do you think it is the decision the firm's president would prefer? We suspect that d_2 or d_3 would be selected to avoid the possibility of incurring a $50,000 loss. In fact, it is reasonable to believe that if a loss as great as even $30,000 could drive Swofford out of business, the president would select d_3, feeling that both investment A and investment B are too risky for Swofford's current financial position.

The way we resolve Swofford's dilemma is first to determine Swofford's utility for the various monetary outcomes. Recall that the utility of any outcome is the total worth of that outcome, taking into account the risks and payoffs involved. If the utilities for the various outcomes are assessed correctly, then the decision alternative with the highest expected utility is the most preferred or best alternative.

Developing Utilities for Payoffs

The procedure we use to establish utility values for the payoffs requires that we first assign a utility value to the best and worst possible payoffs in the decision situation. Any values work as long as the utility assigned to the best payoff is greater than the utility assigned to the worst payoff. In Swofford's case, Table 14.9 shows that $50,000 is the best payoff and −$50,000 is the worst payoff. Suppose, then, that we arbitrarily make the following assignments of these two payoffs:

$$
\begin{aligned}
\text{Utility of } -\$50{,}000 &= U(-\$50{,}000) = 0 \\
\text{Utility of } \$50{,}000 &= U(\$50{,}000) = 10
\end{aligned}
$$

Now let us see how we can determine the utility associated with every other payoff.

Consider the process of establishing the utility of a payoff of \$30,000. First, we ask Swofford's president to state a preference between a guaranteed \$30,000 payoff and the opportunity to engage in the following **lottery,** or bet:

Lottery: Swofford obtains a payoff of \$50,000 with probability p and a payoff of $-$\$50,000 with probability $(1 - p)$.

If p is very close to 1, Swofford's president would prefer the lottery to the certain payoff of \$30,000 because the firm would virtually guarantee itself a payoff of \$50,000. On the other hand, if p is very close to 0, the president would clearly prefer the guarantee of \$30,000. In any event, as p changes continuously from 0 to 1, the preference for the guaranteed payoff of \$30,000 will change at some point into a preference for the lottery. At the change point, the president is indifferent between the guaranteed payoff of \$30,000 and the lottery. For example, let us assume that when $p = 0.95$, the president is indifferent between the certain payoff of \$30,000 and the lottery. Given this value of p, we can compute the utility of a \$30,000 payoff as follows:

$$\begin{aligned} U(\$30{,}000) &= pU(\$50{,}000) + (1 - p)U(-\$50{,}000) \\ &= 0.95(10) + (0.5)(0) \\ &= 9.5 \end{aligned}$$

Obviously, if we started with a different assignment of utilities for payoffs of \$50,000 and $-$\$50,000, we would end up with a different utility for \$30,000. Hence, we must conclude that the utility assigned to each payoff is not unique, but is relative to the initial choice of utilities for the best and worst payoffs. We discuss this factor further at the end of this section. For now, however, we continue to use a value of 10 for the utility of \$50,000 and a value of 0 for the utility of $-$\$50,000.

Before computing the utility for the other payoffs, let us consider the significance of assigning a utility of 9.5 to a payoff of \$30,000. Clearly, when $p = 0.95$, the expected value of the lottery is

$$\begin{aligned} \text{EV(Lottery)} &= 0.95(\$50{,}000) + 0.05(-\$50{,}000) \\ &= \$47{,}500 - \$2{,}500 \\ &= \$45{,}000 \end{aligned}$$

We see that although the expected value of the lottery when $p = 0.95$ is \$45,000, Swofford's president would just as soon take a guaranteed payoff of \$30,000 and thus take a conservative, or risk-avoiding, viewpoint. That is, the president would rather have \$30,000 for certain than risk anything greater than a 5 percent chance of incurring a loss of \$50,000. One can view the difference between the EV of \$45,000 for the lottery and the \$30,000 guaranteed payoff as the risk premium that the president would be willing to pay to avoid the 5 percent chance of losing \$50,000.

To compute the utility associated with a payoff of $-$\$20,000, we must ask Swofford's president to state a preference between a guaranteed $-$\$20,000 payoff and the opportunity to engage in the following lottery.

Lottery: Swofford obtains a payoff of \$50,000 with probability p and a payoff of $-$\$50,000 with probability $(1 - p)$.

Note that it is exactly the same lottery we used to establish the utility of a payoff of \$30,000. In fact, this lottery will be used to establish the utility for any monetary value in the Swofford payoff table. Using this lottery, then, we must ask the president to state the value of p that provides an indifference between a guaranteed payoff of −\$20,000 and the lottery. For example, we might begin by asking the president to choose between a certain loss of \$20,000 and the lottery with a payoff of \$50,000 with probability $p = 0.90$ and a payoff of −\$50,000 with probability $(1 - p) = 0.10$. What answer do you think we would get? Surely, with this high probability of obtaining a payoff of \$50,000, the president would elect the lottery. Next, we might ask if $p = 0.85$ would result in indifference between the loss of \$20,000 for certain and the lottery. Again, the president might tell us that the lottery would be preferred. Suppose that we continue in this fashion until we get to $p = 0.55$, where we find that with this value of p, the president is indifferent between the payoff of −\$20,000 and the lottery. That is, for any value of p less than 0.55, the president would rather take a loss of \$20,000 for certain than risk the potential loss of \$50,000 with the lottery; for any value of p above 0.55, the president would elect the lottery. Thus, the utility assigned to a payoff of −\$20,000 is

$$\begin{aligned} U(-\$20{,}000) &= pU(\$50{,}000) + (1 - p)U(-\$50{,}000) \\ &= 0.55(10) + 0.45(0) \\ &= 5.5 \end{aligned}$$

Again, let us examine the significance of this assignment as compared with the expected value approach. When $p = 0.55$, the expected value of the lottery is

$$\begin{aligned} \text{EV(Lottery)} &= 0.55(\$50{,}000) + 0.45(-\$50{,}000) \\ &= \$27{,}500 - \$22{,}500 \\ &= \$5{,}000 \end{aligned}$$

Thus, the president would just as soon absorb a loss of \$20,000 for certain as take the lottery, even though the expected value of the lottery is \$5000. Once again we see the conservative, or risk-avoiding, point of view of Swofford's president.

In the two preceding examples where we computed the utility for a specific monetary payoff, M, we first found the probability p where the decision maker was indifferent between a guaranteed payoff of M and a lottery with a payoff of \$50,000 with probability p and −\$50,000 with probability $(1 - p)$. The utility of M was then computed as

$$\begin{aligned} U(M) &= pU(\$50{,}000) + (1 - p)U(-\$50{,}000) \\ &= p(10) + (1 - p)0 \\ &= 10p \end{aligned}$$

Using this procedure, utility values for the rest of the payoffs in Swofford's problem were developed. The results are presented in Table 14.10.

After we determine the utility value of each of the possible monetary values, we can write the original payoff table in terms of utility values. Table 14.11 shows the utility for the various outcomes in the Swofford problem. The notation we use for the entries in the utility table is U_{ij}, which denotes the utility associated with decision alternative d_i and state of nature s_j. Using this notation, we see that $U_{23} = 4.0$.

TABLE 14.10 UTILITY OF MONETARY PAYOFFS FOR THE SWOFFORD, INC., PROBLEM

Monetary Value	Indifference Value of *p*	Utility Value
$ 50,000	Does not apply	10.0
30,000	0.95	9.5
20,000	0.90	9.0
0	0.75	7.5
−20,000	0.55	5.5
−30,000	0.40	4.0
−50,000	Does not apply	0.0

TABLE 14.11 UTILITY TABLE FOR SWOFFORD, INC., PROBLEM

	State of Nature		
	Prices Up	Prices Stable	Prices Down
Decision Alternative	s_1	s_2	s_3
Investment A, d_1	9.5	9.0	0.0
Investment B, d_2	10.0	5.5	4.0
Do not invest, d_3	7.5	7.5	7.5

Expected Utility Approach

We can now apply the expected value computations introduced in Section 14.3 to the payoffs in Table 14.11 in order to select an optimal decision alternative for Swofford, Inc. However, because utility values represent such a special case of expected value, we refer to the expected value when applied to utility values as the *expected utility* (EU). In this way, we avoid any possible confusion between the expected value for the original payoff table and the expected value for the payoff table consisting of *utility values.* Thus, the **expected utility approach** requires the analyst to compute the expected utility for each decision alternative and then select the alternative yielding the best expected utility. If there are N possible states of nature, the expected utility of a decision alternative d_i is given by

$$\text{EU}(d_i) = \sum_{j=1}^{N} P(s_j)U_{ij} \tag{14.15}$$

The expected utility for each of the decision alternatives in the Swofford problem is computed as follows:

$$\begin{aligned}
\text{EU}(d_1) &= 0.3(9.5) + 0.5(9.0) + 0.2(0) = 7.35 \\
\text{EU}(d_2) &= 0.3(10) + 0.5(9.0) + 0.2(4.0) = 6.55 \\
\text{EU}(d_3) &= 0.3(7.5) + 0.5(7.5) + 0.2(7.5) = 7.50
\end{aligned}$$

Problem 28 asks you to use the expected utility approach to determine the optimal decision.

We see that the optimal decision using the expected utility approach is d_3, do not invest. The ranking of alternatives according to the president's utility assignments and the associated monetary value is as follows:

Ranking of Decision Alternatives	Expected Utility	Expected Monetary Value
Do not invest	7.50	$ 0
Investment A	7.35	9000
Investment B	6.55	−1000

Note that whereas investment A had the highest expected monetary value of $9000, the analysis indicates that Swofford should decline this investment. The rationale behind not selecting Investment A is that the 0.2 probability of a $50,000 loss was considered by Swofford's president to involve a serious risk. The seriousness of this risk and its associated impact on the company were not adequately reflected by the expected monetary value of investment A. It was necessary to assess the utility for each payoff to adequately take this risk into account.

Unfortunately, the determination of the appropriate utilities is not a trivial task. As we have seen, measuring utility requires a degree of subjectivity on the part of the decision maker, and different decision makers will have different utility functions. This aspect of utility often causes decision makers to feel uncomfortable about using the expected utility approach. However, if we encounter a decision situation in which we are convinced monetary value is not the only relevant measure of performance, utility analysis should be considered.

NOTES AND COMMENTS

1. In the Swofford problem, we used a utility of 10 for the largest possible payoff and 0 for the smallest. Had we chosen 1 for the utility of the largest payoff and 0 for the utility of the smallest, the utility for any monetary value M would have been the value of p at which the decision maker was indifferent between a certain payoff of M and a lottery in which the best payoff is obtained with probability of p and the worst payoff is obtained with probability of $(1 - p)$. Thus, the utility for any monetary value would have been equal to the probability of earning the highest payoff. Often, this choice is made because of the ease in computation. We chose not to do so to emphasize the distinction between the utility values and the indifference probabilities for the lottery.
2. Generally, when the payoffs for a particular decision-making problem fall into a reasonable range—the best is not too good and the worst is not too bad—decision makers tend to express preferences in agreement with the expected monetary value approach. Thus, as a guideline we suggest asking the decision maker to consider the best and worst possible payoffs for a problem and assess their reasonableness. If the decision maker believes they are in the reasonable range, the expected monetary value criterion can be used. However, if the payoffs appear unreasonably large or unreasonably small and if the decision maker feels monetary values do not adequately reflect the true preferences for the payoffs, a utility analysis of the problem should be considered.

SUMMARY

Decision analysis can be used to determine a recommended decision alternative or an optimal decision strategy when a decision maker is faced with an uncertain and risk-filled pattern of future events. The goal of decision analysis is to identify the best decision alternative or the optimal decision strategy given information about the uncertain events and the possible consequences or payoffs. The uncertain future events are called chance events and the outcomes of the chance events are called states of nature.

We showed how influence diagrams, payoff tables, and decision trees could be used to structure a decision problem and describe the relationships among the decisions, the chance events, and the consequences. We presented three approaches to decision making without probabilities: the optimistic approach, the conservative approach, and the minimax regret approach. When probability assessments are provided for the states of nature, the expected value approach can be used to identify the recommended decision alternative or decision strategy.

In cases where sample information about the chance events is available, a sequence of decisions has to be made. First we must decide whether to obtain the sample information. If the answer to this decision is yes, an optimal decision strategy based on the specific sample information must be developed. In this situation, decision trees and the expected value approach can be used to determine the optimal decision strategy.

Even though the expected value approach can be used to obtain a recommended decision alternative or optimal decision strategy, the payoff that actually occurs will usually have a value different from the expected value. A risk profile provides a probability distribution for the possible payoffs and can assist the decision maker in assessing the risks associated with different decision alternatives. Finally, sensitivity analysis can be conducted to determine the effect changes in the probabilities for the states of nature and changes in the values of the payoffs have on the recommended decision alternative.

In the last section, we suggested that the expected utility approach should be used in situations in which monetary value is not the only relevant measure of performance. Unlike monetary value, utility is a measure of the total worth of an outcome resulting from the choice of a decision alternative and the occurrence of a state of nature. As such, utility takes into account the decision maker's attitude toward the profit, loss, and risk associated with an outcome. In the examples, we saw how the use of utility analysis can lead to decision recommendations that differ from those that would be selected using the expected monetary value approach.

Decision analysis has been widely used in practice. The Management Science in Action, Investing in a Transmission System at Oglethorpe Power, describes the use of decision analysis to decide whether to invest in a major transmission system between Georgia and Florida.

MANAGEMENT SCIENCE IN ACTION

INVESTING IN A TRANSMISSION SYSTEM AT OGLETHORPE POWER*

Oglethorpe Power Corporation (OPC) provides wholesale electrical power to consumer-owned cooperatives in the state of Georgia. Florida Power Corporation proposed that OPC join in the building of a major transmission line from Georgia to Florida. Deciding whether to become involved in the building of the transmission line was a major decision for OPC because it would involve the commitment of substantial OPC resources. OPC worked with Applied Decision Analysis, Inc., to conduct a comprehensive decision analysis of the problem.

In the problem formulation step, three decisions were identified: (1) build a transmission line from Georgia to Florida; (2) upgrade existing transmission facilities; and (3) who would control the new facilities. Oglethorpe was faced with five chance events: (1) construction costs, (2) competition, (3) demand in Florida, (4) OPC's share of the operation, and (5) pricing. The consequence or payoff was measured in terms of dollars saved. The influence diagram for the problem had three decision nodes, five chance nodes, a consequence node, and several intermediate nodes that described intermediate calculations. The decision tree for the problem had more than 8000 paths from the starting node to the terminal branches.

An expected value analysis of the decision tree provided an optimal decision strategy for OPC. However, the risk profile for the optimal decision strategy showed that the recommended strategy was very risky and had a significant probability of increasing OPC's cost rather than providing a savings. The risk analysis led to the conclusion that more information about the competition was needed in order to reduce OPC's risk. Sensitivity analysis involving various probabilities and payoffs showed that the value of the optimal decision strategy was stable over a reasonable range of input values. The final recommendation from the decision analysis was that OPC should begin negotiations with Florida Power Corporation concerning the building of the new transmission line.

*Based on Adam Borison, "Oglethorpe Power Corporation Decides about Investing in a Major Transmission System," *Interfaces* (March/April 1995): 25–36.

GLOSSARY

Chance event An uncertain future event affecting the consequence, or payoff, associated with a decision.

Consequence The result obtained when a decision alternative is chosen and a chance event occurs. A measure of the consequence is often called a payoff.

States of nature The possible outcomes for chance events that affect the payoff associated with a decision alternative.

Influence diagram A graphical device that shows the relationship among decisions, chance events, and consequences for a decision problem.

Node An intersection or junction point of an influence diagram or a decision tree.

Decision nodes Nodes indicating points where a decision is made.

Chance nodes Nodes indicating points where an uncertain event will occur.

Payoff A measure of the consequence of a decision such as profit, cost, or time. Each combination of a decision alternative and a state of nature has an associated payoff (consequence).

Payoff table A tabular representation of the payoffs for a decision problem.

Decision tree A graphical representation of the decision problem that shows the sequential nature of the decision-making process.

Branch Lines showing the alternatives from decision nodes and the outcomes from chance nodes.

Optimistic approach An approach to choosing a decision alternative without using probabilities. For a maximization problem, it leads to choosing the decision alternative corresponding to the largest payoff; for a minimization problem, it leads to choosing the decision alternative corresponding to the smallest payoff.

Conservative approach An approach to choosing a decision alternative without using probabilities. For a maximization problem, it leads to choosing the decision alternative that maximizes the minimum payoff; for a minimization problem, it leads to choosing the decision alternative that minimizes the maximum payoff.

Minimax regret approach An approach to choosing a decision alternative without using probabilities. For each alternative, the maximum regret is computed, which leads to choosing the decision alternative that minimizes the maximum regret.

Opportunity loss, or regret The amount of loss (lower profit or higher cost) from not making the best decision for each state of nature.

Expected value approach An approach to choosing a decision alternative based on the expected value of each decision alternative. The recommended decision alternative is the one that provides the best expected value.

Expected value (EV) For a chance node, it is the weighted average of the payoffs. The weights are the state-of-nature probabilities.

Expected value of perfect information (EVPI) The expected value of information that would tell the decision maker exactly which state of nature is going to occur (i.e., perfect information).

Risk analysis The study of the possible payoffs and probabilities associated with a decision alternative or a decision strategy.

Sensitivity analysis The study of how changes in the probability assessments for the states of nature or changes in the payoffs affect the recommended decision alternative.

Risk profile The probability distribution of the possible payoffs associated with a decision alternative or decision strategy.

Prior probabilities The probabilities of the states of nature prior to obtaining sample information.

Sample information New information obtained through research or experimentation that enables an updating or revision of the state-of-nature probabilities.

Posterior (revised) probabilities The probabilities of the states of nature after revising the prior probabilities based on sample information.

Decision strategy A strategy involving a sequence of decisions and chance outcomes to provide the optimal solution to a decision problem.

Expected value of sample information (EVSI) The difference between the expected value of an optimal strategy based on sample information and the "best" expected value without any sample information.

Efficiency The ratio of EVSI to EVPI as a percentage; perfect information is 100% efficient.

Bayes' theorem A theorem that enables the use of sample information to revise prior probabilities.

Conditional probabilities The probability of one event given the known outcome of a (possibly) related event.

Joint probabilities The probabilities of both sample information and a particular state of nature occurring simultaneously.

Utility A measure of the total worth of an outcome reflecting a decision maker's attitude toward considerations such as profit and loss and intangibles such as risk.

Lottery A hypothetical investment alternative with a probability p of obtaining the best possible payoff and a probability of $(1 - p)$ of obtaining the worst possible payoff.

Expected utility approach An approach that considers the expected utility for each decision alternative and then selects the decision alternative yielding the highest expected utility.

PROBLEMS

1. The following payoff table shows profit for a decision analysis problem with two decision alternatives and three states of nature.

Decision Alternative	State of Nature s_1	s_2	s_3
d_1	250	100	25
d_2	100	100	75

   a. Construct a decision tree for this problem.
   b. If the decision maker knows nothing about the probabilities of the three states of nature, what is the recommended decision using the optimistic, conservative, and minimax regret approaches?

2. Suppose that a decision maker faced with four decision alternatives and four states of nature develops the following profit payoff table.

Decision Alternative	State of Nature s_1	s_2	s_3	s_4
d_1	14	9	10	5
d_2	11	10	8	7
d_3	9	10	10	11
d_4	8	10	11	13

   a. If the decision maker knows nothing about the probabilities of the four states of nature, what is the recommended decision using the optimistic, conservative, and minimax regret approaches?
   b. Which approach do you prefer? Explain. Is establishing the most appropriate approach before analyzing the problem important for the decision maker? Explain.
   c. Assume that the payoff table provides *cost* rather than profit payoffs. What is the recommended decision using the optimistic, conservative, and minimax regret approaches?

3. Southland Corporation's decision to produce a new line of recreational products resulted in the need to construct either a small plant or a large plant. The best selection of plant size depends on how the marketplace reacts to the new product line. To conduct an analysis, marketing management has decided to view the possible long-run demand as either low, medium, or high. The following payoff table shows the projected profit in millions of dollars:

Plant Size	Long-Run Demand Low	Medium	High
Small	150	200	200
Large	50	200	500

a. What is the decision to be made, and what is the chance event for Southland's problem?
b. Construct an influence diagram.
c. Construct a decision tree.
d. Recommend a decision based on the use of the optimistic, conservative, and minimax regret approaches.

4. Amy Lloyd is interested in leasing a new Saab and has contacted three automobile dealers for pricing information. Each dealer offered Amy a closed-end 36-month lease with no down payment due at the time of signing. Each lease includes a monthly charge and a mileage allowance. Additional miles receive a surcharge on a per-mile basis. The monthly lease cost, the mileage allowance, and the cost for additional miles follow:

Dealer	Monthly Cost	Mileage Allowance	Cost per Additional Mile
Forno Saab	\$299	36,000	\$0.15
Midtown Motors	\$310	45,000	\$0.20
Hopkins Automotive	\$325	54,000	\$0.15

Amy decided to choose the lease option that will minimize her total 36-month cost. The difficulty is that Amy is not sure how many miles she will drive over the next three years. For purposes of this decision she believes it is reasonable to assume that she will drive 12,000 miles per year, 15,000 miles per year, or 18,000 miles per year. With this assumption Amy estimated her total costs for the three lease options. For example, she figures that the Forno Saab lease will cost her \$10,764 if she drives 12,000 miles per year, \$12,114 if she drives 15,000 miles per year, or \$13,464 if she drives 18,000 miles per year.
a. What is the decision, and what is the chance event?
b. Construct a payoff table for Amy's problem.
c. If Amy has no idea which of the three mileage assumptions is most appropriate, what is the recommended decision (leasing option) using the optimistic, conservative, and minimax regret approaches?
d. Suppose that the probabilities that Amy drives 12,000, 15,000, and 18,000 miles per year are 0.5, 0.4, and 0.1, respectively. What option should Amy choose using the expected value approach?
e. Develop a risk profile for the decision selected in part (d). What is the most likely cost, and what is its probability?
f. Suppose that after further consideration, Amy concludes that the probabilities that she will drive 12,000, 15,000, and 18,000 miles per year are 0.3, 0.4, and 0.3, respectively. What decision should Amy make using the expected value approach?

5. The following profit payoff table was presented in Problem 1. Suppose that the decision maker obtained the probability assessments $P(s_1) = 0.65$, $P(s_2) = 0.15$, and $P(s_3) = 0.20$. Use the expected value approach to determine the optimal decision.

	State of Nature		
Decision Alternative	s_1	s_2	s_3
d_1	250	100	25
d_2	100	100	75

6. The profit payoff table presented in Problem 2 is repeated here.

	State of Nature			
Decision Alternative	s_1	s_2	s_3	s_4
d_1	14	9	10	5
d_2	11	10	8	7
d_3	9	10	10	11
d_4	8	10	11	13

Suppose that the decision maker obtains information that enables the following probability assessments to be made: $P(s_1) = 0.5$, $P(s_2) = 0.2$, $P(s_3) = 0.2$, and $P(s_4) = 0.1$.

a. Use the expected value approach to determine the optimal decision.

b. Now assume that the entries in the payoff table are costs; use the expected value approach to determine the optimal decision.

7. Hudson Corporation is considering three options for managing its data processing operation: continuing with its own staff, hiring an outside vendor to do the managing (referred to as *outsourcing*), or using a combination of its own staff and an outside vendor. The cost of the operation depends on future demand. The annual cost of each option (in thousands of dollars) depends on demand as follows.

	Demand		
Staffing Options	**High**	**Medium**	**Low**
Own staff	650	650	600
Outside vendor	900	600	300
Combination	800	650	500

a. If the demand probabilities are 0.2, 0.5, and 0.3, which decision alternative will minimize the expected cost of the data processing operation? What is the expected annual cost associated with that recommendation?

b. Construct a risk profile for the optimal decision in part (a). What is the probability of the cost exceeding \$700,000?

8. The following payoff table shows the profit for a decision problem with two states of nature and two decision alternatives.

	State of Nature	
Decision Alternative	s_1	s_2
d_1	10	1
d_2	4	3

a. Use graphical sensitivity analysis to determine the range of probabilities of state of nature s_1 for which each of the decision alternatives has the largest expected value.

b. Suppose $P(s_1) = 0.2$ and $P(s_2) = 0.8$. What is the best decision using the expected value approach?

c. Perform sensitivity analysis on the payoffs for decision alternative d_1. Assume the probabilities are as given in part (b) and find the range of payoffs under states of nature s_1 and s_2 that will keep the solution found in part (b) optimal. Is the solution more sensitive to the payoff under state of nature s_1 or s_2?

9. Myrtle Air Express decided to offer direct service from Cleveland to Myrtle Beach. Management must decide between a full-price service using the company's new fleet of jet aircraft and a discount service using smaller capacity commuter planes. It is clear that the best choice depends on the market reaction to the service Myrtle Air offers. Management developed estimates of the contribution to profit for each type of service based upon two possible levels of demand for service to Myrtle Beach: strong and weak. The following table shows the estimated quarterly profits (in thousands of dollars).

	Demand for Service	
Service	**Strong**	**Weak**
Full price	$960	−$490
Discount	$670	$320

a. What is the decision to be made, what is the chance event, and what is the consequence for this problem? How many decision alternatives are there? How many outcomes are there for the chance event?

b. If nothing is known about the probabilities of the chance outcomes, what is the recommended decision using the optimistic, conservative, and minimax regret approaches?

c. Suppose that management of Myrtle Air Express believes that the probability of strong demand is 0.7 and the probability of weak demand is 0.3. Use the expected value approach to determine an optimal decision.

d. Suppose that the probability of strong demand is 0.8 and the probability of weak demand is 0.2. What is the optimal decision using the expected value approach?

e. Use graphical sensitivity analysis to determine the range of demand probabilities for which each of the decision alternatives has the largest expected value.

10. Video Tech is considering marketing one of two new video games for the coming holiday season: Battle Pacific or Space Pirates. Battle Pacific is a unique game and appears to have no competition. Estimated profits (in thousands of dollars) under high, medium, and low demand are as follows:

		Demand	
Battle Pacific	**High**	**Medium**	**Low**
Profit	$1000	$700	$300
Probability	0.2	0.5	0.3

Video Tech is optimistic about its Space Pirates game. However, the concern is that profitability will be affected by a competitor's introduction of a video game viewed as similar to Space Pirates. Estimated profits (in thousands of dollars) with and without competition are as follows:

		Demand	
Space Pirates With Competition	**High**	**Medium**	**Low**
Profit	$800	$400	$200
Probability	0.3	0.4	0.3

Space Pirates Without Competition	Demand		
	High	**Medium**	**Low**
Profit	$1600	$800	$400
Probability	0.5	0.3	0.2

a. Develop a decision tree for the Video Tech problem.
b. For planning purposes, Video Tech believes there is a 0.6 probability that its competitor will produce a new game similar to Space Pirates. Given this probability of competition, the director of planning recommends marketing the Battle Pacific video game. Using expected value, what is your recommended decision?
c. Show a risk profile for your recommended decision.
d. Use sensitivity analysis to determine what the probability of competition for Space Pirates would have to be for you to change your recommended decision alternative.

11. For the Pittsburgh Development Corporation problem in Section 14.3, the decision alternative to build the large condominium complex was found to be optimal using the expected value approach. In Section 14.4 we conducted a sensitivity analysis for the payoffs associated with this decision alternative. We found that the large complex remained optimal as long as the payoff for the strong demand was greater than or equal to $17.5 million and as long as the payoff for the weak demand was greater than or equal to −$19 million.
    a. Consider the medium complex decision. How much could the payoff under strong demand increase and still keep decision alternative d_3 the optimal solution?
    b. Consider the small complex decision. How much could the payoff under strong demand increase and still keep decision alternative d_3 the optimal solution?

12. The distance from Potsdam to larger markets and limited air service have hindered the town in attracting new industry. Air Express, a major overnight delivery service, is considering establishing a regional distribution center in Potsdam. But Air Express will not establish the center unless the length of the runway at the local airport is increased. Another candidate for new development is Diagnostic Research, Inc. (DRI), a leading producer of medical testing equipment. DRI is considering building a new manufacturing plant. Increasing the length of the runway is not a requirement for DRI, but the planning commission feels that doing so will help convince DRI to locate their new plant in Potsdam. Assuming that the town lengthens the runway, the Potsdam planning commission believes that the probabilities shown in the following table are applicable.

	DRI Plant	**No DRI Plant**
Air Express Center	.30	.10
No Air Express Center	.40	.20

For instance, the probability that Air Express will establish a distribution center and DRI will build a plant is .30.

The estimated annual revenue to the town, after deducting the cost of lengthening the runway, is as follows:

	DRI Plant	**No DRI Plant**
Air Express Center	$600,000	$150,000
No Air Express Center	$250,000	−$200,000

If the runway expansion project is not conducted, the planning commission assesses the probability DRI will locate their new plant in Potsdam at 0.6; in this case, the estimated annual revenue to the town will be $450,000. If the runway expansion project is not conducted and DRI does not locate in Potsdam, the annual revenue will be $0 since no cost will have been incurred and no revenues will be forthcoming.

a. What is the decision to be made, what is the chance event, and what is the consequence?

b. Compute the expected annual revenue associated with the decision alternative to lengthen the runway.

c. Compute the expected annual revenue associated with the decision alternative to not lengthen the runway.

d. Should the town elect to lengthen the runway? Explain.

e. Suppose that the probabilities associated with lengthening the runway were as follows:

	DRI Plant	No DRI Plant
Air Express Center	.40	.10
No Air Express Center	.30	.20

What effect, if any, would this change in the probabilities have on the recommended decision?

13. Seneca Hill Winery recently purchased land for the purpose of establishing a new vineyard. Management is considering two varieties of white grapes for the new vineyard: Chardonnay and Riesling. The Chardonnay grapes would be used to produce a dry Chardonnay wine, and the Riesling grapes would be used to produce a semi-dry Riesling wine. It takes approximately four years from the time of planting before new grapes can be harvested. This length of time creates a great deal of uncertainty concerning future demand and makes the decision concerning the type of grapes to plant difficult. Three possibilities are being considered: Chardonnay grapes only; Riesling grapes only; and both Chardonnay and Riesling grapes. Seneca management decided that for planning purposes it would be adequate to consider only two demand possibilities for each type of wine: strong or weak. With two possibilities for each type of wine it was necessary to assess four probabilities. With the help of some forecasts in industry publications management made the following probability assessments.

	Riesling Demand	
Chardonnay Demand	**Weak**	**Strong**
Weak	0.05	0.50
Strong	0.25	0.20

Revenue projections show an annual contribution to profit of $20,000 if Seneca Hill only plants Chardonnay grapes and demand is weak for Chardonnay wine, and $70,000 if they only plant Chardonnay grapes and demand is strong for Chardonnay wine. If they only plant Riesling grapes, the annual profit projection is $25,000 if demand is weak for Riesling grapes and $45,000 if demand is strong for Riesling grapes. If Seneca plants both types of grapes, the annual profit projections are shown in the following table.

	Riesling Demand	
Chardonnay Demand	**Weak**	**Strong**
Weak	\$22,000	\$40,000
Strong	\$26,000	\$60,000

a. What is the decision to be made, what is the chance event, and what is the consequence? Identify the alternatives for the decisions and the possible outcomes for the chance events.
b. Develop a decision tree.
c. Use the expected value approach to recommend which alternative Seneca Hill Winery should follow in order to maximize expected annual profit.
d. Suppose management is concerned about the probability assessments when demand for Chardonnay wine is strong. Some believe it is likely for Riesling demand to also be strong in this case. Suppose the probability of strong demand for Chardonnay and weak demand for Riesling is 0.05 and that the probability of strong demand for Chardonnay and strong demand for Riesling is 0.40. How does this change the recommended decision? Assume that the probabilities when Chardonnay demand is weak are still 0.05 and 0.50.
e. Other members of the management team expect the Chardonnay market to become saturated at some point in the future, causing a fall in prices. Suppose that the annual profit projections fall to \$50,000 when demand for Chardonnay is strong and Chardonnay grapes only are planted. Using the original probability assessments, determine how this change would affect the optimal decision.

14. The following profit payoff table was presented in Problems 1 and 5.

	State of Nature		
Decision Alternative	s_1	s_2	s_3
d_1	250	100	25
d_2	100	100	75

The probabilities for the states of nature are $P(s_1) = 0.65$, $P(s_2) = 0.15$, and $P(s_3) = 0.20$.
a. What is the optimal decision strategy if perfect information were available?
b. What is the expected value for the decision strategy developed in part (a)?
c. Using the expected value approach, what is the recommended decision without perfect information? What is its expected value?
d. What is the expected value of perfect information?

15. The Lake Placid Town Council decided to build a new community center to be used for conventions, concerts, and other public events, but considerable controversy surrounds the appropriate size. Many influential citizens want a large center that would be a showcase for the area. But the mayor feels that if demand does not support such a center, the community will lose a large amount of money. To provide structure for the decision process, the council narrowed the building alternatives to three sizes: small, medium, and large. Everybody agreed that the critical factor in choosing the best size is the number of people who will want to use the new facility. A regional planning consultant provided demand estimates under three scenarios: worst case, base case, and best case. The worst-case scenario corresponds to a situation in which tourism drops significantly; the base-case scenario corresponds to a situation in which Lake Placid continues to attract visitors at current levels; and the best-case scenario corresponds to a significant increase in tourism. The consultant has provided probability assessments of 0.10, 0.60, and 0.30 for the worst-case, base-case, and best-case scenarios, respectively.

The town council suggested using net cash flow over a five-year planning horizon as the criterion for deciding on the best size. The following projections of net cash flow (in thousands of dollars) for a five-year planning horizon have been developed. All costs, including the consultant's fee, have been included.

	Demand Scenario		
Center Size	**Worst Case**	**Base Case**	**Best Case**
Small	400	500	660
Medium	−250	650	800
Large	−400	580	990

a. What decision should Lake Placid make using the expected value approach?
b. Construct risk profiles for the medium and large alternatives. Given the mayor's concern over the possibility of losing money and the result of part (a), which alternative would you recommend?
c. Compute the expected value of perfect information. Do you think it would be worth trying to obtain additional information concerning which scenario is likely to occur?
d. Suppose the probability of the worst-case scenario increases to 0.2, the probability of the base-case scenario decreases to 0.5, and the probability of the best-case scenario remains at 0.3. What effect, if any, would these changes have on the decision recommendation?
e. The consultant has suggested that an expenditure of $150,000 on a promotional campaign over the planning horizon will effectively reduce the probability of the worst-case scenario to zero. If the campaign can be expected to also increase the probability of the best-case scenario to 0.4, is it a good investment?

16. Consider a variation of the PDC decision tree shown in Figure 14.9. The company must first decide whether to undertake the market research study. If the market research study is conducted, the outcome will either be favorable (F) or unfavorable (U). Assume there are only two decision alternatives d_1 and d_2 and two states of nature s_1 and s_2. The payoff table showing profit is as follows:

	State of Nature	
Decision Alternative	s_1	s_2
d_1	100	300
d_2	400	200

a. Show the decision tree.
b. Using the following probabilities, what is the optimal decision strategy?

$$P(F) = 0.56 \quad P(s_1 \mid F) = 0.57 \quad P(s_1 \mid U) = 0.18 \quad P(s_1) = 0.40$$
$$P(U) = 0.44 \quad P(s_2 \mid F) = 0.43 \quad P(s_2 \mid U) = 0.82 \quad P(s_2) = 0.60$$

17. A real estate investor has the opportunity to purchase land currently zoned residential. If the county board approves a request to rezone the property as commercial within the next year, the investor will be able to lease the land to a large discount firm that wants to open a new store on the property. However, if the zoning change is not approved, the investor will have to sell the property at a loss. Profits (in thousands of dollars) are shown in the following payoff table.

	State of Nature	
	Rezoning Approved	**Rezoning Not Approved**
Decision Alternative	s_1	s_2
Purchase, d_1	600	−200
Do not purchase, d_2	0	0

a. If the probability that the rezoning will be approved is 0.5, what decision is recommended? What is the expected profit?

b. The investor can purchase an option to buy the land. Under the option, the investor maintains the rights to purchase the land anytime during the next three months while learning more about possible resistance to the rezoning proposal from area residents. Probabilities are as follows.

Let H = High resistance to rezoning
L = Low resistance to rezoning

$$P(H) = 0.55 \qquad P(s_1 \mid H) = 0.18 \qquad P(s_2 \mid H) = 0.82$$
$$p(L) = 0.45 \qquad P(s_1 \mid L) = 0.89 \qquad P(s_2 \mid L) = 0.11$$

What is the optimal decision strategy if the investor uses the option period to learn more about the resistance from area residents before making the purchase decision?

c. If the option will cost the investor an additional $10,000, should the investor purchase the option? Why or why not? What is the maximum that the investor should be willing to pay for the option?

18. Dante Development Corporation is considering bidding on a contract for a new office building complex. Figure 14.16 shows the decision tree prepared by one of Dante's analysts. At node 1, the company must decide whether to bid on the contract. The cost of preparing the bid is $200,000. The upper branch from node 2 shows that the company has a 0.8 probability of winning the contract if it submits a bid. If the company wins the bid, it will have to pay $2,000,000 to become a partner in the project. Node 3 shows that the company will then consider doing a market research study to forecast demand for the office units prior to beginning construction. The cost of this study is $150,000. Node 4 is a chance node showing the possible outcomes of the market research study.

Nodes 5, 6, and 7 are similar in that they are the decision nodes for Dante to either build the office complex or sell the rights in the project to another developer. The decision to build the complex will result in an income of $5,000,000 if demand is high and $3,000,000 if demand is moderate. If Dante chooses to sell its rights in the project to another developer, income from the sale is estimated to be $3,500,000. The probabilities shown at nodes 4, 8, and 9 are based on the projected outcomes of the market research study.

a. Verify Dante's profit projections shown at the ending branches of the decision tree by calculating the payoffs of $2,650,000 and $650,000 for first two outcomes.

b. What is the optimal decision strategy for Dante, and what is the expected profit for this project?

FIGURE 14.16 DECISION TREE FOR THE DANTE DEVELOPMENT CORPORATION

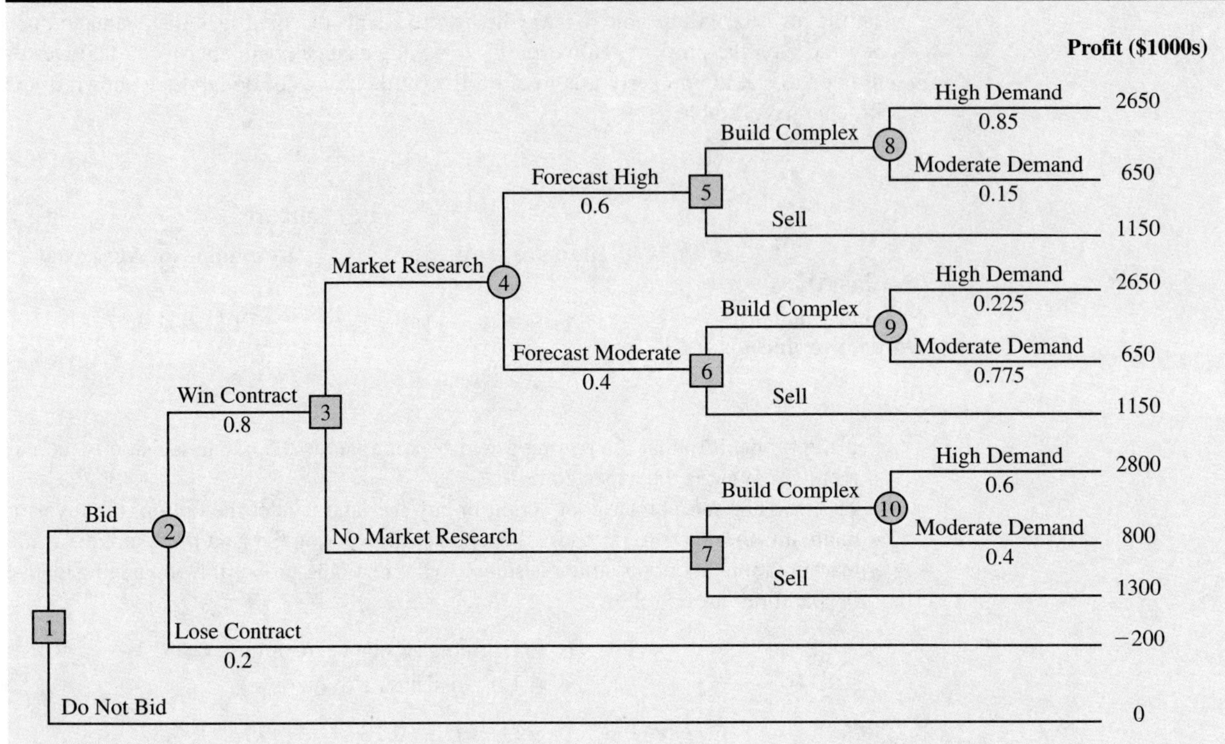

c. What would the cost of the market research study have to be before Dante would change its decision about the market research study?

d. Develop a risk profile for Dante.

19. Hale's TV Productions is considering producing a pilot for a comedy series in the hope of selling it to a major television network. The network may decide to reject the series, but it may also decide to purchase the rights to the series for either one or two years. At this point in time, Hale may either produce the pilot and wait for the network's decision or transfer the rights for the pilot and series to a competitor for $100,000. Hale's decision alternatives and profits (in thousands of dollars) are as follows:

	State of Nature		
Decision Alternative	**Reject, s_1**	**1 Year, s_2**	**2 Years, s_3**
Produce pilot, d_1	−100	50	150
Sell to competitor, d_2	100	100	100

The probabilities for the states of nature are $P(s_1) = 0.20$, $P(s_2) = 0.30$, and $P(s_3) = 0.50$. For a consulting fee of $5000, an agency will review the plans for the comedy series and indicate the overall chances of a favorable network reaction to the series. Assume that the agency review will result in a favorable (F) or an unfavorable (U) review and that the following probabilities are relevant.

$$P(F) = 0.69 \qquad P(s_1 \mid F) = 0.09 \qquad P(s_1 \mid U) = 0.45$$
$$P(U) = 0.31 \qquad P(s_2 \mid F) = 0.26 \qquad P(s_2 \mid U) = 0.39$$
$$P(s_3 \mid F) = 0.65 \qquad P(s_3 \mid U) = 0.16$$

a. Construct a decision tree for this problem.
b. What is the recommended decision if the agency opinion is not used? What is the expected value?
c. What is the expected value of perfect information?
d. What is Hale's optimal decision strategy assuming the agency's information is used?
e. What is the expected value of the agency's information?
f. Is the agency's information worth the $5000 fee? What is the maximum that Hale should be willing to pay for the information?
g. What is the recommended decision?

20. Embassy Publishing Company received a six-chapter manuscript for a new college textbook. The editor of the college division is familiar with the manuscript and estimated a 0.65 probability that the textbook will be successful. If successful, a profit of $750,000 will be realized. If the company decides to publish the textbook and it is unsuccessful, a loss of $250,000 will occur.

Before making the decision to accept or reject the manuscript, the editor is considering sending the manuscript out for review. A review process provides either a favorable (F) or unfavorable (U) evaluation of the manuscript. Past experience with the review process suggests probabilities $P(F) = 0.7$ and $P(U) = 0.3$ apply. Let $s_1 =$ the textbook is successful, and $s_2 =$ the textbook is unsuccessful. The editor's initial probabilities of s_1 and s_2 will be revised based on whether the review is favorable or unfavorable. The revised probabilities are as follows.

$$P(s_1 \mid F) = 0.75 \qquad P(s_1 \mid U) = 0.417$$
$$P(s_2 \mid F) = 0.25 \qquad P(s_2 \mid U) = 0.583$$

a. Construct a decision tree assuming that the company will first make the decision of whether to send the manuscript out for review and then make the decision to accept or reject the manuscript.
b. Analyze the decision tree to determine the optimal decision strategy for the publishing company.
c. If the manuscript review costs $5000, what is your recommendation?
d. What is the expected value of perfect information? What does this EVPI suggest for the company?

21. Lawson's Department Store faces a buying decision for a seasonal product for which demand can be high, medium, or low. The purchaser for Lawson's can order 1, 2, or 3 lots of the product before the season begins but cannot reorder later. Profit projections (in thousands of dollars) are shown.

	State of Nature		
	High Demand	**Medium Demand**	**Low Demand**
Decision Alternative	s_1	s_2	s_3
Order 1 lot, d_1	60	60	50
Order 2 lots, d_2	80	80	30
Order 3 lots, d_3	100	70	10

a. If the prior probabilities for the three states of nature are 0.3, 0.3, and 0.4, respectively, what is the recommended order quantity?

b. At each preseason sales meeting, the vice president of sales provides a personal opinion regarding potential demand for this product. Because of the vice president's enthusiasm and optimistic nature, the predictions of market conditions have always been either "excellent" (E) or "very good" (V). Probabilities are as follows.

$P(E) = 0.70$	$P(s_1 \mid E) = 0.34$	$P(s_1 \mid V) = 0.20$
$P(V) = 0.30$	$P(s_2 \mid E) = 0.32$	$P(s_2 \mid V) = 0.26$
	$P(s_3 \mid E) = 0.34$	$P(s_3 \mid V) = 0.54$

What is the optimal decision strategy?

c. Use the efficiency of sample information and discuss whether the firm should consider a consulting expert who could provide independent forecasts of market conditions for the product.

22. Suppose that you are given a decision situation with three possible states of nature: s_1, s_2, and s_3. The prior probabilities are $P(s_1) = 0.2$, $P(s_2) = 0.5$, and $P(s_3) = 0.3$. With sample information I, $P(I \mid s_1) = 0.1$, $P(I \mid s_2) = 0.05$, and $P(I \mid s_3) = 0.2$. Compute the revised or posterior probabilities: $P(s_1 \mid I)$, $P(s_2 \mid I)$, and $P(s_3 \mid I)$.

23. In the following profit payoff table for a decision problem with two states of nature and three decision alternatives, the prior probabilities for s_1 and s_2 are $P(s_1) = 0.8$ and $P(s_2) = 0.2$.

	State of Nature	
Decision Alternative	s_1	s_2
d_1	15	10
d_2	10	12
d_3	8	20

a. What is the optimal decision?

b. Find the EVPI.

c. Suppose that sample information I is obtained, with $P(I \mid s_1) = 0.20$ and $P(I \mid s_2) = 0.75$. Find the posterior probabilities $P(s_1 \mid I)$ and $P(s_2 \mid I)$. Recommend a decision alternative based on these probabilities.

24. To save on expenses, Rona and Jerry agreed to form a carpool for traveling to and from work. Rona preferred to use the somewhat longer but more consistent Queen City Avenue. Although Jerry preferred the quicker expressway, he agreed with Rona that they should take Queen City Avenue if the expressway had a traffic jam. The following payoff table provides the one-way time estimate in minutes for traveling to or from work.

	State of Nature	
	Expressway Open	**Expressway Jammed**
Decision Alternative	s_1	s_2
Queen City Avenue, d_1	30	30
Expressway, d_2	25	45

Based on their experience with traffic problems, Rona and Jerry agreed on a 0.15 probability that the expressway would be jammed.

In addition, they agreed that weather seemed to affect the traffic conditions on the expressway. Let

$$C = \text{clear}$$
$$O = \text{overcast}$$
$$R = \text{rain}$$

The following conditional probabilities apply.

$$P(C \mid s_1) = 0.8 \quad P(O \mid s_1) = 0.2 \quad P(R \mid s_1) = 0.0$$
$$P(C \mid s_2) = 0.1 \quad P(O \mid s_2) = 0.3 \quad P(R \mid s_2) = 0.6$$

a. Use Bayes' theorem for probability revision to compute the probability of each weather condition and the conditional probability of the expressway open s_1 or jammed s_2 given each weather condition.
b. Show the decision tree for this problem.
c. What is the optimal decision strategy, and what is the expected travel time?

25. The Gorman Manufacturing Company must decide whether to manufacture a component part at its Milan, Michigan, plant or purchase the component part from a supplier. The resulting profit is dependent upon the demand for the product. The following payoff table shows the projected profit (in thousands of dollars).

	State of Nature		
	Low Demand	**Medium Demand**	**High Demand**
Decision Alternative	s_1	s_2	s_3
Manufacture, d_1	−20	40	100
Purchase, d_2	10	45	70

The state-of-nature probabilities are $P(s_1) = 0.35$, $P(s_2) = 0.35$, and $P(s_3) = 0.30$.

a. Use a decision tree to recommend a decision.
b. Use EVPI to determine whether Gorman should attempt to obtain a better estimate of demand.
c. A test market study of the potential demand for the product is expected to report either a favorable (F) or unfavorable (U) condition. The relevant conditional probabilities are as follows:

$$P(F \mid s_1) = 0.10 \quad P(U \mid s_1) = 0.90$$
$$P(F \mid s_2) = 0.40 \quad P(U \mid s_2) = 0.60$$
$$P(F \mid s_3) = 0.60 \quad P(U \mid s_3) = 0.40$$

What is the probability that the market research report will be favorable?

d. What is Gorman's optimal decision strategy?
e. What is the expected value of the market research information?
f. What is the efficiency of the information?

26. Three decision makers have assessed utilities for the following decision problem (payoff in dollars).

	State of Nature		
Decision Alternative	s_1	s_2	s_3
d_1	20	50	−20
d_2	80	100	−100

The indifference probabilities are as follows.

	Indifference Probability (p)		
Payoff	**Risk Avoider**	**Risk Taker**	**Risk Neutral**
100	1.00	1.00	1.00
80	0.95	0.70	0.90
50	0.90	0.60	0.75
20	0.70	0.45	0.60
−20	0.50	0.25	0.40
−100	0.00	0.00	0.00

For the payoff of 20, what is the premium that the risk avoider will pay to avoid risk? What is the premium that the risk taker will pay to have the opportunity of the high payoff?

27. In Problem 26, if $P(s_1) = 0.25$, $P(s_2) = 0.50$, and $P(s_3) = 0.25$, find a recommended decision for each of the three decision makers. Note that for the same decision problem, different utilities can lead to different decisions.

28. A firm has three investment alternatives. The payoff table (in thousands of dollars) and associated probabilities are as follows:

	Economic Condition		
Investment	**Up**	**Stable**	**Down**
d_1	100	25	0
d_2	75	50	25
d_3	50	50	50
Probabilities	0.40	0.30	0.30

a. Using the expected value approach, which decision is preferred?

b. For the lottery having a payoff of \$100,000 with probability p and \$0 with probability $(1 - p)$, two decision makers expressed the following indifference probabilities:

	Indifference Probability (p)	
Profit	**Decision Maker A**	**Decision Maker B**
\$75,000	0.80	0.60
50,000	0.60	0.30
25,000	0.30	0.15

Find the most preferred decision for each decision maker using the expected utility approach.

c. Why don't decision makers A and B select the same decision alternative?

29. In a certain state lottery, a lottery ticket costs \$2. In terms of the decision to purchase or not to purchase a lottery ticket, suppose the following payoff table (in \$) applies:

	State of Nature	
	Win	Lose
Decision Alternative	s_1	s_2
Purchase lottery ticket, d_1	300,000	−2
Do not purchase lottery ticket, d_2	0	0

a. If a realistic estimate of the chances of winning are 1 in 250,000, use the expected value approach to recommend a decision.

b. If a particular decision maker assigns an indifference probability of 0.000001 to the \$0 payoff, would this individual purchase a lottery ticket? Use expected utility to justify your answer.

30. Alexander Industries is considering purchasing an insurance policy for its new office building in St. Louis. The policy has an annual cost of \$10,000. If Alexander Industries does not purchase the insurance and minor fire damage occurs to the office building, a cost of \$100,000 is anticipated; the cost if major or total destruction occurs is \$200,000. The payoff table in (\$), including the state-of-nature probabilities, is as follows:

		Damage	
	None	Minor	Major
Decision Alternative	s_1	s_2	s_3
Purchase insurance, d_1	10,000	10,000	10,000
Do not purchase insurance, d_2	0	100,000	200,000
Probabilities	0.96	0.03	0.01

a. Using the expected value approach, what decision do you recommend?

b. What lottery would you use to assess utilities? (*Note:* The data are costs, which makes the best payoff \$0.)

c. Assume we found the following indifference probabilities for the lottery defined in part (b):

Cost	Indifference Probability (p)
\$ 10,000	0.99
100,000	0.60

What decision would you recommend?

d. Do you favor using expected value or expected utility for this decision problem? Why?

31. Suppose that the point spread for a particular sporting event is 10 points and that with this spread you are convinced you would have a 0.6 probability of winning a bet on your team. However, the local bookie will accept only a $1000 bet. Assuming that such bets are legal, would you bet on your team? (Disregard any commission charged by the bookie.) Remember that you must pay losses out of your own pocket. Your payoff table (in $) is as follows:

	State of Nature	
	You Win	**You Lose**
Decision Alternative	s_1	s_2
Bet, d_1	1000	−1000
Don't bet, d_2	0	0

a. What decision does the expected value approach recommend?
b. What is your indifference probability for the $0 payoff? (Although this determination is not easy, be as realistic as possible. Remember, this calculation is required if we are to do an analysis that reflects your attitude toward risk.)
c. What decision would you make based on the expected utility approach?
d. Would other individuals assess the same utility values you do? Explain.
e. If your decision in part (c) was to place the bet, repeat the analysis, assuming a minimum bet of $10,000.

32. Two different routes can be used to travel between two cities. Route A normally takes 60 minutes, while route B normally takes 45 minutes. If traffic problems are encountered on route A, the travel time increases to 70 minutes; traffic problems on route B increase travel time to 90 minutes. The probability of the delay is 0.2 for route A and 0.3 for route B.
a. Using the expected value approach, what is the recommended route?
b. If utilities are to be assigned to the travel times, what is the appropriate lottery? Note that the smaller times should reflect higher utilities.
c. Using the lottery of part (b), assume the decision maker expresses indifference probabilities of

$p = 0.8$ for 60 minutes
$p = 0.6$ for 70 minutes

What route should this decision maker select?

33. A new product has the following profit projections and associated probabilities:

Profit	**Probability**
150,000	0.10
100,000	0.25
50,000	0.20
0	0.15
−50,000	0.20
−100,000	0.10

a. Use the expected value approach to make the decision of whether to market the new product.

b. Because of the high dollar values involved, especially the possibility of a $100,000 loss, the marketing vice president expressed some concern about the use of the expected value approach. As a consequence, if a utility analysis is performed, what is the appropriate lottery? Assume the following indifference probabilities are assigned:

Profit	Indifference Probability (p)
$100,000	0.95
50,000	0.70
0	0.50
−50,000	0.25

c. Use expected utility to recommend a decision.

d. Should the decision maker feel comfortable with the final decision recommended by the analysis?

34. A Las Vegas roulette wheel has 38 different numerical values. If an individual bets on one number and wins, the payoff is 35 to 1.

a. Show a payoff table for a $10 bet on one number using decision alternatives of bet and do not bet.

b. What is the recommended decision using the expected value approach?

c. What range of utility values would a decision maker have to assign to the $0 payoff to have expected utility justify his or her decision to place the $10 bet?

Case Problem 1 PROPERTY PURCHASE STRATEGY

Glenn Foreman, president of Oceanview Development Corporation, is considering submitting a bid to purchase property that will be sold by sealed bid at a county tax foreclosure. Glenn's initial judgment is to submit a bid of $5 million. Based on his experience, Glenn estimates that a bid of $5 million will have a 0.2 probability of being the highest bid and securing the property for Oceanview. The current date is June 1. Sealed bids for the property must be submitted by August 15. The winning bid will be announced on September 1.

If Oceanview submits the highest bid and obtains the property, the firm plans to build and sell a complex of luxury condominiums. However, a complicating factor is that the property is currently zoned for single-family residences only. Glenn believes that a referendum could be placed on the voting ballot in time for the November election. Passage of the referendum would change the zoning of the property and permit construction of the condominiums.

The sealed-bid procedure requires the bid to be submitted with a certified check for 10% of the amount bid. If the bid is rejected, the deposit is refunded. If the bid is accepted, the deposit is the down payment for the property. However, if the bid is accepted and the bidder does not follow through with the purchase and meet the remainder of the financial obligation within six months, the deposit will be forfeited. In this case, the county will offer the property to the next highest bidder.

To determine whether Oceanview should submit the $5 million bid, Glenn conducted some preliminary analysis. This preliminary work provided an assessment of 0.3 for the probability that the referendum for a zoning change will be approved and resulted in the following estimates of the costs and revenues that will be incurred if the condominiums are built.

Cost and Revenue Estimates	
Revenue from condominium sales	$15,000,000
Cost	
Property	$5,000,000
Construction expenses	$8,000,000

If Oceanview obtains the property and the zoning change is rejected in November, Glenn believes that the best option would be for the firm not to complete the purchase of the property. In this case, Oceanview would forfeit the 10 percent deposit that accompanied the bid.

Because the likelihood that the zoning referendum will be approved is such an important factor in the decision process, Glenn suggested that the firm hire a market research service to conduct a survey of voters. The survey would provide a better estimate of the likelihood that the referendum for a zoning change would be approved. The market research firm that Oceanview Development has worked with in the past has agreed to do the study for $15,000. The results of the study will be available August 1, so that Oceanview will have this information before the August 15 bid deadline. The results of the survey will be either a prediction that the zoning change will be approved or a prediction that the zoning change will be rejected. After considering the record of the market research service in previous studies conducted for Oceanview, Glenn developed the following probability estimates concerning the accuracy of the market research information.

$$P(A \mid s_1) = 0.9 \qquad P(N \mid s_1) = 0.1$$
$$P(A \mid s_2) = 0.2 \qquad P(N \mid s_2) = 0.8$$

where

A = prediction of zoning change approval
N = prediction that zoning change will not be approved
s_1 = the zoning change is approved by the voters
s_2 = the zoning change is rejected by the voters

Managerial Report

Perform an analysis of the problem facing the Oceanview Development Corporation, and prepare a report that summarizes your findings and recommendations. Include the following items in your report:

1. A decision tree that shows the logical sequence of the decision problem
2. A recommendation regarding what Oceanview should do if the market research information is not available
3. A decision strategy that Oceanview should follow if the market research is conducted
4. A recommendation as to whether Oceanview should employ the market research firm, along with the value of the information provided by the market research firm

Include the details of your analysis as an appendix to your report.

Case Problem 2 LAWSUIT DEFENSE STRATEGY

John Campbell, an employee of Manhattan Construction Company, claims to have injured his back as a result of a fall while repairing the roof at one of the Eastview apartment buildings. He filed a lawsuit against Doug Reynolds, the owner of Eastview Apartments, asking for damages of $1,500,000. John claims that the roof had rotten sections and that his fall could have been prevented if Mr. Reynolds had told Manhattan Construction about the problem. Mr. Reynolds notified his insurance company, Allied Insurance, of the lawsuit. Allied must defend Mr. Reynolds and decide what action to take regarding the lawsuit.

Some depositions and a series of discussions took place between both sides. As a result, John Campbell offered to accept a settlement of $750,000. Thus, one option is for Allied to pay John $750,000 to settle the claim. Allied is also considering making John a counteroffer of $400,000 in the hope that he will accept a lesser amount to avoid the time and cost of going to trial. Allied's preliminary investigation shows that John's case is strong; Allied is concerned that John may reject their counteroffer and request a jury trial. Allied's lawyers spent some time exploring John's likely reaction if they make a counteroffer of $400,000.

The lawyers concluded that it is adequate to consider three possible outcomes to represent John's possible reaction to a counteroffer of $400,000: (1) John will accept the counteroffer and the case will be closed; (2) John will reject the counteroffer and elect to have a jury decide the settlement amount; or (3) John will make a counteroffer to Allied of $600,000. If John does make a counteroffer, Allied decided that they will not make additional counteroffers. They will either accept John's counteroffer of $600,000 or go to trial.

If the case goes to a jury trial, Allied considers three outcomes possible: (1) the jury may reject John's claim and Allied will not be required to pay any damages; (2) the jury will find in favor of John and award him $750,000 in damages; or (3) the jury will conclude that John has a strong case and award him the full amount of $1,500,000.

Key considerations as Allied develops its strategy for disposing of the case are the probabilities associated with John's response to an Allied counteroffer of $400,000 and the probabilities associated with the three possible trial outcomes. Allied's lawyers believe the probability that John will accept a counteroffer of $400,000 is 0.10, the probability that John will reject a counteroffer of $400,000 is 0.40, and the probability that John will, himself, make a counteroffer to Allied of $600,000 is 0.50. If the case goes to court, they believe that the probability the jury will award John damages of $1,500,000 is 0.30, the probability that the jury will award John damages of $750,000 is 0.50, and the probability that the jury will award John nothing is 0.20.

Managerial Report

Perform an analysis of the problem facing Allied Insurance and prepare a report that summarizes your findings and recommendations. Be sure to include the following items:

1. A decision tree
2. A recommendation regarding whether Allied should accept John's initial offer to settle the claim for $750,000
3. A decision strategy that Allied should follow if they decide to make John a counteroffer of $400,000
4. A risk profile for your recommended strategy

Appendix 14.1 DECISION ANALYSIS WITH TREEPLAN

TreePlan* is an Excel add-in that can be used to develop decision trees for decision analysis problems. The software package is provided on the CD that accompanies this text. Instructions for installing TreePlan are included with the software. A manual containing additional information on starting and using TreePlan is also included on the CD. In this appendix, we show how to use TreePlan to build a decision tree and solve the PDC problem presented in Section 14.3. The decision tree for the PDC problem is shown in Figure 14.17.

Getting Started: An Initial Decision Tree

We begin by assuming that TreePlan has been installed and an Excel workbook is open. To build a TreePlan version of the PDC decision tree proceed as follows:

Step 1. Select cell A1
Step 2. Select the **Tools** menu and choose **Decision Tree**
Step 3. When the **TreePlan New** dialog box appears:
Click **New Tree**

A decision tree with one decision node and two branches appears as follows:

	A	B	C	D	E	F	G
1							
2				Decision 1			
3							0
4				0	0		
5		1					
6	0						
7				Decision 2			
8							0
9				0	0		

Adding a Branch

The PDC problem has three decision alternatives (small, medium, and large condominium complexes), so we must add another decision branch to the tree.

Step 1. Select cell B5
Step 2. Select the **Tools** menu and choose **Decision Tree**
Step 3. When the **TreePlan Decision** dialog box appears:
Select **Add branch**
Click **OK**

A revised tree with three decision branches now appears in the Excel worksheet.

*TreePlan was developed by Professor Michael R. Middleton at the University of San Francisco and modified for use by Professor James E. Smith at Duke University. The TreePlan Web site is located at http://www.treeplan.com.

FIGURE 14.17 PDC DECISION TREE

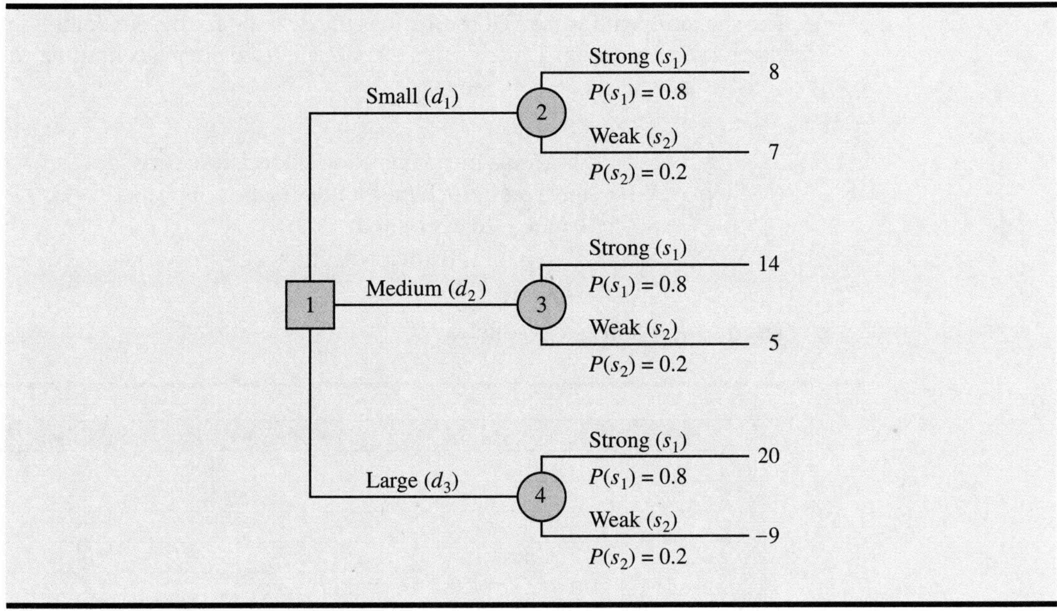

Naming the Decision Alternatives

The decision alternatives can be named by selecting the cells containing the labels Decision 1, Decision 2, and Decision 3, and then entering the corresponding PDC names Small, Medium, and Large. After naming the alternatives, the PDC tree with three decision branches appears as follows:

	A	B	C	D	E	F	G
1							
2				Small			
3							0
4				0	0		
5							
6							
7				Medium			
8		1					0
9	0			0	0		
10							
11							
12				Large			
13							0
14				0	0		

Adding Chance Nodes

The chance event for the PDC problem is the demand for the condominiums, which may be either strong or weak. Thus, a chance node with two branches must be added at the end of each decision alternative branch.

Step 1. Select cell F3
Step 2. Select the **Tools** menu and choose **Decision Tree**
Step 3. When the **TreePlan Terminal** dialog box appears:
Select **Change to event node**
Select **Two** in the **Branches** section
Click **OK**

The tree now appears as follows:

	A	B	C	D	E	F	G	H	I	J	K
1								0.5			
2								Event 4			
3											0
4				Small				0	0		
5											
6				0	0			0.5			
7								Event 5			
8											0
9								0	0		
10											
11		1									
12	0			Medium							
13											0
14				0	0						
15											
16											
17				Large							
18											0
19				0	0						

We next select the cells containing Event 4 and Event 5 and rename them Strong and Weak to provide the proper names for the PDC states of nature. After doing so we can copy the subtree for the chance node in cell F5 to the other two decision branches to complete the structure of the PDC decision tree.

Step 1. Select cell F5
Step 2. Select the **Tools** menu and choose **Decision Tree**
Step 3. When the **TreePlan Event** dialog box appears:
Select **Copy subtree**
Click **OK**
Step 4. Select cell F13
Step 5. Select the **Tools** menu and choose **Decision Tree**
Step 6. When the **TreePlan Terminal** dialog box appears
Select **Paste subtree**
Click **OK**

This copy/paste procedure places a chance node at the end of the Medium decision branch. Repeating the same copy/paste procedure for the Large decision branch completes the structure of the PDC decision tree as shown in Figure 14.18

Inserting Probabilities and Payoffs

TreePlan provides the capability of inserting probabilities and payoffs into the decision tree. In Figure 14.18, we see that TreePlan automatically assigned an equal probability 0.5 to each of the chance outcomes. For PDC, the probability of strong demand is 0.8 and the probability of weak demand is 0.2. We can select cells H1, H6, H11, H16, H21, and H26 and insert the appropriate probabilities. The payoffs for the chance outcomes are inserted in cells H4, H9, H14, H19, H24, and H29. After inserting the PDC probabilities and payoffs, the PDC decision tree appears as shown in Figure 14.19.

Note that the payoffs also appear in the right-hand margin of the decision tree. The payoffs in the right margin are computed by a formula that adds the payoffs on all of the branches leading to the associated terminal node. For the PDC problem, no payoffs are

FIGURE 14.18 PDC DECISION TREE DEVELOPED BY TREEPLAN

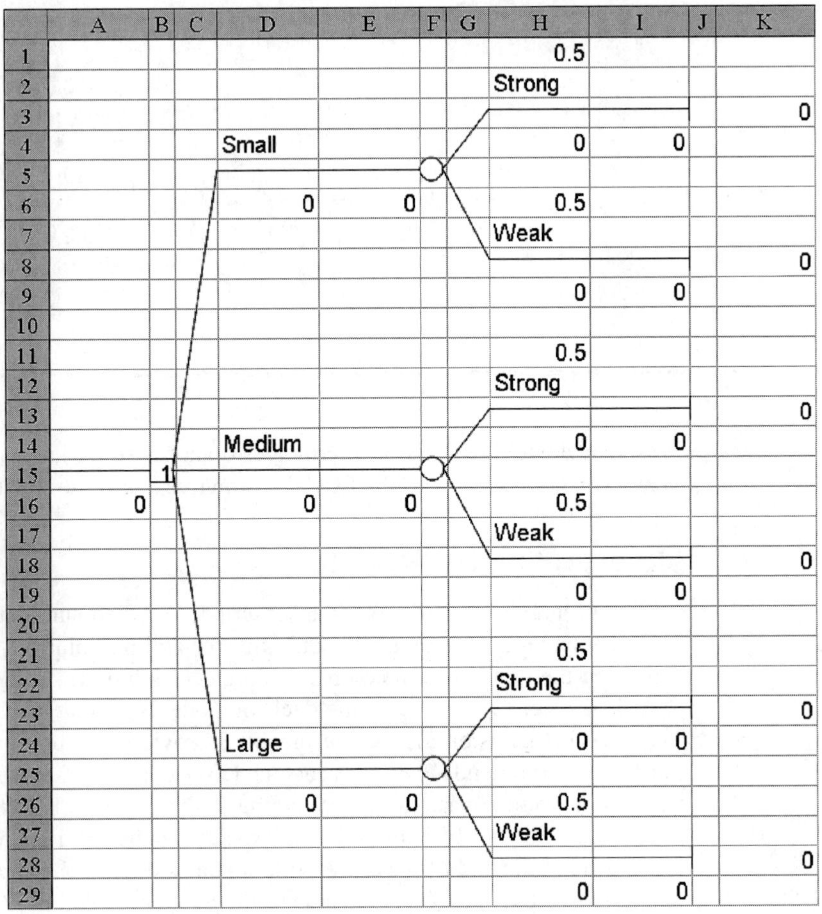

	A	B	C	D	E	F	G	H	I	J	K
1								0.5			
2								Strong			
3											0
4				Small				0	0		
5											
6				0	0			0.5			
7								Weak			
8											0
9								0	0		
10											
11								0.5			
12								Strong			
13											0
14				Medium				0	0		
15		1									
16	0			0	0			0.5			
17								Weak			
18											0
19								0	0		
20											
21								0.5			
22								Strong			
23											0
24				Large				0	0		
25											
26				0	0			0.5			
27								Weak			
28											0
29								0	0		

FIGURE 14.19 PDC DECISION TREE WITH BRANCH PROBABILITIES AND PAYOFFS

	A	B	C	D	E	F	G	H	I	J	K
1								0.8			
2								Strong			
3											8
4				Small				8	8		
5											
6				0	7.8			0.2			
7								Weak			
8											7
9								7	7		
10											
11								0.8			
12								Strong			
13											14
14				Medium				14	14		
15		3									
16	14.2			0	12.2			0.2			
17								Weak			
18											5
19								5	5		
20											
21								0.8			
22								Strong			
23											20
24				Large				20	20		
25											
26				0	14.2			0.2			
27								Weak			
28											-9
29								-9	-9		

associated with the decision alternatives branches so we leave the default values of zero in cells D6, D16, and D24. The PDC decision tree is now complete.

Interpreting the Result

When probabilities and payoffs are inserted, TreePlan automatically makes the backward pass computations necessary to determine the optimal solution. Optimal decisions are identified by the number in the corresponding decision node. In the PDC decision tree in Figure 14.19, cell B15 contains the decision node. Note that a 3 appears in this node, which tells us that decision alternative branch 3 provides the optimal decision. Thus, decision analysis recommends PDC construct the Large condominium complex. The expected value of this decision appears at the beginning of the tree in cell A16. Thus, we see the optimal expected value is \$14.2 million. The expected values of the other decision alternatives are displayed at the end of the corresponding decision branch. Thus, referring to cells E6 and E16, we see that the expected value of the Small complex is \$7.8 million and the expected value of the Medium complex is \$12.2 million.

Other Options

TreePlan defaults to a maximization objective. If you would like a minimization objective, follow these steps:

Step 1. Select the **Tools** menu and choose **Decision Tree**
Step 2. Select **Options**
Step 3. Choose **Minimize (costs)**
Click **OK**

In using a TreePlan decision tree, we can modify probabilities and payoffs and quickly observe the impact of the changes on the optimal solution. Using this "what if" type of sensitivity analysis, we can identify changes in probabilities and payoffs that would change the optimal decision. Also, because TreePlan is an Excel add-in, most of Excel's capabilities are available. For instance, we could use boldface to highlight the name of the optimal decision alternative on the final decision tree solution. A variety of other options TreePlan provides is contained in the TreePlan manual on the CD that accompanies this text. Computer software packages such as TreePlan make it easier to do a thorough analysis of a decision problem.

CHAPTER 15

Multicriteria Decisions

CONTENTS

In previous chapters we showed how a variety of quantitative methods can help managers make better decisions. Whenever we desired an optimal solution, we utilized a single criterion (e.g., maximize profit, minimize cost, minimize time). In this chapter we discuss techniques that are appropriate for situations in which the decision maker needs to consider multiple criteria in arriving at the overall best decision. For example, consider a company involved in selecting a location for a new manufacturing plant. The cost of land and construction may vary from location to location, so one criterion in selecting the best site could be the cost involved in building the plant; if cost were the sole criterion of interest, management would simply select the location that minimizes land cost plus construction cost. Before making any decision, however, management might also want to consider additional criteria such as the availability of transportation from the plant to the firm's distribution centers, the attractiveness of the proposed location in terms of hiring and retaining employees, energy costs at the proposed site, and state and local taxes. In such situations the complexity of the problem increases because one location may be more desirable in terms of one criterion and less desirable in terms of one or more of the other criteria.

To introduce the topic of multicriteria decision making, we consider a technique referred to as **goal programming.** This technique has been developed to handle multiple-criteria situations within the general framework of linear programming. We next consider a *scoring model* as a relatively easy way to identify the best decision alternative for a multicriteria problem. Finally, we introduce a method known as the *analytical hierarchy process (AHP),* which allows the user to make pairwise comparisons among the criteria and a series of pairwise comparisons among the decision alternatives in order to arrive at a prioritized ranking of the decision alternatives.

15.1 GOAL PROGRAMMING: FORMULATION AND GRAPHICAL SOLUTION

To illustrate the goal programming approach to multicriteria decision problems, let us consider a problem facing Nicolo Investment Advisors. A client has $80,000 to invest and, as an initial strategy, would like the investment portfolio restricted to two stocks:

Stock	Price/Share	Estimated Annual Return/Share	Risk Index/Share
U.S. Oil	$25	$3	0.50
Hub Properties	$50	$5	0.25

U.S. Oil, which has a return of $3 on a $25 share price, provides an annual rate of return of 12 percent, whereas Hub Properties provides an annual rate of return of 10 percent. The risk index per share, 0.50 for U.S. Oil and 0.25 for Hub Properties, is a rating Nicolo assigned to measure the relative risk of the two investments. Higher risk index values imply greater risk; hence, Nicolo judged U.S. Oil to be the riskier investment. By specifying a maximum portfolio risk index, Nicolo will avoid placing too much of the portfolio in high-risk investments.

To illustrate how to use the risk index per share to measure the total portfolio risk, suppose that Nicolo chooses a portfolio that invests all $80,000 in U.S. Oil, the higher risk, but higher return, investment. Nicolo could purchase $80,000/$25 = 3200 shares of U.S. Oil, and the portfolio would have a risk index of 3200(0.50) = 1600. Conversely, if Nicolo purchases no shares of either stock, the portfolio will have no risk, but also no return. Thus, the portfolio risk index will vary from 0 (least risk) to 1600 (most risk).

Nicolo's client would like to avoid a high-risk portfolio; thus, investing all funds in U.S. Oil would not be desirable. However, the client agreed that an acceptable level of risk would correspond to portfolios with a maximum total risk index of 700. Thus, considering only risk, one *goal* is to find a portfolio with a risk index of 700 or less.

Another goal of the client is to obtain an annual return of at least $9000. This goal can be achieved with a portfolio consisting of 2000 shares of U.S. Oil [at a cost of 2000($25) = $50,000] and 600 shares of Hub Properties [at a cost of 600($50) = $30,000]; the annual return in this case would be 2000($3) + 600($5) = $9000. Note, however, that the portfolio risk index for this investment strategy would be 2000(0.50) + 600(0.25) = 1150; thus, this portfolio achieves the annual return goal but does not satisfy the portfolio risk index goal.

Thus, the portfolio selection problem is a multicriteria decision problem involving two conflicting goals: one dealing with risk and one dealing with annual return. The goal programming approach was developed precisely for this kind of problem. Goal programming can be used to identify a portfolio that comes closest to achieving both goals. Before applying the methodology, the client must determine which, if either, goal is more important.

Suppose that the client's top-priority goal is to restrict the risk; that is, keeping the portfolio risk index at 700 or less is so important that the client is not willing to trade the achievement of this goal for any amount of an increase in annual return. As long as the portfolio risk index does not exceed 700, the client seeks the best possible return. Based on this statement of priorities, the goals for the problem are as follows:

Primary Goal (Priority Level 1)

Goal 1: Find a portfolio that has a risk index of 700 or less.

Secondary Goal (Priority Level 2)

Goal 2: Find a portfolio that will provide an annual return of at least $9000.

In goal programming with preemptive priorities, we never permit trade-offs between higher and lower level goals.

The primary goal is called a *priority level 1 goal,* and the secondary goal is called a *priority level 2 goal.* In goal programming terminology, these are called **preemptive priorities** because the decision maker is not willing to sacrifice any amount of achievement of the priority level 1 goal for the lower priority goal. The portfolio risk index of 700 is the **target value** for the priority level 1 (primary) goal, and the annual return of $9000 is the target value for the priority level 2 (secondary) goal. The difficulty in finding a solution that will achieve these goals is that only $80,000 is available for investment.

Developing the Constraints and the Goal Equations

We begin by defining the decision variables:

$$U = \text{number of shares of U.S. Oil purchased}$$
$$H = \text{number of shares of Hub Properties purchased}$$

Constraints for goal programming problems are handled in the same way as in an ordinary linear programming problem. In the Nicolo Investment Advisors problem, one constraint corresponds to the funds available. Because each share of U.S. Oil costs $25 and each share of Hub Properties costs $50, the constraint representing the funds available is

$$25U + 50H \leq 80{,}000$$

To complete the formulation of the model, we must develop a **goal equation** for each goal. Let us begin by writing the goal equation for the primary goal. Each share of U.S. Oil has a risk index of 0.50 and each share of Hub Properties has a risk index of 0.25; therefore, the portfolio risk index is $0.50U + 0.25H$. Depending on the values of U and H, the portfolio risk index may be less than, equal to, or greater than the target value of 700. To represent these possibilities mathematically, we create the goal equation

$$0.50U + 0.25H = 700 + d_1^+ - d_1^-$$

where

d_1^+ = the amount by which the portfolio risk index exceeds the target value of 700

d_1^- = the amount by which the portfolio risk index is less than the target value of 700

To achieve a goal exactly, the two deviation variables must both equal zero.

In goal programming, d_1^+ and d_1^- are called **deviation variables.** The purpose of deviation variables is to allow for the possibility of not meeting the target value exactly. Consider, for example, a portfolio that consists of $U = 2000$ shares of U.S. Oil and $H = 0$ shares of Hub Properties. The portfolio risk index is $0.50(2000) + 0.25(0) = 1000$. In this case, $d_1^+ = 300$ reflects the fact that the portfolio risk index exceeds the target value by 300 units; note also that since d_1^+ is greater than zero, the value of d_1^- must be zero. For a portfolio consisting of $U = 0$ shares of U.S. Oil and $H = 1000$ shares of Hub Properties, the portfolio risk index would be $0.50(0) + 0.25(1000) = 250$. In this case, $d_1^- = 450$ and $d_1^+ = 0$, indicating that the solution provides a portfolio risk index of 450 less than the target value of 700.

In general, the letter d is used for deviation variables in a goal programming model. A superscript of plus (+) or minus (−) is used to indicate whether the variable corresponds to a positive or negative deviation from the target value. If we bring the deviation variables to the left-hand side, we can rewrite the goal equation for the primary goal as

$$0.50U + 0.25H - d_1^+ + d_1^- = 700$$

Note that the value on the right-hand side of the goal equation is the target value for the goal. The left-hand side of the goal equation consists of two parts:

1. A function that defines the amount of goal achievement in terms of the decision variables (e.g., $0.50U + 0.25H$)
2. Deviation variables representing the difference between the target value for the goal and the level achieved

To develop a goal equation for the secondary goal, we begin by writing a function representing the annual return for the investment:

$$\text{Annual return} = 3U + 5H$$

Then we define two deviation variables that represent the amount of over- or underachievement of the goal. Doing so, we obtain

d_2^+ = the amount by which the annual return for the portfolio is greater than the target value of \$9000

d_2^- = the amount by which the annual return for the portfolio is less than the target value of \$9000

Using these two deviation variables, we write the goal equation for goal 2 as

$$3U + 5H = 9000 + d_2^+ - d_2^-$$

or

$$3U + 5H - d_2^+ + d_2^- = 9000$$

This step completes the development of the goal equations and the constraints for the Nicolo portfolio problem. We are now ready to develop an appropriate objective function for the problem.

Developing an Objective Function with Preemptive Priorities

The objective function in a goal programming model calls for minimizing a function of the deviation variables. In the portfolio selection problem, the most important goal, denoted P_1, is to find a portfolio with a risk index of 700 or less. This problem has only two goals, and the client is unwilling to accept a portfolio risk index greater than 700 to achieve the secondary annual return goal. Therefore, the secondary goal is denoted P_2. As we stated previously, these goal priorities are referred to as preemptive priorities because the satisfaction of a higher level goal cannot be traded for the satisfaction of a lower level goal.

Goal programming problems with preemptive priorities are solved by treating priority level 1 goals (P_1) first in an objective function. The idea is to start by finding a solution that comes closest to satisfying the priority level 1 goals. This solution is then modified by solving a problem with an objective function involving only priority level 2 goals (P_2); however, revisions in the solution are permitted only if they do not hinder achievement of the P_1 goals. In general, solving a goal programming problem with preemptive priorities involves solving a sequence of linear programs with different objective functions; P_1 goals are considered first, P_2 goals second, P_3 goals third, and so on. At each stage of the procedure, a revision in the solution is permitted only if it causes no reduction in the achievement of a higher priority goal.

We must solve one linear program for each priority level.

The number of linear programs that we must solve in sequence to develop the solution to a goal programming problem is determined by the number of priority levels. One linear program must be solved for each priority level. We will call the first linear program solved the priority level 1 problem, the second linear program solved the priority level 2 problem, and so on. Each linear program is obtained from the one at the next higher level by changing the objective function and adding a constraint.

We first formulate the objective function for the priority level 1 problem. The client stated that the portfolio risk index should not exceed 700. Is underachieving the target value of 700 a concern? Clearly, the answer is no because portfolio risk index values of less than 700 correspond to less risk. Is overachieving the target value of 700 a concern? The answer is yes because portfolios with a risk index greater than 700 correspond to unacceptable levels of risk. Thus, the objective function corresponding to the priority level 1 linear program should minimize the value of d_1^+.

The goal equations and the funds available constraint have already been developed. Thus, the priority level 1 linear program can now be stated.

P_1 Problem

$$\begin{aligned}
&\text{Min} \quad d_1^+ \\
&\text{s.t.} \\
&\quad 25U + 50H &&\leq 80{,}000 \quad \text{Funds available} \\
&\quad 0.50U + 0.25H - d_1^+ + d_1^- &&= 700 \quad P_1 \text{ goal} \\
&\quad 3U + 5H - d_2^+ + d_2^- &&= 9000 \quad P_2 \text{ goal} \\
&\quad U, H, d_1^+, d_1^-, d_2^+, d_2^- \geq 0
\end{aligned}$$

Graphical Solution Procedure

One approach that can often be used to solve a difficult problem is to break the problem into two or more smaller or easier problems. The linear programming procedure we use to solve the goal programming problem is based on this approach.

The graphical solution procedure for goal programming is similar to that for linear programming presented in Chapter 2. The only difference is that the procedure for goal programming involves a separate solution for each priority level. Recall that the linear programming graphical solution procedure uses a graph to display the values for the decision variables. Because the decision variables are nonnegative, we consider only that portion of the graph where $U \geq 0$ and $H \geq 0$. Recall also that every point on the graph is called a *solution point.*

We begin the graphical solution procedure for the Nicolo Investment problem by identifying all solution points that satisfy the available funds constraint:

$$25U + 50H \leq 80{,}000$$

The shaded region in Figure 15.1, feasible portfolios, consists of all points that satisfy this constraint—that is, values of U and H for which $25U + 50H \leq 80{,}000$.

The objective for the priority level 1 linear program is to minimize d_1^+, the amount by which the portfolio index exceeds the target value of 700. Recall that the P_1 goal equation is

$$0.50U + 0.25H - d_1^+ + d_1^- = 700$$

When the P_1 goal is met exactly, $d_1^+ = 0$ and $d_1^- = 0$; the goal equation then reduces to $0.50U + 0.25H = 700$. Figure 15.2 shows the graph of this equation; the shaded region identifies all solution points that satisfy the available funds constraint and also result in the value of $d_1^+ = 0$. Thus, the shaded region contains all the feasible solution points that achieve the priority level 1 goal.

At this point, we solved the priority level 1 problem. Note that alternative optimal solutions are possible; in fact, all solution points in the shaded region in Figure 15.2 maintain a portfolio risk index of 700 or less, and hence $d_1^+ = 0$.

FIGURE 15.1 PORTFOLIOS THAT SATISFY THE AVAILABLE FUNDS CONSTRAINT

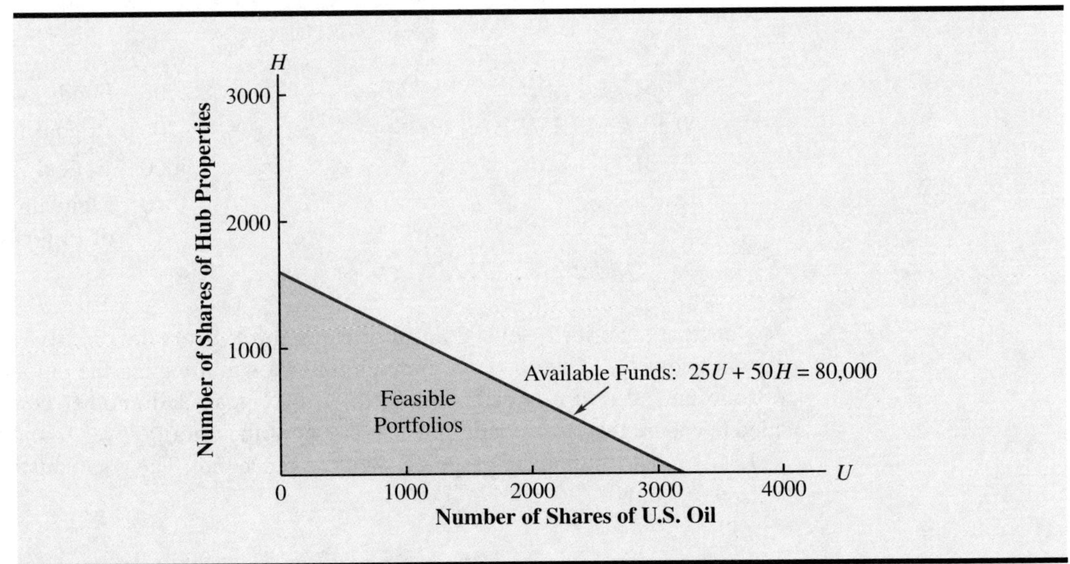

FIGURE 15.2 PORTFOLIOS THAT SATISFY THE P_1 GOAL

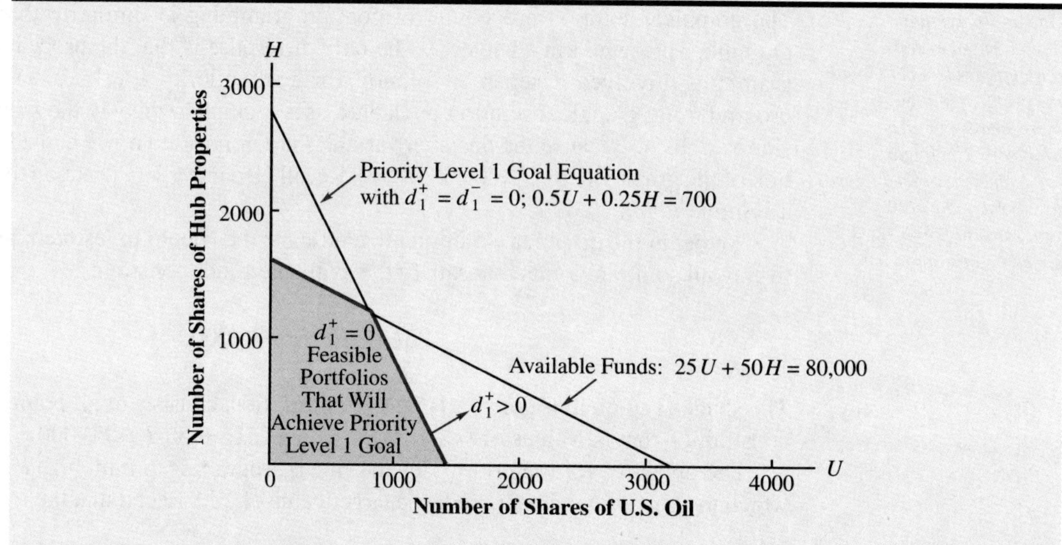

The priority level 2 goal for the Nicolo Investment problem is to find a portfolio that will provide an annual return of at least \$9000. Is overachieving the target value of \$9000 a concern? Clearly, the answer is no because portfolios with an annual return of more than \$9000 correspond to higher returns. Is underachieving the target value of \$9000 a concern? The answer is yes because portfolios with an annual return of less than \$9000 are not acceptable to the client. Thus, the objective function corresponding to the priority level 2 linear program should minimize the value of d_2^-. However, because goal 2 is a secondary goal, the solution to the priority level 2 linear program must not degrade the optimal solution to the priority level 1 problem. Thus, the priority level 2 linear program can now be stated.

P_2 Problem

$$
\begin{aligned}
&\text{Min} \quad d_2^- \\
&\text{s.t.} \\
&\quad 25U + 50H \qquad\qquad\qquad\qquad\qquad \leq 80{,}000 \quad \text{Funds available} \\
&\quad 0.50U + 0.25H - d_1^+ + d_1^- \qquad\quad = 700 \quad P_1 \text{ goal} \\
&\quad 3U + 5H \qquad\qquad\qquad - d_2^+ + d_2^- = 9000 \quad P_2 \text{ goal} \\
&\quad d_1^+ \qquad\qquad\qquad\qquad\qquad\qquad = 0 \quad \text{Maintain achievement of } P_1 \text{ goal} \\
&\quad U, H, d_1^+, d_1^-, d_2^+, d_2^- \geq 0
\end{aligned}
$$

Note that the priority level 2 linear program differs from the priority level 1 linear program in two ways. The objective function involves minimizing the amount by which the portfolio annual return underachieves the level 2 goal, and another constraint has been added to ensure that no amount of achievement of the priority level 1 goal is sacrificed.

Let us now continue the graphical solution procedure. The goal equation for the priority level 2 goal is

$$3U + 5H - d_2^+ + d_2^- = 9000$$

When both d_2^+ and d_2^- equal zero, this equation reduces to $3U + 5H = 9000$; we show the graph with this equation in Figure 15.3.

At this stage, we cannot consider any solution point that will degrade the achievement of the priority level 1 goal. Figure 15.3 shows that no solution points will achieve the priority level 2 goal and maintain the values we were able to achieve for the priority level 1 goal. In fact, the best solution that can be obtained when considering the priority level 2 goal is given by the point ($U = 800, H = 1200$); in other words, this point comes the closest to satisfying the priority level 2 goal from among those solutions satisfying the priority level 1 goal. Because the annual return corresponding to this solution point is \$3(800) + \$5(1200) = \$8400, identifying a portfolio that will satisfy both the priority level 1 and the priority level 2 goals is impossible. In fact, the best solution underachieves goal 2 by $d_2^- =$ \$9000 − \$8400 = \$600.

Thus, the goal programming solution for the Nicolo Investment problem recommends that the \$80,000 available for investment be used to purchase 800 shares of U.S. Oil and 1200 shares of Hub Properties. Note that the priority level 1 goal of a portfolio risk index of 700 or less has been achieved. However, the priority level 2 goal of at least a \$9000 annual return is not achievable. The annual return for the recommended portfolio is \$8400.

In summary, the graphical solution procedure for goal programming involves the following steps.

Step 1. Identify the feasible solution points that satisfy the problem constraints.
Step 2. Identify all feasible solutions that achieve the highest-priority goal; if no feasible solutions will achieve the highest-priority goal, identify the solution(s) that comes closest to achieving it.
Step 3. Move down one priority level, and determine the "best" solution possible without sacrificing any achievement of higher priority goals.
Step 4. Repeat step 3 until all priority levels have been considered.

FIGURE 15.3 BEST SOLUTION WITH RESPECT TO BOTH GOALS (SOLUTION TO P_2 PROBLEM)

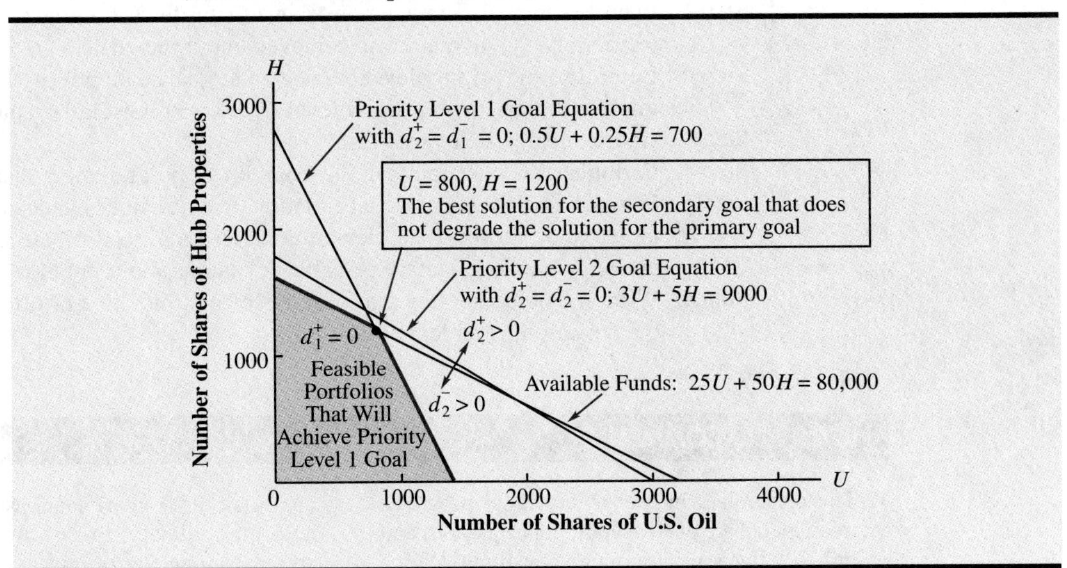

Problem 2 will test your ability to formulate a goal programming model and use the graphical solution procedure to obtain a solution.

Although the graphical solution procedure is a convenient method for solving goal programming problems involving two decision variables, the solution of larger problems requires a computer-aided approach. In Section 15.2 we illustrate how to use a computer software package to solve more complex goal programming problems.

Goal Programming Model

As we stated, preemptive goal programming problems are solved as a sequence of linear programs: one linear program for each priority level. However, notation that permits writing a goal programming problem in one concise statement is helpful.

In writing the overall objective for the portfolio selection problem, we must write the objective function in a way that reminds us of the preemptive priorities. We can do so by writing the objective function as

$$\text{Min} \quad P_1(d_1^+) + P_2(d_2^-)$$

The priority levels P_1 and P_2 are not numerical weights on the deviation variables, but simply labels that remind us of the priority levels for the goals.

We now write the complete goal programming model as

$$\begin{array}{lllll}
\text{Min} & P_1(d_1^+) + P_2(d_2^-) & & & \\
\text{s.t.} & & & & \\
& 25U + 50H & \leq & 80{,}000 & \text{Funds available} \\
& 0.50U + 0.25H - d_1^+ + d_1^- & = & 700 & P_1 \text{ goal} \\
& 3U + 5H - d_2^+ + d_2^- & = & 9000 & P_2 \text{ goal} \\
& U, H, d_1^+, d_1^-, d_2^+, d_2^- \geq 0 & & &
\end{array}$$

With the exception of the P_1 and P_2 priority levels in the objective function, this model is a linear programming model. The solution of this linear program involves solving a sequence of linear programs involving goals at decreasing priority levels.

We now summarize the procedure used to develop a goal programming model.

Step 1. Identify the goals and any constraints that reflect resource capacities or other restrictions that may prevent achievement of the goals.
Step 2. Determine the priority level of each goal; goals with priority level P_1 are most important, those with priority level P_2 are next most important, and so on.
Step 3. Define the decision variables.
Step 4. Formulate the constraints in the usual linear programming fashion.
Step 5. For each goal, develop a goal equation, with the right-hand side specifying the target value for the goal. Deviation variables d_1^+ and d_1^- are included in each goal equation to reflect the possible deviations above or below the target value.
Step 6. Write the objective function in terms of minimizing a prioritized function of the deviation variables.

NOTES AND COMMENTS

1. The constraints in the general goal programming model are of two types: goal equations and ordinary linear programming constraints. Some analysts call the goal equations *goal constraints* and the ordinary linear programming constraints *system constraints.*

2. You might think of the general goal programming model as having "hard" and "soft" constraints. The hard constraints are the ordinary linear programming constraints that cannot be violated. The soft constraints are the ones resulting from the goal equations. Soft constraints can be violated but with a penalty for doing so. The penalty is reflected by the coefficient of the deviation variable in the objective function. In Section 15.2 we illustrate this point with a problem that has a coefficient of 2 for one of the deviation variables.
3. Note that the constraint added in moving from the linear programming problem at one priority level to the linear programming problem at the next lower priority level becomes a hard constraint. No amount of achievement of a higher priority goal may be sacrificed to achieve a lower priority goal.

15.2 GOAL PROGRAMMING: SOLVING MORE COMPLEX PROBLEMS

In Section 15.1 we formulated and solved a goal programming model that involved one priority level 1 goal and one priority level 2 goal. In this section we show how to formulate and solve goal programming models that involve multiple goals within the same priority level. Although specially developed computer programs can solve goal programming models, these programs are not as readily available as general purpose linear programming software packages. Thus, the computer solution procedure outlined in this section develops a solution to a goal programming model by solving a sequence of linear programming models with a general purpose linear programming software package.

Suncoast Office Supplies Problem

The management of Suncoast Office Supplies establishes monthly goals, or quotas, for the types of customers contacted. For the next four weeks, Suncoast's customer contact strategy calls for the salesforce, which consists of four salespeople, to make 200 contacts with established customers who have previously purchased supplies from the firm. In addition, the strategy calls for 120 contacts of new customers. The purpose of this latter goal is to ensure that the salesforce is continuing to investigate new sources of sales.

After making allowances for travel and waiting time, as well as for demonstration and direct sales time, Suncoast allocated two hours of salesforce effort to each contact of an established customer. New customer contacts tend to take longer and require three hours per contact. Normally, each salesperson works 40 hours per week, or 160 hours over the four-week planning horizon; under a normal work schedule, the four salespeople will have $4(160) = 640$ hours of salesforce time available for customer contacts.

Management is willing to use some overtime, if needed, but is also willing to accept a solution that uses less than the scheduled 640 hours available. However, management wants both overtime and underutilization of the workforce limited to no more than 40 hours over the four-week period. Thus, in terms of overtime, management's goal is to use no more than $640 + 40 = 680$ hours of salesforce time; and in terms of labor utilization, management's goal is to use at least $640 - 40 = 600$ hours of salesforce time.

In addition to the customer contact goals, Suncoast established a goal regarding sales volume. Based on its experience, Suncoast estimates that each established customer contacted will generate \$250 of sales and that each new customer contacted will generate \$125 of sales. Management wants to generate sales revenue of at least \$70,000 for the next month.

Given Suncoast's small salesforce and the short time frame involved, management decided that the overtime goal and the labor utilization goal are both priority level 1 goals. Management also concluded that the \$70,000 sales revenue goal should be a priority level 2 goal and that the two customer contact goals should be priority level 3 goals. Based on these priorities, we can now summarize the goals.

Priority Level 1 Goals

Goal 1: Do not use any more than 680 hours of salesforce time.

Goal 2: Do not use any less than 600 hours of salesforce time.

Priority Level 2 Goal

Goal 3: Generate sales revenue of at least $70,000.

Priority Level 3 Goals

Goal 4: Call on at least 200 established customers.

Goal 5: Call on at least 120 new customers.

Formulating the Goal Equations

Next, we must define the decision variables whose values will be used to determine whether we are able to achieve the goals. Let

E = the number of established customers contacted

N = the number of new customers contacted

Using these decision variables and appropriate deviation variables, we can develop a goal equation for each goal. The procedure used parallels the approach introduced in the preceding section. A summary of the results obtained is shown for each goal.

Goal 1

$$2E + 3N - d_1^+ + d_1^- = 680$$

where

d_1^+ = the amount by which the number of hours used by the salesforce is greater than the target value of 680 hours

d_1^- = the amount by which the number of hours used by the salesforce is less than the target value of 680 hours

Goal 2

$$2E + 3N - d_2^+ + d_2^- = 600$$

where

d_2^+ = the amount by which the number of hours used by the salesforce is greater than the target value of 600 hours

d_2^- = the amount by which the number of hours used by the salesforce is less than the target value of 600 hours

Goal 3

$$250E + 125N - d_3^+ + d_3^- = 70{,}000$$

where

d_3^+ = the amount by which the sales revenue is greater than the target value of \$70,000

d_3^- = the amount by which the sales revenue is less than the target value of \$70,000

Goal 4

$$E - d_4^+ + d_4^- = 200$$

where

d_4^+ = the amount by which the number of established customer contacts is greater than the target value of 200 established customer contacts

d_4^- = the amount by which the number of established customer contacts is less than the target value of 200 established customer contacts

Goal 5

$$N - d_5^+ + d_5^- = 120$$

where

d_5^+ = the amount by which the number of new customer contacts is greater than the target value of 120 new customer contacts

d_5^- = the amount by which the number of new customer contacts is less than the target value of 120 new customer contacts

Formulating the Objective Function

To develop the objective function for the Suncoast Office Supplies problem, we begin by considering the priority level 1 goals. When considering goal 1, if $d_1^+ = 0$, we will have found a solution that uses no more than 680 hours of salesforce time. Because solutions for which d_1^+ is greater than zero represent overtime beyond the desired level, the objective function should minimize the value of d_1^+. When considering goal 2, if $d_2^- = 0$, we will have found a solution that uses *at least* 600 hours of salesforce time. If d_2^- is greater than zero, however, labor utilization will not have reached the acceptable level. Thus, the objective function for the priority level 1 goals should minimize the value of d_2^-. Because both priority level 1 goals are equally important, the objective function for the priority level 1 problem is

$$\text{Min} \quad d_1^+ + d_2^-$$

In considering the priority level 2 goal, we note that management wants to achieve sales revenues of at least \$70,000. If $d_3^- = 0$, Suncoast will achieve revenues of *at least* \$70,000, and if $d_3^- > 0$, revenues of less than \$70,000 will be obtained. Thus, the objective function for the priority level 2 problem is

$$\text{Min} \quad d_3^-$$

Next, we consider what the objective function must be for the priority level 3 problem. When considering goal 4, if $d_4^- = 0$, we will have found a solution with *at least* 200 established customer contacts; however, if $d_4^- > 0$, we will have underachieved the goal of contacting at least 200 established customers. Thus, for goal 4 the objective is to minimize d_4^-. When considering goal 5, if $d_5^- = 0$, we will have found a solution with *at least* 120 new customer contacts; however, if $d_5^- > 0$, we will have underachieved the goal of contacting at least 120 new customers. Thus, for goal 5 the objective is to minimize d_5^-. If both goals 4 and 5 are equal in importance, the objective function for the priority level 3 problem would be

$$\text{Min} \quad d_4^- + d_5^-$$

However, suppose that management believes that generating new customers is vital to the long-run success of the firm and that goal 5 should be weighted more than goal 4. If management believes that goal 5 is twice as important as goal 4, the objective function for the priority level 3 problem would be

$$\text{Min} \quad d_4^- + 2d_5^-$$

Combining the objective functions for all three priority levels, we obtain the overall objective function for the Suncoast Office Supplies problem:

$$\text{Min} \quad P_1(d_1^+) + P_1(d_2^-) + P_2(d_3^-) + P_3(d_4^-) + P_3(2d_5^-)$$

As we indicated previously, P_1, P_2, and P_3 are simply labels that remind us that goals 1 and 2 are the priority level 1 goals, goal 3 is the priority level 2 goal, and goals 4 and 5 are the priority level 3 goals. We can now write the complete goal programming model for the Suncoast Office Supplies problem as follows:

$$\begin{array}{ll}
\text{Min} & P_1(d_1^+) + P_1(d_2^-) + P_2(d_3^-) + P_3(d_4^-) + P_3(2d_5^-) \\
\text{s.t.} & \\
& \begin{array}{rlr}
2E + 3N - d_1^+ + d_1^- & = 680 & \text{Goal 1} \\
2E + 3N - d_2^+ + d_2^- & = 600 & \text{Goal 2} \\
250E + 125N - d_3^+ + d_3^- & = 70{,}000 & \text{Goal 3} \\
E - d_4^+ + d_4^- & = 200 & \text{Goal 4} \\
N - d_5^+ + d_5^- & = 120 & \text{Goal 5}
\end{array} \\
& E, N, d_1^+, d_1^-, d_2^+, d_2^-, d_3^+, d_3^-, d_4^+, d_4^-, d_5^+, d_5^- \geq 0
\end{array}$$

Computer Solution

The following computer procedure develops a solution to a goal programming model by solving a sequence of linear programming problems. The first problem comprises all the constraints and all the goal equations for the complete goal programming model; however, the objective function for this problem involves only the P_1 priority level goals. Again, we refer to this problem as the P_1 problem.

Whatever the solution to the P_1 problem, a P_2 problem is formed by adding a constraint to the P_1 model that ensures that subsequent problems will not degrade the solution obtained for the P_1 problem. The objective function for the priority level 2 problem takes into consideration only the P_2 goals. We continue the process until we have considered all priority levels. We illustrate the procedure for the Suncoast Office Supplies problem using the linear programming module of The Management Scientist software package.

To solve the Suncoast Office Supplies problem, we begin by solving the P_1 problem:

$$
\begin{aligned}
\text{Min} \quad & d_1^+ + d_2^- \\
\text{s.t.} \quad & \\
& 2E + 3N - d_1^+ + d_1^- = 680 \quad \text{Goal 1} \\
& 2E + 3N - d_2^+ + d_2^- = 600 \quad \text{Goal 2} \\
& 250E + 125N - d_3^+ + d_3^- = 70{,}000 \quad \text{Goal 3} \\
& E - d_4^+ + d_4^- = 200 \quad \text{Goal 4} \\
& N - d_5^+ + d_5^- = 120 \quad \text{Goal 5} \\
& E, N, d_1^+, d_1^-, d_2^+, d_2^-, d_3^+, d_3^-, d_4^+, d_4^-, d_5^+, d_5^- \geq 0
\end{aligned}
$$

In Figure 15.4 we show The Management Scientist solution for this linear program. Note that D1PLUS refers to d_1^+, D2MINUS refers to d_2^-, D1MINUS refers to d_1^-, and so on. The solution shows $E = 250$ established customer contacts and $N = 60$ new customer contacts. Because D1PLUS = 0 and D2MINUS = 0, we see that the solution achieves both goals 1 and 2. Alternatively, the value of the objective function is 0, confirming that both priority level 1 goals have been achieved. Next, we consider goal 3, the priority level 2 goal, which is to minimize D3MINUS. The solution in Figure 15.4 shows that D3MINUS = 0. Thus, the solution of $E = 250$ established customer contacts and $N = 60$ new customer contacts also achieves goal 3, the priority level 2 goal, which is to generate a sales revenue of at least \$70,000. The fact that D3PLUS = 0 indicates that the current

FIGURE 15.4 THE MANAGEMENT SCIENTIST SOLUTION OF THE P_1 PROBLEM

```
Objective Function Value =      0.000

     Variable              Value              Reduced Costs
  --------------     ---------------       -----------------
       D1PLUS                0.000                  1.000
       D2MINUS               0.000                  1.000
       E                   250.000                  0.000
       N                    60.000                  0.000
       D1MINUS               0.000                  0.000
       D2PLUS               80.000                  0.000
       D3PLUS                0.000                  0.000
       D3MINUS               0.000                  0.000
       D4PLUS               50.000                  0.000
       D4MINUS               0.000                  0.000
       D5PLUS                0.000                  0.000
       D5MINUS              60.000                  0.000
```

solution satisfies goal 3 exactly at $70,000. Finally, the solution in Figure 15.4 shows D4PLUS = 50 and D5MINUS = 60. These values tell us that goal 4 of the priority level 3 goals is overachieved by 50 established customers, but that goal 5 is underachieved by 60 new customers. As this point, both the priority level 1 and 2 goals have been achieved, but we need to solve another linear program to determine whether a solution can be identified that will satisfy both of the priority level 3 goals. Therefore, we go directly to the P_3 problem.

The linear programming model for the P_3 problem is a modification of the linear programming model for the P_1 problem. Specifically, the objective function for the P_3 problem is expressed in terms of the priority level 3 goals. Thus, the P_3 problem objective function becomes minimize D4MINUS + 2D5MINUS. The original five constraints of the P_1 problem appear in the P_3 problem. However, two additional constraints must be added to ensure that the solution to the P_3 problem continues to satisfy the priority level 1 and priority level 2 goals. Thus, we add the priority level 1 constraint D1PLUS + D2MINUS = 0 and the priority level 2 constraint D3MINUS = 0. Making these modifications to the P_1 problem, we obtain the solution to the P_3 problem shown in Figure 15.5.

Referring to Figure 15.5, we see the objective function value of 120 indicates that the priority level 3 goals cannot be achieved. Since D5MINUS = 60, the optimal solution of $E = 250$ and $N = 60$ results in 60 fewer new customer contacts than desired. However, the fact that we solved the P_3 problem tells us the goal programming solution comes as close as possible to satisfying priority level 3 goals given the achievement of both the priority level 1 and 2 goals. Because all priority levels have been considered, the solution procedure is finished. The optimal solution for Suncoast is to contact 250 established customers and 60 new customers. Although this solution will not achieve management's goal of contacting at least 120 new customers, it does achieve each of the other goals specified. If management isn't happy with this solution, a different set of priorities could be considered. Management must keep in mind, however, that in any situation involving multiple goals at different priority levels, rarely will all the goals be achieved with existing resources.

FIGURE 15.5 THE MANAGEMENT SCIENTIST SOLUTION OF THE P_3 PROBLEM

```
Objective Function Value =  120.000

    Variable                  Value               Reduced Costs
  --------------         ---------------        ----------------
    D1PLUS                        0.000                   0.000
    D2MINUS                       0.000                   1.000
    E                           250.000                   0.000
    N                            60.000                   0.000
    D1MINUS                       0.000                   1.000
    D2PLUS                       80.000                   0.000
    D3PLUS                        0.000                   0.008
    D3MINUS                       0.000                   0.000
    D4PLUS                       50.000                   0.000
    D4MINUS                       0.000                   1.000
    D5PLUS                        0.000                   2.000
    D5MINUS                      60.000                   0.000
```

NOTES AND COMMENTS

1. Not all goal programming problems involve multiple priority levels. For problems with one priority level, only one linear program needs to be solved to obtain the goal programming solution. The analyst simply minimizes the weighted deviations from the goals. Trade-offs are permitted among the goals because they are all at the same priority level.
2. The goal programming approach can be used when the analyst is confronted with an infeasible solution to an ordinary linear program. Reformulating some constraints as goal equations with deviation variables allows a solution that minimizes the weighted sum of the deviation variables. Often, this approach will suggest a reasonable solution.
3. The approach that we used to solve goal programming problems with multiple priority levels is to solve a sequence of linear programs. These linear programs are closely related so that complete reformulation and solution are not necessary. By changing the objective function and adding a constraint, we can go from one linear program to the next.

15.3 SCORING MODELS

A scoring model is a relatively quick and easy way to identify the best decision alternative for a multicriteria decision problem. We will demonstrate the use of a scoring model for a job selection application.

Assume that a graduating college student with a double major in finance and accounting received job offers for the following three positions:

- A financial analyst for an investment firm located in Chicago
- An accountant for a manufacturing firm located in Denver
- An auditor for a CPA firm located in Houston

When asked about which job is preferred, the student made the following comments: "The financial analyst position in Chicago provides the best opportunity for my long-run career advancement. However, I would prefer living in Denver rather than in Chicago or Houston. On the other hand, I liked the management style and philosophy at the Houston CPA firm the best." The student's statement points out that this example is clearly a multicriteria decision problem. Considering only the *long-run career advancement* criterion, the financial analyst position in Chicago is the preferred decision alternative. Considering only the *location* criterion, the best decision alternative is the accountant position in Denver. Finally, considering only the *management style* criterion, the best alternative is the auditor position with the CPA firm in Houston. For most individuals, a multicriteria decision problem that requires a trade-off among the several criteria is difficult to solve. In this section, we describe how a **scoring model** can assist in analyzing a multicriteria decision problem and help identify the preferred decision alternative.

The steps required to develop a scoring model are as follows:

A scoring model enables a decision maker to identify the criteria and indicate the weight or importance of each criterion.

Step 1. Develop a list of the criteria to be considered. The criteria are the factors that the decision maker considers relevant for evaluating each decision alternative.

Step 2. Assign a weight to each criterion that describes the criterion's relative importance. Let

$$w_i = \text{the weight for criterion } i$$

Step 3. Assign a rating for each criterion that shows how well each decision alternative satisfies the criterion. Let

$$r_{ij} = \text{the rating for criterion } i \text{ and decision alternative } j$$

Step 4. Compute the score for each decision alternative. Let

$$S_j = \text{score for decision alternative } j$$

The equation used to compute S_j is as follows:

$$S_j = \sum_i w_i r_{ij} \qquad (15.1)$$

Step 5. Order the decision alternatives from the highest score to the lowest score to provide the scoring model's ranking of the decision alternatives. The decision alternative with the highest score is the recommended decision alternative.

Let us return to the multicriteria job selection problem the graduating student was facing and illustrate the use of a scoring model to assist in the decision-making process. In carrying out step 1 of the scoring model procedure, the student listed seven criteria as important factors in the decision-making process. These criteria are as follows:

- Career advancement
- Location
- Management style
- Salary
- Prestige
- Job security
- Enjoyment of the work

In step 2, a weight is assigned to each criterion to indicate the criterion's relative importance in the decision-making process. For example, using a five-point scale, the question used to assign a weight to the career advancement criterion would be as follows:

Relative to the other criteria you are considering, how important is career advancement?

Importance	Weight
Very important	5
Somewhat important	4
Average importance	3
Somewhat unimportant	2
Very unimportant	1

By repeating this question for each of the seven criteria, the student provided the criterion weights shown in Table 15.1. Using this table, we see that career advancement and enjoyment of the work are the two most important criteria, each receiving a weight of 5. The management style and job security criteria are both considered somewhat important, and thus each received a weight of 4. Location and salary are considered average in importance, each

TABLE 15.1 WEIGHTS FOR THE SEVEN JOB SELECTION CRITERIA

Criterion	Importance	Weight (w_i)
Career advancement	Very important	5
Location	Average importance	3
Management style	Somewhat important	4
Salary	Average importance	3
Prestige	Somewhat unimportant	2
Job security	Somewhat important	4
Enjoyment of the work	Very important	5

receiving a weight of 3. Finally, because prestige is considered to be somewhat unimportant, it received a weight of 2.

The weights shown in Table 15.1 are subjective values provided by the student. A different student would most likely choose to weight the criteria differently. One of the key advantages of a scoring model is that it uses the subjective weights that most closely reflect the preferences of the individual decision maker.

In step 3, each decision alternative is rated in terms of how well it satisfies each criterion. For example, using a nine-point scale, the question used to assign a rating for the "financial analyst in Chicago" alternative and the career advancement criterion would be as follows:

To what extent does the financial analyst position in Chicago satisfy your career advancement criterion?

Level of Satisfaction	Rating
Extremely high	9
Very high	8
High	7
Slightly high	6
Average	5
Slightly low	4
Low	3
Very low	2
Extremely low	1

A score of 8 on this question would indicate that the student believes the financial analyst position would be rated "very high" in terms of satisfying the career advancement criterion.

This scoring process must be completed for each combination of decision alternative and decision criterion. Because seven decision criteria and three decision alternatives need to be considered, $7 \times 3 = 21$ ratings must be provided. Table 15.2 summarizes the student's responses. Scanning this table provides some insights about how the student rates each decision criterion and decision alternative combination. For example, a rating of 9, corresponding to an extremely high level of satisfaction, only appears for the management style criterion and the auditor position in Houston. Thus, considering all combinations, the student rates the auditor position in Houston as the very best in terms of satisfying the management criterion. The lowest rating in the table is a 3 that appears for the location criterion

TABLE 15.2 RATINGS FOR EACH DECISION CRITERION AND EACH DECISION ALTERNATIVE COMBINATION

	Decision Alternative		
Criterion	Financial Analyst Chicago	Accountant Denver	Auditor Houston
Career advancement	8	6	4
Location	3	8	7
Management style	5	6	9
Salary	6	7	5
Prestige	7	5	4
Job security	4	7	6
Enjoyment of the work	8	6	5

of the financial analyst position in Chicago. This rating indicates that Chicago is rated "low" in terms of satisfying the student's location criterion. Other insights and interpretations are possible, but the question at this point is how a scoring model uses the data in Tables 15.1 and 15.2 to identify the best overall decision alternative.

Step 4 of the procedure shows that equation (15.1) is used to compute the score for each decision alternative. The data in Table 15.1 provide the weight for each criterion (w_i) and the data in Table 15.2 provide the ratings of each decision alternative for each criterion (r_{ij}). Thus, for decision alternative 1, the score for the financial analyst position in Chicago is

By comparing the scores for each criterion, a decision maker can learn why a particular decision alternative has the highest score.

$$S_1 = \sum_i w_i r_{i1} = 5(8) + 3(3) + 4(5) + 3(6) + 2(7) + 4(4) + 5(8) = 157$$

The scores for the other decision alternatives are computed in the same manner. The computations are summarized in Table 15.3.

From Table 15.3, we see that the highest score of 167 corresponds to the accountant position in Denver. Thus, the accountant position in Denver is the recommended decision al-

TABLE 15.3 COMPUTATION OF SCORES FOR THE THREE DECISION ALTERNATIVES

		Decision Alternative					
		Financial Analyst Chicago		Accountant Denver		Auditor Houston	
Criterion	Weight w_i	Rating r_{i1}	Score $w_i r_{i1}$	Rating r_{i2}	Score $w_i r_{i2}$	Rating r_{i3}	Score $w_i r_{i3}$
Career advancement	5	8	40	6	30	4	20
Location	3	3	9	8	24	7	21
Management style	4	5	20	6	24	9	36
Salary	3	6	18	7	21	5	15
Prestige	2	7	14	5	10	4	8
Job security	4	4	16	7	28	6	24
Enjoyment of the work	5	8	40	6	30	5	25
Score			157		167		149

ternative. The financial analyst position in Chicago, with a score of 157, is ranked second, and the auditor position in Houston, with a score of 149, is ranked third.

The job selection example that illustrates the use of a scoring model involved seven criteria, each of which was assigned a weight from 1 to 5. In other applications the weights assigned to the criteria may be percentages that reflect the importance of each of the criteria. In addition, multicriteria problems often involve additional subcriteria that enable the decision maker to incorporate additional detail into the decision process. For instance, consider the location criterion in the job selection example. This criterion might be further subdivided into the following three subcriteria:

- Affordability of housing
- Recreational opportunities
- Climate

In this case, the three subcriteria would have to be assigned weights, and a score for each decision alternative would have to be computed for each subcriterion. The Management Science in Action, Scoring Model at Ford Motor Company, illustrates how scoring models can be applied for a problem involving four criteria, each of which has several subcriteria. This example also demonstrates the use of percentage weights for the criteria and the wide applicability of scoring models in more complex problem situations.

MANAGEMENT SCIENCE IN ACTION

SCORING MODEL AT FORD MOTOR COMPANY*

Ford Motor Company needed benchmark data in order to set performance targets for future and current model automobiles. A detailed proposal was developed and sent to five suppliers. Three suppliers were considered acceptable for the project.

Because the three suppliers had different capabilities in terms of teardown analysis and testing, Ford developed three project alternatives:

Alternative 1: Supplier C does the entire project alone.

Alternative 2: Supplier A does the testing portion of the project and works with Supplier B to complete the remaining parts of the project.

Alternative 3: Supplier A does the testing portion of the project and works with Supplier C to complete the remaining parts of the project.

For routine projects, selecting the lowest cost alternative might be appropriate. However, because this project involved many nonroutine tasks, Ford incorporated four criteria into the decision process.

The four criteria selected by Ford are as follows:

1. Skill level (effective project leader and a skilled team)
2. Cost containment (ability to stay within approved budget)
3. Timing containment (ability to meet program timing requirements)
4. Hardware display (location and functionality of teardown center and user friendliness)

Using team consensus, a weight of 25% was assigned to each of these criteria; note that these weights indicate that members of the Ford project team considered each criterion to be equally important in the decision process.

Each of the four criteria was further subdivided into subcriteria. For example, the skill-level criterion had four subcriteria: project manager leadership; team structure organization; team players' communication; and past Ford experience. In total, 17 subcriteria were considered. A team-consensus weighting process was used to develop percentage weights for the subcriteria. The weights assigned to the skill-level subcriteria were 40% for project manager leadership; 20% for team structure organization; 20% for team players' communication; and 20% for past Ford experience.

Team members visited all the suppliers and individually rated them for each subcriterion using a 1–10 scale (1-worst, 10-best). Then, in a team

(*continued*)

meeting, consensus ratings were developed. For Alternative 1, the consensus ratings developed for the skill-level subcriteria were 8 for project manager leadership; 8 for team structure organization; 7 for team players' communication; and 8 for past Ford experience. Because the weights assigned to the skill-level subcriteria are 40%, 20%, 20%, and 20%, the rating for Alternative 1 corresponding to the skill-level criterion is

$$\text{Rating} = .4(8) + .2(8) + .2(7) + .2(8) = 7.8$$

In a similar fashion, ratings for Alternative 1 corresponding to each of the other criteria were developed. The results obtained were a rating of 6.8 for cost containment, 6.65 for timing containment, and 8 for hardware display. Using the initial weights of 25% assigned to each criterion, the final rating for Alternative 1 = .25(7.8) + .25(6.8) + .25(6.65) + .25(8) = 7.3. In a similar fashion, a final rating of 7.4 was developed for Alternative 2, and a final rating of 7.5 was developed for Alternative 3. Thus, Alternative 3 was the recommended decision. Subsequent sensitivity analysis on the weights assigned to the criteria showed that Alternative 3 still received equal or higher ratings than Alternative 1 or Alternative 2. These results increased the team's confidence that Alternative 3 was the best choice.

*Based on Senthil A. Gurusami, "Ford's Wrenching Decision," *OR/MS Today* (December 1998): 36–39.

15.4 ANALYTIC HIERARCHY PROCESS

The **analytic hierarchy process (AHP),** developed by Thomas L. Saaty,[1] is designed to solve complex multicriteria decision problems. AHP requires the decision maker to provide judgments about the relative importance of each criterion and then specify a preference for each decision alternative using each criterion. The output of AHP is a prioritized ranking of the decision alternatives based on the overall preferences expressed by the decision maker.

To introduce AHP, we consider a car purchasing decision problem faced by Diane Payne. After a preliminary analysis of the makes and models of several used cars, Diane narrowed her list of decision alternatives to three cars: a Honda Accord, a Saturn, and a Chevrolet Cavalier. Table 15.4 summarizes the information Diane collected about these cars.

Diane decided that the following criteria were relevant for her car selection decision process:

- Price
- Miles per gallon (MPG)
- Comfort
- Style

Data regarding the Price and MPG are provided in Table 15.4. However, measures of the Comfort and Style cannot be specified so directly. Diane will need to consider factors such as the car's interior, type of audio system, ease of entry, seat adjustments, and driver visibility in order to determine the comfort level of each car. The style criterion will have to be based on Diane's subjective evaluation of the color and the general appearance of each car.

AHP allows a decision maker to express personal preferences and subjective judgments about the various aspects of a multicriteria problem.

Even when a criterion such as price can be easily measured, subjectivity becomes an issue whenever a decision maker indicates his or her personal preference for the decision alternatives based on price. For instance, the price of the Accord ($13,100) is $3600 more than the price of the Cavalier ($9500). The $3600 difference might represent a great deal of money to one person, but not much of a difference to another person. Thus, whether the Accord is considered "extremely more expensive" than the Cavalier or perhaps only "moder-

[1]T. Saaty, *Decision Making for Leaders: The Analytic Hierarchy Process for Decisions in a Complex World,* 3d. ed., RWS, 1999.

TABLE 15.4 INFORMATION FOR THE CAR SELECTION PROBLEM

	Decision Alternative		
Characteristics	**Accord**	**Saturn**	**Cavalier**
Price	$13,100	$11,200	$9500
Color	Black	Red	Blue
Miles per gallon	19	23	28
Interior	Deluxe	Above Average	Standard
Body type	4-door midsize	2-door sport	2-door compact
Sound system	AM/FM, tape, CD	AM/FM	AM/FM

ately more expensive" than the Cavalier depends upon the financial status and the subjective opinion of the person making the comparison. An advantage of AHP is that it can handle situations in which the unique subjective judgments of the individual decision maker constitute an important part of the decision-making process.

Developing the Hierarchy

The first step in AHP is to develop a graphical representation of the problem in terms of the overall goal, the criteria to be used, and the decision alternatives. Such a graph depicts the **hierarchy** for the problem. Figure 15.6 shows the hierarchy for the car selection problem. Note that the first level of the hierarchy shows that the overall goal is to select the best car. At the second level, the four criteria (Price, MPG, Comfort, and Style) each contribute to the achievement of the overall goal. Finally, at the third level, each decision alternative—Accord, Saturn, and Cavalier—contributes to each criterion in a unique way.

Using AHP, the decision maker specifies judgments about the relative importance of each of the four criteria in terms of its contribution to the achievement of the overall goal. At the next level, the decision maker indicates a preference for each decision alternative based on each criterion. A mathematical process is used to synthesize the information on

FIGURE 15.6 HIERARCHY FOR THE CAR SELECTION PROBLEM

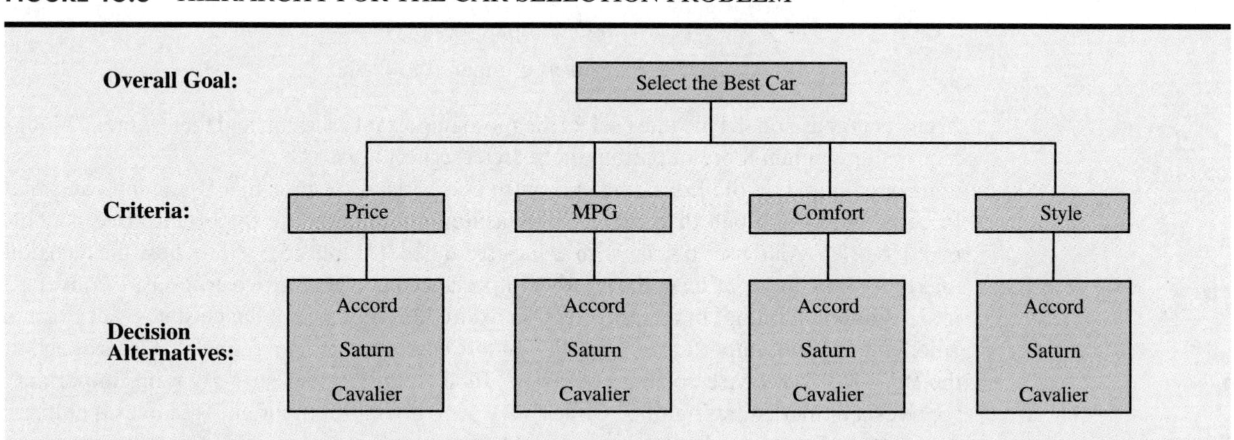

the relative importance of the criteria and the preferences for the decision alternatives to provide an overall priority ranking of the decision alternatives. In the car selection problem, AHP will use Diane's personal preferences to provide a priority ranking of the three cars in terms of how well each car meets the overall goal of being the *best* car.

15.5 ESTABLISHING PRIORITIES USING AHP

In this section we show how AHP uses pairwise comparisons expressed by the decision maker to establish priorities for the criteria and priorities for the decision alternatives based on each criterion. Using the car selection example, we show how AHP determines priorities for each of the following:

1. How the four criteria contribute to the overall goal of selecting the best car
2. How the three cars compare using the Price criterion
3. How the three cars compare using the MPG criterion
4. How the three cars compare using the Comfort criterion
5. How the three cars compare using the Style criterion

In the following discussion, we demonstrate how to establish priorities for the four criteria in terms of how each contributes to the overall goal of selecting the best car. The priorities of the three cars using each criterion can be determined similarly.

Pairwise Comparisons

Pairwise comparisons form the fundamental building blocks of AHP. In establishing the priorities for the four criteria, AHP will require Diane to state how important each criterion is relative to each other criterion when the criteria are compared two at a time (pairwise). That is, with the four criteria (Price, MPG, Comfort, and Style) Diane must make the following pairwise comparisons:

Price compared to MPG
Price compared to Comfort
Price compared to Style
MPG compared to Comfort
MPG compared to Style
Comfort compared to Style

In each comparison, Diane must select the more important criterion and then express a judgment of how much more important the selected criterion is.

For example, in the Price-MPG pairwise comparison, assume that Diane indicates that Price is more important than MPG. To measure how much more important Price is compared to MPG, AHP uses a scale with values from 1 to 9. Table 15.5 shows how the decision maker's verbal description of the relative importance between the two criteria are converted into a numerical rating. In the car selection example, suppose that Diane states that Price is "moderately more important" than MPG. In this case, a numerical rating of 3 is assigned to the Price-MPG pairwise comparison. From Table 15.5, we see "strongly more important" receives a numerical rating of 5, while "very strongly more important" receives a numerical rating of 7. Intermediate judgments such as "strongly to very strongly more important" are possible and would receive a numerical rating of 6.

TABLE 15.5 COMPARISON SCALE FOR THE IMPORTANCE OF CRITERIA USING AHP

Verbal Judgment	Numerical Rating
Extremely more important	9
	8
Very strongly more important	7
	6
Strongly more important	5
	4
Moderately more important	3
	2
Equally important	1

Table 15.6 provides a summary of the six pairwise comparisons Diane provided for the car selection problem. Using the information in this table, Diane has specified that

Price is moderately more important than MPG

Price is equally to moderately more important than Comfort

Price is equally to moderately more important than Style

Comfort is moderately to strongly more important than MPG

Style is moderately to strongly more important than MPG

Style is equally to moderately more important than Comfort

AHP uses the numerical ratings from the pairwise comparisons to establish a priority or importance measure for each criterion.

As shown, the flexibility of AHP can accommodate the unique preferences of each individual decision maker. First, the choice of the criteria that are considered can vary depending upon the decision maker. Not everyone would agree that Price, MPG, Comfort, and Style are the only criteria to be considered in a car selection problem. Perhaps you would want to add safety, resale value, and/or other criteria if you were making the car selection decision. AHP can accommodate any set of criteria specified by the decision maker. Of course, if additional criteria are added, more pairwise comparisons will be necessary. In addition, if you agree with Diane that Price, MPG, Comfort, and Style are the four criteria to use, you would probably disagree with her as to the relative importance of the criteria. Using the format of Table 15.6, you could provide your own assessment of the importance of each pairwise comparison, and AHP would adjust the numerical ratings to reflect your personal preferences.

TABLE 15.6 SUMMARY OF DIANE PAYNE'S PAIRWISE COMPARISONS OF THE FOUR CRITERIA FOR THE CAR SELECTION PROBLEM

Pairwise Comparison	More Important Criterion	How Much More Important	Numerical Rating
Price-MPG	Price	Moderately	3
Price-Comfort	Price	Equally to moderately	2
Price-Style	Price	Equally to moderately	2
MPG-Comfort	Comfort	Moderately to strongly	4
MPG-Style	Style	Moderately to strongly	4
Comfort-Style	Style	Equally to moderately	2

Pairwise Comparison Matrix

To determine the priorities for the four criteria, we need to construct a matrix of the pairwise comparison ratings provided in Table 15.6. Using the four criteria, the **pairwise comparison matrix** will consist of four rows and four columns as shown here:

	Price	MPG	Comfort	Style
Price				
MPG				
Comfort				
Style				

Each of the numerical ratings in Table 15.6 must be entered into the pairwise comparison matrix. As an illustration of this process consider the numerical rating of 3 for the Price-MPG pairwise comparison. Table 15.6 shows that for this pairwise comparison that Price is the most important criterion. Thus, we must enter a 3 into the row labeled Price and the column labeled MPG in the pairwise comparison matrix. In general, the entries in the column labeled Most Important Criterion in Table 15.6 indicate which row of the pairwise comparison matrix the numerical rating must be placed in. As another illustration, consider the MPG-Comfort pairwise comparison. Table 15.6 shows that Comfort is the most important criterion for this pairwise comparison and that the numerical rating is 4. Thus, we enter a 4 into the row labeled Comfort and into the column labeled MPG. Following this procedure for the other pairwise comparisons shown in Table 15.6, we obtain the following pairwise comparison matrix.

	Price	MPG	Comfort	Style
Price		3	2	2
MPG				
Comfort		4		
Style		4	2	

Because the diagonal elements are comparing each criterion to itself, the diagonal elements of the pairwise comparison matrix are always equal to 1. For example, if Price is compared to Price, the verbal judgment would be "equally important" with a rating of 1; thus, a 1 would be placed into the row labeled Price and into the column labeled Price in the pairwise comparison matrix. At this point, the pairwise comparison matrix appears as follows:

	Price	MPG	Comfort	Style
Price	1	3	2	2
MPG		1		
Comfort		4	1	
Style		4	2	1

All that remains is to complete the entries for the remaining cells of the matrix. To illustrate how these values are obtained, consider the numerical rating of 3 for the Price-MPG pairwise comparison. This rating implies that the MPG-Price pairwise comparison should have a rating of ⅓. That is, because Diane already indicated Price is moderately more important than MPG (a rating of 3), we can infer that a pairwise comparison of MPG relative to Price should be ⅓. Similarly, because the Comfort-MPG pairwise comparison has a rating of 4, the MPG-Comfort pairwise comparison would be ¼. Thus, the complete pairwise comparison matrix for the car selection criteria is as follows:

	Price	MPG	Comfort	Style
Price	1	3	2	2
MPG	⅓	1	¼	¼
Comfort	½	4	1	½
Style	½	4	2	1

Synthesization

Using the pairwise comparison matrix, we can now calculate the priority of each criterion in terms of its contribution to the overall goal of selecting the best car. This aspect of AHP is referred to as **synthesization.** The exact mathematical procedure required to perform synthesization is beyond the scope of this text. However, the following three-step procedure provides a good approximation of the synthesization results.

1. Sum the values in each column of the pairwise comparison matrix.
2. Divide each element in the pairwise comparison matrix by its column total; the resulting matrix is referred to as the **normalized pairwise comparison matrix.**
3. Compute the average of the elements in each row of the normalized pairwise comparison matrix; these averages provide the priorities for the criteria.

To show how the synthesization process works, we carry out this three-step procedure for the criteria pairwise comparison matrix.

Step 1. Sum the values in each column.

	Price	MPG	Comfort	Style
Price	1	3	2	2
MPG	⅓	1	¼	¼
Comfort	½	4	1	½
Style	½	4	2	1
Sum	2.333	12.000	5.250	3.750

Step 2. Divide each element of the matrix by its column total.

	Price	MPG	Comfort	Style
Price	0.429	0.250	0.381	0.533
MPG	0.143	0.083	0.048	0.067
Comfort	0.214	0.333	0.190	0.133
Style	0.214	0.333	0.381	0.267

Step 3. Average the elements in each row to determine the priority of each criterion.

	Price	MPG	Comfort	Style	Priority
Price	0.429	0.250	0.381	0.533	0.398
MPG	0.143	0.083	0.048	0.067	0.085
Comfort	0.214	0.333	0.190	0.133	0.218
Style	0.214	0.333	0.381	0.267	0.299

The AHP synthesization procedure provides the priority of each criterion in terms of its contribution to the overall goal of selecting the best car. Thus, using Diane's pairwise comparisons provided in Table 15.6, AHP determines that Price with a priority of 0.398 is the most important criterion in the car selection process. Style with a priority of 0.299 ranks second in importance and is closely followed by Comfort with a priority of 0.218. MPG is the least important criterion with a priority of 0.085.

Consistency

A key step in AHP is the making of several pairwise comparisons as previously described. An important consideration in this process is the **consistency** of the pairwise judgments provided by the decision maker. For example, if criterion A compared to criterion B has a numerical rating of 3 and if criterion B compared to criterion C has a numerical rating of 2, perfect consistency of criterion A compared to criterion C would have a numerical rating of $3 \times 2 = 6$. If the A to C numerical rating assigned by the decision maker was 4 or 5, some inconsistency would exist among the pairwise comparison.

With numerous pairwise comparisons, perfect consistency is difficult to achieve. In fact, some degree of inconsistency can be expected to exist in almost any set of pairwise comparisons. To handle the consistency issue, AHP provides a method for measuring the degree of consistency among the pairwise comparisons provided by the decision maker. If the degree of consistency is unacceptable, the decision maker should review and revise the pairwise comparisons before proceeding with the AHP analysis.

A consistency ratio greater than 0.10 indicates inconsistency in the pairwise comparisons. In such cases, the decision maker should review the pairwise comparisons before proceeding.

AHP provides a measure of the consistency for the pairwise comparisons by computing a **consistency ratio.** This ratio is designed in such a way that a value *greater than* 0.10 indicates an inconsistency in the pairwise judgments. Thus, if the consistency ratio is 0.10 or less, the consistency of the pairwise comparisons is considered reasonable, and the AHP process can continue with the synthesization computations.

Although the exact mathematical computation of the consistency ratio is beyond the scope of this text, an approximation of the ratio can be obtained with little difficulty. The step-by-step procedure for estimating the consistency ratio for the criteria of the car selection problem follows.

Step 1. Multiply each value in the first column of the pairwise comparison matrix by the priority of the first item; multiply each value in the second column of the pairwise comparison matrix by the priority of the second item; continue this process for all columns of the pairwise comparison matrix. Sum the values across the rows to obtain a vector of values labeled "weighted sum." This computation for the car selection problem is as follows:

$$0.398\begin{bmatrix}1\\ 1/3\\ 1/2\\ 1/2\end{bmatrix} + 0.085\begin{bmatrix}3\\ 1\\ 4\\ 4\end{bmatrix} + 0.218\begin{bmatrix}2\\ 1/2\\ 1\\ 2\end{bmatrix} + 0.299\begin{bmatrix}2\\ 1/4\\ 1/2\\ 1\end{bmatrix} =$$

$$\begin{bmatrix}0.398\\ 0.133\\ 0.199\\ 0.199\end{bmatrix} + \begin{bmatrix}0.255\\ 0.085\\ 0.340\\ 0.340\end{bmatrix} + \begin{bmatrix}0.436\\ 0.054\\ 0.218\\ 0.436\end{bmatrix} + \begin{bmatrix}0.598\\ 0.075\\ 0.149\\ 0.299\end{bmatrix} = \begin{bmatrix}1.687\\ 0.347\\ 0.907\\ 1.274\end{bmatrix}$$

Step 2. Divide the elements of the weighted sum vector obtained in step 1 by the corresponding priority for each criterion.

$$\text{Price} \quad \frac{1.687}{0.398} = 4.236$$

$$\text{MPG} \quad \frac{0.347}{0.085} = 4.077$$

$$\text{Comfort} \quad \frac{0.907}{0.218} = 4.163$$

$$\text{Style} \quad \frac{1.274}{0.299} = 4.264$$

Step 3. Compute the average of the values found in step 2; this average is denoted λ_{max}.

$$\lambda_{max} = \frac{(4.236 + 4.077 + 4.163 + 4.264)}{4} = 4.185$$

Step 4. Compute the consistency index (CI) as follows:

$$\text{CI} = \frac{\lambda_{max} - n}{n - 1}$$

where n is the number of items being compared. Thus, we have

$$\text{CI} = \frac{4.185 - 4}{4 - 1} = 0.0616$$

Step 5. Compute the consistency ratio, which is defined as

$$\text{CR} = \frac{\text{CI}}{\text{RI}}$$

where RI is the consistency index of a *randomly* generated pairwise comparison matrix. The value of RI depends on the number of items being compared and is given as follows:

n	3	4	5	6	7	8
RI	0.58	0.90	1.12	1.24	1.32	1.41

Thus, for the car selection problem with $n = 4$ criteria, we have RI $= 0.90$ and a consistency ratio

$$\text{CR} = \frac{0.0616}{0.90} = 0.068$$

Problem 16 will give you practice with the synthesization calculations and determining the consistency ratio.

As mentioned previously, a consistency ratio of 0.10 or less is considered acceptable. Because the pairwise comparisons for the car selection criteria show CR $= 0.068$, we can conclude that the degree of consistency in the pairwise comparisons is acceptable.

Other Pairwise Comparisons for the Car Selection Problem

Continuing with the AHP analysis of the car selection problem, we need to use the pairwise comparison procedure to determine the priorities for the three cars using each of the criteria: Price, MPG, Comfort, and Style. Determining these priorities requires Diane to express pairwise comparison preferences for the cars using each criterion one at a time. For example, using the Price criterion, Diane must make the following pairwise comparisons:

the Accord compared to the Saturn

the Accord compared to the Cavalier

the Saturn compared to the Cavalier

In each comparison, Diane must select the more preferred car and then express a judgment of how much more preferred the selected car is.

For example, using the Price as the basis for comparison, assume that Diane considers the Accord-Saturn pairwise comparison and indicates that the less expensive Saturn is preferred. Table 15.7 shows how AHP uses Diane's verbal description of the preference between the Accord and Saturn to determine a numerical rating of the preference. For example, suppose that Diane states that based on Price, the Saturn is "moderately more preferred" to the Accord. Thus, using the Price criterion, a numerical rating of 3 is assigned to the Saturn row and Accord column of the pairwise comparison matrix.

Table 15.8 shows the summary of the car pairwise comparisons that Diane provided for each criterion of the car selection problem. Using this table and referring to selected pairwise comparison entries, we see that Diane stated the following preferences:

In terms of Price, the Cavalier is moderately to strongly more preferred than the Accord.

In terms of MPG, the Cavalier is moderately more preferred than the Saturn.

In terms of Comfort, the Accord is very strongly to extremely more preferred than the Cavalier.

In terms of Style, the Saturn is moderately more preferred than the Accord.

TABLE 15.7 PAIRWISE COMPARISON SCALE FOR THE PREFERENCE OF DECISION ALTERNATIVES USING AHP

Verbal Judgment	Numerical Rating
Extremely preferred	9
	8
Very strongly preferred	7
	6
Strongly preferred	5
	4
Moderately preferred	3
	2
Equally preferred	1

Practice setting up a pairwise comparison matrix and determine whether judgments are consistent by working Problem 20.

Using the pairwise comparison matrixes in Table 15.8, many other insights may be gained about the preferences Diana expressed for the cars. However, at this point, AHP continues by synthesizing each of the four pairwise comparison matrixes in Table 15.8 in order to determine the priority of each car using each criterion. A synthesization is conducted for each pairwise comparison matrix using the three-step procedure described previously for the criteria pairwise comparison matrix. Four synthesization computations provide the four sets of priorities shown in Table 15.9. Using this table, we see that the Cavalier is the preferred alternative based on Price (0.557), the Cavalier is the preferred alternative based on MPG (0.639), the Accord is the preferred alternative based on Comfort (0.593), and the Saturn is the preferred alternative based on Style (0.656). At this point, no car is the clear, overall best. The next section shows how to combine the priorities for the criteria and the priorities in Table 15.9 to develop an overall priority ranking for the three cars.

TABLE 15.8 PAIRWISE COMPARISON MATRIXES SHOWING PREFERENCES FOR THE CARS USING EACH CRITERION

Price

	Accord	Saturn	Cavalier
Accord	1	1/3	1/4
Saturn	3	1	1/2
Cavalier	4	2	1

MPG

	Accord	Saturn	Cavalier
Accord	1	1/4	1/6
Saturn	4	1	1/3
Cavalier	6	3	1

Comfort

	Accord	Saturn	Cavalier
Accord	1	2	8
Saturn	1/2	1	6
Cavalier	1/8	1/6	1

Style

	Accord	Saturn	Cavalier
Accord	1	1/3	4
Saturn	3	1	7
Cavalier	1/4	1/7	1

15.6 USING AHP TO DEVELOP AN OVERALL PRIORITY RANKING

In Section 15.5, we used Diane's pairwise comparisons of the four criteria to develop the priorities of 0.398 for Price, 0.085 for MPG, 0.218 for Comfort, and 0.299 for Style. We now want to use these priorities and the priorities shown in Table 15.9 to develop an overall priority ranking for the three cars.

The procedure used to compute the overall priority is to weight each car's priority shown in Table 15.9 by the corresponding criterion priority. For example, the Price criterion has a priority of 0.398, and the Accord has a priority of 0.123 in terms of the Price criterion. Thus, $0.398 \times 0.123 = 0.049$ is the priority value of the Accord based on the Price criterion. To obtain the overall priority of the Accord, we need to make similar computations for the MPG, Comfort, and Style criteria and then add the values to obtain the overall priority. This calculation is as follows:

Overall Priority of the Accord:

$$0.398(0.123) + 0.085(0.087) + 0.218(0.593) + 0.299(0.265) = 0.265$$

Repeating this calculation for the Saturn and the Cavalier, we obtain the following results:

Overall Priority of the Saturn:

$$0.398(0.320) + 0.085(0.274) + 0.218(0.341) + 0.299(0.656) = 0.421$$

Overall Priority of the Cavalier:

$$0.398(0.557) + 0.085(0.639) + 0.218(0.065) + 0.299(0.080) = 0.314$$

Ranking these priorities, we have the AHP ranking of the decision alternatives:

Car	Priority
1. Saturn	0.421
2. Cavalier	0.314
3. Accord	0.265

These results provide a basis for Diane to make a decision regarding the purchase of a car. As long as Diane believes that her judgments regarding the importance of the criteria and

TABLE 15.9 PRIORITIES FOR EACH CAR USING EACH CRITERION

	Criterion			
	Price	MPG	Comfort	Style
Accord	0.123	0.087	0.593	0.265
Saturn	0.320	0.274	0.341	0.656
Cavalier	0.557	0.639	0.065	0.080

Work Problem 24 and determine the AHP priorities for the two decision alternatives.

her preferences for the cars using each criterion are valid, the AHP priorities show that the Saturn is preferred. In addition to the recommendation of the Saturn as the best car, the AHP analysis helped Diane gain a better understanding of the trade-offs in the decision-making process and a clearer understanding of why the Saturn is the AHP recommended alternative.

NOTES AND COMMENTS

1. The scoring model in Section 15.3 used the following equation to compute the overall score of a decision alternative.

$$S_j = \sum_i w_i r_{ij}$$

where

w_i = the weight for criterion i

r_{ij} = the rating for criterion i and decision alternative j

In Section 15.5 AHP used the same calculation to determine the overall priority of each decision alternative. The difference between the two approaches is that the scoring model required the decision maker to estimate the values of w_i and r_{ij} directly. AHP used synthesization to compute the criterion priorities w_i and the decision alternative priorities r_{ij} based on the pairwise comparison information provided by the decision maker.

2. The software package Expert Choice® marketed by Decision Support Software provides a user-friendly procedure for implementing AHP on a personal computer. Expert Choice takes the decision maker through the pairwise comparison process in a step-by-step manner. Once the decision maker responds to the pairwise comparison prompts, Expert Choice automatically constructs the pairwise comparison matrix, conducts the synthesization calculations, and presents the overall priorities. Expert Choice is a software package that should warrant consideration by a decision maker who anticipates solving a variety of multicriteria decision problems.

SUMMARY

In this chapter we used goal programming to solve problems with multiple goals within the linear programming framework. We showed that the goal programming model contains one or more goal equations and an objective function designed to minimize deviations from the goals. In situations where resource capacities or other restrictions affect the achievement of the goals, the model will contain constraints that are formulated and treated in the same manner as constraints in an ordinary linear programming model.

In goal programming problems with preemptive priorities, priority level 1 goals are treated first in an objective function to identify a solution that will best satisfy these goals. This solution is then revised by considering an objective function involving only the priority level 2 goals; solution modifications are considered only if they do not degrade the solution obtained for the priority level 1 goals. This process continues until all priority levels have been considered.

We showed how a variation of the linear programming graphical solution procedure can be used to solve goal programming problems with two decision variables. Specialized goal programming computer packages are available for solving the general goal programming problem, but such computer codes are not as readily available as are general purpose linear programming computer packages. As a result, we showed how the linear programming module of The Management Scientist software package can be used to solve a goal programming problem.

We then presented a scoring model as a quick and relatively easy way to identify the most desired decision alternative in a multicriteria problem. The decision maker provides a subjective weight indicating the importance of each criterion. Then the decision maker rates each decision alternative in terms of how well it satisfies each criterion. The end result is a score for each decision alternative that indicates the preference for the decision alternative considering all criteria.

We also presented an approach to multicriteria decision making called the analytic hierarchy process (AHP). We showed that a key part of AHP is the development of judgments concerning the relative importance of, or preference for, the elements being compared. A consistency ratio is computed to determine the degree of consistency exhibited by the decision maker in making the pairwise comparisons. Values of the consistency ratio less than or equal to 0.10 are considered acceptable.

Once the set of all pairwise comparisons has been developed, a process referred to as synthesization is used to determine the priorities for the elements being compared. The final step of the analytic hierarchy process involves multiplying the priority levels established for the decision alternatives relative to each criterion by the priority levels reflecting the importance of the criteria themselves; the sum of these products over all the criteria provides the overall priority level for each decision alternative.

GLOSSARY

Goal programming A linear programming approach to multicriteria decision problems whereby the objective function is designed to minimize the deviations from goals.

Preemptive priorities Priorities assigned to goals that ensure that the satisfaction of a higher level goal cannot be traded for the satisfaction of a lower level goal.

Target value A value specified in the statement of the goal. Based on the context of the problem, management will want the solution to the goal programming problem to result in a value for the goal that is less than, equal to, or greater than the target value.

Goal equation An equation whose right-hand side is the target value for the goal; the left-hand side of the goal equation consists of (1) a function representing the level of achievement and (2) deviation variables representing the difference between the target value for the goal and the level achieved.

Deviation variables Variables that are added to the goal equation to allow the solution to deviate from the goal's target value.

Scoring model An approach to multicriteria decision making that requires the user to assign weights to each criterion that describes the criterion's relative importance and to assign a rating that shows how well each decision alternative satisfies each criterion. The output is a score for each decision alternative.

Analytic hierarchy process (AHP) An approach to multicriteria decision making based on pairwise comparisons for elements in a hierarchy.

Hierarchy A diagram that shows the levels of a problem in terms of the overall goal, the criteria, and the decision alternatives.

Pairwise comparison matrix A matrix that consists of the preference, or relative importance, ratings provided during a series of pairwise comparisons.

Synthesization A mathematical process that uses the preference or relative importance values in the pairwise comparison matrix to develop priorities.

Normalized pairwise comparison matrix The matrix obtained by dividing each element of the pairwise comparison matrix by its column total. This matrix is computed as an intermediate step in the synthesization of priorities.

Consistency A concept developed to assess the quality of the judgments made during a series of pairwise comparisons. It is a measure of the internal consistency of these comparisons.

Consistency ratio A numerical measure of the degree of consistency in a series of pairwise comparisons. Values less than or equal to 0.10 are considered reasonable.

PROBLEMS

1. The RMC Corporation blends three raw materials to produce two products: a fuel additive and a solvent base. Each ton of fuel additive is a mixture of $\frac{2}{5}$ ton of material 1 and $\frac{3}{5}$ ton of material 3. A ton of solvent base is a mixture of $\frac{1}{2}$ ton of material 1, $\frac{1}{5}$ ton of material 2, and $\frac{3}{10}$ ton of material 3. RMC's production is constrained by a limited availability of the three raw materials. For the current production period, RMC has the following quantities of each raw material: material 1, 20 tons; material 2, 5 tons; material 3, 21 tons. Management wants to achieve the following P_1 priority level goals.

   Goal 1: Produce at least 30 tons of fuel additive.

   Goal 2: Produce at least 15 tons of solvent base.

   Assume there are no other goals.

   a. Is it possible for management to achieve both P_1 level goals given the constraints on the amounts of each material available? Explain.

   b. Treating the amounts of each material available as constraints, formulate a goal programming model to determine the optimal product mix. Assume that both P_1 priority level goals are equally important to management.

   c. Use the graphical goal programming procedure to solve the model formulated in part (b).

   d. If goal 1 is twice as important as goal 2, what is the optimal product mix?

2. DJS Investment Services must develop an investment portfolio for a new client. As an initial investment strategy, the new client would like to restrict the portfolio to a mix of two stocks:

Stock	Price/Share	Estimated Annual Return (%)
AGA Products	$ 50	6
Key Oil	100	10

   The client wants to invest $50,000 and established the following two investment goals.

   Priority Level 1 Goal

   Goal 1: Obtain an annual return of at least 9%.

   Priority Level 2 Goal

   Goal 2: Limit the investment in Key Oil, the riskier investment, to no more than 60% of the total investment.

   a. Formulate a goal programming model for the DJS Investment problem.

   b. Use the graphical goal programming procedure to obtain a solution.

3. The L. Young & Sons Manufacturing Company produces two products, which have the following profit and resource requirement characteristics.

Characteristic	Product 1	Product 2
Profit/unit	$4	$2
Dept. A hours/unit	1	1
Dept. B hours/unit	2	5

   Last month's production schedule used 350 hours of labor in department A and 1000 hours of labor in department B.

Young's management has been experiencing workforce morale and labor union problems during the past six months because of monthly departmental workload fluctuations. New hiring, layoffs, and interdepartmental transfers have been common because the firm has not attempted to stabilize workload requirements.

Management would like to develop a production schedule for the coming month that will achieve the following goals.

Goal 1: Use 350 hours of labor in department A.

Goal 2: Use 1000 hours of labor in department B.

Goal 3: Earn a profit of at least \$1300.

a. Formulate a goal programming model for this problem, assuming that goals 1 and 2 are P_1 level goals and goal 3 is a P_2 level goal; assume that goals 1 and 2 are equally important.
b. Solve the model formulated in part (a) using the graphical goal programming procedure.
c. Suppose that the firm ignores the workload fluctuations and considers the 350 hours in department A and the 1000 hours in department B as the maximum available. Formulate and solve a linear programming problem to maximize profit subject to these constraints.
d. Compare the solutions obtained in parts (b) and (c). Discuss which approach you favor, and why.
e. Reconsider part (a) assuming that the priority level 1 goal is goal 3 and the priority level 2 goals are goals 1 and 2; as before, assume that goals 1 and 2 are equally important. Solve this revised problem using the graphical goal programming procedure and compare your solution to the one obtained for the original problem.

4. Industrial Chemicals produces two adhesives used in the manufacturing process for airplanes. The two adhesives, which have different bonding strengths, require different amounts of production time: the IC-100 adhesive requires 20 minutes of production time per gallon of finished product, and the IC-200 adhesive uses 30 minutes of production time per gallon. Both products use 1 pound of a highly perishable resin for each gallon of finished product. Inventory currently holds 300 pounds of the resin, and more can be obtained if necessary. However, because of the shelf life of the material, any amount not used in the next two weeks will be discarded.

The firm has existing orders for 100 gallons of IC-100 and 120 gallons of IC-200. Under normal conditions, the production process operates eight hours per day, five days per week. Management wants to schedule production for the next two weeks to achieve the following goals.

Priority Level 1 Goals

Goal 1: Avoid underutilization of the production process.

Goal 2: Avoid overtime in excess of 20 hours for the two weeks.

Priority Level 2 Goals

Goal 3: Satisfy existing orders for the IC-100 adhesive; that is, produce at least 100 gallons of IC-100.

Goal 4: Satisfy existing orders for the IC-200 adhesive; that is, produce at least 120 gallons of IC-200.

Priority Level 3 Goal

Goal 5: Use all the available resin.

a. Formulate a goal programming model for the Industrial Chemicals problem. Assume that both priority level 1 goals and that both priority level 2 goals are equally important.
b. Use the graphical goal programming procedure to develop a solution for the model formulated in part (a).

5. Standard Pump recently won a \$14 million contract with the U.S. Navy to supply 2000 custom-designed submersible pumps over the next four months. The contract calls for the delivery of 200 pumps at the end of May, 600 pumps at the end of June, 600 pumps at the end of July, and 600 pumps at the end of August. Standard's production capacity is 500 pumps in May, 400 pumps in June, 800 pumps in July, and 500 pumps in August. Management would like to develop a production schedule that will keep monthly ending inventories low while at the same time minimizing the fluctuations in inventory levels from month to month. In attempting to develop a goal programming model of the problem, the company's production scheduler let x_m denote the number of pumps produced in month m and s_m denote the number of pumps in inventory at the end of month m. Here, $m = 1$ refers to May, $m = 2$ refers to June, $m = 3$ refers to July, and $m = 4$ refers to August. Management asks you to assist the production scheduler in model development.
   a. Using these variables, develop a constraint for each month that will satisfy the following demand requirement:

$$\begin{pmatrix}\text{Beginning}\\\text{Inventory}\end{pmatrix} + \begin{pmatrix}\text{Current}\\\text{Production}\end{pmatrix} - \begin{pmatrix}\text{Ending}\\\text{Inventory}\end{pmatrix} = \begin{pmatrix}\text{This Month's}\\\text{Demand}\end{pmatrix}$$

   b. Write goal equations that represent the fluctuations in the production level from May to June, June to July, and July to August.
   c. Inventory carrying costs are high. Is it possible for Standard to avoid carrying any monthly ending inventories over the scheduling period of May to August? If not, develop goal equations with a target of zero for the ending inventory in May, June, and July.
   d. Besides the goal equations developed in parts (b) and (c), what other constraints are needed in the model?
   e. Assuming the production fluctuation and inventory goals are of equal importance, develop and solve a goal programming model to determine the best production schedule.
   f. Can you find a way to reduce the variables and constraints needed in your model by eliminating the goal equations and deviation variables for ending inventory levels? Explain.

6. Michigan Motors Corporation (MMC) just introduced a new luxury touring sedan. As part of its promotional campaign, the marketing department decided to send personalized invitations to test drive the new sedan to two target groups: (1) current owners of an MMC luxury automobile and (2) owners of luxury cars manufactured by one of MMC's competitors. The cost of sending a personalized invitation to each customer is estimated to be \$1 per letter. Based on previous experience with this type of advertising, MMC estimates that 25% of the customers contacted from group 1 and 10% of the customers contacted from group 2 will test drive the new sedan. As part of this campaign, MMC set the following goals.

   Goal 1: Get at least 10,000 customers from group 1 to test drive the new sedan.

   Goal 2: Get at least 5000 customers from group 2 to test drive the new sedan.

   Goal 3: Limit the expense of sending out the invitations to \$70,000.

   Assume that goals 1 and 2 are P_1 priority level goals and that goal 3 is a P_2 priority level goal.
   a. Suppose that goals 1 and 2 are equally important; formulate a goal programming model of the MMC problem.
   b. Use the goal programming computer procedure illustrated in Section 15.2 to solve the model formulated in part (a).
   c. If management believes that contacting customers from group 2 is twice as important as contacting customers from group 1, what should MMC do?

7. A committee in charge of promoting a Ladies Professional Golf Association tournament is trying to determine how best to advertise the event during the two weeks prior to the tournament. The committee obtained the following information about the three advertising media they are considering using.

Category	Audience Reached per Advertisement	Cost per Advertisement	Maximum Number of Advertisements
TV	200,000	\$2500	10
Radio	50,000	\$ 400	15
Newspaper	100,000	\$ 500	20

The last column in this table shows the maximum number of advertisements that can be run during the next two weeks; these values should be treated as constraints. The committee established the following goals for the campaign.

Priority Level 1 Goal

Goal 1: Reach at least 4 million people.

Priority Level 2 Goal

Goal 2: The number of television advertisements should be at least 30% of the total number of advertisements.

Priority Level 3 Goal

Goal 3: The number of radio advertisements should not exceed 20% of the total number of advertisements.

Priority Level 4 Goal

Goal 4: Limit the total amount spent for advertising to \$20,000.

a. Formulate a goal programming model for this problem.
b. Use the goal programming computer procedure illustrated in Section 15.2 to solve the model formulated in part (a).

8. Morley Company is attempting to determine the best location for a new machine in an existing layout of three machines. The existing machines are located at the following x_1, x_2 coordinates on the shop floor.

$$\text{Machine 1: } x_1 = 1, x_2 = 7$$
$$\text{Machine 2: } x_1 = 5, x_2 = 9$$
$$\text{Machine 3: } x_1 = 6, x_2 = 2$$

a. Develop a goal programming model that can be solved to minimize the total distance of the new machine from the three existing machines. The distance is to be measured rectangularly. For example, if the location of the new machine is ($x_1 = 3$, $x_2 = 5$), it is considered to be a distance of $|3 - 1| + |5 - 7| = 2 + 2 = 4$ from machine 1. *Hint:* In the goal programming formulation, let

x_1 = first coordinate of the new machine location
x_2 = second coordinate of the new machine location
d_i^+ = amount by which the x_1 coordinate of the new machine exceeds the x_1 coordinate of machine i ($i = 1, 2, 3$)

d_i^- = amount by which the x_1 coordinate of machine i exceeds the x_1 coordinate of the new machine ($i = 1, 2, 3$)

e_i^+ = amount by which the x_2 coordinate of the new machine exceeds the x_2 coordinate of machine i ($i = 1, 2, 3$)

e_i^- = amount by which the x_2 coordinate of machine i exceeds the x_2 coordinate of the new machine ($i = 1, 2, 3$)

b. What is the optimal location for the new machine?

9. One advantage of using the multicriteria decision-making methods presented in this chapter is that the criteria weights and the decision alternative ratings may be modified to reflect the unique interests and preferences of each individual decision maker. For example, assume that another graduating college student had the same three job offers described in Section 15.3. This student provided the following scoring model information. Rank the overall preference for the three positions. Which position is recommended?

		Ratings		
Criteria	Weight	Analyst Chicago	Accountant Denver	Auditor Houston
Career advancement	5	7	4	4
Location	2	5	6	4
Management style	5	6	5	7
Salary	4	7	8	4
Prestige	4	8	5	6
Job security	2	4	5	8
Enjoyment of the work	4	7	5	5

10. The Kenyon Manufacturing Company is interested in selecting the best location for a new plant. After a detailed study of 10 sites, the three location finalists are Georgetown, Kentucky; Marysville, Ohio; and Clarksville, Tennessee. The Kenyon management team provided the following data on location criteria, criteria importance, and location ratings. Use a scoring model to determine the best location for the new plant.

		Ratings		
Criteria	Weight	Georgetown, Kentucky	Marysville, Ohio	Clarksville, Tennessee
Land cost	4	7	4	5
Labor cost	3	6	5	8
Labor availability	5	7	8	6
Construction cost	4	6	7	5
Transportation	3	5	7	4
Access to customers	5	6	8	5
Long-range goals	4	7	6	5

11. The Davis family of Atlanta, Georgia, is planning its annual summer vacation. Three vacation locations along with criteria weights and location ratings follow. What is the recommended vacation location?

		Ratings		
Criteria	**Weight**	**Myrtle Beach, South Carolina**	**Smoky Mountains**	**Branson, Missouri**
Travel distance	2	5	7	3
Vacation cost	5	5	6	4
Entertainment available	3	7	4	8
Outdoor activities	2	9	6	5
Unique experience	4	6	7	8
Family fun	5	8	7	7

12. A high school senior is considering attending one of the following four colleges or universities. Eight criteria, criteria weights, and school ratings are also shown. What is the recommended choice?

		Ratings			
Criteria	**Weight**	**Midwestern University**	**State College at Newport**	**Handover College**	**Tecumseh State**
School prestige	3	8	6	7	5
Number of students	4	3	5	8	7
Average class size	5	4	5	8	7
Cost	5	5	8	3	6
Distance from home	2	7	8	7	6
Sports program	4	9	5	4	6
Housing desirability	4	6	5	7	6
Beauty of campus	3	5	3	8	5

13. Mr. and Mrs. Brinkley are interested in purchasing condominium property in Naples, Florida. The three most preferred condominiums are listed along with criteria weights and rating information. Which condominium is preferred?

		Ratings		
Criteria	**Weight**	**Park Shore**	**The Terrace**	**Gulf View**
Cost	5	5	6	5
Location	4	7	4	9
Appearance	5	7	4	7
Parking	2	5	8	5
Floor plan	4	8	7	5
Swimming pool	1	7	2	3
View	3	5	4	9
Kitchen	4	8	7	6
Closet space	3	6	8	4

14. Clark and Julie Anderson are interested in purchasing a new boat and have limited their choice to one of three boats manufactured by Sea Ray, Inc.: the 220 Bowrider, the 230 Overnighter, and the 240 Sundancer. The Bowrider weighs 3100 pounds, has no overnight capability, and has a price of $28,500. The 230 Overnighter weighs 4300 pounds, has a reasonable overnight capability, and has a price of $37,500. The 240 Sundancer weighs 4500 pounds, has an excellent overnight capability (kitchen, bath, and bed), and has a price of $48,200. The Andersons provided the scoring model information separately as shown here.

Clark Anderson

		Ratings		
Criteria	**Weight**	**220 Bowrider**	**230 Overnighter**	**240 Sundancer**
Cost	5	8	5	3
Overnight capability	3	2	6	9
Kitchen/bath facilities	2	1	4	7
Appearance	5	7	7	6
Engine/speed	5	6	8	4
Towing/handling	4	8	5	2
Maintenance	4	7	5	3
Resale value	3	7	5	6

Julie Anderson

		Ratings		
Criteria	**Weight**	**220 Bowrider**	**230 Overnighter**	**240 Sundancer**
Cost	3	7	6	5
Overnight capability	5	1	6	8
Kitchen/bath facilities	5	1	3	7
Appearance	4	5	7	7
Engine/speed	2	4	5	3
Towing/handling	2	8	6	2
Maintenance	1	6	5	4
Resale value	2	5	6	6

a. Which boat does Clark Anderson prefer?
b. Which boat does Julie Anderson prefer?

15. Use the pairwise comparison matrix for the price criterion shown in Table 15.8 to verify that the priorities after synthesization are 0.123, 0.320, and 0.557. Compute the consistency ratio and comment on its acceptability.

16. Use the pairwise comparison matrix for the style criterion as shown in Table 15.8 to verify that the priorities after synthesization are 0.265, 0.656, and 0.080. Compute the consistency ratio and comment on its acceptability.

17. Dan Joseph was considering entering one of two graduate schools of business to pursue studies for an MBA degree. When asked how he compared the two schools with respect to reputation, he responded that he preferred school A strongly to very strongly to school B.
a. Set up the pairwise comparison matrix for this problem.
b. Determine the priorities for the two schools relative to this criterion.

18. An organization was investigating relocating its corporate headquarters to one of three possible cities. The following pairwise comparison matrix shows the president's judgments regarding the desirability for the three cities.

	City 1	City 2	City 3
City 1	1	5	7
City 2	1/5	1	3
City 3	1/7	1/3	1

a. Determine the priorities for the three cities.
b. Is the president consistent in terms of the judgments provided? Explain.

19. The following pairwise comparison matrix contains the judgments of an individual regarding the fairness of two proposed tax programs, A and B.

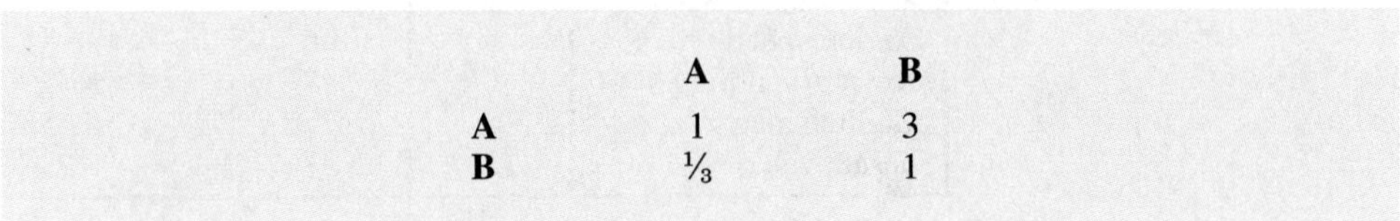

	A	B
A	1	3
B	1/3	1

a. Determine the priorities for the two programs.
b. Are the individual's judgments consistent? Explain.

20. Asked to compare three soft drinks with respect to flavor, an individual stated that

A is moderately more preferable than B.

A is equally to moderately more preferable than C.

B is strongly more preferable than C.

a. Set up the pairwise comparison matrix for this problem.
b. Determine the priorities for the soft drinks with respect to the flavor criterion.
c. Compute the consistency ratio. Are the individual's judgments consistent? Explain.

21. Refer to Problem 20. Suppose that the individual had stated the following judgments instead of those given in Problem 20.

A is strongly more preferable than C.

B is equally to moderately more preferable than A.

B is strongly more preferable than C.

Answer parts (a), (b), and (c) as stated in Problem 20.

22. The national sales director for Jones Office Supplies needs to determine the best location for the next national sales meeting. Three locations have been proposed: Dallas, San Francisco, and New York. One criterion considered important in the decision is the desirability of the location in terms of restaurants, entertainment, and so on. The national sales manager made the following judgments with regard to this criterion.

New York is very strongly more preferred than Dallas.

New York is moderately more preferred than San Francisco.

San Francisco is moderately to strongly more preferred than Dallas.

a. Set up the pairwise comparison matrix for this problem.
b. Determine the priorities for the desirability criterion.
c. Compute the consistency ratio. Are the sales manager's judgments consistent? Explain.

23. A study comparing four personal computers resulted in the following pairwise comparison matrix for the performance criterion.

	1	2	3	4
1	1	3	7	1/3
2	1/3	1	4	1/4
3	1/7	1/4	1	1/6
4	3	4	6	1

a. Determine the priorities for the four computers relative to the performance criterion.
b. Compute the consistency ratio. Are the judgments regarding performance consistent? Explain.

24. An individual was interested in determining which of two stocks to invest in, Central Computing Company (CCC) or Software Research, Inc. (SRI). The criteria thought to be most relevant in making the decision are the potential yield of the stock and the risk associated with the investment. The pairwise comparison matrixes for this problem are

Criterion	Yield	Risk
Yield	1	2
Risk	1/2	1

Yield	CCC	SRI
CCC	1	3
SRI	1/3	1

Risk	CCC	SRI
CCC	1	1/2
SRI	2	1

a. Compute the priorities for each pairwise comparison matrix.
b. Determine the overall priority for the two investments, CCC and SRI. Which investment is preferred based on yield and risk?

25. The vice president of Harling Equipment needs to select a new director of marketing. The two possible candidates are Bill Jacobs and Sue Martin, and the criteria thought to be most relevant in the selection are leadership ability (L), personal skills (P), and administrative skills (A). The following pairwise comparison matrixes were obtained.

Criterion	L	P	A
L	1	1/3	1/4
P	3	1	2
A	4	1/2	1

Leadership	Jacobs	Martin
Jacobs	1	4
Martin	1/4	1

Personal	Jacobs	Martin
Jacobs	1	1/3
Martin	3	1

Administrative	Jacobs	Martin
Jacobs	1	2
Martin	1/2	1

a. Compute the priorities for each pairwise comparison matrix.
b. Determine an overall priority for each candidate. Which candidate is preferred?

26. A woman considering the purchase of a custom sound stereo system for her car looked at three different systems (A, B, and C), which varied in terms of price, sound quality, and FM reception. The following pairwise comparison matrixes were developed.

	Criterion		
	Price	**Sound**	**Reception**
Price	1	3	4
Sound	⅓	1	3
Reception	¼	⅓	1

	Price		
	A	**B**	**C**
A	1	4	2
B	¼	1	⅓
C	½	3	1

	Sound		
	A	**B**	**C**
A	1	½	¼
B	2	1	⅓
C	4	3	1

	Reception		
	A	**B**	**C**
A	1	4	2
B	¼	1	1
C	½	1	1

a. Compute the priorities for each pairwise comparison matrix.
b. Determine an overall priority for each system. Which stereo system is preferred?

Case Problem EZ TRAILERS, INC.

EZ Trailers, Inc., manufactures a variety of general purpose trailers, including a complete line of boat trailers. Two of their best-selling boat trailers are the EZ-190 and the EZ-250. The EZ-190 is designed for boats up to 19 feet in length, and the EZ-250 can be used for boats up to 25 feet in length.

EZ Trailers would like to schedule production for the next two months for these two models. Each unit of the EZ-190 requires four hours of production time, and each unit of the EZ-250 uses six hours of production time. The following orders have been received for March and April.

Model	March	April
EZ-190	800	600
EZ-250	1100	1200

The ending inventory from February was 200 units of the EZ-190 and 300 units of the EZ-250. The total number of hours of production time used in February was 6300 hours.

The management of EZ Trailers is concerned about being able to satisfy existing orders for the EZ-250 for both March and April. In fact, it believes that this goal is the most important one that a production schedule should meet. Next in importance is satisfying existing orders for the EZ-190. In addition, management doesn't want to implement any production schedule that would involve significant labor fluctuations from month to month. In this regard, its goal is to develop a production schedule that would limit fluctuations in labor hours used to a maximum of 1000 hours from one month to the next.

Managerial Report

Perform an analysis of EZ Trailers's production scheduling problem, and prepare a report for EZ's president that summarizes your findings. Include a discussion and analysis of the following items in your report.

1. The production schedule that best achieves the goals as specified by management.
2. Suppose that EZ Trailers's storage facilities would accommodate only a maximum of 300 trailers in any one month. What effect would this have on the production schedule?
3. Suppose that EZ Trailers can store only a maximum of 300 trailers in any one month. In addition, suppose management would like to have an ending inventory in April of at least 100 units of each model. What effect would both changes have on the production schedule?
4. What changes would occur in the production schedule if the labor fluctuation goal was the highest priority goal?

Appendix 15.1 SCORING MODELS WITH EXCEL

Excel provides an efficient way to analyze a multicriteria decision problem that can be described by a scoring model. We will use the job selection application from Section 15.3 to demonstrate this procedure.

A worksheet for the job selection scoring model is shown in Figure 15.7. The criteria weights are placed into cells B6 to B12. The ratings for each criterion and decision alternative are entered into cells C6 to E12.

The calculations used to compute the score for each decision alternative are shown in the bottom portion of the worksheet. The calculation for cell C18 is provided by the cell formula

=$B6*C6

This cell formula can be copied from cell C18 to cells C18:E24 to provide the results shown in rows 18 to 24. The score for the financial analyst position in Chicago is found by placing the following formula in cell C26:

=SUM(C18:C24)

Copying cell C26 to cells D26:E26 provides the scores for the accountant in Denver and the auditor in Houston positions.

FIGURE 15.7 WORKSHEET FOR THE JOB SELECTION SCORING MODEL

EXCELfile
Scoring

	A	B	C	D	E	F
1	**Job Selection Scoring Model**					
2						
3				**Ratings**		
4			**Analyst**	**Accountant**	**Auditor**	
5	**Criteria**	**Weight**	**Chicago**	**Denver**	**Houston**	
6	Career Advancement	5	8	6	4	
7	Location	3	3	8	7	
8	Management	4	5	6	9	
9	Salary	3	6	7	5	
10	Prestige	2	7	5	4	
11	Job Security	4	4	7	6	
12	Enjoy the Work	5	8	6	5	
13						
14						
15	**Scoring Calculations**					
16			**Analyst**	**Accountant**	**Auditor**	
17	**Criteria**		**Chicago**	**Denver**	**Houston**	
18	Career Advancement		40	30	20	
19	Location		9	24	21	
20	Management		20	24	36	
21	Salary		18	21	15	
22	Prestige		14	10	8	
23	Job Security		16	28	24	
24	Enjoy the Work		40	30	25	
25						
26	**Score**		157	167	149	

CHAPTER 16

Forecasting

CONTENTS

An essential aspect of managing any organization is planning for the future. Indeed, the long-run success of an organization depends on how well management is able to anticipate the future and develop appropriate strategies. Good judgment, intuition, and an awareness of the state of the economy may give a manager a rough idea or "feeling" of what is likely to happen in the future. However, converting this feeling into a number that can be used as next quarter's sales volume or next year's raw material cost per unit often is difficult. This chapter introduces several forecasting methods for that purpose.

Suppose that we have been asked to provide quarterly forecasts of the sales volume for a particular product during the coming year. Production schedules, raw material purchasing plans, inventory policies, and sales quotas will be affected by the quarterly forecasts that we provide. Consequently, poor forecasts may result in increased costs for the firm. How should we go about providing the quarterly sales volume forecasts?

Most companies can forecast total demand for all products, as a group, with errors of less than 5 percent. However, forecasting demand for individual products may result in significantly higher errors.

We will certainly want to review the actual sales data for the product in previous periods. Using these historical data, we can identify the general level of sales and any trend such as an increase or decrease in sales volume over time. A further review of the data might reveal a seasonal pattern such as peak sales occurring in the third quarter of each year and sales volume bottoming out during the first quarter. By reviewing historical data, we can often develop a better understanding of the pattern of past sales, leading to better predictions of future sales for the product.

The historical sales data form a time series. A **time series** is a set of observations of a variable measured at successive points in time or over successive periods of time. In this chapter we introduce several procedures for analyzing time series. The objective of such analyses is to provide good **forecasts** or predictions of future values of the time series.

A forecast is simply a prediction of what will happen in the future. Managers must learn to accept the fact that, regardless of the technique used, they will not be able to develop perfect forecasts.

Forecasting methods can be classified as quantitative or qualitative. Quantitative forecasting methods can be used when (1) past information about the variable being forecast is available, (2) the information can be quantified, and (3) a reasonable assumption is that the pattern of the past will continue into the future. In such cases, a forecast can be developed using a time series method or a causal method.

If the historical data are restricted to past values of the variable that we are trying to forecast, the forecasting procedure is called a **time series method.** The objective of time series methods is to discover a pattern in the historical data and then extrapolate this pattern into the future; the forecast is based solely on past values of the variable that we are trying to forecast and/or on past forecast errors. In this chapter we discuss three time series methods: smoothing (moving averages, weighted moving averages, and exponential smoothing), trend projection, and trend projection adjusted for seasonal influence.

Causal forecasting methods are based on the assumption that the variable we are trying to forecast exhibits a cause-effect relationship with one or more other variables. In this chapter we discuss the use of regression analysis as a causal forecasting method. For instance, the sales volume for many products is influenced by advertising expenditures, so regression analysis may be used to develop an equation showing how these two variables are related. Then, once the advertising budget has been set for the next period, we could substitute this value into the equation to develop a prediction or forecast of the sales volume for that period. Note that if a time series method had been used to develop the forecast, advertising expenditures would not even have been considered; that is, a time series method would have based the forecast solely on past sales.

Qualitative methods generally involve the use of expert judgment to develop forecasts. For instance, a panel of experts might develop a consensus forecast of the prime rate for a year from now. An advantage of qualitative procedures is that they can be applied when the information on the variable being forecast cannot be quantified and when historical data ei-

FIGURE 16.1 AN OVERVIEW OF FORECASTING METHODS

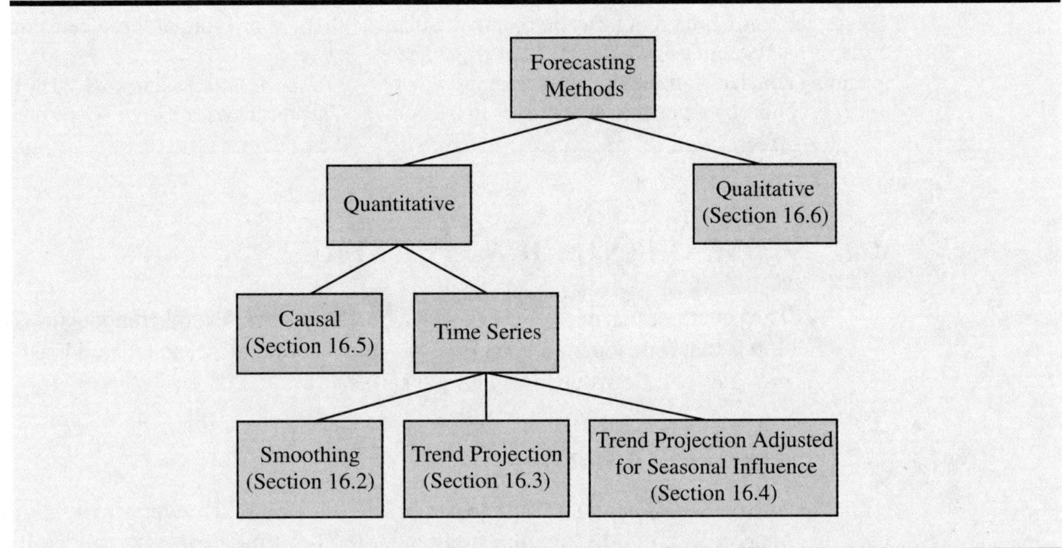

ther are not applicable or available. Figure 16.1 provides an overview of the types of forecasting methods.

Because all companies need to develop forecasts, forecasting is used in a wide variety of applications. For instance, the Management Science in Action, Forecasting Energy Needs at Cincinnati Gas & Electric Company, discusses the use of forecasting in the utility industry and a later Management Science in Action describes the forecasting of spare parts at American Airlines.

MANAGEMENT SCIENCE IN ACTION

FORECASTING ENERGY NEEDS AT CINCINNATI GAS & ELECTRIC COMPANY*

The Cincinnati Gas & Electric Company (CG&E), a subsidiary of Cinergy Corporation, provides gas service to approximately 440,000 gas customers and 720,000 electric customers. As in any modern company, forecasting at CG&E is an integral part of operating and managing the business. Depending on the decision to be made, the forecasting techniques used range from judgment and graphical trend projections to sophisticated statistical models.

Forecasting in the utility industry offers some unique perspectives. Because electricity cannot take the form of finished goods or in-process inventories, this product must be generated to meet the instantaneous requirements of the customers. Electrical shortages are not just lost sales, but "brownouts" or "blackouts." This situation places an unusual burden on the utility forecaster. On the positive side, the demand for energy and the sale of energy are more predictable than for many other products. Also, unlike the situation in a multiproduct firm, a great amount of forecasting effort and expertise can be concentrated on the two products: gas and electricity.

The largest observed electric demand for any given period, such as an hour, a day, a month, or a year, is defined as the peak load. The forecast of the annual electric peak load guides the timing decision for constructing future generating units, and the financial impact of this decision is great. Obviously, a timing decision that leads to having the unit available no sooner than necessary is crucial.

The energy forecasts are important in other ways also. For example, purchases of coal as fuel for the generating units are based on the forecast

(continued)

levels of energy needed. The revenue from the electric operations of the company is determined from forecasted sales, which in turn enters into the planning of rate changes and external financing. These planning and decision-making processes are among the most important managerial activities in the company. It is imperative that the decision makers have the best forecast information available to assist them in arriving at these decisions.

*Based on information provided by Dr. Richard Evans of Cincinnati Gas & Electric Company, Cincinnati, Ohio.

16.1 COMPONENTS OF A TIME SERIES

The pattern or behavior of the data in a time series has several components. The usual assumption is that four separate components—trend, cyclical, seasonal, and irregular—combine to provide specific values for the time series.

Trend Component

In time series analysis, the measurements may be taken every hour, day, week, month, or year, or at any other regular interval. Although time series data generally exhibit random fluctuations, the time series may still show gradual shifts or movements to relatively higher or lower values over a longer period of time. The gradual shifting of the time series is referred to as the **trend** in the time series. This shifting or trend is usually the result of long-term factors such as changes in the population, demographic characteristics of the population, technology, and consumer preferences.

For example, a manufacturer of photographic equipment may observe substantial month-to-month variability in the number of cameras sold. However, in reviewing sales over the past 10 to 15 years, this manufacturer may note a gradual increase in the annual sales volume. Suppose that the sales volume was approximately 1700 cameras per month in 1993, 2300 cameras per month in 1998, and 2500 cameras per month in 2003. Although actual month-to-month sales volumes may vary substantially, this gradual growth in sales shows an upward trend for the time series. Figure 16.2 shows a straight line that may be a good approximation of the trend in camera sales. Although the trend for camera sales appears to be linear and increasing over time, sometimes the trend in a time series can be described better by some other pattern.

Figure 16.3 shows some other possible time series trend patterns. Part (a) shows a nonlinear trend; in this case, the time series shows little growth initially, then a period of rapid growth, and finally a leveling off. This trend pattern might be a good approximation of sales for a product from introduction through a growth period and into a period of market saturation. The linear decreasing trend in part (b) is useful for time series displaying a steady decline over time. The horizontal line in part (c) represents a time series that has no consistent increase or decrease over time and thus no trend.

Cyclical Component

Although a time series may exhibit a trend over long periods of time, all future values of the time series will not fall exactly on the trend line. In fact, time series often show alternating sequences of points below and above the trend line. Any recurring sequence of points above and below the trend line lasting more than one year can be attributed to the **cyclical component** of the time series. Figure 16.4 shows the graph of a time series with an obvious cyclical component. The observations are taken at intervals of one year.

FIGURE 16.2 LINEAR TREND OF CAMERA SALES

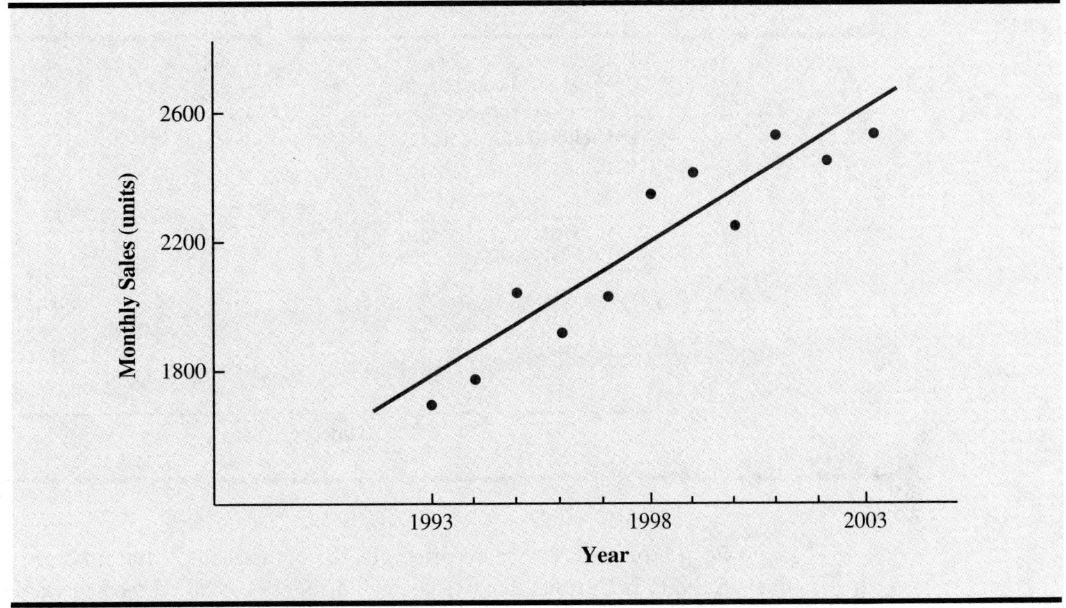

Many time series exhibit cyclical behavior with regular runs of observations below and above the trend line. Generally, this component of the time series results from multiyear cyclical movements in the economy. For example, periods of modest inflation followed by periods of rapid inflation can lead to many time series that alternate below and above a generally increasing trend line (e.g., a time series for housing costs).

Seasonal Component

Whereas the trend and cyclical components of a time series are identified by analyzing multiyear movements in historical data, many time series show a regular pattern over one-year periods. For example, a manufacturer of swimming pools expects low sales activity in the fall and winter months, with peak sales occurring in the spring and summer months. Manufacturers of snow removal equipment and heavy clothing, however, expect just the

FIGURE 16.3 EXAMPLES OF SOME POSSIBLE TIME SERIES TREND PATTERNS

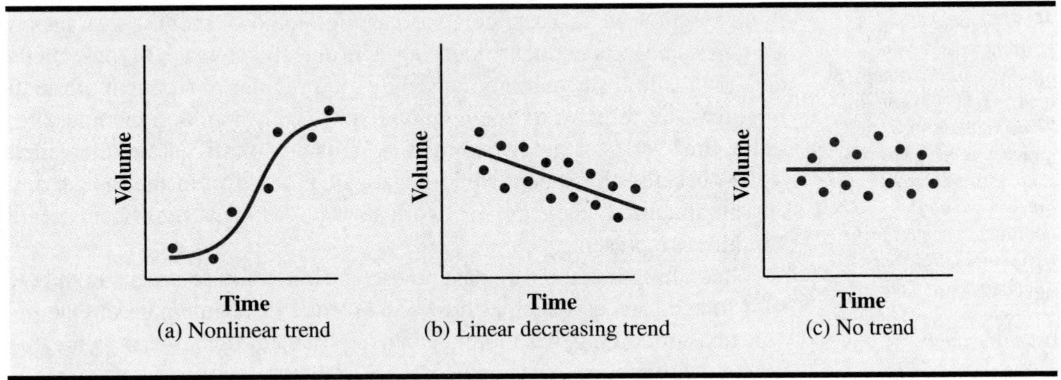

FIGURE 16.4 TREND AND CYCLICAL COMPONENTS OF A TIME SERIES (DATA POINTS ARE ONE YEAR APART)

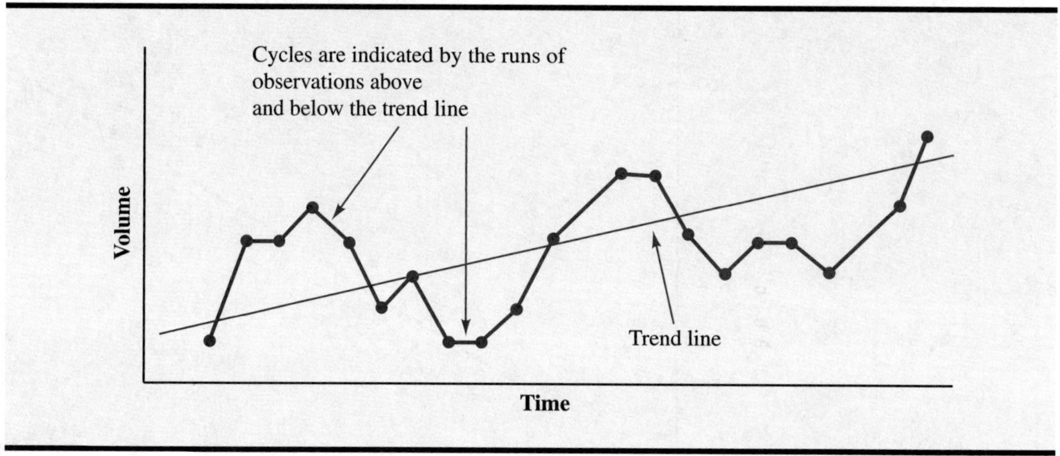

opposite yearly pattern. Not surprisingly, the component of the time series that represents the variability in the data due to seasonal influences is called the **seasonal component.** Although we generally think of seasonal movement in a time series as occurring within one year, the seasonal component also may be used to represent any regularly repeating pattern that is less than one year in duration. For example, daily traffic volume data show within-the-day "seasonal" behavior, with peak levels during rush hours, moderate flow during the rest of the day, and light flow from midnight to early morning.

Irregular Component

The **irregular component** of the time series is the residual or "catchall" factor that includes deviations of actual time series values from those expected given the effects of the trend, cyclical, and seasonal components. It accounts for the random variability in the time series. The irregular component is caused by the short-term, unanticipated, and nonrecurring factors that affect the time series. Because this component accounts for the random variability in the time series, it is unpredictable. We cannot attempt to predict its impact on the time series.

16.2 SMOOTHING METHODS

Many manufacturing environments require forecasts for thousands of items weekly or monthly. Thus, in choosing a forecasting technique, simplicity and ease of use are important criteria. The data requirements for the techniques in this section are minimal, and the techniques are easy to use and understand.

In this section we discuss three forecasting methods: moving averages, weighted moving averages, and exponential smoothing. The objective of each of these methods is to "smooth out" the random fluctuations caused by the irregular component of the time series. Therefore, they are referred to as *smoothing methods.* Smoothing methods are appropriate for a stable time series—that is, one that exhibits no significant trend, cyclical, or seasonal effects—because they adapt well to changes in the level of the time series. However, without modification, they do not work as well when a significant trend and/or seasonal variation are present.

Smoothing methods are easy to use and generally provide a high level of accuracy for short-range forecasts such as a forecast for the next time period. One of the methods, exponential smoothing, has minimal data requirements and thus is a good method to use when forecasts are required for large numbers of items.

Moving Averages

The **moving averages** method uses the average of the *most recent n* data values in the time series as the forecast for the next period. Mathematically,

$$\text{Moving average} = \frac{\Sigma(\text{most recent } n \text{ data values})}{n} \tag{16.1}$$

The term *moving* indicates that, as a new observation becomes available for the time series, it replaces the oldest observation in equation (16.1), and a new average is computed. As a result, the average will change, or move, as new observations become available.

To illustrate the moving averages method, consider the 12 weeks of data presented in Table 16.1 and Figure 16.5. These data show the number of gallons of gasoline sold by a gasoline distributor in Bennington, Vermont, over the past 12 weeks. Figure 16.5 indicates that, although random variability is present, the time series appears to be stable over time. Thus, the smoothing methods of this section are applicable.

To use moving averages to forecast gasoline sales, we must first select the number of data values to be included in the moving average. For example, let us compute forecasts using a three-week moving average. The moving average calculation for the first three weeks of the gasoline sales time series is

$$\text{Moving average (weeks 1–3)} = \frac{17 + 21 + 19}{3} = 19$$

We then use this moving average value as the forecast for week 4. The actual value observed in week 4 is 23, so the forecast error in week 4 is $23 - 19 = 4$. In general, the error associated with a forecast is the difference between the observed value of the time series and the forecast.

The calculation for the second three-week moving average is

$$\text{Moving average (weeks 2–4)} = \frac{21 + 19 + 23}{3} = 21$$

TABLE 16.1 GASOLINE SALES TIMES SERIES

Week	Sales (1000s of gallons)
1	17
2	21
3	19
4	23
5	18
6	16
7	20
8	18
9	22
10	20
11	15
12	22

FIGURE 16.5 GRAPH OF GASOLINE SALES TIME SERIES

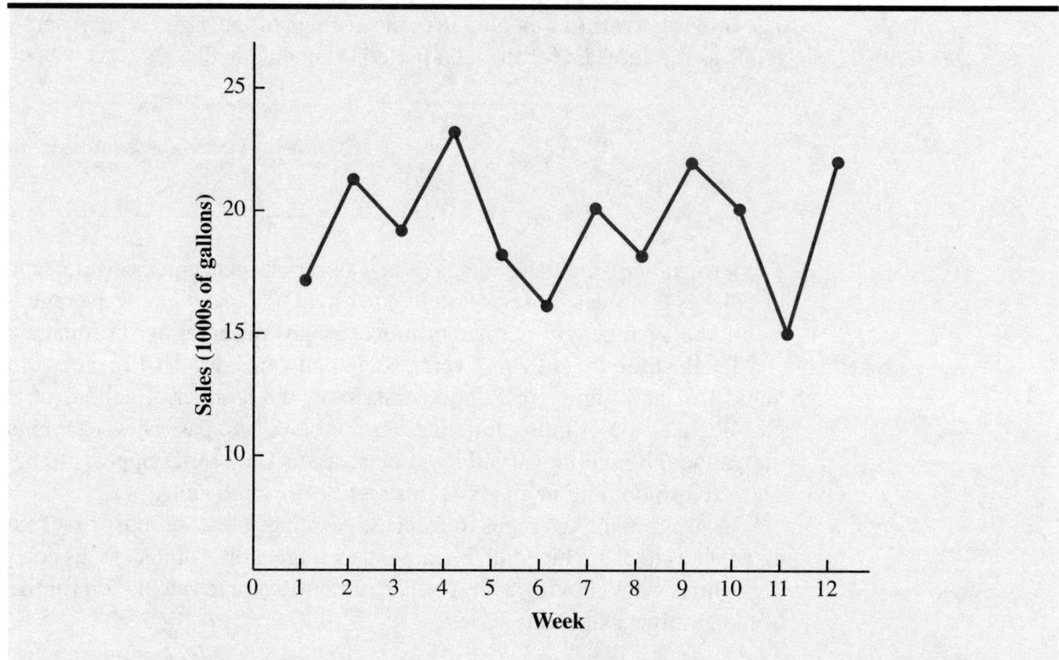

Try Problem 1 for practice in using moving averages to compute a forecast.

Hence, the forecast for week 5 is 21, and the error associated with this forecast is $18 - 21 = -3$. Thus, the forecast error may be positive or negative, depending on whether the forecast is too low or too high. A complete summary of the three-week moving average calculations for the gasoline sales time series is shown in Table 16.2.

To forecast gasoline sales for week 13 using a three-week moving average, we need to compute the average of sales for weeks 10, 11, and 12. The calculation for this moving average is

$$\text{Moving average (weeks 10–12)} = \frac{20 + 15 + 22}{3} = 19$$

Hence, the forecast for week 13 is 19, or 19,000 gallons of gasoline. Figure 16.6 shows a graph of the original time series and the three-week moving average forecasts.

Forecast Accuracy. An important consideration in selecting a forecasting method is the accuracy of the forecast. Clearly, we want forecast errors to be small. The last two columns of Table 16.2, which contain the forecast errors and the forecast errors squared, can be used to develop measures of forecast accuracy.

For the gasoline sales time series, we can use the last column of Table 16.2 to compute the average of the sum of the squared errors. Doing so, we obtain

$$\text{Average of the sum of squared errors} = \frac{92}{9} = 10.22$$

This average of the sum of squared errors is commonly referred to as the **mean squared error (MSE).** The MSE is an often-used measure of the accuracy of a forecasting method and is the one we use in this chapter.

TABLE 16.2 SUMMARY OF THREE-WEEK MOVING AVERAGE CALCULATIONS

Week	Time Series Value	Moving Average Forecast	Forecast Error	Squared Forecast Error
1	17			
2	21			
3	19			
4	23	19	4	16
5	18	21	−3	9
6	16	20	−4	16
7	20	19	1	1
8	18	18	0	0
9	22	18	4	16
10	20	20	0	0
11	15	20	−5	25
12	22	19	3	9
		Totals	0	92

Problem 2 will test your ability to use MSE as a measure of forecast accuracy.

As we indicated previously, to use the moving averages method, we must first select the number of data values to be included in the moving average. Not surprisingly, for a particular time series, different lengths of moving averages will affect the accuracy of the forecast. One possible approach to choosing the number of values to be included is to use trial and error to identify the length that minimizes the MSE. Then, if we assume that the length that is best for the past will also be best for the future, we would forecast the next value in

FIGURE 16.6 GRAPH OF GASOLINE SALES TIME SERIES AND THREE-WEEK MOVING AVERAGE FORECASTS

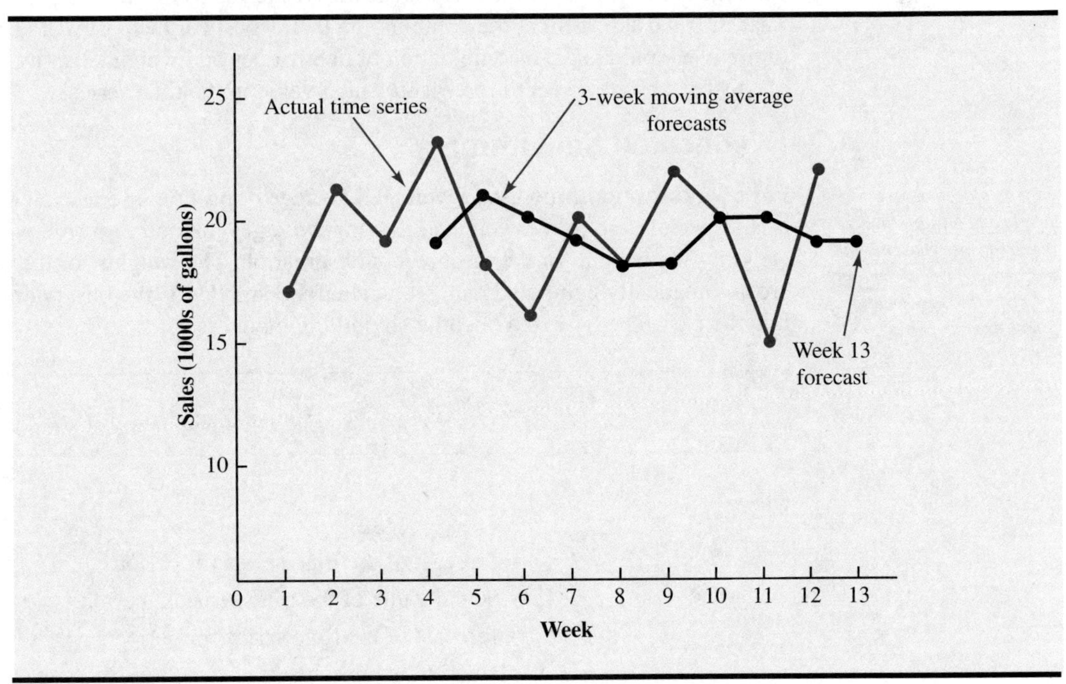

the time series using the number of data values that minimized the MSE for the historical time series.

Weighted Moving Averages

In the moving averages method, each observation in the calculation receives the same weight. One variation, known as **weighted moving averages,** involves selecting different weights for each data value and then computing a weighted average of the most recent n data values as the forecast. In most cases, the most recent observation receives the most weight, and the weight decreases for older data values. For example, we can use the gasoline sales time series to illustrate the computation of a weighted three-week moving average, with the most recent observation receiving a weight three times as great as that given the oldest observation, and the next oldest observation receiving a weight twice as great as the oldest. For week 4 the computation is

$$\text{Weighted moving averages forecast for week 4} = \frac{3}{6}(19) + \frac{2}{6}(21) + \frac{1}{6}(17) = 19.33$$

Note that for the weighted moving average the sum of the weights is equal to 1. Actually, this condition was also true for the simple moving average: Each weight was ⅓. However, recall that the simple or unweighted moving average provided a forecast of 19.

Forecast Accuracy. To use the weighted moving averages method, we must first select the number of data values to be included in the weighted moving average and then choose weights for each of the data values. In general, if we believe that the recent past is a better predictor of the future than the distant past, larger weights should be given to the more recent observations. However, when the time series is highly variable, selecting approximately equal weights for each data value may be best. Note that the only requirement in selecting the weights is that their sum must equal 1. To determine whether one particular combination of data values and weights provides a more accurate forecast than another combination, we will continue to use the MSE criterion as the measure of forecast accuracy. That is, if we assume that the combination that is best for the past will also be best for the future, we would use the combination of data values and weights that minimized MSE for the historical time series to forecast the next value in the time series.

Exponential Smoothing

Exponential smoothing is simple and has few data requirements. Thus, it is an inexpensive, useful approach for firms that make many forecasts each period.

Exponential smoothing uses a weighted average of past time series values as the forecast; it is a special case of the weighted moving averages method in which we select only one weight—the weight for the most recent observation. The weights for the other data values are automatically computed and get smaller and smaller as the observations move farther into the past. The basic exponential smoothing model is

$$F_{t+1} = \alpha Y_t + (1 - \alpha)F_t \qquad (16.2)$$

where

$$\begin{aligned} F_{t+1} &= \text{forecast of the time series for period } t + 1 \\ Y_t &= \text{actual value of the time series in period } t \\ F_t &= \text{forecast of the time series for period } t \\ \alpha &= \text{smoothing constant } (0 \le \alpha \le 1) \end{aligned}$$

Equation (16.2) shows that the forecast for period $t + 1$ is a weighted average of the actual value in period t and the forecast for period t; note in particular that the weight given to the actual value in period t is α and that the weight given to the forecast in period t is $1 - \alpha$. We can demonstrate that the exponential smoothing forecast for any period also is a weighted average of *all the previous actual values* for the time series with a time series consisting of three periods of data: Y_1, Y_2, and Y_3. To start the calculations, we let F_1 equal the actual value of the time series in period 1; that is, $F_1 = Y_1$. Hence, the forecast for period 2

$$\begin{aligned} F_2 &= \alpha Y_1 + (1 - \alpha)F_1 \\ &= \alpha Y_1 + (1 - \alpha)Y_1 \\ &= Y_1 \end{aligned}$$

Thus, the exponential smoothing forecast for period 2 is equal to the actual value of the time series in period 1.

The forecast for period 3 is

$$F_3 = \alpha Y_2 + (1 - \alpha)F_2 = \alpha Y_2 + (1 - \alpha)Y_1$$

Finally, substituting this expression for F_3 in the expression for F_4, we obtain

$$\begin{aligned} F_4 &= \alpha Y_3 + (1 - \alpha)F_3 \\ &= \alpha Y_3 + (1 - \alpha)[\alpha Y_2 + (1 - \alpha)Y_1] \\ &= \alpha Y_3 + \alpha(1 - \alpha)Y_2 + (1 - \alpha)^2 Y_1 \end{aligned}$$

Hence, F_4 is a weighted average of the first three time series values. The sum of the coefficients, or weights, for Y_1, Y_2, and Y_3 equals 1. A similar argument can be made to show that, in general, any forecast F_{t+1} is a weighted average of all the previous time series values.

Despite the fact that exponential smoothing provides a forecast that is a weighted average of all past observations, all the past data do not need to be saved in order to compute the forecast for the next period. In fact, once the **smoothing constant** α has been selected, only two pieces of information are required to compute the forecast. Equation (16.2) shows that with a given α we can compute the forecast for period $t + 1$ simply by knowing the actual and forecast time series values for period t—that is, Y_t and F_t.

To illustrate the exponential smoothing approach to forecasting, consider the gasoline sales time series presented previously in Table 16.1 and Figure 16.5. As indicated, the exponential smoothing forecast for period 2 is equal to the actual value of the time series in period 1. Thus, with $Y_1 = 17$, we set $F_2 = 17$ to get the exponential smoothing computations started. From the time series data in Table 16.1, we find an actual time series value in period 2 of $Y_2 = 21$. Thus, period 2 has a forecast error of $21 - 17 = 4$.

Continuing with the exponential smoothing computations, using a smoothing constant of $\alpha = 0.2$, provides the forecast for period 3:

$$F_3 = 0.2Y_2 + 0.8F_2 = 0.2(21) + 0.8(17) = 17.8$$

Once the actual time series value in period 3, $Y_3 = 19$, is known, we can generate a forecast for period 4:

$$F_4 = 0.2Y_3 + 0.8F_3 = 0.2(19) + 0.8(17.8) = 18.04$$

By continuing the exponential smoothing calculations, we can determine the weekly forecast values and the corresponding weekly forecast errors, as shown in Table 16.3. Note

TABLE 16.3 SUMMARY OF THE EXPONENTIAL SMOOTHING FORECASTS AND FORECAST ERRORS FOR GASOLINE SALES WITH SMOOTHING CONSTANT $\alpha = 0.2$

Week (t)	Time Series Value (Y_t)	Exponential Smoothing Forecast (F_t)	Forecast Error ($Y_t - F_t$)
1	17		
2	21	17.00	4.00
3	19	17.80	1.20
4	23	18.04	4.96
5	18	19.03	−1.03
6	16	18.83	−2.83
7	20	18.26	1.74
8	18	18.61	−0.61
9	22	18.49	3.51
10	20	19.19	0.81
11	15	19.35	−4.35
12	22	18.48	3.52

that we have not shown an exponential smoothing forecast or the forecast error for period 1 because no forecast was made. For week 12, we have $Y_{12} = 22$ and $F_{12} = 18.48$. Can we use this information to generate a forecast for week 13 before the actual value of week 13 becomes known? Using the exponential smoothing model, we have

$$F_{13} = 0.2Y_{12} + 0.8F_{12} = 0.2(22) + 0.8(18.48) = 19.18$$

Can you now use exponential smoothing to develop forecasts? Try Problem 4.

Thus, the exponential smoothing forecast of the amount sold in week 13 is 19.18, or 19,180 gallons of gasoline. With this forecast, the firm can make plans and decisions accordingly. The accuracy of the forecast will not be known until the end of week 13.

Figure 16.7 shows the plot of the actual and the forecast values from Table 16.3. Note in particular how the forecasts "smooth out" the irregular fluctuations in the time series.

Forecast Accuracy. In the preceding exponential smoothing calculations, we used a smoothing constant of $\alpha = 0.2$. Although any value of α between 0 and 1 is acceptable, some values will yield better forecasts than others. Insight into choosing a good value for α can be obtained by rewriting the basic exponential smoothing model as follows:

$$\begin{aligned} F_{t+1} &= \alpha Y_t + (1 - \alpha)F_t \\ &= \alpha Y_t + F_t - \alpha F_t \\ &= \underbrace{F_t}_{\text{Forecast in period } t} + \alpha\underbrace{(Y_t - F_t)}_{\text{Forecast error in period } t} \end{aligned} \tag{16.3}$$

Thus, the new forecast F_{t+1} is equal to the previous forecast F_t plus an adjustment, which is α times the most recent forecast error, $Y_t - F_t$. That is, the forecast in period $t + 1$ is ob-

FIGURE 16.7 GRAPH OF ACTUAL AND FORECAST GASOLINE SALES TIME SERIES WITH SMOOTHING CONSTANT $\alpha = 0.2$

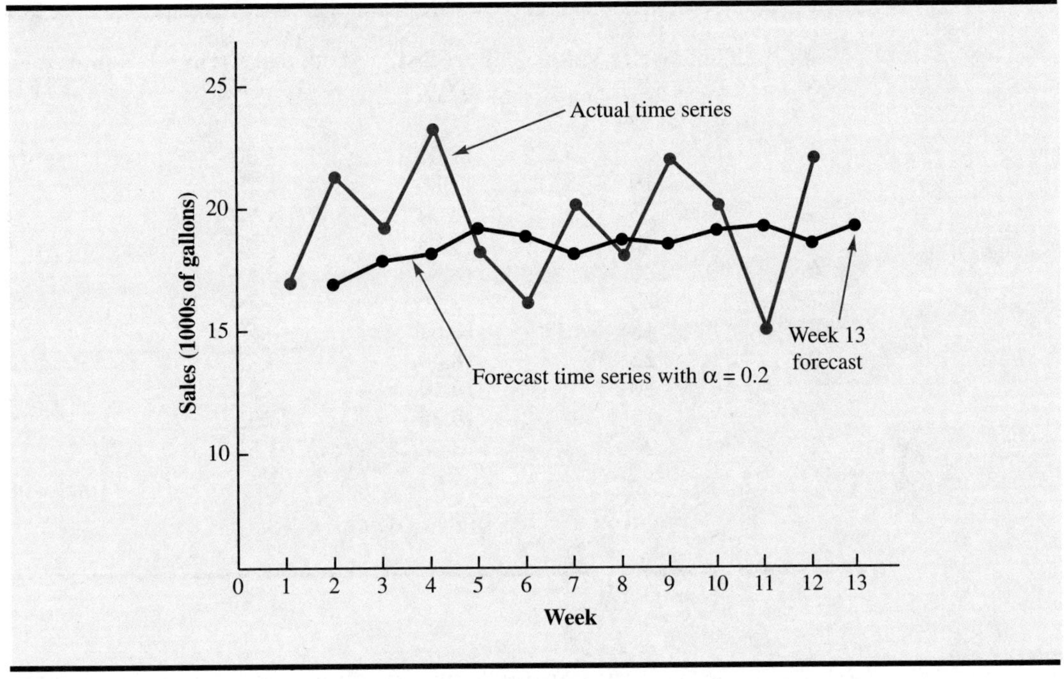

tained by adjusting the forecast in period t by a fraction of the forecast error. If the time series contains substantial random variability, a small value of the smoothing constant is preferred. The reason for this choice is that, because much of the forecast error is due to random variability, we do not want to overreact and adjust the forecasts too quickly. For a time series with relatively little random variability, larger values of the smoothing constant have the advantage of quickly adjusting the forecasts when forecasting errors occur and therefore allowing the forecast to react faster to changing conditions.

Problem 5 asks you to determine whether moving averages or exponential smoothing provides the best forecasts for a given set of data.

The criterion we use to determine a desirable value for the smoothing constant α is the same as the criterion we proposed earlier for determining the number of periods of data to include in the moving averages calculation. That is, we choose the value of α that minimizes the mean squared error. A summary of the MSE calculations for the exponential smoothing forecast of gasoline sales with $\alpha = 0.2$ is shown in Table 16.4. Note that there is one less squared error term than the number of periods of data because we had no past values with which to make a forecast for period 1. Would a different value of α have provided better results in terms of a lower MSE value? Perhaps the most straightforward way to answer this question is simply to try another value for α. We then compare its mean squared error with the MSE value of 8.98, obtained using a smoothing constant of $\alpha = 0.2$.

The exponential smoothing results with $\alpha = 0.3$ are shown in Table 16.5. With MSE = 9.35, a smoothing constant of $\alpha = 0.3$ results in less forecast accuracy than a smoothing constant of $\alpha = 0.2$. Thus, we would be inclined to use the original smoothing constant of 0.2. Using a trial-and-error calculation with other values of α, we can find a "good" value for the smoothing constant. This value can be used in the exponential smoothing model to provide forecasts for the future. At a later date, after new time series observations have been obtained, we analyze the newly collected time series data to determine whether the smoothing constant should be revised to provide better forecasting results.

TABLE 16.4 MEAN SQUARED ERROR COMPUTATIONS FOR FORECASTING GASOLINE SALES WITH $\alpha = 0.2$

Week (t)	Time Series Value (Y_t)	Forecast (F_t)	Forecast Error ($Y_t - F_t$)	Squared Forecast Error $(Y_t - F_t)^2$
1	17			
2	21	17.00	4.00	16.00
3	19	17.80	1.20	1.44
4	23	18.04	4.96	24.60
5	18	19.03	−1.03	1.06
6	16	18.83	−2.83	8.01
7	20	18.26	1.74	3.03
8	18	18.61	−0.61	0.37
9	22	18.49	3.51	12.32
10	20	19.19	0.81	0.66
11	15	19.35	−4.35	18.92
12	22	18.48	3.52	12.39
			Total	98.80

MSE = 98.80/11 = 8.98

TABLE 16.5 MEAN SQUARED ERROR COMPUTATIONS FOR FORECASTING GASOLINE SALES WITH $\alpha = 0.3$

Week (t)	Time Series Value (Y_t)	Forecast (F_t)	Forecast Error ($Y_t - F_t$)	Squared Forecast Error $(Y_t - F_t)^2$
1	17			
2	21	17.00	4.00	16.00
3	19	18.20	0.80	0.64
4	23	18.44	4.56	20.79
5	18	19.81	−1.81	3.28
6	16	19.27	−3.27	10.69
7	20	18.29	1.71	2.92
8	18	18.80	−0.80	0.64
9	22	18.56	3.44	11.83
10	20	19.59	0.41	0.17
11	15	19.71	−4.71	22.18
12	22	18.30	3.70	13.69
			Total	102.83

MSE = 102.83/11 = 9.35

NOTES AND COMMENTS

1. Another commonly used measure of forecast accuracy is the **mean absolute deviation (MAD).** This measure is simply the average of the absolute values of all the forecast errors. Using the errors given in Table 16.2, we obtain

$$\text{MAD} = \frac{4 + 3 + 4 + 1 + 0 + 4 + 0 + 5 + 3}{9} = 2.67$$

One major difference between the MSE and the MAD is that the MSE measure is influenced much more by large forecast errors than by small errors (for the MSE measure the errors are squared). The selection of the best measure of forecasting accuracy is not a simple matter. Indeed, forecasting experts often disagree as to which measure should be used. We use the MSE measure in this chapter.

2. Spreadsheet packages are an effective aid in choosing a good value of α for exponential smoothing and selecting weights for the weighted moving averages method. With the time series data and the forecasting formulas in the spreadsheets, you can experiment with different values of α (or moving average weights) and choose the value(s) providing the smallest MSE or MAD. In the chapter appendix, we show how this process can be done.

16.3 TREND PROJECTION

In this section we show how to forecast the values of a time series that exhibits a long-term linear trend. The type of time series for which the trend projection method is applicable shows a consistent increase or decrease over time. Because this type of time series is not stable, the smoothing methods described in the preceding section are not applicable.

Consider the time series for bicycle sales of a particular manufacturer over the past 10 years, as shown in Table 16.6 and Figure 16.8. Note that 21,600 bicycles were sold in year 1; 22,900 were sold in year 2; and so on. In year 10, the most recent year, 31,400 bicycles were sold. Although Figure 16.8 shows some up-and-down movement over the past 10 years, the time series for the number of bicycles sold seems to have an overall increasing or upward trend.

We do not want the trend component of a time series to follow each and every "up" and "down" movement. Rather, the trend component should reflect the gradual shifting—in this case, growth—of the time series values. After we view the time series data in Table 16.6

TABLE 16.6 BICYCLE SALES TIME SERIES

Year (t)	Sales (1000s) (Y_t)
1	21.6
2	22.9
3	25.5
4	21.9
5	23.9
6	27.5
7	31.5
8	29.7
9	28.6
10	31.4

FIGURE 16.8 GRAPH OF BICYCLE SALES TIME SERIES

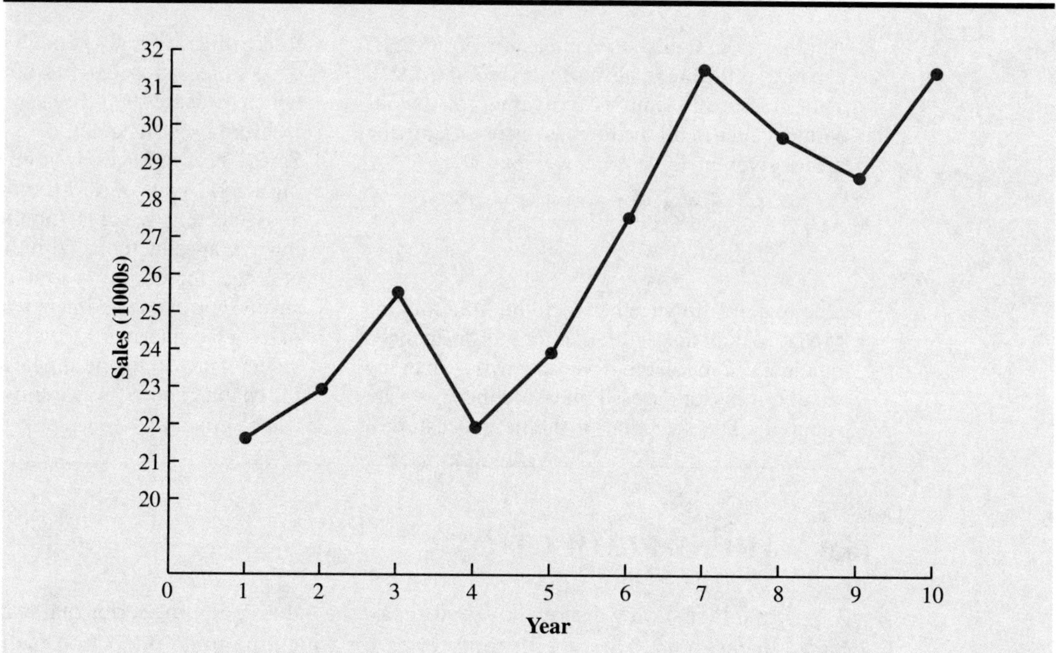

and the graph in Figure 16.8, we might agree that a linear trend as shown in Figure 16.9 provides a reasonable description of the long-run movement in the series.

We use the bicycle sales data to illustrate the calculations involved in applying regression analysis to identify a linear trend. For a linear trend, the estimated sales volume expressed as a function of time is

$$T_t = b_0 + b_1 t \tag{16.4}$$

where

T_t = trend value for bicycle sales in period t
b_0 = intercept of the trend line
b_1 = slope of the trend line

Note that, for the time series on bicycle sales, $t = 1$ corresponds to the oldest time series value and $t = 10$ corresponds to the most recent time series value. The equations for computing b_1 and b_0 are

$$b_1 = \frac{\Sigma tY_t - (\Sigma t \Sigma Y_t)/n}{\Sigma t^2 - (\Sigma t)^2/n} \tag{16.5}$$

$$b_0 = \bar{Y} - b_1 \bar{t} \tag{16.6}$$

FIGURE 16.9 TREND REPRESENTED BY A LINEAR FUNCTION FOR BICYCLE SALES

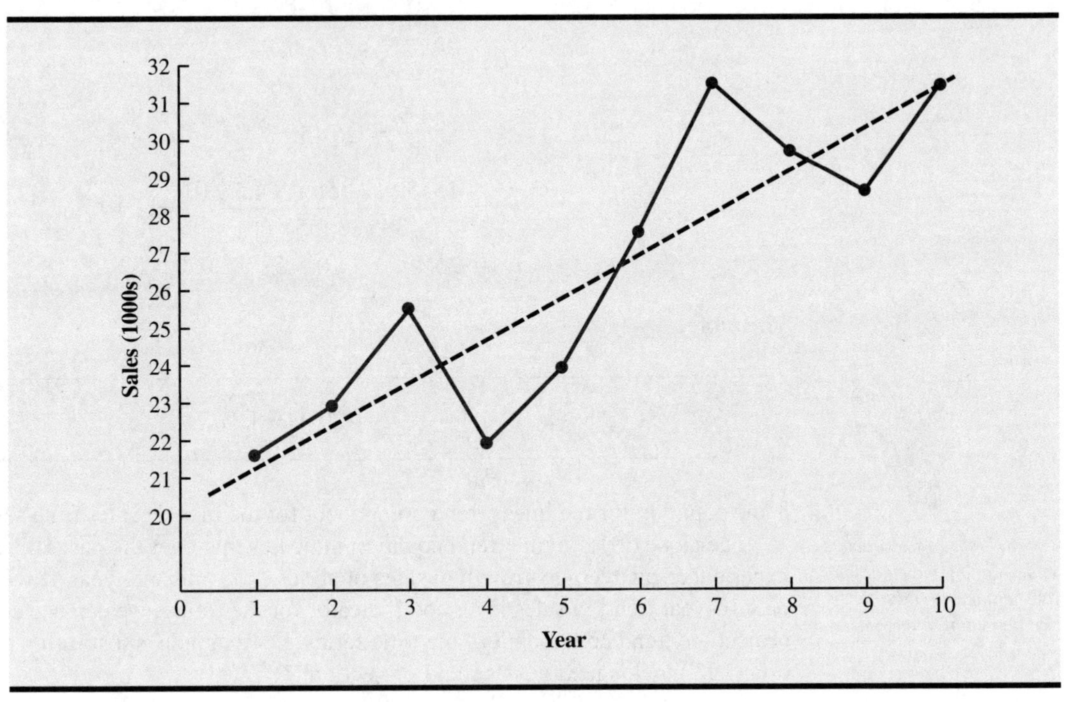

where

Y_t = actual value of the time series in period t
n = number of periods
$\bar{Y}$ = average value of the time series; that is, $\bar{Y} = \sum Y_t/n$
$\bar{t}$ = average value of t; that is, $\bar{t} = \sum t/n$

	t	Y_t	tY_t	t^2
	1	21.6	21.6	1
	2	22.9	45.8	4
	3	25.5	76.5	9
	4	21.9	87.6	16
	5	23.9	119.5	25
	6	27.5	165.0	36
	7	31.5	220.5	49
	8	29.7	237.6	64
	9	28.6	257.4	81
	10	31.4	314.0	100
Totals	55	264.5	1545.5	385

Using these relationships for b_0 and b_1 and the bicycle sales data of Table 16.6, we obtain the following calculations.

$$\bar{t} = \frac{55}{10} = 5.5$$

$$\bar{Y} = \frac{264.5}{10} = 26.45$$

$$b_1 = \frac{1545.5 - (55)(264.5)/10}{385 - (55)^2/10} = 1.10$$

$$b_0 = 26.45 - 1.10(5.5) = 20.4$$

Therefore,

$$T_t = 20.4 + 1.1t \qquad (16.7)$$

is the equation for the linear trend component for the bicycle sales time series.

Try Problem 14 for practice in developing the equation for the linear trend component of a time series.

The slope of 1.1 in the trend equation indicates that over the past 10 years the firm has experienced an average growth in sales of about 1100 units per year. If we assume that the past 10-year trend in sales is a good indicator for the future, we can use equation (16.7) to project the trend component of the time series. For example, substituting $t = 11$ into equation (16.7) yields next year's trend projection, T_{11}:

$$T_{11} = 20.4 + 1.1(11) = 32.5$$

Thus, the trend component yields a sales forecast of 32,500 bicycles for next year.

We can also use the trend line to forecast sales farther into the future. For instance, using equation (16.7), we develop forecasts for an additional 2 and 3 years into the future as follows:

$$T_{12} = 20.4 + 1.1(12) = 33.6$$
$$T_{13} = 20.4 + 1.1(13) = 34.7$$

The use of a linear function to model the trend is common. However, as we discussed earlier, sometimes time series exhibit a curvilinear (nonlinear) trend similar to those shown in Figure 16.10. More advanced texts discuss how to develop models for these more complex relationships.

16.4 TREND AND SEASONAL COMPONENTS

We have shown how to forecast the values of a time series that has a trend component. In this section we extend the discussion by showing how to forecast the values of a time series that has both trend and seasonal components.

Many situations in business and economics involve period-to-period comparisons. For instance, we might be interested to learn that unemployment is up 2 percent compared to last month, steel production is up 5 percent over last month, or that the production of electric power is down 3 percent from the previous month. Care must be exercised in using such information, however, because whenever a seasonal influence is present, such comparisons

FIGURE 16.10 SOME POSSIBLE FORMS OF NONLINEAR TREND PATTERNS

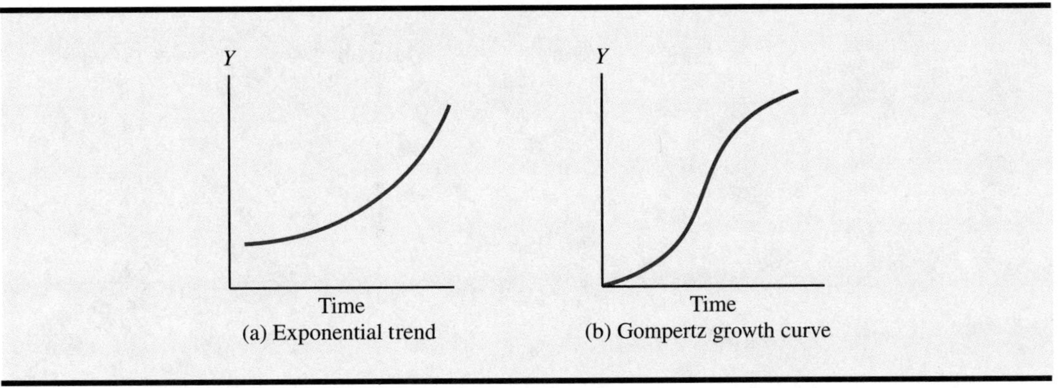

usually are not especially meaningful. For instance, the fact that electric power consumption is down by 3 percent from August to September might be only the seasonal effect associated with a decrease in the use of air conditioning and not because of a long-term decline in the use of electric power. Indeed, after adjusting for the seasonal effect, we might even find that the use of electric power has increased.

Removing the seasonal effect from a time series is known as *deseasonalizing the time series.* After we do so, period-to-period comparisons are more meaningful and can help identify whether a trend exists. The approach we take in this section is appropriate in situations when only seasonal effects are present or in situations when both seasonal and trend components are present. The first step is to compute seasonal indexes and use them to deseasonalize the data. Then, if a trend is apparent in the deseasonalized data, we use regression analysis on the deseasonalized data to estimate the trend.

Multiplicative Model

In addition to a trend component T and a seasonal component S, we assume that the time series also has an irregular component I. The irregular component accounts for the random effects in the time series that cannot be explained by the trend and seasonal components. Using T_t, S_t, and I_t to identify the trend, seasonal, and irregular components at time t, we assume that the actual time series value, denoted by Y_t, can be described by the **multiplicative time series model.**

$$Y_t = T_t \times S_t \times I_t \tag{16.8}$$

In this model, T_t is the trend measured in units of the item being forecast. However, the S_t and I_t components are measured in relative terms, with values above 1.00 indicating effects above the trend, and values below 1.00 indicating effects below the trend.

We illustrate the use of the multiplicative model with trend, seasonal, and irregular components by working with the quarterly data presented in Table 16.7 and Figure 16.11. These data show television set sales (in thousands of units) for a particular manufacturer over the past four years. We begin by showing how to identify the seasonal component of the time series.

TABLE 16.7 QUARTERLY DATA FOR TELEVISION SET SALES

Year	Quarter	Sales (1000s)
1	1	4.8
	2	4.1
	3	6.0
	4	6.5
2	1	5.8
	2	5.2
	3	6.8
	4	7.4
3	1	6.0
	2	5.6
	3	7.5
	4	7.8
4	1	6.3
	2	5.9
	3	8.0
	4	8.4

FIGURE 16.11 GRAPH OF QUARTERLY TELEVISION SET SALES TIME SERIES

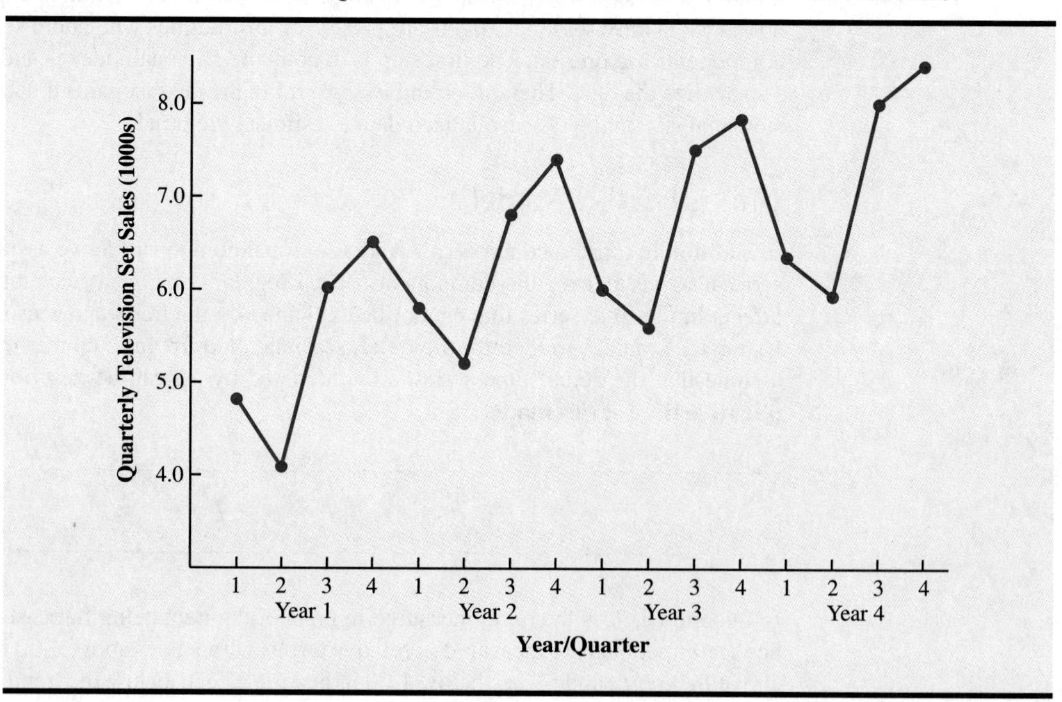

Calculating the Seasonal Indexes

Figure 16.11 indicates that sales are lowest in the second quarter of each year, followed by higher sales levels in quarters 3 and 4. Thus, we conclude that a seasonal pattern exists for television set sales. We begin the computational procedure used to identify each quarter's seasonal influence by computing a moving average to isolate the combined seasonal and irregular components, S_t and I_t.

To do so, we use one year of data in each calculation. Because we are working with a quarterly series, we use four data values in each moving average. The moving average calculation for the first four quarters of the television set sales data is

$$\text{First moving average} = \frac{4.8 + 4.1 + 6.0 + 6.5}{4} = \frac{21.4}{4} = 5.35$$

Note that the moving average calculation for the first four quarters yields the average quarterly sales over year 1 of the time series. Continuing the moving average calculation, we next add the 5.8 value for the first quarter of year 2 and drop the 4.8 for the first quarter of year 1. Thus, the second moving average is

$$\text{Second moving average} = \frac{4.1 + 6.0 + 6.5 + 5.8}{4} = \frac{22.4}{4} = 5.6$$

Similarly, the third moving average calculation is $(16.0 + 6.5 + 5.8 + 5.2)/4 = 5.875$.

Before we proceed with the moving average calculations for the entire time series, we return to the first moving average calculation, which resulted in a value of 5.35. The 5.35 value represents an average quarterly sales volume (across all seasons) for year 1. As we look back at the calculation of the 5.35 value, associating 5.35 with the "middle" quarter of the moving average group makes sense. Note, however, that we encounter some difficulty in identifying the middle quarter; four quarters in the moving average allow for no middle quarter. The 5.35 value corresponds to the last half of quarter 2 and the first half of quarter 3. Similarly, if we go to the next moving average value of 5.60, the middle corresponds to the last half of quarter 3 and the first half of quarter 4.

Recall that the reason for computing moving averages is to isolate the combined seasonal and irregular components. However, the moving average values we computed do not correspond directly to the original quarters of the time series. We can resolve this difficulty by using the midpoints between successive moving average values. For example, because 5.35 corresponds to the first half of quarter 3 and 5.60 corresponds to the last half of quarter 3, we can use $(5.35 + 5.60)/2 = 5.475$ as the moving average value for quarter 3. Similarly, we associate a moving average value of $(5.60 + 5.875)/2 = 5.738$ with quarter 4. The result is a *centered moving average.* Table 16.8 shows a complete summary of the moving average and centered moving average calculations for the television set sales data.

If the number of data points in a moving average calculation is an odd number, the middle point will correspond to one of the periods in the time series. In such cases, we would not have to center the moving average values to correspond to a particular time period, as we did in the calculations in Table 16.8.

What do the centered moving averages in Table 16.8 tell us about this time series? Figure 16.12 shows plots of the actual time series values and the corresponding centered moving average. Note particularly how the centered moving average values tend to "smooth out" both the seasonal and irregular fluctuations in the time series. The moving average values computed for four quarters of data do not include the fluctuations due to seasonal in-

TABLE 16.8 CENTERED MOVING AVERAGE CALCULATIONS FOR THE TELEVISION SET SALES TIME SERIES

Year	Quarter	Sales (1000s)	Four-Quarter Moving Average	Centered Moving Average
1	1	4.8		
	2	4.1		
			5.350	
	3	6.0		5.475
			5.600	
	4	6.5		5.738
			5.875	
2	1	5.8		5.975
			6.075	
	2	5.2		6.188
			6.300	
	3	6.8		6.325
			6.350	
	4	7.4		6.400
			6.450	
3	1	6.0		6.538
			6.625	
	2	5.6		6.675
			6.725	
	3	7.5		6.763
			6.800	
	4	7.8		6.838
			6.875	
4	1	6.3		6.938
			7.000	
	2	5.9		7.075
			7.150	
	3	8.0		
	4	8.4		

FIGURE 16.12 GRAPH OF QUARTERLY TELEVISION SET SALES TIME SERIES AND CENTERED MOVING AVERAGE

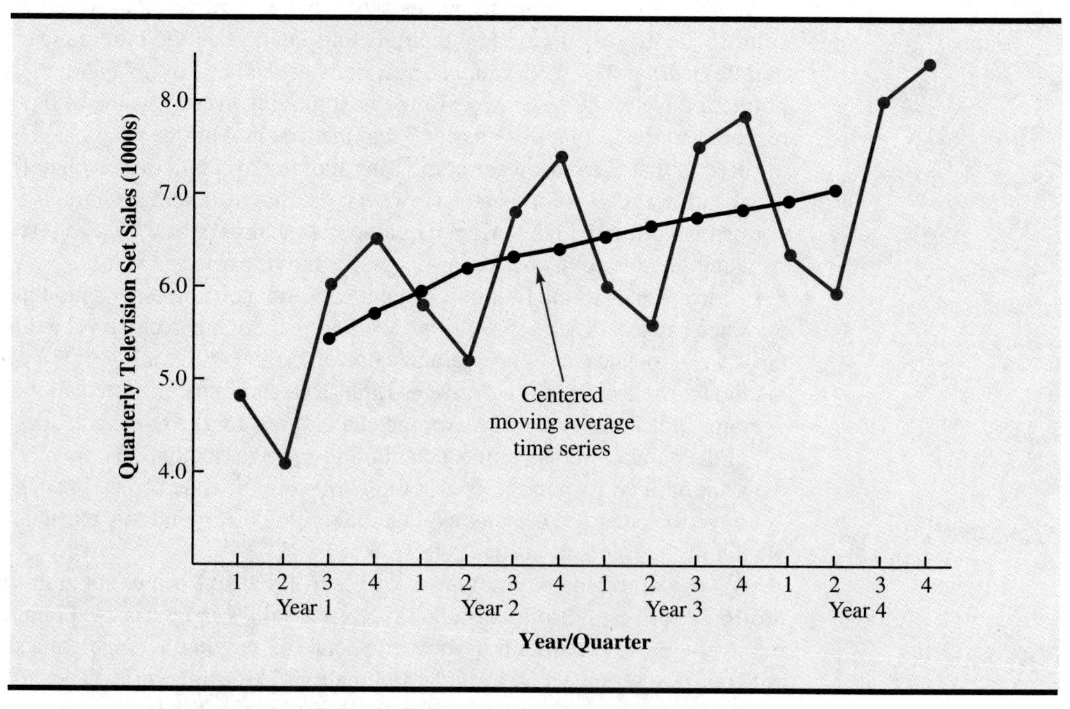

fluences because the seasonal effect has been averaged out. Each point in the centered moving average represents what the value of the time series would be without seasonal or irregular influences.

By dividing each time series observation by the corresponding centered moving average value, we can identify the seasonal-irregular effect in the time series. For example, the third quarter of year 1 shows 6.0/5.475 = 1.096 as the combined seasonal-irregular component. Table 16.9 summarizes the resulting seasonal-irregular values for the entire time series.

Consider the third quarter. The results from years 1, 2, and 3 show third-quarter values of 1.096, 1.075, and 1.109, respectively. Thus, in all cases the seasonal-irregular component appears to have an above average influence in the third quarter. The fluctuations over the three years can be attributed to the irregular component, so we can average the computed values to eliminate the irregular influence and obtain an estimate of the third-quarter seasonal influence:

$$\text{Seasonal effect of third quarter} = \frac{1.096 + 1.075 + 1.109}{3} = 1.09$$

We refer to 1.09 as the **seasonal index** for the third quarter. In Table 16.10 we summarize the calculations involved in computing the seasonal indexes for the television set sales time series. Thus, the seasonal indexes for all four quarters are: quarter 1, 0.93; quarter 2, 0.84; quarter 3, 1.09; and quarter 4, 1.14.

Interpretation of the values in Table 16.10 provides some observations about the "seasonal" component in television set sales. The best sales quarter is the fourth quarter, with sales averaging 14 percent above the average quarterly value. The worst, or slowest, sales quarter is the second quarter, with its seasonal index at 0.84, showing the sales average 16 percent below the average quarterly sales. The seasonal component corresponds to the intuitive expectation that television viewing interest and thus television purchase patterns tend to

TABLE 16.9 SEASONAL-IRREGULAR VALUES FOR THE TELEVISION SET SALES TIME SERIES

Year	Quarter	Sales (1000s)	Centered Moving Average	Seasonal-Irregular Value
1	1	4.8		
	2	4.1		
	3	6.0	5.475	1.096
	4	6.5	5.738	1.133
2	1	5.8	5.975	0.971
	2	5.2	6.188	0.840
	3	6.8	6.325	1.075
	4	7.4	6.400	1.156
3	1	6.0	6.538	0.918
	2	5.6	6.675	0.839
	3	7.5	6.763	1.109
	4	7.8	6.838	1.141
4	1	6.3	6.938	0.908
	2	5.9	7.075	0.834
	3	8.0		
	4	8.4		

TABLE 16.10 SEASONAL INDEX CALCULATIONS FOR THE TELEVISION SET SALES TIME SERIES

Quarter	Seasonal-Irregular Component Values (S_tI_t)	Seasonal Index (S_t)
1	0.971, 0.918, 0.908	0.93
2	0.840, 0.839, 0.834	0.84
3	1.096, 1.075, 1.109	1.09
4	1.133, 1.156, 1.141	1.14

peak in the fourth quarter, with its coming winter season and fewer outdoor activities. The low second-quarter sales reflect the reduced television interest resulting from the spring and presummer activities of the potential customers.

Can you now compute and interpret seasonal indexes for a time series? Try Problem 25.

One final adjustment may be necessary in obtaining the seasonal indexes. The multiplicative model requires that the average seasonal index equal 1.00, so the sum of the four seasonal indexes in Table 16.10 must equal 4.00. In other words, the seasonal effects must even out over the year. The average of the seasonal indexes in our example is equal to 1.00, and hence, this type of adjustment is not necessary. In other cases, a slight adjustment may be necessary. To make the adjustment, multiply each seasonal index by the number of seasons divided by the sum of the unadjusted seasonal indexes. For instance, for quarterly data, multiply each seasonal index by 4/(sum of the unadjusted seasonal indexes). Some of the problems at the end of the chapter require this adjustment.

With deseasonalized data, comparing sales in successive periods makes sense. With data that have not been deseasonalized, relevant comparisons can often be made between sales in the current period and sales in the same period one year ago.

Deseasonalizing the Time Series

The purpose of finding seasonal indexes is to remove the seasonal effects from a time series. This process is referred to as *deseasonalizing* the time series. Economic time series adjusted for seasonal variations (**deseasonalized time series**) are reported in the *Survey of Current Business, The Wall Street Journal,* and *Business Week.* Using the notation of the multiplicative model, we have

$$Y_t = T_t \times S_t \times I_t$$

By dividing each time series observation by the corresponding seasonal index, we remove the effect of season from the time series. The deseasonalized time series for television set sales is summarized in Table 16.11. A graph of the deseasonalized television set sales time series is shown in Figure 16.13.

Using Deseasonalized Time Series to Identify Trend

Although the graph in Figure 16.13 shows some up-and-down movement over the past 16 quarters, the time series seems to have an upward linear trend. To identify this trend, we use the same procedure as in the preceding section; in this case, the data used are quarterly deseasonalized sales values. Thus, for a linear trend, the estimated sales volume expressed as a function of time is

$$T_t = b_0 + b_1 t$$

TABLE 16.11 DESEASONALIZED VALUES FOR THE TELEVISION SET SALES TIMES SERIES

Year	Quarter	Sales (1000s) (Y_t)	Seasonal Index (S_t)	Deseasonalized Sales ($Y_t/S_t = T_tI_t$)
1	1	4.8	0.93	5.16
	2	4.1	0.84	4.88
	3	6.0	1.09	5.50
	4	6.5	1.14	5.70
2	1	5.8	0.93	6.24
	2	5.2	0.84	6.19
	3	6.8	1.09	6.24
	4	7.4	1.14	6.49
3	1	6.0	0.93	6.45
	2	5.6	0.84	6.67
	3	7.5	1.09	6.88
	4	7.8	1.14	6.84
4	1	6.3	0.93	6.77
	2	5.9	0.84	7.02
	3	8.0	1.09	7.34
	4	8.4	1.14	7.37

FIGURE 16.13 DESEASONALIZED TELEVISION SET SALES TIME SERIES

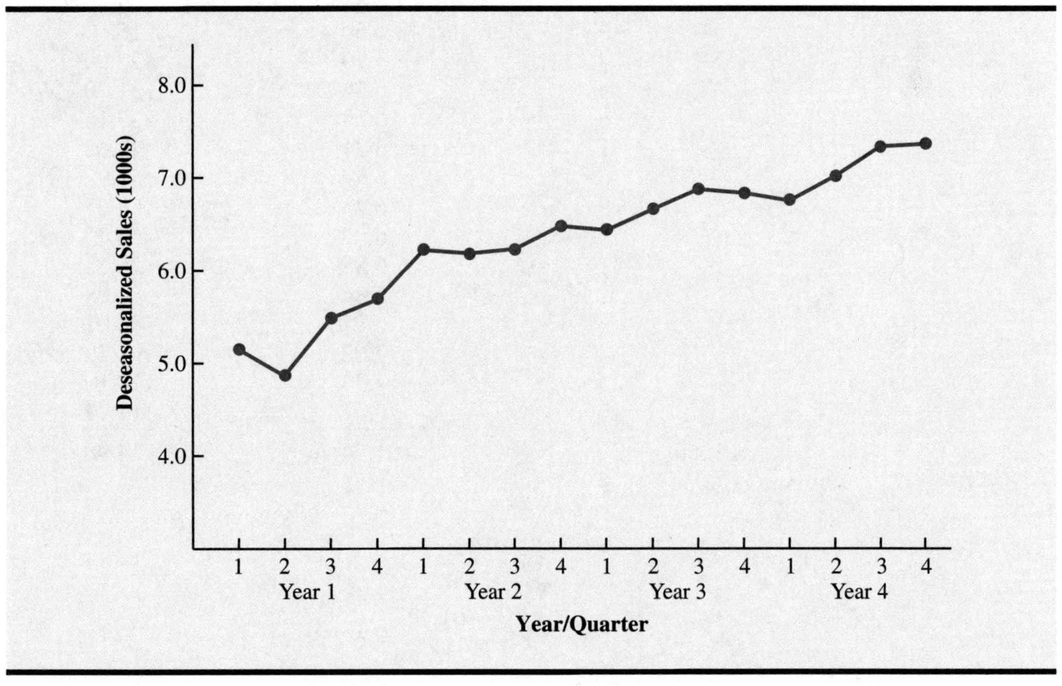

where

$$T_t = \text{trend value for television set sales in period } t$$
$$b_0 = \text{intercept of the trend line}$$
$$b_1 = \text{slope of the trend line}$$

As before, $t = 1$ corresponds to the time of the first observation for the time series, $t = 2$ corresponds to the time of the second observation, and so on. Thus, for the deseasonalized television set sales time series, $t = 1$ corresponds to the first deseasonalized quarterly sales value and $t = 16$ corresponds to the most recent deseasonalized quarterly sales value. The equations for computing the values of b_0 and b_1 are

$$b_1 = \frac{\Sigma tY_t - (\Sigma t \Sigma Y_t)/n}{\Sigma t^2 - (\Sigma t)^2/n} \quad \text{and} \quad b_0 = \bar{Y} - b_1\bar{t}$$

Note, however, that Y_t now refers to the deseasonalized time series value at time t and not to the actual value of the time series. Using the given relationships for b_0 and b_1 and the deseasonalized sales data of Table 16.11, we make the following calculations.

	t	Y_t (deseasonalized)	tY_t	t^2
	1	5.16	5.16	1
	2	4.88	9.76	4
	3	5.50	16.50	9
	4	5.70	22.80	16
	5	6.24	31.20	25
	6	6.19	37.14	36
	7	6.24	43.68	49
	8	6.49	51.92	64
	9	6.45	58.05	81
	10	6.67	66.70	100
	11	6.88	75.68	121
	12	6.84	82.08	144
	13	6.77	88.01	169
	14	7.02	98.28	196
	15	7.34	110.10	225
	16	7.37	117.92	256
Totals	136	101.74	914.98	1496

$$\bar{t} = \frac{136}{16} = 8.5$$

$$\bar{Y} = \frac{101.74}{16} = 6.359$$

$$b_1 = \frac{914.98 - (136)(101.74)/16}{1496 - (136)^2/16} = 0.148$$

$$b_0 = 6.359 - 0.148(8.5) = 5.101$$

Therefore,

$$T_t = 5.101 + 0.148t$$

is the equation for the linear trend component of the time series.

The slope of 0.148 indicates that over the past 16 quarters the firm has experienced an average deseasonalized growth in sales of about 148 sets per quarter. If we assume that the past 16-quarter trend in sales data is a reasonably good indicator of the future, we can use this equation to project the trend component of the time series for future quarters. For example, substituting $t = 17$ into the equation yields next quarter's trend projection, T_{17}:

$$T_{17} = 5.101 + 0.148(17) = 7.617$$

Thus, the trend component yields a sales forecast of 7617 television sets for the next quarter. Similarly, the trend component produces sales forecasts of 7765, 7913, and 8061 television sets in quarters 18, 19, and 20, respectively.

Seasonal Adjustments

The final step in developing the forecast when both trend and seasonal components are present is to use the seasonal index to adjust the trend projection. Returning to the television set sales example, we have a trend projection for the next four quarters. Now we must adjust the forecast for the seasonal effect. The seasonal index for the first quarter of year 5 ($t = 17$) is 0.93, so we obtain the quarterly forecast by multiplying the forecast based on trend ($T_{17} = 7617$) times the seasonal index (0.93). Thus, the forecast for the next quarter is $7617(0.93) = 7084$. Table 16.12 shows the quarterly forecast for quarters 17–20. The forecasts show the high-volume fourth quarter with a 9190-unit forecast and the low-volume second quarter with a 6523-unit forecast.

Models Based on Monthly Data

In the preceding television set sales example we used quarterly data to illustrate the computation of seasonal indexes. However, many businesses use monthly rather than quarterly forecasts. In such cases, the procedures introduced in this section can be applied with minor modifications. First, a 12-month moving average replaces the 4-quarter moving average; second, 12 monthly seasonal indexes, rather than the 4 quarterly indexes, must be computed. Other than these changes, the computational and forecasting procedures are identical.

TABLE 16.12 QUARTERLY FORECASTS FOR THE TELEVISION SET SALES TIME SERIES

Year	Quarter	Trend Forecast	Seasonal Index (see Table 16.10)	Quarterly Forecast
5	1	7617	0.93	(7617)(0.93) = 7084
	2	7765	0.84	(7765)(0.84) = 6523
	3	7913	1.09	(7913)(1.09) = 8625
	4	8061	1.14	(8061)(1.14) = 9190

Cyclical Component

Mathematically, the multiplicative model of equation (16.8) can be expanded to include a cyclical component as follows:

$$Y_t = T_t \times C_t \times S_t \times I_t \tag{16.9}$$

The cyclical component is attributable to multiyear cycles in the time series. It is analogous to the seasonal component but over a longer period of time. However, because of the length of time involved, obtaining enough relevant data to estimate the cyclical component often is difficult. Another difficulty is that the length of cycles usually varies. We leave further discussion of the cyclical component to texts on forecasting methods.

16.5 REGRESSION ANALYSIS

Regression analysis is a statistical technique that can be used to develop a mathematical equation showing how variables are related. In regression terminology, the variable that is being predicted is called the *dependent* or *response* variable. The variable or variables being used to predict the value of the dependent variable are called the *independent* or *predictor* variables. Regression analysis involving one independent variable and one dependent variable for which the relationship between the variables is approximated by a straight line is called *simple linear regression.* Regression analysis involving two or more independent variables is called *multiple regression analysis.* In Section 16.3 we utilized simple linear regression to fit a linear trend to the bicycle sales time series. Recall that we developed a linear equation relating bicycle sales to the time period. The number of bicycles sold isn't actually causally related to time; instead, time is a surrogate for variables to which the number of bicycles sold is actually related but which are either unknown or too difficult or costly to measure. Thus, the use of regression analysis for trend projection is not a causal forecasting method because only past values of sales, the variable being forecast, were used.

When we use regression analysis to relate the variable that we want to forecast to other variables that are supposed to influence or explain that variable, it becomes a causal forecasting method. The Management Science in Action, Spare Parts Forecasting at American Airlines, explains why that company uses regression analysis as a causal forecasting method to estimate the demand for spare parts.

MANAGEMENT SCIENCE IN ACTION

SPARE PARTS FORECASTING AT AMERICAN AIRLINES*

American Airlines developed the Rotables Allocation and Planning System (RAPS) to provide demand forecasts for spare parts, assist in allocating spare parts to airports, and calculate the availability level of each spare part. The demand forecasting module of RAPS provides monthly demand forecasts for more than 5000 parts, ranging from coffee makers to landing gears. The average price for parts covered by RAPS is approximately $5000.

Prior to RAPS, American Airlines used time series methodology to forecast spare parts demand. The time series methodology was slow to respond to external factors such as changes in aircraft utilization and major fleet expansions. To correct for these deficiencies, the forecasting component of RAPS involves the use of regression analysis "to establish a relationship between monthly part removals and various functions of monthly flying hours." The RAPS system generates the monthly demand forecasts in less than an hour.

Nearly all the parts covered by the RAPS system are essential to the operation of an aircraft. A part shortage can even result in cancellation of a flight, so the cost can be substantial. The materials management group at American Airlines estimated "that using RAPS has provided a one-time savings of $7 million and recurring annual savings of nearly $1 million."

*Based on Mark J. Tedone, "Repairable Part Management," *Interfaces* 19, no. 4 (July/August 1989): 61–68.

Using Regression Analysis as a Causal Forecasting Method

To illustrate how regression analysis is used as a causal forecasting method, we consider the sales forecasting problem faced by Armand's Pizza Parlors, a chain of Italian restaurants doing business in a five-state area. The most successful locations have been near college campuses. The managers believe that quarterly sales for these restaurants (denoted by y) are related positively to the size of the student population (denoted by x); that is, restaurants near campuses with a large population tend to generate more sales than those located near campuses with a small population. Using regression analysis we can develop an equation showing how the dependent variable y is related to the independent variable x. This equation can then be used to forecast quarterly sales for restaurants located near college campuses given the size of the student population.

In situations where time series data are not available, regression analysis can still be used to develop a forecast. For instance, suppose that management wanted to forecast sales for a new restaurant they were considering opening near a college campus. Because no historical data are available on sales for a new restaurant, Armand's cannot use time series data to develop the forecast. But, as we will now illustrate, regression analysis can still be used to forecast quarterly sales.

To develop the equation relating quarterly sales and the size of the student population, Armand's collected data from a sample of 10 of its restaurants located near college campuses. These data are summarized in Table 16.13. For example, restaurant 1, with $y = 58$

TABLE 16.13 DATA ON QUARTERLY SALES AND STUDENT POPULATION FOR 10 RESTAURANTS

Restaurant	y = Quarterly Sales ($1000s)	x = Student Population (1000s)
1	58	2
2	105	6
3	88	8
4	118	8
5	117	12
6	137	16
7	157	20
8	169	20
9	149	22
10	202	26

FIGURE 16.14 SCATTER DIAGRAM OF QUARTERLY SALES VERSUS STUDENT POPULATION

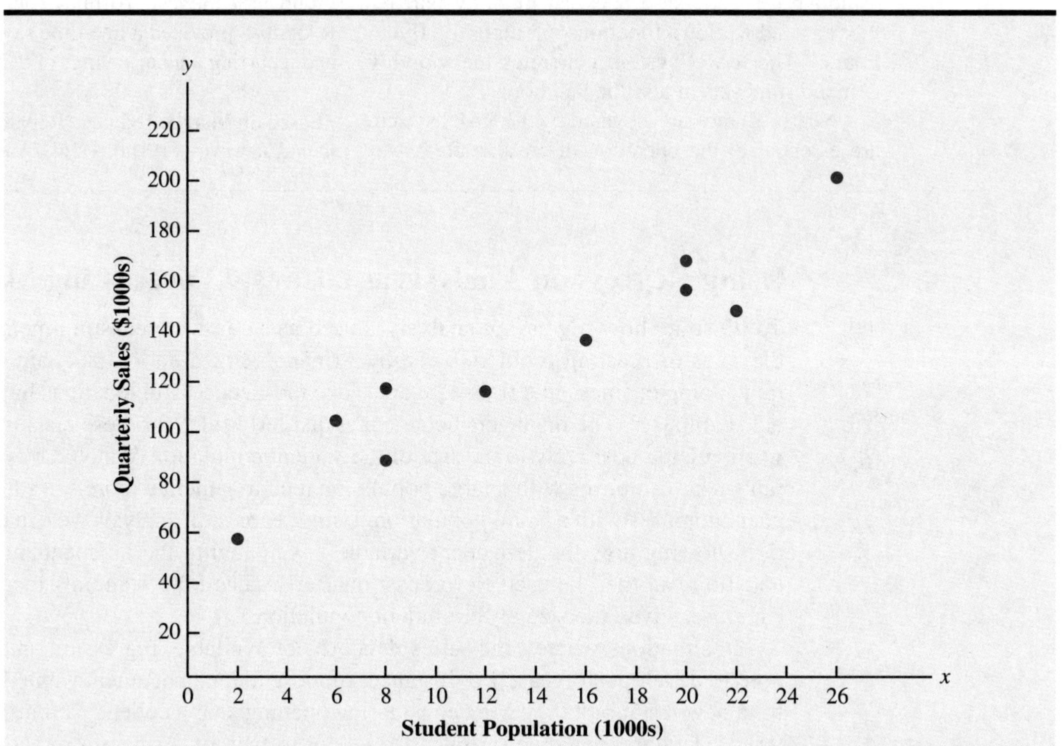

and $x = 2$, had \$58,000 in quarterly sales and is located near a campus with 2000 students. Figure 16.14 shows graphically the data presented in Table 16.13. The size of the student population is shown on the horizontal axis, with quarterly sales shown on the vertical axis. This type of graph is called a *scatter diagram.* Usually the independent variable is plotted on the horizontal axis, and the dependent variable is plotted on the vertical axis. The advantage of a scatter diagram is that it provides an overview of the data and enables us to draw preliminary conclusions about a possible relationship between the variables.

What preliminary conclusions can we draw from Figure 16.14? Sales appear to be higher at campuses with larger student populations. Also, it appears that the relationship between the two variables can be approximated by a straight line; indeed, x and y appear to be positively related. In Figure 16.15 we can draw a straight line through the data that appears to provide a good linear approximation of the relationship between the variables. Observe that the relationship isn't perfect. Indeed, few, if any, of the data fall exactly on the line. However, if we can develop the mathematical expression for this line, we may be able to use it to forecast the value of y corresponding to each possible value of x. The resulting equation of the line is called the *estimated regression equation.*

Using the least-squares method of estimation, the estimated regression equation is

$$\hat{y} = b_0 + b_1x \tag{6.10}$$

FIGURE 16.15 STRAIGHT-LINE APPROXIMATION FOR DATA ON QUARTERLY SALES AND STUDENT POPULATION

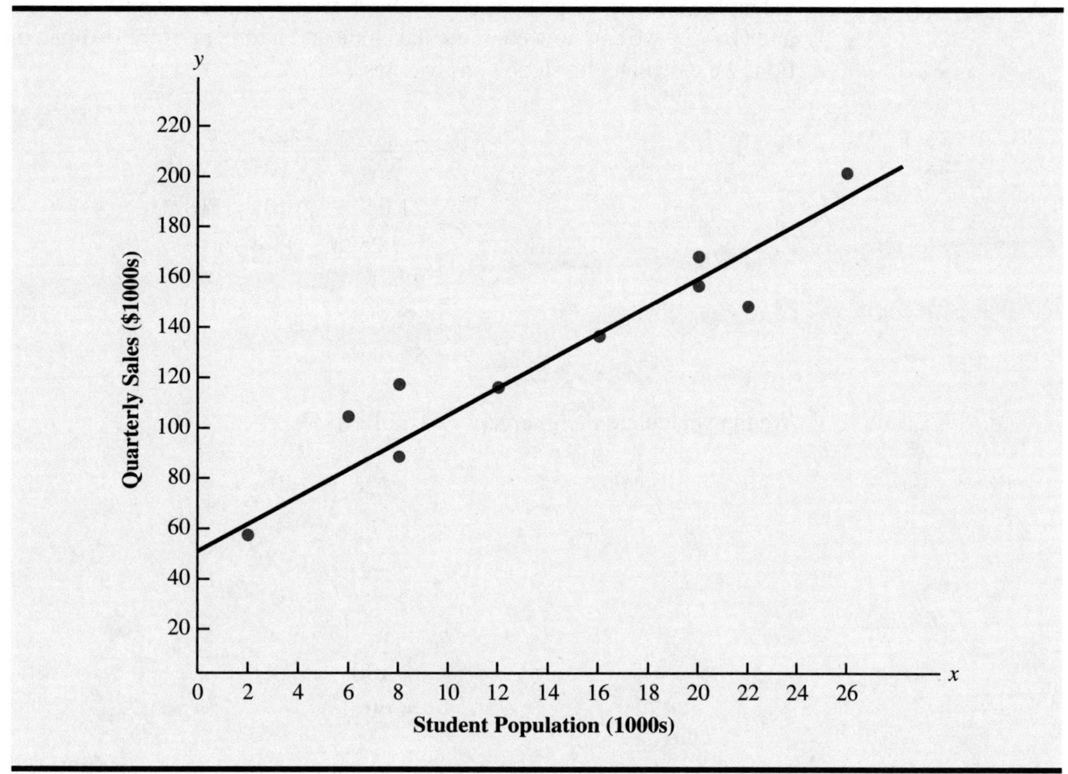

where

$\hat{y}$ = estimated value of the dependent variable (quarterly sales)
b_0 = intercept of the estimated regression equation
b_1 = slope of the estimated regression equation
x = value of the independent variable (student population)

We use the sample data and the following equations to compute the intercept b_0 and slope b_1:

$$b_1 = \frac{\sum x_i y_i - (\sum x_i \sum y_i)/n}{\sum x_i^2 - (\sum x_i)^2/n} \tag{16.11}$$

$$b_0 = \bar{y} - b_1\bar{x} \tag{16.12}$$

where

x_i = value of the independent variable for the ith observation
y_i = value of the dependent variable for the ith observation
$\bar{x}$ = mean value for the independent variable
$\bar{y}$ = mean value for the dependent variable
n = total number of observations

Some of the calculations necessary to develop the least-squares estimated regression equation for the data on student population and quarterly sales are shown in Table 16.14. Our example contains 10 restaurants or observations; hence, $n = 10$. Using equations (16.11) and (16.12), we can now compute the slope and intercept of the estimated regression equation. We calculate the slope b_1 as follows:

$$\begin{aligned} b_1 &= \frac{\Sigma x_i y_i - (\Sigma x_i \Sigma y_i)/n}{\Sigma x_i^2 - (\Sigma x_i)^2/n} \\ &= \frac{21{,}040 - (140)(1300)/10}{2528 - (140)^2/10} \\ &= \frac{2840}{568} \\ &= 5 \end{aligned}$$

We then calculate the intercept b_0 as follows:

$$\begin{aligned} \bar{x} &= \frac{\Sigma x_i}{n} = \frac{140}{10} = 14 \\ \bar{y} &= \frac{\Sigma y_i}{n} = \frac{1300}{10} = 130 \\ b_0 &= \bar{y} - b_1 \bar{x} \\ &= 130 - 5(14) \\ &= 60 \end{aligned}$$

Thus, the estimated regression equation found by using the method of least squares is

$$\hat{y} = 60 + 5x$$

We show the graph of this equation in Figure 16.16.

TABLE 16.14 CALCULATIONS FOR THE LEAST-SQUARES ESTIMATED REGRESSION EQUATION FOR ARMAND'S PIZZA PARLORS

Restaurant (i)	y_i	x_i	$x_i y_i$	x_i^2
1	58	2	116	4
2	105	6	630	36
3	88	8	704	64
4	118	8	944	64
5	117	12	1,404	144
6	137	16	2,192	256
7	157	20	3,140	400
8	169	20	3,380	400
9	149	22	3,278	484
10	202	26	5,252	676
Totals	1300	140	21,040	2528

FIGURE 16.16 THE ESTIMATED REGRESSION EQUATION FOR ARMAND'S PIZZA PARLORS

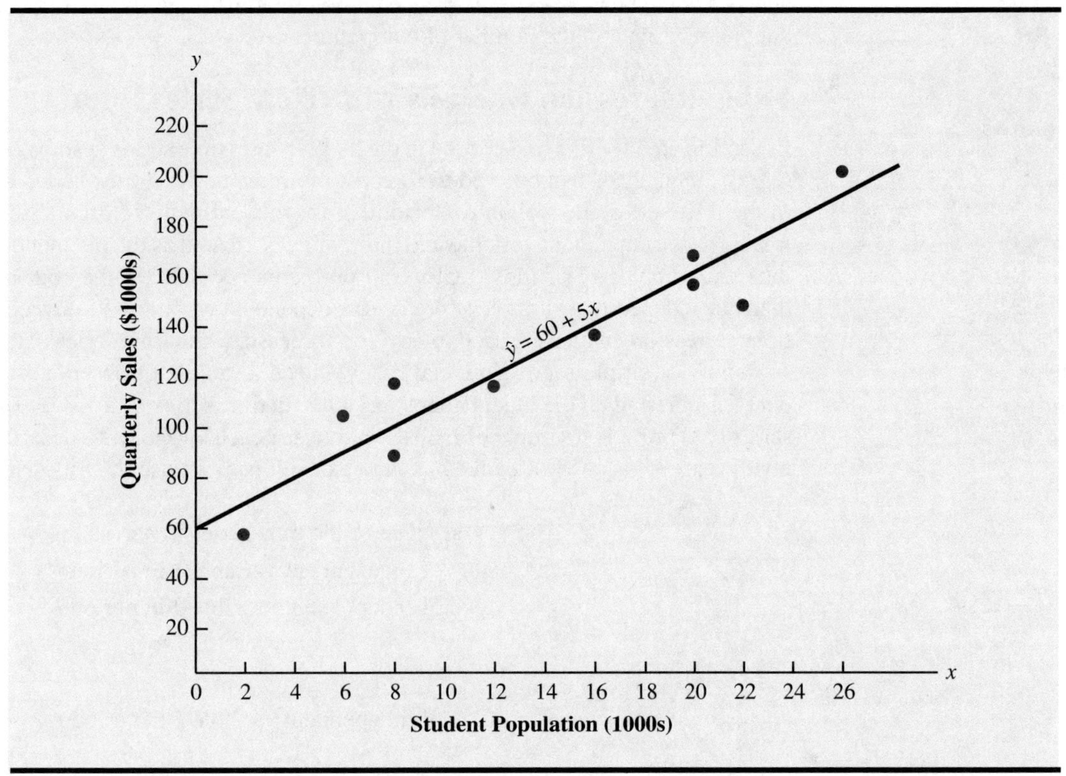

The slope of the estimated regression equation ($b_1 = 5$) is positive, implying that, as student population increases, quarterly sales increase. In fact, we can conclude (because sales are measured in thousands of dollars and student population in thousands) that an increase in the student population of 1000 is associated with an increase of $5000 in expected quarterly sales; that is, quarterly sales are expected to increase by $5 per student.

If we believe that the least-squares estimated regression equation adequately describes the relationship between x and y, using the estimated regression equation to forecast the value of y for a given value of x seems reasonable. For example, if we wanted to forecast quarterly sales for a new restaurant to be located near a campus with 16,000 students, we would compute

Practice using regression analysis to develop a forecast by working Problem 33.

$$\begin{aligned} \hat{y} &= 60 + 5(16) \\ &= 140 \end{aligned}$$

Hence, we would forecast quarterly sales of $140,000.

The sales forecasting problem facing Armand's Pizza Parlors illustrates how simple linear regression analysis can be used to develop forecasts when time series data are not available. Multiple regression analysis also can be applied in these situations if additional data for other independent variables are available. For example, suppose that the management of Armand's Pizza Parlors also believes that the number of competitors near the college campus is related to quarterly sales. Intuitively, management believes that restaurants located near campuses with fewer competitors generate more sales revenue than those located near campuses with more competitors. With additional data, multiple regression analysis could be used to develop an equation relating quarterly sales to the size of the student population and the number of competitors.

Using Regression Analysis with Time Series Data

In Section 16.3 we fit a linear trend to the bicycle sales time series to show how simple linear regression analysis can be used to forecast future values of a time series when past values of the time series are available. Recall that for this problem the annual sales in year t was treated as the dependent variable and the year t was treated as the independent variable. The inherent complexity of most real-world problems necessitates the consideration of more than one independent variable to predict the dependent variable. We now consider how multiple regression analysis is used to develop forecasts when time series data are available.

To use multiple regression analysis, we need a sample of observations for the dependent variable and all the independent variables. In time series analysis, the n periods of time series data provide a sample of n observations for each variable. To describe the wide variety of regression-based models that can be developed, we use the following notation:

$$
\begin{aligned}
Y_t &= \text{actual value of the time series in period } t \\
x_{1t} &= \text{value of independent variable 1 in period } t \\
x_{2t} &= \text{value of independent variable 2 in period } t \\
&\;\;\vdots \\
x_{kt} &= \text{value of independent variable } k \text{ in period } t
\end{aligned}
$$

The n periods of data necessary to develop the estimated regression equation would appear as follows.

	Dependent Variable	Independent Variables						
Period	Y_t	x_{1t}	x_{2t}	x_{3t}	·	·	·	x_{kt}
1	Y_1	x_{11}	x_{21}	x_{31}	·	·	·	x_{k1}
2	Y_2	x_{12}	x_{22}	x_{32}	·	·	·	x_{k2}
·	·	·	·	·	·	·	·	·
·	·	·	·	·	·	·	·	·
·	·	·	·	·	·	·	·	·
n	Y_n	x_{1n}	x_{2n}	x_{3n}	·	·	·	x_{kn}

As you might imagine, a number of choices can be made when selecting the independent variables in a forecasting model. One possible choice is simply time. We made this choice in Section 16.3 when we estimated the trend of the time series using a linear function of the independent variable time. Letting

$$x_{1t} = t$$

we obtain an estimated regression equation of the form

$$\hat{Y}_t = b_0 + b_1 t$$

where $\hat{Y}_t$ is the estimate of the time series value Y_t and where b_0 and b_1 are the estimated regression coefficients. In a more complex model, additional terms could be added corresponding to time raised to other powers. For example, if

$$x_{2t} = t^2 \quad \text{and} \quad x_{3t} = t^3$$

the estimated regression equation would become

$$\begin{aligned} \hat{Y}_t &= b_0 + b_1 x_{1t} + b_2 x_{2t} + b_3 x_{3t} \\ &= b_0 + b_1 t + b_2 t^2 + b_3 t^3 \end{aligned}$$

Note that this model provides a forecast of a time series with curvilinear characteristics over time.

Other regression-based forecasting models involve the use of a mixture of economic and demographic independent variables. For example, in forecasting the sale of refrigerators, we might select independent variables such as

x_{1t} = price in period t

x_{2t} = total industry sales in period $t - 1$

x_{3t} = number of building permits for new houses in period $t - 1$

x_{4t} = population forecast for period t

x_{5t} = advertising budget for period t

According to the usual multiple regression procedure, an estimated regression equation with five independent variables would be used to develop forecasts in this case.

Spyros Makridakis, a noted forecasting expert, conducted research showing that simple techniques usually outperform more complex procedures for short-term forecasting. Using a more sophisticated and expensive procedure will not guarantee better forecasts.

Whether a regression approach provides a good forecast depends largely on how well we are able to identify and obtain data for independent variables that are closely related to the time series. Generally, during the development of an estimated regression equation, we will want to consider many possible sets of independent variables. Thus, part of the regression analysis procedure should focus on the selection of the set of independent variables that provides the best forecasting model.

In the chapter introduction we stated that causal forecasting methods are based on the assumption that the variable we are trying to forecast exhibits a cause-effect relationship with one or more other variables. Regression analysis is the tool most often used in developing causal models. The related time series become the independent variables, and the time series being forecast is the dependent variable.

Another type of regression-based forecasting model occurs whenever all the independent variables are previous values of the same time series. For example, if the time series values are denoted $Y_1, Y_2, \ldots, Y_n$, we might try to find an estimated regression equation relating Y_t to the most recent time series values, Y_{t-1}, Y_{t-2}, and so on. For instance, if we use the actual values of the time series for the three most recent periods as independent variables, the estimated regression equation would be

$$\hat{Y}_t = b_0 + b_1 Y_{t-1} + b_2 Y_{t-2} + b_3 Y_{t-3}$$

Regression models such as this one in which the independent variables are previous values of the time series are referred to as **autoregressive models.**

Finally, another regression-based forecasting approach is one that incorporates a mixture of the independent variables previously discussed. For example, we might select a combination of time variables, some economic/demographic variables, and some previous values of the time series variable itself.

16.6 QUALITATIVE APPROACHES

If historical data are not available, managers may use a qualitative technique to develop forecasts. But the cost of using qualitative techniques can be high because of the time commitment required from the people involved.

In the preceding sections we discussed several types of quantitative forecasting methods. Most of these techniques require historical data on the variable of interest, so they cannot be applied when no historical data are available. Furthermore, even when such data are available, a significant change in environmental conditions affecting the time series may make the use of past data questionable in predicting future values of the time series. For example, a government-imposed gasoline rationing program would raise questions about the validity of a gasoline sales forecast based on historical data. Qualitative forecasting techniques offer an alternative in these and other cases.

Delphi Method

One of the most commonly used qualitative forecasting techniques is the **Delphi method.** This technique, originally developed by a research group at the Rand Corporation, attempts to develop forecasts through "group consensus." In its usual application, the members of a panel of experts—all of whom are physically separated from and unknown to each other—are asked to respond to a series of questionnaires. The responses from the first questionnaire are tabulated and used to prepare a second questionnaire that contains information and opinions of the entire group. Each respondent is then asked to reconsider and possibly revise his or her previous response in light of the group information provided. This process continues until the coordinator feels that some degree of consensus has been reached. The goal of the Delphi method is not to produce a single answer as output, but instead to produce a relatively narrow spread of opinions within which the majority of experts concurs.

Expert Judgment

Empirical evidence and theoretical arguments suggest that between 5 and 20 experts should be used in judgmental forecasting.

Qualitative forecasts often are based on the judgment of a single expert or represent the consensus of a group of experts. For example, each year a group of experts at Merrill Lynch gather to forecast the level of the Dow Jones Industrial Average and the prime rate for the next year. In doing so, the experts individually consider information that they believe will influence the stock market and interest rates; then they combine their conclusions into a forecast. No formal model is used, and no two experts are likely to consider the same information in the same way.

Expert judgment is a forecasting method that is often recommended when conditions in the past are not likely to hold in the future. Even though no formal quantitative model is used, expert judgment provides good forecasts in many situations.

Scenario Writing

The qualitative procedure referred to as **scenario writing** consists of developing a conceptual scenario of the future based on a well-defined set of assumptions. Different sets of assumptions lead to different scenarios. The job of the decision maker is to decide how likely each scenario is and then to make decisions accordingly.

Intuitive Approaches

Subjective, or *intuitive qualitative approaches,* are based on the ability of the human mind to process information that, in most cases, is difficult to quantify. These techniques are often used in group work, wherein a committee or panel seeks to develop new ideas or solve complex problems through a series of "brainstorming sessions." In such sessions, individuals are freed from the usual group restrictions of peer pressure and criticism because they can present any idea or opinion without regard to its relevancy and, even more importantly, without fear of criticism.

SUMMARY

In this chapter we discussed how forecasts can be developed to help managers develop appropriate strategies for the future. We began by defining a time series as a set of observations on a variable measured at successive points in time or over successive periods of time. A time series may involve four separate components: trend, seasonal, irregular, and cyclical. By isolating these components and measuring their apparent effects, future values of the time series can be forecast.

Quantitative forecasting methods include time series methods and causal methods. A time series method is appropriate when the historical data are restricted to past values of the variable being forecast. The three time series methods discussed in the chapter are smoothing (moving averages, weighted moving averages, and exponential smoothing), trend projection, and trend projection adjusted for seasonal influence.

Smoothing methods are appropriate for a stable time series; that is, one that exhibits no significant trend, cyclical, or seasonal effects. The moving averages approach consists of computing an average of past values and then using this average as the forecast for the next period. The weighted moving averages method allows for the possibility of unequal weights for the data; thus, the moving averages method is a special case of the weighted moving averages method in which all the weights are equal. Exponential smoothing also is a special case of the weighted moving averages method involving only one parameter: the weight for the most recent observation.

When a time series consists of random fluctuations around a long-term trend line, a linear equation may be used to estimate the trend. When seasonal effects are present, seasonal indexes can be computed and used to deseasonalize the data and to develop forecasts. When both seasonal and long-term trend effects are present, a trend line is fitted to the deseasonalized data; the seasonal indexes are then used to adjust the trend projections.

Causal forecasting methods are based on the assumption that the variable being forecast exhibits a cause-effect relationship with one or more other variables. A causal forecasting method is one that relates the variable being forecast to other variables that are thought to influence or explain it. Regression analysis is a causal forecasting method that can be used to develop forecasts when time series data are not available.

Qualitative forecasting methods may be used when little or no historical data are available. Qualitative forecasting methods also are considered most appropriate when the historical pattern of the time series is not expected to continue into the future.

GLOSSARY

Time series A set of observations of a variable measured at successive points in time or over successive periods of time.

Forecast A projection or prediction of future values of a time series.

Time series method Forecasting method that is based on the use of historical data that are restricted to past values of the variable we are trying to forecast..

Causal forecasting methods Forecasting methods that are based on the assumption that the variable we are trying to forecast exhibits a cause-effect relationship with one or more other variables.

Trend The gradual shift or movement of the time series to relatively higher or lower values over a longer period of time.

Cyclical component The component of the time series that accounts for the periodic above-trend and below-trend behavior of the time series lasting more than one year.

Seasonal component The component of the time series that represents the variability in the data due to seasonal influences.

Irregular component The component of the time series that accounts for the random variability in the time series.

Moving averages A smoothing method that uses the average of the most recent n data values in the time series as the forecast for the next period.

Mean squared error (MSE) An approach to measuring the accuracy of a forecasting model. This measure is the average of the sum of the squared differences between the actual time series values and the forecasted values.

Weighted moving averages A smoothing method that uses a weighted average of the most recent n data values as the forecast.

Exponential smoothing A smoothing method that uses a weighted average of past time series values as the forecast; it is a special case of the weighted moving averages method in which we select only one weight—the weight for the most recent observation.

Smoothing constant In the exponential smoothing model, the smoothing constant is the weight given to the actual value of the time series in period t.

Mean absolute deviation (MAD) A measure of forecast accuracy. The average of the absolute values of the forecast errors.

Multiplicative time series model A model that assumes that the separate components of the time series can be multiplied together to identify the actual time series value. When the four components of trend, cyclical, seasonal, and irregular are assumed present, we obtain $Y_t = T_t \times C_t \times S_t \times I_t$. When cyclical effects are not modeled, we obtain $Y_t = T_t \times S_t \times I_t$.

Seasonal index A measure of the seasonal effect on a time series. A seasonal index above 1 indicates a positive effect, a seasonal index of 1 indicates no seasonal effect, and a seasonal index less than 1 indicates a negative effect.

Deseasonalized time series A time series that has had the effect of season removed by dividing each original time series observation by the corresponding seasonal index.

Regression analysis A statistical technique used to develop a mathematical equation showing how variables are related.

Autoregressive model A regression model in which the independent variables are previous values of the time series.

Delphi method A qualitative forecasting method that obtains forecasts through group consensus.

Scenario writing A qualitative forecasting method that consists of developing a conceptual scenario of the future based on a well-defined set of assumptions.

PROBLEMS

1. Corporate Triple A Bond interest rates for 12 consecutive months are 9.5, 9.3, 9.4, 9.6, 9.8, 9.7, 9.8, 10.5, 9.9, 9.7, 9.6, and 9.6.
   a. Develop three- and four-month moving averages for this time series. Which moving average provides the better forecasts? Explain.
   b. What is the moving average forecast for the next month?

2. Refer to the gasoline sales time series data in Table 16.1.
   a. Compute four- and five-week moving averages for the time series.
   b. Compute the MSE for the four- and five-week moving average forecasts.
   c. What appears to be the best number of weeks of past data to use in the moving average computation? Remember that the MSE for the three-week moving average is 10.22.

3. Refer again to the gasoline sales time series data in Table 16.1.
   a. Use a weight of ½ for the most recent observation, ⅓ for the second most recent, and ⅙ for the third most recent to compute a three-week weighted moving average for the time series.
   b. Compute the MSE for the weighted moving average in part (a). Do you prefer this weighted moving average to the unweighted moving average? Remember that the MSE for the unweighted moving average is 10.22.
   c. Suppose that you are allowed to choose any weights as long as they sum to 1. Could you always find a set of weights that would make the MSE smaller for a weighted moving average than for an unweighted moving average? Why or why not?

4. Use the gasoline sales time series data from Table 16.1 to show the exponential smoothing forecasts using $\alpha = 0.1$. Using the mean squared error criterion, would you prefer a smoothing constant of $\alpha = 0.1$ or $\alpha = 0.2$?

5. For the Hawkins Company, the monthly percentages of all shipments that were received on time over the past 12 months are 80, 82, 84, 83, 83, 84, 85, 84, 82, 83, 84, and 83.
   a. Compare a three-month moving average forecast with an exponential smoothing forecast for $\alpha = 0.2$. Which provides the better forecasts?
   b. What is the forecast for next month?

6. With a smoothing constant of $\alpha = 0.2$, equation (16.2) shows that the forecast for the 13th week of the gasoline sales data from Table 16.1 is given by $F_{13} = 0.2Y_{12} + 0.8F_{12}$. However, the forecast for week 12 is given by $F_{12} = 0.2Y_{11}10.8F_{11}$. Thus, we could combine these two results to write the forecast for the 13th week as

$$F_{13} = 0.2Y_{12} + 0.8(0.2Y_{11} + 0.8F_{11}) = 0.2Y_{12} + 0.16Y_{11} + 0.64F_{11}$$

   a. Make use of the fact that $F_{11} = 0.2Y_{10} + 0.8F_{10}$ (and similarly for F_{10} and F_9) and continue to expand the expression for F_{13} until you have written it in terms of the past data values Y_{12}, Y_{11}, Y_{10}, Y_9, and Y_8, and the forecast for period 8.
   b. Refer to the coefficients or weights for the past data values Y_{12}, Y_{11}, Y_{10}, Y_9, and Y_8; what observation can you make about how exponential smoothing weights past data values in arriving at new forecasts? Compare this weighting pattern with the weighting pattern of the moving averages method.

7. Alabama building contracts for a 12-month period (in millions of dollars) are 240, 350, 230, 260, 280, 320, 220, 310, 240, 310, 240, and 230.
   a. Compare a three-month moving average forecast with an exponential smoothing forecast using $\alpha = 0.2$. Which provides the better forecasts?
   b. What is the forecast for the next month?

8. Moving averages often are used to identify movements in stock prices. Daily closing prices (in dollars per share) for SanDisk for August 16, 2002, through September 3, 2002, follow (http://www.finance.yahoo.com).

Day	Price ($)	Day	Price ($)
August 16	14.45	August 26	16.45
August 19	15.75	August 27	15.60
August 20	16.45	August 28	15.09
August 21	17.40	August 29	16.42
August 22	17.32	August 30	16.21
August 23	15.96	September 3	15.22

a. Use a five-day moving average to smooth the time series. Forecast the closing price for September 4, 2002.
b. Use a four-day weighted moving average to smooth the time series. Use a weight of 0.4 for the most recent period, 0.3 for the next period back, 0.2 for the third period back, and 0.1 for the fourth period back. Forecast the closing price for September 4, 2002.
c. Use exponential smoothing with a smoothing constant of $\alpha = 0.7$ to smooth the time series. Forecast the closing price for September 4, 2002.
d. Which of the three methods do you prefer? Why?

9. The following data represent 15 quarters of manufacturing capacity utilization (in percentages).

Quarter/Year	Utilization	Quarter/Year	Utilization
1/2000	82.5	1/2002	78.8
2/2000	81.3	2/2002	78.7
3/2000	81.3	3/2002	78.4
4/2000	79.0	4/2002	80.0
1/2001	76.6	1/2003	80.7
2/2001	78.0	2/2003	80.7
3/2001	78.4	3/2003	80.8
4/2001	78.0		

a. Compute three- and four-quarter moving averages for this time series. Which moving average provides the better forecast for the fourth quarter of 2003?
b. Use smoothing constants of $\alpha = 0.4$ and $\alpha = 0.5$ to develop forecasts for the fourth quarter of 2003. Which smoothing constant provides the better forecast?
c. Based on the analyses in parts (a) and (b), which method—moving averages or exponential smoothing—provides the better forecast? Explain.

10. For the 2001–2002 National Basketball Association season, Philadelphia 76ers Allen Iverson was the scoring leader with an average of 31.4 points per game. The following data show the average number of points per game for the scoring leader from the 1991–1992 season to the 2001–2002 season (*The World Almanac 2002* and http://www.nba.com).

Season	Average	Season	Average
1991–1992	30.1	1997–1998	28.7
1992–1993	32.6	1998–1999	26.8
1993–1994	29.8	1999–2000	29.7
1994–1995	29.3	2000–2001	31.1
1995–1996	30.4	2001–2002	31.4
1996–1997	29.6		

a. Use exponential smoothing to forecast this time series. Consider smoothing constants of $\alpha = 0.1$ and 0.2. What value of the smoothing constant provides the best forecast?
b. What is the forecast of the leading scoring average for the 2002–2003 season?

11. The percentage of individual investors' portfolios committed to stock depends on the state of the economy. As of April 1997, a typical portfolio consisted of cash (19%), stocks (30%), stock funds (37%), bonds (8%), and bond funds (6%) (*AAII Journal,* June 1997). The following table reports the percentage of stocks in a typical portfolio in nine quarters from 1995 to 1997.

Quarter	Stock %	Quarter	Stock %
1st—1995	29.8	2nd—1996	31.5
2nd—1995	31.0	3rd—1996	32.0
3rd—1995	29.9	4th—1996	31.9
4th—1995	30.1	1st—1997	30.0
1st—1996	32.2		

a. Use exponential smoothing to forecast this time series. Consider smoothing constants of $\alpha = 0.2$, 0.3, and 0.4. What value of the smoothing constant provides the best forecast?
b. What is the forecast of the percentage of assets committed to stocks for the second quarter of 1997?

12. United Dairies, Inc., supplies milk to several independent grocers throughout Dade County, Florida. Management wants to develop a forecast of the number of half-gallons of milk sold per week. Sales data (in units) for the past 12 weeks are as follows.

Week	Sales	Week	Sales
1	2750	7	3300
2	3100	8	3100
3	3250	9	2950
4	2800	10	3000
5	2900	11	3200
6	3050	12	3150

Use exponential smoothing, with $\alpha = 0.4$, to develop a forecast of demand for week 13.

13. Ten weeks of data on the Commodity Futures Index are 7.35, 7.40, 7.55, 7.56, 7.60, 7.52, 7.52, 7.70, 7.62, and 7.55.
a. Compute the exponential smoothing values for $\alpha = 0.2$.
b. Compute the exponential smoothing values for $\alpha = 0.3$.
c. Which exponential smoothing model provides the better forecasts? Forecast week 11.

14. The enrollment data (figures in thousands) for a state college for the past six years are shown.

Year	1	2	3	4	5	6
Enrollment	20.5	20.2	19.5	19.0	19.1	18.8

Develop the equation for the linear trend component for this time series. Comment on what is happening to enrollment at this institution.

15. Automobile sales at B. J. Scott Motors, Inc., provided the following 10-year time series.

Year	Sales	Year	Sales
1	400	6	260
2	390	7	300
3	320	8	320
4	340	9	340
5	270	10	370

Plot the time series, and comment on the appropriateness of a linear trend. What type of functional form would be best for the trend pattern of this time series?

16. The president of a small manufacturing firm has been concerned about the continual growth in manufacturing costs over the past several years. The following is a time series of the cost per unit (in dollars) for the firm's leading product over the past eight years.

Year	Cost per Unit ($)	Year	Cost per Unit ($)
1	20.00	5	26.60
2	24.50	6	30.00
3	28.20	7	31.00
4	27.50	8	36.00

a. Graph this time series. Does a linear trend appear?

b. Develop the equation for the linear trend component for the time series. What is the average cost increase per year?

17. TV ratings provided by Nielsen Media Research show the percentage of TV-owning households tuned in to a particular program. The following data show the rating for the top-rated TV show of each season, from 1987–1988 to 2000–2001 (*The New York Times Almanac 2002*).

Season	Rating	Season	Rating
1987–1988	27.8	1994–1995	20.5
1988–1989	25.5	1995–1996	22.0
1989–1990	23.4	1996–1997	21.2
1990–1991	21.6	1997–1998	22.0
1991–1992	21.7	1998–1999	17.8
1992–1993	21.6	1999–2000	16.6
1993–1994	21.9	2000–2001	17.4

a. Graph this time series. Does a linear trend appear?

b. Develop a linear trend equation for this time series.

c. Use the trend equation to estimate the rating for the 2001–2002 season.

18. The Federal Election Commission maintains data showing the voting age population, the number of registered voters, and the turnout for federal elections. The following table shows the national voter turnout in presidential elections as a percentage of the voting age population from 1964 to 2000 (http://www.fec.gov).

Year	Percentage Voting	Year	Percentage Voting
1964	61.92	1984	53.11
1968	60.84	1988	50.11
1972	55.21	1992	55.09
1976	53.55	1996	49.08
1980	52.56	2000	51.30

a. Graph this time series. Does a linear trend appear?

b. Develop the equation for the linear trend component for the time series. What is the average decrease in the percentage voting per presidential election?

c. Use the trend equation to forecast the percentage voting in 2004.

19. The following data show the time series of the most recent quarterly capital expenditures (in billions of dollars) for the 1000 largest manufacturing firms: 24, 25, 23, 24, 22, 26, 28, 31, 29, 32, 37, and 42.

a. Develop a linear trend equation for the time series.
b. Graph the time series and the linear trend equation.
c. What appears to be happening to capital expenditures? What is the forecast one year, or four quarters, into the future?

20. The Costello Music Company has been in business for five years. During that time, the sales of electric organs have grown from 12 units in the first year to 76 units in the most recent year. Fred Costello, the firm's owner, wants to develop a forecast of organ sales for the coming year based on the historical data shown.

Year	1	2	3	4	5
Sales	12	28	34	50	76

a. Graph this time series. Does a linear trend appear?
b. Develop the equation for the linear trend component for the time series. What is the average increase in sales per year for the firm?

21. Hudson Marine has been an authorized dealer for C&D marine radios for the past seven years. The number of radios sold each year is shown.

Year	1	2	3	4	5	6	7
Number Sold	35	50	75	90	105	110	130

a. Graph this time series. Does a linear trend appear?
b. Develop the equation for the linear trend component for the time series.
c. Use the linear trend developed in part (b) to prepare a forecast for sales in year 8.

22. The League of American Theatres and Producers, Inc., collects a variety of statistics for Broadway plays, such as gross revenue, playing time, and number of new productions. The following data show the season attendance (in millions) for Broadway shows from 1990 to 2001 (*The World Almanac 2002*).

Season	**Attendance (in millions)**	**Season**	**Attendance (in millions)**
1990–1991	7.3	1996–1997	10.6
1991–1992	7.4	1997–1998	11.5
1992–1993	7.9	1998–1999	11.7
1993–1994	8.1	1999–2000	11.4
1994–1995	9.0	2000–2001	11.9
1995–1996	9.5		

a. Plot the time series and comment on the appropriateness of a linear trend.
b. Develop the equation for the linear trend component for this time series.
c. What is the average increase in attendance per season?
d. Use the trend equation to forecast attendance for the 2001–2002 season.

23. The Garden Avenue Seven sells tapes of its musical performances. The following data show sales for the past 18 months. The group's manager wants an accurate method for forecasting future sales.

Month	Sales	Month	Sales	Month	Sales
1	293	7	381	13	549
2	283	8	431	14	544
3	322	9	424	15	601
4	355	10	433	16	587
5	346	11	470	17	644
6	379	12	481	18	660

a. Use exponential smoothing, with $\alpha = 0.3, 0.4$, and 0.5. Which value of α provides the best forecasts?
b. Use trend projection to provide a forecast. What is the value of MSE?
c. Which method of forecasting would you recommend to the manager? Why?

24. The Mayfair Department Store in Davenport, Iowa, is trying to determine the amount of sales lost while it was shut down because of summer floods. Sales data for January through June are shown.

Month	Sales ($1000s)
January	185.72
February	167.84
March	205.11
April	210.36
May	255.57
June	261.19

a. Use exponential smoothing, with $\alpha = 0.4$, to develop a forecast for July and August. (*Hint:* Use the forecast for July as the actual sales in July in developing the August forecast.) Comment on the use of exponential smoothing for forecasts more than one period into the future.
b. Use trend projection to forecast sales for July and August.
c. Mayfair's insurance company proposed a settlement based on lost sales of $240,000 in July and August. Is this amount fair? If not, what amount would you counter with?

25. The quarterly sales data (number of copies sold) for a college textbook over the past three years are as follows.

Quarter	Year 1	Year 2	Year 3
1	1690	1800	1850
2	940	900	1100
3	2625	2900	2930
4	2500	2360	2615

a. Show the four-quarter moving average values for this time series. Plot both the original time series and the moving averages on the same graph.
b. Compute seasonal indexes for the four quarters.
c. When does the textbook publisher experience the largest seasonal index? Does this result appear to be reasonable? Explain.

26. Identify the monthly seasonal indexes for the following three years of expenses for a six-unit apartment house in southern Florida. Use a 12-month moving average calculation.

Month	Year 1	Year 2	Year 3
January	170	180	195
February	180	205	210
March	205	215	230
April	230	245	280
May	240	265	290
June	315	330	390
July	360	400	420
August	290	335	330
September	240	260	290
October	240	270	295
November	230	255	280
December	195	220	250

27. Air pollution control specialists in southern California monitor the amount of ozone, carbon dioxide, and nitrogen dioxide in the air on an hourly basis. The hourly time series data exhibit seasonality, with the levels of pollutants showing similar patterns over the hours in the day. On July 15, 16, and 17, the observed levels of nitrogen dioxide in a city's downtown area for the 12 hours from 6:00 A.M. to 6:00 P.M. were as follows.

July 15	25	28	35	50	60	60	40	35	30	25	25	20
July 16	28	30	35	48	60	65	50	40	35	25	20	20
July 17	35	42	45	70	72	75	60	45	40	25	25	25

a. Identify the hourly seasonal indexes for the 12 hourly daily readings.
b. Based on the seasonal indexes in part (a), the trend equation developed for the deseasonalized data is $T_t = 32.983 + 0.3922t$. Using only the trend equation, develop forecasts for the 12 hours for July 18.
c. Use the seasonal indexes from part (a) to adjust the trend forecasts in part (b).

28. Refer to Problem 21. Suppose that the following are the quarterly sales data for the past seven years.

Year	Quarter 1	Quarter 2	Quarter 3	Quarter 4	Total Sales
1	6	15	10	4	35
2	10	18	15	7	50
3	14	26	23	12	75
4	19	28	25	18	90
5	22	34	28	21	105
6	24	36	30	20	110
7	28	40	35	27	130

a. Show the four-quarter moving average values for this time series. Plot both the original time series and the moving averages on the same graph.
b. Compute the seasonal indexes for the four quarters.
c. When does Hudson Marine experience the largest seasonal effect? Does this result seem reasonable? Explain.

29. Consider the Costello Music Company scenario presented in Problem 20 and the following quarterly sales data.

Year	Quarter 1	Quarter 2	Quarter 3	Quarter 4	Total Yearly Sales
1	4	2	1	5	12
2	6	4	4	14	28
3	10	3	5	16	34
4	12	9	7	22	50
5	18	10	13	35	76

a. Compute the seasonal indexes for the four quarters.
b. When does Costello Music experience the largest seasonal effect? Does this result appear to be reasonable? Explain.

30. Refer to the Hudson Marine data in Problem 28.
a. Deseasonalize the data, and use the deseasonalized time series to identify the trend.
b. Use the results of part (a) to develop a quarterly forecast for next year based on trend.
c. Use the seasonal indexes developed in Problem 28 to adjust the forecasts developed in part (b) to account for the effect of season.

31. Consider the Costello Music Company time series in Problem 29.
a. Deseasonalize the data, and use the deseasonalized time series to identify the trend.
b. Use the results of part (a) to develop a quarterly forecast for next year based on trend.
c. Use the seasonal indexes developed in Problem 29 to adjust the forecasts developed in part (b) to account for seasonal effects.

32. Electric power consumption is measured in kilowatt-hours (kWh). The local utility company has an interrupt program, whereby commercial customers who participate receive favorable rates but must agree to cut back consumption if the utility requests them to do so. Timko Products cut back consumption at 12:00 noon Thursday. To assess the savings, the utility must estimate Timko's usage without the interrupt. The period of interrupted service was from noon to 8:00 P.M. Data on electric consumption for the past 72 hours is available.

Time Period	Monday	Tuesday	Wednesday	Thursday
12–4 A.M.	—	19,281	31,209	27,330
4–8 A.M.	—	33,195	37,014	32,715
8–12 noon	—	99,516	119,968	152,465
12–4 P.M.	124,299	123,666	156,033	
4–8 P.M.	113,545	111,717	128,889	
8–12 midnight	41,300	48,112	73,923	

a. Is there a seasonal effect over the 24-hour period? Compute seasonal indexes for the six 4-hour periods.
b. Use trend adjusted for seasonal factors to estimate Timko's normal usage over the period of interrupted service.

33. Eddie's Restaurants collected the following data on the relationship between advertising and sales at a sample of five restaurants.

Advertising Expenditures ($1000s)	1.0	4.0	6.0	10.0	14.0
Sales ($1000s)	19.0	44.0	40.0	52.0	53.0

a. Let x represent advertising expenditures and y represent sales. Use the method of least squares to develop a straight-line approximation of the relationship between the two variables.

b. Use the equation developed in part (a) to forecast sales for an advertising expenditure of $8000.

34. The management of a chain of fast-food restaurants wants to investigate the relationship between the daily sales volume (in dollars) of a company restaurant and the number of competitor restaurants within a 1-mile radius. The following data have been collected.

Number of Competitors Within 1 Mile	**Sales ($)**
1	3600
1	3300
2	3100
3	2900
3	2700
4	2500
5	2300
5	2000

a. Develop the least-squares estimated regression equation that relates daily sales volume to the number of competitor restaurants within a 1-mile radius.

b. Use the estimated regression equation developed in part (a) to forecast the daily sales volume for a particular company restaurant that has four competitors within a 1-mile radius.

35. The supervisor of a manufacturing process believed that assembly-line speed (in feet/minute) affected the number of defective parts found during on-line inspection. To test this theory, management had the same batch of parts inspected visually at a variety of line speeds. The following data were collected.

Line Speed	**Number of Defective Parts Found**
20	21
20	19
40	15
30	16
60	14
40	17

a. Develop the estimated regression equation that relates line speed to the number of defective parts found.

b. Use the equation developed in part (a) to forecast the number of defective parts found for a line speed of 50 feet per minute.

Case Problem 1 FORECASTING SALES

The Vintage Restaurant is located on Captiva Island, a resort community near Fort Myers, Florida. The restaurant, which is owned and operated by Karen Payne, just completed its third year of operation. During this time, Karen sought to establish a reputation for the restaurant as a high-quality dining establishment that specializes in fresh seafood. The efforts made by Karen and her staff proved successful, and her restaurant is currently one of the best and fastest-growing restaurants on the island.

Karen concluded that, to plan better for the growth of the restaurant in the future, she needs to develop a system that will enable her to forecast food and beverage sales by month for up to one year in advance. Karen compiled the following data on total food and beverage sales for the three years of operation.

Food and Beverage Sales for the Vintage Restaurant ($1000s)

Month	First Year	Second Year	Third Year
January	242	263	282
February	235	238	255
March	232	247	265
April	178	193	205
May	184	193	210
June	140	149	160
July	145	157	166
August	152	161	174
September	110	122	126
October	130	130	148
November	152	167	173
December	206	230	235

Managerial Report

Perform an analysis of the sales data for the Vintage Restaurant. Prepare a report for Karen that summarizes your findings, forecasts, and recommendations. Include the following:

1. A graph of the time series.
2. An analysis of the seasonality of the data. Indicate the seasonal indexes for each month, and comment on the high seasonal and low seasonal sales months. Do the seasonal indexes make intuitive sense? Discuss.
3. Forecast sales for January through December of the fourth year.
4. Assume that January sales for the fourth year turned out to be $295,000. What was your forecast error? If this error is large, Karen may be puzzled about the difference between your forecast and the actual sales value. What can you do to resolve her uncertainty in the forecasting procedure?
5. Recommendations as to when the system that you developed should be updated to account for new sales data that will occur.
6. Include detailed calculations of your analysis in an appendix to your report.

Case Problem 2 FORECASTING LOST SALES

The Carlson Department Store suffered heavy damage when a hurricane struck on August 31, 2003. The store was closed for four months (September 2003 through December 2003), and Carlson is now involved in a dispute with its insurance company concerning the amount of lost sales during the time the store was closed. Two key issues must be resolved: (1) the amount of sales Carlson would have made if the hurricane had not struck; and (2) whether Carlson is entitled to any compensation for excess sales from increased business activity after the storm. More than $8 billion in federal disaster relief and insurance money came into the county, resulting in increased sales at department stores and numerous other businesses.

Table 16.15 shows the sales data for the 48 months preceding the storm. Table 16.16 reports total sales for the 48 months preceding the storm for all department stores in the

TABLE 16.15 SALES FOR CARLSON DEPARTMENT STORE, SEPTEMBER 1999 THROUGH AUGUST 2003

Month	1999	2000	2001	2002	2003
January		1.45	2.31	2.31	2.56
February		1.80	1.89	1.99	2.28
March		2.03	2.02	2.42	2.69
April		1.99	2.23	2.45	2.48
May		2.32	2.39	2.57	2.73
June		2.20	2.14	2.42	2.37
July		2.13	2.27	2.40	2.31
August		2.43	2.21	2.50	2.23
September	1.71	1.90	1.89	2.09	
October	1.90	2.13	2.29	2.54	
November	2.74	2.56	2.83	2.97	
December	4.20	4.16	4.04	4.35	

TABLE 16.16 DEPARTMENT STORE SALES FOR THE COUNTY, SEPTEMBER 1999 THROUGH DECEMBER 2003

Month	1999	2000	2001	2002	2003
January		46.8	46.8	43.8	48.0
February		48.0	48.6	45.6	51.6
March		60.0	59.4	57.6	57.6
April		57.6	58.2	53.4	58.2
May		61.8	60.6	56.4	60.0
June		58.2	55.2	52.8	57.0
July		56.4	51.0	54.0	57.6
August		63.0	58.8	60.6	61.8
September	55.8	57.6	49.8	47.4	69.0
October	56.4	53.4	54.6	54.6	75.0
November	71.4	71.4	65.4	67.8	85.2
December	117.6	114.0	102.0	100.2	121.8

county, as well as the total sales in the county for the four months the Carlson Department Store was closed. Management asks you to analyze these data and develop estimates of the lost sales at the Carlson Department Store for the months of September through December 2003. Management also wants to determine whether a case can be made for excess storm-related sales during the same period. If such a case can be made, Carlson is entitled to compensation for excess sales it would have earned in addition to ordinary sales.

Managerial Report

Prepare a report for the management of the Carlson Department store that summarizes your findings, forecasts, and recommendations. Include the following:

1. An estimate of sales had there been no hurricane.
2. An estimate of countywide department store sales had there been no hurricane.
3. An estimate of lost sales for the Carlson Department Store for September through December 2003.

Appendix 16.1 USING EXCEL FOR FORECASTING

In this appendix we show how Excel can be used to develop forecasts using three forecasting methods: moving averages, exponential smoothing, and trend projection.

Moving Averages

To show how Excel can be used to develop forecasts using the moving averages method, we will develop a forecast for the gasoline sales time series in Table 16.1 and Figure 16.5. We assume that the user has entered the sales data for the 12 weeks into worksheet rows 1 through 12 of column A. The following steps can be used to produce a three-week moving average.

Step 1. Select the **Tools** menu
Step 2. Select the **Data Analysis** option
Step 3. When the **Data Analysis Tools** dialog box appears, choose **Moving Average**
Step 4. When the **Moving Average** dialog box appears:
Enter A1:A12 in the **Input Range** box
Enter 3 in the **Interval** box
Enter B1 in the **Output Range** box
Click **OK**

The three-week moving average forecasts will appear in column B of the worksheet. Note that forecasts for periods of other lengths can be computed easily by entering a different value in the **Interval** box.

Exponential Smoothing

To show how Excel can be used for exponential smoothing, we again develop a forecast for the gasoline sales time series in Table 16.1 and Figure 16.5. We assume that the user has entered the sales data for the 12 weeks into worksheet rows 1 through 12 of column A and that the smoothing constant is $\alpha = 0.2$. The following steps can be used to produce a forecast.

Step 1. Select the **Tools** menu
Step 2. Select the **Data Analysis** option

Step 3. When the **Data Analysis Tools** dialog box appears, choose **Exponential Smoothing**

Step 4. When the **Exponential Smoothing** dialog box appears:
Enter A1:A12 in the **Input Range** box
Enter 0.8 in the **Damping factor** box
Enter B1 in the **Output Range** box
Click **OK**

The exponential smoothing forecasts will appear in column B of the worksheet. Note that the value we entered in the **Damping factor** box is $1 - \alpha$; forecasts for other smoothing constants can be computed easily by entering a different value for $1 - \alpha$ in the **Damping factor** box.

Trend Projection

To show how Excel can be used for trend projection, we develop a forecast for the bicycle sales time series in Table 16.6 and Figure 16.8. We assume that the user has entered the year (1–10) for each observation into worksheet rows 1 through 10 of column A and the sales values into worksheet rows 1 through 10 of column B. The following steps can be used to produce a forecast for year 11 by trend projection.

Step 1. Select an empty cell in the worksheet

Step 2. Select the **Insert** menu

Step 3. Choose the **Function** option

Step 4. When the **Insert Function** dialog box appears:
Choose **Statistical** in the **Select a category** box
Choose **Forecast** in the **Select a function** box
Click **OK**

Step 5. When the **Function Arguments** dialog box appears:
Enter 11 in the **x** box
Enter B1:B10 in the **Known y's** box
Enter A1:A10 in the **Known x's** box
Click **OK**

The forecast for year 11, in this case 32.5, will appear in the cell selected in step 1.

CHAPTER 17

Markov Processes

CONTENTS

Markov process models are useful in studying the evolution of systems over repeated trials. The repeated trials are often successive time periods where the state of the system in any particular period cannot be determined with certainty. Rather, transition probabilities are used to describe the manner in which the system makes transitions from one period to the next. Hence, we are interested in the probability of the system being in a particular state at a given time period.

Markov process models can be used to describe the probability that a machine that is functioning in one period will continue to function or will break down in the next period. Models can also be used to describe the probability that a consumer purchasing brand A in one period will purchase brand B in the next period. The Management Science in Action, Benefit of Health Care Services, describes how a Markov process model was used to determine the health status probabilities for persons aged 65 and older. Such information was helpful in understanding the future need for health care services and the benefits of expanding current health care programs.

In this chapter we present a marketing application that involves an analysis of the store-switching behavior of supermarket customers. As a second illustration, we consider an accounting application that is concerned with the transitioning of accounts receivable dollars to different account-aging categories. Because an in-depth treatment of Markov processes is beyond the scope of this text, the analysis in both illustrations is restricted to situations consisting of a finite number of states, the transition probabilities remaining constant over time, and the probability of being in a particular state at any one time period depending only on the state in the immediately preceding time period. Such Markov processes are referred to as *Markov chains with stationary transition probabilities.*

MANAGEMENT SCIENCE IN ACTION

BENEFIT OF HEALTH CARE SERVICES*

The U.S. General Accounting Office (GAO) is an independent, nonpolitical audit organization in the legislative branch of the federal government. GAO evaluators obtained data on the health conditions of individuals aged 65 and older. The individuals were identified as being in three possible states:

- **Best:** Able to perform daily activities without assistance
- **Next Best:** Able to perform some daily activities without assistance
- **Worst:** Unable to perform daily activities without assistance

Using a two-year period, the evaluators developed estimates of the transition probabilities among the three states. For example, a transition probability that a person in the Best state is still in the Best state one year later was 0.80, while the transition probability that a person in the Best state moves to the Next Best state one year later is 0.10. The Markov analysis of the full set of transition probabilities determined the steady-state probabilities that individuals would be in each state. Thus, for a given population aged 65 and older, the steady-state probabilities would indicate the percentage of the population that would be in each state in future years.

The GAO study further subdivided individuals into two groups: those receiving appropriate health care and those not receiving appropriate health care. For individuals not receiving appropriate health care, the kind of additional care and the cost of that care were estimated. The revised transition probabilities showed that with appropriate health care, the steady-state probabilities indicated the larger percentage of the population that would be in the Best and Next Best health states in future years. Using these results, the model provided evidence of the future benefits that would be achieved by expanding current health care programs.

*Based on information provided by Bill Ammann, U.S. General Accounting Office.

17.1 MARKET SHARE ANALYSIS

Suppose we are interested in analyzing the market share and customer loyalty for Murphy's Foodliner and Ashley's Supermarket, the only two grocery stores in a small town. We focus on the sequence of shopping trips of one customer and assume that the customer makes one shopping trip each week to either Murphy's Foodliner or Ashley's Supermarket, but not both.

Using the terminology of Markov processes, we refer to the weekly periods or shopping trips as the **trials of the process.** Thus, at each trial, the customer will shop at either Murphy's Foodliner or Ashley's Supermarket. The particular store selected in a given week is referred to as the **state of the system** in that period. Because the customer has two shopping alternatives at each trial, we say the system has two states. With a finite number of states, we identify the states as follows:

State 1. The customer shops at Murphy's Foodliner.
State 2. The customer shops at Ashley's Supermarket.

If we say the system is in state 1 at trial 3, we are simply saying that the customer shops at Murphy's during the third weekly shopping period.

As we continue the shopping trip process into the future, we cannot say for certain where the customer will shop during a given week or trial. In fact, we realize that during any given week, the customer may be either a Murphy's customer or an Ashley's customer. However, using a Markov process model, we will be able to compute the probability that the customer shops at each store during any period. For example, we may find a 0.6 probability that the customer will shop at Murphy's during a particular week and a 0.4 probability that the customer will shop at Ashley's.

To determine the probabilities of the various states occurring at successive trials of the Markov process, we need information on the probability that a customer remains with the same store or switches to the competing store as the process continues from trial to trial or week to week.

Suppose that, as part of a market research study, we collect data from 100 shoppers over a 10-week period. Suppose further that these data show each customer's weekly shopping trip pattern in terms of the sequence of visits to Murphy's and Ashley's. To develop a Markov process model for the sequence of weekly shopping trips, we need to express the probability of selecting each store (state) in a given period solely in terms of the store (state) that was selected during the previous period. In reviewing the data, suppose that we find that of all customers who shopped at Murphy's in a given week, 90 percent shopped at Murphy's the following week while 10 percent switched to Ashley's. Suppose that similar data for the customers who shopped at Ashley's in a given week show that 80 percent shopped at Ashley's the following week while 20 percent switched to Murphy's. Probabilities based on these data are shown in Table 17.1. Because these probabilities indicate that a customer moves, or makes a transition, from a state in a given period to each state in the following period, these probabilities are called **transition probabilities.**

TABLE 17.1 TRANSITION PROBABILITIES FOR MURPHY'S AND ASHLEY'S GROCERY SALES

Current Weekly Shopping Period	Next Weekly Shopping Period	
	Murphy's Foodliner	**Ashley's Supermarket**
Murphy's Foodliner	0.9	0.1
Ashley's Supermarket	0.2	0.8

An important property of the table of transition probabilities is that the sum of the probabilities in each row is 1; each row of the table provides a probability distribution. For example, a customer who shops at Murphy's one week must shop at either Murphy's or Ashley's the next week. The entries in row 1 give the probabilities associated with each of these events. The 0.9 and 0.8 probabilities in Table 17.1 can be interpreted as measures of store loyalty in that they indicate the probability of a repeat visit to the same store. Similarly, the 0.1 and 0.2 probabilities are measures of the store-switching characteristics of the customers. In developing a Markov process model for this problem, we are assuming that the transition probabilities will be the same for any customer and that the transition probabilities will not change over time.

The chapter appendix contains a review of matrix notation and operations.

Note that Table 17.1 has one row and one column for each state of the system. We will use the symbol p_{ij} to represent the transition probabilities and the symbol P to represent the matrix of transition probabilities; that is,

$$p_{ij} = \text{probability of making a transition from state } i \text{ in a given period to state } j \text{ in the next period}$$

For the supermarket problem, we have

A quick check for a valid matrix of transition probabilities is to make sure the sum of the probabilities in each row equals 1.

$$P = \begin{bmatrix} p_{11} & p_{12} \\ p_{21} & p_{22} \end{bmatrix} = \begin{bmatrix} 0.9 & 0.1 \\ 0.2 & 0.8 \end{bmatrix}$$

Using the matrix of transition probabilities, we can now determine the probability that a customer will be a Murphy's customer or an Ashley's customer at some period in the future. Let us begin by assuming that we have a customer whose last weekly shopping trip was to Murphy's. What is the probability that this customer will shop at Murphy's on the next weekly shopping trip, period 1? In other words, what is the probability that the system will be in state 1 after the first transition? The matrix of transition probabilities indicates that this probability is $p_{11} = 0.9$.

Now let us consider the state of the system in period 2. A useful way of depicting what can happen on the second weekly shopping trip is to draw a tree diagram of the possible outcomes (see Figure 17.1). Using this tree diagram, we see that the probability that the customer shops at Murphy's during both the first and the second weeks is (0.9)(0.9) = 0.81. Also, note that the probability of the customer switching to Ashley's on the first trip and then switching back to Murphy's on the second trip is (0.1)(0.2) = 0.02. Because these options are the only two ways that the customer can be in state 1 (shopping at Murphy's) during the second period, the probability of the system being in state 1 during the second period is 0.81 + 0.02 = 0.83. Similarly, the probability of the system being in state 2 during the second period is 0.09 + 0.08 = 0.17.

As desirable as the tree diagram approach may be from an intuitive point of view, it becomes cumbersome when we want to extend the analysis to three or more periods. Fortunately, we have an easier way to calculate the probabilities of the system being in state 1 or state 2 for any subsequent period. First, we introduce a notation that will allow us to represent these probabilities for any given period. Let

$$\pi_i(n) = \text{probability that the system is in state } i \text{ in period } n$$

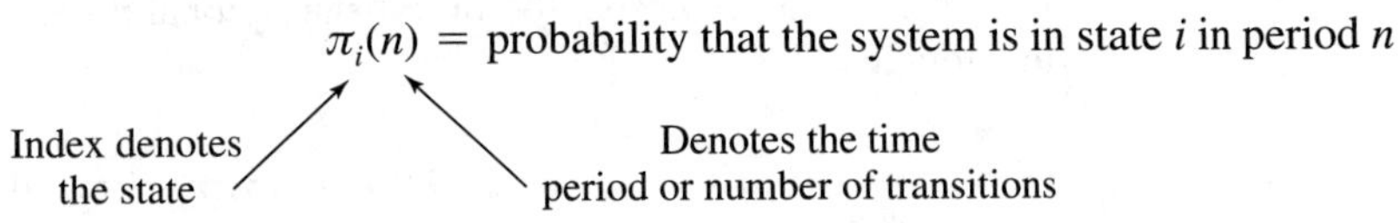

FIGURE 17.1 TREE DIAGRAM DEPICTING TWO WEEKLY SHOPPING TRIPS OF A CUSTOMER WHO SHOPPED LAST AT MURPHY'S

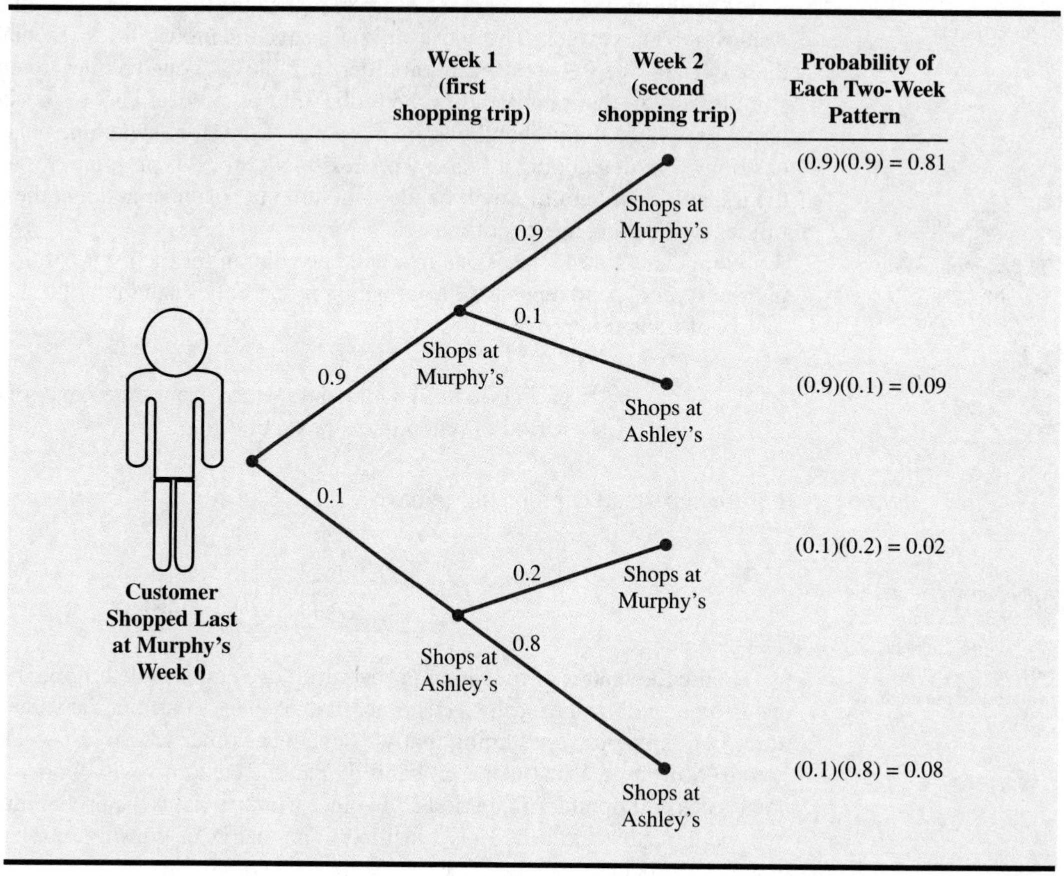

For example, $\pi_1(1)$ denotes the probability of the system being in state 1 in period 1, while $\pi_2(1)$ denotes the probability of the system being in state 2 in period 1. Because $\pi_i(n)$ is the probability that the system is in state i in period n, this probability is referred to as a **state probability.**

The terms $\pi_1(0)$ and $\pi_2(0)$ will denote the probability of the system being in state 1 or state 2 at some initial or starting period. Week 0 represents the most recent period, when we are beginning the analysis of a Markov process. If we set $\pi_1(0) = 1$ and $\pi_2(0) = 0$, we are saying that as an initial condition the customer shopped last week at Murphy's; alternatively, if we set $\pi_1(0) = 0$ and $\pi_2(0) = 1$, we would be starting the system with a customer who shopped last week at Ashley's. In the tree diagram of Figure 17.1, we consider the situation in which the customer shopped last at Murphy's. Thus,

$$[\pi_1(0) \quad \pi_2(0)] = [1 \quad 0]$$

is a vector that represents the initial state probabilities of the system. In general, we use the notation

$$\Pi(n) = [\pi_1(n) \quad \pi_2(n)]$$

to denote the vector of state probabilities for the system in period n. In the example, $\Pi(1)$ is a vector representing the state probabilities for the first week, $\Pi(2)$ is a vector representing the state probabilities for the second week, and so on.

Using this notation, we can find the state probabilities for period $n + 1$ by simply multiplying the known state probabilities for period n by the transition probability matrix. Using the vector of state probabilities and the matrix of transition probabilities, the multiplication[1] can be expressed as follows:

$$\Pi(\text{next period}) = \Pi(\text{current period})P$$

or

$$\Pi(n + 1) = \Pi(n)P \tag{17.1}$$

Beginning with the system in state 1 at period 0, we have $\Pi(0) = [1 \ 0]$. We can compute the state probabilities for period 1 as follows:

$$\Pi(1) = \Pi(0)P$$

or

$$\begin{aligned}[\pi_1(1) \quad \pi_2(1)] &= [\pi_1(0) \quad \pi_2(0)]\begin{bmatrix} p_{11} & p_{12} \\ p_{21} & p_{22} \end{bmatrix} \\ &= [1 \quad 0]\begin{bmatrix} 0.9 & 0.1 \\ 0.2 & 0.8 \end{bmatrix} \\ &= [0.9 \quad 0.1]\end{aligned}$$

The state probabilities $\pi_1(1) = 0.9$ and $\pi_2(1) = 0.1$ are the probabilities that a customer who shopped at Murphy's during week 0 will shop at Murphy's or at Ashley's during week 1.

Using equation (17.1), we can compute the state probabilities for the second week as follows:

$$\Pi(2) = \Pi(1)P$$

or

$$\begin{aligned}[\pi_1(2) \quad \pi_2(2)] &= [\pi_1(1) \quad \pi_2(1)]\begin{bmatrix} p_{11} & p_{12} \\ p_{21} & p_{22} \end{bmatrix} \\ &= [0.9 \quad 0.1]\begin{bmatrix} 0.9 & 0.1 \\ 0.2 & 0.8 \end{bmatrix} \\ &= [0.83 \quad 0.17]\end{aligned}$$

We see that the probability of shopping at Murphy's during the second week is 0.83, while the probability of shopping at Ashley's during the second week is 0.17. These same results

[1]Appendix 17.1 provides the step-by-step procedure for vector and matrix multiplication.

were previously obtained using the tree diagram of Figure 17.1. By continuing to apply equation (17.1), we can compute the state probabilities for any future period; that is,

$$\begin{aligned} \Pi(3) &= \Pi(2)P \\ \Pi(4) &= \Pi(3)P \\ &\vdots \\ \Pi(n+1) &= \Pi(n)P \end{aligned}$$

Table 17.2 shows the result of carrying out these calculations for 10 periods.

The vectors $\Pi(1)$, $\Pi(2)$, $\Pi(3)$, . . . contain the probabilities that a customer who started out as a Murphy customer will be in state 1 or state 2 in the first period, the second period, the third period, and so on. In Table 17.2 we see that after a few periods these probabilities do not change much from one period to the next.

If we had started with 1000 Murphy customers—that is, 1000 customers who last shopped at Murphy's—our analysis indicates that during the fifth weekly shopping period, 723 would be customers of Murphy's, and 277 would be customers of Ashley's. Moreover, during the tenth weekly shopping period, 676 would be customers of Murphy's, and 324 would be customers of Ashley's.

Now let us repeat the analysis, but this time we will begin the process with a customer who shopped last at Ashley's. Thus,

$$\Pi(0) = [\pi_1(0) \quad \pi_2(0)] = [0 \quad 1]$$

Using equation (17.1), the probability of the system being in state 1 or state 2 in period 1 is given by

$$\Pi(1) = \Pi(0)P$$

or

$$\begin{aligned} [\pi_1(1) \quad \pi_2(1)] &= [\pi_1(0) \quad \pi_2(0)]\begin{bmatrix} p_{11} & p_{12} \\ p_{21} & p_{22} \end{bmatrix} \\ &= [0 \quad 1]\begin{bmatrix} 0.9 & 0.1 \\ 0.2 & 0.8 \end{bmatrix} \\ &= [0.2 \quad 0.8] \end{aligned}$$

Proceeding as before, we can calculate subsequent state probabilities. Doing so, we obtain the results shown in Table 17.3.

TABLE 17.2 STATE PROBABILITIES FOR FUTURE PERIODS BEGINNING INITIALLY WITH A MURPHY'S CUSTOMER

State	Period (n)										
Probability	**0**	**1**	**2**	**3**	**4**	**5**	**6**	**7**	**8**	**9**	**10**
$\pi_1(n)$	1	0.9	0.83	0.781	0.747	0.723	0.706	0.694	0.686	0.680	0.676
$\pi_2(n)$	0	0.1	0.17	0.219	0.253	0.277	0.294	0.306	0.314	0.320	0.324

TABLE 17.3 STATE PROBABILITIES FOR FUTURE PERIODS BEGINNING INITIALLY WITH AN ASHLEY'S CUSTOMER

State	Period (n)										
Probability	**0**	**1**	**2**	**3**	**4**	**5**	**6**	**7**	**8**	**9**	**10**
$\pi_1(n)$	0	0.2	0.34	0.438	0.507	0.555	0.589	0.612	0.628	0.640	0.648
$\pi_2(n)$	1	0.8	0.66	0.562	0.493	0.445	0.411	0.388	0.372	0.360	0.352

In the fifth shopping period, the probability that the customer will be shopping at Murphy's is 0.555, and the probability that the customer will be shopping at Ashley's is 0.445. In the tenth period, the probability that a customer will be shopping at Murphy's is 0.648, and the probability that a customer will be shopping at Ashley's is 0.352.

As we continue the Markov process, we find that the probability of the system being in a particular state after a large number of periods is independent of the beginning state of the system. The probabilities that we approach after a large number of transitions are referred to as the **steady-state probabilities.** We shall denote the steady-state probability for state 1 with the symbol π_1 and the steady-state probability for state 2 with the symbol π_2. In other words, in the steady-state case, we simply omit the period designation from $\pi_i(n)$ because it is no longer necessary.

Analyses of Tables 17.2 and 17.3 indicate that as n gets larger, the difference between the state probabilities for the nth period and the $(n + 1)$th period becomes increasingly smaller. This analysis leads us to the conclusion that as n gets large, the state probabilities at the $(n + 1)$th period are very close to those at the nth period. This observation provides the basis of a simple method for computing the steady-state probabilities without having to actually carry out a large number of calculations.

In general, we know from equation (17.1) that

$$[\pi_1(n+1) \quad \pi_2(n+1)] = [\pi_1(n) \quad \pi_2(n)]\begin{bmatrix} p_{11} & p_{12} \\ p_{21} & p_{22} \end{bmatrix}$$

Because for sufficiently large n the difference between $\Pi(n + 1)$ and $\Pi(n)$ is negligible, we see that in the steady state $\pi_1(n + 1) = \pi_1(n) = \pi_1$, and $\pi_2(n + 1) = \pi_2(n) = \pi_2$. Thus, we have

$$\begin{aligned}[\pi_1 \quad \pi_2] &= [\pi_1 \quad \pi_2]\begin{bmatrix} p_{11} & p_{12} \\ p_{21} & p_{22} \end{bmatrix} \\ &= [\pi_1 \quad \pi_2]\begin{bmatrix} 0.9 & 0.1 \\ 0.2 & 0.8 \end{bmatrix}\end{aligned}$$

After carrying out the multiplications, we obtain

$$\pi_1 = 0.9\pi_1 + 0.2\pi_2 \tag{17.2}$$

and

$$\pi_2 = 0.1\pi_1 + 0.8\pi_2 \tag{17.3}$$

However, we also know the steady-state probabilities must sum to 1 with

$$\pi_1 + \pi_2 = 1 \tag{17.4}$$

Using equation (17.4) to solve for π_2 and substituting the result in equation (17.2), we obtain

$$\begin{aligned} \pi_1 &= 0.9\pi_1 + 0.2(1 - \pi_1) \\ \pi_1 &= 0.9\pi_1 + 0.2 - 0.2\pi_1 \\ \pi_1 - 0.7\pi_1 &= 0.2 \\ 0.3\pi_1 &= 0.2 \\ \pi_1 &= \tfrac{2}{3} \end{aligned}$$

Can you now compute the steady-state probabilities for Markov processes with two states? Problem 3 provides an application.

Then, using equation (17.4), we can conclude that $\pi_2 = 1 - \pi_1 = \frac{1}{3}$. Thus, using equations (17.2) and (17.4), we can solve for the steady-state probabilities directly. You can check for yourself that we could have obtained the same result using equations (17.3) and (17.4).[2]

Thus, if we have 1000 customers in the system, the Markov process model tells us that in the long run, with steady-state probabilities $\pi_1 = \frac{2}{3}$ and $\pi_2 = \frac{1}{3}$, $\frac{2}{3}(1000) = 667$ customers will be Murphy's and $\frac{1}{3}(1000) = 333$ customers will be Ashley's. The steady-state probabilities can be interpreted as the market shares for the two stores.

Market share information is often quite valuable in decision making. For example, suppose Ashley's Supermarket is contemplating an advertising campaign to attract more of Murphy's customers to its store. Let us suppose further that Ashley's believes this promotional strategy will increase the probability of a Murphy's customer switching to Ashley's from 0.10 to 0.15. The revised transition probabilities are given in Table 17.4.

Given the new transition probabilities, we can modify equations (17.2) and (17.4) to solve for the new steady-state probabilities or market shares. Thus, we obtain

$$\pi_1 = 0.85\pi_1 + 0.20\pi_2$$

With three states, the steady-state probabilities are found by solving three equations for the three unknown steady-state probabilities. Try Problem 7 as a slightly more difficult problem involving three states.

Substituting $\pi_2 = 1 - \pi_1$ from equation (17.4), we have

$$\begin{aligned} \pi_1 &= 0.85\pi_1 + 0.20(1 - \pi_1) \\ \pi_1 &= 0.85\pi_1 + 0.20 - 0.20\pi_1 \\ \pi_1 - 0.65\pi_1 &= 0.20 \\ 0.35\pi_1 &= 0.20 \\ \pi_1 &= 0.57 \end{aligned}$$

[2]Even though equations (17.2) and (17.3) provide two equations and two unknowns, we must include equation (17.4) when solving for π_1 and π_2 to ensure that the sum of steady-state probabilities will equal 1.

TABLE 17.4 REVISED TRANSITION PROBABILITIES FOR MURPHY'S AND ASHLEY'S GROCERY STORES

Current Weekly Shopping Period	Next Weekly Shopping Period	
	Murphy's Foodliner	**Ashley's Supermarket**
Murphy's Foodliner	0.85	0.15
Ashley's Supermarket	0.20	0.80

and

$$\pi_2 = 1 - 0.57 = 0.43$$

Other examples of Markov processes include the promotion of managers to various positions within an organization, the migration of people into and out of various regions of the country, and the progression of students through the years of college, including eventually dropping out or graduating.

We see that the proposed promotional strategy will increase Ashley's market share from $\pi_2 = 0.33$ to $\pi_2 = 0.43$. Suppose that the total market consists of 6000 customers per week. The new promotional strategy will increase the number of customers doing their weekly shopping at Ashley's from 2000 to 2580. If the average weekly profit per customer is $10, the proposed promotional strategy can be expected to increase Ashley's profits by $5800 per week. If the cost of the promotional campaign is less than $5800 per week, Ashley should consider implementing the strategy.

This example demonstrates how a Markov analysis of a firm's market share can be useful in decision making. Suppose that instead of trying to attract customers from Murphy's Foodliner, Ashley's directed a promotional effort at increasing the loyalty of its own customers. In this case, p_{22} would increase, and p_{21} would decrease. Once we knew the amount of the change, we could calculate new steady-state probabilities and compute the impact on profits.

NOTES AND COMMENTS

1. The Markov processes presented in this section have what is called the *memoryless property*: the current state of the system together with the transition probabilities contain all the information necessary to predict the future behavior of the system. The prior states of the system do not have to be considered. Such Markov processes are considered first-order Markov processes. Higher-order Markov processes are ones in which future states of the system depend on two or more previous states.
2. Analysis of a Markov process model is not intended to optimize any particular aspect of a system. Rather, the analysis predicts or describes the future and steady-state behavior of the system. For instance, in the grocery store example, the analysis of the steady-state behavior provided a forecast or prediction of the market shares for the two competitors. In other applications, quantitative analysts have extended the study of Markov processes to what are called *Markov decision processes.* In these models, decisions can be made at each period, which affect the transition probabilities and hence influence the future behavior of the system. Markov decision processes have been used in analyzing machine breakdown and maintenance operations, planning the movement of patients in hospitals, developing inspection strategies, determining newspaper subscription duration, and analyzing equipment replacement.

17.2 ACCOUNTS RECEIVABLE ANALYSIS

An accounting application in which Markov processes have produced useful results involves the estimation of the allowance for doubtful accounts receivable. This allowance is an estimate of the amount of accounts receivable that will ultimately prove to be uncollectible (i.e., bad debts).

Let us consider the accounts receivable situation for Heidman's Department Store. Heidman's uses two aging categories for its accounts receivable: (1) accounts that are classified as 0–30 days old, and (2) accounts that are classified as 31–90 days old. If any portion of an account balance exceeds 90 days, that portion is written off as a bad debt. Heidman's follows the procedure of aging the total balance in any customer's account according to the oldest unpaid bill. For example, suppose that one customer's account balance on September 30 is as follows:

Date of Purchase	Amount Charged
August 15	$25
September 18	10
September 28	50
Total	$85

An aging of accounts receivable on September 30 would assign the total balance of $85 to the 31–90-day category because the oldest unpaid bill of August 15 is 46 days old. Let us assume that one week later, October 7, the customer pays the August 15 bill of $25. The remaining total balance of $60 would now be placed in the 0–30-day category since the oldest unpaid amount, corresponding to the September 18 purchase, is less than 31 days old. This method of aging accounts receivable is called the *total balance method* because the total account balance is placed in the age category corresponding to the oldest unpaid amount.

Note that under the total balance method of aging accounts receivable, dollars appearing in a 31–90-day category at one point in time may appear in a 0–30-day category at a later point in time. In the preceding example, this movement between categories was true for $60 of September billings, which shifted from a 31–90-day to a 0–30-day category after the August bill had been paid.

Let us assume that on December 31 Heidman's shows a total of $3000 in its accounts receivable and that the firm's management would like an estimate of how much of the $3000 will eventually be collected and how much will eventually result in bad debts. The estimated amount of bad debts will appear as an allowance for doubtful accounts in the year-end financial statements.

Let us see how we can view the accounts receivable operation as a Markov process. First, concentrate on what happens to *one* dollar currently in accounts receivable. As the firm continues to operate into the future, we can consider each week as a trial of a Markov process with a dollar existing in one of the following states of the system:

State 1. Paid category
State 2. Bad debt category
State 3. 0–30-day category
State 4. 31–90-day category

Thus, we can track the week-by-week status of one dollar by using a Markov analysis to identify the state of the system at a particular week or period.

Using a Markov process model with the preceding states, we define the transition probabilities as follows:

$$p_{ij} = \text{probability of a dollar in state } i \text{ in one week moving to state } j \text{ in the next week}$$

Based on historical transitions of accounts receivable dollars, the following matrix of transition probabilities, P, has been developed for Heidman's Department Store:

$$P = \begin{bmatrix} p_{11} & p_{12} & p_{13} & p_{14} \\ p_{21} & p_{22} & p_{23} & p_{24} \\ p_{31} & p_{32} & p_{33} & p_{34} \\ p_{41} & p_{42} & p_{43} & p_{44} \end{bmatrix} = \begin{bmatrix} 1.0 & 0.0 & 0.0 & 0.0 \\ 0.0 & 1.0 & 0.0 & 0.0 \\ 0.4 & 0.0 & 0.3 & 0.3 \\ 0.4 & 0.2 & 0.3 & 0.1 \end{bmatrix}$$

Note that the probability of a dollar in the 0–30-day category (state 3) moving to the paid category (state 1) in the next period is 0.4. Also, this dollar has a 0.3 probability it will remain in the 0–30-day category (state 3) one week later, and a 0.3 probability that it will be in the 31–90-day category (state 4) one week later. Note also that a dollar in a 0–30-day account cannot make the transition to a bad debt (state 2) in one week.

When absorbing states are present, each row of the transition matrix corresponding to an absorbing state will have a single 1 and all other probabilities will be 0.

An important property of the Markov process model for Heidman's accounts receivable situation is the presence of *absorbing states.* For example, once a dollar makes a transition to state 1, the paid state, the probability of making a transition to any other state is zero. Similarly, once a dollar is in state 2, the bad debt state, the probability of a transition to any other state is zero. Thus, once a dollar reaches state 1 or state 2, the system will remain in this state forever. We can conclude that all accounts receivable dollars will eventually be absorbed into either the paid or the bad debt state, and hence the name **absorbing state.**

Fundamental Matrix and Associated Calculations

Whenever a Markov process has absorbing states, we do not compute steady-state probabilities because each unit ultimately ends up in one of the absorbing states. With absorbing states present, we are interested in knowing the probability that a unit will end up in each of the absorbing states. For the Heidman's Department Store problem, we want to know the probability that a dollar currently in the 0–30-day age category will end up paid (absorbing state 1) as well as the probability that a dollar in this age category will end up a bad debt (absorbing state 2). We also want to know these absorbing-state probabilities for a dollar currently in the 31–90-day age category.

The computation of the absorbing-state probabilities requires the determination and use of what is called a **fundamental matrix.** The mathematical logic underlying the fundamental matrix is beyond the scope of this text. However, as we show, the fundamental matrix is derived from the matrix of transition probabilities and is relatively easy to compute for Markov processes with a small number of states. In the following example, we show the computation of the fundamental matrix and the determination of the absorbing-state probabilities for Heidman's Department Store.

We begin the computations by partitioning the matrix of transition probabilities into the following four parts:

$$P = \left[\begin{array}{cc|cc} 1.0 & 0.0 & 0.0 & 0.0 \\ 0.0 & 1.0 & 0.0 & 0.0 \\ \hline 0.4 & 0.0 & 0.3 & 0.3 \\ 0.4 & 0.2 & 0.3 & 0.1 \end{array}\right] = \left[\begin{array}{cc|cc} 1.0 & 0.0 & 0.0 & 0.0 \\ 0.0 & 1.0 & 0.0 & 0.0 \\ \hline \multicolumn{2}{c|}{R} & \multicolumn{2}{c}{Q} \end{array}\right]$$

where

$$R = \begin{bmatrix} 0.4 & 0.0 \\ 0.4 & 0.2 \end{bmatrix} \qquad Q = \begin{bmatrix} 0.3 & 0.3 \\ 0.3 & 0.1 \end{bmatrix}$$

A matrix N, called a *fundamental matrix,* can be calculated using the following formula:

$$N = (I - Q)^{-1} \tag{17.5}$$

where I is an identity matrix with 1s on the main diagonal and 0s elsewhere. The superscript -1 is used to indicate the inverse of the matrix $(I - Q)$. In Appendix 17.1 we present formulas for finding the inverse of a matrix with two rows and two columns.

Before proceeding, we note that to use equation (17.5), the identity matrix I must be chosen such that it has the *same size or dimensionality* as the matrix Q. In our example problem, Q has two rows and two columns, so we must choose

$$I = \begin{bmatrix} 1.0 & 0.0 \\ 0.0 & 1.0 \end{bmatrix}$$

Let us now continue with the example problem by computing the fundamental matrix.

$$\begin{aligned} I - Q &= \begin{bmatrix} 1.0 & 0.0 \\ 0.0 & 1.0 \end{bmatrix} - \begin{bmatrix} 0.3 & 0.3 \\ 0.3 & 0.1 \end{bmatrix} \\ &= \begin{bmatrix} 0.7 & -0.3 \\ -0.3 & 0.9 \end{bmatrix} \end{aligned}$$

and (see Appendix 17.1)

$$N = (I - Q)^{-1} = \begin{bmatrix} 1.67 & 0.56 \\ 0.56 & 1.30 \end{bmatrix}$$

If we multiply the fundamental matrix N times the R portion of the P matrix, we obtain the probabilities that accounts receivable dollars initially in states 3 or 4 will eventually reach each of the absorbing states. The multiplication of N times R for the Heidman's Department Store problem provides the following results (again, see Appendix 17.1 for the steps of this matrix multiplication):

$$NR = \begin{bmatrix} 1.67 & 0.56 \\ 0.56 & 1.30 \end{bmatrix} \begin{bmatrix} 0.4 & 0.0 \\ 0.4 & 0.2 \end{bmatrix} = \begin{bmatrix} 0.89 & 0.11 \\ 0.74 & 0.26 \end{bmatrix}$$

The first row of the product NR is the probability that a dollar in the 0–30-day age category will end up in each absorbing state. Thus, we see a 0.89 probability that a dollar in the 0–30-day category will eventually be paid and a 0.11 probability that it will become a bad debt. Similarly, the second row shows the probabilities associated with a dollar in the 31–90-day category; that is, a dollar in the 31–90-day category has a 0.74 probability of eventually being paid and a 0.26 probability of proving to be uncollectible. Using this information, we can predict the amount of money that will be paid and the amount that will be lost as bad debts.

Establishing the Allowance for Doubtful Accounts

Let B represent a two-element vector that contains the current accounts receivable balances in the 0–30-day and the 31–90-day categories; that is,

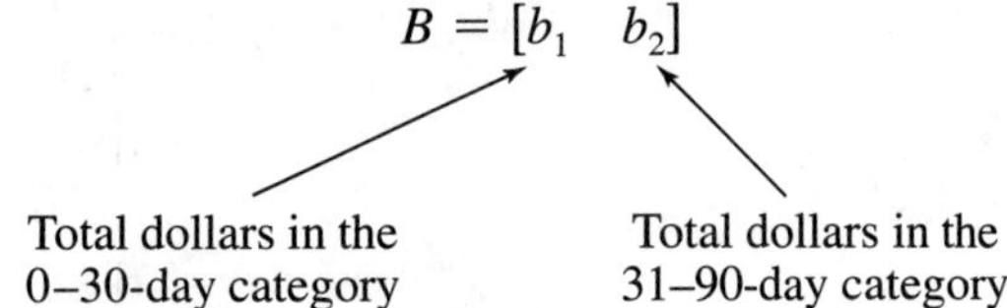

Suppose that the December 31 balance of accounts receivable for Heidman's shows \$1000 in the 0–30-day category (state 3) and \$2000 in the 31–90-day category (state 4).

$$B = [1000 \quad 2000]$$

We can multiply B times NR to determine how much of the \$3000 will be collected and how much will be lost. For example

$$\begin{aligned} BNR &= [1000 \quad 2000]\begin{bmatrix} 0.89 & 0.11 \\ 0.74 & 0.26 \end{bmatrix} \\ &= [2370 \quad 630] \end{aligned}$$

Thus, we see that \$2370 of the accounts receivable balances will be collected and \$630 will be written off as a bad debt expense. Based on this analysis, the accounting department would set up an allowance for doubtful accounts of \$630.

The matrix multiplication of BNR is simply a convenient way of computing the eventual collections and bad debts of the accounts receivable. Recall that the NR matrix showed a 0.89 probability of collecting dollars in the 0–30-day category and a 0.74 probability of collecting dollars in the 31–90-day category. Thus, as was shown by the BNR calculation, we expect to collect a total of $(1000)0.89 + (2000)0.74 = 890 + 1480 = \$2370$.

Suppose that on the basis of the previous analysis Heidman's would like to investigate the possibility of reducing the amount of bad debts. Recall that the analysis indicated that a 0.11 probability or 11 percent of the amount in the 0–30-day age category and 26 percent of the amount in the 31–90-day age category will prove to be uncollectible. Let us assume that Heidman's is considering instituting a new credit policy involving a discount for prompt payment.

Management believes that the policy under consideration will increase the probability of a transition from the 0–30-day age category to the paid category and decrease the probability of a transition from the 0–30-day to the 31–90-day age category. Let us assume that a careful study of the effects of this new policy leads management to conclude that the following transition matrix would be applicable:

$$P = \left[\begin{array}{cc|cc} 1.0 & 0.0 & 0.0 & 0.0 \\ 0.0 & 1.0 & 0.0 & 0.0 \\ \hline 0.6 & 0.0 & 0.3 & 0.1 \\ 0.4 & 0.2 & 0.3 & 0.1 \end{array}\right]$$

We see that the probability of a dollar in the 0–30-day age category making a transition to the paid category in the next period has increased to 0.6 and that the probability of a dollar in the 0–30-day age category making a transition to the 31–90-day category has decreased to 0.1. To determine the effect of these changes on bad debt expense, we must calculate N, NR, and BNR. We begin by using equation (17.5) to calculate the fundamental matrix N:

$$\begin{aligned} N = (I - Q)^{-1} &= \left\{ \begin{bmatrix} 1.0 & 0.0 \\ 0.0 & 1.0 \end{bmatrix} - \begin{bmatrix} 0.3 & 0.1 \\ 0.3 & 0.1 \end{bmatrix} \right\}^{-1} \\ &= \begin{bmatrix} 0.7 & -0.1 \\ -0.3 & 0.9 \end{bmatrix}^{-1} \\ &= \begin{bmatrix} 1.5 & 0.17 \\ 0.5 & 1.17 \end{bmatrix} \end{aligned}$$

By multiplying N times R, we obtain the new probabilities that the dollars in each age category will end up in the two absorbing states:

$$\begin{aligned} NR &= \begin{bmatrix} 1.5 & 0.17 \\ 0.5 & 1.17 \end{bmatrix} \begin{bmatrix} 0.6 & 0.0 \\ 0.4 & 0.2 \end{bmatrix} \\ &= \begin{bmatrix} 0.97 & 0.03 \\ 0.77 & 0.23 \end{bmatrix} \end{aligned}$$

We see that with the new credit policy we would expect only 3 percent of the funds in the 0–30-day age category and 23 percent of the funds in the 31–90-day age category to prove to be uncollectible. If, as before, we assume a current balance of \$1000 in the 0–30-day age category and \$2000 in the 31–90-day age category, we can calculate the total amount of accounts receivable that will end up in the two absorbing states by multiplying B times NR. We obtain

$$\begin{aligned} BNR &= [1000 \quad 2000] \begin{bmatrix} 0.97 & 0.03 \\ 0.77 & 0.23 \end{bmatrix} \\ &= [2510 \quad 490] \end{aligned}$$

Problem 11, which provides a variation of Heidman's Department Store problem, will give you practice in analyzing Markov processes with absorbing states.

Thus, the new credit policy shows a bad debt expense of \$490. Under the previous credit policy, we found the bad debt expense to be \$630. Thus, a savings of \$630 − \$490 = \$140 could be expected as a result of the new credit policy. Given the total accounts receivable balance of \$3000, this savings represents a 4.7 percent reduction in bad debt expense. After considering the costs involved, management can evaluate the economics of adopting the new credit policy. If the cost, including discounts, is less than 4.7 percent of the accounts receivable balance, we would expect the new policy to lead to increased profits for Heidman's Department Store.

SUMMARY

In this chapter we presented Markov process models as well as examples of their application. We saw that a Markov analysis could provide helpful decision-making information about a situation that involves a sequence of repeated trials with a finite number of possible states on each trial. A primary objective is obtaining information about the probability of each state after a large number of transitions or time periods.

A market share application showed the computational procedure for determining the steady-state probabilities that could be interpreted as market shares for two competing supermarkets. In an accounts receivable application, we introduced the notion of absorbing states; for the two absorbing states, referred to as the paid and bad debt categories, we showed how to determine the percentage of an accounts receivable balance that would be absorbed in each of these states.

Markov process models have also been used to analyze strategies in sporting events. The Management Science in Action, Markov Processes and Canadian Curling, describes the advantage gained in the sport of curling from winning the opening coin toss.

MANAGEMENT SCIENCE IN ACTION

MARKOV PROCESSES AND CANADIAN CURLING*

Curling is a sport played on a strip of ice 14 feet wide and 146 feet long—about half the length of a football field. At the end of each strip is a "house" composed of four concentric circles etched in the ice, much like the target in a dartboard. The object is to slide a curling stone—called a rock—down the strip of ice and have it finish as close to the center of the house (the bulls-eye) as possible. A game consists of 10 ends. In an end, each team slides eight rocks down the strip and then the score is tallied. The team with the rock closest to the center of the house wins one or more points. A point is scored for every rock inside the closest rock for the other team. No rocks in the house means no score for the end.

The team that goes last has an advantage. For instance, that team has the opportunity to execute a "take out" by knocking the other team's rock(s) out of the house with their last shot. The team that goes last in an end is said to have the hammer. At the beginning of the game a coin toss determines which team starts with the hammer. As the game progresses, the hammer switches sides after any end in which the team with the hammer scores. If no score is made in an end, the hammer does not switch sides.

A Markov model was developed to determine the expected value of winning the coin toss to start the game with the hammer. Data were obtained for 8421 games played in the Canadian Men's Curling Championship over the 13 years from 1985 to 1997. The transition probabilities were based on the probability distributions for points scored in each of the 10 ends. An interesting finding was that the transition probabilities for the first end and the last end (and any extra ends) differed from those for the middle ends (ends 2 through 9).

Results of the Markov analysis showed that the expected score differential in favor of the team winning the opening coin toss was 1.115 when using three separate sets of transition probabilities. When one set of aggregate transition probabilities was used for all ends, the expected score differential in favor of the team winning the opening toss was 1.006. These results clearly indicate a significant advantage in winning the opening toss.

*Based on Kent J. Kostuk and Keith A. Willoughby, "OR/MS 'Rocks' the 'House'," *OR/MS Today* (December 1999): 36–39.

GLOSSARY

Trials of the process The events that trigger transitions of the system from one state to another. In many applications, successive time periods represent the trials of the process.

State of the system The condition of the system at any particular trial or time period.

Transition probability Given that the system is in state i during one period, the transition probability p_{ij} is the probability that the system will be in state j during the next period.

State probability The probability that the system will be in any particular state. (That is, $\pi_i(n)$ is the probability of the system being in state i in period n.)

Steady-state probability The probability that the system will be in any particular state after a large number of transitions. Once steady state has been reached, the state probabilities do not change from period to period.

Absorbing state A state is said to be absorbing if the probability of making a transition out of that state is zero. Thus, once the system has made a transition into an absorbing state, it will remain there.

Fundamental matrix A matrix necessary for the computation of probabilities associated with absorbing states of a Markov process.

PROBLEMS

1. In the market share analysis of Section 17.1, suppose that we are considering the Markov process associated with the shopping trips of one customer, but we do not know where the customer shopped during the last week. Thus, we might assume a 0.5 probability that the customer shopped at Murphy's and a 0.5 probability that the customer shopped at Ashley's at period 0; that is, $\pi_1(0) = 0.5$ and $\pi_2(0) = 0.5$. Given these initial state probabilities, develop a table similar to Table 17.2 showing the probability of each state in future periods. What do you observe about the long-run probabilities of each state?

2. Management of the New Fangled Softdrink Company believes that the probability of a customer purchasing Red Pop or the company's major competition, Super Cola, is based on the customer's most recent purchase. Suppose that the following transition probabilities are appropriate:

	To	
From	**Red Pop**	**Super Cola**
Red Pop	0.9	0.1
Super Cola	0.1	0.9

   a. Show the two-period tree diagram for a customer who last purchased Red Pop. What is the probability that this customer purchases Red Pop on the second purchase?
   b. What is the long-run market share for each of these two products?
   c. A Red Pop advertising campaign is being planned to increase the probability of attracting Super Cola customers. Management believes that the new campaign will increase to 0.15 the probability of a customer switching from Super Cola to Red Pop. What is the projected effect of the advertising campaign on the market shares?

3. The computer center at Rockbottom University has been experiencing computer downtime. Let us assume that the trials of an associated Markov process are defined as one-hour periods and that the probability of the system being in a running state or a down state is based on the state of the system in the previous period. Historical data show the following transition probabilities:

	To	
From	**Running**	**Down**
Running	0.90	0.10
Down	0.30	0.70

a. If the system is initially running, what is the probability of the system being down in the next hour of operation?
b. What are the steady-state probabilities of the system being in the running state and in the down state?

4. One cause of the downtime in Problem 3 was traced to a specific piece of computer hardware. Management believes that switching to a different hardware component will result in the following transition probabilities:

	To	
From	**Running**	**Down**
Running	0.95	0.05
Down	0.60	0.40

a. What are the steady-state probabilities of the system being in the running and down states?
b. If the cost of the system being down for any period is estimated to be $500 (including lost profits for time down and maintenance), what is the breakeven cost for the new hardware component on a time-period basis?

5. A major traffic problem in the Greater Cincinnati area involves traffic attempting to cross the Ohio River from Cincinnati to Kentucky using Interstate 75. Let us assume that the probability of no traffic delay in one period, given no traffic delay in the preceding period, is 0.85 and that the probability of finding a traffic delay in one period, given a delay in the preceding period, is 0.75. Traffic is classified as having either a delay or a no-delay state, and the period considered is 30 minutes.
a. Assume that you are a motorist entering the traffic system and receive a radio report of a traffic delay. What is the probability that for the next 60 minutes (two time periods) the system will be in the delay state? Note that this result is the probability of being in the delay state for two consecutive periods.
b. What is the probability that in the long run the traffic will not be in the delay state?
c. An important assumption of the Markov process models presented in this chapter has been the constant or stationary transition probabilities as the system operates in the future. Do you believe this assumption should be questioned for this traffic problem? Explain.

6. Data collected from selected major metropolitan areas in the eastern United States show that 2% of individuals living within the city limits move to the suburbs during a one-year period while 1% of individuals living in the suburbs move to the city during a one-year period. Answer the following questions assuming that this process is modeled by a Markov process with two states: city and suburbs.
a. Prepare the matrix of transition probabilities.
b. Compute the steady-state probabilities.
c. In a particular metropolitan area, 40% of the population lives in the city, and 60% of the population lives in the suburbs. What population changes do your steady-state probabilities project for this metropolitan area?

7. Assume that a third grocery store, Quick Stop Groceries, enters the market share and customer loyalty situation described in Section 17.1. Quick Stop Groceries is smaller than either Murphy's Foodliner or Ashley's Supermarket. However, Quick Stop's convenience with faster service and gasoline for automobiles can be expected to attract some customers

who currently make weekly shopping visits to either Murphy's or Ashley's. Assume that the transition probabilities are as follows:

	To		
From	**Murphy's**	**Ashley's**	**Quick Stop**
Murphy's Foodliner	0.85	0.10	0.05
Ashley's Supermarket	0.20	0.75	0.05
Quick Stop Groceries	0.15	0.10	0.75

a. Compute the steady-state probabilities for this three-state Markov process.
b. What market share will Quick Stop obtain?
c. With 1000 customers, the original two-state Markov process in Section 17.1 projected 667 weekly customer trips to Murphy's Foodliner and 333 weekly customer trips to Ashley's Supermarket. What impact will Quick Stop have on the customer visits at Murphy's and Ashley's? Explain.

8. The purchase patterns for two brands of toothpaste can be expressed as a Markov process with the following transition probabilities:

	To	
From	**Special B**	**MDA**
Special B	0.90	0.10
MDA	0.05	0.95

a. Which brand appears to have the most loyal customers? Explain.
b. What are the projected market shares for the two brands?

9. Suppose that in Problem 8 a new toothpaste brand enters the market such that the following transition probabilities exist:

	To		
From	**Special B**	**MDA**	**T-White**
Special B	0.80	0.10	0.10
MDA	0.05	0.75	0.20
T-White	0.40	0.30	0.30

What are the new long-run market shares? Which brand will suffer most from the introduction of the new brand of toothpaste?

10. Given the following transition matrix with states 1 and 2 as absorbing states, what is the probability that units in states 3 and 4 end up in each of the absorbing states?

$$P = \begin{bmatrix} 1.0 & 0.0 & 0.0 & 0.0 \\ 0.0 & 1.0 & 0.0 & 0.0 \\ 0.2 & 0.1 & 0.4 & 0.3 \\ 0.2 & 0.2 & 0.1 & 0.5 \end{bmatrix}$$

11. In the Heidman's Department Store problem of Section 17.2, suppose that the following transition matrix is appropriate:

$$P = \begin{bmatrix} 1.0 & 0.0 & 0.0 & 0.0 \\ 0.0 & 1.0 & 0.0 & 0.0 \\ 0.5 & 0.0 & 0.25 & 0.25 \\ 0.5 & 0.2 & 0.05 & 0.25 \end{bmatrix}$$

If Heidman's has \$4000 in the 0–30-day category and \$5000 in the 31–90-day category, what is your estimate of the amount of bad debts the company will experience?

12. The KLM Christmas Tree Farm owns a plot of land with 5000 evergreen trees. Each year KLM allows retailers of Christmas trees to select and cut trees for sale to individual customers. KLM protects small trees (usually less than 4 feet tall) so that they will be available for sale in future years. Currently, 1500 trees are classified as protected trees, while the remaining 3500 are available for cutting. However, even though a tree is available for cutting in a given year, it may not be selected for cutting until future years. Most trees not cut in a given year live until the next year, but some diseased trees are lost every year.

In viewing the KLM Christmas tree operation as a Markov process with yearly periods, we define the following four states:

State 1. Cut and sold

State 2. Lost to disease

State 3. Too small for cutting

State 4. Available for cutting but not cut and sold

The following transition matrix is appropriate:

$$P = \begin{bmatrix} 1.0 & 0.0 & 0.0 & 0.0 \\ 0.0 & 1.0 & 0.0 & 0.0 \\ 0.1 & 0.2 & 0.5 & 0.2 \\ 0.4 & 0.1 & 0.0 & 0.5 \end{bmatrix}$$

How many of the farm's 5000 trees will be sold eventually, and how many will be lost?

13. A large corporation collected data on the reasons both middle managers and senior managers leave the company. Some managers eventually retire, but others leave the company prior to retirement for personal reasons including more attractive positions with other firms. Assume that the following matrix of one-year transition probabilities applies with the four states of the Markov process being retirement, leaves prior to retirement for personal reasons, stays as a middle manager, stays as a senior manager.

	Retirement	Leaves—Personal	Middle Manager	Senior Manager
Retirement	1.00	0.00	0.00	0.00
Leaves—Personal	0.00	1.00	0.00	0.00
Middle Manager	0.03	0.07	0.80	0.10
Senior Manager	0.08	0.01	0.03	0.88

a. What states are considered absorbing states? Why?

b. Interpret the transition probabilities for the middle managers.

c. Interpret the transition probabilities for the senior managers.
d. What percentage of the current middle managers will eventually retire from the company? What percentage will leave the company for personal reasons?
e. The company currently has 920 managers: 640 middle managers and 280 senior managers. How many of these managers will eventually retire from the company? How many will leave the company for personal reasons?

14. Data for the progression of college students at a particular college are summarized in the following matrix of transition probabilities.

	Graduate	Drop Out	Freshman	Sophomore	Junior	Senior
Graduate	1.00	0.00	0.00	0.00	0.00	0.00
Drop Out	0.00	1.00	0.00	0.00	0.00	0.00
Freshman	0.00	0.20	0.15	0.65	0.00	0.00
Sophomore	0.00	0.15	0.00	0.10	0.75	0.00
Junior	0.00	0.10	0.00	0.00	0.05	0.85
Senior	0.90	0.05	0.00	0.00	0.00	0.05

a. What states are absorbing states?
b. Interpret the transition probabilities for a sophomore.
c. Use The Management Scientist software package to compute the probabilities that a sophomore will graduate and that a sophomore will drop out.
d. In an address to the incoming class of 600 freshmen, the dean asks the students to look around the auditorium and realize that about 50% of the freshmen present today will not make it to graduation day. Does your Markov process analysis support the dean's statement? Explain.
e. Currently, the college has 600 freshmen, 520 sophomores, 460 juniors, and 420 seniors. What percentage of the 2000 students attending the college will eventually graduate?

Appendix 17.1 MATRIX NOTATION AND OPERATIONS

Matrix Notation

A *matrix* is a rectangular arrangement of numbers. For example, consider the following matrix that we have named D:

$$D = \begin{bmatrix} 1 & 3 & 2 \\ 0 & 4 & 5 \end{bmatrix}$$

The matrix D is said to consist of six elements, where each element of D is a number. To identify a particular element of a matrix, we have to specify its location. Therefore, we introduce the concepts of rows and columns.

All elements across some horizontal line in a matrix are said to be in a row of the matrix. For example, elements 1, 3, and 2 in D are in the first row, and elements 0, 4, and 5 are in the second row. By convention, we refer to the top row as row 1, the second row from the top as row 2, and so on.

All elements along some vertical line are said to be in a column of the matrix. Elements 1 and 0 in D are elements in the first column, elements 3 and 4 are elements of the second column, and elements 2 and 5 are elements of the third column. By convention, we refer to the leftmost column as column 1, the next column to the right as column 2, and so on.

We can identify a particular element in a matrix by specifying its row and column position. For example, the element in row 1 and column 2 of D is the number 3. This position is written as

$$d_{12} = 3$$

In general, we use the following notation to refer to the specific elements of D:

$$d_{ij} = \text{element located in the } i\text{th row and } j\text{th column of } D$$

We always use capital letters for the names of matrixes and the corresponding lowercase letters with two subscripts to denote the elements.

The *size* of a matrix is the number of rows and columns in the matrix and is written as the number of rows $\times$ the number of columns. Thus, the size of D is 2×3.

Frequently we will encounter matrixes that have only one row or one column. For example,

$$G = \begin{bmatrix} 6 \\ 4 \\ 2 \\ 3 \end{bmatrix}$$

is a matrix that has only one column. Whenever a matrix has only one column, we call the matrix a *column vector.* In a similar manner, any matrix that has only one row is called a *row vector.* Using our previous notation for the elements of a matrix, we would refer to specific elements in G by writing g_{ij}. However, since G has only one column, the column position is unimportant, and we need only specify the row the element of interest is in. That is, instead of referring to elements in a vector using g_{ij}, we specify only one subscript, which denotes the position of the element in the vector. For example,

$$g_1 = 6 \qquad g_2 = 4 \qquad g_3 = 2 \qquad g_4 = 3$$

Matrix Operations

Matrix Transpose The transpose of a matrix is formed by making the rows in the original matrix the columns in the transpose matrix, and by making the columns in the original matrix the rows in the transpose matrix. For example, the transpose of the matrix

$$D = \begin{bmatrix} 1 & 3 & 2 \\ 0 & 4 & 5 \end{bmatrix}$$

is

$$D^t = \begin{bmatrix} 1 & 0 \\ 3 & 4 \\ 2 & 5 \end{bmatrix}$$

Note that we use the superscript t to denote the transpose of a matrix.

Matrix Multiplication We demonstrate how to perform two types of matrix multiplication: (1) multiplying two vectors, and (2) multiplying a matrix times a matrix.

The product of a row vector of size $1 \times n$ times a column vector of size $n \times 1$ is the number obtained by multiplying the first element in the row vector times the first element in the column vector, the second element in the row vector times the second element in the column vector, and continuing on through the last element in the row vector times the last element in the column vector, and then summing the products. Suppose, for example, that we wanted to multiply the row vector H times the column vector G, where

$$H = [2 \quad 1 \quad 5 \quad 0] \text{ and } G = \begin{bmatrix} 6 \\ 4 \\ 2 \\ 3 \end{bmatrix}$$

The product HG, referred to as a vector product, is given by

$$HG = 2(6) + 1(4) + 5(2) + 0(3) = 26$$

The product of a matrix of size $p \times n$ and a matrix of size $n \times m$ is a new matrix of size $p \times m$. The element in the ith row and jth column of the new matrix is given by the vector product of the ith row of the $p \times n$ matrix times the jth column of the $n \times m$ matrix. Suppose, for example, that we want to multiply D times A, where

$$D = \begin{bmatrix} 1 & 3 & 2 \\ 0 & 4 & 5 \end{bmatrix} \qquad A = \begin{bmatrix} 1 & 3 & 5 \\ 2 & 0 & 4 \\ 1 & 5 & 2 \end{bmatrix}$$

Let $C = DA$ denote the product of D times A. The element in row 1 and column 1 of C is given by the vector product of the first row of D times the first column of A. Thus

$$c_{11} = [1 \quad 3 \quad 2] \begin{bmatrix} 1 \\ 2 \\ 1 \end{bmatrix} = 1(1) + 3(2) + 2(1) = 9$$

The element in row 2 and column 1 of C is given by the vector product of the second row of D times the first column of A. Thus,

$$c_{21} = [0 \quad 4 \quad 5] \begin{bmatrix} 1 \\ 2 \\ 1 \end{bmatrix} = 0(1) + 4(2) + 5(1) = 13$$

Calculating the remaining elements of C in a similar fashion, we obtain

$$C = \begin{bmatrix} 9 & 13 & 21 \\ 13 & 25 & 26 \end{bmatrix}$$

Clearly, the product of a matrix and a vector is just a special case of multiplying a matrix times a matrix. For example, the product of a matrix of size $m \times n$ and a vector of size $n \times 1$ is a new vector of size $m \times 1$. The element in the ith position of the new vector is given by the vector product of the ith row of the $m \times n$ matrix times the $n \times 1$ column vector. Suppose, for example, that we want to multiply D times K, where

$$D = \begin{bmatrix} 1 & 3 & 2 \\ 0 & 4 & 5 \end{bmatrix} \quad K = \begin{bmatrix} 1 \\ 4 \\ 2 \end{bmatrix}$$

The first element of DK is given by the vector product of the first row of D times K. Thus,

$$[1 \quad 3 \quad 2] \begin{bmatrix} 1 \\ 4 \\ 2 \end{bmatrix} = 1(1) + 3(4) + 2(2) = 17$$

The second element of DK is given by the vector product of the second row of D and K. Thus,

$$[0 \quad 4 \quad 5] \begin{bmatrix} 1 \\ 4 \\ 2 \end{bmatrix} = 0(1) + 4(4) + 5(2) = 26$$

Hence, we see that the product of the matrix D times the vector K is given by

$$DK = \begin{bmatrix} 1 & 3 & 2 \\ 0 & 4 & 5 \end{bmatrix} \begin{bmatrix} 1 \\ 4 \\ 2 \end{bmatrix} = \begin{bmatrix} 17 \\ 26 \end{bmatrix}$$

Can any two matrixes be multiplied? The answer is no. To multiply two matrixes, the number of the columns in the first matrix must equal the number of rows in the second. If this property is satisfied, the matrixes are said to *conform for multiplication.* Thus, in our example, D and K could be multiplied because D had three columns and K had three rows.

Matrix Inverse. The inverse of a matrix A is another matrix, denoted A^{-1}, such that $A^{-1}A = \text{I}$ and $AA^{-1} = \text{I}$. The inverse of any square matrix A consisting of two rows and two columns is computed as follows:

$$A = \begin{bmatrix} a_{11} & a_{12} \\ a_{21} & a_{22} \end{bmatrix}$$

$$A^{-1} = \begin{bmatrix} a_{22}/d & -a_{12}/d \\ -a_{21}/d & a_{11}/d \end{bmatrix}$$

where $d = a_{11}a_{22} - a_{21}a_{12}$ is the determinant of the 2×2 matrix A. For example, if

$$A = \begin{bmatrix} 0.7 & -0.3 \\ -0.3 & 0.9 \end{bmatrix}$$

then

$$d = (0.7)(0.9) - (-0.3)(-0.3) = 0.54$$

and

$$A^{-1} = \begin{bmatrix} 0.9/0.54 & 0.3/0.54 \\ 0.3/0.54 & 0.7/0.54 \end{bmatrix} = \begin{bmatrix} 1.67 & 0.56 \\ 0.56 & 1.30 \end{bmatrix}$$

CHAPTER 18

Dynamic Programming

CONTENTS

Dynamic programming is an approach to problem solving that decomposes a large problem that may be difficult to solve into a number of smaller problems that are usually much easier to solve. Moreover, the dynamic programming approach allows us to break up a large problem in such a way that once all the smaller problems have been solved, we have an optimal solution to the large problem. We shall see that each of the smaller problems is identified with a stage of the dynamic programming solution procedure. As a consequence, the technique has been applied to decision problems that are multistage in nature. Often, multiple stages are created because a sequence of decisions must be made over time. For example, a problem of determining an optimal decision over a one-year horizon might be broken into 12 smaller stages, where each stage requires an optimal decision over a one-month horizon. In most cases, each of these smaller problems cannot be considered to be completely independent of the others, and it is here that dynamic programming is helpful. Let us begin by showing how to solve a shortest-route problem using dynamic programming.

18.1 A SHORTEST-ROUTE PROBLEM

In Chapter 9 we studied a labeling algorithm for solving the shortest-route problem. Let us now illustrate the dynamic programming approach by using it to solve a shortest-route problem. Consider the network presented in Figure 18.1. Assuming that the numbers above each arc denote the direct distance in miles between two nodes, find the shortest route from node 1 to node 10.

Before attempting to solve this problem, let us consider an important characteristic of all shortest-route problems. This characteristic is a restatement of Richard Bellman's famous **principle of optimality** as it applies to the shortest-route problem.[1]

The Principle of Optimality

If a particular node is on the optimal route, then the shortest path from that node to the end is also on the optimal route.

The dynamic programming approach to the shortest-route problem essentially involves treating each node as if it were on the optimal route and making calculations accordingly. In doing so, we will work backward by starting at the terminal node, node 10, and calculating the shortest route from each node to node 10 until we reach the origin, node 1. At this point, we will have solved the original problem of finding the shortest route from node 1 to node 10.

As we stated in the introduction to this chapter, dynamic programming decomposes the original problem into a number of smaller problems that are much easier to solve. In the shortest-route problem for the network in Figure 18.1, the smaller problems that we will create define a four-stage dynamic programming problem. The first stage begins with nodes that are exactly one arc away from the destination, and ends at the destination node. Note from Figure 18.1 that only nodes 8 and 9 are exactly one arc away from node 10. In dynamic programming terminology, nodes 8 and 9 are considered to be the input nodes for stage 1, and node 10 is considered to be the output node for stage 1.

The second stage begins with all nodes that are exactly two arcs away from the destination and ends with all nodes that are exactly one arc away. Hence, nodes 5, 6, and 7 are the input nodes for stage 2, and nodes 8 and 9 are the output nodes for stage 2. Note that the output nodes

[1]S. Dreyfus, *Dynamic Programming and the Calculus of Variations* (New York: Academic Press, 1965).

FIGURE 18.1 NETWORK FOR THE SHORTEST-ROUTE PROBLEM

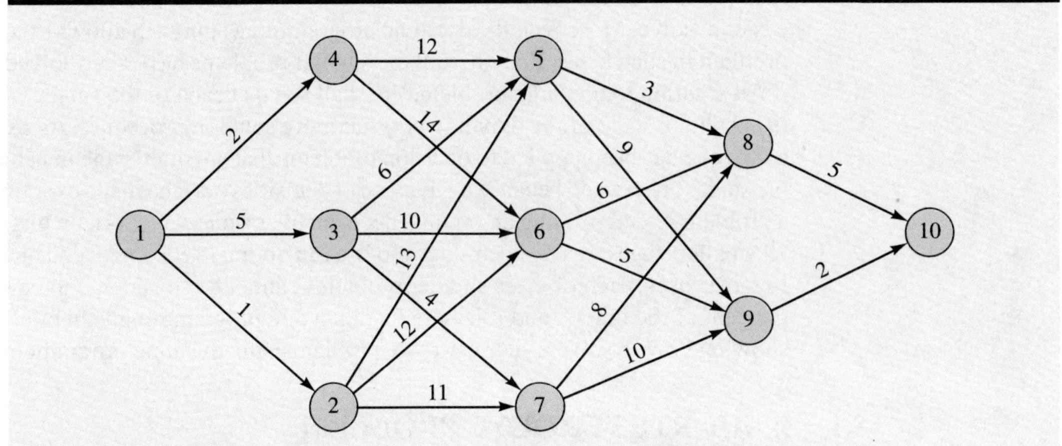

for stage 2 are the input nodes for stage 1. The input nodes for the third-stage problem are all nodes that are exactly three arcs away from the destination—that is, nodes 2, 3, and 4. The output nodes for stage 3, all of which are one arc closer to the destination, are nodes 5, 6, and 7. Finally, the input node for stage 4 is node 1, and the output nodes are 2, 3, and 4. The decision problem we shall want to solve at each stage is, Which arc is best to travel over in moving from each particular input node to an output node? Let us consider the stage 1 problem.

We arbitrarily begin the stage 1 calculations with node 9. Because only one way affords travel from node 9 to node 10, this route is obviously shortest and requires us to travel a distance of 2 miles. Similarly, only one path goes from node 8 to node 10. The shortest route from node 8 to the end is thus the length of that route, or 5 miles. The stage 1 decision problem is solved. For each input node, we have identified an optimal decision—that is, the best arc to travel over to reach the output node. The stage 1 results are summarized here:

Stage 1

Input Node	Arc (decision)	Shortest Distance to Node 10
8	8–10	5
9	9–10	2

To begin the solution to the stage 2 problem, we move to node 7. (We could have selected node 5 or 6; the order of the nodes selected at any stage is arbitrary.) Two arcs leave node 7 and are connected to input nodes for stage 1: arc 7–8, which has a length of 8 miles, and arc 7–9, which has a length of 10 miles. If we select arc 7–8, we will have a distance from node 7 to node 10 of 13 miles, that is, the length of arc 7–8, 8 miles, plus the shortest distance to node 10 from node 8, 5 miles. Thus, the decision to select arc 7–8 has a total associated distance of $8 + 5 = 13$ miles. With a distance of 10 miles for arc 7–9 and stage 1 results showing a distance of 2 miles from node 9 to node 10, the decision to select arc 7–9 has an associated distance of $10 + 2 = 12$ miles. Thus, given we are at node 7, we should select arc 7–9 because it is on the path that will reach node 10 in the shortest distance

(12 miles). By performing similar calculations for nodes 5 and 6, we can generate the following stage 2 results:

Stage 2

Input Node	Arc (decision)	Output Node	Shortest Distance to Node 10
5	5–8	8	8
6	6–9	9	7
7	7–9	9	12

In Figure 18.2 the number in the square above each node considered so far indicates the length of the shortest route from that node to the end. We have completed the solution to the first two subproblems (stages 1 and 2). We now know the shortest route from nodes 5, 6, 7, 8, and 9 to node 10.

To begin the third stage, let us start with node 2. Note that three arcs connect node 2 to the stage 2 input nodes. Thus, to find the shortest route from node 2 to node 10, we must make three calculations. If we select arc 2–7 and then follow the shortest route to the end, we will have a distance of $11 + 12 = 23$ miles. Similarly, selecting arc 2–6 requires $12 + 7 = 19$ miles, and selecting arc 2–5 requires $13 + 8 = 21$ miles. Thus, the shortest route from node 2 to node 10 is 19 miles, which indicates that arc 2–6 is the best decision, given that we are at node 2. Similarly, we find that the shortest route from node 3 to node 10 is given by Min $\{4 + 12, 10 + 7, 6 + 8\} = 14$; the shortest route from node 4 to node 10 is given by Min $\{14 + 7, 12 + 8\} = 20$. We complete the stage 3 calculations with the following results:

Stage 3

Input Node	Arc (decision)	Output Node	Shortest Distance to Node 10
2	2–6	6	19
3	3–5	5	14
4	4–5	5	20

In solving the stage 4 subproblem, we find that the shortest route from node 1 to node 10 is given by Min $\{1 + 19, 5 + 14, 2 + 20\} = 19$. Thus, the optimal decision at stage 4 is the selection of arc 1–3. By moving through the network from stage 4 to stage 3 to stage 2 to stage 1, we can identify the best decision at each stage and therefore the shortest route from node 1 to node 10.

Stage	Arc (decision)
4	1–3
3	3–5
2	5–8
1	8–10

FIGURE 18.2 INTERMEDIATE SOLUTION TO THE SHORTEST-ROUTE PROBLEM USING DYNAMIC PROGRAMMING

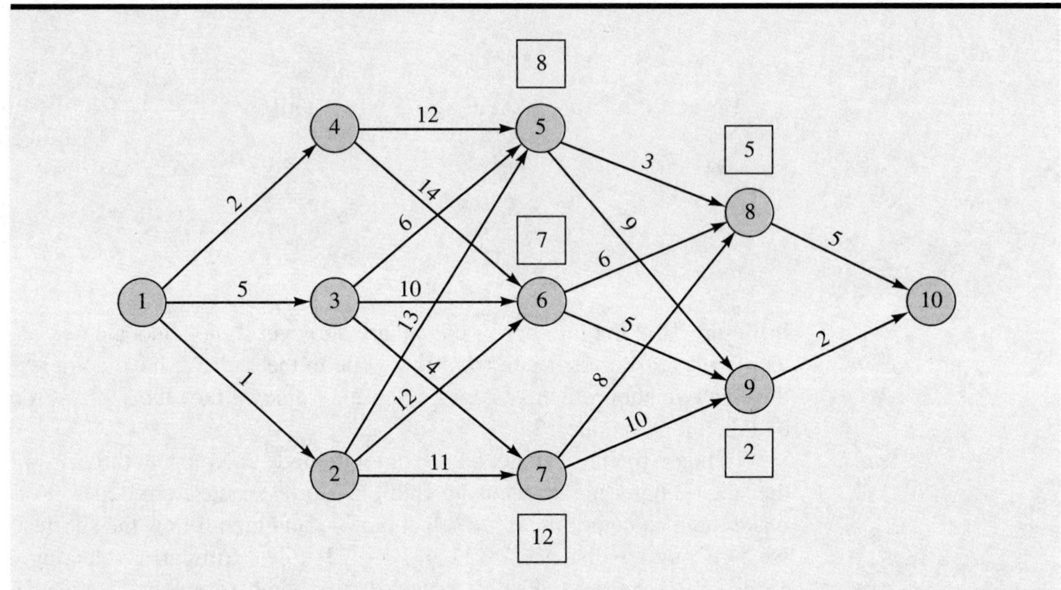

Thus, the shortest route is through nodes 1–3–5–8–10 with a distance of 5 + 6 + 3 + 5 = 19 miles.

Note how the calculations at each successive stage make use of the calculations at prior stages. This characteristic is an important part of the dynamic programming procedure. Figure 18.3 illustrates the final network calculations. Note that in working back through the stages we have now determined the shortest route from every node to node 10.

Dynamic programming, while enumerating or evaluating several paths at each stage, does not require us to enumerate all possible paths from node 1 to node 10. Returning to the stage 4 calculations, we consider three alternatives for leaving node 1. The complete route associated with each of these alternatives is presented as follows:

Arc Alternatives at Node 1	Complete Path to Node 10	Distance	
1–2	1–2–6–9–10	20	
1–3	1–3–5–8–10	19	← Selected as best
1–4	1–4–5–8–10	22	

Try Problem 2, part (a), for practice solving a shortest-route problem using dynamic programming.

When you realize that there are a total of 16 alternate routes from node 1 to node 10, you can see that dynamic programming has provided substantial computational savings over a total enumeration of all possible solutions.

The fact that we did not have to evaluate all the paths at each stage as we moved backward from node 10 to node 1 is illustrative of the power of dynamic programming. Using dynamic programming, we need only make a small fraction of the number of calculations

FIGURE 18.3 FINAL SOLUTION TO THE SHORTEST-ROUTE PROBLEM USING DYNAMIC PROGRAMMING

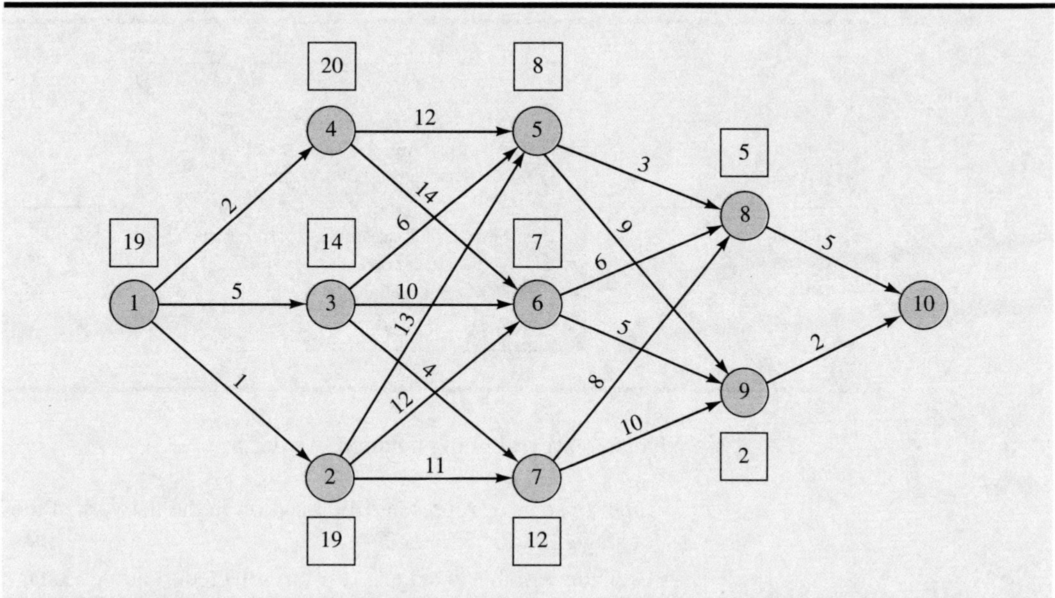

that would be required using total enumeration. If the example network had been larger, the computational savings provided by dynamic programming would have been even greater.

18.2 DYNAMIC PROGRAMMING NOTATION

Perhaps one of the most difficult aspects of learning to apply dynamic programming involves understanding the notation. The notation we will use is the same as that used by Nemhauser[2] and is fairly standard.

The **stages** of a dynamic programming solution procedure are formed by decomposing the original problem into a number of subproblems. Associated with each subproblem is a stage in the dynamic programming solution procedure. For example, the shortest-route problem introduced in the preceding section was solved using a four-stage dynamic programming solution procedure. We had four stages because we decomposed the original problem into the following four subproblems:

1. **Stage 1 Problem:** Where should we go from nodes 8 and 9 so that we will reach node 10 along the shortest route?
2. **Stage 2 Problem:** Using the results of stage 1, where should we go from nodes 5, 6, and 7 so that we will reach node 10 along the shortest route?
3. **Stage 3 Problem:** Using the results of stage 2, where should we go from nodes 2, 3, and 4 so that we will reach node 10 along the shortest route?
4. **Stage 4 Problem:** Using the results of stage 3, where should we go from node 1 so that we will reach node 10 along the shortest route?

[2]G. L. Nemhauser, *Introduction to Dynamic Programming* (New York: Wiley, 1966).

Let us look closely at what occurs at the stage 2 problem. Consider the following representation of this stage:

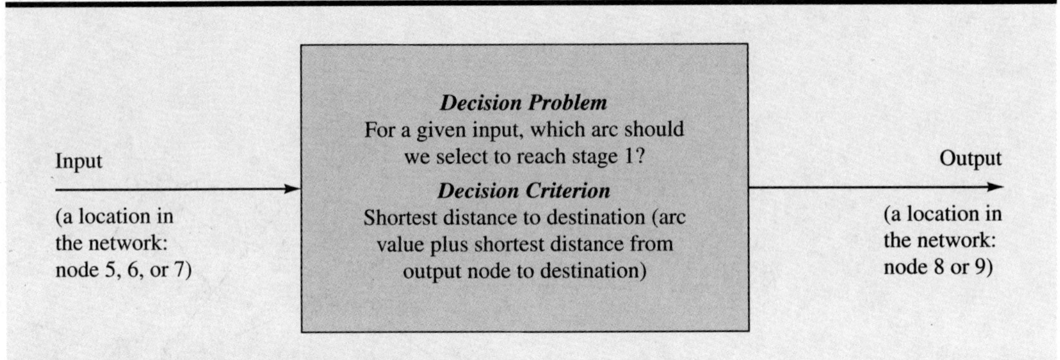

Using dynamic programming notation, we define

x_2 = input to stage 2; represents the location in the network at the beginning of stage 2 (node 5, 6, or 7)

d_2 = decision variable at stage 2 (the arc selected to move to stage 1)

x_1 = output for stage 2; represents the location in the network at the end of stage 2 (node 8 or 9)

Using this notation, the stage 2 problem can be represented as follows:

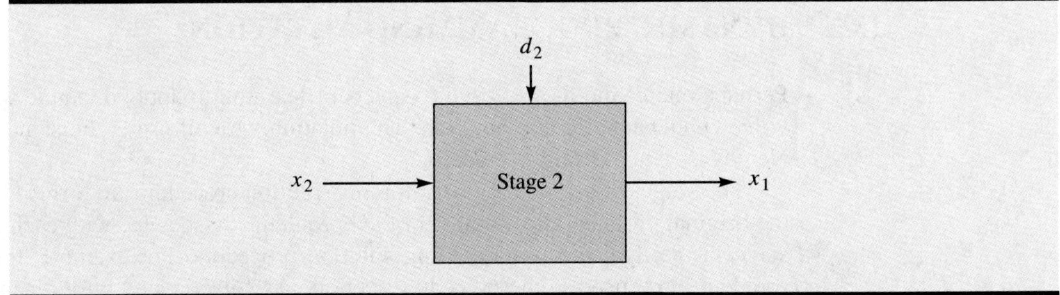

Recall that using dynamic programming to solve the shortest-route problem, we worked backward through the stages, beginning at node 10. When we reached stage 2, we did not know x_2 because the stage 3 problem had not yet been solved. The approach used was to consider *all* alternatives for the input x_2. Then we determined the best decision d_2 for each of the inputs x_2. Later, when we moved forward through the system to recover the optimal sequence of decisions, we saw that the stage 3 decision provided a specific x_2, node 5, and from our previous analysis we knew the best decision (d_2) to make as we continued on to stage 1.

Let us consider a general dynamic programming problem with N stages and adopt the following general notation:

x_n = input to stage n (output from stage $n + 1$)

d_n = **decision variable** at stage n

The general N-stage problem is decomposed as follows:

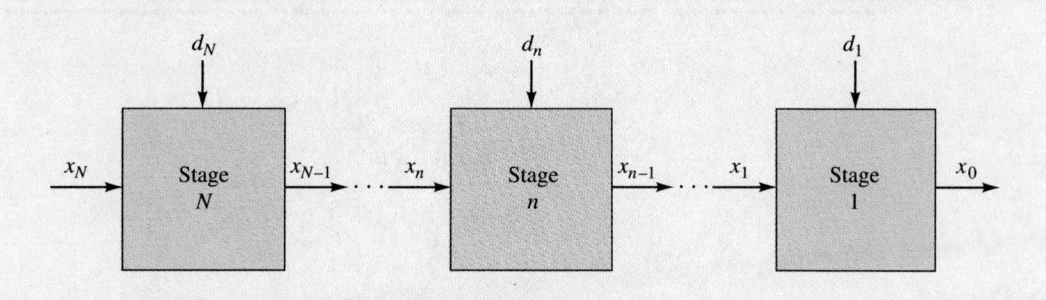

The four-stage shortest-route problem can be represented as follows:

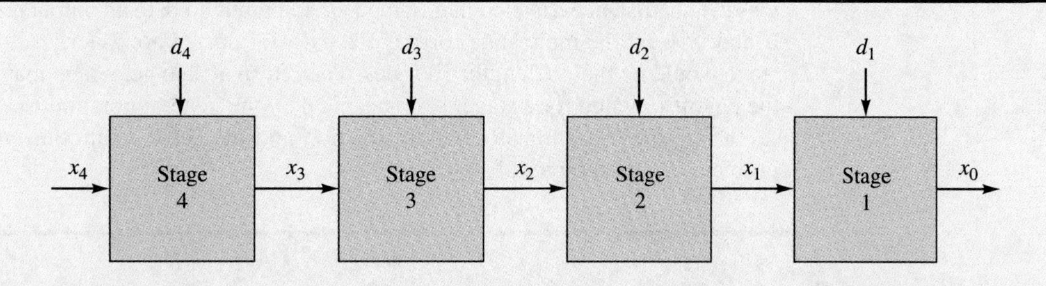

The values of the input and output variables x_4, x_3, x_2, x_1, and x_0 are important because they join the four subproblems together. At any stage, we will ultimately need to know the input x_n to make the best decision d_n. These x_n variables can be thought of as defining the *state* or condition of the system as we move from stage to stage. Accordingly, these variables are referred to as the **state variables** of the problem. In the shortest-route problem, the state variables represented the location in the network at each stage (i.e., a particular node).

At stage 2 of the shortest-route problem, we considered the input x_2 and made the decision d_2 that would provide the shortest distance to the destination. The output x_1 was based on a combination of the input and the decision; that is, x_1 was a function of x_2 and d_2. In dynamic programming notation, we write:

$$x_1 = t_2(x_2, d_2)$$

where $t_2(x_2, d_2)$ is the function that determines the stage 2 output. Because $t_2(x_2, d_2)$ is the function that "transforms" the input to the stage into the output, this function is referred to as the **stage transformation function.** The general expression for the stage transformation function is

$$x_{n-1} = t_n(x_n, d_n)$$

The mathematical form of the stage transformation function is dependent on the particular dynamic programming problem. In the shortest-route problem, the transformation function was based on a tabular calculation. For example, Table 18.1 shows the stage transformation function $t_2(x_2, d_2)$ for stage 2. The possible values of d_2 are the arcs selected in the body of the table.

TABLE 18.1 STAGE TRANSFORMATION $x_1 = t_2(x_2, d_2)$ FOR STAGE 2 WITH THE VALUE OF x_1 CORRESPONDING TO EACH VALUE OF x_2

x_2 Input State	x_1 Output State 8	9
5	5–8	5–9
6	6–8	6–9
7	7–8	7–9

Each stage also has a return associated with it. In the shortest-route problem, the return was the arc distance traveled in moving from an input node to an output node. For example, if node 7 were the input state for stage 2 and we selected arc 7–9 as d_2, the return for that stage would be the arc length, 10 miles. The return at a stage, which may be thought of as the payoff or value for a stage, is represented by the general notation $r_n(x_n, d_n)$.

Using the stage transformation function and the **return function,** the shortest-route problem can be shown as follows.

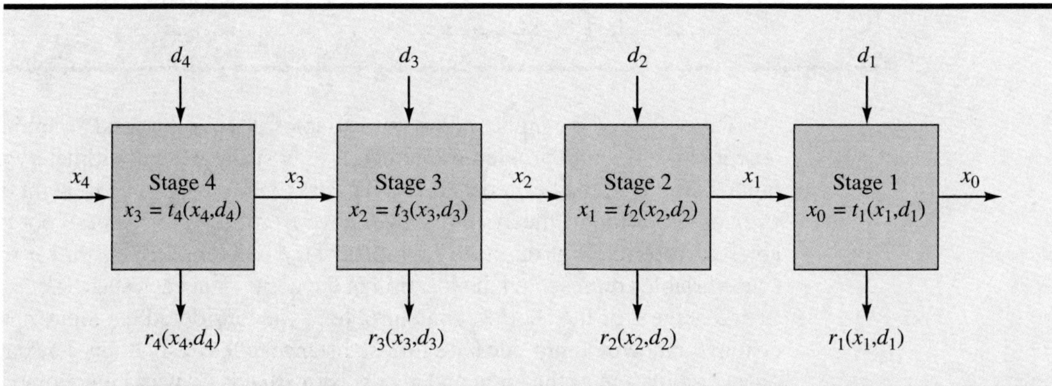

If we view a system or a process as consisting of N stages, we can represent a dynamic programming formulation as follows:

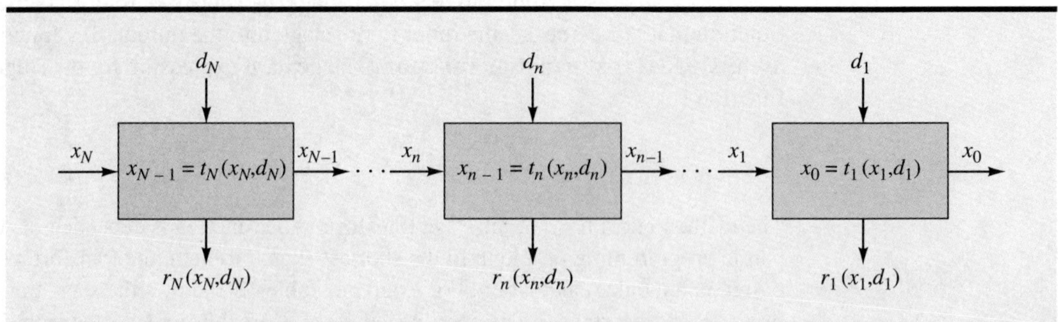

Each of the rectangles in the diagram represents a stage in the process. As indicated, each stage has two inputs: the state variable and the decision variable. Each stage also has two outputs: a new value for the state variable and a return for the stage. The new value for the state variable is determined as a function of the inputs using $t_n(x_n, d_n)$. The value of the return for a stage is also determined as a function of the inputs using $r_n(x_n, d_n)$.

The optimal total return depends only on the state variable.

In addition, we will use the notation $f_n(x_n)$ to represent the optimal total return from stage n and all remaining stages, given an input of x_n to stage n. For example, in the shortest-route problem, $f_2(x_2)$ represents the optimal total return (i.e., the minimum distance) from stage 2 and all remaining stages, given an input of x_2 to stage 2. Thus, we see from Figure 18.3 that $f_2(x_2 = \text{node } 5) = 8$, $f_2(x_2 = \text{node } 6) = 7$, and $f_2(x_2 = \text{node } 7) = 12$. These values are the ones indicated in the squares at nodes 5, 6, and 7.

NOTES AND COMMENTS

1. The primary advantage of dynamic programming is its "divide and conquer" solution strategy. Using dynamic programming, a large, complex problem can be divided into a sequence of smaller interrelated problems. By solving the smaller problems sequentially, the optimal solution to the larger problem is found. Dynamic programming is a general approach to problem solving; it is not a specific technique such as linear programming, which can be applied in the same fashion to a variety of problems. Although some characteristics are common to all dynamic programming problems, each application requires some degree of creativity, insight, and expertise to recognize how the larger problems can be broken into a sequence of interrelated smaller problems.
2. Dynamic programming has been applied to a wide variety of problems including inventory control, production scheduling, capital budgeting, resource allocation, equipment replacement and maintenance. In many of these applications, periods such as days, weeks, and months provide the sequence of interrelated stages for the larger multiperiod problem.

18.3 THE KNAPSACK PROBLEM

The basic idea of the **knapsack problem** is that N different types of items can be put into a knapsack. Each item has a certain weight associated with it as well as a value. The problem is to determine how many units of each item to place in the knapsack to maximize the total value. A constraint is placed on the maximum weight permissible.

To provide a practical application of the knapsack problem, consider a manager of a manufacturing operation who must make a biweekly selection of jobs from each of four categories to process during the following two-week period. A list showing the number of jobs waiting to be processed is presented in Table 18.2. The estimated time required for completion and the value rating associated with each job are also shown.

The value rating assigned to each job category is a subjective score assigned by the manager. A scale from 1 to 20 is used to measure the value of each job, where 1 represents jobs of the least value, and 20 represents jobs of most value. The value of a job depends on such things as expected profit, length of time the job has been waiting to be processed, priority, and so on. In this situation, we would like to select certain jobs during the next two weeks such that all the jobs selected can be processed within 10 working days and the total value of the jobs selected is maximized. In knapsack problem terminology, we are in essence selecting the best jobs for the two-week (10 working days) knapsack, where the knapsack has a capacity equal to the 10-day production capacity. Let us formulate and solve this problem using dynamic programming.

TABLE 18.2 JOB DATA FOR THE MANUFACTURING OPERATION

Job Category	Number of Jobs to Be Processed	Estimated Completion Time per Job (days)	Value Rating per Job
1	4	1	2
2	3	3	8
3	2	4	11
4	2	7	20

This problem can be formulated as a dynamic programming problem involving four stages. At stage 1, we must decide how many jobs from category 1 to process; at stage 2, we must decide how many jobs from category 2 to process; and so on. Thus, we let

d_n = number of jobs processed from category n (decision variable at stage n)
x_n = number of days of processing time remaining at the beginning of stage n (state variable for stage n)

Thus, with a two-week production period, $x_4 = 10$ represents the total number of days available for processing jobs. The stage transformation functions are as follows:

Stage 4. $x_3 = t_4(x_4, d_4) = x_4 - 7d_4$
Stage 3. $x_2 = t_3(x_3, d_3) = x_3 - 4d_3$
Stage 2. $x_1 = t_2(x_2, d_2) = x_2 - 3d_2$
Stage 1. $x_0 = t_1(x_1, d_1) = x_1 - 1d_1$

The return at each stage is based on the value rating of the associated job category and the number of jobs selected from that category. The return functions are as follows:

Stage 4. $r_4(x_4, d_4) = 20d_4$
Stage 3. $r_3(x_3, d_3) = 11d_3$
Stage 2. $r_2(x_2, d_2) = 8d_2$
Stage 1. $r_1(x_1, d_1) = 2d_1$

Figure 18.4 shows a schematic of the problem.

FIGURE 18.4 DYNAMIC PROGRAMMING FORMULATION OF THE JOB SELECTION PROBLEM

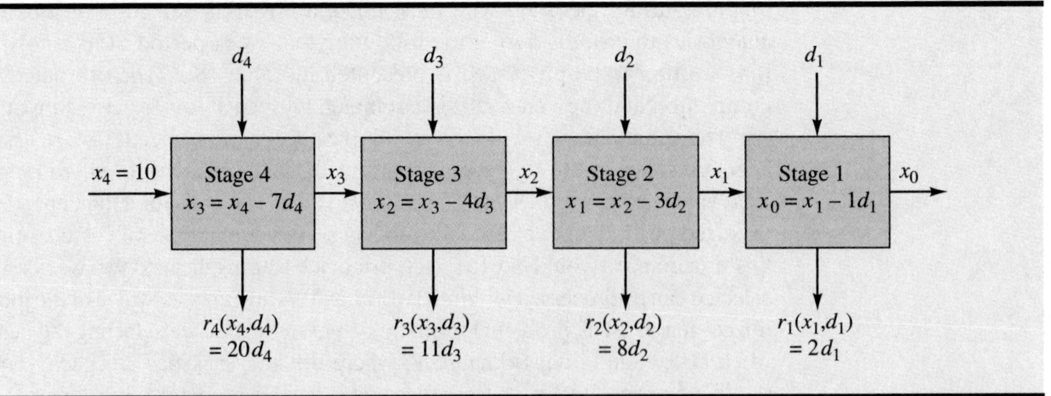

As with the shortest-route problem in Section 18.1, we will apply a backward solution procedure; that is, we will begin by assuming that decisions have already been made for stages 4, 3, and 2 and that the final decision remains (how many jobs from category 1 to select at stage 1). A restatement of the principle of optimality can be made in terms of this problem. That is, regardless of whatever decisions have been made at previous stages, if the decision at stage n is to be part of an optimal overall strategy, the decision made at stage n must necessarily be optimal for all remaining stages.

Let us set up a table that will help us calculate the optimal decisions for stage 1.

Stage 1. Note that stage 1's input (x_1), the number of days of processing time available at stage 1, is unknown because we have not yet identified the decisions at the previous stages. Therefore, in our analysis at stage 1, we will have to consider all possible values of x_1 and identify the best decision d_1 for each case; $f_1(x_1)$ will be the total return after decision d_1 is made. The possible values of x_1 and the associated d_1 and $f_1(x_1)$ values are as follows:

x_1	d_1^*	$f_1(x_1)$
0	0	0
1	1	2
2	2	4
3	3	6
4	4	8
5	4	8
6	4	8
7	4	8
8	4	8
9	4	8
10	4	8

The d_1^* column gives the optimal values of d_1 corresponding to a particular value of x_1, where x_1 can range from 0 to 10. The specific value of x_1 will depend on how much processing time has been used by the jobs in the other categories selected in stages 2, 3, and 4. Because each stage 1 job requires one day of processing time and has a positive return of two per job, we always select as many jobs at this stage as possible. The number of category 1 jobs selected will depend on the processing time available, but cannot exceed four.

Recall that $f_1(x_1)$ represents the value of the optimal total return from stage 1 and all remaining stages, given an input of x_1 to stage 1. Therefore, $f_1(x_1) = 2x_1$ for values of $x_1 \leq 4$, and $f_1(x_1) = 8$ for values of $x_1 > 4$. The optimization of stage 1 is accomplished. We now move on to stage 2 and carry out the optimization at that stage.

Stage 2. Again, we will use a table to help identify the optimal decision. Because stage 2's input (x_2) is unknown, we have to consider all possible values from 0 to 10. Also, we have to consider all possible values of d_2 (i.e., 0, 1, 2, or 3). The entries under the heading $r_2(x_2, d_2) + f_1(x_1)$ represent the total return that will be forthcoming from the final two stages, given the input of x_2 and the decision of d_2. For example, if stage 2 were entered with $x_2 = 7$ days of processing time remaining, and if a decision were made to select two jobs from category 2 (i.e., $d_2 = 2$), the total return for stages 1 and 2 would be 18.

x_2 \ d_2	$r_2(x_2, d_2) + f_1(x_1)$						$x_1 = t_2(x_2, d_2^*)$
	0	1	2	3	d_2^*	$f_2(x_2)$	$= x_2 - 3d_2^*$
0	(0)	—	—	—	0	0	0
1	(2)	—	—	—	0	2	1
2	(4)	—	—	—	0	4	2
3	6	(8)	—	—	1	8	0
4	8	(10)	—	—	1	10	1
5	8	(12)	—	—	1	12	2
6	8	14	(16)	—	2	16	0
7	8	16	(18)	—	2	18	1
8	8	16	(20)	—	2	20	2
9	8	16	22	(24)	3	24	0
10	8	16	24	(26)	3	26	1

The return for stage 2 would be $r_2(x_2, d_2) = 8d_2 = 8(2) = 16$, and with $x_2 = 7$ and $d_2 = 2$, we would have $x_1 = x_2 - 3d_2 = 7 - 6 = 1$. From the previous table, we see that the optimal return from stage 1 with $x_1 = 1$ is $f_1(1) = 2$. Thus, the total return corresponding to $x_2 = 7$ and $d_2 = 2$ is given by $r_2(7,2) + f_1(1) = 16 + 2 = 18$. Similarly, with $x_2 = 5$, and $d_2 = 1$, we get $r_2(5,1) + f_1(2) = 8 + 4 = 12$. Note that some combinations of x_2 and d_2 are not feasible. For example, with $x_2 = 2$ days, $d_2 = 1$ is infeasible because category 2 jobs each require 3 days to process. The infeasible solutions are indicated by a dash.

After all the total returns in the rectangle have been calculated, we can determine an optimal decision at this stage for each possible value of the input or state variable x_2. For example, if $x_2 = 9$, we can select one of four possible values for d_2: 0, 1, 2, or 3. Clearly $d_3 = 3$ with a value of 24 yields the maximum total return for the last two stages. Therefore, we record this value in the column. For additional emphasis, we circle the element inside the rectangle corresponding to the optimal return. The optimal total return, given that we are in state $x_2 = 9$ and must pass through two more stages, is thus 24, and we record this value in the $f_2(x_2)$ column. Given that we enter stage 2 with $x_2 = 9$ and make the optimal decision there of $d_2^* = 3$, we will enter stage 1 with $x_1 = t_2(9, 3) = x_2 - 3d_2 = 9 - 3(3) = 0$. This value is recorded in the last column in the table. We can now go on to stage 3.

Stage 3. The table we construct here is much the same as for stage 2. The entries under the heading $r_3(x_3, d_3) + f_2(x_2)$ represent the total return over stages 3, 2, and 1 for all possible inputs x_3 and all possible decisions d_3.

x_3 \ d_3	$r_3(x_3, d_3) + f_2(x_2)$: 0	1	2	d_3^*	$f_3(x_3)$	$x_2 = t_3(x_3, d_3^*) = x_3 - 4d_3^*$
0	(0)	—	—	0	0	0
1	(2)	—	—	0	2	1
2	(4)	—	—	0	4	2
3	(8)	—	—	0	8	3
4	10	(11)	—	1	11	0
5	12	(13)	—	1	13	1
6	(16)	15	—	0	16	6
7	18	(19)	—	1	19	3
8	20	21	(22)	2	22	0
9	(24)	23	(24)	0,2	24	9,1
10	26	(27)	26	1	27	6

Some features of interest appear in this table that were not present at stage 2. We note that if the state variable $x_3 = 9$, then two possible decisions will lead to an optimal total return from stages 1, 2, and 3; that is, we may elect to process no jobs from category 3, in which case, we will obtain no return from stage 3, but will enter stage 2 with $x_2 = 9$. Because $f_2(9) = 24$, the selection of $d_3 = 0$ would result in a total return of 24. However, a selection of $d_3 = 2$ also leads to a total return of 24. We obtain a return of $11(d_3) = 11(2) = 22$ for stage 3 and a return of 2 for the remaining two stages because $x_2 = 1$. To show the available alternative optimal solutions at this stage, we have placed two entries in the d_3^* and $x_2 = t_3(x_3, d_3^*)$ columns. The other entries in this table are calculated in the same manner as at stage 2. Let us now move on to the last stage.

Stage 4. We know that 10 days are available in the planning period; therefore, the input to stage 4 is $x_4 = 10$. Thus, we have to consider only one row in the table, corresponding to stage 4.

x_4 \ d_4	$r_4(x_4, d_4) + f_3(x_3)$: 0	1	d_4^*	$f_4(x_4)$	$x_3 = t_4(x_4, d_4^*) = 10 - 7d_4^*$
10	27	(28)	1	28	3

The optimal decision, given $x_4 = 10$, is $d_4^* = 1$.

We have completed the dynamic programming solution of this problem. To identify the overall optimal solution, we must now trace back through the tables, beginning at stage 4, the last stage considered. The optimal decision at stage 4 is $d_4^* = 1$. Thus, $x_3 = 10 - 7d_4^* = 3$, and we enter stage 3 with 3 days available for processing. With $x_3 = 3$, we see that the best decision at stage 3 is $d_3^* = 0$. Thus, we enter stage 2 with $x_2 = 3$. The optimal decision at stage 2 with $x_2 = 3$ is $d_2^* = 1$, resulting in $x_1 = 0$. Finally, the decision at stage 1 must be $d_1^* = 0$. The optimal strategy for the manufacturing operation is as follows:

	Decision	Return
	$d_1^* = 0$	0
	$d_2^* = 1$	8
	$d_3^* = 0$	0
	$d_4^* = 1$	20
	Total	28

We should schedule one job from category 2 and one job from category 4 for processing over the next 10 days.

Another advantage of the dynamic programming approach can now be illustrated. Suppose we wanted to schedule the jobs to be processed over an eight-day period only. We can solve this new problem simply by making a recalculation at stage 4. The new stage 4 table would appear as follows:

x_4 \ d_4	$r_4(x_4, d_4) + f_3(x_3)$: 0	1	d_4^*	$f_4(x_4)$	$x_3 = t_4(x_4, d_4^*) = 8 - 7d_4^*$
8	(22)	(22)	0,1	22	8,1

Actually, we are testing the sensitivity of the optimal solution to a change in the total number of days available for processing. We have here the case of alternative optimal solutions. One solution can be found by setting $d_4^* = 0$ and tracing through the tables. Doing so, we obtain the following:

	Decision	Return
	$d_1^* = 0$	0
	$d_2^* = 0$	0
	$d_3^* = 2$	22
	$d_4^* = 0$	0
	Total	22

A second optimal solution can be found by setting $d_4^* = 1$ and tracing back through the tables. Doing so, we obtain another solution (which has exactly the same total return):

	Decision	Return
	$d_1^* = 1$	2
	$d_2^* = 0$	0
	$d_3^* = 0$	0
	$d_4^* = 1$	20
	Total	22

Can you now solve a knapsack problem using dynamic programming? Try Problem 3.

From the shortest-route and the knapsack examples you should be familiar with the stage-by-stage solution procedure of dynamic programming. In the next section we show how dynamic programming can be used to solve a production and inventory control problem.

18.4 A PRODUCTION AND INVENTORY CONTROL PROBLEM

Suppose we developed forecasts of the demand for a particular product over several periods, and we would like to decide on a production quantity for each of the periods so that demand can be satisfied at a minimum cost. Two costs need to be considered: production costs and holding costs. We will assume that one production setup will be made each period; thus, setup costs will be constant. As a result, setup costs are not considered in the analysis.

We allow the production and holding costs to vary across periods. This provision makes the model more flexible because it also allows for the possibility of using different facilities for production and storage in different periods. Production and storage capacity constraints, which may vary across periods, will be included in the model. We adopt the following notation:

N = number of periods (stages in the dynamic programming formulation)
D_n = demand during stage n; $n = 1, 2, \ldots, N$
x_n = a state variable representing the amount of inventory on hand at the beginning of stage n; $n = 1, 2, \ldots, N$
d_n = production quantity for stage n; $n = 1, 2, \ldots, N$
P_n = production capacity in stage n; $n = 1, 2, \ldots, N$
W_n = storage capacity at the end of stage n; $n = 1, 2, \ldots, N$
C_n = production cost per unit in stage n; $n = 1, 2, \ldots, N$
H_n = holding cost per unit of ending inventory for stage n; $n = 1, 2, \ldots, N$

We develop the dynamic programming solution for a problem covering three months of operation. The data for the problem are presented in Table 18.3. We can think of each month as a stage in a dynamic programming formulation. Figure 18.5 shows a schematic of such a formulation. Note that the beginning inventory in January is one unit.

In Figure 18.5 we numbered the periods backward; that is, stage 1 corresponds to March, stage 2 corresponds to February, and stage 3 corresponds to January. The stage transformation functions take the form of ending inventory = beginning inventory + production − demand. Thus, we have

$$\begin{aligned} x_3 &= 1 \\ x_2 &= x_3 + d_3 - D_3 = x_3 + d_3 - 2 \\ x_1 &= x_2 + d_2 - D_2 = x_2 + d_2 - 3 \\ x_0 &= x_1 + d_1 - D_1 = x_1 + d_1 - 3 \end{aligned}$$

The return functions for each stage represent the sum of production and holding costs for the month. For example, in stage 1 (March), $r_1(x_1, d_1) = 200d_1 + 40(x_1 + d_1 - 3)$ represents the total production and holding costs for the period. The production costs are \$200 per unit, and the holding costs are \$40 per unit of ending inventory. The other return functions are

$$\begin{aligned} r_2(x_2, d_2) &= 150d_2 + 30(x_2 + d_2 - 3) \qquad \text{Stage 2, February} \\ r_3(x_3, d_3) &= 175d_3 + 30(x_3 + d_3 - 2) \qquad \text{Stage 3, January} \end{aligned}$$

TABLE 18.3 PRODUCTION AND INVENTORY CONTROL PROBLEM DATA

		Capacity		Cost per Unit	
Month	**Demand**	**Production**	**Storage**	**Production**	**Holding**
January	2	3	2	$175	$30
February	3	2	3	150	30
March	3	3	2	200	40

The beginning inventory for January is one unit.

This problem is particularly interesting because three constraints must be satisfied at each stage as we perform the optimization procedure. The first constraint is that the ending inventory must be less than or equal to the warehouse capacity. Mathematically, we have

$$x_n + d_n - D_n \leq W_n$$

or

$$x_n + d_n \leq W_n + D_n \tag{18.1}$$

The second constraint is that the production level in each period may not exceed the production capacity. Mathematically, we have

$$d_n \leq P_n \tag{18.2}$$

FIGURE 18.5 PRODUCTION AND INVENTORY CONTROL PROBLEM AS A THREE-STAGE DYNAMIC PROGRAMMING PROBLEM

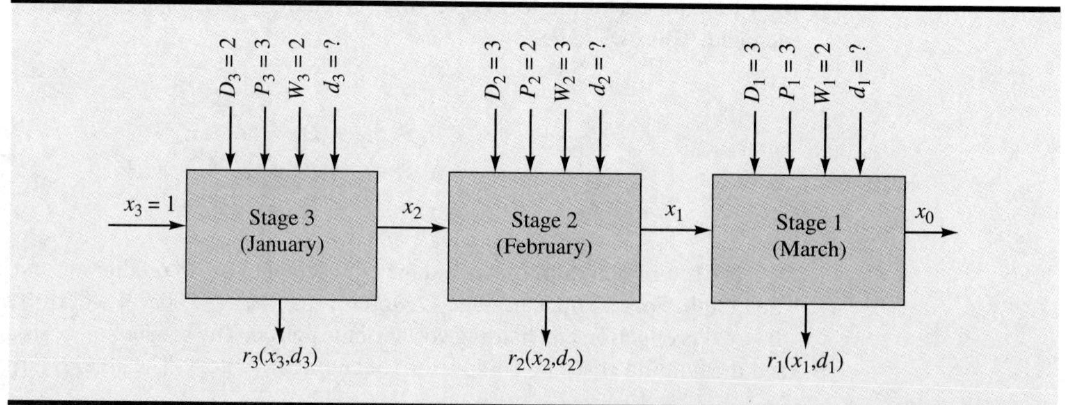

In order to satisfy demand, the third constraint is that the beginning inventory plus production must be greater than or equal to demand. Mathematically, this constraint can be written as

$$x_n + d_n \geq D_n \tag{18.3}$$

Let us now begin the stagewise solution procedure. At each stage, we want to minimize $r_n(x_n, d_n) + f_{n-1}(x_{n-1})$ subject to the constraints given by equations (18.1), (18.2), and (18.3).

Stage 1. The stage 1 problem is as follows:

$$\begin{aligned}
\text{Min} \quad & r_1(x_1, d_1) = 200d_1 + 40(x_1 + d_1 - 3) \\
\text{s.t.} \quad & \\
& x_1 + d_1 \leq 5 \quad \text{Warehouse constraint} \\
& d_1 \leq 3 \quad \text{Production constraint} \\
& x_1 + d_1 \geq 3 \quad \text{Satisfy demand constraint}
\end{aligned}$$

Combining terms in the objective function, we can rewrite the problem:

$$\begin{aligned}
\text{Min} \quad & r_1(x_1, d_1) = 240d_1 + 40x_1 - 120 \\
\text{s.t.} \quad & \\
& x_1 + d_1 \leq 5 \\
& d_1 \leq 3 \\
& x_1 + d_1 \geq 3
\end{aligned}$$

Following the tabular approach we adopted in Section 18.3, we will consider all possible inputs to stage 1 (x_1) and make the corresponding minimum-cost decision. Because we are attempting to minimize cost, we will want the decision variable d_1 to be as small as possible and still satisfy the demand constraint. Thus, the table for stage 1 is as follows:

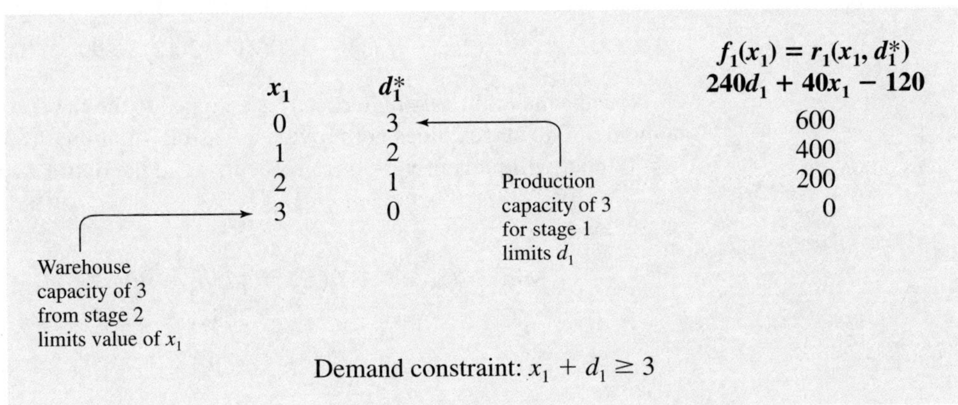

x_1	d_1^*	$f_1(x_1) = r_1(x_1, d_1^*)$ $240d_1 + 40x_1 - 120$
0	3	600
1	2	400
2	1	200
3	0	0

Now let us proceed to stage 2.

Stage 2.

$$\text{Min} \quad r_2(x_2, d_2) + f_1(x_1) = 150d_2 + 30(x_2 + d_2 - 3) + f_1(x_1)$$
$$= 180d_2 + 30x_2 - 90 + f_1(x_1)$$

s.t.

$$x_2 + d_2 \leq 6$$
$$d_2 \leq 2$$
$$x_2 + d_2 \geq 3$$

The stage 2 calculations are summarized in the following table:

x_2 \ d_2	$r_2(x_2, d_2) + f_1(x_1)$: 0	1	2	d_2^*	$f_2(x_2)$	$x_1 = x_2 + d_2^* - 3$
0	—	—	—	—	M	—
1	—	—	(900)	2	900	0
2	—	750	(730)	2	730	1

Production capacity of 2 for stage 2 (column d_2 = 2)

Warehouse capacity of 2 from stage 3 (rows x_2)

Check demand constraint $x_2 + d_2 \geq 3$ for each x_2, d_2 combination (– indicates an infeasible solution)

The detailed calculations for $r_2(x_2, d_2) + f_1(x_1)$ when $x_2 = 1$ and $d_2 = 2$ are as follows:

$$r_2(1,2) + f_1(0) = 180(2) + 30(1) - 90 + 600 = 900$$

For $r_2(x_2, d_2) + f_1(x_1)$ when $x_2 = 2$ and $d_2 = 1$, we have

$$r_2(2,1) + f_1(0) = 180(1) + 30(2) - 90 + 600 = 750$$

For $x_2 = 2$ and $d_2 = 2$, we have

$$r_2(2,2) + f_1(1) = 180(2) + 30(2) - 90 + 400 = 730$$

Note that an arbitrarily high cost M is assigned to the $f_2(x_2)$ column for $x_2 = 0$. Because an input of 0 to stage 2 does not provide a feasible solution, the M cost associated with the $x_2 = 0$ input will prevent $x_2 = 0$ from occurring in the optimal solution.

Stage 3.

$$\text{Min} \quad r_3(x_3, d_3) + f_2(x_2) = 175d_3 + 30(x_3 + d_3 - 2) + f_2(x_2)$$
$$= 205d_3 + 30x_3 - 60 + f_2(x_2)$$

s.t.

$$x_3 + d_3 \leq 4$$
$$d_3 \leq 3$$
$$x_3 + d_3 \geq 2$$

With $x_3 = 1$ already defined by the beginning inventory level, the table for stage 3 becomes

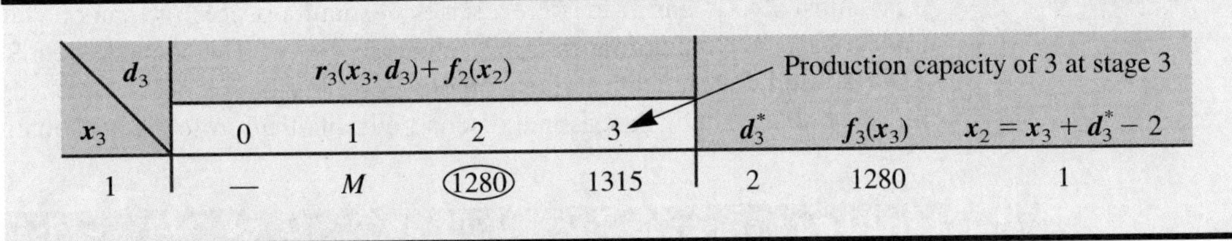

d_3 / x_3	$r_3(x_3, d_3) + f_2(x_2)$						
	0	1	2	3	d_3^*	$f_3(x_3)$	$x_2 = x_3 + d_3^* - 2$
1	—	M	(1280)	1315	2	1280	1

Try Problem 10 for practice using dynamic programming to solve a production and inventory control problem.

Thus, we find that the total cost associated with the optimal production and inventory policy is \$1280. To find the optimal decisions and inventory levels for each period, we trace back through each stage and identify x_n and d_n^* as we go. Table 18.4 summarizes the optimal production and inventory policy.

TABLE 18.4 OPTIMAL PRODUCTION AND INVENTORY CONTROL POLICY

Month	Beginning Inventory	Production	Production Cost	Ending Inventory	Holding Cost	Total Monthly Cost
January	1	2	\$ 350	1	\$30	\$ 380
February	1	2	300	0	0	300
March	0	3	600	0	0	600
		Totals	\$1250		\$30	\$1280

NOTES AND COMMENTS

1. With dynamic programming, as with other management science techniques, the computer can be a valuable computational aid. However, because dynamic programming is a general approach with stage decision problems differing substantially from application to application, no one algorithm or computer software package is available for solving dynamic programs. Some software packages exist for specific types of problems; however, most new applications of dynamic programming will require specially designed software if a computer solution is to be obtained.
2. The introductory illustrations of dynamic programming presented in this chapter are deterministic and involve a finite number of decision alternatives and a finite number of stages. For these types of problems, computations can be organized and carried out in a tabular form. With this structure, the optimization problem at each stage can usually be solved by total enumeration of all possible outcomes. More complex dynamic programming models may include probabilistic components, continuous decision variables, or an infinite number of stages. In cases where the optimization problem at each stage involves continuous decision variables, linear programming or calculus-based procedures may be needed to obtain an optimal solution.

SUMMARY

Dynamic programming is an attractive approach to problem solving when it is possible to break a large problem into interrelated smaller problems. The solution procedure then proceeds recursively, solving one of the smaller problems at each stage. Dynamic programming is not a specific algorithm, but rather an approach to problem solving. Thus, the recursive optimization may be carried out differently for different problems. In any case, it is almost always easier to solve a series of smaller problems than one large one. Through this process, dynamic programming obtains its power. The Management Science in Action, The EPA and Water Quality Management, describes how the EPA uses a dynamic programming model to establish seasonal discharge limits that protect water quality.

MANAGEMENT SCIENCE IN ACTION

THE EPA AND WATER QUALITY MANAGEMENT*

The U.S. Environmental Protection Agency (EPA) is an independent agency of the executive branch of the federal government. The EPA administers comprehensive environmental protection laws related to the following areas:

- Water pollution control, water quality, and drinking water
- Air pollution and radiation
- Pesticides and toxic substances
- Solid and hazardous waste, including emergency spill response and Superfund site remediation

The EPA administers programs designed to maintain acceptable water quality conditions for rivers and streams throughout the United States. To guard against polluted rivers and streams, the government requires companies to obtain a discharge permit from federal or state authorities before any form of pollutants can be discharged into a body of water. These permits specifically notify each discharger as to the amount of legally dischargeable waste that can be placed in the river or stream. The discharge limits are determined by ensuring that water quality criteria are met even in unusually dry seasons when the river or stream has a critically low-flow condition. Most often, this condition is based on the lowest flow recorded over the past 10 years. Ensuring that water quality is maintained under the low-flow conditions provides a high degree of reliability that the water quality criteria can be maintained throughout the year.

A goal of the EPA is to establish seasonal discharge limits that enable lower treatment costs while maintaining water quality standards at a prescribed level of reliability. These discharge limits are established by first determining the design stream flow for the body of water receiving the waste. The design stream flows for each season interact to determine the overall reliability that the annual water quality conditions will be maintained. The Municipal Environmental Research Laboratory in Cincinnati, Ohio, developed a dynamic programming model to determine design stream flows, which in turn could be used to establish seasonal waste discharge limits. The model chose the design stream flows that minimized treatment cost subject to a reliability constraint that the probability of no water quality violation was greater than a minimal acceptable probability. The model contained a stage for each season, and the reliability constraint established the state variability for the dynamic programming model. With the use of this dynamic programming model, the EPA is able to establish seasonal discharge limits that provide a minimum-cost treatment plan that maintains EPA water quality standards.

*Based on information provided by John Convery of the Environmental Protection Agency.

GLOSSARY

Dynamic programming An approach to problem solving that permits decomposing a large problem that may be difficult to solve into a number of interrelated smaller problems that are usually easier to solve.

Principle of optimality Regardless of the decisions made at previous stages, if the decision made at stage n is to be part of an overall optimal solution, the decision made at stage n must be optimal for all remaining stages.

Stages When a large problem is decomposed into a number of subproblems, the dynamic programming solution approach creates a stage to correspond to each of the subproblems.

Decision variable d_n A variable representing the possible decisions that can be made at stage n.

State variables x_n and x_{n-1} An input state variable x_n and an output state variable x_{n-1} together define the condition of the process at the beginning and end of stage n.

Stage transformation function $t_n(x_n, d_n)$ The rule or equation that relates the output state variable x_{n-1} for stage n to the input state variable x_n and the decision variable d_n.

Return function $r_n(x_n, d_n)$ A value (such as profit or loss) associated with making decision d_n at stage n for a specific value of the input state variable x_n.

Knapsack problem Finding the number of N items, each of which has a different weight and value, that can be placed in a knapsack with limited weight capacity so as to maximize the total value of the items placed in the knapsack.

PROBLEMS

1. In Section 18.1 we solved a shortest-route problem using dynamic programming. Find the optimal solution to this problem by total enumeration; that is, list all 16 possible routes from the origin, node 1, to the destination, node 10, and pick the one with the smallest value. Explain why dynamic programming results in fewer computations for this problem.

2. Consider the following network. The numbers above each arc represent the distance between the connected nodes.

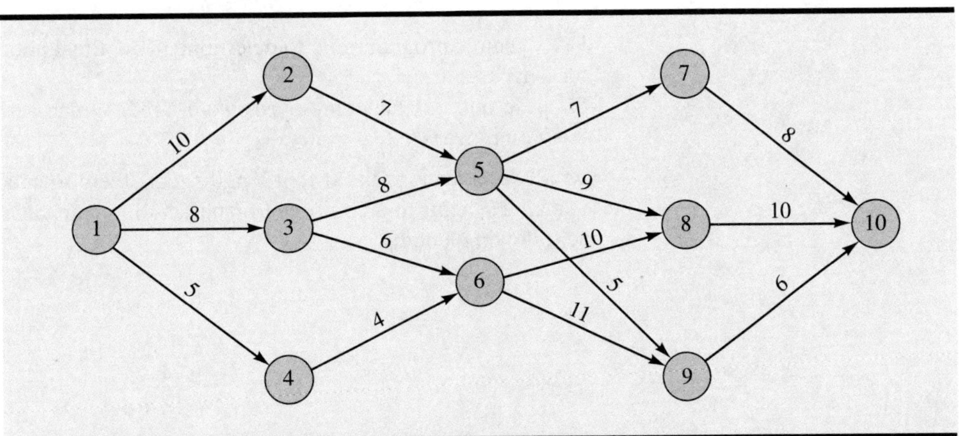

   a. Find the shortest route from node 1 to node 10 using dynamic programming.
   b. What is the shortest route from node 4 to node 10?
   c. Enumerate all possible routes from node 1 to node 10. Explain how dynamic programming reduces the number of computations to fewer than the number required by total enumeration.

3. A charter pilot has additional capacity for 2000 pounds of cargo on a flight from Dallas to Seattle. A transport company has four types of cargo in Dallas to be delivered to Seattle. The number of units of each cargo type, the weight per unit, and the delivery fee per unit are shown.

Cargo Type	Units Available	Weight per Unit (100 pounds)	Delivery Fee ($100s)
1	2	8	22
2	2	5	12
3	4	3	7
4	3	2	3

a. Use dynamic programming to find how many units of each cargo type the pilot should contract to deliver.
b. Suppose the pilot agrees to take another passenger and the additional cargo capacity is reduced to 1800 pounds. How does your recommendation change?

4. A firm just hired eight new employees and would like to determine how to allocate their time to four activities. The firm prepared the following table, which gives the estimated profit for each activity as a function of the number of new employees allocated to it:

	Number of New Employees								
Activities	**0**	**1**	**2**	**3**	**4**	**5**	**6**	**7**	**8**
1	22	30	37	44	49	54	58	60	61
2	30	40	48	55	59	62	64	66	67
3	46	52	56	59	62	65	67	68	69
4	5	22	36	48	52	55	58	60	61

a. Use dynamic programming to determine the optimal allocation of new employees to the activities.
b. Suppose only six new employees were hired. Which activities would you assign to these employees?

5. A sawmill receives logs in 20-foot lengths, cuts them to smaller lengths, and then sells these smaller lengths to a number of manufacturing companies. The company has orders for the following lengths:

$$l_1 = 3 \text{ ft}$$
$$l_2 = 7 \text{ ft}$$
$$l_3 = 11 \text{ ft}$$
$$l_4 = 16 \text{ ft}$$

The sawmill currently has an inventory of 2000 logs in 20-foot lengths and would like to select a cutting pattern that will maximize the profit made on this inventory. Assuming the sawmill has sufficient orders available, its problem becomes one of determining the cutting pattern that will maximize profits. The per-unit profit for each of the smaller lengths is as follows:

Length (feet)	3	7	11	16
Profit ($)	1	3	5	8

Any cutting pattern is permissible as long as

$$3d_1 + 7d_2 + 11d_3 + 16d_4 \leq 20$$

where d_i is the number of pieces of length l_i cut, $i = 1, 2, 3, 4$.

a. Set up a dynamic programming model of this problem, and solve it. What are your decision variables? What is your state variable?

b. Explain briefly how this model can be extended to find the best cutting pattern in cases where the overall length l can be cut into N lengths, $l_1, l_2, \ldots, l_N$.

6. A large manufacturing company has a well-developed management training program. Each trainee is expected to complete a four-phase program, but at each phase of the training program a trainee may be given a number of different assignments. The following assignments are available with their estimated completion times in months at each phase of the program.

Phase I	Phase II	Phase III	Phase IV
A–13	E–3	H–12	L–10
B–10	F–6	I–6	M–5
C–20	G–5	J–7	N–13
D–17		K–10	

Assignments made at subsequent phases depend on the previous assignment. For example, a trainee who completes assignment A at phase I may only go on to assignment F or G at phase II—that is, a precedence relationship exists for each assignment.

Assignment	Feasible Succeeding Assignments	Assignment	Feasible Succeeding Assignments
A	F, G	H	L, M
B	F	I	L, M
C	G	J	M, N
D	E, G	K	N
E	H, I, J, K	L	Finish
F	H, K	M	Finish
G	J, K	N	Finish

a. The company would like to determine the sequence of assignments that will minimize the time in the training program. Formulate and solve this problem as a dynamic programming problem. (*Hint:* Develop a network representation of the problem where each node represents completion of an activity.)

b. If a trainee just completed assignment F and would like to complete the remainder of the training program in the shortest possible time, which assignment should be chosen next?

7. Crazy Robin, the owner of a small chain of Robin Hood Sporting Goods stores in Des Moines and Cedar Rapids, Iowa, just purchased a new supply of 500 dozen top-line golf balls. Because she was willing to purchase the entire amount of a production overrun, Robin was able to buy the golf balls at one-half the usual price.

Three of Robin's stores do a good business in the sale of golf equipment and supplies, and, as a result, Robin decided to retail the balls at these three stores. Thus, Robin is faced with the problem of determining how many dozen balls to allocate to each store. The following estimates show the expected profit from allocating 100, 200, 300, 400, or 500 dozen to each store:

	Number of Dozens of Golf Balls				
Store	**100**	**200**	**300**	**400**	**500**
1	\$600	\$1100	\$1550	\$1700	\$1800
2	500	1200	1700	2000	2100
3	550	1100	1500	1850	1950

Assuming the lots cannot be broken into any sizes smaller than 100 dozen each, how many dozen golf balls should Crazy Robin send to each store?

8. The Max X. Posure Advertising Agency is conducting a 10-day advertising campaign for a local department store. The agency determined that the most effective campaign would possibly include placing ads in four media: daily newspaper, Sunday newspaper, radio, and television. A total of \$8000 has been made available for this campaign, and the agency would like to distribute this budget in \$1000 increments across the media in such a fashion that an advertising exposure index is maximized. Research conducted by the agency permits the following estimates to be made of the exposure per each \$1000 expenditure in each of the media.

	Thousands of Dollars Spent							
Media	**1**	**2**	**3**	**4**	**5**	**6**	**7**	**8**
Daily newspaper	24	37	46	59	72	80	82	82
Sunday newspaper	15	55	70	75	90	95	95	95
Radio	20	30	45	55	60	62	63	63
Television	20	40	55	65	70	70	70	70

a. How much should the agency spend on each medium to maximize the department store's exposure?
b. How would your answer change if only \$6000 were budgeted?
c. How would your answers in parts (a) and (b) change if television were not considered as one of the media?

9. Suppose we have a three-stage process where the yield for each stage is a function of the decision made. In mathematical notation, we may state our problem as follows:

$$\begin{aligned} \text{Max} \quad & r_1(d_1) + r_2(d_2) + r_3(d_3) \\ \text{s.t.} \quad & \\ & d_1 + d_2 + d_3 \leq 1000 \end{aligned}$$

The possible values the decision variables may take on at each stage and the corresponding returns are as follows:

Stage 1		Stage 2		Stage 3	
d_1	$r_1(d_1)$	d_2	$r_2(d_2)$	d_3	$r_3(d_3)$
0	0	100	120	100	175
100	110	300	400	500	700
200	300	500	650		
300	400	600	700		
400	425	800	975		

a. Use total enumeration to list all feasible sequences of decisions for this problem. Which one is optimal [i.e., maximizes $r_1(d_1) + r_2(d_2) + r_3(d_3)$]?

b. Use dynamic programming to solve this problem.

10. Recall the production and inventory control problem of Section 18.4. Mills Manufacturing Company has just such a production and inventory control problem for an armature the company manufactures as a component for a generator. The available data for the next 3-month planning period are as follow:

		Capacity		Cost per Unit	
Month	Demand	Production	Warehouse	Production	Holding
1	20	30	40	$2.00	$0.30
2	30	20	30	1.50	0.30
3	30	30	20	2.00	0.20

Use dynamic programming to find the optimal production quantities and inventory levels in each period for the Mills Manufacturing Company. Assume an inventory of 10 units on hand at the beginning of month 1 and production runs are completed in multiples of 10 units (i.e., 10, 20, or 30 units).

Case Problem PROCESS DESIGN

The Baker Chemical processing plant is considering introducing a new product. However, before making a final decision, management requests estimates of profits associated with different process designs. The general flow process is represented:

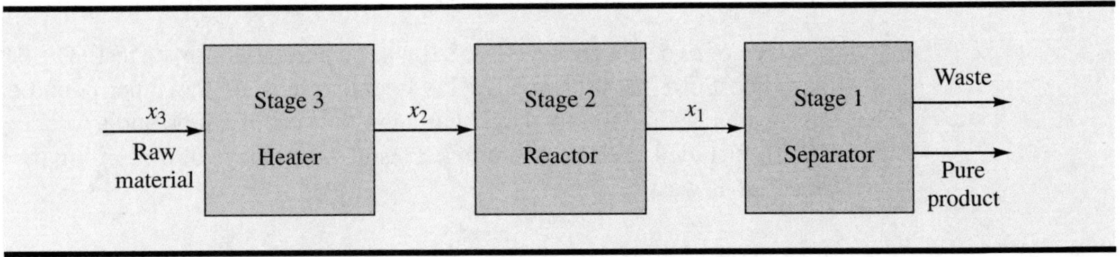

Raw material is fed into a heater at the rate of 4500 pounds per week. The heated material is routed to a reactor where a portion of the raw material is converted to pure product. A separator then withdraws the finished product for sale. The unconverted material is discarded as waste.

Profit considerations are to be based on a two-year payback period on investments; that is, all capital expenditures must be recovered in two years (100 weeks). All calculations will be based on weekly operations. Raw material costs are expected to stay fixed at $1 per pound, and the forecasted selling price for the finished product is $6 per pound.

It is your responsibility to determine the process design that will yield maximum profit per week. You and your coworkers collect the following preliminary data.

One heater with an initial cost of $12,000 is being considered at stage 3. Two temperatures, 700°F and 800°F, are feasible. The operating costs for the heater depend directly on the temperature to be attained. These costs are as follows:

Operating Costs at Stage 3

	Decisions at Stage 3	
Input x_3	**700°F**	**800°F**
4500 lb	$280/week	$380/week

Stage 3's output x_2, which is also the input to stage 2, may be expressed as 4500 pounds of raw material heated to either 700°F or 800°F. One of the decisions you must make is to choose the temperature for heating the raw material.

A reactor, which can operate with either of two catalysts, C1 or C2, is to be used for stage 2. The initial cost of this reactor is $50,000. The operating costs of this reactor are independent of the input x_2 and depend only on the catalyst selected. The costs of the catalysts are included in the operating costs. The output will be expressed in pounds of converted (or pure) material. The percentage of material converted depends on the incoming temperature and the catalyst used. The following tables summarize the pertinent information. Thus, a second decision you must make is to specify which catalyst should be used.

Percent Conversion

	Decisions at Stage 2	
x_2	**C1**	**C2**
(4500 lb, 700°F)	20	40
(4500 lb, 800°F)	40	60

Operating Costs Decisions at Stage 2

C1	**C2**
$450/week	$650/week

One of two separators, S1 or S2, will be purchased for stage 1. The S1 separator has an initial cost of $20,000 and a weekly operating cost of $0.10 per pound of pure product to be separated. Comparatively, S2 has an initial cost of $5000 and a weekly operating cost of $0.20. Included in these operating costs is the expense of discarding the unconverted raw material as waste.

Managerial Report

1. Develop a dynamic programming model for the Baker Chemical process design.
2. Make specific recommendations on the following:
   - Best temperature for the heater
   - Best catalyst to use with the reactor
   - Best separator to purchase
3. What is the weekly profit?

APPENDIXES

Appendix A Areas for the Standard Normal Distribution

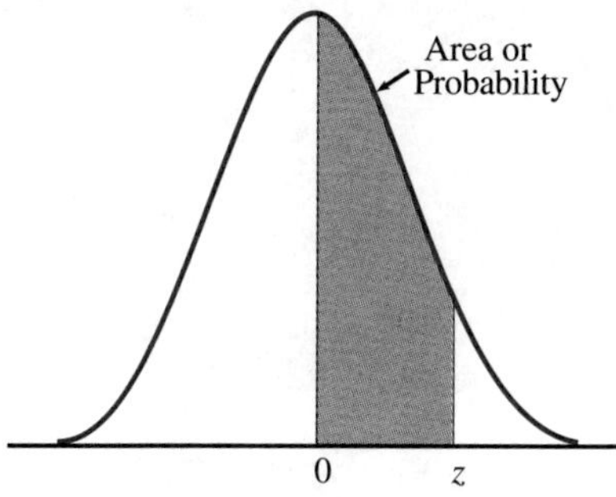

Entries in the following table give the area under the curve between the mean and z standard deviations above the mean. For example, for $z = 1.25$ the area under the curve between the mean and z is 0.3944.

z	**0.00**	**0.01**	**0.02**	**0.03**	**0.04**	**0.05**	**0.06**	**0.07**	**0.08**	**0.09**
0.0	0.0000	0.0040	0.0080	0.0120	0.0160	0.0199	0.0239	0.0279	0.0319	0.0359
0.1	0.0398	0.0438	0.0478	0.0517	0.0557	0.0596	0.0636	0.0675	0.0714	0.0753
0.2	0.0793	0.0832	0.0871	0.0910	0.0948	0.0987	0.1026	0.1064	0.1103	0.1141
0.3	0.1179	0.1217	0.1255	0.1293	0.1331	0.1368	0.1406	0.1443	0.1480	0.1517
0.4	0.1554	0.1591	0.1628	0.1664	0.1700	0.1736	0.1772	0.1808	0.1844	0.1879
0.5	0.1915	0.1950	0.1985	0.2019	0.2054	0.2088	0.2123	0.2157	0.2190	0.2224
0.6	0.2257	0.2291	0.2324	0.2357	0.2389	0.2422	0.2454	0.2486	0.2517	0.2549
0.7	0.2580	0.2611	0.2642	0.2673	0.2704	0.2734	0.2764	0.2794	0.2823	0.2852
0.8	0.2881	0.2910	0.2939	0.2967	0.2995	0.3023	0.3051	0.3078	0.3106	0.3133
0.9	0.3159	0.3186	0.3212	0.3238	0.3264	0.3289	0.3315	0.3340	0.3365	0.3389
1.0	0.3413	0.3438	0.3461	0.3485	0.3508	0.3531	0.3554	0.3577	0.3599	0.3621
1.1	0.3643	0.3665	0.3686	0.3708	0.3729	0.3749	0.3770	0.3790	0.3810	0.3830
1.2	0.3849	0.3869	0.3888	0.3907	0.3925	0.3944	0.3962	0.3980	0.3997	0.4015
1.3	0.4032	0.4049	0.4066	0.4082	0.4099	0.4115	0.4131	0.4147	0.4162	0.4177
1.4	0.4192	0.4207	0.4222	0.4236	0.4251	0.4265	0.4279	0.4292	0.4306	0.4319
1.5	0.4332	0.4345	0.4357	0.4370	0.4382	0.4394	0.4406	0.4418	0.4429	0.4441
1.6	0.4452	0.4463	0.4474	0.4484	0.4495	0.4505	0.4515	0.4525	0.4535	0.4545
1.7	0.4554	0.4564	0.4573	0.4582	0.4591	0.4599	0.4608	0.4616	0.4625	0.4633
1.8	0.4641	0.4649	0.4656	0.4664	0.4671	0.4678	0.4686	0.4693	0.4699	0.4706
1.9	0.4713	0.4719	0.4726	0.4732	0.4738	0.4744	0.4750	0.4756	0.4761	0.4767
2.0	0.4772	0.4778	0.4783	0.4788	0.4793	0.4798	0.4803	0.4808	0.4812	0.4817
2.1	0.4821	0.4826	0.4830	0.4834	0.4838	0.4842	0.4846	0.4850	0.4854	0.4857
2.2	0.4861	0.4864	0.4868	0.4871	0.4875	0.4878	0.4881	0.4884	0.4887	0.4890
2.3	0.4893	0.4896	0.4898	0.4901	0.4904	0.4906	0.4909	0.4911	0.4913	0.4916
2.4	0.4918	0.4920	0.4922	0.4925	0.4927	0.4929	0.4931	0.4932	0.4934	0.4936
2.5	0.4938	0.4940	0.4941	0.4943	0.4945	0.4946	0.4948	0.4949	0.4951	0.4952
2.6	0.4953	0.4955	0.4956	0.4957	0.4959	0.4960	0.4961	0.4962	0.4963	0.4964
2.7	0.4965	0.4966	0.4967	0.4968	0.4969	0.4970	0.4971	0.4972	0.4973	0.4974
2.8	0.4974	0.4975	0.4976	0.4977	0.4977	0.4978	0.4979	0.4979	0.4980	0.4981
2.9	0.4981	0.4982	0.4982	0.4983	0.4984	0.4984	0.4985	0.4985	0.4986	0.4986
3.0	0.4987	0.4987	0.4987	0.4988	0.4988	0.4989	0.4989	0.4989	0.4990	0.4990

Appendix B Values of $e^{-\lambda}$

λ	$e^{-\lambda}$	λ	$e^{-\lambda}$	λ	$e^{-\lambda}$
0.05	0.9512	2.05	0.1287	4.05	0.0174
0.10	0.9048	2.10	0.1225	4.10	0.0166
0.15	0.8607	2.15	0.1165	4.15	0.0158
0.20	0.8187	2.20	0.1108	4.20	0.0150
0.25	0.7788	2.25	0.1054	4.25	0.0143
0.30	0.7408	2.30	0.1003	4.30	0.0136
0.35	0.7047	2.35	0.0954	4.35	0.0129
0.40	0.6703	2.40	0.0907	4.40	0.0123
0.45	0.6376	2.45	0.0863	4.45	0.0117
0.50	0.6065	2.50	0.0821	4.50	0.0111
0.55	0.5769	2.55	0.0781	4.55	0.0106
0.60	0.5488	2.60	0.0743	4.60	0.0101
0.65	0.5220	2.65	0.0707	4.65	0.0096
0.70	0.4966	2.70	0.0672	4.70	0.0091
0.75	0.4724	2.75	0.0639	4.75	0.0087
0.80	0.4493	2.80	0.0608	4.80	0.0082
0.85	0.4274	2.85	0.0578	4.85	0.0078
0.90	0.4066	2.90	0.0550	4.90	0.0074
0.95	0.3867	2.95	0.0523	4.95	0.0071
1.00	0.3679	3.00	0.0498	5.00	0.0067
1.05	0.3499	3.05	0.0474	5.05	0.0064
1.10	0.3329	3.10	0.0450	5.10	0.0061
1.15	0.3166	3.15	0.0429	5.15	0.0058
1.20	0.3012	3.20	0.0408	5.20	0.0055
1.25	0.2865	3.25	0.0388	5.25	0.0052
1.30	0.2725	3.30	0.0369	5.30	0.0050
1.35	0.2592	3.35	0.0351	5.35	0.0047
1.40	0.2466	3.40	0.0334	5.40	0.0045
1.45	0.2346	3.45	0.0317	5.45	0.0043
1.50	0.2231	3.50	0.0302	5.50	0.0041
1.55	0.2122	3.55	0.0287	5.55	0.0039
1.60	0.2019	3.60	0.0273	5.60	0.0037
1.65	0.1920	3.65	0.0260	5.65	0.0035
1.70	0.1827	3.70	0.0247	5.70	0.0033
1.75	0.1738	3.75	0.0235	5.75	0.0032
1.80	0.1653	3.80	0.0224	5.80	0.0030
1.85	0.1572	3.85	0.0213	5.85	0.0029
1.90	0.1496	3.90	0.0202	5.90	0.0027
1.95	0.1423	3.95	0.0193	5.95	0.0026
2.00	0.1353	4.00	0.0183	6.00	0.0025
				7.00	0.0009
				8.00	0.000335
				9.00	0.000123
				10.00	0.000045

Appendix C References and Bibliography

Chapter 1 Introduction

Churchman, C. W., R. L. Ackoff, and E. L. Arnoff. *Introduction to Operations Research.* Wiley, 1957.

Horner, Peter. "The Sabre Story," *OR/MS Today* (June 2000).

Leon, Linda, Z. Przasnyski, and K. C. Seal. "Spreadsheets and OR/MS Models: An End-User Perspective," *Interfaces* (March/April 1996).

Powell, S. G. "Innovative Approaches to Management Science," *OR/MS Today* (October 1996).

Savage, S. "Weighing the Pros and Cons of Decision Technology and Spreadsheets," *OR/MS Today* (February 1997).

Winston, W. L. "The Teachers' Forum: Management Science with Spreadsheets for MBAs at Indiana University," *Interfaces* (March/April 1996).

Chapters 2 to 8 Linear Programming, Transportation, Assignment, Transshipment, and Integer Programming Problems

Bazarra, M. S., J. J. Jarvis, and H. D. Sherali. *Linear Programming and Network Flows,* 2d ed. Wiley, 1990.

Carino, H. F., and C. H. Le Noir, Jr. "Optimizing Wood Procurement in Cabinet Manufacturing," *Interfaces* (March/April 1988): 10–19.

Dantzig, G. B. *Linear Programming and Extensions.* Princeton University Press, 1963.

Geoffrion, A., and G. Graves. "Better Distribution Planning with Computer Models," *Harvard Business Review* (July/August 1976).

Greenberg, H. J. "How to Analyze the Results of Linear Programs—Part 1: Preliminaries," *Interfaces* 23, no. 4 (July/August 1993): 56–67.

Greenberg, H. J. "How to Analyze the Results of Linear Programs—Part 2: Price Interpretation," *Interfaces* 23, no. 5 (September/October 1993): 97–114.

Greenberg, H. J. "How to Analyze the Results of Linear Programs—Part 3: Infeasibility Diagnosis," *Interfaces* 23, no. 6 (November/December 1993): 120–139.

Lillien, G., and A. Rangaswamy. *Marketing Engineering: Computer-Assisted Marketing Analysis and Planning.* Addison-Wesley, 1998.

Nemhauser, G. L., and L. A. Wolsey. *Integer and Combinatorial Optimization.* Wiley, 1999.

Schrage, Linus. *Optimization Modeling with LINDO,* 4th ed. LINDO Systems Inc., 2000.

Sherman, H. D. "Hospital Efficiency Measurement and Evaluation," *Medical Care* 22, no. 10 (October 1984): 922–938.

Winston, W. L., and S. C. Albright. *Practical Management Science,* 2d ed. Duxbury Press, 2001.

Chapter 9 Network Models

Bazaraa, M. S., J. J. Jarvis, and H. D. Sherali. *Linear Programming and Network Flows,* 2d ed. Wiley, 1990.

Evans, J. R., and E. Minieka. *Optimization Algorithms for Networks and Graphs,* 2d ed. Marcel Dekker, 1992.

Ford, L. R., and D. R. Fulkerson. *Flows and Networks.* Princeton University Press, 1962.

Glover, F., and D. Klingman. "Network Applications in Industry and Government," *AIIE Transactions* (December 1977).

Jensen, P. A., and W. J. Barnes. *Network Flow Programming.* Krieger, 1987.

Chapter 10 Project Scheduling: PERT/CPM

Moder, J. J., C. R. Phillips, and E. W. Davis. *Project Management with CPM, PERT and Precedence Diagramming,* 3d ed. Blitz, 1995.

Wasil, E. A., and A. A. Assad. "Project Management on the PC: Software, Applications, and Trends," *Interfaces* 18, no. 2 (March/April 1988): 75–84.

Wiest, J., and F. Levy. *Management Guide to PERT-CPM,* 2d ed. Prentice Hall, 1977.

Chapter 11 Inventory Models

Fogarty, D. W., J. H. Blackstone, and T. R. Hoffman. *Production and Inventory Management,* 2d ed. South-Western, 1990.

Hillier, F., and G. J. Lieberman. *Introduction to Operations Research,* 7th ed. McGraw-Hill, 2000.

Narasimhan, S. L., D. W. McLeavey, and P. B. Lington. *Production Planning and Inventory Control,* 2d ed. Prentice Hall, 1995.

Orlicky, J., and G. W. Plossi. *Orlicky's Material Requirements Planning.* McGraw-Hill, 1994.

Vollmann, T. E., W. L. Berry, and D. C. Whybark. *Manufacturing Planning and Control Systems,* 4th ed. McGraw-Hill, 1997.

Chapter 12 Waiting Line Models

Bunday, B. D. *An Introduction to Queueing Theory.* Wiley, 1996.

Gross, D., and C. M. Harris. *Fundamentals of Queueing Theory,* 3d ed. Wiley, 1997.

Hall, R. W. *Queueing Methods: For Services and Manufacturing.* Prentice Hall, 1997.

Hillier, F., and G. J. Lieberman. *Introduction to Operations Research,* 7th ed. McGraw-Hill, 2000.

Kao, E. P. C. *An Introduction to Stochastic Processes.* Duxbury, 1996.

Chapter 13 Simulation

Banks, J., J. S. Carson, and B. L. Nelson. *Discrete-Event System Simulation,* 2d ed. Prentice Hall, 1995.

Fishwick, P. A. *Simulation Model Design and Execution: Building Digital Worlds.* Prentice Hall, 1995.

Harrell, C. R., and K. Tumau. *Simulation Made Easy: A Manager's Guide.* Institute of Industrial Engineers, 1996.

Kelton, W. D., R. P. Sadowski, and D. A. Sadowski. *Simulation with Arena.* McGraw-Hill, 1998.

Law, A. M., and W. D. Kelton. *Simulation Modeling and Analysis,* 3d ed. McGraw-Hill, 1999.

Pidd, M. *Computer Simulation in Management Science,* 4th ed. Wiley, 1998.

Thesen, A., and L. E. Travis. *Simulation for Decision Making.* Wadsworth, 1992.

Chapter 14 Decision Analysis

Berger, J. O. *Statistical Decision Theory and Bayesian Analysis,* 2d ed. Springer-Verlag, 1985.

Chernoff, H., and L. E. Moses. *Elementary Decision Theory.* Dover, 1987.

Clemen, R. T., and T. Reilly. *Making Hard Decisions with Decision Tools.* Duxbury, 2001.

Goodwin, P., and G. Wright. *Decision Analysis for Management Judgment,* 2d ed. Wiley, 1999.

Gregory, G. *Decision Analysis.* Plenum, 1988.

Pratt, J. W., H. Raiffa, and R. Schlaifer. *Introduction to Statistical Decision Theory.* MIT Press, 1995.

Raiffa, H. *Decision Analysis.* McGraw-Hill, 1997.

Schlaifer, R. *Analysis of Decisions Under Uncertainty.* Krieger, 1978.

Chapter 15 Multicriteria Decisions

Dyer, J. S. "A Clarification of Remarks on the Analytic Hierarchy Process," *Management Science* 36, no. 3 (March 1990): 274–275.

Dyer, J. S. "Remarks on the Analytic Hierarchy Process," *Management Science* 36, no. 3 (March 1990): 249–258.

Harker, P. T., and L. G. Vargas. "Reply to Remarks on the Analytic Hierarchy Process by J. S. Dyer," *Management Science* 36, no. 3 (March 1990): 269–273.

Harker, P. T., and L. G. Vargas. "The Theory of Ratio Scale Estimation: Saaty's Analytic Hierarchy Process," *Management Science* 33, no. 11 (November 1987): 1383–1403.

Ignizio, J. *Introduction to Linear Goal Programming.* Sage, 1986.

Keeney, R. L., and H. Raiffa. *Decisions with Multiple Objectives: Preferences and Value Tradeoffs.* Cambridge, 1993.

Saaty, T. *Decision Making for Leaders: The Analytic Hierarchy Process for Decisions in a Complex World,* 3d ed. RWS, 1999.

Saaty, T. *Multicriteria Decision Making,* 2d ed. RWS, 1996.

Saaty, T. L. "An Exposition of the AHP in Reply to the Paper Remarks on the Analytic Hierarchy Process," *Management Science* 36, no. 3 (March 1990): 259–268.

Saaty, T. L. "Rank Generation, Preservation, and Reversal in the Analytic Hierarchy Decision Process," *Decision Sciences* 18 (1987): 157–177.

Winkler, R. L. "Decision Modeling and Rational Choice: AHP and Utility Theory," *Management Science* 36, no. 3 (March 1990): 247–248.

Chapter 16 Forecasting

Bowerman, B. L., and R. T. O'Connell. *Forecasting and Time Series: An Applied Approach,* 3d ed. Duxbury, 2000.

Box, G. E. P., G. M. Jenkins, and G. C. Reinsel. *Time Series Analysis: Forecasting and Control,* 3d ed. Prentice Hall, 1994.

Hanke, J. E., and A. G. Reitsch. *Business Forecasting,* 6th ed. Prentice Hall, 1998.

Makridakis, S. G., S. C. Wheelwright, and R. J. Hyndman. *Forecasting: Methods and Applications,* 3d ed. Wiley, 1997.

Wilson, J. H., and B. Keating. *Business Forecasting,* 3d ed. Irwin, 1998.

Chapter 17 Markov Processes

Bharucha-Reid, A. T. *Elements of the Theory of Markov Processes and Their Applications.* Dover, 1997.

Bhat, U. N. *Elements of Applied Stochastic Processes,* 2d ed. Wiley, 1984.

Filar, J. A., and K. Vrieze. *Competitive Markov Decision Processes.* Springer-Verlag, 1996.

Norris, J. *Markov Chains.* Cambridge, 1997.

Chapter 18 Dynamic Programming

Bellman, R. E. *Dynamic Programming and Modern Control.* Academic Press, 1966.

Bertsekas, D. P. *Dynamic Programming and Optimal Control,* vols. 1 and 2. Athena Scientific, 1995.

Dreyfus, S. E. *The Art and Theory of Dynamic Programming.* Academic Press, 1977.

Nemhauser, G. L. *Introduction to Dynamic Programming.* Wiley, 1966.

Appendix D Self-Test Solutions and Answers to Even-Numbered Problems

Chapter 1

2. Define the problem; identify the alternatives; determine the criteria; evaluate the alternatives; choose an alternative

4. A quantitative approach should be considered because the problem is large, complex, important, new, and repetitive

6. Quicker to formulate, easier to solve, and/or more easily understood

8. **a.** Max $10x + 5y$

   s.t.

   $$5x + 2y \le 40$$
   $$x \ge 0, y \ge 0$$

   b. Controllable inputs: x and y
   Uncontrollable inputs: profit (10,5), labor-hours (5,2), and labor-hour availability (40)

   c. See Figure 1.8c

   d. $x = 0, y = 20$; Profit $= \$100$ (Solution by trial and error)

   e. Deterministic

10. **a.** Total units received $= x + y$

    b. Total cost $= 0.20x + 0.25y$

    c. $x + y = 5000$

    d. $x \le 4000$ Kansas City
    $y \le 3000$ Minneapolis

    e. Min $0.20x + 0.25y$

    s.t.

    $$x + y = 5000$$
    $$x \le 4000$$
    $$y \le 3000$$
    $$x, y \ge 0$$

FIGURE 1.8c SOLUTION

Profit: $10/unit for x, $5/unit for y
Labor-hours: 5/unit for x, 2/unit for y
40 labor-hour capacity
Uncontrollable Inputs

Production quantities x and y
Controllable Input

Max $10x + 5y$
s.t.
$5x + 2y \le 40$
$x \ge 0$
$y \ge 0$
Mathematical Model

Projected profit and check on production time constraint
Output

12. **a.** $TC = 1000 + 30x$

    b. $P = 40x - (1000 + 30x) = 10x - 1000$

    c. Break even when $P = 0$
    Thus, $10x - 1000 = 0$
    $$10x = 1000$$
    $$x = 100$$

14. **a.** 4706

    b. Loss of $12,000

    c. $23

    d. $11,800

16. **a.** Max $6x + 4y$

    b. $50x + 30y \le 80{,}000$
    $$50x \le 50{,}000$$
    $$30y \le 45{,}000$$

Chapter 2

1. Parts (a), (b), and (e) are acceptable linear programming relationships
   Part (c) is not acceptable because of $-2x_2^2$
   Part (d) is not acceptable because of $3\sqrt{x_1}$
   Part (f) is not acceptable because of $1x_1x_2$
   Parts (c), (d), and (f) could not be found in a linear programming model because they contain nonlinear terms

2. **a.**

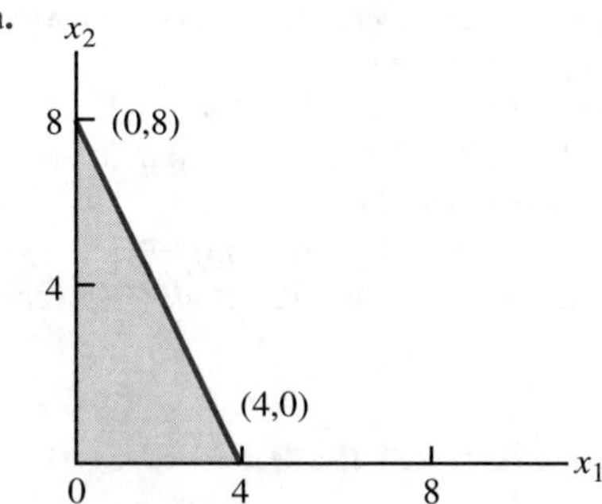

   b.

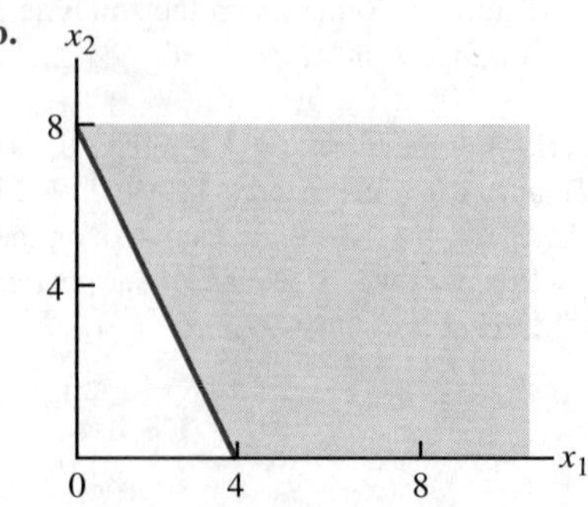

c.

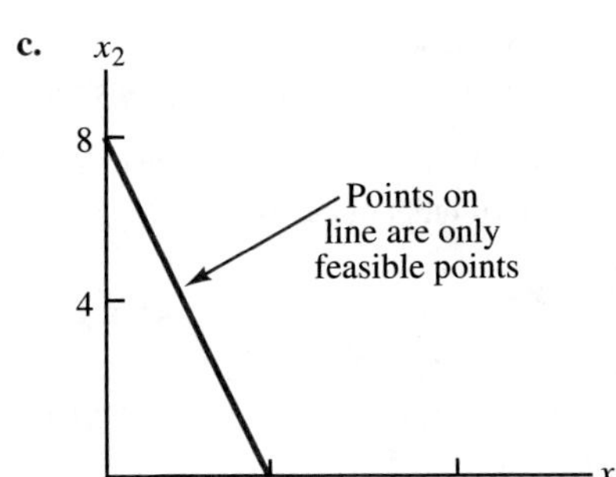

4. a.

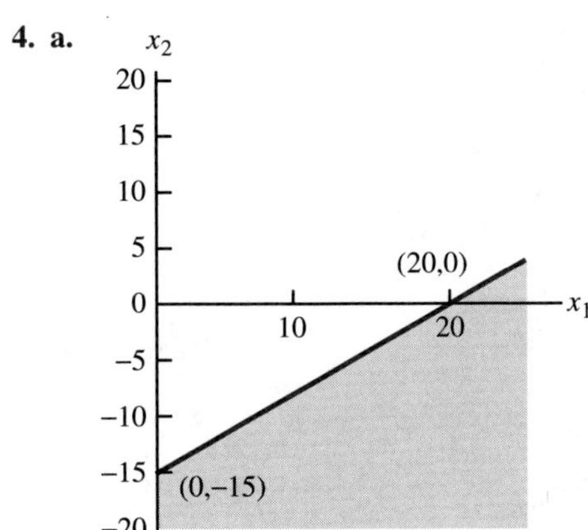

b.

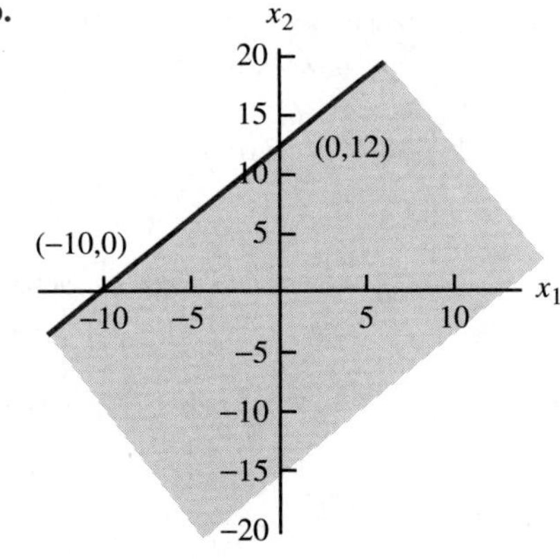

c.

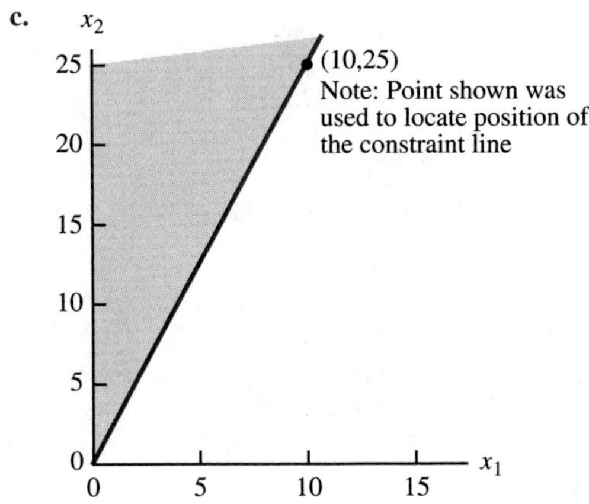

6.

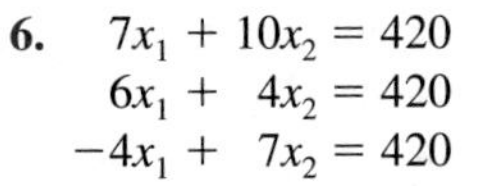

$$
\begin{aligned}
7x_1 + 10x_2 &= 420 \\
6x_1 + 4x_2 &= 420 \\
-4x_1 + 7x_2 &= 420
\end{aligned}
$$

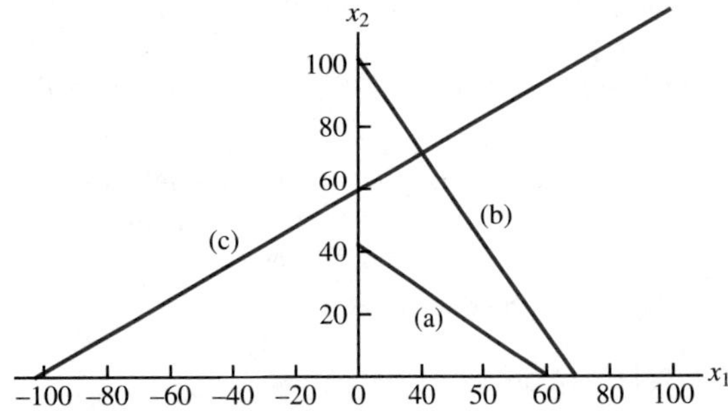

7.

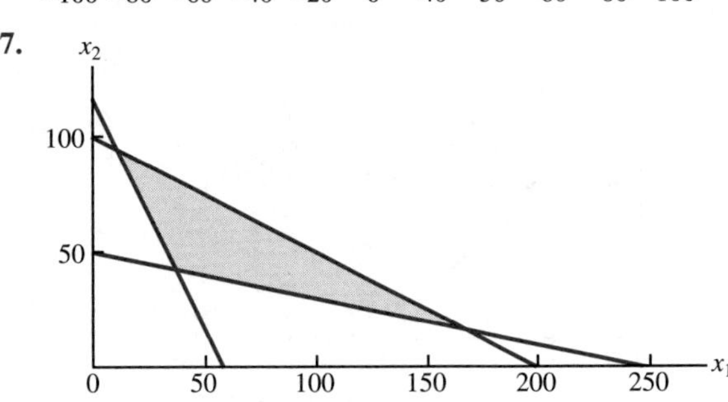

8.

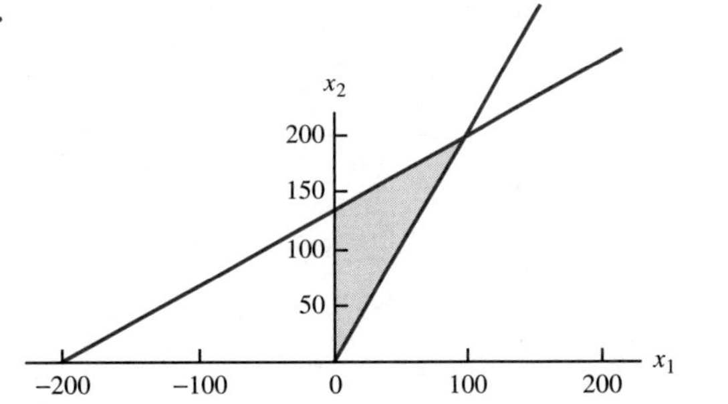

10.

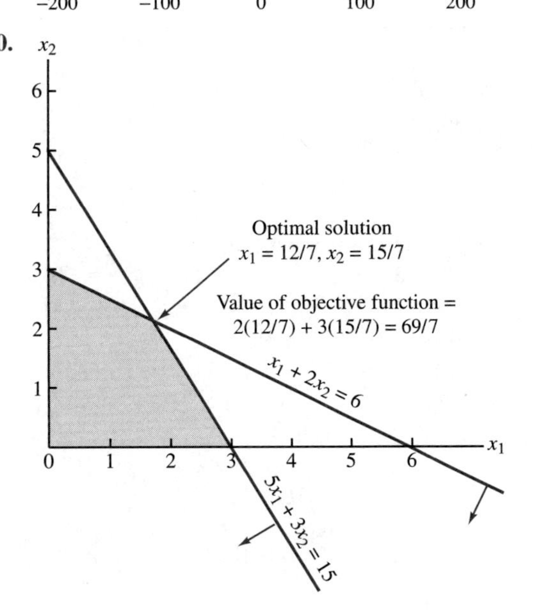

$$\begin{aligned} x_1 + 2x_2 &= 6 \quad (1) \\ 5x_1 + 3x_2 &= 15 \quad (2) \end{aligned}$$

Equation (1) times 5: $5x_1 + 10x_2 = 30$ (3)

Equation (2) minus equation (3): $-7x_2 = -15$

$x_2 = 15/7$

From equation (1): $x_1 = 6 - 2(15/7)$

$= 6 - 30/7 = 12/7$

12. a. $x_1 = 3, x_2 = 1.5$; Value of optimal solution = 13.5

b. $x_1 = 0, x_2 = 3$; Value of optimal solution = 18

c. four: (0, 0), (4, 0), (3, 1.5), and (0.3)

14. a.

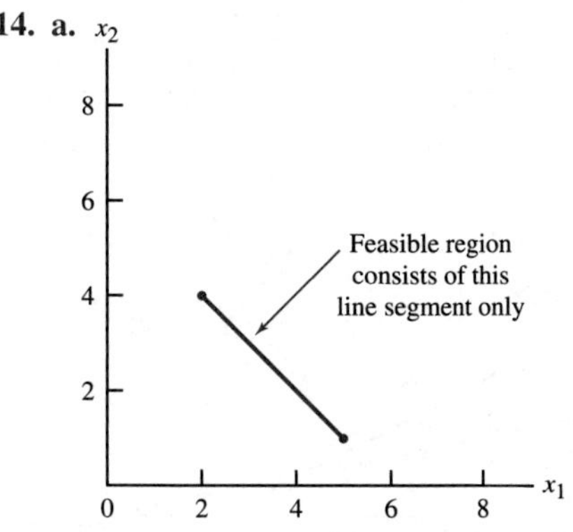

b. The extreme points are (5,1) and (2,4)

c.

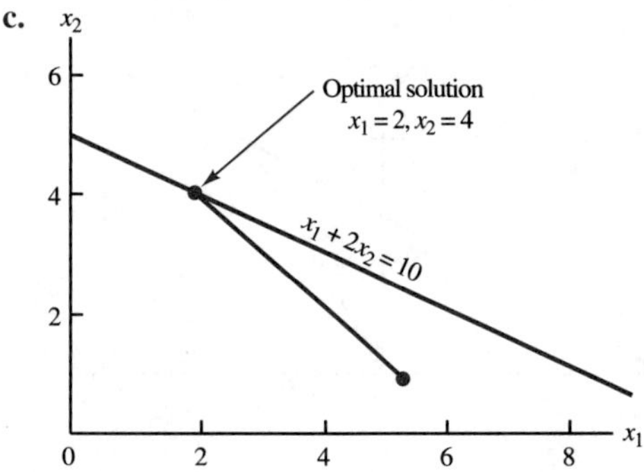

16. a. $3S + 9D$

b. (0,540)

c. 90, 150, 348, 0

17. Max $5x_1 + 2x_2 + 8x_3 + 0s_1 + 0s_2 + 0s_3$

s.t.

$$\begin{aligned} 1x_1 - 2x_2 + 0.5x_3 + 1s_1 \qquad\qquad &= 420 \\ 2x_1 + 3x_2 - 1x_3 \qquad + 1s_2 \qquad &= 610 \\ 6x_1 - 1x_2 + 3x_3 \qquad\qquad + 1s_3 &= 125 \\ x_1, x_2, x_3, s_1, s_2, s_3 &\ge 0 \end{aligned}$$

18. b. $x_1 = 18/7, x_2 = 15/7$

c. 0, 0, 4/7

20. a. Max $2400E + 1800L$

s.t.

$$\begin{aligned} 6E + 3L &\le 2100 \\ 1L &\le 280 \\ 2E + 2.5L &\le 1000 \\ E, L &\ge 0 \end{aligned}$$

b. $E = 250, L = 200$, \$960,000

c. Engine manufacturing time and assembly/testing time

22. a. Let R = number of units of regular model

C = number of units of catcher's model

Max $5R + 8C$

$1R + \frac{3}{2}C \le 900$ Cutting and sewing

$\frac{1}{2}R + \frac{1}{3}C \le 300$ Finishing

$\frac{1}{8}R + \frac{1}{4}C \le 100$ Packaging and shipping

$R, C \ge 0$

b.

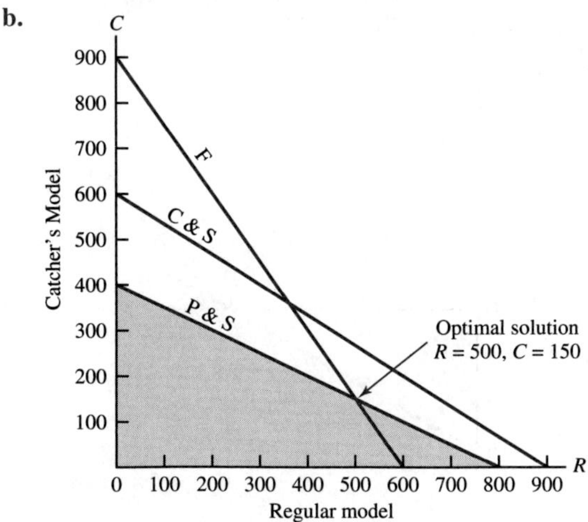

c. 5(500) + 8(150) = \$3,700

d. C & S $1(500) + \frac{3}{2}(150) = 725$

F $\frac{1}{2}(500) + \frac{1}{3}(150) = 300$

P & S $\frac{1}{8}(500) + \frac{1}{4}(150) = 100$

e.

Department	Capacity	Usage	Slack
Cutting and sewing	900	725	175 hours
Finishing	300	300	0 hours
Packaging and shipping	100	100	0 hours

24. a. Max $50N + 80R$

s.t.

$$\begin{aligned} N + R &= 1000 \\ N &\ge 250 \\ R &\ge 250 \\ N - 2R &\ge 0 \\ N, R &\ge 0 \end{aligned}$$

b. $N = 666.67, R = 333.33$; Audience exposure = 60,000

26. a. Max $1W + 1.25M$

s.t.

$$\begin{aligned} 5W + 7M &\le 4480 \\ 3W + 1M &\le 2080 \\ 2W + 2M &\le 1600 \\ W, M &\ge 0 \end{aligned}$$

b. $W = 560, M = 240$; Profit = 860

28. a. Max $15E + 18C$

s.t.

$$\begin{aligned} 40E + 25C &\leq 50{,}000 \\ 40E \quad &\geq 15{,}000 \\ 25C &\geq 10{,}000 \\ 25C &\leq 25{,}000 \\ E, C &\geq 0 \end{aligned}$$

c. (375, 400); (1000, 400); (625, 1000); (375, 1000)

d. $E = 625$, $C = 1000$

Total return = $27,375

29.

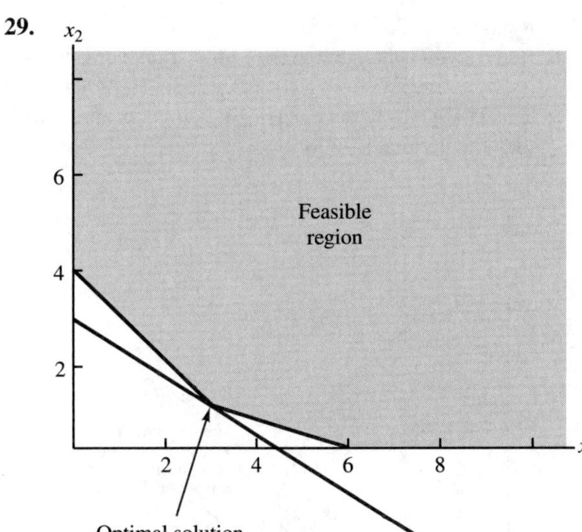

Objective function value = 13

30.

Extreme Points	Objective Function Value	Surplus Demand	Surplus Total Production	Slack Processing Time
(250, 100)	800	125	—	—
(125, 225)	925	—	—	125
(125, 350)	1300	—	125	—

32. a.

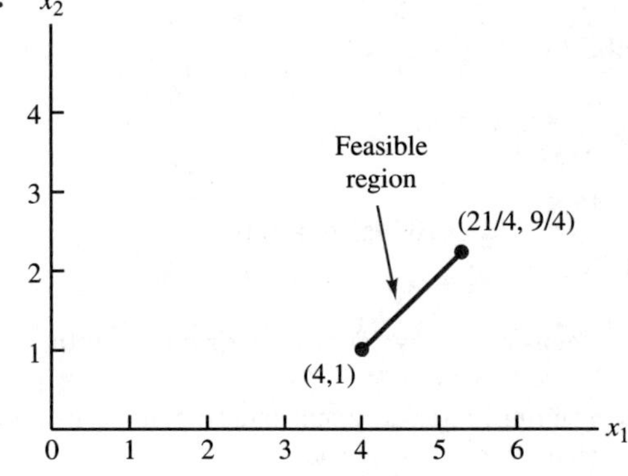

b. The two extreme points are

$(x_1 = 4, x_2 = 1)$ and $(x_1 = 21/4, x_2 = 9/4)$

c. The optimal solution [see part (a)] is $x_1 = 4$, $x_2 = 1$

33. a. Min $6x_1 + 4x_2 + 0s_1 + 0s_2 + 0s_3$

s.t.

$$\begin{aligned} 2x_1 + 1x_2 - s_1 \quad &= 12 \\ 1x_1 + 1x_2 \quad - s_2 \quad &= 10 \\ 1x_2 \quad + s_3 &= 4 \\ x_1, x_2, s_1, s_2, s_3 &\geq 0 \end{aligned}$$

b. The optimal solution is $x_1 = 6$, $x_2 = 4$

c. $s_1 = 4$, $s_2 = 0$, $s_3 = 0$

34. a. Min $10{,}000T + 8{,}000P$

s.t.

$$\begin{aligned} T \quad &\geq 8 \\ P &\geq 10 \\ T + \quad P &\geq 25 \\ 3T + \quad 2P &\leq 84 \end{aligned}$$

c. (15, 10); (21.33, 10); (8, 30); (8, 17)

d. $T = 8$, $P = 17$

Total cost = $216,000

36. a. Min $7.50S + 9.00P$

s.t.

$$\begin{aligned} 0.10S + 0.30P &\geq 6 \\ 0.06S + 0.12P &\leq 3 \\ S + \quad P &= 30 \\ S, P &\geq 0 \end{aligned}$$

c. Optimal solution is $S = 15$, $P = 15$

d. No

e. Yes

38. $P_1 = 30$, $P_2 = 25$, Cost = $55

40.

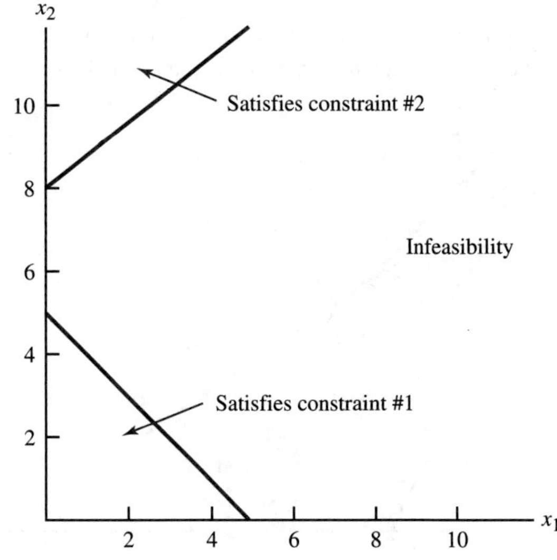

41.

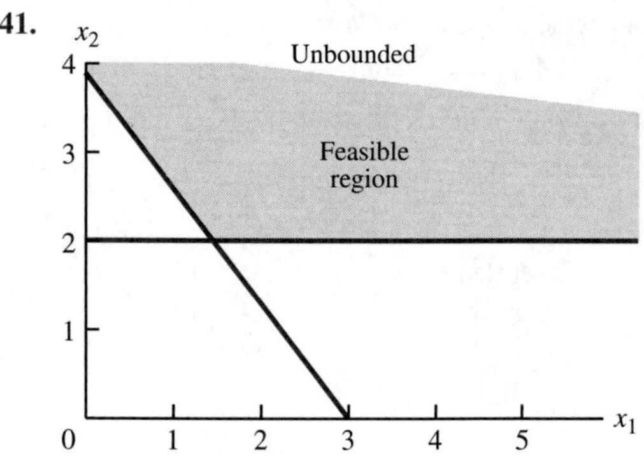

42. a. $x_1 = 30/16$, $x_2 = 30/16$; Value of optimal solution $= 60/16$
b. $x_1 = 0$, $x_2 = 3$; Value of optimal solution $= 6$

44. a. 180, 20
b. Alternative optimal solutions
c. 120, 80

46. No feasible solution; several possible actions can be taken, such as reduce total production to $A = 125$ and $B = 350$

48. a. No feasible solution
b. Need an additional 1.5 tons of material 3

50. $M = 65.45$, $R = 261.82$; Profit = \$45,818

52. $S = 384$, $O = 80$

54. a. Max $160M_1 + 345M_2$

s.t.

$$\begin{aligned} M_1 \quad &\leq 15 \\ M_2 &\leq 10 \\ M_1 \quad &\geq 5 \\ M_2 &\geq 5 \\ 40M_1 + 50M_2 &\leq 1000 \\ M_1, M_2 &\geq 0 \end{aligned}$$

b. $M_1 = 12.5$, $M_2 = 10$

Chapter 3

2. New optimal solution is $F = 100/3$ and $S = 40/3$
Dual price for the material 3 constraint is \$44.44

3. a.

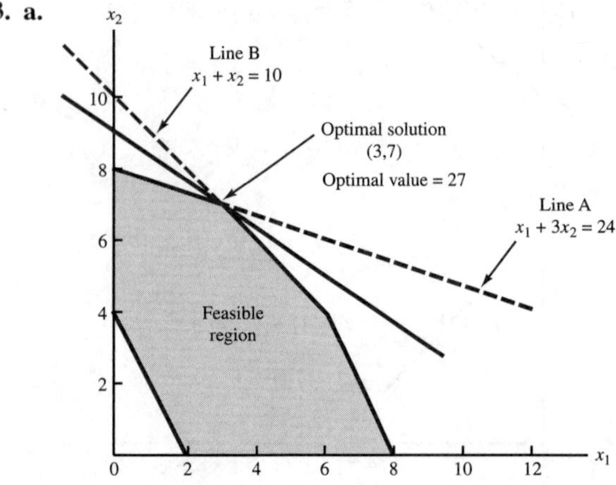

b. Slope of line B $= -1$
Slope of line A $= -1/3$
Let C_1 = objective function coefficient of x_1
C_2 = objective function coefficient of x_2
$-1 \leq -C_1/3 \leq -1/3$
$1 \geq C_1/3 \quad C_1/3 \geq 1/3$
$C_1 \leq 3 \quad C_1 \geq 1$
Range: $1 \leq C_1 \leq 3$

c. $-1 \leq -2/C_2 \leq -1/3$
$1 \geq 2/C_2 \quad 2/C_2 \geq 1/3$
$C_2 \geq 2 \quad C_2 \leq 6$
Range: $2 \leq C_2 \leq 6$

d. Because this change leaves C_1 in its range of optimality, the same solution ($x_1 = 3$, $x_2 = 7$) is optimal

e. This change moves C_2 outside its range of optimality; the new optimal solution is

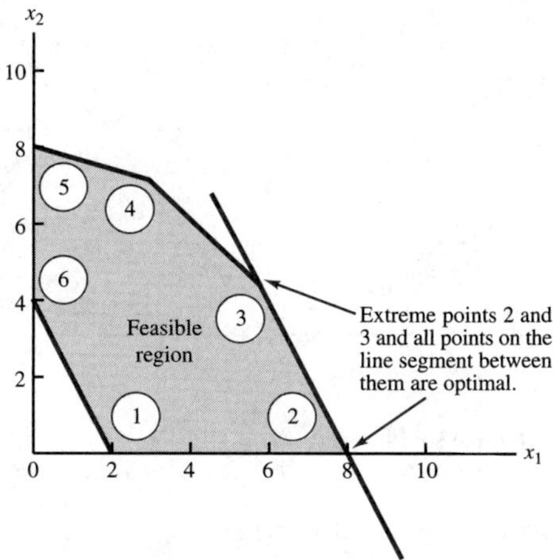

Alternative optimal solutions exist; extreme points 2 and 3 and all points on the line segment between them are optimal

4. By making a small increase in the right-hand side of constraint 1 and resolving, we find a dual price of 1.5 for the constraint, which means the objective function will improve at the rate of 1.5 per unit increase in the right-hand side; because constraint 2 is not binding, its dual price is zero

6. -0.333, -0.333, 0

8. a. $x_1 = 9$, $x_2 = 4$
b. 0, 0.0769

10. a. $x_1 = 0$, $x_2 = 10$, Value $= 100$
b. No change

11. a. Regular glove = 500; Catcher's mitt = 150; Value = 3700
b. The finishing, packaging, and shipping constraints are binding; there is no slack

c. Cutting and sewing = 0
Finishing = 3
Packaging and shipping = 28
Additional finishing time is worth $3 per unit, and additional packaging and shipping time is worth $28 per unit

d. In the packaging and shipping department, each additional hour is worth $28

12. a. 4 to 12
3.33 to 10

b. As long as the profit contribution for the regular glove is between $4.00 and $12.00, the current solution is optimal. As long as the profit contribution for the catcher's mitt stays between $3.33 and $10.00, the current solution is optimal. The optimal solution is not sensitive to small changes in the profit contributions for the gloves

c. The dual prices for the resources are applicable over the following ranges:

Constraint	Right-Hand-Side Range
Cutting and sewing	725 to No Upper Limit
Finishing	133.33 to 400
Packaging and shipping	75 to 135

d. Amount of increase = (28)(20) = $560

14. a. More than $7.00
b. More than $3.50
c. None

16. a. S = 4000, M = 10,000, Total risk = 62,000

b.

Variable	Range of Optimality
S	3.75 to No Upper Limit
M	No Lower Limit to 6.4

c. 5(4000) + 4(10,000) = $60,000
d. 60,000/1,200,000 = 0.05 or 5%
e. 0.057 risk units
f. 0.057(100) = 5.7%

18. a. $E = 80$, $S = 120$, $D = 0$
Profit = $16,440
b. Fan motors and cooling coils
c. Labor hours; 320 hours available
d. Objective function coefficient range of optimality

No Lower Limit to 159

Since $150 is in this range, the optimal solution would not change

19. a. Range of optimality

E 47.5 to 75
S 87 to 126
D No Lower Limit to 159

b.

Model	Profit	Change	Allowable Increase/Decrease	%
E	$ 63	Increase $6(100)	$75 − $63 = $12	$\frac{6}{12}(100) = 50$
S	$ 95	Decrease $2	$95 − $87 = $8	$\frac{2}{8}(100) = 25$
D	$135	Increase $4	$159 − $135 = $24	$\frac{4}{24}(100) = 17$
				92

Because changes are 92% of allowable changes, the optimal solution of $E = 80$, $S = 120$, $D = 0$ will not change

The change in total profit will be

E 80 units @ +$6 = $480
S 120 units @ −$2 = −240
$240

∴ Profit = $16,440 + $240 = $16,680

c. Range of feasibility

Constraint 1 160 to 280
Constraint 2 200 to 400
Constraint 3 2080 to No Upper Limit

d. Yes, Fan motors = 200 + 100 = 300 is outside the range of feasibility; the dual price will change

20. a. Manufacture 100 cases of A and 60 cases of B, and purchase 90 cases of B; Total cost = $2170
b. Demand for A, demand for B, assembly time
c. −12.25, −9.0, 0, .375
d. Assembly time constraint

22. a. 100 suits, 150 sport coats
Profit = $40,900
40 hours of cutting overtime
b. Optimal solution will not change
c. Consider ordering additional material
$34.50 is the maximum price
d. Profit will improve by $875

24. a. Max $0.07H + 0.12P + 0.09A$
s.t.

$$H + P + A = 1{,}000{,}000$$
$$0.6H - 0.4P - 0.4A \geq 0$$
$$P - 0.6A \leq 0$$
$$H, P, A \geq 0$$

b. H = $400,000, P = $225,000, A = $375,000
Total annual return = $88,750
Annual percentage return = 8.875%
c. No change
d. Increase of $890
e. Increase of $312.50 or 0.031%

26. a. Min $30L + 25D + 18S$

s.t.

$$\begin{aligned} L + D + S &= 100 \\ 0.6L - 0.4D &\geq 0 \\ -0.15L - 0.15D + 0.85S &\geq 0 \\ -0.25L - 0.25D + S &\leq 0 \\ L &\leq 50 \\ L, D, S &\geq 0 \end{aligned}$$

b. $L = 48, D = 72, S = 30$
Total cost = \$3780

c. No change

d. No change

28. a. 333.3, 0, 833.3; Risk = 14,666.7; Return = 18,000 or 9%

b. 1000, 0, 0, 2500; Risk = 18,000; Return = 22,000 or 11%

c. \$4000

30. a. Let M_1 = units of component 1 manufactured
M_2 = units of component 2 manufactured
M_3 = units of component 3 manufactured
P_1 = units of component 1 purchased
P_2 = units of component 2 purchased
P_3 = units of component 3 purchased

Min $4.50M_1 + 5.00M_2 + 2.75M_3 + 6.50P_1 + 8.80P_2 + 7.00P_3$

s.t.

$$\begin{aligned} 2M_1 + 3M_2 + 4M_3 &\leq 21{,}600 && \text{Production} \\ 1M_1 + 1.5M_2 + 3M_3 &\leq 15{,}000 && \text{Assembly} \\ 1.5M_1 + 2M_2 + 5M_3 &\leq 18{,}000 && \text{Testing/Packaging} \\ 1M_1 + 1P_1 &= 6{,}000 && \text{Component 1} \\ 1M_2 + 1P_2 &= 4{,}000 && \text{Component 2} \\ 1M_3 + 1P_3 &= 3{,}500 && \text{Component 3} \\ M_1, M_2, M_3, P_1, P_2, P_3 &\geq 0 \end{aligned}$$

b.

Source	Component 1	Component 2	Component 3
Manufacture	2000	4000	1400
Purchase	4000		2100

Total Cost \$73,550

c. Production: \$54.36 per hour
Testing & Packaging: \$ 7.50 per hour

d. Dual prices = −\$7.969; it would cost Benson \$7.969 to add a unit of component 2

32. b. $G = 120{,}000$; $S = 30{,}000$; $M = 150{,}000$

c. 0.15 to 0.60; No Lower Limit to 0.122; 0.02 to 0.20

d. 4668

e. $G = 48{,}000$; $S = 192{,}000$; $M = 60{,}000$

f. The client's risk index and the amount of funds available

34. a. $L = 3, N = 7, W = 5, S = 5$

b. Each additional minute of broadcast time increases cost by \$100

c. If local coverage is increased by 1 minute, total cost will increase by \$100

d. If the time devoted to local and national news is increased by 1 minute, total cost will increase by \$100

e. Increasing the sports by 1 minute will have no effect because the dual price is 0

Chapter 4

1. a. Let T = number of television advertisements
R = number of radio advertisements
N = number of newspaper advertisements

Max $100{,}000T + 18{,}000R + 40{,}000N$

s.t.

$$\begin{aligned} 2000T + 300R + 600N &\leq 18{,}200 && \text{Budget} \\ T &\leq 10 && \text{Max TV} \\ R &\leq 20 && \text{Max radio} \\ N &\leq 10 && \text{Max news} \\ -0.5T + 0.5R - 0.5N &\leq 0 && \text{Max 50\% radio} \\ 0.9T - 0.1R - 0.1N &\geq 0 && \text{Min 10\% TV} \\ T, R, N &\geq 0 \end{aligned}$$

Solution:		Budget \$
	$T = 4$	\$ 8000
	$R = 14$	4200
	$N = 10$	6000
		\$18,200

Audience = 1,052,000

b. The dual price for the budget constraint is 51.30; thus, a \$100 increase in the budget should provide an increase in audience coverage of approximately 5130. The right-hand-side range for the budget constraint will show that this interpretation is correct

2. a. $x_1 = 77.89, x_2 = 63.16$, \$3284.21

b. Department A \$15.79; Department B \$47.37

c. $x_1 = 87.21, x_2 = 65.12$, \$3341.34
Department A 10 hours; Department B 3.2 hours

4. a. $x_1 = 500, x_2 = 300, x_3 = 200$, \$550

b. \$0.55

c. Aroma, 75; Taste, 84.4

d. −\$0.60

6. 50 units of product 1; 0 units of product 2; 300 hours department A; 600 hours department B

8. Schedule 19 officers as follows:
3 begin at 8:00 A.M.; 3 begin at noon; 7 begin at 4:00 P.M.; 4 begin at midnight; 2 begin at 4:00 A.M.

9. a. Decision variables A, P, M, H, and G represent the fraction or proportion of the total investment in each alternative

$$\begin{aligned}
\text{Max} \quad & 0.073A + 0.103P + 0.064M + 0.075H + 0.045G \\
\text{s.t.} \quad & \\
& A + P + M + H + G = 1 \\
& 0.5A + 0.5P - 0.5M - 0.5H \leq 0 \\
& -0.5A - 0.5P + 0.5M + 0.5H \leq 0 \\
& -0.25M - 0.25H + G \geq 0 \\
& -0.6A + 0.4P \leq 0 \\
& A, P, M, H, G \geq 0
\end{aligned}$$

Objective function = 0.079; $A = 0.178$; $P = 0.267$; $M = 0.000$; $H = 0.444$; $G = 0.111$

b. Multiplying A, P, M, H, and G by the $100,000 invested provides the following

Atlantic Oil	$ 17,800
Pacific Oil	26,700
Huber Steel	44,400
Government bonds	11,100
	$100,000

c. 0.079($100,000) = $7900

d. The marginal rate of return is 0.079

10. a. 40.9%, 14.5%, 14.5%, 30.0%
Annual return = 5.4%

b. 0.0%, 36.0%, 36.0%, 28.0%
Annual return = 2.52%

c. 75.0%, 0.0%, 15.0%, 10.0%
Annual return = 8.2%

b. Yes

12.

Week	Buy	Sell	Store
1	80,000	0	100,000
2	0	0	100,000
3	0	100,000	0
4	25,000	0	25,000

14. b.

Quarter	Production	Ending Inventory
1	4000	2100
2	3000	1100
3	2000	100
4	1900	500

15. Let x_{11} = gallons of crude 1 used to produce regular
x_{12} = gallons of crude 1 used to produce high octane
x_{21} = gallons of crude 2 used to produce regular
x_{22} = gallons of crude 2 used to produce high octane

$$\begin{aligned}
\text{Min} \quad & 0.10x_{11} + 0.10x_{12} + 0.15x_{21} + 0.15x_{22} \\
\text{s.t.} \quad &
\end{aligned}$$

Each gallon of regular must have at least 40% A

$$\begin{aligned}
x_{11} + x_{21} &= \text{amount of regular produced} \\
0.4(x_{11} + x_{21}) &= \text{amount of A required for regular} \\
0.2x_{11} + 0.50x_{21} &= \text{amount of A in } (x_{11} + x_{21}) \text{ gallons of regular gas} \\
\therefore 0.2x_{11} + 0.50x_{21} &\geq 0.4x_{11} + 0.40x_{21} \\
\therefore -0.2x_{11} + 0.10x_{21} &\geq 0
\end{aligned}$$

Each gallon of high octane can have at most 50% B

$$\begin{aligned}
x_{12} + x_{22} &= \text{amount high octane} \\
0.5(x_{12} + x_{22}) &= \text{amount of B required for high octane} \\
0.60x_{12} + 0.30x_{22} &= \text{amount of B in } (x_{12} + x_{22}) \text{ gallons of high octane} \\
\therefore 0.60x_{12} + 0.30x_{22} &\leq 0.5x_{12} + 0.5x_{22} \\
\therefore 0.1x_{12} - 0.2x_{22} &\leq 0 \\
x_{11} + x_{21} &\geq 800{,}000 \\
x_{12} + x_{22} &\geq 500{,}000 \\
x_{11}, x_{12}, x_{21}, x_{22} &\geq 0
\end{aligned}$$

Optimal solution: $x_{11} = 266{,}667$, $x_{12} = 333{,}333$, $x_{21} = 533{,}333$, $x_{22} = 166{,}667$
Cost = $165,000

16. x_i = number of 10-inch rolls processed by cutting alternative i

a. $x_1 = 0$, $x_2 = 125$, $x_3 = 500$, $x_4 = 1500$, $x_5 = 0$, $x_6 = 0$, $x_7 = 0$; 2125 rolls with waste of 750 inches

b. 2500 rolls with no waste; however, 1½-inch size is overproduced by 3000 units

18. a. 5 Super, 2 Regular, and 3 Econo-Tankers
Total cost $583,000; monthly operating cost $4650

19. a. Let x_{11} = amount of men's model in month 1
x_{21} = amount of women's model in month 1
x_{12} = amount of men's model in month 2
x_{22} = amount of women's model in month 2
s_{11} = inventory of men's model at end of month 1
s_{21} = inventory of women's model at end of month 1
s_{12} = inventory of men's model at end of month 2
s_{22} = inventory of women's model at end of month 2

$$\begin{aligned}
\text{Min} \quad & 120x_{11} + 90x_{21} + 120x_{12} + 90x_{22} + 2.4s_{11} + 1.8s_{21} + 2.4s_{12} + 1.8s_{22} \\
\text{s.t.} \quad & \\
& \left.\begin{aligned} x_{11} - s_{11} &= 130 \\ x_{21} - s_{21} &= 95 \\ s_{11} + x_{12} - s_{12} &= 200 \\ s_{21} + x_{22} - s_{22} &= 150 \end{aligned}\right\} \text{Satisfy demand} \\
& \left.\begin{aligned} s_{12} &\geq 25 \\ s_{22} &\geq 25 \end{aligned}\right\} \text{Ending inventory requirement}
\end{aligned}$$

Labor-hours: Men's 2.0 + 1.5 = 3.5
Women's 1.6 + 1.0 = 2.6

$$\left.\begin{aligned}
3.5x_{11} + 2.6x_{21} &\geq 900 \\
3.5x_{11} + 2.6x_{21} &\leq 1100 \\
3.5x_{11} + 2.6x_{21} - 3.5x_{12} - 2.6x_{22} &\leq 100 \\
-3.5x_{11} - 2.6x_{21} + 3.5x_{12} + 2.6x_{22} &\leq 100
\end{aligned}\right\} \text{Labor smoothing}$$

$$x_{11}, x_{12}, x_{21}, x_{22}, s_{11}, s_{12}, s_{21}, s_{22} \geq 0$$

Solution: $x_{11} = 193$; $x_{21} = 95$; $x_{12} = 162$; $x_{22} = 175$
Total cost = \$67,156
Inventory levels: $s_{11} = 63$; $s_{12} = 25$; $s_{21} = 0$; $s_{22} = 25$
Labor levels: Previous 1000 hours
Month 1 922.25 hours
Month 2 1022.25 hours

b. To accommodate the new policy, the right-hand sides of the four labor-smoothing constraints must be changed to 950, 1050, 50, and 50, respectively; the new total cost is \$67,175

20. Produce 10,250 units in March, 10,250 units in April, and 12,000 units in May

22. 5, 515, 887 sq. in. of waste
Machine 3: 492 minutes

24. Investment strategy: 45.8% of A and 100% of B
Objective function = \$4340.40
Savings/Loan Schedule

	Period			
	1	2	3	4
Savings	242.11	—	—	341.04
Funds from loan	—	200.00	127.58	—

26. b. Solution does not indicate that General Hospital is relatively inefficient
c. General Hospital

28. c. No; E = 1 indicates that all the resources used by Hospital E are required to produce the outputs of Hospital E
d. Hospital E

30. a. Newark
b. Five ODIFs change: $PMQ = 23$; $POQ = 43$; $NMQ = 56$; $CMQ = 32$; and $COQ = 46$; the allocations for the other ODIFs remain the same as in the original solution
c. Four ODIFs change: $POQ = 45$; $NMQ = 56$; $CMQ = 37$; and $COQ = 44$; the allocations for the other ODIFs remain the same as in the original solution
d. *COY*, with a bid price of \$443

32. c.

Type	Value
Convention/two-night package	36
Convention/Friday only	12
Convention/Saturday only	15
Regular/Two-night package	20
Regular/Friday only	28
Regular/Saturday only	25

d. \$50

Chapter 5

1. a. With $x_1 = 0$, we have

$$x_2 = 6 \quad (1)$$
$$4x_2 + x_3 = 12 \quad (2)$$

From (1), we have $x_2 = 6$; substituting for x_2 in (2) yields

$$4(6) + x_3 = 12$$
$$x_3 = 12 - 24 = -12$$

Basic solution: $x_1 = 0, x_2 = 6, x_3 = -12$

b. With $x_2 = 0$, we have

$$3x_1 = 6 \quad (3)$$
$$2x_1 + x_3 = 12 \quad (4)$$

From (3), we find $x_1 = 2$; substituting for x_1 in (4) yields

$$2(2) + x_3 = 12$$
$$x_3 = 12 - 4 = 8$$

Basic solution: $x_1 = 2, x_2 = 0, x_3 = 8$

c. With $x_3 = 0$, we have

$$3x_1 + x_2 = 6 \quad (5)$$
$$2x_1 + 4x_2 = 12 \quad (6)$$

Multiplying (6) by $3/2$ and subtracting from (5) yields

$$3x_1 + x_2 = 6$$
$$-(3x_1 + 6x_2) = -18$$
$$-5x_2 = -12$$
$$x_2 = 12/5$$

Substituting $x_2 = 12/5$ into (5) yields

$$3x_1 + 12/5 = 6$$
$$3x_1 = 18/5$$
$$x_1 = 6/5$$

Basic solution: $x_1 = 6/5, x_2 = 12/5, x_3 = 0$

d. The basic solutions found in parts (b) and (c) are basic feasible solutions. The one in part (a) is not because $x_3 = -12$.

2. a. Max $x_1 + 2x_2$
s.t.

$$x_1 + 5x_2 + s_1 = 10$$
$$2x_1 + 6x_2 + s_2 = 16$$
$$x_1, x_2, s_1, s_2 \geq 0$$

b. 2

c. $x_1 = 0, x_2 = 0, s_1 = 10, s_2 = 16$; feasible
$x_1 = 0, x_2 = 2, s_1 = 0, s_2 = 4$; feasible
$x_1 = 0, x_2 = 8/3, s_1 = -10/3, s_2 = 0$; not feasible
$x_1 = 10, x_2 = 0, s_1 = 0, s_2 = -4$; not feasible
$x_1 = 8, x_2 = 0, s_1 = 2, s_2 = 0$; feasible
$x_1 = 5, x_2 = 1, s_1 = 0, s_2 = 0$; feasible

d. $x_1 = 8, x_2 = 0$; Value = 8

4. a. Standard form:

$$\begin{aligned} \text{Max} \quad & 60x_1 + 90x_2 \\ \text{s.t.} \quad & \\ & 15x_1 + 45x_2 + s_1 = 90 \\ & 5x_1 + 5x_2 + s_2 = 20 \\ & x_1, x_2, s_1, s_2 \geq 0 \end{aligned}$$

b. Partial initial simple tableau:

x_1	x_2	s_1	s_2	
60	90	0	0	
15	45	1	0	**90**
5	5	0	1	**20**

5. a. Initial tableau:

		x_1	x_2	s_1	s_2	
Basis	c_B	5	9	0	0	
s_1	0	10	9	1	0	**90**
s_2	0	−5	3	0	1	**15**
z_j		0	0	0	0	**0**
$c_j - z_j$		5	9	0	0	

b. Introduce x_2 at the first iteration

c.

$$\begin{aligned} \text{Max} \quad & 5x_1 + 9x_2 \\ \text{s.t.} \quad & \\ & 10x_1 + 9x_2 \leq 90 \\ & -5x_1 + 3x_2 \leq 15 \\ & x_1, x_2 \geq 0 \end{aligned}$$

6. a.

z_j	0	0	0	0	0	0	**0**
$c_j - z_j$	5	20	25	0	0	0	

b.

$$\begin{aligned} \text{Max} \quad & 5x_1 + 20x_2 + 25x_3 + 0s_1 + 0s_2 + 0s_3 \\ \text{s.t.} \quad & \\ & 2x_1 + 1x_2 + 1s_1 = 40 \\ & 2x_2 + 1x_3 + 1s_2 = 30 \\ & 3x_1 - \tfrac{1}{2}x_3 + 1s_3 = 15 \\ & x_1, x_2, x_3, s_1, s_2, s_3 \geq 0 \end{aligned}$$

c. s_1, s_2, s_3; it is the origin
d. 0
e. x_3 enters, s_2 leaves
f. 30, 750
g. $x_1 = 10, s_1 = 20$
$x_2 = 0, s_2 = 0$, Value = 800
$x_3 = 30, s_3 = 0$

8. a. $x_1 = 540, x_2 = 252$
b. \$7668
c. 630, 480, 708, 117
d. 0, 120, 0, 18

10. $x_2 = 250, x_3 = 150, s_2 = 4000$
Value = 4850

12. A = 0, B = 0, C = 33⅓; Profit = 500

14. a. $x_1 = 0, x_2 = 50, x_3 = 75$; Profit = \$210
c. Grade B grapes and labor

15.

$$\begin{aligned} \text{Max} \quad & 4x_1 + 2x_2 - 3x_3 + 5x_4 + 0s_1 - Ma_1 + 0s_2 - Ma_3 \\ \text{s.t.} \quad & \\ & 2x_1 - 1x_2 + 1x_3 + 2x_4 - 1s_1 + 1a_1 = 50 \\ & 3x_1 - 1x_3 + 2x_4 + 1s_2 = 80 \\ & 1x_1 + 1x_2 + 1x_4 + 1a_3 = 60 \\ & x_1, x_2, x_3, x_4, s_1, s_2, a_1, a_3 \geq 0 \end{aligned}$$

16.

$$\begin{aligned} \text{Max} \quad & -4x_1 - 5x_2 - 3x_3 + 0s_1 + 0s_2 + 0s_4 - Ma_1 - Ma_2 - Ma_3 \\ \text{s.t.} \quad & \\ & 4x_1 + 2x_3 - 1s_1 + 1a_1 = 20 \\ & -1x_2 + 1x_3 - 1s_2 + 1a_2 = 8 \\ & -1x_1 + 2x_2 + 1a_3 = 5 \\ & 2x_1 + 1x_2 + 1x_3 + 1s_4 = 12 \\ & x_1, x_2, x_3, s_1, s_2, s_4, a_1, a_2, a_3 \geq 0 \end{aligned}$$

17. Converting to a max problem and solving using the simplex method, the final simplex tableau is

		x_1	x_2	x_3	s_1	s_2	
Basis	c_B	−3	−4	−8	0	0	
x_1	−3	1	0	−1	−¼	⅛	**1**
x_2	−4	0	1	2	0	−¼	**4**
z_j		−3	−4	−5	¾	⅝	**−19**
$c_j - z_j$		0	0	−3	−¾	−⅝	

18. $x_2 = 60, x_3 = 60, s_3 = 20$; Value = 2040

20. 2400 boxes of 33 gallon bags
Profit = \$480

22. $x_1 = 480, x_4 = 480, x_6 = 800$; Value = 46,400

23. Final simplex tableau:

		x_1	x_2	s_1	s_2	a_2	
Basis	c_B	4	8	0	0	$-M$	
x_2	8	1	1	½	0	0	**5**
a_2	$-M$	−2	0	−½	−1	1	**3**
z_j		$8 + 2M$	8	$4 + M/2$	$+M$	$-M$	$\mathbf{40 - 3M}$
$c_j - z_j$		$-4 - 2M$	0	$-4 - M/2$	$-M$	0	

Infeasible; optimal solution condition is reached with the artificial variable a_2 still in the solution

24. Alternative optimal solutions:

		x_1	x_2	s_1	s_2	s_3	
Basis	c_B	−3	−3	0	0	0	
s_2	0	0	0	−4/3	1	1/6	**4**
x_1	−3	1	0	−2/3	0	1/12	**4**
x_2	−3	0	1	2/3	0	−1/3	**4**
z_j		−3	−3	0	0	¾	**−24**
$c_j - z_j$		0	0	0	0	−¾	

↑ (under s_1) Indicates alternative optimal solutions exist:
$x_1 = 4, x_2 = 4, z = 24$
$x_1 = 8, x_2 = 0, z = 24$

25. Unbounded solution:

Basis	c_B	x_1	x_2	s_1	s_2	s_3	
		1	1	0	0	0	
s_3	0	$8/3$	0	$-1/3$	0	1	**4**
s_2	0	4	0	-1	1	0	**36**
x_2	1	$4/3$	1	$-1/6$	0	0	**4**
z_j		$4/3$	1	$-1/6$	0	0	**4**
$c_j - z_j$		$-1/3$	0	$1/6$	0	0	

↑ Incoming column (under s_1)

26. Alternative optimal solution: $x_1 = 4, x_2 = 0, x_3 = 0$
$x_1 = 0, x_2 = 0, x_3 = 8$

28. Infeasible

30. a. Infeasible solution; not enough sewing time
b. Alternative optimal solutions: $x_1 = 1000, x_2 = 0, x_3 = 250$ or $x_1 = 1000, x_2 = 200, x_3 = 0$
Profit = \$4000

Chapter 6

1. a. Recomputing the $c_j - z_j$ values for the nonbasic variables with c_1 as the coefficient of x_1 leads to the following inequalities that must be satisfied:
For x_2, we get no inequality because of the zero in the x_2 column for the row in which x_1 is a basic variable
For s_1, we get

$$0 + 4 - c_1 \le 0$$
$$c_1 \ge 4$$

For s_2, we get

$$0 - 12 + 2c_1 \le 0$$
$$2c_1 \le 12$$
$$c_1 \le 6$$
$$\text{Range: } 4 \le c_1 \le 6$$

b. Because x_2 is nonbasic, we have

$$c_2 \le 8$$

c. Because s_1 is nonbasic, we have

$$c_{s_1} \le 1$$

2. a. $31.25 \le c_2 \le 83.33$
b. $-43.33 \le c_{s_2} \le 8.75$
c. $c_{s_3} \le 26/5$
d. Variables do not change; Value = \$1920

3. a. It is the z_j value for s_1; dual price = 1
b. It is the z_j value for s_2; dual price = 2
c. It is the z_j value for s_3; dual price = 0
d.
$$s_3 = 80 + 5(-2) = 70$$
$$x_3 = 30 + 5(-1) = 25$$
$$x_1 = 20 + 5(1) = 25$$
$$\text{Value} = 220 + 5(1) = 225$$

e.
$$s_3 = 80 - 10(-2) = 100$$
$$x_3 = 30 - 10(-1) = 40$$
$$x_1 = 20 - 10(1) = 10$$
$$\text{Value} = 220 - 10(1) = 210$$

4. a.
$$80 + \Delta b_1(-2) \ge 0 \qquad \Delta b_1 \le 40$$
$$30 + \Delta b_1(-1) \ge 0 \qquad \Delta b_1 \le 30$$
$$20 + \Delta b_1(1) \ge 0 \qquad \Delta b_1 \ge -20$$
$$-20 \le \Delta b_1 \le 30$$
$$100 \le b_1 \le 150$$

b.
$$80 + \Delta b_2(7) \ge 0 \qquad \Delta b_2 \ge -80/7$$
$$30 + \Delta b_2(3) \ge 0 \qquad \Delta b_2 \ge -10$$
$$20 + \Delta b_2(-2) \ge 0 \qquad \Delta b_2 \le 10$$
$$-10 \le \Delta b_2 \le 10$$
$$40 \le b_2 \le 60$$

c.
$$80 - \Delta b_3(1) \ge 0 \rightarrow \Delta b_3 \le 80$$
$$30 - \Delta b_3(0) \ge 0$$
$$20 - \Delta b_3(0) \ge 0$$
$$\Delta b_3 \le 80$$
$$b_3 \le 110$$

6. a. $6.3 \le c_1 \le 13.5$
b. $6\frac{2}{3} \le c_2 \le 14\frac{2}{7}$
c. Variables do not change; Value = \$7164
d. Below $6\frac{2}{3}$ or above $14\frac{2}{7}$
e. $x_1 = 300, x_2 = 420$; Value = \$9300

8. a. $x_1 = 5220/11, x_2 = 3852/11$; Value = 86,868/11
b. No, s_1 would enter the basis

10. a. Increase in profit
b. No

12. a. $14 \le b_1 \le 21\frac{1}{2}$
b. $4 \le b_2$
c. $18\frac{3}{4} \le b_3 \le 30$
d. Dual price = 400/9; Range: $18\frac{3}{4} \le b_3 \le 30$

14. a. $400/3 \le b_1 \le 800$
b. $275 \le b_2$
c. $275/2 \le b_3 \le 625$

16. a. $x_1 = 4000, x_2 = 10{,}000$; Total risk = 62,000
b. Increase it by 2.167 per unit
c. $48{,}000 \le b_2 \le 102{,}000$
d. $x_1 = 5667, x_2 = 9167$; Total risk = 72,833
e. Variables do not change; Total risk = 66,000

17. a. The dual is given by:

$$\text{Min} \quad 550u_1 + 700u_2 + 200u_3$$
s.t.
$$1.5u_1 + 4u_2 + 2u_3 \ge 4$$
$$2u_1 + 1u_2 + 3u_3 \ge 6$$
$$4u_1 + 2u_2 + 1u_3 \ge 3$$
$$3u_1 + 1u_2 + 2u_3 \ge 1$$
$$u_1, u_2, u_3 \ge 0$$

b. Optimal solution: $u_1 = 3/10$; $u_2 = 0$, $u_3 = 54/30$
The z_j values for the four surplus variables of the dual show $x_1 = 0, x_2 = 25, x_3 = 125$, and $x_4 = 0$

c. Because $u_1 = 3/10$, $u_2 = 0$, and $u_3 = 54/30$, machines A and C ($u_j > 0$) are operating at capacity; machine C is the priority machine since each hour is worth 54/30

18. The dual is given by

$$\begin{aligned} \text{Max} \quad & 5u_1 + 5u_2 + 24u_3 \\ \text{s.t.} \quad & \\ & 15u_1 + 4u_2 + 12u_3 \le 2800 \\ & 15u_1 + 8u_2 \le 6000 \\ & u_1 + 8u_3 \le 1200 \\ & u_1, u_2, u_3 \ge 0 \end{aligned}$$

19. The canonical form is

$$\begin{aligned} \text{Max} \quad & 3x_1 + x_2 + 5x_3 + 3x_4 \\ \text{s.t.} \quad & \\ & 3x_1 + 1x_2 + 2x_3 \le 30 \\ & -3x_1 - 1x_2 - 2x_3 \le -30 \\ & -2x_1 - 1x_2 - 3x_3 - x_4 \le -15 \\ & 2x_2 + 3x_4 \le 25 \\ & x_1, x_2, x_3, x_4 \ge 0 \end{aligned}$$

The dual is

$$\begin{aligned} \text{Min} \quad & 30u_1' - 30u_1'' - 15u_2 + 25u_3 \\ \text{s.t.} \quad & \\ & 3u_1' - 3u_1'' - 2u_2 \ge 3 \\ & u_1' - u_1'' - u_2 + 2u_3 \ge 1 \\ & 2u_1' - 2u_1'' - 3u_2 \ge 5 \\ & - u_2 + 3u_3 \ge 3 \\ & u_1', u_1'', u_2, u_3 \ge 0 \end{aligned}$$

20. a.

$$\begin{aligned} \text{Max} \quad & 30u_1 + 20u_2 + 80u_3 \\ \text{s.t.} \quad & \\ & u_1 + u_3 \le 1 \\ & u_2 + 2u_3 \le 1 \\ & u_1, u_2, u_3 \ge 0 \end{aligned}$$

b. $x_1 = 30$, $x_2 = 25$

c. Reduce cost by \$0.50

22. a.

$$\begin{aligned} \text{Max} \quad & 10x_1 + 5x_2 \\ \text{s.t.} \quad & \\ & x_1 \ge 20 \\ & x_2 \ge 20 \\ & x_1 \le 100 \\ & x_2 \le 100 \\ & 3x_1 + x_2 \le 175 \\ & x_1, x_2 \ge 0 \end{aligned}$$

b.

$$\begin{aligned} \text{Min} \quad & -20u_1 - 20u_2 + 100u_3 + 100u_4 + 175u_5 \\ \text{s.t.} \quad & \\ & -u_1 + u_3 + 3u_5 \ge 10 \\ & - u_2 + u_4 + u_5 \ge 5 \\ & u_1, u_2, u_3, u_4, u_5 \ge 0 \end{aligned}$$

Solution: $u_4 = 5/3$, $u_5 = 10/3$

c. $x_1 = 25$, $x_2 = 100$; commission = \$750

24. Check both constraints with $x_1 = 10$, $x_2 = 30$, $x_3 = 15$
Both constraints are satisfied; solution remains optimal

Chapter 7

1.

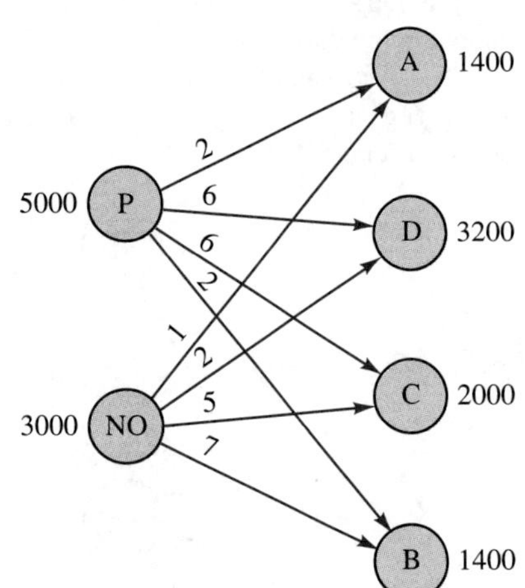

2. a. Let x_{11} = amount shipped from Jefferson City to Des Moines

x_{12} = amount shipped from Jefferson City to Kansas City

.
.
.

x_{23} = amount shipped from Omaha to St. Louis

$$\begin{aligned} \text{Min} \quad & 14x_{11} + 9x_{12} + 7x_{13} + 8x_{21} + 10x_{22} + 5x_{23} \\ \text{s.t.} \quad & \\ & x_{11} + x_{12} + x_{13} \le 30 \\ & x_{21} + x_{22} + x_{23} \le 20 \\ & x_{11} + x_{21} = 25 \\ & x_{12} + x_{22} = 15 \\ & x_{13} + x_{23} = 10 \\ & x_{11}, x_{12}, x_{13}, x_{21}, x_{22}, x_{23} \ge 0 \end{aligned}$$

b.

Optimal Solution	Amount	Cost
Jefferson City–Des Moines	5	70
Jefferson City–Kansas City	15	135
Jefferson City–St. Louis	10	70
Omaha–Des Moines	20	160
	Total	435

4. b. $x_{12} = 300$, $x_{21} = 100$, $x_{22} = 100$, $x_{23} = 300$, $x_{31} = 100$
Cost = 10,400

6. b.

Seattle–Denver	4000	Seattle–Los Angeles	5000
Columbus–Mobile	4000	New York–Pittsburgh	3000
New York–Mobile	1000	New York–Los Angeles	1000
New York–Washington	3000		

Cost = \$150,000

c.

Seattle–Denver	4000	Seattle–Los Angeles	5000
Columbus–Mobile	5000	New York–Pittsburgh	4000
New York–Los Angeles	1000	New York–Washington	3000

Cost actually decreases by \$9000

8. The network model, the linear programming formulation and the optimal solution are shown; note that the third constraint corresponds to the dummy origin; the variables x_{31}, x_{32}, x_{33}, and x_{34} are the amounts shipped out of the dummy origin and do not appear in the objective function since they are given a coefficient of zero

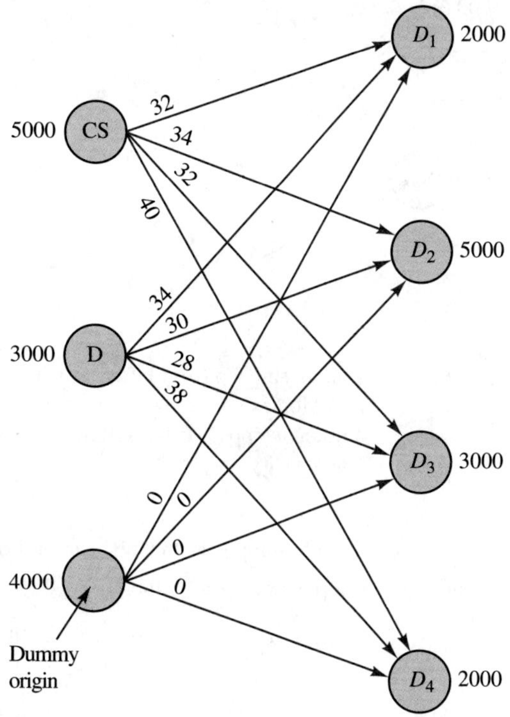

$$
\begin{array}{l}
\text{Max } 32x_{11} + 34x_{12} + 32x_{13} + 40x_{14} + 34x_{21} + 30x_{22} + 28x_{23} + 38x_{24} \\
\text{s.t.} \\
\quad x_{11} + x_{12} + x_{13} + x_{14} \le 5000 \\
\quad x_{21} + x_{22} + x_{23} + x_{24} \le 3000 \\
\quad x_{31} + x_{32} + x_{33} + x_{34} \le 4000 \\
\quad x_{11} + x_{21} + x_{31} = 2000 \\
\quad x_{12} + x_{22} + x_{32} = 5000 \\
\quad x_{13} + x_{23} + x_{33} = 3000 \\
\quad x_{14} + x_{24} + x_{34} = 2000 \\
\quad x_{ij} \ge 0 \quad \text{for all } i, j
\end{array}
$$

Optimal Solution	Units	Cost
Clifton Springs-D_2	4,000	$136,000
Clifton Springs-D_4	1,000	40,000
Danville-D_1	2,000	68,000
Danville-D_4	1,000	38,000
	Total	$282,000

Customer 2 demand has a shortfall of 1000; customer 3 demand of 3000 is not satisfied

10. 1–A 300; 1–C 1200; 2–A 1200; 3–A 500; 3–B 500

12. a.

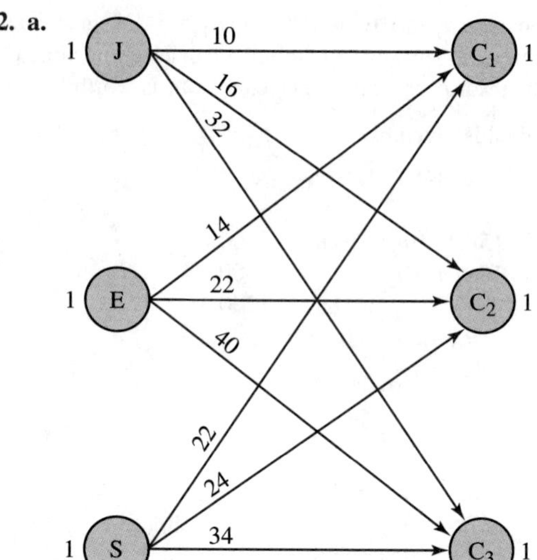

b.

$$
\begin{array}{l}
\text{Min } 10x_{11} + 16x_{12} + 32x_{13} + 14x_{21} + 22x_{22} + 40x_{23} + 22x_{31} + 24x_{32} + 34x_{33} \\
\text{s.t.} \\
\quad x_{11} + x_{12} + x_{13} \le 1 \\
\quad x_{21} + x_{22} + x_{23} \le 1 \\
\quad x_{31} + x_{32} + x_{33} \le 1 \\
\quad x_{11} + x_{21} + x_{31} = 1 \\
\quad x_{12} + x_{22} + x_{32} = 1 \\
\quad x_{13} + x_{23} + x_{33} = 1 \\
\quad x_{ij} \ge 0 \quad \text{for all } i, j
\end{array}
$$

Solution $x_{12} = 1, x_{21} = 1, x_{33} = 1$; total completion time = 64

14. b. Green – 1; Brown – 2; Red – 3; Blue – 4; White – 5
Cost = $16,200

16. b. Toy to 2, Auto Parts to 4, Housewares to 3, Video to 1

18. a. Plano: Kansas City and Dallas
Flagstaff: Los Angeles
Springfield: Chicago, Columbus, and Atlanta
Boulder: Newark and Denver
Cost = $216,000

b. Nashville

c. Columbus is switched from Springfield to Nashville
Cost = $227,000

20. A to MS, B to Ph.D., C to MBA, D to undergrad
Maximum total rating = 13.3

22. a.

	Supplier					
Division	**1**	**2**	**3**	**4**	**5**	**6**
1	614	660	534	680	590	630
2	603	639	702	693	693	630
3	865	830	775	850	900	930
4	532	553	511	581	595	553
5	720	648	684	693	657	747

b. Optimal solution:

Supplier 1–Division 2	\$ 603
Supplier 2–Division 5	648
Supplier 3–Division 3	775
Supplier 5–Division 1	590
Supplier 6–Division 4	553
Total	\$3169

23. a.

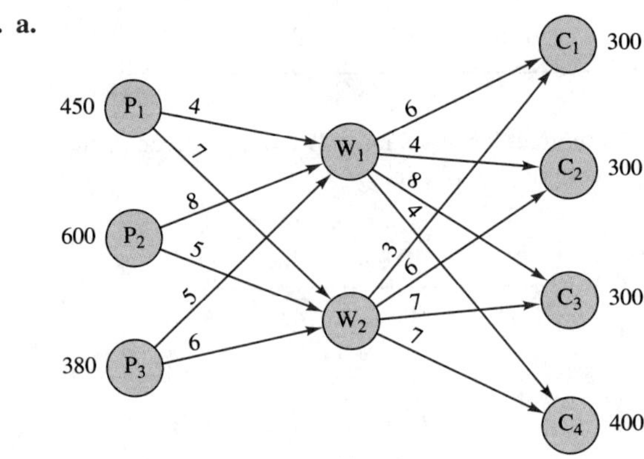

b.

$$\text{Min } 4x_{14}+7x_{15}+8x_{24}+5x_{25}+5x_{34}+6x_{35}+6x_{46}+4x_{47}+8x_{48}+4x_{49}+3x_{56}+6x_{57}+7x_{58}+7x_{59}$$

s.t.

$$\begin{aligned}
x_{14} + x_{15} &\le 450\\
x_{24} + x_{25} &\le 600\\
x_{34} + x_{35} &\le 380\\
-x_{14} - x_{24} - x_{34} + x_{46} + x_{47} + x_{48} + x_{49} &= 0\\
-x_{15} - x_{25} - x_{35} + x_{56} + x_{57} + x_{58} + x_{59} &= 0\\
x_{46} + x_{56} &= 300\\
x_{47} + x_{57} &= 300\\
x_{48} + x_{58} &= 300\\
x_{49} + x_{59} &= 400
\end{aligned}$$

c.

	Warehouse	
Plant	**1**	**2**
1	450	—
2	—	600
3	250	—

Total cost = \$11,850

	Customer			
Warehouse	**1**	**2**	**3**	**4**
1	—	300	—	400
2	300	—	300	—

24. c. $x_{14} = 320$, $x_{25} = 600$, $x_{47} = 300$, $x_{49} = 20$, $x_{56} = 300$, $x_{58} = 300$, $x_{39} = 380$
Cost = \$11,220

26. c. Note: Augusta: 1, Tupper Lake: 2, Albany: 3, Portsmouth: 4, Boston: 5, New York: 6, Philadelphia: 7

Variable	Value	Variable	Value
x_{13}	50	x_{36}	0
x_{14}	250	x_{37}	150
x_{23}	100	x_{45}	150
x_{24}	0	x_{46}	100
x_{35}	0	x_{47}	0

Objective function = 4300

28.

Optimal Solution	Units Shipped	Cost
Muncie-Cincinnati	1	6
Cincinnati-Concord	3	84
Brazil-Louisville	6	18
Louisville-Macon	2	88
Louisville-Greenwood	4	136
Xenia-Cincinnati	5	15
Cincinnati-Chatham	3	72
	Total	419

Two rail cars must be held at Muncie until a buyer is found

32. c. Regular-month 1: 275; overtime-month 1: 25; inventory at end of month 1: 150
Regular-month 2: 200; overtime-month 2: 50; inventory at end of month 2: 150
Regular-month 3: 100; overtime-month 3: 50; inventory at end of month 3: 0

34. a. An initial solution is

	Los Angeles	San Francisco	San Diego
San Jose	4 100	10	6
Las Vegas	8 100	16	6 200
Tucson	14	18 300	10

Total cost = \$7800

b. Note that the initial solution is degenerate because only 4 cells are occupied; a zero is assigned to the cell in row 3 and column 1 so that the row and column indexes can be computed

u_i	v_j: 4	8	2
0	[4] 100	[10] ②	[6] ④
4	[8] 100	[16] ④	[6] 200
10	[14] 0	[18] 300	[10] (−2)

Cell in row 3 and column 3 is identified as an incoming cell; however, 0 units can be added to this cell. Initial solution remains optimal

c.

San Jose–San Francisco:	100
Las Vegas–Los Angeles:	200
Las Vegas–San Diego:	100
Tucson–San Francisco:	200
Tucson–San Diego	100
Total Cost = $7800	

Note that this total cost is the same as for part (a); thus, we have alternative optimal solutions

d. The final transportation tableau is shown; the total transportation cost is $8000, an increase of $200 over the solution to part (a)

u_i	v_j: 2	10	2	
0	[4] ②	[10] 100	[6] ④	100
6	[8] 200	[16] 100	[M] (M−8)	300
8	[14] ④	[18] 100	[10] 200	300
	200	300	200	700

36. See Problem 4

40. Subtract 10 from row 1, 14 from row 2, and 22 from row 3 to obtain:

	1	2	3
Jackson	0	6	22
Ellis	0	8	26
Smith	0	2	12

Subtract 0 from column 1, 2 from column 2, and 12 from column 3 to obtain:

	1	2	3
Jackson	0	④	10
Ellis	0	6	14
Smith	0	0	0

Two lines cover the zeros; the minimum unlined element is 4; step 3 yields:

	1	2	3
Jackson	0	[0]	6
Ellis	[0]	2	10
Smith	0	0	[0]

Optimal solution: Jackson–2
Ellis–1
Smith–3
Time requirement is 64 days

42. Terry 2; Carle 3; MacClymonds 1; Higley unassigned
Time = 26 days

43. We start with the opportunity loss matrix:

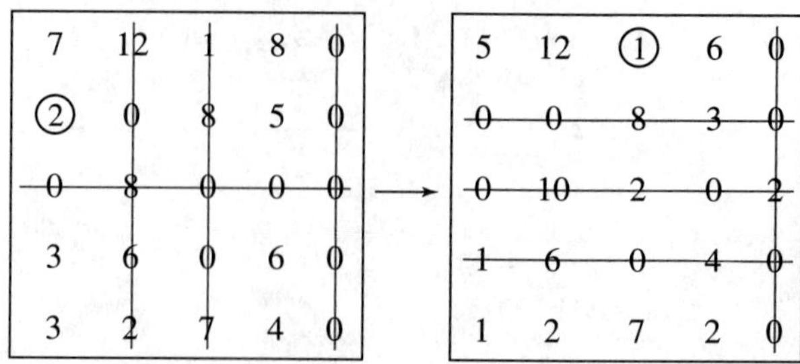

7	12	1	8	0
②	0	8	5	0
0	8	0	0	0
3	6	0	6	0
3	2	7	4	0

→

5	12	①	6	0
0	0	8	3	0
0	10	2	0	2
1	6	0	4	0
1	2	7	2	0

	1	2	3	4	D*
Shoe	4	11	0	5	0
Toy	0	0	8	3	1
Auto	0	10	2	0	3
Houseware	1	6	0	4	1
Video	0	1	6	1	0

*D = Dummy

	Optimal Solution	Profit
Toy	2	18
Auto	4	16
Housewares	3	13
Video	1	14
	Total	61

44. Toy – 2; Auto – 4; Housewares – 3; Video – 1

Chapter 8

2. a.

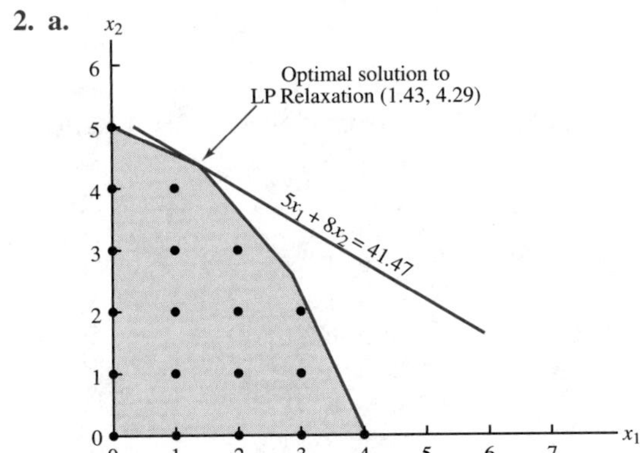

b. The optimal solution to the LP Relaxation is given by $x_1 = 1.43$, $x_2 = 4.29$ with an objective function value of 41.47. Rounding down gives the feasible integer solution $x_1 = 1$, $x_2 = 4$; its value is 37

c.

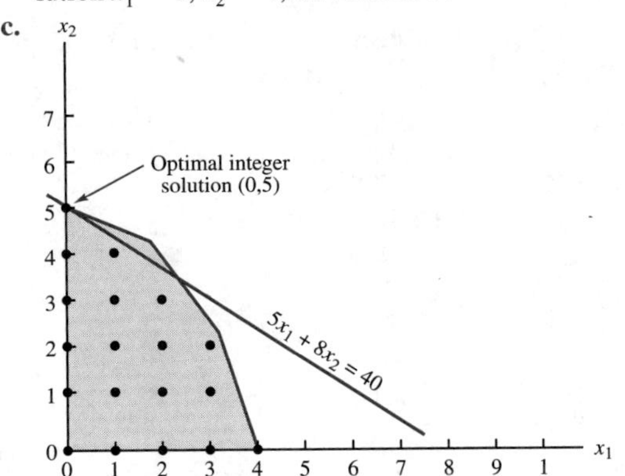

The optimal solution is given by $x_1 = 0$, $x_2 = 5$; its value is 40. It is not the same solution as found by rounding down; it provides a 3-unit increase in the value of the objective function

4. a. $x_1 = 3.67$, $x_2 = 0$; Value = 36.7
Rounded: $x_1 = 3$, $x_2 = 0$; Value = 30
Lower bound = 30; Upper bound = 36.7

b. $x_1 = 3$, $x_2 = 2$; Value = 36

c. Alternative optimal solutions: $x_1 = 0$, $x_2 = 5$
$x_1 = 2$, $x_2 = 4$

5. a. The feasible mixed-integer solutions are indicated by the boldface vertical lines in the graph

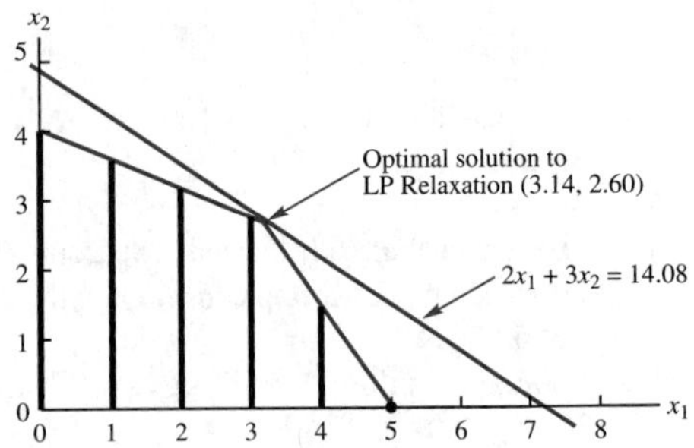

b. The optimal solution to the LP Relaxation is given by $x_1 = 3.14$, $x_2 = 2.60$; its value is 14.08
Rounding down the value of x_1 to find a feasible mixed-integer solution yields $x_1 = 3$, $x_2 = 2.60$ with a value of 13.8; this solution is clearly not optimal; with $x_1 = 3$, x_2 can be made larger without violating the constraints

c. The optimal solution to the MILP is given by $x_1 = 3$, $x_2 = 2.67$; its value is 14 as shown in the following figure

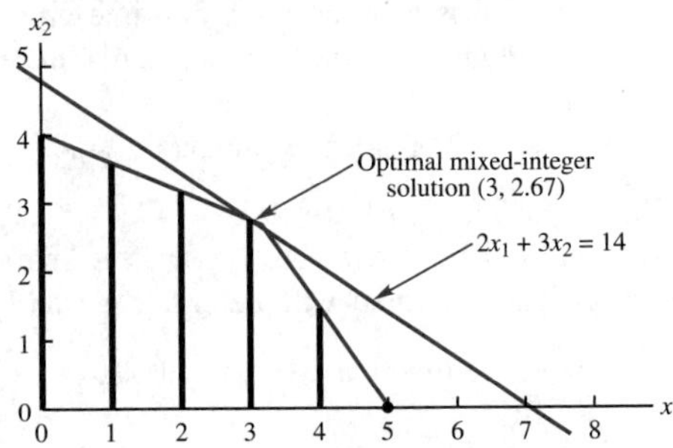

6. b. $x_1 = 1.96$, $x_2 = 5.48$; Value = 7.44
Rounded: $x_1 = 1.96$, $x_2 = 5$; Value = 6.96
Lower bound = 6.96; Upper bound = 7.44

c. $x_1 = 1.29$, $x_2 = 6$; Value = 7.29

7. a. $x_1 + x_3 + x_5 + x_6 = 2$

b. $x_3 - x_5 = 0$

c. $x_1 + x_4 = 1$

d. $x_4 \leq x_1$
$x_4 \leq x_3$

e. $x_4 \leq x_1$
$x_4 \leq x_3$
$x_4 \geq x_1 + x_3 - 1$

8. a. $x_3 = 1, x_4 = 1, x_6 = 1$; Value = 17,500
b. Add $x_1 + x_2 \leq 1$
c. Add $x_3 - x_4 = 0$

10. b. Choose locations B and E

12. a. $P \leq 15 + 15Y_P$
$D \leq 15 + 15Y_D$
$J \leq 15 + 15Y_J$
$Y_P + Y_D + Y_J \leq 1$
b. $P = 15, D = 15, J = 30$
$Y_P = 0, Y_D = 0, Y_J = 1$; Value = 50

13. a. Add the following multiple-choice constraint to the problem
$y_1 + y_2 = 1$
New optimal solution: $y_1 = 1,\ y_3 = 1,\ x_{12} = 10,\ x_{31} = 30, x_{52} = 10, x_{53} = 20$
Value = 940
b. Because one plant is already located in St. Louis, it is only necessary to add the following constraint to the model
$y_3 + y_4 \leq 1$
New optimal solution: $y_4 = 1,\ x_{42} = 20,\ x_{43} = 20,\ x_{51} = 30$
Value = 860

14. b. Modernize plants 1 and 3 or plants 4 and 5
d. Modernize plants 1 and 3

16. b. Use all part-time employees
Bring on as follows: 9:00 A.M.–6, 11:00 A.M.–2, 12:00 noon–6, 1:00 P.M.–1, 3:00 P.M.–6
Cost = $672
c. Same as in part (b)
d. New solution is to bring on 1 full-time employee at 9:00 A.M., 4 more at 11:00 A.M. and part-time employees as follows:
9:00 A.M.–5, 12:00 noon–5, and 3:00 P.M.–2

18. a. 52, 49, 36, 83, 39, 70, 79, 59
b. Thick crust, cheese blend, chunky sauce, medium sausage. Six of eight consumers will prefer this pizza (75%)

20. a. New objective function: Min $25x_1 + 40x_2 + 40x_3 + 40x_4 + 25x_5$
b. $x_4 = x_5 = 1$; modernize the Ohio and California plants
c. Add the constraint $x_2 + x_3 = 1$
d. $x_1 = x_3 = 1$

22. $x_1 + x_2 + x_3 = 3y_1 + 5y_2 + 7y_3$
$y_1 + y_2 + y_3 = 1$

24. a. $x_{111}, x_{112}, x_{121}$
b. $x_{111} + x_{112} + x_{121} \leq 1$
c. $x_{531} + x_{532} + x_{533} + x_{541} + x_{542} + x_{543} + x_{551} + x_{552} + x_{561} \leq 1$
d. Only two screens are available
e. $x_{213} + x_{222} + x_{231} + x_{422} + x_{431} + x_{531} + x_{532} + x_{533} + x_{631} + x_{632} + x_{633} \leq 2$

Chapter 9

1.

Node	Shortest Route from Node 1	Distance
2	1–2	7
3	1–3	9
4	1–2–5–6–4	17
5	1–2–5	12
6	1–2–5–6	14
7	1–2–5–6–7	17

2.

Node	Shortest Route from Node 7	Distance
1	7–6–5–3–1	22
2	7–4–2	11
3	7–6–5–3	12
4	7–4	5
5	7–5–6	8
6	7–6	6

4. 1–4–5–6–8; distance = 10

6.

Node	Shortest Route from Node C	Distance
1	C–1	35
2	C–2	20
3	C–3	20
4	C–4	30
5	C–3–5	55
6	C–3–6	50
7	C–3–8–7	100
8	C–3–8	80
9	C–4–10–9	85
10	C–4–10	70

8. 1–2–8–10–11

10.

Connect	Distance
1–6	2
6–7	3
7–8	1
7–10	2
10–9	3
9–4	2
9–3	3
3–2	1
4–5	3
7–11	4
8–13	4

Connect	Distance
14–15	2
15–12	3
14–13	4
Total	37

12. 1–2, 2–5, 5–6, 6–3, 6–8, 3–4, 8–7
Total length = 2900 feet

14. 1–4, 2–3, 3–4, 4–5, 4–6, 6–7, 7–8, 8–9, 9–11, 11–10
Minimum length = 28 miles

15. The capacitated transshipment problem to solve is given

Max x_{61}
s.t.

$$
\begin{aligned}
&x_{12} + x_{13} + x_{14} - x_{61} = 0 \\
&x_{24} + x_{25} - x_{12} - x_{42} = 0 \\
&x_{34} + x_{36} - x_{13} - x_{43} = 0 \\
&x_{42} + x_{43} + x_{45} + x_{46} - x_{14} - x_{24} - x_{34} - x_{54} = 0 \\
&x_{54} + x_{56} - x_{25} - x_{45} = 0 \\
&x_{61} - x_{36} + x_{46} - x_{56} = 0 \\
&x_{12} \le 2 \quad x_{13} \le 6 \quad x_{14} \le 3 \\
&x_{24} \le 1 \quad x_{25} \le 4 \\
&x_{34} \le 3 \quad x_{36} \le 2 \\
&x_{42} \le 1 \quad x_{43} \le 3 \quad x_{45} \le 1 \quad x_{46} \le 3 \\
&x_{54} \le 1 \quad x_{56} \le 6 \\
&x_{ij} \ge 0 \text{ for all } i, j
\end{aligned}
$$

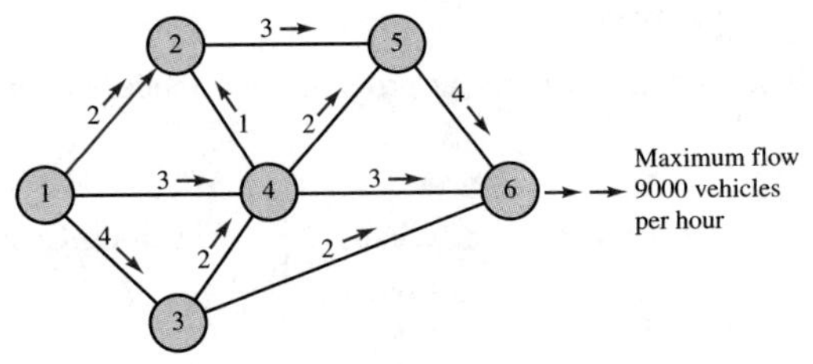

16. Maximal flow = 11,000 vehicles per hour

18. a. 10 hours; 10,000 gallons per hour
b. 11.1 hours; flow reduced to 9000 gallons per hour

20. Maximal flow = 23 gallons/minute
The total flow from 3 to 5 must be 5 gallons/minute

Chapter 10

2.

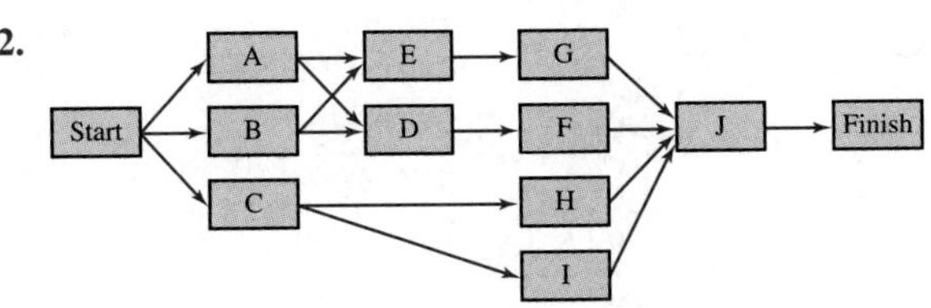

3.

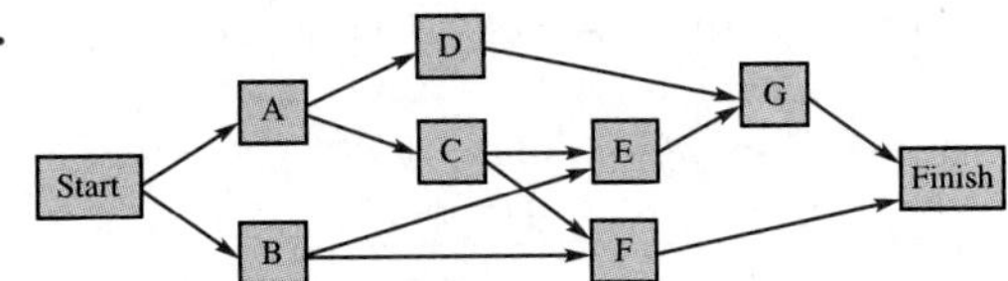

4. a. A–D–G
b. No; Time = 15 months

6. a. Critical path: A–D–F–H
b. 22 weeks
c. No, it is a critical activity
d. Yes, 2 weeks
e. Schedule for activity E:

Earliest start	3
Latest start	4
Earliest finish	10
Latest finish	11

8. b. B–C–E–F–H
d. Yes, time = 49 weeks

10. a.

Activity	Optimistic	Most Probable	Pessimistic	Expected Times	Variance
A	4	5.0	6	5.00	0.11
B	8	9.0	10	9.00	0.11
C	7	7.5	11	8.00	0.44
D	7	9.0	10	8.83	0.25
E	6	7.0	9	7.17	0.25
F	5	6.0	7	6.00	0.11

b. Critical activities: B–D–F
Expected project completion time: 9.00 + 8.83 + 6.00 = 23.83
Variance of projection completion time: 0.11 + 0.25 + 0.11 = 0.47

12. a. A–D–H–I
b. 25.66 days
c. 0.2578

13.

Activity	Expected Time	Variance
A	5	0.11
B	3	0.03
C	7	0.11
D	6	0.44
E	7	0.44
F	3	0.11
G	10	0.44
H	8	1.78

From Problem 6, A–D–F–H is the critical path, so
$E(T) = 5 + 6 + 3 + 8 = 22$
$\sigma^2 = 0.11 + 0.44 + 0.11 + 1.78 = 2.44$

$$z = \frac{\text{Time} - E(T)}{\sigma} = \frac{\text{Time} - 22}{\sqrt{2.44}}$$

		Area
a. Time = 21:	$z = -0.64$	0.2389

$P(21 \text{ weeks}) = 0.5000 - 0.2389 = 0.2611$

		Area
b. Time = 22:	$z = 0$	0.0000

$P(22 \text{ weeks}) = 0.5000$

		Area
c. Time = 25:	$z = +1.92$	0.4726

$P(25 \text{ weeks}) = 0.5000 + 0.4726 = 0.9726$

14. a. A–D–F–G
b. 1.5 days
c. 29.5, 2.36
d. 0.6293

16. a.

$E(T)$	Variance
16	3.92
13	2.03
10	1.27

b. 0.9783, approximately 1.00, approximately 1.00

18. c. A–B–D–G–H–I, 14.17 weeks
d. 0.0951, yes

20. b. Crash B(1 week), D(2 weeks), E(1 week), F(1 week), G(1 week)
Total cost = \$2427
c. All activities are critical

21. a.

Activity	Earliest Start	Latest Start	Earliest Finish	Latest Finish	Slack	Critical Activity
A	0	0	3	3	0	Yes
B	0	1	2	3	1	
C	3	3	8	8	0	Yes
D	2	3	7	8	1	
E	8	8	14	14	0	Yes
F	8	10	10	12	2	
G	10	12	12	14	2	

Critical Path: A–C–E
Project completion time = $t_A + t_C + t_E = 3 + 5 + 6 =$ 14 days
b. Total cost = \$8400

22. a.

Activity	Max Crash Days	Crash Cost/Day
A	1	\$600
B	1	700
C	2	400
D	2	400
E	2	500
F	1	400
G	1	500

$$\begin{aligned}
\text{Min} \quad & 600Y_A + 700Y_B + 400Y_C + 400Y_D + 500Y_E + 400Y_F + 400Y_G \\
\text{s.t.} \quad & \\
& X_A + Y_A \geq 3 \\
& X_B + Y_B \geq 2 \\
& -X_A + X_C + Y_C \geq 5 \\
& -X_B + X_D + Y_D \geq 5 \\
& -X_C + X_E + Y_E \geq 6 \\
& -X_D + X_E + Y_E \geq 6 \\
& -X_C + X_F + Y_F \geq 2 \\
& -X_D + X_F + Y_F \geq 2 \\
& -X_F + X_G + Y_G \geq 2 \\
& -X_E + X_{FIN} \geq 0 \\
& -X_G + X_{FIN} \geq 0 \\
& X_{FIN} \leq 12 \\
& Y_A \leq 1 \\
& Y_B \leq 1 \\
& Y_C \leq 2 \\
& Y_D \leq 2 \\
& Y_E \leq 2 \\
& Y_F \leq 1 \\
& Y_G \leq 1 \\
& \text{All } X, Y \geq 0
\end{aligned}$$

b. Solution of the linear programming model in part (a) shows

Activity	Crash	Crashing Cost
C	1 day	\$400
E	1 day	500
	Total	\$900

c. Total cost = Normal cost + Crashing cost
= \$8400 + \$900 = \$9300

24. c. A–B–C–F, 31 weeks
d. Crash A(2 weeks), B(2 weeks), C(1 week), D(1 week), E(1 week)
e. All activities are critical
f. \$112,500

Chapter 11

1. a. $Q^* = \sqrt{\dfrac{2DC_0}{C_h}} = \sqrt{\dfrac{2(3600)(20)}{0.25(3)}} = 438.18$

b. $r = dm = \dfrac{3600}{250}(5) = 72$

c. $T = \frac{250Q^*}{D} = \frac{250(438.18)}{3600} = 30.43$ days

d. $TC = \frac{1}{2}QC_h + \frac{D}{Q}C_0$

$= \frac{1}{2}(438.18)(0.25)(3) + \frac{3600}{438.18}(20) = \$328.63$

2. \$164.32 for each; Total cost = \$328.64

4. a. 1095.45
b. 240
c. 22.82 days
d. \$273.86 for each; Total cost = \$547.72

6. a. 15.95
b. \$2106
c. 15.04
d. 16.62 days

8. $Q^* = 11.73$, use 12
5 classes per year
\$225,200

10. $Q^* = 1414.21$
$T = 28.28$ days
Production runs of 7.07 days

12. $Q^* = 1000$; Total cost = \$1200
Yes, the change saves \$300 per year

13. a. $Q^* = \sqrt{\frac{2DC_0}{(1 - D/P)C_h}}$

$= \sqrt{\frac{2(7200)(150)}{(1 - 7200/25{,}000)(0.18)(14.50)}} = 1078.12$

b. Number of production runs $= \frac{D}{Q^*} = \frac{7200}{1078.12} = 6.68$

c. $T = \frac{250Q}{D} = \frac{250(1078.12)}{7200} = 37.43$ days

d. Production run length $= \frac{Q}{P/250}$

$= \frac{1078.12}{25{,}000/250} = 10.78$ days

e. Maximum inventory $= \left(1 - \frac{D}{P}\right)Q$

$= \left(1 - \frac{7200}{25{,}000}\right)(1078.12)$

$= 767.62$

f. Holding cost $= \frac{1}{2}\left(1 - \frac{D}{P}\right)QC_h$

$= \frac{1}{2}\left(1 - \frac{7200}{25{,}000}\right)(1078.12)(0.18)(14.50)$

$= \$1001.74$

Ordering cost $= \frac{D}{Q}C_0 = \frac{7200}{1078.12}(150) = \$1001.74$

Total cost = \$2003.48

g. $r = dm = \left(\frac{D}{250}\right)m = \frac{7200}{250}(15) = 432$

14. New $Q^* = 4509$

15. a. $Q^* = \sqrt{\frac{2DC_0}{C_h}\left(\frac{C_h + C_b}{C_b}\right)}$

$= \sqrt{\frac{2(12{,}000)(25)}{0.50}\left(\frac{0.50 + 5}{0.50}\right)} = 1148.91$

b. $S^* = Q^*\left(\frac{C_h}{C_h + C_b}\right) = 1148.91\left(\frac{0.50}{0.50 + 5}\right) = 104.45$

c. Max inventory $= Q^* - S^* = 1044.46$

d. $T = \frac{250Q^*}{D} = \frac{250(1148.91)}{12{,}000} = 23.94$ days

e. Holding $= \frac{(Q - S)^2}{2Q}C_h = \$237.38$

Ordering $= \frac{D}{Q}C_0 = \$261.12$

Backorder $= \frac{S^2}{2Q}C_b = \$23.74$

Total cost = \$522.24

The total cost for the EOQ model in Problem 4 was \$547.72; allowing backorders reduces the total cost

16. 135.55; $r = dm - S$; less than

18. 64, 24.44

20. $Q^* = 100$; Total cost = \$3,601.50

21. $Q = \sqrt{\frac{2DC_0}{C_h}}$

$Q_1 = \sqrt{\frac{2(500)(40)}{0.20(10)}} = 141.42$

$Q_2 = \sqrt{\frac{2(500)(40)}{0.20(9.7)}} = 143.59$

Because Q_1 is over its limit of 99 units, Q_1 cannot be optimal (see Problem 23); use $Q_2 = 143.59$ as the optimal order quantity

Total cost $= \frac{1}{2}QC_h + \frac{D}{Q}C_0 + DC$

$= 139.28 + 139.28 + 4850.00 = \$5128.56$

22. $Q^* = 300$; Savings = \$480

24. a. 500
b. 580.4

25. a. $c_o = 80 - 50 = 30$

$c_u = 125 - 80 = 45$

$P(D \le Q^*) = \frac{c_u}{c_u + c_o} = \frac{45}{45 + 30} = 0.60$

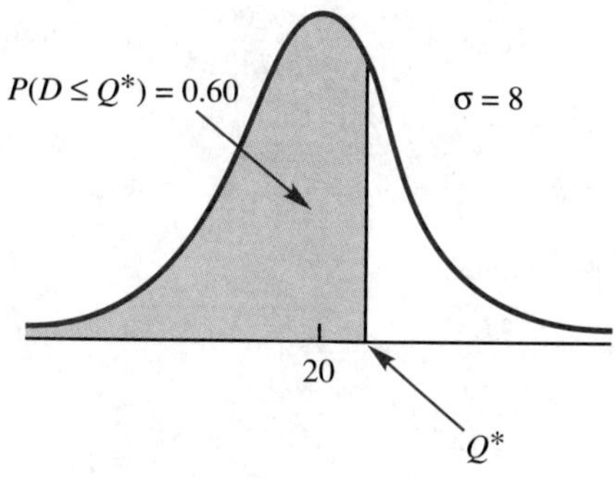

For an area of 0.60 below Q^*, $z = 0.25$
$Q^* = 20 + 0.25(8) = 22$

b. $P(\text{Sell all}) = P(D \ge Q^*) = 1 - 0.60 = 0.40$

26. a. $150
b. $240 − $150 = $90
c. 47
d. 0.625

28. a. 440
b. 0.60
c. 710
d. c_u = $17

29. a. $r = dm = (200/250)15 = 12$

b. $\frac{D}{Q} = \frac{200}{25} = 8$ orders/year
The limit of 1 stock-out per year means that
$P(\text{Stock-out/cycle}) = 1/8 = 0.125$

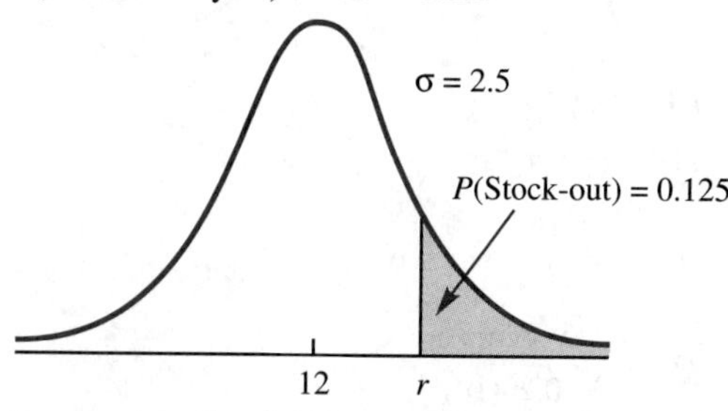

For area in tail = 0.125, $z = 1.15$

$$z = \frac{r - 12}{2.5} = 1.15$$

or

$$r = 12 + 1.15(2.5) = 14.875 \approx 15$$

c. Safety stock = 3 units
Added cost = 3($5) = $15/year

30. a. 13.68 (14)
b. 17.83 (18)
c. 2, $10; 6, $30

32. a. 31.62
b. 19.86 (20); 0.2108
c. 5, $15

33. a. 1/52 = 0.0192
b. $M = \mu + z\sigma = 60 + 2.07(12) = 85$
c. $M = 35 + (0.9808)(85 - 35) = 84$

34. a. 243
b. 93, $54.87
c. 613
d. 163, $96.17
e. Yes, added cost only $41.30 per year
f. Yes, added cost would be $4130 per year

36. a. 40
b. 62.25; 7.9
c. 54
d. 36

Chapter 12

2. a. 0.4512
b. 0.6988
c. 0.3012

4. 0.3333, 0.2222, 0.1481, 0.0988, 0.1976

5. a. $P_0 = 1 - \frac{\lambda}{\mu} = 1 - \frac{10}{12} = 0.1667$

b. $L_q = \frac{\lambda^2}{\mu(\mu - \lambda)} = \frac{10^2}{12(12 - 10)} = 4.1667$

c. $W_q = \frac{L_q}{\lambda} = 0.4167$ hour (25 minutes)

d. $W = W_q + \frac{1}{\mu} = 0.5$ hour (30 minutes)

e. $P_w = \frac{\lambda}{\mu} = \frac{10}{12} = 0.8333$

6. a. 0.3750
b. 1.0417
c. 0.8333 minutes (50 seconds)
d. 0.6250
e. Yes

8. 0.20, 3.2, 4, 3.2, 4, 0.80
Slightly poorer service

10. a. New: 0.3333, 1.3333, 2, 0.6667, 1, 0.6667
Experienced: 0.50, 0.50, 1, 0.25, 0.50, 0.50
b. New $74; experienced $50; hire experienced

11. a. $\lambda = 2.5;\quad \mu = \frac{60}{10} = 6$ customers per hour

$$L_q = \frac{\lambda^2}{\mu(\mu - \lambda)} = \frac{(2.5)^2}{6(6 - 2.5)} = 0.2976$$

$$L = L_q + \frac{\lambda}{\mu} = 0.7143$$

$$W_q = \frac{L_q}{\lambda} = 0.1190 \text{ hours (7.14 minutes)}$$

$$W = W_q + \frac{1}{\mu} = 0.2857 \text{ hours}$$

$$P_w = \frac{\lambda}{\mu} = \frac{2.5}{6} = 0.4167$$

b. No; $W_q = 7.14$ minutes; firm should increase the mean service rate (μ) for the consultant or hire a second consultant

c. $\mu = \frac{60}{8} = 7.5$ customers per hour

$$L_q = \frac{\lambda^2}{\mu(\mu - \lambda)} = \frac{(2.5)^2}{7.5(7.5 - 2.5)} = 0.1667$$

$$W_q = \frac{L_q}{\lambda} = 0.0667 \text{ hour (4 minutes)}$$

The service goal is being met

12. a. 0.25, 2.25, 3, 0.15 hours, 0.20 hours, 0.75
b. The service needs improvement

14. a. 8
b. 0.3750
c. 1.0417
d. 12.5 minutes
e. 0.6250
f. Add a second consultant

16. a. 0.50
b. 0.50
c. 0.10 hours (6 minutes)
d. 0.20 hours (12 minutes)
e. Yes, $W_q = 6$ minutes is most likely acceptable for a marina

18. a. $k = 2$; $\lambda/\mu = 14/10 = 1.4$; $P_0 = 0.1765$

b. $$L_q = \frac{(\lambda/\mu)^2\lambda\mu}{1!(2\mu - \lambda)^2}P_0 = \frac{(1.4)^2(14)(10)}{(20 - 14)^2}(0.1765) = 1.3451$$

$$L = L_q + \frac{\lambda}{\mu} = 1.3451 + \frac{14}{10} = 2.7451$$

c. $$W_q = \frac{L_q}{\lambda} = \frac{1.3453}{14} = 0.0961 \text{ hours (5.77 minutes)}$$

d. $$W = W_q + \frac{1}{\mu} = 0.0961 + \frac{1}{10} = 0.1961 \text{ hours (11.77 minutes)}$$

e. $P_0 = 0.1765$

$$P_1 = \frac{(\lambda/\mu)^1}{1!}P_0 = \frac{14}{10}(0.1765) = 0.2470$$

$$P(\text{wait}) = P(n \geq 2) = 1 - P(n \leq 1) = 1 - 0.4235 = 0.5765$$

20. a. Use $k = 2$
$W = 3.7037$ minutes
$L = 4.4444$
$P_w = 0.7111$

b. For $k = 3$
$W = 7.1778$ minutes
$L = 15.0735$ customers
$P_w = 0.8767$
Expand post office

21. From Problem 11, a service time of 8 minutes has $\mu = 60/8 = 7.5$

$$L_q = \frac{\lambda^2}{\mu(\mu - \lambda)} = \frac{(2.5)^2}{7.5(7.5 - 2.5)} = 0.1667$$

$$L = L_q + \frac{\lambda}{\mu} = 0.50$$

Total cost $= \$25L + \$16$
$= 25(0.50) + 16 = \$28.50$

Two channels: $\lambda = 2.5$; $\mu = 60/10 = 6$
With $P_0 = 0.6552$,

$$L_q = \frac{(\lambda/\mu)^2\lambda\mu}{1!(2\mu - \lambda)^2}P_0 = 0.0189$$

$$L = L_q + \frac{\lambda}{\mu} = 0.4356$$

Total cost $= 25(0.4356) + 2(16) = \$42.89$

Use one consultant with an 8-minute service time

22.

Characteristic	A	B	C
a. P_0	0.2000	0.5000	0.4286
b. L_q	3.2000	0.5000	0.1524
c. L	4.0000	1.0000	0.9524
d. W_q	0.1333	0.0208	0.0063
e. W	0.1667	0.0417	0.0397
f. P_w	0.8000	0.5000	0.2286

The two-channel System C provides the best service

24. a. 0.0466, 0.05
b. 1.4
c. 11:00 A.M.

25. $\lambda = 4$, $W = 10$ minutes
a. $\mu = ½ = 0.5$
b. $W_q = W - 1/\mu = 10 - 1/0.5 = 8$ minutes
c. $L = \lambda W = 4(10) = 40$

26. a. 0.2668, 10 minutes, 0.6667
b. 0.0667, 7 minutes, 0.4669
c. \$25.33; \$33.34; one-channel

27. a. $2/8$ hours $= 0.25$ per hour
b. $1/3.2$ hours $= 0.3125$ per hour

c. $$L_q = \frac{\lambda^2\sigma^2 + (\lambda/\mu)^2}{2(1 - \lambda/\mu)} = \frac{(0.25)^2(2)^2 + (0.25/0.3125)^2}{2(1 - 0.25/0.3125)} = 2.225$$

d. $$W_q = \frac{L_q}{\lambda} = \frac{2.225}{0.25} = 8.9 \text{ hours}$$

e. $$W = W_q + \frac{1}{\mu} = 8.9 + \frac{1}{0.3125} = 12.1 \text{ hours}$$

f. Same as $P_w = \frac{\lambda}{\mu} = \frac{0.25}{0.3125} = 0.80$

80% of the time the welder is busy

28. a. 10, 9.6
b. Design A with $\mu = 10$
c. 0.05, 0.01
d. A: 0.5, 0.3125, 0.8125, 0.0625, 0.1625, 0.5
B: 0.4792, 0.2857, 0.8065, 0.0571, 0.1613, 0.5208
e. Design B has slightly less waiting time

30. a. $\lambda = 42$; $\mu = 20$

i	$(\lambda/\mu)^i/i!$
0	1.0000
1	2.1000
2	2.2050
3	1.5435
Total	6.8485

j	P_j
0	1/6.8485 = 0.1460
1	2.1/6.8485 = 0.3066
2	2.2050/6.8485 = 0.3220
3	1.5435/6.8485 = 0.2254
	1.0000

b. 0.2254
c. $L = \lambda/\mu(1 - P_k) = 42/20(1 - 0.2254) = 1.6267$
d. Four lines will be necessary; the probability of denied access is 0.1499

32. a. 31.03%
b. 27.59%
c. 0.2759, 0.1092, 0.0351
d. 3, 10.92%

34. $N = 5$; $\lambda = 0.025$; $\mu = 0.20$; $\lambda/\mu = 0.125$
a.

n	$\dfrac{N!}{(N-n)!}\left(\dfrac{\lambda}{\mu}\right)^n$
0	1.0000
1	0.6250
2	0.3125
3	0.1172
4	0.0293
5	0.0037
Total	2.0877

$P_0 = 1/2.0877 = 0.4790$

b. $L_q = N - \left(\dfrac{\lambda + \mu}{\lambda}\right)(1 - P_0)$
$= 5 - \left(\dfrac{0.225}{0.025}\right)(1 - 0.4790) = 0.3110$

c. $L = L_q + (1 - P_0) = 0.3110 + (1 - 0.4790)$
$= 0.8321$

d. $W_q = \dfrac{L_q}{(N - L)\lambda} = \dfrac{0.3110}{(5 - 0.8321)(0.025)}$
$= 2.9854$ minutes

e. $W = W_q + \dfrac{1}{\mu} = 2.9854 + \dfrac{1}{0.20} = 7.9854$ minutes

f. Trips/day = (8 hours)(60 minutes/hour)(λ)
= (8)(60)(0.025) = 12 trips
Time at copier: 12 × 7.9854 = 95.8 minutes/day
Wait time at copier: 12 × 2.9854 = 35.8 minutes/day

g. Yes, five assistants × 35.8 = 179 minutes (3 hours/day), so 3 hours per day are lost to waiting
(35.8/480)(100) = 7.5% of each assistant's day is spent waiting for the copier

Chapter 13

2. a. c = variable cost per unit
x = demand
Profit = $(50 - c)x - 30{,}000$
b. Base: Profit = (50 − 20)1200 − 30,000 = 6,000
Worst: Profit = (50 − 24)300 − 30,000 = −22,200
Best: Profit = (50 − 16)2100 − 30,000 = 41,400
c. Simulation will be helpful in estimating the probability of a loss

4. a. 0.00–0.08, 0.08–0.20, 0.20–0.48, 0.48–0.72, 0.72–0.86, 0.86–0.96, 0.96–1.00
b. 2, 5, 2, 3, 2, 4, 2, 1, 1, 2
c. 24 units

5. a.

Stock Price Change	Interval
−2	0.00 but less than 0.05
−1	0.05 but less than 0.15
0	0.15 but less than 0.40
Stock Price Change	**Interval**
+1	0.40 but less than 0.60
+2	0.60 but less than 0.80
+3	0.80 but less than 0.90
+4	0.90 but less than 1.00

b. Beginning price \$39
0.1091 indicates −1 change; \$38
0.9407 indicates +4 change; \$42
0.1941 indicates 0 change; \$42
0.8083 indicates +3 change; \$45 (ending price)

6. a. 0.00–0.83, 0.83–0.89, 0.89–0.94, 0.94–0.96, 0.96–0.98, 0.98–0.99, 0.99–1.00
b. 4 claims paid; Total = \$22,000

8. a. Atlanta wins each game if random number is in interval 0.00–0.60, 0.00–0.55, 0.00–0.48, 0.00–0.45, 0.00–0.48, 0.00–0.55, 0.00–0.50
b. Atlanta wins games 1, 2, 4, and 6
Atlanta wins series 4 to 2
c. Repeat many times; record % of Atlanta wins

9. a. Base-case based on most likely;
Time = 6 + 5 + 14 + 8 = 33 weeks
Worst: Time = 8 + 7 + 18 + 10 = 43 weeks
Best: Time = 5 + 3 + 10 + 8 = 26 weeks
b. 0.1778 for A: 5 weeks
0.9617 for B: 7 weeks
0.6849 for C: 14 weeks
0.4503 for D: 8 weeks; Total = 34 weeks
c. Simulation will provide an estimate of the probability of 35 weeks or less

10. a. 0.4737
b. Win if Rand < 0.4737
c. Wins $50; Loses $250
d. Simulation run needed

12. a. $7, $3, $12
b. Purchase: 0.00–0.25, 0.25–0.70, 0.70–1.00
Labor: 0.00–0.10, 0.10–0.35, 0.35–0.70, 0.70–1.00
Transportation: 0.00–0.75, 0.75–1.00
c. $5
d. $7
e. Provide probability profit less than $5/unit

14. Selected cell formulas for the worksheet shown in Figure F13.14 are as follows:

Cell	Formula
B13	=$C$7+RAND()*($C$8−$C$7)
C13	=NORMINV(RAND(),$G$7,$G$8)
D13	=($C$3−B13)*C13−$C$4

a. The mean profit should be approximately $6000; simulation results will vary with most simulations having a mean profit between $5500 and $6500
b. 120 to 150 of the 500 simulation trials should show a loss; thus, the probability of a loss should be between 0.24 and 0.30
c. This project appears too risky

16. a. About 36% of simulation runs will show $130,000 as the winning bid
b. $150,000; $10,000
c. Recommend $140,000

18. Selected cell formulas for the worksheet shown in Figure F13.18 are as follows:

Cell	Formula
B11	=$C$4 + RAND()*($C$5−$C$4)
C11	=NORMINV(RAND(),$H$4,$H$5)
D11	=MAX(B11:C11)
G11	=COUNTIF(D11:D1010,"<750")
H11	=G11/COUNT(D11:D1010)

a. $750,000 should win roughly 600 to 650 of the 1000 times; the probability of winning the bid should be between 0.60 and 0.65
b. The probability of $775,000 winning should be roughly 0.82, and the probability of $785,000 winning should be roughly 0.88; a contractor's bid of $775,000 is recommended

20. a. Results vary with each simulation run
Approximate results: 50,000 provided $230,000
60,000 provided $190,000
70,000 less than $100,000
b. Recommend 50,000 units
c. Roughly 0.75

FIGURE F13.14 WORKSHEET FOR THE MADEIRA MANUFACTURING COMPANY

	A	B	C	D	E	F	G
1	**Madeira Manufacturing Company**						
2							
3	Selling Price per Unit		$50				
4	Fixed Cost		$30,000				
5							
6	**Variable Cost (Uniform Distribution)**				**Demand (Normal Distribution)**		
7	Smallest Value		$16		Mean		1200
8	Largest Value		$24		Standard Deviation		300
9							
10	**Simulation trials**						
11		Variable					
12	Trial	Cost per Unit	Demand	Profit			
13	1	$17.81	788	($4,681)			
14	2	$18.86	1078	$3,580			

FIGURE F13.18 WORKSHEET FOR THE CONTRACTOR BIDDING

	A	B	C	D	E	F	G	H
1	**Contractor Bidding**							
2								
3	**Contractor A (Uniform Distribution)**					**Contractor B (Normal Distribution)**		
4	Smallest Value		$600			Mean		$700
5	Largest Value		$800			Standard Deviation		$50
6								
7								
8								
9								
10	**Simulation**					**Results**		
11		Contractor	Contractor	Highest		Contractor's	Number	Probability
12	Trial	A's Bid	B's Bid	Bid		Bid	of Wins	of Winning
13	1	$673.00	$720	$720		750	629	0.629
14	2	$757.00	$655	$757		775	824	0.824
15	3	$706	$791	$791		785	887	0.887
16	4	$638	$677	$677				

22. Very poor operation; some customers wait 30 minutes or more

24. **b.** Mean waiting time approximately 0.8 minutes
c. 30% to 35% of customers have to wait

Chapter 14

1. **a.**

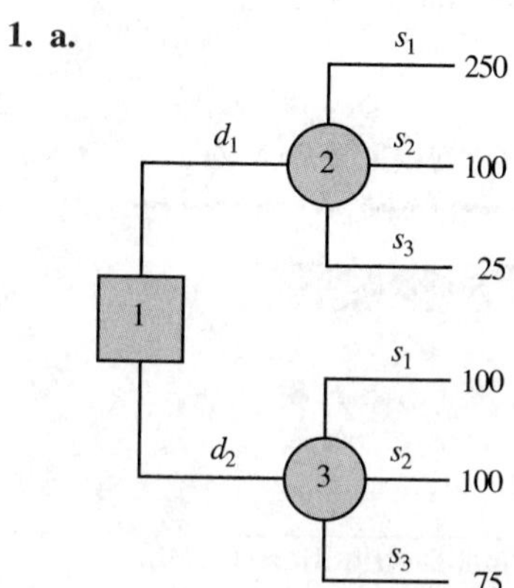

b.

Decision	Maximum Profit	Minimum Profit
d_1	250	25
d_2	100	75

Optimistic approach: Select d_1
Conservative approach: Select d_2

Regret or opportunity loss table:

Decision	s_1	s_2	s_3
d_1	0	0	50
d_2	150	0	0

Maximum regret: 50 for d_1 and 150 for d_2; select d_1

2. **a.** Optimistic: d_1
Conservative: d_3
Minimax regret: d_3
c. Optimistic: d_1
Conservative: d_2 or d_3
Minimax regret: d_2

3. **a.** Decision: Choose the best plant size from the two alternatives: a small plant and a large plant
Chance event: Market demand for the new product line with three possible outcomes (states of nature): low, medium, and high
b. Influence Diagram:

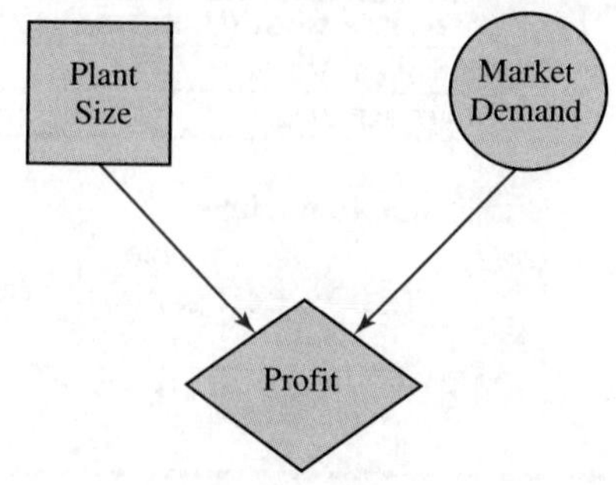

c.

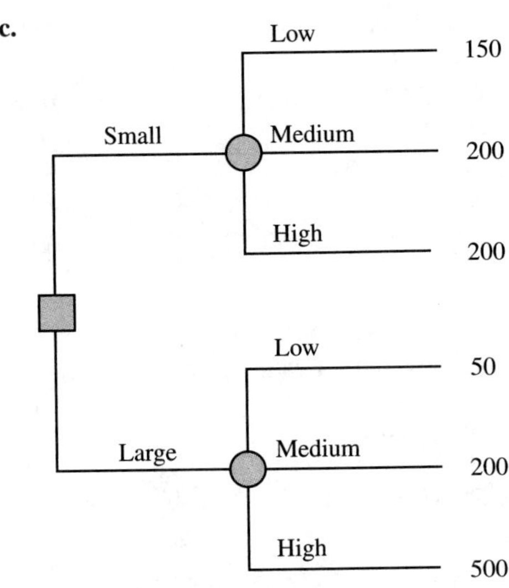

d.

Decision	Maximum Profit	Minimum Profit	Maximum Regret
Small	200	150	300
Large	500	50	100

Optimistic Approach: Large Plant
Conservative Approach: Small Plant
Minimax Regret: Large Plant

4. a. Decision: Which lease option to choose
Chance event: Miles driven

b.

	Annual Miles Driven		
	12,000	15,000	18,000
Forno	10,764	12,114	13,464
Midtown	11,160	11,160	12,960
Hopkins	11,700	11,700	11,700

c. Optimistic: Forno Saab
Conservative: Hopkins Automotive
Minimax: Hopkins Automotive

d. Midtown Motors

e. Most likely: \$11,160; Probability = 0.9

f. Midtown Motors or Hopkins Automotive

5. a. $EV(d_1) = 0.65(250) + 0.15(100) + 0.20(25) = 182.5$
$EV(d_2) = 0.65(100) + 0.15(100) + 0.20(75) = 95$
The optimal decision is d_1

6. a. d_1
b. d_4

7. a. EV(own staff) = 0.2(650) + 0.5(650) + 0.3(600) = 635
EV(outside vendor) = 0.2(900) + 0.5(600) + 0.3(300) = 570
EV(combination) = 0.2(800) + 0.5(650) + 0.3(500) = 635
Optimal decision: Hire an outside vendor with an expected cost of \$570,000

b.

	Cost	Probability
Own staff	300	0.3
Outside vendor	600	0.5
Combination	900	0.2
		1.0

8. a. $EV(d_1) = p(10) + (1 - p)(1) = 9p + 1$
$EV(d_2) = p(4) + (1 - p)(3) = 1p + 3$

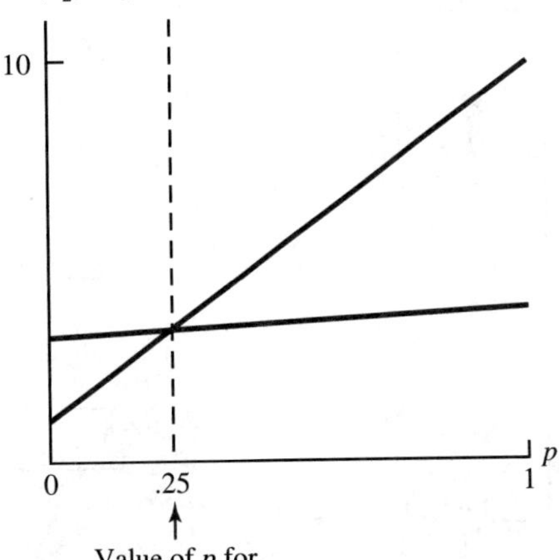

$9p + 1 = 1p + 3$ and hence $p = 0.25$
d_2 is optimal for $p \leq 0.25$, d_1 is optimal for $p \geq 0.25$

b. d_2

c. As long as the payoff for $s_1 \geq 2$, then d_2 is optimal

10. b. Space Pirates
EV = \$724,000
\$84,000 better than Battle Pacific

c.

\$200	0.18
\$400	0.32
\$800	0.30
\$1600	0.20

d. $P(\text{Competition}) > 0.7273$

12. a. Decision: Whether to lengthen the runway
Chance event: The location decisions of Air Express and DRI
Consequence: Annual revenue

b. \$255,000

c. \$270,000

d. No

e. Lengthen the runway

14. a. If s_1, then d_1; if s_2, then d_1 or d_2; if s_3, then d_2

b. $EVwPI = 0.65(250) + 0.15(100) + 0.20(75) = 192.5$

c. From the solution to Problem 5, we know that EV(d_1) = 182.5 and EV(d_2) = 95; thus, recommended decision is d_1; hence, EVwoPI = 182.5

d. EVPI = EVwPI − EVwoPI = 192.5 − 182.5 = 10

16. a.

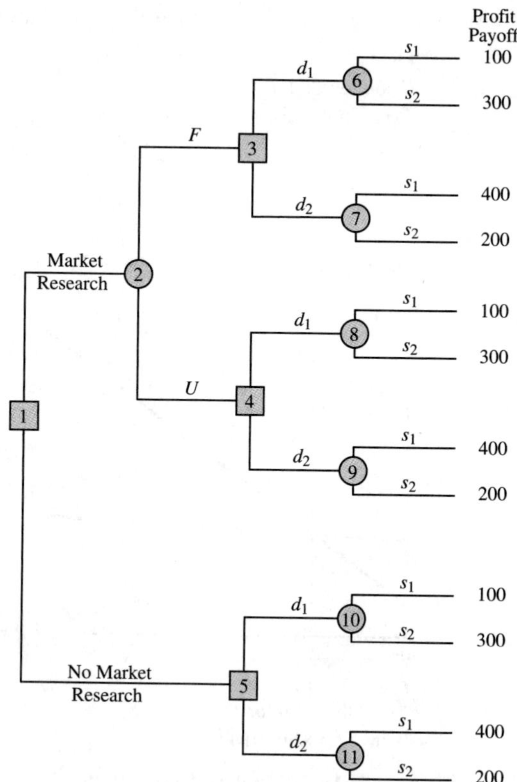

b. EV (node 6) = 0.57(100) + 0.43(300) = 186
EV (node 7) = 0.57(400) + 0.43(200) = 314
EV (node 8) = 0.18(100) + 0.82(300) = 264
EV (node 9) = 0.18(400) + 0.82(200) = 236
EV (node 10) = 0.40(100) + 0.60(300) = 220
EV (node 11) = 0.40(400) + 0.60(200) = 280

EV (node 3) = Max(186,314) = 314 d_2
EV (node 4) = Max(264,236) = 264 d_1
EV (node 5) = Max(220,280) = 280 d_2

EV (node 2) = 0.56(314) + 0.44(264) = 292
EV (node 1) = Max(292,280) = 292

∴ Market Research
If favorable, decision d_2
If unfavorable, decision d_1

18. a. 5000 − 200 − 2000 − 150 = 2650
3000 − 200 − 2000 − 150 = 650

b. Expected values at nodes

8: 2350	5: 2350	9: 1100
6: 1150	10: 2000	7: 2000
4: 1870	3: 2000	2: 1560
1: 1560		

c. Cost would have to decrease by at least $130,000

d.

Payoff (in millions)	Probability
−$200	.20
800	.32
2800	.48
	1.00

20. b. If Do Not Review, Accept
If Review and *F*, Accept
If Review and *U*, Accept
Always Accept

c. Do not review; EVSI = $0

d. $87,500; better method of predicting success

22.

State of Nature	$P(s_j)$	$P(I/s_j)$	$P(I \cap s_j)$	$P(s_j/I)$
s_1	0.2	0.10	0.020	0.1905
s_2	0.5	0.05	0.025	0.2381
s_3	0.3	0.20	0.060	0.5714
	1.0		$P(I)$ = 0.105	1.0000

24. a. 0.695, 0.215, 0.090
0.98, 0.02
0.79, 0.21
0.00, 1.00

c. If *C*, Expressway
If *O*, Expressway
If *R*, Queen City
26.6 minutes

26. Risk-avoider, at $20 payoff $p = 0.70$
EV(Lottery) = 0.70(100) + 0.30(−100) = $40
Will Pay 40 − 20 = $20
Risk-taker, at $20 payoff $p = 0.45$
EV(Lottery) = 0.45(100) + 0.55(−100) = −$10
Will Pay 20 − (−10) = $30

28. a.
$$\left.\begin{aligned} EV(d_1) &= 0.40(100) + 0.30(25) + 0.30(0) = 47.5 \\ EV(d_2) &= 0.40(75) + 0.30(50) + 0.30(25) = 52.5 \\ EV(d_3) &= 0.40(50) + 0.30(50) + 0.30(50) = 50.0 \end{aligned}\right\} d_2$$

b. Using utilities

Decision Maker A	Decision Maker B
EU(d_1) = 4.9	EU(d_1) = 4.45 Best
EU(d_2) = 5.9	EU(d_2) = 3.75
EU(d_3) = 6.0 Best	EU(d_3) = 3.00

c. Difference in attitude toward risk; decision maker A tends to avoid risk, whereas decision maker B tends to take a risk for the opportunity of a large payoff

30. a. d_2; EV(d_2) = \$5,000
b. p = probability of a \$0 cost
$1 - p$ = probability of a \$200,000 cost
c. d_1; EV(d_1) = 9.9
d. Expected utility approach; it avoids risk of large loss

32. a. Route B; EV = 58.5
b. p = probability of a 45-minute travel time
$1 - p$ = probability of a 90-minute travel time
c. Route A; EV = 7.6; risk-avoider

34. a.

	Win	Lose
Bet	350	−10
Do not bet	0	0

b. d_2
c. Risk takers
d. Between 0 and 0.26

Chapter 15

2. a. Let x_1 = number of shares of AGA Products purchased
x_2 = number of shares of Key Oil purchased
To obtain an annual return of exactly 9%:

$$0.06(50)x_1 + 0.10(100)x_2 = 0.09(50{,}000)$$
$$3x_1 + 10x_2 = 4500$$

To have exactly 60% of the total investment in Key Oil:

$$100x_2 = 0.60(50{,}000)$$
$$x_2 = 300$$

Therefore, we can write the goal programming model as follows:

$$\begin{aligned} &\text{Min } P_1(d_1^-) + P_2(d_2^+) \\ &\text{s.t.} \\ &50x_1 + 100x_2 \le 50{,}000 \quad \text{Funds available} \\ &3x_1 + 10x_2 - d_1^+ + d_1^- = 4{,}500 \quad P_1 \text{ goal} \\ &x_2 - d_2^+ + d_2^- = 300 \quad P_2 \text{ goal} \\ &x_1, x_2, d_1^+, d_1^-, d_2^+, d_2^- \ge 0 \end{aligned}$$

b. In the following graphical solution, $x_1 = 250$ and $x_2 = 375$

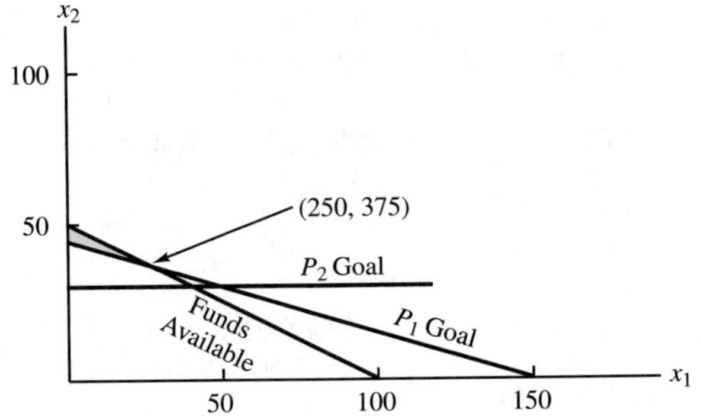

4. a.
$$\begin{aligned} &\text{Min } P_1(d_1^-) + P_1(d_2^+) + P_2(d_3^-) + P_2(d_4^-) + P_3(d_5^-) \\ &\text{s.t.} \\ &20x_1 + 30x_2 - d_1^+ + d_1^- = 4800 \\ &20x_1 + 30x_2 - d_2^+ + d_2^- = 6000 \\ &x_1 - d_3^+ + d_3^- = 100 \\ &x_2 - d_4^+ + d_4^- = 120 \\ &x_1 + x_2 - d_5^+ + d_5^- = 300 \\ &x_1, x_2, \text{all deviation variables} \ge 0 \end{aligned}$$

b. $x_1 = 120$, $x_2 = 120$

6. a. Let x_1 = number of letters mailed to group 1 customers
x_2 = number of letters mailed to group 2 customers

$$\begin{aligned} &\text{Min } P_1(d_1^-) + P_1(d_2^-) + P_2(d_3^+) \\ &\text{s.t.} \\ &x_1 - d_1^+ + d_1^- = 40{,}000 \\ &x_2 - d_2^+ + d_2^- = 50{,}000 \\ &x_1 + x_2 - d_3^+ + d_3^- = 70{,}000 \\ &x_1, x_2, \text{all deviation variables} \ge 0 \end{aligned}$$

b. $x_1 = 40{,}000$, $x_2 = 50{,}000$
c. Optimal solution does not change

8. a.
$$\begin{aligned} &\text{Min } d_1^- + d_1^+ + e_1^- + e_1^+ + d_2^- + d_2^+ + e_2^- + e_2^+ + d_3^- + d_3^+ + e_3^- + e_3^+ \\ &\text{s.t.} \\ &x_1 + d_1^- - d_1^+ = 1 \\ &x_2 + e_1^- - e_1^+ = 7 \\ &x_1 + d_2^- - d_2^+ = 5 \\ &x_2 + e_2^- - e_2^+ = 9 \\ &x_1 + d_3^- - d_3^+ = 6 \\ &x_2 + e_3^- - e_3^+ = 2 \\ &\text{all variables} \ge 0 \end{aligned}$$

b. $x_1 = 5$, $x_2 = 7$

9. Scoring calculations

Criterion	Analyst Chicago	Accountant Denver	Auditor Houston
Career advancement	35	20	20
Location	10	12	8
Management	30	25	35
Salary	28	32	16
Prestige	32	20	24
Job security	8	10	16
Enjoyment of the work	28	20	20
Totals	171	139	139

The analyst position in Chicago is recommended

10. 178, 184, 151
Marysville

12. 170, 168, 190, 183
Handover College

14. a. 220 Bowrider (194)
b. 240 Sundancer (144)

16. Step 1: Column totals are 17/4, 31/21, and 12
Step 2:

Style	Accord	Saturn	Cavalier
Accord	4/17	7/31	4/12
Saturn	12/17	21/31	7/12
Cavalier	1/17	3/31	1/12

Step 3:

Style	Accord	Saturn	Cavalier	Row Average
Accord	0.235	0.226	0.333	0.265
Saturn	0.706	0.677	0.583	0.656
Cavalier	0.059	0.097	0.083	0.080

Consistency Ratio
Step 1:

$$0.265\begin{bmatrix}1\\3\\1/4\end{bmatrix} + 0.656\begin{bmatrix}1/3\\1\\1/7\end{bmatrix} + 0.080\begin{bmatrix}4\\7\\1\end{bmatrix}$$

$$\begin{bmatrix}0.265\\0.795\\0.066\end{bmatrix} + \begin{bmatrix}0.219\\0.656\\0.094\end{bmatrix} + \begin{bmatrix}0.320\\0.560\\0.080\end{bmatrix} = \begin{bmatrix}0.802\\2.007\\0.239\end{bmatrix}$$

Step 2: 0.802/0.265 = 3.028
2.007/0.656 = 3.062
0.239/0.080 = 3.007

Step 3: λ_{max} = (3.028 + 3.062 + 3.007)/3 = 3.032
Step 4: CI = (3.032 − 3)/2 = 0.016
Step 5: CR = 0.016/0.58 = 0.028
Because CR = 0.028 is less than 0.10, the degree of consistency exhibited in the pairwise comparison matrix for style is acceptable

18. a. 0.724, 0.193, 0.083
b. CR = 0.057, yes

20. a.

Flavor	A	B	C
A	1	3	2
B	1/3	1	5
C	1/2	1/5	1

b. Step 1: Column totals are 11/6, 21/5, and 8
Step 2:

Flavor	A	B	C
A	6/11	15/21	2/8
B	2/11	5/21	5/8
C	3/11	1/21	1/8

Step 3:

Flavor	A	B	C	Row Average
A	0.545	0.714	0.250	0.503
B	0.182	0.238	0.625	0.348
C	0.273	0.048	0.125	0.148

c. Step 1:

$$0.503\begin{bmatrix}1\\1/3\\1/2\end{bmatrix} + 0.348\begin{bmatrix}3\\1\\1/5\end{bmatrix} + 0.148\begin{bmatrix}2\\5\\1\end{bmatrix}$$

$$\begin{bmatrix}0.503\\0.168\\0.252\end{bmatrix} + \begin{bmatrix}1.044\\0.348\\0.070\end{bmatrix} + \begin{bmatrix}0.296\\0.740\\0.148\end{bmatrix} = \begin{bmatrix}1.845\\1.258\\0.470\end{bmatrix}$$

Step 2: 1.845/0.503 = 3.668
1.258/0.348 = 3.615
0.470/0.148 = 3.123

Step 3: λ_{max} = (3.668 + 3.615 + 3.123)/3 = 3.469
Step 4: CI = (3.469 − 3)/2 = 0.235
Step 5: CR = 0.235/0.58 = 0.415
Because CR = 0.415 is greater than 0.10, the individual's judgments are not consistent

22. a.

	D	S	N
D	1	1/4	1/7
S	4	1	1/3
N	7	3	1

b. 0.080, 0.265, 0.656
c. CR = 0.028, yes

24. Criteria: Yield and Risk
Step 1: Column totals are 1.5 and 3
Step 2:

	Yield	Risk	Priority
Yield	0.667	0.667	0.667
Risk	0.333	0.333	0.333

With only two criteria, CR = 0; no need to compute CR
Preceding calculations for Yield and Risk provide

Stocks	Yield Priority	Risk Priority
CCC	0.750	0.333
SRI	0.250	0.667

Overall Priorities:
CCC 0.667(0.750) + 0.333(0.333) = 0.611
SRI 0.667(0.250) + 0.333(0.667) = 0.389
CCC is preferred

26. a. Criterion: 0.608, 0.272, 0.120
Price: 0.557, 0.123, 0.320
Sound: 0.137, 0.239, 0.623
Reception: 0.579, 0.187, 0.046
b. 0.446, 0.162, 0.392
System A is preferred

Chapter 16

1. a.

Month	Time Series Value	3-Month Moving Average Forecast	(Error)^2	4-Month Moving Average Forecast	(Error)^2
1	9.5				
2	9.3				
3	9.4				
4	9.6	9.40	0.04		
5	9.8	9.43	0.14	9.45	0.12
6	9.7	9.60	0.01	9.53	0.03
7	9.8	9.70	0.01	9.63	0.03
8	10.5	9.77	0.53	9.73	0.59
9	9.9	10.00	0.01	9.95	0.00
10	9.7	10.07	0.14	9.98	0.08
11	9.6	10.03	0.18	9.97	0.14
12	9.6	9.73	0.02	9.92	0.10
		Totals	1.08		1.09

MSE(three-month) = 1.08/9 = 0.12
MSE(four-month) = 1.09/8 = 0.14
Use a three-month moving average

b. Forecast = (9.7 + 9.6 + 9.6)/3 = 9.63

2. a.

Week	Time Series Value	4-Week Moving Average Forecast	(Error)^2	5-Week Moving Average Forecast	(Error)^2
1	17				
2	21				
3	19				
4	23				
5	18	20.00	4.00		
6	16	20.25	18.06	19.60	12.96
7	20	19.00	1.00	19.40	0.36
8	18	19.25	1.56	19.20	1.44
9	22	18.00	16.00	19.00	9.00
10	20	19.00	1.00	18.80	1.44
11	15	20.00	25.00	19.20	17.64
12	22	18.75	10.56	19.00	9.00
		Totals	77.18		51.84

b. MSE(four-week) = 77.18/8 = 9.65
MSE(five-week) = 51.84/7 = 7.41

c. For the limited data provided, the five-week moving average provides the smallest MSE

4.

Week	Time Series Value	Forecast	Error	(Error)^2
1	17			
2	21	17.00	4.00	16.00
3	19	17.40	1.60	2.56
4	23	17.56	5.44	29.59
5	18	18.10	−0.10	0.01
6	16	18.09	−2.09	4.37
7	20	17.88	2.12	4.49
8	18	18.10	−0.10	0.01
9	22	18.09	3.91	15.29
10	20	18.48	1.52	2.31
11	15	18.63	−3.63	13.18
12	22	18.27	3.73	13.91
			Total	101.72

MSE = 101.72/11 = 9.25
$\alpha = 0.2$ provided a lower MSE
therefore, $\alpha = 0.2$ is better than $\alpha = 0.1$

5. a.

Month	Y_t	3-Month Moving Average Forecast	(Error)^2	$\alpha = 2$ Forecast	(Error)^2
1	80				
2	82			80.00	4.00
3	84			80.40	12.96
4	83	82.00	1.00	81.12	3.53
5	83	83.00	0.00	81.50	2.25
6	84	83.33	0.45	81.80	4.84
7	85	83.33	2.79	82.24	7.62
8	84	84.00	0.00	82.79	1.46
9	82	84.33	5.43	83.03	1.06
10	83	83.67	0.45	82.83	0.03
11	84	83.00	1.00	82.86	1.30
12	83	83.00	0.00	83.09	0.01
		Totals	11.12		39.06

MSE(three-month) = 11.12/9 = 1.24
MSE($\alpha = 0.2$) = 39.06/11 = 3.55
Use a three-month moving average

b. (83 + 84 + 83)/3 = 83.3

6. b. The more recent data receive the greater weight or importance in determining the forecast

8. a. 15.71
b. 15.74
c. 15.51
d. Moving averages; it has the smallest MSE (0.60)

10. a. $\alpha = 0.1$
b. 29.99

12. 3117.01

14. $\sum t = 21; \sum t^2 = 91; \sum Y_t = 117.1;$
$\sum tY_t = 403.7; n = 6$

$$b_1 = \frac{\sum tY_t - (\sum t \sum Y_t)/n}{\sum t^2 - (\sum t)^2/n}$$
$$= \frac{403.7 - (21)(117.1)/6}{91 - (21)^2/6}$$
$$= -0.3514$$

$b_0 = \bar{Y} - b_1\bar{t} = 19.5167 - (-.3514)(3.5) = 20.7466$
$T_t = 20.7466 - 0.3514t$

Conclusion: Enrollment appears to be decreasing by an average of approximately 351 students per year

16. a. Linear trend appears to be reasonable
b. $T_t = 19.993 + 1.774t$
Average cost increase of \$1.77 per unit per year

18. a. The graph shows a linear trend
b. $T_t = 60.553 - 1.141t$; 1.14%
c. 48.0%

20. a. A linear trend appears to exist
b. $T_t = -5 + 15t$
Average increase in sales is 15 units per year

22. a. A linear trend appears to be appropriate
b. $T_t = 6.4564 + 0.5345t$
c. .5345 million
d. 2001–2002 season: $T_{13} = 6.4564 + 0.5345(12) =$ 12.87 million

24. a. Forecast for July is 236.97; forecast for August is 236.97
b. Forecast for July is 278.88; forecast for August is 297.33
c. Not fair; it does not account for upward trend in sales

25. a. Four-quarter moving averages beginning with (1690 + 940 + 2625 + 2500)/4 = 1938.75
Other moving averages are

1966.25	2002.50
1956.25	2052.50
2025.00	2060.00
1990.00	2123.75

b.

Quarter	Seasonal-Irregular Component Values		Seasonal Index	Adjusted Seasonal Index
1	0.904	0.900	0.9020	0.900
2	0.448	0.526	0.4970	0.486
3	1.344	1.453	1.3985	1.396
4	1.275	1.164	1.2195	1.217
		Total	4.0070	

Note: Adjustment for seasonal index = 4.000/4.007 = 0.9983

c. The largest seasonal effect is in the third quarter, which corresponds to the back-to-school demand during July, August, and September of each year

26. 0.707, 0.777, 0.827, 0.966, 1.016, 1.305, 1.494, 1.225, 0.976, 0.986, 0.936, 0.787

28. a. Selected centered moving averages for t = 5, 10, 15, and 20 are 11.125, 18.125, 22.875, and 27.000
b. 0.899, 1.362, 1.118, 0.621
c. Quarter 2, prior to summer boating season

30. a. $T_t = 6.329 + 1.055t$
b. 36.92, 37.98, 39.03, 40.09
c. 33.23, 51.65, 43.71, 24.86

32. a. Yes, there is a seasonal effect; seasonal indexes are 1.696, 1.458, 0.711, 0.326, 0.448, 1.362
b. Forecast for 12–4 is 166,761.13; forecast for 4–8 is 146,052.99

33. a.

Restaurant (i)	x_i	y_i	$x_i y_i$	x_i^2
1	1	19	19	1
2	4	44	176	16
3	6	40	240	36
4	10	52	520	100
5	14	53	742	196
Totals	35	208	1697	349

$$\bar{x} = \frac{35}{5} = 7$$
$$\bar{y} = \frac{208}{5} = 41.6$$
$$b_1 = \frac{\sum x_i y_i - (\sum x_i \sum y_i)/n}{\sum x_i^2 - (\sum x_i)^2/n}$$
$$= \frac{1697 - (35)(208)/5}{349 - (35)^2/5}$$
$$= \frac{241}{104} = 2.317$$

$b_0 = \bar{y} - b_1\bar{x} = 41.6 - 2.317(7) = 25.381$
$\hat{y} = 25.381 + 2.317x$

b. $\hat{y} = 25.381 + 2.317(8) = 43.917$, or \$43,917

34. a. $\hat{y} = 37.666 - 3.222x$
b. \$3444

Chapter 17

2. a. 0.82
b. $\pi_1 = 0.5, \pi_2 = 0.5$
c. $\pi_1 = 0.6, \pi_2 = 0.4$

3. a. 0.10 as given by the transition probability

b. $\pi_1 = 0.90\pi_1 + 0.30\pi_2$ (1)

$\pi_2 = 0.10\pi_1 + 0.70\pi_2$ (2)

$\pi_1 + \pi_2 = 1$ (3)

Using (1) and (3),

$$0.10\pi_1 - 0.30\pi_2 = 0$$
$$0.10\pi_1 - 0.30(1 - \pi_1) = 0$$
$$0.10\pi_1 - 0.30 + 0.30\pi_1 = 0$$
$$0.40\pi_1 = 0.30$$
$$\pi_1 = 0.75$$
$$\pi_2 = (1 - \pi_1) = 0.25$$

4. a. $\pi_1 = 0.92, \pi_2 = 0.08$

b. $85

6. a.

	City	Suburbs
City	0.98	0.02
Suburbs	0.01	0.99

b. $\pi_1 = 0.333, \pi_2 = 0.667$

c. City will decrease from 40% to 33%; suburbs will increase from 60% to 67%

7. a. $\pi_1 = 0.85\pi_1 + 0.20\pi_2 + 0.15\pi_3$ (1)

$\pi_2 = 0.10\pi_1 + 0.75\pi_2 + 0.10\pi_3$ (2)

$\pi_3 = 0.05\pi_1 + 0.05\pi_2 + 0.75\pi_3$ (3)

$\pi_1 + \pi_2 + \pi_3 = 1$ (4)

Using (1), (2), and (4) provides three equations with three unknowns; solving provides $\pi_1 = 0.548$, $\pi_2 = 0.286$, and $\pi_3 = 0.166$

b. 16.6% as given by π_3

c. Quick Stop should take

667 − 0.548(1000) = 119 Murphy's customers

and 333 − 0.286(1000) = 47 Ashley's customers

Total 166 Quick Stop customers

It will take customers from Murphy's and Ashley's

8. a. MDA

b. $\pi = 1/3, \pi_2 = 2/3$

10. 3 − 1(0.59), 4 − 1(0.52)

11. $I = \begin{bmatrix} 1 & 0 \\ 0 & 1 \end{bmatrix}$ $Q = \begin{bmatrix} 0.25 & 0.25 \\ 0.05 & 0.25 \end{bmatrix}$

$$(I - Q) = \begin{bmatrix} 0.75 & -0.25 \\ -0.05 & 0.75 \end{bmatrix}$$

$$N = (I - Q)^{-1} = \begin{bmatrix} 1.3636 & 0.4545 \\ 0.0909 & 1.3636 \end{bmatrix}$$

$$NR = \begin{bmatrix} 1.3636 & 0.4545 \\ 0.0909 & 1.3636 \end{bmatrix}\begin{bmatrix} 0.5 & 0.0 \\ 0.5 & 0.2 \end{bmatrix} = \begin{bmatrix} 0.909 & 0.091 \\ 0.727 & 0.273 \end{bmatrix}$$

$$BNR = [4000 \quad 5000]\begin{bmatrix} 0.909 & 0.091 \\ 0.727 & 0.273 \end{bmatrix} = [7271 \quad 1729]$$

Estimate $1729 in bad debts

12. 3580 will be sold eventually; 1420 will be lost

14. a. Graduate and drop out

b. P(Drop Out) = 0.15, P(Sophomore) = 0.10, P(Junior) = 0.75

c. 0.706, 0.294

d. Yes; P(Graduate) = 0.54

P(Drop Out) = 0.46

e. 1479 (74%) will graduate

Chapter 18

2. a. The numbers in the squares above each node represent the shortest route from the node to node 10

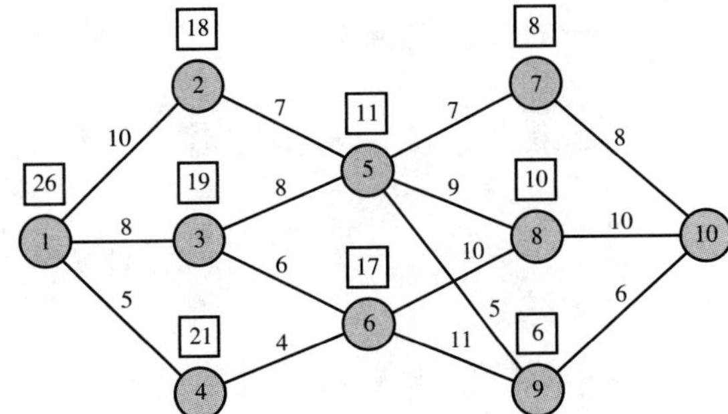

The shortest route is given by the sequence of nodes (1–4–6–9–10)

b. The shortest route from node 4 to node 10 is given by (4–6–9–10)

c.

Route	Value	Route	Value
(1–2–5–7–10)	32	(1–3–6–8–10)	34
(1–2–5–8–10)	36	(1–3–6–9–10)	31
(1–2–5–9–10)	28	(1–4–6–8–10)	29
(1–3–5–7–10)	31	(1–4–6–9–10)	26
(1–3–5–8–10)	35		
(1–3–5–9–10)	27		

3. Use four stages (one for each type of cargo); let the state variable represent the amount of cargo space remaining
   a. In hundreds of pounds, we have up to 20 units of capacity available

Stage 1 (Cargo Type 1):

x_1	0	1	2	d_1^*	$f_1(x_1)$	x_0
0–7	0	—	—	0	0	0–7
8–15	0	22	—	1	22	0–7
16–20	0	22	44	2	44	0–4

Stage 2 (Cargo Type 2):

x_2	0	1	2	d_2^*	$f_2(x_2)$	x_1
0–4	0	—	—	0	0	0–4
5–7	0	12	—	1	12	0–2
8–9	22	12	—	0	22	8–9
10–12	22	12	24	2	24	0–2
13–15	22	34	24	1	34	8–10
16–17	44	34	24	0	44	16–17
18–20	44	34	46	2	46	8–10

Stage 3 (Cargo Type 3):

x_3	0	1	2	3	4	d_3^*	$f_3(x_3)$	x_2
0–2	0	—	—	—	—	0	0	0–2
3–4	0	7	—	—	—	1	7	0–1
5	12	7	—	—	—	0	12	5
6–7	12	7	14	—	—	2	14	0–1
8	22	19	14	—	—	0	22	8
9	22	19	14	21	—	0	22	9
10	24	19	14	21	—	0	24	10
11	24	29	26	21	—	1	29	8
12	24	29	26	21	28	1	29	9
13	34	31	26	21	28	0	34	13
14–15	34	31	36	33	28	2	36	8–9
16	44	41	38	33	28	0	44	16
17	44	41	38	43	40	0	44	17
18	46	41	38	43	40	0	46	18
19	46	51	48	45	40	1	51	16
20	46	51	48	45	50	1	51	17

Stage 4 (Cargo Type 4):

x_4	0	1	2	3	d_4^*	$f_4(x_4)$	x_3
20	51	49	50	45	0	51	20

Tracing back through the tables, we find

Stage	State Variable Entering	Optimal Decision	State Variable Leaving
4	20	0	20
3	20	1	17
2	17	0	17
1	17	2	1

Load 1 unit of cargo type 3 and 2 units of cargo type 1 for a total return of $5100

   b. Only the calculations for stage 4 need to be repeated; the entering value for the state variable is 18

x_4	0	1	2	3	d_4^*	$f_4(x_4)$	x_3
18	46	47	42	38	1	47	16

Optimal solution: $d_4 = 1, d_3 = 0, d_2 = 0, d_1 = 2$
Value = 47

4. a. Alternative optimal solutions: value = 186
   Solution 1: A1–3, A2–2, A3–0, A4–3
   Solution 2: A1–2, A2–3, A3–0, A4–3
   b. Value = 172; A1–1, A2–2, A3–0, A4–3

6. a. A–G–J–M
   b. Choose H

8. a. Daily news–1, Sunday news–3, radio–1, TV-3; Max exposure = 169
   b. 1, 2, 1, 2; Max exposure = 139
   c. For part (a): 2, 3, 3; Max exposure = 152
   For part (b): 2, 3, 1; Max exposure = 127

10. The optimal production schedule is as follows:

Month	Beginning Inventory	Production	Ending Inventory
1	10	20	10
2	10	20	0
3	0	30	0

Index

A

B

C

D

H

I

J

K

L

M

N

O

P

Q

R

S

T

U

V

W

Y

Z

QUICK GUIDE TO CABLE SELECTION

NOTE: INFORMATION BELOW APPLIES TO COPPER WIRE ONLY

Confirm the right cable for your project using the illustration above. Distance may impact the appropriate gauge of wire in the cable. Cables are labeled with two numbers. The first indicates wire size and the second how many wires are in the cable. For example, 12/2 cable means 12-gauge wire and two wires plus a ground wire.

CHOOSE THE RIGHT GAUGE WIRE

GAUGE GUIDE FOR MAXIMUM ALLOWABLE WIRE LENGTH, 2% NOMINAL VOLTAGE DROP

		COPPER CONDUCTORS							
AMPS	WATTS	UP TO 50'	UP TO 100'	UP TO 150'	UP TO 200'	UP TO 250'	UP TO 300'	UP TO 400'	UP TO 500'
15	1800	14 Gauge	12 Gauge	10 Gauge	6 Gauge	6 Gauge	6 Gauge	4 Gauge	4 Gauge
20	2400	12 Gauge	10 Gauge	8 Gauge	6 Gauge	6 Gauge	4 Gauge	4 Gauge	2 Gauge
30	3000	10 Gauge	8 Gauge	6 Gauge	6 Gauge	4 Gauge	4 Gauge	2 Gauge	2 Gauge
40	4800	8 Gauge	6 Gauge	4 Gauge	4 Gauge	2 Gauge	2 Gauge	1 Gauge	1/0 Gauge
50	6000	6 Gauge	6 Gauge	4 Gauge	4 Gauge	2 Gauge	1 Gauge	1/0 Gauge	2/0 Gauge

This information is provided as a general guideline only. For safe wiring practices consult the National Electric Code®, local building codes and regulations, and your local building inspector. Always remember that installation of electrical wire can be hazardous and, if done improperly, can result in personal injury or property damage.

The correct wire gauge (size) for your project is based on the amperage, or power, required and the distance the wire travels. The chart at left helps you determine what gauge wire you need. Remember, the smaller the number, the larger the wire. For example, a 6-gauge wire is larger than an 8-gauge wire.

Canadian codes differ from the above charts, and typically require a 14/2 cable on most household circuits. Check your provincial codes before completing your project.

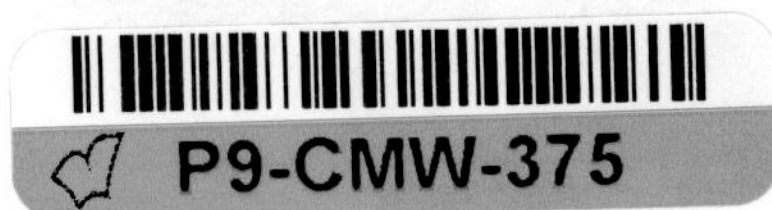
P9-CMW-375

Wiring 1-2-3™

Meredith® Books Development Team
Project Editor: Catherine M. Staub
Art Director: John Eric Seid
Copy Chief: Catherine Hamrick
Copy and Production Editor: Terri Fredrickson
Managers, Book Production: Pam Kvitne, Marjorie J. Schenkelberg
Contributing Copy Editor: Margaret Smith
Contributing Proofreaders: John C. Edwards, Steve Hallam, Raymond L. Kast, Ralph Selzer
Contributing Designers: Tim Abramowitz, Joyce E. DeWitt
Electronic Production Coordinator: Paula Forest
Editorial Assistants: Renee E. McAtee, Karen Schirm

Meredith® Books
Editor in Chief: James D. Blume
Design Director: Matt Strelecki
Managing Editor: Gregory H. Kayko
Executive Editor, Home Depot Books: Benjamin W. Allen

Director, Retail Sales and Marketing: Terry Unsworth
Director, Sales, Special Markets: Rita McMullen
Director, Sales, Premiums: Michael A. Peterson
Director, Sales, Retail: Tom Wierzbicki
Director, Book Marketing: Brad Elmitt
Director, Operations: George A. Susral
Director, Production: Douglas M. Johnston

Vice President, General Manager: Jamie L. Martin

Meredith Publishing Group
President, Publishing Group: Christopher M. Little
Vice President, Finance & Administration: Max Runciman

Meredith Corporation
Chairman and Chief Executive Officer: William T. Kerr

Chairman of the Executive Committee: E. T. Meredith III

The Home Depot®
Senior Vice President, Marketing and Communications: Dick Hammill
Project Director: Hugh Miskel

Greenleaf Publishing, Inc.
Editor: Dave Toht
Writer: Steve Cory
Art Director: Jean De Vaty
Associate Art Director: Rebecca Jon Michaels
Photography: Dan Stultz
Studio Assistant: Jeanine Jankovsky
Illustrator: Jim Swanson
Copy Editors: Barbara Webb, Dawn Kotapish
Technical Consultant: Joe Hansa
Intern: Kathryn Millhorn
With thanks to: Dave's Electric, Batavia, IL and Tech Lighting, Inc., Chicago, IL

Library of Congress Catalog Control Number: 00-133272
ISBN: 0-696-21184-x
Distributed by Meredith Corporation

Note to the Reader: Due to differing conditions, tools, and individual skills, Meredith Corporation and The Home Depot assume no responsibility for any damages, injuries suffered, or losses incurred as a result of following the information published in this book. Before beginning any project, review the instructions carefully, and if any doubts or questions remain, consult local experts or authorities. Because codes and regulations vary greatly, you always should check with authorities to ensure that your project complies with all applicable local codes and regulations. Always read and observe all of the safety precautions provided by any tool or equipment manufacturer, and follow all accepted safety procedures.

The editors of *Wiring 1-2-3*™ are dedicated to providing accurate and helpful do-it-yourself information. We welcome your comments about improving this book and ideas for other books we might offer to home improvement enthusiasts.
Contact us by any of these methods:

1. Leave a voice message at **800/678-2093**
2. Write to **Meredith Books, Home Depot Books, 1716 Locust Street, Des Moines, IA 50309–3023**
3. Send e-mail to **hi123@mdp.com**. Visit The Home Depot website at **homedepot.com**

Wiring 1-2-3™

Install, Upgrade, Repair, and Maintain Your Home's Electrical System

Wiring 1-2-3™ TABLE OF CONTENTS

HOW TO USE THIS BOOK

Wiring 1-2-3 is filled with practical home wiring projects you can do! Professional electricians from The Home Depot stores across the United States and Canada provided projects that people like you want to do. They helped make sure the book has all the steps for you to successfully complete each project.

Start by reading **Safety First**. It walks you through basic rules for working with electricity. Pay close attention to **bold red type** and safety tips marked with stop signs.

If you're new to wiring projects, check out **Understanding Wiring**. It provides you with knowledge of what you're working with before you start a project.

To discover what electrical upgrades you may need in your home, turn to the chapter on **Inspecting Your Home**.

Ready to start a project? Check out **Top 10 Projects**. We've gathered projects The Home Depot electrical associates report are the most common for do-it-yourselfers.

Basic Tools and Skills will help you prepare for the projects in the following chapters: **Electrical Repairs, Planning Lighting,** and **Easy Upgrades**.

Electrical Repairs covers common repair jobs, such as rewiring lamps, replacing plugs and cords, and resetting breakers.

Good lighting does more than illuminate. Turn to **Planning Lighting** for help using lights to create indoor and outdoor areas with style and function.

Easy Upgrades shows you how to complete simple tasks that involve detaching old wires and attaching new wires. Projects include installing track lighting and grounding receptacles.

Once you've completed some easy upgrades or top 10 projects, you'll have the skills to move on to **Planning New Electrical Service**. Learn what tools you need and how to draw plans. Now you should be ready to tackle **Running New Cable**, **Installing New Services**, and **Major Projects**.

Running New Cable provides directions for installing lines in new framing and existing homes.

Turn to **Installing New Services** when you're ready to install a new electrical device or fixture such as a wall light, attic fan, or outdoor receptacle.

Major Projects covers installations that involve adding new circuits. Work through the projects in this chapter only after you've successfully completed projects throughout the book. If your local or provincial codes don't allow homeowners to add new circuits, this chapter will provide you with information to understand the project you're hiring an electrician to complete.

If you have a project involving telephone wire, coaxial cable, door chimes, or thermostats, turn to **Low-Voltage Wiring**.

If you prefer to hire a pro, this book will provide you with the knowledge to make the right choice and help you judge the work that's done.

For the do-it-yourselfer, *Wiring 1-2-3* provides step-by-step directions, tips from the pros, lighting design ideas, and safety information to help you safely, easily, and accurately complete your home wiring projects and stylishly light your home.

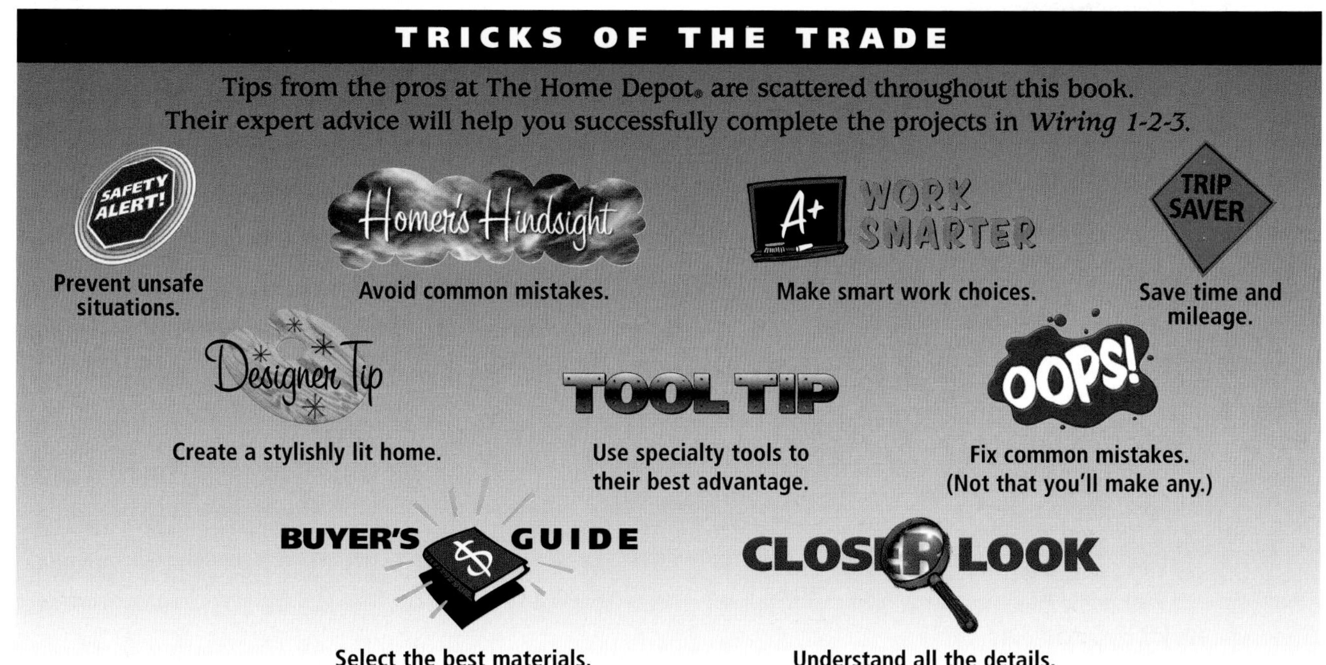
TRICKS OF THE TRADE
Tips from the pros at The Home Depot® are scattered throughout this book.
Their expert advice will help you successfully complete the projects in *Wiring 1-2-3*.
SAFETY ALERT!
Prevent unsafe situations.
Homer's Hindsight
Avoid common mistakes.
A+ WORK SMARTER
Make smart work choices.
TRIP SAVER
Save time and mileage.
Designer Tip
Create a stylishly lit home.
TOOL TIP
Use specialty tools to their best advantage.
OOPS!
Fix common mistakes. (Not that you'll make any.)
BUYER'S GUIDE
Select the best materials.
CLOSER LOOK
Understand all the details.

SAFETY FIRST

Electricians and others who have done a lot of electrical work know they always have to follow safety precautions. They've heard hair-raising stories about what happens to people who ignore safe work habits. This book is loaded with safety reminders to help you stay safe while you work. Follow them.

Electricity deserves your respect. Consider how household current can affect the human body. If your feet are dry and you are wearing rubber-soled shoes, receiving a shock from a 120-volt circuit will definitely hurt, but it will probably not cause you serious harm. However, if conditions are wet or your feet are not protected with rubber-soled shoes and you are standing on the ground or on a metal ladder, 120 volts can cause the muscles in your hands to contract so that you grasp the source of current involuntarily. The current will cause your heart to beat wildly, very likely to the point of heart failure. Expect the same consequence if you touch both live wires of a 240-volt current, even if your feet are dry and protected. Children are in even greater danger.

SHUT OFF THE POWER. For most electrical projects, it is essential that you shut off power at the service panel. Flip a breaker off, or unscrew and remove a fuse.

TEST FOR POWER. Confirm that the power is off. (See pages 44–45 for how to use testers.) If you are using any type of neon tester, test the tester to be sure it is not showing power only because its bulb is out.

The wiring in a modern home should have safety features, such as grounding and ground-fault circuit interruption. (See pages 51–57 for how to inspect your home for these and other safety considerations.) Both greatly reduce the possibility of dangerous shock, but they don't offer complete protection to a person who is working on exposed wires and devices. This is why professional electricians work very carefully. So should you.

Here are a few basic rules for safe electrical work. Follow them at all times, even when you are doing "just a little" electrical job.

SHUT OFF THE POWER

If there is no electrical current, you cannot receive a shock. Always shut off power to the circuit you are working on. Do this by flipping a circuit breaker or completely unscrewing a fuse. Then test for the presence of power (see pages 44–45).

TEST FOR POWER

Be aware that more than one circuit may be running in a box. Test all the wires in an open box for power, not just the wires you will be working on. Test everything twice.

Regularly test your tester to make sure it will indeed tell you when power is present. Touch it to a live circuit and see that it glows just before every test. Many a war story tells of someone turning off the power, only to have a family member or co-worker turn it back on while work is in progress. Post a sign telling people not to restore power; lock the service panel if possible.

STAY FOCUSED

Most electrical mishaps occur because of small mental mistakes. Remove all distractions. Keep people, especially children, well out of the way. Turn the radio off. Even after turning off the power, work as if the wires are live. Work methodically, and double-check all connections before restoring power.

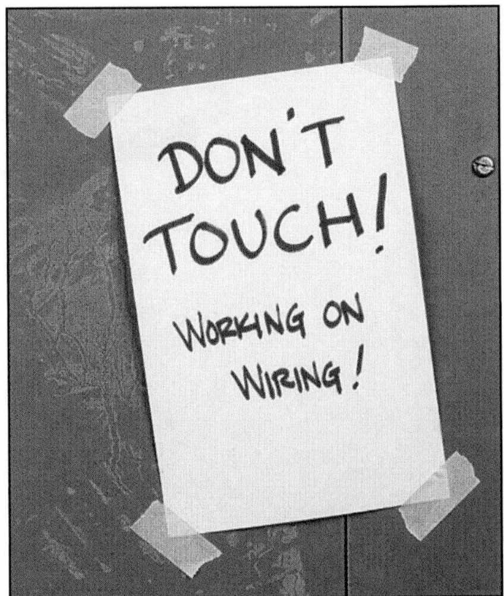

POST A SIGN ON THE PANEL. Take steps to make absolutely certain that no one will turn the power back on while you are working. If possible, lock the service panel.

USE PROTECTIVE TOOLS AND CLOTHING

Rubber grips offer more protection than simple plastic or wood handles, so always use rubber-gripped tools when wiring. Get in the habit of using them correctly: Grab by the handle, not the metal shaft. Make sure your pliers and cutting tools have rubber grips that are long enough so you will not be tempted to touch the metal while working. Replace a tool when the rubber is damaged.

Wear rubber-soled shoes, such as athletic shoes, and perhaps rubber gloves, so that electrical current will not travel easily through you and into the ground. Never work with wet feet or while standing on a wet surface. Do not wear jewelry or a watch—anything that could possibly get snagged on wires. Use a fiberglass or wood ladder; an aluminum ladder conducts electricity.

ASK QUESTIONS

Electricians consult with each other all the time, even when they are 99 percent sure they already understand. Never proceed with an installation or repair unless you are completely sure you know what you are doing. Don't hesitate to ask "stupid" questions of electrical experts in a Home Depot or an electrical supply store.

BE PROTECTED FROM THE GROUND UP. Always keep your feet protected with rubber soles, to lessen the effects of a possible shock. In damp areas, stand on dry boards.

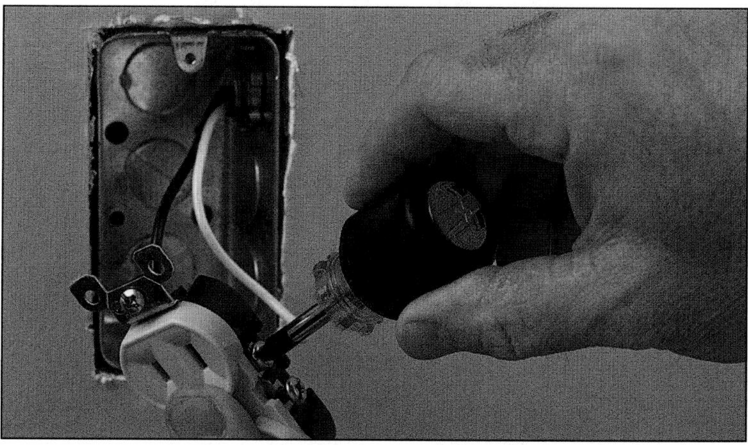

USE RUBBER-GRIPPED TOOLS. Don't use tools with plastic or wood handles unless they also have rubber sleeves to provide extra protection against electrical shock.

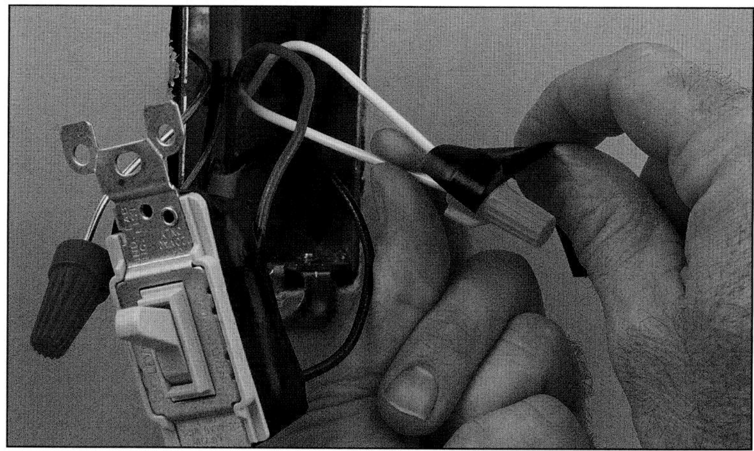

USE ELECTRICIAN'S TAPE. Electrician's tape provides extra protection against dangerous ground faults and shorts. Even if not required by code, wrap wire nuts and terminals with tape (see pages 43 and 50).

1 UNDERSTANDING WIRING

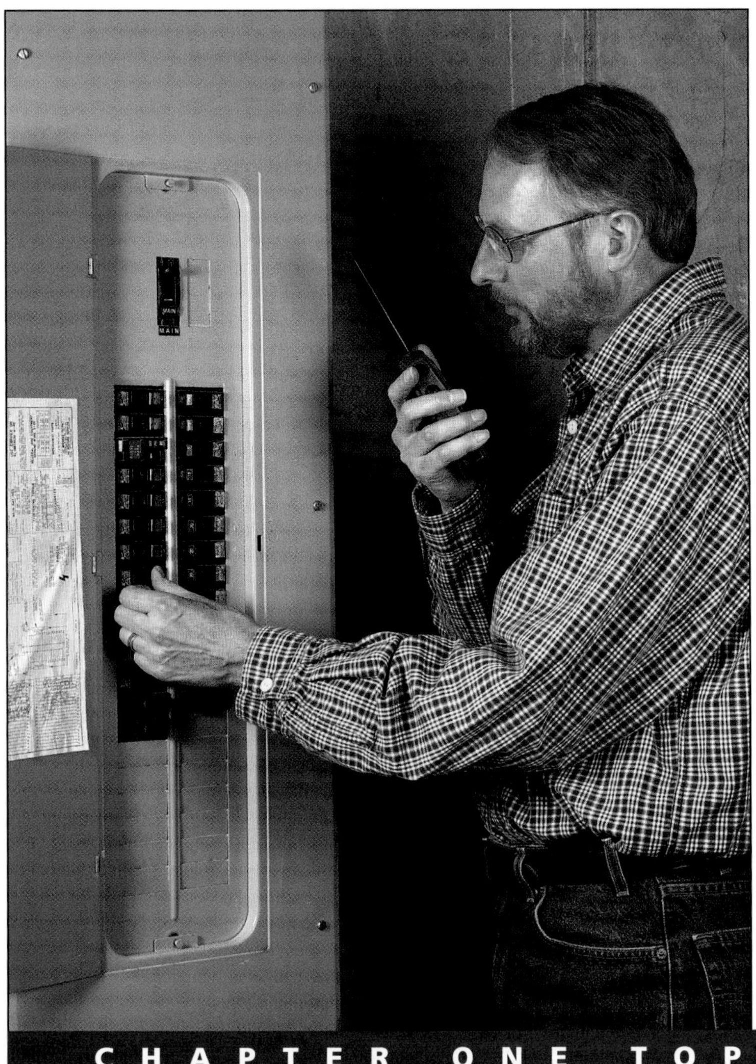

Wiring contributes to the convenience of life. Flip a switch or turn a knob, and electricity instantly goes to work. Occasionally, however, a lamp flickers or a receptacle goes dead. Many electrical procedures are well within the range of most homeowners, but because electricity can be dangerous to work with, it may be tempting to call a professional electrician.

This chapter equips you with the basic knowledge you need to safely work on your home's wiring. It introduces you to the purpose and function of every wire and every device in your home. Take the time to become knowledgeable about how your home circuits work. Familiarize yourself with standard safeguards against electrical shocks and fire. For many projects, you may decide to call in a pro, but this chapter will prepare you to understand what makes a job safe and reliable—useful information whether or not you do it yourself.

CHAPTER ONE TOPICS

HOW POWER GETS DISTRIBUTED

Electricity is the flow of electrons through a **conductor**—copper or aluminum wires in household construction. Electricity must travel in a loop, called a **circuit.** In most cases, power travels out to a fixture or device through a hot wire—usually coated with black or red insulation—and back through a neutral wire, which has white insulation. When the circuit is broken at any point, power ceases to flow.

Newer homes are grounded. Grounding connects all outlets to the earth and is an essential safety feature (pages 11–13). Ungrounded outlets can give a serious shock if there is a short circuit due to a damaged wire or device. Ground wires are either bare copper or have green insulation. Polarization is a similar safety feature found in older homes (page 11).

VOLTAGE AND AMPS

Voltage is the electrical pressure exerted by the power source. Most household fixtures use 120 volts. Large items such as ranges and central air conditioners require 240 volts. On the packaging of electrical devices or in manufacturer's instructions, you may see voltage figures, such as 115, 125, 220, or even 250 volts. These numbers reflect the fact that voltage can vary; a 115-volt receptacle is interchangeable with a receptacle rated at 125 volts. **Here, we'll refer to 120-volt and 240-volt circuits.**

The pressure on all wires is approximately 120 or 240 volts, but the amount of electricity used by each fixture or appliances varies. This is because wires, fixtures, and appliances have different resistance to the voltage. Simply put, the thicker the wire, the more electricity travels through it. The terms **amperes** (or **amps**) and **watts** refer to the amount of electrical current that specific elements of a system use (pages 62–63).

FROM UTILITY TO HOME

Electrical power flows into neighborhoods through overhead (or underground) high-voltage wires. Transformers reduce the amount of power so that the wires entering homes carry a relatively safe load of 120 volts per wire. Through a **service head,** these wires enter a **meter.** The meter records how much power a home uses for billing purposes. The wires then enter the home's **service panel,** which divides the power into branch **circuits** (see opposite page).

Most homes have three wires—two "hot" wires to carry power into the house and one neutral wire to carry power back to complete the circuit. Having two hot wires means that a home can run **120-volt circuits** and **240-volt circuits** (for large appliances). Older homes with only two wires entering the home—a hot and a neutral—can run only 120-volt outlets. Some appliances, such as electric water heaters, are **hard-wired** to the circuit (wires are attached directly to the unit without the use of a plug or receptacle).

Underground electrical service to homes is usually provided by three wires—black, red, and white—that travel through a pipe called conduit. Overhead service is usually

CLOSER LOOK

TECHNICAL TERMS.
If you need to plug in a lamp, you find an outlet, right? Well, almost. Technically, an electrical outlet is anyplace where electricity leaves the wires to perform a service—such as at a light fixture. A receptacle is a type of outlet; it is where electricity exits the system through, say, a toaster plug. A device is something that carries, but does not use, electricity itself; receptacles and switches are devices. A fixture is an electrical outlet that is permanently fixed in place, and an appliance is a user of electricity that can be moved. Thus an overhead light is a fixture, and a microwave oven is an appliance.

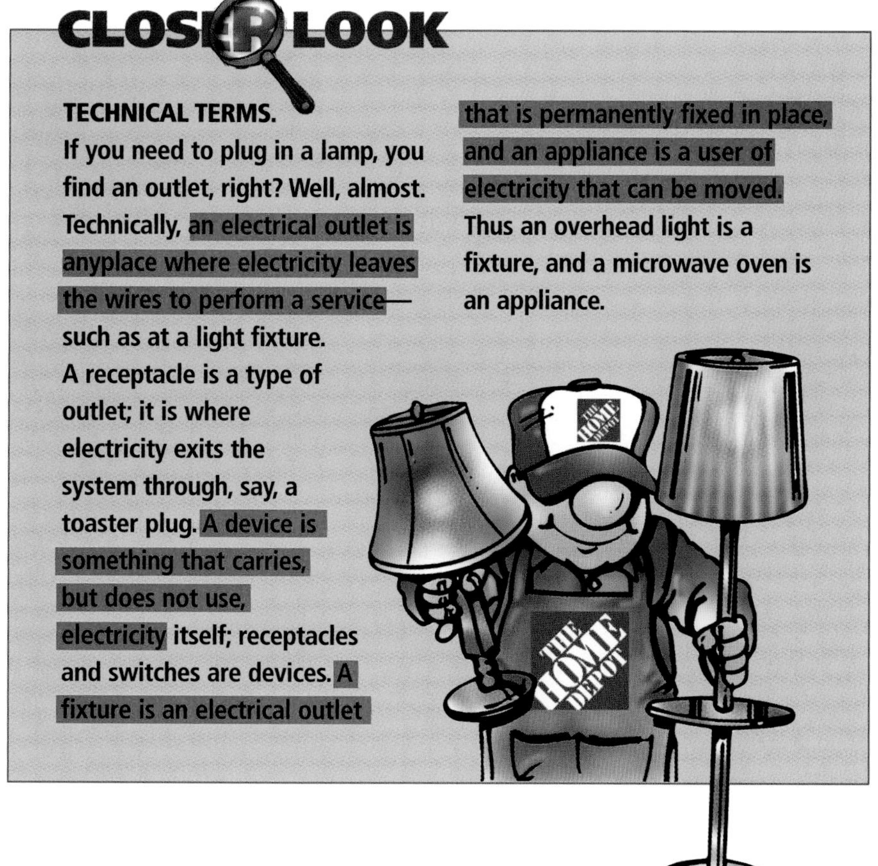

provided by three wires, one of which may be bare. They all connect to the house at a service head. These wires must not be damaged. If an overhead wire rubs against a tree or if an underground line seems exposed, call your utility company.

KNOW YOUR LIMITS

You can perform most repairs and installations on wires, devices, and fixtures in the home, but do not touch anything outside the home. Never touch wires leading to the service panel or wires upstream from the main shutoff (pages 14–15). If you have questions about the wires entering your house or leading from the meter to the service panel, call your utility company. These wires are usually their legal responsibility.

FROM SERVICE HEAD TO RECEPTACLE

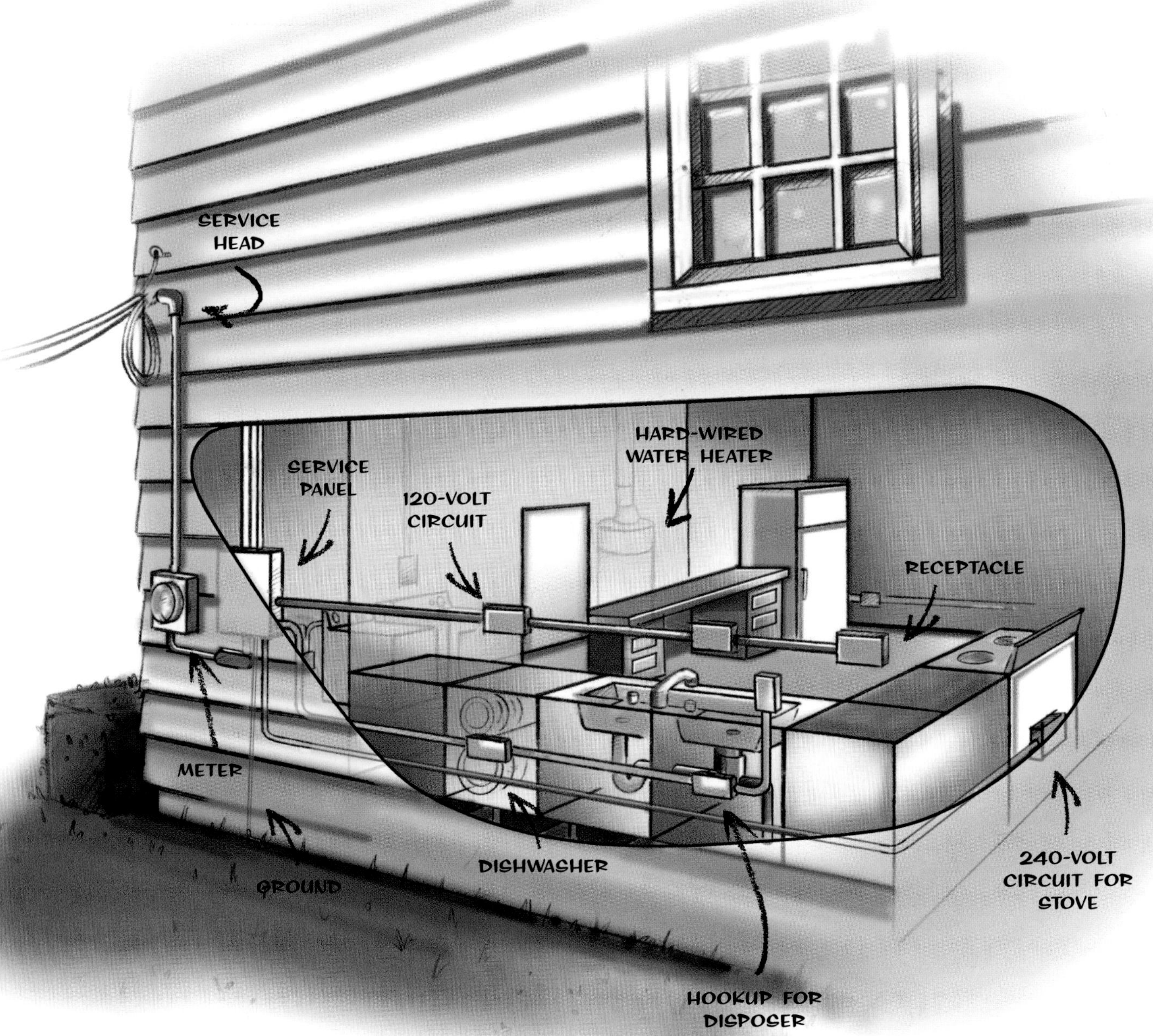

HOW A CIRCUIT WORKS

Service panels, whether they have breakers or fuses, divide household current into several circuits. Each circuit carries power from the service panel via hot (usually black or red) wires to various outlets in the house, and then back to the service panel via a neutral (usually white) wire.

TYPES OF CIRCUITS

Most household circuits carry 120 volts. There also may be several 240-volt circuits. Circuits are rated according to amps. If the outlets on a circuit draw too many amps, the circuit overloads. When this happens, a fuse will blow or a breaker will trip (pages 80–81), preventing an unsafe condition.

A 120-volt circuit usually serves a number of outlets. For instance, it may supply power to a series of lights, a series of receptacles, or some of each. Heavy-use items, such as dishwashers and refrigerators, may have their own dedicated circuits. A 240-volt circuit is always dedicated to one outlet. A standard 120-volt 15-amp circuit uses #14 wire; a 20-amp circuit uses thicker #12 wire. Until recently, 240-volt circuits used three wires—two hot and one neutral. Recent codes require four wires, as shown below; the added wire is for grounding.

Circuits provide convenience as well as safety. If a repair or new installation is under way, you can shut off power to an individual circuit instead of the entire house.

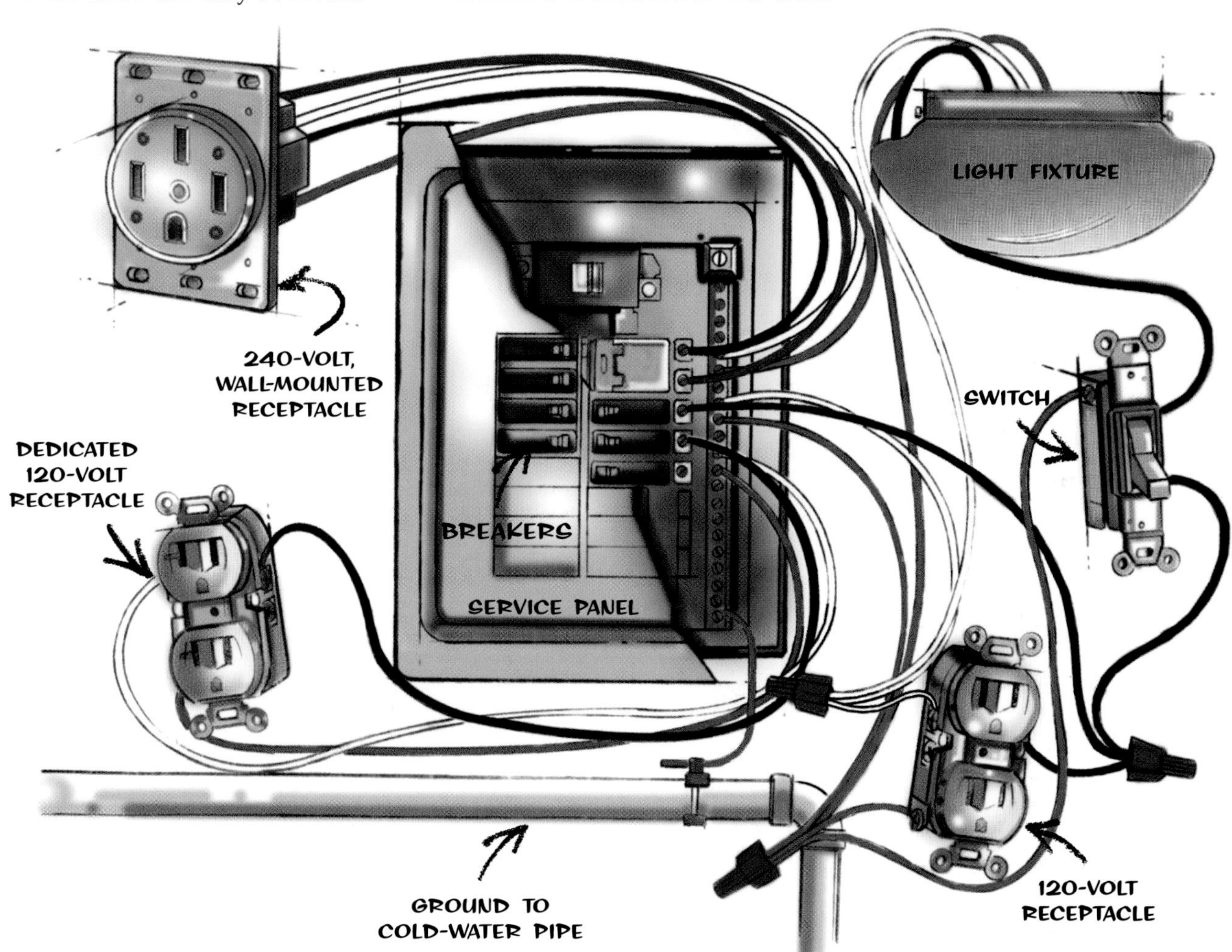

A SERVICE PANEL HAS 120- AND 240-VOLT CIRCUITS. Your service panel distributes power according to the needs of a circuit. For example, a 240-volt circuit is designed to supply electricity to a heavy-duty user of power, such as an electric range or a dryer. The single receptacle on a dedicated 120-volt circuit might feed a refrigerator or a large microwave, while another 120-volt circuit feeds a series of receptacles and switched overhead light fixtures.

GROUNDING AND POLARIZATION

Normally, electricity travels in insulated wires and exits through a light fixture into a bulb, for example. If a wire comes loose or if a device cracks, a short circuit **(ground fault)** results, energizing something you don't want to be energized. A short can occur if a loose wire inside a dryer touches the dryer's frame or if cracked insulation allows bare wire to touch a metal electrical box. If you touch energized metal, you'll get a dangerous shock. Grounding and polarization protect against this. Here's how they work:

GROUNDING

Grounding minimizes the possibility that a short circuit will cause a shock. A grounded device, fixture, or appliance is usually connected to a grounding wire—either bare or green—which leads to the neutral bar in the service panel. This bar is connected to the earth by one or a combination of these:

- cold-water pipe
- grounding rods driven deep in the ground
- metal plate sunk in a footing.

Another method uses the metal sheathing of armored cable or conduit (page 16)—not a ground wire—as the ground path to the service panel.

When a ground fault occurs, the ground path carries the power to the service panel. This extra path lowers resistance, causing a great deal of power to flow back to the panel. This in turn trips a circuit breaker or blows a fuse. At the same time, power is directed harmlessly into the earth.

Whether your system uses grounding wires or sheathing as the ground path, it must be unbroken. A single disconnected ground wire or a loose connection in the sheathing or conduit can make the grounding system useless. To check whether a receptacle is grounded, plug in a receptacle analyzer (page 44).

POLARIZATION

Polarization is a way of making sure that electricity goes where you want it to go. Because a polarized plug has one prong wider than the other, there is only one way that the plug can be inserted into a polarized receptacle. If the receptacle is wired correctly and an appliance plug is polarized, the hot wire, and not the neutral wire, will always be controlled by the appliance switch. If the receptacle or plug isn't polarized, the neutral wire might be connected to the appliance switch instead, and power would be present in the appliance even when it is switched off. For extra protection against shock, install GFCI protection (page 27).

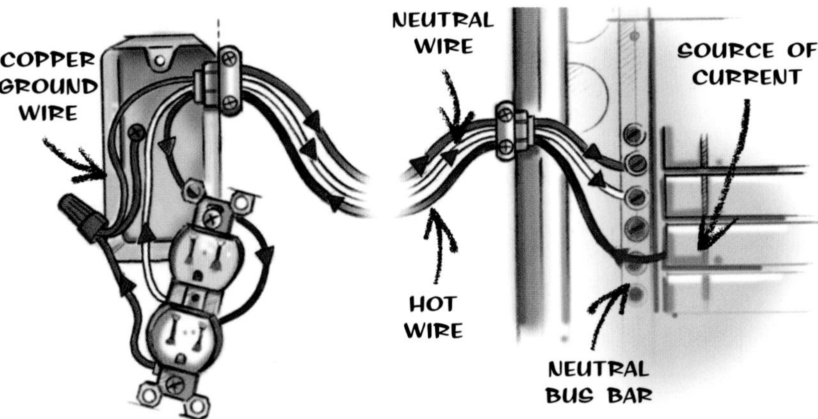

HOW A GROUNDED RECEPTACLE WORKS. To ground a receptacle, a ground wire (either bare or green) is attached to the receptacle (and to the box, if it is metal) and leads to the neutral bus bar in the service panel. The panel itself is grounded (page 10). This receptacle is also polarized.

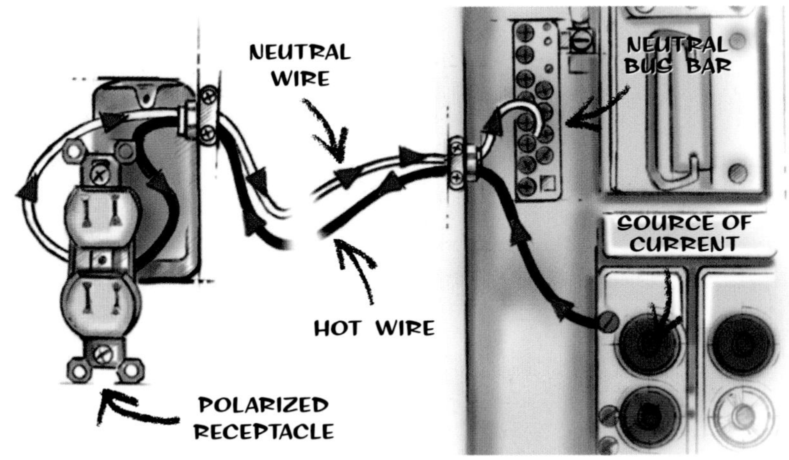

HOW A POLARIZED RECEPTACLE WORKS. The black wire is connected to the receptacle's brass terminal at one end and to the circuit breaker or fuse at the other end. The white wire runs from the silver terminal screw to the service panel's neutral bus bar.

GROUNDING METHODS

Before you begin any electrical work, find out how your system is grounded. First, plug a receptacle analyzer (page 44) into every receptacle to make sure they are grounded. Then check your service panel to make sure it's grounded—perhaps to a pipe or to grounding rods. Finally, look at the wiring of your receptacles or fixtures to see how they're grounded (opposite page).

If you have an older home without grounding, you should ground any new circuits you install. It is also possible to ground individual receptacles (page 107). A GFCI that is ungrounded can offer substantial protection for individual circuits (page 13).

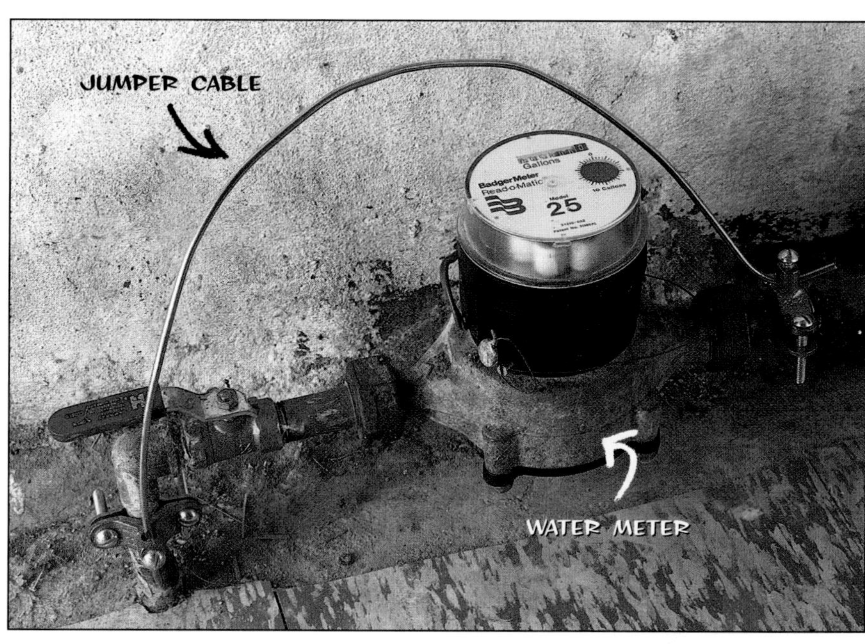

JUMP A WATER METER. Provide an unbroken path for a ground that uses a water pipe. A water meter, for instance, breaks the path. Make sure that the ground wire is connected on the upstream side of the meter (toward the street, not the house) or that there is a tightly clamped jumper cable, as shown.

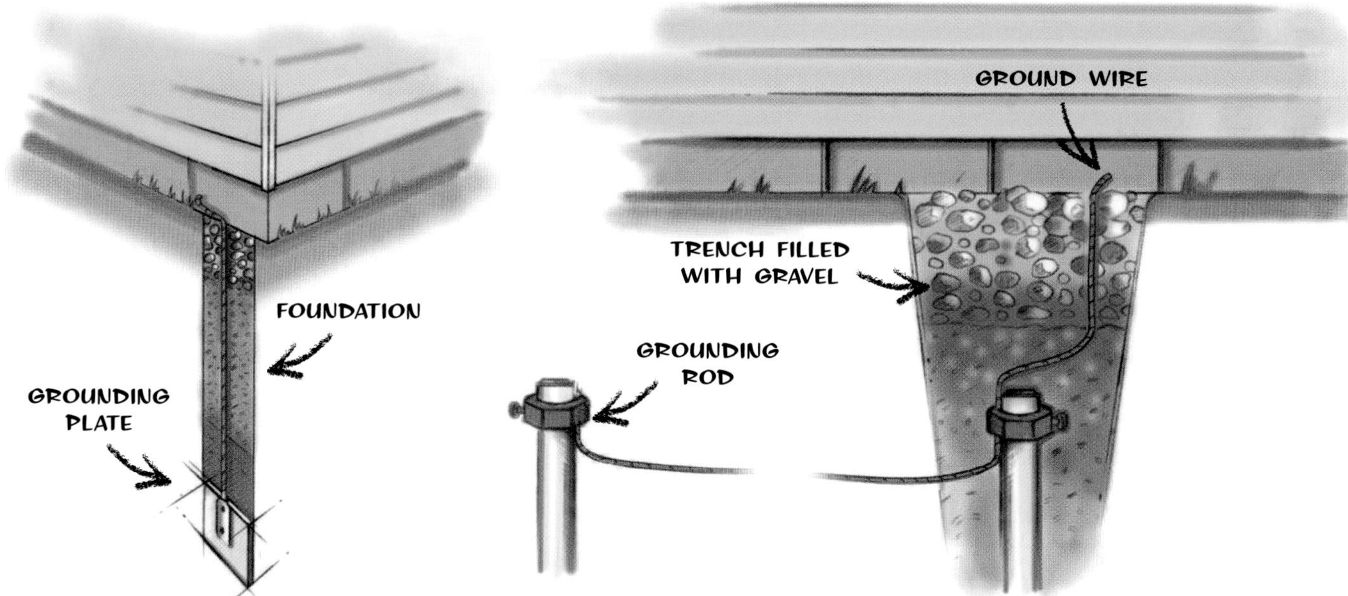

GROUNDING IN ROCKY SOIL. A house's ground wire may be attached to a grounding plate embedded in the concrete of a footing or foundation. To avoid subterranean rocks, the rod may be driven at an angle. Another solution is to connect the ground wire to rebar embedded in the foundation.

GROUNDING RODS. Usually, a standard grounding rod or two provide the best connection into the earth. Many systems use a single rod, but most codes require at least two connected rods, spaced at least 6 feet apart. A rod must be driven at least 8 feet into the ground. Damp soil provides better grounding conditions than dry soil. If you have dry soil, add another rod or two to improve the connection. The grounding wire must be connected firmly to the rod, either with a special clamp or by welding. Local codes specify how deep the top of the rod should be buried.

HOW RECEPTACLES ARE GROUNDED

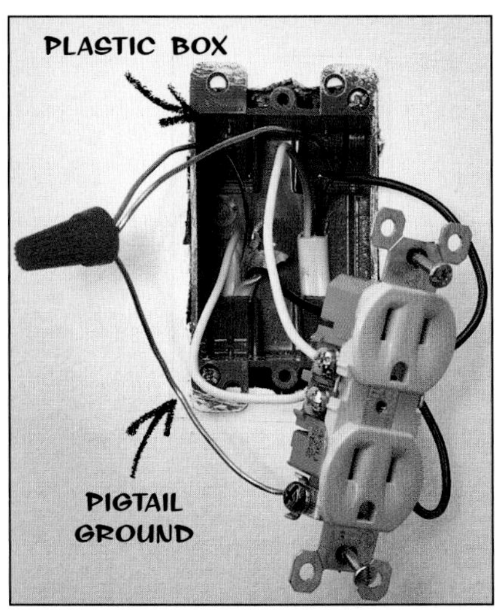

GROUNDING IN A PLASTIC BOX. Because plastic boxes do not conduct electricity, most codes require only that the receptacle be grounded. Check that bare copper grounding wires are spliced together and are attached to the grounding screw of the receptacle. Make sure that all the connections are tight.

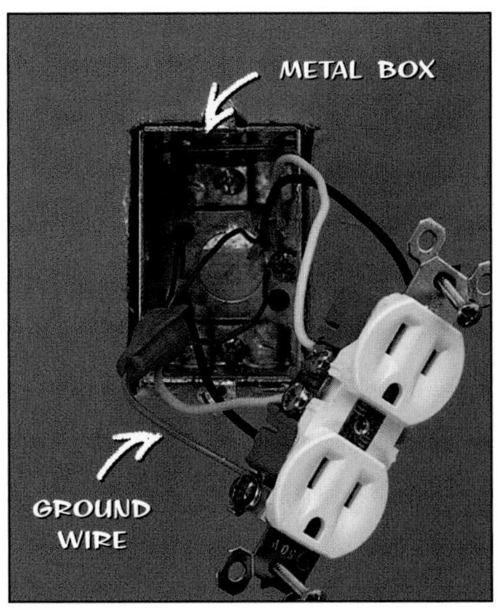

DOUBLE-GROUND A METAL BOX. Tightly splice the ground wires together with a wire nut, and attach them to the receptacle and to the box. This ensures that the box is grounded even if the receptacle is not tightly connected to the box. You get double protection!

GROUND 'EM FIRST!

Always connect the ground wires first. Once you are sure all the ground connections are firm, connect the neutral wire, then the hot wire. To ensure a solid connection between the receptacle and the box, remove the cardboard washer from the receptacle's screws. If you forget to ground a device, you may not detect the resulting danger because the ungrounded device or fixture will work just fine.

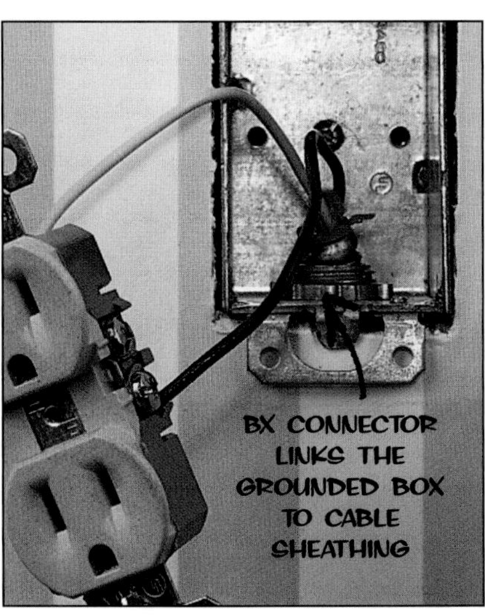

USING SHEATHING AS A GROUND. When BX is installed the sheathing is used as a ground. Metal conduit (page 126) serves as a ground when a grounding wire is not present. Be sure the metal sheathing is clamped tightly to the box so a grounding connection is made between the box and the tabs of the receptacle. Recent codes call for metal-clad (MC) cable, which includes a grounding wire.

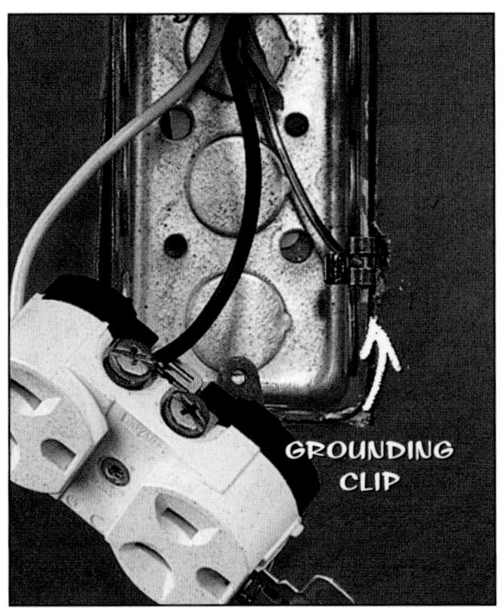

USING GROUNDING CLIPS. Many electricians frown upon using grounding clips because they can easily be pulled off. If yours is loose, replace it with a clip that really grabs. Or, if the grounding wire is long enough, anchor it to the back of the box with a screw (see above).

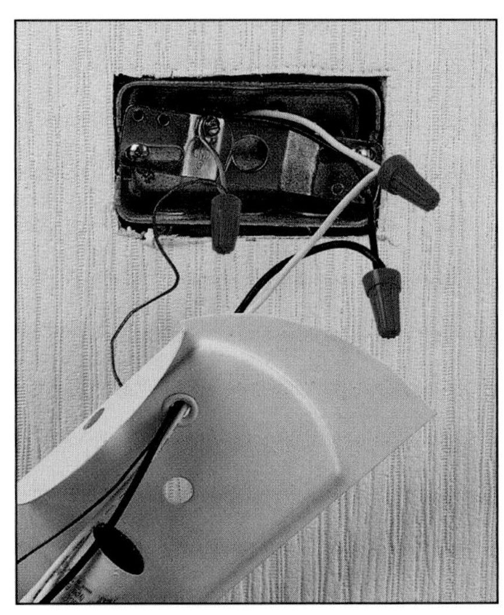

GROUNDING LIGHT FIXTURES. Your light fixtures should be grounded. Whether a light fixture box is metal or plastic, a grounding wire should be connected to the fixture. The ground connection may be made to a fixture's thin ground wire or to a screw on the mounting strap. If the box is metal, it should also be connected to a ground wire.

KNOW YOUR SERVICE PANEL

Find your home's service panel and learn how it works before you start wiring inspections, repairs, or installations. It's where you'll turn off power to circuits that you are working on and where you will run to when a circuit blows.

HOW A SERVICE PANEL WORKS

A service panel is the nerve center of your household's electrical system. It routes power to the circuits in your home and shuts down any circuit that gets overloaded. Every adult in your house should know how to safely reach the service panel to turn off or restore electricity.

Power from the utility company enters the panel through three thick main wires—two hots and one neutral. The main neutral wire connects to a neutral bus bar, and the two hot mains connect to the main power shutoff—either a large circuit breaker or a pull-out fuse. Some panels use fuses (below left); some use breakers (below right).

Some very old homes have only two main wires, one hot and one neutral. Such a system is usually considered adequate if left alone, but if you add service to it you will be violating code. However, it will likely be inadequate for the electrical appliances in the average household. If this describes your home, get an electrician to install new service.

From the main shutoff, two hot bus bars (also called legs) run most of the length down the panel. Each bar carries 120 volts. Circuit breakers or fuses connect to these bars. (This is easier to see in a breaker box than in a fuse box.) Fuses and breakers rated at 120 volts are attached to a single hot bar; 240-volt breakers or fuses are attached to both hot bars.

Each 120-volt circuit has a black or color wire connected to a circuit breaker or fuse, and a white wire

A 100-AMP FUSE BOX. A large fuse box with a capacity of 100 amps provides adequate electrical service for most medium-sized homes, though it will be less convenient to use than a breaker box. This box is well organized, with plenty of space and unimpeded paths for all the wires.

A 100-AMP BREAKER BOX. You can see the two hot bus bars more clearly on a breaker box. This 100-amp box has ample room for the wires, which are carefully laid out so you easily can see the path for each one.

connected to a neutral bus bar. Ground wires also lead to the neutral bar. Neutral bars (usually two) connect to a system ground wire. Some systems that use metal conduit or BX sheathing do not use grounding wires. (See page 13 for more about grounding.)

Power runs through each fuse or breaker and then out of the panel via a hot wire to whatever receptacles, lights, or appliances are on the circuit. White neutral wires bring power back to a neutral bus bar in the service panel, completing the loop.

WHEN CIRCUITS OVERLOAD

If a circuit becomes overloaded and is in danger of overheating, the circuit breaker will trip or the fuse will blow, disconnecting power to the entire circuit. The same thing happens during a ground fault (page 11) or a short circuit, when a hot wire accidentally touches a neutral wire. *If a circuit shuts down frequently, you have a faulty appliance, device, or, most likely, an overloaded circuit (pages 62–63).*

WHEN TO UPGRADE A PANEL

If your panel seems cramped or confusing, have an electrician make sure it is safe. Some panels are too small for the number of circuits they serve, crowding the wires. Others have the neutral bars too near the hot bus bars, so that hot and neutral wires are dangerously close to each other. Others have the neutral bar too far away, so neutral wires have to travel around the panel.

RESPECT YOUR SERVICE PANEL. ***Even seasoned electricians are very careful when working on service panels. If you have reservations about working on your service panel yourself, hire help. If you decide to inspect or work on the panel yourself, follow these safety tips.***

- **ALWAYS KNOW WHAT'S HOT.** A shutoff device—a switch, a breaker, or a fuse—turns off power only to the wires beyond the device. The wires entering the shutoff device are hot at all times. Be sure you know which wires are upstream of the shutoff (prior to the device and therefore not controlled by it) and which are downstream (after it, and therefore controlled by it). If you turn off the main breaker or remove the main fuse, the whole house will go dead and all the circuits will be de-energized, but not all of the service panel will be safe. Unless the utility company turns them off, the thick wires entering the panel are always hot.
- **KEEP YOUR HANDS OFF THE BUS BAR.** When you turn off a breaker or remove a fuse, the wires to the circuit will be dead, but the bus bar will still be hot. The bus bars are always energized unless the main breaker has been turned off or the main fuse has been removed.
- **KEEP THE COVER ON.** Unless you are working on or inspecting a service panel, keep the cover attached so that there is no possibility that you will accidentally touch wires.
- **MAKE A MAP OF YOUR CIRCUITS** (page 61) and post it on the inside panel door so you can easily see which breaker or fuse needs to be disabled.
- **STORE STUFF AWAY FROM THE PANEL.** Keep flammable objects, including hanging clothes, at least 2 feet away. Have a flashlight handy (with fresh batteries).
- **ALWAYS WEAR RUBBER-SOLED SHOES.** If the floor by the panel is at all damp, lay down some boards and lay a rubber mat on top of the boards.
- **NEVER LET ANYONE CLIP TEMPORARY LINES INTO THE PANEL.** Welders and floor sanders sometimes want to clip 240-volt extension lines directly onto your hot and neutral bars. This is dangerous!

WIRES AND CABLES

Use the right wire and cable to avoid creating a dangerous situation that you'll have to tear out and redo. Here are the basics:

WIRES

Wire is usually made of a single, solid strand of metal encased in insulation. For flexibility and ease of pulling, some wire is stranded (above right). Wire is sized according to American Wire Gauge (AWG) categories. Size determines how much amperage the wire will carry. Common household wires and their ratings are:

- **#14 wire** (also called 14-gauge) carries 15 amps
- **#12 wire** carries 20 amps
- **#10 wire** carries 30 amps.

If a wire carries more amperage than it is rated for, it will dangerously overheat. Older wires have rubber insulation, which lasts about 30 years. New wires have longer-lasting polyvinyl insulation. Insulation color often tells the function of wire: **Black, red,** or other colors indicate hot wire. **White** or **off-white** generally is neutral. **Green** or **bare** wire is ground.

TYPES OF ELECTRICAL CABLE

Cable is two or more wires wrapped together in plastic or metal sheathing. **Nonmetallic (NM) cable** is permitted inside wall, ceiling, and floor cavities. Special metal plates must be added to the framing to protect the cable from puncture (page 129). Printing on **NM cable** tells you what is inside: 12/3 means there are three #12 wires, not counting the ground wire. "G" means that there is a ground wire. For underground installations and in damp areas, use **underground-feed (UF) cable (also called NMWU cable).** UF cable encases the wires in solid plastic. **Telephone cable** is being supplanted by **Cat 5 cable,** suitable for telephones, modems, and computer networking. **Coaxial cable** carries television signals. **Armored cable** (pages 124–125) has a flexible metal sheathing. **BX,** also called **AC,** has no ground wire—the sheathing is used for grounding. (The thin metal bonding strip cannot be used as a ground wire.) **Metal-clad (MC) cable** has a insulated green grounding wire. (A similar material, Greenfield, or flexible conduit, is armored sheathing without wires. Install it, then pull wires through it.) **Conduit** is a solid pipe through which individual wires are run (pages 126–127). Metal conduit is often required in commercial installations. Most building departments require it only where the wiring is exposed.

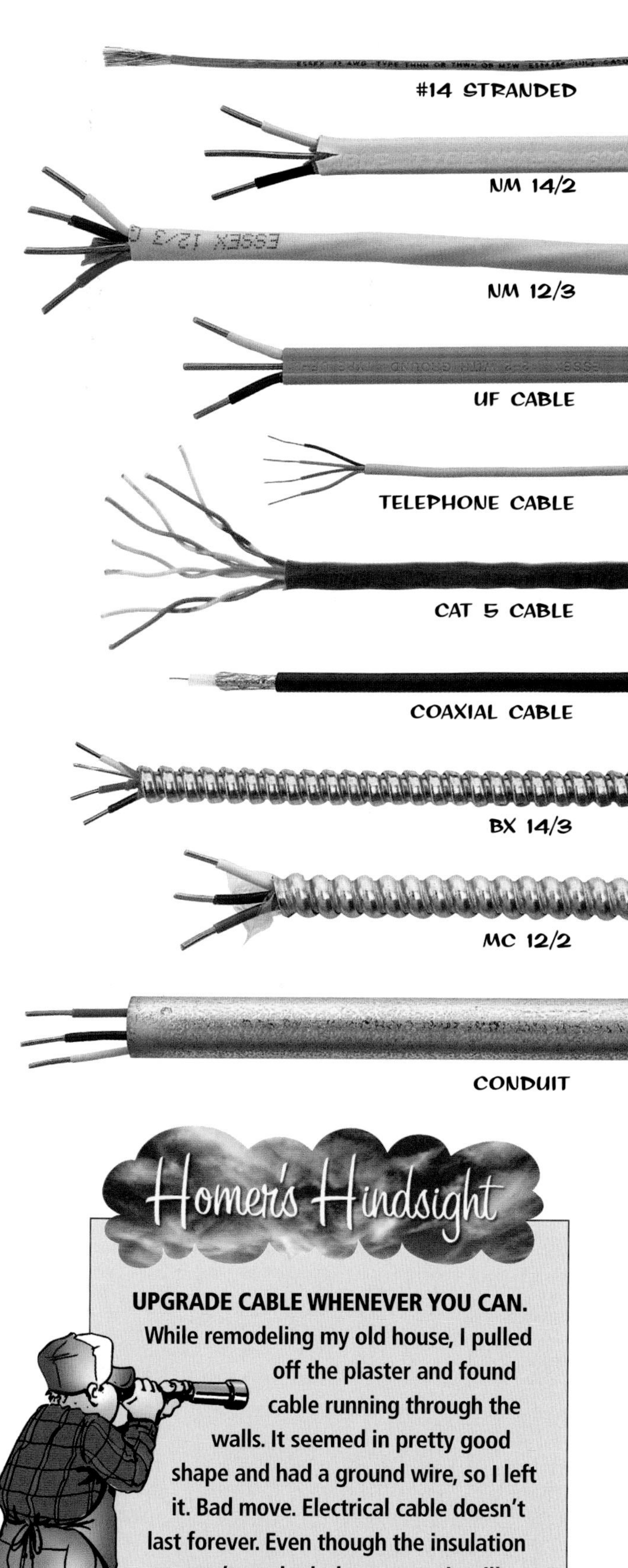

Homer's Hindsight

UPGRADE CABLE WHENEVER YOU CAN. While remodeling my old house, I pulled off the plaster and found cable running through the walls. It seemed in pretty good shape and had a ground wire, so I left it. Bad move. Electrical cable doesn't last forever. Even though the insulation wasn't cracked, chances are it will deteriorate within the next 20 years. I blew the chance to replace it easily.

RECEPTACLES AND SWITCHES

Switches and receptacles usually provide trouble-free operation for decades. However, they are not indestructible. If one of yours is cracked, singed, or seems too loose, replace it (pages 22, 26).

WIRES AND AMPS

Most switches and receptacles in a home are designed to carry 15 amps. To confirm yours, look on the metal plate for the amperage rating. Any 15-amp device should be connected to #14 wire (opposite page), which should lead to a 15-amp fuse or circuit breaker in the service panel. If the wires are #12 or thicker, or if a 15-amp device is connected to a fuse or breaker that is 20-amp or greater, hire an electrician: This is a potentially dangerous situation.

Be sure that the amperage of a 240-volt receptacle is rated no lower than that of the appliance. If you are unsure as to which receptacle to use, check with your building department or ask an electrician.

GROUND HOLE UP OR DOWN?

In many areas, electricians install receptacles with the ground holes down (when the receptacles are vertical) or to the right (when they're horizontal). In other locales, the practice is just the opposite—up, or to the left.

Some professionals have complicated notions about why one way is better than the rest. Most of their theories involve making sure the ground prong is the last to be pulled out of a receptacle, so the appliance remains grounded until it is plugged in. Ground down seems to be more common, but there is no harm in reversing this. Choose one way or the other, and then stick with it throughout your house.

CHOOSING A 120-VOLT RECEPTACLE

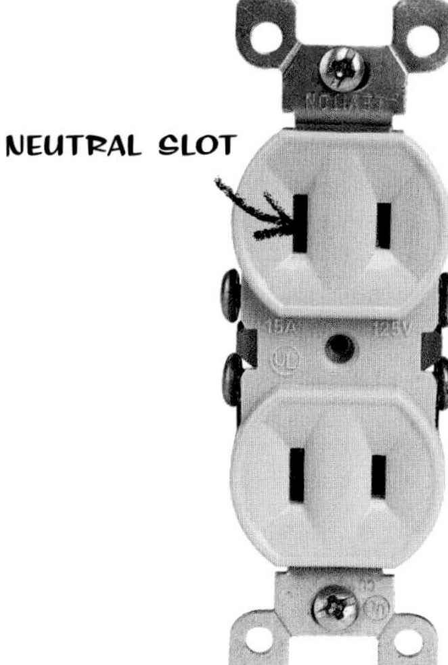

UNGROUNDED 120-VOLT RECEPTACLE. This type of receptacle has two slots, with no hole for a grounding prong. This one is polarized (page 11), with one slot longer than the other so that a polarized plug can be inserted only one way.

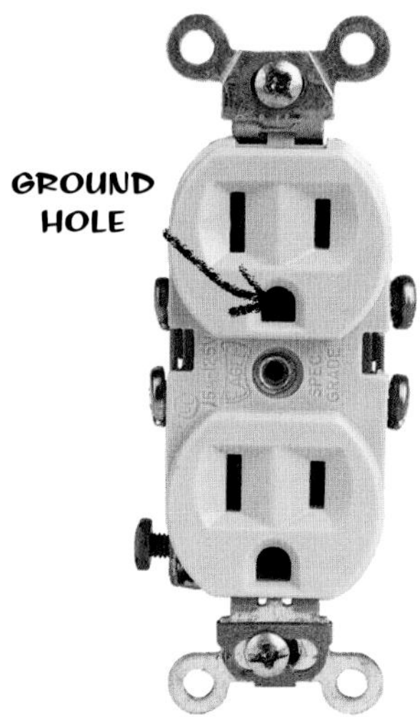

GROUNDED 15-AMP, 120-VOLT RECEPTACLE. This receptacle is the most common household electrical device. It will serve most lamps and appliances and will overload if you plug in two heavy-use items that total more than 15 amps.

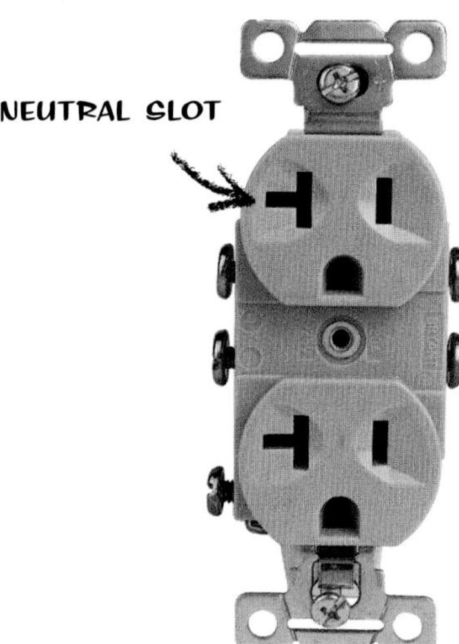

20-AMP, 120-VOLT RECEPTACLE. This receptacle has a neutral slot shaped like a sideways T so you can confidently plug in large appliances or heavy-use tools. It should connect to #12 wires that lead to a 20-amp circuit or fuse in the service panel.

CHOOSING A 240-VOLT RECEPTACLE

WALL-MOUNTED 240-VOLT RECEPTACLE. Appliances using 240 volts have different plug designs so they can't be plugged into the wrong receptacle. To be safe, check the information plate on the appliance to confirm that the amperage matches that of the receptacle.

SURFACE-MOUNTED 120/240-VOLT RECEPTACLE. Some heavy-duty appliances require receptacles with both standard voltage and high voltage. For example, a range commonly uses 240 volts for its burners and 120 volts for the light and the clock. A 120/240-volt receptacle provides both levels of power.

WALL-MOUNTED 120/240-VOLT RECEPTACLE. This wall-mounted receptacle is typically used with a stove. Install it in a standard electrical box.

CHOOSING A SWITCH

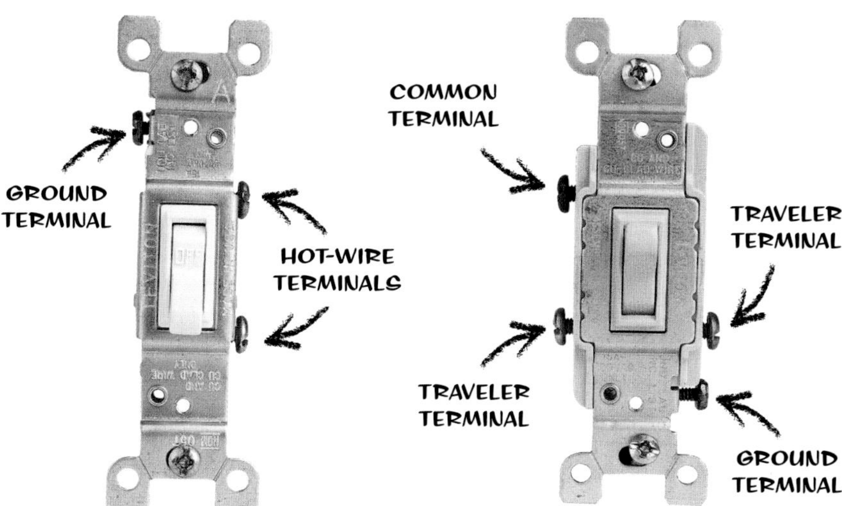

SINGLE-POLE SWITCH. This is the workhorse switch in your home. It has two terminals for hot wires and may also have a green terminal for a ground wire. The toggle is labeled ON and OFF and should be connected to two #14 wires. These wires should be two black wires or a black wire and a white wire that has been marked (page 20). Check local codes.

THREE-WAY SWITCH. Three-ways are always installed in pair—both switches control the same light(s). There are no ON and OFF markings on the toggle. The common terminal is where you attach the wire bearing power from the source or to the fixture. (See page 24 for how to wire a three-way switch.)

THREE OR FOUR?

Until recently, it was common to wire high-voltage receptacles with three wires—two hot and one neutral for a 120/240 receptacle; two hot and one ground wire for a 240-volt receptacle. Current codes, however, often require a fourth wire so that the receptacle has both a ground and a neutral for added protection (page 77). You are probably not required to upgrade existing three-wire receptacles.

RECEPTACLE AND SWITCH WIRING

When you remove an electrical cover plate and pull out a switch or receptacle, you may find an arrangement involving a few wires going directly to the device. Or, you may find a multicolored tangle of wires, some related to the switch or receptacle and some not. Here are some of the most common wiring configurations you'll find behind electrical cover plates.

(The pictures on these pages emphasize the wiring for the hot and neutral wires. For various options on connecting ground wires, see pages 12–13.)

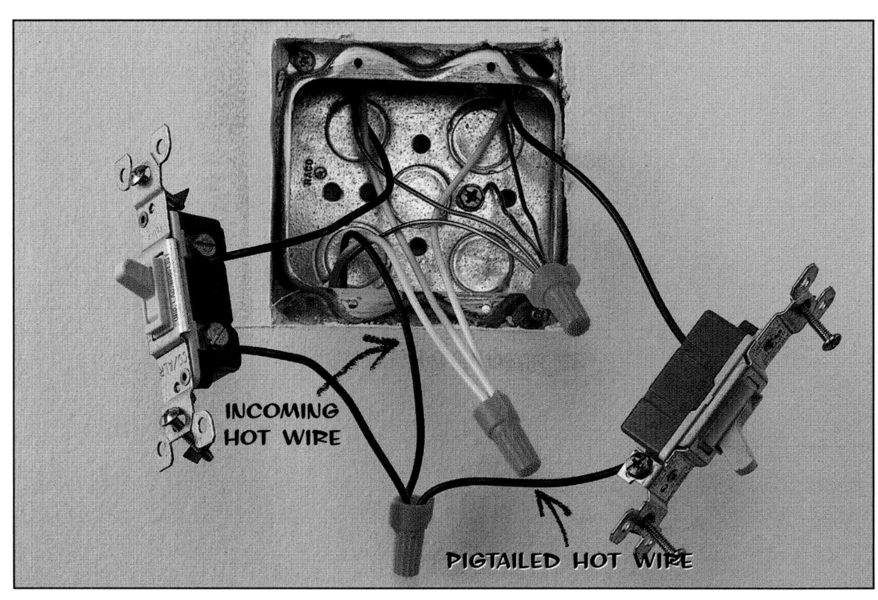

SWITCHES SHARING A HOT WIRE. Switches that share a hot wire are on the same circuit. Two pigtails (page 49) branch off from the incoming hot wire and connect to each switch. Another hot wire runs from each switch to a light. White wires are spliced.

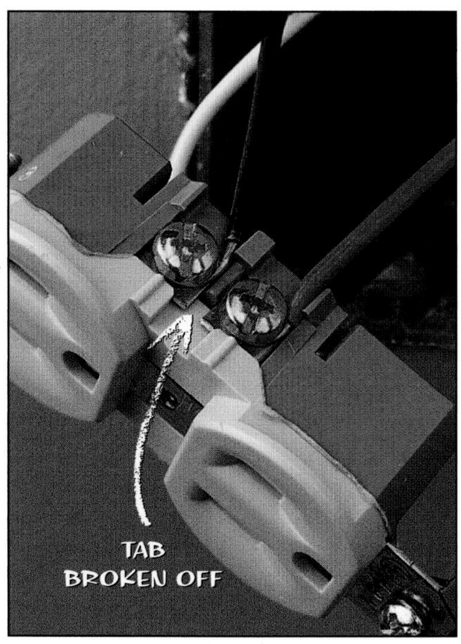

A SPLIT RECEPTACLE. Also known as a "half-hot" receptacle, this is connected to two hot wires. The brass tab joining the brass terminals has been broken off. With the tab broken, each hot wire energizes one plug. Some split-circuit receptacles have each plug energized by a different circuit so that you can plug in two high-amperage appliances without the danger of tripping a breaker. Others are wired so that half the receptacle is controlled by a wall switch, while the other half is hot all the time. See page 144 for more information.

CLOSER LOOK

MIDDLE-OF-THE-RUN RECEPTACLE.
A receptacle with one cable that carries power into the receptacle and one that carries it to another device is called a "middle-of-the-run receptacle." Usually, two black wires are connected to the brass terminals and two white wires to the silver terminals. Or, the blacks and the whites may be joined, with a pigtail at each splice. Each pigtail is attached to the receptacle. If only one cable enters the box, the receptacle is at the end of the run. The black wire is attached to the brass terminal, the white wire is attached to the silver terminal, and the ground wire is attached to the receptacle.

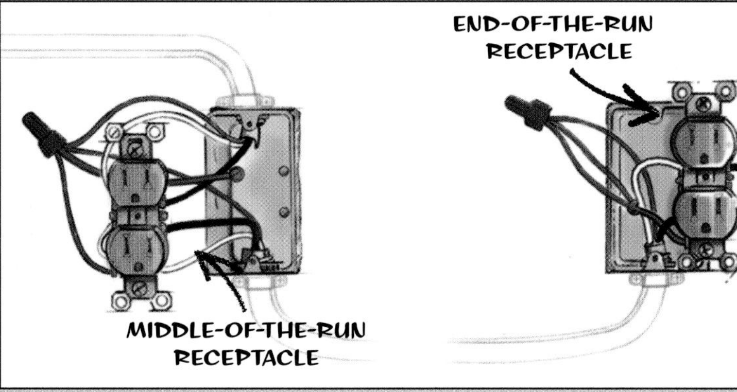

RECEPTACLE AND SWITCH WIRING (CONTINUED)

WIRES STRIPPED MIDWAY. You may find wires that have 1 inch of insulation stripped along the lengths, rather than being cut and each end stripped. Some electricians use this technique to save time. If the connections are tight, this is a safe arrangement. However, for your own work, avoid this shortcut. Wire often gets nicked or scraped in the process. Use pigtails instead (page 49).

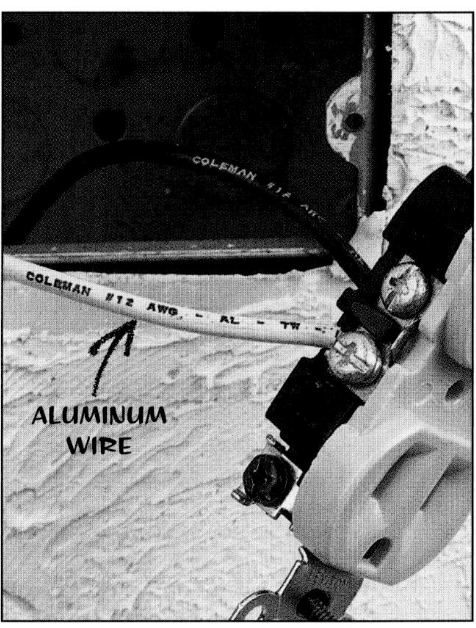

ALUMINUM WIRE. Aluminum wire, which is silver in color and thicker than copper wire, is not widely used because it expands and contracts, loosening connections. (See page 64 for how to keep an aluminum system safe.)

SHOCK DEFENSE:
MAKE SURE ALL CIRCUITS TO THE DEVICE ARE OFF.
Test for power (pages 44–45), or flip a light switch. Boxes may contain wires from more than one circuit. Trace the cables back to the service panel to turn off the circuit. Test all wires for power with a voltage detector (pages 5, 44, and 45).
HANDLE WITH CARE.
When removing the plate, grasp only the rubber handle of the screwdriver. When removing the device, pull gently, holding the plastic rather than metal parts. Don't dislodge wires. Wear rubber-soled shoes.

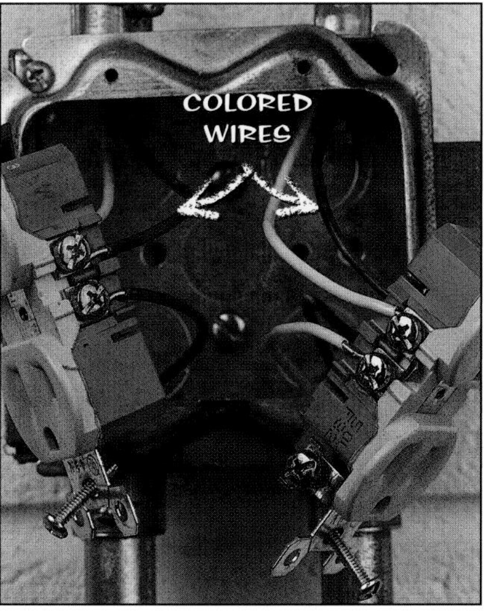

WHAT COLORED WIRES MEAN. Colored wires are sometimes used by electricians to indicate different circuits. When this is done correctly, a circuit uses its own wire color—say, brown or purple. By turning off the breaker attached to the brown wire, you turn off power to all devices attached to brown wires. (Do not assume yours is wired this way. Always test to make sure power is off.)

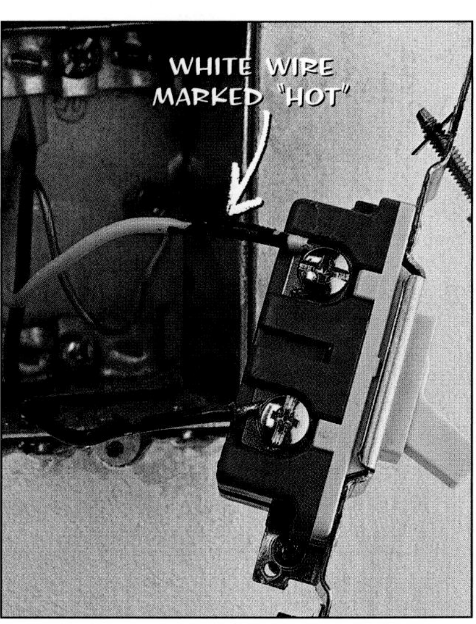

WHY WHITE WIRES ARE MARKED. When power runs into the fixture box rather than the switch box, another cable brings a black and a white wire into the switch box. When the switch is on, both wires are hot, so the white wire is painted black with a marker or wrapped with a bit of electrician's tape. Do not remove the tape or scrape away the paint, or you will give the false—and dangerous—signal that the white wire is neutral.

2 TOP 10 PROJECTS

Home Depot associates across the United States and Canada report that the projects in this chapter are the most popular. You probably bought this book with one or more of these projects in mind. Some you might tackle out of necessity: One of your home's receptacles, switches, or light fixtures may be malfunctioning and therefore must be replaced. Other projects are upgrades that will make your home a safer and more enjoyable place to be.

Before beginning any of these projects, read Chapter 1, **Understanding Wiring,** for important background information. If you get into a project and find techniques that are new to you, follow the page references provided. They'll take you to the section that covers the subject in greater detail.

CHAPTER TWO PROJECTS

REPLACING A SWITCH

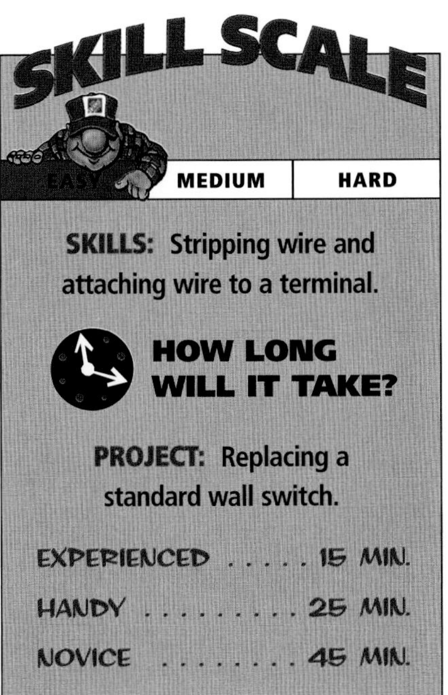

SKILL SCALE
EASY
MEDIUM
HARD
SKILLS: Stripping wire and attaching wire to a terminal.
HOW LONG WILL IT TAKE?
PROJECT: Replacing a standard wall switch.
EXPERIENCED . . . . . 15 MIN.
HANDY . . . . 25 MIN.
NOVICE . . . . 45 MIN.

STUFF YOU'LL NEED
TOOLS: Tester, combination stripper, lineman's pliers, longnose pliers, side-cutting pliers, screwdriver
MATERIALS: New switch, electrician's tape, wire nuts

BUYER'S GUIDE
STURDY DEVICES FOR HEAVY USE.
If a switch is used constantly, pay a little extra for a device labeled "commercial" or "spec-rated." It has stronger contacts and is sturdier.

If your switch pops when you turn it on, if it seems loose, or if your light fixture doesn't switch on even with a new bulb, it's time to replace the switch. Switches are easy and quick to test and install.

CHOOSING A REPLACEMENT

If the switch has two wires connected to it (it might also have a ground wire) and a toggle marked ON and OFF, it is a single-pole switch—the most common type.
If three wires connect to it (not counting the ground wire), it is a three-way switch (page 18).

You may choose to replace your switch with a dimmer. If so, it's *not* necessary to change the wiring entering the box, but you do have to connect wires to leads with wire nuts rather than screw wires to terminals (page 50).

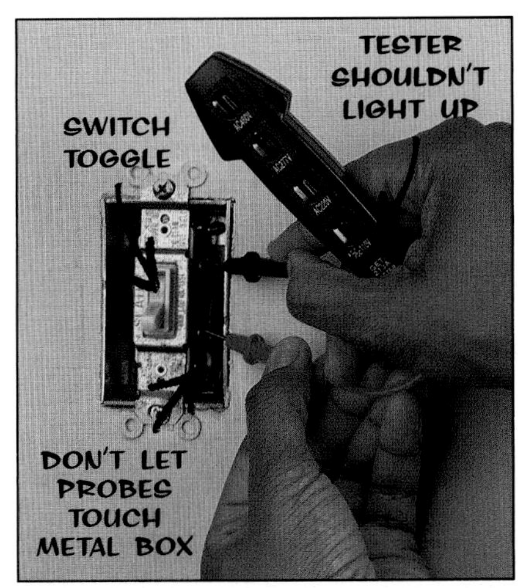

TESTER SHOULDN'T LIGHT UP

DON'T LET PROBES TOUCH METAL BOX

1 **TEST FOR POWER.** At the service panel, shut off power to the circuit supplying the switch. Remove the two screws above and below the switch toggle, and pull off the cover plate. (If it is painted over, first score around it with a utility knife.) Test with a 4-level voltage tester (page 44) or multitester (page 45) to make sure that power is off.

2 **INSPECT THE WIRING.** Remove the two screws holding the switch to the box. Gently pry out the switch. Pull on the wires to ensure that they're firmly connected to the terminals. If a wire is loose or broken, you've probably found the problem.

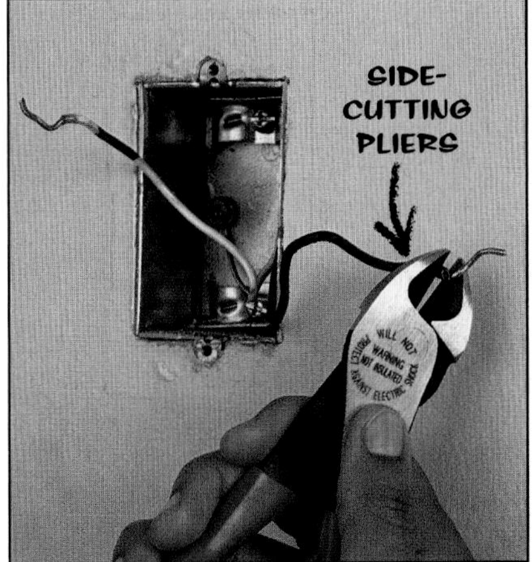

3 **TRIM DAMAGED WIRE.** Unscrew the terminal screws on the switch about ¼ inch (stop when they get hard to turn), and remove the wires. If a stripped wire end appears nicked or twisted, snip off the damage.

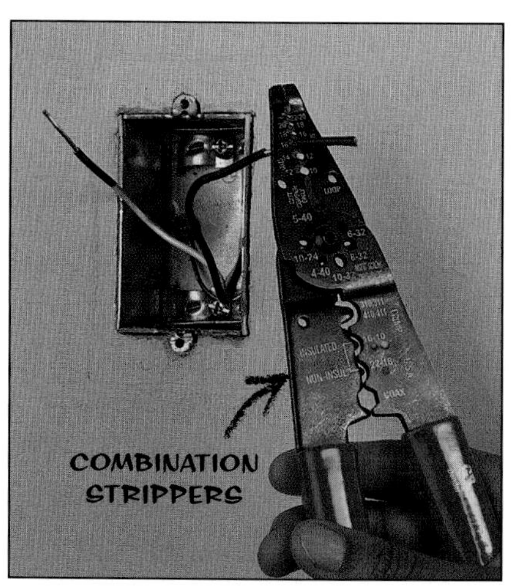

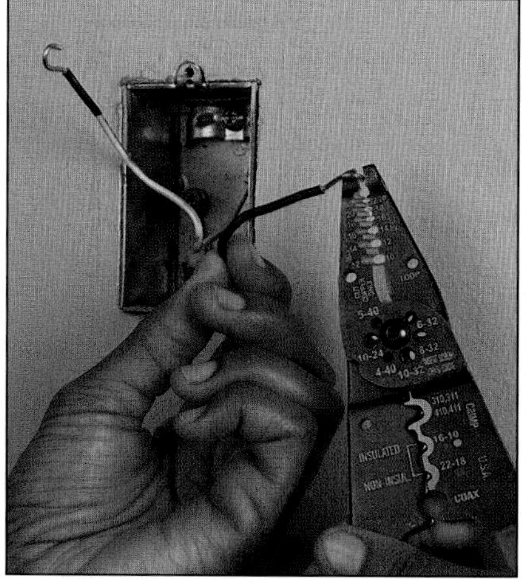

4 RESTRIP TRIMMED WIRE. Using combination strippers, strip about ¾ inch of insulation from the end of any wires that you snipped (pages 46–47). If you strip a white wire that has been painted black or marked with black tape, remark it.

5 TWIST A LOOP. Form a question mark at the end of each wire, using the tip of combination strippers (page 46) or longnose pliers . Make the loop tight enough so that it just fits around the shank of the terminal screw.

LOOP THOSE WIRES RIGHT THE FIRST TIME 'ROUND.

Replacing a switch should be a no-brainer, shouldn't it? When my light fixture went on the fritz, I figured it had to be the switch. I replaced it but didn't loop the wires clockwise around the terminals. The fixture still didn't work, so I replaced it again. Still no light. Only then did I notice that a wire had spun off the switch terminal! I attached the wire the right way, and the light worked like a charm.

Even if your local codes don't require that a switch be grounded to a metal box, do it anyway.

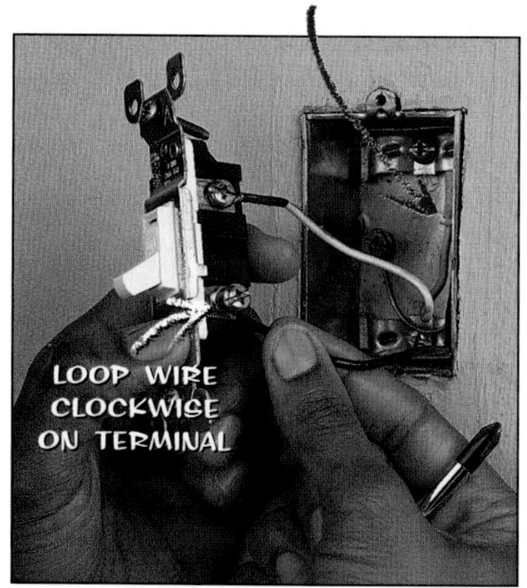

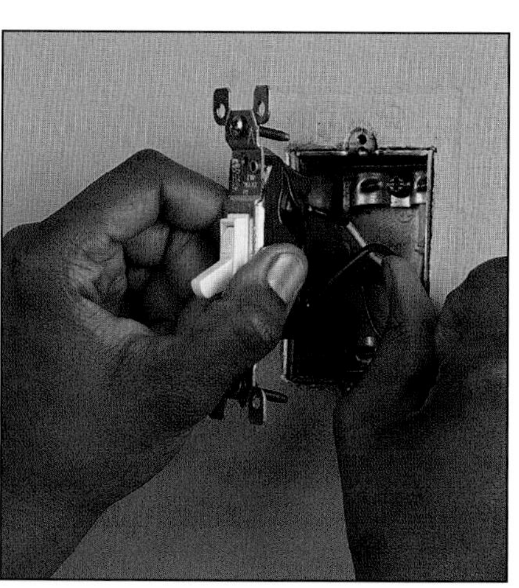

6 ATTACH THE WIRES. On new switches, the terminals are screwed down tight. Unscrew each until it gets hard to turn. Slip a looped wire end under the screw head, with the end of the loop pointing *clockwise.* Squeeze the wire end tight around the terminal with longnose pliers (page 48) or the tip of a combination tool. Tighten the screw.

7 WRAP THE SWITCH BODY. For extra protection, wrap the switch with electrician's tape so that all terminals and bare wires are covered. This also ensures that wires won't come off the terminal screws.

8 INSTALL THE SWITCH. Gently push the wires back into the box as you push the switch back into position. Aim the mounting screws at the screw holes. Tighten the screws and check that the switch is plumb (straight up and down). The elongated holes allow for adjustments. Replace the cover plate, restore power, and try the switch.

REPLACING A THREE-WAY SWITCH

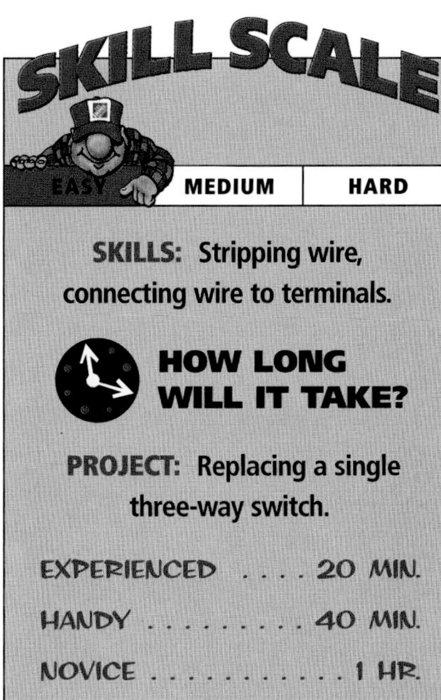

SKILL SCALE
EASY
MEDIUM
HARD
SKILLS: Stripping wire, connecting wire to terminals.
HOW LONG WILL IT TAKE?
PROJECT: Replacing a single three-way switch.
EXPERIENCED .... 20 MIN.
HANDY .... 40 MIN.
NOVICE .... 1 HR.

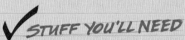

STUFF YOU'LL NEED

TOOLS: Tester, screwdriver, combination strippers, longnose pliers, lineman's pliers

MATERIALS: Three-way switch, electrician's tape, masking tape

BUYER'S GUIDE

THREE-WAY DIMMER.
Replace only one of your paired three-way switches with a dimmer: Two dimmers won't work. The remaining switch requires a standard three-way toggle. (Fluorescent fixtures also require special dimmers.)

Three-way switches work in pairs to control a light from two locations—handy for controlling a light from the top and the bottom of stairways, or from either end of hallways. The toggle isn't marked OFF and ON. Either up or down can be ON depending on the position of the toggle of the other three-way. (For more on three-way switches, see pages 148–150.)

Before you begin, shut off power to the circuit (page 5). Disconnect wires from terminals, and restrip any damaged wires (page 22). Most of the steps for replacing a three-way switch are the same as for a single-pole switch; but with three-ways, be sure to mark the wires before you remove the old device.

1 TAG THE COMMON WIRE. Shut off power, remove the cover plate, and test to make sure there is no power in the box. Label the common wire with a piece of masking tape. The common terminal (page 149) is colored differently than the others (it's not the green ground screw) and may be marked "common" on the switch body.

2 OPTION A:
WIRING ONE CABLE. When only one cable enters the box, it will have three wires plus a ground. Identify the hot wire using a voltage detector (pages 42, 45), or by touching one prong of a voltage tester to a ground and the other to each wire in turn. Attach the hot wire to the common terminal, which is a different color. Attach the other two wires to the traveler terminals. Connect the grounds.

OPTION B:
WIRING TWO CABLES. If two cables enter the box, one cable will have two wires and the other will have three wires (plus ground wires). But despite all the extra wires, you'll find only three wire ends. Proceed just as you would for a one-cable installation (left).

REPLACING A DIMMER SWITCH

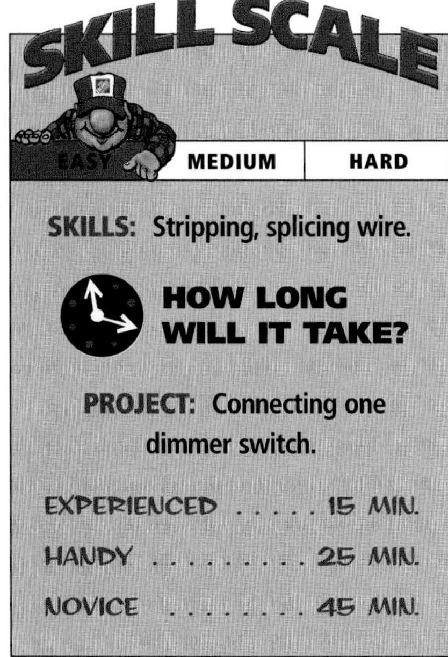

STUFF YOU'LL NEED
TOOLS: Screwdriver, side-cutting pliers, strippers
MATERIALS: Dimmer switch, wire nuts, electrician's tape

Make sure the new dimmer switch is rated for the total wattage of the fixture. A chandelier with eight 100-watt bulbs is too much for a 600-watt dimmer to handle. Don't use a standard dimmer for a fan, or you will burn out the motor. Install no more than one three-way dimmer; the other switch must be a three-way toggle. You can buy rotary dimmers (the least expensive), dimmers that look like standard switches, or models with a separate ON-OFF switch so the dimmer will turn on at the level of your choice.

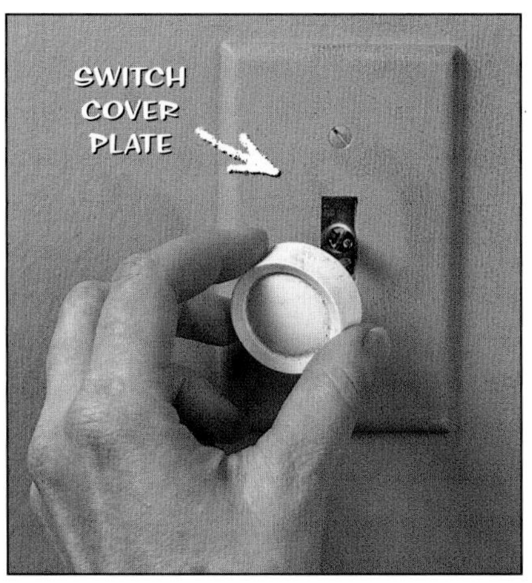

1 REMOVE THE KNOB. Shut off power at the service panel. Pull off the rotary knob with firm outward pressure. Underneath is a standard switch cover plate. Remove the cover plate. Remove the mounting screws and carefully pull out the switch body.

2 TEST FOR POWER. A dimmer has wire leads instead of terminals. Remove the wire nuts and test for power by touching the probes of the tester to both wires, or to either wire and the metal box, or to one wire and the ground wire. If power is detected, shut off the correct circuit in the service panel. (To test for continuity, see page 74.)

3 OPTION A: INSTALLING A STANDARD DIMMER. Attach the ground wire if there is one. Strip $\frac{3}{4}$ inch of insulation from each solid house wire and 1 inch from each stranded dimmer lead. Wrap a lead around a wire with your fingers, so that the lead protrudes past the wire about $\frac{1}{8}$ inch. Slip on a wire nut and twist until tight. Test the strength of the connection by gently tugging on both wires.

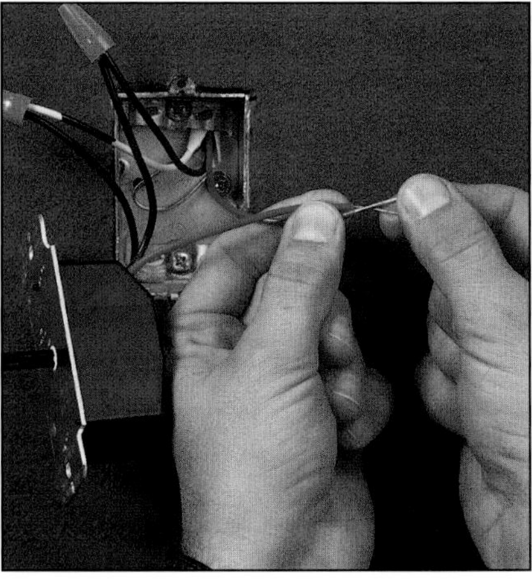

OPTION B: INSTALLING A THREE-WAY DIMMER. If you replace a three-way dimmer, tag the existing lead wires to connect the new dimmer in the same way as the old dimmer. If only one cable enters the box, attach the black wire to the common terminal and the other two wires to the traveler terminals. If you replace a three-way toggle switch with a dimmer, tag the wire that leads to the common terminal. The other two wires are interchangeable.

REPLACING A RECEPTACLE

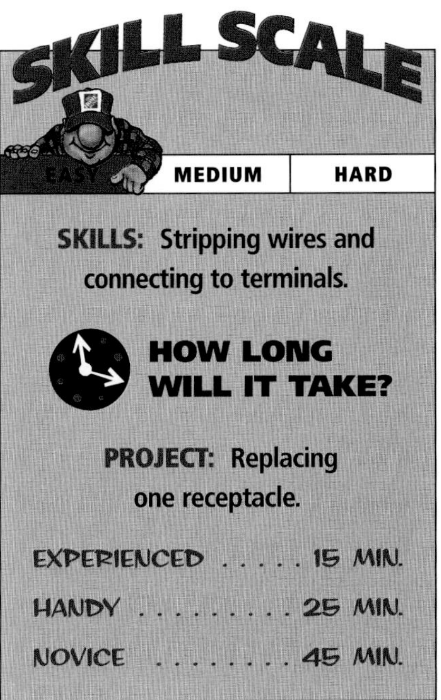

SKILL SCALE
EASY
MEDIUM
HARD
SKILLS: Stripping wires and connecting to terminals.
HOW LONG WILL IT TAKE?
PROJECT: Replacing one receptacle.
EXPERIENCED . . . . . 15 MIN.
HANDY . . . . 25 MIN.
NOVICE . . . . 45 MIN.

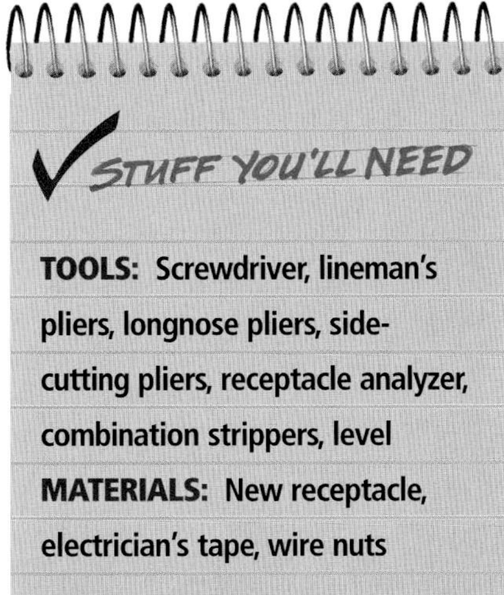

If a receptacle doesn't seem to work, first check that whatever is plugged into it works properly. Replace any receptacle that is cracked. Before buying a replacement receptacle, check the wiring. Usually, the wires leading to a receptacle will be #14 and the circuit breaker or fuse will be 15 amp. In that case, install a 15-amp receptacle. Install a 20-amp receptacle only if the wires are #12 and the circuit breaker or fuse is 20 amps or greater.

1 CHECK THAT POWER IS OFF. Turn off power to the circuit (page 5). Test to confirm. If the tester shows current, check your service panel and turn off another likely circuit. Test again, and proceed only if power is off. Remove the cover plate and unscrew the mounting screws. Being careful not to touch wires or terminals, pull out the receptacle.

2 TEST WIRES FOR POWER. In a damaged receptacle, wires may be hot even though testing shows no power. Touch tester probes to the terminals. If more than two wires enter the box, test all the wires (page 5). If you have old wiring and both wires are black, use a receptacle analyzer (page 44) to check that the neutral wire is connected to the silver terminal and the hot wire to the brass.

3 SNIP AND RESTRIP DAMAGED WIRE ENDS. Once you're sure the power is off, unscrew the terminals and pull away the wires, taking care not to twist them too much. If a wire end appears nicked or damaged or if it looks like it's been twisted several times, snip off the end and restrip it (pages 22–23).

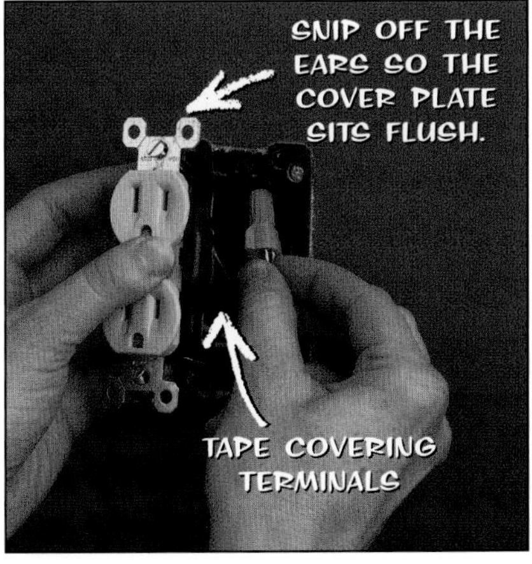

4 INSTALL THE RECEPTACLE. Wire the new receptacle the same as the old, with each white wire connected to a silver terminal and each black or color wire connected to a brass terminal. Wrap electrician's tape to cover all terminals and bare wires. Gently push the outlet into the box. Tighten the mounting screws, and check that the receptacle is straight. Replace the cover plate, restore power, and test with a receptacle analyzer.

ADDING GFCI PROTECTION

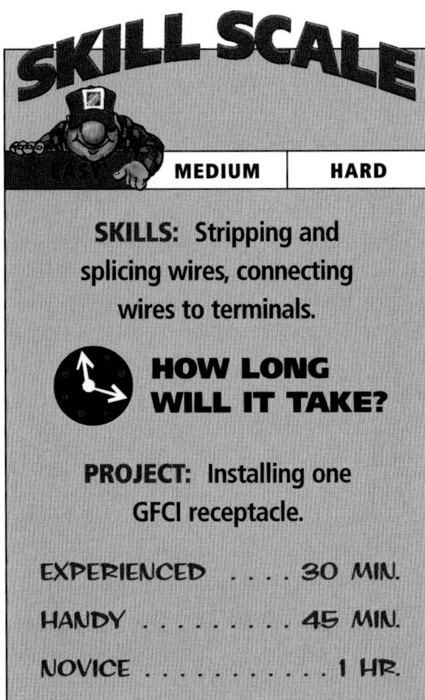

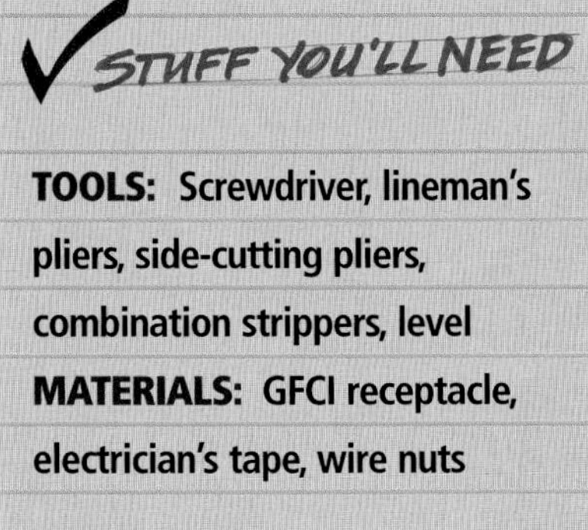

STUFF YOU'LL NEED
TOOLS: Screwdriver, lineman's pliers, side-cutting pliers, combination strippers, level
MATERIALS: GFCI receptacle, electrician's tape, wire nuts

A ground-fault circuit interrupter (GFCI) shuts down power in milliseconds when it detects the tiniest change in current flow. Codes require GFCIs in bathrooms, in kitchens near sinks, outdoors, and in garages. GFCIs are inexpensive and simple to install.

A single GFCI can protect up to four receptacles, switches, and lights on the same circuit. A GFCI circuit breaker can protect an entire circuit (page 100). If your home has ungrounded receptacles (pages 11–13), installing GFCIs will provide protection, but won't ground your circuits.

Check your GFCIs at least once a month by pushing in the test button. (The reset button should pop out. Push it back in.) A GFCI may provide power even though it has lost its ability to protect.

Don't use a GFCI as a receptacle for a refrigerator, freezer, or any other appliance that must stay on all the time—it may trip off without your knowing. Also, do not attempt to control a GFCI with a switch.

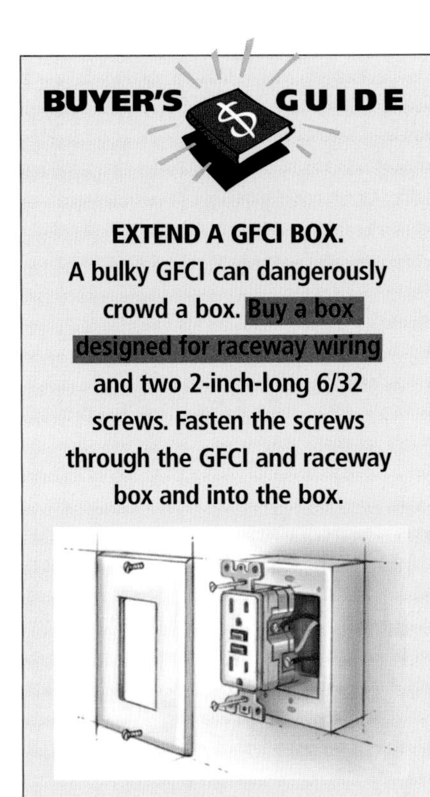

BUYER'S GUIDE
EXTEND A GFCI BOX.
A bulky GFCI can dangerously crowd a box. Buy a box designed for raceway wiring and two 2-inch-long 6/32 screws. Fasten the screws through the GFCI and raceway box and into the box.

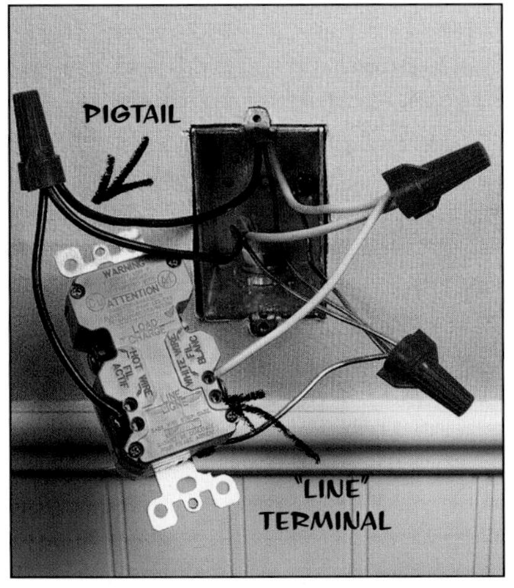

INSTALLING A SINGLE GFCI. Shut off the power. Make connections only to the LINE terminals. For an end-of-the-run box, connect the wires to the terminals. If the box is middle-of-the-run (shown), for each connection, make a pigtail by stripping either end of a 6-inch-long wire. Splice each pigtail to the wire(s) with a wire nut, and connect it to the GFCI terminals. Put the white wire on the silver terminal and the black or color wire on the brass terminal.

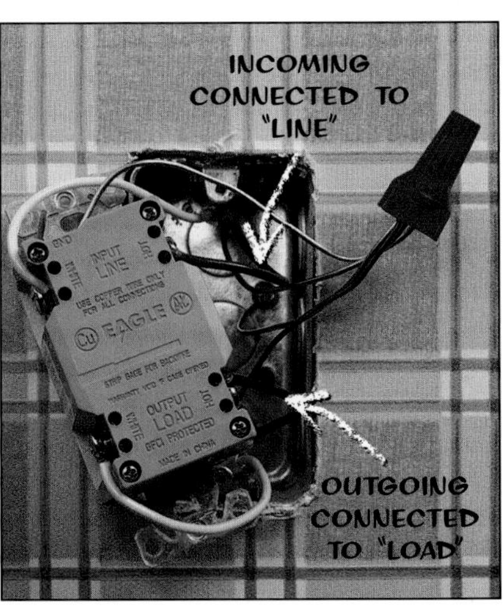

PROTECTING OTHER OUTLETS. Shut off the power. Connect the wires carrying power into the box to the LINE terminals. Then connect the wires leading out of the box (to other receptacles or lights) to the LOAD terminals. If you're unsure which wires come from the service panel, pull the wires out of the box and position them so they will not touch each other, restore power, and use a tester to see which pair of wires is hot; connect these to the LINE terminals.

UPGRADING A CEILING FIXTURE

SKILLS: Stripping and splicing wires, connecting wires to terminals, attaching a fixture.

HOW LONG WILL IT TAKE?

PROJECT: Attaching a new fixture to an existing box. Allow more time if you need to buy the correct mounting parts, replace incoming cable damaged by heat, or patch the ceiling.

EXPERIENCED . . . . 20 MIN.
HANDY . . . . 40 MIN.
NOVICE . . . . 1 HR.

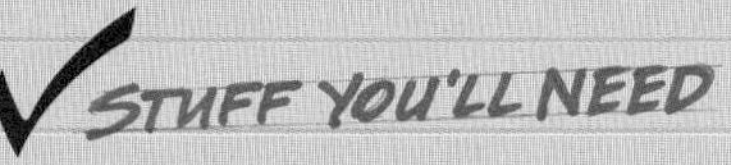

TOOLS: Voltage tester or multitester, combination strippers, lineman's pliers, longnose pliers, side-cutting pliers, screwdriver, stepladder

MATERIALS: New light fixture, electrician's tape, wire nuts

Before you replace the fixture, check that the canopy of the new fixture (the part that snugs up to the ceiling) will cover any imperfections in the drywall or plaster. If you have a thin "pancake" box, replace it with a remodeling box (pages 133–134).

Determine which mounting hardware you'll need before buying a new fixture. Turn off the power at the service panel (page 5) and remove the fixture. Enlist a helper to support the fixture while you remove the mounting screws that hold the canopy in place. Gently pull down the fixture. Working as if the wires are hot, unscrew the wire nuts. Test that the power is off, and then undo the wires. Note the type of mounting hardware, or remove it and take it along when buying a new fixture.

The new fixture will probably include mounting hardware (usually, a strap). You may be able to reuse existing hardware.

Always push the house wires up into the box. Never place them in the fixture's canopy, where they may be harmed by heat.

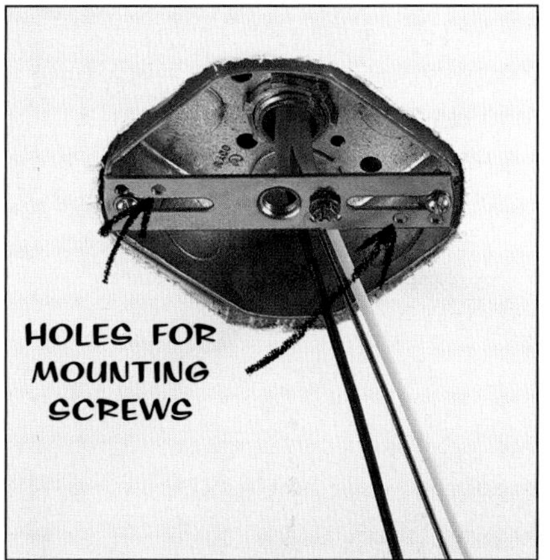

1 WIRE A FLUSH-MOUNTED FIXTURE. Tug on the hardware to make sure the box is firmly attached. Don't depend on the wires and wire nuts to support it while you work. Rest the fixture on a stepladder, or make a hook from a wire coat hanger and temporarily suspend the fixture from the mounting strap. With the power off, splice white to white wires and black to black wires, using wire nuts (page 47). Tuck the house wires up into the box.

2 MOUNT THE FIXTURE. Slide a mounting screw through the fixture and up into the threaded hole in the strap. Start one mounting screw, fastening it halfway in, then start the other screw. With a screwdriver or a drill and screwdriver bit, drive the mounting screws tight.

SAVE THAT INSULATION. **Don't remove the fiberglass insulation at the top of a ceiling fixture, even if it seems to get in the way. It's there to protect the wires from overheating.**

SPECIAL ALIGNMENT

1 ADD A SWIVEL STRAP. Use a swivel strap (also called an offset crossbar) if you need to twist the canopy into exact alignment. This is most often a consideration when installing a fixture with a geometric canopy.

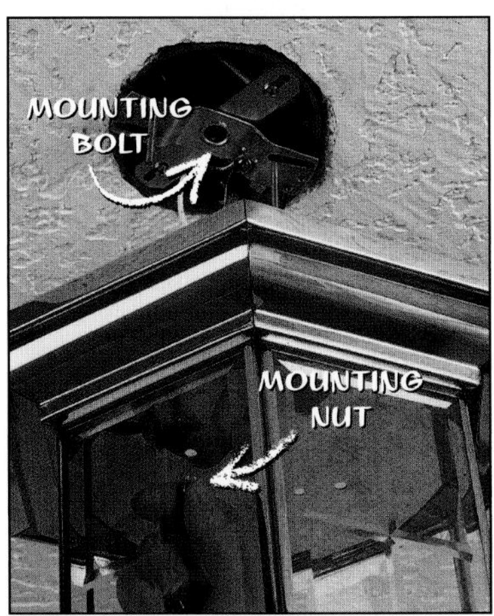

2 MOUNT A FIXTURE THAT NEEDS ALIGNMENT. Wire the fixture, and tuck the house wires up into the box. Screw both mounting bolts into the threaded holes of the strap. Line up the fixture-mounting holes with the bolts and attach the fixture, using the decorative mounting nuts.

CENTER-MOUNTED

1 USE A CENTER STUD FOR CENTER-MOUNTED FIXTURES. A center stud, sometimes called a nipple, may have wires running through it (for a pendant fixture) or around it (for a center-mounted fixture). A variation uses a center nipple, which screws into the strap.

2 INSTALL A CENTER-MOUNTED FIXTURE. The center stud should be long enough to go through the strap and the fixture, but not so long that it pokes into the box or hits the globe. Attach the wires and fold them into the box as you slide the canopy up and over the stud. Snugly secure the canopy with the nut.

OLDER INSTALLATION

1 ADD A HICKEY IN OLDER INSTALLATIONS. An older home may have a $\frac{3}{8}$-inch pipe running through the middle of the ceiling box. To install a pendant fixture, add a hickey to make the transition from the pipe to a new fixture. Feed the fixture leads through the hickey, and tuck the house wires up into the box.

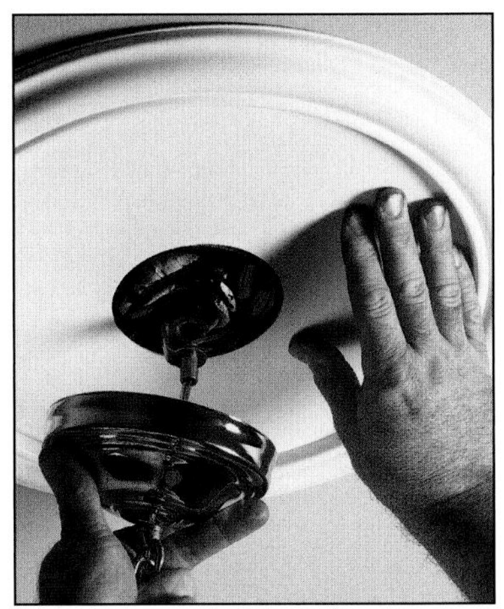

2 ADD A MEDALLION. Hickeys are found in old houses with plaster and lath ceilings. The fixture canopy usually won't cover damaged plaster around the ceiling box. Adding a medallion saves you the trouble of patching and painting while adding a decorative feature.

ADDING UNDER-CABINET LIGHTS

SKILLS: Running new cable and connecting to power, attaching light fixtures, stripping and splicing wires, wiring a switch.

HOW LONG WILL IT TAKE?

PROJECT: Removing the backsplash, cutting holes, running cable, wiring four lights, and reinstalling the backsplash.

EXPERIENCED . . . . . . 1 DAY
HANDY . . . . 1 1/2 DAYS
NOVICE . . . . 2 DAYS

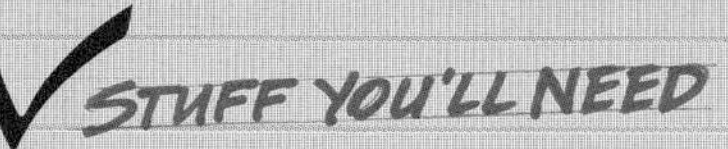

TOOLS: Mulitester or voltage tester, lineman's pliers, side-cutting pliers, longnose pliers, combination strippers, drywall saw, screwdriver, drill with spade bit, utility knife, flat pry bar

MATERIALS: Under-cabinet fluorescent lights, armored or NM cable, electrician's tape, wire nuts, cable clamps, cable staples, switch box, nailing plates

Under-cabinet lighting brightens work surfaces and adds pleasing visual depth to kitchens. Fluorescent lighting is a cool, low-energy light source. If you need only one or two lights, consider buying small fluorescent fixtures with cords and switches. However, you won't want to turn on three or more lights every time you walk into the kitchen. If you want a series of lights controlled by a wall switch, buy fixtures without cords or switches. Lights that are only 1 inch thick are sleeker than standard 1 1/2-inch lights, but they are more difficult to wire and require special reducing cable clamps. Get the longest lights possible for the available under-cabinet spaces; you'll probably need several sizes.

Some codes require that you run armored cable or conduit through walls; others allow exposed armored or nonmetallic (NM) cable. Codes may require you to pull power from a source other than a countertop receptacle. Check with your building department.

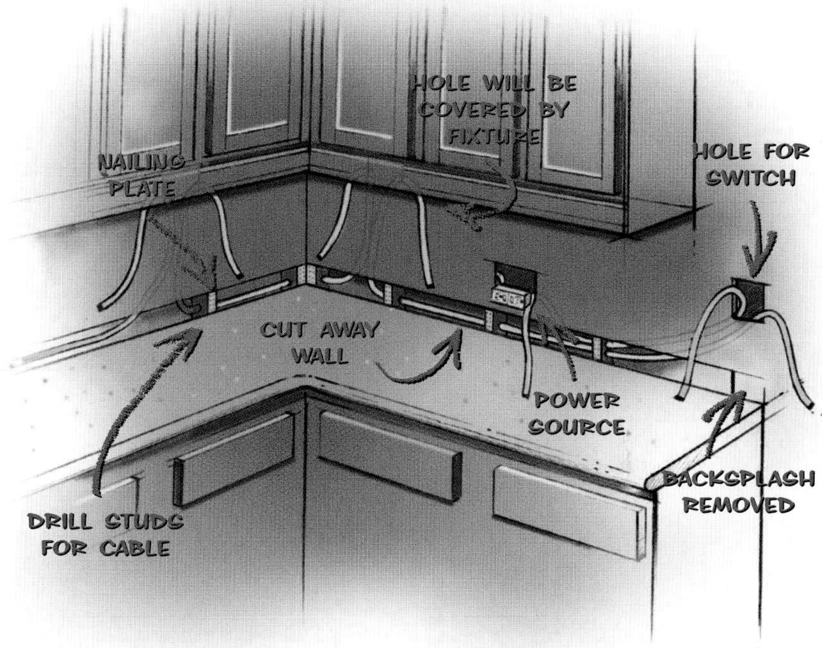

1 **RUN CABLE.** Plan the wiring so as many holes as possible will be covered when you're done. If the countertop backsplash is removable, remove it and cut a channel in the drywall or plaster that will be completely covered by the backsplash. Drill holes in the studs to accommodate cable (pages 128–132). (If you can't remove a backsplash, allow time for patching and painting the wall afterward. Or, install tile between the countertop and the wall cabinets.) Examine each light to determine exactly where the cable will enter and exit. Cut narrow holes in the wall where the cable will enter the lights. Cut carefully so the hole will be covered when the light is installed. Cut a hole for the switch box, and run cable into it from a power source—perhaps a nearby receptacle (pages 141–142). Do not connect the cable to power. Run cable from the switch box to the hole for the first light, then from the first to the second light, and so on. Let about 16 inches of cable hang from the holes so you'll have plenty of slack to make connections. Most local codes allow fluorescent lights to be used as junction boxes, so you can string the wire from light to light. Check to be sure.

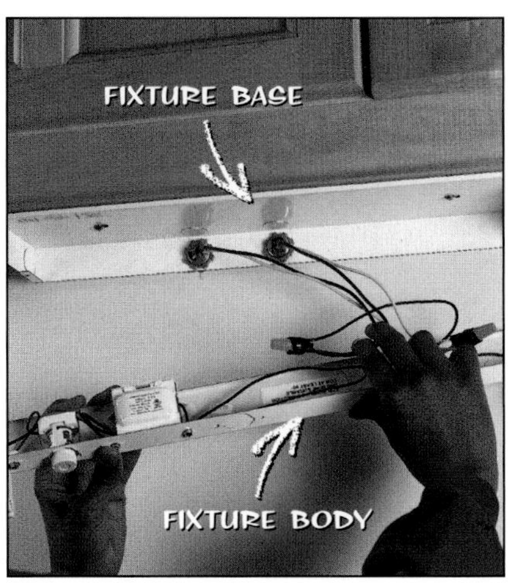

2 **ATTACH THE LIGHTS.** Disassemble the lights, and remove the lens and fluorescent tubes. Clamp each cable to the light as you would clamp cable to a box (pages 123 and 125). Have a helper hold the light as close to the rear wall as possible while you drive screws through the light and into the underside of the cabinet. Be sure that the screws won't poke through to the inside of the cabinet.

3 **WIRE THE LIGHTS.** Plan so that wires will not come within an inch of the ballast. Splice wires with the leads inside the light, black to black and white to white. Position the wires flat in the base so they will not get in the way when you add the fixture body. Gently push the bottom portion of the light into position. If it does not go in easily, take it down and realign the wires for an easier fit. Attach the fixture base.

Designer Tip

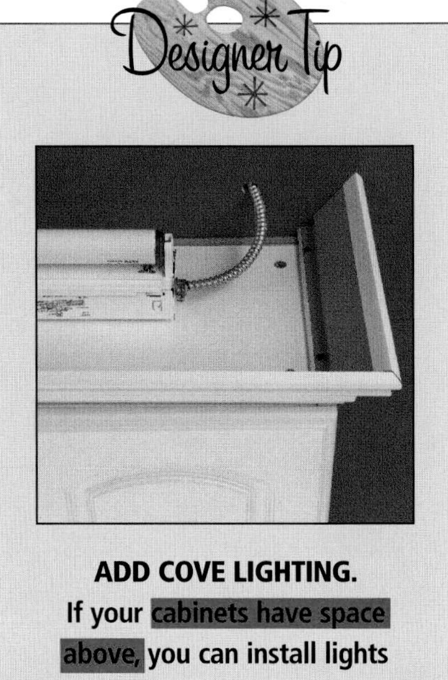

ADD COVE LIGHTING.
If your cabinets have space above, you can install lights there without hiding the cable.

4 **WIRE THE SWITCH.** Install a switch box with the cables clamped to it (page 122–123). Splice the white wires together. Attach each of the black wires to a single-pole switch (don't use a dimmer with fluorescents). Connect the ground wire to the switch and to the box if it is metal. Wrap the body of the switch with tape so the terminals are covered. Shut off power to the receptacle or junction box that will supply the power. Splice white to white and black to a black or color wire (page 47). Restore power.

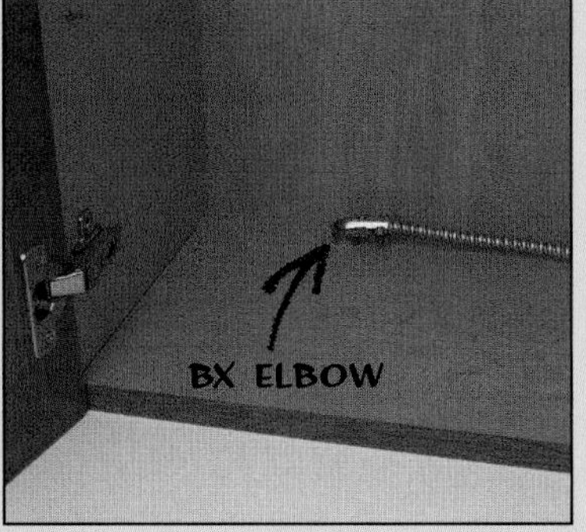

CABLE INSIDE THE CABINET.
Cut holes in the cabinets. Lay BX or MC cable on the inside. Plan exactly where the cable will enter each light below the cabinet. Because you can't slip excess cable into the wall cabinet, you'll have to cut the cable precisely. (See pages 124–125 about working with armored cable.)

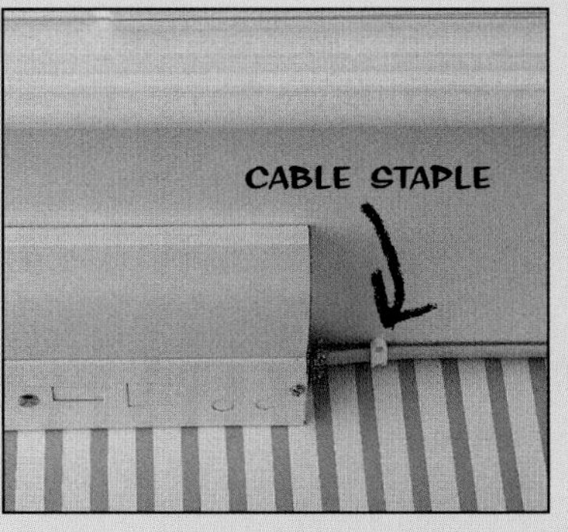

CABLE UNDER THE CABINET.
Attach the lights under the cabinets, string cable under the cabinet, and staple the cable in place using cable staples. Measure and cut carefully so the cable is flat along the length. Check your local code before doing this; it is not allowed in some areas.

HANGING A CEILING FAN

SKILLS: Removing an old box, installing a fan box, attaching a fixture, stripping and splicing wires, wiring a switch.

HOW LONG WILL IT TAKE?

PROJECT: Replacing a light fixture with a new ceiling fan.

EXPERIENCED . . . . . 2 HRS.
HANDY . . . . 4 HRS.
NOVICE . . . . 8 HRS.

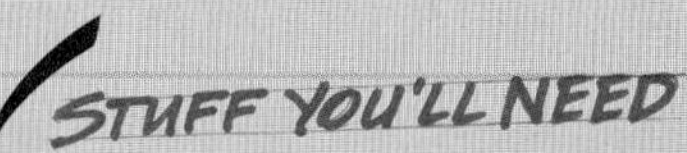

STUFF YOU'LL NEED

TOOLS: Drywall saw, hammer, voltage tester or multitester, combination strippers, linesman's pliers, longnose pliers, crescent wrench, side-cutting pliers, screwdriver, reciprocating saw or metal-cutting keyhole saw

MATERIALS: Fan, fan-rated box, downrod extender, light kit, fan/light switch (can be remote-controlled), electrician's tape, wire nuts

Ceiling fans circulate air downward to cool rooms in the summer and upward to evenly disperse heat in the winter. Observe the following guidelines to install a fan, and it will effectively circulate the air in your home without hissing, wobbling, or pulling away from the ceiling.

PLANNING FOR A FAN

Before installing a fan, consider these issues:

- Decide whether to wire the switch to control the fan and the light separately (page 34).
- Buy a separate light kit if your unit doesn't inlude one; some fans include lights so check to be sure.
- Plan how you'll cover the hole once you remove the old ceiling box. Buy a light with a canopy that's wide enough to cover the hole, or get a medallion to hide ceiling imperfections (page 29).
- Decide how many blades you want. Four-blade fans move more air than five-blade models.
- Avoid "ceiling hugger" fans—they do not circulate air well. Fans should have downrods long enough (you can buy downrod extenders) to position fan blades at least 10 inches from the ceiling, but check that the blades are no lower than 7 feet from the floor.
- Use only a fan-rated dimmer if you install one; a standard dimmer will burn out the fan motor.

REMOVING AND REPLACING THE BOX

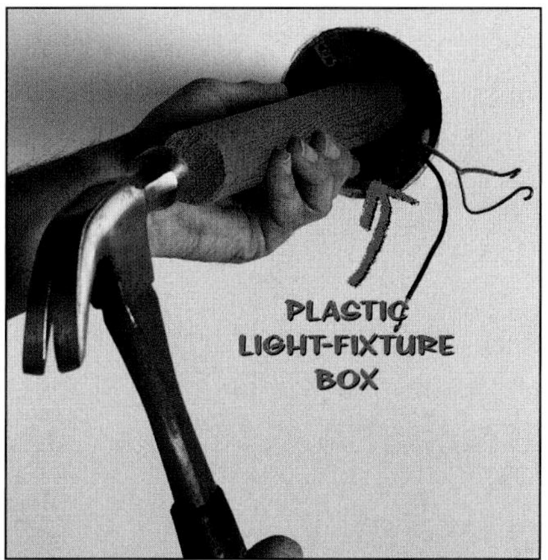

REMOVING A CEILING BOX. Shut off the power. Sometimes, you can remove screws or nails and pry out the box. Or, you may have to carefully cut away drywall or plaster to get to fasteners. If the box is nailed to a joist, cut around the box to enlarge the hole, and tap the box loose using a piece of wood and a hammer. You may be able to cut through fasteners with a reciprocating saw or a metal-cutting keyhole saw. Take great care not to slice through any cable.

SCREWING A FAN BOX TO A JOIST FROM BELOW. If you have a joist in the middle of the hole (as may be the case if you removed a thin "pancake" ceiling box), attaching a fan box from below will be easy. Buy a thin fan-rated box, and clamp the cable to it. Hold it in place and drill pilot holes; then drive in 2-inch wood screws. (Don't use drywall screws or "all-purpose" screws—they break too easily.)

ADDING A NEW CEILING BOX

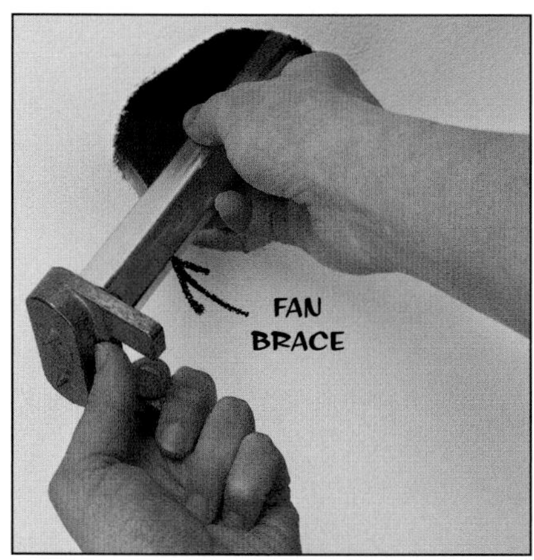

1 **SLIP IN THE BRACE.** Assemble the box on the brace to understand how it goes together; then take it apart again. Push the brace in through the hole and spread it apart until it touches the joists on both sides. The legs of the brace at each end should rest on top of the drywall or plaster.

2 **TIGHTEN THE BRACE.** Measure to make sure that the brace is centered in the hole. Position it on the joists at the correct height so the box will be flush with the surface of the ceiling. Use a crescent wrench or channel-type pliers to tighten the brace until it is firm.

USE A FAN-RATED BOX.

A ceiling fan box is different than an ordinary ceiling box in two ways: First, it is designed to attach very firmly, either directly to a joist or with a support bar. Second, it is equipped with deep-threaded holes or strong bolts so that you can tightly clamp the fan to it. You'll never get this kind of strength from an ordinary ceiling box.

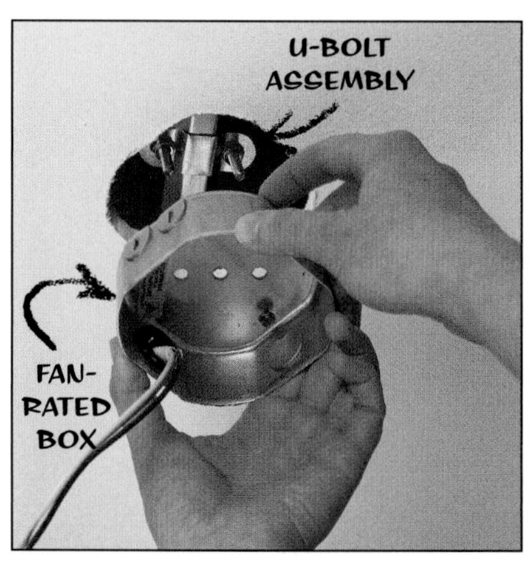

3 **ATTACH THE BOX.** Attach the U-bolt assembly to the brace so that the assembly is centered in the hole and the bolts face down. Thread cable through the cable connector and into the fan-rated box. Slip the box up so the bolts slide through it, and tighten the nuts to secure the box.

WORK SMARTER

WHEN FRAMING IS ACCESSIBLE, ATTACH A CEILING BOX TO A JOIST.

Install this type of box in unfinished ceilings or ceilings with a large hole. Drill pilot holes and drive in 1¼-inch wood screws to attach it to a joist.

OR INSTALL A BRACED BOX FROM ABOVE.

Buy a new-work ceiling fan box with a brace. Slide the box along the brace to position it. Tighten the clamp. Attach the brace by driving in 1¼-inch wood screws.

HANGING A CEILING FAN (CONTINUED)

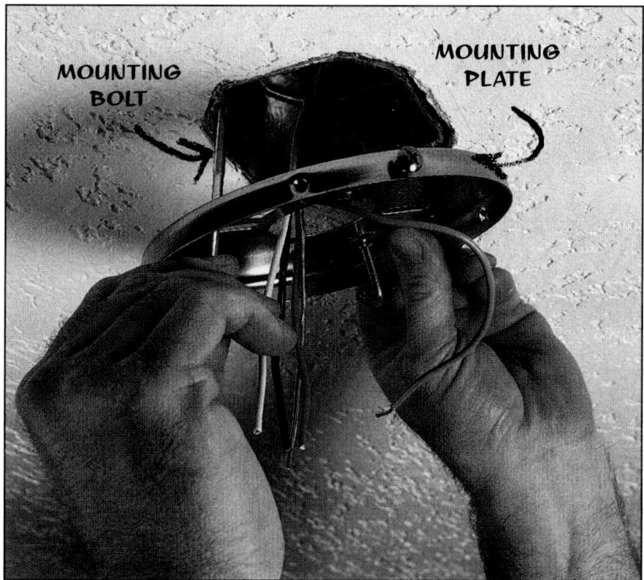

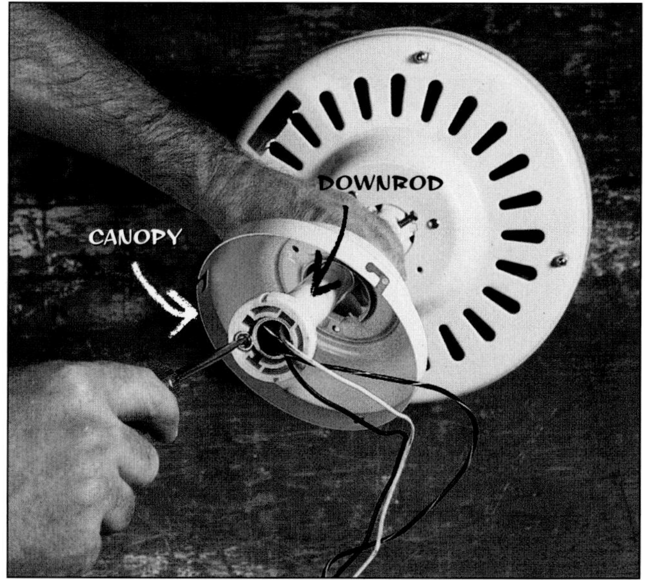

4 **INSTALL THE MOUNTING PLATE.** Thread the wires through the center of the mounting plate. If the box has mounting bolts that poke through the plate, fit the mounting plate over the bolts and fasten it with the nuts provided. If separate bolts are provided, push each one through the mounting plate as shown. When both bolts are in place, tighten the plate onto the ceiling.

5 **ASSEMBLE THE DOWNROD AND CANOPY.** On a work table, ready the fan for installation, following manufacturer's instructions. Run the fan leads through the downrod (or downrod extender), and tightly screw on the downrod. Remember to tighten the setscrews. Slip on the canopy, then install the bulb-shape fitting at the top of the downrod. It will rest in the canopy when the canopy is attached to the ceiling. Be careful not to mangle the wires. Do not attach the fan blades yet.

CLOSER LOOK

SWITCHING THE FAN AND LIGHT.
You probably have two-wire cable (not counting the ground wire) running into the ceiling fixture. If so, you have four options to control the fan and the light:

- **Hook the fan to the two wires so the wall switch turns the fan and the light on or off at the same time. Use the pull chains on the fixture to control the fan and light individually. This is convenient enough if you don't need to change fan speeds often.**
- **Purchase a fan that has a special fan/light switch that requires only two wires. These fans are expensive, however, and the switches have been known to turn the fan on by themselves — a dangerous situation if you're away for a few days.**
- **Install a remote-control switch, as shown on page 35. This is rather costly, but far less work than running new cable.**
- **Run three-wire cable from the fixture to the switch and hook it up as shown on page 22. You can conveniently control the fan and light separately by using a special wall switch.**

6 **WIRE THE FAN.** Temporarily hang the fan from the hook on the mounting ring. Connect the copper ground wire to the green wire attached to the fan base. If you have only two wires, connect both the black lead (for the fan motor) and the blue or striped lead (for the light) to the black house wire, and the white lead to the white house wire. If you have three-wire cable, connect black to black, white to white, and red to the blue or striped light lead. Check the manufacturer's directions. You may choose to install a remote control unit (right).

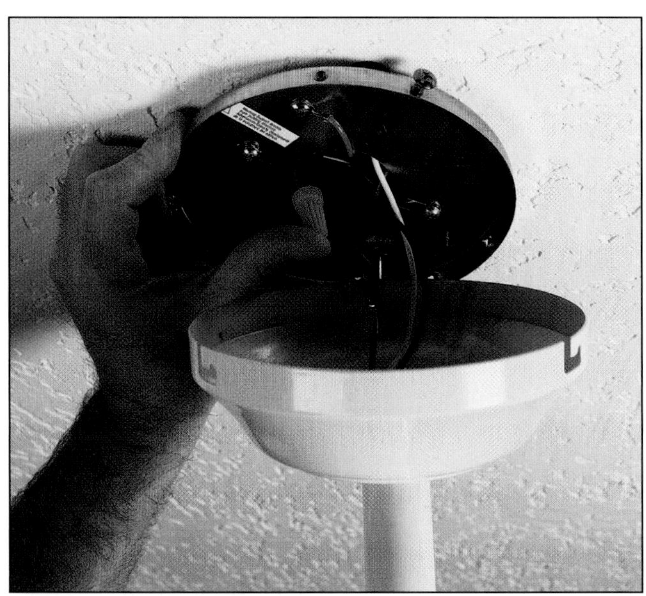

7 **ATTACH THE CANOPY TO THE MOUNTING PLATE.** Use a helper to support the fan motor while you drive the screws. Push the wires and wire nuts up into the box to keep them from vibrating against the canopy when the fan is running. Clip the canopy onto the mounting plate and tighten the screws.

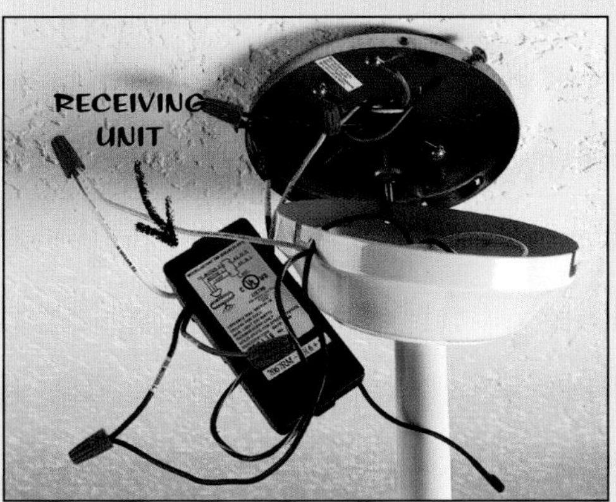

WIRELESS REMOTE SWITCH.

If you have only two wires running from the switch to the fan box, a remote control will let you control the fan and light separately. Before you install the canopy, hook up the receiving unit with both fan and light leads (black and blue or striped) spliced with the remote's black lead, and the white wire spliced to the white lead. Make sure the little dip switches are set the same on the switch unit and the receiving unit. Install the canopy. Put a battery in the sending unit, and attach a hanging bracket on a wall.

If the ceiling fixture was originally switched, the two wires sending power to the fan are still controlled by that switch. The sending unit controls the fan or light, or both, only when the wall switch is on.

HANGING A CEILING FAN (CONTINUED)

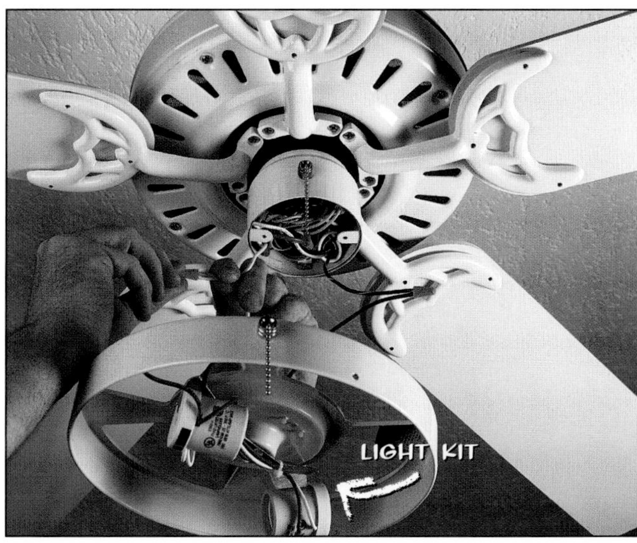

8 **ATTACH THE BLADES.** If the brackets are not all of uniform shape, return them and get replacements. Screw a bracket to each fan blade. Make sure the side of the blade that you want to show faces down. Attach each bracket to the motor with two screws. Drive the screws slowly to avoid stripping. Don't bend the brackets as you work.

9 **WIRE THE LIGHT KIT.** When you remove the plate on the bottom of the fan, you may see a tangle of wires. Don't worry; just find the blue or striped lead and the white lead, and connect them to the light kit leads. Screw the light kit up to the fan. Some light kits require a spacer ring between the fan and the light. The spacer ring should come with the kit or the fan.

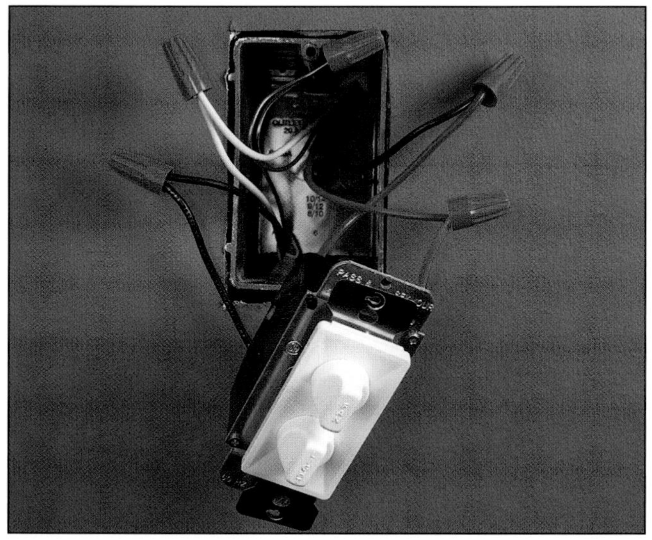

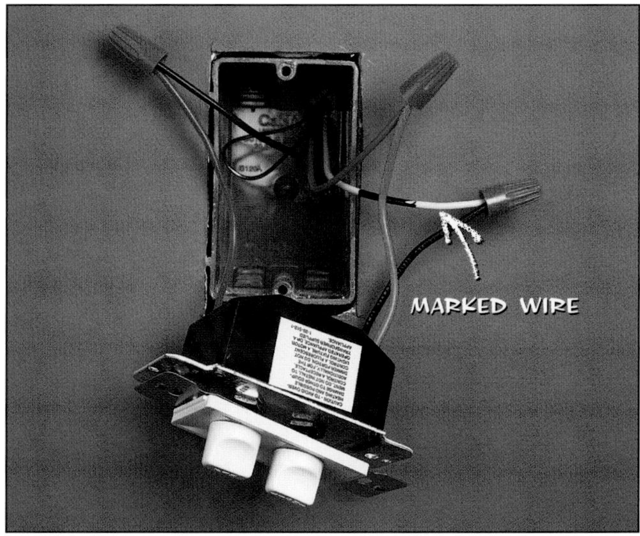

10 **OPTION A:**
IF POWER RUNS TO THE SWITCH. Shut off power to the switch. A three-wire cable usually runs from the fan to the switch, and a two-wire cable brings power to the switch. Follow the manufacturer's instructions; wire colors vary. Most likely you'll splice the black wire bringing power to the black switch lead, and splice the two white wires together. Then splice the black wire from the fan and the red wire from the light to the switch's fan and light leads.

OPTION B:
IF POWER RUNS TO THE CEILING BOX. If the switch box has only one cable—the one from the fan—then power runs to the ceiling box. Usually you'll find a black-marked white wire that brings power from the fan to the switch; however, the previous installer may not have marked it. If unmarked, wrap tape around its end and splice it with the switch's black lead. Splice the red wire (from the light) and the black wire (from the fan) to the switch's light and fan leads.

INSTALLING RECESSED LIGHTING

SKILLS: Installing cable, connecting to power, wiring a switch, and stripping and splicing wire.

HOW LONG WILL IT TAKE?

PROJECT: Running cable and installing 4 lights with a switch, in a finished ceiling.

EXPERIENCED . . . . . . 1 DAY

HANDY . . . . $1\frac{1}{2}$ DAYS

NOVICE . . . . 2 DAYS

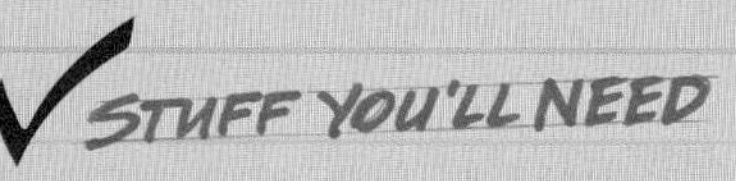

TOOLS: Stud finder, drill with long bit, drywall saw or hole-cutting drill attachment, voltage tester or multitester, combination strippers, lineman's pliers, screwdriver, safety glasses

MATERIALS: Can lights and trims, switch box and switch, cable and clamps, electrician's tape, wire nuts

Can lights, also called "pot lights," are recessed lights that use 60- to 150-watt floodlight bulbs. They're ideal for task lighting, highlighting artwork, or grouped to illuminate whole rooms. (See page 93 for tips on planning.) Cans get hot. Position them at least 1 inch away from wood and other flammables. Always follow manufacturer's instructions.

If the joists are exposed, use a new-work can light (page 39). For ceilings already covered by drywall or plaster and lath, buy a remodel can (below) that clips into a hole cut in the ceiling, (It's also called an old-work, or retrofit, can.) To install a remodel can, follow the steps beginning on page 38.

CHOOSING CANISTER LIGHTS

Can lights are designed to suit specific situations. Here's how to choose the right one:

- If there's insulation in the ceiling, buy IC (Insulation Compatible) lights. Standard recessed lights will dangerously overheat when surrounded with insulation.
- Buy tiny low-voltage can lights. They're stylish accent lights, but they are expensive. They're wired in the same way as standard can lights.
- Use bulbs of the recommended wattage or lower. Bulbs with too-high wattage will dangerously overheat. When putting a number of cans on a dimmer, add up all the wattage and make sure your dimmer is rated to handle the load.
- If you have less than 8 inches of vertical space above the ceiling, purchase a low-clearance canister.

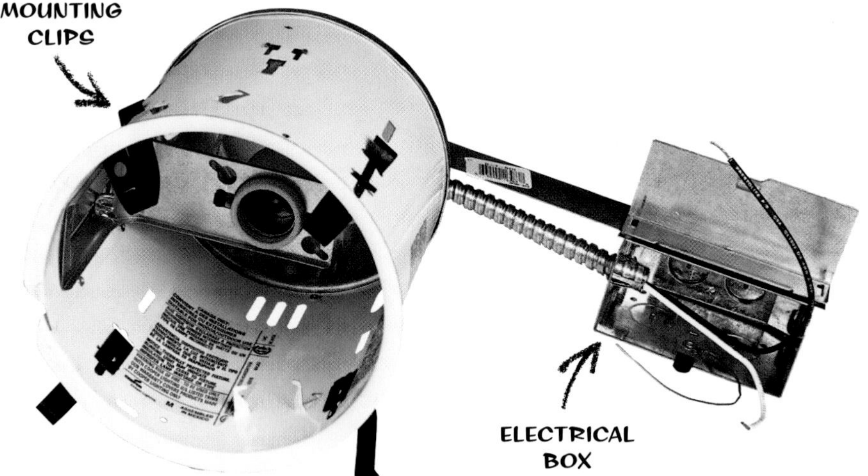

ANATOMY OF A CAN LIGHT. A standard remodel canister fixture has an approved electrical box, suspended far enough from the light so it will not overheat. A thermal protector shuts the light off if it becomes too hot (for example, if you use a bulb of too-high voltage. If you have less than 8 inches of vertical space above your ceiling, purchase special cans designed to fit into this smaller space. Be sure they are IC (Insulation Compatible) rated, so there will be no danger of overheating.

INSTALLING RECESSED LIGHTING (CONTINUED)

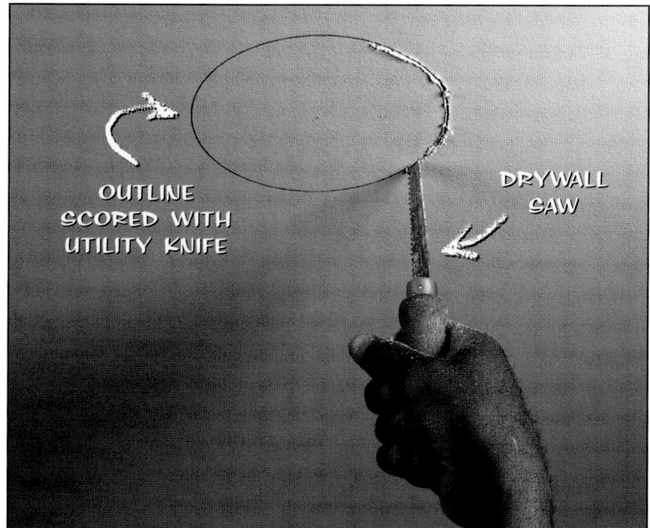

1 **OPTION A:**
CUT THE HOLE. Lightly mark all light locations. Use a stud finder to make sure they do not overlap a joist. Or, drill a hole and poke a bent wire up into it to make sure the hole is entirely between joists. Use the template provided with the light to draw a circle on the ceiling. Draw and cut each hole precisely. If it is even a little too big, the can may not clamp tightly. Wearing safety glasses, cut the line lightly with a utility knife; then cut along the inside of the knife line with a drywall saw. Take care not to snag any wires that may be in the ceiling cavity.

OPTION B:
USE A HOLE-CUTTING SAW. This tool saves time and cuts holes precisely. You don't have to draw the outline of the hole on the ceiling; just mark the center point. Check to see that you will not run into a joist. Check that the lights fit snugly without having to be forced into place. Note: This tool is costly (the saw and the arbor are sold separately), but it's worth the price if you have more than six holes to cut through plaster. A less-expensive tool (inset) is available for cutting through drywall only.

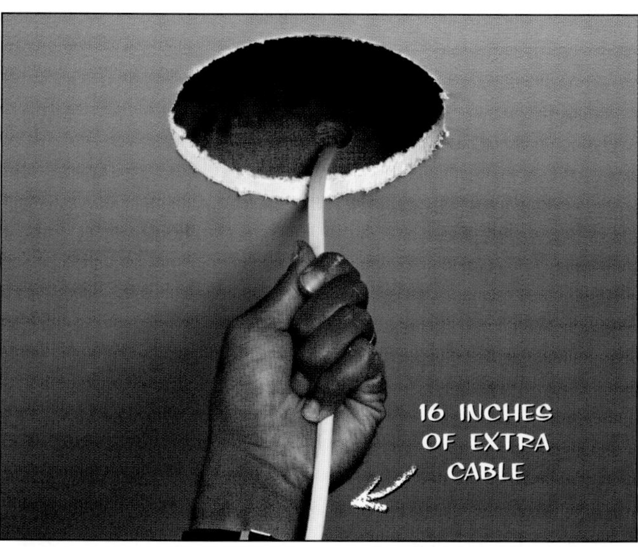

2 **ROUGH-IN THE WIRING.** Run cable from a power source to a switch box, and then to the first hole, allowing at least 16 inches of extra cable to make wiring easy. (See pages 122–131 for how to run cable.) Work carefully and use a drill with a long bit to avoid cutting additional access holes (pages 133–138) that will need patching later.

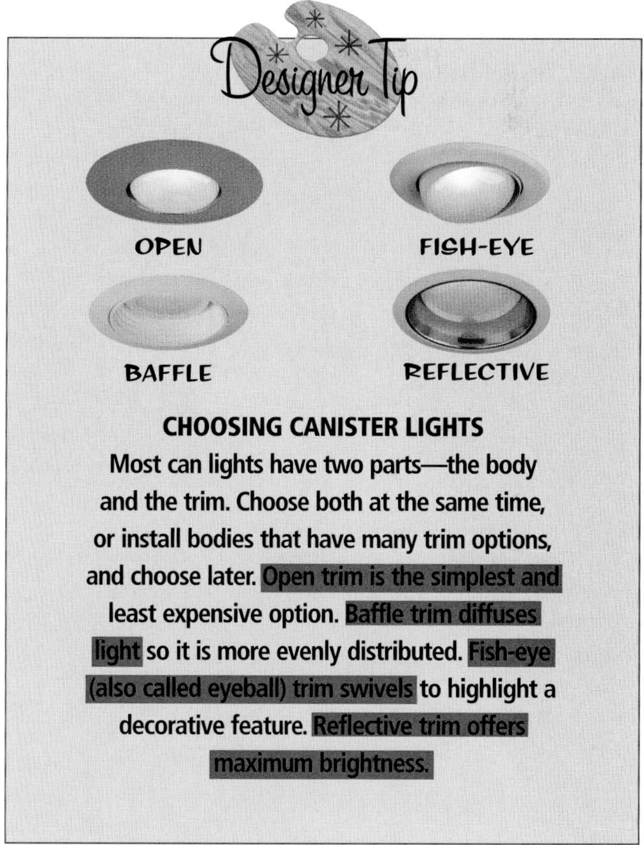

CHOOSING CANISTER LIGHTS

Most can lights have two parts—the body and the trim. Choose both at the same time, or install bodies that have many trim options, and choose later. Open trim is the simplest and least expensive option. Baffle trim diffuses light so it is more evenly distributed. Fish-eye (also called eyeball) trim swivels to highlight a decorative feature. Reflective trim offers maximum brightness.

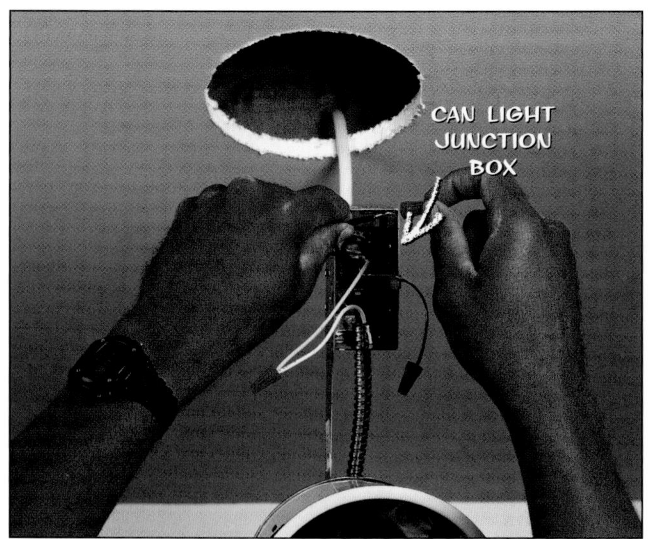

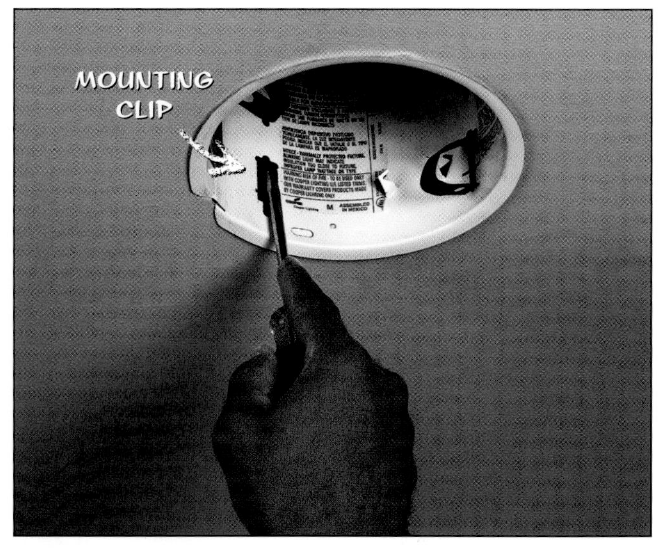

3 **WIRE THE LIGHT.** Open the light's junction box. Usually, there's a plate that pops off. Run cable into the box and clamp it. Strip insulation and make wire splices—black to black, white to white, and ground to ground (pages 46–47). Fold the wires into the box and replace the cover.

4 **MOUNT THE LIGHT.** Most remodel cans have four clips that clamp the can to the ceiling by pushing down on the top of the drywall or plaster. Pull the clips in so they do not protrude outside the can. Slip the can's box into the hole; then push the can body up into the hole until its flange is tight to the ceiling. With your thumb or a screwdriver, push each clip up and outward until it clicks and clamps the fixture.

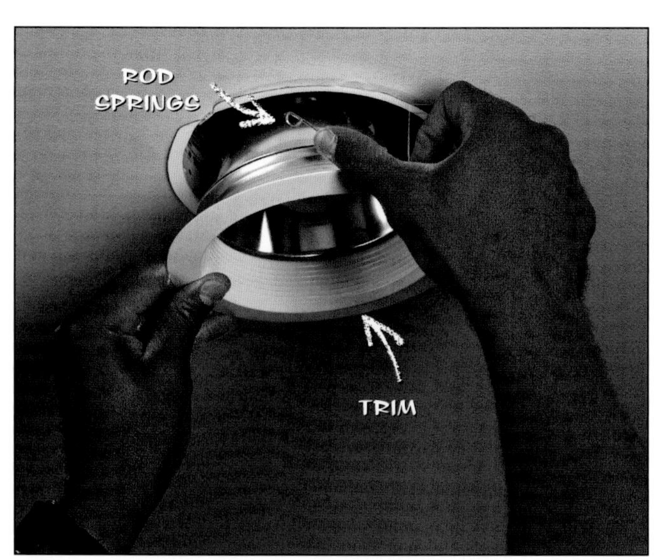

5 **ADD THE TRIM.** Most trims are mounted with coil springs or squeezable rod springs (as shown). If you have coil springs: Hook each spring to its assigned hole inside the can (if it is not already there). Pull out each spring and hook it to the trim; then carefully guide the trim into position. If you have rod springs, squeeze and insert both ends of each spring into their assigned holes; then push the trim up.

CLOSER LOOK

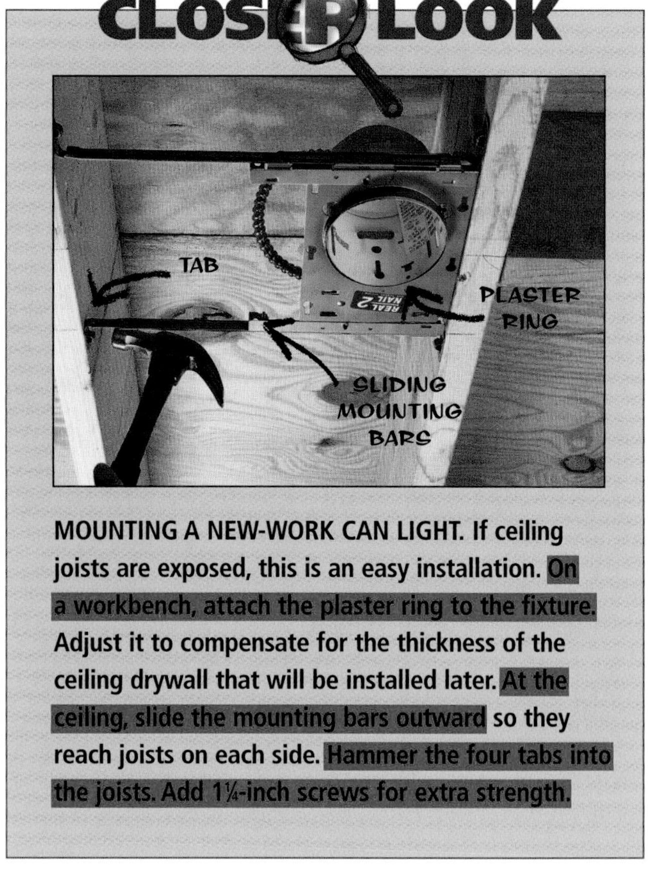

MOUNTING A NEW-WORK CAN LIGHT. If ceiling joists are exposed, this is an easy installation. On a workbench, attach the plaster ring to the fixture. Adjust it to compensate for the thickness of the ceiling drywall that will be installed later. At the ceiling, slide the mounting bars outward so they reach joists on each side. Hammer the four tabs into the joists. Add 1¼-inch screws for extra strength.

INSTALLING LOW-VOLTAGE LANDSCAPE LIGHTING

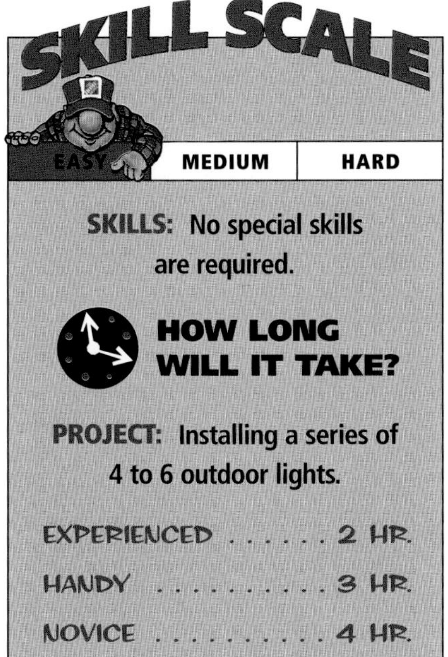

SKILLS: No special skills are required.

HOW LONG WILL IT TAKE?

PROJECT: Installing a series of 4 to 6 outdoor lights.

EXPERIENCED . . . . . . 2 HR.
HANDY . . . . 3 HR.
NOVICE . . . . 4 HR.

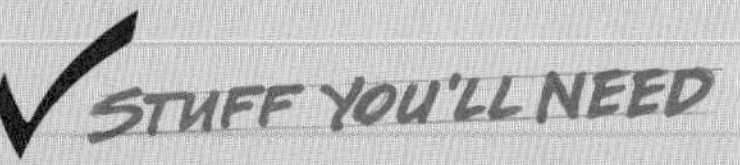

STUFF YOU'LL NEED

TOOLS: Screwdriver, drill, tool for trenching, lineman's pliers

MATERIALS: Set of lights with a transformer and timer

Installing outdoor lights is simple and quick. And low-voltage cable carries so little power that there is no danger of shock. The most economical approach is to buy a set that includes lights, cable, and transformer/timer. Avoid the very cheapest models, which have unreliable connections.

Make sure the cable is long enough for your needs. If you need to extend a line beyond the recommended length, use #14 or #12 low-voltage wire from beginning to end. The system plugs into a standard 120-volt receptacle. If you don't have an outdoor receptacle, you can plug the transformer into an indoor receptacle and run the low-voltage cable out through a small hole in the wall. (To install an outdoor receptacle, see pages 162–163.) See pages 94–96 for planning outdoor lighting.

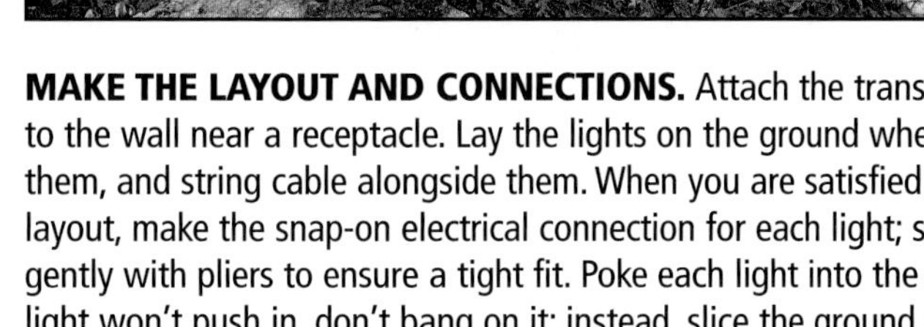

MAKE THE LAYOUT AND CONNECTIONS. Attach the transformer/timer to the wall near a receptacle. Lay the lights on the ground where you want them, and string cable alongside them. When you are satisfied with the layout, make the snap-on electrical connection for each light; squeeze each gently with pliers to ensure a tight fit. Poke each light into the ground. If a light won't push in, don't bang on it; instead, slice the ground with a shovel or flat pry bar, then poke into the slice. Dig a shallow trench for the cable, or cover it with mulch.

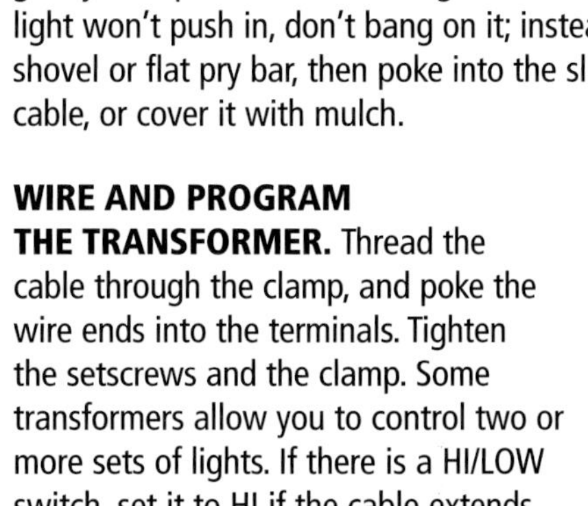

WIRE AND PROGRAM THE TRANSFORMER. Thread the cable through the clamp, and poke the wire ends into the terminals. Tighten the setscrews and the clamp. Some transformers allow you to control two or more sets of lights. If there is a HI/LOW switch, set it to HI if the cable extends very far; see the manufacturer's instructions. Program the timer according to the directions.

3 BASIC TOOLS AND SKILLS

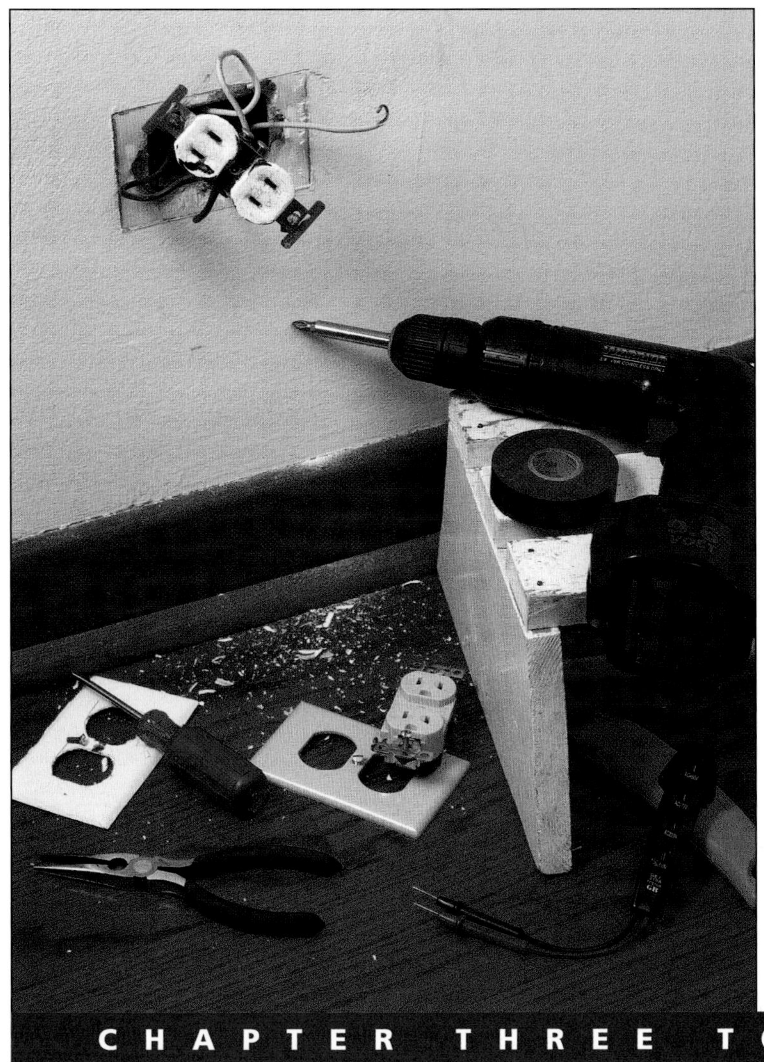

Equipped with a basic understanding of household electricity, you may be tempted to dive right into your project. After all, how hard can it be? Grab a utility knife, some tape, and a pair of pliers, and start splicing and twisting, right?

Some homeowners who tackle wiring projects with this attitude successfully complete the repairs they set out to make. But there's no guarantee that their work will meet the standard requirements for safety and longevity.

Professional electricians perform their highly detailed work accurately and safely. They ensure the tightness of connections so there's no chance of them coming apart. They cover all bare wires to avoid the danger of shorts.

With the help of this book, the right tools, and some practice, you can maintain and upgrade your home's electrical system with the confidence and reliability that rival the pros'.

CHAPTER THREE TOPICS

TOOL TIP

THE RIGHT STUFF.
Although you'll need carpentry tools to cut and patch holes for installing cable and boxes, don't use them as substitutes for tools designed specifically for electrical work. The right tools protect you from shocks, result in secure splices and connections, and make the job more enjoyable.

BASIC TOOL KIT

Compared to power tools used for carpentry work, the cost of electrical tools is a drop in the tool bucket. Buy everything you need. If you spend a little more to buy professional-quality tools, you'll find that they'll help you work faster and produce better connections.

The following section describes the tools you'll need to make all the inspections, repairs, and installations described in this book through page 108. (You may also need a few basic household tools such as a hammer, standard pliers, and a keyhole saw.) More advanced tools required for installing new electrical lines are described on pages 110–111. Be sure all your metal tools have insulated grips.

TOOLS YOU'LL NEED

With **combination strippers,** you can remove insulation from wires neatly and without nicking the metal. This tool is far superior to cheap adjustable strippers, which are a struggle to use and often damage the wire.

A **wire stripper/cutter** cuts wire like a pair of scissors and has a hole for stripping wire. Professional electricians often use this tool, or lineman's pliers, to strip wires instead of using combination strippers. It takes practice to do this without damaging the wire. **Side-cutting pliers,** or diagonal cutters, make it easy to cut wire and to snip off stripped plastic sheathing.

With **Lineman's pliers** you can cut wire and easily twist them together. Buy a high-quality pair that is fairly heavy in the hand, smooth-operating, with precisely aligned cutting edges for easy snipping of wires. Use **longnose pliers** to twist a tight loop in a wire end before attaching it to a terminal. Make sure the one you buy is sturdy enough to handle household wiring—some are intended for finer wires used in electronics.

Among the many precautions you can take to protect against electrical shock, using **rubber-grip**

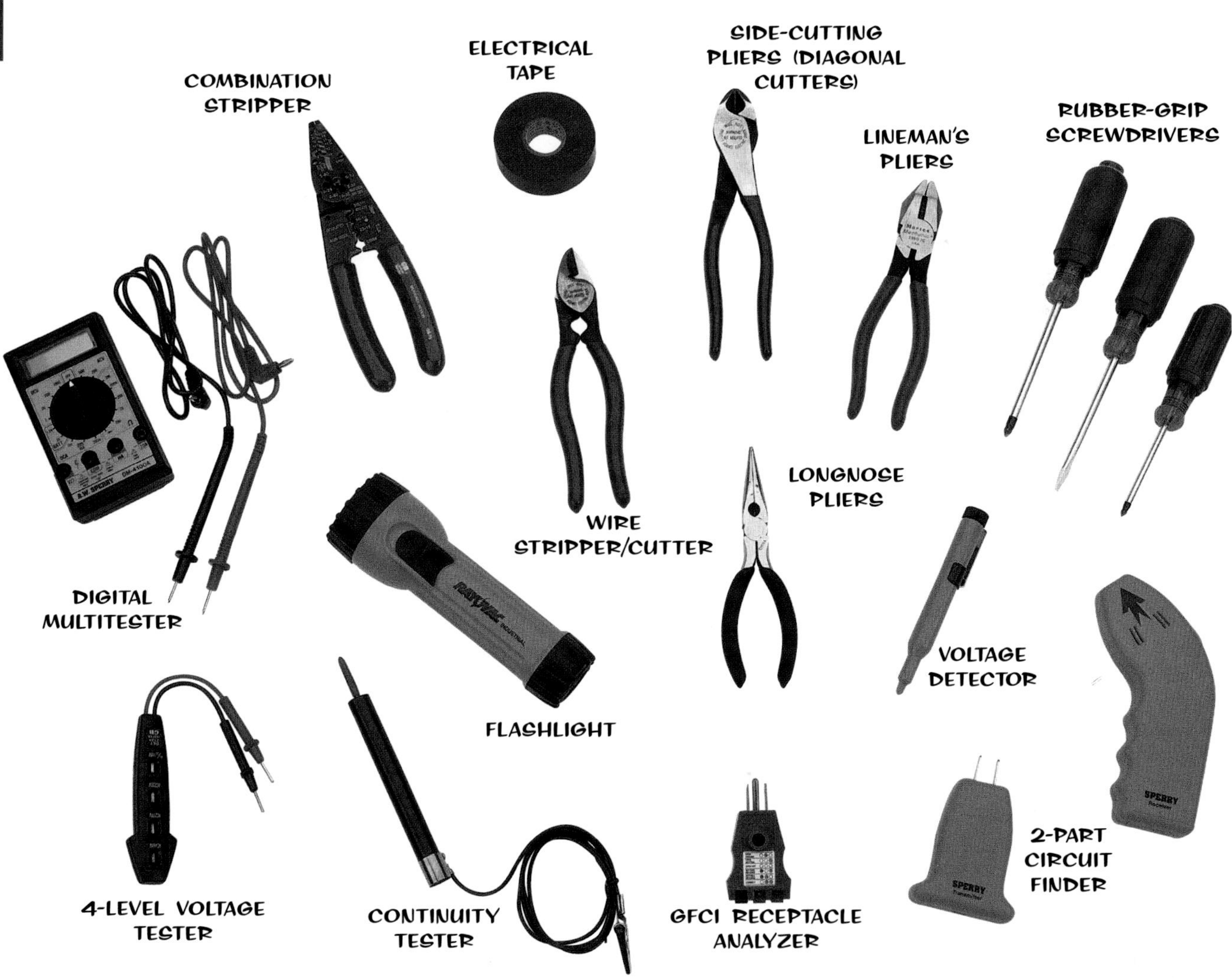

screwdrivers when doing electrical work is one of the most important. Don't use screwdrivers with plastic handles only. They can crack, creating a shock hazard. The handles should be large enough so that you will not be tempted to grab the metal shaft while you work. (Four-in-one screwdrivers are especially unsuited to electrical work because they have a metal shaft that runs through the handle.)

Keep a reliable **flashlight** handy because you may have to work in the dark.

Every home center has a bin of inexpensive **electrical tape.** It'll do the job, but far better is the more expensive, better-quality tape—it's thicker, more adhesive, and longer lasting.

SELECTING TESTERS

Even if you do not plan to do much electrical work, buy a **GFCI (Ground-Fault Circuit Interrupter) receptacle analyzer** (it handles standard receptacles as well). It will quickly tell you whether the receptacles are safe.

There are a variety of tools you can use to test for the existence of power. A **continuity tester** checks the reliability of fuses, switches, and sockets with the power off. A **four-level voltage tester**—better than the cheaper, single-level version—indicates if the power is on or off. A **digital multitester** is useful for appliance repair as well as electrical work. It performs the tasks of both a continuity tester and a voltage tester.

A **voltage detector** senses power, even through wire and cable insulation, so you can see whether wires are live before you work with them. With a **two-part circuit finder,** you can easily find out which circuit a receptacle is on. (Testers are described in detail on pages 44–45.)

BASIC TOOL CARE

Protect tools from moisture; rust causes them to lose their effectiveness. Make sure that the plastic insulation on each tool is in good shape so that your hand does not touch any metal part. If a cutting tool loses its edge so it's a struggle to cut wire, replace the tool.

TOOL TIP

ELECTRICIAN'S TOOL BELT.
Though a basic carpentry tool belt will keep your electrical tools close at hand, an electrician's tool belt is specially designed for keeping often-used electrical items within easy reach. Even if you work on only a half-dozen boxes and devices, a belt will save time.

FIBERGLASS STEPLADDER.
Never stand on a metal ladder while working with or near electricity. Use a fiberglass ladder, like the one shown above, or a wood ladder that's labeled "nonconductive." Not only do these items protect you from shock, they are also heavier than aluminum ladders and are more stable.

USING TESTERS

Reliable testing is essential to electrical work. Testers tell you whether the wires you are working on are hot; whether a switch, receptacle, or fixture is in working order; and whether a receptacle is wired safely.

Don't skimp on electrical testing tools. You might not need a fancy multitester, but avoid inexpensive tools such as single neon testers. They can quickly burn out or easily break, making you think there is no power when there really is.

If you buy a multitester, invest in a digital model rather than one with a dial. A digital tester is easier to use and is far less likely to give the wrong reading.

Examine your tester regularly to be sure it provides accurate information. To confirm that it's working, poke the probes of a voltage tester into a receptacle you know to be live, and make sure the tester lights up. Touch the probes of a continuity tester together. If the tester lights up, it's working. If it doesn't light up, it may need a battery or a bulb. Keep testers dry and safe from harm.

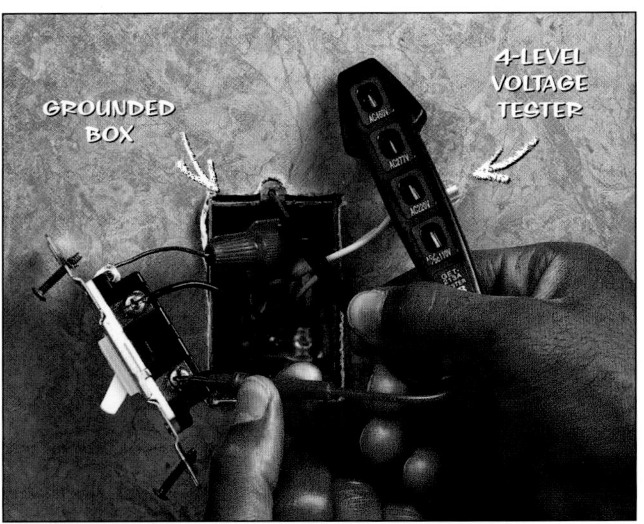

A VOLTAGE TESTER INDICATES THE PRESENCE OF POWER. A four-level voltage tester is safer and more reliable than one-level versions. Always confirm that a voltage tester is working by trying it on a circuit that you know to be live. Touch the tester's probes to a hot wire and a grounded box, to a hot wire and a neutral wire, or insert them into the slots of a receptacle. If the tester light doesn't come on, the circuit is shut off.

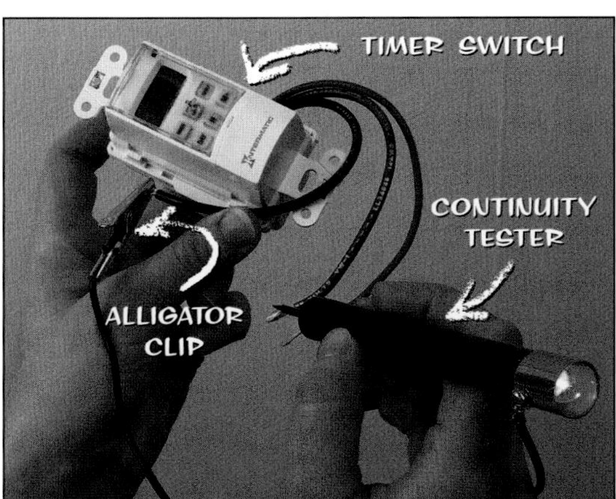

A CONTINUITY TESTER TELLS YOU WHETHER A DEVICE OR FUSE IS DEFECTIVE. Disconnect the device from all household wires. Attach the tester's alligator clip to one terminal and touch the probe to the other terminal. If the device switch is working, the tester light will glow when the switch is turned on and go out when the switch is turned off. To test the wiring in an appliance or lamp, touch both ends of each wire. The tester light will glow if the wire is unbroken. (To test a fuse, see page 81.)

A RECEPTACLE ANALYZER TELLS YOU WHETHER YOUR RECEPTACLES ARE SAFE. When you plug this analyzer into a receptacle, one or more of three lights will glow, telling you whether the receptacle is working, grounded, and polarized (page 11). Red analyzers will test ground-fault circuit interrupter (GFCI) receptacles as well as standard receptacles. Yellow analyzers test standard receptacles only.

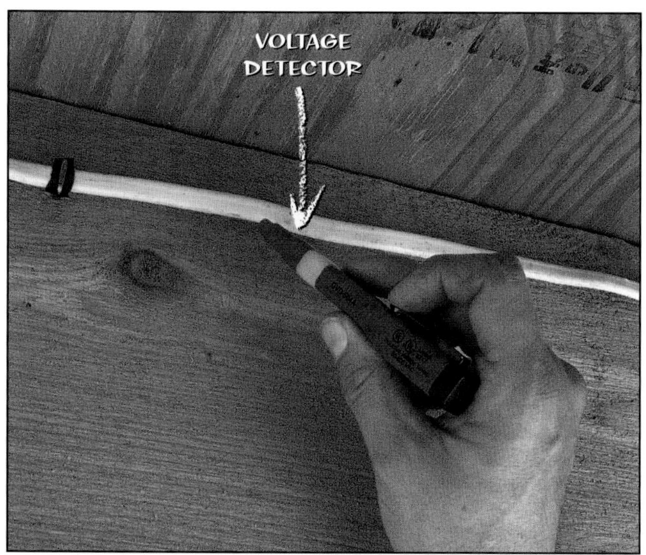

A VOLTAGE DETECTOR SENSES POWER—EVEN THROUGH WIRE AND CABLE INSULATION. This handy tester lets you check whether wires are live before you work on them. The probe doesn't need to touch a bare wire or terminal. Press the detector button and hold it on or near an insulated wire or cable to see if power is present. If there's power, a light comes on.

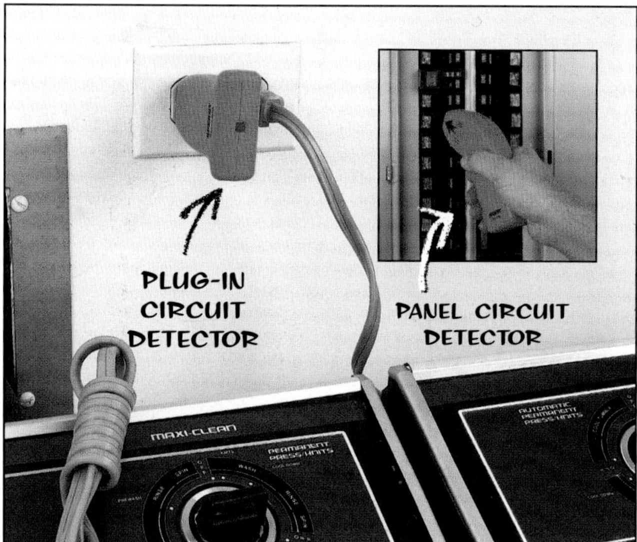

CIRCUIT DETECTORS INDICATE WHICH CIRCUIT A RECEPTACLE IS ON. Plug one part of the circuit detector into the receptacle. Open the service panel door and point the other part of the tester at the circuit breakers. The detector will glow to indicate the correct circuit. Even after switching off the circuit, check for power at the receptacle before working.

TOOL TIP

MULTITESTERS

TO TEST FOR VOLTAGE. A multitester tests 120-volt, 240-volt, or low-voltage circuitry. Multitesters have negative and positive probes. Test for voltage by touching each probe to a wire, terminal, or receptacle slot. You can also touch one probe to the black wire and the other to a ground, such as a metal box. The display should show between 108 and 132 volts for a 120-volt circuit, and between 216 and 264 volts for a 240-volt circuit. Low-voltage circuitry can register as low as 4 volts.

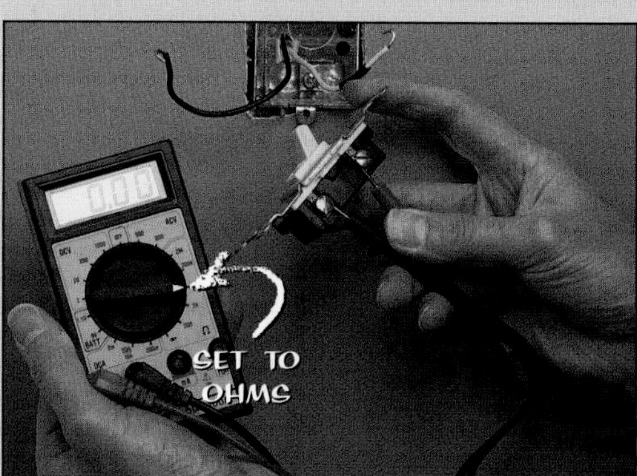

TO TEST FOR CONTINUITY. A multitester can test a switch, receptacle, fuse, or light fixture to see whether its circuitry is damaged. Shut off the power and remove the device. Test for continuity by turning the dial to an "ohms" setting and touching each probe to a terminal on the device. If you test a switch, turn it ON. If the multitester needle shows zero resistance, the device is in good shape. An infinity reading means that the device is defective.

STRIPPING AND SPLICING WIRE

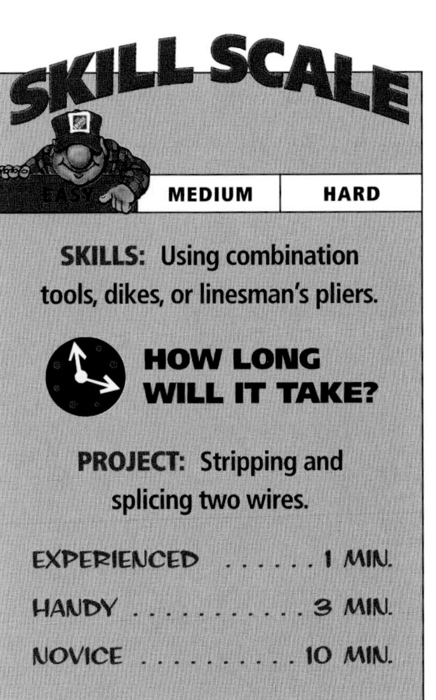

SKILL SCALE
EASY
MEDIUM
HARD
SKILLS: Using combination tools, dikes, or linesman's pliers.
HOW LONG WILL IT TAKE?
PROJECT: Stripping and splicing two wires.
EXPERIENCED ...... 1 MIN.
HANDY .... 3 MIN.
NOVICE .... 10 MIN.

With practice, you'll soon learn to remove insulation and connect wires with ease. Keep in mind that cutting into metal wire while stripping will weaken it. If wires are not joined tightly, the electrical connection will be compromised and could cause a short.

To work with new cable, you'll first have to remove the sheathing. (See pages 122–125 to see how to remove sheathing from various types of cable.)

Use a wire nut (page 50) to join wires. Twist the wires together before adding the wire nut.

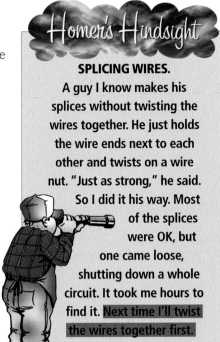

SPLICING WIRES.
A guy I know makes his splices without twisting the wires together. He just holds the wire ends next to each other and twists on a wire nut. "Just as strong," he said. So I did it his way. Most of the splices were OK, but one came loose, shutting down a whole circuit. It took me hours to find it. Next time I'll twist the wires together first.

✓ **STUFF YOU'LL NEED**

TOOLS: Combination strippers, lineman's pliers, or side-cutting pliers

MATERIALS: Wire, electrician's tape, wire nuts

When splicing two wires together, strip about 1 inch of insulation. If the wire will be joined to a terminal, remove about 3/4 inch.

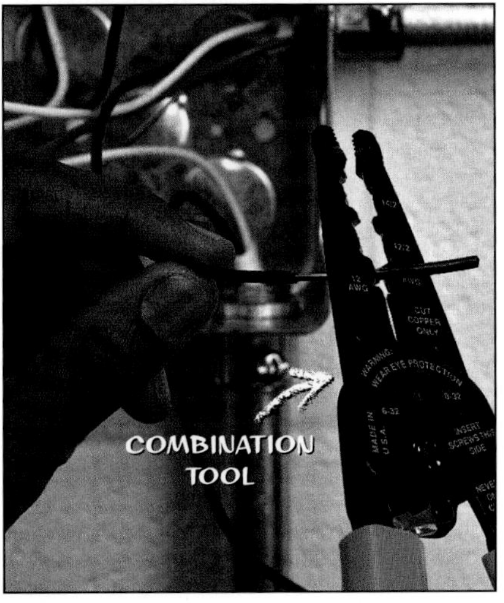

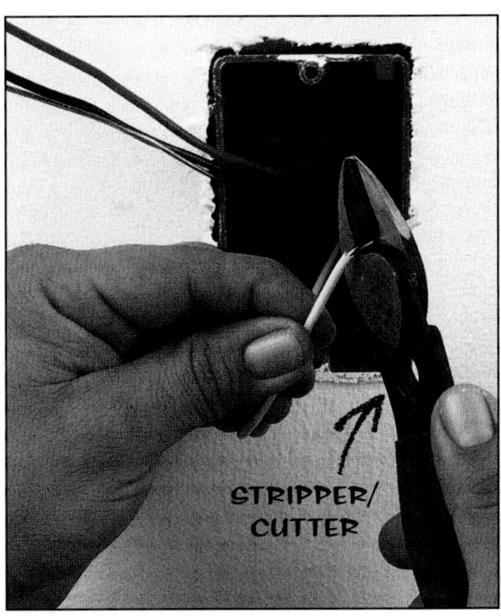

1 OPTION A:
STRIP WIRES WITH A COMBINATION TOOL. Don't use a utility knife; it will probably nick the wire. Choose a pair of wire strippers you are comfortable with, and practice with them until you're comfortable using them. To use a combination tool, slip the wire into the correct hole, squeeze, twist, and pull off the insulation. The insulation should come off easily.

OPTION B:
USE A WIRE STRIPPER/CUTTER. Many electricians consider combination strippers too slow. They prefer tools that are sometimes call "dikes." These include lineman's pliers, side-cutting pliers, or a stripper/cutter, with a single stripping hole. It takes time to learn to use these tools without nicking the wire. Press down with just the right amount of pressure to cut through the insulation and not the wire. Maintain the same pressure and twist until the insulation is cut all the way around. Ease up on the squeezing pressure, and pull off the insulation.

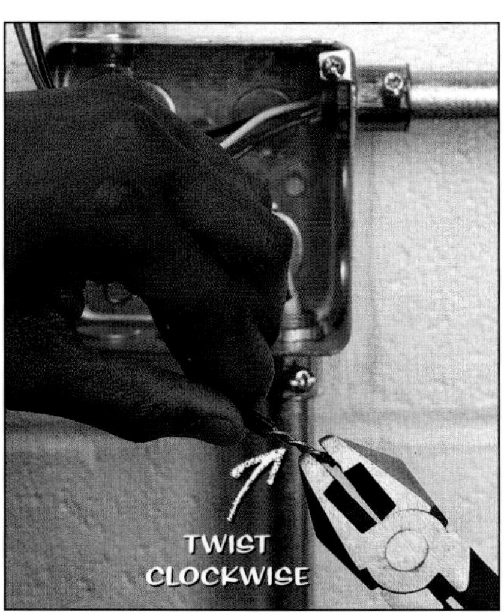

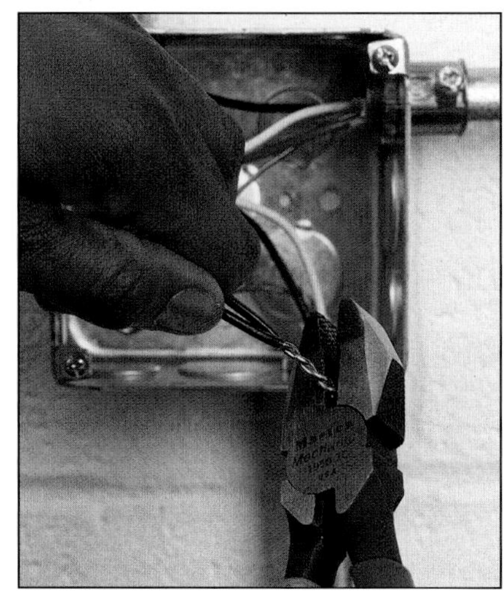

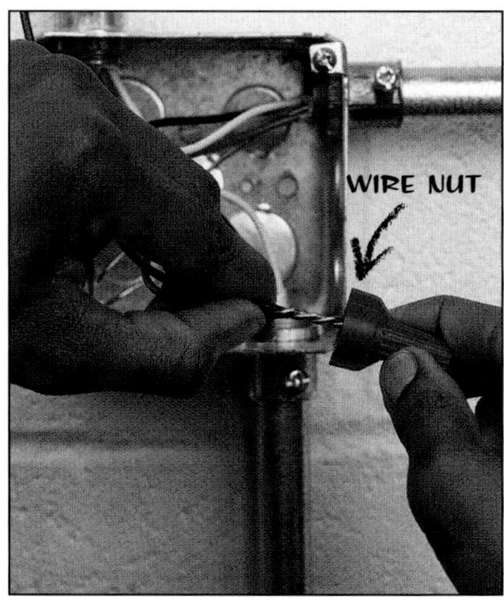

2 **TWIST WIRES TOGETHER.** Hold the stripped wires side by side. Grab the ends of both with linesman's pliers. Twist clockwise, making sure that both wires turn. Twist them together like a candy cane; don't twist one around the other. The wires should form a neat-looking spiral. Twist several times, but don't overtwist or you might break the wires.

3 **CUT THE END.** Using the lineman's pliers or side-cutting pliers, snip off the end of the twist. Leave enough exposed metal so that the wire nut will just cover it—about ½ inch usually does it.

4 **CAP WITH A WIRE NUT.** Select a wire nut designed for the number and size of wires you have spliced (page 50). Slip the nut on as far as it will go, and twist clockwise until tight. Test the connection by tugging on the nut—it should hold securely for extra protection. Wrap electrician's tape around the bottom of the cap.

SPLICING THREE OR FOUR WIRES. When twisting three or four wires together, hold them parallel and twist them all at once with linesman's pliers. (Don't twist two together and then try to add a third.) Choose a wire nut designed to accommodate the number and size of wires you have spliced (page 50) and twist the nut on as shown in Step 4.

WORK SMARTER

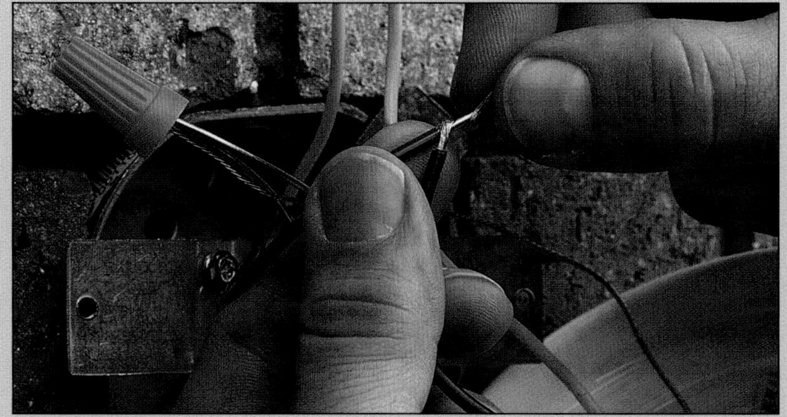

JOINING SOLID TO STRANDED WIRE.

To join stranded wire (often found on light fixtures and specialty switches) to solid-core wire, give the strands several twists between your thumb and forefinger to consolidate the strands. Then wrap the stranded wire around the solid wire, again with your fingers. Check that the stranded wire protrudes past the solid wire ⅛ inch or so. Twist on a wire nut, and tug both wires to make sure you have a solid connection. Finally, wrap the bottom of the wire nut with electrician's tape.

JOINING WIRE TO A TERMINAL

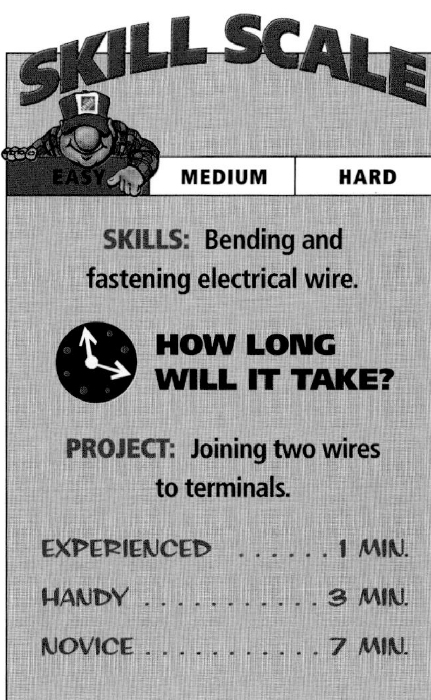

SKILL SCALE
EASY
MEDIUM
HARD
SKILLS: Bending and fastening electrical wire.
HOW LONG WILL IT TAKE?
PROJECT: Joining two wires to terminals.
EXPERIENCED ...... 1 MIN.
HANDY .... 3 MIN.
NOVICE .... 7 MIN.

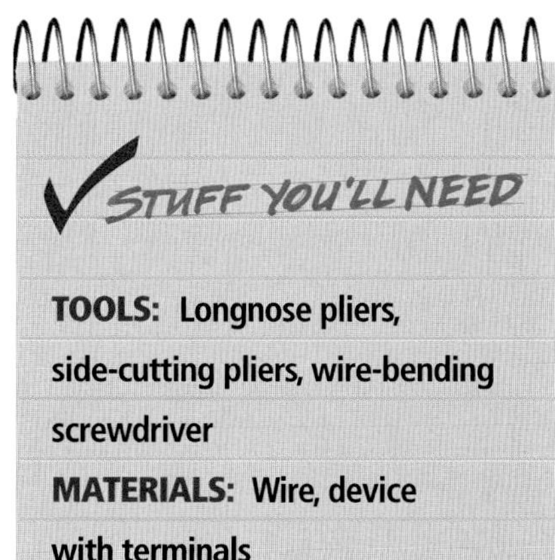

STUFF YOU'LL NEED
TOOLS: Longnose pliers, side-cutting pliers, wire-bending screwdriver
MATERIALS: Wire, device with terminals

Joining wire to a terminal is an important skill and a key step in most electrical projects. Do this step properly to ensure the device works and doesn't develop a short.

MAKING THE RIGHT CONNECTION

Electricians wrap the wire nearly all the way around the screw to make a connection that is completely reliable. With some practice, you can make joints just as strong. Bend a wire in a quarter circle, slip it under the screw head, and tighten the screw.

Many devices come with terminal screws unscrewed. Screw in any unused terminal screws so they won't stick out dangerously, creating a shock hazard should the terminal touch a metal box.

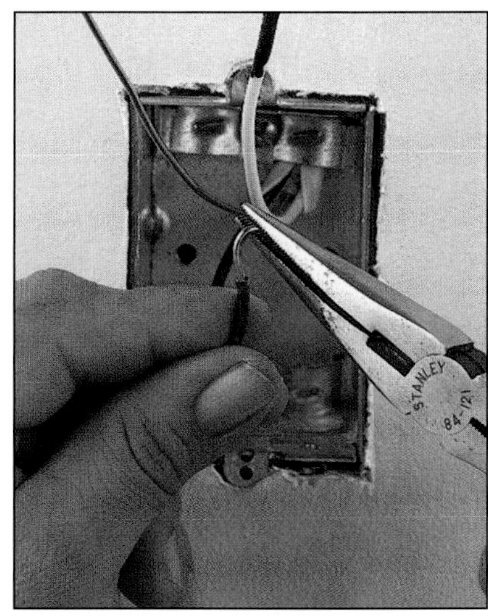

1 START A LOOP. Check that power is shut off. Strip about ¾ inch of insulation from a wire end (page 46). Using longnose pliers or the tip of a pair of combination strippers, grab the wire just above the insulation and bend it back at about a 45-degree angle. Move the pliers up about ¼ inch beyond the insulation, and bend again in the opposite direction, about 90 degrees.

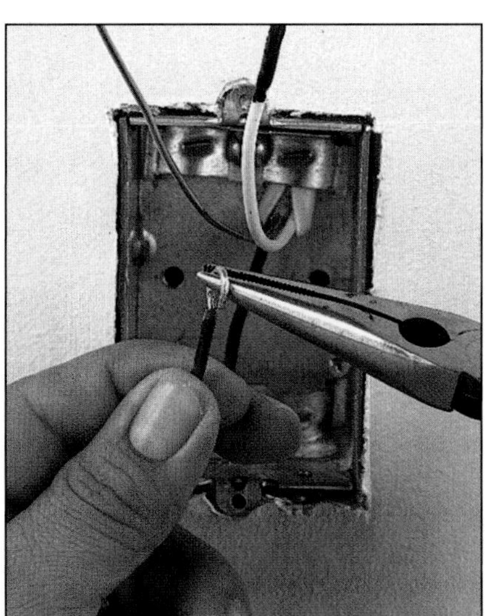

2 OPTION A: BEND A QUESTION MARK. Use a longnose pliers to form a near-loop with an opening just wide enough to slip over the threads of a terminal screw. Move the pliers another ¼ inch away from the insulation, and bend again to form a shape that looks like a question mark.

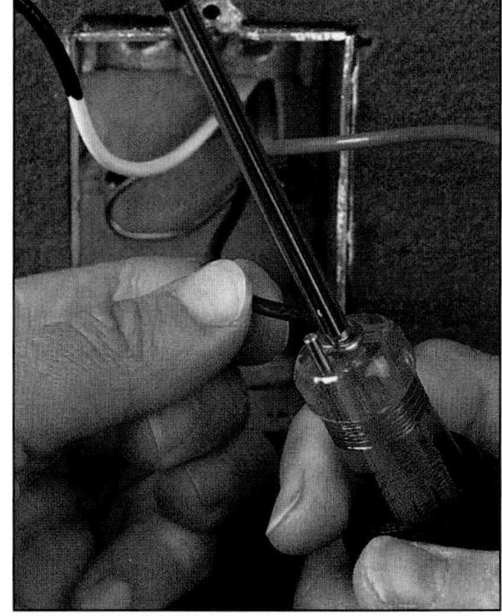

OPTION B: USE A WIRE-BENDING SCREWDRIVER. This simple tool makes perfect hooks every time. Just push the stripped wire between the screwdriver shaft and the stud at the base of the handle. Twist the handle to make a perfect loop.

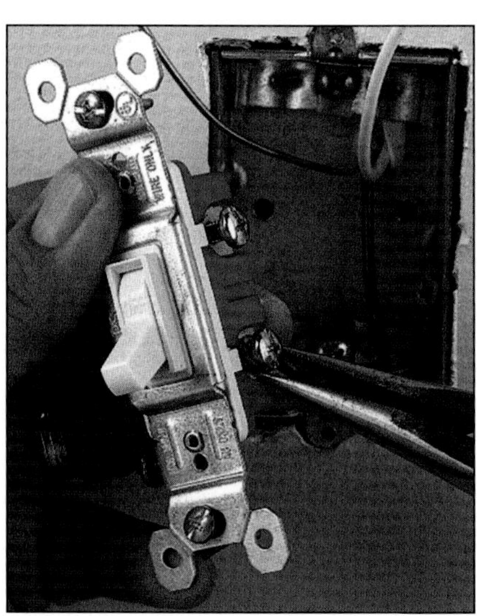

3 SQUEEZE THE LOOP AROUND THE SCREW. Make sure the terminal screw is unscrewed enough to become hard to turn. Slip the loop over the screw threads, with the loop running clockwise. Use longnose pliers or combination strippers to squeeze the loop around the terminal, then tighten the screw.

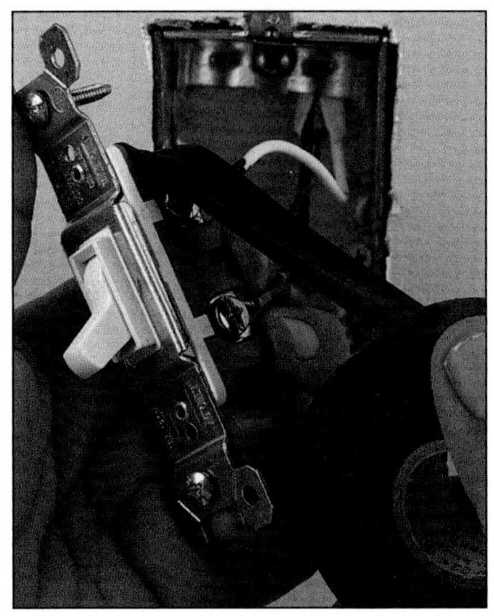

4 WRAP WITH TAPE. After all the wires are connected to a switch or receptacle, wrap electrician's tape around the body of the device to cover the screw heads and any exposed wires. The tape not only ensures that the wires stay attached, it keeps the terminals from touching the box.

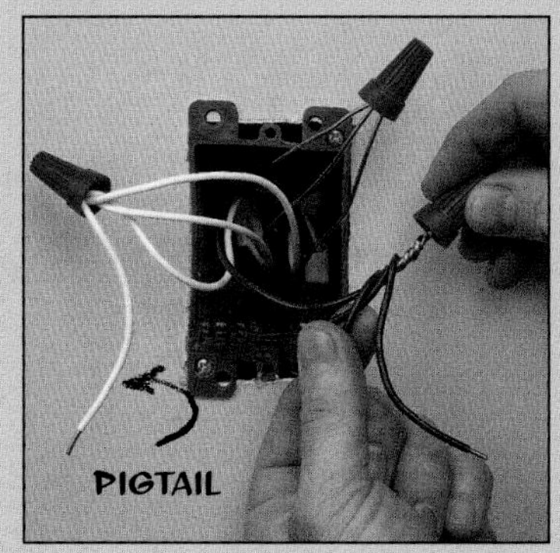

USING PIGTAILS. Codes prohibit attaching two wires to one terminal. If you need to attach two wires to one terminal, cut a "pigtail" wire 6 inches long, and strip both ends. Splice the two wires to the pigtail, and join the pigtail to the terminal.

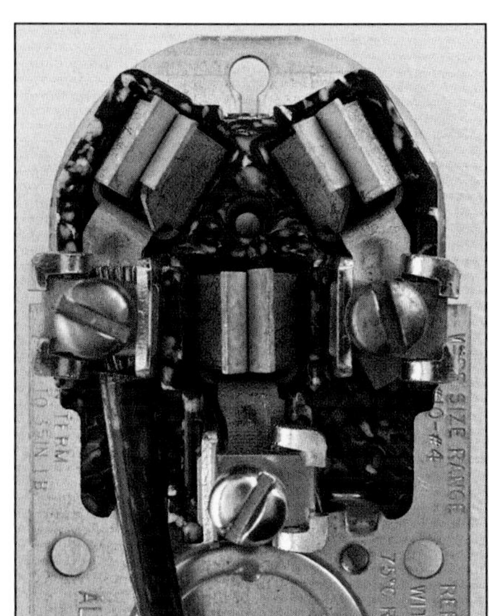

CONNECTING TO A 240-VOLT RECEPTACLE. Be certain that power is shut off—there is a dangerous level of power here. Strip about ½ inch of insulation from the wire end. The wire should be straight, not looped. Loosen the setscrew, poke the wire into the hole, and tighten the screw. (See page 145 for installing a 240-volt receptacle.)

SAFETY ALERT!

SKIP THE PUSH-IN OPTION. Most professionals don't trust this method even though it saves time. Many receptacles and switches have holes in the back for easy connection of wires. Once you've stripped the insulation (a strip gauge shows you how much), you poke the wire in. To remove a wire, insert a small screwdriver into a nearby slot. The wire releases. The system works, but the resulting electrical connection is not as secure as a connection made using a terminal screw. Take the extra minute to do it right.

WIRE NUTS AND TAPE

Wire nuts must cap all wire splices. These nuts come in several sizes, identified by color. On the package you will find a chart telling how many wires of a given size the nut can handle.

In older homes, you may find spliced wire ends wrapped with rubberized tape that is covered with cloth friction tape. Electricians often wrapped these well, so you may find them difficult to unwrap. (Slice with a utility knife before unwinding.)

Small, colored wire nuts are often included with light fixtures. If they are all plastic (with no metal threads inside) or if it is a challenge to get them to twist on because they are too small, use orange nuts instead. Use **yellow** connectors for splices as small as two #14s or as large as three #12s. **Orange** nuts handle combinations ranging from two #16 wires up to two #14s. Use **green** wire nuts for ground wires only. The hole in the top allows you to make an instant pigtail, with one wire poking out. **Red** wire nuts will grab splices as small as two #12s and as large as four #12s.

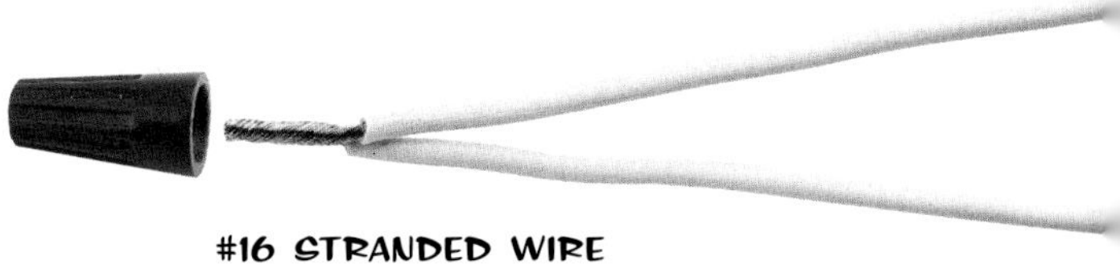

GET THE GOOD TAPE.
The inexpensive tape often found in large bins at a home center will do the job, but many electricians prefer to use professional-quality tape. It's thicker and has better adhesive.

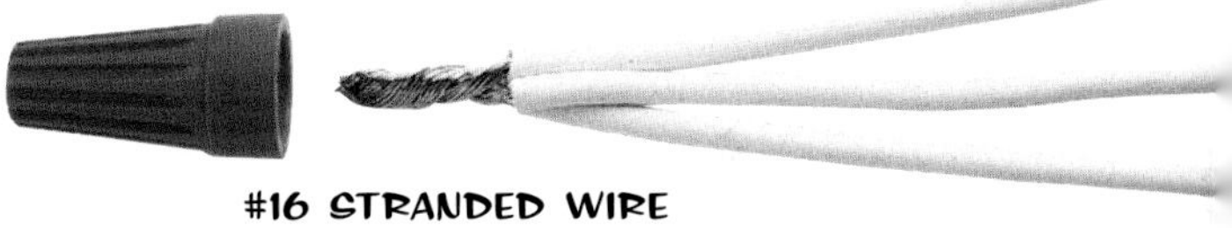

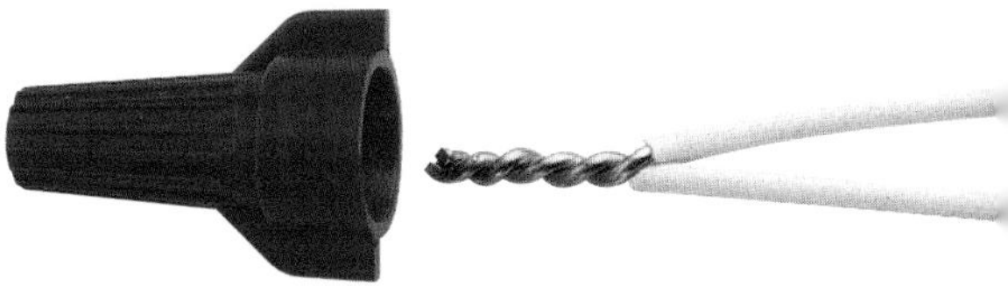

#16 STRANDED WIRE

#14 SOLID WIRE

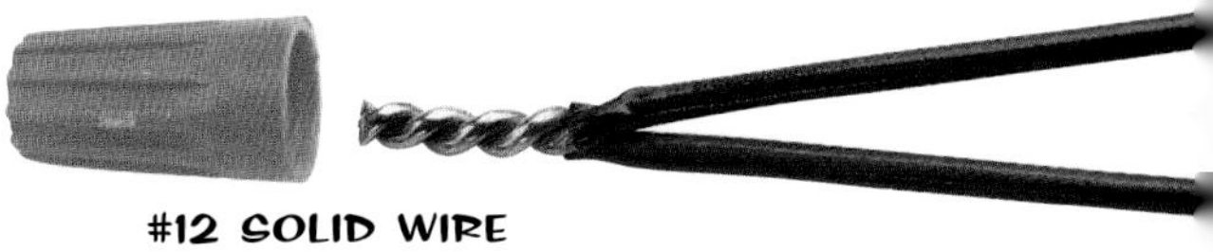

#12 SOLID WIRE

#16 STRANDED WIRE

#14 SOLID WIRE

#14 STRANDED WIRE

#14 SOLID WIRE

#14 SOLID WIRE

#12 SOLID WIRE

4 INSPECTING YOUR HOME

You don't have to be a professional electrician with a clipboard and a head full of electrical codes to correctly assess the safety of your home. Many problems that inspectors can find will be just as obvious to you once you learn how to find them.

This chapter begins with a simple "walk-around" inspection of your home, instructing you to examine fixtures, receptacles, and switches in plain sight. Later, the chapter demonstrates how to open your service panel and electrical boxes to inspect wires and terminals.

Each section identifies common household problems and refers you to a page describing how they can be fixed.

CHAPTER FOUR TOPICS

CHASE DOWN LIGHT FLICKERS.
Did you ever sit down to read a magazine only to have your floor lamp flicker off and on? Besides being annoying, such flickering indicates a poor connection or a damaged switch, causing a dangerous electricity arc. Don't live with it. Check the bulb, switch, cord, and plug.

MEETING CODE

Local building codes and regulations are imposed to protect you and your family from shock and fire, and to make sure your wiring works reliably for decades.

WHEN YOU DON'T NEED CODE

Codes change over the years as new hazards are discovered and new products are introduced. It's possible that some of the wiring in your home fails to conform to current regulations. Usually, that's not a problem, as long as it conforms to the rules that existed when the wiring was installed. But any new work, even if it connects to old work, must meet code.

If you repair a fixture or replace one fixture with another without running new cable, there's no need to consult codes. Even if local regulations require you to get a permit for every fixture replacement, most inspectors will not want to be bothered with such small changes.

WHEN TO CONSULT CODE

If, during the course of an installation or inspection, you see wiring that's improperly connected and you don't know how to fix it, or if you see wiring that you do not understand, call in a pro or check with your local building inspection department.

Whenever you install new service in your home (make an installation that involves running new cable) you must get a permit and be sure to work according to code. (See page 112 for tips on working with inspectors.)

THE NEC AND LOCAL CODES

Codes vary from area to area. In fact, sometimes the regulations in two neighboring cities differ. However, all local codes are based on the National Electrical Code (NEC). Published by the nonprofit National Fire Protection Association, the NEC is a massive book that provides more detail than you'll ever need about a particular problem. Check out a copy from your local library. The NEC is updated every few years. (In Canada, look for the Canadian Electrical Code.)

As you consult these books, remember that local codes prevail. Your local building inspection department will have brochures that describe the most common electrical codes for residences.

BUYER'S GUIDE

HIRING A PRO.

Most professional electricians are qualified, are honest, and charge fairly. Unfortunately, a few take advantage of homeowners' lack of knowledge and general fear of electricity. Too often, unscrupulous contractors target the elderly.

Word-of-mouth can be a great way to find a reliable contractor, but even sharp consumers may be unaware that they have overpaid or have paid for shoddy work. For a large job, get quotes from at least three contractors. Their bids should include a list of "specs"—everything that will be installed and how it will be installed.

Check that the contractor is licensed for your area and is covered by insurance. This way, if there is a fire or if a worker is injured on your property, you will not be held liable. If the work involves running new cable, the contractor—not the customer—should get a permit.

Read the section in this book about the installation you will pay for. Don't be afraid to ask the electrician to explain what he or she is doing. Question everything that looks substandard. In particular, have the contractor explain how the installation is grounded.

A WALK-AROUND INSPECTION

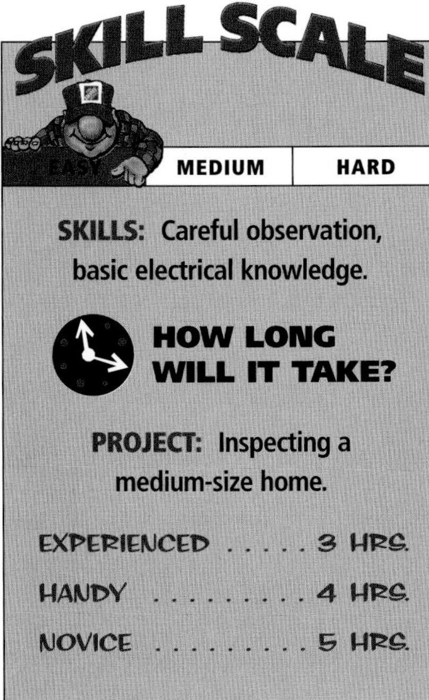

SKILLS: Careful observation, basic electrical knowledge.

HOW LONG WILL IT TAKE?

PROJECT: Inspecting a medium-size home.

EXPERIENCED . . . . . 3 HRS.
HANDY . . . . 4 HRS.
NOVICE . . . . 5 HRS.

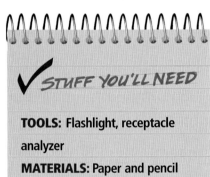

STUFF YOU'LL NEED

TOOLS: Flashlight, receptacle analyzer

MATERIALS: Paper and pencil

Once you know what to look for, most household wiring problems are easy to find and fix. Make a whole-house inspection by checking closets, the attic, the basement or crawl space, and the garage. Globes for light fixtures will be the only things you have to remove. Prioritize everything that needs to be done and immediately take care of all potentially hazardous problems.

INSPECTING RECEPTACLES FOR PROBLEMS

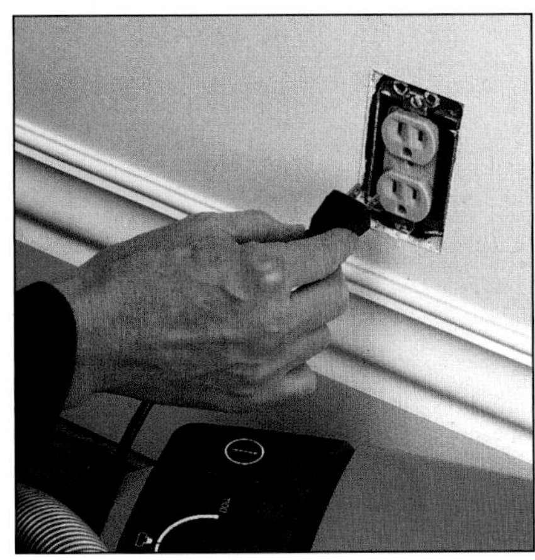

1 LOOK FOR DEVICES THAT LACK COVER PLATES. If the cover plate to a switch or receptacle is missing, replace it immediately. Lack of cover plates presents a dangerous situation: Children might reach into the electrical box, where live wires lurk. An adult fumbling for the switch at night could receive a shock as well. Replace any missing cover plates.

2 CHECK GROUNDING. A two-hole receptacle is ungrounded (page 17). If the metal tab of an adapter is connected to the screw in the middle of the receptacle, it may be grounded. But often, this adapter is plugged in without being connected to ground, providing a false sense of security. In many areas, an adapter is actually illegal. Use a receptacle analyzer to test. See page 13 for how to protect the circuit.

3 BEWARE OF CRACKED RECEPTACLES. A crack on the outside may mean that a receptacle's inner circuitry is in danger of shorting out. New receptacles are inexpensive and easy to replace (page 26).

4 UPGRADE UNGROUNDED RECEPTACLES. Receptacles with only two slots and no grounding hole are ungrounded. Homeowners got by with ungrounded wiring for decades, but grounding provides a necessary level of protection. If you can't install grounded receptacles, add ground-fault circuit interrupter (GFCI) receptacles (page 27).

INSPECTING RECEPTACLES FOR PROBLEMS (CONTINUED)

5 WIGGLE SWITCH TOGGLES. If there seems to be too much play in the switch toggle—especially if you hear a pop when the switch is turned on or off—the device should be replaced (pages 22–24).

6 TEST A GFCI. Just because a ground-fault circuit interrupter (GFCI) receptacle is supplying power doesn't mean it will protect against shock. A GFCI can lose its protecting capacity. Test each GFCI by pushing the test button. The reset button should pop out. If it doesn't, replace the GFCI receptacle (page 27).

7 STANDARD RECEPTACLES IN DAMP AREAS. A wet receptacle is a shock hazard, so current codes call for ground-fault circuit interrupters (GFCIs) in bathrooms, near sinks, and outdoors. See page 27 for instructions on installing a GFCI. (Canada: GFCIs are not allowed on kitchen counters. Use split receptacles instead. See pages 144, 175.)

8 CHECK FOR GROUNDING AND POLARIZATION. If a receptacle analyzer indicates that a receptacle is not grounded, shut off the power and remove the cover plate and the receptacle (page 26). Compare the wiring with the examples shown on pages 11 and 13. If a wire is loose, reattach it. If a receptacle is not polarized, switch wires so that the hot wire is connected to the brass terminal and the neutral wire is connected to the silver terminal. If you are not sure what is wrong, call a pro.

SAFETY ALERT!

KID-SAFE RECEPTACLES. Although kids sometimes pull them out, the simplest and cheapest protection is to push a plastic insert (above left) into each unused outlet. For more reliable protection, install a special cover plate (above right) that must be twisted before inserting the plug. Most importantly, teach children to respect electricity and to stay away from all receptacles.

INSPECTING FIXTURES AND BOXES FOR PROBLEMS

1 **CHECK FOR UNSECURED GLOBES.** After replacing a light bulb, it's easy to tighten a setscrew before the globe is properly nested into place. With a little vibration, the globe could crash to the floor. When replacing a globe, unscrew the setscrews a bit more than necessary for removing the globe. Slip the globe up and make sure its lip is above all the screws before you tighten them. Check again after tightening.

2 **DETERMINE IF THE BULB WATTAGE MATCHES THE FIXTURE.** It's easy to overlook the stickers inside light fixtures that state the maximum allowable wattage. Bulbs with too-high wattage will overheat fixtures. At best, you'll have to change bulbs more often; at worst, overheating can cause a fire. If you need more light, install a new fixture (pages 28–29) with a higher wattage allowance.

CHECK YOUR INSURANCE. Some insurance policies have exclusions stating that the insurer does not have to pay for fire damage if the home had certain defects in its wiring. It's in your financial interest, as well as in the interest of safety, to make sure your electrical system is free of obvious defects.

If you find a problem, be sure to shut off the power before fixing it.

3 **AVOID BARE LIGHT BULBS IN CLOSETS.** Too often, light fixtures in closets don't have globes. Sweaters, comforters, cardboard boxes, and other flammables placed too near bare bulbs can catch fire. The best solution is to replace your closet light with a fixture that has a globe covering the bulb. Or install a surface-mounted fluorescent light (page 104).

4 **MAKE SPACE IN CROWDED BOXES.** If a junction box is so crowded that it prevents the cover plate from being tightened all the way, install a box extender (page 82), or replace the box with a larger one.

CHECKING CORDS AND WIRES FOR PROBLEMS

1 CHECK FOR BROKEN OR BENT GROUNDING PRONGS. Appliance and tool grounding plugs are installed for your safety. Do not remove or bend back grounding prongs—you will negate an important safety feature. (See page 11 for an explanation of grounding.) Replace a plug that has a bad prong (pages 72–73).

2 DON'T OVERLOAD RECEPTACLES. This many-armed monster is awkward and unsafe. Using too many appliances at once can overheat the receptacle. Install another receptacle (page 141).

Don't just tape a damaged wire — be sure to replace it!

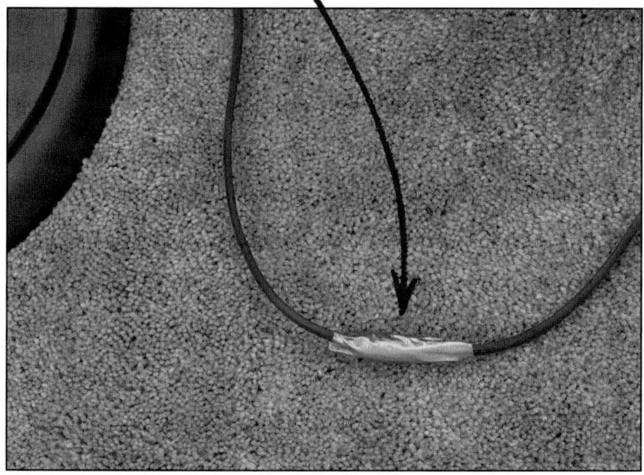

3 WATCH OUT FOR DAMAGED CORDS. A cord with less-than-perfect insulation can cause shock or start a fire. All lamp cords and appliance cords should be free of nicks; you should see no bare wire. Run your fingers along each unplugged cord. If you feel cracks or if the cord is brittle, replace it (pages 68–69). Pay special attention to the cord near the plug, where insulation is most often damaged.

BUYER'S GUIDE

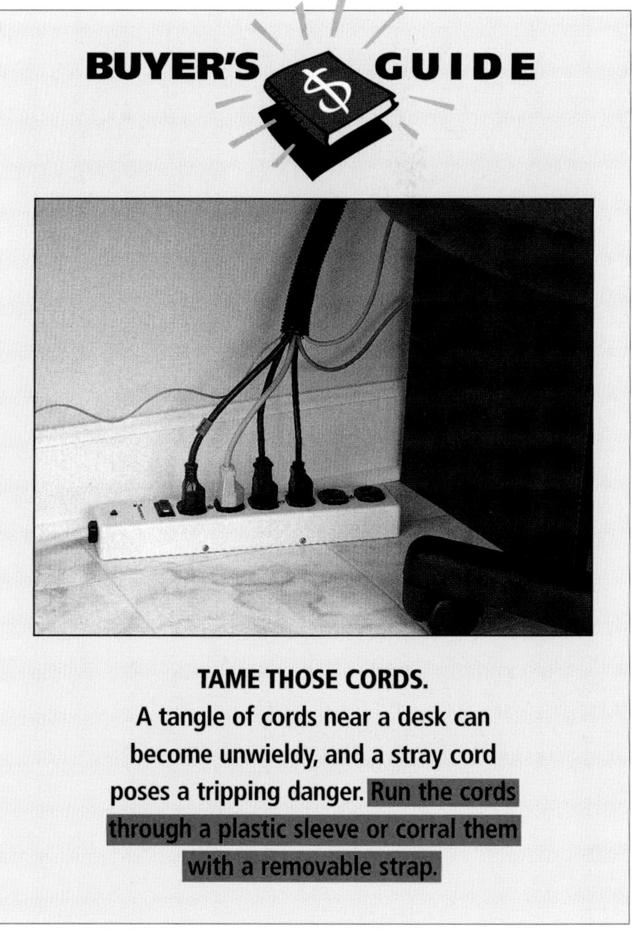

TAME THOSE CORDS.
A tangle of cords near a desk can become unwieldy, and a stray cord poses a tripping danger. Run the cords through a plastic sleeve or corral them with a removable strap.

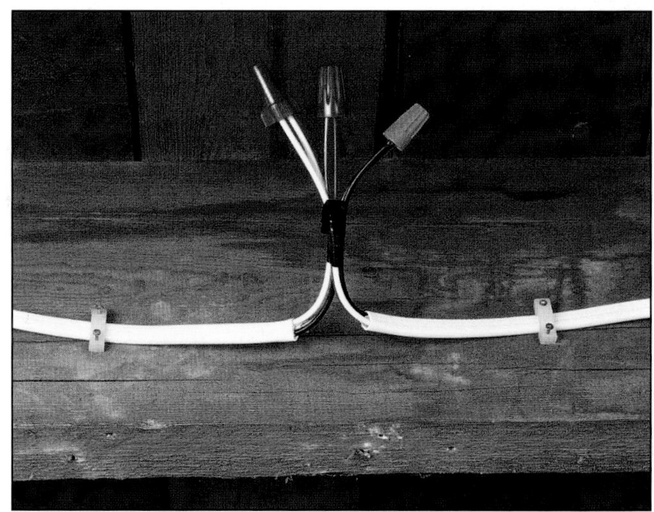

4 CHECK CABLE ENTERING A BOX WITHOUT A CLAMP. Cable and wire must be firmly held, because vibration can cause rubbing—which can harm insulation. Metal boxes in particular have sharp edges that can nick insulation. (Plastic boxes do not usually require clamps. Staple the cable to a stud or joist within 12 inches of the box.) Shut off power to the box, unhook the wires, and attach the cable with a cable clamp (pages 123 and 125).

5 FIX EXPOSED SPLICES. Exposed connections can easily be bumped and loosened, running the risk of a short or fire. That's one of the reasons all wire and cable splices must be within an approved electrical box—either a junction box, a switch or receptacle box, or a fixture that is designed to be used as an electrical box. (To add a box, see pages 118–119 and 137.)

6 SECURE LOOSE CABLE. NEVER USE CABLE AS A HANGING ROD. Codes in some areas permit exposed NM (nonmetallic) cable in basements and garages, while other areas require armored cable or metal conduit. Whatever type of cable you have, it should be tightly stapled to a surface so it cannot accidentally be pulled out.

7 CHECK KNOB-AND-TUBE WIRING. This old style of wiring is still in use in many homes. As long as the wires are completely undisturbed and the wire insulation is in good shape, it can be used. But the insulation can get brittle and easily damaged. Have a pro evaluate it for safety. If you ever replace or extend this type of wiring, do not use more knob-and-tube hardware. Instead, use standard cable clamped to electrical boxes (pages 122–127).

INSPECTING INSIDE BOXES

SKILLS: Shutting off power.

HOW LONG WILL IT TAKE?

PROJECT: Inspecting one box.

EXPERIENCED ...... 5 MIN.
HANDY .... 10 MIN.
NOVICE .... 15 MIN.

TOOLS: Voltage tester or multitester, screwdriver, flashlight
MATERIALS: None required

Be cautious and careful when opening and inspecting a box. Kill power to a box by shutting off power at the service panel. However, there is always the potential that more than one circuit goes to a box. Work carefully. Use rubber-gripped tools, wear rubber-soled shoes, and do not touch bare wires. See pages 22 and 26 for instructions on opening a switch box and a receptacle box.

1 LOOK FOR OVERCROWDING. Using a rubber-handled screwdriver, back out the screws holding the box cover plate until the cover is loose enough to remove. Too many wires crammed into too small a box can lead to shorts. See pages 118–119 to select the right size box.

2 CHECK FOR OLD, CRACKED INSULATION. If wire insulation is hard and brittle, shut off the circuit and wrap the damaged insulation with a hot-shrink sleeve (page 82). If all the wiring in your house has brittle insulation, you may need to hire an electrician to rewire your house.

WORK SMARTER

OPENING A JUNCTION BOX.
Junction boxes have flat metal cover plates and are usually found in basements, garages, or utility rooms. They generally hold six or more wires spliced with wire nuts. If possible, trace the cables from the junction box back to the service panel. Follow the hot wires in the service panel to figure out which circuit or circuits need to be shut off.

It may not be possible for you to shut off the power before opening a junction box, if, for example, you can't follow the cable. Also, wires from two or more circuits may run through a single junction box. So, even if you've shut off power, act as if power is still on. Loosen the two screws holding the cover plate, and ease off the plate. If you need to test for power, gently pull out wires so that no two splices are closer together than 1 inch. Unscrew the wire nuts and touch the probes of a multitester or voltage tester to both neutral (white) and hot (black or colored) wires (pages 44–45).

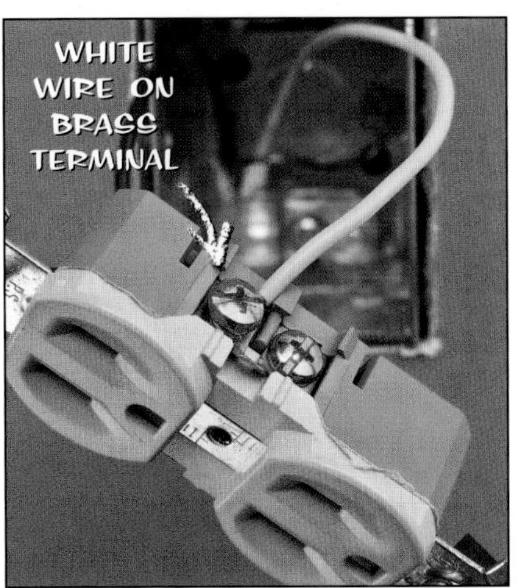

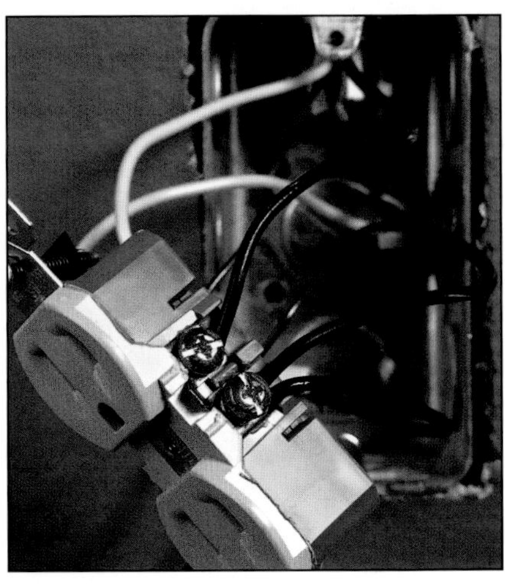

3 LOOK FOR EXPOSED WALL MATERIAL AROUND BOXES. An electrical box should be flush with the finished wall; if not, it poses a fire hazard. To solve this problem, replace the box or install a box extender (page 82).

4 CONFIRM POLARIZATION. If the white wire is connected to a brass terminal and the black one is connected to a silver terminal, the receptacle isn't polarized. An appliance or light plugged into it may be energized even when switched off. Reverse the wires so white goes to silver and black goes to brass. (See page 11 to learn how polarization works.)

5 ENSURE SAFETY WITH A PIGTAIL CONNECTION. Two wires should not be attached to the same terminal: Not only do they make a poor connection, they can pop off and short. Remove the two wires and make a pigtail connection (page 49).

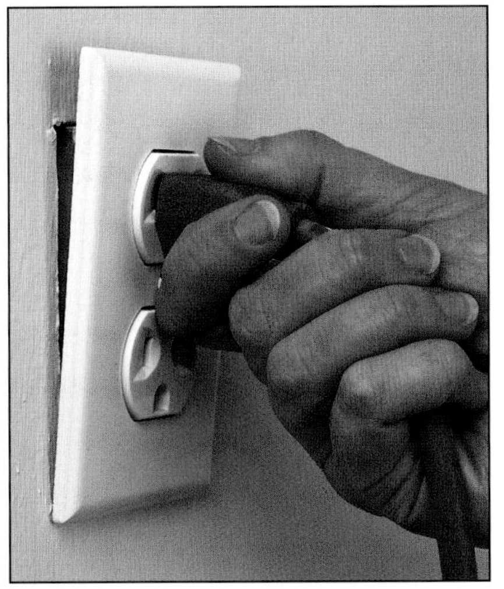

6 CHECK ARMORED CABLE CONNECTORS. The cut ends of armored cable are sharp and can slice through wire insulation. Even if no damage has been done, install a plastic bushing (page 125) wherever one is missing. If a wire has been nicked, cover it with a hot-shrink sleeve (page 82).

7 ENSURE THAT BOXES ARE SECURE. When electrical boxes are not securely anchored, wiring or connections can be damaged. If a loose switch or receptacle box is next to a stud, pull out the device, drill a hole through the side of the box, and drive a screw through the box and into the stud. If it is not near a stud, replace the box with an "old-work" box that clamps to the drywall or plaster (pages 133–134).

8 CHECK THAT GFCI RECEPTACLES ARE CORRECTLY WIRED. The wires coming from the power source should connect to the LINE terminals, and the wires leading out to other receptacles or fixtures should connect to the LOAD terminals (page 27).

INSPECTING A SERVICE PANEL

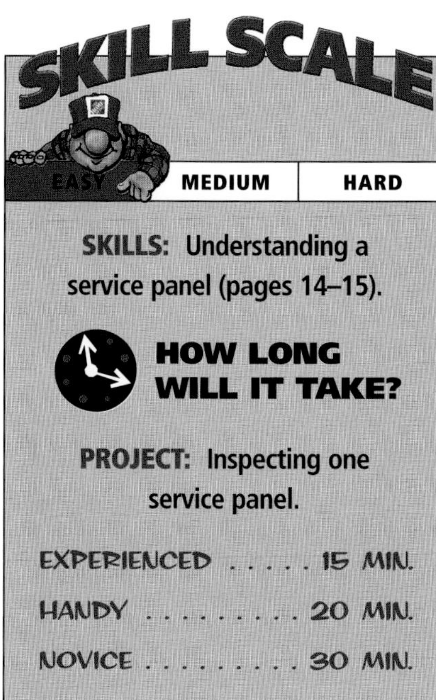

SKILLS: Understanding a service panel (pages 14–15).

HOW LONG WILL IT TAKE?

PROJECT: Inspecting one service panel.

EXPERIENCED . . . . . 15 MIN.
HANDY . . . . 20 MIN.
NOVICE . . . . 30 MIN.

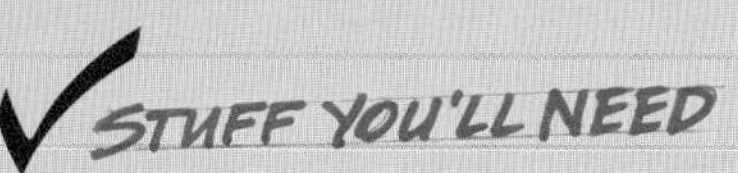

TOOLS: Screwdriver, flashlight, voltage detector
MATERIALS: None required

Even if your service panel was installed correctly, substandard wiring may have been added later. Inspect the entire panel, but pay special attention to new additions. Look for a melted breaker, burned wires, or a burned bus bar. Call an electrician if you see any sign of scorching or overheating. If you can't read the size of an old wire, carefully compare the thickness of its copper with newer wires. If you see three or more wires attached to a breaker, call in an electrician: Codes might allow you to make a pigtail connection (page 49) inside a panel.

CHECK WIRE THICKNESS. A #14 wire connected to a 20-amp breaker poses a very dangerous situation. A 20-amp breaker is designed for a #12 wire or larger. A #14 wire can overheat and even melt insulation or start a fire before the 20-amp breaker trips. Replace the breaker with one that is 15 amps. Consult a professional electrician if this causes the breaker to trip often.

OPENING A PANEL.
Study the safety precautions on page 15 before opening a panel. Switch off the main power in the box before attempting any work. The outer cover includes the door. Loosen or remove screws at the bottom, sides, and top. Lift out the cover.
You'll probably see the wires and their connections to the breakers and the neutral bar. Remove the second cover if you need to remove a breaker. Don't touch any wires.

TROUBLESHOOTING YOUR FUSE BOX

Check your service panel for these signs of trouble:

- **Rust** in the fuse or breaker box may indicate that the box is getting wet. This can be very dangerous. Make sure the box is dry at all times.
- A **30-amp fuse** may indicate that a higher-than-recommended fuse was installed because that circuit kept blowing fuses. Also, check 20-amp fuses to make sure they shouldn't be 15-amps. If the wire leading to the fuse is not #10 or thicker, the fuse should be lower in amperage—15 amps for #14 wire and 20 amps for #12 wire.
- Constantly **blown fuses** are an annoyance—and they indicate that a circuit is overstressed. See pages 62–63 for tips on balancing circuit loads.
- Without an **index**, or circuit map, it can be challenging to figure out which circuit to shut off or turn back on. See opposite page for how to map circuits.
- In some areas, a panel attached to a **flammable surface** is considered a fire hazard; nonflammable material is required between the panel and wood.
- **Open knockouts** also present a fire danger. Buy push-in "goof plugs" designed to fill open knockouts.

MAPPING CIRCUITS

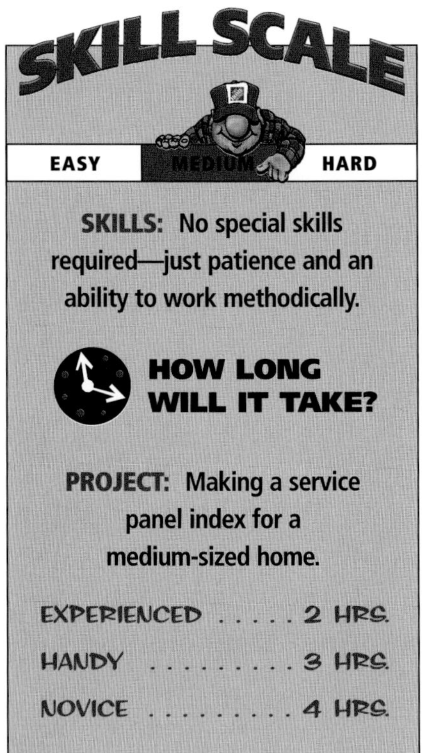

SKILL SCALE
EASY
MEDIUM
HARD
SKILLS: No special skills required—just patience and an ability to work methodically.
HOW LONG WILL IT TAKE?
PROJECT: Making a service panel index for a medium-sized home.
EXPERIENCED . . . . . 2 HRS.
HANDY . . . . 3 HRS.
NOVICE . . . . 4 HRS.

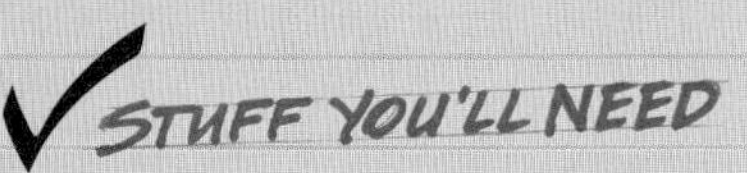

TOOLS: 2 cordless phones or walkie-talkies, circuit finder

MATERIALS: Masking tape, marker, pencil, and paper

When making a repair or new installation, knowing which circuit controls which outlet speeds the job and makes working safer. That's why electrical codes require service panels to have an index telling which receptacles, lights, and appliances are on which circuit. If your panel has no index, creating one will take some time. Prepare by turning on all the lights in the house. Plug a light, fan, or radio into as many receptacles as possible, and switch them on. Turn on the dishwasher and open the door of the microwave oven. With the whole house switched on, you are ready to map.

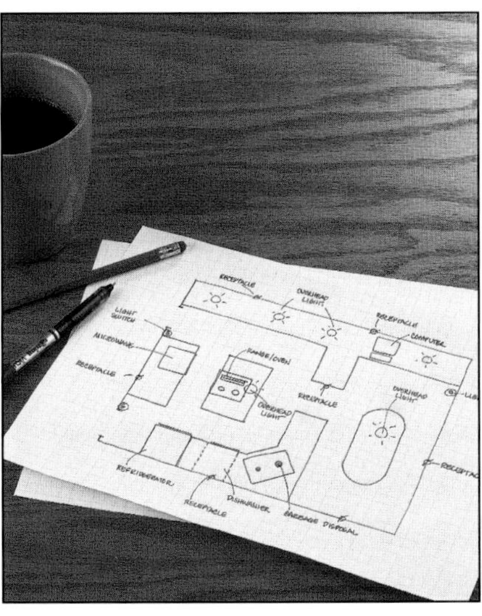

1 MAP THE LOCATIONS OF ALL OUTLETS. Draw a rough sketch of each floor in your house, noting the location of every receptacle, switch, light, and appliance. (You may want to use the symbols shown on page 114.) On the service panel, place a numbered piece of tape next to each breaker or switch.

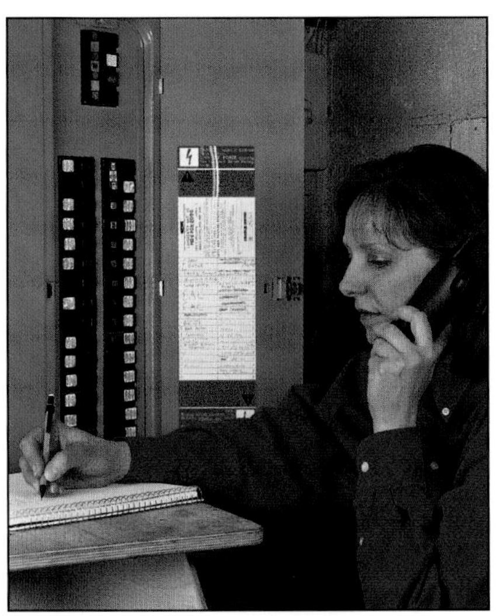

2 IDENTIFY CIRCUITS. To communicate with your helper, use a pair of walkie-talkies or two cellular phones. Start at the top of the panel. Switch off the circuit and have your helper identify the room without power. On the map, jot down the number of the circuit next to each outlet that is turned off. Repeat these steps for each circuit.

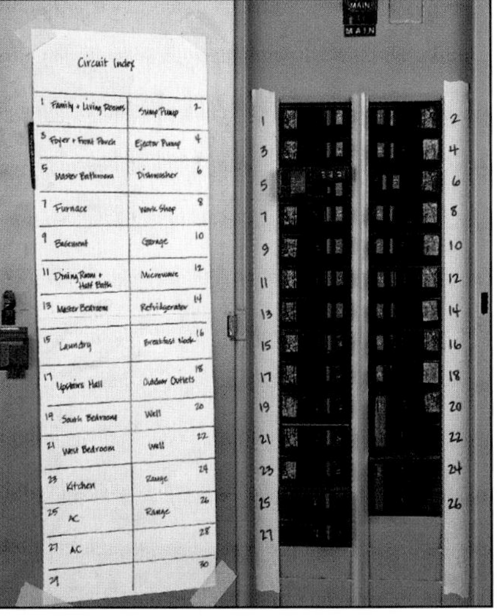

3 DRAW UP THE INDEX. Write an index that accounts for all the fixtures, receptacles, and hardwired appliances in your home. Attach the index to the inside door panel. You may be surprised to find that some circuits wander through several rooms. This can be confusing, but it is not dangerous.

AVOIDING CIRCUIT OVERLOADS

The total power used by all of a home's light fixtures, lamps, appliances, and tools is called "demand." When demand exceeds the safe capacity of a circuit, the circuit is overloaded.

BREAKERS AND FUSES

It's usually easy to tell if a circuit is overloaded: The breaker trips frequently or the fuse keeps blowing. This probably means that wires are overheating, posing a threat to your home.

Sometimes the solution is simple: Move one high-amperage appliance (such as a microwave oven or toaster) to a receptacle on another circuit. If the overloads stop, then the problem is solved. If not, you may need to install a new circuit (pages 168–169).

Overloading problems often occur on 120-volt circuits, which serve multiple receptacles and lights. Most 240-volt circuits serve only one receptacle or appliance. If a 240-volt circuit regularly overloads, change the wiring.

To better understand troublesome circuits and to prepare for adding new electrical lines, the chart below shows how close the circuits are to being overloaded.

CHECKING WATTS AND AMPS

If the service panel does not have an accurate index, map the house and add an index (page 61). Find a circuit's amperage rating by looking at the circuit breaker or fuse. Add up the wattage of every light bulb on the circuit. Note the amperage or watt rating for every appliance and tool plugged into receptacles as well. This information should be printed somewhere on the appliance. Examples are illustrated opposite. Some appliances vary widely in ratings, so check appliances individually. Older appliances usually have a higher rating.

SAFE CAPACITY

Codes require that appliances and fixtures on a circuit do not exceed "safe capacity," usually defined as the total capacity minus 20 percent. (See the chart, below left.) If the total demand exceeds a circuit's safe capacity and you can't solve the problem by plugging an appliance into a receptacle on another circuit, install a new circuit (pages 168–169). If a circuit suddenly becomes touchy—tripping the breaker at the slightest provocation—check to see if the breaker is functioning correctly (page 81).

CALCULATING CIRCUIT CAPACITY

Here are two ways to calculate circuit capacity. First, if you know the amperage and voltage of the circuit, you can determine the total capacity by doing this calculation:

Amps × Volts = Watts

For example, if you have a 15-amp, 120-volt circuit, total capacity in watts is 15 × 120, or 1800 watts (15 × 120 = 1800). With a 20-amp, 120-volt circuit, total capacity is 2400 watts (20 × 120).

Or work the other way around:

Watts ÷ Volts = Amps

If all the bulbs in a pendant light fixture add up to 600 watts, the light is using 5 amps (600 ÷ 120 = 5). If such a fixture hangs in your kitchen, don't run a toaster (at 6–13 amps) on the same 15-amp circuit or you might overload the circuit.

Some electricians use this general rule: Allow 100 watts for each amp. That means allowing no more than 1500 watts on a 15-amp circuit and no more than 2000 watts on a 20-amp circuit.

A+ WORK SMARTER

SAFE CAPACITY FOR 120-VOLT CIRCUITS. To be sure your circuit won't overload, check individual appliances to determine the watts required by each appliance and fixture on a circuit. Total the usage to make sure it is within the safe capacity shown here.

AMPS	TOTAL CAPACITY	SAFE CAPACITY
15A	1800 watts	1440 watts/12 amps
20A	2400 watts	1920 watts/16 amps
25A	3000 watts	2400 watts/20 amps
30A	3600 watts	2880 watts/24 amps

WATTAGE AND AMPERAGE RATINGS

These ratings are examples only. Check appliances individually.

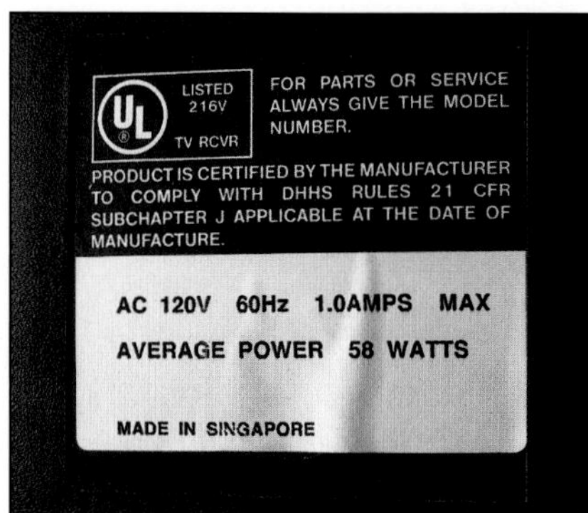

TELEVISION
50–300 watts/ 0.4–2.5 amps

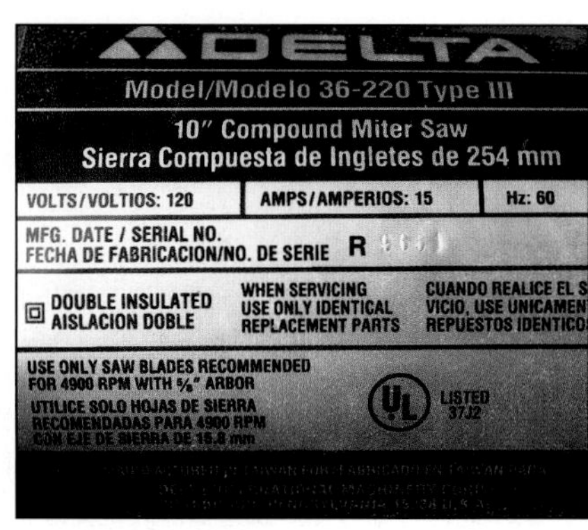

CIRCULAR SAW
1200 watts/ 10 amps

REFRIGERATOR
700–1200 watts/ 5.8–10 amps

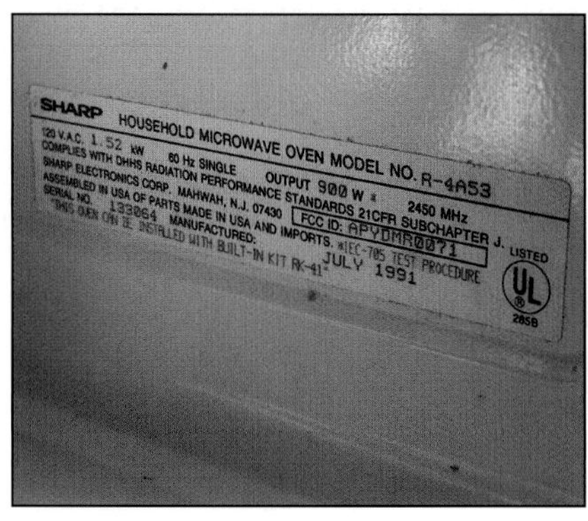

MICROWAVE OVEN
900–1500 watts/ 7.5–12.5 amps

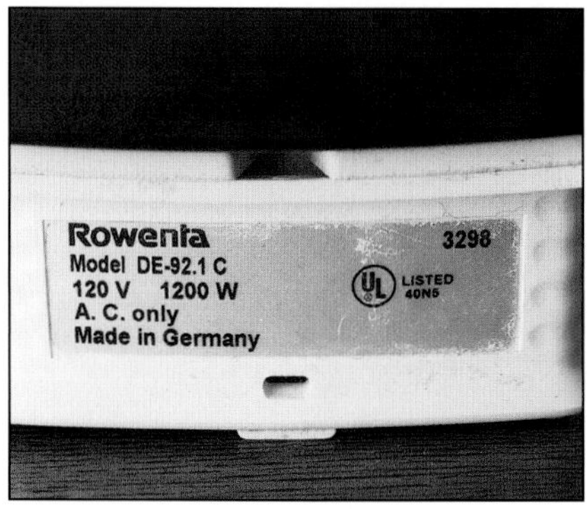

IRON
1000–1200 watts/ 8.3–10 amps

TOASTER
800–1600 watts/ 6.6–13.3 amps

ALLOW FOR MOTOR SURGE.
During the first few seconds a motor is started, it uses significantly more power than during normal operation. A circuit supplying appliances with motors—a refrigerator, freezer, air-conditioner, or fan, for instance—needs extra capacity to handle occasional power surges. Window air-conditioners and refrigerators should probably be plugged into receptacles that have their own circuits.

WATT CHEER!
I covered the house with Christmas lights last year, and without realizing it, really created an overload. I plugged in the extension cord for the lights and the whole circuit blew. I added up the demand and found that my 10 strings of lights pulled 1800 watts. And I was about to hook them to a 600-watt timer! I switched to another circuit. This summer, I'm installing an outdoor circuit just for decorative lights.

ALUMINUM WIRING

When copper prices increased in the early 1970s, builders in many areas switched to aluminum wire. Homeowners soon discovered, however, that aluminum posed a fire hazard, especially when connected to brass or copper terminals or wires. By the time aluminum wire was banned, thousands of homes had been wired. Because aluminum expands and contracts over time, it can loosen from terminals, causing faults. Also, where aluminum is attached to brass or copper, it oxidizes, degrading the connection.

Consider replacing aluminum wires with copper if the wires run through conduit or Greenfield. You (or an electrician) can install new wires by attaching them to the old wires and pulling them through the conduit (page 127). However, if the aluminum is encased in NM or armored cable, replacing it will be difficult and costly.

CHECK WIRING: Aluminum wire is marked "AL." The stripped wire is a dull silver color. Aluminum is a soft metal and strains easily. Look for cracks in the bare wire.

PREVENTIVE MAINTENANCE FOR ALUMINUM WIRING

To check the condition of your aluminum wiring, you'll need to systematically open every switch box, receptacle box, fixture, hardwired appliance, and junction box in your home.

Shut off power to a circuit and open its boxes. If a switch or receptacle has CO/ALR written on it (center right), it is safe to connect aluminum wires to it. If the device is a standard receptacle, replace it with a CO/ALR device. (Buy them at electrical supply stores if your home centers do not carry them.) How to replace devices is described on pages 22–23 and 26.

Or, use a more time-consuming but less costly method (bottom right): Disconnect an aluminum wire from its terminal, and connect it to a short pigtail made of copper. Squirt antioxidant from its tubular container (below right) onto the wire ends. Then, twist the wires together and attach an Al/Cu wire nut, which is made for this purpose. Connect the copper pigtail to the standard switch or receptacle.

Make sure that throughout the house all aluminum-to-copper or aluminum-to-brass connections are brushed clean of corrosion (look for a powdery white coating, especially on devices near damp areas); coat the connections with antioxidant. Check each device, backing off the terminal screws, adding the antioxidant, and firmly retightening the screws. Aluminum breaks easily. If a wire end is cracked, snip it off and restrip.

Check all connections to terminals annually, and tighten them as needed.

CHECK DEVICES. All switches and receptacles should have CO/ALR stamped on them. If not, replace them with a CO/ALR device. Check every switch and receptacle.

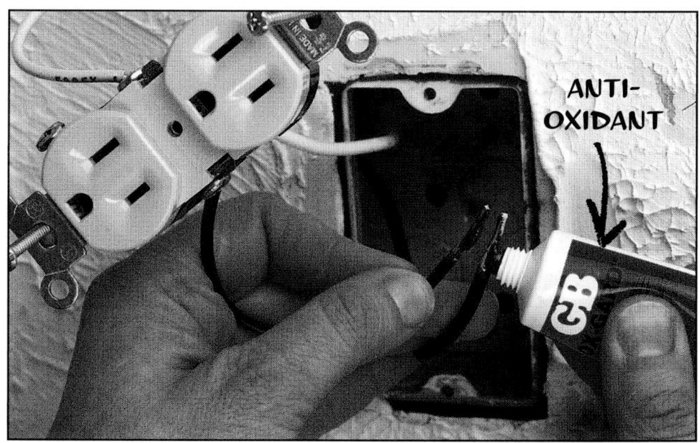

APPLY ANTIOXIDANT. To keep the aluminum from developing a nonconductive layer of oxidant, especially where aluminum is joined to copper, snip off bare wire ends, restrip, and coat the wires with antioxidant. Use Al/Cu wire nuts, and attach to copper pigtails.

INSPECTING YOUR HOME

5 ELECTRICAL REPAIRS

When electrical devices and fixtures no longer work, often the logical solution is to replace rather than repair them. Switches, receptacles, lamps, and overhead lights may not cost enough to warrant the time it takes to diagnose and repair them.

Some repairs, however, are quick and easy. You may be able to get your lamp to work again by simply pulling up the tab on the light socket (see page 66). If you have a valuable antique lamp or overhead light—a treasured part of your home—you certainly have a vested interest in getting it back into working order.

CHAPTER FIVE TOPICS

FIXING LAMP SOCKETS

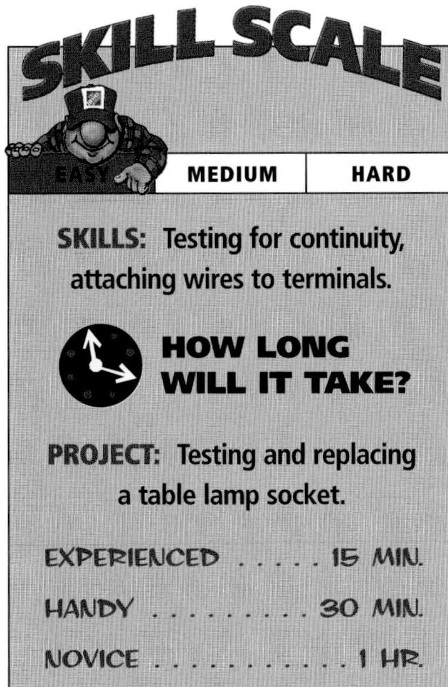

SKILL SCALE
EASY
MEDIUM
HARD
SKILLS: Testing for continuity, attaching wires to terminals.
HOW LONG WILL IT TAKE?
PROJECT: Testing and replacing a table lamp socket.
EXPERIENCED . . . . . 15 MIN.
HANDY . . . . 30 MIN.
NOVICE . . . . 1 HR.

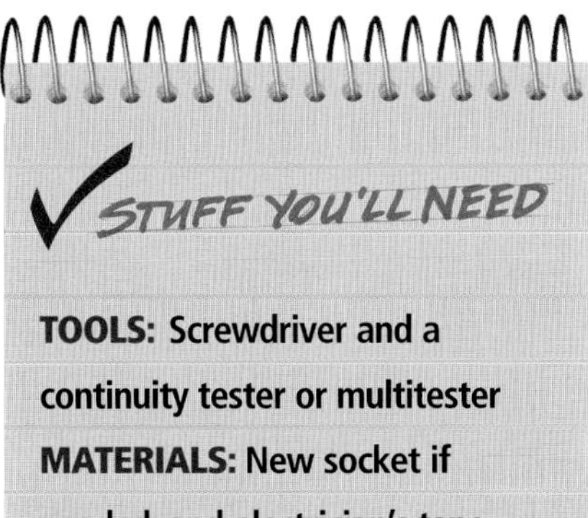

STUFF YOU'LL NEED
TOOLS: Screwdriver and a continuity tester or multitester
MATERIALS: New socket if needed, and electrician's tape

If a lamp doesn't work, eliminate the obvious causes first. Make sure the lamp is plugged in. Make sure the bulb is OK. A burned-out bulb usually makes a tinkling sound when you shake it. Screw in a fresh bulb if necessary.

Check that the receptacle's circuit hasn't blown a fuse or popped a breaker. If the lamp still doesn't work, test by plugging in a lamp that you know is in working order. If it lights up, you've isolated the problem to the lamp itself. Before replacing the cord or switch, take a look at the socket.

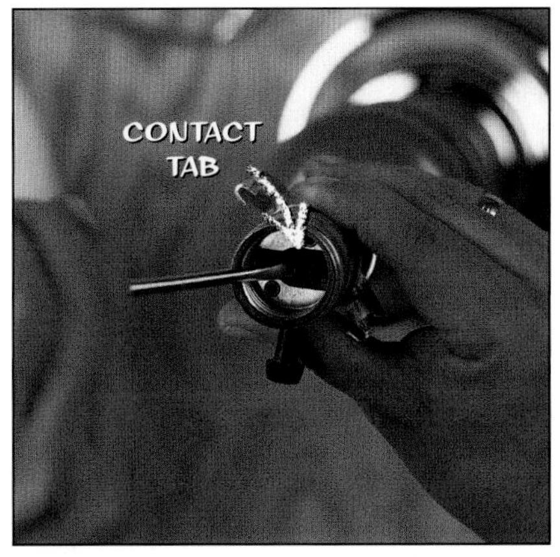

1 PRY UP THE CONTACT TAB. Unplug the lamp and remove the bulb. If the contact tab is corroded or rusty, scrape it with a screwdriver. If the tab lays flat, it may not be making solid contact with the base of the bulb. Gently pry up the tab about ⅛ inch and retest. If the lamp still doesn't work, go to the next step.

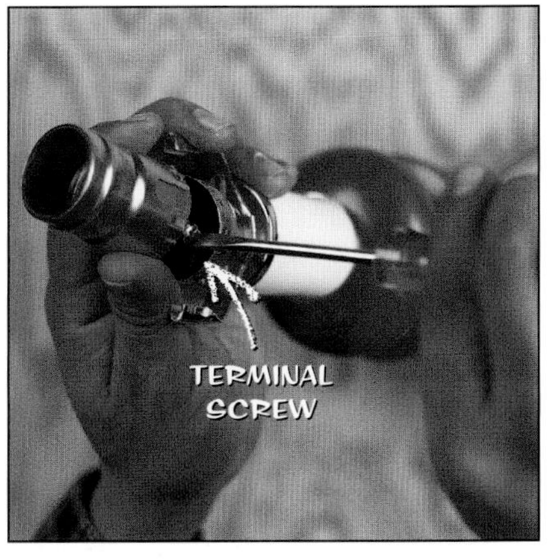

2 REMOVE THE SOCKET. Look for the word PRESS on the socket shell. Push there with your thumb as you squeeze the shell and wiggle it up and out. If there is a cardboard sleeve, remove it, too. Loosen the two terminal screws and pull out the socket.

Connect the ridged (neutral) wire to the silver terminal and the smooth (hot) wire to the brass terminal.

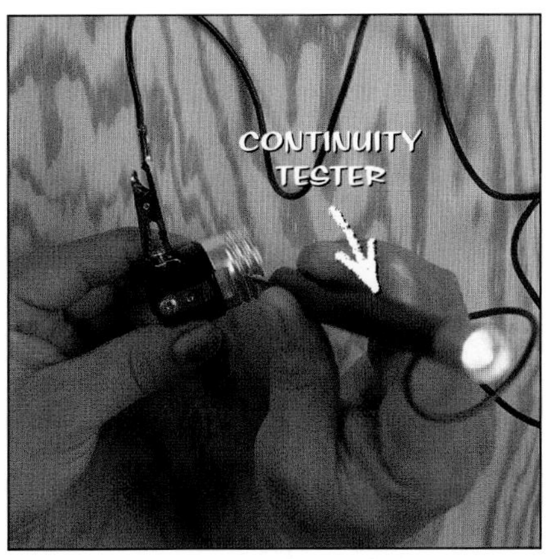

3 TEST THE SOCKET AND SWITCH. Test the socket with a continuity tester (shown) or a multitester (pages 44–45). Touch one probe to the neutral (silver) screw and the other to the threaded metal of the socket. If the tester bulb doesn't light, replace the socket. If the socket has a switch, touch the clips to the brass terminal and to the contact tab. If the switch is defective, replace it. If it is not, test the cord and plug (page 68).

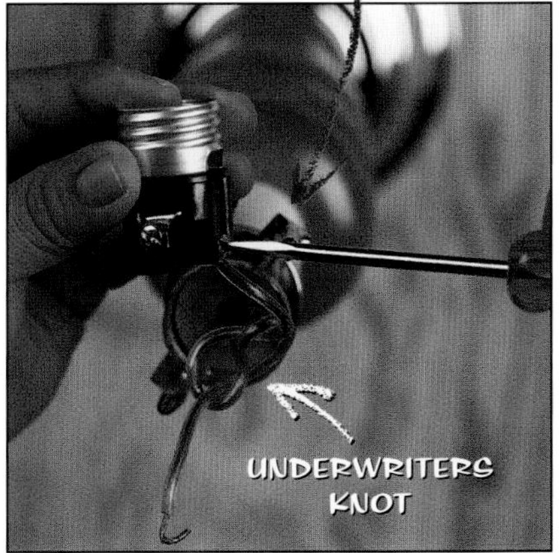

4 REPLACE THE SOCKET. You may need to loosen a small setscrew in order to unscrew the old socket base. Install the new base, threading the cord carefully so you don't nick the insulation. Tie the wires with an Underwriters knot as shown. Twist the strands together with your fingers, and form a partial loop. Wrap each wire clockwise around a terminal, and tighten its terminal screw. Slip on the cardboard sleeve, and snap down the socket shell into position.

REPLACING LAMP SWITCHES

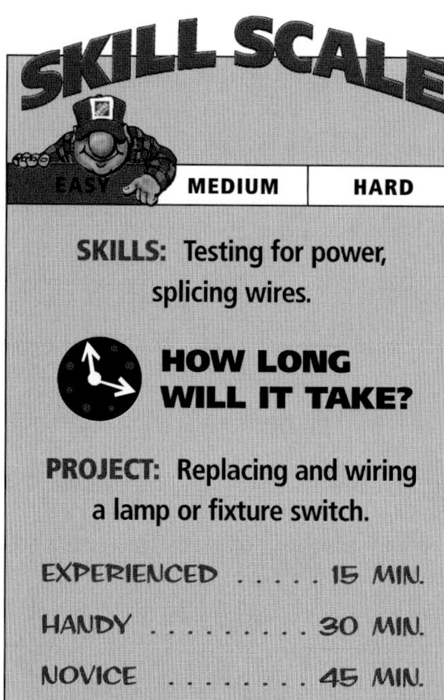

SKILLS: Testing for power, splicing wires.

HOW LONG WILL IT TAKE?

PROJECT: Replacing and wiring a lamp or fixture switch.

EXPERIENCED ..... 15 MIN.
HANDY .... 30 MIN.
NOVICE .... 45 MIN.

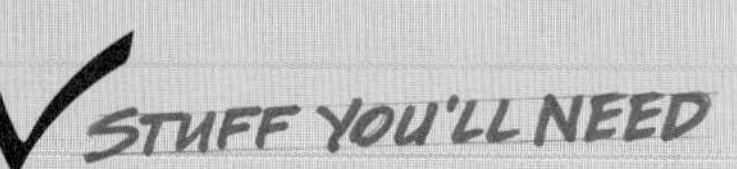

TOOLS: Voltage tester, combination strippers, pliers
MATERIALS: New switch, electrician's tape, wire nuts

A toggle, pull-chain, or twist switch is not an integral part of the lamp or the fixture on which it's mounted. It's an inexpensive switch that can be easily replaced—and may need to be replaced yearly, if heavily used.

There's one universal hole size, so you can interchange twist switches with toggles or pull-chains.

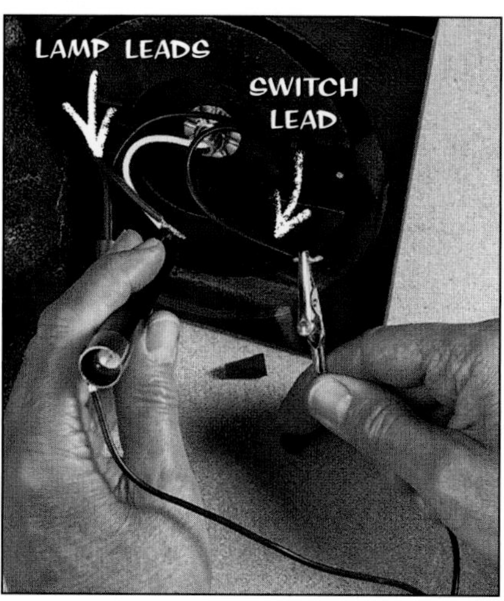

1 TEST THE SWITCH. Unplug the lamp. Remove the bottom of the lamp to access the wiring. Remove one of the wire nuts that connects a lead from the switch to the lamp wires. Clip one probe of a continuity tester to the switch lead and the other to the lamp wires. Try the switch several times. If the continuity detector doesn't light, the switch is defective.

2 REPLACE THE SWITCH. Unplug the lamp. Unscrew the switch retaining nut—you may need to use pliers. Unravel the wires, then pull out the switch. If the wires on the lamp are damaged, snip off the stripped portion and restrip the insulation. Insert the switch into the hole, and tightly screw in the retaining nut. Splice the switch leads to the lamp, and twist on the wire nuts.

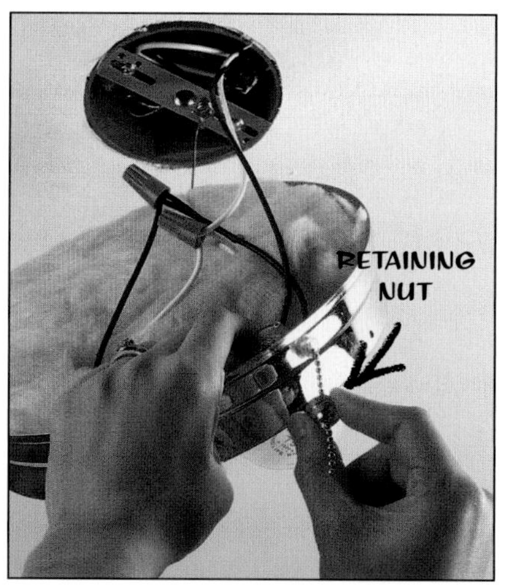

REPLACING A PULL-CHAIN SWITCH. Test a switch like this (common on ceiling lights and fans) in the same way as a toggle or twist switch. It mounts with a retaining nut. Some porcelain ceiling fixtures have built-in switches; these can't be repaired.

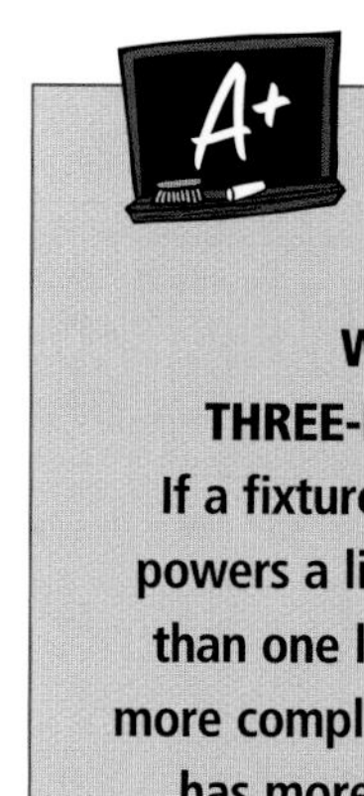

WORK SMARTER

WIRING A THREE-LEVEL SWITCH. If a fixture-mounted switch powers a light or fan at more than one level, the wiring is more complicated. If the switch has more than two leads, carefully tag the lamp or fixture wires with pieces of marked tape so you know which wire goes where when you install the replacement. Take the old switch with you to the hardware store or home center to buy an exact replacement.

REWIRING LAMPS

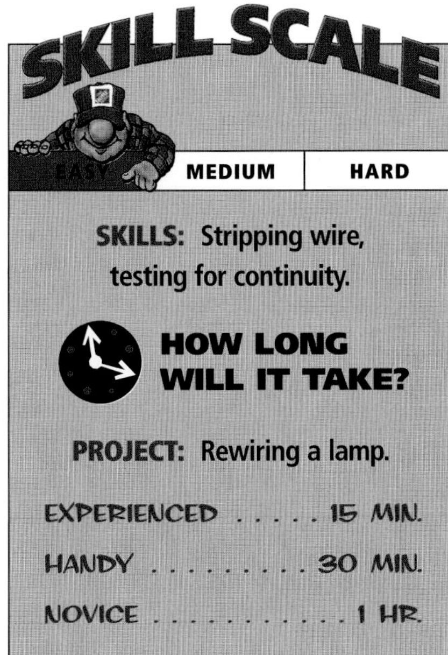

SKILL SCALE
EASY
MEDIUM
HARD
SKILLS: Stripping wire, testing for continuity.
HOW LONG WILL IT TAKE?
PROJECT: Rewiring a lamp.
EXPERIENCED . . . . . 15 MIN.
HANDY . . . . 30 MIN.
NOVICE . . . . 1 HR.

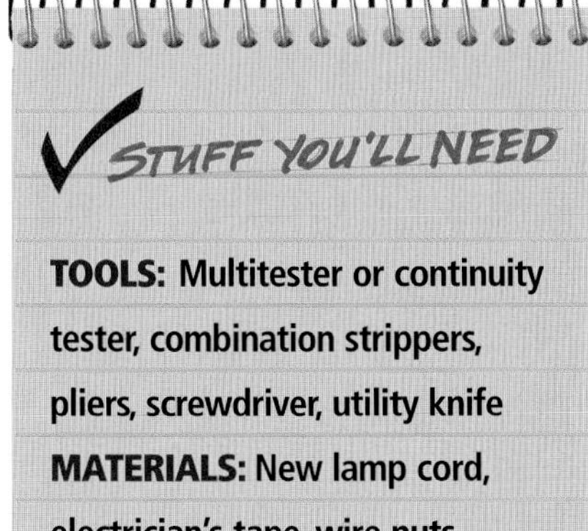

STUFF YOU'LL NEED
TOOLS: Multitester or continuity tester, combination strippers, pliers, screwdriver, utility knife
MATERIALS: New lamp cord, electrician's tape, wire nuts

Wiring lamps is simple work. Electricity travels up through the lamp body through a cord until it reaches the socket. If the tests show that the socket works okay (page 66), the problem is probably with the cord. Don't repair a section of a cord: Cord splices never look good and they unravel easily. Install a new replacement lamp cord, which has a molded plug.

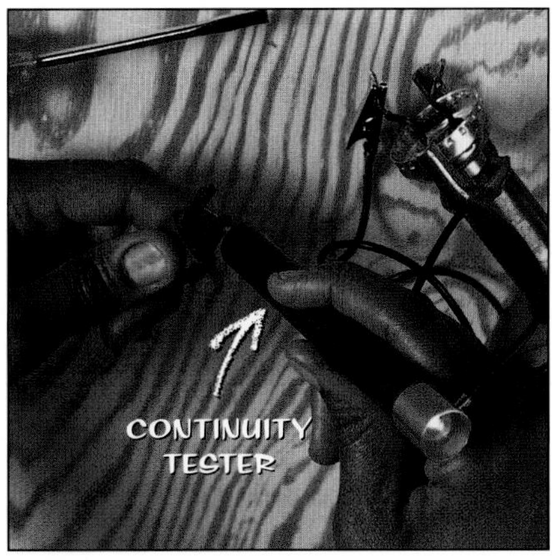

1 TEST WIRES FOR CONTINUITY. With the socket removed (page 66), touch the probes of a continuity tester or multitester (pages 44–45) to the end of the ridged (neutral) wire and the wide prong of the plug. Then touch the probes to the smooth (hot) wire and the narrow prong. If either test fails to show continuity, replace the cord and plug. If the prongs are the same size, test each wire with both prongs. The meter should show continuity on one prong only.

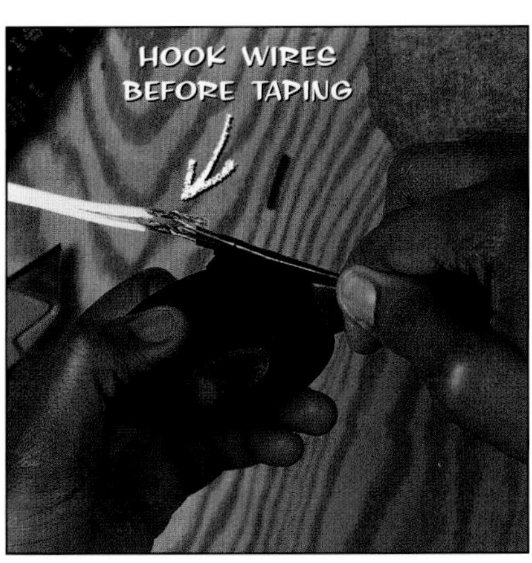

2 TO PULL THE NEW CORD THROUGH THE LAMP, HOOK THE NEW CORD TO THE OLD. Cut the old cord about 8 inches past the lamp base. Strip the ends of the old and new cords. Twist all the strands clockwise with your fingers so that no strands are loose. Bend the old wires and the new wires. Hook them together as shown. Wrap the joint tightly with electrician's tape.

3 PULL THE NEW CORD THROUGH. This step is easier with a helper. While pulling up on the old cord at the top of the lamp, feed the new cord into the hole at the base. If the tape gets stuck, pull the cord out and wrap the tape more tightly. Keep pulling until the new cord emerges from the top. Unwrap the tape. Tie an Underwriters knot, and connect the new cord to the socket (page 66).

EXTRACTING A BROKEN BULB.

If a bulb is broken and stuck in the socket, don't try to unscrew it by hand. Unplug the lamp. Press a potato onto the broken glass and then twist. Or, insert the end of a wooden broom handle into the middle of the socket and twist.

REPAIRING A TWO-SOCKET LAMP

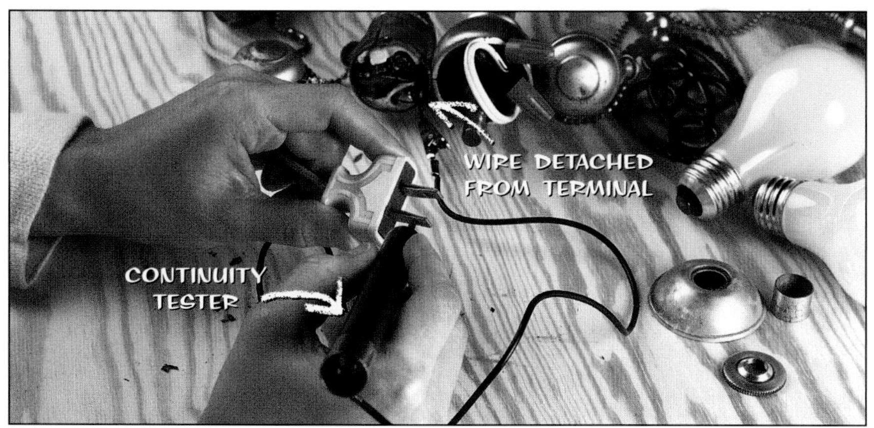

1 REMOVE THE COVER AND TEST THE LAMP. If a lamp has two or more sockets and only one doesn't operate, test and replace the defective one as you would a one-socket lamp (page 66). Remove the cover plate and make sure the wire connections are tight. With the lamp switch on, use a multitester or continuity tester to check for continuity (pages 44–45). If only one socket fails to light, the wire between the splice and the socket is probably the culprit. If all the sockets fail to work, then the cord between the plug and the splice is bad.

2 REWIRE THE LAMP. Replace one cord at a time. For the sockets, cut and strip pieces of cord to the length of the old pieces. Connect the ridged (neutral) wire to the silver socket terminal and the smooth (hot) wire to the brass terminal. When splicing, always connect ridged wire to ridged and smooth to smooth.

DIVIDING AND STRIPPING LAMP CORD

1 DIVIDING THE LAMP CORD. Separate part of a lamp cord into two wires before making connections. Stick the tip of a knife blade into the little valley between the two cords, and push down until it jabs firmly into the work surface below.

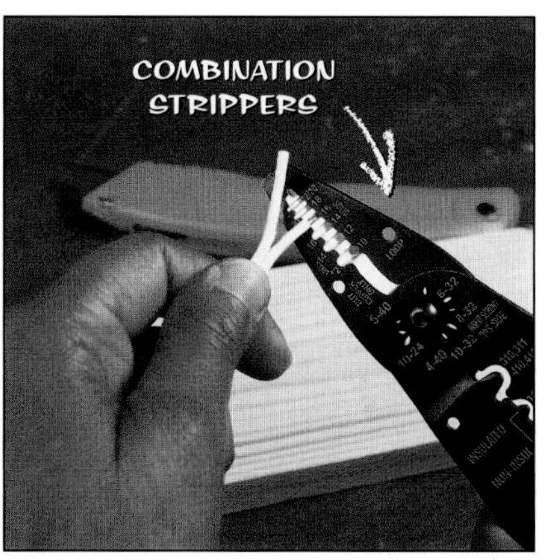

2 STRIPPING THE LAMP CORD. Pull the cord—not the knife—to separate the wires. Once you have made this cut, pull the wires farther apart if needed. Use combination strippers to remove insulation. Work carefully so that you don't pull off more than a couple of wire strands with the insulation.

A LAMP REWIRE KIT.
Some lamps have special components—such as washers or plastic stoppers. Replace them while you are rewiring. A lamp rewire kit contains the cord with plug and the little parts unique to that kind of lamp. The kit shown is for a bottle-type lamp.

REWIRING DESK LAMPS

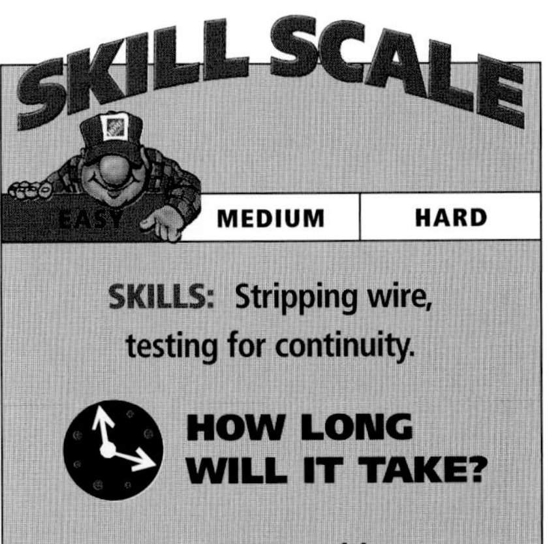

SKILLS: Stripping wire, testing for continuity.

HOW LONG WILL IT TAKE?

PROJECT: Repairing a typical desk lamp.

EXPERIENCED .... 30 MIN.
HANDY .... 1 HR.
NOVICE .... 2 HRS.

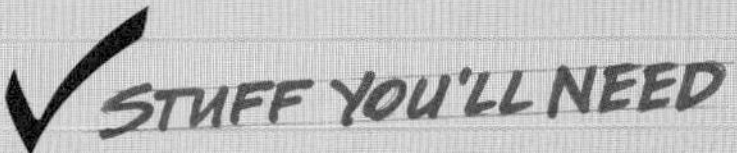

✓ STUFF YOU'LL NEED

TOOLS: Voltage tester, continuity tester, combination strippers, pliers, screwdriver

MATERIALS: Electrician's tape, replacement lamp wire

Repairing incandescent desk lamps is similar to floor and table lamp repair. If a lamp goes out, first check that the bulb is good, that the cord is plugged in, and that the receptacle is getting power. (See page 78 to repair fluorescents.)

If a lamp has a fixture-mounted switch, check that it is working (page 67). Gently pry up the tab inside the socket (page 66) and try the lamp again. Test the cord for continuity (pages 44–45). Replace it if it fails the test or appears damaged. Then test the socket.

If you have an old fluorescent lamp, you probably won't find any replacement parts other than new bulbs. Parts vary according to the brand and model of the lamp. New sockets, starters, and ballasts simply aren't widely available.

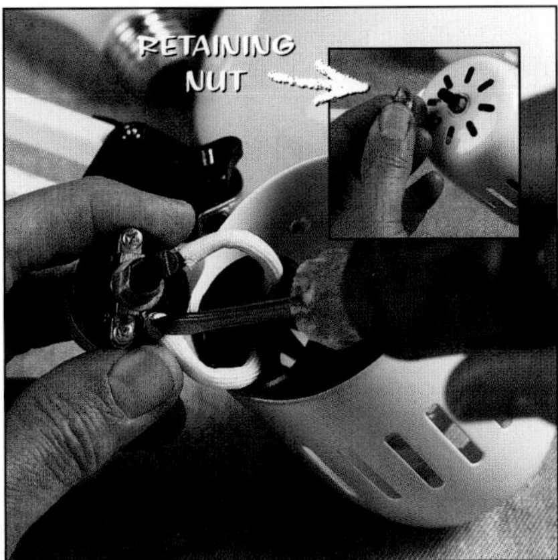

1 DISCONNECT THE SOCKET ON AN INCANDESCENT LAMP. Unplug the lamp. If there is a twist switch at the top of the shade, unscrew its retaining nut (see inset) and gently pull out the socket. If possible, push or pull wire for some slack to make it easier to get at the terminal screws. On some types of lamps, the socket can come out. Test the socket as shown on page 66.

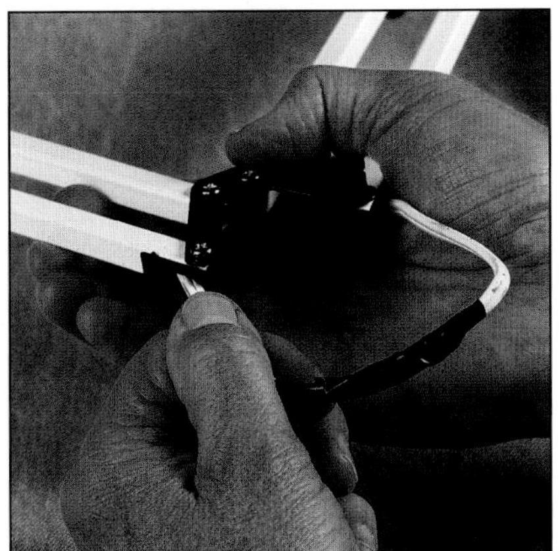

2 REWIRE. See pages 68–69 for general rewiring instructions. In the case of a desk lamp, there may be extra twists and turns. Feed the cord carefully through each one. Some models allow you to temporarily loosen joints to make it easier to pull the wire through. You may want to use a small amount of pulling lubricant (page 127).

CLOSER LOOK

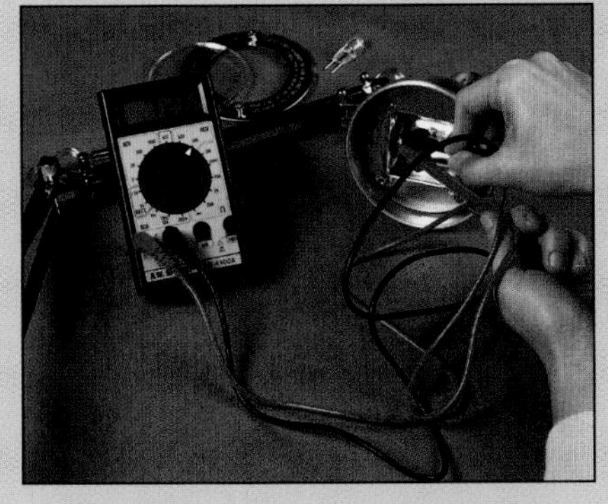

REPAIRING HALOGENS. Halogen bulbs get extremely hot, so allow each to cool before removing it. Use a cloth—oil from your fingers can damage the bulbs. (If you touch the bulb, clean it with alcohol.) With the lamp plugged in and turned on, test the socket. Set a multitester to test low voltage, and test the socket terminals where the bulb prongs connect. If you get the correct voltage, replace the bulb. If the reading is low, see if the lamp fuse is blown. If the these steps don't fix it, the transformer or the wiring is faulty; buy a new lamp.

REPAIRING PENDANT FIXTURES

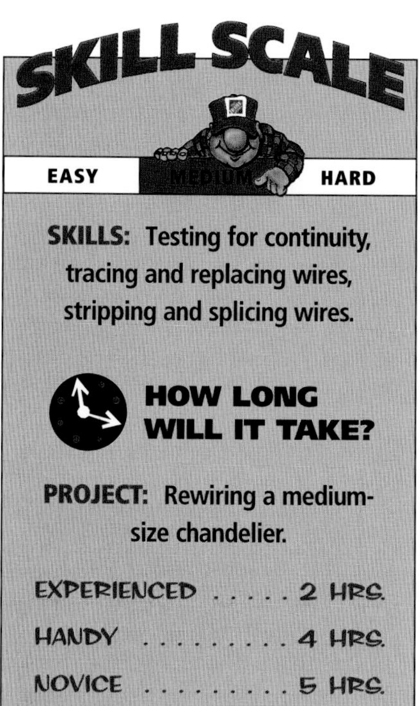

SKILLS: Testing for continuity, tracing and replacing wires, stripping and splicing wires.

HOW LONG WILL IT TAKE?

PROJECT: Rewiring a medium-size chandelier.

EXPERIENCED ..... 2 HRS.
HANDY .... 4 HRS.
NOVICE .... 5 HRS.

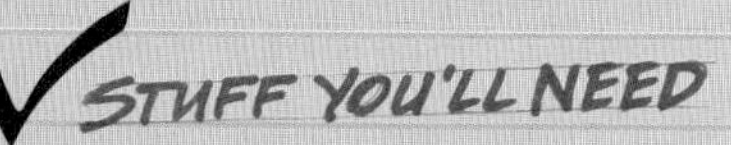

TOOLS: Voltage tester, continuity tester, combination strippers, longnose pliers, side-cutting pliers, screwdriver

MATERIALS: Lamp core, electrician's tape, wire nuts

Regular flush-mounted ceiling fixtures rarely need repair, and when they do, the wiring is straightforward. Pendent fixtures or chandeliers, however, often have a tangle of wires running through narrow tubes. When old insulation cracks, pendent lights start to fail and sparks may fly.

If one wire has brittle insulation, replace all the wires; the others are just as old.

If only one light malfunctions, turn off the switch and test its socket. Replace the socket if it is defective (page 66).

To get ready, shut off power to the circuit at the service panel. Have a helper hold the fixture, or bend the ends of a coat hanger to support it. Loosen the screws holding the canopy in place.

1 OPEN THE FIXTURE. Slide down the canopy. Pull out and separate the wires. Carefully remove the wire nuts. Test for the presence of power in the box (pages 44–45). If any wires are live, shut off the correct circuit. Disconnect the wires and take down the fixture. Remove the cover near the bottom of the fixture to expose the connections.

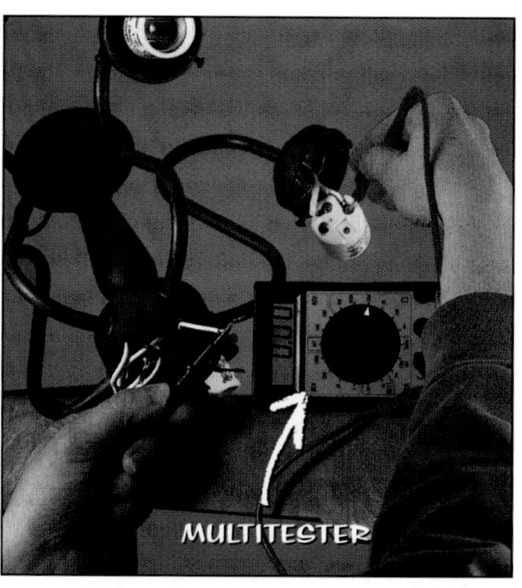

2 TEST THE SOCKET WIRES. If some of the sockets do not light, test each wire for continuity. To find out which cord goes where, tug on the cord at the socket end while holding the wires at the base. Unscrew the wire nuts at the base, and test both the ridged (neutral) wire and the smooth wire for continuity. If you do not get a positive reading for both wires, replace the cord. Test and repair all malfunctioning light sockets.

3 TEST THE STEM WIRES. If all the lights fail to come on, the stem wires probably need replacing. To make sure, twist the stem wires together at the base. Touch tester probes to both wires at the top of the fixture. If no continuity is indicated, replace the stem wires as shown on page 68.

REPLACING PLUGS AND SWITCHES

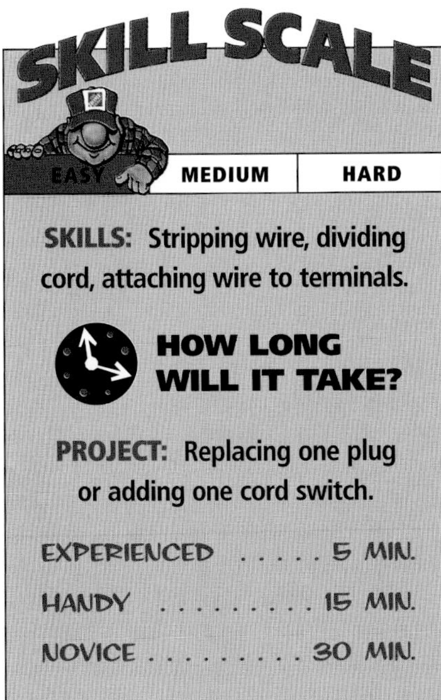

SKILL SCALE
EASY
MEDIUM
HARD
SKILLS: Stripping wire, dividing cord, attaching wire to terminals.
HOW LONG WILL IT TAKE?
PROJECT: Replacing one plug or adding one cord switch.
EXPERIENCED ..... 5 MIN.
HANDY .... 15 MIN.
NOVICE .... 30 MIN.

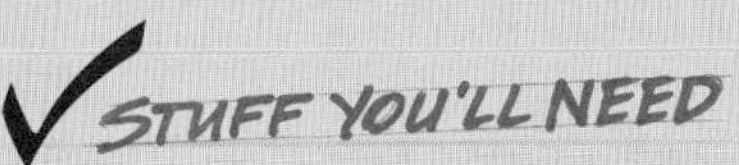

TOOLS: Combination strippers, utility knife, screwdriver

MATERIALS: Replacement plug or cord switch

A plug with loose prongs or a cracked body is dangerous and should be replaced. If the cord and the plug are damaged, rewire the lamp or appliance with a one-piece cord and plug (page 68). If only the plug is damaged, save yourself the chore of rewiring the entire device by using one of the replacement plugs shown here.

A cord switch, which is almost as easy to install, is ideal for lamps that have hard-to-reach switches. You can add a cord switch in minutes.

INSTALLING FLAT REPLACEMENT PLUGS

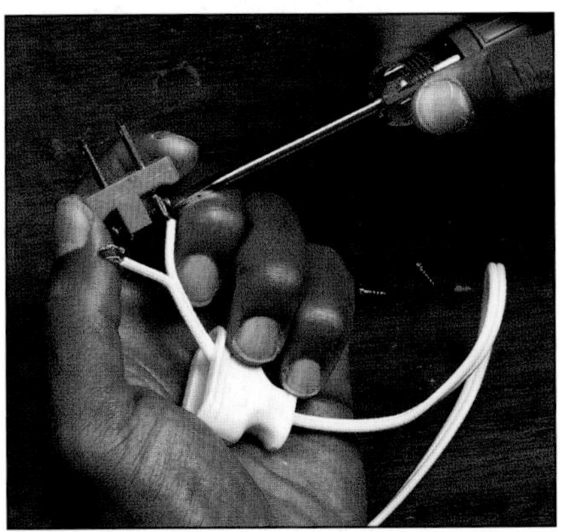

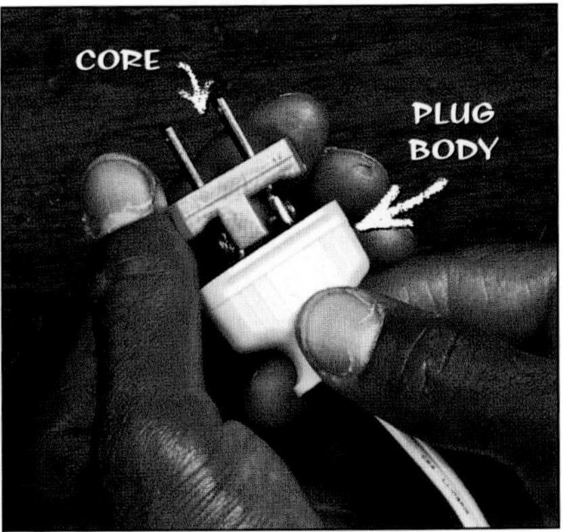

1 **JOIN THE WIRES TO A FLAT REPLACEMENT PLUG.** Cut the cord near the old plug. Slide the cord through the replacement plug body. Separate and strip the cord wires (page 69). Twist the wire strands tightly with your fingers, and wrap the strands clockwise around the core terminals. Tighten the screws.

2 **SNAP ON THE BODY.** Make sure the connections to the terminals are tight. Hold the core with one hand and push the body onto it with the other hand until the two pieces snap together.

INSTALLING A QUICK-CONNECT PLUG

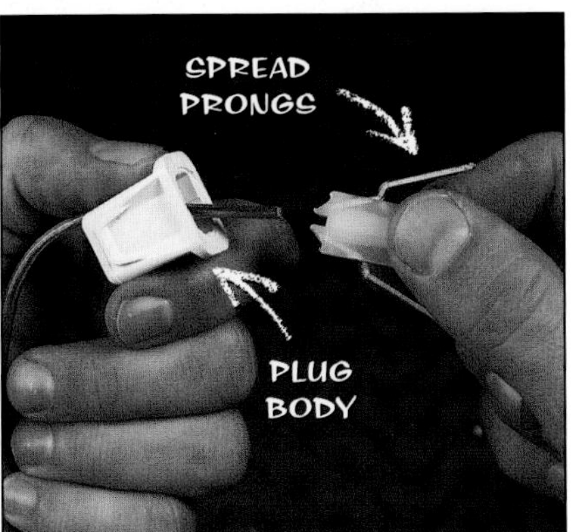

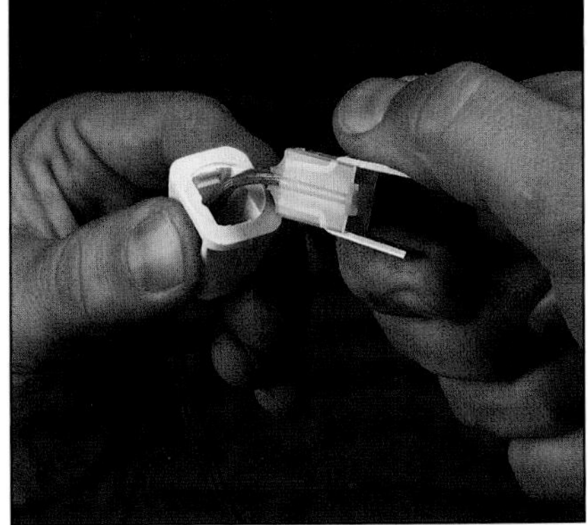

1 **INSERT THE WIRES.** With this type of plug, you do not have to divide or strip the cord. Cut off the old plug. Thread the cord through the plug body. Spread the prongs apart, and push the cord into the core. Connect the ridged (neutral) wire to the wider prong.

2 **SQUEEZE AND SLIDE TOGETHER.** Squeeze the prongs together so they bite down on the cord. While still squeezing, slip the body onto the core until it snaps into place.

INSTALLING A ROUND PLUG

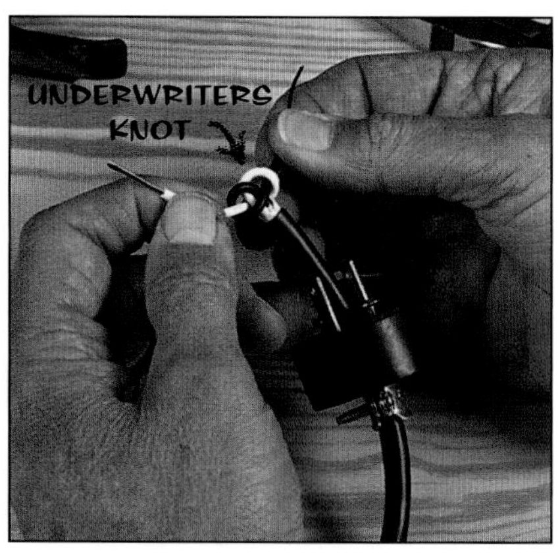

1 INSERT AND TIE THE WIRES FOR A ROUND PLUG. Cut the old cord near the plug. Separate the replacement plug core and body. Thread the cord through the plug body. Use a utility knife to strip 1½ inches of sheathing, being careful not to nick the insulation of the three wires inside. Strip about ½ inch of insulation from each of the wires. Tie the black and white wires in an Underwriters knot.

2 MAKE THE CONNECTIONS. Twist the wires together with your fingers so there are no loose strands. Wrap each wire clockwise around a terminal on the core: black wire to the narrow prong, white wire to the wider prong, and green wire to the round grounding prong. Tighten the screws, snap the body onto the core, and tighten the clamp screws to the cord.

RATE THE WIDTH OF YOUR APPLIANCE CORDS.

Most lamp cords are a standard thickness, but appliance cords vary. When you buy an appliance cord, make sure it is rated to handle the appliance amperage (page 62-63). A cord that's too thin will dangerously overheat. To see whether a cord needs to be replaced, bend it at several points. If the insulation cracks or feels like it's about to crack, replace the cord.

ELECTRICAL REPAIRS

BUYER'S GUIDE

QUICK-INSTALL CORD SWITCHES. Choose the location of the switch carefully: You won't be able to move it after it is installed. An inexpensive rotating switch (below left) will not last long if the switch is used daily but is fine for occasional use. To install one, use a utility knife to cut a 1-inch-long slit to divide the cord; then snip the smooth (hot) wire, but do not strip it. Insert the wire into the switch, and screw the two halves of the switch together.

A rocker switch (below center) is more solidly built and will last longer. It will fit with a flat lamp cord or a round appliance cord. It takes a few minutes longer to install: Cut and strip the smooth (hot) wire, and connect the ends to terminals.

A toe-button switch (below right) is ideal for torchiers and plant lights that are otherwise hard to reach. It installs like on-cord rotating and rocker switches.

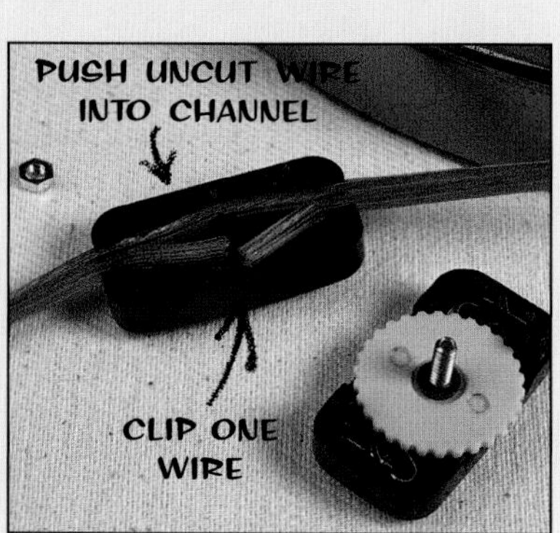

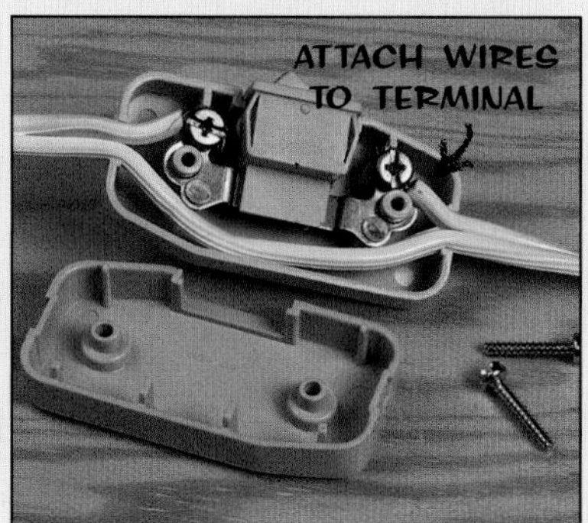

TESTING SWITCHES

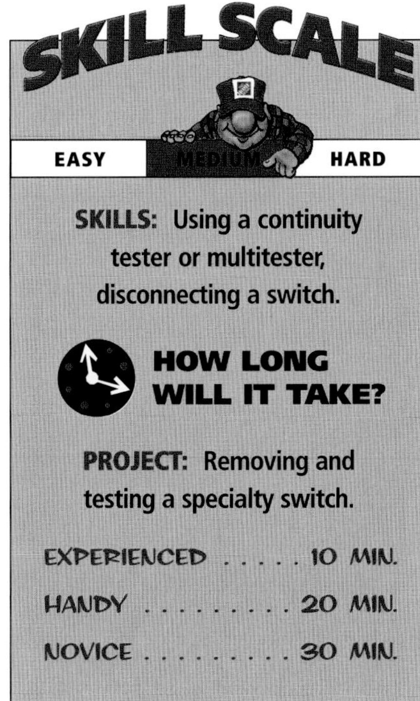

SKILL SCALE
EASY
MEDIUM
HARD
SKILLS: Using a continuity tester or multitester, disconnecting a switch.
HOW LONG WILL IT TAKE?
PROJECT: Removing and testing a specialty switch.
EXPERIENCED . . . . . 10 MIN.
HANDY . . . . 20 MIN.
NOVICE . . . . 30 MIN.

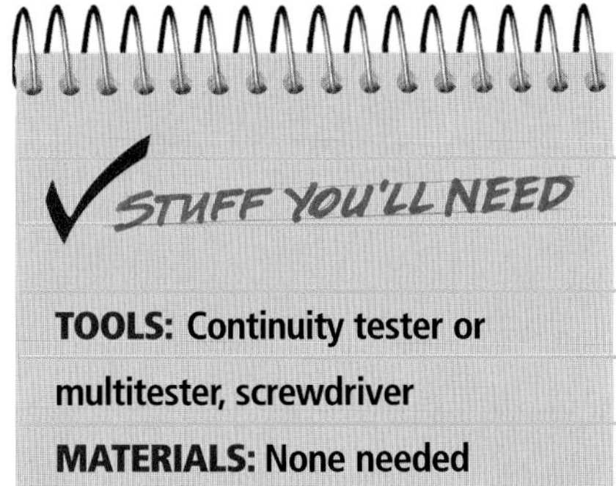

STUFF YOU'LL NEED
TOOLS: Continuity tester or multitester, screwdriver
MATERIALS: None needed

A switch should show continuity when turned on and no continuity when turned off. With some specialty switches, however, it might be hard to know when the switch is on and when it is off. Some of the more common specialty switches are expensive enough to warrant testing before you replace them. (You may want to replace single-pole switches without testing—they're cheap to replace.) Do not test a switch while it is wired. Shut off power to the circuit, and remove the switch.

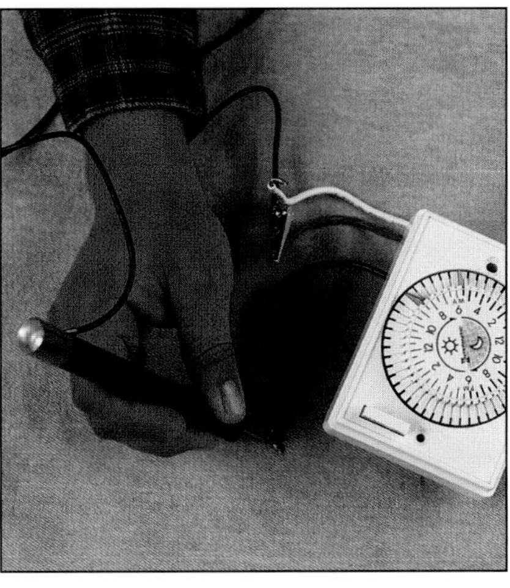

TESTING A TIMER SWITCH. Turn the dial until the red ON tab just passes the indicator arrow and clicks on. Touch one probe to the red lead and the other probe to the black lead. If there is no continuity, the switch is defective; replace it. Also turn the dial until the OFF tab passes the arrow and clicks off. Touch the red and black leads again. If the tester shows continuity, the switch is defective; replace it.

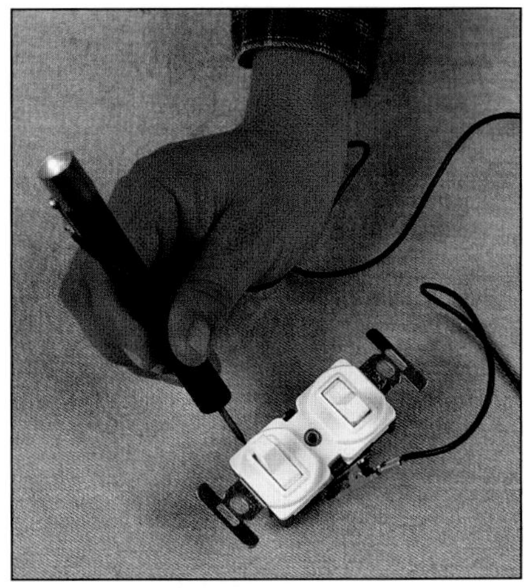

TESTING A DOUBLE SWITCH. Test each of the switches in the same way: Touch the probes to the terminals on each side of the switch. If the tester indicates continuity with the switch ON and no continuity with the switch OFF, then the switch is working. If you get any other result from either switch, replace the device.

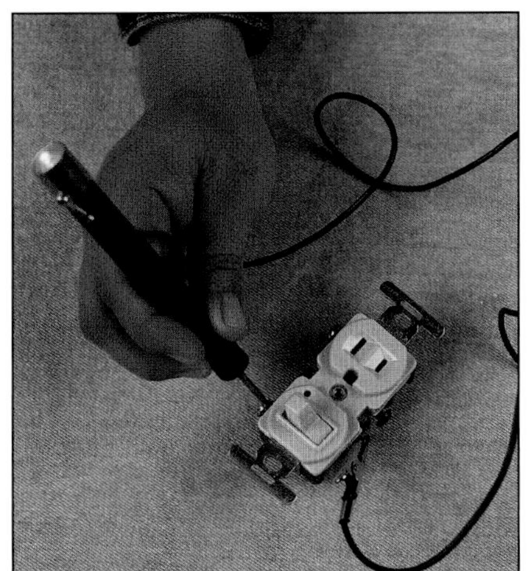

TESTING A SWITCH/RECEPTACLE. Begin by testing the switch. With probes touching the terminal on each side, the tester should show continuity with the switch ON and no continuity with the switch OFF. If you get different results, replace the device.

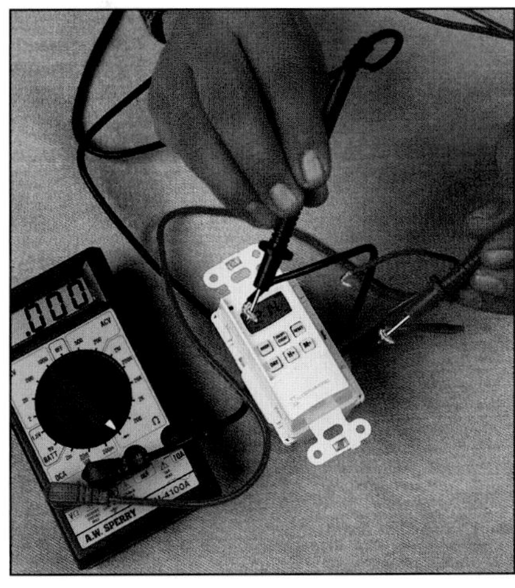

TESTING A PROGRAMMABLE SWITCH. Turn the manual override switch to ON, and touch the probes to both leads. Use a digital multitester as shown or a continuity tester (pages 44–45) to test for continuity. Then test with the switch turned OFF. The tester should show no continuity. If your results differ, replace the switch.

TESTING A THREE-WAY SWITCH

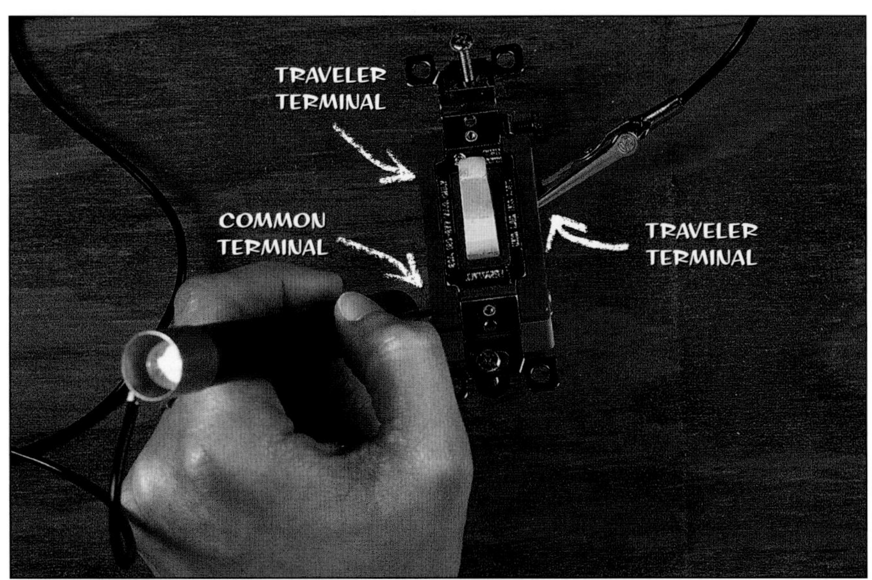

TESTING A THREE-WAY SWITCH. Touch one probe to the common terminal (it is a different color and may have "common" printed next to it) and one to either of the other "traveler" terminals. Flip the switch. The tester should show continuity when the toggle is either up or down, but not in both positions. Keep the toggle in the ON position (the position that shows continuity) for the first traveler terminal, and move one probe from the first traveler terminal to the second. The tester should show no continuity. Flip the switch, and the tester should show continuity. If any of the test results differ, replace the switch. (See pages 148–150 for more about three-way switches.)

UNDERSTANDING AND TESTING A FOUR-WAY SWITCH

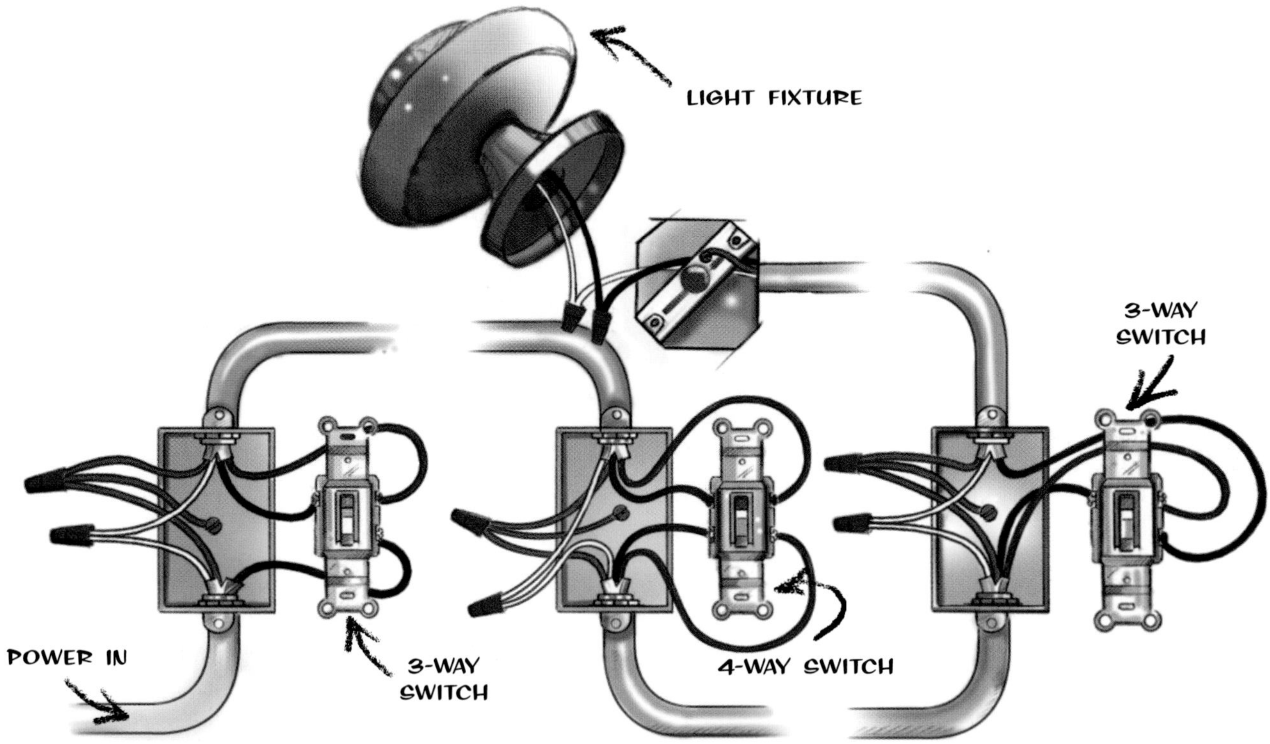

A FOUR-WAY SYSTEM CONTROLS A SINGLE LIGHT WITH THREE OR MORE SWITCHES. The first and last switches are three-ways, and the switch or switches between them are four-ways. Carefully tag all the wires before removing any of the switches. This schematic will help if you get confused. Test the three-way switches as described above, but you'll have to take the four-way to an electrical supply store for testing. What's so complicated about a four-way? The switch should have four paths for continuity. The direction of the paths depends on the manufacturer that made the switch. The paths of continuity may run crosswise or diagonally from any of the four terminals to any of the others.

CHECKING 240-VOLT RECEPTACLES

SKILLS: Confidence working on high-voltage devices, connecting to terminals, using a tester.

HOW LONG WILL IT TAKE?

PROJECT: Replacing a 240-volt receptacle.

EXPERIENCED ...... 1 HR.
HANDY .... 2 HRS.
NOVICE .... 3 HRS.

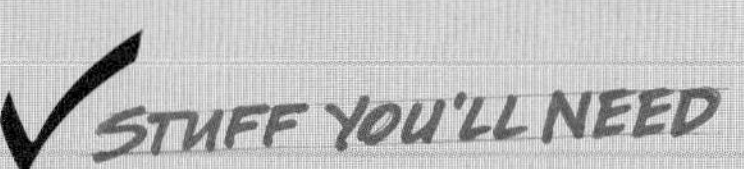

TOOLS: Screwdriver, continuity tester or multitester, longnose pliers

MATERIALS: None needed

TAKE EXTRA PRECAUTIONS. 240 volts can do a lot more damage than 120. When doing a live test, wear rubber-soled shoes and, if kneeling, use a rubber pad. Do not touch the metal parts of the tester probes. (See pages 5–6 for other important safety tips.)

Stationary 240-volt appliances, such as electric water heaters, central air-conditioning units, and electric furnaces, are "hardwired." Instead of having cords with plugs, a cable runs directly from the appliance to a junction box.

Movable 240-volt appliances, such as window air conditioners and electric ranges, are plugged into 240-volt receptacles.

Some receptacles deliver both 240-volt and 120-volt power (page 145). These are used for electric ranges and clothes dryers that need heavy voltage for heating elements and standard voltage for motors and clocks.

Specific types of receptacles are available, each with a different hole configuration so only one type of plug can fit. Ranges usually use 120/240-volt, 50-amp receptacles; dryers plug into 120/240-volt, 30-amp receptacles; air conditioners use 240-volt, 30-amp receptacles.

TESTING A 240-VOLT RECEPTACLE. If an appliance plugged into a 240-volt receptacle gets no power or only partial power, first check the service panel to make sure that the breaker hasn't tripped or the fuse hasn't blown. To make a live test, turn on the circuit, and carefully insert the probes of a four-level voltage tester or a multitester (pages 44–45) into the two vertical slots. The meter should register around 240 volts. With one probe in a vertical slot and one in a neutral or ground slot, you should get a reading of 120 volts. If your readings differ, shut off power to the circuit and remove the receptacle. Make sure the wiring connections are tight. If they are not, tighten and retest. Otherwise, replace the receptacle with a duplicate (page 145). If the receptacle is working correctly, but the appliance is not, you may need to replace the appliance cord.

SWITCHING FROM THREE-WIRE TO FOUR-WIRE

1 SWITCHING FROM A THREE-WIRE TO A FOUR-WIRE DRYER RECEPTACLE AND CORD. In many areas, codes require that electric dryer receptacles have four holes connected to four wires—two hot, one neutral, and one ground. But you may have a four-hole receptacle and an old dryer that has a three-prong plug. If so, replace the dryer cord and plug. Buy the correct type of cord with plug at a home center or electrical supply store. Unplug the dryer. Open the access panel on the back of the dryer.

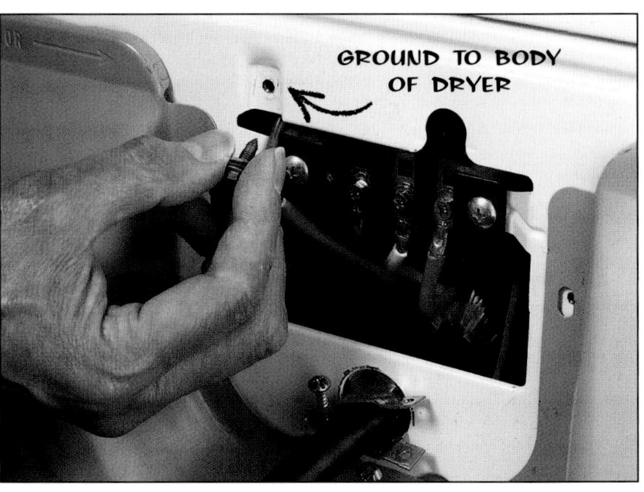

2 ATTACH THE WIRES. Kneel on a foam pad while you work. Note how the three-wire cord is attached, and wire the new cord the same way. A ground for the dryer motor often attaches to the dryer body near where the plug wires attach. Attach the cord's ground wire to it.

3 TIGHTEN THE STRAIN-RELIEF BRACKET. Don't neglect this important piece of hardware; if the dryer cord gets yanked, the bracket will protect the connections and help avoid a possible short. Fit it into the cord access hole and evenly tighten both screws firmly onto the cord.

CLOSER LOOK

MOVE UP TO A GROUNDED RECEPTACLE.

If your system is grounded (look for a copper wire fastened to the box and check for grounding at your service panel), give yourself a safety edge by installing a four-wire receptacle. Attach black to black, white to white, and red to red. With #10 wire, pigtail to the ground. If you need to run new cable for a new receptacle, see pages 121-132.

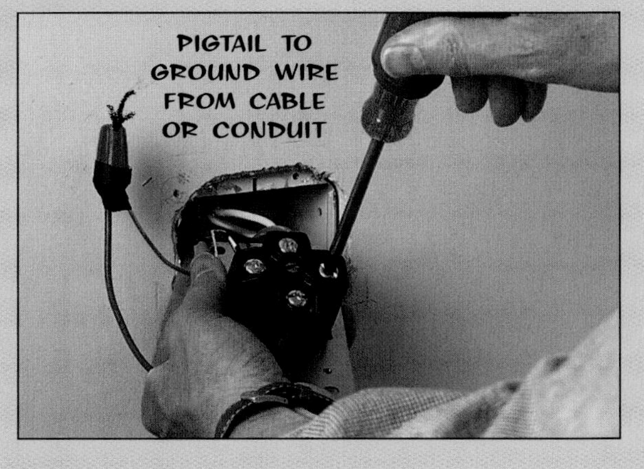

ELECTRICAL REPAIRS

REPAIRING FLUORESCENTS

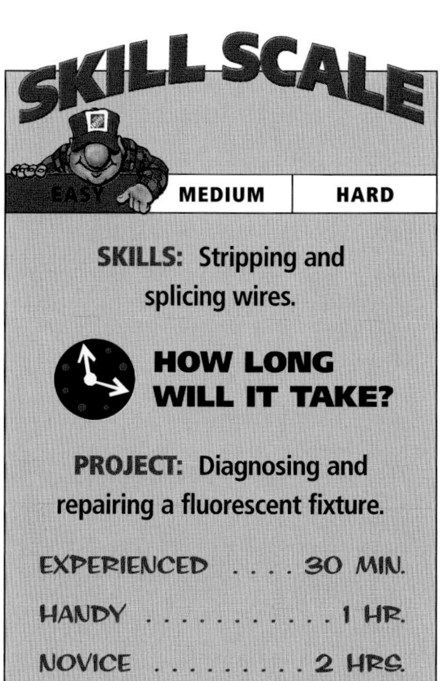

SKILL SCALE
EASY
MEDIUM
HARD
SKILLS: Stripping and splicing wires.
HOW LONG WILL IT TAKE?
PROJECT: Diagnosing and repairing a fluorescent fixture.
EXPERIENCED . . . . 30 MIN.
HANDY . . . . 1 HR.
NOVICE . . . . 2 HRS.

TOOLS: Combination strippers, longnose pliers, screwdriver
MATERIALS: Replacement parts, electrician's tape, wire nuts

Fluorescent lights use less energy and last longer than incandescent lights, but they can be finicky to repair. The greatest challenge can be finding the right replacement parts. Starters will need replacing on older fixtures (newer fixtures don't need them). Consider replacing starters when you replace tubes. Sockets can loosen or crack; ballasts are particularly troublesome and expensive to replace. Save yourself time and trouble by taking down the fixture to repair it on a bench.

TROUBLESHOOTING

A **flickering** or **partially lighted** tube is the most common problem. Take these steps to troubleshoot:
- Rotate it for a better connection.
- Replace the starter.
- Replace the ballast or the fixture.

If a tube has **very dark spots** at either end:
- Replace it, even if it works. It may cause the ballast to wear out.

If the tube **does not light** at all:
- Rotate the tube to get a better connection.
- Check the ballast for a temperature rating. Some fixtures will not start in cold or hot temperatures.
- Make sure the circuit is getting power. Test, then replace the wall switch (pages 22–23) if necessary.
- Replace the tube, especially if it's dark at the ends or if a pin is bent.
- Replace the socket if it is cracked or if the tube does not seat tightly.
- Replace the ballast or the fixture.

If the **ballast hums:**
- Try turning off a nearby radio or heavy-use electrical appliance.
- Tighten the ballast-mounting screws.
- Replace the ballast.

If the ballast is **oozing a thick black substance:**
- Replace the fixture or, wearing protective gloves, replace the ballast.

KNOW YOUR FIXTURE. It takes an initial burst of voltage to light a fluorescent tube. Once it's lighted, current is cut back because the tube can "coast" on very little voltage. The ballast, a transformer, steps down the voltage. In older models, the ballast is a bulky and heavy rectangular object. Newer models have electronic ballasts. In a rapid-start fixture (below left), the ballast performs this two-level delivery of power. In a starter-type fixture (below right), a small cylindrical starter acts as a switch, sending a greater amount of current to the tube until it lights.

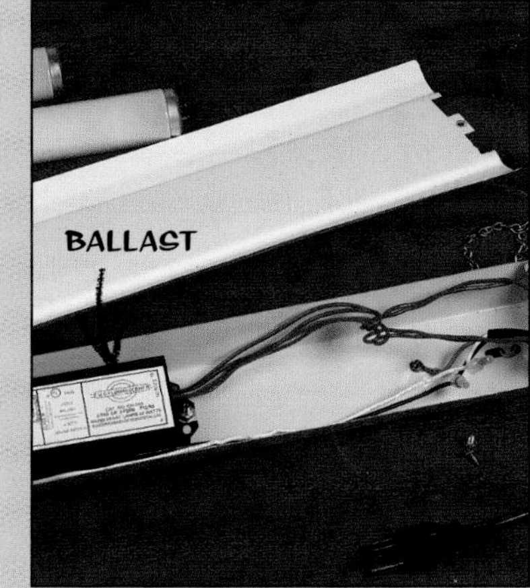

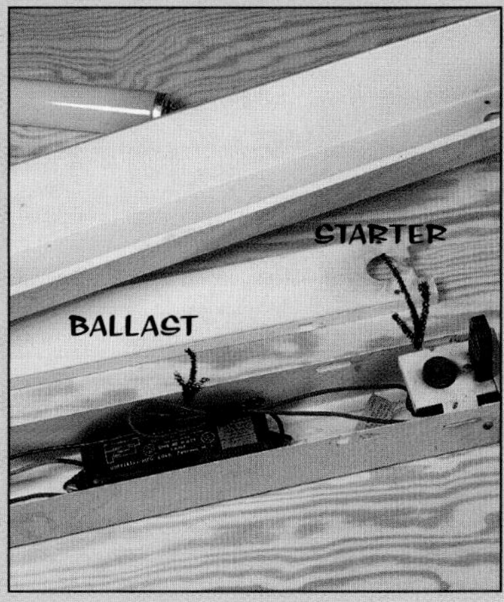

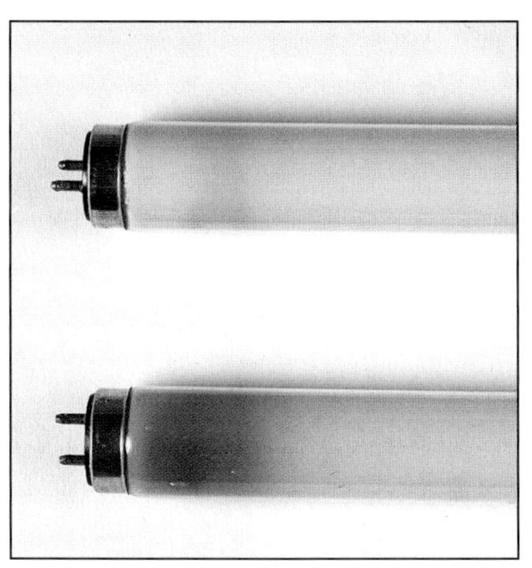

IDENTIFYING SIGNS OF TUBE WEAR. If a tube suddenly stops lighting and is not blackened at the ends, gently rotate it while the fixture is turned on and see whether that brings it back to life. Gray spots near the ends of a tube (top) are signs of normal aging. If the ends are black or dark gray (bottom), you should replace the tube. If a fixture has two tubes, always replace both at the same time.

REPLACING A TUBE. To remove a tube, hold it at each end and twist carefully until you feel it loosen. Remove it, being careful not to damage the tube pins or the sockets. Replace it with a tube of the same size and wattage. With dual lamps, replace both bulbs at the same time.

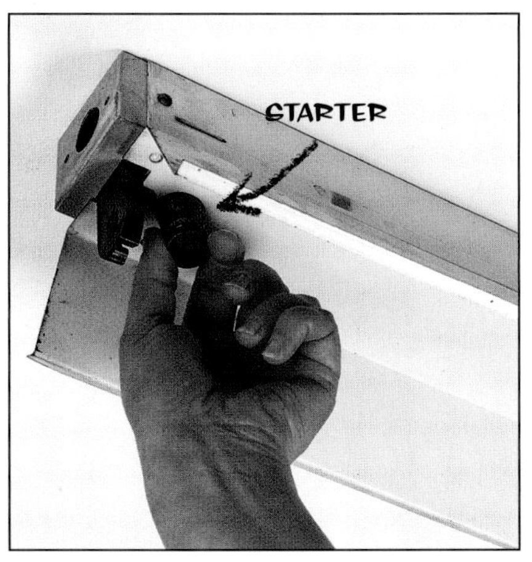

REPLACING A STARTER. If it takes more than a few seconds for a starter-type fixture to light up, remove the tube and twist the starter to see whether you can seat the starter more firmly. If the ends of a tube light up but the center doesn't, replace the starter. Press in the starter and twist counterclockwise to remove it. Buy a starter with the same part number as the old one. Push in and twist clockwise to install it.

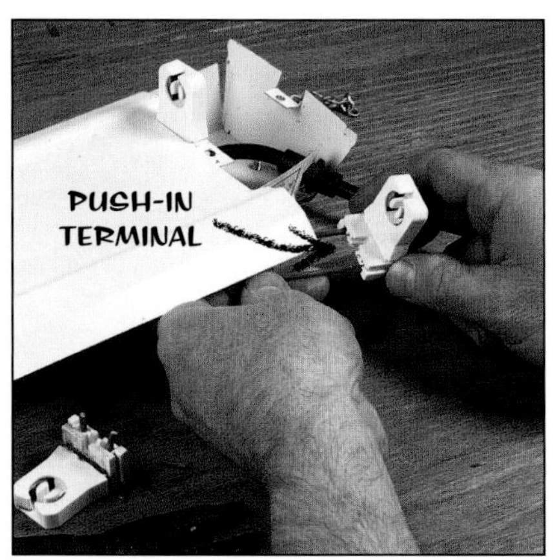

REPLACING A SOCKET. These crack easily, especially if you are not careful when removing or installing a tube. Unscrew the bracket holding the socket in place, or slide the socket out of the groove. If the socket has push-in terminals, poke the slot to release the wire. If the socket has attached wires, cut the wires and strip off about ½ inch of insulation. Install a new socket with push-in terminals or screw terminals.

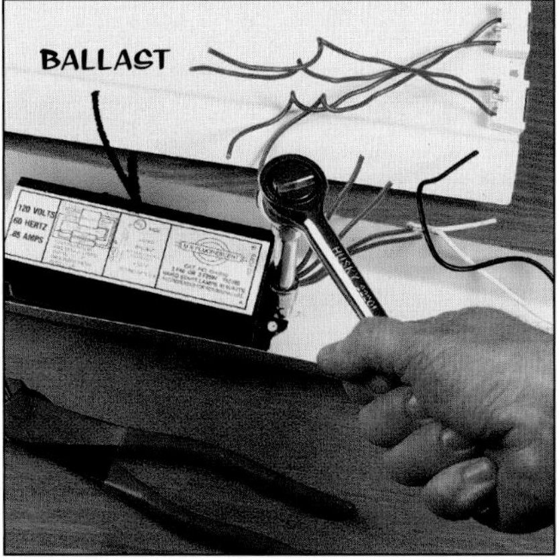

REPLACING A BALLAST. Shut off power to the circuit supplying the light, and check for the presence of power. Disconnect the wires if possible. If it's not possible, cut them close to the ballast. Either way, tag the remaining wires so you'll remember which wire goes where. Unscrew the ballast, and take it to a home center or electrical supply store for a replacement. Install the new ballast in just the same way as the old one was installed. You may prefer to replace the fixture entirely.

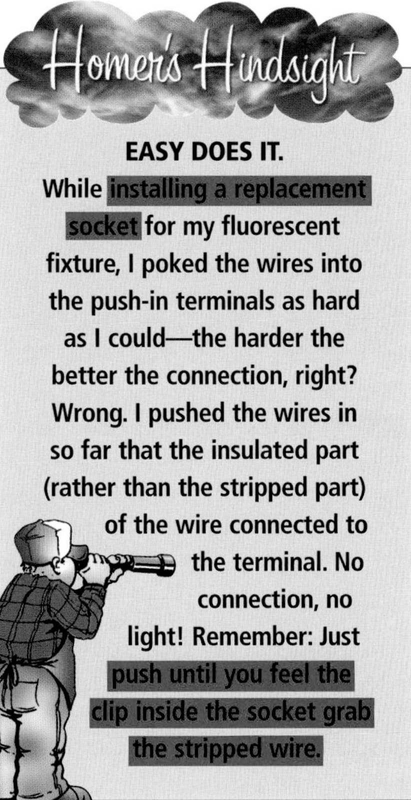

Homer's Hindsight

EASY DOES IT.

While installing a replacement socket for my fluorescent fixture, I poked the wires into the push-in terminals as hard as I could—the harder the better the connection, right? Wrong. I pushed the wires in so far that the insulated part (rather than the stripped part) of the wire connected to the terminal. No connection, no light! Remember: Just push until you feel the clip inside the socket grab the stripped wire.

RESETTING BREAKERS

The fuses or circuit breakers in the service panel form the first line of defense for your home, protecting you and your family from fire and shock. If a house is wired correctly, with no circuits overloaded, you may never have to open your service panel except to shut off power while working on an electrical project.

If a circuit in your home frequently blows a fuse or trips a breaker, check pages 62–63 for tips on how to eliminate circuit overloads.

Learn how to shut off and restore power from the service panel. Map your circuits and tape an index in your service panel (page 61). Always leave a clear pathway to the service panel.

If a circuit breaker trips often, even though you don't seem to be running too many appliances or lights, the problem may be the wiring or the circuit breaker. It's easy to test a breaker (see below).

TESTING A BREAKER

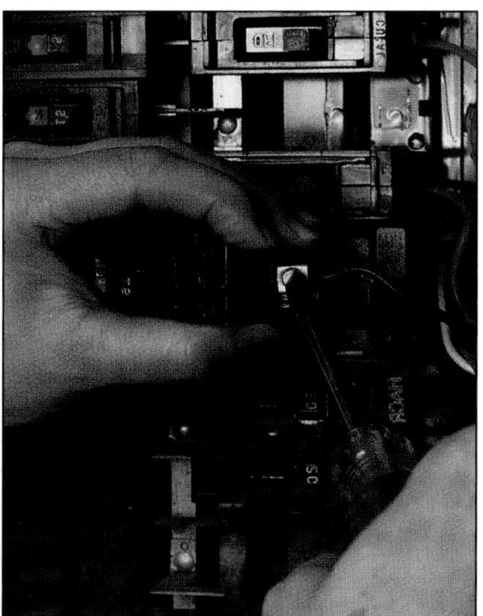

1 TEST THE CIRCUIT BREAKER. If you suspect that a faulty breaker is tripping for no apparent reason, touch the prongs of a voltage tester to the breaker's terminal screw and a ground. If there is no power, the breaker is faulty. Or try this test: Shut off the main breaker. Loosen the setscrews on the suspected breaker and a nearby breaker of the same amperage. Switch the wires, tighten the setscrews, and flip the main breaker back on. If the original breaker trips unreasonably while connected to a different circuit, replace the breaker.

2 REPLACE THE BREAKER. Shut off the main breaker to be safe. Loosen the setscrew on the damaged breaker, then pull out the wire. Pull out the breaker by hand. Make sure you touch only plastic, never anything metal. Pull out one end of the breaker to loosen it, and then pull out the whole breaker. Buy a new breaker of the same amperage and size, made by the same manufacturer. Slip the wire into the new breaker and tighten the setscrew. Push the breaker in until it snaps place like the ones around it. Restore power.

CLOSER LOOK

HOW BREAKERS TRIP

Service panels and breakers are made by a number of manufacturers, so there are various ways to reset breakers. Here are some common types of breakers.

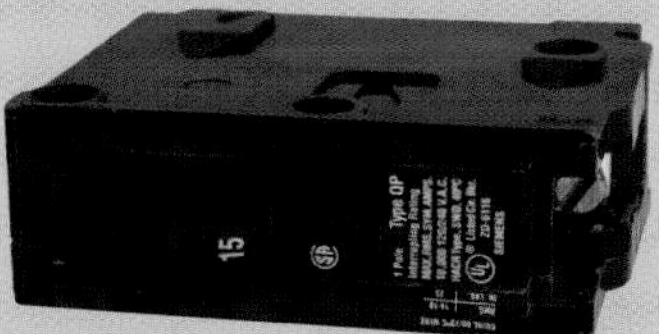

This type flips halfway toward OFF when it trips. To reset it, turn it off, then on.

This breaker flips off all the way. Just flip it back on to reset it. On some, a red button displays or pops out, showing that the breaker has tripped.

This breaker model has a button that pops out when it trips. Push the button in to reset.

CHANGING FUSES

Always replace a blown fuse with a fuse of amperage appropriate for the circuit. A living area usually requires a 15-amp fuse; an appliance area needs a 20-amp fuse. A 30-amp fuse is used only for a range or dryer circuit, or for a line to a subpanel. Installing a fuse of higher amperage may get the circuit going again, but it puts your house at risk because the fuse won't blow when wires get dangerously hot.

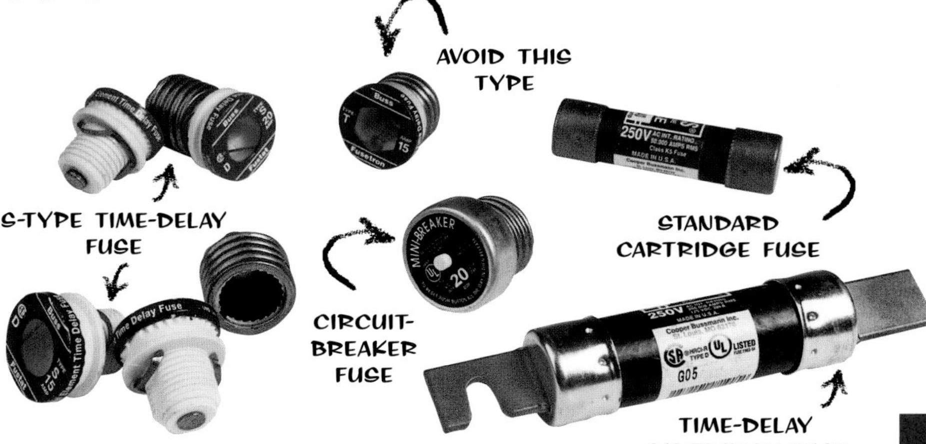

TYPES OF FUSES

A time-delay fuse holds itself together for a second or so during a momentary surge of power—for example, when a refrigerator motor turns on. The fuse will blow if the circuit remains overloaded.

An S-type fuse has a socket adapter that screws into the fuse box socket, where it becomes permanently lodged. Once screwed in, it is impossible to install a fuse of a different amperage.

A circuit-breaker fuse has a push button that pops out when the circuit overloads. Instead of replacing the fuse, you push the button back in to restore power. Many electricians don't think they're reliable; others consider them safe.

WHY A FUSE BLEW

If the metal strip inside the fuse is broken completely, the circuit overloaded: Too many appliances and lights were running at the same time. If the fuse window is blackened, the cause is a short circuit—meaning that somewhere wires are touching each other or a wire is making contact with metal. Inspect switches, receptacles, and fixtures—and fix the problem right away.

SHORT

OVERLOAD

ELECTRICAL REPAIRS

WORKING WITH CARTRIDGE FUSES

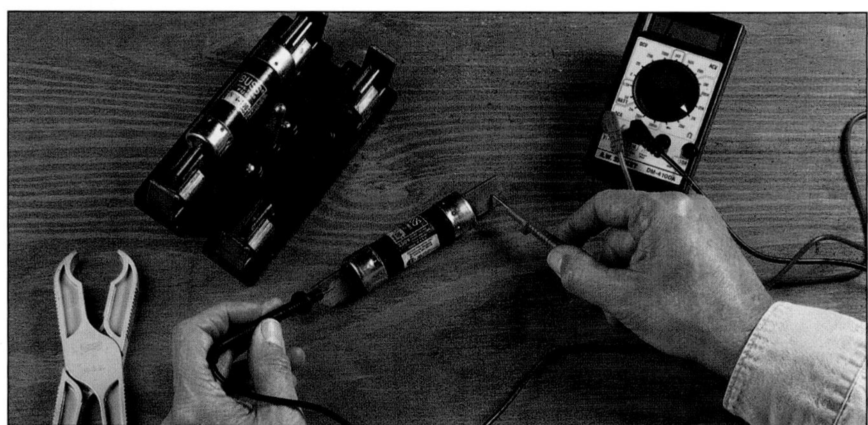

1 REMOVE THE FUSE FROM THE BLOCK. If a 240-volt circuit in a fuse box blows, the fuses are probably located inside a fuse block. Turn off the power. Grab the wire handle and pull out the block. Use a fuse puller to remove each cartridge fuse.

2 TEST THE CARTRIDGE FUSE. (Be careful. If you have just removed the fuse, its metal parts may be hot.) To see whether a cartridge fuse has failed, touch both ends with the probes of a continuity tester or multitester (pages 44–45). If the fuse tests positive for continuity, it is good. If not, it has blown. Take it to a home center or hardware store and buy an exact replacement.

REPAIRING WIRES IN BOXES

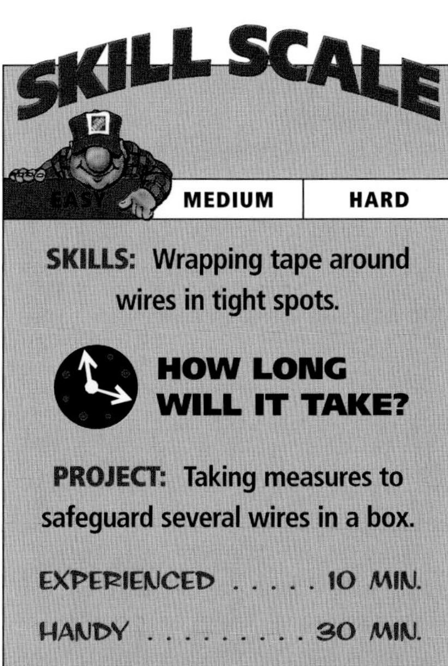

SKILLS: Wrapping tape around wires in tight spots.

HOW LONG WILL IT TAKE?

PROJECT: Taking measures to safeguard several wires in a box.

EXPERIENCED . . . . . 10 MIN.
HANDY . . . . 30 MIN.
NOVICE . . . . 45 MIN.

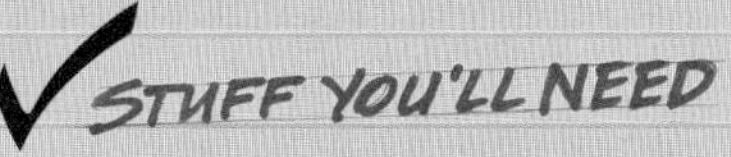

STUFF YOU'LL NEED

TOOLS: Screwdriver

MATERIALS: Electrician's tape, BX bushings

You open a box in your older home and find old wiring with insulation that is cracked and frayed. Very likely, all the hidden wires in the house are in equally bad shape. What can you do?

Rewiring is the safest solution. It is not too big a job if all the wires run through conduit or Greenfield flexible conduit (pages 126–127), but many homes are wired with cable. Replacing cable means making holes in walls, followed by time-consuming, expensive patching and redecorating.

Wires wrapped tightly in cable are likely to be in better condition than wires exposed to air. Insert a plastic bushing and tape the wires to protect the circuit until you rewire. Better yet, protect the wire with a hot-shrink sleeve (above right).

While the box is open, take the following precautions as well. A box recessed behind the wall surface poses a fire danger and is out of code. Slip in an extender ring (below right), and add the cover plate. Debris that collects in an electrical box, especially sawdust, poses a fire hazard; vacuum it out immediately.

PROTECT A WIRE WITH A HOT-SHRINK SLEEVE. If a wire has cracked, brittle, or otherwise damaged insulation, buy a small bag of plastic sleeves made to protect wires. Shut off power to the circuit. Disconnect the damaged wire, and slip a sleeve down over it. Point a hair dryer or heat gun at the sleeve until it shrinks, forming a long-lasting protective coating.

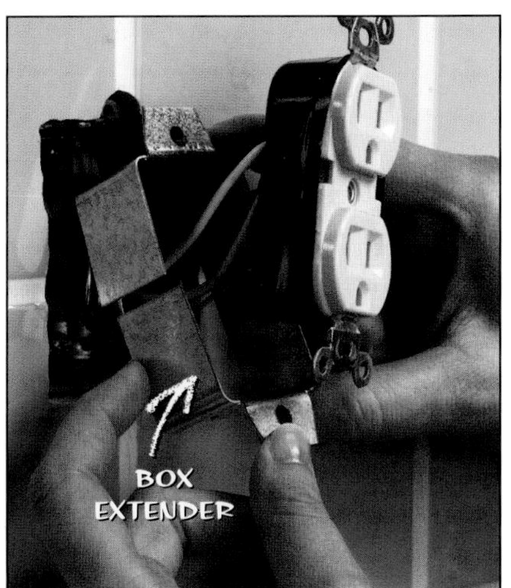

EXTEND A RECESSED BOX. If a box is recessed from a wall surface, there is a danger of fire—especially if the wall surface is wood paneling. However, even tile edges or drywall should be covered. Purchase a box extender sized to fit your box, and slip it on.

CLOSER LOOK

LEAKY WIRES.
Wiring with cracked insulation can leak small amounts of electricity. Known as a high-resistance short circuit, this power loss won't blow a fuse or trip a breaker, but it can overheat wires. To test for this problem, completely shut down the house. Remove all lightbulbs, unplug all lamps and appliances, and disconnect hardwired appliances such as electric water heaters and whole-house fans. Turn on all the switches. Then watch your electric meter. If it shows power usage, then you have a high-resistance short.

Test circuits one by one to narrow down the source of the leak. It may be a bad connection or damaged wire insulation in an electrical box. If you can't find the source, call in a professional.

6 PLANNING LIGHTING

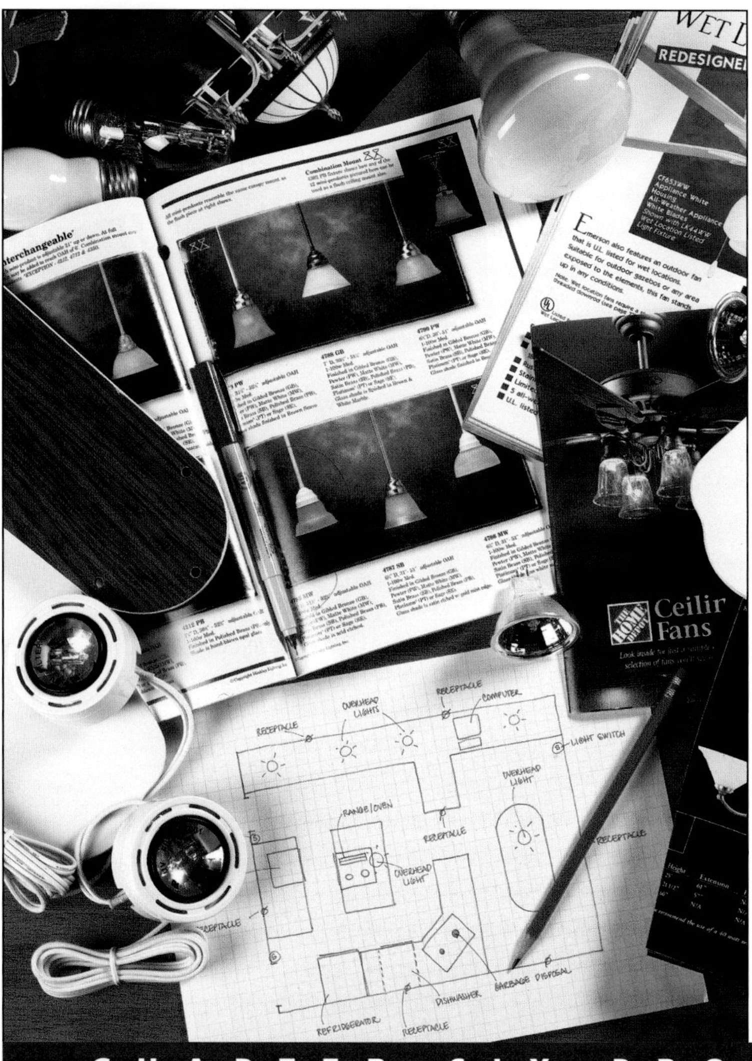

Before you choose light fixtures, draw up a lighting plan. Keep in mind that lighting does more than just illuminate. Lighting also:

- **Enhances activities.** Reading, food preparation—even cleaning—is easier and more pleasurable when the lighting is ample but not glaring.
- **Highlights decorative features.** By changing or redirecting lights, you can emphasize artwork, favorite pieces of furniture, or other decorative features. You can even position lights to make a room seem larger. Outdoor lighting can dramatize built-ins and plantings.
- **Sets a mood.** By building versatility into a room with a variety of fixtures and dimmer switches, you can easily adjust the lighting to suit the occasion.
- **Provides safety.** Well-placed lights help make stairs and hallways safer; outdoors, lighting can even discourage intruders.

CHAPTER SIX PROJECTS

CHOOSING CEILING FIXTURES

The broad range of overhead fixtures can be roughly divided into ones with eye-catching decorative features (like the ones shown on this page) and ones that are hardly noticeable but provide general illumination (like the flush ceiling fixtures shown opposite below). Track lights (opposite) fall in between. All come in a wide variety of styles. Here are the basic types and features to choose from.

PENDANT LIGHTS

Lights that hang down from the ceiling are called pendants. Use them for general lighting, to illuminate a dining room table, or to light up a work surface.

A chandelier or other type of pendant usually can't illuminate a large room on its own. That's because a chandelier often hangs at eye level and would produce an unpleasant glare if it were bright enough to light an entire room.

- **Pendant shades.** Use a pendant shade to focus light on a specific space, such as a small table, a countertop, or a narrow work area. A pendant light with a glass shade will provide general lighting as well as directed light. A metal shade focuses light more directly. Older styles of pendant lights hang by decorative brass chains, with neutral-colored lamp cord running through the chain. Newer fixtures use a plain chrome-colored wire for support, with the cord running alongside.
- **Pendant lanterns.** These lights resemble the old glass lanterns that protected candles from wind. Use them in narrow areas like foyers and stairways. Hang these at least 6½ feet from the ground so that people can walk under them. Center a pendant lantern widthwise in a narrow room. If it is near a large window, place it so it will look centered from the outside.
- **Chandeliers.** Originally designed as candleholders, chandeliers usually have five or more light bulbs. Look for a model that is easy to clean; complex designs can be difficult to dust. Keep it in scale—a chandelier that is too small will appear to be dwarfed by the room. When choosing a unit to hang over a dining room table, select one that is about 12 inches narrower than the table. If it is any wider, people may bump their heads on it when they stand up from the table.

In an entryway, maintain proportion by installing a chandelier that is 2 inches wide for every foot of room width—for example, use a 20-inch-wide light in a 10-foot-wide room.

Get the height right. A common mistake is to hang a chandelier too low. A chandelier should hang about 30 inches above a table top. The length of the chain will depend on your ceiling height.

TRACK CEILING FIXTURES

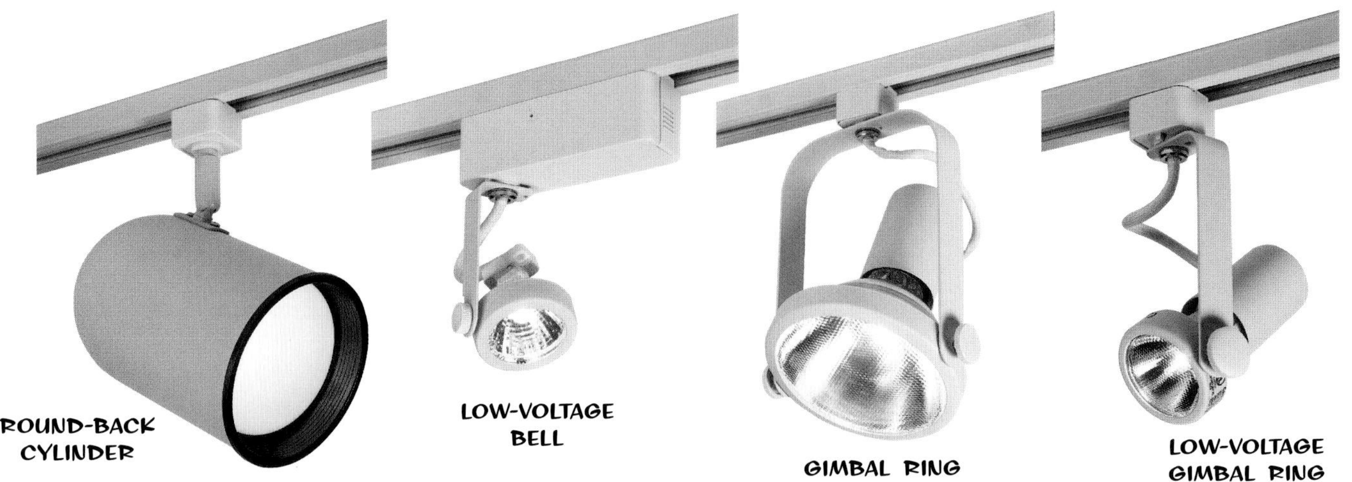

CHOOSING TRACK LIGHTS. A single track lighting system can combine general lighting and accent lighting. When choosing a lamp, make sure it can handle the light bulb of your choice and that it will fit onto your track. Incandescent lamps such as a **round-back cylinder** or a **gimbal ring** produce a broad, intense beam. Low-voltage halogen track lights such as a **low-voltage bell** or **low-voltage gimbal ring** produce a more intense, less broad area of light. They have their own transformer, so they can attach to a standard-voltage track. (However, these low-voltage lights require a special dimmer switch; a standard dimmer will damage the lamps.) A track that partially encircles a room at a distance of 6 feet or so from the walls will disperse light more effectively than a single track running through the middle of the room.

FLUSH CEILING FIXTURES

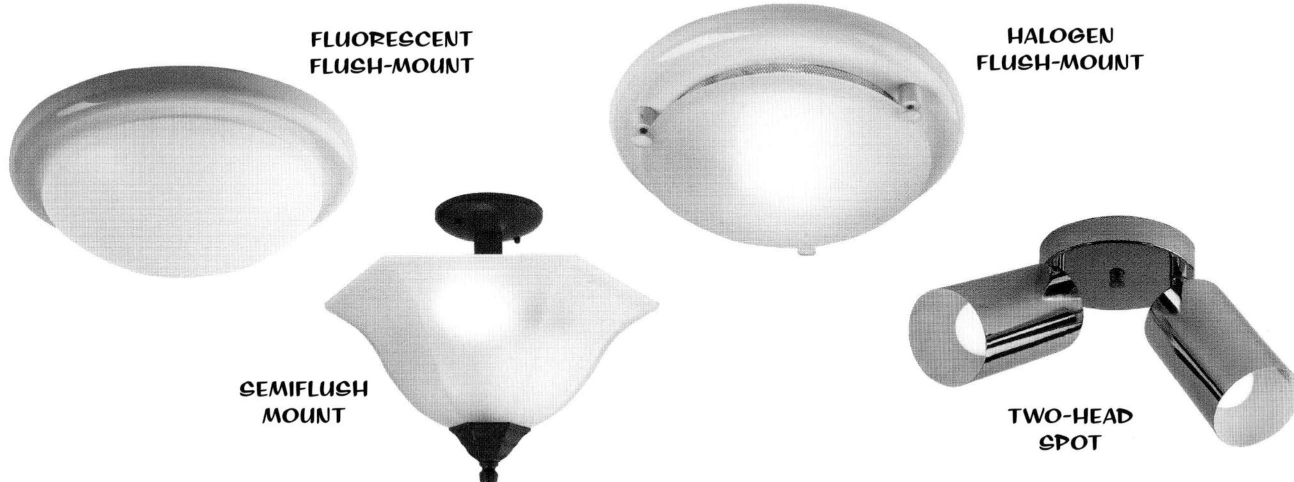

CHOOSING FLUSH FIXTURES. A **single flush fixture** in the middle of the ceiling is the most common way to light a room. These fixtures usually produce enough light to adequately illuminate a 12×12-foot room with an 8-foot ceiling or a 16×16-foot room with a 10-foot ceiling (the higher the fixture, the broader the spread of its light). They hug the ceiling, consistently distributing light. Newer **fluorescent ceiling fixtures** with electronic ballasts look like incandescents, save energy, and have tubes that rarely burn out. A **semiflush** fixture hangs down a foot or so from the ceiling. It diffuses light through the globe as well as upward like a cove light, evenly illuminating a room. **Halogens** offer more intense light. **Two- or three-head spotlights** provide some of track lighting's versatility. Point the lights horizontally for general lighting, or angle them downward to highlight certain areas of the room.

SELECTING BULBS AND TUBES

The color of a light bulb or a light fixture globe or shade significantly affects the mood of a room. Lighting that is slightly red or yellow is considered "warm," while blue-tinged light is "cool." Incandescent bulbs produce warm light; many fluorescents are cool—if not downright cold.

Choose the color of your home's lighting according to the color of your furnishings. If you have pure white walls or cabinetry, warm lighting will make them beige. Cool light directed at brownish natural wood may give it a green tinge.

Fortunately, whether you have a fluorescent or an incandescent fixture, you can switch from cool to warm light, or vice versa, by changing the bulbs or tubes.

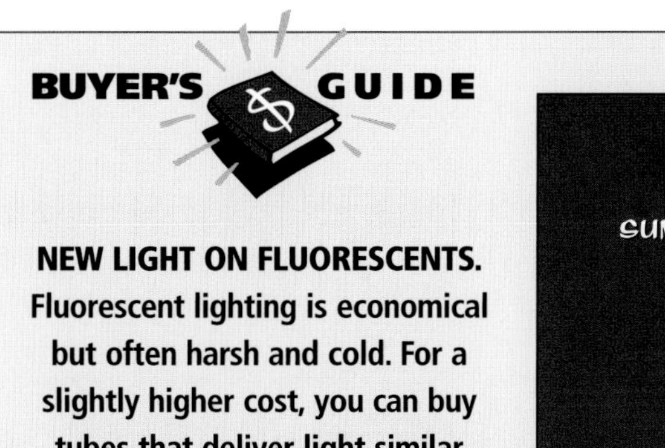

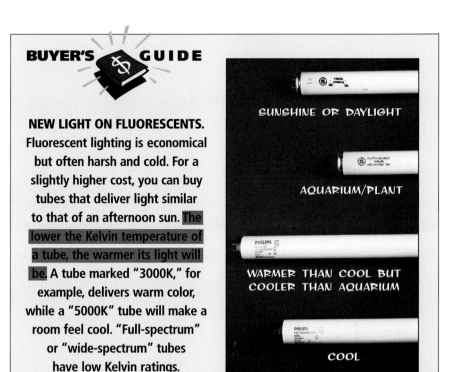

NEW LIGHT ON FLUORESCENTS. **Fluorescent lighting is economical but often harsh and cold. For a slightly higher cost, you can buy tubes that deliver light similar to that of an afternoon sun. The lower the Kelvin temperature of a tube, the warmer its light will be. A tube marked "3000K," for example, delivers warm color, while a "5000K" tube will make a room feel cool. "Full-spectrum" or "wide-spectrum" tubes have low Kelvin ratings.**

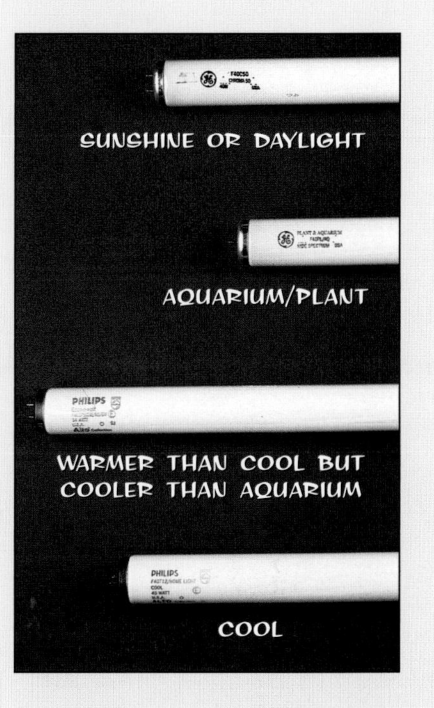

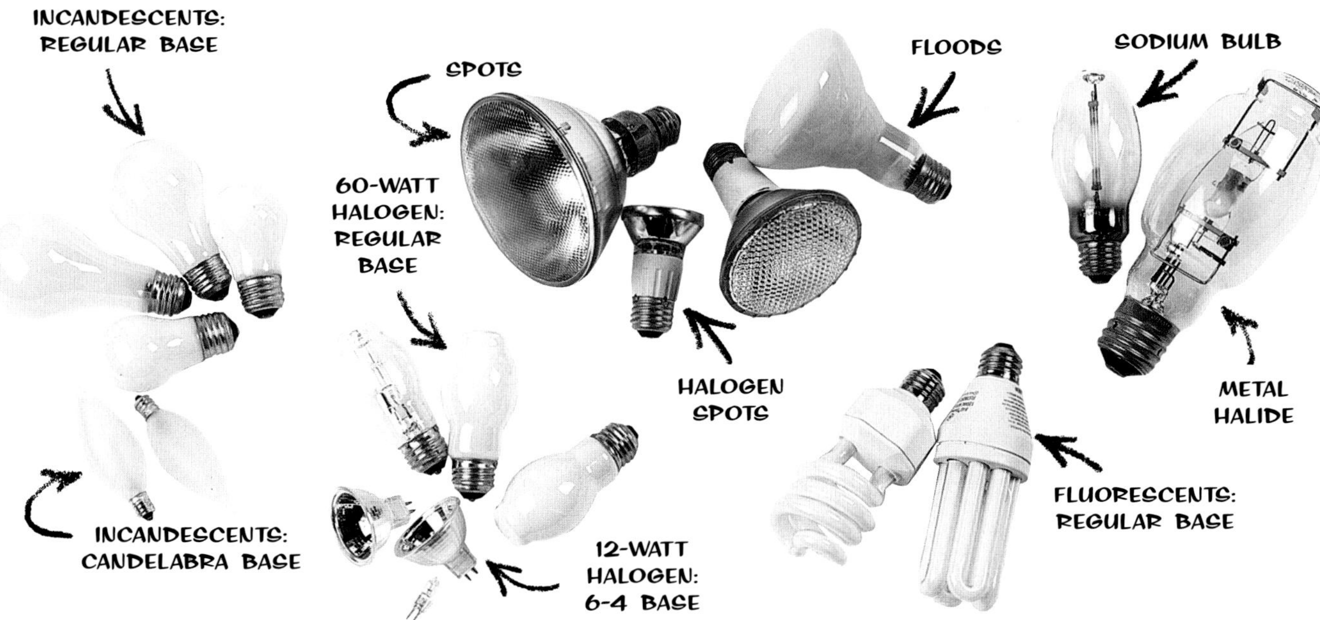

LIGHTBULB OPTIONS.

- **Incandescent bulbs** are the most common but have comparatively short lives and are not very energy efficient.
- **Low-voltage halogen bulbs** last longer than incandescents and use far less energy, but they burn hot. Halogens come in so many styles, so make sure the bulb base fits in your fixture.
- **Reflector bulbs** direct either a wide or narrow beam of light, depending on the bulb. A "spot" bulb projects a flashlight-like beam. A "flood" bulb illuminates a wider area.The second number on the stamped label indicates the degree of the beam spread.
- **Fluorescent tubes** that screw into incandescent sockets save money in the long run. Choose from among several shapes and degrees of warmth.
- **HID (High-Intensity Discharge) lamps** such as sodium, metal halide, and mercury vapor produce very bright, economical light outdoors.

PLANNING KITCHEN LIGHTING

The right lighting plan can make your kitchen more cheerful and inviting, increase the safety of food preparation, and highlight cabinetry and other design features. As you plan, remember that surfaces like ceramic tiles and semigloss paint reflect light. This can be a beneficial, but in the wrong place they can bounce bright light into your eyes.

- **Ambient lighting** produces a daylight effect. Flush ceiling fixtures or track lights spread light more evenly than recessed can lights or pendants. Cove lighting creates ambient light originating from several directions. Windows and skylights are great sources of light during daylight hours, but they need help in the evening or in gloomy weather. A dimmer switch or two on your ambient lighting will make it easier to strike the right balance.
- **Task lights** under kitchen cabinets or in other strategic areas illuminate common kitchen tasks like food preparation and dish washing. A range hood with a light eases stove-top cooking as it vents odors.
- **In-between lights** illuminate kitchen work spaces while providing generous amounts of ambient light. These lights include recessed can lights over a sink, pendant fixtures above an eating area, and track lights in a semicircle near cabinetry.

PLANNING KITCHEN LIGHTING (CONTINUED)

LIGHTING YOUR EATING AND PREP AREAS. Ensure that ambient lighting is positioned so that it amply illuminates work areas. To supplement ambient light, install fluorescent or under-cabinet halogen lights over work surfaces. If there are no cabinets above, use track lighting, sconces, recessed can lights in the ceiling, or halogen trapeze lights. Pendant lights work well for task lighting but are not practical above a sink because they hang down too low.

Strings of rope lights placed along the kickplate add an accent and highlight your flooring.

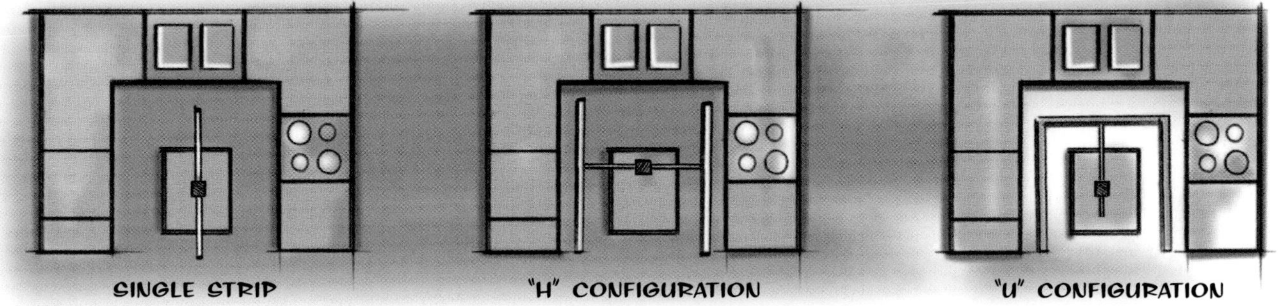

SHAPING UP WITH TRACK LIGHTING. Many kitchens feature a single strip of track lighting running through the center of the ceiling. This kind of light provides adequate illumination but can sometimes bounce off wall cabinets and produce an uncomfortable glare—especially if the cabinets are shiny or light in color. The lights can cast a shadow over a person preparing food at the countertop, contributing to poor visibility.

Instead of installing a single strip of track lighting along the ceiling, wrap the tracks around the room in an "H" or a "U" pattern. Install the tracks about 3 feet out from the wall and 2 feet out from the wall cabinets. The lamps will then shine down over the shoulders of people working at counters, or toward the center of the room—providing both task lighting and ambient light.

LIGHTING UP CABINETS. Achieve a stunning effect with lights placed inside glass-doored cabinets. If the shelves are also glass, the light will glimmer as it filters down. Use small fluorescent fixtures—which stay cool—and control them with a special fluorescent dimmer switch.

CHOOSING A BEDSIDE LIGHT. For bedtime reading, a swivel light that mounts on a wall has great advantages over a table lamp. You can point the light directly at your book, and it won't take up space on the end table.

INSTALLING SCONCE LIGHTING. Lights that mount on the wall can make a room feel larger and a hallway wider. Use sconces for accents rather than for ambient lighting. Place low-wattage bulbs in them, unless you want to highlight the wall above.

LIGHTING ROOM BY ROOM

Provide very bright light in areas used for work and study. In rooms designed for entertaining, less light is called for.

- **Eating/dining areas.** A bright pendant light is appropriate for a breakfast nook or other informal eating area, but a table used for fine dining should have indirect, subtle light. Point recessed or track lights away from the table. Position a chandelier so it does not shine in diners' eyes.
- **Hallways and stairways.** These areas require enough light so people won't trip. You may need lights at the bottom and top of a stairway. A 75-watt ceiling fixture every 12 feet is sufficient for a hallway. Increase the wattage if elderly people live in your home. Wall sconces work well in these areas.
- **Study.** A single reading lamp can create an uncomfortable glare on book pages. Provide one or two additional sources of light, such as ample overhead lighting or a second lamp.
- **Work rooms/hobby areas.** Start with overhead lighting that distributes light evenly throughout the room. Then add nonglare lights above work surfaces and flexible lamps for specific tasks.

LIGHTING LIVING AREAS

Living rooms, dining rooms, great rooms, and large bedrooms all benefit from both ambient and task lighting. Rather than installing a single lighting component, think in terms of the total effect of the room. "Layering" several types of lights makes a room more comforting and inviting. The goal is flexibility, so you can set a variety of moods by brightening or dimming the entire room or part of the room.

- **Highlight a piece of art or cabinetry** or accentuate wall texture with lights to give the room warmth and interest.
- **Put at least one of the components on a dimmer switch,** and install several lights that are optional, but not necessary. Don't be afraid to install too many lights; you don't have to have all of them on at the same time.
- **Install an in-between light** such as a dining-area chandelier to brighten the dinner table and provide some ambient light.

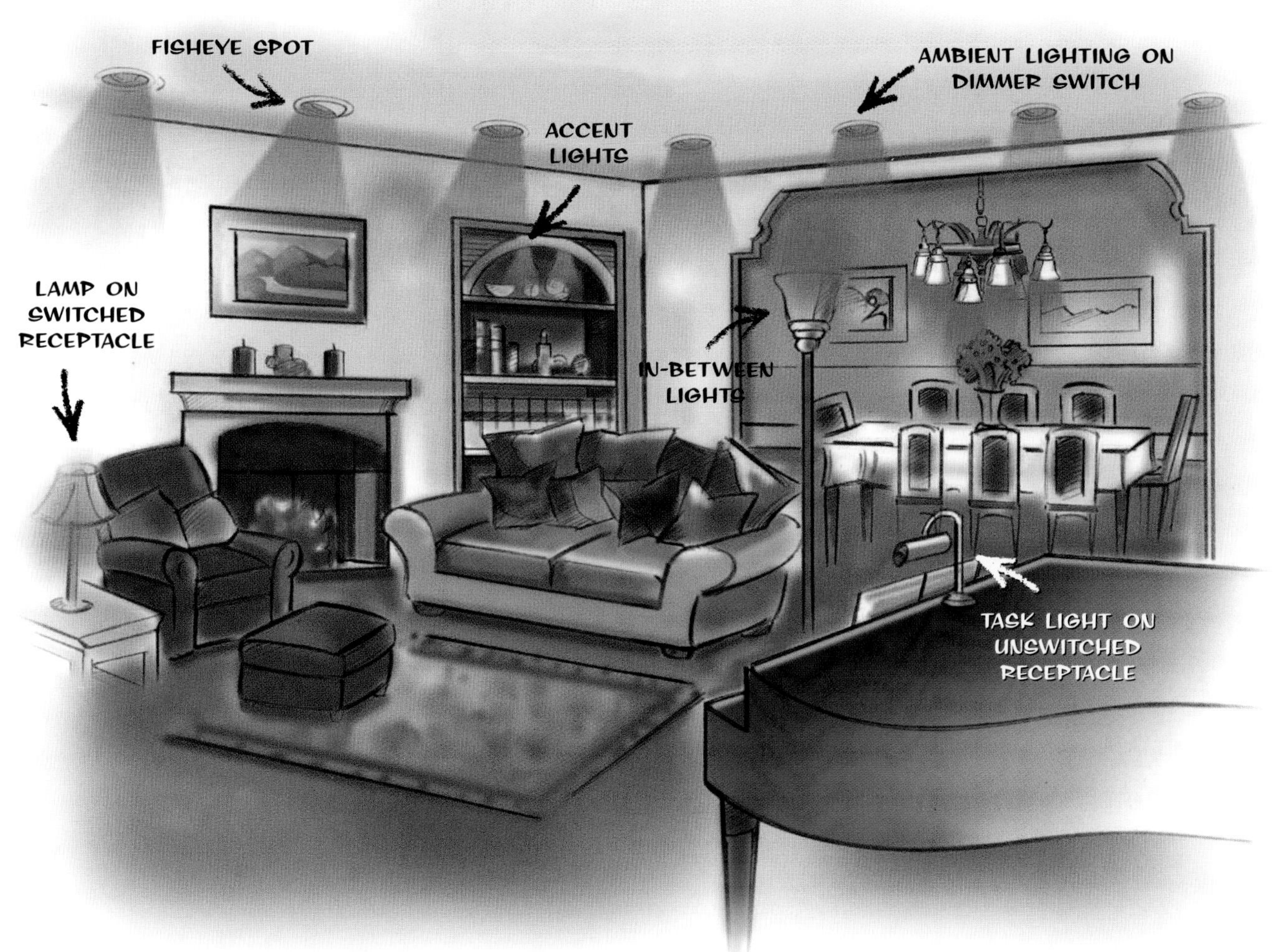

SHOWING OFF A GREAT ROOM WITH GREAT LIGHTING. The lighting plan for this large family room includes a grid of recessed canister lights for general lighting and a centrally located chandelier over the dining table. A recessed light with fisheye trim spotlights a wall painting. The table lamp and floor lamp are controlled by wall switches. Accent lights brighten shelves. The task light on the piano is on an unswitched receptacle.

PLANNING LIGHTING

LIGHTING A BATHROOM

An average-size bathroom needs a ceiling fan/light in the center of the main room, a moisture-proof ceiling light over the shower/bath, and lights over the sink.

- **Ambient lighting** is typically provided by an overhead light combined with a vent fan. Make sure the fan's blower is powerful enough to adequately vent your bathroom (pages 156–158). For a little more money, you can also purchase a low-watt night-light or a fan-forced heater unit. Some people prefer a heat lamp near the tub or shower for additional heat while drying off after bathing.
- **Bathroom mirror lighting** deserves careful thought. A horizontal strip of decorative light bulbs above the mirror provides lots of light but may shine in your eyes. A fluorescent fixture with a lens provides more even light but may lack warmth. Sconce lights placed on either side of the mirror are the best source for lighting your face for shaving or applying makeup. When planning circuits, don't forget to install a Ground-Fault Circuit Interrupter (GFCI) receptacle near the sink.
- **Shower lighting supplements** what little light comes through the shower curtain or glass door. Consider installing a recessed canister light with a watertight lens placed directly above the shower.

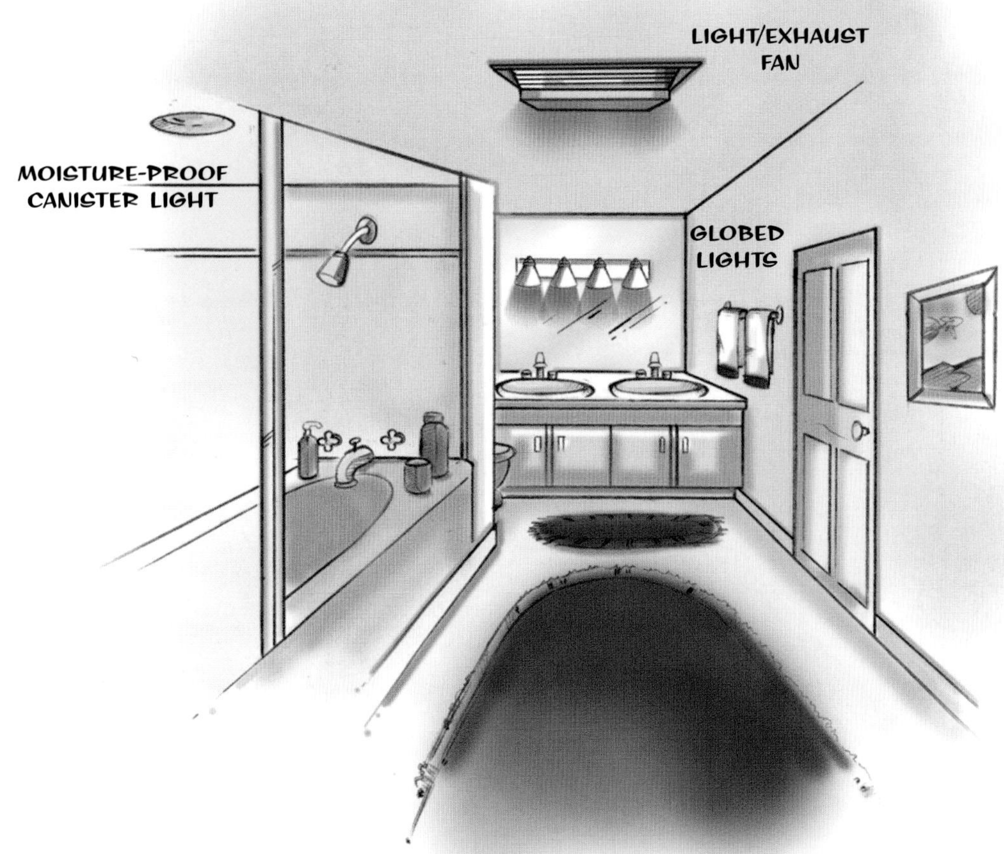

LIGHTING UP YOUR BATHROOM. The darker the color of your bathroom walls and fixtures, the more light you need. Natural light from a window may be sufficient for daytime use. But for nighttime and early-morning use, the shower, in particular, might need one or two moisture-proof canister lights. (Codes limit them to 60 watts each if the shower is enclosed.) Above the sink, install moisture-resistant globed lights that won't shine in your eyes. Overhead, install a single fixture that efficiently and stylishly combines a light, exhaust fan, and perhaps a night-light and a heater.

LIGHTING COUNTERTOPS. Place fluorescent or halogen under-cabinet lights so they will illuminate the countertop but not shine in a person's eyes. If the light fixtures are chunky, consider installing a 2-inch strip of wood along the underside of the cabinet to shield the glare.

USING COVE LIGHTING. This is an easy and inexpensive way to add an elegant lighting touch to a kitchen. Fluorescent fixtures placed on the top of a wall cabinet wash the wall and ceiling in a glow that disperses even light throughout the kitchen.

LIGHTING FOR HEALTHY PLANTS

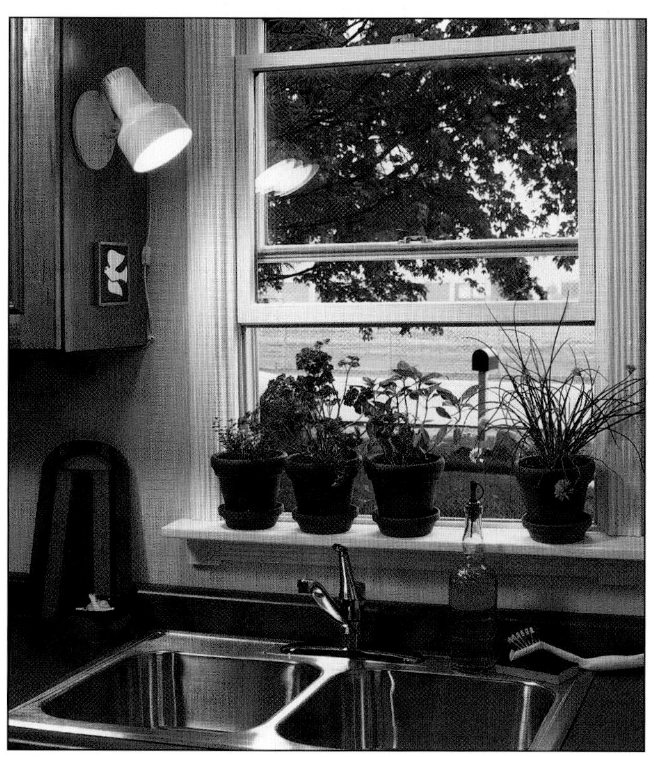

SUPPLEMENTING NATURAL LIGHT. Nothing brightens a kitchen window like potted flowers or herbs. Most plants need at least 4 hours of direct sunlight a day. Unless your window provides this kind of exposure, you may need to supplement your room's natural light with artificial rays. Install incandescent or fluorescent bulbs or tubes that are labeled full- or wide-spectrum. As supplements to filtered window light, these lights only need to be on for several hours a day. Keep them a foot or more away from your plants to avoid drying out the leaves.

If your room provides little natural sunlight or none at all, you will have to install supplemental lighting at close range. To grow healthy plants, train these lights on your plants and leave them on for all or most of the day.

PLANNING FOR CAN LIGHTING

Can lights vary in intensity and angle. The higher your ceiling, the more floor space a light will illuminate. In general, recessed cans should be 6 feet from each other. Of course, most rooms are not sized to accommodate this, so you'll have to adjust your calculations. In the example below, most of the lights are 5 feet apart. Make a similar plan for your own installation, experimenting with several configurations. Take your plans with you to your home center for advice.

Once you start installing can lights, you'll find that many have to be moved several inches from their ideal locations in order to avoid hitting joists (ceiling framing). Fortunately, this will not make a big difference in the overall effect.

SPECIAL TECHNIQUES

In addition to providing general lighting, recessed can lights can enhance decorating strategies with:

- **Wall washing.** To light up a large wall area, install cans with wall-wash trims that are 24 to 30 inches apart, and the same distance from the wall.
- **Accent lighting.** Spotlight a painting, fireplace mantle, or other feature with a can that has an eyeball trim. Place it 18 to 24 inches from the wall, centered on the object.
- **Grazing.** To dramatize an unusual vertical surface, such as a fireplace or a textured wall, place cans 6 to 12 inches from the wall and 12 to 18 inches apart. Wire them with a separate dimmer switch.

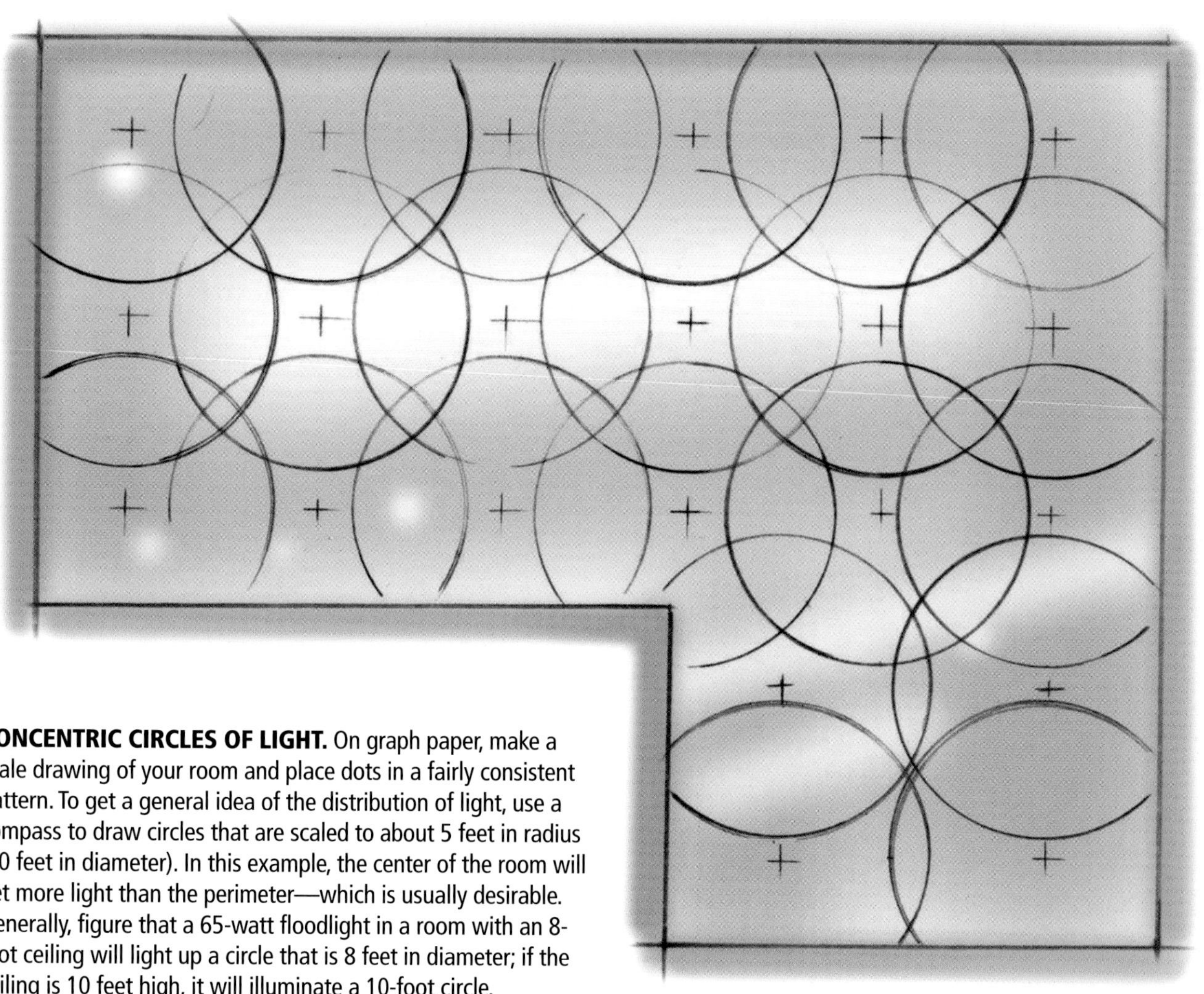

CONCENTRIC CIRCLES OF LIGHT. On graph paper, make a scale drawing of your room and place dots in a fairly consistent pattern. To get a general idea of the distribution of light, use a compass to draw circles that are scaled to about 5 feet in radius (10 feet in diameter). In this example, the center of the room will get more light than the perimeter—which is usually desirable. Generally, figure that a 65-watt floodlight in a room with an 8-foot ceiling will light up a circle that is 8 feet in diameter; if the ceiling is 10 feet high, it will illuminate a 10-foot circle.

PLANNING SECURITY LIGHTING

Outdoor lighting may be your home's most important security feature. It may even deter intruders more effectively than additional door locks or an alarm system.

- **Keep areas brightly lit** so there are no dark pathways. Ideally, two or more lights should be pointed at a potential intruder who approaches your home.
- **Install two light fixtures at each door of entry**—or at least one fixture equipped with two bulbs in case one bulb burns out. Control these lights with motion sensors or timers (page 99) rather than an inside switch.
- **Install motion-sensor-controlled spotlights** over the garage door and under the eaves. These not only discourage intruders, but also make it easier to carry in the groceries at night.
- **Place light posts or path lights along walkways**. Control bright lights with motion sensors and low-voltage lights with a timer or photocell so they stay on all night.
- **Make it difficult to extinguish lights.** Casual trespassers will usually be deterred by bright lights, but a professional thief will look for ways to shut off your security lights. Seven feet may be an attractive height for placing porch lights, but an intruder can easily reach that high. Place outdoor lights 9 or more feet above the ground.
- **Add standard-voltage light posts** to fortify your property. Low-voltage path lighting can be easily disconnected.
- **Install bright lights on motion-sensor switches** indoors behind a sliding glass door or large window. These will surprise intruders and alert you as well.

BRIGHT AND SECURE. This grouping of lights makes intruders uncomfortable but it appears decorative enough not to broadcast its security function. Outside entry lights, spots, eave lights, and light posts allow no place to hide. A timer-controlled indoor light behind a large window makes it appear as if the occupants are home even when they're not. For ease of use, control the light with timers or motion sensors.

LIGHTING YOUR YARD

Lighting can emphasize your yard's best features. Begin by making a sketch of your property, including plantings, pathways, and outdoor structures. Spend an evening or two with a worklight and extension cord to try out some ideas. Vary the positioning. Outdoor lights may be suspended, mounted on poles, installed on the side of a deck or house, or placed under foliage. Consider these other options:

- **Try outdoor-rated rope lights.** Some rope lights (page 105) are designed for exterior use. Hang them loosely from post to post on a railing, stretch them taut along a fascia board, or spiral-wrap them—barber-shop style—around a pole or post.
- **Incorporate holiday lights.** Outdoor holiday lights—whether large and colorful or tiny white pinpricks—can be used year-round. Hang them high and fire them up for a party.
- **Use both standard-voltage and low-voltage lights.** Keep some standard-voltage lights around for times when you want to see clearly at night, but give yourself the option of using low-voltage lighting as well.
- **Experiment with color.** Use outdoor lenses and lightbulbs in various colors to set just the right mood. The results can be surprising, so take the time to experiment. Blue light resembles the cast of a full moon's light. Green light cast on a tree or shrub can give foliage a special luminescence. Reds, oranges, and yellows can evoke a warm, inviting feel.

LIGHTS THAT EMPHASIZE FOLIAGE. Aim illumination toward attractive features of your yard, such as trees and plantings. Be sure these lights don't create an unpleasant glare for passersby. Bright under-eave lights are less harsh if blue lenses or bulbs are used. A tree can appear lit from within by an in-ground spotlight shining upward. Romanticize in-ground lights by simply dropping a few leaves on top of them. Lights that shine through flowering plants cast interesting shadows and highlight the colors of petals. Brick lighting defines the borders of a patio or driveway. All these elements can add to your home's security (opposite page) while they beautify your lot.

DECK AND PATIO LIGHTING

You'll find many light fixtures designed specifically for decks and patios at your home center. Position these lights to shine up from a patio surface, point down at a deck or stair treads, or sit atop posts and provide general illumination. The simplest way to add outdoor lighting is to plug in a string of low-voltage lights. However, keep in mind that these lights look temporary and are easily damaged.

120-VOLT FIXTURES

A flexible lighting system should combine low-voltage lights with standard 120-volt fixtures. Run standard-voltage cable or conduit in trenches (pages 164–165), hide it under decking or railing pieces, or drill long holes through posts and fish it through (page 166). Plan these installations to complement security lighting (page 94).

ROPE LIGHTS

Exterior-grade rope lights can be strung in fanciful patterns or in orderly straight lines. Unless you use a lot of them, they will be more decorative than bright. Plug them directly into a receptacle, or use an extension cord approved for outdoor use. Fasten them to wood posts and railings with galvanized fence staples.

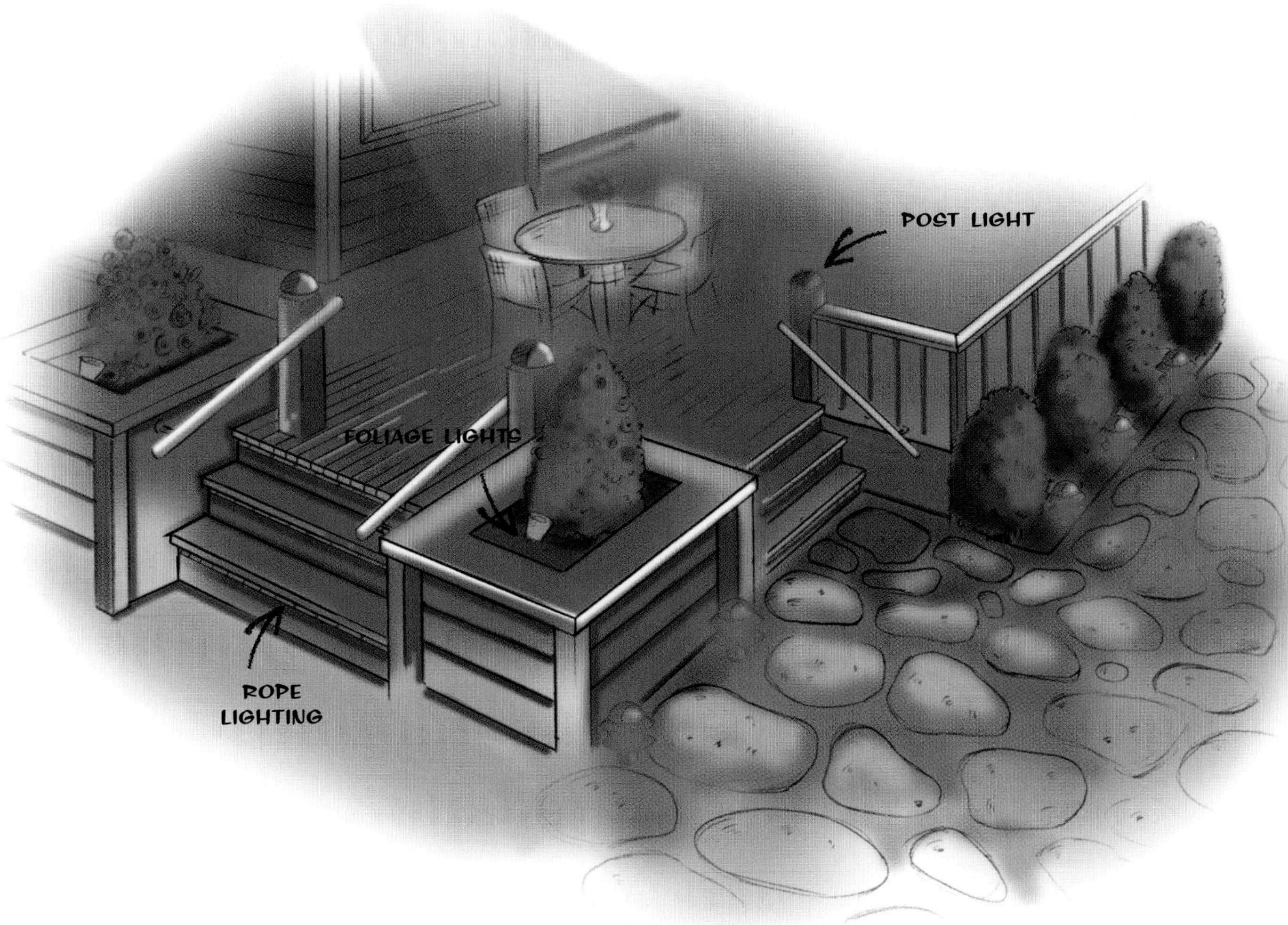

LIGHTING TO SUIT EVERY MOOD AND PURPOSE. Treat outdoor diners to the same even lighting you would expect them to enjoy inside. Point several eave lights at the table, positioning them as high as possible. Rope lights are great as accents and to illuminate steps to help reduce the possibility of tripping. Post lights offer gentle highlights, while other lights give emphasis to specific features, such as plantings and flowers.

7 EASY UPGRADES

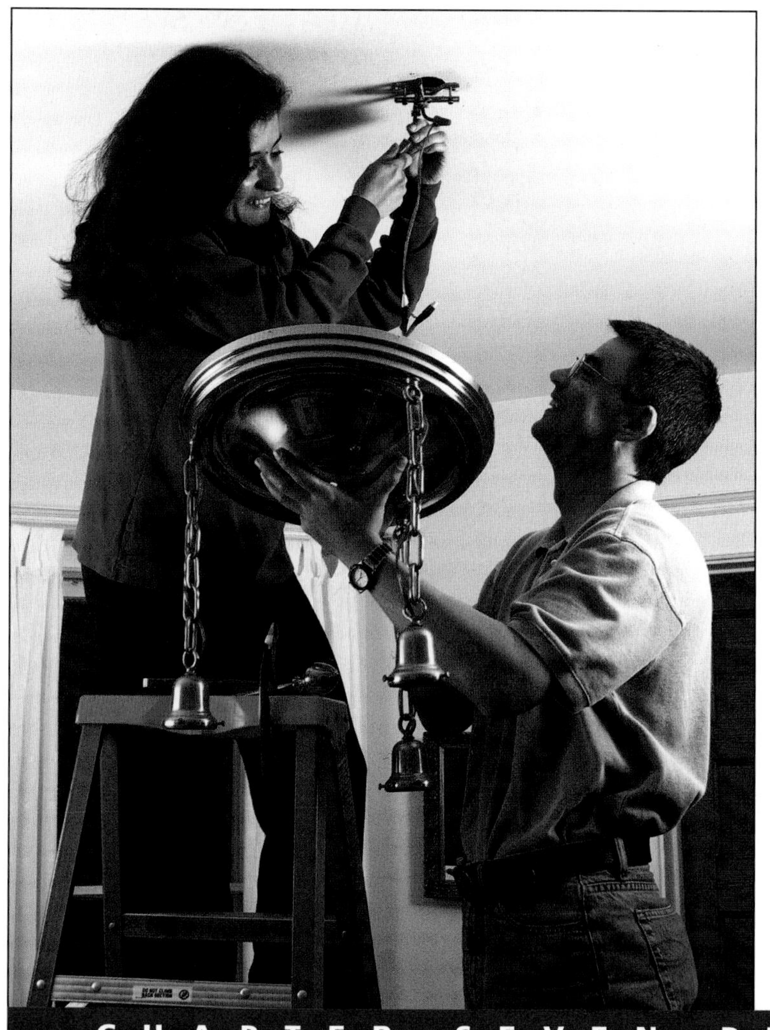

Electrical components come in standard, interchangeable sizes. So, with little difficulty, you can remove an old fixture and replace it with one that has the style or features you want. Most of the fixture and device upgrades in this chapter can be done in less than a day. None of them calls for running new cable or changing electrical boxes. You won't have to calculate loads, make drawings, or tear apart your walls.

Typically, the only wiring you'll have to do involves detaching old wires and attaching new wires or leads. This is simple stuff, but don't be tempted to "hot-wire"—making connections without switching off the power. **Always shut off the power and test for the presence of power before starting these upgrades.**

CHAPTER SEVEN PROJECTS

INSTALLING SPECIAL SWITCHES

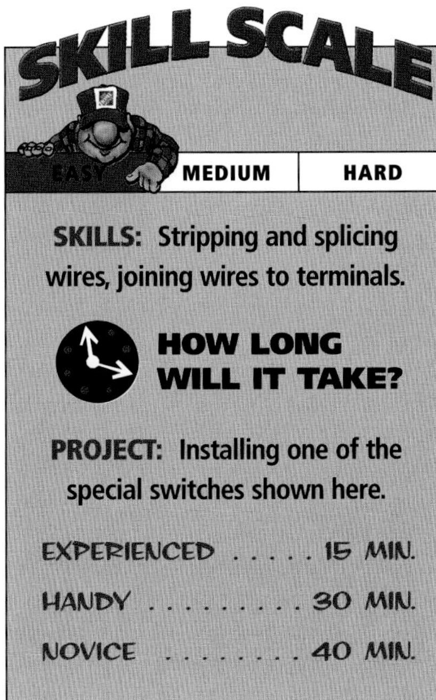

SKILLS: Stripping and splicing wires, joining wires to terminals.

HOW LONG WILL IT TAKE?

PROJECT: Installing one of the special switches shown here.

EXPERIENCED ..... 15 MIN.

HANDY .... 30 MIN.

NOVICE .... 40 MIN.

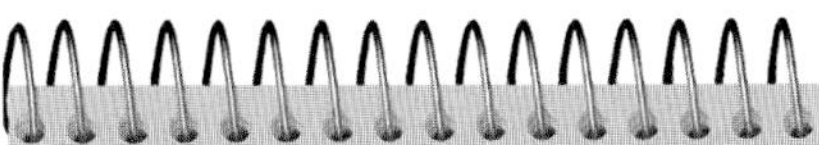

TOOLS: Combination tool, lineman's pliers, screwdriver

MATERIALS: Specialty switch, wire nuts

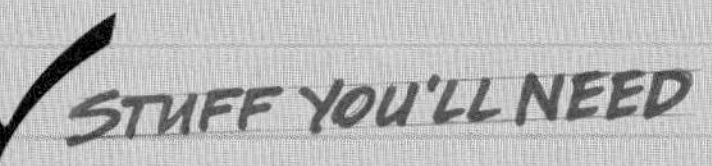

Within an hour, you can install any of several clever switches that do everything from control a circuit at a preset time to switch on a light as you walk into a room. Instead of the familiar screw-down terminals on toggle switches, most special switches have **leads**—short lengths of stranded wire. Shut off power to the circuit. To splice leads, follow the directions on page 47.

TOUCH-SENSITIVE DIMMER. With this switch, you dim or brighten a light by continuing to press the switch, rather than by turning a knob or operating a toggle. Connect the black lead to the black feed wire and the red lead to the black wire (or to the white wire painted black) running to the fixture. Connect the green lead to ground (page 13).

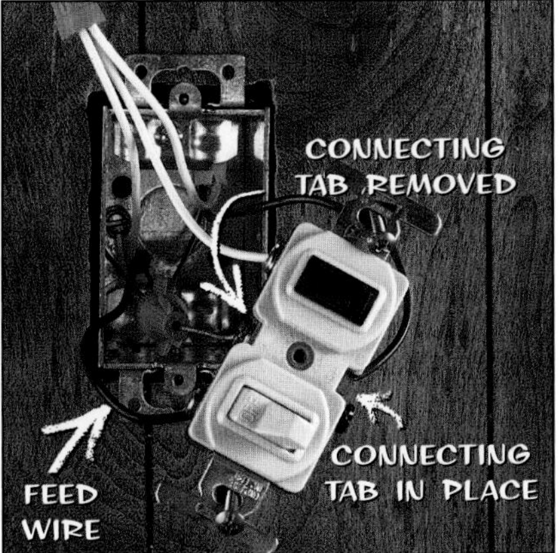

PILOT-LIGHT SWITCH. Use one of these for a garage light or an attic fan—anywhere you can't see the fixture while operating the switch. When the light glows, the fixture is on. Connect the black feed wire to the brass terminal where there is no connecting tab, and the other black wire to a brass terminal on the other side. Pigtail the neutral wires, and connect one to the silver terminal.

ANYWHERE SWITCH.

This switch lets you control a fixture without having to run electrical cable. Wire the receiver inside the fixture, attach the sending switch "anywhere" on a wall, and put in a battery. You can even use these switches in a three-way setup (pages 148–150), and dimmers are also available.

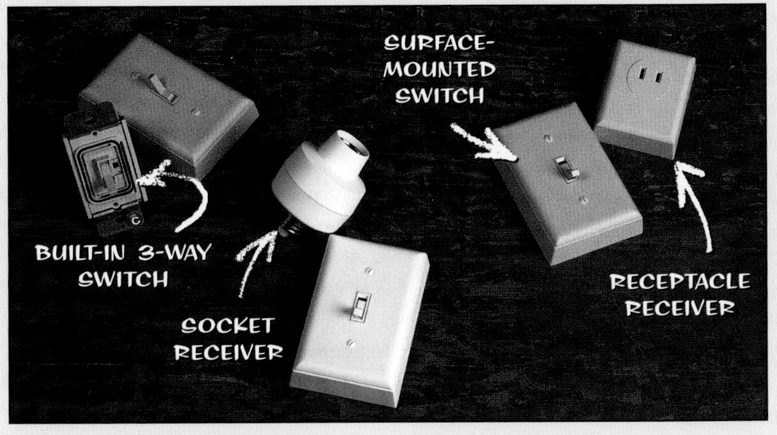

TIMER SWITCH. This switch turns outdoor lights on and off one or more times a day. Install one only if two cables (four wires, not counting the grounds) enter the box. (If only two wires exist, use a programmable switch instead.) Connect the black feed wire to the black lead and the other black wire (which goes to the fixture) to the red lead. Pigtail the whites, and connect them to the white lead.

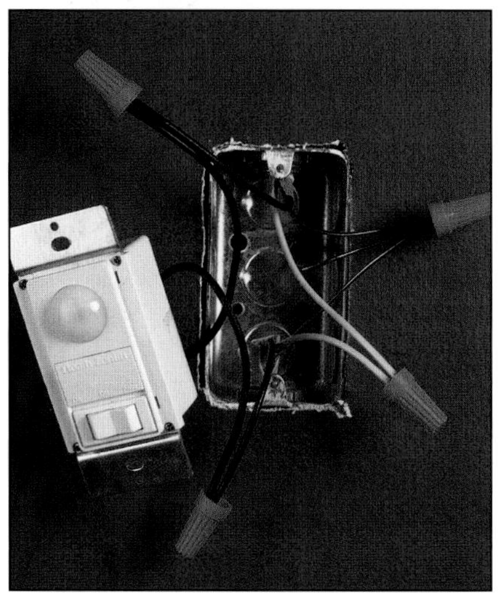

MOTION-SENSOR SWITCH. This switch turns on when its infrared beam senses movement. Adjust the time-delay feature to control how long the light will stay on. Wiring is the same as for a standard single-pole switch (pages 22–23), except that you connect to leads rather than to terminals.

CLOSER LOOK

ONE OR TWO?
If only one cable enters a switch box, then power runs to the fixture. Two wires—a black, and a white wire painted black—run from the fixture to the switch. If two cables enter the switch box, one brings power and the other runs to the fixture. With one cable, the black wire is the feed wire and the black-painted white wire leads to the fixture (page 20). Timer, combination, and pilot-light switches are among those that can be installed only if you have two cables in the box; there must be an unmarked white neutral wire.

EASY UPGRADES

COMBO SWITCHES

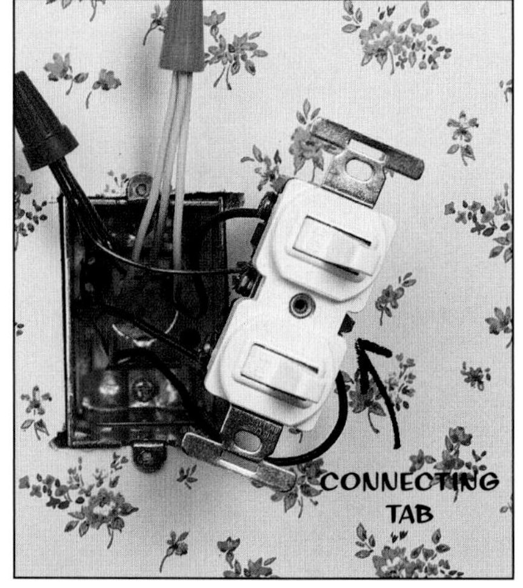

DOUBLE SWITCH. This device allows you to control two fixtures from a single switch box. Three cables enter the box: One brings power and the other two run to fixtures. Hook the feed wire to a terminal on the side that has a connecting tab. Hook the other two black wires to the terminals on the other side of the switch. Splice the white wires and the grounds.

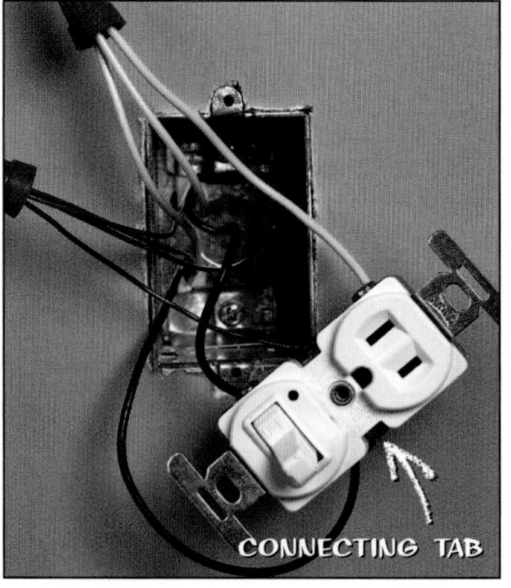

SWITCH/RECEPTACLE. This combines a switch and a grounded receptacle plug in a single switch box. The device usually is wired so the receptacle is hot all the time. Hook the feed wire to a terminal on the side with a connecting tab. Hook the other black wire to a brass terminal on the other side. Pigtail the white wires and hook to the silver terminal.

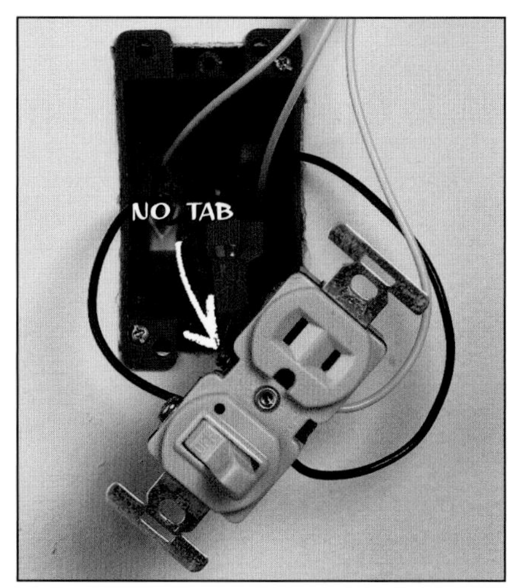

SWITCH/RECEPTACLE WITH RECEPTACLE CONTROLLED BY SWITCH. If you want the receptacle to turn off when the switch is off, reverse the positions of the black wires so the feed wire is on the side that does not have a connecting tab.

INSTALLING A GFCI BREAKER

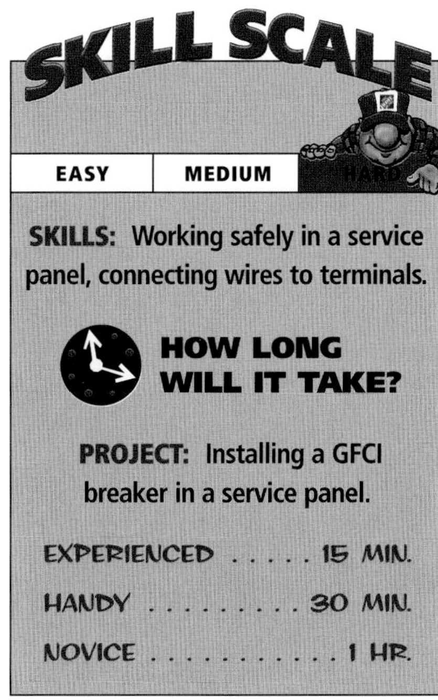

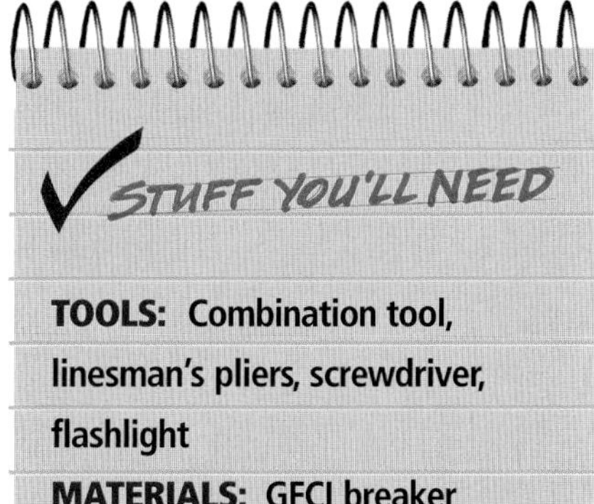

STUFF YOU'LL NEED
TOOLS: Combination tool, linesman's pliers, screwdriver, flashlight
MATERIALS: GFCI breaker

The least expensive way to give a circuit GFCI protection is to install a GFCI receptacle. It can be wired to protect up to four additional receptacles (page 27). However, GFCI receptacles are notoriously short-lived. Because they will continue to provide power even when their ability to protect is lost, test them regularly.

For more reliable protection, install a GFCI circuit breaker. It's expensive, but it protects all the outlets on a circuit. Although you must feel comfortable about working on a service panel, installing a GFCI breaker can be easier than installing a GFCI receptacle. The latter is bulky and often requires a box extender.

See pages 14–15 for general safety instructions for working in a service panel. Always shut off power to the main breaker before you begin working.

LIGHTNING PROTECTION. Lightning will seriously damage a roof, and if it hits the power line coming into your home, lightening may fry your service panel. Nothing will protect your home or electrical system from a direct hit, but some surge protectors will protect against nearby strikes. Or install an arrester system, which is basically an old-fashioned lightning rod. One or more rods are fastened to the highest points on the house, and a thick cable leads from them to the ground. The rod will conduct a reduced charge into the earth.

INSTALLING A GFCI BREAKER. Shut off the main breaker. (This de-energizes all the wires and circuitry after the main breaker, but the wires leading into the service panel will still be live.) Have a flashlight handy. Pull out the existing circuit breaker, loosen the terminal screw, and pull the wire out. Insert that wire into the GFCI breaker, and tighten the screw to clamp the wire tight. Detach the line's white wire from the neutral bus, and attach it to the breaker. Push the GFCI breaker into place as you would a standard breaker (page 80). Attach the curly white wire to the neutral bus bar, and restore power.

ADDING SURGE PROTECTION

SKILLS: Installing an arrester, stripping and connecting wires.

HOW LONG WILL IT TAKE?

PROJECT: Installing a surge arrester in a service panel.

EXPERIENCED . . . . 20 MIN.
HANDY . . . . 40 MIN.
NOVICE . . . . 1 HR.

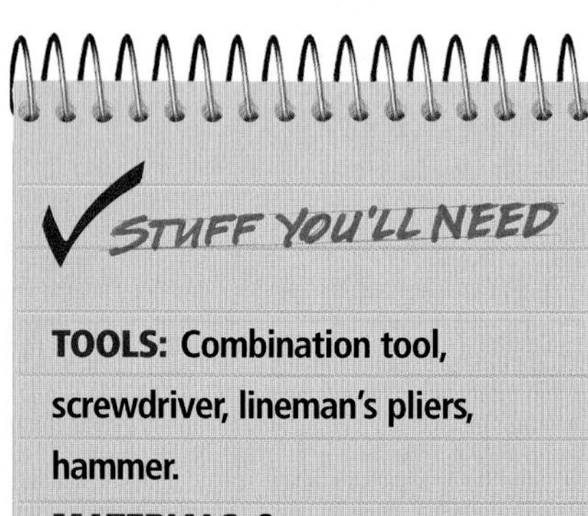

TOOLS: Combination tool, screwdriver, lineman's pliers, hammer.

MATERIALS: Surge arrester

Once in a while, power supplied by your utility company may suddenly increase for a few milliseconds. This "surge" does not affect most electrical components, but it can damage sensitive electronic equipment, such as computers and televisions. A surge on your telephone line can destroy your modem and damage your computer. So buy surge protection. The higher a device's "joule" (a unit of strength of energy) rating, the better the protection. A surge arrester or protector will work only if the electrical system is grounded.

POWER STRIP SURGE SUPPRESSOR. An inexpensive device like this not only protects against surges but makes it easy to organize all those cords in a home office. Just plug it in. To protect a modem and computer, spend a little more for a device with a phone connection.

SURGE-PROTECTING CONSOLE. Available at stores that sell computers, under-monitor devices protect electronic equipment and phone lines from surges. They also help you organize the tangle of cords behind your desk.

WORK SMARTER

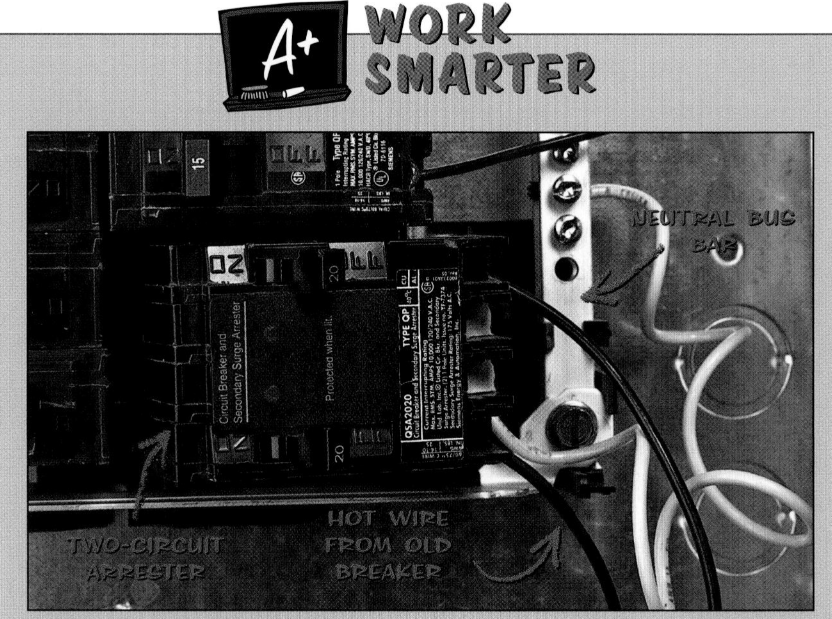

ARRESTER IN BREAKER BOX. To install an arrester that covers two circuits, shut off the main breaker. Remove two circuit breakers. Switch the breaker toggles to OFF. Push the breaker into place (page 80). Transfer the black wires from the old breakers to the terminals of the arrester. Attach the curly white wire to the neutral bus bar (make sure there are no kinks). Restore power and switch the arrester breakers on. Another type of surge arrester protects the entire panel.

EASY UPGRADES

INSTALLING TRACK LIGHTING

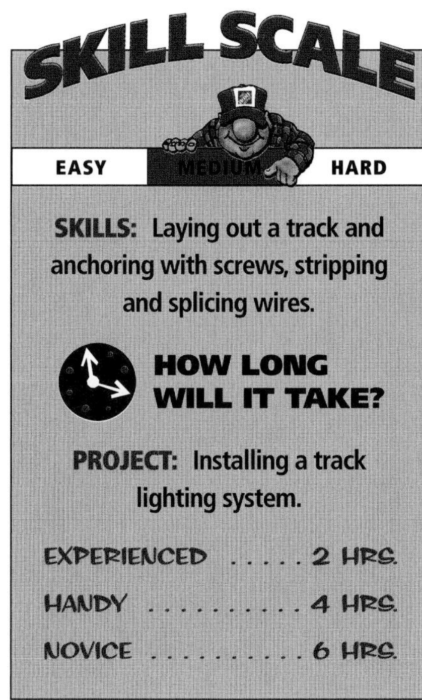

SKILL SCALE
EASY
MEDIUM
HARD
SKILLS: Laying out a track and anchoring with screws, stripping and splicing wires.
HOW LONG WILL IT TAKE?
PROJECT: Installing a track lighting system.
EXPERIENCED . . . . . 2 HRS.
HANDY . . . . 4 HRS.
NOVICE . . . . 6 HRS.

STUFF YOU'LL NEED
TOOLS: Combination tool, lineman's pliers, drill with screwdriver bit, tape measure, hacksaw
MATERIALS: Track system with lights, wire nuts, screws, plastic anchors

A track system is the most versatile of all ceiling fixtures. You can configure it in many ways (page 88), choose from several lamp styles, and position the lamps to suit your needs. To begin installation, remove the existing ceiling fixture to locate the track. If you don't have an existing ceiling fixture that is switched, see pages 146–147 for how to install a new one.

PURCHASING A TRACK SYSTEM. Work with a salesperson; explain the size and configuration you want. Buy a kit that includes track, mounting plate, end cap, and canopy. You also may have to buy additional track and end caps, as well as L- or T- fittings for the corners. Choose the lights and bulbs when you buy the tracks. You can put different types of lamps on the same track, but be sure to purchase lamps made by the same manufacturer as the track—otherwise the two may be incompatible.

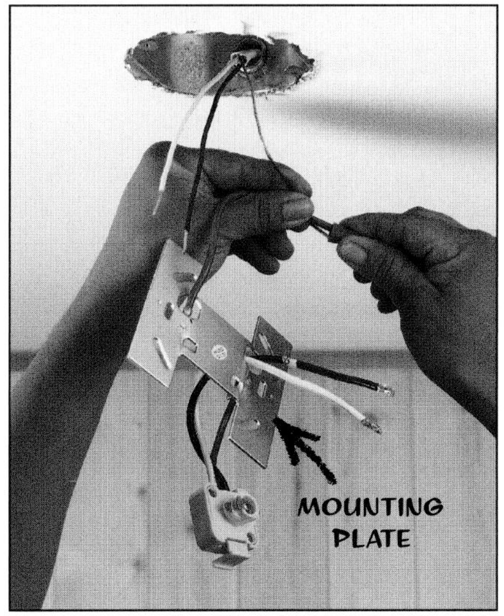

1 INSTALL THE MOUNTING PLATE. Shut off power at the service panel. Use wire nuts to splice the house wires to the plate leads. Connect the ground wire to the plate and to the box if it is metal (pages 32–33). Push the wires into the box, and screw the plate to the box so it is snug against the ceiling.

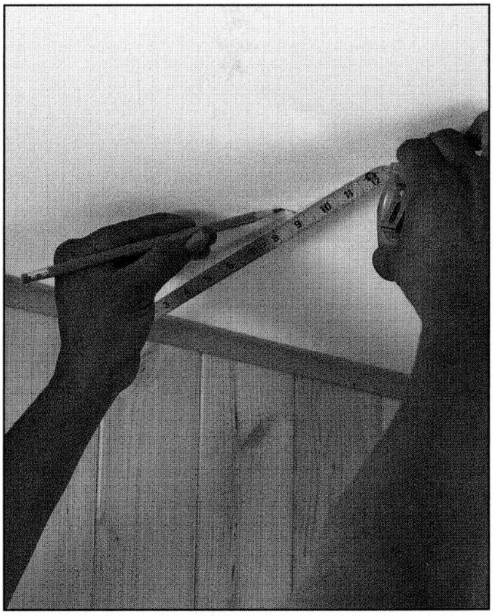

2 MEASURE AND MARK FOR THE TRACK. At the mounting plate, measure to see how far the side of the track will be from the nearest wall. Mark the ceiling so the track will be consistently parallel to the wall. Use a framing square to draw lines if the track turns a corner.

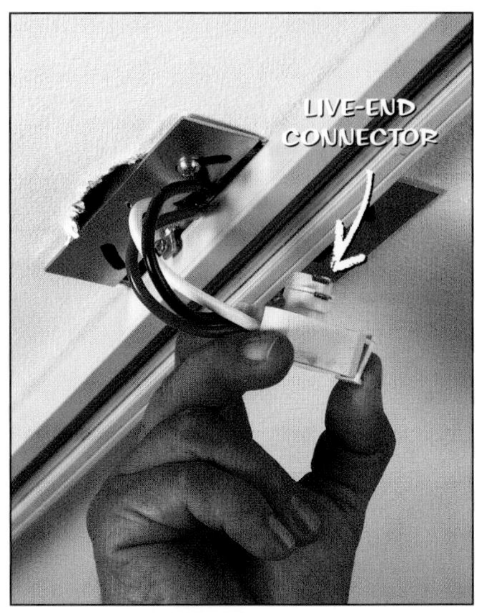

3 ATTACH THE TRACK TO THE MOUNTING PLATE. Have a helper hold the track in place against the ceiling and centered on the mounting plate. Drive the setscrews to anchor the track to the plate.

4 SECURE THE TRACK. Use a stud finder to locate joists. If the track is more than 4 feet long, have a helper hold one end while you work. Snap the track onto the plate, and drive a screw into every available joist. If there are no joists, drill holes every foot or so, insert plastic anchors, and drive screws into the anchors.

5 TWIST ON THE LIVE-END CONNECTOR. Insert the live-end connector and turn it 90 degrees until it snaps into place. Align the connector's two copper tabs with the two copper bars inside the track. Snap the plastic canopy over the track and mounting plate.

6 ATTACH A CORNER. You can buy connectors to make 90-degree turns, T- shapes, or odd-angled turns. Slide the connector into the track that is already installed, slide the next track onto the connector, and attach that track to the ceiling. Cover all open track ends with end caps.

7 TWIST ON A LIGHT. This type of light twists into place in the same way as the live-end connector (Step 5). Another type has a metal arm that is twisted to tighten. Restore power, turn on the switch, and swivel the lights to position them for the best effect.

CLOSER LOOK

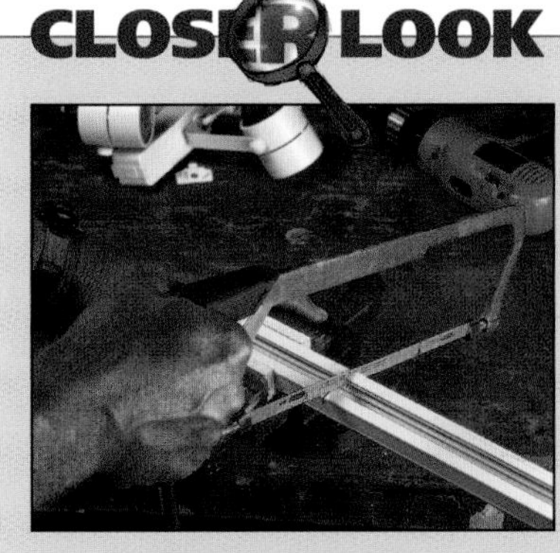

CUTTING TRACK.

Tracks are available in standard lengths of 2, 4, 6, and 8 feet. If these sizes do not fit your needs, cut a track with a hacksaw or a sabersaw equipped with a fine-toothed metal-cutting blade. Clamp the track in a vice or hold it firmly with your hand as you cut. Cut slowly and take care not to bend the track while cutting. Reattach the plastic end piece.

INSTALLING FLUORESCENT LIGHTING

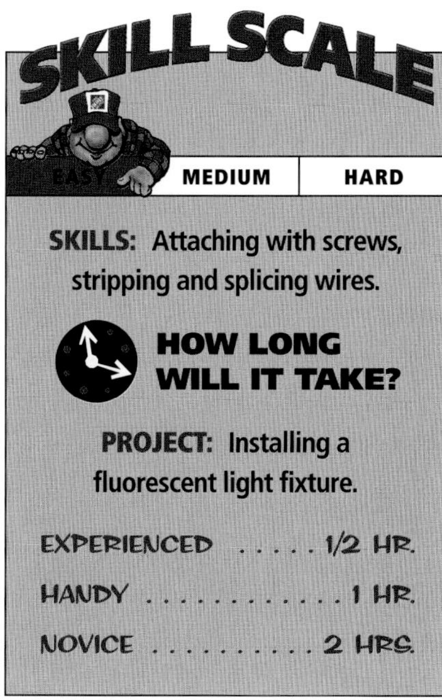

SKILLS: Attaching with screws, stripping and splicing wires.

HOW LONG WILL IT TAKE?

PROJECT: Installing a fluorescent light fixture.

EXPERIENCED ..... 1/2 HR.
HANDY .... 1 HR.
NOVICE .... 2 HRS.

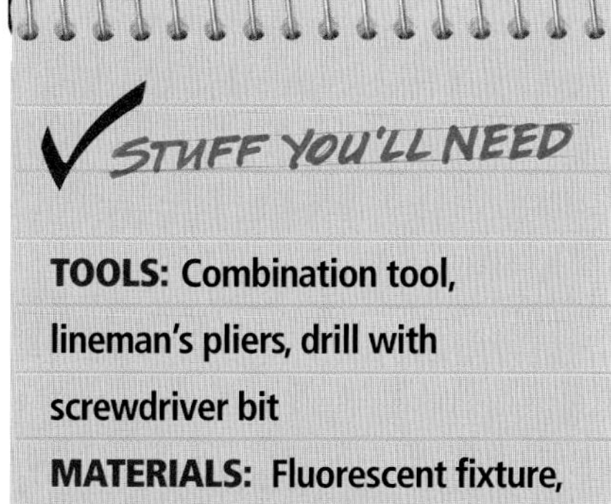

STUFF YOU'LL NEED

TOOLS: Combination tool, lineman's pliers, drill with screwdriver bit

MATERIALS: Fluorescent fixture, wire nuts, screws

Fluorescent lights often are installed without a ceiling box: Cable is clamped to the fixture, which substitutes for a box. However, some codes require that fluorescent lights be attached to ceiling boxes. Suspend the fixture or set it in a suspended ceiling grid and make the connections. Square or rectangular fixtures with long tubes are the most common. Other fluorescent fixtures are shaped like incandescents and use circular or U-shape tubes.

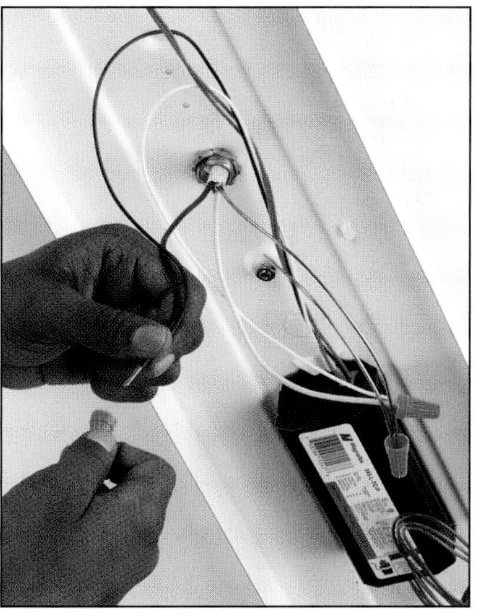

INSTALLING A FLUORESCENT. Shut off power at the service panel. Remove the old fixture. Clamp the cable to a knockout in the new fixture and attach the fixture directly to the ceiling by driving screws into joists. Splice the fixture's wires to the incoming wires. Attach the cover plate.

CONSIDER FLUORESCENT LIGHTING OPTIONS.

- **If an old fluorescent light needs a new ballast (page 78), consider replacing the fixture. Newer fluorescents with electronic ballasts are trouble-free for decades.**
- **Save energy costs by replacing an incandescent ceiling light with a fluorescent.**
- **Fluorescent tubes offer a greater variety of light than ever (page 86). A diffusing lens further softens the light.**

INSTALLING FLUORESCENTS IN A SUSPENDED CEILING. Fluorescent fixtures fit into the ceiling grid, taking up the space of a 2×2–foot (shown) or 2×4–foot ceiling tile. For smaller fixtures, install additional metal grid pieces and cut ceiling tiles to fit in either side. When you've established your power source for the lights (see pages 128–129 for how to extend the incoming line), install the grid, then attach the cable to the fixture, leaving more than enough cable to reach the power source. Connect to the power source before adding the tiles.

INSTALLING HALOGEN LIGHTING

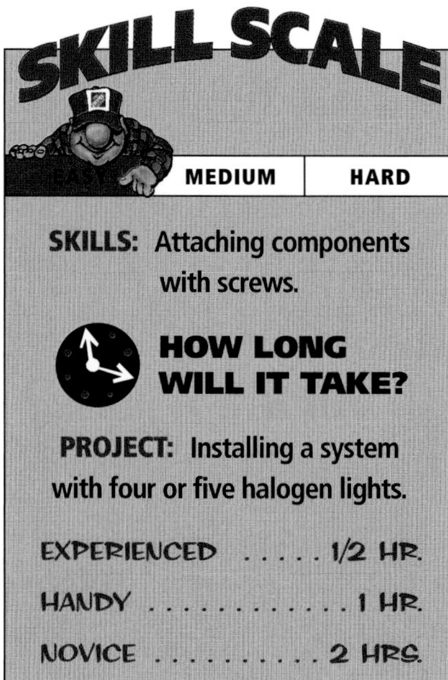

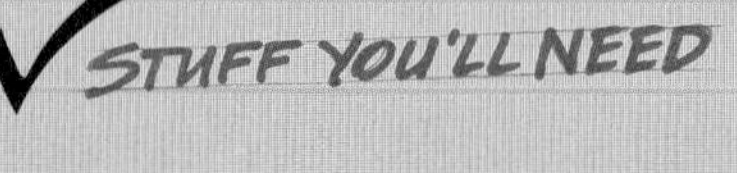

TOOLS: Drill with screwdriver bit, combination tool, hammer

MATERIALS: Halogen kit (wire, lights, terminal block, transformer, cord switch), insulated staples

To light counters or display shelves, consider a halogen puck light kit that plugs into a receptacle. A typical kit includes a transformer, cord, cord switch, several hockey-puck-shape lights that are attached to the underside of shelves or cabinets, and detailed instructions. If you don't like using a cord switch, plug the kit into a receptacle controlled by a switch (page 99), or alter a receptacle and run cable so one outlet can be switched off and on (page 143).

HALOGEN SAFETY TIPS

Halogens provide intense, almost glittering light and they get hot. Position them where people won't brush against them. Don't attach them to particleboard that may scorch. Use halogens in a closet only if you are sure they will always be 18 inches or more away from clothing or boxes. If you use them in small, enclosed spaces, such as shelves with glass doors, reduce the heat by replacing a 20-watt bulb with a 10-watt bulb. Drill ¼-inch air vent holes in the cabinet above the puck lights.

- Halogens are very bright. Position them so they will be out of sight.
- Never use a halogen without the lens, which filters UV rays.
- Do not touch a bulb with your skin; natural oils will damage a bulb. Always handle halogen bulbs with a soft cloth.

INSTALLING HALOGEN ROPE LIGHTS. To install rope lights, simply staple a rope into place and plug it in. It's bright enough to use as under-cabinet countertop lighting and doesn't get as hot as "puck" lighting. Install rope lights in a straight line, or drape them in soft loops.

A round-top stapler (page 180) makes it easier to attach the wires.

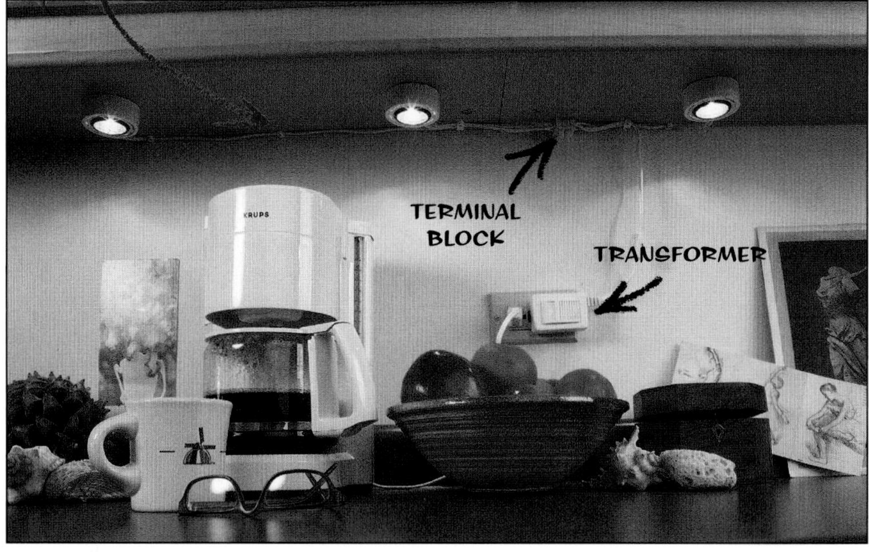

INSTALLING PUCK LIGHTING. Drill ¼-inch holes to run wires, or plan to staple wires to the surface. Remove the covers from the lights, and mount the light bodies with screws. Snap on the trim rings, threading the wires through any holes. Attach a terminal block at a central location. Cut the transformer wires to length, strip the ends, and insert them into the terminal block. Plug the transformer into the wall. Staple down any loose wires.

INSTALLING TRAPEZE LIGHTS

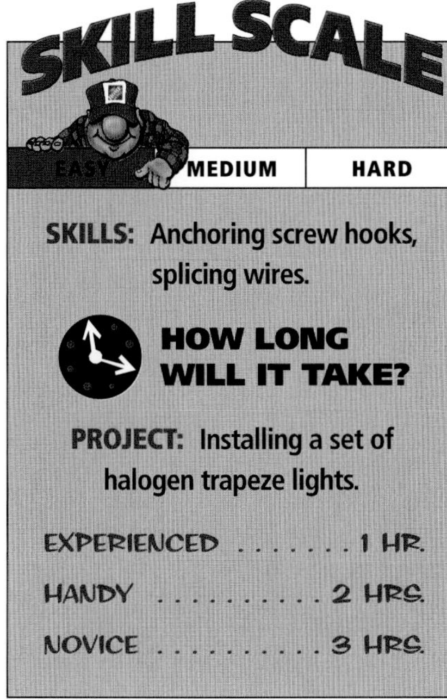

SKILLS: Anchoring screw hooks, splicing wires.

HOW LONG WILL IT TAKE?

PROJECT: Installing a set of halogen trapeze lights.

EXPERIENCED .... 1 HR.
HANDY .... 2 HRS.
NOVICE .... 3 HRS.

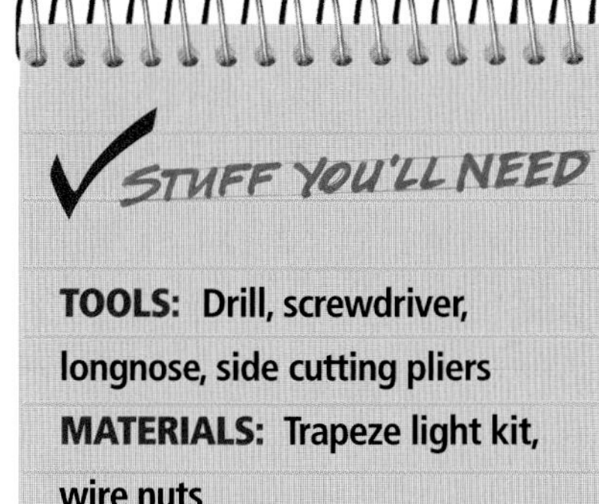

✓ STUFF YOU'LL NEED

TOOLS: Drill, screwdriver, longnose, side cutting pliers
MATERIALS: Trapeze light kit, wire nuts

These halogen fixtures are stylish, energy efficient, and—because you can easily point them to do the most good—versatile. The exposed wires are not dangerous because they carry very low voltage. Remove an existing ceiling light and attach a canopy transformer to the ceiling box (as shown in Step 2), or insert a plug-in transformer into a switched receptacle (page 143).

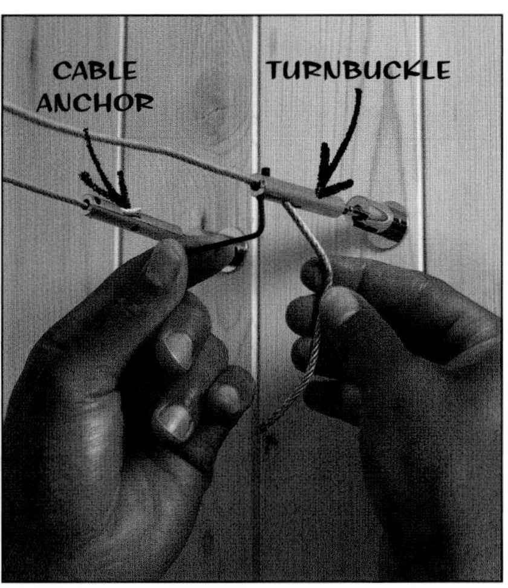

1 STRETCH THE CABLES. Shut off power. Remove the light fixture (page 28) or install and run cable to a ceiling box (pages 122–132) where you plan to install the lights. Attach two cable anchors on the walls between which the unit will hang. Cut two lengths of cable to span the length of the installation. Fasten cables to the anchors and tighten the turnbuckle until the cables are taut.

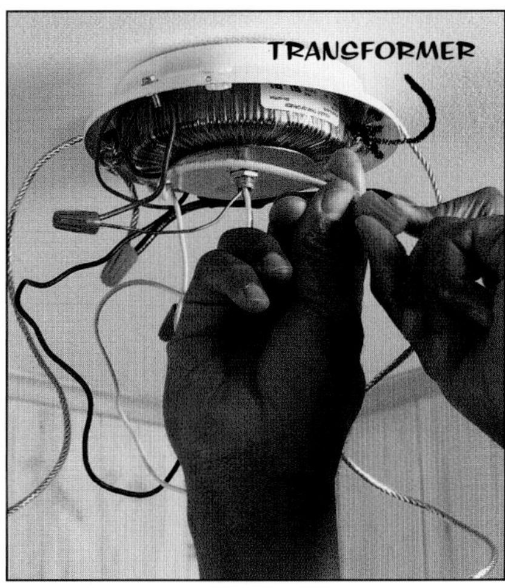

2 INSTALL THE TRANSFORMER. Install a strap on the ceiling box (pages 28–29). Mount the transformer onto the strap. Splice the canopy transformer's red lead to the house's black wire, and splice white to white wires. Connect the green lead to the ground (page 13).

Go ahead and adjust the lights while the power is on. The voltage is so low you won't feel a thing.

3 CONNECT THE LOW-VOLTAGE WIRES. You may have to cut the low-voltage leads to the right length, restrip the clear insulation, and reattach the leads to the transformer. Clamp the leads onto the stretched cables using the fasteners provided with the kit. Attach the cover to the transformer.

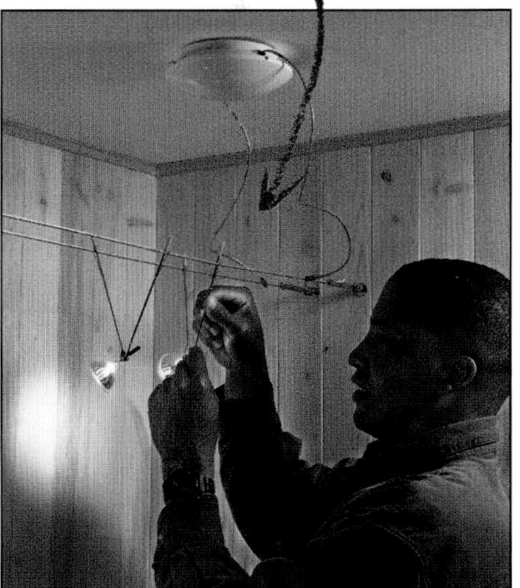

4 HANG THE LIGHTS. Hold a halogen with a cloth (oil from your skin will damage it), and push the pins into a light arm. Slip the spring clamp over a wire, position the light arm on the cable, and clip the spring clamp onto the cable. Restore power and test.

GROUNDING RECEPTACLES

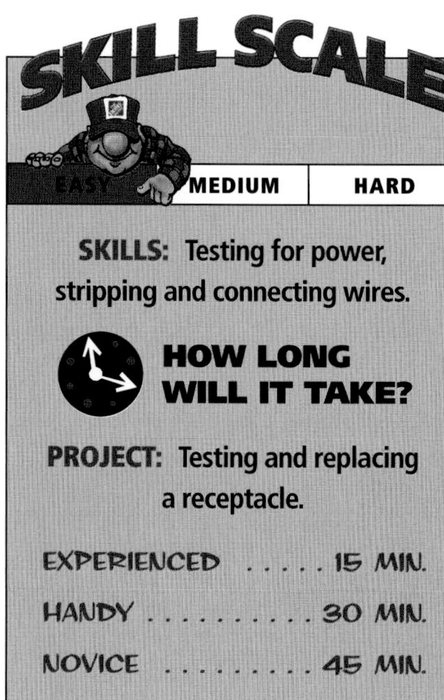

SKILL SCALE
EASY
MEDIUM
HARD
SKILLS: Testing for power, stripping and connecting wires.
HOW LONG WILL IT TAKE?
PROJECT: Testing and replacing a receptacle.
EXPERIENCED ..... 15 MIN.
HANDY .... 30 MIN.
NOVICE .... 45 MIN.

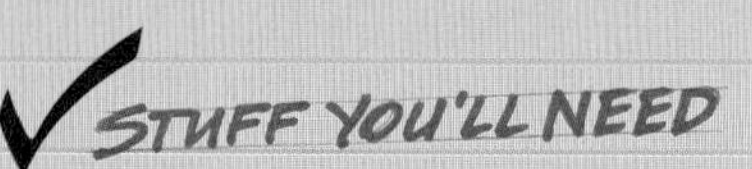

✓ STUFF YOU'LL NEED

TOOLS: Voltage tester or multitester, combination tool, screwdriver, longnose pliers

MATERIALS: Grounded receptacle, electrician's tape

If a receptacle is ungrounded (with two slots only, and no grounding hole), its box may actually be grounded. If so, simply install a grounded receptacle. Do not install a grounded receptacle if the box is not grounded—you'll give the false impression the box is grounded when it is not. (For a description of grounding, see pages 11–13.)

If a box is ungrounded, ground it by running a #12 green insulated or bare copper wire to a cold-water pipe. Or, install a GFCI receptacle (page 27), which will provide greater protection than grounding.

1 TEST AN UNGROUNDED RECEPTACLE FOR GROUND. Scrape off any paint from the mounting screw. Insert one probe of a voltage tester or multitester into one receptacle slot, and touch the other to the mounting screw. Repeat test for other slot. If voltage is present, the box is grounded and you can install a three-hole receptacle.

2 TEST AGAIN. If the first test is negative, remove the cover plate and repeat the first test, but touch the metal box, rather than the mounting screw, with one probe. If power is now indicated, you can install a grounded receptacle.

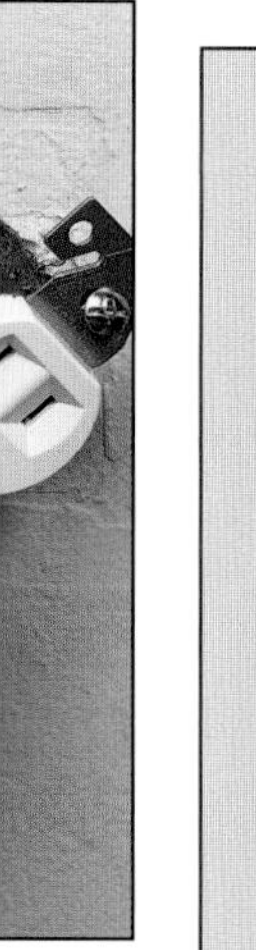

3 INSTALL A GROUNDED RECEPTACLE. Snip off the stripped wire ends, which could break if they are bent again, and restrip. See page 20 for wiring directions. Be sure to test with a receptacle analyzer. If the test shows the receptacle is not polarized, switch the wires.

SAFETY ALERT!

AVOID GROUNDING ADAPTERS. This type of adapter works if it is connected to the mounting screw of a grounded box. But it's not much work to install a grounded receptacle, so there's no good reason to use an adapter. It's prohibited by some local codes and illegal in Canada.

INSTALLING MOTION-SENSOR LIGHTS

SKILL SCALE
EASY
MEDIUM
HARD
SKILLS: Stripping and splicing wires.
HOW LONG WILL IT TAKE?
PROJECT: Installing and adjusting a motion-sensor light.
EXPERIENCED .... 1 HR.
HANDY .... 1 1/2 HRS.
NOVICE .... 2 HRS.

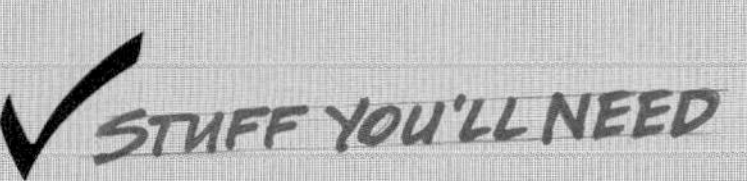

STUFF YOU'LL NEED

TOOLS: Combination tool, screwdriver

MATERIALS: Motion sensor light, wire nuts, electrician's tape, perhaps a mounting strap

Motion-sensor lights greet you when you come home at night, and they discourage potential burglars. If you have an existing floodlight, they are easy to install. (To install an exterior box for a new light, see pages 162–163.)

Choose a fixture that lets you control the time and the sensitivity to motion. If the light is connected to a switch inside the house, you can override the motion sensor so the light stays on or off.

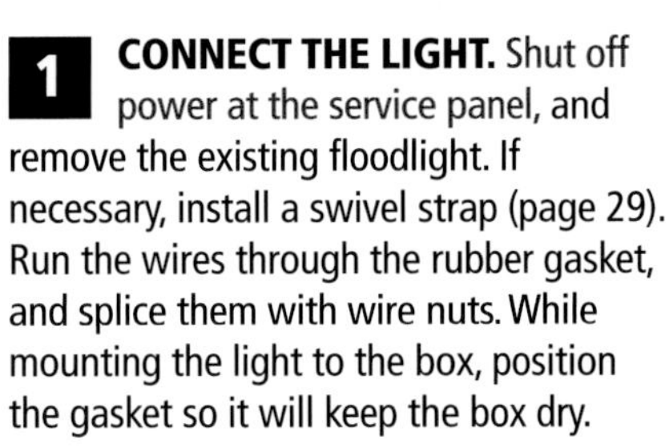

1 CONNECT THE LIGHT. Shut off power at the service panel, and remove the existing floodlight. If necessary, install a swivel strap (page 29). Run the wires through the rubber gasket, and splice them with wire nuts. While mounting the light to the box, position the gasket so it will keep the box dry.

2 POSITION THE LIGHT. Restore power. Loosen the locknuts and twist the light until it is directed where you want it. Tighten the locknuts. At night, turn the light on permanently by flipping off the wall switch, then on again.

3 MAKE ADJUSTMENTS. To activate the motion sensor, manufacturer's instructions will probably tell you to turn off the wall switch, wait a few seconds, and turn it back on. Choose how long you want the light to stay on (ON TIME). There may be a control that keeps the light less bright for the amount of time you choose (DUAL BRIGHT). Set the RANGE to the middle position, and test how sensitive the motion sensor is by walking around near it. Adjust if necessary.

Homer's Hindsight

BE KIND TO YOUR NEIGHBORS. I positioned my floodlight and adjusted the sensitivity so the light would shine on any intruder who set foot on my property. Unfortunately, everyone walking on the sidewalk at night set off the light, making them feel like they were making a prison break! To keep peace with my neighbors, I readjusted the light.

CHAPTER 8 PLANNING FOR NEW SERVICES

Once you are comfortable with projects like replacing devices and fixtures, you're ready to go—not boldly, but carefully—where few homeowners dare to tread. You're ready to add new electrical service. "New service" refers to running new cable. It can be as simple as tapping into a receptacle to add a new line (page 141) or as complex as installing several new circuits in a subpanel (pages 168–171).

This chapter helps you ask the right questions and come up with the best solutions so your new installation will do what you want it to do, and do it safely. You'll learn which tools and materials to buy, how to balance loads on a circuit and draw plans, and how to anticipate code requirements.

CHAPTER EIGHT TOPICS

BUYING TOOLS TO RUN NEW LINES

The money you pay for quality electrical tools will be minor compared to how much you'll save by doing the work yourself. To run new lines, you will need most of the tools shown here, as well as those on pages 42–43. Buy everything you need; the job will go easier.

FOR CUTTING INTO WALLS

These tools pave the way for installing electrical cable and boxes. The right tools, along with sharp bits and blades, will do the least damage to walls, saving you patching time afterwards. Consider buying a **corded power drill** with a 3/8-inch chuck for large bits. (A cordless drill may not have the power or capacity to drill numerous holes in walls and framing.) Have several 5/8-inch and 3/4-inch **spade bits** on hand; they dull quickly. A **fishing bit** drills holes in hard-to-reach joists and studs. The **bender** helps you aim the bit where you want it to go. Once the hole is drilled, the bender has a **pulling attachment** that allows you to pull the cable with the bit.

Use a **drywall saw** to cut small holes in drywall. To cut through plaster and lath, use a **saber saw** with a fine-cutting blade, or use a **rotary-cutting tool.** A **flat pry bar** is ideal for trim removal and modest demolition. A **utility knife** is an essential all-purpose tool.

RENT A RIGHT-ANGLE DRILL. If you need to drill, say, 20 holes or more through studs or joists, you probably should rent a 1/2-inch right-angle drill.

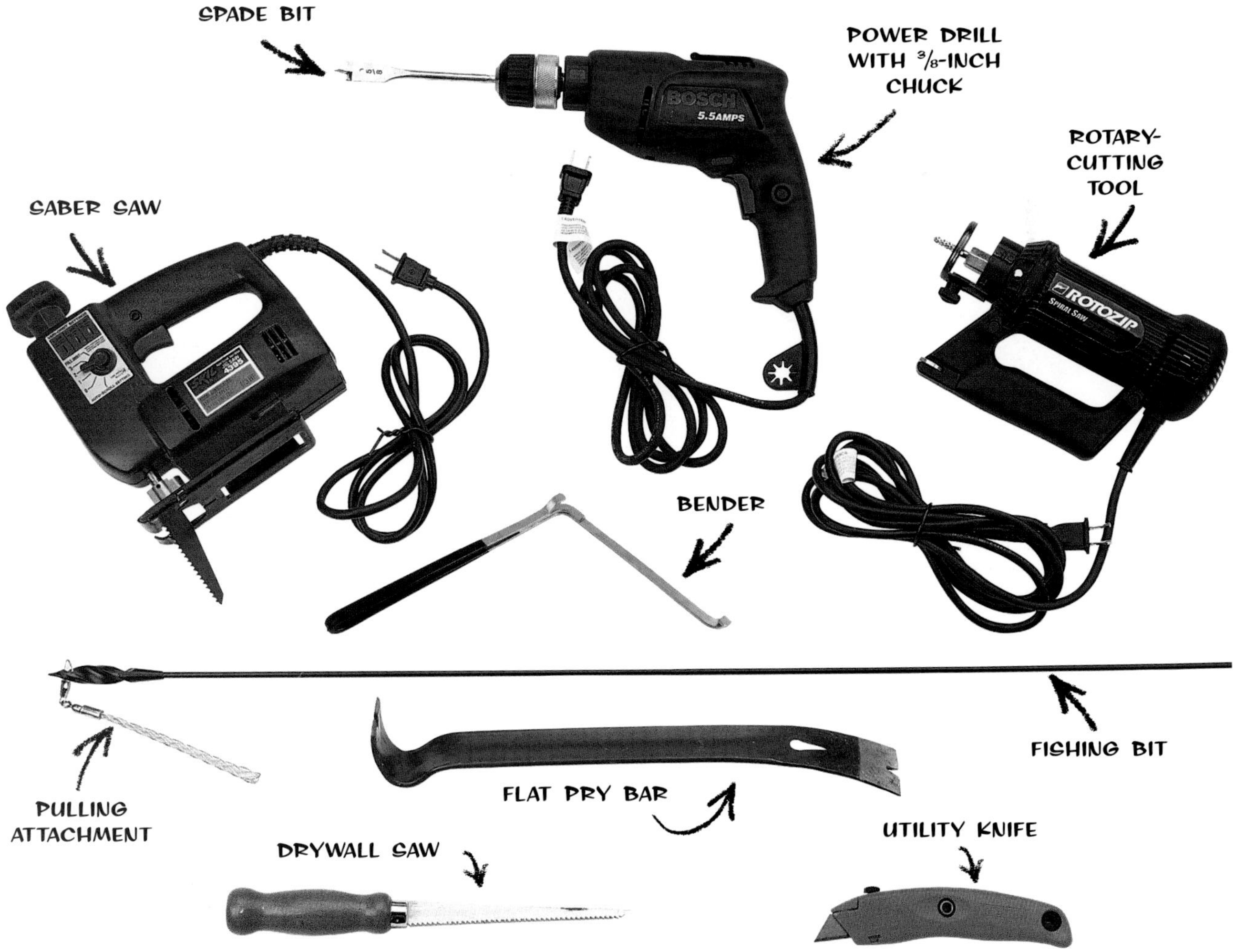

SPADE BIT

POWER DRILL WITH 3/8-INCH CHUCK

ROTARY-CUTTING TOOL

SABER SAW

BENDER

FISHING BIT

PULLING ATTACHMENT

FLAT PRY BAR

UTILITY KNIFE

DRYWALL SAW

MAPPING A JOB

Building departments require detailed drawings and comprehensive lists of materials before issuing permits. To save yourself and the inspector aggravation, do your best to make your drawing clear and complete.

DRAW A PLAN

If you'll be wiring existing space, measure the rooms and make a scale drawing on graph paper. If you have blueprints for a new addition, use those. Make several copies of the floor plan so you can start over if you make mistakes. Include windows, doors, cabinets, and other obstructions.

Begin by drawing in all the switches, receptacles, and fixtures, using the symbols below. Then use color pencils to draw the cable runs. Use a different color for each circuit. Mark each cable—for example, "14/2 WG" for a cable with two #14 wires and a ground wire.

As you draw, make a list of materials, tallying the number of boxes, devices, and fixtures, and roughly figuring how much cable you will need.

DON'T FORGET

Check and double-check your drawing and your list.

- Make sure none of the circuits is overloaded (pages 116–117).
- See that switches are conveniently placed to easily turn on lights.
- Consider how each room will be used, and add devices where necessary. For instance, a home office with a computer should have a dedicated circuit.
- Make sure all your boxes will be large enough (page 116).
- Remember that if you add circuits, you may need to expand service with a subpanel (pages 170–171), a new service panel (page 172), or even a new line from the utility to your house. Determine how to run cable to the service panel or subpanel.

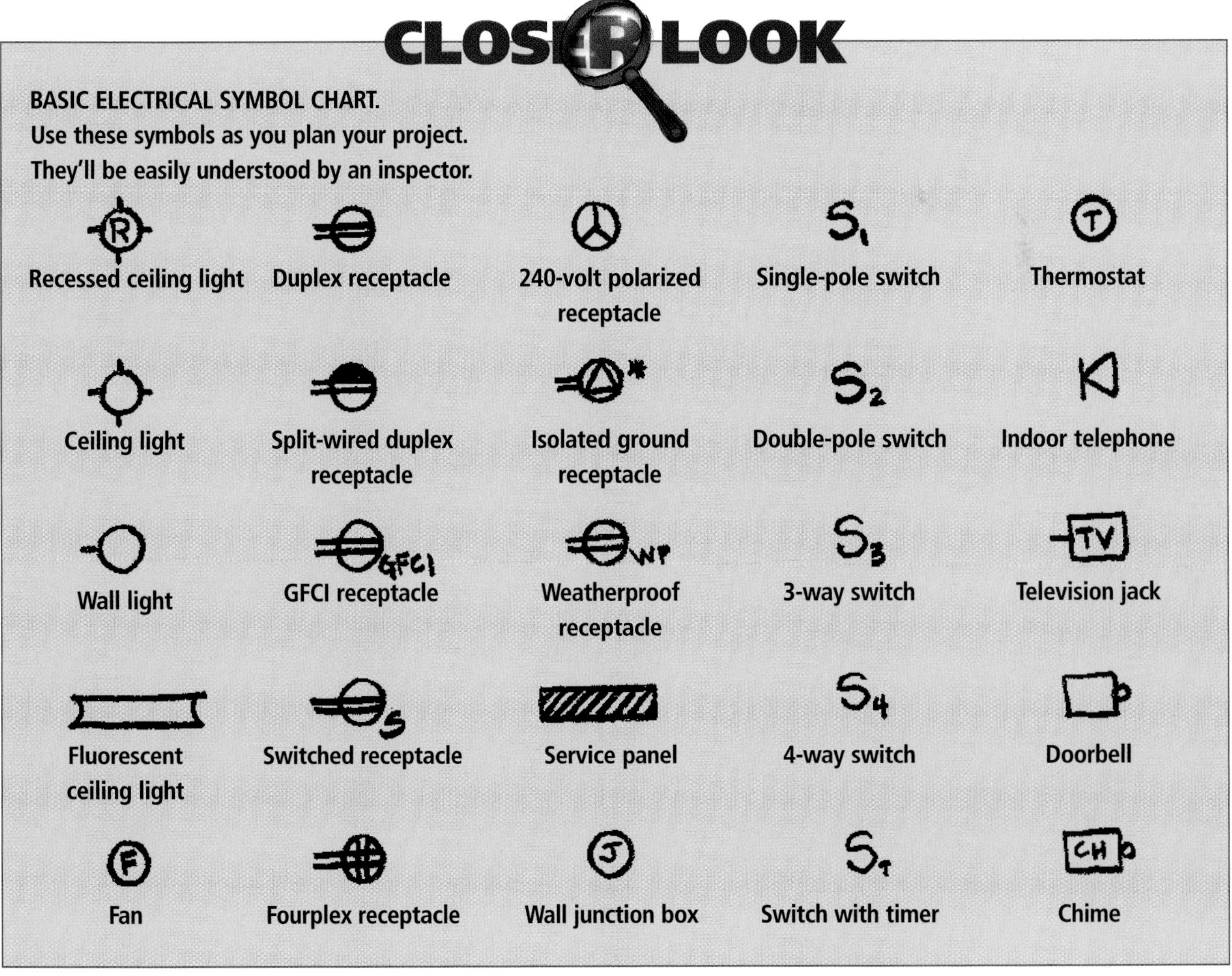

CODES YOU MAY ENCOUNTER

Here's a quick summary of codes that are typical for household wiring projects. Follow them as you work up your plans and write your materials list.

These guidelines should satisfy most requirements, but keep in mind that your local codes might have different requirements. You probably will want to exceed requirements in order to provide your family with sufficient and safe electrical service.

The more you communicate your specific plans and techniques to your inspector, the less chance that you will have to tear out and do the job over again. It's better to be set straight by your inspector when the job is still on paper.

CABLE TYPE

Most locales allow NM (nonmetallic) cable for all installations where the cable runs inside walls or ceilings. Some areas require armored cable or conduit. If the cable will be exposed, many local codes require armored cable or conduit.

WIRE GAUGE

Use #14 wire for 15-amp circuits, and #12 wire for 20-amp circuits.

PLASTIC AND METAL BOXES

Many locales allow plastic boxes for receptacles, switches, and fixtures; but some require metal boxes. Boxes must be flush with the finished drywall, plaster, or paneling. Make sure boxes are large enough for their conductors (page 116).

RUNNING CABLE

NM and armored cable must be run through holes in the center of studs or joists so that a drywall or trim nail cannot reach it. Most codes require metal nail guards as well. Some inspectors want cable for receptacles to be run about 10 inches above the receptacles. NM cable should be stapled to a stud or joist within 8 inches of the box it enters. Once the cable is clamped to a box, at least ¼ inch of sheathing should be visible in the box, and at least 8 inches of wire should be available for connecting to the device or fixture.

CIRCUIT CAPACITY

Make sure usage does not exceed "safe capacity" (pages 62–63). Local codes may be stricter.

LIVING ROOM, DINING ROOM, FAMILY ROOM, AND BEDROOM SPECS

Space receptacles no more than 12 feet apart along each wall. If a small section of wall (between two doors, for example) is more than 2 feet wide, it should have a receptacle. For most purposes, use 15-amp receptacles. Every room should have at least one light controlled by a wall switch near the entry door. The switch may control an overhead light or one outlet of a receptacle, into which you can plug a lamp. Attach a ceiling fan to an approved ceiling fan box, not a standard box. Ceiling lights must be controlled by wall switches, never by pull chain switches.

HALLWAY AND STAIRWAY SPECS

A stairway should have an overhead light controlled by three-way switches at the bottom and top of the stairs. If a hallway is more than 10 feet long, it must have at least one receptacle.

KITCHEN SPECS

Above countertops, space receptacles no more than 4 feet apart. All countertop receptacles must be GFCI. However, some codes call for split-circuit receptacles above a countertop, which cannot be GFCI. Install one 15-amp circuit for lighting, two 20-amp circuits for receptacles, and separate circuits for the dishwasher and refrigerator. (Canada: Kitchens must have split 15-amp circuits only—no 20-amp circuits.)

BATHROOM SPECS

Any GFCI receptacle should be on its own circuit. Install the lights and fan on a separate 15- or 20-amp circuit.

GARAGE AND WORKSHOP SPECS

Install a 15-amp circuit for lights and a 20-amp circuit for tools. Install two 20-amp circuits if you have many power tools. Many areas require GFCIs in garages. Check your local code.

COMMON CODE REQUIREMENTS

It's your house and you're doing the work yourself. Why should a city inspector come around and tell you what to do? Codes and inspections are a sort of collective wisdom based on the experience of nearly a century of living with electricity. Those lessons have been incorporated into electrical codes. These codes exist to prevent house fires and injury from shocks, and to keep your electrical system running well.

MEETING NATIONAL, PROVINCIAL, AND LOCAL CODES

Whenever you run new electrical cable, your local building department will require you to get a permit and have the work approved by one of its inspectors. Inspectors and building departments use the *National Electrical Code* (NEC) as the basis for most of their regulations. However, local standards often supplement or modify these basic rules.

You'll find some of the most common code requirements in the chart (opposite). The list is not complete, however, and you may need other sources of information.

You can buy a copy of the NEC, but it costs about $50 and is difficult to wade through. Most of its many pages deal with such items as commercial installations that homeowners will never encounter. Many useful handbooks on the NEC are available. Buy one, or borrow one from a library, that emphasizes residential installations.

COORDINATING THE TASKS

If you are building an addition to your house or gutting walls to remodel a kitchen or bathroom, you'll need to juggle carpentry, plumbing, and wall and floor finishing. Whether you do all or some of the work yourself, it's important that the various jobs are coordinated so that workers do not get in the way of each other and so that inspectors can see what they need to inspect. Aim for this sequence: **(1)** Install framing or gut the walls. **(2)** Run the rough plumbing, install electrical cable and boxes, and then call in the inspector. **(3)** Cover the walls with drywall, and paint. **(4)** Install the finish plumbing and electrical, and have it inspected.

WORKING WITH INSPECTORS

Inspectors usually work with professional electricians who know codes and what is expected at inspections. Inspectors usually have a tight schedule and can't take time to educate you about what is needed. Their job is to inspect, not to help you plan your project. Take these steps to assure that the inspections go smoothly.

- Before scheduling an inspection, ask the building department for printed information about your type of electrical project. Make neat, readable, and complete drawings (pages 114–115), and provide a list of the materials.
- When you present your plans, accept criticisms and directives graciously. It usually does no good to argue—and the inspector does know more than you do. Make it clear that you want to do things the right way. Take notes while the inspector talks to you so you can remember every detail of what needs to be done.
- Be clear on when the inspections will take place and exactly what needs to be done before each inspection. Before calling for an inspection, double-check that everything required is complete—don't make the inspector come back again. Don't cover up wiring that the inspector needs to see. If you install drywall before the inspection, you may have to rip it out and reinstall it after the inspection.
- Some building departments limit the kinds of work that a homeowner can do; you may have to hire a professional for at least part of a job. Others will let you take on advanced work only if you can pass an oral or written test.

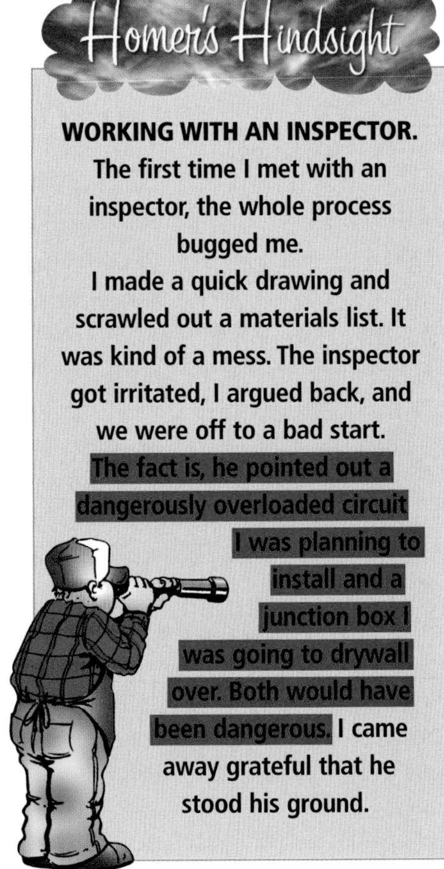

Homer's Hindsight
WORKING WITH AN INSPECTOR.
The first time I met with an inspector, the whole process bugged me.
I made a quick drawing and scrawled out a materials list. It was kind of a mess. The inspector got irritated, I argued back, and we were off to a bad start.
The fact is, he pointed out a dangerously overloaded circuit I was planning to install and a junction box I was going to drywall over. Both would have been dangerous. I came away grateful that he stood his ground.

PLANNING FOR NEW SERVICES

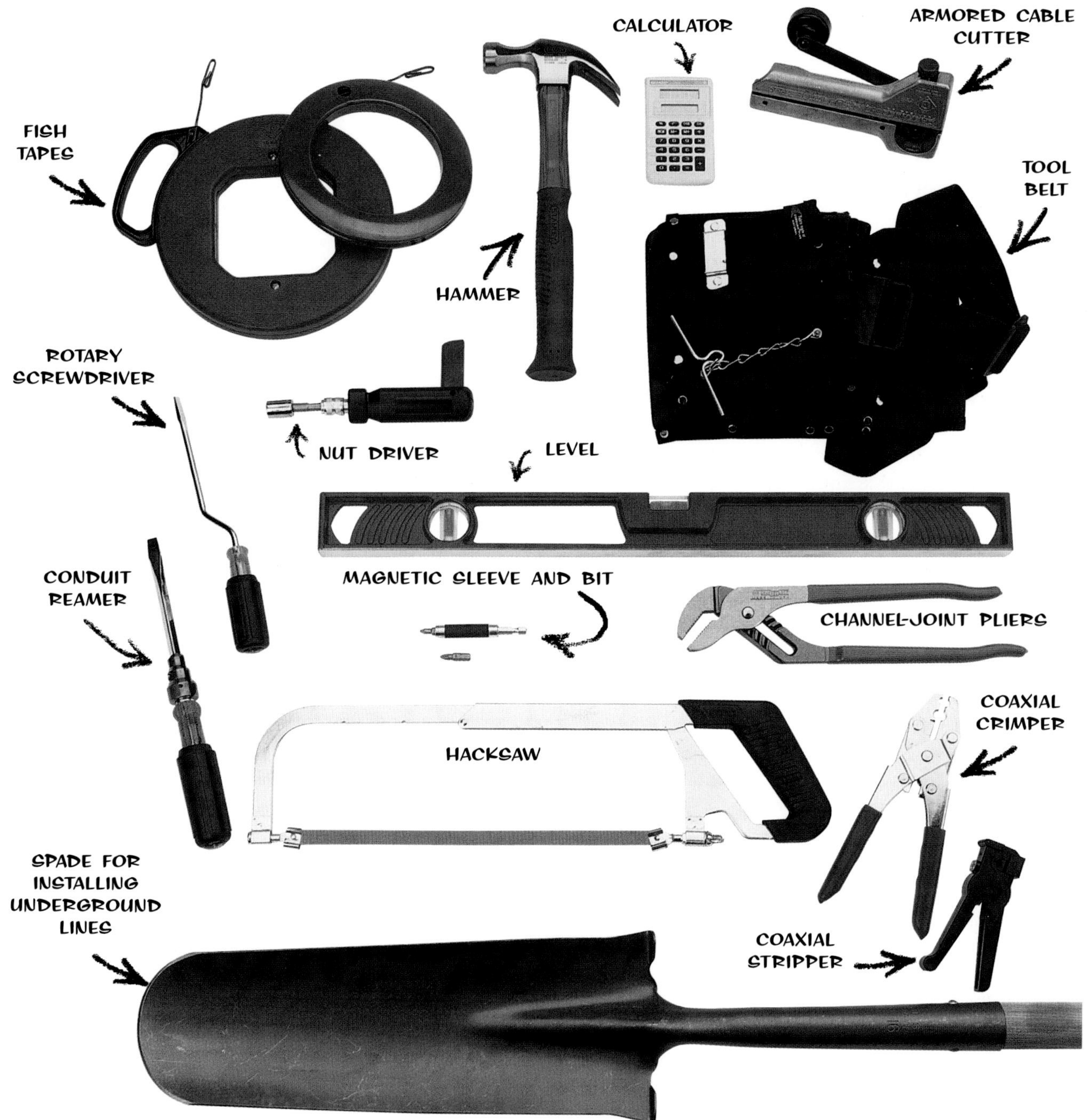

FOR RUNNING NEW LINES

Complete your kit with these relatively inexpensive tools. When working with armored cable, you may want to use an **armored cable cutter** (see page 124 for other options). For figuring circuit loads, use a small hand-held **calculator.** A **fish tape** helps you to run cable through finished walls and pull wires through conduit. Sometimes you need two tapes so that you can hook them together (page 131).

Buy an electrician's **tool belt** so you won't fumble around for tools. You'll use a **hammer** to tap locknuts tight onto cable clamps. If a box or fixture has bolts instead of screws, you'll need a **nut driver.** Use a **level** to mark cutouts on walls and square up boxes.

To drive screws quickly and firmly, nothing beats a drill with a **magnetic sleeve.** Insert small screwdriver bits into its tip, and they will be magnetized so you can drive screws with one hand. With a **rotary screwdriver,** you can drive or remove small screws on cover plates, switches, and receptacles in a flash.

You may need a pair of **channel-joint pliers** for handling connectors. Cut conduit with a **hacksaw** equipped with a professional-quality blade that will last longer. After cutting the conduit, remove burrs with a **conduit reamer.** For coaxial cable, use a **crimper** and a **stripper.** Use a **narrow spade** to excavate for outdoor cable.

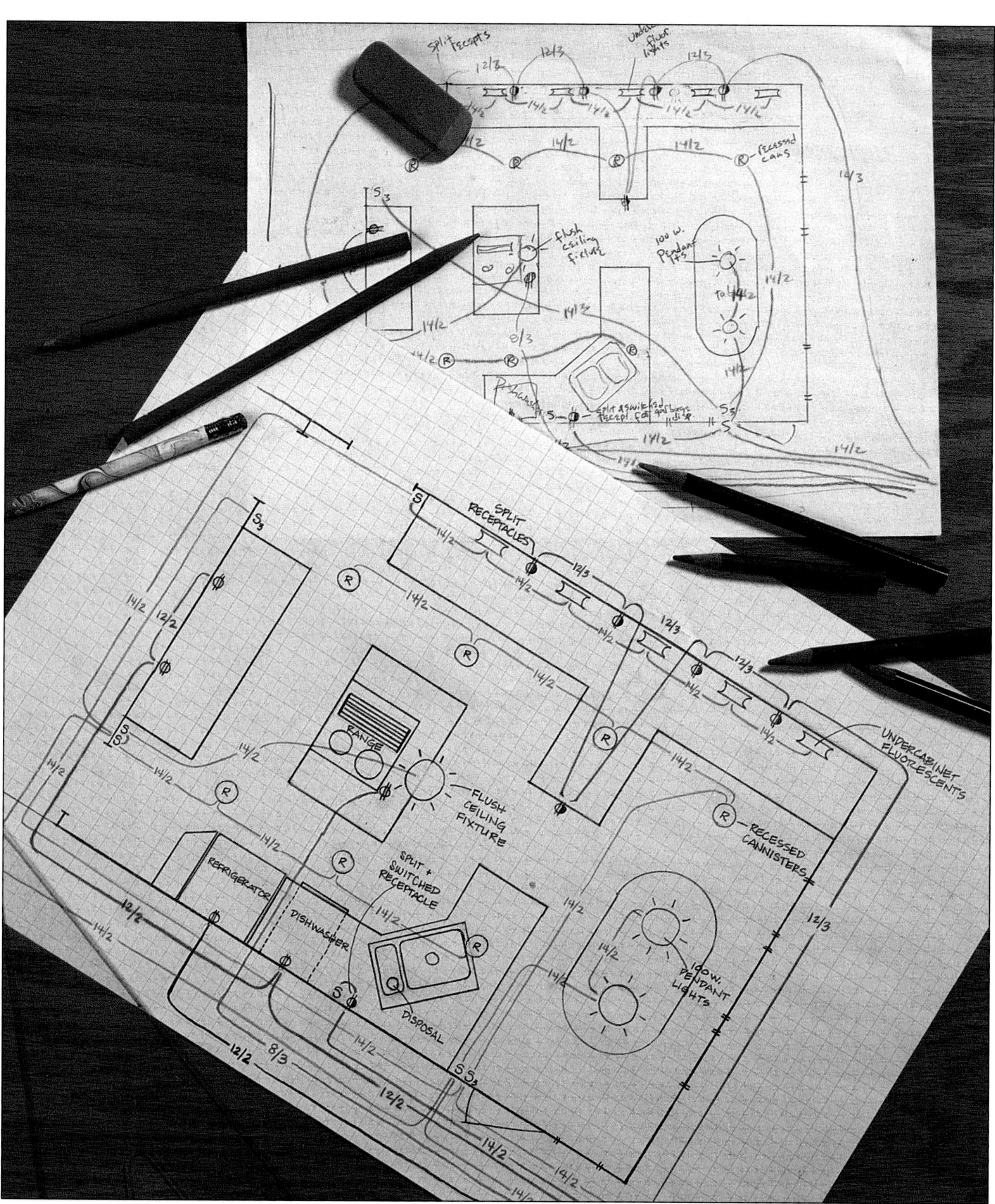

MAKE A PLAN. Draw a floor plan of your project and make an extra copy or two. Use color pencils to distinguish your circuits. Add symbols for the various devices (they'll be useful when making your materials list). When you're satisfied with your plan, make a clean version to copy for the city and for your own use.

LOADING CIRCUITS CORRECTLY

When planning to add new service to your home, ask three important questions: First, will any individual circuit become overloaded as a result of adding service? Second, is your service panel large enough to accommodate any new circuits you will be adding? And finally, is the power entering your home from the utility company sufficient for your needs?

LOADING INDIVIDUAL CIRCUITS

If you will be extending an existing circuit to add a receptacle or a light fixture, make sure you won't overload that circuit. List all the receptacles, fixtures, and appliances on that circuit, and then add the wattage of the new service to determine whether you will be within "safe usage." (See pages 62–63 to make this calculation.)

SIZING UP A SERVICE PANEL

If existing circuits are not large enough to accommodate the new service you want to install, or if you will be wiring an addition, install new circuits.

Open your service panel (see page 60). If you see available blank slots, adding a circuit will be easy. If all the spaces are taken up, you may be able to add service by installing a tandem breaker (page 117).

Older homes with fuse boxes often receive 60-amp service from the utility company. If your wiring is less than 40 years old, your home probably has 100-amp service. Larger homes built in the last 15 years may have 200-amp service. The total amperage for your home is usually written on the main breaker or fuse.

GOT ENOUGH POWER?

If you add up the amperage of all the breakers in the box, you will probably find that the total is more than the overall rating of the service panel. For example, a 100-amp service panel may have breakers totaling 220 amps. This does not mean that it is over capacity.

The amperage rating tells you how much amperage each hot **bus bar** (page 14–15) delivers. So each vertical row of breakers on a 100-amp box delivers 100 amps. And the breakers on a single bar can exceed the total capacity, because all the lights, fixtures, receptacles, and

SIZING ELECTRICAL BOXES

Electrical codes calculate the cubic-inch capacity of boxes and then determine how many wires—and of what size—each box can accommodate.

A #14 wire occupies 2 cubic inches; a #12 wire occupies 2.25 cubic inches. (Canada: Use 1.5 cubic inches per #14 wire and 2 cubic inches per #12 wire.)

When counting the number of wires in a box, count a switch, receptacle, or any portion of a fixture that extends into the box as one wire.

As a general rule, buy large boxes unless you don't have room in your wall or ceiling. The bigger boxes don't cost much more, and they will give you room for upgrades in the future.

A METAL BOX used for a three-way switch holds nine #14 "wires"—two blacks, two whites, one red, three grounds, and one switch, for a total of 18 cubic inches.

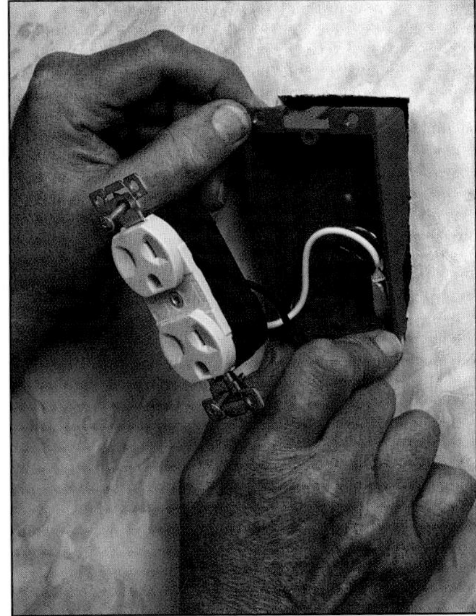

A PLASTIC BOX used for an end-of-the-line receptacle has only four #14 wires—a white, a black, a ground, and the receptacle, for a total of only 8 cubic inches.

appliances will never run at the same time.

A home with more than 2000 square feet will probably need more than 60-amp service. A house with less than 4,000 square feet that doesn't have electric heat or central air-conditioning probably needs no more than 100-amp service.

COMPUTING YOUR EXACT POWER NEEDS

To more accurately determine whether you have enough service, compute your home's electrical usage in watts. (Remember, watts = volts × amps; page 62). The *National Electric Code (NEC)* uses this formula (also see chart below).

- Multiply the overall square footage of your home by 3 to determine lighting and receptacle needs.
- For each kitchen appliance circuit and the laundry room circuit, add 1500 watts. Or add the total wattage used by all permanent appliances, such as the dishwasher, clothes dryer, and electric range.
- Add it all up. Because you'll never use every outlet at full tilt at once, the NEC figures the first 10,000 watts at 100 percent and then adds 40 percent of the rest.
- Add the wattage of either the central air-conditioning or the heating unit, whichever is greater.
- Divide by 230 to figure how many amps you need. In the example below, 85 amps is needed, so 100-amp service is adequate.

If you need more power, consult with the utility company. They may need to install new wires, an expensive proposition.

CLOSER LOOK

SAMPLE WORKSHEET FOR AN 1,800-SQUARE-FOOT HOME.

CIRCUITS	WATTS × CIRCUITS OR ITEMS	TOTALS
Basic lighting and receptacle load, in watts:	1,800 × 3 =	5,400
Two kitchen appliance circuits, one laundry circuit:	1,500 × 3 =	4,500
Dedicated circuits:		
Range	11,500	
Dishwasher	1,100	
Garbage Disposal	900	
Others	+ 3,300 =	16,800
	Subtotal:	26,700
First 10,000 at 100 percent	10,000 × 100%	10,000
Balance of subtotal at 40 percent	+ 16,700 × 40%	6,680
	=	16,680
Air-conditioner or heating unit (greater of two)	+ 2,800 =	19,480
Determine amps by dividing watts by 230	19,480 ÷ 230 =	85 amps
Conclusion: 100-amp service is sufficient.		

NEED MORE CIRCUITS?
Here are some options if you need more circuits than your service panel can provide.

ADD A TANDEM BREAKER. You may be able to install a tandem breaker, which supplies two circuits but uses only one slot. Check local codes to see whether tandem breakers are allowed for your service panel. You may need to install a subpanel or a new service panel instead (pages 170–172).

USE A BREAKER BOX EQUIPPED FOR NEW CIRCUITS. This box has plenty of room for new circuits. A standard 120-volt breaker will take up one slot, and a 240-volt breaker will use two spaces.

CHOOSING BOXES

All electrical connections must be contained inside a box. And all boxes—including junction boxes—must be accessible. Never cover a box with drywall or paneling. Some fixtures, such as recessed cans and fluorescent lights, contain their own boxes so connections can be made inside them.

Be sure to buy boxes large enough to avoid crowding the wires (page 116).

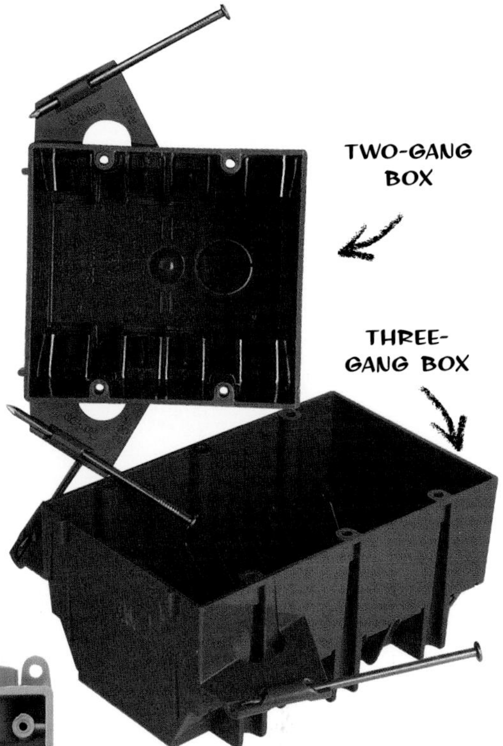

TWO-GANG BOX

THREE-GANG BOX

PVC OUTDOOR BOX

CEILING REMODEL BOX

PLASTIC BOXES

In many areas, plastic boxes are the norm for all indoor residential wiring. They are inexpensive and quick to install. To install most new-work boxes, position and drive in the two nails. To install **remodel boxes** (boxes installed in walls already covered by drywall or plaster), see page 133–134.

Of course, you cannot ground a plastic box. For that reason, some local codes do not allow them, or they allow them only for certain purposes.

Some plastic boxes have holes with knockout tabs, so the cable is not held in place by the box. In that case, you must use cable clamps and staple the cable within 8 inches of the box. Other boxes have built-in metal or plastic cable clamps. Check local codes to see whether clamps are required.

Plastic boxes are easier to damage than metal boxes. When installing a new-work box, all it takes is one wrong swing with your hammer to crack the box. Never install a box that is cracked. Buy several extra boxes just in case.

Most plastic boxes are brittle, so don't use them where they are not built into the wall. The exception is an outdoor box made of especially strong PVC plastic.

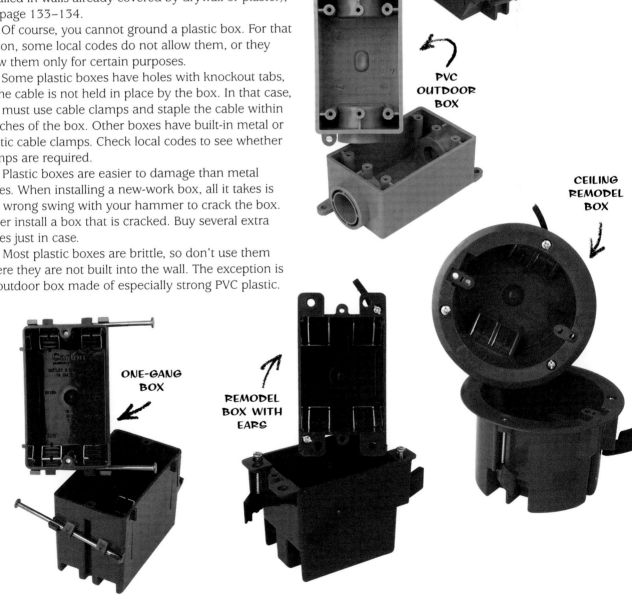

ONE-GANG BOX

REMODEL BOX WITH EARS

METAL BOXES

Even if the local building department does not require metal boxes, you may prefer them because they are stronger and provide a better ground connection. Many codes require that all junction boxes—and all exposed boxes—be metal (with the exception of an outdoor PVC box, shown opposite). If a system uses conduit or armored cable and does not have a ground wire, the boxes must be metal in to provide a grounding path to the cable or conduit.

New-work metal boxes often have nailing brackets. Position the box, and drive screws or nails through the holes and into a stud or joist.

To open a knockout hole in a metal box, punch it with a hammer and screwdriver; then grab the slug from the inside with linesman's pliers and twist it off. Install a cable clamp if the box does not have built-in clamps.

Gangable boxes can be dismantled and ganged together to make space for two or more devices.

Install most switch boxes and ceiling boxes flush with the finished wall or ceiling surface. Install a junction box ½ inch behind the wall surface and add a **mud ring**—also called an adapter plate—which has screw holes for the cover plate. Choose a 4×4 junction box or a larger 4¹¹⁄₁₆-inch box. Make sure the cover plate or mud ring will fit the box. If a junction box holds only spliced wires and no device, cover it with a metal blank plate if it is exposed and a plastic blank plate if it will be enclosed in a wall.

Use round-cornered junction boxes called **handy boxes** if the box will be exposed on a basement or garage wall. Use metal cover plates. For a ceiling fan, use a fan-rated box (page 33).

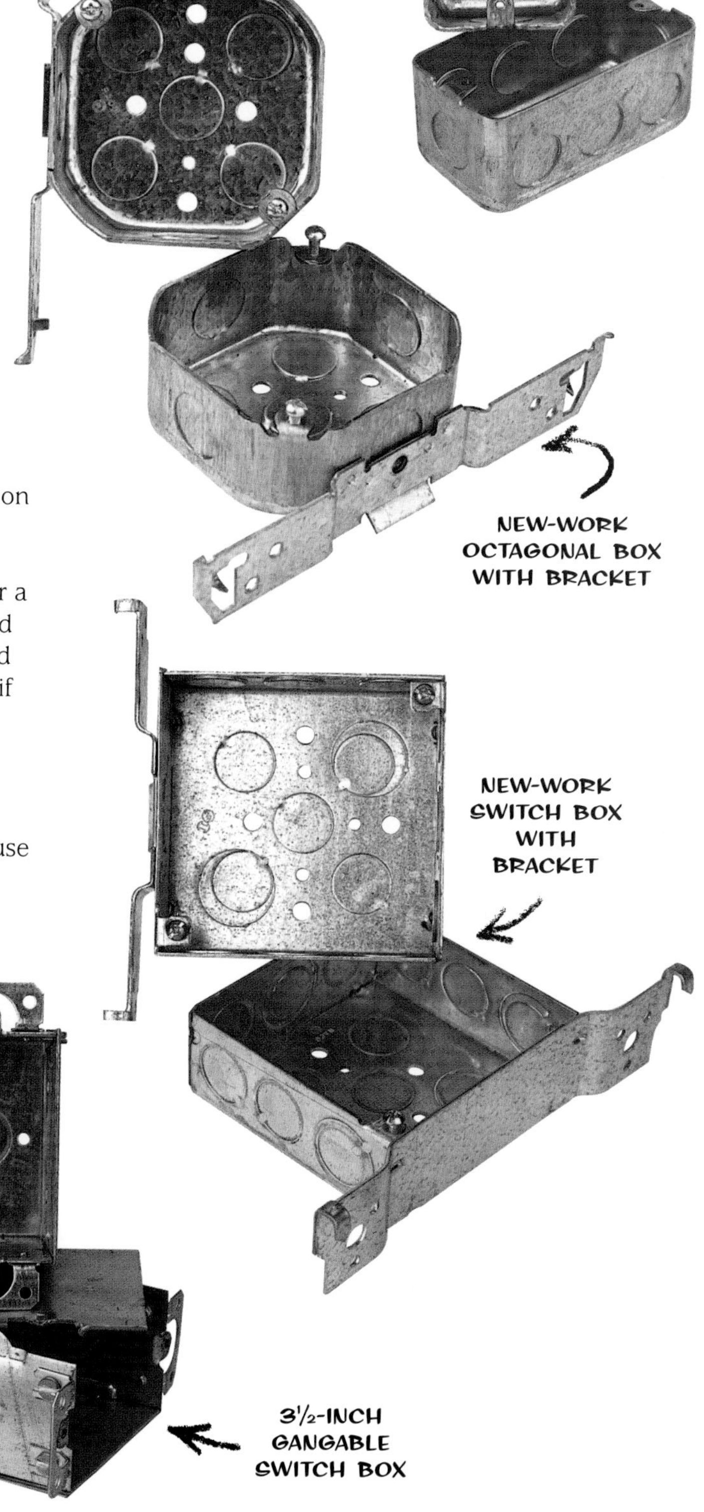

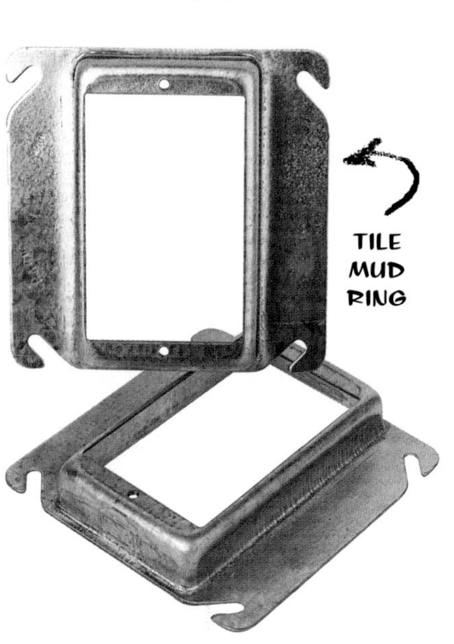

PLANNING FOR NEW SERVICES

INSTALLING STRAPS AND STAPLES

Cable, whether hidden in a wall or exposed, must be installed carefully to keep it from being damaged. Codes specify how and where each type of cable must be anchored. A **staple** holds the cable firmly without damaging its sheathing. Staples with plastic parts are better because they are less likely to damage the sheathing than the once-popular metal staples. Choose the right size staples to fit the cable.

When running cable along joists or studs, secure NM or armored cable at least 1¼ inches back from the front edge of the framing member (to protect it from drywall screws), using a plastic staple every 3 to 4 feet. Staple cable within 12 inches of a box that has a clamp and within 8 inches of a box that does not have a clamp. Never secure two cables with a single staple.

Use **drive straps** (below) for conduit; you can use **one- or two-hole straps** (below right) for either armored cable or conduit. When attaching a one-hole or a two-hole strap to wood, use a drill to drive in 1¼-inch screws. To anchor a strap to concrete, block, or brick, drill holes with a masonry bit and drive masonry screws into the holes.

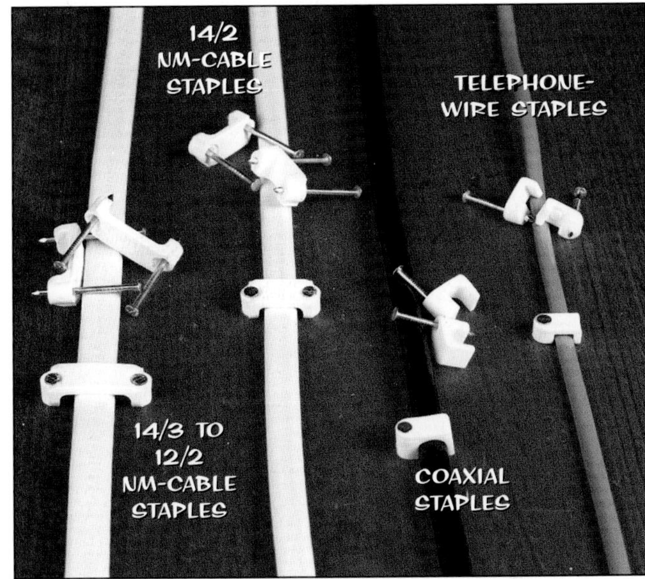

CHOOSING THE RIGHT STAPLE. A staple should hug the cable tightly without denting it. To attach it, position the staple over the cable, taking care that the nails do not touch the cable, and hammer in the nails. If you have a lot of telephone cable to install, purchase a staple gun that drives in round-topped staples (page 180).

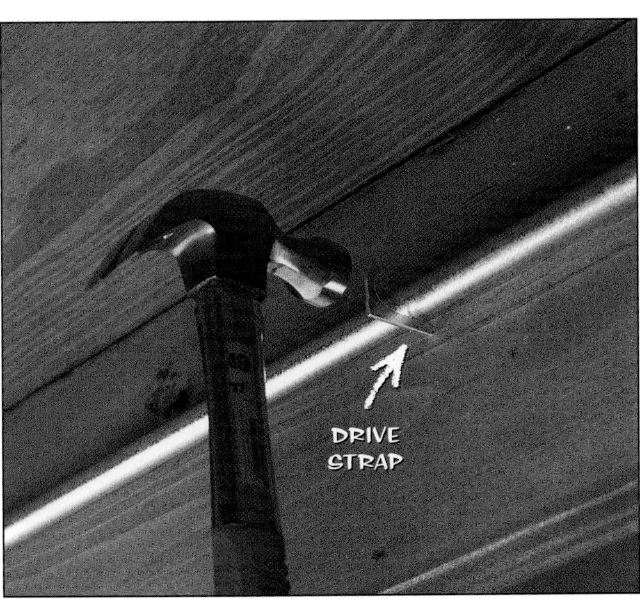

ANCHORING CONDUIT TO WOOD. Use hook-like drive straps to attach conduit to wood. Hold the drive strap next to the conduit, and pound the strap in until it firmly grips the conduit. Place straps every 4 feet and within 12 inches of a box.

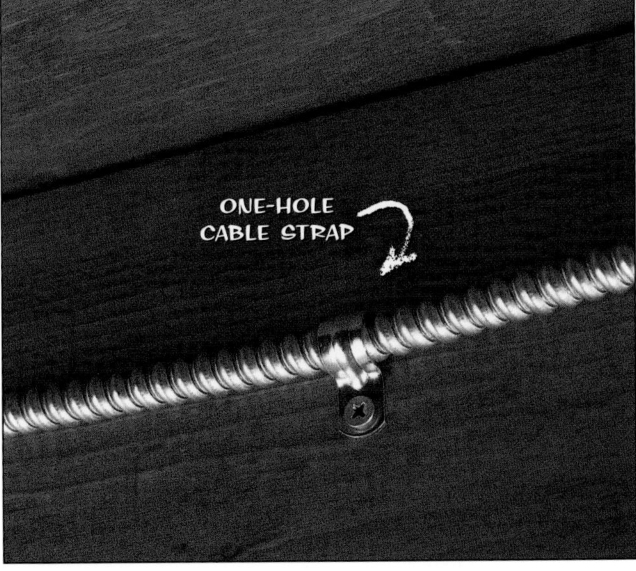

ANCHORING ARMORED CABLE TO WOOD. Fasten a strap in place with a 1¼-inch general-purpose screw. Use two-hole straps to install two parallel lines. Place the cable straps every 3 to 4 feet.

9 RUNNING NEW CABLE

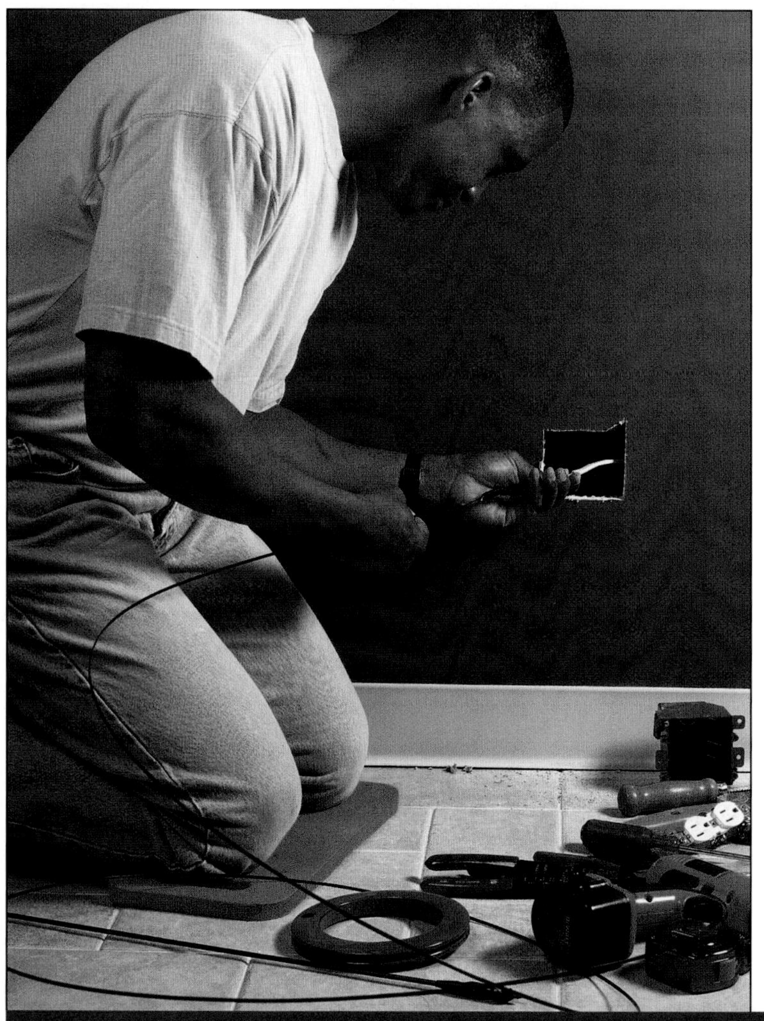

Before you start to run new lines, complete your wiring plan (Chapter 8) and get city approval for your project. Next, be sure to have a basic understanding of your home's electrical system (Chapter 1) and be comfortable with basic wiring techniques (Chapter 3). You'll find that installing boxes and cable in new framing is straightforward—even fun—once you've mastered the techniques. Running new lines in old walls is more challenging, especially if there isn't an attic or crawl space in which to run the lines. With planning, a few new skills, and the right tools, you'll get the job done right.

CHAPTER NINE PROJECTS

WORKING WITH NM CABLE

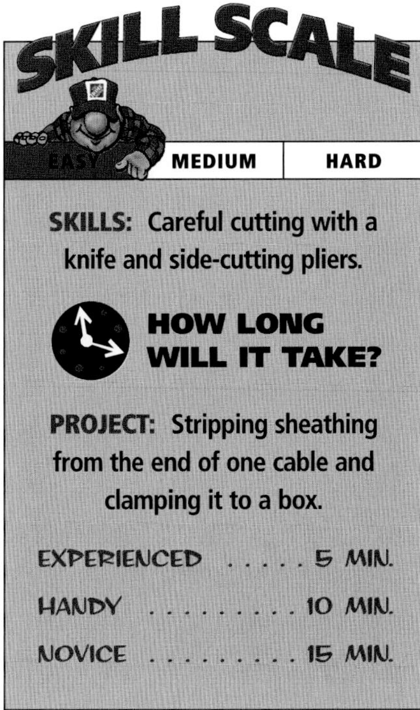

SKILLS: Careful cutting with a knife and side-cutting pliers.

HOW LONG WILL IT TAKE?

PROJECT: Stripping sheathing from the end of one cable and clamping it to a box.

EXPERIENCED . . . . . 5 MIN.
HANDY . . . . 10 MIN.
NOVICE . . . . 15 MIN.

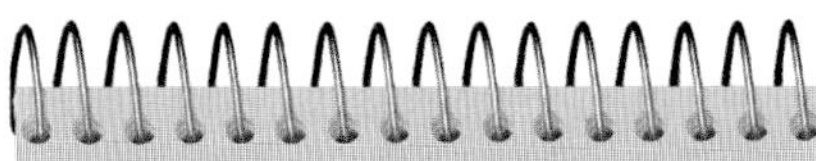

STUFF YOU'LL NEED

TOOLS: Knife, lineman's pliers, side-cutting pliers

MATERIALS: Nonmetallic (NM) cable

You'll find nonmetallic (NM) cable easy to cut and quick to install. Just be careful when you remove the sheathing so you don't accidently slit the wire insulation. If you do, cut off the damage and start again; otherwise you will get a short or a shock.

Whenever possible, strip sheathing before cutting the cable to length. That way, if you make a mistake you can try again.

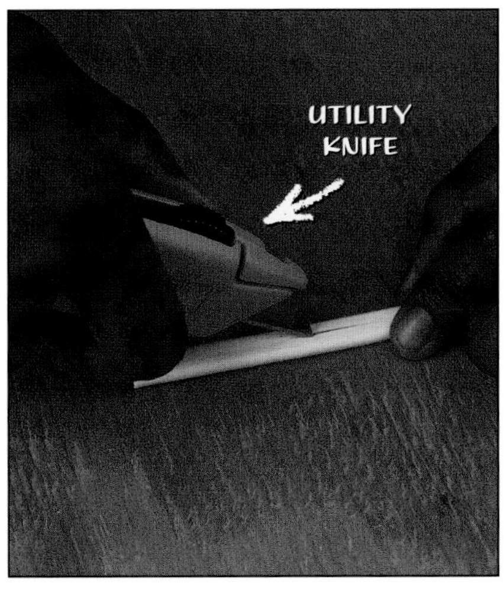

1 SLIT THE CABLE WITH A KNIFE. Flatten one end of the cable on a work surface. One side of the cable has a slight valley. With that side up, use a utility knife to start a cut about 3 inches from the cable end. Insert the blade into the middle of the valley (directly above the bare ground wire) so the blade just pierces through the sheathing. Slit to the end of the cable.

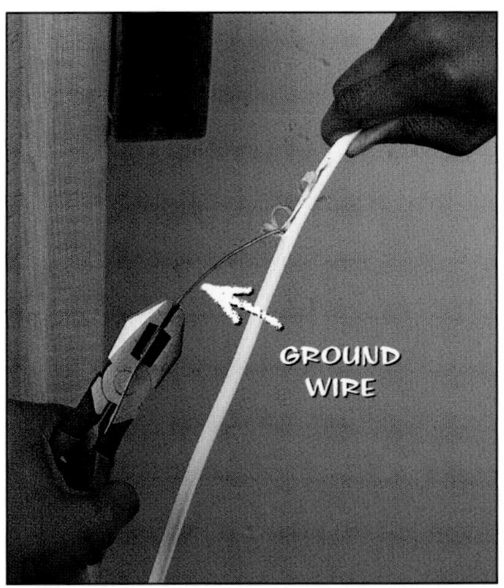

2 PULL THE GROUND WIRE. Cut or pull back the sheathing so you can grab the end of the ground wire with lineman's pliers. Hold the cable end in the other hand, and pull back the ground wire until you have made a slit in the sheathing about 12 inches long.

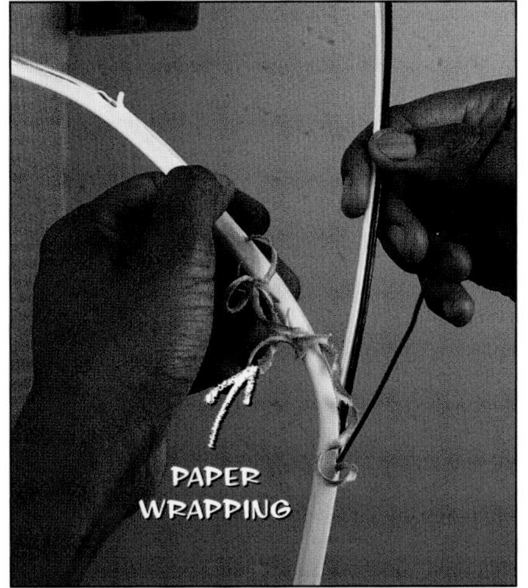
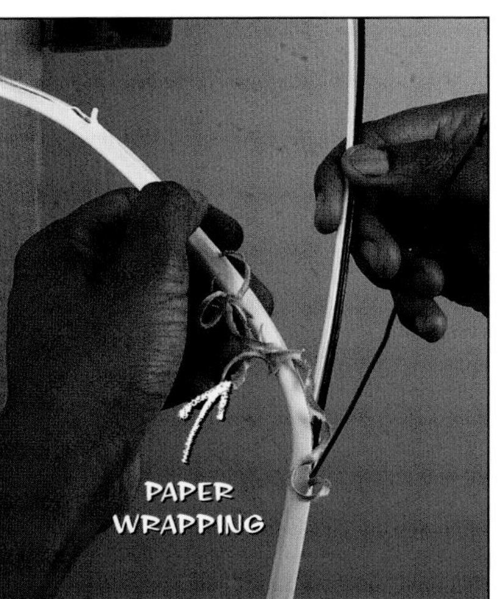

3 REMOVE THE WRAPPING. Pull the plastic sheathing back. Peel off any protective paper wrapping or thin strips of plastic, and cut them off.

TOOL TIP

USING A CABLE RIPPER. Use this tool to strip cable that is already installed in a box. Practice on scrap cable first to make sure the ripper doesn't cut too deeply and damage wire insulation.

RUNNING NEW CABLE

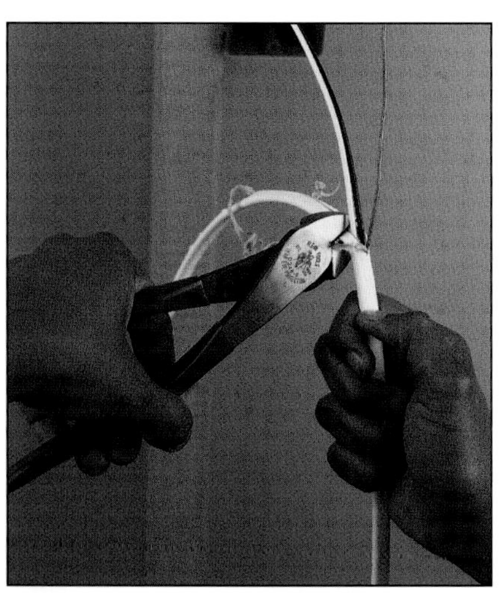

4 **SNIP THE SHEATHING.** Use side-cutting pliers, a combination tool, or the cutting portion of lineman's pliers to cut the sheathing.

5 **PULL THE CABLE INTO THE BOX.** Push the wires through the clip or clamp on the box (see right for the types you'll find). Pull the cable into the box so at least ¼ inch of sheathing shows inside.

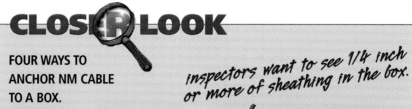

FOUR WAYS TO ANCHOR NM CABLE TO A BOX.

inspectors want to see 1/4 inch or more of sheathing in the box.

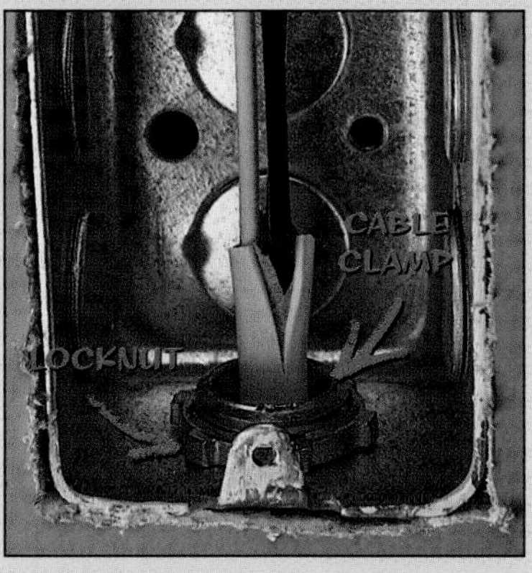

CABLE CLAMP. Buy clamps made for NM cable. Remove the knockout. Screw the clamp to the cable, then slip it through the hole and screw on the locknut. Tighten the locknut by tapping with a hammer and screwdriver. Or attach to the box first, slide the cable through the clamp, then tighten the screws.

POKE AND STAPLE. To run cable into many plastic boxes, you may need to push the cable past a plastic flap or knock out a plastic tab. Once you've inserted the cable into the box, staple the cable on a framing member within 8 inches of the box.

BUILT-IN CLAMP. Plastic boxes large enough to hold more than one device have internal clamps, as do most remodel boxes. Tighten the screw to firmly clamp the cable.

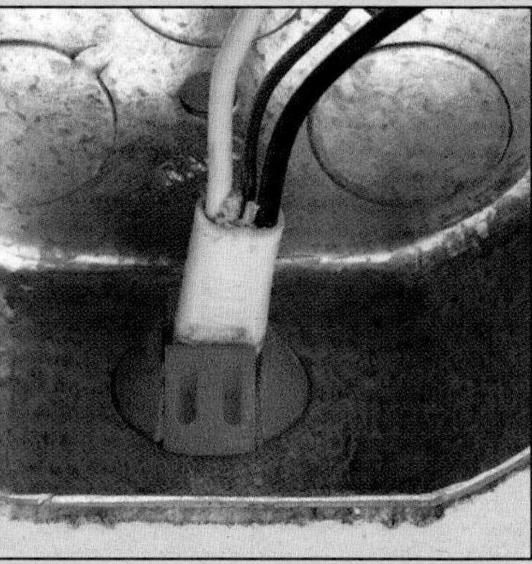

POP-IN PLASTIC CONNECTOR. Remove the knockout and push this connector in place. Then push the cable through and, if accessible, staple the cable within 8 inches of the box.

WORKING WITH ARMORED CABLE

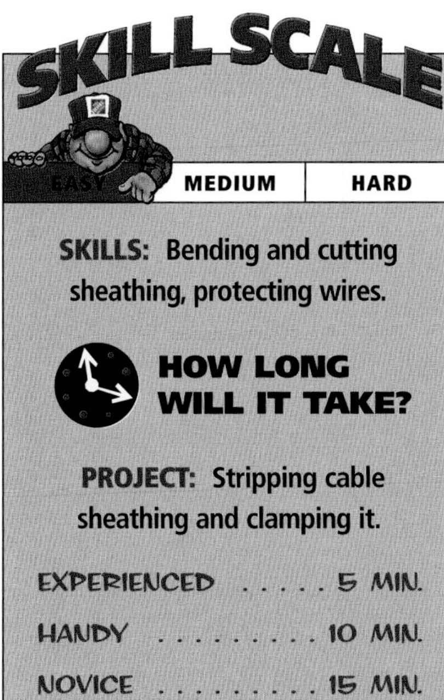

SKILLS: Bending and cutting sheathing, protecting wires.

HOW LONG WILL IT TAKE?

PROJECT: Stripping cable sheathing and clamping it.

EXPERIENCED ..... 5 MIN.
HANDY .... 10 MIN.
NOVICE .... 15 MIN.

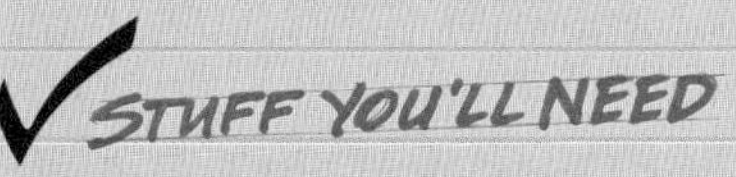

TOOLS: Side-cutting pliers, screwdriver, hammer, channel-joint pliers, perhaps an armored cable cutter

MATERIALS: BX or MC cable, protective bushings

The features of flexible armored cable fall midway between NM and conduit. Armored cable is easier to install than conduit and less flexible than NM. It protects wires better than NM but won't turn away nails as well as conduit.

TYPES OF ARMORED CABLE

There are two types of armored cable. BX cable has no ground wire; the sheathing itself provides the path for ground. (Its thin metal bonding strip is sometimes improperly used as a ground. The strip is easily broken and is intended only to ensure a conductive connection to a metal box.) Older BX used heavy steel sheathing. Today's cable uses aluminum, which is lighter, is a better conductor, and is much easier to cut.

MC cable is like BX but with a green-insulated grounding wire. Some new building codes require using MC instead of BX for a sure ground.

WHERE TO USE IT

Some codes call for armored cable instead of NM. Others require NM or conduit where the cable is exposed. Run armored cable inside walls, and protect it from nails as you would NM cable. Armored cable will bend only so far, so use NM around wall corners (page 128) and around door jambs (page 131).

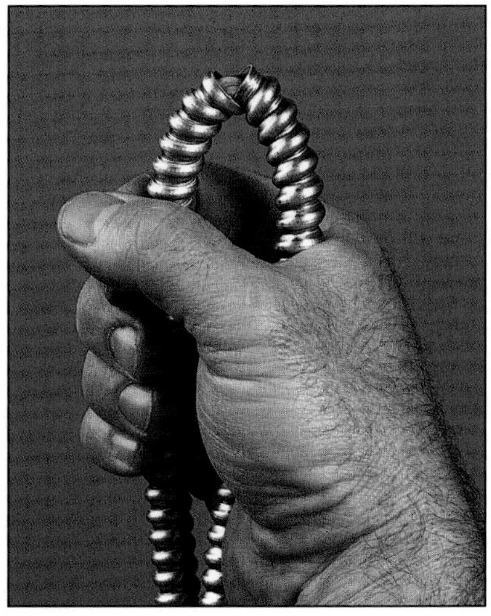

1 BEND AND SQUEEZE THE CABLE. About 1 foot from the end, bend the cable and then squeeze the bend until the armor breaks apart slightly. If you have trouble doing this by hand, use a pair of channel-joint pliers.

TOOL TIP

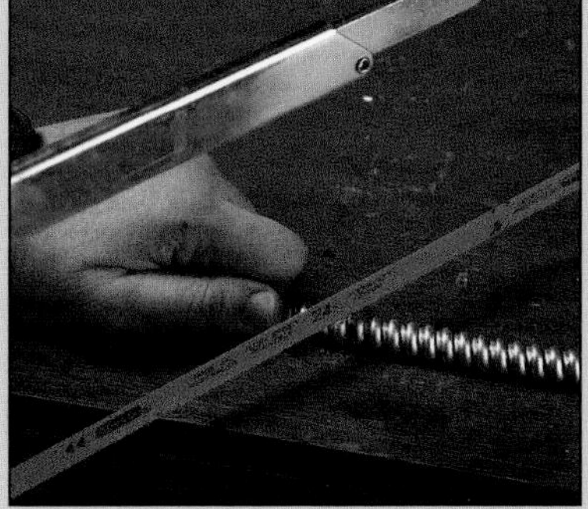

NIPPING WITH A HACKSAW. Some people find stripping armored cable easier if they cut it with a hacksaw first. Barely slice through one of the ridges so you can see the wires but are sure you haven't nicked them.

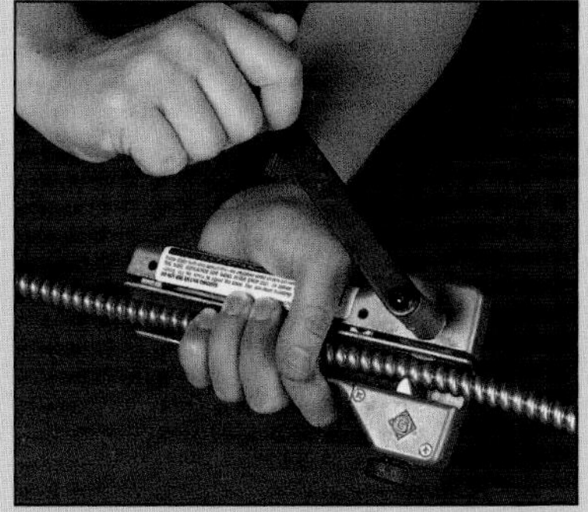

USING AN ARMORED CABLE CUTTER. For large jobs, you may want to invest in this tool. Adjust the cutter for cable size, slip in the cable, and turn the handle to make a lengthwise cut.

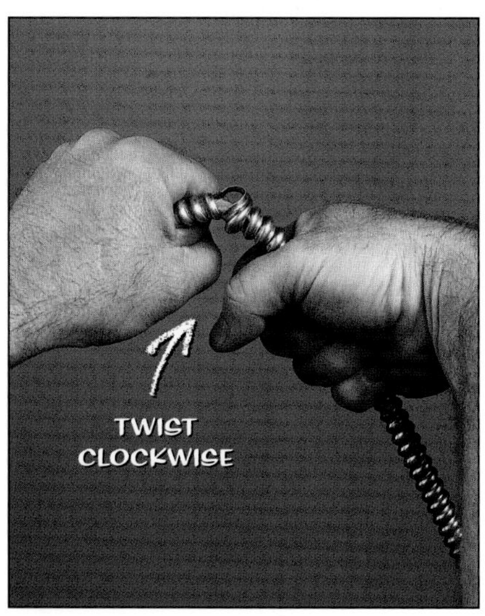

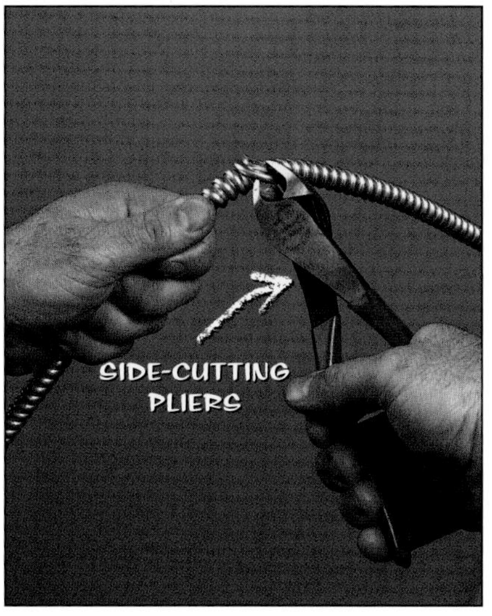

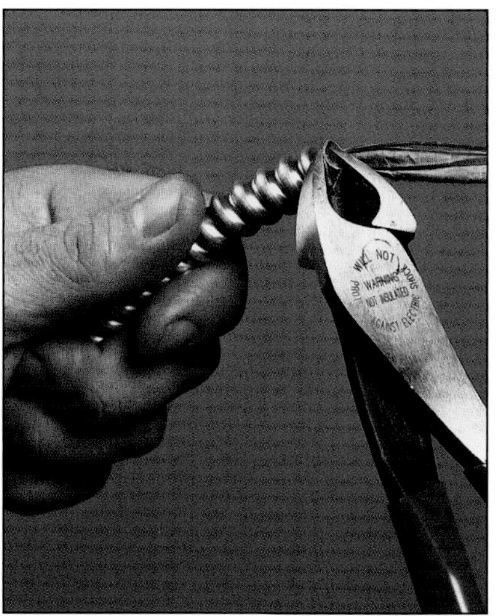

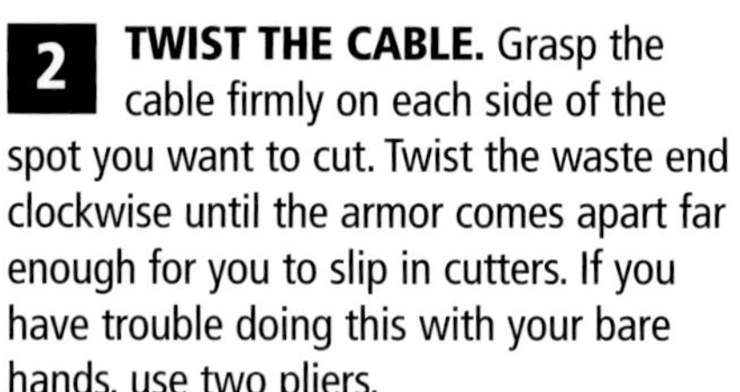

2 TWIST THE CABLE. Grasp the cable firmly on each side of the spot you want to cut. Twist the waste end clockwise until the armor comes apart far enough for you to slip in cutters. If you have trouble doing this with your bare hands, use two pliers.

3 SNIP AND REMOVE THE ARMOR. Cut through one rib of the armor with a pair of side-cutting pliers. Slide the waste armor off the wires. Keep your hands clear of sharp edges.

4 TRIM SHARP ENDS. Remove paper wrapping and plastic strips. Leave the thin metal bonding strip alone. Use side-cutting pliers to snip away pointed ends of sheathing that could nick wire insulation.

if bushings did not come with your cable, buy them separately.

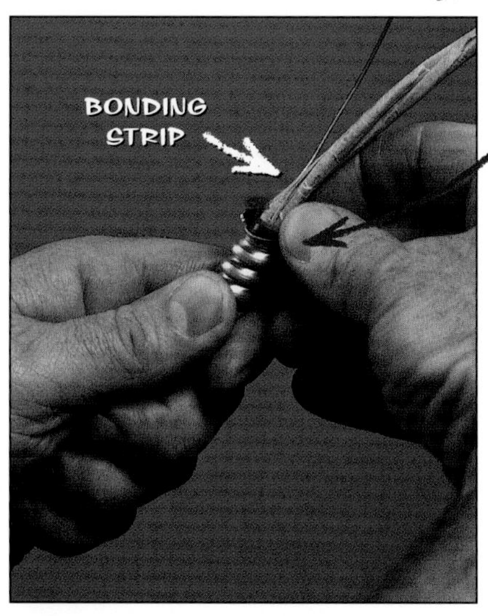

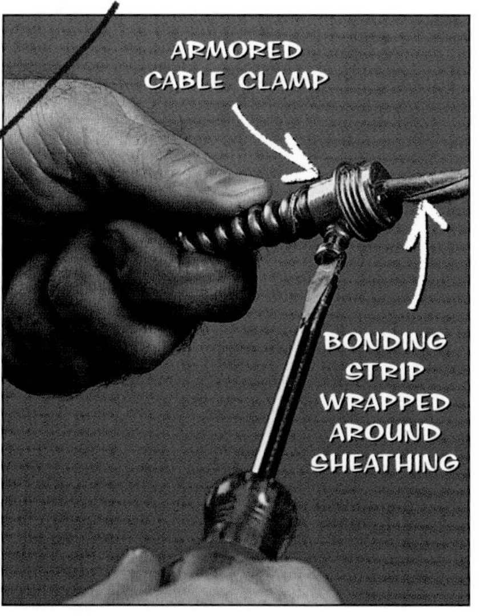

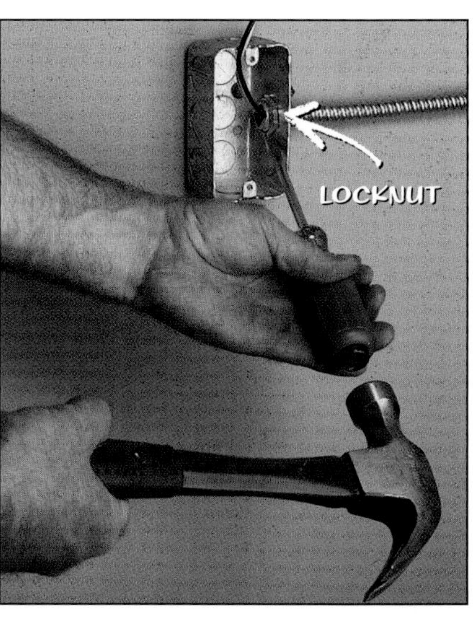

5 SLIP ON THE BUSHING. Slip a bushing over the wires. Slide it down into the armor so the bushing protects the wires from the sharp edges of the armor. If there is a bonding strip, ask your inspector what to do with it. Most inspectors want you to cut it to about 2 inches and wrap it over the bushing and around the armor, helping to ensure conductive contact between the armor and the box.

6 ATTACH THE CLAMP. Remove the locknut from an armored cable clamp. Slide the clamp down over the bushing as far as it will go, and tighten the screw. Double-check to make sure that none of the wires are in danger of being nicked by the armor.

7 CONNECT TO THE BOX. Remove a knockout slug from a metal box, and poke the connector into the hole. Slide the locknut over the wires, and tighten it onto the cable clamp. On BX cable, this connection is the ground—use a hammer and a screwdriver to tap the locknut tight.

RUNNING CONDUIT

SKILL SCALE
EASY
MEDIUM
HARD
SKILLS: Measuring and cutting conduit, assembling parts.
HOW LONG WILL IT TAKE?
PROJECT: To install and wire 50 feet of conduit with five bends.
EXPERIENCED ..... 3 HRS.
HANDY .... 5 HRS.
NOVICE .... 8 HRS.

STUFF YOU'LL NEED
TOOLS: Conduit and fittings, wire, lubricant
MATERIALS: Screwdriver, lineman's pliers, hacksaw, conduit reamer, fish tape

Conduit is the most durable product for running wire. It's more expensive and time-consuming to install than cable, but it is no longer necessary to learn how to bend conduit. Ready-made parts make installation easier than ever. Use conduit on unfinished walls and ceilings where wiring will be exposed. Use electrical metallic tubing (EMT), or "thinwall" conduit, for most indoor installations and thicker intermediate metal conduit (IMC) for outdoor jobs. Plastic rigid nonmetallic conduit (PVC) is also used outdoors.

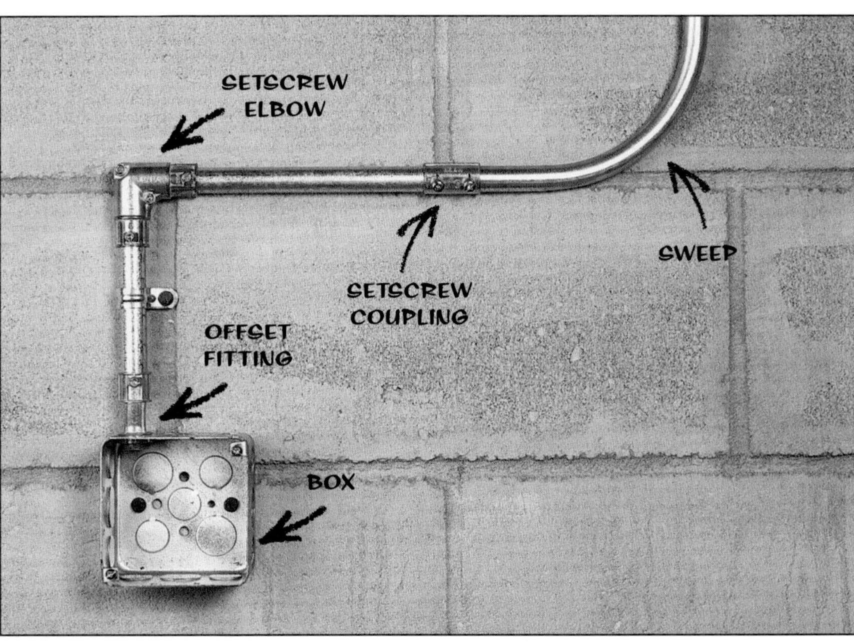

ASSEMBLING THE PARTS. Take a rough drawing of your installation to a home center or electrical supply store. Ask a salesperson to help you gather all the pieces you need. Generally, use ½-inch conduit for up to five #12 wires or six #14 wires, and ¾-inch conduit for more wires. (Larger conduit will make pulling easier, so consider buying ¾-inch in any case.)

Use **setscrew couplings and elbows** for indoor installations (you'll have to use compression fittings outdoors). If the conduit and the box are installed flush against a wall, you'll need an **offset fitting**. Use a **sweep** to turn most corners. At every four bends, provide access to the wires by installing a box or a pulling elbow (Step 5).

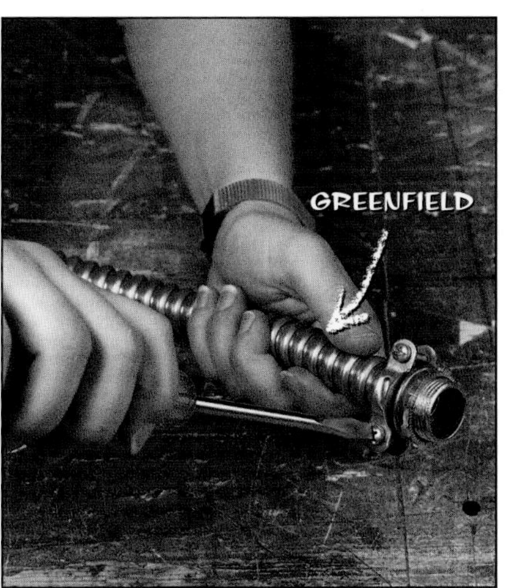

GREENFIELD. Also called flexible metal conduit, Greenfield is essentially armored cable without the wires. It is expensive, so use it sparingly in places where rigid conduit would be difficult to install.

PVC CONDUIT. In many areas, PVC is acceptable for indoor and outdoor installations. Cut it with a backsaw or hacksaw and a miter box. Glue the pieces together using PVC cement approved by an inspector.

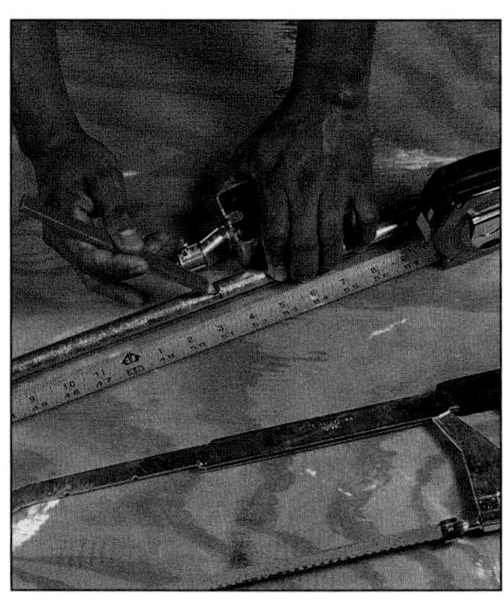

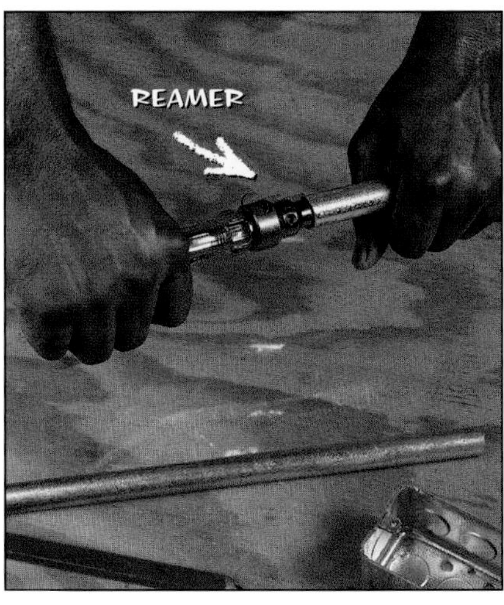

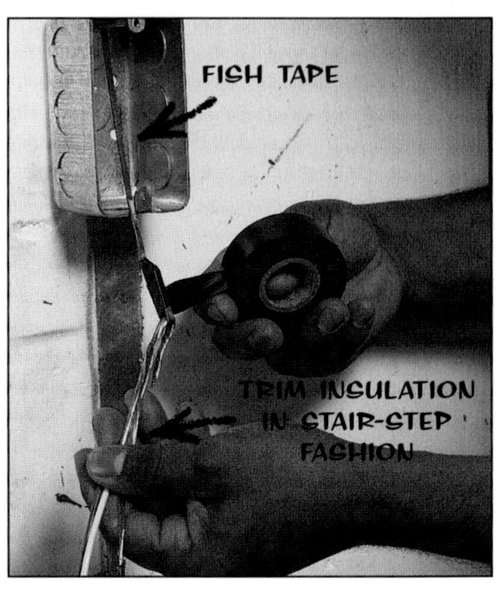

1 **MEASURE AND CUT.** Install the boxes first, then cut conduit to fit between them. At a corner, have a helper hold a sweep in place while you mark the conduit for cutting. Use a hacksaw with a fine-tooth blade to cut.

2 **REMOVE BURRS.** Ream out all burrs with a conduit reamer so the wires can slide smoothly past joints without damaging the sheathing.

3 **RUN FISH TAPE AND ATTACH THE WIRES.** Feed the fish tape through the conduit in the opposite direction from which you will pull the wires. Poke the wire ends through the fish tape's loop and bend them over in stair-step fashion. Wrap firmly and neatly with electrician's tape so the joint will not bind when it goes through a sweep.

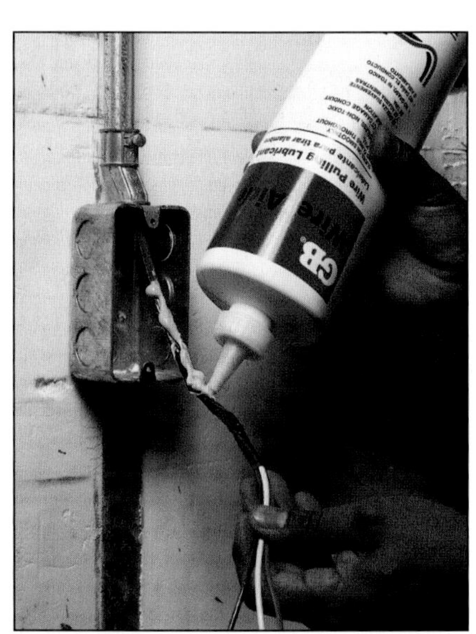

4 **SQUIRT LUBRICANT.** To make pulling easier on long runs, pour a bit of pulling lubricant on the wires. (Don't risk using substitute lubricants like dishwashing liquid or hand soap. Some can dangerously degrade wire insulation over time.)

5 **PULL THE WIRES.** Have someone feed the wires through one end while you pull the fish tape on the other end. Pull with steady pressure. Try to keep the wires moving, rather than starting and stopping. If you get stuck, back up a few inches to gain a running start.

CLOSER LOOK

INSTALL PULLING ELBOWS. If the conduit will make more than three turns between boxes, install a pulling elbow to make fishing easier. Don't splice wires here; just use the opening to pull the wires through.

WIRING IN UNFINISHED FRAMING

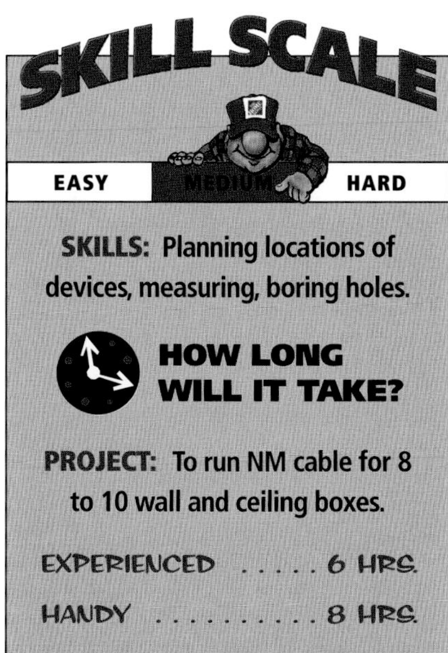

SKILLS: Planning locations of devices, measuring, boring holes.

HOW LONG WILL IT TAKE?

PROJECT: To run NM cable for 8 to 10 wall and ceiling boxes.

EXPERIENCED . . . . . 6 HRS.
HANDY . . . . 8 HRS.
NOVICE . . . . .10 HRS.

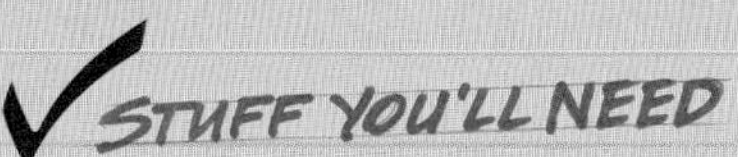

TOOLS: Drill with ⅝-inch or ¾-inch bits, hammer, tape measure, level, longnose pliers, utility knife
MATERIALS: NM or armored cable, electrical boxes, protective nailing plates, cable staples, safety goggles

Running cable through bare framing members is far easier than fishing it through a wall finished with drywall or plaster and lath (pages 130–134). If the existing wall surface is flawed or if you also are installing plumbing in a remodeling job, it usually saves work to tear off all the drywall. Start anew, rather than living with a roomful of small wall patches.

INSTALLING CABLE THAT IS SAFE AND SECURE

Installing NM cable with plastic boxes is quick and easy—drill holes, run the cable through, and poke it into boxes. But don't run cable any old way. Safety concerns and codes dictate that it must be positioned out of harm's way, which means precise measuring and installing.

Choosing boxes and cable. Check local codes before buying materials. Codes may call for metal boxes, although plastic is fine in most areas. Assuming you will be installing ½-inch drywall after wiring, buy boxes that are easy to install ½ inch out from a stud or joist. Plan wiring carefully (Chapter 8), so you'll install the correct cables. For instance, use 14/2 for most general lighting and receptacles, 12-gauge for 20-amp circuits, and three-wire cable for three-way switches and split receptacles.

Placing holes. Local codes may specify the height at which cable for receptacles should be run, as well as where to put staples.

If an unfinished attic is above or a basement is below, run some of the cables there (page 132).

1 **INSTALL THE BOXES.** Attach all the boxes before running cable. Receptacle boxes are usually positioned 12 inches above the floor and switch boxes 45 inches above the floor. (Many electricians set their hammer head down on the floor, using a hammer length to position floor-level receptacles.) Hold a nail-on box with its front edge positioned out from the stud the thickness of the drywall, and drive the two nails. Double-check to see that you've installed all the boxes. Walk around the room pretending to use all the switches.

SAFETY ALERT!

NEVER NOTCH.
In a tight spot like this, you may be tempted to whip out the hammer and chisel and chop notches in the face of the studs so the cable runs easier. But the cable would then be dangerously exposed and severely bent at the corner. Instead, drill slightly larger holes, bend the cable before poking it in, and grab it with longnose pliers.

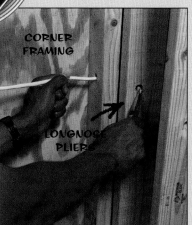

CORNER FRAMING
LONGNOSE PLIERS

2 DRILL THE HOLES. Wherever possible, use a tape measure and level to mark studs and joists. Mark so holes will be in a straight horizontal line. Drill 5/8-inch holes for most NM cable and 3/4-inch holes for three-wire cable or armored cable. A 3/8-inch drill works fine for small jobs, but give it a rest if it overheats.

A TYPICAL CABLE ROUGH-IN. Run cable in a straight horizontal line, 1 foot above the receptacles (areas under windows are an exception) or according to local code. To keep cable out of the reach of nails, drill all holes in the center of studs and at least 1¼ inches up from the bottom of joists. Nail on protective nailing plates for extra safety (they may be required for every hole). Even if you will only hang a light, install a ceiling fan box in case you choose to add a ceiling fan later.

3 PULL THE CABLE. To avoid kinks, keep the cable straight and untwisted as you work. When possible, pull the cable first and then cut it to length. If you must cut it first, allow plenty of extra length. Pull the cable fairly tight, but loose enough so there is an inch or so of play.

4 PROTECT THE CABLE WITH NAILING PLATES. These are inexpensive and quick to install. Be sure to nail one of these wherever the cable is within 1¼ inches of the front edge of the framing member. For added safety (and to satisfy some local codes), install nailing plates over every hole.

5 STAPLE THE CABLE AND RUN IT INTO THE BOXES. Staple cable tightly wherever it runs along a joist so it is out of the reach of nails. Staple within 8 inches of a plastic box and within 12 inches of a metal box. See pages 123 and 125 for clamping methods.

WIRING FINISHED ROOMS

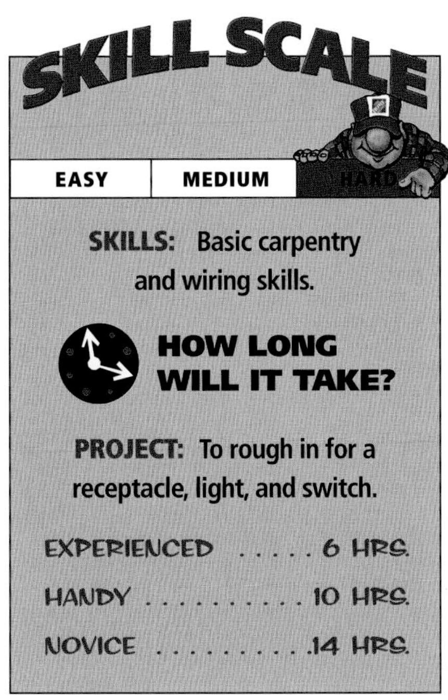

You need the patience of a surgeon to run wiring through walls that are finished with drywall or plaster. At times, you'll feel like grabbing a hammer and knocking big holes in the wall to get at that darned cable. But remember that patching and painting walls are tedious and time-consuming tasks, so any steps you can take to minimize wall or ceiling damage will save you work in the long run.

FOLLOW THE EASIEST PATH

If you have an unfinished attic or a basement, run as much of the cable there as possible. If a basement or attic is finished, run armored cable instead of NM.

Use an electronic stud finder to locate joists and studs that may be in the way. You may be able to move a box a few inches to avoid an obstruction. Wherever possible, run cable parallel to studs or joists.

First, cut holes for the boxes (pages 133–134); then run the cable. Reach into the box holes with your hand, a fish tape, or a long drill bit in order to reach the cable.

If you plan to take power from an existing receptacle for your new service, make sure you will not overload the circuit.

1 DRILL A LOCATOR HOLE. Directly below a box from which you want to grab power, remove the base shoe and drill a ¼-inch hole through the floor. Poke a wire down through the hole.

2 DRILL UP THROUGH THE BOTTOM PLATE. Using the wire as a reference point, drill a 1-inch hole through the middle of the wall's bottom plate (a 2×4 lying flat on top of the flooring above).

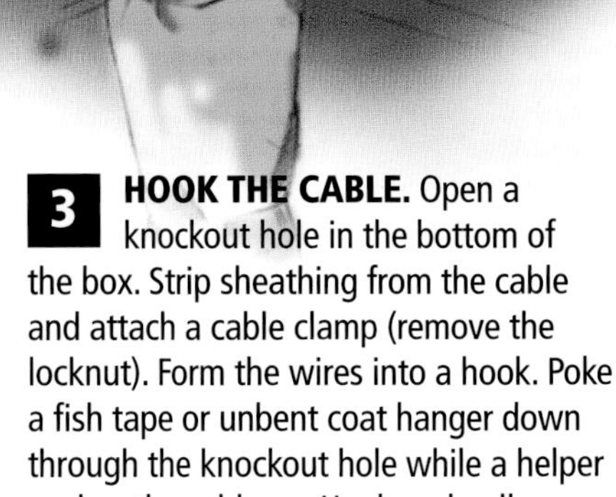

3 HOOK THE CABLE. Open a knockout hole in the bottom of the box. Strip sheathing from the cable and attach a cable clamp (remove the locknut). Form the wires into a hook. Poke a fish tape or unbent coat hanger down through the knockout hole while a helper pushes the cable up. Hook and pull up.

RUNNING CABLE BEHIND A BASEBOARD. Use a flat prybar to remove baseboard molding. With a drywall saw, cut a channel in the drywall at least 1 inch shorter than the baseboard. Drill holes through the centers of the studs and run cable through the holes. Protect all holes with nail plates.

TOOL TIP

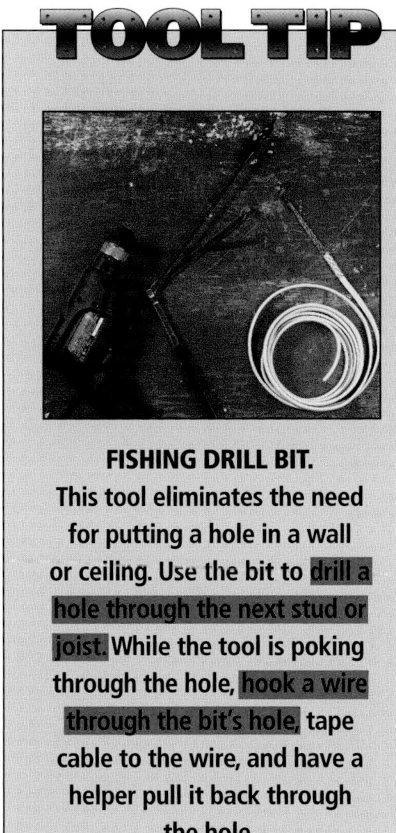

FISHING DRILL BIT.
This tool eliminates the need for putting a hole in a wall or ceiling. Use the bit to drill a hole through the next stud or joist. While the tool is poking through the hole, hook a wire through the bit's hole, tape cable to the wire, and have a helper pull it back through the hole.

RUNNING CABLE THROUGH A WALL. If the new box will be more or less directly behind the existing box from which you will grab power, you can avoid wall patching. Cut the hole for the remodel box. Remove the existing receptacle and punch out a knockout in the back or bottom of its box. Run one fish tape through the existing box and one through the new hole. Hook them together. Pull the tape back through the hole, and you're ready to pull cable from the hole to the box.

RUNNING CABLE AROUND A DOOR. If you have a slab floor and no access to the ceiling, this may be your only option. But check to see if this is OK with local codes. Remove casing from around a door and snake cable around. You may be able to slip the cable between the jamb and the stud. Or, drill a hole and run the cable in the cavity on the other side of the stud.

WIRING FINISHED ROOMS (CONTINUED)

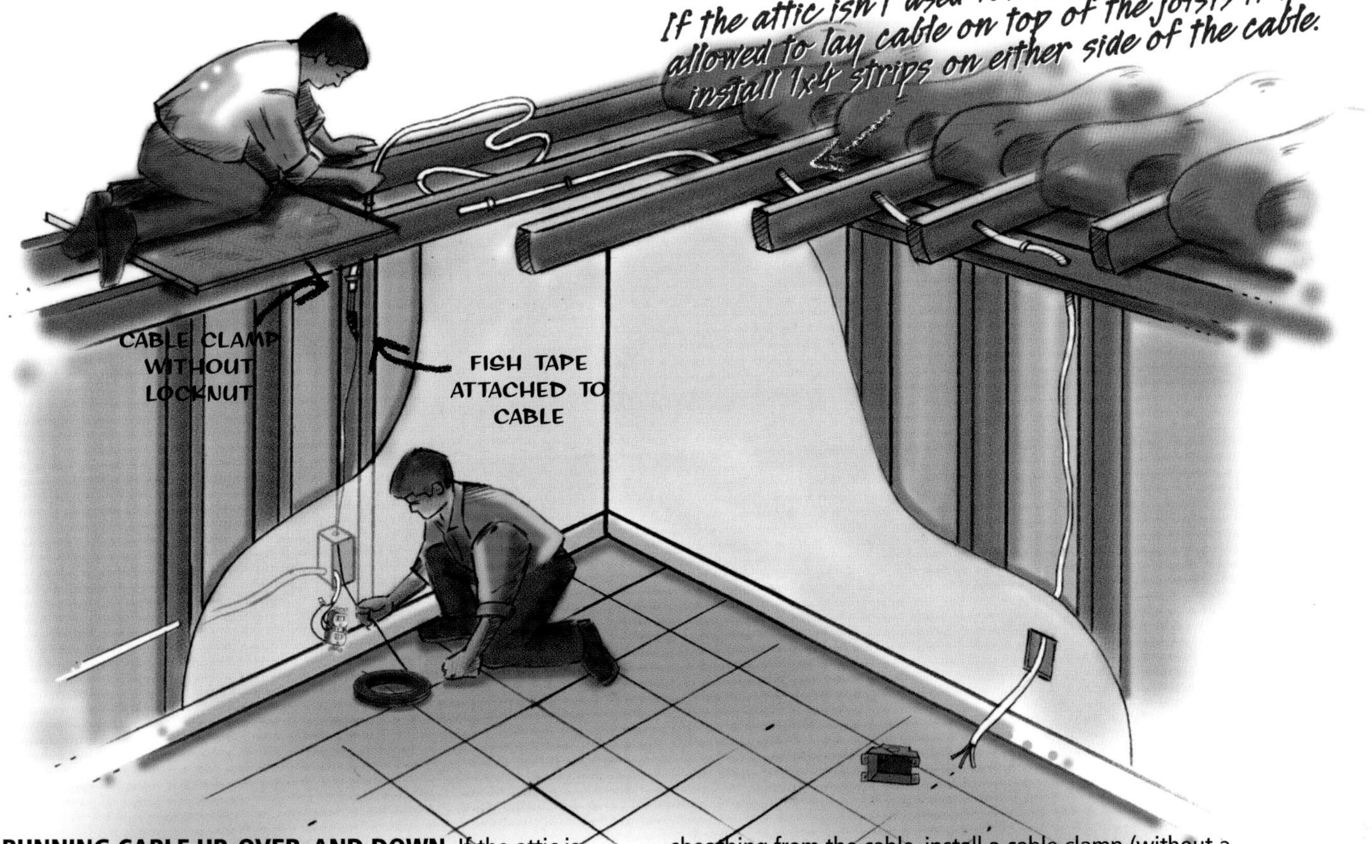

If the attic isn't used for storage, you may be allowed to lay cable on top of the joists if you install 1x4 strips on either side of the cable.

CABLE CLAMP WITHOUT LOCKNUT

FISH TAPE ATTACHED TO CABLE

RUNNING CABLE UP, OVER, AND DOWN. If the attic is accessible, drill a hole through the top plate. Run cable down through it to the hole for the new box directly below. Drill holes and run cable through the joists, over to the spot directly above the existing box from which you want to run power. Strip sheathing from the cable, install a cable clamp (without a locknut), and form the wires into a hook. Punch out a knockout hole and run a fish tape up the wall. Jiggle and slide the tape back and forth until it goes through the hole in the ceiling plate. Have a helper hook the cable to the tape and pull it into the box.

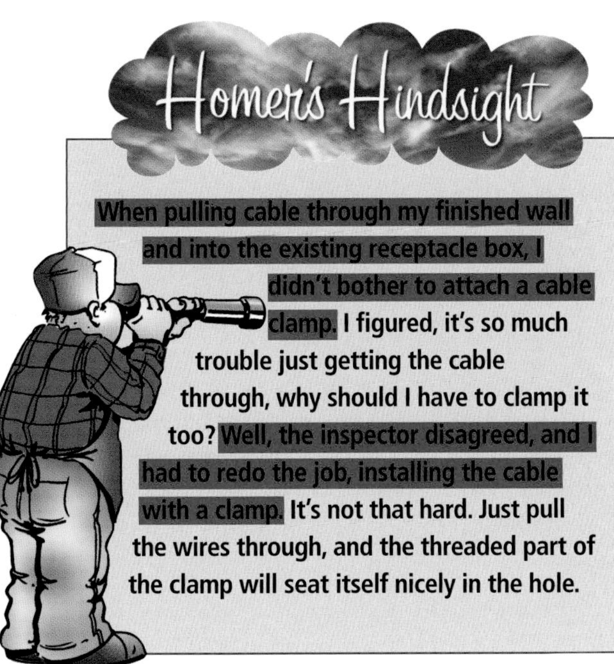

Homer's Hindsight

When pulling cable through my finished wall and into the existing receptacle box, I didn't bother to attach a cable clamp. I figured, it's so much trouble just getting the cable through, why should I have to clamp it too? Well, the inspector disagreed, and I had to redo the job, installing the cable with a clamp. It's not that hard. Just pull the wires through, and the threaded part of the clamp will seat itself nicely in the hole.

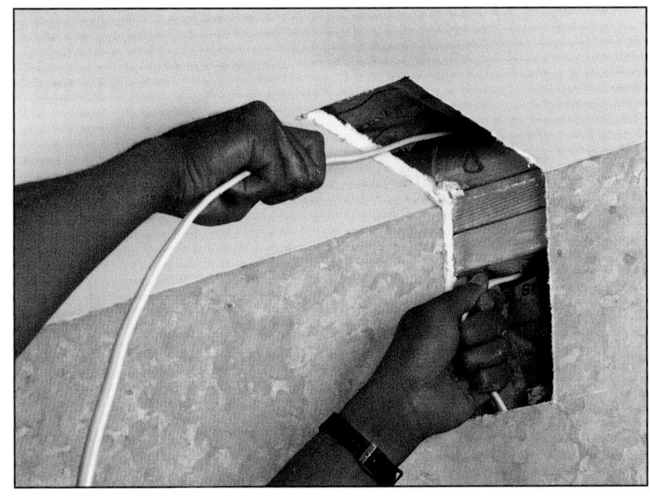

WHERE THE CEILING AND WALL MEET. When there is no access from above or below, cut notches in the drywall and plaster, like this. Drill a 1-inch hole up through the center of the top plate. Bend the cable, poke it up through the hole, and grab it from the other side.

INSTALLING REMODELING BOXES

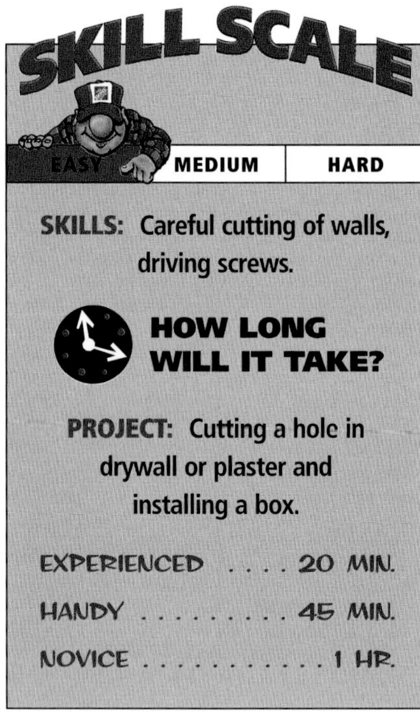

SKILL SCALE
EASY
MEDIUM
HARD
SKILLS: Careful cutting of walls, driving screws.
HOW LONG WILL IT TAKE?
PROJECT: Cutting a hole in drywall or plaster and installing a box.
EXPERIENCED .... 20 MIN.
HANDY .... 45 MIN.
NOVICE .... 1 HR.

STUFF YOU'LL NEED
TOOLS: Electronic stud finder, utility knife, drywall saw, saber saw or rotary cutter, screwdriver, drill
MATERIALS: Remodeling (old-work) box, screws

When you run cable to install new devices in an old wall, you have several handy self-attaching boxes at your service. To use these **remodeling** boxes (also called **old-work** or **cut-in** boxes), you need only cut a hole, run the cable, clamp the cable to the box, and install the remodeling box.

To make sure you won't hit a stud or joist, before cutting a hole, drill a small bore in the wall, and probe with a piece of wire.

Cut the hole carefully, using one of the methods shown on this page. The hole will probably not be rectangular (page 141). The box should fit into the hole snugly, but not so tightly that you have to force it. If the hole is too wide, the box may not effectively attach to the drywall or plaster.

CUTTING A HOLE IN PLASTER WITH A SABER SAW. Cutting through a lath and plaster wall is difficult and often results in cracked plaster. Drill holes at each corner, and score the face of the plaster with a utility knife. Cut with a saber saw equipped with a fine-tooth blade. Press hard against the wall to reduce lath vibration.

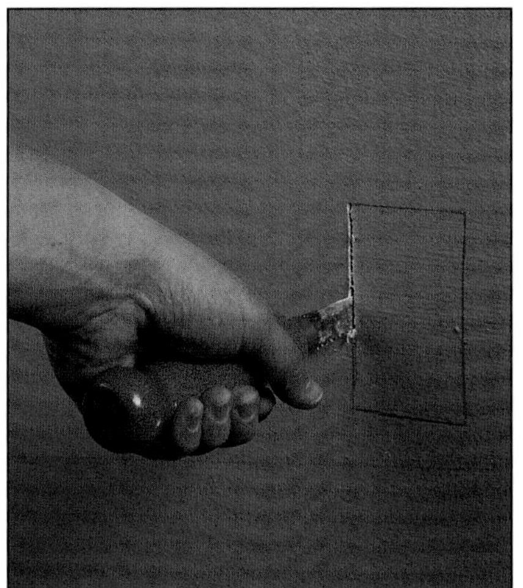

CUTTING A HOLE IN DRYWALL. Use a pencil to mark the location of the hole, and score the paper surface with a utility knife. Cut along the inside of the knife-cut with a drywall saw. The resulting hole will be free of ragged edges.

CUTTING A HOLE IN PLASTER WITH A SPIRAL CUTTING TOOL. Because of its rapidly rotating blade, this tool won't rattle your lath and loosen the plaster. To use this tool, set the base on the wall and tip the blade away from the surface while you let it come to full speed. Then tilt the blade gently into the wall. Have extra blades on hand; they dull quickly on plaster.

ATTACHING THE BOXES

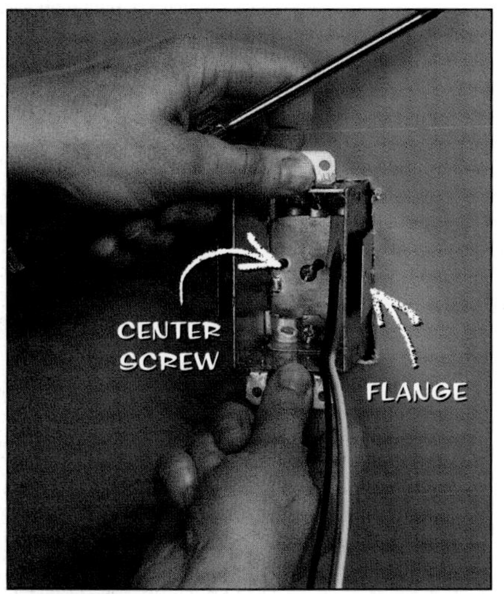

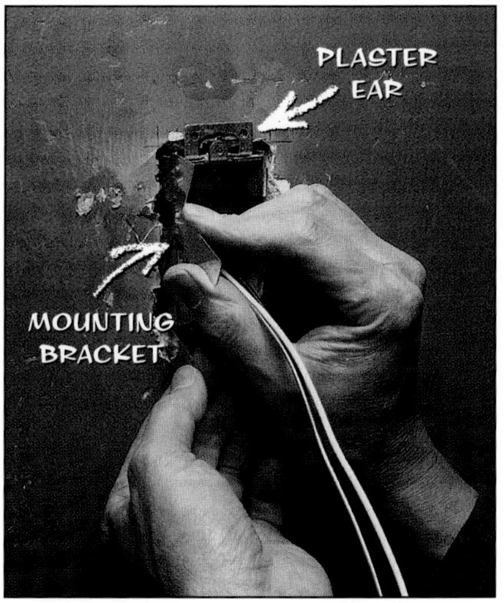

INSTALLING A BOX WITH SPRING FLANGES. If you buy this kind of box, make sure both flanges spring out firmly from the box. Push the box into the hole until the flanges are free to spring outward. As you tighten the center screw, the flanges should move toward you until they fit snugly against the back of the drywall or plaster.

INSTALLING A BOX WITH SIDE CLAMPS. After pushing the box into the hole, tighten the screw on each side. Each clamp extends behind the wall to hold the box in place.

USING MOUNTING BRACKETS. Push a metal box with plaster ears into the hole, then slip a bracket in on each side. Center each bracket behind the wall. Pull the bracket toward you until it's tight, push the box tightly against the wall, then fold the tabs into the box with your thumb. Tighten the tabs with pliers.

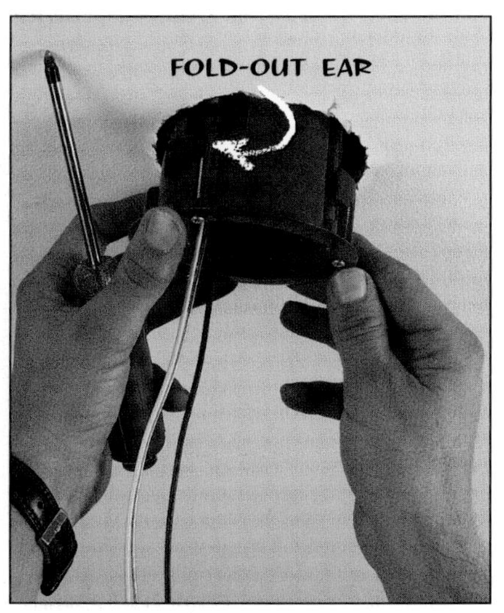

INSTALLING A BOX WITH FOLD-OUT EARS. These plastic remodeling boxes have ears that swing out behind the drywall or plaster. Push the box into the hole, then turn the screws clockwise until the ears clamp onto the back of the drywall or plaster. Switch boxes are also available with this same wall-grabbing mechanism.

CLOSER LOOK

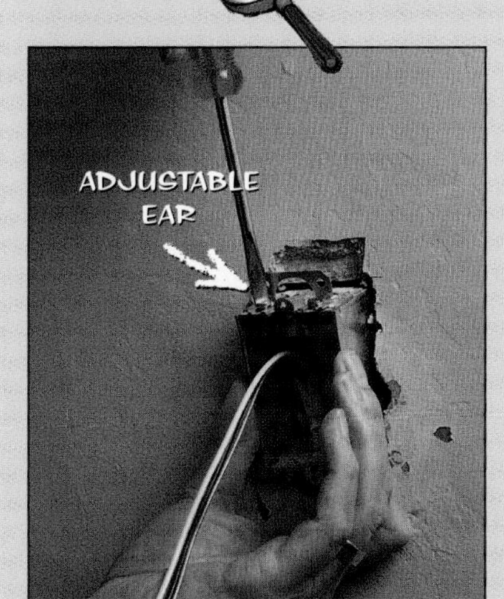

1 ADJUST THE PLASTER EARS. Many metal boxes have adjustable ears. Cut the hole and chip out the plaster above and below so the ears will fit. Loosen the two screws and adjust each ear so the face of the box is flush with the wall surface. Tighten the screws.

2 ANCHOR THE BOX TO THE LATH. Lath cracks easily, so work carefully. Drill pilot holes, and drive short screws to anchor the ears to the lath. Expect to do some patching after using this method.

PATCHING WALLS

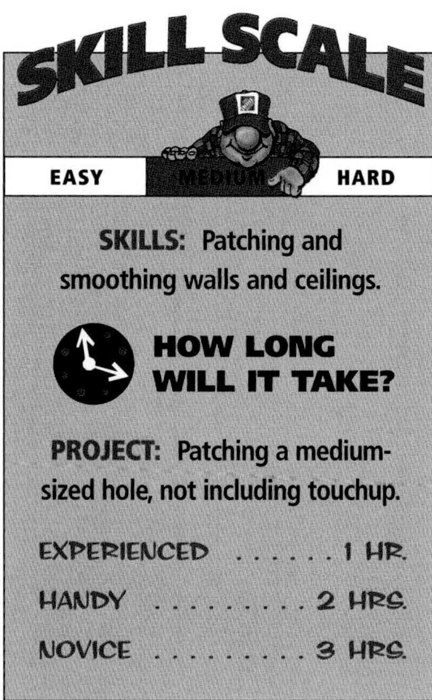

✓ STUFF YOU'LL NEED

TOOLS: Putty knife, 4-inch and 8-inch taping blades, utility knife, sanding block

MATERIALS: Drywall, mesh patching tape, joint compound, spackling compound

The techniques shown on pages 130–132 help you minimize damage to walls, but patching drywall or plaster will probably be the finishing step in running cable.

Most homes built after the 1950s have walls covered with drywall—also called Sheetrock or wallboard. It's usually ½ inch thick and is fairly easy to patch. The time-consuming part is patching and smoothing the joint between the old and the new surfaces.

An older home may have lath-and-plaster walls. The lath often splits or loosens and the plaster crumbles, making patching a challenge. Older homes may have a combination of the two: Old plaster walls are often covered with ¼- or ⅜-inch drywall.

HANDLING TEXTURED WALLS

Some drywall surfaces have a textured surface that is difficult to duplicate. You can cut out the pieces carefully and replace them with the original pieces when you are done wiring. You might get away with simply caulking the joints.

If a ceiling has a cottage-cheese-like appearance, a foam product has been blown onto it. You can buy a special patching compound to repair or recoat the ceiling, or hire a pro to recoat it.

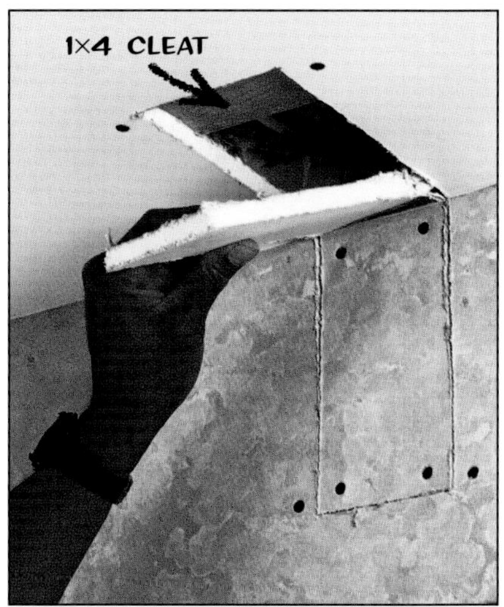

1 PATCH A SMALL HOLE IN DRYWALL. Cut a new piece of drywall to fit the hole, or reuse the piece you cut out. If you do not have a stud or joist to screw to, cut a 1×4 about 4 inches longer than the hole. Place the piece behind the hole as shown. Drive 1¼-inch drywall screws to secure the patch.

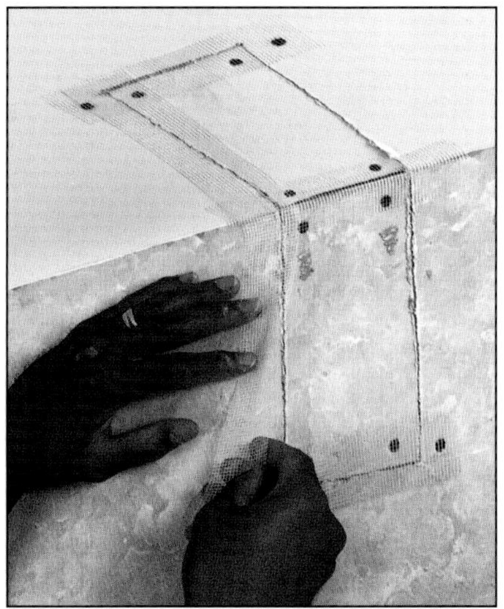

2 TAPE THE JOINTS. Cut pieces of fiberglass mesh patching tape and lay them over the joints. Apply joint compound and smooth it with a drywall taping knife. (Ready-mix joint compound is easy to use, but dry-mix compound is stronger and sets faster.)

3 SAND THE PATCH. Allow the compound to dry. Reapply the compound, feathering the edges. It will take several coats to smooth the joint. Sand the patch smooth with a drywall-sanding block. Prime and paint.

1 CUT A HOLE FOR A DRYWALL PATCH. Use a level or framing square to mark out a rectangle around the damage. Your marks should span from stud to stud or joist to joist. Cut with a drywall saw. Cut 2×2 or 2×4 cleats a few inches longer than the hole. Hold them against the back of the drywall as you drive 3-inch drywall screws into the framing.

2 INSTALL THE PATCH. Cut a patch to fit, about 1/4 inch smaller than the hole in each direction. Attach the patch with 1 1/4-inch drywall screws. Cover the joints with tape, apply joint compound (below), and sand (page 135).

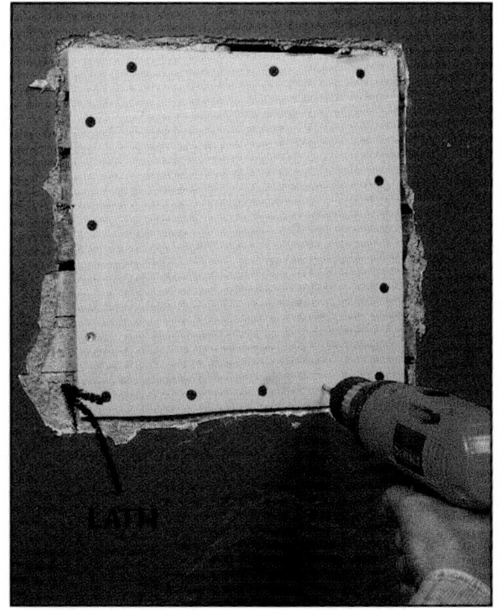

1 PATCH PLASTER WITH DRYWALL. Remove loose plaster. Tap with a hammer to excavate a rough rectangular shape. If the lath is solid, don't expose studs or joists. For the patch, use drywall that is the same thickness as the plaster. Cut the patch roughly to size, and attach it to the lath with 1 1/4-inch drywall screws.

2 FILL THE GAP WITH JOINT COMPOUND. You can mix it with perlited gypsum (see "Cutting a Channel in a Plaster Wall," above). Apply mesh tape to the joints, then apply joint compound. For best results, apply several feathering coats of joint compound, scraping and sanding between coats.

A+ WORK SMARTER

CUTTING A CHANNEL IN A PLASTER WALL. You might cut a narrow channel through a plaster wall to slip a cable through. To fill the gap, combine dry-mix joint compound ("90" or "45") with an equal amount of perlited gypsum. Mix the two with water, and you'll have a paste that won't sag when you apply it. Force the paste into the cavity with a putty knife. Allow it to dry, then apply subsequent coats of joint compound.

Homer's Hindsight

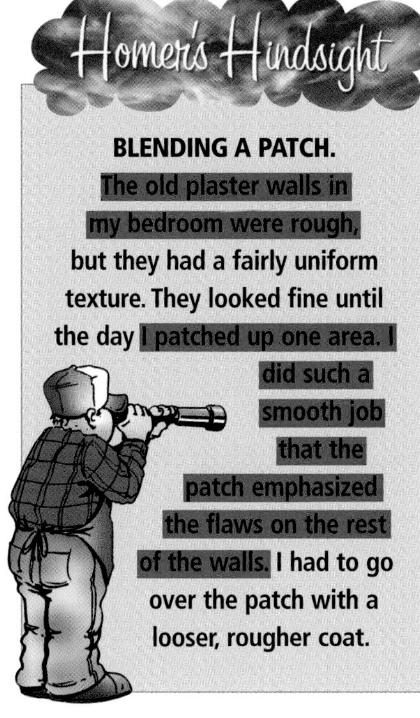

BLENDING A PATCH. **The old plaster walls in my bedroom were rough, but they had a fairly uniform texture. They looked fine until the day I patched up one area. I did such a smooth job that the patch emphasized the flaws on the rest of the walls. I had to go over the patch with a looser, rougher coat.**

INSTALLING A JUNCTION BOX

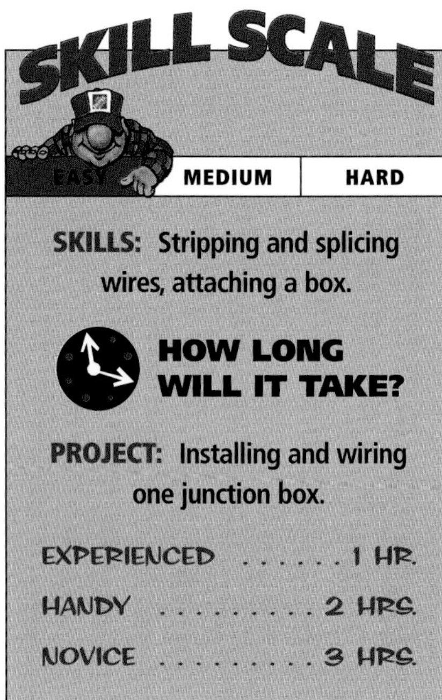

SKILLS: Stripping and splicing wires, attaching a box.

HOW LONG WILL IT TAKE?

PROJECT: Installing and wiring one junction box.

EXPERIENCED ...... 1 HR.
HANDY .... 2 HRS.
NOVICE .... 3 HRS.

STUFF YOU'LL NEED

TOOLS: Combination tool, lineman's pliers, screwdriver, drill, voltage tester

MATERIALS: Junction box with cover, wire nuts, screws

Install a junction box wherever wires must be spliced. Keep the box accessible—never bury it in a wall or ceiling. Junction boxes are usually flush-mounted to walls or attached to attic, basement, or crawl-space framing. But you can set one inside a wall as you would a switch box. Cover the junction box with a blank plastic cover plate.

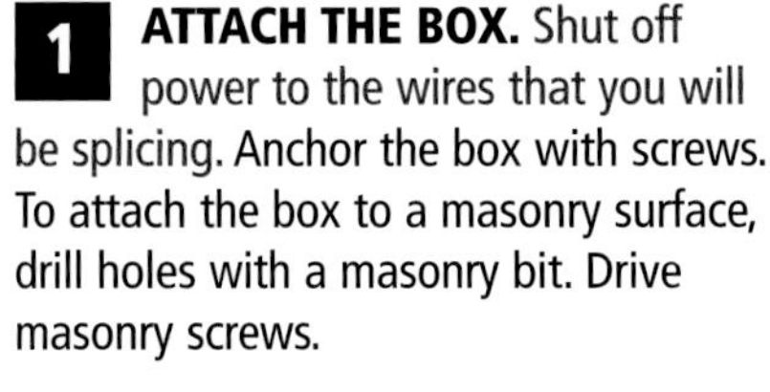

1 ATTACH THE BOX. Shut off power to the wires that you will be splicing. Anchor the box with screws. To attach the box to a masonry surface, drill holes with a masonry bit. Drive masonry screws.

2 WIRE THE BOX. Strip cable sheathing and clamp the cable, or connect conduit. Strip wires and connect them with wire nuts. If the box is metal, make a grounding pigtail and connect it to the green grounding screw.

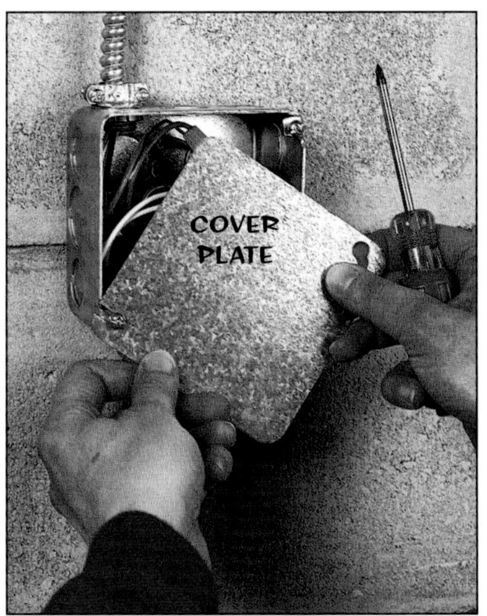

3 COVER THE BOX. Fold the wires into the box and attach the cover plate. To do so, loosen the screws at two corners of the box, hook the cover plate on first one screw and then the other, and tighten the screws.

A+ WORK SMARTER

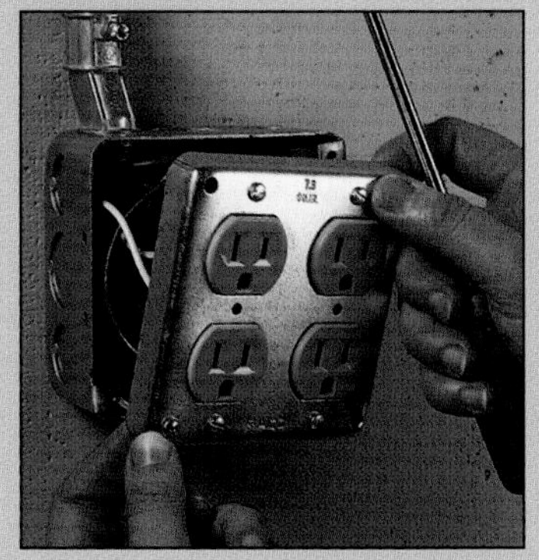

USE A METAL COVER PLATE IN UTILITY AREAS.

If a receptacle or switch is in an exposed box, use a metal rather than a plastic cover plate. You may need to break off the device's metal "ears". Attach the devices to the cover plate first, and then attach the cover plate to the box.

INSTALLING RACEWAY WIRING

SKILL SCALE
EASY
MEDIUM
HARD
SKILLS: Connecting with screws, stripping and joining wires.
HOW LONG WILL IT TAKE?
PROJECT: Installing a switch and fixture, or several receptacles.
EXPERIENCED . . . . . 3 HRS.
HANDY . . . . 5 HRS.
NOVICE . . . . 8 HRS.

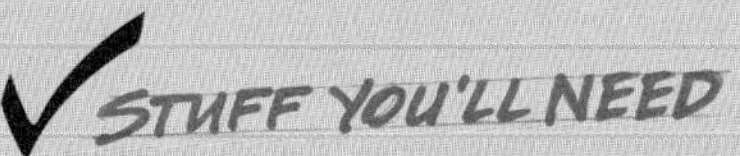

✓ STUFF YOU'LL NEED

TOOLS: Drill, screwdriver, hacksaw, combination tool, longnose pliers

MATERIALS: Box extender with cover plate, channel, fittings, fixture bases, fixture box, wire, clips, new devices, plastic anchors

Raceway wiring is an easy way to install a switch, fixture, or receptacle when cutting into a wall is difficult or appearances aren't important. It will spare you the hassle of cutting into walls, drilling holes, fishing cable, and patching the walls.

GATHERING THE PARTS

Take a drawing of your proposed installation to a home center or electrical supply source, and ask a salesperson to help you assemble all the parts. Choose metal, which is paintable, or plastic, which is not.

You'll need a starter box for each device, channel, L and T connectors, receptacle or switch boxes, and perhaps a fixture box. Buy plenty of wire. Use green-insulated wire for the ground, never bare copper.

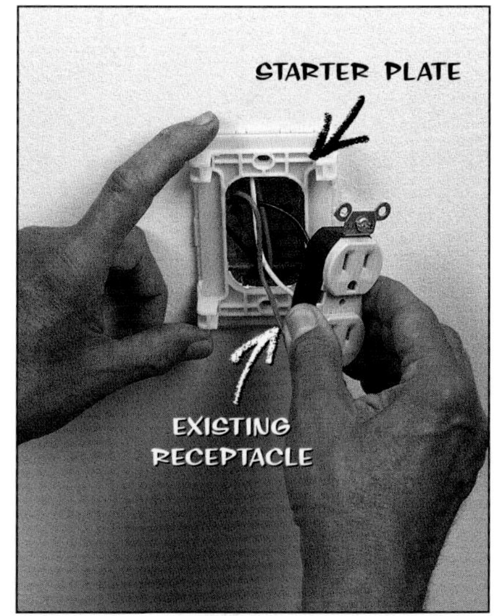

1 INSTALL THE STARTER BOX. Shut off power to the circuit. Pull out a receptacle, and mount a starter plate on the wall behind it. Install new raceway boxes for receptacles, switches, and fixtures in the same way.

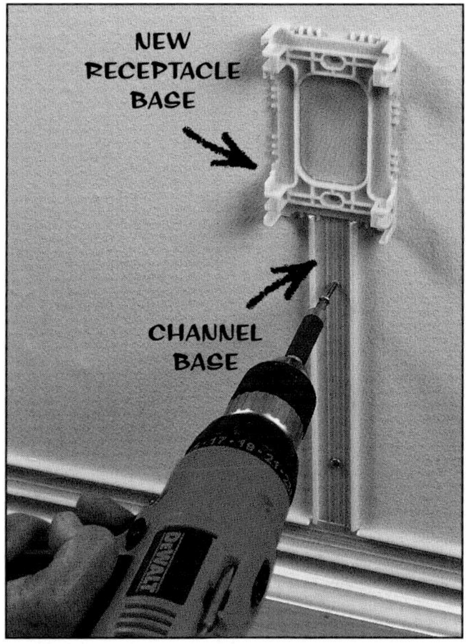

2 CUT AND ATTACH THE CHANNEL BASE. Use a hacksaw to cut pieces of channel to fit between the boxes. Attach the channel base to the wall with screws driven into studs or plastic anchors. Use fittings at all corners.

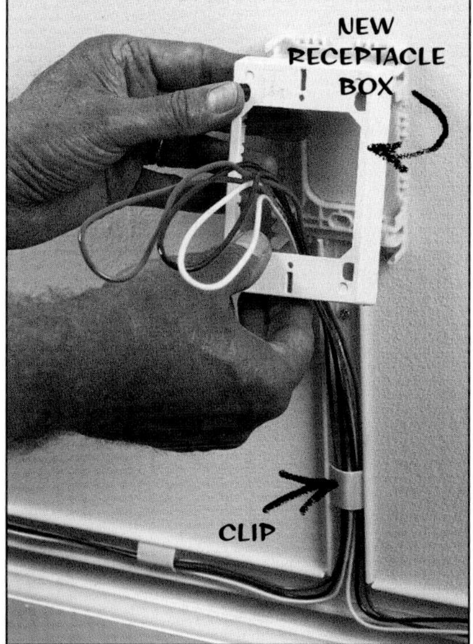

3 RUN THE WIRES. Place wires in the channel base and secure them with clips about every foot. Leave 8 inches of wire at each box to make connections. Snap any device boxes onto the bases and fasten them with screws driven into studs or plastic anchors.

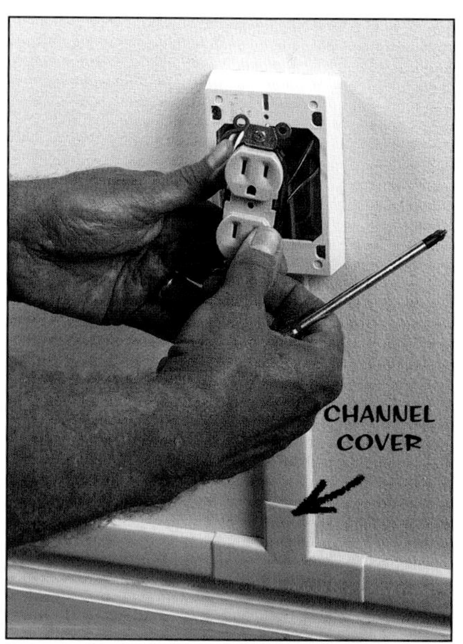

4 **WIRE THE DEVICES AND FIXTURES.** Snap the covers onto the channel base and the corner pieces. Strip the wire ends and connect them to the terminals just as you would for standard wiring. Install cover plates, restore power, and test.

FISHING WIRES IN METAL RACEWAY. Metal channels do not come apart in two pieces. Install clips on the wall, and snap the channel into the clips. Fish wires through the channel. If you can't shove the wires through, you might have to use a fish tape.

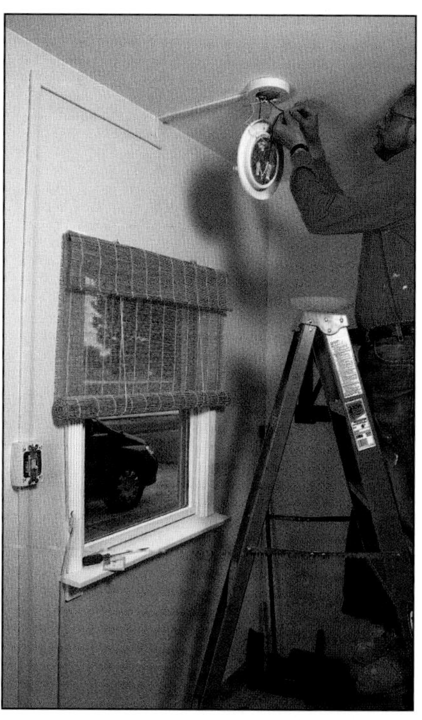

ADDING A LIGHT AND WALL SWITCH USING RACEWAY WIRING. To add a switched ceiling light to a room, you need a nearby receptacle. Install a ceiling fixture base, making sure that it is firmly attached to joists in the ceiling. Install the raceway switch base, and run a channel from the receptacle to the switch base and on to the fixture base. Run wiring and add the boxes. Make wiring connections as shown on page 142, and install the devices.

Use a similar arrangement to add a wall switch to a pull-chain light fixture. Install a raceway switch box at a convenient height. Remove the ceiling fixture, and install a raceway fixture box onto the ceiling box. Run the channel and two black wires from the switch to the fixture, making connections as shown on page 146.

TRY THESE QUICK AND EASY PRODUCT OPTIONS. **Cord channel (above left) encases and protects lamp cord that must be run along a wall. A multi-outlet strip (above right) is a sort of super extension cord, with a grounded receptacle every foot or so. No wiring is required to install these products. The channels mount to clips, or they stick to the wall with tape backing.**

CHAPTER 10 INSTALLING NEW SERVICES

Few construction projects are more satisfying than adding electrical devices or fixtures to your home. Most of these jobs take less than a day, yet make big improvements in your family's quality of life. The installations in this chapter rely on the skills and knowledge taught in the first two-thirds of the book. Refer to earlier chapters for specific instructions on the projects that follow.

Whenever adding new services, follow these important guidelines:

- Turn off power to the circuit you are working on, and test all open boxes to make sure no is power present.
- Be sure the new service will not overload your circuit.
- Follow local codes for running cable and installing boxes. Obtain a permit from your building department every time you install new cable.

CHAPTER TEN PROJECTS

INSTALLING A NEW RECEPTACLE

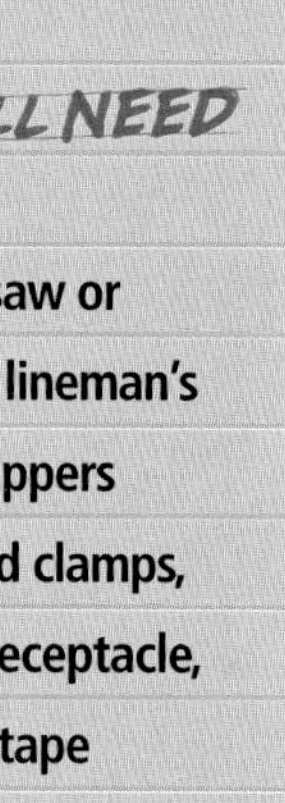

✓ STUFF YOU'LL NEED

TOOLS: Drill, drywall saw or sabersaw, screwdriver, lineman's pliers, combination strippers
MATERIALS: Cable and clamps, remodel box, staples, receptacle, wire nuts, electrician's tape

The easiest way to install a new receptacle is to tap an existing receptacle for power, as shown here. Before you do this, make sure you will not overload the existing receptacle's circuit (page 116–117).

If you can't pull power from a nearby receptacle, you may be able to tap into a junction box above or below the room. You also can pull power from a light fixture or switch—whichever has power entering its box.

As a last resort, you may have to run cable all the way back to the service panel and install a new circuit breaker (pages 168–169).

As with many electrical projects, patching and painting walls afterward can be more trouble than the wiring. See pages 130–132 for tips on reducing damage to your walls.

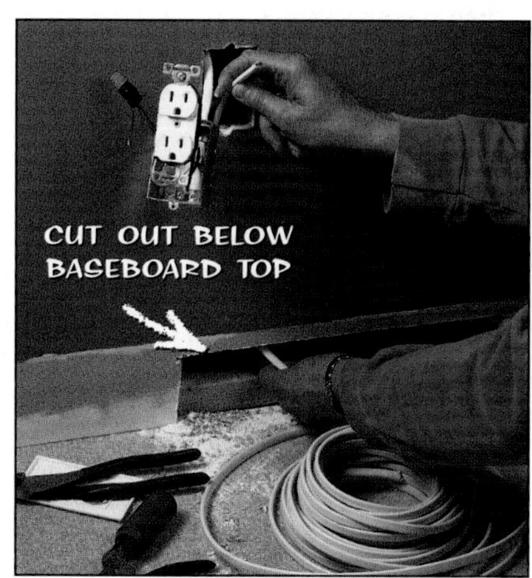

1 PLAN A PATH FOR THE CABLE. Choose a path that will cause minimal damage to the walls, such as running cable behind a baseboard (shown). Remove the baseboard and cut away the drywall. Shut off power to the circuit. Remove a knockout in the receptacle's box from where you'll take power, add a connector, then fish the cable.

2 RUN THE CABLE THROUGH THE HOLES. Cut a hole for the new receptacle box. Drill holes in the centers of studs for the cable to pass through. Strip 6 to 8 inches of sheathing from either end of the cable. Punch out a knockout hole and clamp the cable to the existing box. Run the cable into a remodel box and attach the box to the wall (pages 130–134). Either clamp the cable to the box or staple the cable near the box.

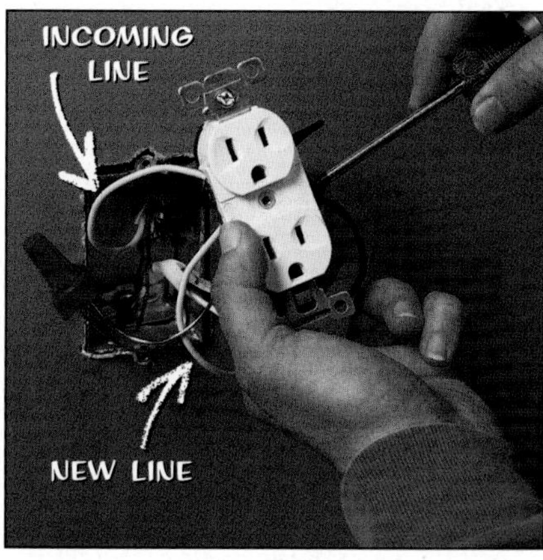

3 WIRE THE RECEPTACLES. If the existing receptacle is at the end of the run (shown), attach the black wire to the brass terminal and the white wire to the silver terminal. If the receptacle is in the middle of the run, no terminals will be available; use pigtails to connect to power (page 49). Wire the new receptacle—white to silver, black to brass. Connect the grounds (pages 12–13). Restore power, then test.

ADDING A WALL SWITCH

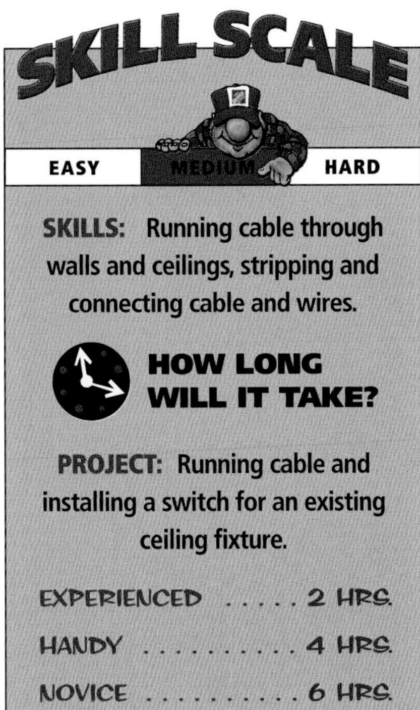

SKILLS: Running cable through walls and ceilings, stripping and connecting cable and wires.

HOW LONG WILL IT TAKE?

PROJECT: Running cable and installing a switch for an existing ceiling fixture.

EXPERIENCED . . . . . 2 HRS.
HANDY . . . . 4 HRS.
NOVICE . . . . 6 HRS.

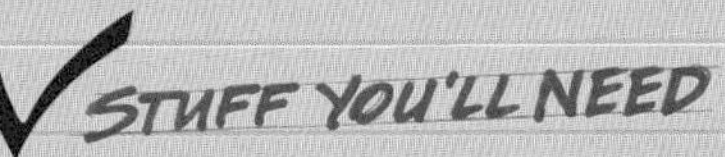

✓ STUFF YOU'LL NEED

TOOLS: Drill, drywall saw or saber saw, fish tape, screwdriver, lineman's pliers, strippers
MATERIALS: Cable and clamps, remodel box, staples, receptacle, wire nuts, electrician's tape, cover plates

Wiring a wall switch to a pull-chain ceiling fixture is simple; the challenge is running cable from the fixture to the switch. You will probably need to cut a hole near the fixture so that you can reach behind its box and clamp cable to it. Consider covering the hole with a medallion (page 29).

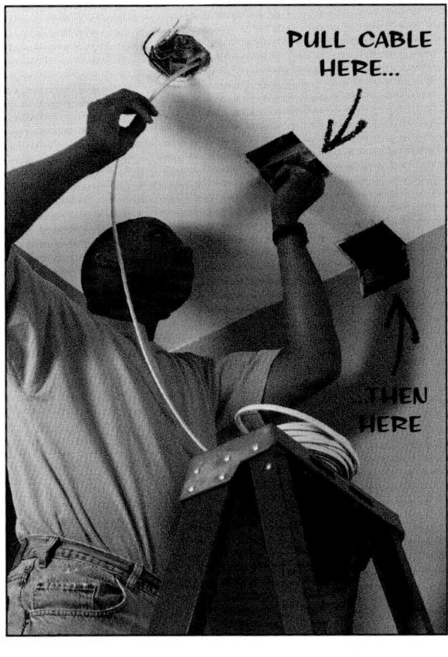

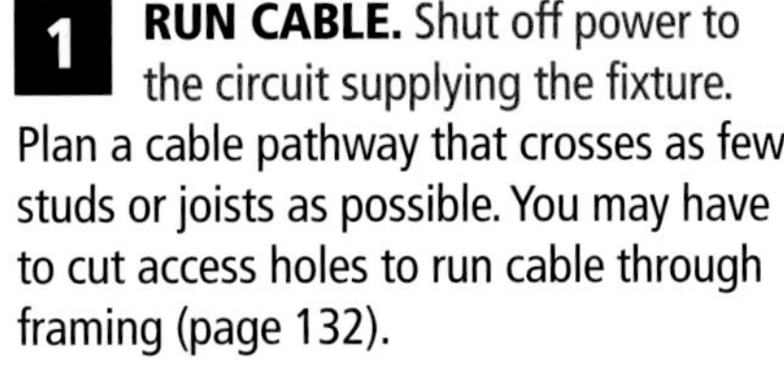

1 RUN CABLE. Shut off power to the circuit supplying the fixture. Plan a cable pathway that crosses as few studs or joists as possible. You may have to cut access holes to run cable through framing (page 132).

2 RUN CABLE TO THE SWITCH BOX. Add nailing plates where you bore holes in framing. Cut a hole for a remodel switch box and pull the cable through. Strip the wires.

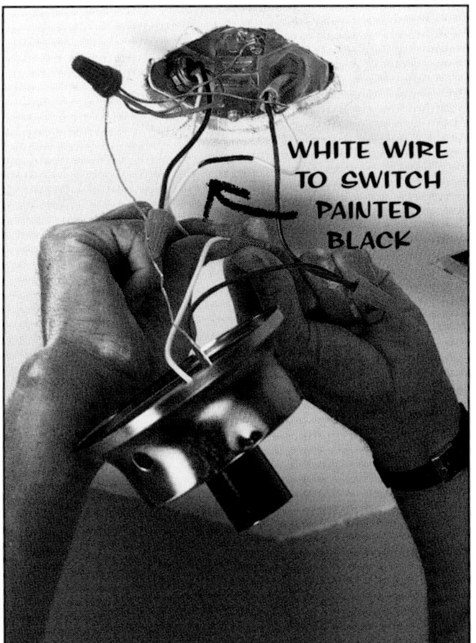

3 WIRE THE FIXTURE. First, connect the ground (pages 12–13). Remove the old black wire from the fixture lead, and splice it to the new white wire and mark it black. Splice the new black wire to the fixture's black lead.

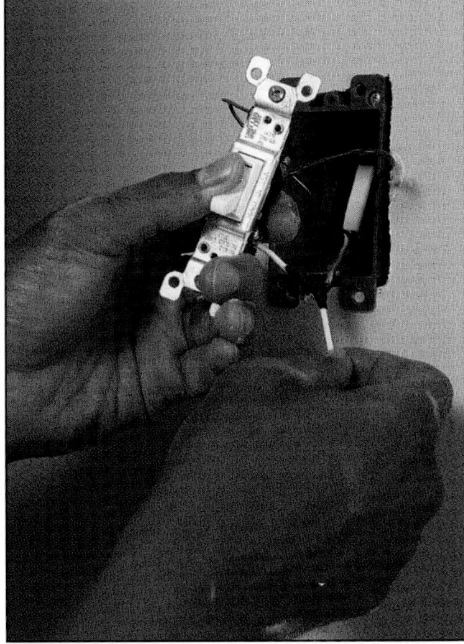

4 CONNET THE GROUND AT THE SWITCH. Attach both wires to the terminals and mark the white wire black. Restore power to the circuit, and test.

SWITCHING A RECEPTACLE

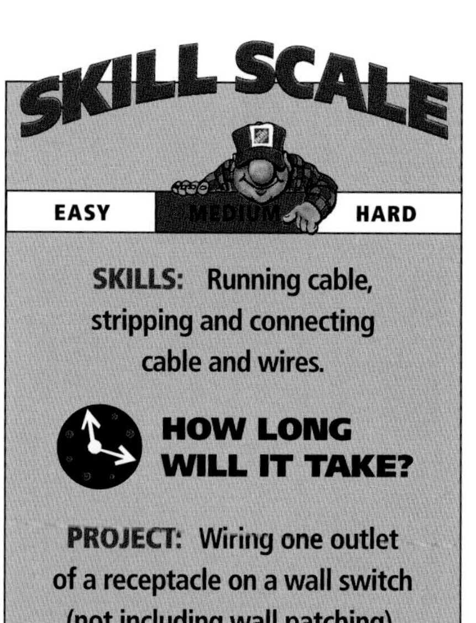

When you assign one outlet of a duplex receptacle to a wall switch, you can control a floor or table lamp from a doorway. The second outlet will remain hot all the time.

To run cable through finished walls and install a remodel box for the switch, see pages 130–134. See pages 12–13 for grounding methods.

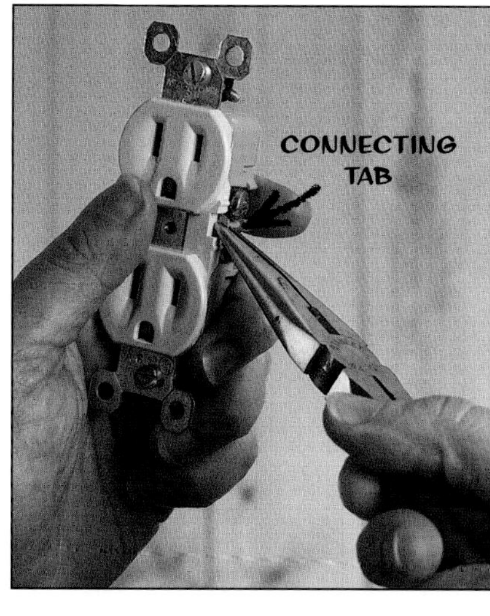

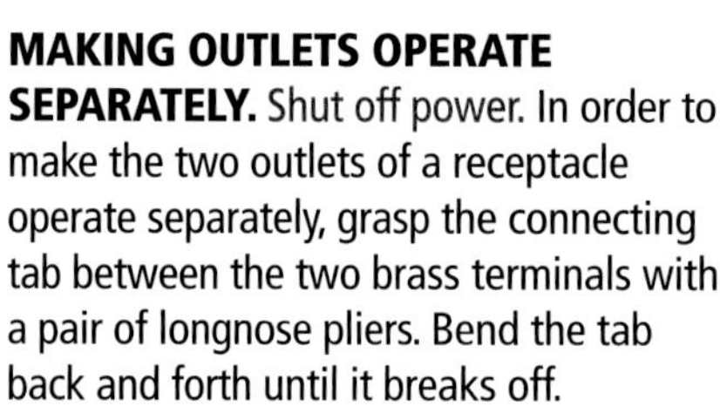

MAKING OUTLETS OPERATE SEPARATELY. Shut off power. In order to make the two outlets of a receptacle operate separately, grasp the connecting tab between the two brass terminals with a pair of longnose pliers. Bend the tab back and forth until it breaks off.

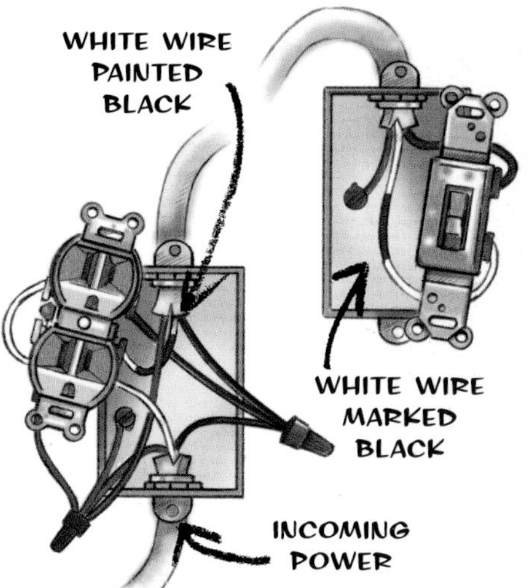

WORKING WITH AN END-OF-THE-RUN RECEPTACLE. Shut off power. Run two-wire cable from the switch to the receptacle. Paint both ends of the white wires black. Connect the grounds. At the receptacle, remove the old black wire and splice it to the new white wire (marked black) and a black pigtail. Connect the pigtail to the always-hot terminal and the other black wire to the other terminal. Attach both wires to the switch.

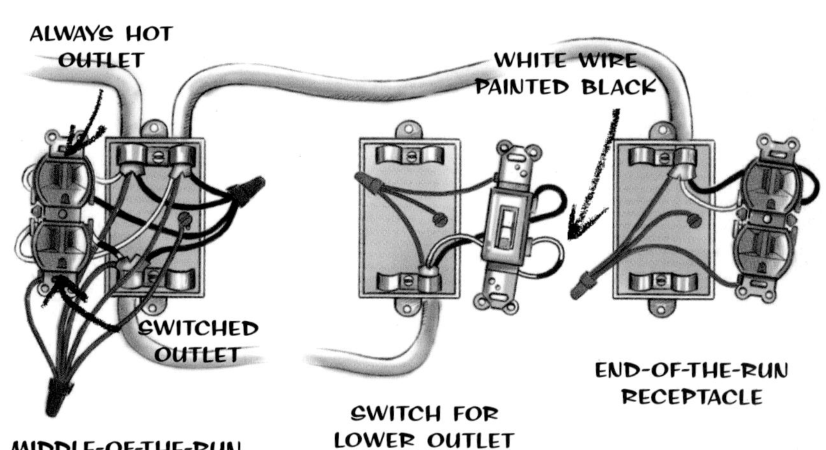

WORKING WITH A RECEPTACLE IN THE MIDDLE OF A RUN. Shut off power. This project will be complicated if the receptacle you want to switch has wires attached to all four terminals. At the receptacle to be switched, remove both old black wires. Splice them with the new white wire (marked black) and a black pigtail. Connect the pigtail to the always-hot outlet and the new black wire to the switched outlet. Wire the switch and connect the grounds.

SPLITTING A RECEPTACLE

SKILLS: Running cable, stripping and splicing cable and wire.

HOW LONG WILL IT TAKE?

PROJECT: Installing four split or alternating receptacles.

EXPERIENCED . . . . . 3 HRS.
HANDY . . . . 4 HRS.
NOVICE . . . . 6 HRS.

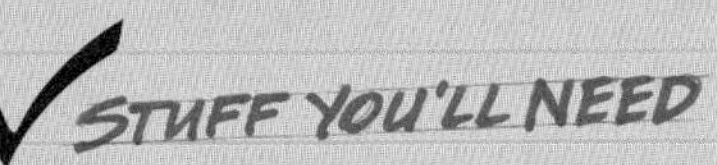

STUFF YOU'LL NEED

TOOLS: Drill, drywall saw or saber saw, fish tape, screwdriver, lineman's pliers, strippers

MATERIALS: Cable and clamps, receptacles, boxes, wire nuts, electrician's tape, cover plates

SWITCHING OPTIONS. Install raceway wiring to avoid the hassles of cutting and patching walls (page 138–139). Or, if a fixture's housing is large enough, install an "anywhere" switch (page 98).

Wherever you're likely to plug in more than one high-amp appliance, you run the risk of overloading a circuit. In some cases, two appliances or tools plugged into the same receptacle can add up to more than the circuit can handle.

That's why some building departments require kitchen counter receptacles to be split, so that each outlet is on a separate circuit (right). (In this case, the receptacles cannot be GFCIs.) Other municipalities prefer alternating the receptacles so that every other one is on the same circuit (below). Either of these configurations may be used in a workshop.

Use 20-amp receptacles and breakers and #12 wire for countertops and shop areas. (Canada: 15 amps maximum.)

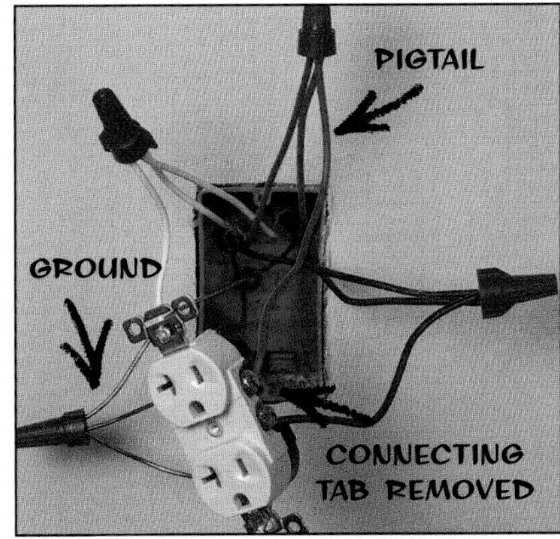

WIRING SPLIT RECEPTACLES. Run three-wire cable, with the black and red wires connected to separate circuit breakers or to the two poles of a double-pole breaker. Break off the connecting tabs on each receptacle (page 143). Using pigtails, connect the white wire to a silver terminal, the red wire to a brass terminal, and the black wire to the other brass terminal. Connect the grounds. Wire the other receptacles the same way.

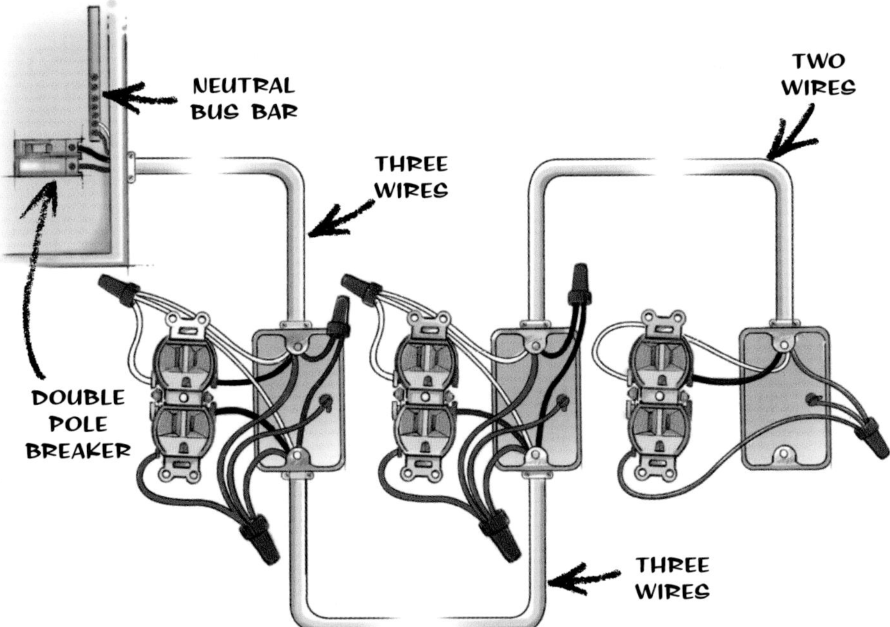

ALTERNATING CIRCUITS. Some codes call for a double-pole breaker, as shown, rather than two separate breakers. When one circuit is turned off, the other is off as well. Use three-wire cable. The black wire brings power to every other receptacle, and the red wire energizes the others. All receptacles share the same neutral wire.

ADDING A 240-VOLT RECEPTACLE

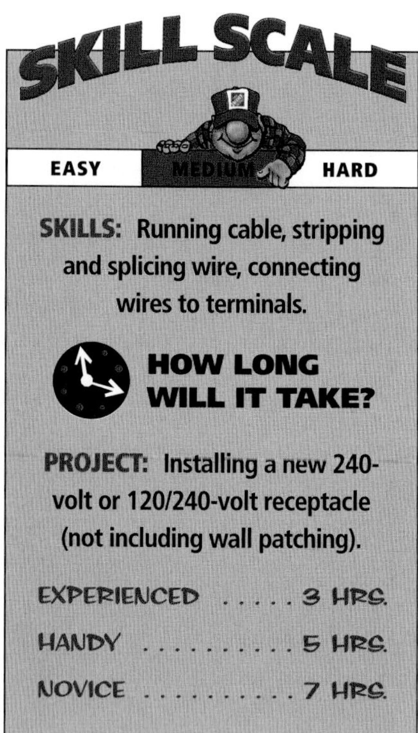

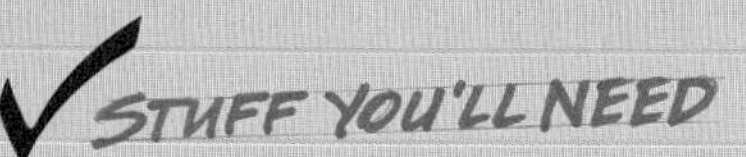

TOOLS: Drill, saw, fish tape, screwdriver, lineman's pliers, combination strippers

MATERIALS: 240- or 240/120-volt receptacle, cable, box, wire nuts, electrician's tape

Wiring a high-voltage receptacle is slightly more complicated than wiring a standard 120-volt receptacle. Follow safety precautions strictly, however, because this amount of voltage is dangerous.

Choose a receptacle that matches the appliance you will plug into it, both in hole configuration and amperage rating. Recent codes require four-wire receptacles; three-wire receptacles were once acceptable (page 76-77). Be sure the wires are thick enough. Use #10 wire for a 30-amp receptacle and #8 wire for a 40- or 50-amp receptacle.

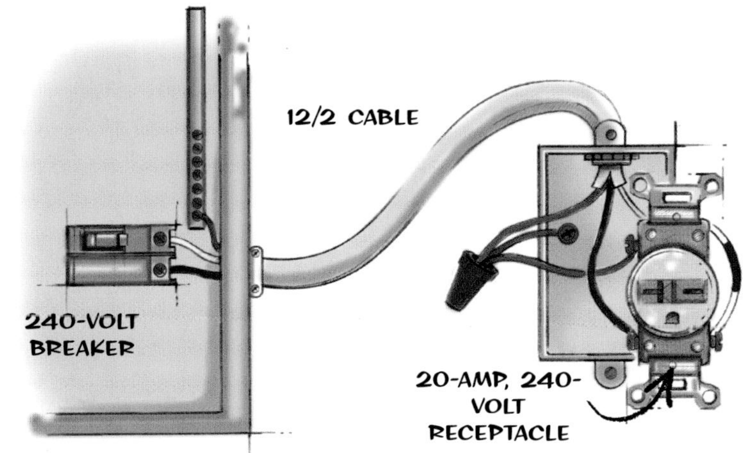

240-VOLT AIR-CONDITIONER RECEPTACLE. A 20-amp, 240-volt receptacle for a window air conditioner or other appliance requires only 12/2 cable, not the heftier #8 wire most 240-volt receptacles require. Connect the grounds. Mark the white wire black at both ends. Connect the two wires to a 240-volt breaker in the service panel and to the receptacle terminals.

120/240-VOLT RECEPTACLE

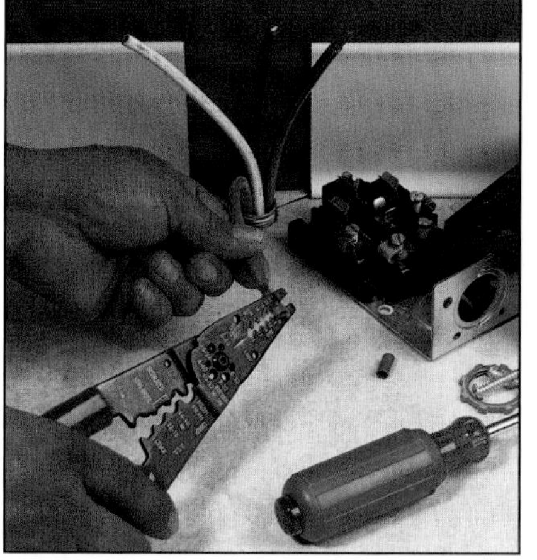

1 RUN THE WIRE. Though some codes allow a 40-amp circuit for a 50-amp range, many electricians prefer a 50-amp circuit so that the range will be protected when all burners are on at the same time (say, at Thanksgiving). Run three-wire cable with #8 wire and strip ¾ inch of insulation from each wire. Some codes require four-wire cable (page 77); check with your building department.

2 INSTALL THE RECEPTACLE. Fasten the receptacle base to the floor or wall with general purpose screws. Connect the black and red wires to the 240-volt breaker, and the white and green to the neutral bus bar. Connect the black, red, and white wires to the receptacle, and connect the ground. Attach the cover housing.

ADDING A FIXTURE WITH SWITCH

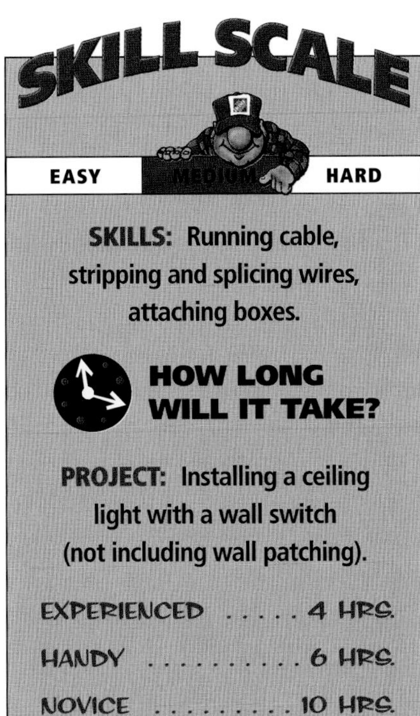

SKILLS: Running cable, stripping and splicing wires, attaching boxes.

HOW LONG WILL IT TAKE?

PROJECT: Installing a ceiling light with a wall switch (not including wall patching).

EXPERIENCED . . . . . 4 HRS.
HANDY . . . . 6 HRS.
NOVICE . . . . 10 HRS.

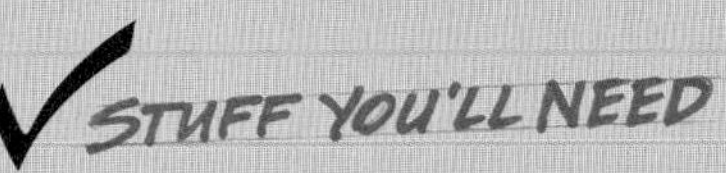

TOOLS: Drill, fish tape, screwdriver, lineman's pliers, combination strippers

MATERIALS: Light fixture and box, switch and box, electrician's tape, cable, staples, wire nuts

When planning to install a new light with a switch, decide whether to send power into the switch box (above) or to the fixture box (below). Shut off power to the box from which you will run power. See pages 130–134 for instructions on installing boxes and running cable, and pages 12–13 for grounding methods.

POWER TO SWITCH BOX

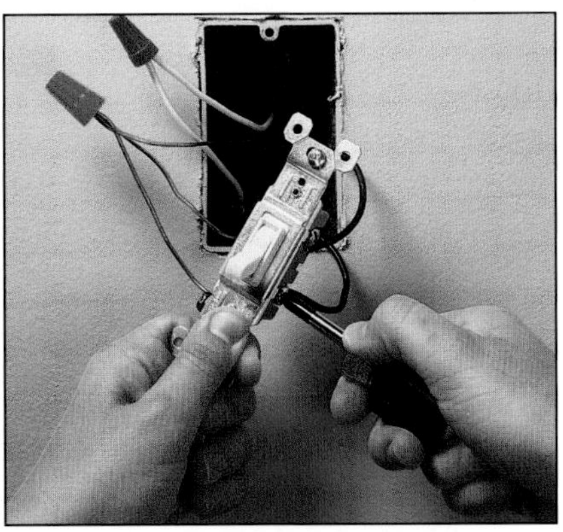

1 RUN WIRE FROM THE POWER SOURCE TO THE SWITCH BOX. Run two-wire cable from a power source to a wall switch box, and from there to a ceiling box. Connect the ground. Splice the white wires and connect the black wires to the switch terminals.

2 WIRE THE FIXTURE. Connect the ground. Splice the white wire to the white fixture lead, and splice the black wire to the black fixture lead. Restore power and test.

POWER TO FIXTURE

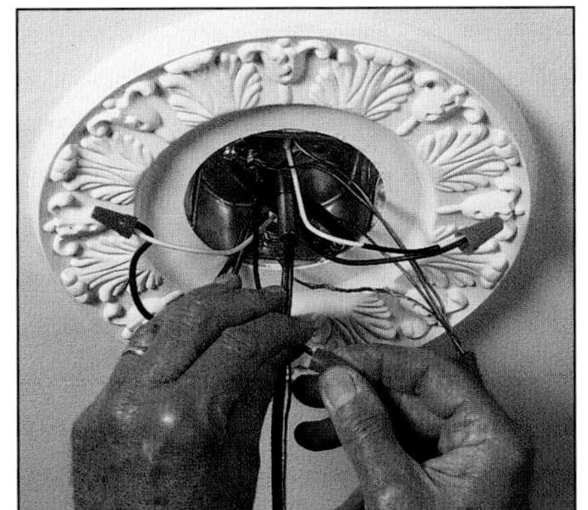

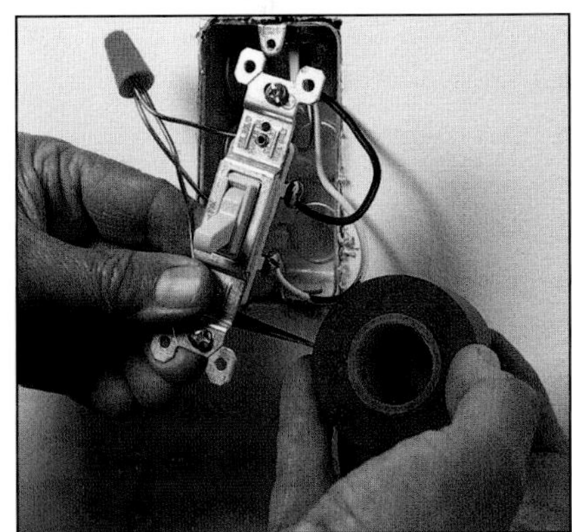

1 RUN POWER TO THE FIXTURE. Run two-wire cable from the power source to the fixture box. Run two-wire cable from the fixture box to the switch, and mark the white wire black at both ends. Connect the ground at the fixture box. Splice the black feed wire (from the power source) to the white wire that is marked black. Splice the other black wire to the fixture's black lead, and splice the white wire to the white lead.

2 WIRE THE SWITCH. Connect the ground. Connect the black wire and the white wire (painted black) to the switch terminals. Restore power and test.

TWO FIXTURES WITH SEPARATE SWITCHES

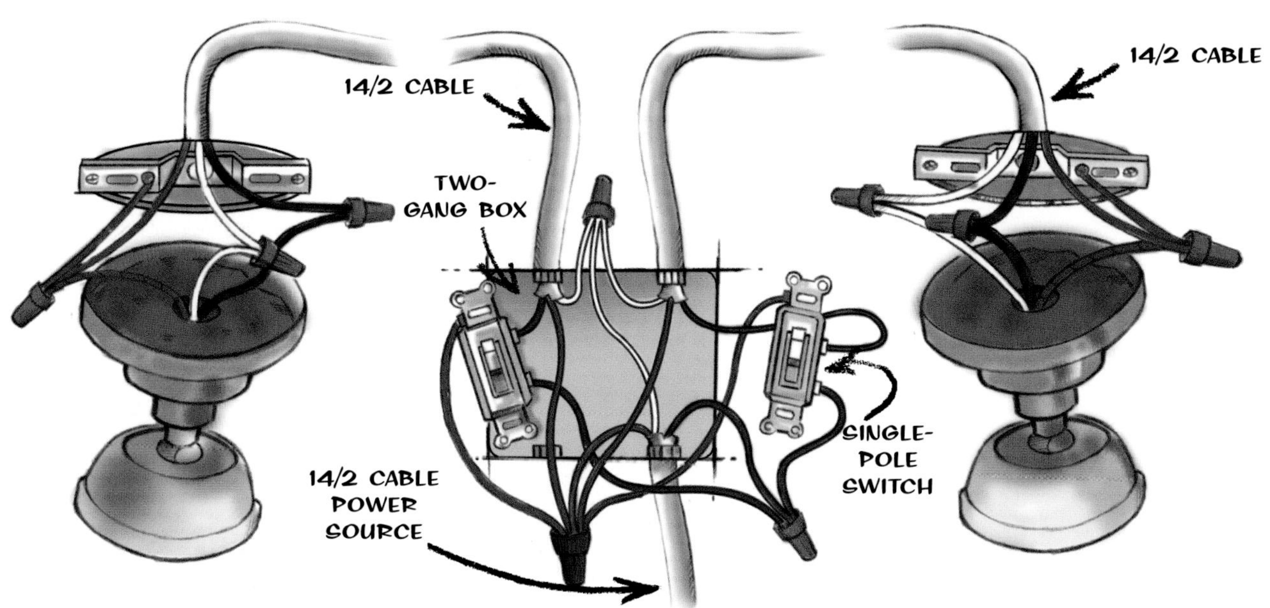

WHEN POWER ENTERS THE SWITCH BOX. Shut off power to the circuit. Run one two-wire cable from the power source into a two-gang switch box, and additional two-wire cables from the switch box to each fixture box. At the switch box, connect the grounds. Splice all the white wires together and splice two black pigtails to the feed wire. Connect one black pigtail and one black wire to each switch. At each fixture box, connect the grounds. Splice the white lead to the white wire and the black lead to the black wire. Restore power and test.

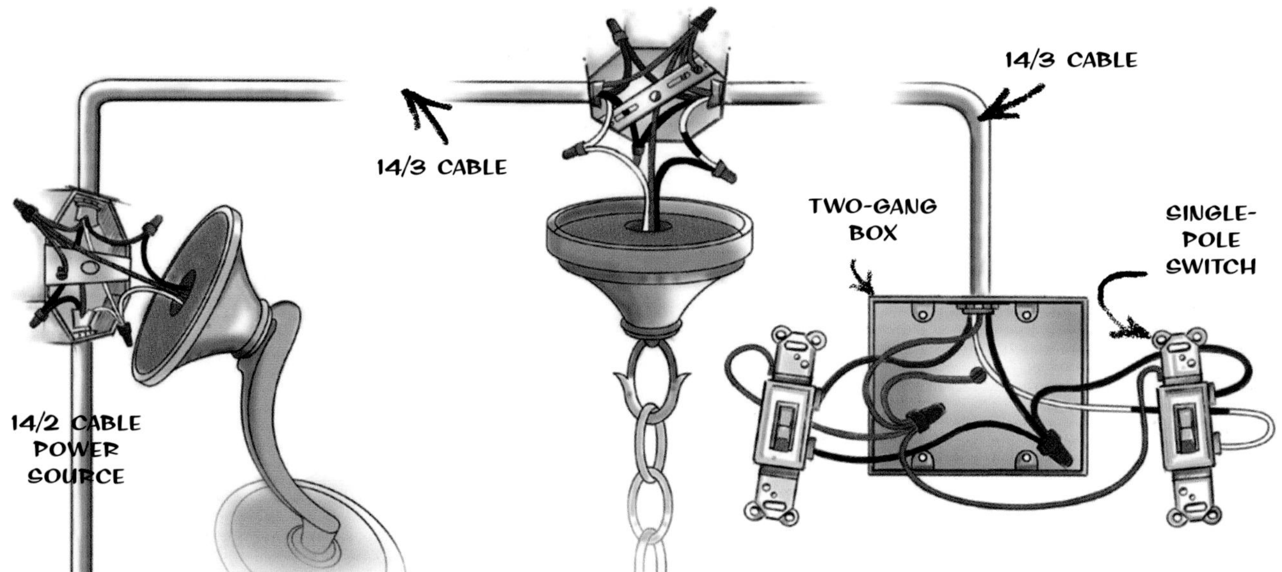

WHEN POWER ENTERS THE FIXTURE. Shut off power to the circuit. Run two-wire cable from a power source to one fixture box. Run three-wire cable from there to the second fixture box. Run three-wire cable from the second fixture box to the two-gang switch box and mark the white wire black at both ends. At the fixture box farthest from the switches, connect the grounds. Splice the two white wires to the fixture's white lead and splice the fixture's black lead to the red wire. Splice the remaining black wires. At the second fixture box, connect the grounds. Splice the marked white wire to the fixture's black lead and the unmarked white wire to the fixture's white lead. Splice the red wires together and splice the black wires together. At the switch box, splice two pigtails to the black wire. Connect the red wire and one pigtail to one switch and the marked white wire and a pigtail to the other switch. Restore power and test.

WIRING THREE-WAY SWITCHES

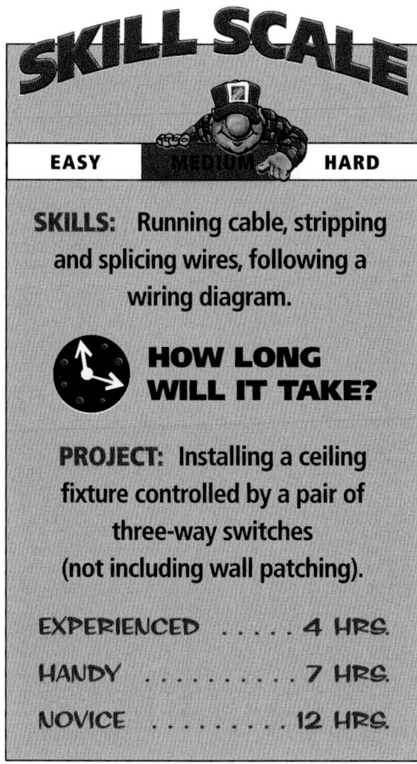

STUFF YOU'LL NEED
TOOLS: Drill, fish tape, lineman's pliers, screwdriver, combination strippers
MATERIALS: Two three-way switches, ceiling fixture, cable and clamps, wire nuts, staples, electrician's tape

Three-way switches are so named because there are three components: two switches and the light fixture. That means you can turn a stairwell light on or off from the top or bottom of the stairs. In long hallways, three-way switches allow you to conveniently control light fixtures from both ends of the hall. In attics, basements, and garages, they spare you from having to grope in the dark looking for the light switch, and they are particularly useful in households with young children who have a tendency to forget to turn off the lights.

See pages 130–134 for tips on running cable and installing boxes and pages 12–13 for grounding methods.

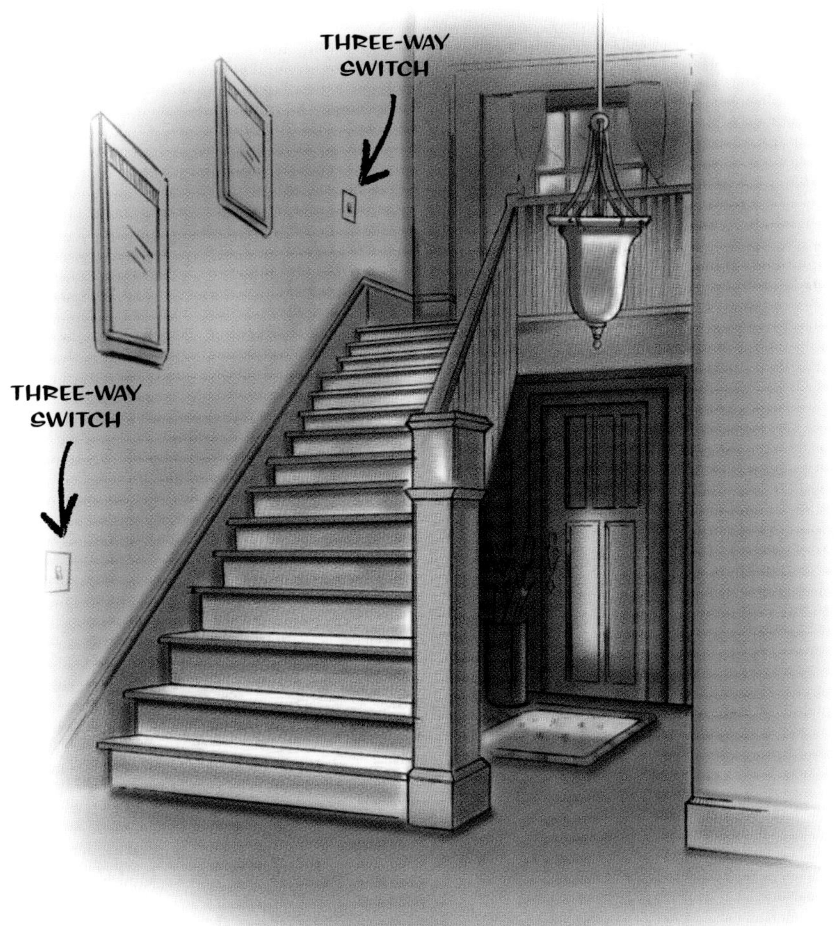

THREE-WAY SWITCHES ON STAIRS. Codes—and common sense—dictate that stairway lighting should be controlled by one switch at the bottom of the stairs and one at the top.

CLOSER LOOK

HOW THREE-WAYS WORK. Three-way switches have three terminals. The light they control is turned on when the two switches provide a continuous pathway for power. When either switch creates a gap in that pathway, the light is off.

In a three-way system, a pair of "traveler" wires travel from switch to switch, never to the fixture itself. It is the "common" wire that carries power to the fixture. When you wire a three-way switch, keep in mind that the traveler terminals are interchangeable—it doesn't matter which traveler wire goes to which traveler terminal. Connect either the feed wire (which brings power) or a wire that attaches to the fixture's black lead to a switch's common terminal.

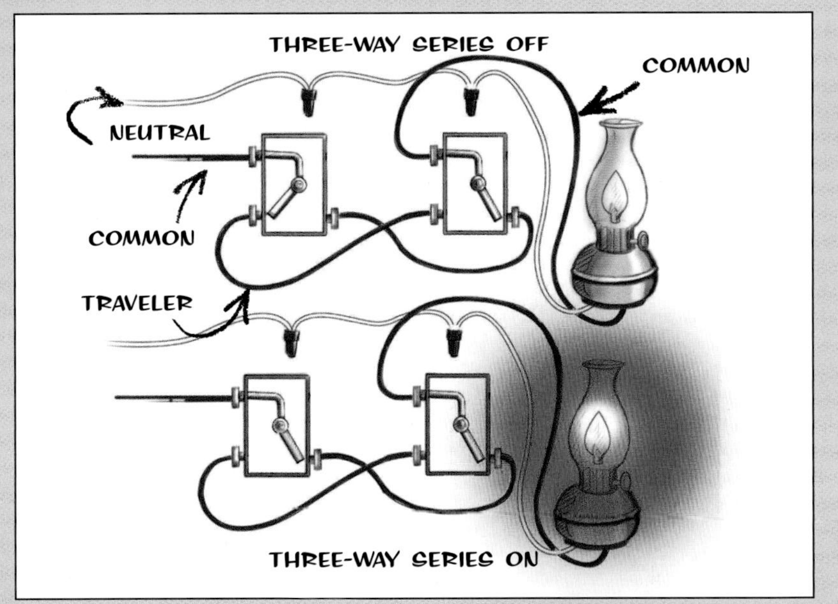

WHEN POWER RUNS FIXTURE-SWITCH-SWITCH

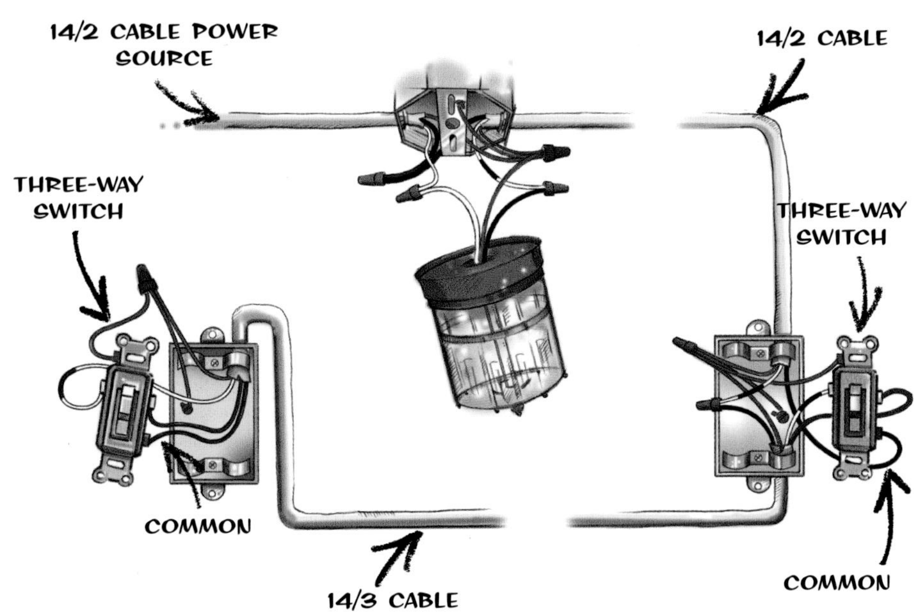

WHEN POWER RUNS TO THE FIXTURE FIRST. Shut off power to the circuit. Run two-wire cable from the power source to the fixture box. Run two-wire cable from the fixture box to the first switch box and mark the white wire black at both ends. Run three-wire cable between the two switch boxes, and mark the white wire black at both ends. Connect the grounds in all three boxes.

At the fixture box, splice the black wires together. Splice the unmarked white wire to the fixture's white lead and splice the marked white wire to the black lead. At the first switch box, connect the marked white wire that comes from the other switch and the red wire to the traveler terminals. Connect the black wire that comes from the fixture to the common terminal. Splice together the remaining wires (one black and one white marked black).

At the second switch box, attach the black-marked white wire and the red wire to the traveler terminals. Attach the black wire to the common terminal. Restore power and test.

WHEN POWER RUNS SWITCH-SWITCH-FIXTURE

WHEN POWER RUNS TO THE SWITCHES FIRST. This is the simplest way to wire three-ways. Shut off power to the circuit. Run two-wire cable from the power source to the first switch box, three-wire cable between the switch boxes, and two-wire cable from the second switch box to the fixture box. Connect the grounds. At the first switch box, splice the white wires. Connect the black feed wire to the common terminal and the other two wires to the traveler terminals. At the second switch box, connect the black wire coming from the fixture to the common terminal (in this case, the lead marked "common" from a three-way dimmer switch). Splice the white wires. Connect the remaining black and red wires to the traveler terminals. At the fixture box, splice the black wire to the black lead and the white wire to the white lead. Restore power and test.

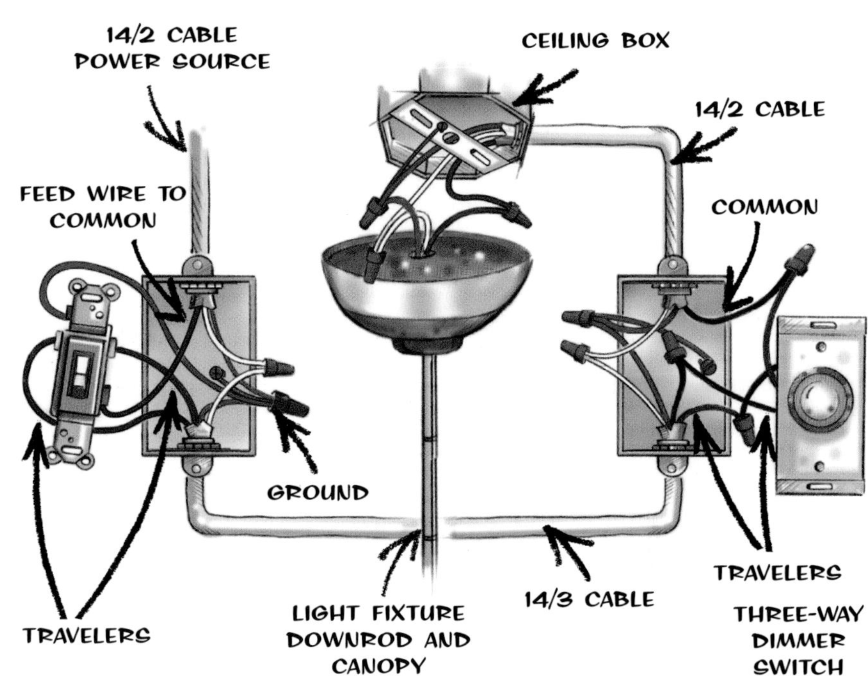

WHEN POWER RUNS SWITCH-FIXTURE-SWITCH

WHEN POWER RUNS SWITCH-FIXTURE-SWITCH. This is the most complicated three-way wiring configuration, but it is sometimes the easiest way to run the cable. Shut off power to the circuit. Run two-wire cable from a power source to the first switch box and three-wire cable from there to the fixture box. Run three-wire cable from the fixture box to the second switch and mark the white wire black at both ends. Connect the grounds in all three boxes. At the first switch box, splice the white wires together. Attach the feed wire to the common terminal and the remaining wires to the traveler terminals. At the fixture box, splice the red wires together. Splice the black wire that comes from the first switch to the white wire that is marked black. Splice the remaining black wire to the black lead and the white wire to the white lead. At the second switch, attach the black wire to the common terminal and the remaining wires to the traveler terminals. Restore power and test.

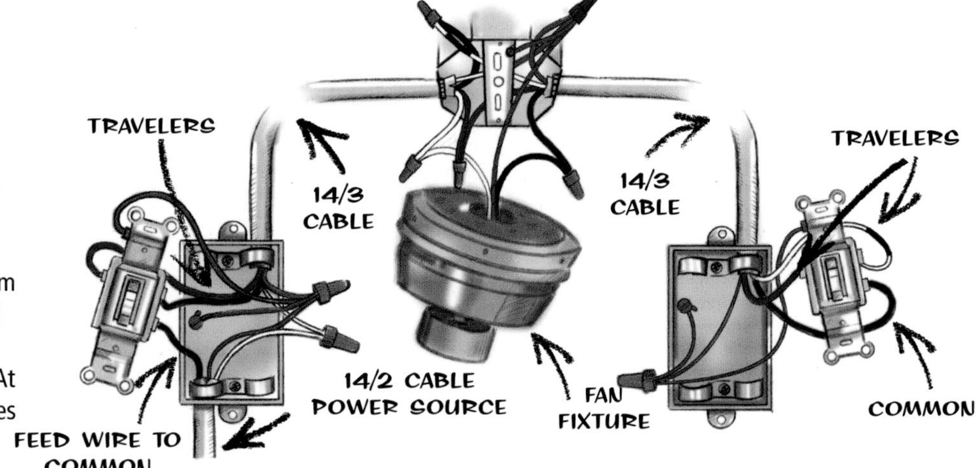

WIRING FOUR-WAY SWITCHES

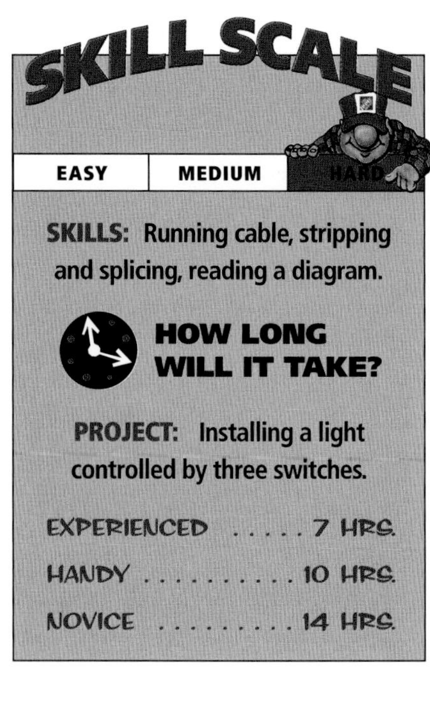

SKILL SCALE
EASY
MEDIUM
HARD
SKILLS: Running cable, stripping and splicing, reading a diagram.
HOW LONG WILL IT TAKE?
PROJECT: Installing a light controlled by three switches.
EXPERIENCED . . . . . 7 HRS.
HANDY . . . . 10 HRS.
NOVICE . . . . 14 HRS.

STUFF YOU'LL NEED

TOOLS: Drill, fish tape, lineman's pliers, screwdriver, combination strippers

MATERIALS: Light fixture, one 4-way and two 3-way switches, cable and clamps, staples, wire nuts, electrician's tape

To control a fixture from three or more locations, install a pair of three-way switches at either end and one or more four-way switches in between. The wiring for this setup can get complex, so you may want to hire an electrician. Shown below is a switch-switch-switch fixture; four-way switches also can be wired with power entering the fixture first.

Install as many four-way switches as you like, as long as the first and last switches are three-ways.

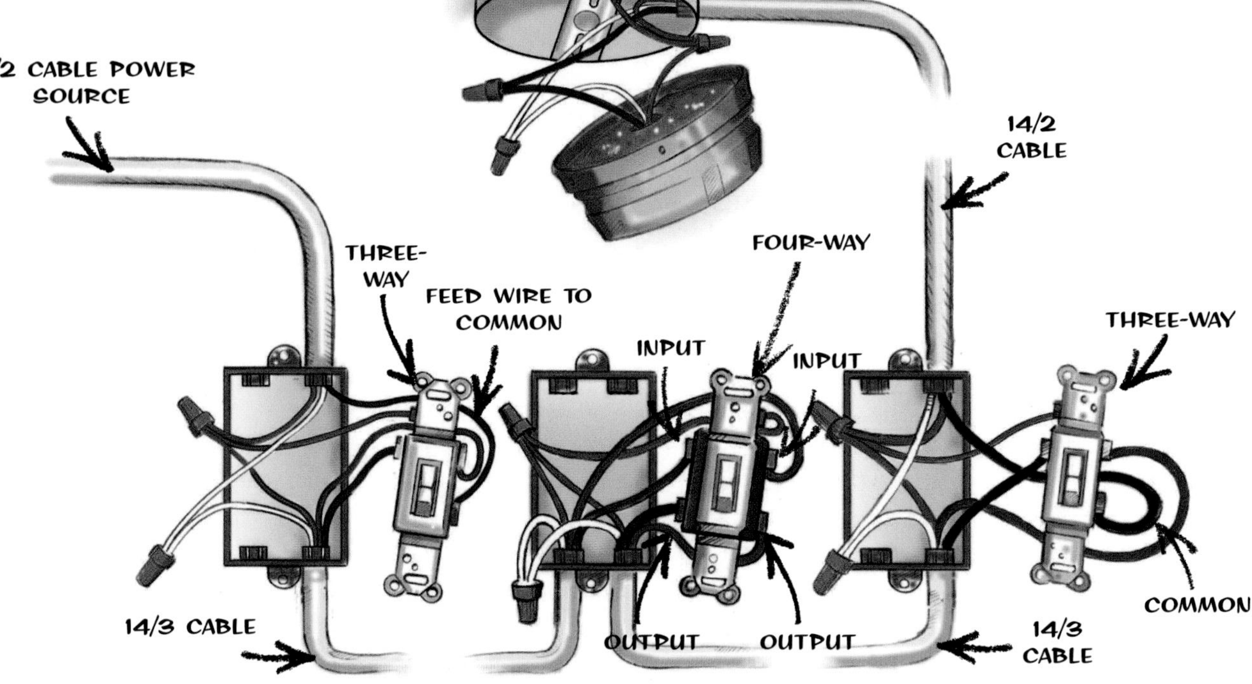

WIRING A FOUR-WAY SETUP. Shut off power to the circuit. Run two-wire cable from a power source to the first switch box. Run three-wire cable from the first switch box to the second and from the second to the third switch box. Run two-wire cable from the third switch box to the fixture box. Connect all the grounds.

At the first switch box, connect the black feed wire to the common terminal of a three-way switch. Splice the white wires and connect the remaining wires to the traveler terminals. At the second switch box, splice the white wires.

Connect the remaining wires to a four-way switch (which has only traveler terminals, no common terminal), as shown. One set of wires should be on the input terminals and the other set on the output terminals.

At the third switch box, splice the white wires. Connect the black wire that comes from the fixture to the common terminal of a three-way switch and the other two wires to the traveler terminals.

At the fixture box, splice white wire to white lead and black wire to black lead. Restore power and test.

ADDING A WALL LIGHT

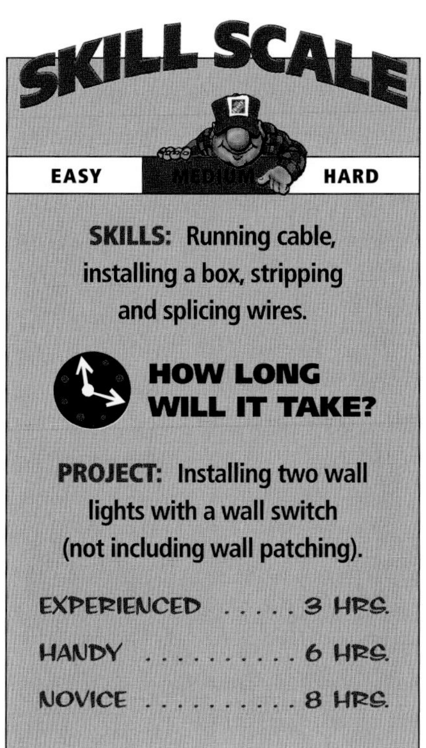

SKILLS: Running cable, installing a box, stripping and splicing wires.

HOW LONG WILL IT TAKE?

PROJECT: Installing two wall lights with a wall switch (not including wall patching).

EXPERIENCED ..... 3 HRS.
HANDY .... 6 HRS.
NOVICE .... 8 HRS.

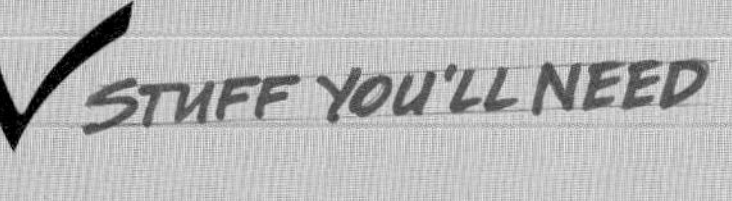

TOOLS: Drill, saw, fish tape, screwdriver, lineman's pliers, combination strippers, level

MATERIALS: Wall sconces or bathroom wall fixture, boxes, cable with clamps, staples, wire nuts, electrician's tape

The methods for installing wall fixtures are the same as those for wiring ceiling lights (page 146). The difference, of course, is that you're working on a vertical surface.

Wall sconces are ideal for hallways and stairwells. Consider wiring them using three-way switches (pages 148–150).

Most wall fixtures attach to a ceiling box. However, check the hardware to make sure you will be able to install the sconce plumb. Buy a swivel strap (page 29) so you can easily adjust the fixture. A fluorescent fixture (for use over a bathroom mirror, for example) may not require a box (page 104).

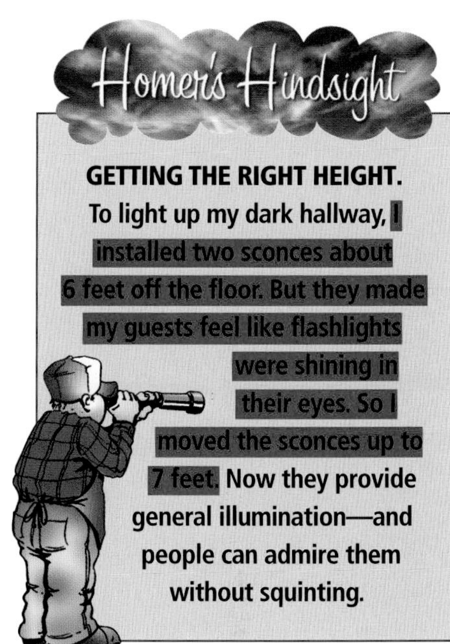

GETTING THE RIGHT HEIGHT. To light up my dark hallway, I installed two sconces about 6 feet off the floor. But they made my guests feel like flashlights were shining in their eyes. So I moved the sconces up to 7 feet. Now they provide general illumination—and people can admire them without squinting.

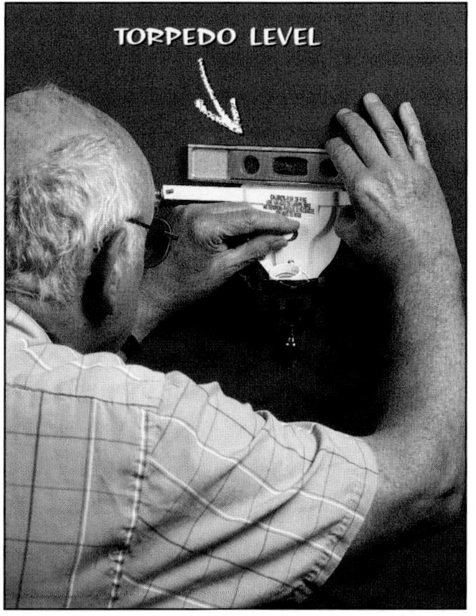

INSTALLING A SCONCE. Run cable from a nearby receptacle or other power source into a switch box and then to a box mounted on the wall. The swivel strap lets you adjust the base until it is level. Depending on the sconce, use either a ceiling fixture box or a switch box. Wire as you would for a ceiling fixture (page 146).

WIRING A VANITY LIGHT. Installing a light over a mirror or medicine cabinet calls for no special wiring techniques. Some fixtures require a box, while others can be wired and then attached directly to the wall. If you will be installing a mirror that reaches to the ceiling, give the glass company exact dimensions for cutting a hole to attach the fixture to a box mounted in the wall behind the mirror.

INSTALLING AN ATTIC FAN

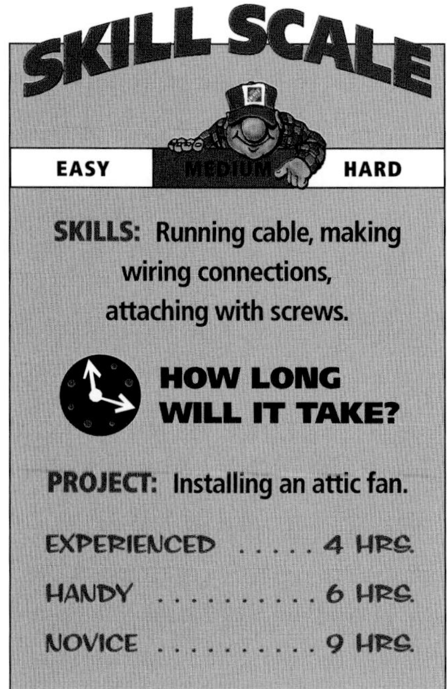

SKILL SCALE

EASY | MEDIUM | HARD

SKILLS: Running cable, making wiring connections, attaching with screws.

HOW LONG WILL IT TAKE?

PROJECT: Installing an attic fan.

EXPERIENCED . . . . . 4 HRS.
HANDY . . . . 6 HRS.
NOVICE . . . . 9 HRS.

✓ STUFF YOU'LL NEED

TOOLS: Drill, fish tape, screwdriver, lineman's pliers, combination strippers

MATERIALS: Attic fan, cable with clamps, wire nuts, electrician's tape

Temperatures in an attic can reach 150 degrees in the summer, making it difficult (and expensive) to keep a home cool. An attic fan, a whole-house fan (page 154–155), or a roof fan (page 155) slashes energy costs and reduces temperatures.

The manufacturer should provide a chart detailing how powerful a fan you need based on the size of your attic. Depending on the size of your house, you may require more than one fan.

1 BRING POWER INTO THE ATTIC. Before tapping into a receptacle or junction box for power, check the amperage on your attic fan and make sure you will not overload the circuit (pages 116–117). Shut off power to the circuit. See pages 130-132 for tips on running cable into the attic. Check with local codes to see whether you need to use armored cable instead of NM cable.

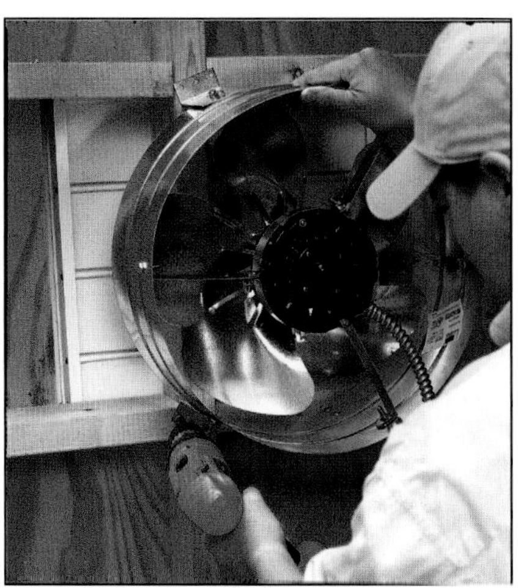

2 MOUNT THE FAN. At a louvered opening in the attic, secure the fan by driving screws through its mounting brackets and into studs. If the studs do not allow you to center the fan in the opening, attach horizontal 2×4s that span between the studs. Attach the fan to the studs. You may choose to install louvers that close when the fan is not operating.

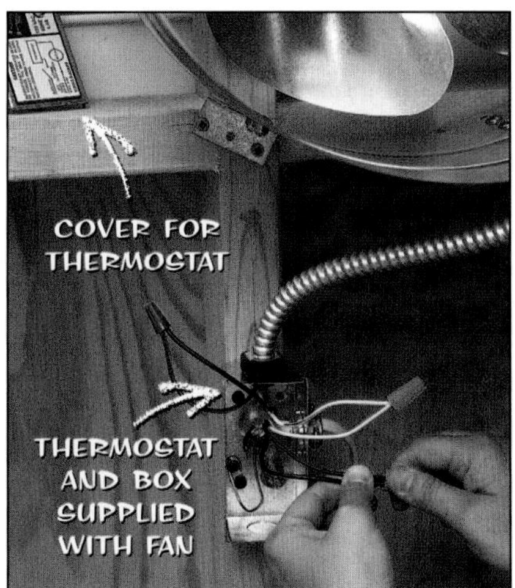
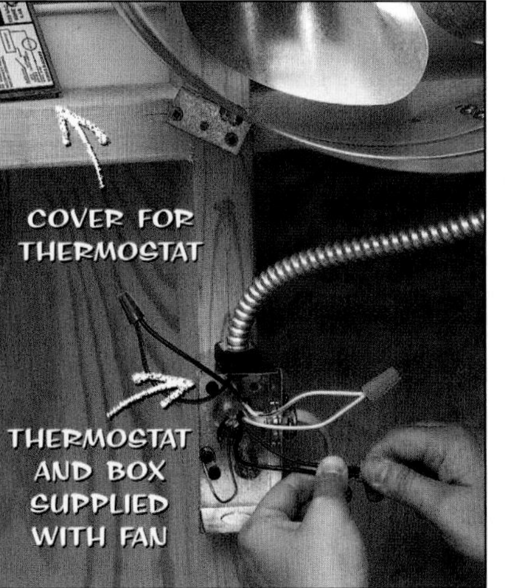

3 MAKE THE ELECTRICAL CONNECTIONS. The fan has its own thermostat switch. Mount the thermostat box to a framing member. Follow the manufacturer's instructions for connecting wires. Restore power, and adjust the temperature control. Or, you can control the fan with a pilot-light switch (page 98) located in the hallway.

CLOSER LOOK

AN ATTIC MUST BREATHE.
An attic fan, whole-house fan, or roof fan moves air efficiently only if the attic is properly ventilated. Usually, a house needs vents near the bottom of the attic (usually under the eaves) and vents near the roof peak, such as turbine vents, gable vents, or a continuous vent running along the ridge. Check that eave vents are not clogged with insulation. If you are not sure that your attic is properly vented, have it inspected by a professional roofer.

INSTALLING A WHOLE-HOUSE FAN

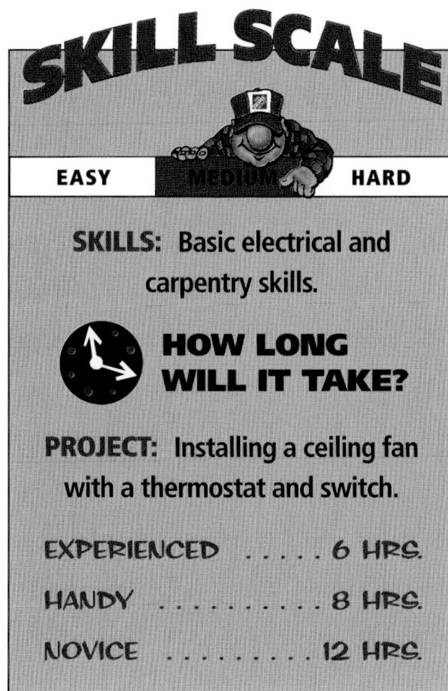

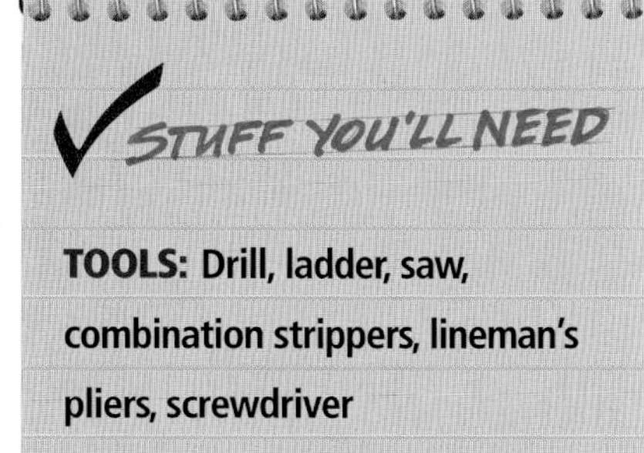

STUFF YOU'LL NEED
TOOLS: Drill, ladder, saw, combination strippers, lineman's pliers, screwdriver
MATERIALS: Whole-house fan, screws, junction box, switch box, cable with clamps, wire nuts, electrician's tape

Find a powerful yet quiet whole-house fan to pull up air through the house and into your attic. A whole-house fan is ideal for spring and fall cooling in hot climates; it may be the only means of cooling you need in moderate climates. For the fan to work, the attic must have adequate ventilation (page 153) and windows on the first floor must be open. Measure your home's square footage to choose the right size fan.

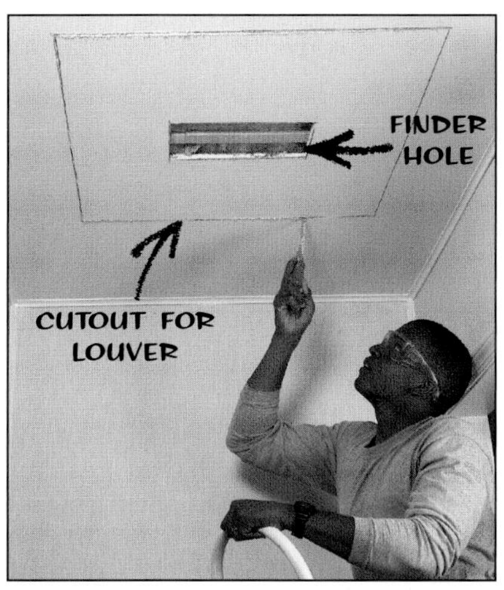

1 CUT A HOLE. Fans are designed to be positioned over one joist so you don't have to compromise ceiling framing. Cut a 1×2-foot finder hole to confirm that the fan will center on a joist. Mark the cutout for the louver and cut through the drywall or lath and plaster. The fan manufacturer will specify dimensions for the hole.

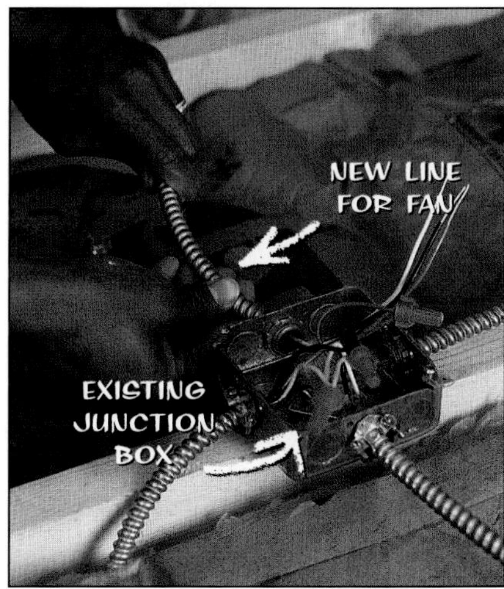

2 BRING POWER TO THE FAN. After making sure that you will not overload a circuit (pages 116–117), shut off power to the circuit. Tap into a junction box or run cable up into the attic (see pages 130–132). Local codes may require you to use armored cable instead of NM cable.

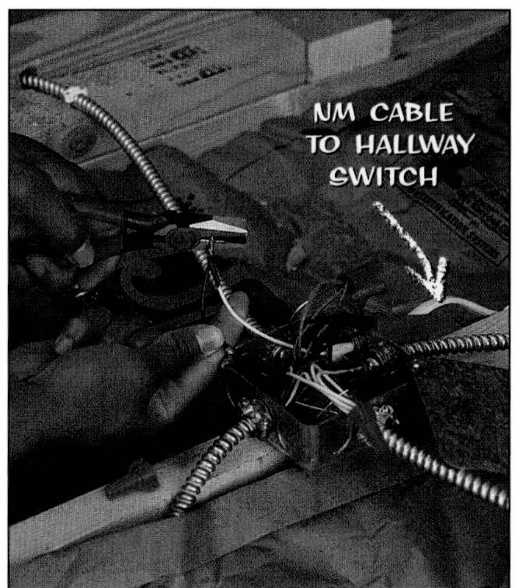

3 WIRE FOR THE SWITCH. A fan-rated rheostat switch lets you vary the fan speed. Bring the two-wire switch cable to the box, marking the white wire black at both ends. Splice it to the black wires in the box. Splice the other switch wire to the fan's black wire and the fan's white to the white wires in the box. Connect the ground.

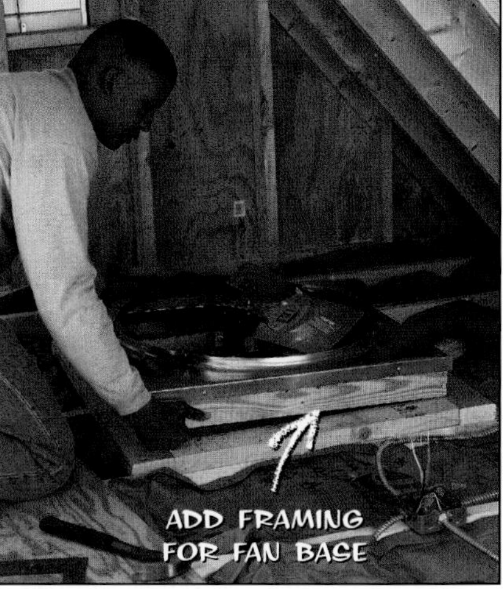

4 MOUNT THE FAN. With a helper, lift the fan up through the opening and into the attic. Add framing as needed so the fan is securely centered over a joist. Attach brackets to the fan frame and position them so they will slip over the exposed joist. Center the fan over the opening and secure the brackets with bolts.

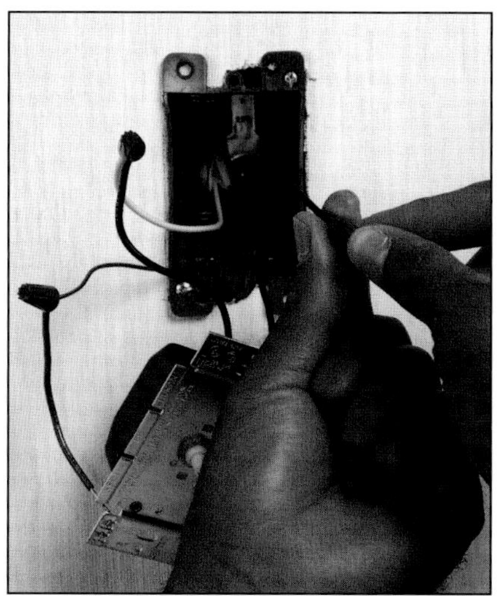

5 **ENCLOSE THE FAN.** Pull back the insulation and cut pieces of 2× blocking to fill gaps at either side of the fan. At each side, cut two pieces to fit between the joists (shown) or one notched piece that fits over the joist. (Some manufacturers supply blocking.) Attach the wood to the joists by drilling pilot holes and attaching with 3-inch screws or 16-penny nails.

6 **WIRE THE RHEOSTAT SWITCH.** Install a fan-rated rheostat switch in the hallway, connecting it to the cable you have run through the wall from the attic junction box. Wire as shown or use the manufacturer's directions.

7 **ATTACH THE LOUVERS.** Hold the louver panel against the ceiling so it covers the hole. Attach the panel by driving screws into the joists and blocking. Restore power and test the fan.

CLOSER LOOK

A FAN TO PULL THE AIR OUT OF YOUR ATTIC.

If your attic does not have a vertical wall to accommodate an attic fan (page 153), this is the next most efficient way to pull air out of an attic. The most difficult part of this installation is not the electrical work, but the roofing. The shingles must be laid correctly over the fan flashing, or the roof will leak. If you have an existing passive roof vent the same size as your fan, you can install the fan in that spot without much trouble. Call a roofer if you aren't sure how to seal the fan.

1 **CUT THE HOLE AND ROOFING.** Follow the manufacturer's directions for cutting a hole through the roof and for cutting back shingles from around the hole. Carefully fold back the shingles.

2 **INSTALL THE FAN.** Slide the fan under the shingles and apply roofing cement as directed. Wire the fan as you would an attic fan (page 153).

INSTALLING A BATHROOM VENT FAN

SKILLS: Advanced electrical skills, carpentry, and roofing.

HOW LONG WILL IT TAKE?

PROJECT: Installing a bathroom fan that vents air through the roof or wall.

EXPERIENCED . . . . . 8 HRS.
HANDY . . . . 12 HRS.
NOVICE . . . . 16 HRS.

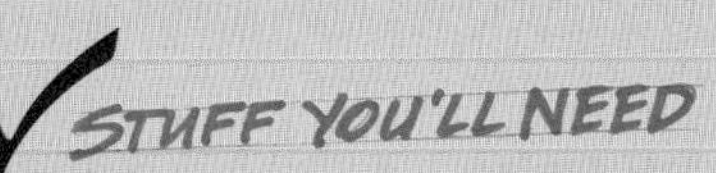

TOOLS: Drill, fish tape, keyhole saw or reciprocating saw, hammer, combination tool, lineman's pliers, screwdriver
MATERIALS: Bathroom vent fan, ducts, end cap or roof jack, straps and screws, roofing cement, shingles, roofing nails, duct tape, caulk, wire nuts, cable with clamps, electrician's tape

A vent fan considerably improves the atmosphere in a bathroom by pulling out moisture, odors, and heat. Codes require bathrooms to have vent fans if there is no natural ventilation, such as a window. You may opt for a fan even if you have a window, so you can clear the air in rainy or cold weather. When choosing a fan, use these guidelines:

- **Make sure the fan will move the air.** Unfortunately, many bathroom fans do little more than make noise. This happens when either the fan is not strong enough or the path through the ductwork is not free and clear. Measure your room and determine how far the ductwork has to travel. Then ask a home center salesperson to help you choose a fan and the ductwork to do the job (page 158). Keep in mind that air travels more freely through solid ducts than through flexible hoses.
- **Consider a fan equipped with a light.** Some units have a fan only, while others include a ceiling light, a low-wattage night-light, and even a forced-air heating unit.
- **Consider the wiring options.** At times, local codes require that the fan come on whenever the overhead light is turned on. Some people prefer separate switches for the bathroom fan and light.

INSTALLING DUCTWORK

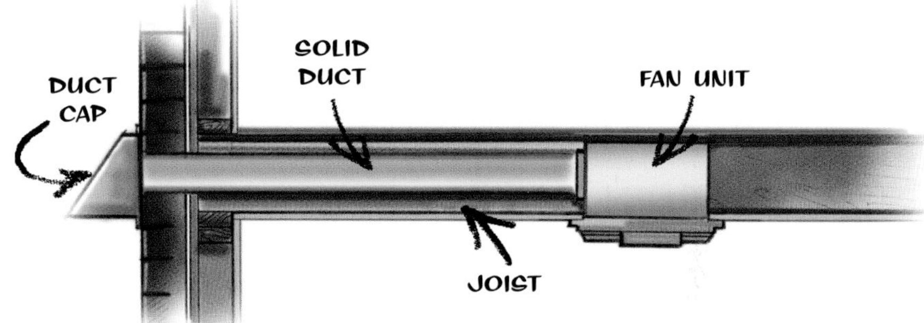

RUNNING DUCT THROUGH A WALL. Choose the shortest and straightest route. A wall vent is the easiest to install because there is no roofing involved. However, it may be difficult to run ductwork between joists.

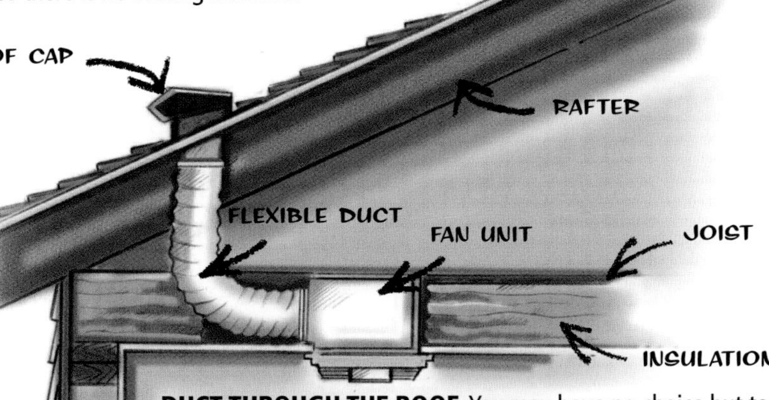

DUCT THROUGH THE ROOF. You may have no choice but to run ductwork through an attic and out the roof. Choose a short, straight path and cut the roof and shingles correctly to avoid leaks. Moist air inside the ducts can condense and drip onto insulation; you may want to cover the duct with pipe insulation.

1 CUT THE HOLE. From the attic above, hold the fan against a joist and mark its outline with a pencil. Cut out the opening. If there is no attic above, use a stud sensor to locate a joist and cut the opening from below. Shut off power to the circuit and provide power if none is present (pages 128–132).

2 ATTACH THE FAN AND DAM OFF INSULATION. Attach the fan to the joist with screws. Some models require a 6-inch gap between the unit and insulation. Cut or push back the insulation; then cut pieces of 2× lumber to fit between the joists and attach the lumber with screws or nails.

3 CUT A HOLE IN THE ROOF. On the underside of the roof, trace a circle just large enough for the roof cap tailpiece. Drill a hole large enough for the saw blade, then cut with a reciprocating saw, saber saw, or keyhole saw. (If you run the ductwork out the wall, see page 158.)

4 CUT AWAY SHINGLES. Remove shingles from around the cutout without damaging the underlying roofing paper. The lower part of the roof cap flange will rest on top of the shingles, and the top part will slip under the shingles.

5 INSTALL THE ROOF CAP. Smear roofing cement on the underside of the cap flange. Slip the upper flange under the shingles as you insert the cap into the hole. Install the shingles on the side, smearing the undersides with roofing cement. Attach the flange with roofing nails and cover the heads with roofing cement.

NOISE CONTROL.
A label on the fan packaging will indicate how many square feet of bathroom space the fan can successfully clear. If there's any doubt, or if your ductwork will be more than 5 feet long, get a slightly more powerful fan than you need. (However, don't overdo it. Keep the power of the fan appropriate to the size of the room.) The SONE rating on a fan indicates its sound-level rating. A 3 SONE rating is quiet; a 7 will be very noisy.

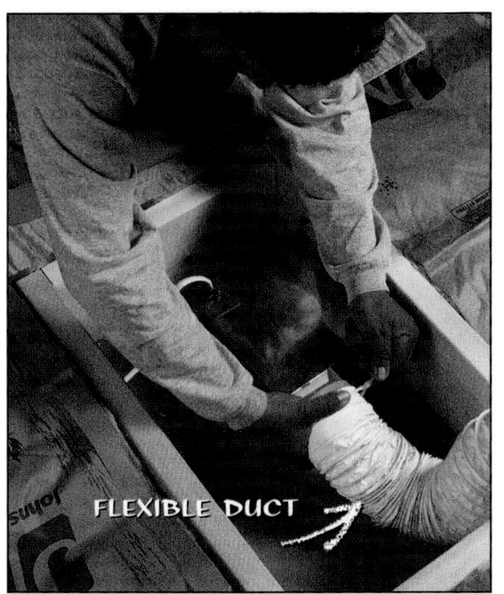

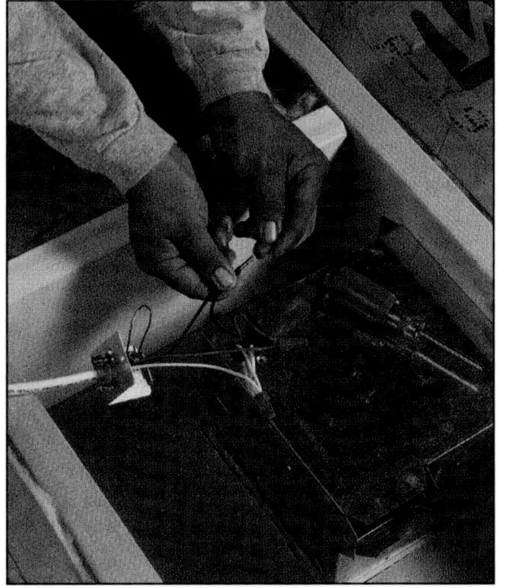

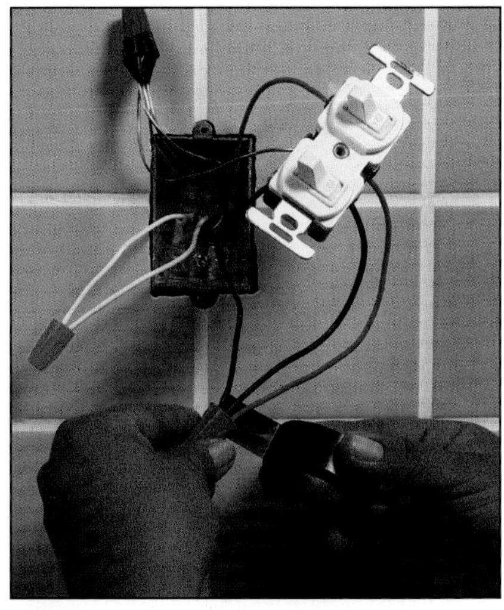

6 **CONNECT THE DUCTWORK.** Flexible ductwork is the easiest to run, but solid ducts are quieter and more efficient. At both the roof cap and the fan, slide a clamp over the duct and slip the duct over the tailpiece. Slide the clamp back over the tailpiece and tighten the clamp. Wrap the joint with duct tape.

7 **WIRE THE FAN.** If wiring does not exist, run cable to the fan and to a switch. If you are installing a fan/light, run three-wire cable from the switch to the fan. Connect the wiring according to the manufacturer's directions. Plug the motor into the built-in receptacle.

8 **WIRE THE SWITCH.** For a fan/light switch that has power entering the switch box, splice the white wires and connect the grounds. Connect power to both switches through two pigtails spliced to the feed wire. Connect the red wire to one switch terminal and the black wire to the other terminal.

WORK SMARTER

INSTALLING A WALL VENT.
If a bathroom is not located directly beneath an attic, you must vent air out through a wall. Even if there is an attic above, it may be easier to run the vent out through a gable wall rather than through the roof. When running ductwork through a ceiling cavity, it is sometimes easier to shove a piece of solid ductwork through rather than snaking flexible ducting. From inside the attic, drill a locator hole through to the outside, then cut out the siding with a reciprocating saw, saber saw, or keyhole saw.

1 **MAKE A TAILPIECE.** Press the duct pipe into the cap. Use sheet-metal screws to attach a piece of solid duct to the cap, then caulk the joint or wrap it with duct tape. Apply a bead of caulk to the back of the flange so it will seal against the siding.

2 **ATTACH THE VENT.** Caulk around the hole and push in the tailpiece. Secure it with four screws. Caulk around the edge of the vent. Complete the connection to the fan indoors using solid or flexible ductwork.

ADDING A RANGE HOOD

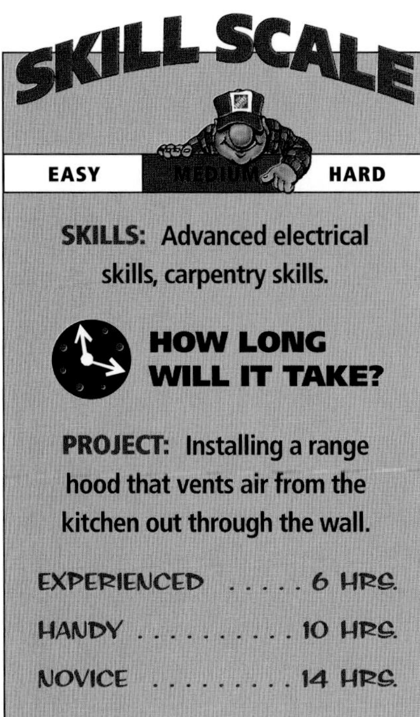

Most residential range hoods, if correctly installed, remove smoke, odor, and heat from the kitchen. To draw out cooking grease, you need a powerful commercial model.

For the best range hood efficiency, run the duct through the wall directly behind the range hood, in as straight a line as possible. You can run the vents of most hoods out the back or the top of the unit.

If a wall stud is in the way of the ductwork, you could do carpentry work to change the framing. An easier solution is to purchase a hood with an extra-strong motor and run the duct around the stud.

Before you purchase a fan, check its "cfm" rating—which indicates the number of cubic feet of air it pulls per minute. Choose a fan with a cfm rating that is double the square footage of your kitchen.

DUCTLESS RANGE HOODS. Cutting a hole in the wall and running ductwork is the most time-consuming and difficult part of installing a range hood. Save yourself the hassle by installing a ductless hood, which runs air through a filter and back into the kitchen rather than moving it outside. This unit will not be as effective at removing smoke and odors, however, and you'll need to change filters fairly often.

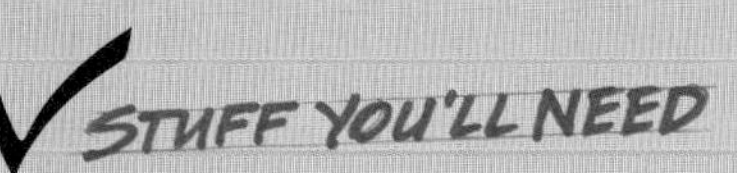

TOOLS: Drill, fish tape, saber saw or reciprocating saw, hammer and cold chisel, screwdriver, combination strippers, lineman's pliers

MATERIALS: Range hood, solid duct, wall cap, masonry screws, cable and clamps, wire nuts, electrician's tape, caulk, safety goggles

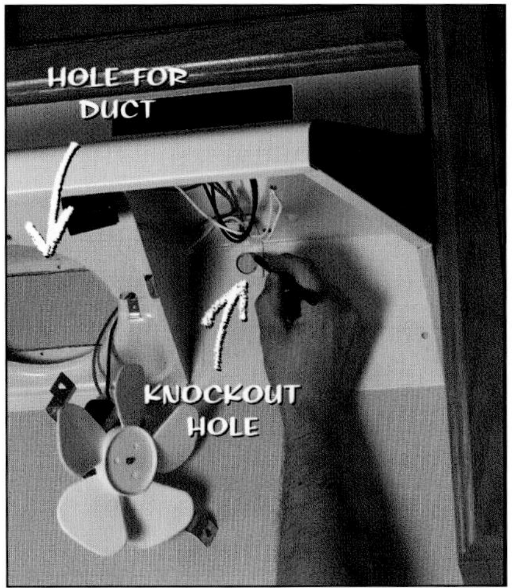

1 **MARK FOR HOLES.** Remove the filter, fan, and electrical housing cover from the range hood. Use a hammer and screwdriver to remove the knockouts for the electrical cable and the duct. Hold the hood in place and mark the holes for the duct and the cable.

2 **CUT THE INSIDE AND DRILL A LOCATOR HOLE.** Cut holes through the drywall or plaster. Using a long bit, drill holes at each corner all the way through the outside wall. (If your exterior is brick or block, see page 160.)

3 **CUT THE SIDING.** Connect the dots between the holes on the outside to mark the outline of the hole. Using a reciprocating saw, saber saw with an extra-long blade, or keyhole saw, cut the outline. Remove insulation or debris that would interfere with installing the duct.

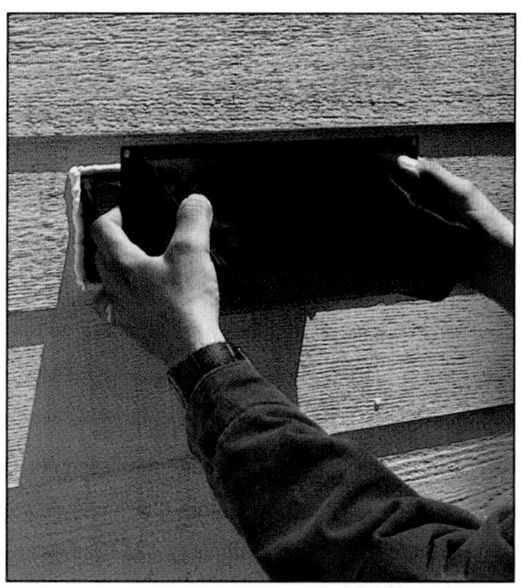

4 **ATTACH THE DUCT CAP.** Push the wall cap into the wall to see if the duct is long enough to reach the range hood. If not, purchase an extension and attach it with sheet-metal screws and duct tape. Apply caulk to the siding where the cap flange will rest. Push the cap into place and fasten with screws. Caulk the perimeter of the flange.

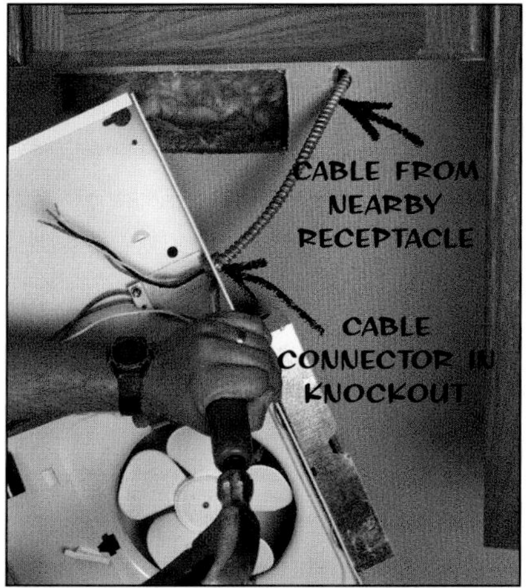

5 **RUN POWER TO THE HOOD.** Shut off power to the circuit. Run cable from a nearby receptacle or junction box through the hole in the wall (pages 130–132). Strip the sheathing and clamp the cable to the range hood electrical knockout. Mount the hood securely by driving screws into studs or adjacent cabinets.

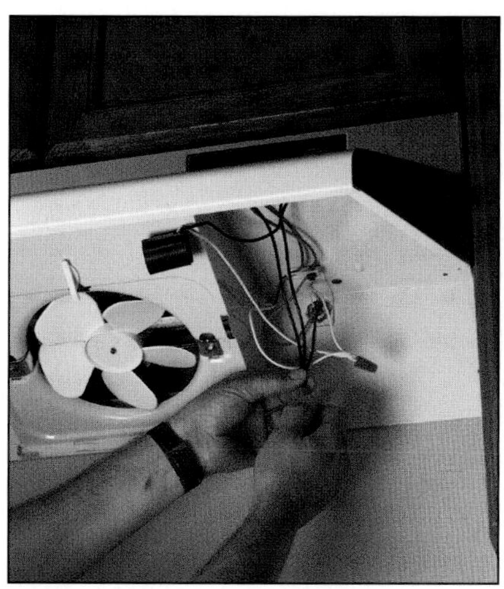

6 **CONNECT THE WIRES.** Splice the white wire to the white fixture lead, black wire to black lead, and the ground wire to the green lead. Fold the wires into place and replace the electrical cover. Reattach the fan and filter. Restore power and test.

CLOSER LOOK

VENTING THROUGH A MASONRY WALL. Use a long masonry bit to drill the locator holes (see Step 2, page 159). Draw the outline carefully, double-checking that you can slip in the vent with room to spare. Drill holes about every inch along the outline; then use a hammer and cold chisel to chip between the holes. To attach the duct cap, drill holes and drive masonry screws. Older homes may have double-thick brick walls—a real challenge!

INSTALLING A SMOKE DETECTOR

SKILLS: Running cable, stripping and splicing wires.

HOW LONG WILL IT TAKE?

PROJECT: Installing one hard-wired smoke detector.

EXPERIENCED . . . . . 3 HRS.
HANDY . . . . 5 HRS.
NOVICE . . . . 8 HRS.

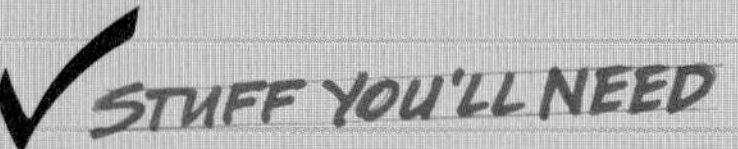

TOOLS: Drill, fish tape, combination tool, lineman's pliers, screwdriver

MATERIALS: Smoke detector (hard-wired with battery backup), cable with clamps, ceiling box, wire nuts, electrician's tape

Many homes have battery-powered smoke detectors that fail to perform when the batteries die. Other homes have hard-wired detectors that don't work if the wiring gets damaged—which often happens in a fire. For the best protection, install hard-wired detectors that have battery backup.

Most codes allow you to install battery-only detectors. These are fine as long as you test them regularly and immediately replace failing batteries.

Many detectors are wired with two-wire cable. As an added safety precaution, install detectors in a series, using three-wire cable. That way, when one is triggered, all will sound. (See pages 128–132 for running cable and pages 133–134 for installing remodeling boxes.)

WHERE TO PUT DETECTORS. If your detectors were installed more than 5 years ago, chances are you have too few to satisfy current codes. For instance, detectors are now required both in the hall and inside bedrooms to warn you in case of a bedroom fire. Ask your building or fire department for recommendations.

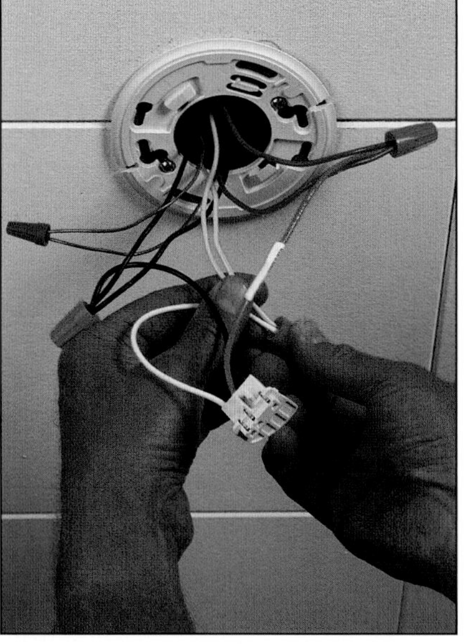

WIRING FOR A SERIES OF DETECTORS. Run three-wire cable to all the detectors so that when one senses smoke, they all screech in unison. (Detectors wired with two-wire cable work independently of one another.) Wire each as shown, following manufacturer's directions.

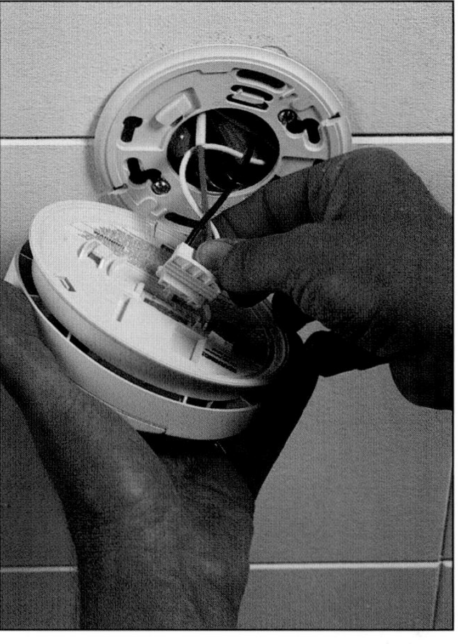

INSTALLING A DETECTOR. Carefully pack the spliced cables into the ceiling box. Clip the connector onto the back of the detector and install the unit.

ADDING AN OUTDOOR RECEPTACLE

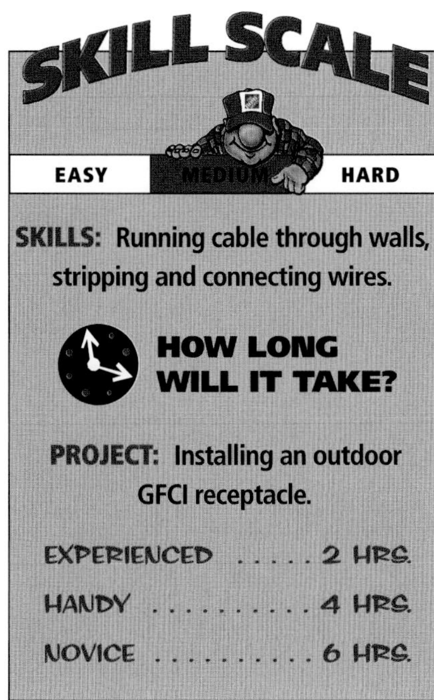

SKILLS: Running cable through walls, stripping and connecting wires.

HOW LONG WILL IT TAKE?

PROJECT: Installing an outdoor GFCI receptacle.

EXPERIENCED ..... 2 HRS.
HANDY .... 4 HRS.
NOVICE .... 6 HRS.

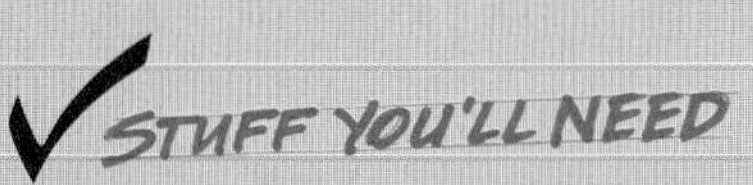

✓ STUFF YOU'LL NEED

TOOLS: Drill with long bit, sabersaw or keyhole saw, combination strippers, screwdriver, lineman's pliers, hammer, (for masonry walls, a masonry bit and cold chisel)

MATERIALS: GFCI receptacle, cable with clamps, remodel box, wire nuts, electrician's tape

Unless you need an outdoor receptacle in a particular location, plan the easiest path for the cable. One option is to install it nearly (but not exactly) back-to-back with an indoor receptacle. Or, run cable through the basement ceiling and out the rim joist.

Even if you install a weatherproof cover, place the receptacle in a dry location and at least 16 inches above the ground. Codes require that an outdoor receptacle be a ground-fault circuit interrupter (GFCI).

Ensure that you will not be overloading a circuit when installing the outdoor receptacle (pages 116–117). If you plug in too many Christmas lights or plan to use heavy-duty power tools, you may need to place the receptacle on its own circuit (pages 168–169). Local codes may require that you have a separate circuit for outdoor electrical service. See pages 130–132 for tips on fishing cable through walls.

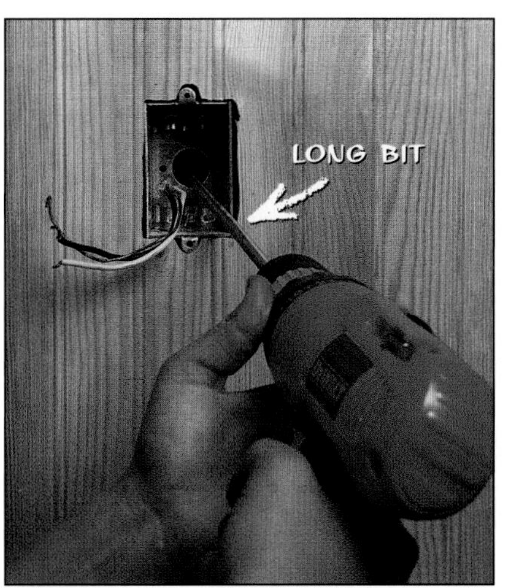

1 DRILL A LOCATOR HOLE. Shut off power to the circuit. Pull out an interior receptacle and detach it. Using a hammer and screwdriver, open a knockout hole in the back of the receptacle box. Put a long bit or a bit extension in your drill. (Use a masonry bit if your exterior is brick.) Poke the bit through the hole in the box. The wall may not be thick enough to fit back-to-back receptacles, so aim the drill bit at an angle. Drill through to the outside.

2 CUT THE HOLE FOR THE RECEPTACLE. On the outside, cut a hole for a receptacle box. Drill a second hole as an entry point and use a saber saw with an extra-long blade, a reciprocating saw, or a keyhole saw. If the exterior is masonry, see page 160 for tips on cutting the hole.

3 **RUN THE CABLE.** Cut cable about 2 feet longer than you need, and strip the sheathing from both ends. Have a helper push the cable from indoors as you pull it out through the hole. Clamp the cable to the remodel box and mount the box (pages 133–134). Install a new GFCI receptacle outside (page 27). Connect to power in the interior box.

4 **INSTALL AN IN-USE COVER.** This kind of cover will keep the receptacle dry even when it has a cord plugged into it, and it can be locked shut. In addition to the plastic cover, install the rubber gasket behind the plate. Restore the power and test the receptacle.

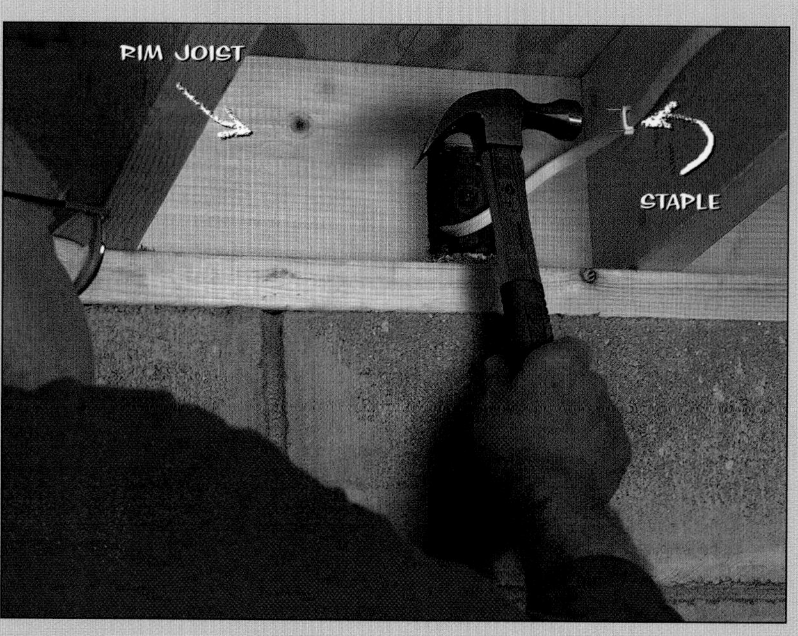

RUNNING CABLE THROUGH A BASEMENT WALL. If your basement ceiling is unfinished, this is probably the easiest method. Shut off power to the circuit and tap into a receptacle or junction box. Cut a hole through the rim joist and siding, and staple the cable to the joist.

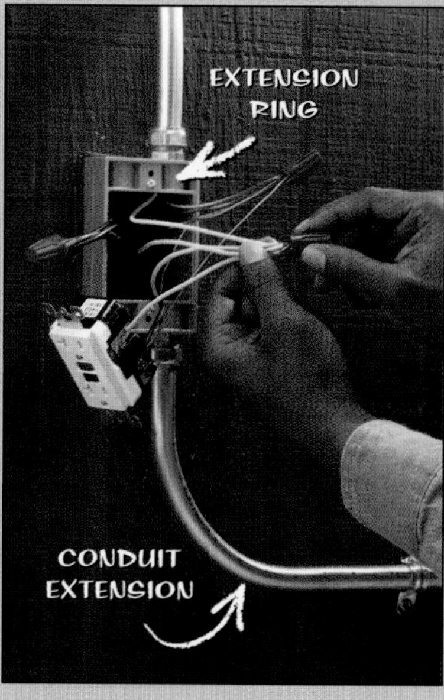

EXTENDING SERVICE FROM AN OUTDOOR RECEPTACLE. Adding an extension ring to the receptacle box allows you to run cable or conduit from the receptacle to supply outdoor lights and other receptacles. Two screws attach the extension ring to the box. Remove one or more knockouts in the ring to extend the circuit.

RUNNING AN OUTDOOR LINE

SKILLS: Advanced wiring, excavating and carpentry.

HOW LONG WILL IT TAKE?

PROJECT: Installing 50 feet of outdoor line, three lights.

EXPERIENCED ..... 10 HRS.
HANDY .... 12 HRS.
NOVICE .... 14 HRS.

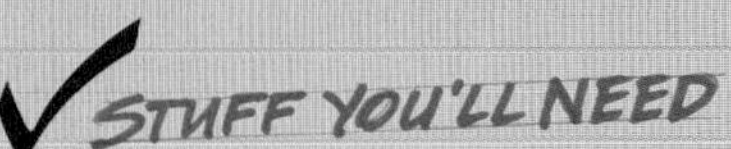

TOOLS: Spade, post-hole digger, hammer, screwdriver, lineman's pliers, combination tool, hacksaw, crescent wrench, drill

MATERIALS: Conduit, fittings, wire or UF cable, string, stakes, outdoor boxes, 4×4 post, concrete

CONDUIT OPTIONS.

Outdoor conduit must be watertight. Use rigid metal conduit with threaded fittings or schedule 40 PVC plastic conduit. (Glue the PVC with cement approved by your local building department.) Take a sketch of your wiring to your supplier for help gathering the parts.

Low-voltage lights (page 40) are quick and easy to install, but if you need outdoor receptacles or strong lighting, roll up your sleeves and prepare to dig trenches and run cable or conduit.

OUTDOOR WIRING OPTIONS

Check with your building department to learn the requirements for outdoor wiring. In some areas, UF (underground feed) cable is fine; elsewhere you must run wires through conduit. Codes also specify whether to use metal or PVC conduit. Codes specify how deep the wiring must be buried and whether you must protect the cable with a 2×6 plank. Conduit usually has to be 18 inches deep and cable must be 24 inches deep.

If you want to install continuous conduit (instead of the conduit-and-cable system shown on the next page), run individual wires—rather than cable—through the conduit.

If you will install only a couple of lights and a receptacle, you may be able to tap into an existing circuit (pages 116–117). However, it is often nearly as easy to run a new circuit for outdoor service (pages 168–169). Your building department may require a separate circuit. If you run more than 50 feet of cable, use #12.

Before digging, call the toll-free numbers for utilities to make sure you won't hit a power, water, gas, phone, or cable line.

1 DIG THE TRENCH. Use a string line to mark the path of the underground cable. Cut the sod neatly and place it right-side-up on the ground so you can reuse it later. Dig to the depth required by codes. If you have a lot of digging to do, consider renting a power trencher. Codes may allow the trench to be more shallow if you cover the cable with a 2×6 plank.

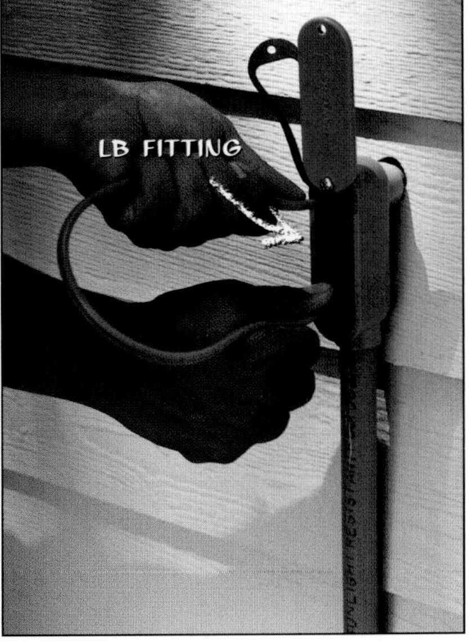

2 START WITH AN LB FITTING. You can begin service with a receptacle (pages 162–163) or with an LB fitting, which makes pulling the wire easier. Start with a short length of conduit sticking out of the house. Attach the LB fitting to it, then a length of conduit downward, then a sweep (a curved piece of conduit) into the trench. Do not splice wires in this fitting.

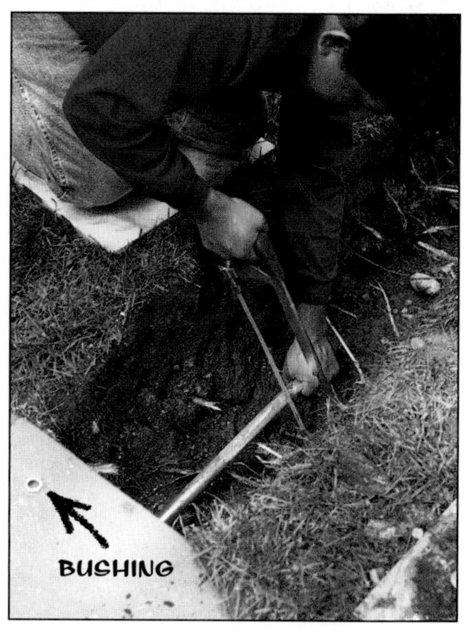

3 TAP CONDUIT UNDER SIDEWALK. Use this method whether running cable or conduit. Cut a piece of metal conduit 2 feet longer than the sidewalk width and flatten one end with a hammer to make a sharp point. Drive the pipe under the sidewalk with a hammer and a block of wood. If required, install conduit for the entire run. In many areas, however, you can run underground-feed (UF) cable.

4 CUT OFF THE SHARP END OF THE CONDUIT WITH A HACKSAW. When using metal conduit, install a plastic bushing at the end of the sweep so the cable won't get nicked as it's pulled through the conduit.

5 ANCHOR A POST FOR A FREESTANDING LIGHT. Use a clamshell digge to, dig a post hole about 3 feet deeper than the trench. Insert a pressure-treated 4×4 post (make sure it is about 1 foot longer than you need), check it for plumb in both directions, and brace it with 1×4s from two sides. Fill the hole with concrete or well-tamped soil. Once the concrete has set, trim the post to the desired height. Continue your run of underground cable or conduit. Either way, finish with metal conduit, running a sweep out of the trench and up the post to the box.

6 INSTALL A BOX. Attach a weatherproof box to the conduit near the top of the post. Mount the conduit to the post with clamps and screws. Run cable into the box or fish wires through the conduit (page 127). Install a GFCI receptacle (page 27).

INSTALLING OUTDOOR LIGHTING

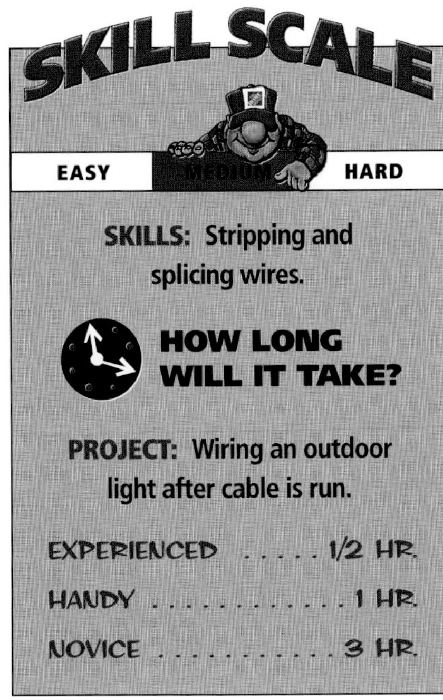

SKILLS: Stripping and splicing wires.

HOW LONG WILL IT TAKE?

PROJECT: Wiring an outdoor light after cable is run.

EXPERIENCED ..... 1/2 HR.
HANDY .... 1 HR.
NOVICE .... 3 HR.

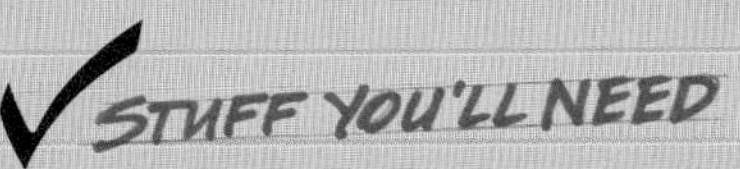

TOOLS: Screwdriver, lineman's pliers, combination tool, drill, saber saw, router
MATERIALS: Outdoor light fixture, photocell switch, box

Final connections for outdoor fixtures are about the same as for indoor fixtures. The main difference is that the outdoor components are heftier and have watertight gaskets.

Some lights come with their own posts, and for others you have to get 4×4 posts separately. Others attach to the tops of railings, under eaves, or to the sides of posts. Incandescents and halogens are typical for residential use; mercury-vapor and metal halide lights are more suited for commercial use. High-output fluorescent tubes operate down to minus 40 degrees Fahrenheit; screw-in fluorescent bulbs will work down to minus 10 degrees Fahrenheit.

Make sure each light's compression fitting fits over the metal or plastic conduit. You may need to buy an adapter to ensure a tight fit. Shut off power to the circuit before connecting wires.

BUYER'S GUIDE

PHOTOCELL SWITCH. This switch turns on a light at dusk and off at dawn. Position the photocell where it can sense daylight and out of the path of artificial light—including the lights controlled by the photocell.

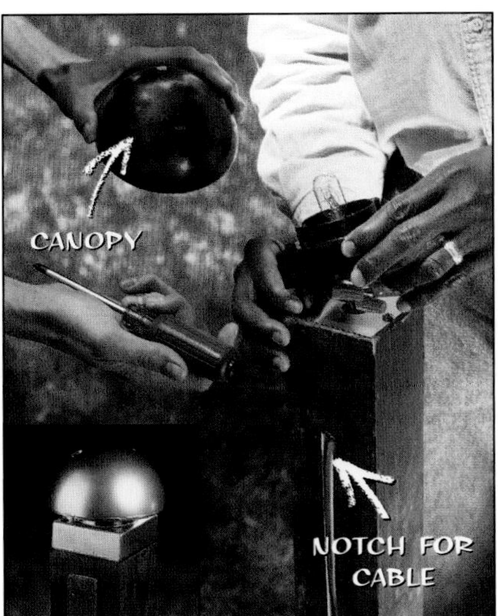

ADDING A POST LIGHT. The subtle illumination (inset) of this 120-volt light illuminates paths and decorates decks. Notch the post with a router and bore a hole from the top to meet the notch. Run cable to the base, wire it white to white and black to black. Pigtail the ground to the base. Install the canopy and cover the notch with a piece of lattice.

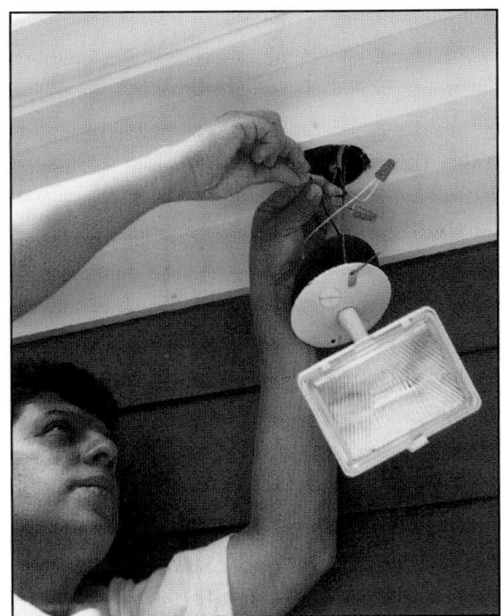

WIRING AN UNDER-EAVE LIGHT. Cable for this kind of light sometimes can be run through the attic. Cut a round hole in the eave, run cable into a remodel box, and attach the box. If you want to install a motion-sensor light (page 108), ask a salesperson to recommend one that will work well on a horizontal surface.

CHAPTER

11 MAJOR PROJECTS

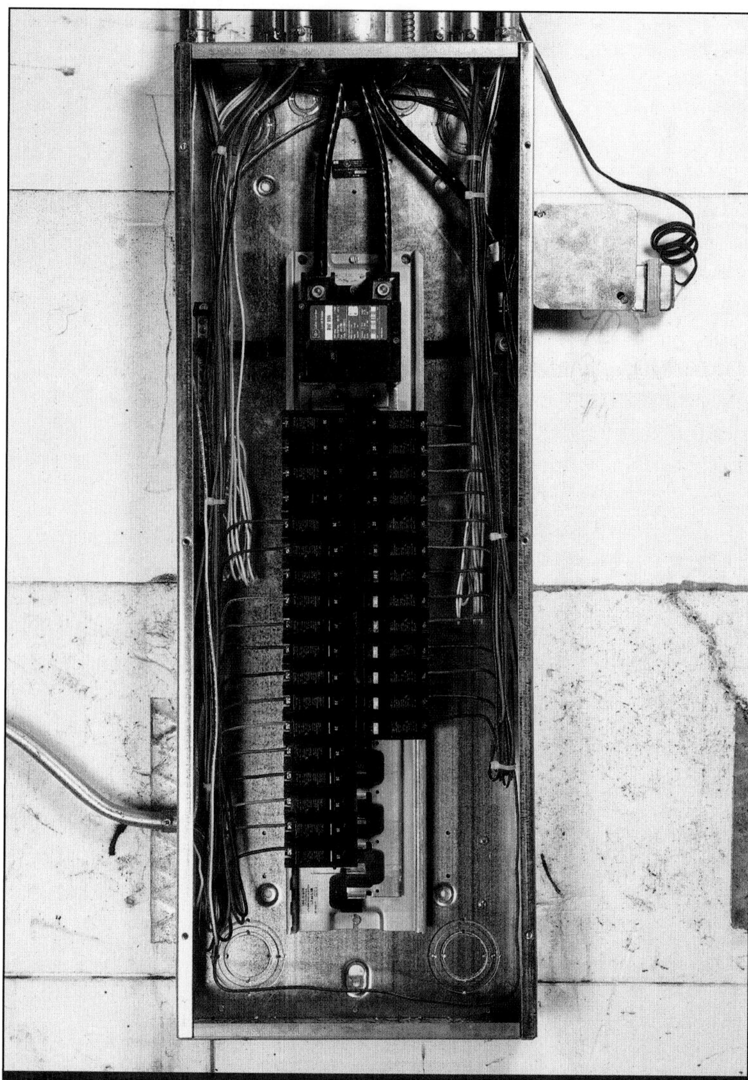

The installations described in this chapter involve adding new circuits. Once you have learned how electricity works and how to calculate loads, and have successfully completed several electrical installations, you are ready for the serious business of installing new circuits.

Your local building department may not allow unlicensed homeowners to run new circuits, install panels or subpanels, or wire entire rooms. If you hire out the work, use this chapter to understand what is involved and how to judge the quality of the work being done.

Before attempting any of the projects in this chapter, be sure you have a thorough understanding of the wiring principles presented in Chapter 1.

CHAPTER ELEVEN PROJECTS

ADDING A NEW CIRCUIT

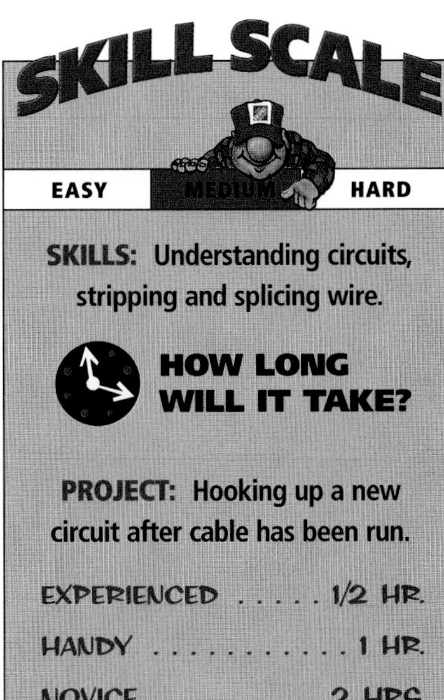

SKILLS: Understanding circuits, stripping and splicing wire.

HOW LONG WILL IT TAKE?

PROJECT: Hooking up a new circuit after cable has been run.

EXPERIENCED ..... 1/2 HR.
HANDY .... 1 HR.
NOVICE .... 2 HRS.

TOOLS: Hammer, screwdriver, lineman's pliers, combination strippers

MATERIALS: Cable and clamp, new circuit breaker

FIRE PROTECTION

Beginning January, 2002, the NEC will require the use of Arc Fault Circuit Interrupters (AFCI) for bedroom circuits. AFCIs provide greater fire protection than a regular breaker. Regular breakers trip for overloads and short circuits. AFCIs offer protection when arcing occurs because of frayed and overheated cords, and impaired wire insulation.

The physical work of installing a new electrical circuit is simple and calls for no special skills. Most of the work is completed outside the service panel. To get a breaker that will fit in your panel, jot down the brand and model number, or bring a sample breaker to the store.

First, determine whether your service panel can accommodate a new breaker, and then plan a circuit that will not be overloaded (pages 116–117). Install the new boxes. Run cable from the boxes back to the service panel (pages 128–132). (Electricians call this practice a "home run.") Hook up the devices and fixtures. Now you're ready to energize the new circuit by installing a new breaker and connecting the wires to it.

1 **SHUT OFF MAIN POWER.** Work during the daytime and have a reliable flashlight on hand. Turn off the main circuit breaker. All the wires and circuit breakers in the panel are now de-energized except for the thick wires that come from the outside and connect to the main breaker. **Do not touch them.**

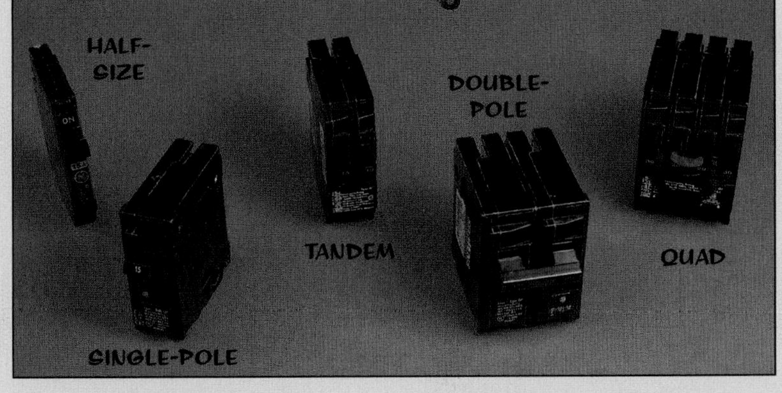

BREAKER OPTIONS. If the service panel has room, install full-size, **single-pole** breakers. If you're out of space, see if your panel can accommodate **half-size or "skinny"** breakers, or **tandem** breakers. In some panels, these breakers only fit in slots near the bottom. Your building department limits the number of breakers that can be installed. If you add too many, they will require you to put in a new panel or a subpanel (pages 170–171). You'll need double-pole breakers for 240-volt circuits. A **quad** breaker can supply two 240-volt circuits.

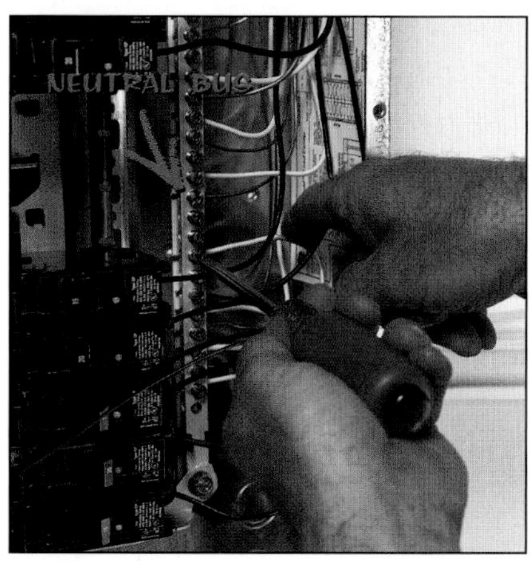

2 **REMOVE A KNOCKOUT.** Remove the service panel cover (page 14). Remove a knockout slug from the side of the service panel and install a cable clamp. Also, remove a knockout tab from the panel cover. (For a double-pole breaker, remove two knockouts.)

3 **CLAMP THE CABLE.** Determine how far the wires must travel to reach the breaker and the neutral bus bar. To avoid tangles, plan a path around the box perimeter. Strip about a foot more sheathing than you think you need. Thread the wires through the clamp and secure the cable. Don't overtighten.

4 **CONNECT THE NEUTRAL WIRE.** Run the neutral wire toward an open terminal in the neutral bus bar, bending the wire carefully so it will easily fit behind the panel cover. Cut the wire to length and strip off about ½ inch of insulation. Poke the end into the terminal and tighten the setscrew. Connect the ground wire to the ground bar (or neutral bar if there is no ground bar).

5 **WIRE THE NEW BREAKER.** Run the hot wire, bending it carefully so it will easily fit behind the panel cover. Cut the wire to length. Strip off ½ inch of insulation. Poke the wire into the new breaker terminal. If bare wire is visible, remove the wire, snip it a little shorter, and reinsert it. Tighten the setscrew.

6 **SNAP THE BREAKER INTO PLACE.** Slip one side of the breaker under a tab to the right or left of the hot bus bar. Push the other side onto the bus bar until the new breaker is flush with the other breakers. (Some brands of breakers may require a slightly different installation method. Check the instructions.) Restore power and test.

INSTALLING DOUBLE-POLE BREAKERS. Shut off the power. Wire a 240/120-volt circuit with the black and red wires connected to the breaker terminals. Connect the white wire to the neutral bus bar. Wire split circuits the same way (page 144). To wire a straight 240-volt circuit (page 145), connect the two hot wires to the breaker and the ground wire to the ground bar (or neutral bar if there is no ground bar).

INSTALLING A SUBPANEL

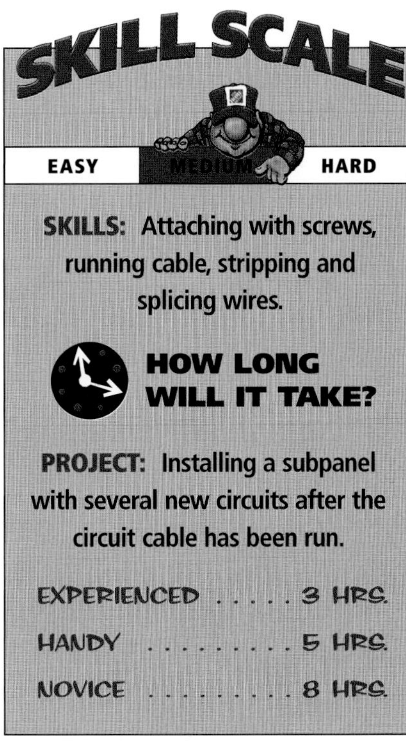

SKILL SCALE
EASY
MEDIUM
HARD
SKILLS: Attaching with screws, running cable, stripping and splicing wires.
HOW LONG WILL IT TAKE?
PROJECT: Installing a subpanel with several new circuits after the circuit cable has been run.
EXPERIENCED . . . . . 3 HRS.
HANDY . . . . 5 HRS.
NOVICE . . . . 8 HRS.

STUFF YOU'LL NEED

TOOLS: Drill, hammer, screwdriver, combination strippers, lineman's pliers

MATERIALS: Subpanel, screws, cable with clamps, staples

An experienced homeowner can tackle a subpanel, but hire a pro if a new service panel is needed (page 172).

WHEN TO ADD A SUBPANEL

Install a subpanel to handle new circuits if the existing service panel does not have open breaker slots and you cannot use half-size breakers (page 168).

A subpanel doesn't add to the total amount of power entering the home. If you have 100-amp service and the new circuits you are installing will require more than that (see page 62 for how to add up your requirements), call an electrician. Electricians working with the utility company can bring 200-amp service to your service head and can install a new service panel.

GETTING READY

Purchase a subpanel. Unlike a main service panel, it has separate bus bars for neutral and ground wires.

Figuring the size of the subpanel, feeder cable, and feeder breaker can be complicated, so consult an electrician or your building department.

In most cases, to add up to six new circuits with a total of 6000 watts or less (pages 116–117), you'll need a 30-amp, 240-volt subpanel. Open two spaces in the main panel and install a 30-amp double-pole feeder breaker. Run 10/3 feeder cable between the main panel and the subpanel. Or install a 40-amp subpanel and feeder breaker, and use #8 wire. Once your plan is approved, get a permit.

1 **MOUNT THE SUBPANEL.** Position the subpanel for easy access but out of reach of small children. As with a main panel, there must be drywall or other nonflammable material between the subpanel and wood framing. Anchor it firmly by driving screws into studs. On a masonry wall, drill holes and drive masonry screws.

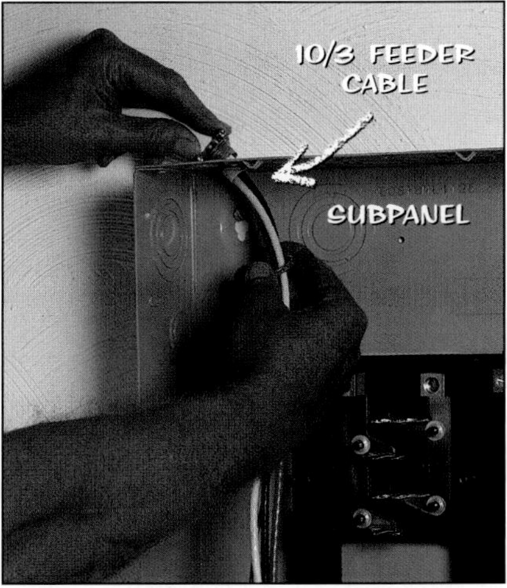

2 **CLAMP THE CABLE TO THE SUBPANEL.** Ask the building department what kind of feeder cable or conduit to use. Punch out the slug from a knockout. Install a cable clamp in the hole. Strip plenty of sheathing so that the wires can run around the perimeter of the subpanel. Clamp the cable to the box.

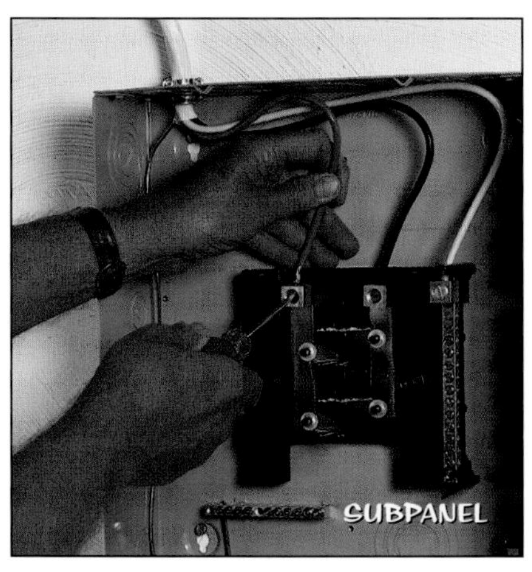

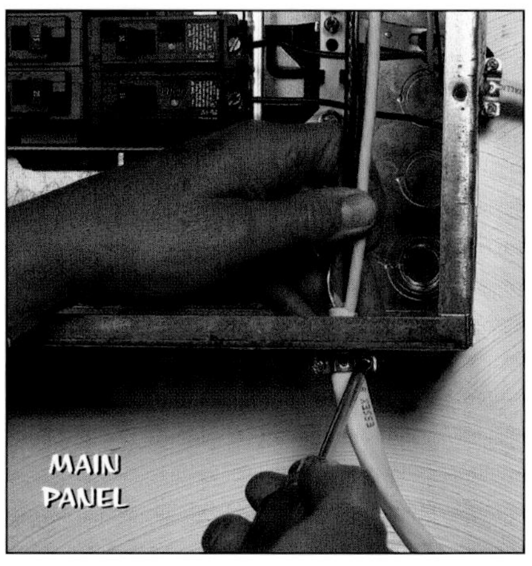

3 **CONNECT THE WIRES IN THE SUBPANEL.** Carefully bend the feeder wires so they run around the perimeter of the subpanel. Run the white wire to the main terminal on the neutral bar and run the ground wire to the ground bar. Run the red and black wires to each of the main terminals on the hot bars. Snip each wire to length and strip off ½-inch of insulation. Poke the wires into the terminals and tighten the setscrews.

4 **MAKE ROOM FOR THE FEEDER BREAKER IN THE MAIN PANEL.** Shut off the main breaker in the main service panel. If you do not have two open slots for the feeder breaker, replace four full-size breakers with two tandem breakers. You may have to remove two breakers and the wires and later connect them to the subpanel.

5 **CLAMP THE CABLE TO THE MAIN PANEL.** Run the feeder cable to the service panel. Strip plenty of sheathing, punch out a knockout slug, and clamp the cable.

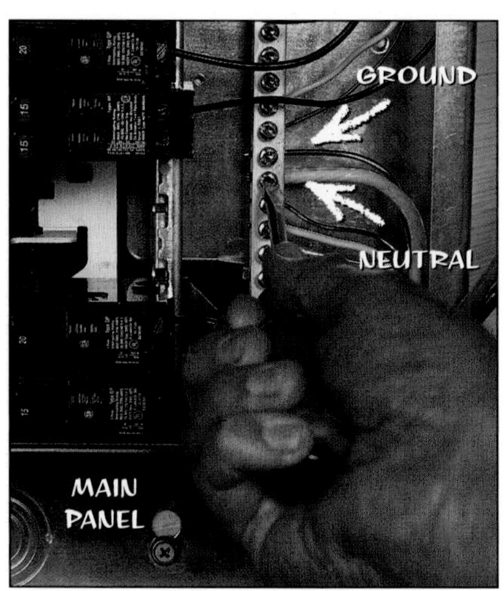

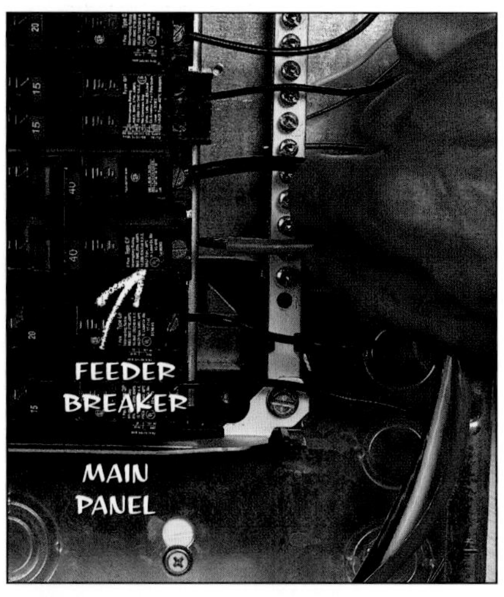

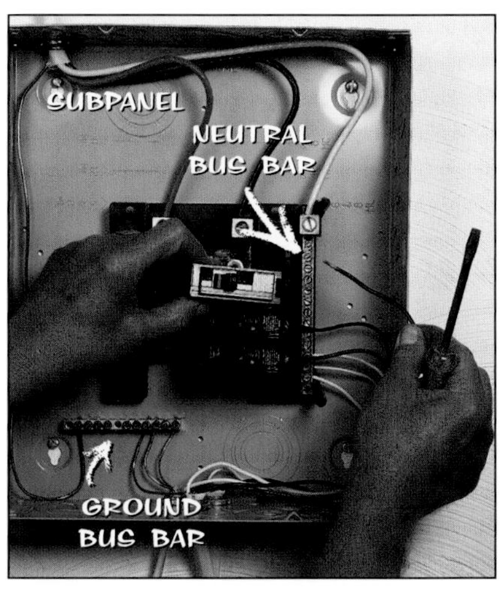

6 **CONNECT THE GROUND AND NEUTRAL WIRES AT THE MAIN PANEL.** Bend the ground wire and the neutral wire around the perimeter of the service panel to open terminals on the neutral bar, and snip them to length. Strip ½-inch of insulation from the neutral wire. Poke the wires into the terminals and tighten the setscrews.

7 **CONNECT THE WIRES TO THE FEEDER BREAKER AT THE MAIN PANEL.** Cut the red and black wires to length. Strip ½-inch of insulation from each and connect them to the two setscrew terminals of a double-pole feeder breaker. Snap the feeder breaker into place. Turn off the feeder breaker and turn on the main breaker.

8 **WIRE NEW BREAKERS TO THE SUBPANEL.** Run cable for new circuits into the subpanel. Connect the wires to new circuit breakers as you would in a main service panel (pages 168–169), but connect the neutral and ground wires to separate bus bars. Turn on the feeder breaker in the main panel to energize the subpanel.

REPLACING A SERVICE PANEL

Although homeowners sometimes install new service panels themselves, many building departments insist that the job be done only by licensed and bonded electricians. **Because the job is complex and potentially dangerous, tackle it only if you have an excellent source of professional advice.**

WHEN TO INSTALL A NEW PANEL

If your service panel is an old-fashioned fuse box, you may want to update it by installing a breaker panel. However, if your circuits rarely blow fuses, the box is not damaged, and you do not plan to add new circuits, there is no compelling reason to upgrade it.

If you need to add new circuits and the service panel cannot accept additional breakers, the easiest solution is to add a subpanel (pages 170–171). A professional electrician—who is used to working with live electricity and sorting out tangles of wires—may prefer to replace the old service panel with a larger one.

If your existing electrical service is insufficient—for example, if you have 60-amp service and need 100 amps or if you have 100-amp service and need 200 amps—you need a new service panel. You also may need to have the utility company change the wires that enter your home.

WHAT'S INVOLVED

An electrician or the utility company must first disconnect the power coming to the house—often by cutting live wires near the service entrance. The electrician can then provide temporary electrical service by tapping the live wires. Obviously, all this is too dangerous for a homeowner.

If your service amperage needs to be increased, the utility company may need to install thicker wires. If you have very old electrical service with only two wires, the utility company must run three wires to your home.

Replacing the service panel is now primarily a matter of managing a tangle of wires. All the wires running to the panel must be disconnected, tagged, and pulled out of the panel. Then the panel must be removed and another one mounted. It's important to position the new panel so that all the wires can reach the breakers and bus bars. When the wires are attached, power can be reconnected.

IT'S A TANGLE. Sorting out the incoming circuits and hooking them up properly is a job best left to the pros. It's not a highly technical job, but it does require clear thinking and the skills that come with practice. Hire a professional electrician to do this.

WIRING A BATHROOM

Bathrooms are usually small, with only a few electrical fixtures and devices. Because they are damp places, specific code requirements apply. You'll need at least two circuits—one for the lights and one for the receptacles.

A bathroom must have at least one ground-fault circuit interrupter (GFCI) receptacle on a 20-amp circuit. The receptacle must be within 12 inches of a sink. If the sink has two bowls, place a single receptacle between the bowls or put one receptacle on each side of the sink. Some codes allow bathroom receptacles to share a circuit with another receptacle elsewhere in the house.

Codes usually require a vent fan. Usually, a vent fan supplies light as well as ventilation. Unless the fan is very powerful or has a heating unit, a vent fan can share a circuit with other bathroom lights.

All overhead lights must be approved for moist rooms. Install lights over the sink, in the main area, and over the tub/shower. Codes may require that you install GFCI protection for the light circuit, especially to protect the light over the tub/shower. (Canada: All bathroom wiring must be GFCI protected.)

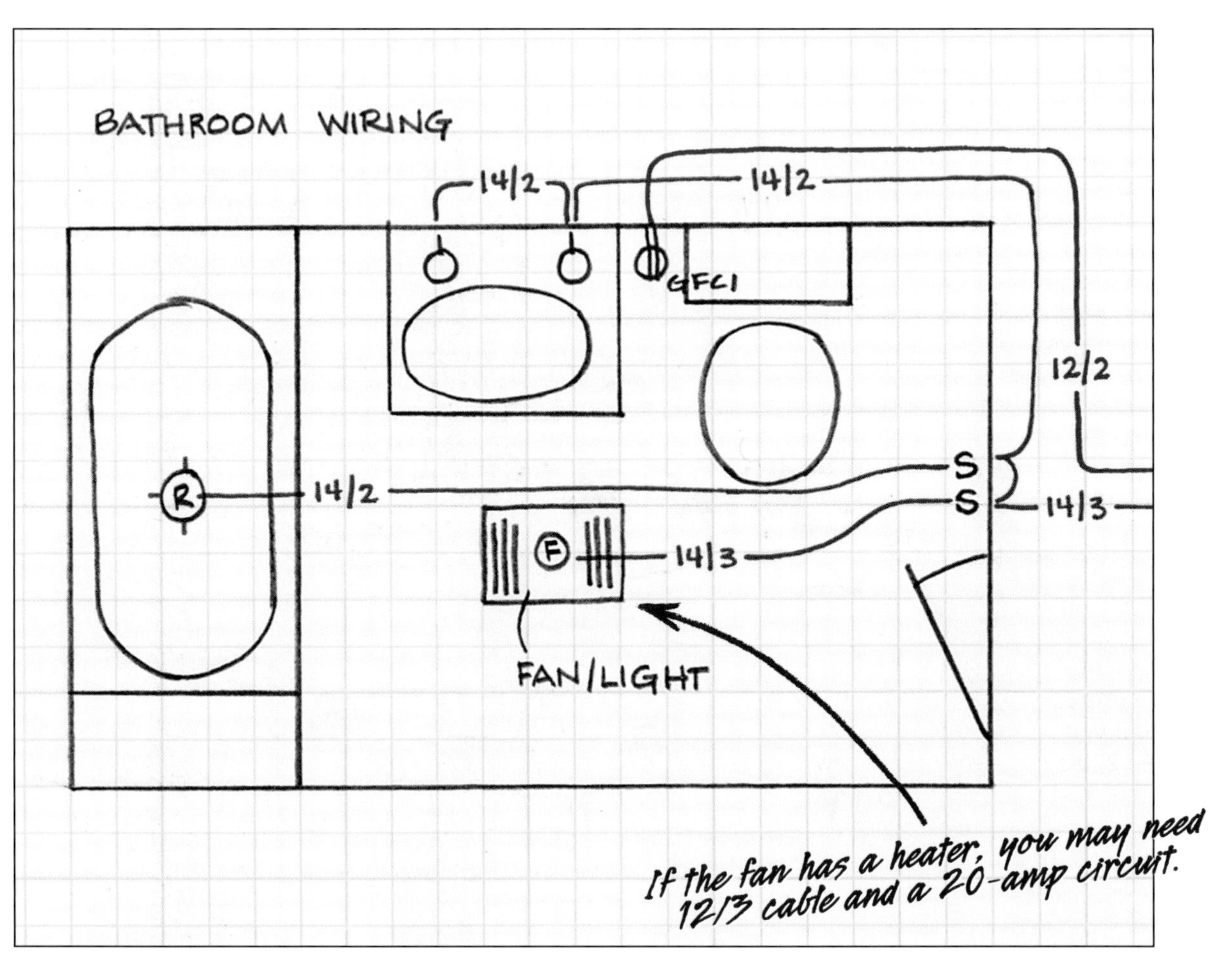

A TYPICAL BATHROOM. Only one receptacle is usually needed in a bathroom. Here, a single GFCI is on its own 20-amp circuit. One 15-amp circuit supplies waterproof can lights over the tub/shower, the lights beside the mirror, and the fan/light. If you install a fan/light with a heating unit, it may pull as much as 1500 watts and will require a separate 20-amp circuit. Switches are conveniently positioned beside the door.

WIRING A KITCHEN

A kitchen is the room that has the most electrical devices and fixtures. It's not unusual to have eight or more circuits in a large kitchen, an organizational challenge.

- **Receptacles.** Position small-appliance receptacles over the counter no more than 4 feet apart and a couple of inches above the countertop backsplash. Have at least two 20-amp circuits for these. Plan the placement of the toaster, mixer, and other appliances. Avoid a potential tangle of cords. Islands and peninsulas also need appliance receptacles, which can be mounted on the sides of cabinets.

  Older microwaves are heavy users of electricity. Many kitchens have a dedicated 20-amp circuit supplying the microwave receptacle. But most new microwaves use far less power and can be safely plugged into any small-appliance receptacle.

  A refrigerator receptacle needs its own 15-amp circuit. Wire a split and switched receptacle (pages 143–144) for the garbage disposal, and place the switch on the wall above the countertop or on a base cabinet. This receptacle has an always-hot outlet that can be used for another appliance.

- **Appliances.** A dishwasher is hard-wired, meaning you run cable directly into it. Hard-wire a range hood as well (pages 159–160). An electric range needs a 240/120-volt receptacle; however, a gas range needs only a 120-volt receptacle.

- **Lights.** A kitchen with many lights might need more than one 15-amp circuit; add up the kitchen's total wattage to find out. Position switches for maximum convenience. A large kitchen may need three-way switches. Codes in some areas, require at least one fluorescent fixture for ambient lighting.

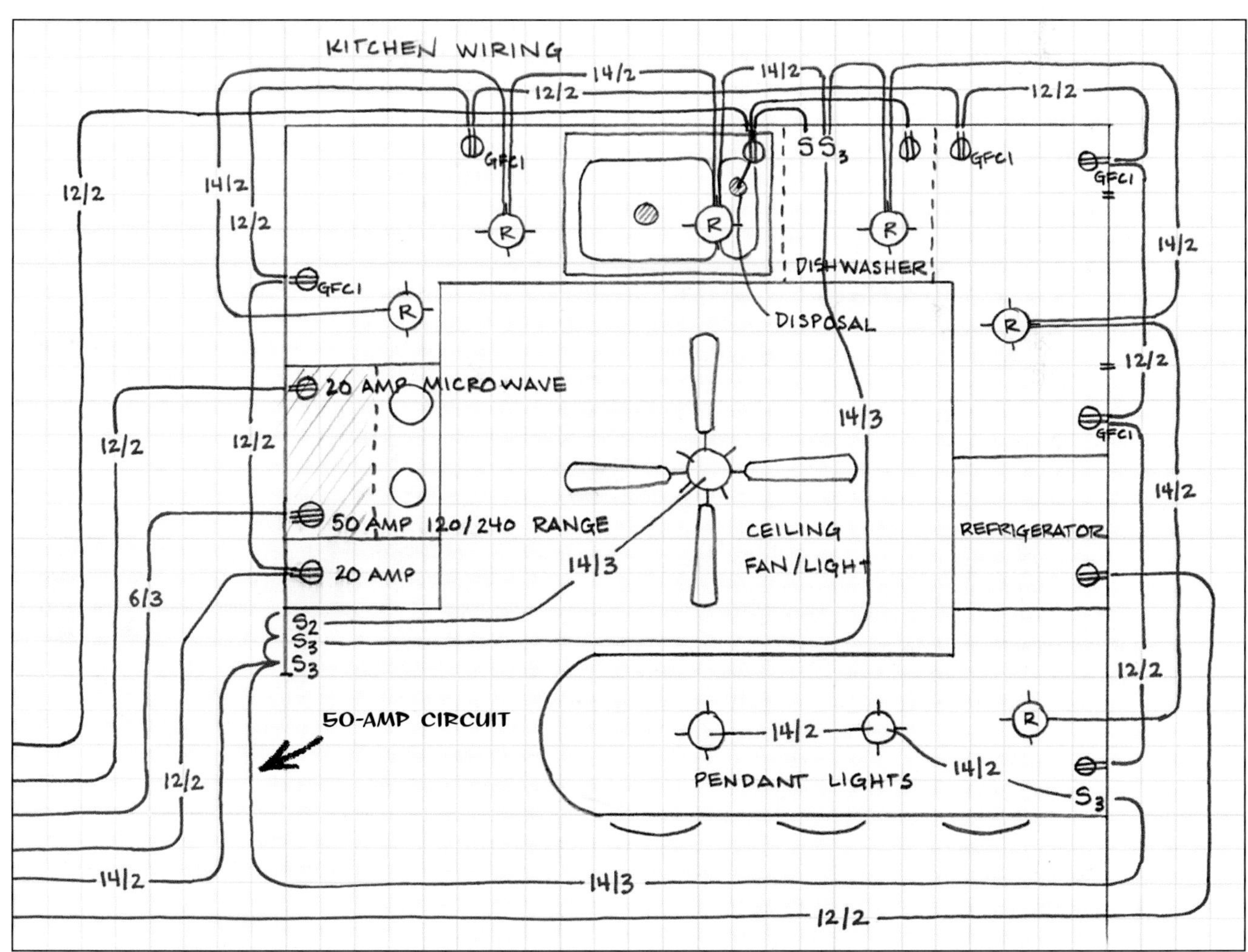

A MODEST-SIZE KITCHEN. A 15-amp lighting circuit supplies a single ceiling fan/light, pendant lights, and recessed can lights; many lights are controlled by 3-way switches. The dishwasher and disposer share a circuit; the microwave and refrigerator each have their own circuit. Over-the-countertop receptacles are GFCI protected. If they're split (page 144), as required in some areas, none could be GFCI. The electric range has its own 50-amp, 240-volt circuit. (For a larger kitchen, see pages 114–115.)

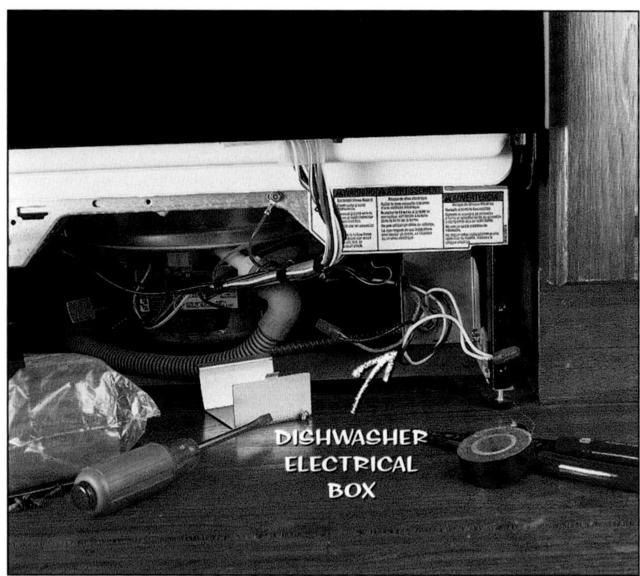

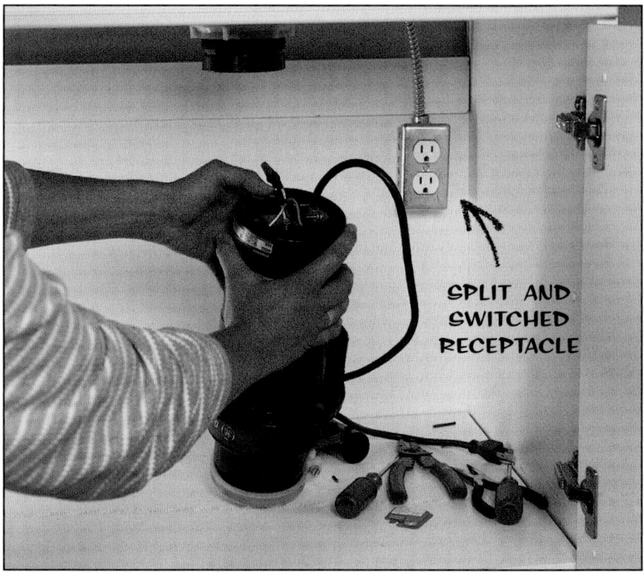

WIRING A DISHWASHER. Run two-wire cable into the space, leaving plenty of slack. Slide in the dishwasher and connect the plumbing. Remove the electrical cover and clamp the cable to the dishwasher electrical box. Splice white to white and black to black wires. Fold back the wires and snap on the cover.

WIRING A GARBAGE DISPOSAL. Install a receptacle box in the wall under the sink and a switch box in an easy-to-reach place above the countertop. Wire for a split and switched receptacle (pages 143–144). Remove the electrical cover from the disposal, strip the ends of an appliance cord, and wire the cord to the disposal. After completing plumbing connections, plug the disposal into the switched outlet.

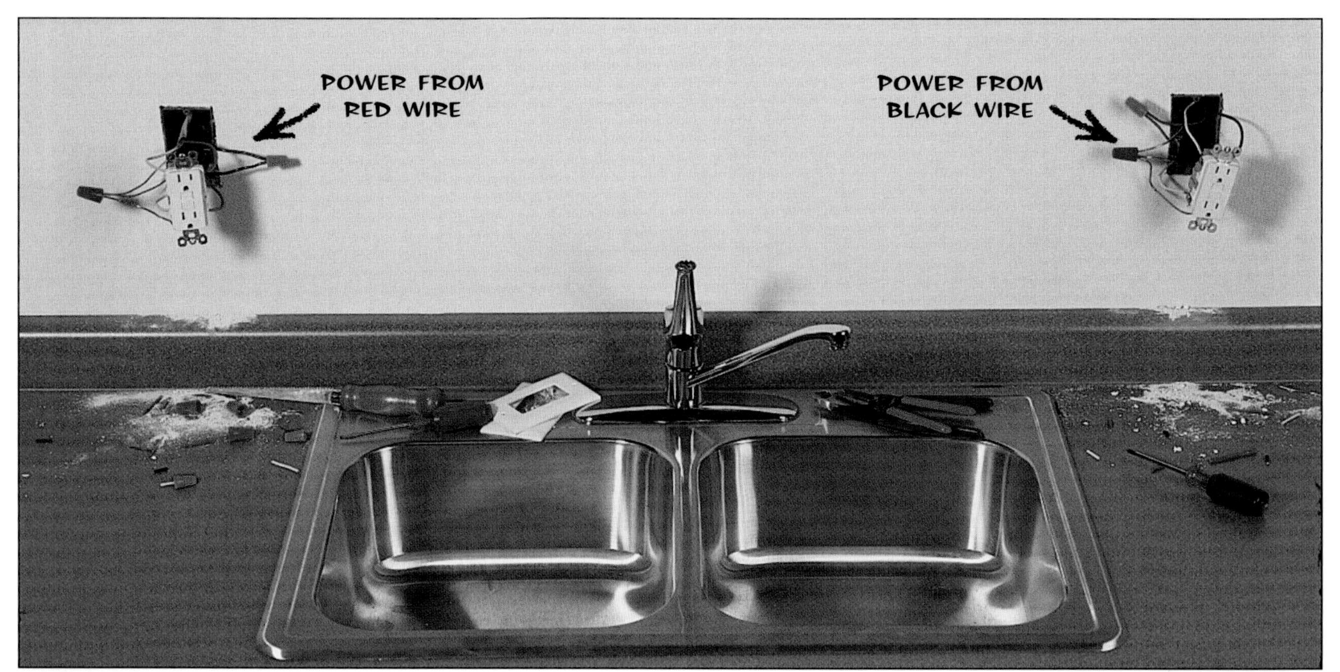

ADDING SMALL-APPLIANCE RECEPTACLES. Run 12/3 cable from a double-pole 20-amp breaker into the first receptacle box and then on to the other boxes. Here the receptacles are wired in an alternating pattern (page 144), with every other receptacle on the red wire and the others on the black wire. The white wire connects to all the receptacles. This arrangement allows you to install GFCIs. Keep in mind that if local codes require split receptacles, you can't install GFCIs.

WIRING A BEDROOM

Most bedrooms have either an overhead switched light or one switched receptacle, plus a receptacle or two on each wall. You can go beyond the basic necessities and supply your bedroom with electrical service to outfit a small office or to add a few creature comforts. NOTE: AFCIs (page 168) will be required beginning January, 2002. For your safety, install one for each bedroom circuit.

- **Receptacles.** Codes typically allow bedroom receptacles to be up to 12 feet apart. If you cut this distance in half, you'll improve receptacle accessibility and give yourself more options for arranging bedroom furniture.To provide a computer with maximum protection against power surges, wire an isolated-ground receptacle. For comfortable TV viewing while in bed, install a wall bracket for a TV with a nearby receptacle, about 6½ feet above the floor.

  Avoid placing a receptacle directly below a window: it may get wet if the window is open during a rainstorm. If you use a window air-conditioner, install a receptacle near the window. An average window unit does not pull heavy amperage, so you can use a 15-amp receptacle on the same circuit as the rest of the bedroom receptacles. A heavy-duty air-conditioner may need a dedicated 20-amp receptacle.
- **Lights.** To control an overhead fan/light, run three-wire cable from the ceiling box to the switch box and install a fan/light switch (page 36). Consider installing three-way switches at the door and by the bed for convenience. Or, install a remote-control switch (page 98). Place a reading lamp at both sides of the bed, each with its own switch.

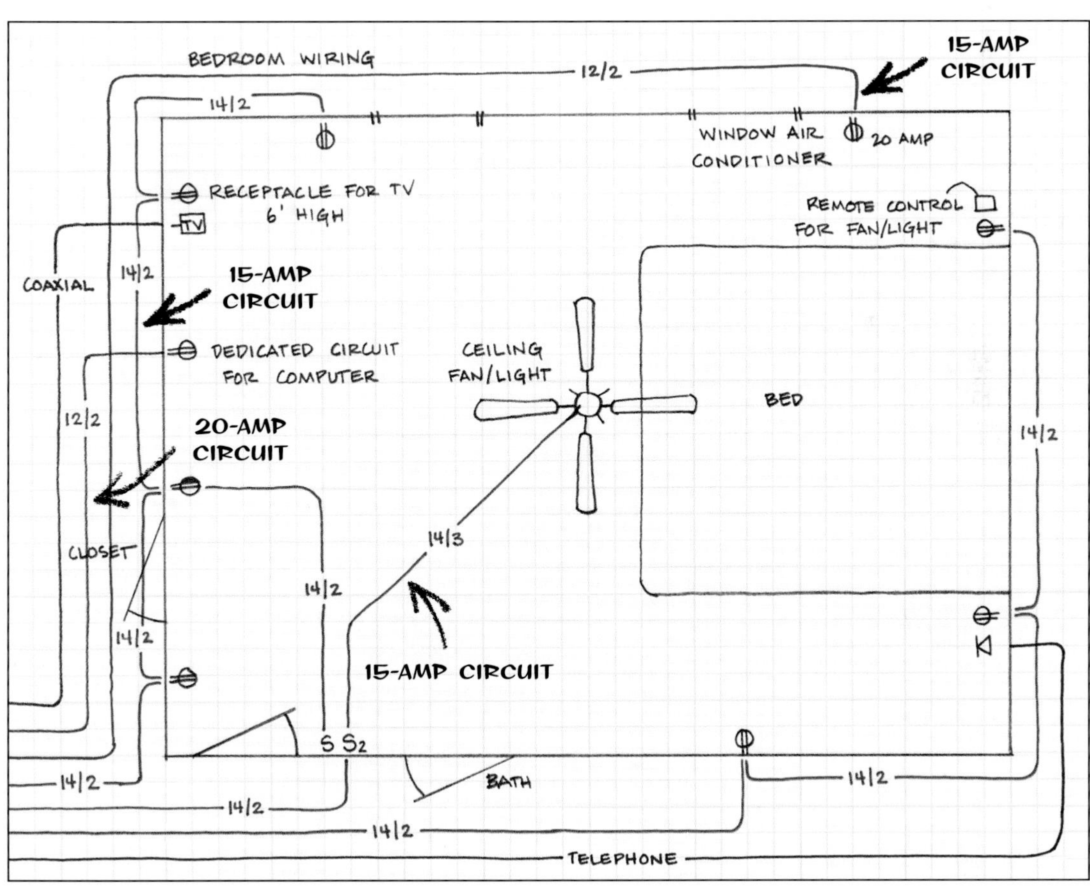

A MULTI-USE BEDROOM. Separate reading lights on each side of the bed each have conveniently placed switches. A receptacle with its own dedicated circuit guards a computer against damage caused by power surges (page 101). A receptacle 6 feet from the floor supplies power to a wall-mounted TV and VCR, and eliminates unsightly dangling cords. The fan/light is controlled by a wall switch and a remote control. (Wire the fan and light separately, using the three-way wiring described on pages 148–150.) A receptacle placed higher than usual near the window accommodates a window air-conditioner.

WIRING A LAUNDRY ROOM

In a laundry room, receptacles that feed the washing machine, gas dryer, and other appliances must be on 20-amp circuits that are not used by any other room. The receptacles must be ground-fault circuit interrupter (GFCI) protected.

If the dryer is electric, you also will need a 30-amp, 120/240-volt receptacle. Use 10-gauge wire and connect the dryer directly to a 30-amp, 240-volt breaker or fuse (page 145). In this example, the washer is on its own circuit. A washing machine could share a circuit with a gas dryer.

Because these machines vibrate, fasten the wiring securely. Local codes may allow NM or armored cable, but conduit is more secure. See pages 126–127 for conduit installation instructions.

Laundry room lights don't need their own circuits. But you shouldn't put them on circuits other than receptacle circuits so you won't be without light if a faulty appliance causes a circuit overload.

LIGHTING CLOSETS AND STORAGE SPACES. The days of exposed lightbulbs on pull-chain switches are past. Lights in closets, attics, crawlspaces, and other storage areas must now be recessed or enclosed, controlled by wall switches, and positioned at least 18 inches away from flammable materials. Wherever there is equipment that must be serviced—such as a sump pump or a water heater—there must be a light controlled by a wall switch.

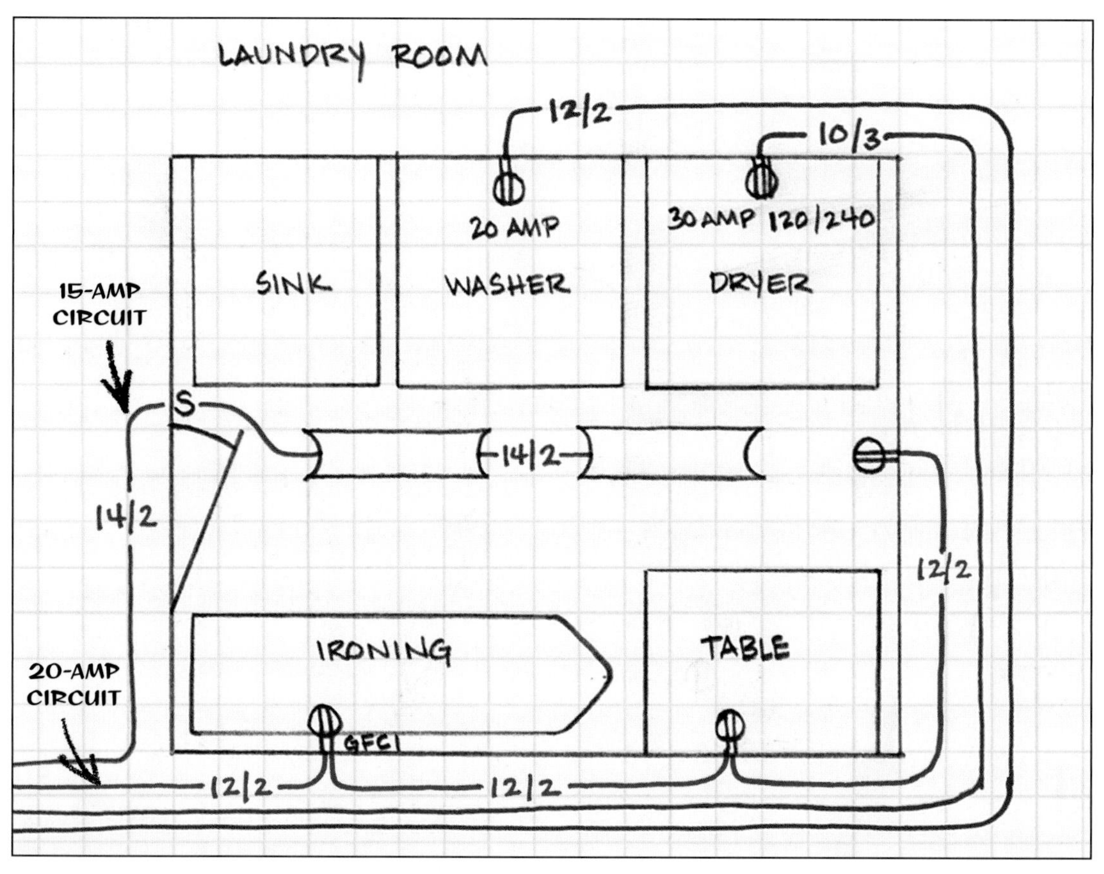

A HARD-WORKING LAUNDRY AREA. The dryer has a dedicated 30-amp, 240-volt circuit, and the washer has its own 20-amp, 120-volt circuit. Because this area could become damp, use ground fault circuit interrupter (GFCI) receptacles throughout (page 27). Fluorescent lights are on a 15-amp circuit, which they may share with lights in other rooms.

CHAPTER

12 LOW-VOLTAGE WIRING

In addition to having miles of standard-voltage wiring, your home likely has hundreds of yards of thin wires that carry little or no power. These wires lead to telephones, thermostats, door chimes, VCRs, and TVs.

These wires and cable carry voltage that is so low it cannot harm you. Still, you should respect low-voltage wiring. Once the wiring is damaged, it can be difficult to diagnose the problem and to repair it. Hide low-voltage wiring inside walls or behind moldings when possible. If wires must be exposed, pull them taut and staple them firmly.

CHAPTER TWELVE PROJECTS

Homer's Hindsight

DRILL NEW HOLES.

When running a new telephone line through my basement, I saved a little time by threading the cable through the same hole as was used by electrical cable. The result: static and buzzing on the line. Always keep phone and TV cable 2 inches apart from electrical cable when running parallel, and 1 inch apart wherever they cross.

INSTALLING TELEPHONE WIRING

SKILLS: Attaching with screws; stapling, stripping, and connecting thin wires.

HOW LONG WILL IT TAKE?

PROJECT: Running about 50 feet of phone cable and installing two jacks.

EXPERIENCED ..... 2 HRS.
HANDY .... 4 HRS.
NOVICE .... 6 HRS.

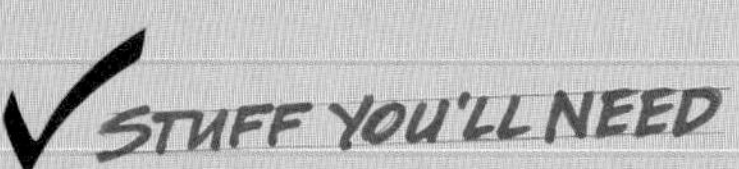

STUFF YOU'LL NEED

TOOLS: Drill, screwdriver, lineman's pliers, combination strippers

MATERIALS: Solid-core telephone cable, phone jacks, staples

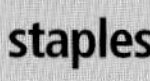

FRAGILE WIRES.
Category 5 cable and telephone wire are fragile. Don't bend, flatten, or otherwise compromise these wires. A damaged wire can result in a distorted connection, especially for computers.

Adding a new telephone jack is straightforward work. Just run cable and connect wires to terminals labeled with their colors. The most difficult part is hiding the cable.

Depending on your service arrangement, it may be less expensive to have the phone company install new service for you. The lines they install will be under warranty—all future repairs will be free.

Cheap telephone cable has wires that are difficult to strip and splice. Spend a little more for "24-AWG" cable with solid-core wires.

Make all connections in a jack or junction box. Plan cable paths so as little of the cable as possible can be seen. For instance, going through a wall (page 180) saves you from running unsightly cable around door moldings. Use these same techniques to run speaker wire.

BUYER'S GUIDE

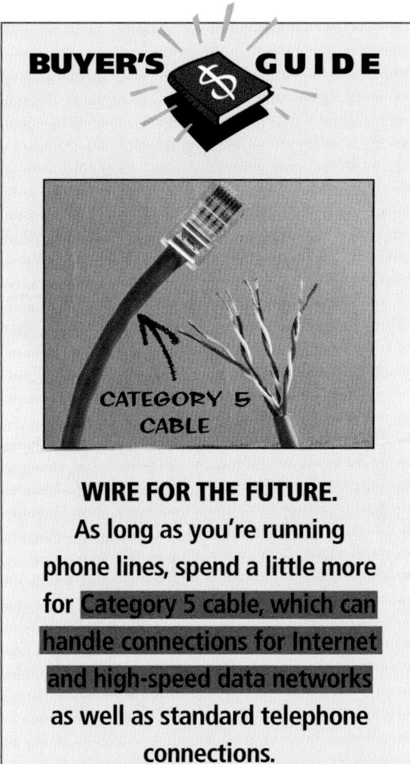

WIRE FOR THE FUTURE.
As long as you're running phone lines, spend a little more for Category 5 cable, which can handle connections for Internet and high-speed data networks as well as standard telephone connections.

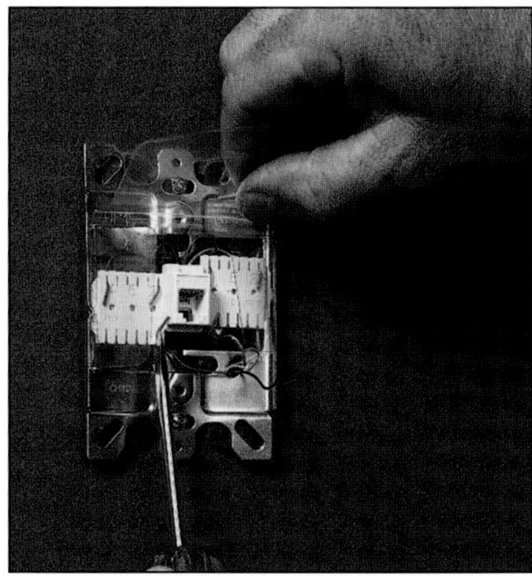

1 OPTION A:
TAP INTO A PHONE JACK. Unscrew the cover from a phone jack or a phone junction box. Strip about 2 inches of sheathing and ½ inch insulation from each wire. (Standard phones use only two of the wires, but it doesn't hurt to connect all the wires.) Loosen each terminal screw. Bend the wire end in a clockwise loop, slip it under the screw head, and tighten the screw.

OPTION B:
USE PUSH-ON CONNECTORS. Some jacks have terminals that clamp onto the wire so you don't have to strip it. Just push the wire down into the slot until it snaps into place.

INSTALLING TELEPHONE WIRING (CONTINUED)

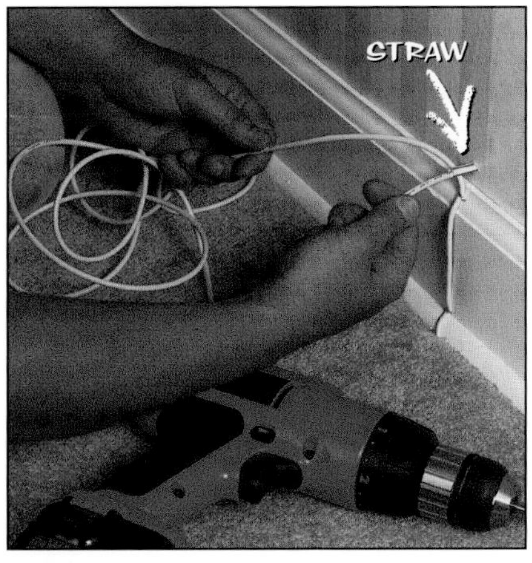

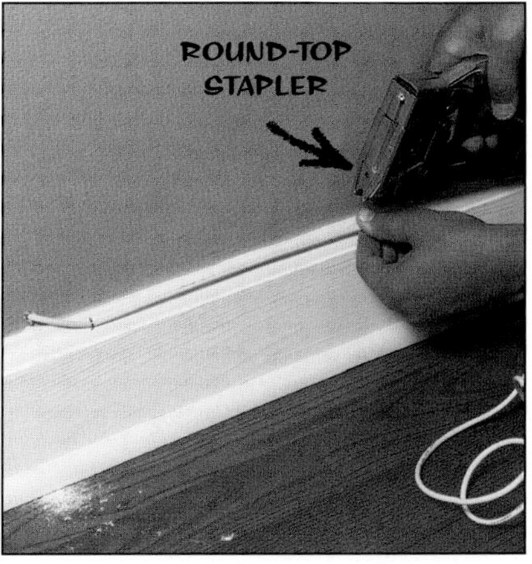

2 **HIDE CABLE.** Use any trick you can think of to tuck away unsightly cable. Pry moldings away from the wall, slip the cable in behind, and renail the molding. Or, pull carpeting back one short section at a time, run cable along the floor behind the tack strip, and push the carpet back into place.

3 **RUN CABLE THROUGH A WALL.** To go through a wall, drill a hole using a long, ¼-inch drill bit, then insert a large drinking straw. Fish the cable through the straw. When you're finished, split and remove the straw.

4 **STAPLE EXPOSED CABLE.** When there is no choice but to leave cable exposed, staple it in place every foot or so along the top of the baseboard. Use a round-top stapler or plastic-shielded staples that hammer into place. (Square-cornered staples damage the cable sheathing.)

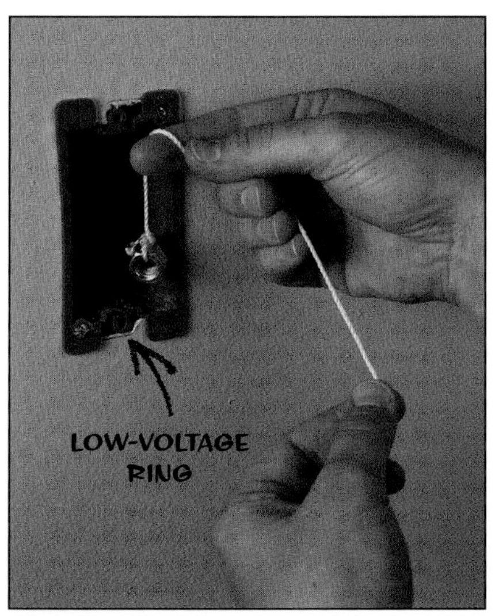

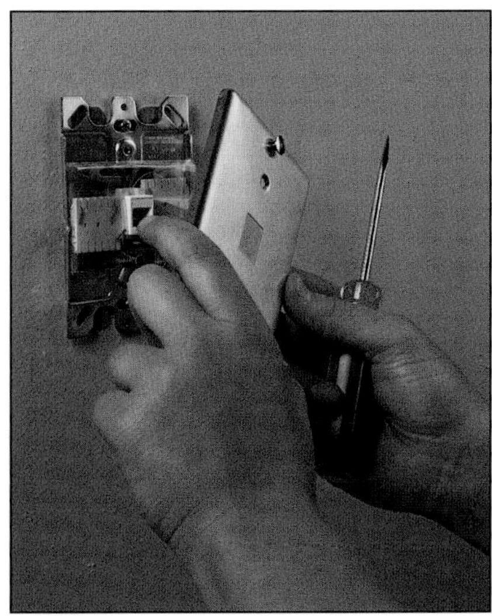

5 **INSTALL A WALL BOX.** A wall jack can attach to a low-voltage ring (as shown) or to an electrical remodel box. Cut a hole in the wall and install the ring. Tie a small weight to a string and lower it through the hole until you feel it hit the floor.

6 **PULL THE CABLE.** Drill a ⅜-inch hole at the bottom of the wall where you want the wire to go. Bend a piece of wire into a hook, slip it into the hole, and pull out a loop of the string. Tape the string to the cable and pull the cable up through the remodel box.

7 **INSTALL A WALL JACK.** Attach the base of the jack and make the connections. Install the cover plate.

RUNNING COAXIAL CABLE

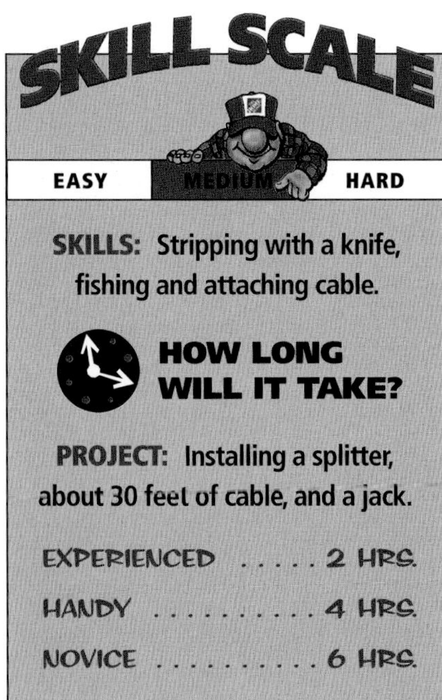

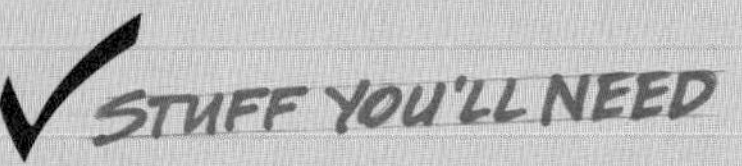

STUFF YOU'LL NEED

TOOLS: Drill, screwdriver, knife, combination strippers
MATERIALS: RG6 coaxial cable, splitter, male connectors, wall jack, staples

Cable TV companies will run new lines and install jacks. Some do simple installations for free; for longer runs, they may charge and may not hide as much of the cable as you like. They also may increase your monthly fee after installing a second or third jack. Still, it's worth checking out the service options before doing your own installations.

Purchase RG6 coaxial cable for all runs through the house. Don't use RG59, which has less substantial wire wrapping. Coaxial cable is thick and ugly, so fish it through walls when possible (pages 130–132).

If your cable signal is weak after adding new lines, install a signal booster to solve the problem. The booster attaches to the coaxial cable and plugs into a receptacle.

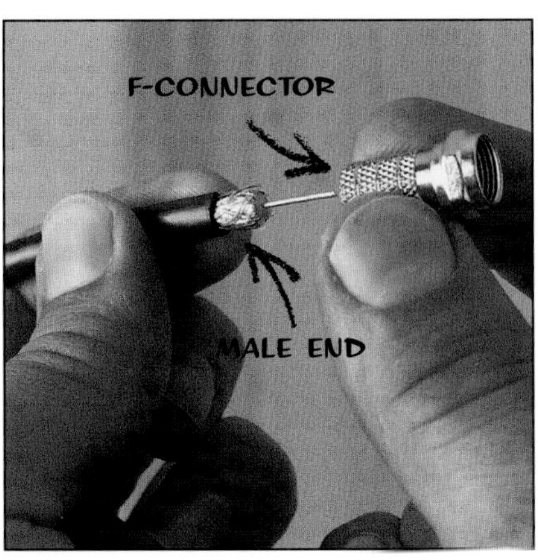

1 MAKE A MALE END. Use combination strippers to strip $\frac{3}{4}$ inch of insulation, exposing the bare wire. Do not bend the exposed wire. With a knife, carefully strip $\frac{3}{8}$ inch of the thin outer sheathing only—do not cut through the metal mesh wrapping. Firmly twist a screw-on F-connector. For best results, purchase a special coaxial crimping tool and attach a crimp-on F-connector.

2 SPLIT A LINE. Cut the line you want to tap into. Install male ends on both ends of the cut line and the end of the new line. Insert and twist all three male connectors onto a signal splitter. Anchor the splitter with screws.

3 INSTALL A JACK. Cut a hole in the wall and run cable to it using the technique shown on page 180. (A regular electrical box can be used, though a low-voltage ring is preferable. See opposite page.) Strip the insulation to make a male end in the cable. Clamp the mounting brackets in the hole. Attach the cable end to the back of the jack by twisting on the F-connector. Tighten the connection with pliers or a wrench. Attach the jack to the wall by driving screws into the mounting brackets.

TROUBLESHOOTING A DOOR CHIME

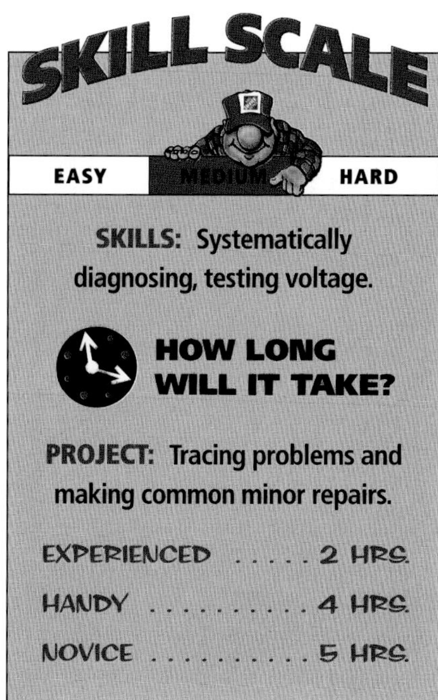

A doorbell or chime system is supplied with low-voltage power—between 8 and 24 volts—by a transformer. When the button is pressed, the circuit closes and sends power to the chime or bell.

FIXING COMMON PROBLEMS

Because the voltage associated with doorbells and chimes is low, there is no need to shut off power unless you are working on the transformer. Here's how to troubleshoot most problems.

- **If a bell or chime develops a fuzzy sound,** remove the chime cover and vacuum out any dust and debris and brush off the bell or chimes.
- **If you get only one tone** when the front (or only) button is pushed, check the wiring in the chime to see that the button is connected to the "front." On many two-button systems, the chime is supposed to "ding dong" when the front button is pushed, and only "ding" when the rear button is pushed.
- **If the chime suddenly stops working** at the same time you blow a fuse or trip a breaker, restore power to the circuit supplying the transformer.
- **If the chime stops working altogether,** conduct a systematic investigation, moving from the simplest to the most complex repairs. First check out the button(s), then the chime, and then the transformer. If none of these reveals a problem, the wiring may be damaged.

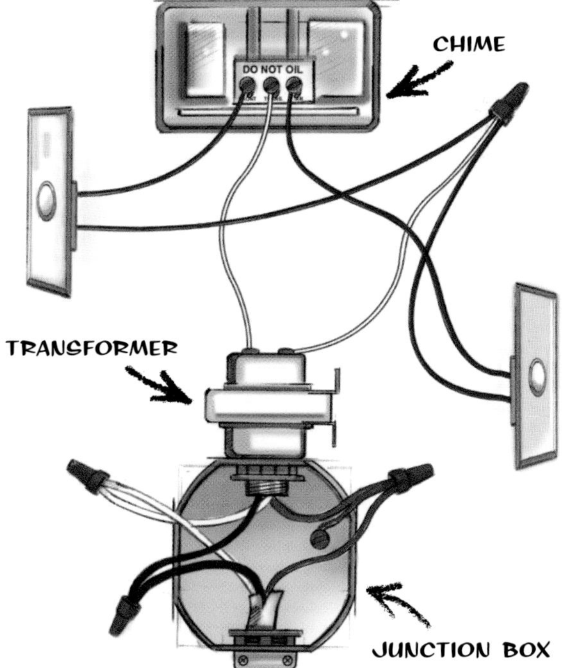

A TYPICAL TWO-BUTTON SETUP. The transformer—usually located in an out-of-the-way spot such as the basement, crawlspace, or cabinet interior—sends low-voltage power to the chime. There, one wire is connected to the chime. Another wire is spliced to two different wires, each of which travels through a button and back to the chime. When either button is pressed, the circuit is completed, power travels to the chime, and the chime rings.

1 **EXAMINE THE BUTTON.** Remove the screws while holding the button in place, and gently pull out the button. (Make sure the wires do not slide back into the hole.) Use a toothbrush to clean away any debris, cocoons, or corrosion, and tighten the screws. If either wire is broken, restrip and reconnect it. Retest the button.

2 **TOUCH WIRES TOGETHER.** If the button still doesn't work, loosen the terminal screws and remove the wires. Holding each wire by its insulation, touch the bare ends together. If the chime sounds, the button is faulty and needs to be replaced. If you see or hear a tiny spark but the chime does not sound, the chime may be faulty (Step 3). If there is no sound and no spark, check the transformer (Step 4, page 184).

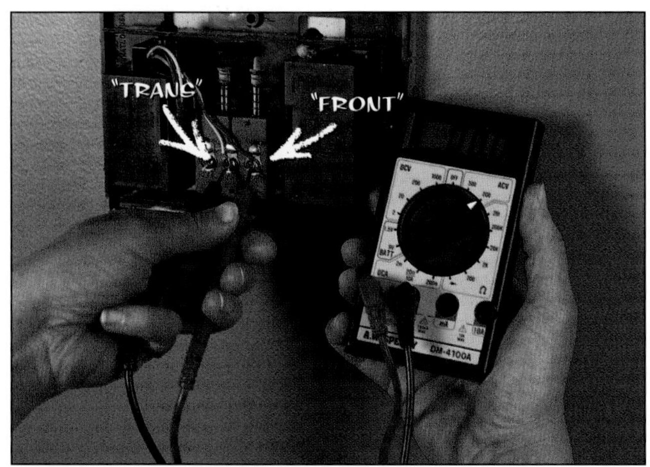

3 **TEST THE CHIME.** Remove the chime cover and ensure that all the wires are securely connected to terminals. Vacuum out any dust and scrape away any corrosion near the terminals. When you pull back a plunger and release it, the chime should sound. If not, clean any greasy buildup that may be gumming up the springs. If the chime still does not work, touch the probes of a multitester to the "front" and "trans" terminals, and to the "rear" and "trans" terminals. If power is present within two volts of the chime's printed voltage rating, then the chime is faulty and should be replaced.

BUYER'S GUIDE

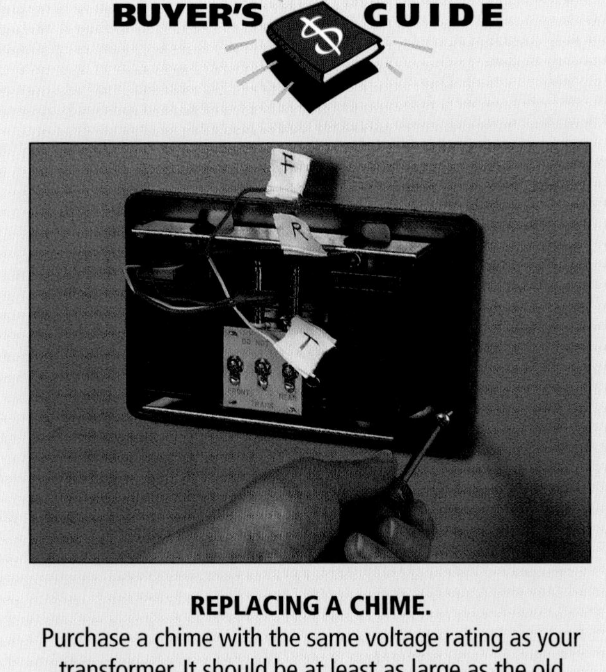

REPLACING A CHIME.

Purchase a chime with the same voltage rating as your transformer. It should be at least as large as the old chime so that you don't have to paint the wall around it. Label the wires with pieces of tape, unscrew the terminal screws, and remove them. Remove the screws holding the chime to the wall and pull it away. Thread the wires through the new chime and fasten the chime to the wall. Connect the wires to the terminals.

TROUBLESHOOTING A DOOR CHIME (CONTINUED)

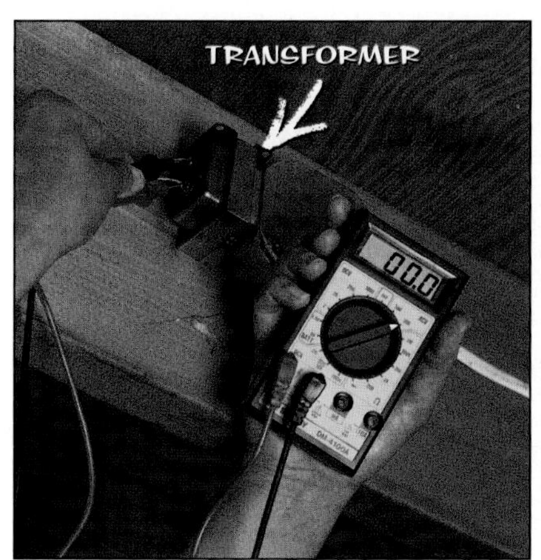

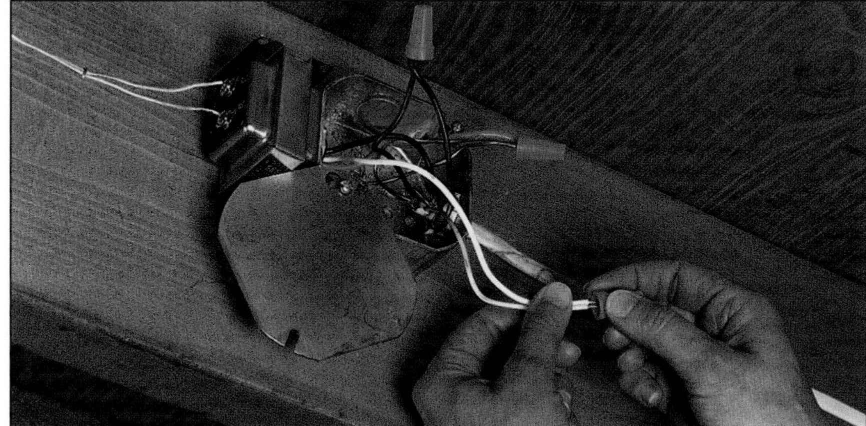

4 TEST THE TRANSFORMER. Look for an exposed electrical box with the transformer attached. Tighten loose connections. Touch the probes of a multitester to both transformer terminals. If you get a reading of more than 2 volts below the transformer rating, the transformer is faulty and should be replaced.

5 REPLACING A TRANSFORMER. Purchase a transformer with the same voltage rating as the old one. Shut off power to the circuit and open the adjacent junction box. Label the bell wires and disconnect them. Disconnect the transformer leads inside the junction box and disconnect the transformer. Thread the new transformer leads into the junction box, fasten the transformer to the box, and splice the leads to the wires. Connect the bell wires and test.

INSTALLING WIRELESS CHIMES

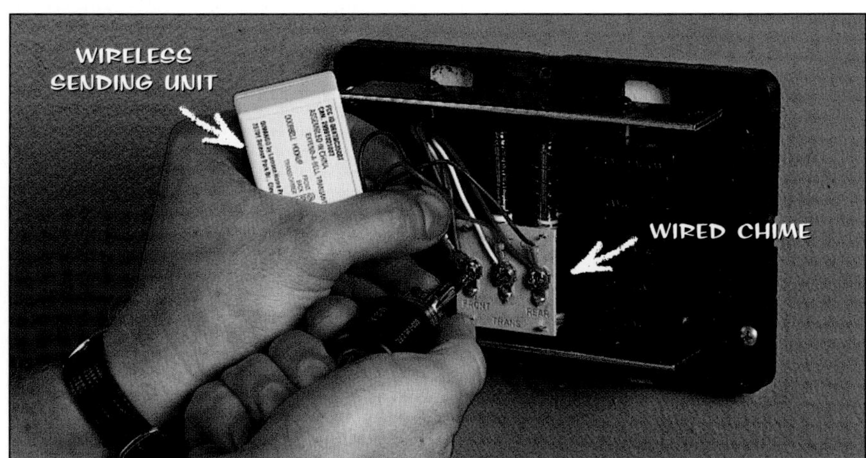

INSTALLING THE CHIME. Rather than going through the trouble of replacing defective bell wire, buy a wireless chime system. Installation is simple: Plug the chime into a standard receptacle., power the button with a battery, and attach the button to the house.

ADDING A WIRELESS CHIME TO AN EXISTING CHIME SYSTEM. If you can't hear your door chime everywhere in your home, add a wireless chime to your wired system. Remove the cover from the existing chime and loosen the terminal screws. Take the leads of the wireless chime's sending unit and insert them under the screws. Tighten the screws. Using its double-sided tape, stick the sending unit to the chime housing. Plug the wireless chime into a receptacle.

TROUBLESHOOTING A THERMOSTAT

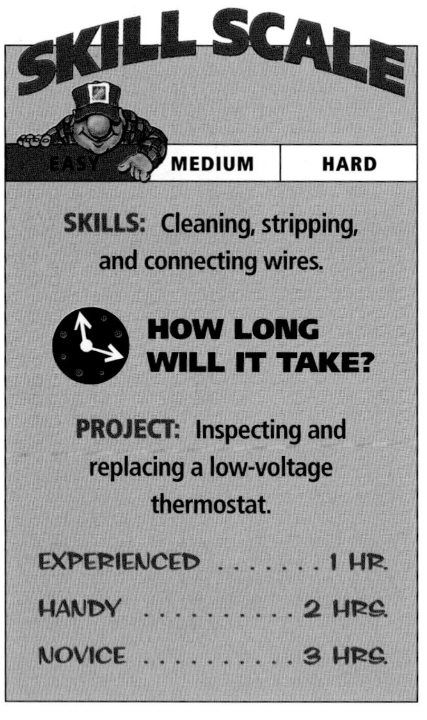

SKILL SCALE
EASY
MEDIUM
HARD
SKILLS: Cleaning, stripping, and connecting wires.
HOW LONG WILL IT TAKE?
PROJECT: Inspecting and replacing a low-voltage thermostat.
EXPERIENCED .... 1 HR.
HANDY .... 2 HRS.
NOVICE .... 3 HRS.

✓ STUFF YOU'LL NEED

TOOLS: Small brush, screwdriver, combination strippers

MATERIALS: Short length of wire, replacement thermostat, scrap of bond paper

The round, low-voltage unit featured in most of these pictures is the most common type of thermostat in use. Yours may be rectangular, but its functions are the same.

If your furnace or air-conditioner fails to operate, check the thermostat for simple mechanical problems. The cover may be jammed in too far, disrupting the mechanism. A wire may have broken or come loose. Or, the parts may be covered with dust, inhibiting electrical contact.

If cleaning and adjusting do not solve the problem, replacing a thermostat is a simple job. Consider installing a programmable unit for more control options. Remember that a thermostat contains mercury, so dispose of it properly.

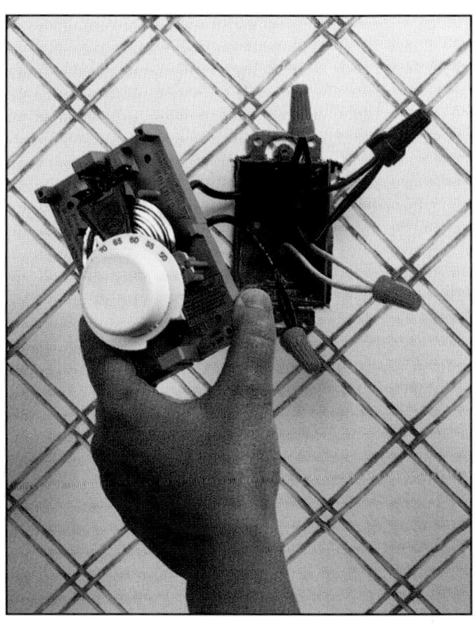

CHECKING A LINE-VOLTAGE THERMOSTAT. If your thermostat uses household current, always shut off power to the circuit before pulling it out. If it fails, disconnect it and take it to a dealer for service or replacement.

REVIEWING THE ANATOMY OF A LOW-VOLTAGE THERMOSTAT. Thin wires come from a transformer and connect to the thermostat base. You'll probably find one wire for the transformer, one for heat, one for air-conditioning, and one for a fan. (A heat pump uses six or more wires and has a special thermostat. Contact a dealer for repairs.) To protect circuitry, shut off power before you start to work.

SEAL OFF DRAFTS.
Even if your thermostat is on an interior wall, air coming through a hole behind it may throw its temperature readings out of whack, resulting in erratic heating. Remove the thermostat base from the wall and fill the hole with insulation or caulk.

CLEANING THE CONTACTS WITH A BRUSH. Pull off the outer cover and use a soft, clean, dry brush to remove dust from the bimetal coil. Turn the dial to get at all the nooks and crannies.

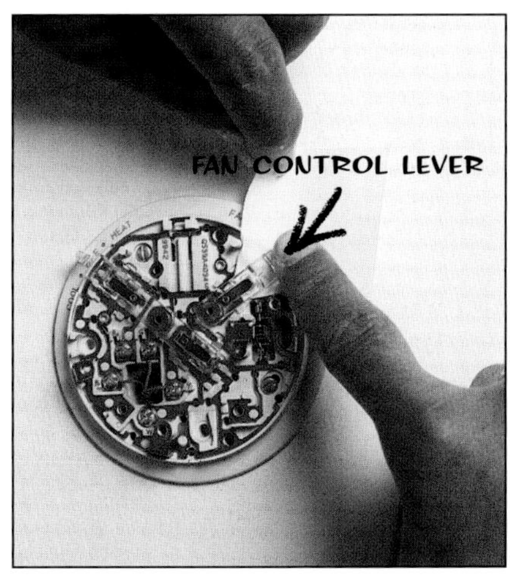

CLEANING THE SWITCH CONTACTS. Remove the screws holding the thermostat body and pull out the body. Gently pull back on the fan control lever, slip a piece of white bond paper behind it, and slide the paper back and forth to clean the contact behind it. Do the same for the mode control lever, if there is one.

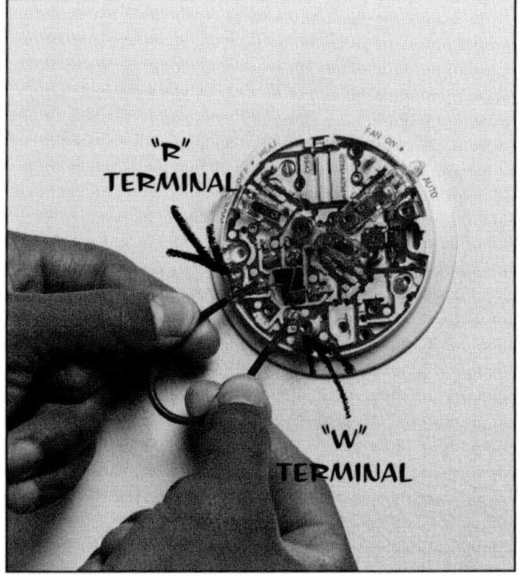

CONDUCTING A HOT-WIRE TEST. If heat does not come on, test to see if power is getting to the thermostat. Cut a short length of wire and strip both ends. Holding only the insulated portion, touch the bare ends to the terminals marked W and R. If the heating system starts to run, replace the thermostat. If nothing happens, troubleshoot or replace the transformer (page 184).

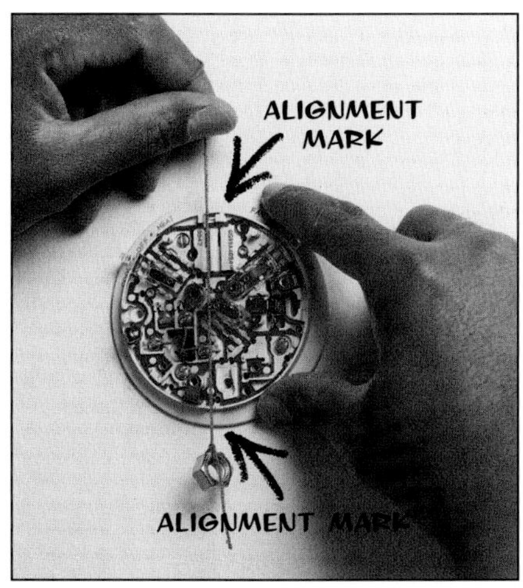

LEVELING A THERMOSTAT. If the temperature is always warmer or cooler than the thermostat setting, the thermostat may be out of level. Hold a level or a weighted string in front of the thermostat to see if the two alignment marks line up. If not, remove the mounting screws, realign the thermostat, and drive new screws.

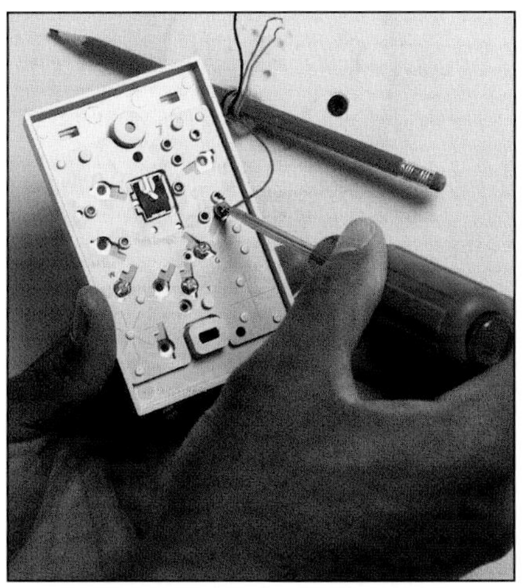

REPLACING A LOW-VOLTAGE THERMOSTAT. Loosen the terminal screws and pull out the wires. Remove the mounting screws and pull out the plate. Clip the wires so they cannot slide back through the hole. Thread the wires through the new thermostat and hook the wires to the terminals. Check for leveling and attach the base to the wall with screws.

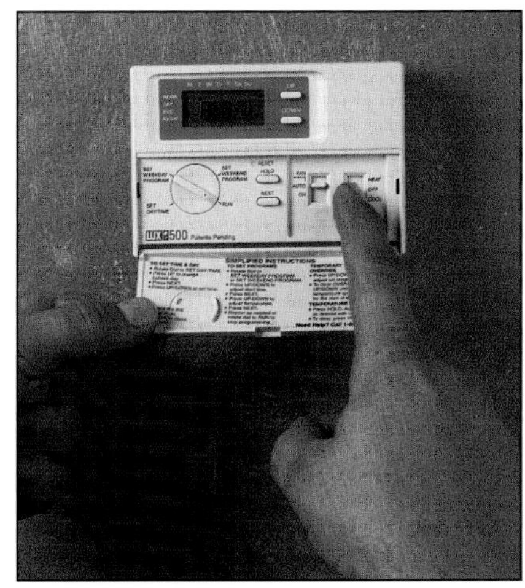

INVESTING IN A PROGRAMMABLE THERMOSTAT. Spend a little more and save money in the long run with a thermostat that adjusts heating or cooling several times a day.

GLOSSARY

Amp. A measurement of the amount of electrical current in a circuit at any moment. *See also* Volt *and* Watt.

Antioxidant. A paste applied to aluminum wires to inhibit corrosion and maintain safe connections.

Armored cable. Two or more insulated wires wrapped in a protective metal sheathing.

Ballast. A transformer that regulates the voltage in a fluorescent lamp.

Bell wire. A thin, typically 18-gauge wire used for doorbells.

Box. A metal or plastic enclosure within which electrical connections are made.

Bus bar. A main power terminal to which circuits are attached in a fuse or breaker box. One bus bar serves the circuit's hot side; the other, the neutral side. Some service panels and all subpanels have separate neutral and ground bus bars.

BX. Armored cable containing insulated wires but no ground wire.

Cable. Two or more insulated wires wrapped in metal or plastic sheathing.

Circuit. The path of electrical flow from a power source through an outlet and back to ground.

Circuit breaker. A switch that automatically interrupts electrical flow in a circuit in case of an overload or short.

Codes. Local laws governing safe wiring practices. *See* National Electrical Code.

Common. A terminal on a three-way switch, usually with a dark-colored screw and marked COM.

Conductor. A wire or anything else that carries electricity.

Conduit. Rigid (metal or PVC) or flexible plastic tubing through which wires are run.

Continuity tester. An instrument that tells whether a device is capable of carrying electricity.

Dimmer. A rotary or sliding switch that lets you vary the intensity of a light.

Duplex receptacle. A device that includes two plug outlets. Most receptacles in homes are duplexes.

Electrical metallic tubing (EMT). Thin-walled, rigid conduit suitable for indoor use.

End-of-the-run. A device located at the end of a circuit. No wires continue from its box to other devices.

Feed wire. A wire that brings household current to a device.

Fishing. Pulling cables through finished walls and ceilings.

Fish tape. A hooked strip of spring steel used for fishing cables through walls and for pulling wires through conduit.

Fixture. Any light or other electrical device permanently attached to a home's wiring.

Flexible metal conduit. Tubing that can be easily bent by hand. *See also* Greenfield.

Fluorescent tube. A light source that uses an ionization process to produce ultraviolet radiation. This radiation becomes visible light when it hits the coated inner surface of the tube.

Four-way switch. A type of switch used to control a light from three or more locations.

Fuse. A safety device designed to stop electrical flow if a circuit shorts or is overloaded. Like a circuit breaker, a fuse protects against fire from overheated wiring.

Ganging. Assembling two or more electrical components into a single unit. Boxes, switches, and receptacles are often ganged.

Greenfield. Flexible metal conduit through which wires are pulled.

Ground. Refers to the fact that electricity always seeks the shortest possible path to the earth. Neutral wires carry electricity to ground in all circuits. An additional grounding wire, or the sheathing of metal-clad cable or conduit, protects against shock from a malfunctioning device.

Ground-fault circuit interrupter (GFCI). A safety device that senses any shock hazard and shuts off a circuit or receptacle.

High-intensity discharge (HID). A type of lighting, including lamps such as halogen, mercury vapor, metal halide, and sodium. All HIDs produce a bright, economical light.

Hot wire. The conductor of current to a receptacle or other outlet. *See also* Neutral wire *and* Ground.

Incandescent bulb. A light source with an electrically charged metal filament that burns at white heat.

Insulation. A nonconductive covering that protects wires and other electricity carriers.

Junction box. An enclosure used for splitting circuits into different branches. In a junction box, wires connect only to each other, never to a switch, receptacle, or fixture.

Kilowatt (kW). One thousand watts. A kilowatt hour is the standard measure of electrical consumption.

Knockouts. Tabs that can be removed to make openings in a box for cable or conduit connectors.

LB connector or fitting. An elbow for conduit with access for pulling wires. Connections cannot be made within this fitting.

Lead. A short wire coming from a fixture, typically stranded, to which a household wire is spliced. It is used instead of a terminal.

MC cable. Armored cable containing at least two insulated wires and an insulated ground wire.

Middle-of-the-run. A device located between two other devices on a circuit. Wires continue from its box to other devices.

Multitester. A device that measures voltage in a circuit and performs other tests.

National Electrical Code (NEC). A set of rules governing safe wiring methods, drafted by the National Fire Protection Association. Local codes sometimes differ from and take precedence over the NEC.

Neutral wire. A conductor that carries current from an outlet back to ground, clad in white insulation. *See also* Hot wire *and* Ground.

New-work box. A metal or plastic box attached to framing members before the wall material is installed.

Nonmetallic (NM) sheathed cable. Two or more insulated wires and a bare ground wire clad in a plastic covering.

Outlet. Any potential point of use in a circuit, including receptacles, switches, and light fixtures.

Old-work box. *See* Remodel box.

Overload. A condition that exists when a circuit is carrying more amperage than it was designed to handle. Overloading causes wires to heat up, which in turn blows fuses or trips circuit breakers.

Pigtail. A length of wire, stripped at both ends, spliced with one or more other wires. It is used instead of attaching two or more wires to a terminal, an unsafe connection.

Polarized plugs. Plugs designed so the hot and neutral sides of a circuit can't be accidentally reversed. One prong of the plug is a different shape than the other.

Raceway wiring. Surface-mounted channels for extending circuits.

Receptacle. An outlet that supplies power for lamps and other plug-in devices.

Recessed can light. A light fixture set into a wall cavity so the lens and trim are flush with the ceiling.

Remodel box. A metal or plastic box, sometimes called an "old-work" box, designed for a hole cut in drywall or plaster and lath.

Rigid conduit. Wire-carrying metal tubing that can be bent only with a special tool.

Romex. A trade name for nonmetallic sheathed cable. *See* Nonmetallic sheathed cable.

Service entrance. The point where power enters a home.

Service panel. The main fuse box or breaker box in a home.

Short circuit. A condition that occurs when hot and neutral wires contact each other. Fuses and breakers protect against fire, which can result from a short.

Stripping. Removing insulation from wire, or sheathing from cable.

Subpanel. A subsidiary fuse box or breaker box linked to a service panel that has no room for additional circuits.

System ground. A wire connecting a service panel to the earth. It may be attached to a main water pipe, to a rod driven into the ground, or to a plate embedded along a footing.

Three-way switch. Operates a light from two locations.

Time-delay fuse. A fuse that does not break the circuit during the momentary overload that can happen when an electric motor starts up. If the overload continues, the fuse blows, shutting off the circuit.

Transformer. A device that reduces or increases voltage. In home wiring, transformers step down current for use with low-voltage equipment such as thermostats and doorbell systems.

Travelers. Two of the three conductors that run between switches in a 3-way installation.

Underwriters knot. A knot used as a strain relief for wires in a lamp socket.

Underwriters Laboratories (UL). An independent testing agency that examines electrical components for safety hazards.

Volt. A measure of electrical pressure. Volts × amps = watts.

Watt. A measure of the power an electrical device consumes. *See also* Volt, Amp, *and* Kilowatt.

Wire nut. A screw-on device used to splice two or more wires.

INDEX

INDEX